The Ultimate Cook Book

The
ULTIMATE COOK BOOK

900 New Recipes, Thousands of Ideas

Bruce Weinstein and Mark Scarbrough

WILLIAM MORROW
An Imprint of HarperCollinsPublishers

HarperCollins books may be purchased for educational, business, or sales promotional use. For information please write: Special Markets Department, HarperCollins Publishers, 10 East 53rd Street, New York, NY 10022.

FIRST EDITION

Designed by Leah Carlson-Stanisic

Library of Congress Cataloging-in-Publication Data

Weinstein, Bruce, 1960–
    The ultimate cook book: 900 new recipes, thousands of ideas / Bruce Weinstein and Mark Scarbrough.
        p. cm.
    ISBN: 978-0-06-083383-1
    ISBN-10: 0-06-083383-1
    1. Cookery. I. Scarbrough, Mark. II. Title.

TX714.W33155 2007
641'.5—dc22

2006046150

---

07 08 09 10 11 WBC/RRD 10 9 8 7 6 5 4 3 2 1

Contents

Acknowledgments

I T TOOK US A YEAR TO DEVELOP NINE HUNDRED NEW RECIPES. AND NO ONE can keep up that pace—almost three a day, every day, seven days a week!—without a lot of help.

Our greatest debt is twofold: to Harriet Bell, our editor and publisher at William Morrow; and to Susan Ginsburg, our agent at Writer's House. Harriet pushes us to avoid cliché, to see the modern food scene through the lens of the modern supermarket, and to forgo the obvious in favor of originality. Susan has championed us and our work over many years, helping us understand the dynamics of the market and making sure we were poised when the door opened. Both of them (along with their husbands, Charlie Allenson and Jerry Webman) have also proven wonderful dinner companions over the years.

Several people took chapters in draft, overlooked the typos, and tested the recipes. These brave folks all had the same assignment: make whatever you want and tell us what happened. Their notes have proven invaluable; we've learned lots by seeing what they made—and what they didn't! Many thanks to Esther Lou Scarbrough, Debbie Weinstein, Julie Weinstein, Amy Kull, Dale Brown, Suzie Hukill, and Jo Booher.

Where would we be without our dedicated coterie of New York eaters? They've been game to taste anything—and have rarely turned down a late afternoon invitation to dinner. They offered notes, encouragement, and good humor in the face of the daunting task of eating "the six chicken dishes from today." We're so lucky to have Steve Rodgers, Marianne Macy, Leora Perlman and Meredith Greenburg, Steve and Melanie Schwartz, Eric Darton and Katie Kehrig as well as their fabulous daughter Gwen, Paula and Benny Yarkoni, Bill Poock and Felix Lao-Batiz, David Sisson and Scott Stevens, and Phyllis Howe and Richard Bradspies at our dinner table and thus in our lives. Special thanks to Jennifer Chang, who has eaten more of this book than anyone else and who, when she tasted the Autumn Lasagna, said, "You ought to make a year's worth of these things."

We can't say enough about the generosity of Ariane Daguin at D'Artagnan. She sent boxes of meat, fowl, and even foie gras. When they showed up at our apartment, we were briefly the envy of every foodie we know.

Thanks as well to Oliviers & Co. for a wonderful range of aromatic olive oils that have become an outright addiction. And thanks to SerendipiTea for a big box of exotic teas. Stephanie Teuwen at Teuwen One Image arranged all these marvels; her support has proved invaluable.

Rival provided us with rice cookers, slow cookers, vacuum sealers, and a range of kitchen appliances that have never left our counters. Thanks to Diane Coffey at The Holmes Group for making that possible.

And OXO offered us kitchen tools that proved indispensable in preparing these recipes. Thanks to Gretchen Holt and Stephanie Karlis for sending us so many goodies.

Finally, we have gorgeous KitchenAid equipment and appliances thanks to Brian Maynard and to Kim Roman at Digitas. Sometimes, it seems we live in a dream.

Over the years, the apparently tireless Beth Shepard at Beth Shepard Communications has worked to provide us with many spokespeople opportunities, among them those with the California Milk Advisory Board, JIF, Smucker's, Splenda, the National Honey Board, and the U.S. Potato Board.

We've had a blast cooking recipes from this book at various cooking schools around the country. Our thanks to Cynthia Liu and Kathleen Taggart at Draeger's Markets in San Mateo and Menlo Park, California; Phyllis Vaccarelli at Let's Get Cookin' in Los Angeles; and the wonderful staff at the Publix Cooking Schools in Tampa and Sarasota, Florida. Thanks to Alicia Laury at Kaplow Communications who helped set up the Florida classes.

Ron and Debbie Eisenberg have given us boundless opportunities. We have great fun at our regular cooking demos in their stores, the Chef's Centrals in Hartsdale, New York, and in Paramus, New Jersey. We are indulged by their staff and made welcome by all the people who come back time and again to see us.

In honing our craft, we'd be lost without our magazine editors: Jim Romanoff at *Eating Well,* Tim Cebula and Ann Pittman at *Cooking Light,* Lisa Chernick at weightwatchers.com, Jill Melton and Candace Floyd at *Relish,* and Clare Lewis at *Today's Health and Wellness.* They have spurred us on to write the best. Plus, Jim brings the best maple syrup from Vermont when he meets us for Chinatown runs.

We're also grateful to Dave Durian and Mallory Pinkard at WBAL in Baltimore for giving us a chance to strut our stuff on air every Tuesday morning at 7:55.

A book is not only an author's work; it's also the work of a publishing house. Lucy Baker and Stephanie Fraser handled all the rarefied and not-so-rarefied details. Sonia Greenbaum did a wonderful job catching all of our pesky errors and straightening out any contorted prose. Once again, Leah Carlson-Stanisic designed a winner and Ann Cahn, as always, kept the whole production schedule moving along. Roberto de Vicq de Cumptich has kept the entire *Ultimate* series looking beautiful in its design; Carrie Bachman and Milena Perez have worked tirelessly promoting this book and its series. Ken Berger has done wonders with special sales. And many thanks to Emily Saladino, our agent's assistant, who has the most underrated job in the business. How many panicked author calls can one person field and still remain cool and professional?

And finally, our deep gratitude to our parents who taught us that the good life is always in reach—and, like an apple, to be relished.

Introduction

WHAT, BESIDES CHUTZPAH, MAKES A COOKBOOK THE ULTIMATE? SIX kinds of deviled eggs (pages 59–60), a year of lasagne (pages 203–208), or a way to make just about every fruit pie (pages 594–597)? The sheer weight of nine hundred recipes and thousands of variations? Or the fact that two food writers said, "to blazes with our waistlines," and spent two years cooking and eating our way through the modern supermarket?

No, what makes this cookbook the ultimate is the philosophy we developed in 1999 with *The Ultimate Ice Cream Book*. In a nutshell, this book takes solid, basic recipes and allows you to customize them endlessly to your taste. You get the best of both worlds: hundreds of recipes from two established food writers, combined with thousands of ways to make the dishes exactly as you want them.

We don't have employees, we don't farm the recipes out, and we don't subcontract their development. We work in our small New York City kitchen (it's four feet wide, including the appliances) and test every recipe ourselves. Needless to say, our friends eat well.

And the recipes in this book are all original content. We've written plenty of single-subject ultimate books. Ten, to be exact—from brownies to chocolate cookies, ice cream to peanut butter, shrimp to potatoes. But this volume isn't a compilation. Rather, *The Ultimate Cook Book* picks up where the other single-subject ultimate books left off.

It's the ultimate expression of our ultimate philosophy: hundreds of base recipes, thousands of variations, nothing complicated, a compendium for all your cooking needs—and a way to take just about every dish and either follow our lead or turn it into something that reflects your taste.

How Did This Ultimate Philosophy Get Started?

It got started (where else?) in New York City. We were talking about (what else?) food. More specifically, our first cookbook. How would we choose between Chocolate Ice Cream, Chocolate Cheesecake Ice Cream, German Chocolate Ice Cream, and Chocolate Banana Chip Ice Cream?

It hit us like a bolt. Most of the time, we want the creamiest, fudgiest chocolate ice cream. After that, we may twist it up a bit and that's easy enough: just an addition here, a substitution there. But we want solid recipes that we can eventually dress up, take beyond their inception to something more personal.

Who Is an Ultimate Cook?

Everyone, we reckon. We developed and tested the recipes ourselves, then we packed them off in draft to see how well we were doing—never to chefs, culinary professionals, or people in the food business; instead, we sent them to our mothers, cousins, friends, and people we'd never met but who volunteered via e-mail. We gave everyone the same task: make two or three recipes from the chapter, any you choose, and tell us exactly what you did.

Many stuck to the base, but others played with the recipes. "Cinnamon makes me sneeze." "I hate crunchy peanut butter." "Who has port?" They liked knowing where to start: a solid, fairly easy recipe with bold flavors using everyday ingredients. They also liked finishing on their own, adding their own nuances to the dish. And that's the very heart of the ultimate philosophy.

So How Do These Variations and Customizations Work?

In almost all the recipes, it's a matter of small additions, substitutions, and changes: spices, flavorings, and the like. Some variations may switch out the centerpiece of the dish—say substituting chicken thighs for pork chops. But most are small changes that can add up to big flavors in the dish. In other words, you can choose the dish by its title with the confidence that this is in fact what you'll get. The nuances can then be rearranged as you like.

In some recipes, the variations are a nutritional matter, best decided by your preference: for example, "1 cup milk (regular, low-fat, or fat-free)." The challenge was to create, say, French toast that lived up to all three options. (See page 35 for the answer.)

A few recipes are road maps that will lead you through various choices to create many different versions of a dish—for example, The Ultimate Granola (page 11), Bacon-Wrapped Anything (page 56), or Creamy Vegetable Soup (page 131).

Finally, some recipes are choices in and of themselves: Spice Rubs for Steaks (pages 385–386) or No-Fail Roast Turkey with Four Wet Rubs (pages 284–286).

What's Inside This Book?

Breakfast to dessert, the full range. Some recipes are for the experienced cook and some are for those just starting out. For example, there's a paella for every season (pages 496–499), but there are also tips on how to make perfect Scrambled Eggs (page 14). There's a passel of easy chicken or fish sautés, skillet wonders that'll have dinner on the table in minutes as well as blow-out dinner-party dishes that showcase some of the best of modern American cooking. How about Braised Beef Short Ribs with Cabbage, Port, and Vanilla (page 396)? Sure, there's homey chicken pot pie (page 282) and lots of ways to make just about every good-ol'-American cobbler the market can afford (pages 623–625); but there are also international dishes like Jerk Chicken Thighs and Plantains (page 281) or Vietnamese-Inspired Spiced Pork Soup (page 153).

By the way, most of those international dishes are listed as "inspired" (Thai-inspired, Greek-inspired, etc.). The authentic preparation of international dishes often requires obscure ingredients not readily available to home cooks. Anyone for the rind of a Buddha's hand, a sinewy Malaysian citrus? Our international recipes are reinterpreted with the modern supermarket in mind.

One other thing we should confess up front: we have a preference for food that can be quickly prepared. We shy away from six-hour smoker roasts, triple-raised yeast doughs, and two-day brines. A few are here, but they're not the norm. Over and over, we've asked the same question: how can we get dinner on the table as soon as possible?

The answer, of course, lies in recipes without pitfalls and complicated tricks, recipes that come from two food writers who've wandered those supermarket aisles for years, looked at the astounding array of food that's available, and then tried to come up with a meal that's satisfying, straightforward, and yet somehow a matter of personal taste.

Overall Tips for Success

• **Read the recipe from start to finish.** You'll understand a dish's flow, discover any quirks, and find out if there's an unfamiliar ingredient or term you should look up before you start.

• **Read around the recipe.** There may be alternative recipes before or after the one you're looking at. Root Vegetable Soup (page 140) is followed by Potato and Roasted Chile Soup (page 141). Is the second recipe more your speed?

• **Choose, then shop.** Cookbooks work best as planning guides. Yes, we love to experiment. We've walked through Chinatown, seen some unfamiliar vegetable, and tried to make dinner out of it. But that's the exception, not the rule. It's better to choose a recipe, then shop for what it requires. Spontaneity is overrated at 6:30 p.m.

• **Know your ingredients.** For any that are unfamiliar, check the Glossary starting on page 654.

• **Know your options.** We're all about variations, but we ask you to be sensible and know what you're doing. We once had someone write to complain that our piecrust was a disaster; on further questioning, she told us that she'd substituted cornstarch for flour. ("They're both white," she wrote.) Simple additions like this vinegar instead of that or one spice substituted for another will probably not affect the final dish, but larger substitutions that change the essential chemistry of the cooking may well compromise the results.

• **Prep your ingredients before you cook.** Of course, this isn't a hard-and-fast rule. If you've read the recipe through, you might know, for example, that there's a thirty-minute break between steps 4 and 5. But cooking will go more quickly—and be more fun—if you're prepared. Would you go to war without a gun?

• **Visual cues mean more than temporal ones.** Always treat timings as estimates. Your stove may have more BTUs than ours; our flour may be drier than yours; our bread crumbs, moister. There's no way to account for the variables, so pay close attention to the visual cues—"until soft," "until slightly thickened," "until an instant-read meat thermometer registers . . ."

✺ Thirty-One Examples of Culinary Shorthand ✺

Although recipes in a cookbook are more expansive than those in a magazine, both are written with culinary chestnuts. If you're a longtime cook, you know the drill. If not, these verbal ticks can sound like a foreign language. Here are the most common.

1. **Preheat the oven to . . .** A conventional oven takes 10 to 15 minutes to come to a stable temperature. In most cases, start preheating the oven even before you lay out your ingredients.

2. **Preheat a gas grill or prepare a charcoal grill.** Like ovens, grills need time to come to the required temperature—although the actual degree called for in a recipe is less precise: usually "high heat," but sometimes "medium" or "low heat." Preheating a gas grill is usually no more than opening a valve and pressing a button (check the manufacturer's instructions). However, creating heat in a charcoal grill involves building the coal bed, then making sure the temperature's right. (Again, follow the manufacturer's instructions.) In general, low heat is 300°F, medium heat is 375°F, and high heat is between 450°F and 500°F. A less scientific approach is to place your open palm 5 inches above the grill grate. The fire is high if you must move your hand in 2 seconds, medium in 4 seconds, and low in 8 seconds.

3. **Roughly chopped, chopped, cubed, finely chopped, diced, minced.** These gradations represent the range for cutting up vegetables, fruits, herbs, and meats. Here are the general parameters.

Roughly chopped: the largest cut with the widest latitude, uneven pieces up to 1 inch wide.
Chopped: slightly smaller, more uniform, 1/2-inch pieces
Cubed: like "chopped" but more exact—small, 1/2-inch cubes
Finely chopped: smaller still but less precise, about 1/4 inch
Diced: a small cube, about 1/4 inch on all sides
Minced: the smallest cuts of all, about 1/8 inch. Mince items by rocking your knife back and forth through them, rather than slicing them into tiny pieces.

4. **Plus additional for greasing the pan.** Sometimes, a little extra fat is called for to grease a pan before it goes into the oven. To grease or oil a cool baking pan, place a small amount of butter or oil on a paper towel and run it around the inside surface of the pan, paying special attention to the corners and creases.

5. **Plus additional for dusting the pan.** Sometimes, you need a barrier of flour (as well as fat) between the batter and the heat. To dust a pan with flour, add a couple of teaspoons to the pan, then tilt and tap it so that the flour covers the surfaces, corners, and edges. Tap out the excess flour by standing the pan on one

edge and rapping it against the side of the sink so the flour can be washed down the drain.

6. **Toasted pecans, walnuts, pine nuts, etc.** Nuts and seeds lose their sometimes cloying softness and have a more intense flavor if the natural oils and sugars have been caramelized, resulting in a golden brown sheen and a nutty aroma. To toast nuts and seeds, place them in a large skillet over medium-low heat and cook, stirring occasionally, until they are light brown and quite aromatic, anywhere from 5 to 8 minutes. Or spread them on a large lipped baking sheet and roast them in a preheated 350°F oven, stirring occasionally, until golden and aromatic, anywhere from 8 to 18 minutes. Peanuts and cashews are often sold "roasted" and so do not need this extra step in the kitchen. Do not use salted nuts or seeds unless the recipe specifically calls for them.

7. **Cut in with a pastry cutter or a fork until . . .** Solid butter or shortening (that is, not softened or melted) must often be mixed into dry ingredients. To do so, cut the fat into chunks, then work these into the flour in the bowl through the tines of a fork or through a pastry cutter, a half-moon tool with parallel curved, dull blades. Work around the bowl, continually repositioning the fat and flour before you press it through the tines, until the mixture looks like coarse, powdery sand.

8. **Roll until . . .** Use a heavy rolling pin, not one of Goliath proportions but one that will flatten the dough. Let the pin's weight flatten and smooth the dough as you roll across it. Often, you roll between sheets of plastic wrap or wax paper; the directions will always tell you which to use. If the pin is touching the dough directly, you may have to dust both with flour.

9. **Set aside . . .** Only set something in the refrigerator if the recipe specifically asks you to do so. Otherwise, set the bowl or plate aside at room temperature, covering it with plastic wrap if the recipe calls for it.

10. **In a warm, dry, draft-free place . . .** In other words, set the dough or batter away from any heating or cooling vents, away from the stove, and never on top of the refrigerator. Our kitchen has a certain nook—farthest from the window, several feet away from the oven—that we've christened our "warm, dry place." Investigate and claim your own. A pantry shelf? A back corner of the counter?

11. **Until doubled in bulk.** Yeast must produce carbon dioxide for a dough to rise, but doubling is not an exact science. You're looking for a dough that has risen a little less than twice its original height in the bowl (the bowl does widen toward the top) and has a gently rounded puff. Another way to tell: if you press your fingers into the dough, the indentation you make will stay put.

12. **Heat a skillet, saucepan, or pot . . .** Do not heat a pan for a prolonged period of time; you may get the pan so hot that you ignite the oil when it's poured in. Use common sense: you want the food to come in contact with a hot surface.

13. **Swirl in the oil.** In 99 out of 100 cases, the oil should be added after the pan has heated. Drizzle the oil all over the pan, then pick the pan up and tilt it back and forth to get the best coverage across the cooking surface.

14. **Cook . . .** To cook is to bring food into contact with heat. Once the food's in the pan, keep everything as close to the heat as possible; don't lift the pan off the heating element.

15. Until softened, until soft, or until translucent. Less a series of gradations than a set of visual cues, these directions refer to the way certain vegetables—onions, shallots, and celery, in particular—transform as they lose moisture over the heat. In most cases, lower the heat if you notice the vegetables turning brown at their edges before they've softened.

16. Stir . . . Use a wooden spoon, a pair of kitchen tongs, or a heat-safe silicone spatula. If you're working with nonstick cookware, use only utensils approved for that surface.

17. With a fork. Whether stirring or fluffing, the point here is to break up clumps or grains so that the texture is coarse but uniform. A spoon will not do the job.

18. Whisk . . . Use a whisk. A good kitchen has at least two, a thin one for working in saucepans and a large, balloon-shaped one for whipping ingredients in bowls.

19. Mop . . . A term for the grill, "to mop" is to slather generously with sauce. Grilling mops, sold in cookware stores, are thick, coarse brushes that hold lots of sauce.

20. Stirring once in a while, occasionally, frequently, often, or constantly. These are the various gradations for how much attention you should pay to a mixture over the heat. None is a call to leave a pan unattended. Stir by moving a wooden spoon in arcs across the bottom of the pan, thereby scraping ingredients off the hot surface and exchanging them with those that have not been in direct contact with the heat. In a stew, the point is to keep elements (usually in suspension) from dropping to the bottom and sticking to the hot surface under the simmering liquid.

21. Until uniform. In other words, until the various components of the mixture are evenly distributed without, say, a pocket of cinnamon or a streak of salt.

22. Until aromatic. Spices and some oils need to be heated so that they'll release their flavors; cook them until you can smell them. But do remember that chili oils will volatilize and the resulting vapors can burn your eyes. As a precaution, do not lean directly over the pot.

23. Until they give off their liquid and it reduces to a glaze. Mushrooms are a tight pack of moisture, held in fibrous chambers that quickly break down over heat. In most cases, the liquid would make a dish watery, so you want the mushrooms to give off most of their liquid (the mixture in the pan will be a little soupy); then you reduce this liquid to a thick glaze to concentrate its flavors before continuing.

24. Scraping up the browned bits on the bottom of the pan. Bits of herbs, protein, or other ingredients get stuck on the pan's bottom, glued there by natural sugars. These browned bits often carry most of the flavor in a soup, stew, or sauce. Once you've added a liquid to a pan, let it come to a simmer, then use a wooden spoon or heat-safe tongs to scrape these caramelized bits off the bottom. The simmering itself should help lift them free, although some are resistant enough to need several seconds to come loose.

25. Simmer slowly, simmer, boil, or bring to a full boil. A slow simmer is just a few bubbles at a time; you can count them as they appear. A simmer is slightly faster, but still gentle. A boil is more vigorous: the ingredients roil in the pot. A full boil means that even heavier ingredients are tossed in the swirl. You may be able to stir down a simmer (in other words, constant stirring will cause the liquid to stop simmering); you should not be able to stir down a boil.

26. Until lightly browned, golden, or dark brown. Color gradations are caused by sugars caramelizing on the outside of food, but the exact color achieved is a matter of time over the heat—and a matter of personal taste. By and large, the darker the color, the more prominent the taste. However, the line between browned and burned is faint but exacting.

27. Coats the back of a wooden spoon. Puddings and custards must be cooked until the flour or cornstarch thickens the liquid. Dip a wooden spoon into the mixture, stir it a couple of times, and lift it out. The back of the spoon should be coated in an opaque film. If you run your finger through the mixture adhering to the back of the spoon, the line you make should have firm borders that do not run or sag.

28. Until an instant-read meat thermometer inserted into . . . reaches . . . An instant-read meat thermometer will give you the temperature in seconds, without its having to be left in the roast for hours. Gently press the thermometer's probe into the cut as directed in the recipe and wait a few seconds for the temperature to register. Never place an instant-read meat thermometer in the oven. Always wash an instant-read thermometer before a subsequent use.

29. Refresh under cool water until room temperature. To keep vegetables crisp, you have to stop the cooking process. When they're in the colander in the sink, run cool—not cold—water over them, tossing occasionally until they're no longer hot to the touch.

30. Transfer to . . . Use a utensil large enough to hold the food securely when you pick it up and bring it to a plate, platter, or rack. Small tools mean broken, chipped, or torn food.

31. Cool on a wire rack until . . . A wire rack is essential for cooling foods; otherwise, they'll sit on a solid surface and turn gummy as they cool. Invest in a large rack, one with feet that lift it up slightly. Also consider buying one with a crosshatch of wires so that smaller foods don't fall through the slats.

Breakfast and Brunch

WE KNOW A MANHATTAN GALLERY OWNER, SHE OF HIGH-CONCEPT glasses, who has renovated her kitchen almost out of existence. Cupboards and drawers? Gone. There's only one small shelf and a half-sized refrigerator shoved in a corner. The only other thing? A single burner so she can make herself an omelet every morning. Even she, a fashionista of the highest order, wants to wake up to breakfast.

A morning routine is so satisfying. Perhaps it's nothing more than a cup of coffee and a piece of toast, but there's something sacred about the day's first moments. It's no wonder that U. S. egg consumption has topped 250 per person a year. No wonder that bakeries have enjoyed a renaissance across the country. And no wonder that while kitchen remodeling remains our nationwide preoccupation, stats show that the number-one meal cooked in these new kitchens is . . . yes, breakfast.

This chapter starts with the simple breakfasts: smoothies and cereals. Then it turns to more substantial fare, brunch for many of us, but a welcome treat—or a fresh start at 7:00 a.m. There's a section devoted to eggs—from the simplest scrambled concoctions to make-ahead casseroles. Then come the reasons God made maple syrup: pancakes, French toast, and the like. Finally, there's a set of easy sides.

Simply put, breakfast's worth the effort—no matter if you've cut your designer life down to a single burner or it's a weekend morning and you've got no plans other than a waffle, the paper, and a cup of coffee.

❋ Breakfast Smoothies ❋

No wonder smoothies have taken over breakfast: they're fast, flavorful, and nutritious. Unfortunately, like muffins, they have also gotten supersized. So keep the servings within reason and use fat-free yogurt or skim milk.

How to Make a Smoothie

Put the ingredients in a blender in the order listed; blend until smooth. Each recipe makes one smoothie; any can be doubled or tripled, depending on your blender's capacity. For a brighter taste, add ⅛ teaspoon salt. For a colder drink, start with an ice cube or two.

Banana Mango Smoothie

1 ripe banana, peeled and broken into pieces
½ cup chopped peeled pitted mango
¼ cup yogurt (regular, plain, or fat-free)
¼ cup orange juice
2 teaspoons honey
⅛ teaspoon ground cinnamon

Lemon Berry Smoothie

½ cup sliced fresh strawberries
½ cup lemon sherbet or sorbet
¼ cup fresh or frozen blueberries
¼ cup fresh or frozen raspberries

Banana Melon Smoothie

1 ripe banana, peeled and broken into
   chunks
¾ cup chopped, peeled, seeded honeydew or
   cantaloupe
¼ cup yogurt (regular, low-fat, or fat-free)
2 tablespoons frozen orange juice concentrate
1 teaspoon vanilla extract

Fruit and Berry Smoothie

4 medium apricots, pitted and halved
4 hulled strawberries, sliced
1 cup yogurt (regular, low-fat, or fat-free)
¼ cup white grape juice
1 tablespoon wheat germ

Peach Melba Smoothie

1 medium ripe peach, pitted and cut into
   wedges
½ cup vanilla frozen yogurt (regular, low-
   fat, or fat-free)
½ cup fresh or frozen raspberries
1 tablespoon lime juice
⅛ teaspoon almond extract

Peanut Butter Smoothie

4 to 5 ice cubes
1 ripe banana, peeled and broken into chunks
½ cup milk (regular, low-fat, or fat-free)
1 tablespoon creamy peanut butter
2 teaspoons honey
½ teaspoon vanilla
⅛ teaspoon grated nutmeg

Strawberry Melon Protein Smoothie

6 hulled strawberries, sliced
¾ cup peeled, seeded cantaloupe or
   honeydew chunks
⅓ cup pineapple juice
2 tablespoons unflavored protein powder

Chocolate Banana Protein Smoothie

3 ice cubes
1 ripe banana, peeled and broken into chunks
1 cup yogurt (regular, low-fat, or fat-free)
2 tablespoons chocolate syrup
2 tablespoons unflavored protein powder
½ teaspoon vanilla extract

Savory Cucumber Smoothie

½ cup peeled, seeded, and chopped cucumber
½ cup blackberries
½ cup apple juice
3 torn basil leaves

Pear Smoothie

1 small ripe pear, peeled, cored, and roughly
   chopped
1 ripe banana, peeled and broken into
   chunks
⅓ cup white cranberry or white grape juice
1 teaspoon lemon juice
⅛ teaspoon almond extract

❁ *Cereals* ❁

Although most of us pour it out of a box, homemade cereal is a treat, especially since it's lacking the preservatives and chemical enhancements often laced into our morning staple.

A road map for
The Ultimate Granola

Granola is endlessly variable, bound only by your whims. Here's a road map to creating your signature version. *Makes about 10 cups*

① Start by positioning the racks in the top and bottom thirds of the oven and preheating the oven to 350°F.

② Spread

   6 cups rolled oats (do not use quick-cooking
      or steel-cut oats)

on a very large baking sheet. Toast in the top third of the oven for 10 minutes. Transfer to a very large bowl. (Maintain the oven's heat.)

③ Next, mix one item from each of the following two lists in a small saucepan set over medium heat.

(a) ⅔ cup of any one of these sweeteners:

   Honey
   Maple syrup
   Unsweetened apple juice concentrate,
      thawed
   Unsweetened white grape juice concentrate,
      thawed
   Sweetened cranberry juice concentrate,
      thawed
   Cane syrup, such as Lyle's Golden
      Syrup
   Agave nectar

   and

(b) 2/3 cup of any one of these fats:

> Walnut oil
> Almond oil
> Canola oil
> Safflower oil
> Grapeseed oil

4 The moment the mixture starts to steam, take the pan off the heat. Stir in

> 1 tablespoon vanilla extract

and set aside to cool for 5 minutes.

5 As that mixture cools, stir all of the following into the toasted oats:

> ½ cup wheat germ
> ¼ cup packed light brown sugar
> 2 teaspoons ground cinnamon
> 1 teaspoon salt

6 **Also add one item from each of the following two lists to the toasted oats mixture:**

(a) ½ cup nuts, seeds, or coconut:

> Finely chopped walnut pieces
> Finely chopped pecan pieces
> Chopped unsalted cashews
> Sliced or slivered almonds
> Unsalted shelled sunflower seeds
> Shredded unsweetened coconut

and

(b) ½ cup fortifier:

> Powdered dry milk
> Powdered fat-free dry milk
> Powdered fat-free dry whey

7 Finally, stir in the prepared cooked sweetening and oil mixture.

8 Spray two large baking sheets with nonstick spray or grease them with a little oil dabbed on a paper towel. Divide the oat mixture between the two baking sheets, spreading it to the corners. Place the trays in the top and bottom thirds of the oven and bake for 10 minutes, stirring once.

9 Reverse the trays top to bottom and back to front, and continue cooking until lightly browned and fragrant, about 10 more minutes, tossing and stirring once or twice.

10 Place the baking sheets on wire racks. Stir 1 cup of any one of the following or any combination into the mixture on the trays (½ cup into each tray):

> Chopped dried apples, chopped dried apricots, chopped dried figs, chopped dried pineapple, chopped dried strawberries, dried blueberries, dried cranberries, dried currants, raisins

11 Cool to room temperature on the trays without disturbing, about 1½ hours.

To store: Break up and seal in plastic bags or containers; the granola will keep in a dark, dry place at room temperature for up to 2 months.

Why Take Time for Breakfast?

Recent research indicates that people who skip breakfast are more likely to have problems with obesity. On average, those who forgo the morning meal eat an additional 100 calories per day. Worse yet, their insulin levels are out of whack by lunch, leading to higher cholesterol and suggesting a range of problems from diabetes to heart disease. Put simply, if you want to gain weight, skip breakfast.

Muesli

Although not traditionally cooked, this breakfast favorite is made better by toasting rolled oats and nuts, then mixing them with quick-cooking oats and the other ingredients. Serve with yogurt or milk, topped with fresh berries. *Makes 9 cups*

1 cup rolled oats (do not use quick-cooked or steel-cut)
1 cup sliced almonds
4 cups quick-cooking oats
1 cup wheat germ
½ cup unsalted sunflower seeds
½ cup raisins
½ cup chopped pitted dates
½ cup shredded unsweetened coconut

1 Position the rack in the center of the oven; preheat the oven to 350°F. Spread the rolled oats and almonds on a large, lipped baking sheet; bake until lightly browned, tossing occasionally, about 7 minutes. Cool on a wire rack to room temperature, about 1 hour.

2 Toss the toasted oats and almonds with the quick-cooking oats, wheat germ, sunflower seeds, raisins, dates, and coconut in a large bowl.

To store: Seal in plastic bags or a large plastic container and keep at room temperature for up to 2 months.

Variations: Substitute chopped walnut pieces or chopped pecan pieces for the almonds.
Substitute dried blueberries, dried cranberries, dried raspberries, or chopped dried strawberries for the raisins.
Substitute chopped dried apples, chopped dried apricots, or chopped dried figs for the dates.

Breakfast Rice Pudding

This rice porridge is like a breakfast risotto. There are two ways to make it: a pressure cooker and a traditional method. *Makes 4 servings*

4 cups milk (regular, low-fat, or fat-free)
1½ cups Arborio rice (see page 494)
1 cup raisins, chopped
2 tablespoons maple syrup
One 4-inch cinnamon stick
¼ teaspoon grated nutmeg
¼ teaspoon salt
⅛ teaspoon ground cloves

Pressure cooker method:
1 Place all the ingredients in a pressure cooker, set it over medium-high heat, and bring to a simmer, stirring all the while.

2 Lock on the lid according to the manufacturer's instructions; bring the cooker to high pressure. Adjust the heat so that the cooker releases steam at a steady rate (this will be indicated by the pressure valve or another feature listed in the manufacturer's instructions); cook at high pressure for 7 minutes.

3 Release the lid using the quick-release method—that is, placing the sealed pressure cooker under cold running water until the locking mechanism releases or until another signal for released pressure happens.

4 Uncover the cooker and return to medium-high heat. Cook, stirring constantly, until creamy and somewhat thickened but just until the rice still has some tooth left, about 1 minute. Remove the cinnamon stick before serving.

Traditional method:
1 Bring the milk to a very low simmer in a medium saucepan set over medium heat. Reduce the heat so the milk stays this hot but does not boil.

2 Ladle ¾ cup hot milk into a large saucepan just now set over medium-low heat; stir in the rice, raisins, maple syrup, cinnamon stick, nutmeg, salt, and cloves. Cook, stirring constantly, until the rice's outer shell turns translucent, about 2 minutes.

3 Add ¾ cup warm milk and cook, stirring constantly, until it has been absorbed, about 3 more minutes.

4 Reduce the heat even further so that the rice cooks very slowly; add ¼ cup milk. Cook, stir-ring constantly, adding more milk in ¼-cup increments only after the pan is almost dry from the last addition, until very creamy and thickened. The total cooking time for this step should be about 30 minutes. Remove the cinnamon stick before serving.

Variations: Substitute 1 cup finely chopped dried fruit, such as apricots or pears, for the raisins.

Substitute honey or packed light brown sugar for the maple syrup.

❋ *Eggs Every Which Way* ❋

Nature's nutritional miracle, an egg is a tight pack of protein, amino acids, fat, vitamins, and minerals—a pack so tight that many cultures find eggs too big a wallop for breakfast and save them for later in the day. In the United States, we like our protein early and often. The myth about old-timers and eggs may be shopworn ("My grandfather started every day with two fried eggs and . . ."), but there's no doubt that eggs have long provided the spark that gets our bodies running.

Scrambled Eggs

It's easy to make good scrambled eggs. As with most things, simpler is better. *Makes 1 serving (see Note)*

> 1 teaspoon unsalted butter, olive oil, or
>   nonstick spray
> 2 large eggs
> 1 tablespoon milk (regular, low-fat, or
>   fat-free), half-and-half, or heavy cream
> Salt and freshly ground black pepper to taste

1 Either heat the butter or olive oil in a small non-stick skillet over medium heat or spray the skillet with nonstick spray and set it over medium heat.

2 While the skillet heats, crack the eggs into a small bowl. Use a fork to whisk in the milk, half-and-half, or cream until almost uniformly yellow.

3 Pour the mixture into the skillet, tilting it so that the mixture coats the bottom. Set the pan over the heat, count to ten, then use a heat-safe rubber spatula to lift the fluffy bits off the pan's bottom, working gently so as not to break up these cloudlike curds.

4 Tilt the skillet to bring more of the unset egg into contact with the hot surface. Once almost all the unset egg has come into contact with the pan and the moment it has set enough to look like loose pudding, gently scoop the curds onto a serving plate; season with salt and pepper.

Note: You can make two, three, or four servings at one time. Use a larger skillet, but don't be fooled by the greater quantity of egg mixture: it's fragile and should be treated gently.

Tips for Success

• Use a seasoned cast-iron or nonstick skillet.

• Lift the curds gently off the skillet's bottom in long, slow arcs with a heat-safe rubber spatula designed for use on nonstick cookware.

• Take the curds out of the pan the moment they lose their runniness. Eggs can break over prolonged heat (that is, the liquid can fall out of suspension).

Variations: Add any of the following with the milk:

1 small plum tomato, seeded and chopped; ½ ounce purchased lump crabmeat; ½ teaspoon capers, drained and rinsed; ½ teaspoon chile powder; ¼ teaspoon mild or hot paprika; ¼ teaspoon curry powder; ¼ teaspoon dried oregano, crumbled or ½ teaspoon minced oregano leaves; ¼ teaspoon dried thyme or ½ teaspoon stemmed thyme; ¼ teaspoon garam masala; or ¼ teaspoon finely grated lemon zest.

You can also add ¼ ounce cheese, finely shredded or grated, per egg scrambled. (That's about 1 tablespoon per egg.) Add the cheese late in the process, during the last 10 or 15 seconds, just so it melts without its fat falling out of suspension.

Three Things to Do with Scrambled Eggs

I. Breakfast Burritos

Heat flour tortillas in the microwave on high until warm, about 20 seconds, then lay them on your work surface. Add a single recipe of Scrambled Eggs (page 14) to each tortilla as well as any of the following combinations before rolling the tortillas up:

1. Salsa, grated Monterey Jack, and chopped fresh cilantro

2. Warmed refried beans and seeded, cored, thinly sliced bell peppers

3. Tapenade and chopped fresh rosemary

4. Jelly and crème fraîche or sour cream

5. Chopped pitted black or green olives, sliced radishes, and warmed canned black beans

6. Guacamole and pickled or fresh sliced jalapeño chiles

7. Dijon mustard, sprouts, and some thinly sliced red onion

8. Corn kernels, scallions, and chopped parsley

9. Thawed frozen peas, chopped mint, and sour cream

10. A couple of slices of lox or smoked salmon and some chopped red onion

Salt eggs when they come out of the pan. Salting early can make them rubbery.

II. Scrambled Egg Sandwich

Toast 2 slices of whole wheat, rye, or oat bread, lightly butter them, and place a single recipe of scrambled eggs on one half. Top with tomato slices, lettuce leaves, and/or sliced or shredded Cheddar, queso blanco, Taleggio, Brie, or even blue cheese; close the sandwich.

To dress the sandwich up, add any fruit chutney, homemade (page 388) or purchased; or any salsa, homemade (page 47) or purchased. Or forgo the butter and use Tapenade (page 42), Hummus (page 43), Aïoli (page 45), Sun-Dried Tomato and Roasted Garlic Pesto (page 48) or Dijon mustard.

III. Migas

This Tex-Mex favorite is made by layering tortillas, scrambled eggs, and Chile con Queso on a plate. If you like, serve tortilla chips and some cooked sausage, preferably Mexican chorizo, on the side. *Makes 4 servings*

> 4 large corn or flour tortillas, warmed
> A quadruple batch of Scrambled Eggs
>   (page 14)
> Chile con Queso (recipe follows)
> ½ cup homemade salsa (see page 47) or
>   purchased salsa
> ¼ cup chopped cilantro leaves

1 Lay a warm tortilla on each serving plate. Top with a quarter of the eggs (that is, 2 eggs per person).

2 Pour ¼ cup Chile con Queso over the eggs, then top with 2 tablespoons salsa and 1 tablespoon chopped cilantro. Serve at once.

Chile con Queso

Double or triple this Mexican cheese sauce to make an appetizer dip. *Makes a little more than 1 cup*

> 2 tablespoons unsalted butter
> 1 small onion, finely chopped
> 2 garlic cloves, minced
> ½ cup diced canned green chiles, drained
>   (hot, medium, or mild)
> ¼ cup white wine or dry vermouth
> 6 ounces Cheddar, shredded
> 3 ounces Monterey Jack, shredded
> 2 ounces regular or low-fat cream cheese,
>   cubed
> About ½ cup (8 tablespoons) heavy cream,
>   at room temperature
> 1½ teaspoons ground cumin
> ½ teaspoon salt, or to taste
> ¼ teaspoon freshly ground pepper,
>   preferably white pepper
> Several dashes of hot red pepper sauce
>   to taste

1 Melt the butter in a large saucepan set over medium-low heat. The moment the foaming subsides, add the onion and cook, stirring often, until translucent, about 3 minutes. Add the garlic and chiles; cook for 20 seconds.

2 Pour in the wine or vermouth and scrape up any bits on the bottom of the pan. Continue cooking until the liquid in the pan has reduced to a glaze.

3 Add the cheese all at once, stir two or three times, and immediately remove the pan from the heat. Stir until the cheese melts, then begin adding cream in 1-tablespoon increments until a smooth, velvety sauce forms. Stir in the cumin, salt, pepper, and hot red pepper sauce.

Eggs, Lox, and Onions

This deli version of scrambled eggs is made milder by adding the lox at the end of cooking, rather than frying it in the fat. *Makes 4 servings*

6 large eggs
½ teaspoon freshly ground black pepper
2 tablespoons unsalted butter or olive oil
1 large onion, diced
8 ounces lox or thickly sliced smoked
    salmon, chopped (see Note)
Salt to taste

1 Whisk the eggs and pepper in a medium bowl until well beaten; set aside.

2 Melt the butter in a large nonstick skillet set over medium-low heat, tipping the skillet to coat the bottom thoroughly; or heat the skillet over medium-low heat and then swirl in the olive oil. Toss in the onion, reduce the heat to low, and cook slowly, stirring often, until golden and quite soft, about 8 minutes.

3 Pour in the eggs and wait for 15 seconds. Use a heat-safe rubber spatula to lift the fluffy curds off the pan's bottom, piling them up without breaking them up. All the while, tip and tilt the skillet to let more of the beaten eggs come into contact with the hot surface.

4 When the last of the liquid egg comes into direct contact with the hot pan, add the lox, stir once, and remove the pan from the heat. Scrape up the curds a couple more times, just to get the lox heated through and well combined but taking care to keep the fluffy eggs intact. Transfer to a serving plate or individual plates; season with salt, but remember that lox or smoked salmon is quite salty—taste the final dish before salting it.

Note: Spraying your knife with nonstick spray helps keep the salmon from sticking to it.

Eggs, Gravlax, and Onions: For a milder dish, substitute Gravlax (page 75) for the lox.

Eggs, Smoked Trout, and Onions: Substitute smoked trout for the smoked salmon.

Herbed Eggs, Lox, and Onions: Add 1 tablespoon chopped parsley leaves, 1 tablespoon minced fresh chives, 1 tablespoon stemmed thyme, or 2 teaspoons chili powder with the lox or smoked salmon.

Fried Eggs

Using a metal spatula against a fried egg invites a broken yolk. If you're going to flip it, do so up the pan's side with a deft flick. *Makes 1 fried egg*

> 1 large egg
> 1 teaspoon unsalted butter, 1 teaspoon olive oil, or 1 teaspoon walnut oil
> Salt and freshly ground black pepper to taste

1 Crack the egg into a small bowl, custard cup, or ramekin. Doing so will prevent egg shells in the skillet and will help you keep the egg from spreading across the pan.

2 Melt the butter or heat one of the oils in a small nonstick skillet over medium heat. Swirl the skillet around so that the fat coats the pan's bottom. Make sure you also coat the pan's side farthest from the handle (you will use this area to shape the fried egg).

3 Tip the hot skillet up slightly from the burner at a 10-degree angle. Pour the egg into the side of the skillet closest to the burner, into the shallow well created by the sides and the bottom as the skillet is tipped up. Count to 5, waiting just until the white starts to harden at the edges, then place the skillet back flat on the burner.

4 Cook until the white has turned opaque, about 25 seconds, then continue with one of these steps.

To make a sunny-side-up fried egg, slide the egg onto a plate and season with salt and pepper.

To make other kinds of fried eggs, gently flip the egg over by quickly but steadily moving the skillet away from you and then back toward you, so that the egg travels up the skillet's curved side and is caught by its bottom on the way down. Do so with a gentle, even stroke so as to preserve the yolk. (To practice beforehand, put a thin slice of tomato or onion in a cold skillet and flip away.)

For over-easy eggs, cook for 5 seconds, then slide the egg out of the skillet onto a plate by tilting the skillet until the egg slides off. Season with salt and pepper.

For over-hard eggs, continue cooking for about 20 seconds until the yolk feels hard when pressed with your finger. Slide the egg out of the pan and onto a serving plate before seasoning with salt and pepper.

Tips for Success

• Use a nonstick skillet with rounded edges (not straight sides).

• Even though you're working on a nonstick surface, add a bit of butter or other fat so the egg slides gracefully across the surface.

Poached Eggs

Simmering eggs very slowly renders them smooth, almost velvety. *Makes 2 poached eggs (can be doubled or tripled—see Notes)*

> 1 teaspoon vinegar (see Notes)
> 2 large eggs
> Salt and freshly ground black pepper to taste

1 Fill a medium saucepan about halfway with water, add the vinegar, and set over high heat just until the water comes to a bare simmer—a few spritzes, but not big bubbles. Meanwhile, crack the eggs into small, individual bowls, custard cups, or ramekins.

❷ Slip the eggs into the pan, then reduce the heat so that the water barely dances in the pan, never bubbles or boils.

❸ Cook undisturbed for 1 minute, just until the whites are somewhat set; then gently turn the eggs over with a slotted spoon and continue cooking just until you can see that the white has set, about 1 minute more. (If you prefer harder yolks, cook up to 1 additional minute.) Remove the eggs one at a time with the slotted spoon, holding each over the pan for a second or two to let water drain off before transferring to a serving bowl. Season with salt and pepper.

Notes: If you increase the yield, use a saucepan large enough that the eggs do not touch or overlap.

Do not necessarily increase the vinegar. Use the stated amount for up to 3 eggs. If you use a larger pot for 4 or more eggs, use 2 teaspoons vinegar.

Vinegar helps set the egg whites without their becoming feathery. Do not use balsamic or rice vinegar; neither has enough acid to do the job.

Eggs Poached in Red Wine: Use the technique above for poaching eggs, but omit the vinegar and substitute red wine for the water. Also add 1 minced shallot, 2 parsley sprigs, 1 thyme sprig, and 1 bay leaf in the saucepan. Bring the mixture to a low simmer and cook the eggs as directed. Season with salt and pepper after you've transferred the eggs to a serving bowl.

Egg Safety

While salmonella in eggs has become a fact of modern life, follow these steps to ensure that the eggs you buy are as safe as they can be:

❶ Keep eggs cool. Get them home from the store quickly. If the day's warm, put a cooler with a bag of ice in your trunk for the eggs (and other perishables).

❷ Set your refrigerator at 40°F. Store eggs in their carton (which has been designed to minimize carbon dioxide and moisture loss, both of which compromise freshness) on a lower shelf of your refrigerator (not on the door where the temperature swings are the most pronounced, thanks to its opening and closing all day).

❸ Crack an egg on a counter or other flat surface. Although eggs are washed at processing facilities, the shell can have residual contaminants. Cracking an egg on the counter prevents tiny pieces of the shell from being driven up into the white and yolk.

❹ Don't use the shell to separate eggs. Rather, wash your hands, then crack the egg into one cupped palm, letting the white slip through your fingers while you cradle the yolk. (Admittedly, this takes practice and a strong stomach.) Or buy a plastic or metal egg separator, available at most kitchenware stores.

❺ Serve egg dishes promptly. Bacteria proliferate between 40°F and 140°F.

❻ If you have leftover whites or yolks, freeze them separately for up to 1 year. Place the whites in a plastic container, seal it, and label it so you know when it was put in the freezer. Yolks, because of their high protein structure, coagulate when frozen; to prevent this, whisk ⅛ teaspoon salt into 4 large egg yolks before freezing. Thaw the whites or yolks overnight in your refrigerator and use at once following these formulas: 2½ tablespoons thawed egg white equals 1 large egg white; 1½ tablespoons thawed egg yolk equals 1 large egg yolk.

Two Streamlined Ways to Use Poached Eggs

I. Eggs Benedict

Hollandaise sauce, ham, eggs? What could be better? Nothing—except streamlining the whole thing so that it takes much less time and can be made any weekend morning. If you have concerns about the undercooked eggs in the Streamlined Hollandaise Sauce, seek out pasteurized eggs in their shells, now available at most supermarkets. *Makes 6 servings*

4 homemade (see page 227) or purchased
    English muffins, split open
8 slices Canadian bacon
8 large eggs
Streamlined Hollandaise Sauce (recipe follows)

1 Toast the English muffin halves and place them on four individual serving plates; set aside.

2 Heat the Canadian bacon either by putting the slices in a nonstick skillet set over medium heat until sizzling and lightly browned, or by placing them on a large plate, covering them with a paper towel, and microwaving on high until sizzling, about 2 minutes. Place one piece of Canadian bacon on each English muffin half.

3 Meanwhile, poach the eggs according to the recipe on page 18. It may be easier to divide the eggs, using two saucepans and poaching four in each. Use a slotted spoon to transfer the poached eggs to the plates, setting one on top of each piece of Canadian bacon. Pour the Streamlined Hollandaise Sauce over the eggs and serve at once.

Streamlined Hollandaise Sauce

The sauce can easily be doubled for a larger dish—or pour it over steamed asparagus or broccoli as a side dish for dinner. *Makes about ½ cup*

3 large egg yolks, preferably from
    pasteurized eggs
1 tablespoon lemon juice
¼ teaspoon salt
⅛ teaspoon cayenne
4 tablespoons (½ stick) unsalted butter

1 Place the egg yolks, lemon juice, salt, and cayenne in a blender but do not blend. Set aside.

2 Melt the butter in a small saucepan set over medium-low heat until the butter foams and then begins to subside. The moment it does, turn the blender on low speed and drizzle in the melted butter in the slightest, smallest stream while the blades are running. Once all the butter's been added, blend until smooth, about 15 seconds.

Cast-Iron Cookware: A Natural Nonstick

Cast-iron cookware is an excellent conductor of heat and a marvel of nonstick efficiency. However, its surface is full of tiny holes and gashes, so it must be "seasoned" before use (that is, those gaps must be filled with fat). To do so, coat the pan in vegetable oil, then place it in a preheated 300°F oven for 1 hour. Cool to room temperature, then repeat twice.

Never clean seasoned cast iron with detergent (which gets lodged in the pores) or steel wool (which rubs off the coating). Instead, pour kosher salt into the skillet and use its graininess and a paper towel to rub off any baked-on bits under warm running water. Afterward, sterilize the surface and prevent rust by heating the skillet to smoking over high heat before cooling it back to room temperature. Store cast-iron cookware uncovered so moisture doesn't build up during humid weather.

II. Eggs Florentine

For a streamlined version of the classic brunch dish, poached eggs are set on a bed of creamed spinach, topped with a bread crumb mixture, and broiled. *Makes 6 servings*

    3 tablespoons plain dried bread crumbs
    3 tablespoons finely grated Parmigiano-
        Reggiano
    2 teaspoons minced oregano leaves or
        1 teaspoon dried oregano
    1 teaspoon minced rosemary leaves or
        ½ teaspoon crushed dried rosemary
    ¼ teaspoon freshly ground black pepper
    6 large eggs
    Unsalted butter, for greasing the baking dish
    Streamlined Florentine Sauce
        (recipe follows)
    Salt to taste

1 Mix the bread crumbs, Parmigiano-Reggiano, oregano, rosemary, and pepper in a small bowl; set aside.

2 Poach the eggs according to the recipe for Poached Eggs on page 18.

3 Preheat the broiler. Lightly butter a 9-inch broiler-safe baking dish or casserole; pour the warmed Streamlined Florentine Sauce into it.

4 Use a slotted spoon to transfer the eggs to the baking dish, placing them on top of the spinach sauce. (Remove the eggs well before the yolks set; they will be broiled and continue to cook.) Sprinkle the prepared bread crumb mixture over the eggs.

5 Broil until the bread crumbs are browned and crisp and the sauce is lightly bubbling at the edges of the dish, about 1 minute. Use a large serving spoon to scoop up the eggs, topping, and sauce, transferring them to individual serving plates. Salt lightly to taste.

Streamlined Florentine Sauce
Makes about ¾ cup

You can also use this simple sauce as a "creamed spinach" side to almost any egg dish—or even as a side to steaks or roast chicken.

    One 10-ounce package frozen chopped
        spinach, thawed and squeezed of any
        excess moisture
    ½ cup half-and-half or heavy cream
    2 tablespoons unsalted butter, melted and
        cooled
    2 tablespoons grated Parmigiano-Reggiano
    ½ teaspoon finely grated lemon zest
    ½ teaspoon salt

1 Place the spinach, half-and-half or cream, melted butter, Parmigiano-Reggiano, lemon zest, and salt in a blender. Cover and blend until smooth, scraping down the sides of the canister as necessary.

2 Pour into a small saucepan, set over very low heat, and bring to the first bubble, just heated through, stirring occasionally. Cover and set aside to keep warm.

Variation: Substitute frozen, chopped broccoli for the spinach. Open the package and thaw the broccoli in a colander to remove excess moisture.

Want hard-boiled eggs for breakfast? Use the technique for hard-cooking eggs in the Deviled Eggs recipe (page 59).

Looking for breakfast breads? Check out the muffins, English muffins, quick loaves, and raised sticky buns in the bread chapter (page 215).

Soft-Boiled Eggs

Soft-boiled eggs cry out for toast: a runny yolk encased by a creamy white. *Makes 1 soft-boiled egg*

1 large egg
Salt and freshly ground black pepper to taste

1 Place the egg in its shell in a medium saucepan and cover with cold water to a depth of 1 inch. Place the pan over medium-high heat and bring to a gentle boil.

2 Cover the pan and set it aside off the heat for 2 minutes for soft centers, 4 minutes for harder ones.

3 Drain and refresh the egg with lukewarm running water until the shell is warm, not hot.

4 To serve, crack the small end of the shell with the back of a flatware spoon, peel off the top, and scoop the egg into a bowl; season with salt and pepper and eat at once.

Alternatively, place the egg in an egg cup and use a sharp knife to lop off about ½ inch from the top, season the egg inside with salt and pepper, and use a small spoon to mine the egg from its shell.

Shirred Eggs

Pronounced "sherd eggs," this British staple requires heat-safe ramekins or custard cups to bake the eggs into a slightly firmer version of poached eggs. *Makes 4 shirred eggs*

Unsalted butter or nonstick spray, for
    greasing the ramekins or cups
¼ cup whole milk, half-and-half, or heavy
    cream (see Note)
2 tablespoons minced chives or the green
    part of a scallion
2 tablespoons minced parsley leaves
4 large eggs
Salt and freshly ground black pepper to taste

1 Position the rack in the center of the oven and preheat it to 350°F. Lightly butter four 1-cup heatproof custard cups or ramekins or spray them with nonstick spray; set aside.

2 Warm the milk, half-and-half, or cream in a small saucepan over very low heat until a few puffs of steam come off the surface; do not simmer. Stir in the chives and parsley. Cover and set aside off the heat for 10 minutes.

3 Place 1 teaspoon cream-and-herb mixture in each custard cup or ramekin; break an egg into each. Divide the remaining cream mixture among the cups (a scant 1 tablespoon in each).

4 Place the ramekins or cups on a large, lipped baking sheet, spacing them at least 2 inches apart for even heat flow. Bake just until the whites begin to set. At 8 minutes, the whites should be set but the yolks still runny; at 12 to 14 minutes, the yolks should be set, too. Remove from the oven, season with salt and pepper, and let stand for 2 minutes at room temperature before serving. (Be forewarned: the cups or ramekins are still quite hot.)

Note: Direct heat toughens egg whites considerably, so you need a small barrier of fat to protect them in the oven. Do not use low-fat or fat-free milk.

Variations: Substitute oregano, tarragon, marjoram, or thyme for the parsley.

Sprinkle a little homemade salsa (see page 47), purchased salsa, or Asian chili sauce over the eggs when they come out of the oven.

Prosciutto-Wrapped Shirred Eggs: Cut 4 paper-thin slices of prosciutto in half the short way. Butter or spray the cups or ramekins, then line each with the prosciutto slices, making sure the strips cover the inside surface without any prosciutto sticking out over the top. Place these lined cups or ramekins on a large, lipped baking sheet and bake in the 350°F oven for 10 minutes. Remove, cool for 10 minutes, and continue with the main recipe from step 2. The eggs will cook faster in these prosciutto cups: about 6 minutes for runny-set and 10 minutes for hard-set.

Omelet

A fluffy omelet is a simple pleasure, provided you have a nonstick skillet. *Makes 1 omelet*

> 1 teaspoon unsalted butter or olive oil
> 3 large eggs, lightly whisked in a small bowl until almost uniform
> Salt and freshly ground black pepper to taste

1 Melt the butter in a medium nonstick skillet over medium heat; or heat a medium nonstick skillet over medium heat, then swirl in the olive oil. Make sure the fat coats the skillet's bottom.

2 Pour in the eggs and immediately tip the pan so that they evenly coat it. Wait for 10 seconds, then use a heat-safe rubber spatula to push the done eggs, the parts nearest the pan's rim, toward the center, tilting the pan to let more of the liquid egg come into contact with the hot surface. Keep doing this for about 1 minute, continually loosening the cooked egg from the pan's surface. Do not mound the curds as you would for scrambled eggs; keep the omelet flat in the skillet by continually pouring more of the liquid egg to the edges and pushing the cooked parts back from the edges, like crumpling up a tablecloth back from a table's edge.

3 Once the omelet is almost set, tilt the pan up by the handle; loosen the "highest" part of the omelet from the edge. Continue lifting the pan up and use the heat-safe spatula to guide the flat omelet as it falls down over itself, the flap you created from the upper edge rolling down as you raise the pan higher and loosen more of the omelet.

4 Place the pan over the serving plate and tip it all the way up so the handle is straight up over the plate. Gently turn the omelet out onto the plate, letting the last bit flop over the top of the omelet on the plate. Season with salt and pepper.

Three Ways to Gussy Up Omelets

I. Herbed Omelets

Sprinkle any of the following or any combination of the following over the omelet just as it's set, just before you start to roll it out of the pan: 1 to 2 tablespoons chopped parsley leaves, 1 to 2 tablespoons minced chives or the minced green part of a scallion, 2 teaspoons chopped fresh oregano leaves, 2 teaspoons chopped fresh tarragon leaves, 2 teaspoons chopped fresh rosemary, 1 to 2 teaspoons stemmed thyme, or ¼ teaspoon garlic powder.

II. Filled Omelets

Add any of the following in a line down the middle of the omelet once it's almost set, before you start rolling it out of the skillet: 1 ounce grated cheese, ¼ cup jam or jelly; ¼ cup Ragù (page 190), Marinara Sauce (page 182), or purchased pasta sauce; ¼ cup purchased cooked lump crabmeat; 2 tablespoons Blackberry-Rhubarb Chutney (page 388) or purchased chutney; 2 to 3 tablespoons Sage Pesto (page 293), Sun-Dried Tomato and Roasted Garlic Pesto (page 48), or purchased pesto; 6 cooked medium cocktail shrimp and Classic Cocktail Sauce (page 61); 3 strips fried bacon, crumbled; 3 cooked asparagus spears; 2 shallots, softened in a small skillet with 1 teaspoon olive oil or unsalted butter over medium heat; 1 or 2 jarred whole roasted red peppers or pimientos.

III. Sauced Omelets

Top an omelet on the serving plate with any of the following: Streamlined Hollandaise Sauce (page 20); Streamlined Florentine Sauce (page 21); Salsa, either homemade (page 47) or purchased; or Salsa Cruda (page 179).

Frittata

A frittata is like a flat omelet cut into wedges for serving. It's easier to make since you just bake the whole thing in the oven. *Makes 4 servings*

6 large eggs
¼ cup milk (regular, low-fat, or fat-free) or
    half-and-half
One of the five fillings (recipes follow),
    made in an oven-safe skillet
Salt and freshly ground black pepper
    to taste

1 Position the rack in the center of the oven and preheat the oven to 400°F. Whisk the eggs and milk or half-and-half in a medium bowl until smooth; set aside.

2 Prepare one of the fillings below.

3 The moment the filling has been made, pour the eggs over that filling in the hot skillet, place it in the oven, and bake until the top is no longer runny and the eggs are puffed, about 15 minutes. Season with salt and pepper before serving.

Bacon, Potato, and Chive Filling
    2 medium yellow potatoes, such as Yukon
        golds, peeled and cut into ½-inch chunks
    6 ounces thick-cut bacon
    1 medium onion, chopped
    2 tablespoons chopped chives or the green
        part of a scallion

1 Place the potatoes in a medium saucepan, cover with cool water to the depth of 1 inch, set the pan over high heat, and bring to a boil. Reduce the heat to medium and cook until tender when pierced with a fork, about 8 minutes. Drain in a colander set in the sink.

2 Fry the bacon in a 10-inch, oven-safe skillet set over medium heat until crisp, turning occasionally, about 4 minutes. Transfer to a paper towel–lined plate and drain off all but 1 tablespoon of the fat in the pan.

3 Return the skillet to medium heat and add the onion. Cook, stirring frequently, until soft, about 3 minutes.

4 Add the potatoes and chives, stir well, then crumble in the bacon. Continue with step 3 of the main recipe to bake the frittata.

Crab and Scallion Filling
    1 tablespoon olive oil
    6 medium scallions, cut into 1-inch
        chunks
    1 green bell pepper, cored, seeded, and
        thinly sliced
    8 ounces purchased cooked lump crabmeat,
        picked over for shell and cartilage
    1 ounce Parmigiano-Reggiano, grated

1 Heat a 10-inch, oven-safe skillet over medium heat. Swirl in the olive oil, then add the scallions and bell pepper. Cook, stirring frequently, until soft and aromatic, about 3 minutes.

2 Sprinkle the crab and cheese evenly into the pan. Continue with step 3 of the main recipe above to bake the frittata.

Southwestern Filling

1 tablespoon canola oil
1 medium shallot, thinly sliced into rings
1 red bell pepper, cored, seeded, and thinly
    sliced
8 ounces smoked deli ham, chopped
½ cup frozen corn kernels, thawed
1 garlic clove, minced
8 cherry tomatoes, quartered
1 tablespoon chopped parsley leaves
Several dashes of hot red pepper sauce to
    taste

1 Heat a 10-inch, oven-safe skillet over medium heat. Swirl in the canola oil, then add the shallot and bell pepper. Cook, stirring frequently, until soft, about 2 minutes. Stir in the ham, corn, and garlic; cook for 30 seconds.

2 Add the tomatoes and cook until softened, about 1 minute. Stir in the parsley and hot red pepper sauce; flatten the filling out across the skillet's entire surface. Continue with step 3 of the main recipe to bake the frittata.

Spinach Filling

1 tablespoon olive oil
1 medium onion, diced
2 garlic cloves, minced
One 10-ounce package frozen
    spinach, thawed and squeezed
    of all moisture
2 ounces Parmigiano-Reggiano,
    Pecorino Romano, or Asiago,
    grated
¼ teaspoon grated nutmeg

1 Heat a 10-inch, oven-safe skillet over medium heat, then swirl in the olive oil and add the onion. Cook, stirring often, until translucent, about 4 minutes. Add the garlic and cook for 15 seconds.

2 Add the spinach, stir well, then sprinkle the cheese and nutmeg over the dish. Flatten the filling out to cover the skillet. Continue with step 3 of the main recipe to bake the frittata.

Pea and Mint Filling

1 tablespoon unsalted butter
2 medium shallots, thinly sliced into
    rings
1½ cups frozen peas
1 tablespoon chopped mint leaves
½ cup sour cream (regular, low-fat, or
    fat-free)

1 Heat a 10-inch, oven-safe skillet over medium heat, then melt the butter, add the shallots, and cook until softened, stirring often, about 2 minutes. Stir in the peas and mint; cook for 15 seconds. Continue with step 3 of the main recipe to bake the frittata.

2 When the frittata comes out the oven, cool for a few minutes, then dot the top with sour cream before serving.

Cheese Topping for a Frittata

Once the frittata is set, remove it from the oven and preheat the broiler. Sprinkle 2 to 3 ounces finely grated Parmigiano-Reggiano, Jarlsberg, Emmentaler, Gruyère, Gouda, Edam, or Asiago over the top of the dish. Place under the broiler, about 4 inches from the heat source, and cook until the cheese melts and browns lightly, about 2 minutes. (If your skillet has a wooden handle, wrap it in aluminum foil to protect it.)

Baked Huevos Rancheros

Most versions of this Tex-Mex classic use either raw, overpowering salsa poured over poached eggs or a thick tomato sauce, reminiscent of pasta sauce. We prefer to poach the eggs right in the sauce. Have plenty of warm tortillas on the side (see page 241). *Makes 6 servings*

1 tablespoon canola oil
1 medium onion, diced
2 small tomatillos, diced, or ¼ cup canned diced tomatillos
2 garlic cloves, minced
1 fresh jalapeño chile, seeded and minced
6 plum or Roma tomatoes, chopped
1 teaspoon ground cumin
½ teaspoon dried oregano
½ teaspoon salt
½ teaspoon freshly ground black pepper
6 large eggs
1 ounce Cheddar, preferably a hard, aged Cheddar, finely grated

1 Position the rack in the lower third of the oven and preheat the oven to 375°F.

2 Heat a large oven-safe skillet over medium heat, then swirl in the canola oil. Add the onion and tomatillos; cook, stirring frequently, until softened, about 3 minutes. Add the garlic and jalapeño; cook for 15 seconds.

3 Pour the tomatoes into the pan, stir well, and bring the mixture to a simmer. Stir in the cumin, oregano, salt, and pepper. Cook, uncovered, until the tomatoes break down and start to form a sauce, stirring occasionally, about 7 minutes.

4 Remove the skillet from the heat. Make six shallow indentations in the salsa, just little nests that will hold the eggs. Crack the eggs into cups or ramekins and slide the eggs from these onto the top of the cooked salsa, placing them in the indentations. Once the eggs are in the pan, gently spoon a little of the sauce (perhaps 2 teaspoons) over each egg, then sprinkle the grated cheese over them and the sauce.

5 Bake until the eggs are set, about 10 minutes. To serve, spoon the eggs and some of the cooked salsa onto individual plates.

Variations: Substitute 1 small green bell pepper, cored, seeded, and chopped, for the tomatillos.
Substitute 1 chile in adobo, minced; 1 poblano chile, seeded and minced; or one 3-ounce can mild chopped green chiles for the fresh jalapeño.

Cheese Fondue Egg Casserole

Here's the ultimate take on a big-crowd, holiday-favorite breakfast. You must make it the night before so that it can set up in the refrigerator before it bakes. *Makes 6 servings (see Note)*

2 tablespoons unsalted butter, plus additional for greasing the baking dish
1 medium onion, finely chopped
12 ounces white button mushrooms, cleaned and thinly sliced
2 teaspoons stemmed thyme or 1 teaspoon dried thyme
½ teaspoon ground allspice
½ teaspoon salt
½ teaspoon freshly ground black pepper
6 ounces Gruyère, finely grated
6 ounces Emmentaler or Jarlsberg, finely grated
One 12-inch loaf day-old French or Italian bread, cut into ½-inch slices
¼ cup dry white wine
8 large eggs
¾ cup milk (regular, low-fat, or fat-free) or half-and-half

1 Melt the butter in a large skillet over medium heat. Add the onion; sauté until softened, about 3 minutes. Add the mushrooms and cook, stirring frequently, until they give off their liquid and it evaporates to a glaze, about 5 minutes.

2 Stir in the thyme, allspice, salt, and pepper. Set the pan off the heat to cool for 10 minutes.

3 Lightly butter a 10-inch round or a 9-inch square baking dish. Mix both cheeses in a medium bowl.

4 Place half the bread in the baking dish, cutting the slices to cover the pan's surface completely. Brush with 2 tablespoons wine. Top with half the mushroom mixture, then half the cheese mixture.

5 Lay the second layer of bread slices as before over all this, brush these slices with the remaining wine, then top them with the remaining mushroom mixture. Sprinkle the remaining cheese over the dish.

6 Whisk the eggs and milk or half-and-half in a medium bowl until smooth. Pour this mixture over the casserole. Cover and refrigerate for at least 8 hours or overnight.

7 Position the rack in the center of the oven and preheat the oven to 375°F.

8 Bake the casserole uncovered until puffed and brown, about 40 minutes. Cool on a wire rack for 5 minutes before serving.

Note: You can double this recipe; if you do, use an 11 × 17-inch baking dish.

Sausage and Cheese Fondue Casserole: Cook ½ pound crumbled sausage meat or sausage-style textured soy protein in the pan with the mushrooms.

Seafood and Cheese Fondue Casserole: Add 6 ounces small "salad" shrimp to the pan with the mushrooms during the last minute of cooking. Once you take the pan off the heat, stir in 4 ounces crabmeat, picked over for shell and cartilage.

Prosciutto and Cheese Fondue Casserole: Layer 2 ounces thinly sliced prosciutto in the casserole just before you add the second layer of bread slices. Omit the salt.

Spinach and Cheese Fondue Casserole: Thaw a 10-ounce package frozen chopped spinach and then squeeze it dry of all excess water. Layer this spinach in the casserole before you add the second layer of bread slices.

Know Your Egg Anatomy!

Shell. A calcium carbonate casing. The color, variable with chicken breeds, indicates nothing about nutritive value.

Albumen. The layers of translucent material that surround the yolk; the major sources of protein and riboflavin. In fresh eggs, a thick layer mounds up around the yolk.

Yolk. The yellow center, one of the few natural sources for Vitamin D, outside of sunlight. In a fresh egg, it's high and perky. The color may change based on a chicken's diet, but these variations do not necessarily indicate a nutritive change.

Chalazae. The edible, ropey strands that anchor the yolk in the shell. Since they dissolve over time, their absence reflects poorly on the egg's freshness.

Blood Spot. A red mark on the yolk, caused by a rupture of blood vessels in the hen as the egg forms. It is not the embryonic beginnings of a chicken.

Mushroom Cheddar Quiche
on a Potato Crust

Instead of standard pastry, grated potatoes make a crunchy crust for this creamy quiche. Use only Russets: they have the right amount of starch for a stable crust. *Makes 6 servings*

2 large Russet potatoes, peeled

1 small onion

5 large eggs, at room temperature

½ teaspoon salt

1 tablespoon unsalted butter, plus additional for greasing the baking dish

12 ounces white button or cremini mushrooms, thinly sliced

¼ teaspoon grated nutmeg

1½ cups milk (regular, low-fat, or fat-free)

1 teaspoon Dijon mustard

½ teaspoon freshly ground black pepper

8 ounces Cheddar, grated

1 Position the rack in the middle of the oven and preheat the oven to 400°F. Lightly butter a 9-inch pie plate and set it aside.

2 Grate the potatoes through the medium holes of a box grater into a large bowl. Once they're grated, pick them up by the handfuls and squeeze out any excess moisture over the sink.

3 Grate the onion into the potatoes, again using the small holes of the box grater. Stir in 1 egg and the salt. Press this mixture into the prepared pie plate.

4 Bake until lightly browned, about 35 minutes. Remove from the oven and cool on a wire rack for at least 10 minutes. (The crust can be made in advance; once cooled to room temperature, cover it with plastic wrap and store it at room temperature for up to 1 day.)

5 Reduce the oven temperature to 375°F. Melt the butter in a large skillet set over medium heat. Add the mushrooms and cook, stirring frequently, until they give off their liquid and it reduces to a glaze, about 8 minutes. Sprinkle the nutmeg over the mushrooms and set aside.

6 Whisk the remaining 4 eggs, milk, mustard, and pepper in a medium bowl until fairly smooth.

7 Sprinkle half the grated cheese over the potato crust. Pour the contents of the skillet over the cheese, then top with the remaining cheese. Pour the prepared egg mixture over the cheese, evenly coating it.

8 Bake until browned and puffed, about 35 minutes. Cool on a wire rack for 5 minutes before serving.

For a quicker quiche, use a basic piecrust. Follow the instructions on page 592 for making the crust and on page 602 for prebaking it. Follow this recipe from step 5.

Or use a store-bought pie crust, following the instructions on the package for prebaking it.

Spinach Cheddar Quiche in a Potato Crust: Omit the mushrooms. Sauté one 10-ounce package frozen chopped spinach and 2 garlic cloves, minced, in the butter until hot and aromatic, about 2 minutes.

Scallop Cheddar Quiche in a Potato Crust: Omit the butter, mushrooms, and nutmeg. Slice 8 ounces large scallops in half so each becomes two disks. Lay these over the first layer of grated cheese.

❋ *The Real Reasons for Maple Syrup* ❋

If it doesn't involve eggs, breakfast should be an excuse for maple syrup. None of these dishes is dusted with confectioners' sugar or garnished with fruit. Why waste calories?

A road map for
Five Kinds of Pancakes

There's only one trick to perfect pancakes: never let the batter sit around. Of course, you can save time by mixing the dry and wet separately the night before; keep the dry on the counter and store the wet, covered, in the refrigerator. *Makes about eighteen 4-inch pancakes*

1 **Start with two large bowls,** one for the wet ingredients and one for the dry. Whisk each together separately.

1. Traditional Pancakes

Wet Ingredients
3 large eggs
2¼ cups milk
6 tablespoons unsalted butter, melted and cooled
2 teaspoons vanilla extract

Dry Ingredients
3 cups all-purpose flour
5 tablespoons sugar
1 tablespoon baking powder
½ teaspoon salt

2. Buttermilk Pancakes

Wet Ingredients
3 large eggs
2 cups buttermilk
4 tablespoons (½ stick) unsalted butter, melted and cooled

Dry Ingredients
2 cups all-purpose flour
¼ cup sugar
2 teaspoons baking soda
½ teaspoon salt

3. Buckwheat Pancakes

Wet Ingredients
4 large eggs
2¾ cups milk
6 tablespoons honey
¼ cup canola oil

Dry Ingredients
2¾ cups buckwheat flour
2 teaspoons baking powder
½ teaspoon salt

4. Gingerbread Pancakes

Wet Ingredients
2 large eggs
1¼ cups milk
1 cup sour cream
¼ cup molasses
4 tablespoons (½ stick) unsalted butter, melted and cooled
2 teaspoons vanilla extract

Dry Ingredients
2 cups all-purpose flour
2 tablespoons sugar
2 teaspoons baking powder
2 teaspoons ground ginger
½ teaspoon ground cinnamon
½ teaspoon salt

5. Multigrain Pancakes

Wet Ingredients
2 large eggs
2 cups milk
3 tablespoons walnut oil
1 teaspoon vanilla extract

Dry Ingredients
1 cup all-purpose flour
1 cup whole wheat flour
⅓ cup sugar
¼ cup wheat germ
1 tablespoon baking powder
½ teaspoon salt

2 Rub a large skillet or flat griddle, preferably nonstick, with a paper towel moistened with a little canola or vegetable oil and set it over medium heat; or spray it with nonstick spray and set it over medium heat; or melt 1 tablespoon unsalted butter in the pan over medium heat, tilting it to coat the bottom thoroughly (see Note).

3 Mix the wet ingredients into the dry with a fork, just until the lumps are gone—the batter should still be a little grainy with some undissolved flour.

4 Scoop up ¼ cup batter and pour it into a neat circle in the pan. Add more ¼-cup circles, as many as can fit without crowding. Cook just until permanent bubbles dot the surface of the cakes, about 2 minutes; then flip with a nonstick-safe spatula and continue cooking until lightly browned, about 1 more minute. You can transfer the cooked pancakes to a heat-safe platter and keep them warm in a 225°F oven while you make more (but for no more than 10 minutes).

Note: You may need to regrease the skillet or griddle between batches.

Blueberry Pancakes: You'll need a little less than 1 pint of fresh berries in total. Once the batter is scooped into the skillet or griddle, dot each cake with 6 to 9 fresh blueberries. Cook as directed.

(Frozen berries are too wet and mushy; they will turn the pancakes blue.)

Nutty Pancakes: Coarsely chop about 1 cup walnut pieces, pecan pieces, or skinned hazelnuts. Stir these into the dry ingredients before you mix in the wet ingredients.

Banana Nut Pancakes: Before mixing the wet into the dry, chop 1 peeled ripe banana and stir it into the wet ingredients. Also, stir about ¾ cup chopped walnut or pecan pieces into the dry ingredients.

Maple Syrup

Although maple syrup may call up images of autumn in New England, maple trees are actually tapped when the sap first runs, while there's still snow on the ground. Early in the season, it takes about 20 gallons of sap to make a gallon of syrup. As the season goes on and the sap gets diluted (more ground water, spring rains), it can take more than 50 gallons to make a gallon of syrup.

Maple syrup is sold by grades, marked on the bottle. In Vermont, the largest U. S. producer, it's divided into five grades: Grade A fancy light amber, Grade A medium amber, Grade A dark amber, Grade B (only for baking), and Grade C (almost like molasses and sold to commercial manufacturers). Although light amber is prized for its delicacy, we prefer medium amber, slightly stronger and more herbaceous.

Canadian syrup—85 percent of the global supply—is graded like Vermont's with Grade 1 divided into three subsets, followed by Grades 2 and 3. Most other U. S. states grade with fewer categories, but those marked Grade A or AA are always preferred. Breakfast demands the best. Why else would anyone get out of bed?

Apple Upside-Down Skillet Pancake

Use a cast-iron skillet or a high-sided sauté pan to hold this large, puffed pancake as it rises. *Makes 4 servings*

2 large eggs plus 2 large egg yolks
½ cup milk (regular, low-fat, or fat-free)
3 tablespoons unsalted butter, melted and cooled, plus 1 additional tablespoon unsalted butter
½ teaspoon vanilla extract
½ cup plus 1 tablespoon flour
3 tablespoons sugar
½ teaspoon baking powder
½ teaspoon baking soda
¼ teaspoon salt
4 tart apples, such as Rome or Granny Smith, peeled, cored, and thinly sliced
½ teaspoon ground cinnamon
Maple syrup for garnish

1 Position the rack in the center of the oven and preheat the oven to 400°F. Whisk the eggs and egg yolks, milk, melted butter, and vanilla in a medium bowl. In a large bowl, stir the flour, 1 tablespoon sugar, the baking powder, baking soda, and salt until uniform. Set both bowls aside until step 4.

2 Melt the remaining 1 tablespoon butter in a 10-inch cast-iron skillet or high-sided sauté pan set over medium heat. Add the apples and cook just until they begin to soften, about 2 minutes.

3 Stir in the remaining 2 tablespoons sugar and the cinnamon; reduce the heat to medium-low and continue cooking until the sugar melts, forms a sticky sauce, and starts to caramelize, about 5 minutes.

4 Use a fork to stir the egg mixture into the flour mixture—there should be no flour visible, but the batter may still be grainy with undissolved flour.

Pour over the apples, then place the skillet or sauté pan in the oven and bake until puffed and brown, about 20 minutes. Cool for 5 minutes before cutting into quarters and passing the syrup on the side.

Variations: Add ½ teaspoon rum extract or maple extract with the vanilla.

Add 1 teaspoon finely grated lemon zest with the salt.

Add ¼ teaspoon grated nutmeg or ground mace with the cinnamon.

Pear Upside-Down Pancake: Substitute 3 ripe pears, peeled, cored, and thinly sliced, for the apples.

Apple Matzo Brei Pancake

At Passover, kosher families cannot have leavened bread in the house and so use matzo, an unleavened bread, sort of like a cracker. Here, it's mixed with apples and eggs for a single skillet-sized pancake. *Makes 4 servings*

Four 6¼-inch × 6¼-inch squares matzo
2 cups boiling water
1 large apple, peeled, cored, and thinly sliced
3 large eggs
½ cup milk (regular, low-fat, or fat-free)
1 tablespoon sugar
½ teaspoon ground cinnamon
¼ teaspoon salt
1 tablespoon canola oil or unsalted butter
Maple syrup for garnish

1 Crumble the matzos into a large bowl, pour in the boiling water, and soak for 1 minute. Drain by holding a small plate over the bowl and tipping the bowl up to pour off the water. Stir in the apple slices. Set aside to cool for 5 minutes.

2 Meanwhile, whisk the eggs, milk, sugar, cinnamon, and salt in a medium bowl.

❸ Stir the egg mixture into the matzo mixture with a wooden spoon.

❹ Heat a 10-inch skillet, preferably nonstick, over medium heat and swirl in the canola oil; or melt the butter in the skillet over medium heat, tilting the pan to make sure the bottom is thoroughly coated with the butter. Add the batter, spreading it evenly to form a cake that takes up the whole skillet. Cook for 1 minute, shaking the skillet repeatedly to keep the matzo from sticking. Cover and cook for 4 minutes.

❺ Uncover, place a large plate over the skillet, then pick up the skillet and invert the whole thing, so that the matzo pancake flips onto the plate. Return the skillet to the heat and slide the matzo pancake back into the pan, uncooked side down. Cook until set and slightly browned, 1 to 2 minutes. To serve, cut into quarters and pass the syrup on the side.

Malt Waffles

These are the best of all worlds: crunch from cornmeal, flavor from malted milk powder. *Makes about six 8-inch waffles*

Canola oil, vegetable oil, or nonstick spray,
    for greasing the waffle iron
2 large eggs
1¼ cups milk (regular, low-fat, or fat-free)
4 tablespoons (½ stick) unsalted butter,
    melted and cooled
1 teaspoon vanilla extract
1½ cups plus 2 tablespoons all-purpose flour
⅓ cup yellow cornmeal
3 tablespoons sugar
3 tablespoons malted milk powder
1 tablespoon baking powder
1 teaspoon salt

❶ Lightly oil or spray a waffle iron, then preheat it according to the manufacturer's instructions.

❷ Whisk the eggs, milk, melted butter, and vanilla in a medium bowl until smooth; set aside.

❸ In a large bowl, whisk the flour, cornmeal, sugar, malted milk powder, baking powder, and salt in a large bowl until the cornmeal is even throughout the mixture.

❹ Use a fork to stir the wet ingredients into the dry, just until any lumps disappear and the batter is fairly smooth.

❺ Spoon about ½ cup waffle batter into the preheated iron, or as much batter as is indicated by the manufacturer's instructions. Close the iron and bake until lightly browned or crispy, depending on your taste (again, check the manufacturer's instructions for exact timing and any indicator lights or sounds). You can place the baked waffles on a large baking sheet and keep them warm in a preheated 225°F oven for up to 10 minutes.

Buttermilk Malt Waffles: Substitute buttermilk for the milk; omit the baking powder and use 2 teaspoons baking soda instead.

Spiced Malt Waffles: Stir in 1½ teaspoons ground ginger, 1 teaspoon ground cinnamon, and/or ¼ teaspoon grated nutmeg with the salt.

✲ Three Flavored Syrups ✲

For the best taste, never boil the syrup—it has been boiled in production—but serve it warm. Choose a medium or dark amber.

I. Vanilla Cinnamon Maple Syrup

Makes about 2 cups

2 cups maple syrup
One 4-inch cinnamon stick
1 vanilla bean

❶ Place the syrup and cinnamon stick in a small saucepan set over very low heat. Split open the vanilla bean and toss it into the syrup.

❷ Heat slowly, just until a couple of tiny bubbles fizz around the pan's inner rim and a puff or two of smoke rises from the surface. Remove the pan from the heat, cover, and set aside for 30 minutes. Remove the cinnamon stick and vanilla bean before serving.

To store: Transfer to a glass or plastic container, cover, and refrigerate for up to 2 weeks; reheat in a small saucepan or in the microwave before serving.

II. Blueberry Maple Syrup

Makes about 3 cups

1 tablespoon unsalted butter
1 cup fresh blueberries
2 cups maple syrup

❶ Melt the butter in a medium saucepan set over medium-low heat. Add the blueberries; cook, stirring occasionally, just until they start to break down, about 2 minutes.

❷ Remove the pan from the heat and stir in the maple syrup until the simmering stops. Cover and set aside off the heat for 20 minutes before serving.

To store: Transfer to a glass or plastic container, cover, and refrigerate for up to 3 days; reheat in a small saucepan or in the microwave before serving.

III. Walnut Butter Rum Maple Syrup

Makes a little over 3 cups

2 tablespoons unsalted butter
1 cup chopped walnut pieces
2 cups maple syrup
2 tablespoons dark rum, such as Myers's

1 Melt the butter in a medium saucepan over medium-low heat; add the walnut pieces. Cook, stirring often, until lightly toasted, about 2 minutes.

2 Stir in the maple syrup and remove the pan from the heat. Stir in the rum, cover, and set aside off the heat for 15 minutes before serving.

To store: Place in a glass or plastic container, cover, and refrigerate for up to 2 weeks; rewarm in a saucepan or in the microwave before serving.

Whole Wheat Banana Waffles

Whole wheat waffles can get heavy, but these are lightened up with mashed bananas. *Makes eight 8-inch waffles*

Canola oil, vegetable oil, or nonstick spray, for greasing the waffle iron
2 large eggs
2 ripe bananas, finely diced
1 cup milk (regular, low-fat, or fat-free)
2 tablespoons canola oil
1 teaspoon vanilla extract
1 cup all-purpose flour
1 cup whole wheat flour
3 tablespoons sugar
1 tablespoon baking powder
1 teaspoon ground cinnamon
½ teaspoon salt

1 Lightly oil or spray a waffle iron, then preheat it according to the manufacturer's instructions.

2 Whisk the eggs, bananas, milk, oil, and vanilla in a medium bowl until the eggs are lightly beaten; set aside.

3 Stir both flours, the sugar, baking powder, cinnamon, and salt in a large bowl. Use a fork to stir in the egg mixture just until a slightly grainy but thick batter forms (see Note).

4 Place about ½ cup batter in the heated waffle iron or as much batter as is indicated by the manufacturer's instructions. Close the iron and cook as directed until browned. You can place the cooked waffles on a large baking sheet in a preheated 225°F oven to keep warm until you've made all of them.

Note: Alternatively, place all the ingredients in a food processor fitted with the chopping blade; pulse several times to blend, then scrape down the sides of the bowl and process until fairly smooth. This method will give you a smoother batter, without any banana "lumps" in it.

Honey Wheat Waffles: Reduce the sugar to 1 tablespoon; whisk 2 tablespoons honey into the wet ingredients with the eggs.

Whole Wheat Peach Waffles: Omit the bananas and use 2 ripe medium peaches, peeled, pitted, and finely diced. (Do not use the food processor method to make the batter.)

Whole Wheat Banana Nut Waffles: Stir ½ cup chopped toasted pecan or walnut pieces into the dry ingredients with the flour. (Do not use the food processor method to make the batter.)

Oat Waffles

Soaking the oats in advance makes exceptionally creamy waffles. *Makes six 8-inch waffles*

1½ cups all-purpose flour
3 tablespoons sugar
2 teaspoons baking soda
½ teaspoon salt
¾ cup regular or low-fat buttermilk (do not use fat-free)
½ cup rolled oats (do not use quick-cooking or steel-cut)
2 large eggs, lightly beaten
¾ cup milk (regular, low-fat, or fat-free)
¼ cup canola oil, plus additional for greasing the waffle iron
1 teaspoon vanilla extract

❶ Whisk the flour, sugar, baking soda, and salt together in a large bowl; set aside.

❷ Whisk the buttermilk and oats in a medium bowl and set aside for 5 minutes. Meanwhile, lightly oil or spray a waffle iron, then preheat it according to the manufacturer's instructions.

❸ Whisk the eggs, milk, canola oil, and vanilla into the buttermilk mixture. Then stir this mixture into the flour mixture with a fork.

❹ Spoon ¼ cup batter into the iron, or as much batter as recommended by the manufacturer. Close the iron and bake until crispy, perhaps 2 minutes. To keep warm, place on a large baking sheet in a preheated 225°F oven while you make more waffles.

For lighter waffles, separate the yolks from the egg whites. Add the yolks where you would have added the whole eggs; beat the egg whites to stiff peaks with an electric mixer at high speed in a separate bowl, then fold them into the batter after the flour mixture.

Baked French Toast

French toast started out as a baked dessert, a way to turn day-old bread into bread pudding. So here's an old technique for a breakfast favorite: a make-ahead baked casserole—best with maple syrup, of course. *Makes about 8 servings*

Unsalted butter, for greasing the pan
One 8-ounce plain Italian bread, challah, or brioche, preferably day-old, cut into 1-inch slices
6 large eggs
2½ cups milk (regular, low-fat, or fat-free)
2 tablespoons sugar
2 teaspoons vanilla extract
½ teaspoon ground cinnamon
¼ teaspoon salt

❶ Lightly butter a 13 × 9-inch baking pan. Lay the bread slices in the pan, fitting them in fairly snugly without any overlap. If there are some gaps, the bread will eventually expand to fill them.

❷ Whisk the eggs, milk, sugar, vanilla, cinnamon, and salt in a large bowl until fairly smooth; pour over the bread in the pan. Cover and refrigerate for at least 8 hours or overnight.

❸ Position the rack in the center of the oven and preheat the oven to 325°F. Set the casserole out on the counter for 10 minutes to bring it back to room temperature.

❹ Bake, uncovered, until puffed and brown, about 45 minutes. Cool for 5 minutes on a wire rack before serving.

Variations: Wedge ¼ cup dried raisins, cranberries, currants, blueberries, or chopped dried apples among the bread slices, taking care to distribute them evenly in the pan.

Reduce the milk to 2¼ cups; add ¼ cup gold rum with the remaining milk.

Add ¼ teaspoon grated nutmeg with the cinnamon.

Baked Blintzes

We prefer these stuffed crepes baked because the filling has more time to melt and meld. We also like them with maple syrup on the side, an utterly untraditional approach. *Makes 18 blintzes*

4 large eggs

2 cups milk (regular, low-fat, or fat-free)

6 tablespoons unsalted butter, melted and cooled, plus additional for greasing the skillet and the baking dish

1 teaspoon salt

1½ cups all-purpose flour

1 cup regular or low-fat ricotta (do not use fat-free)

8 ounces regular or low-fat cream cheese (do not use fat-free), softened to room temperature

3 tablespoons sugar

2 teaspoons vanilla extract

2 large egg yolks, at room temperature

Maple syrup for garnish

1 First, to make the crepes, place the whole eggs, milk, 2 tablespoons melted butter, and the salt in a large blender or in a food processor fitted with the chopping blade; cover and blend or process until smooth. Add the flour; cover again and blend or process until smooth, scraping down the sides of the bowl or canister once or twice to make sure all the flour is incorporated. Alternatively, make this batter in a large bowl with a whisk; once you've whisked together the egg mixture, whisk in the flour in small increments,

just 1 or 2 tablespoons at a time, to create the smoothest, airiest batter.

2 Place a dab of butter on a paper towel or piece of wax paper and use it to grease a 10-inch skillet, preferably nonstick. Set the skillet over medium-low heat for 1 minute. Pour 3 tablespoons of the batter into the skillet; tilt and tip the skillet until the batter completely coats the bottom. Cook until lightly mottled, about 30 seconds. Peel up the crepe, preferably with nonstick-safe tongs, and flip it. Cook about 30 more seconds, just until blond and set. Remove the crepe to a plate and continue making more, greasing the skillet after every two or three and stacking the crepes on the plate as they come out of the skillet.

3 Position the rack in the center of the oven and preheat the oven to 350°F. Lightly butter a 13 × 9-inch baking dish.

4 Use a fork to mix the ricotta, cream cheese, sugar, vanilla, and the egg yolks in a medium bowl until smooth.

5 Place one of the crepes on your work surface; spoon 2 tablespoons of the cheese filling in a long log shape in the middle of the crepe. Fold the crepe over the ends of the log, then roll it up. Place it seam side down in the prepared baking dish and continue filling more crepes.

6 Once they're all filled and in the pan, brush them generously with some of the remaining melted butter. Bake until lightly browned, about 20 minutes, brushing every 5 minutes or so with more of the remaining melted butter. Cool on a wire rack for 5 minutes before serving with maple syrup on the side.

No wimpy sides! Some of these are substantial enough to stand on their own. All are fit for celebration mornings.

Hash Browns

The best hash browns are made with Yukon gold potatoes, a yellow-fleshed varietal with a great balance of starch and moisture. Our version is actually a take on röesti, a classic Swiss dish of buttery fried potatoes. *Makes 6 servings*

> 3 large Yukon gold potatoes (about 1¼ pounds), peeled
> 1 small onion
> ½ teaspoon salt
> ½ teaspoon freshly grated black pepper
> 6 tablespoons unsalted butter

1 Grate the potatoes and onion through the large holes of a box grater or with a food processor fitted with the grating attachment. Stir in the salt and pepper.

2 Melt 2 tablespoons of the butter in a 12-inch skillet, preferably nonstick, set over medium heat. The moment the foam starts to subside, add the potato mixture, pressing down with the back of a wooden spoon or a rubber spatula. Cook undisturbed until the bottom begins to brown, about 6 minutes.

3 Place a large plate over the skillet, then invert the skillet and plate together, so that the potato pancake falls onto the plate. Return the skillet to the heat, add 2 more tablespoons butter, and slip the potato pancake back into the skillet, "raw" side down. Cook undisturbed for another 4 minutes.

4 Break up the potato cake with a wooden spoon into chunks. Add the remaining 2 tablespoons butter and continue cooking, stirring often, until crispy outside and tender inside the potato chunks, about 5 more minutes.

Variations: Substitute olive oil or walnut oil for the butter. (Do not use toasted walnut oil.)

Stir any of the following into the potato mixture with the salt and pepper:

1 tablespoon chopped rosemary leaves or 2 teaspoons crumbled dried rosemary, 1 tablespoon chopped tarragon leaves or 2 teaspoons dried tarragon, 2 teaspoons curry powder, 2 teaspoons minced sage leaves or 1 teaspoon rubbed sage, or 2 teaspoons stemmed thyme or 1 teaspoon dried thyme.

Sweet Potato Hash

This hash is made with a combination of red-skinned potatoes and sweet potatoes—both of which have been cut into small, even cubes. Have your butcher slice the Canadian bacon thicker than the usual packaged variety, about ½ inch thick. Sweet potatoes break down easily, so stir the hash just enough to keep it from sticking. *Makes 6 main-course or 10 side servings*

> ¾ pound red-skinned potatoes (about 2 large), scrubbed and cut into ½-inch pieces
> ¾ pound sweet potato (about 1 medium), peeled and cut into ½-inch pieces
> 4 tablespoons (½ stick) unsalted butter

1 large onion, diced
1 large green bell pepper, cored, seeded, and finely chopped
3 garlic cloves, minced
1 pound Canadian bacon, cut into ½-inch cubes
⅔ cup chicken or vegetable broth
2 tablespoons vegetable oil
¼ pound fresh spinach leaves, stemmed and coarsely chopped
1 tablespoon apple cider vinegar
Freshly ground black pepper to taste

1 Place the potatoes in a pot, cover with cool water to a depth of 1 inch, set over high heat, and bring to a boil. Reduce the heat and simmer for 5 minutes. Drain in a colander set in the sink.

2 Melt the butter in a very large skillet, preferably nonstick, over medium-low heat. Add the onion and bell pepper; cook until soft, about 4 minutes, stirring frequently. Add the garlic and cook for 15 seconds.

3 Add the Canadian bacon and cook, stirring constantly, for 1 minute. Add about ½ cup of the broth, the partially cooked potatoes, and the vegetable oil. Reduce the heat to very low and cook, stirring frequently but gently, until the broth has been absorbed and the potatoes are starting to get tender and a little crispy, 10 to 12 minutes.

4 Stir in the remaining broth, the spinach, and vinegar. Cook until the spinach wilts, about 2 minutes; season with pepper as desired. (The hash can be made in advance: cool to room temperature, place in a baking dish, cover, and refrigerate for up to 2 days; reheat, covered, in a preheated 350°F oven for 10 minutes.)

Corned Beef Hash: Omit the Canadian bacon and spinach. Add ½ pound cooked corned beef, cut into ½ cubes, with the vinegar.

Brie Grits

The sweetest, creamiest cheese grits are made with soft, ripe cheese. *Makes 6 servings*

2 cups vegetable broth
2 cups water
¼ cup milk (regular, low-fat, or fat-free)
¼ cup dry white wine or dry vermouth
1 cup quick-cooking grits
4 ounces Brie, rind removed, cut into ½-inch chunks (see Note)
¼ teaspoon grated nutmeg

1 Combine the broth, water, milk, and wine or vermouth in a medium saucepan and bring it to a simmer over medium-high heat.

2 Slowly whisk in the grits, reduce the heat to very low, cover, and cook at the lowest simmer until thickened, until most of the liquid has been absorbed, 10 to 12 minutes.

3 Remove the pan from the heat; stir in the cheese just until it melts. Stir in the nutmeg, cover, and set aside for 5 minutes before serving.

Note: To make the cheese easier to cut, place it in the freezer for about 20 minutes.

Variations: Substitute any soft goat cheese, such as Montrachet, for the Brie.
For a stronger taste, substitute Taleggio or even Camembert for the Brie.
Substitute coarsely grated Asiago or Parmigiano-Reggiano for the Brie.
Stir in 1 tablespoon chopped fresh rosemary with the cheese.

Creamy Cantaloupe and Mint Salad

With some yogurt and honey, a fresh melon salad makes a fine breakfast side. You can't make this easy side in advance because the yogurt and salt will cause the melon to weep too much. Always smell cantaloupes when buying to make sure they're sweet. *Makes 6 servings*

1 cup yogurt (regular, low-fat, or fat-free)
2 tablespoons honey
1 teaspoon vanilla extract
1 teaspoon ginger juice
¼ teaspoon salt
Two 3-pound cantaloupes, cut in half and seeded—then cut into wedges, peeled, and cut into 1-inch cubes; or scooped into 1-inch balls with a melon baller
2 tablespoons chopped mint leaves

❶ Whisk the yogurt, honey, vanilla, ginger juice, and salt in a small bowl.

❷ Place the melon chunks and mint in a bowl. Pour the dressing over the top and toss gently.

Variations: Substitute lemon juice for the ginger juice.

Add 1 tablespoon poppy seeds with the yogurt.

Omit the ginger juice and mint; stir in 1 teaspoon ground cinnamon with the vanilla.

Substitute honeydew for the cantaloupe—or use a combination of the two.

Substitute 1 quart strawberries, sliced, for one of the melons.

Dried Fruit Compote

This compote makes a great starter—or a wintry breakfast on its own alongside a batch of Buttermilk Muffins (page 234). Look for soft, pliable dried fruits, without brown spots. You can also serve this easy compote as a dessert with Sweetened Whipped Cream (page 522). *Makes 6 servings*

6 whole cloves
4 whole allspice berries
3 cardamom pods
1 star anise pod
3½ cups water, plus additional as needed
1 cup sugar
¼ cup honey
Two 4-inch cinnamon sticks
12 pitted prunes
10 dried red plum halves
8 dried peach halves, each halved
6 dried pear halves, each halved
6 dried figs, stemmed
6 dried pineapple rings, quartered
¼ teaspoon salt

❶ Seal the cloves, allspice berries, cardamom pods, and star anise pods in a tea ball. Or wrap in a small piece of cheesecloth, tie with butcher's twine, and set aside.

❷ Stir the water, sugar, and honey in a large saucepan over medium-high heat until the sugar dissolves. Drop in the cinnamon sticks and the prepared spice ball, then bring the mixture to a simmer, undisturbed.

❸ Stir in the prunes, dried plums, peaches, pears, figs, and pineapple rings; bring the liquid back to a simmer.

❹ Cover, reduce the heat to low, and simmer until the fruit is soft, about 30 minutes. If the liquid gets absorbed (because the dried fruit was especially dry), add more water in ¼-cup increments. When done, the compote should have enough liquid to act as a sauce when it's served.

5 Remove the pan from the heat and set aside, covered, until the mixture is at room temperature, about 1 hour. Remove the spice ball. Stir in the salt before serving.

To store: Transfer to a glass or plastic container, cover, and store in the refrigerator for up to 3 days; let it return to room temperature before serving.

Appetizers, Nibbles, and Snacks

WE USUALLY SERVE THESE BITES AND NIBBLES IN THE LIVING ROOM AND SO have come to refer to them as "coffee-table food."

Ever wonder why people gather in the kitchen at a party? Because the food's there. Move the food to the coffee table and nine times out of ten, you'll move the party to the living room, too.

A good appetizer is a momentary thing, barely noticed in the gap between "here" and "gone." You can spend hours on the main course, but you'll set a mood of grace and ease with a simple starter. If an appetizer's too deliberate, it's broken its promise: to give everyone time to settle in with a round of drinks. If you have to break out a full set of cutlery, what's the point?

There was once a classic distinction between *amuse-bouche* (French for "mouth fun") and first courses. In our modern world, the difference has largely vanished, except at high-end restaurants. Nowadays, appetizers are finger and fork foods before dinner—although we admit we've made a meal out of them many a night. Put together five or six, a range of flavors and textures, and you've got a party that can last well past the dinner hour.

◉ *No-Cook Spreads, Dips, and Salsas* ◉

These are the easiest of all: just a little chopping—and a lot of that can be done in a food processor or a blender. While most of these should be stored in the refrigerator, bring them to room temperature before serving because the flavors will have a chance to develop in ways that are impossible at colder temperatures.

Tapenade

This chunky olive paste is perfect on toasted bread. Be careful: there's a fine line between chopped and mushed. Use a high-quality, cold-pressed extra virgin olive oil. *Makes about 1 cup*

    2 cups pitted black olives, preferably
        Kalamata or niçoise olives
    2 garlic cloves, quartered
    1 tablespoon capers, drained
    1 teaspoon stemmed thyme
    ⅓ cup extra virgin olive oil
    2 tablespoons lemon juice
    ½ to 1 teaspoon freshly ground black pepper

Quick method:
Place all the ingredients in a food processor fitted with the chopping blade; pulse until coarsely chopped.

Traditional method:
Place the olives, garlic, capers, and thyme on a large cutting board, preferably one with a small trough at the edges. Rock a chef's knife through the ingredients, rotating the knife slowly so that it cuts everything into small chunks. Gather the mixture together several times and continue chopping until minced. Place in a serving bowl; stir in the olive oil, lemon juice, and pepper.

To store: Spoon into a nonreactive container, cover, and refrigerate for up to 4 days; allow the spread to return to room temperature before using.

Green Olive Tapenade: Substitute pitted green olives, preferably a tart Greek olive, for the black olives.

Roasted Garlic Tapenade: Wrap 4 unpeeled garlic cloves in a small foil packet, then roast in a preheated 400°F oven until soft, about 25 minutes. Squeeze the pulp into the food processor or onto the cutting board before you chop the olives. Reduce the olive oil to ¼ cup and the lemon juice to 1 tablespoon.

Sun-Dried Tomato Tapenade: Replace half the black olives with sun-dried tomatoes packed in oil, drained and rinsed. Reduce the olive oil to 3 tablespoons.

Nonreactive Bowls

A nonreactive bowl is one that will not form harmful chemical compounds when the acid in some foods comes in touch with its surface. Nonreactive materials include heat-safe glass, stainless steel, enameled iron, enameled steel, or some ceramics (certain glazes are reactive). Reactive cookware is made of tin, copper, and nonanodized aluminum, as well as certain dyes and chemicals in decorative glass and pottery.

Hummus

Tahini, a sesame seed paste, is a nutty foil to the chickpeas in this easy Middle Eastern dip. *Makes about 2 cups*

1⅔ cups canned chickpeas or garbanzo
    beans, drained and rinsed
2 garlic cloves
¼ cup tahini
¼ cup extra virgin olive oil
¼ cup lemon juice
1 teaspoon salt
½ teaspoon freshly ground black pepper

Place all the ingredients in a food processor fitted with the chopping blade or in a large blender. Pulse or blend a few times to get everything chopped, then scrape down the sides of the bowl and puree or blend until smooth.

To store: Transfer to a nonreactive bowl, cover, and refrigerate for up to 2 days.

Variations: Substitute peanut butter for the tahini.
    Substitute any toasted nut oil for the olive oil.
    Add 2 teaspoons dried dill, 1 teaspoon ground cumin, 1 teaspoon lemon pepper, or ¼ teaspoon cayenne pepper with the other ingredients.
    Roasted Red Pepper Hummus: Reduce the tahini and lemon juice to 2 tablespoons each; add 1 whole jarred roasted red pepper or pimiento.
    Roasted Garlic Hummus: Omit the garlic and use the pulp from a whole head of roasted garlic (see page 460).

Serving Suggestions: After you've spooned the hummus into a serving bowl, drizzle extra virgin olive oil, toasted walnut oil, toasted pumpkin seed oil, or syrupy balsamic vinegar over the spread.

Red Pepper Almond Dip

Almonds blend into a creamy silkiness in this quick dip. *Makes about 2 cups*

2 large jarred whole roasted red peppers or
    pimientos
1 cup whole raw almonds
1 garlic clove, slivered
1 teaspoon balsamic vinegar
½ teaspoon salt
½ teaspoon freshly ground black pepper
¼ teaspoon fennel seeds
⅛ teaspoon ground cinnamon

Place all the ingredients in a food processor fitted with the chopping blade; process until smooth, scraping down the sides of the bowl as necessary.

To store: Cover and refrigerate in a nonreactive bowl for up to 3 days, but allow the dip to come back to room temperature before serving.

Variations: Add 1 teaspoon dried oregano, ¼ teaspoon grated nutmeg, and/or ⅛ teaspoon cayenne pepper.

Guacamole

Good guacamole is all about technique: make a paste, then stir in the avocados. *Makes about 3 cups*

2 garlic cloves, quartered
½ teaspoon kosher or coarse-grained salt
½ teaspoon freshly ground black pepper
1 small shallot, minced
2 tablespoons lime juice
1 teaspoon chili powder
½ teaspoon ground cumin
2 or more dashes of hot red pepper sauce
3 very ripe, almost black Hass avocados
16 cherry tomatoes, quartered

① Place the garlic, salt, and pepper in a mortar and crush them into a paste with the pestle. Alternatively, place them in a medium bowl and use a sturdy fork to make a paste out of them, crushing the garlic against the salt grains.

② Mix in the shallot, lime juice, chili powder, cumin, and hot red pepper sauce, using the pestle or fork to make a chunky paste out of the mixture.

③ Cut all the avocados in half through the stem remnant, taking care to slice around the large pit. Gently twist the two halves apart, then remove the pits. Use a sharp paring knife to make crosshatch cuts through the flesh while it's still in the cuplike skin. Take care not to cut through the skin (especially if you're holding the avocado in your hand).

④ Hold four of the avocado halves over the mortar or bowl and turn the skin inside out, thereby letting the pieces fall into the spice mixture. Use a fork to stir and gently mash the avocado into the mixture, creating a chunky dip.

⑤ Turn the remaining two avocado halves inside out over the mortar or the bowl, letting the chunks fall in. Add the cherry tomatoes, too. Stir gently with a wooden spoon. (We do not recommend making guacamole ahead.)

Variations: Omit the hot red pepper sauce and add 1 small canned chipotle in adobo, stemmed and seeded, with the garlic cloves.

Substitute ¼ cup minced red onion for the shallot.

Substitute lemon juice for the lime juice.

Margarita Guacamole: Add 2 tablespoons high-quality tequila with the garlic, kosher salt, and pepper as you make the paste. Also add 2 teaspoons grated orange zest with the lime juice.

Black Bean Dip

Always rinse canned beans to rid them of the slippery residue left over from the canning process. We've added vinegar and orange zest for a flavorful kick. *Makes about 2 cups*

1¾ cups canned black beans, drained and
  rinsed
1 red or yellow bell pepper, cored, seeded,
  and roughly chopped
1 canned chipotle in adobo, stemmed
  (see Note)
2 tablespoons olive oil
2 tablespoons red wine vinegar
2 teaspoons finely grated orange zest
1 teaspoon ground cumin
½ teaspoon salt

Food processor method:
Place all the ingredients in a food processor fitted with the chopping blade; pulse until coarsely chopped, then process until fairly smooth.

Hand-ground method:
Place the beans in a large bowl and mash with a pastry cutter or a fork; finely chop the bell pepper and chipotle and add them to the mixture. Use the pastry cutter or fork to mash in the remaining ingredients.

To store: Transfer to a nonreactive bowl, cover, and refrigerate for up to 3 days.

Note: Seed the chipotle for a milder dip.

Variations: Substitute 1 fresh jalapeño chile, seeded, or 2 serrano chiles, seeded, for the chipotle in adobo.

Substitute 1 small red onion, roughly chopped, for the bell pepper.

Substitute walnut oil for the olive oil and add ¼ cup chopped toasted walnut pieces with the black beans.

White Bean and Sun-Dried Tomato Dip

This chunky Italian bean dip is often served on Tomato Bruschetta (page 57). It's also a good sandwich spread, a mayonnaise substitute. Working by hand will produce a chunkier spread—more traditional but also more work. *Makes about 2 cups*

1⅔ cups canned cannellini or Great
     Northern white beans, drained and
     rinsed
12 pitted black olives, roughly chopped
4 anchovy fillets, roughly chopped
¼ cup sun-dried tomatoes packed in oil,
     drained and roughly chopped
2 tablespoons olive oil
2 tablespoons lemon juice
2 tablespoons chopped parsley leaves
¼ teaspoon freshly ground black pepper

Food processor method:
Place all the ingredients in a food processor fitted with the chopping blade; pulse just until combined, then process just until chunky.

Hand-ground method:
First, mince the anchovy fillets. Then place them and the beans in a bowl; mash with a pastry cutter or two forks. Stir in the remaining ingredients.

To store: Transfer to a nonreactive bowl, cover, and refrigerate for up to 2 days.

Variations: Stir 2 chopped Roma or plum tomatoes into the finished dip.
     Add 1 tablespoon chopped rosemary leaves and/or 2 teaspoons stemmed thyme with the parsley.
     Substitute red pepper flakes for the pepper.

Want breadsticks for the coffee table? See page 227.

Aïoli with Crudités

This Provençal mayonnaise is best as a dip for raw vegetables, although you can use it as a spread for sandwiches, a sauce with grilled fish, or a substitute for tartar sauce with fried seafood. We prefer light and healthy almond oil, but you can use olive oil for a more traditional taste. Crudités (crew-dee-TAY) is just French for cut-up vegetables. *Makes about 1 cup*

2 large egg yolks (see Note, page 46)
2 to 3 anchovy fillets
2 garlic cloves, quartered
2 tablespoons lemon juice
¼ teaspoon cayenne pepper
¾ cup almond oil or extra virgin olive oil
Thick cucumber rounds, celery ribs, baby
     carrots, cauliflower florets, and other raw
     vegetables for dipping

❶ Place the egg yolks, anchovy fillets, garlic, lemon juice, and cayenne in a food processor fitted with the chopping blade or in a large blender. Pulse or blend a few times until the anchovies are well chopped.

❷ With the machine running, add the oil in the slowest drizzle, just a dribble at a time, either through the feed tube or through the center opening in the blender lid. It's imperative that you add the oil slowly so that it has a chance to emulsify.

❸ Once all the oil has been added, continue processing or blending until thick and smooth, about 30 seconds. Serve with raw vegetables on the side for dipping.

To store: Spoon the aïoli into a sealable container and refrigerate for up to 3 days.

Note: If you're concerned about raw egg yolks, use whole, in-the-shell, pasteurized eggs, found in the refrigerator case of most high-end markets.

Variations: Substitute 2 tablespoons minced peeled fresh ginger for the anchovies and garlic.

Substitute 1 teaspoon prepared wasabi paste for the anchovies and the garlic.

Tzatziki with Toasted Pita Rounds

This classic Greek dip has been cooling down Mediterranean palates for hundreds of years. Look for thick, ricotta-like Greek yogurt at high-end markets or specialty food stores. *Makes about 2 cups*

8 ounces Greek yogurt (see Note)
1 medium cucumber, peeled, seeded, and minced
2 garlic cloves, crushed
1 tablespoon extra virgin olive oil, plus extra for brushing the pita rounds
2 teaspoons minced mint leaves or minced dill fronds
1 to 2 teaspoons lemon juice
¼ teaspoon salt
¼ teaspoon freshly ground black pepper
Round pita pockets

1 Mix the yogurt, cucumber, garlic, olive oil, mint or dill, lemon juice, salt, and pepper in a large bowl until smooth. Cover and refrigerate for at least 2 hours.

2 Preheat the broiler. Open the pita pockets, then split them apart, creating two rounds. Brush the smooth side of each with a little olive oil, then slice the rounds into pie-shaped wedges. Place these on

the broiler rack or a baking sheet and toast 4 inches from the heat source until lightly browned, a little less than 1 minute. Serve with the chilled Tzatziki.

To store: Cover the dip and refrigerate for up to 5 days.

Note: If you can't find Greek yogurt, line a colander with cheesecloth or a large coffee filter, put 12 ounces plain yogurt in it, and place the whole thing over a bowl to catch the drips. Refrigerate for at least 8 hours or overnight. Discard the watery material in the bowl; use the thickened yogurt in the colander.

Dip Vehicles

Toasted pita wedges
Toasted sliced baguette rounds
Corn or flour tortillas
Chips and crackers of all sorts
Rice cakes
Pretzel rods
Thick-cut waffle potato chips or Gaufrettes (page 77)
Celery ribs, baby carrots, and seeded bell pepper spears (see Note)
Broccoli and cauliflower florets
Sugar snap peas (see page 113)
Endive spears
Braised or grilled asparagus spears (see page 453—stand them up in a vase for a gorgeous presentation)
Thick-cut cucumber rounds
Grilled chicken wings or tenders
Crunchy apple slices, lightly washed with lemon juice
Note: If you don't want to cut up your own vegetables, check the salad bar at your supermarket; these vegetables are there and ready to go (but pricier than the do-it-yourself varieties).

The Ultimate Salsa

Simply put, salsa is a raw dip, a mixture of two contrasting flavors, spiked with aromatics and a little heat. Oil is optional. That said, there's no reason to stand on ceremony—just as there's no reason not to experiment, especially since the bright flavors of fruits and vegetables match so well with aromatics and spices. Here's a chart to get you going on your own customized salsa. Mix and match items from each column.

Basic Flavor (choose 1)	Complementary Flavor (choose 1)	Aromatic (choose 1 or 2)	Heat (choose 1, to taste)	Oil (choose 1, optional)
2 cups chopped tomato	1/4 cup minced shallot	3 tablespoons chopped cilantro leaves	Chopped seeded jalapeño chile	1 tablespoon extra virgin olive oil
2 cups chopped tomatillo	1/3 cup minced red onion	2 tablespoons chopped mint leaves	Chopped seeded serrano chile	1 tablespoon canola oil
2 cups chopped pitted peaches	1/2 cup minced celery	2 tablespoons chopped parsley leaves	Chopped seeded poblano chile	1 tablespoon mustard oil
2 cups chopped pitted nectarines	1/2 cup minced, cored, seeded bell pepper	1 tablespoon chopped oregano leaves	Red pepper flakes	2 teaspoons almond oil
2 cups chopped, peeled, and cored pineapple	1/2 cup minced seeded tart green apple	1 tablespoon stemmed thyme	Bottled hot red pepper sauce	2 teaspoons walnut oil
2 cups chopped strawberries	1/2 cup diced seeded cucumber	1/2 teaspoon ground cinnamon		
2 cups chopped peeled pitted mango	1/2 cup peeled and diced jicama	1/4 teaspoon ground allspice		
Chopped seeded watermelon, honeydew, or cantaloupe				

To season: Salt just before serving the salsa. Start with 1/2 teaspoon salt and taste. If you salt it ahead of time, the fruit and vegetables will weep and the salsa will turn watery in storage.

To store: Place in a nonreactive bowl, cover, and refrigerate for up to 2 days.

Our Favorite Combinations

Traditional Salsa: Tomatoes, red onion, oregano, jalapeño, and canola oil

Pineapple Salsa: Pineapple, red onion, thyme, mint, and serrano

Peach Salsa: Peaches, shallot, thyme, allspice, hot red pepper sauce, and almond oil

Tomatillo Salsa: Tomatillos, apple, thyme, oregano, jalapeño, and olive oil

Not all of these dips are served hot, but they all do involve turning the stove or oven on. That said, most of them are as easy as their no-cook kin.

Sun-Dried Tomato and Roasted Garlic Pesto

Hardly traditional, this pizza-sauce pesto makes an excellent dip for bread, crackers, pita wedges, or chips. *Makes about 2 cups*

16 sun-dried tomato halves
   (see Note)
2 cups boiling water
⅓ cup grated aged Asiago
3 tablespoons olive oil
1 tablespoon packed oregano leaves
1 teaspoon red wine vinegar
¼ teaspoon salt
2 roasted garlic heads (see page 460)

① Place the sun-dried tomatoes in a medium bowl, pour the boiling water over them, and soak until soft, about 20 minutes.

② Place the softened tomatoes and 6 tablespoons of their soaking liquid in a food processor fitted with the chopping blade or in a large blender. Add the grated cheese, olive oil, oregano, vinegar, and salt.

③ Squeeze the pulp from each roasted garlic clove into the processor or blender. Pulse a few times, then process or blend until smooth.

To store: Transfer to a nonreactive bowl, cover, and refrigerate for up to 3 days; serve at room temperature.

Note: Use pliable, soft, sun-dried tomatoes, often found in the produce section of your market. Don't use sun-dried tomatoes packed in oil.

Variations: Add ¼ teaspoon red pepper flakes with the salt.

Substitute rosemary, tarragon, or thyme leaves for the oregano.

Substitute Parmigiano-Reggiano, Pecorino Romano, or hard, aged goat cheese for the Asiago.

Pesto

Pesto is a no-cook, Italian sauce, a favorite since Roman times and often thought to come from either Genoa or Sicily, but in fact probably of African origins. Although traditionally made of basil, pine nuts, Parmigiano-Reggiano, olive oil, garlic, and salt, pesto can truly be made from a range of ingredients, including this version with no nuts and oregano standing in for the basil. We've included it here among the cooked dips because the sun-dried tomatoes must be softened with boiling water (thus, the stove must be turned on and the garlic, roasted). Other pestos in this book, equally good as coffee-table dips, are Sage Pesto (page 293), Pecan Pesto (page 179), and Mint Pesto (page 443). See page 46 for a host of things that'll get the pesto from the bowl to your mouth.

Eggplant Caviar

This classic dip—sometimes called "Poor Man's Caviar" because of the creamy, tiny caviar-like eggplant seeds—is enhanced by the sour spike of pomegranate molasses, a Middle Eastern condiment. *Makes about 3 cups*

  1 medium eggplant (about 1 pound)
  2 tablespoons olive oil
  2 medium shallots, chopped
  1 jarred whole roasted red pepper or
    pimiento, drained, rinsed, and minced
  2 tablespoons pomegranate molasses
  1 teaspoon white wine vinegar
  ½ teaspoon salt
  ¼ teaspoon freshly ground black pepper

1 Prick the eggplant in several places with a fork. Wrap it in heavy-duty aluminum foil or a couple of layers of regular foil. Place it directly over a low gas flame and roast until soft, turning often, about 30 minutes. Alternatively, prick the eggplant, wrap it in the foil, and roast in a preheated 375°F oven on a lipped baking sheet until soft, about 40 minutes. In either case, cool at room temperature until easily handled, about 15 minutes.

2 Meanwhile, heat a medium skillet over medium heat. Swirl in the oil, then add the shallots and reduce the heat to very low. Cook, stirring often, until golden, about 15 minutes.

3 Unwrap the eggplant and cut it in half. Scoop the flesh into a medium nonreactive bowl. Stir in the softened shallots, minced red pepper or pimiento, pomegranate molasses, vinegar, salt, and pepper with a fork, mashing the eggplant slightly as you do so.

To store: Cover and refrigerate for up to 3 days; serve at room temperature.

Variations: Substitute 1 medium yellow onion, chopped, for the shallots.

Substitute frozen orange juice concentrate, thawed, or frozen cranberry juice concentrate, thawed, for the pomegranate molasses.

Stir in 1 tablespoon minced oregano leaves, 1 tablespoon minced parsley leaves, or 2 teaspoons stemmed thyme with the salt.

Omit the black pepper and add a few dashes of hot red pepper sauce.

Stir ¼ cup sour cream into the dip.

Artichoke Dip

We prefer fresh baby artichokes, rather than canned hearts, which often make the dip gummy. It's even better the next day, after the flavors have had a chance to meld. *Makes about 3 cups*

  12 baby artichokes (about 2 pounds—for
    selecting tips, see page 452)
  1 lemon, quartered
  3 large egg yolks (see Note on pasteurized
    eggs, page 46)
  ½ cup homemade mayonnaise (see page 121)
    or purchased mayonnaise (do not use fat-
    free)
  ½ cup dry vermouth or dry white wine
  1 ounce Parmigiano-Reggiano, finely grated
    (about ¼ cup)
  2 tablespoons chopped chives or 2
    tablespoons minced scallions, green part
    only
  2 teaspoons Dijon mustard
  1 teaspoon Worcestershire sauce
  A few dashes of hot red pepper sauce
    to taste

1 Bring a medium pot of salted water to a boil over high heat. Meanwhile, trim off the tough outer leaves from the artichokes; trim off any woody stems as well. Cut the trimmed artichokes in half.

2 Drop the artichokes and the quartered lemon into the boiling water; cook until the artichokes are tender, about 12 to 15 minutes. While they're cooking, position the rack in the middle of the oven and preheat the oven to 350°F.

3 Drain the artichokes in a colander set in the sink, discard the lemon quarters, and refresh the artichokes under cool running water until room temperature.

4 Place the artichokes, egg yolks, mayonnaise, vermouth or wine, Parmigiano-Reggiano, chives, mustard, Worcestershire sauce, and hot red pepper sauce in a food processor fitted with the chopping blade. Pulse a few times, then scrape down the sides of the bowl and process until smooth.

5 Spoon the dip into an oven-safe crock or a small, deep baking dish. Bake until set, bubbling, and lightly browned, about 40 minutes. Set aside at room temperature for 5 minutes before serving.

Variations: You can use frozen baby artichokes—do not defrost; drop them straight into the water and cook until tender, about 10 minutes.

Substitute Asiago, Pecorino Romano, or Grana Padano for the Parmigiano-Reggiano.

For an Asian take, substitute 2 teaspoons minced peeled fresh ginger and 1 teaspoon sesame oil for the mustard.

Asparagus Dip: Substitute 2 pounds asparagus spears for the artichokes. To cook, trim the spears with a vegetable peeler to get rid of any stringy bits, cut the spears into 2-inch sections, and boil until tender, about 5 minutes.

Borscht on a Cracker

Borscht is traditionally beet soup, but this borscht-style dip is a great starter—provided you don't have white carpeting. *Makes 6 servings*

8 medium beets, peeled
⅔ cup sour cream (regular, low-fat, or fat-free)
2 tablespoons minced dill fronds
2 tablespoons olive oil
1 tablespoon white wine vinegar
1 tablespoon prepared horseradish
½ teaspoon salt
¼ teaspoon freshly ground black pepper
24 to 30 small crackers, such as table water crackers

1 Position the rack in the center of the oven and preheat the oven to 400°F. Wrap the beets tightly in aluminum foil.

2 Bake until tender, about 1 hour. Cool in the foil packet for 15 minutes.

3 Carefully unwrap the packet; save any liquid. Cool the beets until you can handle them, then shred through the large holes of a box grater into a large bowl. Alternatively, feed them through the shredding blade into a food processor. Stir in any liquid from the packet.

4 Stir in the sour cream, dill, oil, vinegar, horseradish, salt, and pepper. Cover and refrigerate until chilled, at least 2 hours or up to 24 hours. Spoon in small mounds onto crackers to serve.

Variations: Substitute golden beets for the regular beets.

Substitute peeled turnips or peeled parsnips for half the beets.

These do double service: they're welcome on the coffee table where they can be picked up with a small fork or a toothpick, but they can also put in an appearance as a condiment with roasts or barbecue, or as a spark alongside salads or noodles.

Roasted Peppers with Balsamic Vinegar and Basil

The trick to this classic Italian antipasto is the quality of the balsamic vinegar. We suggest using an aged balsamic—five years maybe, not fifteen or twenty—not too syrupy, but with character and depth. *Makes about 6 servings (about 4 cups)*

3 red bell peppers
3 yellow bell peppers
12 basil leaves, finely shredded
1 tablespoon aged balsamic vinegar
½ teaspoon salt, preferably kosher or coarse-grained salt
½ teaspoon freshly ground black pepper

1 Char the bell peppers, either by holding and turning them one at a time with tongs over an open gas flame so that the outer skin bubbles and blackens, or by placing them on a large lipped baking sheet set 4 inches from a preheated broiler and turning occasionally until blackened all over, about 6 minutes. In either case, transfer to a paper bag and seal tightly or put them all in a large bowl and seal with plastic wrap. Set aside for 10 minutes.

2 Gently remove the peppers from the bag or bowl and peel off the blackened skin while holding the peppers over a clean medium bowl. (You want to catch any juice.) Don't peel the peppers under running water; you'll rinse off a good deal of their flavor. There's no harm if a few black specks remain.

3 Stem, core, and seed the peppers on a large cutting board, again preserving as much juice as possible. Cut the peppers into ½-inch strips and place them in the medium bowl along with any reserved juice.

4 Toss with the basil, balsamic vinegar, salt, and pepper. Cover and set aside at room temperature for at least 2 hours.

To store: Cover and refrigerate for up to 3 days; serve at room temperature.

Variation: Substitute 2 tablespoons minced mint, parsley, rosemary, tarragon, or thyme for the basil.

Trushee

These no-canning pickles are traditional in Sephardic homes at Passover. You'll need at least 2 days to let them marinate. Try them alongside toasted walnut halves. *Makes about 20 servings*

2 small cauliflower heads, stemmed and cut into small florets (see page 457)
10 carrots, peeled and thinly sliced into rings
1 pound green beans, trimmed
4 cups white vinegar
4 cups water

⅓ cup sugar

2 tablespoons plus 2 teaspoons salt,
preferably kosher salt

4 garlic cloves, peeled

3 bay leaves

1 Fill a large pot or Dutch oven halfway with water and bring it to a boil over high heat. Add the cauliflower florets; cook for 1 minute. Add the carrots; cook for 2 more minutes. Add the beans; cook for 1 minute. Drain everything in a large colander set in the sink—work in batches if you need to—then refresh under cool, running water until room temperature. Set aside to drain.

2 Return the pot or Dutch oven to medium-high heat; add the vinegar, water, sugar, salt, garlic, and bay leaves, stirring until the sugar dissolves. Leave the pot untouched until it comes to a full boil—the moment it does, remove it from the heat and cool at room temperature for 10 minutes.

3 Place the drained vegetables in a very large nonreactive crock, bowl, or glass jar. Pour the vinegary syrup over them. Cool to room temperature, then cover and refrigerate for at least 2 days, turning the vegetables occasionally in the marinade. Discard the bay leaves before serving. Serve by scooping out the trushee with a slotted spoon, draining them, and placing them on a small platter, or by placing the whole crock on the coffee table and allowing your guests to spear their own with bamboo skewers.

To store: Refrigerate, covered, for up to 3 weeks.

Variations: Add 3 tablespoons chopped fresh dill with the vinegar.

Add 3 small red chiles with the vinegar; discard the chiles before serving.

Candied Garlic

Serve these spicy/sweet cloves with cocktails; have toothpicks at the ready. *Makes 40 candied cloves*

40 garlic cloves, peeled

1½ cups water

Vegetable oil, for greasing the plate

2 tablespoons sugar

¼ teaspoon salt

1 Bring the garlic and water to a boil in a large skillet set over high heat. Cook until the water has evaporated, about 15 minutes. Meanwhile, lightly oil a pie plate.

2 Sprinkle the sugar over the garlic and reduce the heat to medium. Toss until the sugar melts, caramelizes, coats the cloves, and browns lightly. Spread the garlic in the caramelized syrup onto the prepared pie plate. Sprinkle with salt. Set aside to cool, about 1 hour.

To store: Cover and refrigerate for up to 3 days; return to room temperature before serving.

Five Things to Do with Candied Garlic

1 Place a small dot of Taleggio in endive spears; add a candied garlic clove to each.

2 Place a wheel of Brie in a small baking dish, then add several candied garlic cloves, maybe a dozen or so. Cover with aluminum foil and bake in a preheated 400°F oven until the cheese is soft and gooey, about 15 minutes.

3 Top a baked Focaccia (page 80) with candied garlic.

4 Toss in salads or green vegetable sides.

5 Add two or three diced, candied garlic cloves to an omelet (see page 23).

Oven-Dried Tomatoes

If you have time but not a lot of energy, here's the perfect nibble: you simply let the oven do the work. *Makes 24 pieces*

    Nonstick spray or vegetable oil
    12 Roma or plum tomatoes, cut in
        half lengthwise
    Sea salt or other coarse-grained
        salt

1 Position the rack in the middle of the oven and preheat the oven to 200°F. Generously spray or oil an oven-safe wire rack. Place the tomato halves, cut side up, on the prepared rack, then set the rack on a lipped baking sheet. Sprinkle the tomatoes with salt.

2 Bake until dark red, shriveled, but still moist, about 8 hours. Remove from the oven and cool to room temperature on the wire rack.

Serving Suggestions: Drizzle the dried tomatoes with extra virgin olive oil, aged balsamic vinegar, white balsamic vinegar, toasted pumpkin seed oil, toasted walnut oil, toasted sesame oil, avocado oil, or any infused olive oil.

Spread a little Tapenade (page 42), Pecan Pesto (page 179), Sun-Dried Tomato and Roasted Garlic Pesto (page 48), or softened goat cheese on each tomato.

Place a small dollop of crème fraîche or sour cream on each tomato after it's cooled. You can also spoon a little caviar or salmon roe onto the crème fraîche or sour cream.

Once you've topped the tomatoes with crème fraîche or sour cream, sprinkle them with toasted sesame seeds, finely chopped toasted walnuts, or any chopped green herb from parsley to tarragon.

Baby Squash and Zucchini Boats

Choose squash and zucchini that are relatively the same size so that they cook evenly. *Makes 48 appetizers*

    24 baby pattypan squash (about 1½ inches
        in diameter), stemmed
    24 baby zucchini (about 2 inches long),
        stemmed
    1⅔ cups canned white beans, drained and
        rinsed
    12 black olives, preferably Kalamata olives,
        pitted
    2 tablespoons extra virgin olive oil
    1 tablespoon lemon juice
    ½ teaspoon ground cumin
    ½ teaspoon ground cinnamon
    ½ teaspoon salt
    ¼ teaspoon freshly ground black pepper
    Small dill sprigs for garnish

1 Bring a large pot of salted water to a boil over high heat. Add the squash and zucchini; blanch for 2 minutes or until crisp-tender. Drain in a colander set in the sink, then refresh under cold, running water until room temperature.

2 Cut off the top of each squash, only about ½ inch or so; also cut a small strip down one side of each zucchini. Hollow out the squash and zucchini with a very small melon baller or a very small spoon, taking care to keep the sides intact.

3 Puree the beans, olives, olive oil, lemon juice, cumin, cinnamon, salt, and pepper in a food processor fitted with the processing blade or a large blender. Alternatively, grind the mixture in a large mortar with a pestle.

4 Place this mixture in a plastic ziplock bag, snip off a tiny corner, seal, and pipe into the squash and zucchini. Alternatively, use a very small spoon to

mound a little of the mixture into each vegetable. Garnish each with a sprig of dill.

To store: Cover and refrigerate for up to 1 day; return to room temperature before serving.

You can also make the white bean filling up to 3 days in advance and store it, tightly covered, in the refrigerator until you're ready to cook the vegetables.

❋ The Classic Cocktails ❋

We prefer smaller, '50ish drinks, rather than their gargantuan, modern kin, which turn depressingly warm and diluted. All these make one drink; you can double at will. If the drink is served up—that is, not over ice—chill the serving glass with ice while you shake the drink, then toss out the ice in the glass and strain the drink into the now-chilled glass. If you don't have a 1-ounce jigger measure, remember that 1/4 ounce equals 1/2 tablespoon, 1/2 ounce equals 1 tablespoon, 3/4 ounce equals 1 1/2 tablespoons, and 1 ounce equals 2 tablespoons.

Cosmopolitan

Shake 1½ ounces vodka, ¾ ounce Cointreau, ¾ ounce lime juice, and ¼ ounce thawed cranberry juice concentrate with ice in a cocktail shaker, then strain into a chilled martini glass.

Daiquiri

Shake 1½ ounces white rum, ½ ounce lime juice, and 1 teaspoon confectioners' sugar with ice in a cocktail shaker, then strain into a chilled martini glass.

Gimlet

Shake 1½ ounces gin and ¾ ounce sweetened lime juice (such as Rose's) with ice in a cocktail shaker, then strain over ice into a glass; serve with a lime wedge.

Manhattan

Shake 1½ ounces Canadian whisky (or rye) and ¾ ounce sweet vermouth with ice in a cocktail shaker, then strain into a chilled martini glass; garnish with a maraschino cherry.

Margarita

Shake 1 ounce tequila, 1 ounce orange-flavored liqueur (such as Cointreau), 1 ounce lime juice, and ¼ teaspoon superfine sugar with ice in a cocktail shaker, then strain over ice into a glass.

Martini

Shake 1½ ounces gin and ¼ ounce dry vermouth with ice in a cocktail shaker, then strain into a chilled martini glass; garnish with an olive.

Mint Julep

Place 6 fresh mint leaves, 1 teaspoon superfine sugar, and 1 teaspoon water in a highball glass; crush and muddle until pastelike. Fill the glass with crushed ice cubes and a few fresh mint leaves; add 2 ounces bourbon and serve with a long spoon.

Mojito

Place 6 fresh mint leaves and 1 teaspoon superfine sugar in a cocktail shaker; muddle and bruise to bring out the mint's flavor. Fill the shaker with ice, then add 1½ ounces light rum, ¾ ounce lime juice, and a dash of bitters. Shake well, then strain into a chilled martini glass; garnish with fresh mint leaves.

Old-Fashioned

Place a sugar cube in a highball glass; dot with 2 dashes of bitters and 1 teaspoon water. Crush and muddle with the back of a spoon, then add a few ice cubes, 2 ounces blended whiskey, and a lemon twist.

Sidecar

Shake 1½ ounces brandy, ¾ ounce orange-flavored liqueur (such as Cointreau), ¾ ounce lemon juice, and ¼ teaspoon superfine sugar with ice in a cocktail shaker; strain into a chilled martini glass.

❀ *Easy Nibbles* ❀

Most of these can stand on their own. Taken together, they make a meal. Best of all, many can be made ahead so you're not in the kitchen at the last minute.

Glazed Bacon

Salty bacon with a maple-syrup shine—frankly, heaven. *Makes 6 to 8 appetizer servings*

   1 pound thick-cut bacon, preferably pepper
      bacon (do not use turkey or soy bacon)
   ¼ cup maple syrup

❶ Position the rack in the center of the oven and preheat the oven to 450°F. Line a large baking sheet with a silicone baking mat or parchment paper.

❷ Spread the bacon strips on the prepared baking sheet. Brush them with the maple syrup.

❸ Bake until golden and crisp, about 25 minutes. Cool for 5 minutes, then cut into bite-sized bits and serve with toothpicks.

Variations: Substitute ¼ cup honey mixed with 1 tablespoon hot water for the maple syrup.
   Substitute ⅓ cup apricot jam or orange marmalade, stirred and melted in a small saucepan over low heat, for the maple syrup.

A road map for
Bacon-Wrapped Anything

Everything may be better with bacon, but appetizers, most of all. You'll need half as many strips of bacon as items you want to wrap.

1 Start with any of the following:

Sea scallops, halved into 2 disks, each sprinkled with a few drops of hot red pepper sauce

Medium shrimp (about 35 per pound), peeled and deveined, marinated in white wine in the refrigerator for 1 hour

Chicken livers, halved and marinated in dry sherry in the refrigerator for 1 hour or topped with a small dollop of bottled chili sauce

Large pitted dates, preferably Medjools, split open, stuffed with a blanched almond, and closed again

Very ripe plantains (the peel almost black), peeled and cut into 1-inch disks

Shucked oysters

Candied Garlic (page 52)

2 Wrap as many of these as you want with

thin-cut bacon strips, each sliced in half the short way

The strips will go around the pieces just a couple of times.

3 Heat a large skillet, preferably nonstick, over medium-high heat. Swirl in

1 tablespoon olive, canola, or vegetable oil

4 Add the bacon-wrapped bits, seam side down, and cook until the bacon is crispy, about 3 to 5 minutes, turning occasionally. Transfer to a wire rack set over a large baking sheet to drain, then serve at room temperature.

Drunken Cucumbers

Since cucumbers pick up the taste of whatever they're in, they ought to be in vodka. *Makes about 12 servings*

One 1-liter bottle vodka

2 teaspoons sugar

4 large cucumbers, peeled and cut into ½-inch rounds

1 to 2 serrano or Thai hot chiles, cut in half lengthwise

1 Stir the vodka and sugar in a large bowl, pitcher, glass container, or food-safe crock until the sugar dissolves.

2 Add the cucumber slices and chiles. Cover and refrigerate for at least 4 days and up to 2 months. To serve, remove the cucumber slices with a slotted spoon.

Variations: Substitute any of the following for the chiles: 2 lemons, cut into quarters; ½ cup dried cranberries; 2 tablespoons chopped mint leaves; 2 tablespoons chopped dill fronds; 1 tablespoon cracked black peppercorns.

Serving Suggestions: Remove the cucumber rounds with a slotted spoon and serve them on crackers topped with a little smear of softened cream cheese or soft goat cheese. Or use a toothpick to spear a pitted olive to each slice. Or use slices as a garnish for a vodka cocktail.

Once the cucumbers are gone from the vodka, use it for mixed drinks or store it in the freezer for ice-cold shots.

Tomato Bruschetta

Make sure you buy the ripest tomatoes possible for these open-faced appetizers. *Makes 30 bruschetta*

One 16-inch loaf Italian bread or French baguette
4 large garlic cloves, peeled and halved the long way
4 to 6 tablespoons extra virgin olive oil
8 plum or Roma tomatoes, chopped
8 basil leaves, shredded
1 small red onion, minced
1½ tablespoons lemon juice
¼ teaspoon sugar
Salt and freshly ground black pepper to taste

1 Preheat the broiler. Slice the bread into ½-inch-thick rounds, discarding the crusty ends.

2 Place the rounds on a large baking sheet and toast them on one side only, 4 inches from the heat, until quite browned and very crunchy, 1 to 2 minutes. Transfer to a wire rack and cool for 5 minutes.

3 Rub the toasted side of the rounds with the cut garlic. (It takes about 4 pieces of bread to use up a halved clove. Don't tear the bread, but do get the garlic oils and some of the garlic meat into the bread's surface.) Lightly brush the toasted sides with the olive oil.

4 Mix the tomatoes, basil, onion, lemon juice, and sugar in a medium bowl. You can cover the tomato topping and keep it in the refrigerator for up to 8 hours; simply leave the toasted rounds out on the counter until you're ready to use them.

5 Just before serving, season the tomato mixture with salt and pepper; spoon some over the toasted rounds.

Variations: Substitute red wine vinegar for the lemon juice.

Omit the sugar and substitute aged balsamic vinegar for the lemon juice.

Substitute fresh oregano or rosemary for the basil.

Omit the basil and add 2 teaspoons capers, drained and rinsed, with the tomatoes.

Other Bruschetta: Once you toast the bread and season it (steps 1 to 3), you can use an array of toppings, including Tapenade (page 42); Sage Pesto (page 293); White Bean and Sun-Dried Tomato Dip (page 45); Sun-Dried Tomato and Roasted Garlic Pesto (page 48); Roasted Peppers with Balsamic Vinegar and Basil (page 51); mascarpone cheese, softened to room temperature, then dotted with chutney (page 388); or cream cheese, softened to room temperature, topped with chutney.

Radish Sandwiches

These buttery tea sandwiches are always welcome before a meal. *Makes 12 small tea sandwiches*

Unsalted butter, softened, to taste
6 slices white bread
6 radishes, trimmed and thinly sliced
Coarse-grained or kosher salt to taste

1 Lightly butter one side of each of the slices of bread. Lay them, buttered side up, on the work surface; then divide the radishes among 3 of the slices, layering the rings across with the bread while keeping them back about ½ inch from the crust. Sprinkle with salt.

2 Top each of the open-faced sandwiches with another slice of bread, buttered side down; trim off the crusts. Cut each sandwich on the diagonal into 4 small, triangular sandwiches.

Variations: Toast the bread.

Lay arugula or basil leaves on top of the radish rings before closing the sandwiches.

Sprinkle a few drops of hot red pepper sauce over the radish rings before closing the sandwiches.

Chicken Wings, Three Ways

U.S. restaurant-goers ordered over 7 billion pounds of chicken wings in 2004! No wonder: there's something splendid about the skin-to-meat-to-bone ratio. *Makes 8 to 10 appetizer servings*

1. Lemon Wings

3 pounds chicken wings, tips removed and discarded, drumlet and winglet sections separated
¼ cup lemon juice
6 garlic cloves, crushed
1 teaspoon salt
½ teaspoon freshly ground black pepper

2. Sesame Wings

3 pounds chicken wings, tips removed and discarded, drumlet and winglet sections separated
6 tablespoons unsalted butter, melted and cooled
½ cup toasted sesame seeds
1 tablespoon toasted sesame oil
1 teaspoon ground ginger
½ teaspoon salt

3. Buffalo Wings

3 pounds chicken wings, tips removed and discarded, drumlet and winglet sections separated
4 tablespoons (½ stick) unsalted butter, melted and cooled
½ cup bottled chili sauce, such as Heinz (or ketchup for slightly milder wings)

¼ cup hot red pepper sauce or Asian red pepper sauce
4 garlic cloves, crushed
½ teaspoon salt

❶ For any recipe, mix all the ingredients together in a large bowl. Cover and refrigerate for 1 hour, stirring occasionally. (The Sesame and Buffalo Wings can be stored up to 12 hours; the Lemon Wings should not be kept more than 2 hours.)

❷ Prepare the grill by preheating a gas grill to medium heat or building a medium-heat ashed coal bed in a charcoal grill; or preheat the broiler. (If desired, line the broiler pan with aluminum foil to make cleanup easier.)

❸ Grill the marinated wings directly over medium heat until crispy and brown, about 15 minutes, turning once or twice. Or broil 4 inches from the heat source until crispy, about 12 minutes, turning a couple of times.

Chicken Wings

Each chicken has two wings; each wing has three parts. There's the pointed tip, called the "flapper" in industry parlance. It's usually removed and discarded in American kitchens but is highly prized in Asian ones. The two meatier sections are the drumlet (so named because it looks like a little drumstick) and the double-boned winglet.

To divide the parts of a wing, hold them against a cutting board and pull any two of the three sections gently apart until the joint is revealed. With the cutting edge toward you, insert the tip of a knife into the joint, pressing the tip straight down to the board; then bring the cutting edge down toward the board, slicing through the ligaments and tendons until the joint snaps apart. Finally, slice through the skin to separate. Repeat with the other joint in the wing.

"Deviled" Eggs, Eight Ways

Filled, hard-cooked eggs never last long on the coffee table. Here are eight versions for your next party. *Makes 12 filled egg halves (can be doubled or tripled)*

6 large eggs
One of the eight fillings that follows

❶ Place the eggs in a saucepan large enough to hold them comfortably in one layer. Fill the pan with cool water so that it comes 1 inch over the eggs. Cover, place over high heat, and bring the water to a full boil.

❷ Remove the pan from the heat, cover, and set aside for 15 minutes. Pour off most of the water in the pan, add a few ice cubes, and run cold water into the pan to cool the eggs quickly to room temperature.

❸ Tap the shells against a counter to crack them in several places, then roll them gently between your palms. Peel off the shells, starting at the large ends.

❹ Cut the eggs in half the long way, then scoop the yolks into a bowl. Set the whites aside while you make one of the fillings.

❺ Spoon the filling back into the whites. For a fancier presentation, place the filling in a pastry bag fitted with a small, star-shaped tip and pipe into the whites—or place the filling in a resealable plastic bag, snip off a tiny bit of one corner, and squeeze the filling through the hole into the whites.

To store: Place the filled eggs on a serving platter, cover loosely with plastic wrap, and refrigerate for up to 24 hours; allow them to stand at room temperature for 10 minutes before serving.

||||||||||||||||||||||||||||||||||||||||||||||||||||||||||||||||||||||||||

Tip for Success

If your appetizer buffet is going to last for an hour or so, consider making a double batch and keeping half the eggs in the fridge until the first batch has been eaten.

||||||||||||||||||||||||||||||||||||||||||||||||||||||||||||||||||||||||||

The Eight Fillings

For any of these, add the ingredients to a medium bowl; and stir and mash with a fork until creamy. Use either homemade mayonnaise (see page 121) or purchased (regular, low-fat, or fat-free).

1. *Classic Deviled Eggs*

6 hard-cooked egg yolks
2 tablespoons unsalted butter, softened
1 tablespoon mayonnaise
1 teaspoon white wine vinegar
¼ teaspoon dry mustard
¼ teaspoon salt
A few dashes of hot red pepper sauce
    to taste

2. *Ginger Eggs*

6 hard-cooked egg yolks
1 small shallot, minced
2 tablespoons mayonnaise
1 tablespoon minced peeled fresh
    ginger
1 teaspoon chili paste
¼ teaspoon salt

3. *Curried Eggs*

6 hard-cooked egg yolks
2 tablespoons mayonnaise
2 teaspoons dry mustard
2 teaspoons curry powder
2 teaspoons lemon juice
¼ teaspoon salt

4. *Wasabi Eggs*

6 hard-cooked egg yolks

3 tablespoons mayonnaise

2 teaspoons prepared wasabi paste

½ teaspoon soy sauce

5. *French Onion Dip Eggs*

6 hard-cooked egg yolks

1½ tablespoons sour cream

1 tablespoon mayonnaise

1 tablespoon minced chives or 1 tablespoon
    minced scallion, green part only

½ teaspoon onion powder

½ teaspoon salt

6. *Cocktail Sauce Eggs*

6 hard-cooked egg yolks

2 tablespoons ketchup

1 to 2 teaspoons prepared horseradish

1 teaspoon lemon juice

¼ teaspoon salt

A few dashes of hot red pepper sauce to
    taste

7. *Southwestern Eggs*

6 hard-cooked egg yolks

3 tablespoons mayonnaise

2 teaspoons chili powder

1 teaspoon ground cumin

1 teaspoon lime juice

¼ teaspoon salt

8. *Quiche Lorraine Eggs*

6 hard-cooked egg yolks

3 strips bacon, fried until crisp and crumbled
    into very small bits

2 tablespoons sour cream (regular, low-fat,
    or fat-free)

2 tablespoons minced scallion, green
    part only

½ teaspoon freshly ground black pepper

Cold Sake-and-Ginger Mussels

Here, you steam the mussels in sake, then chill them in a ginger broth. For tips on handling mussels, see page 360. *Makes 6 appetizer servings (can be doubled)*

½ cup sake

3 garlic cloves, quartered

36 large mussels, cleaned and debearded

1 small shallot, minced

¼ cup soy sauce

2 tablespoons minced peeled fresh ginger

2 tablespoons minced cilantro leaves

1 tablespoon toasted sesame oil

Pickled sushi ginger for garnish

1 Bring the sake and garlic to a boil in a large pot over high heat. Add the mussels, cover, and reduce the heat to medium. Simmer until the mussels open, about 5 minutes. Drain in a large colander set in the sink and cool for a few minutes.

2 Collect any mussels from the colander that have fallen out of their shells, then pull the remainder out of their shells. Place the mussel meat in a medium bowl and gently stir in the shallot, soy sauce, ginger, cilantro, and sesame oil. Cover and refrigerate for at least 1 hour or up to 48 hours. Place the shells in a large bowl, cover, and refrigerate separately as well.

3 Return one mussel to each shell half along with some of the marinade. (Of course, you will have twice as many shell halves as mussels; choose the largest and prettiest ones.) Top each with a small piece of pickled sushi ginger for garnish.

Variations: Substitute Japanese beer, such as Kirin or Ichiban, for the sake.

Add up to 1 teaspoon Chinese chili paste with the soy sauce.

Steamed Shrimp with Classic Cocktail Sauce

There's nothing better than this American favorite. Feel free to adjust the horseradish or hot sauce to your taste. For an elegant presentation, place the shrimp in martini glasses and top with this classic American sauce. *Makes about 6 appetizer servings (with 1½ cups sauce)*

1 cup ketchup
¼ cup prepared horseradish
2 tablespoons lemon juice
2 tablespoons chopped dill fronds
1 tablespoon Worcestershire sauce
A few dashes of hot red pepper sauce to taste
1 pound medium shrimp (35 to 40 per pound), deveined but unpeeled

1 Mix the ketchup, horseradish, lemon juice, dill, Worcestershire sauce, and hot red pepper sauce in a small nonreactive bowl. (The sauce can be made in advance and stored in the refrigerator for up to 3 days.)

2 Place the shrimp in the layers of a tiered bamboo steamer. Alternatively, use a conventional vegetable steamer. Fill a large pot—one whose width matches the bamboo steamer or that accommodates the vegetable steamer—with 2 inches of water. Bring to a boil over high heat.

3 Place the steamer or basket over the water and cook until the shrimp are pink and firm, about 5 minutes. Remove the shrimp immediately from the heat to stop their cooking. Be forewarned—they are very hot. Serve warm or chill first in an ice-water bath, then in the refrigerator, before serving with Classic Cocktail Sauce on the side.

Shrimp Yakitori

Although *yakitori* means "grilled poultry" in Japanese, we think this classic, sweet, sticky sauce goes exceptionally well with shrimp. Consider standing the skewered shrimp up in a vase as a "bouquet." *Makes 18 shrimp on skewers*

½ cup dry sake or white wine
¼ cup soy sauce (see Note)
1 tablespoon mirin
1 tablespoon molasses
1 teaspoon Worcestershire sauce
1 teaspoon sugar
18 large shrimp, preferably those that measure 15 to 20 per pound, peeled and deveined
18 bamboo skewers
2 tablespoons toasted sesame seeds

1 Whisk the sake, soy sauce, mirin, molasses, Worcestershire sauce, and sugar in a small saucepan set over medium heat. Bring the mixture to a simmer, reduce the heat, and simmer for 1 minute. Remove from the heat and cool to room temperature, about 1 hour. (The sauce can be made in advance and stored, covered, in the refrigerator for up to 3 days.)

2 Stir the shrimp into the cooled marinade and set aside for 15 minutes. Meanwhile, soak the skewers in a baking pan filled with water for 15 minutes to ensure they don't burn over the fire. Also preheat the broiler or prepare the grill for a medium-heat fire.

3 Thread a shrimp onto each skewer, starting at the tail end of the shrimp and threading it back and forth onto the skewer so that it straightens out, its natural curve bent open as the skewer pierces it three or four times. Reserve the marinade.

④ Broil the shrimp 6 inches from the heat source for 2 minutes or grill over medium heat for 2 minutes. Brush with the reserved marinade, turn, and continue cooking until the shrimp are pink and firm, 2 to 3 minutes, basting once more with the marinade. If you place the skewer ends to the side of the heat source, they will not burn—or wrap the ends in aluminum foil. Place the skewered shrimp on a serving plate and sprinkle with the sesame seeds.

Note: Yakitori sauce is usually made with tamari, a thick, dark Japanese soy sauce that proves hard to find in the United States. Here, we've crafted a mélange to replicate tamari; should you get a bottle, omit the soy sauce, molasses, and Worcestershire sauce and use 1/3 cup.

Variations: Substitute chicken tenders or sea scallops for the shrimp.

Use the yakitori sauce as a marinade and/or barbecue mop for boneless skinless chicken breasts or boneless pork loin chops on the grill.

Crab Sage Puffs

Serve these light, airy bundles with Blue Cheese Dressing (page 105), purchased ranch dressing, or mango chutney. *Makes about 18 puffs*

1/2 cup water
1 1/2 tablespoons olive oil, plus additional for greasing the baking sheet
1/4 teaspoon salt
1/4 teaspoon freshly ground black pepper
1/2 cup all-purpose flour
1 large egg plus 1 egg white
1 ounce Parmigiano-Reggiano, finely grated
2 teaspoons minced sage leaves
A couple of dashes hot red pepper sauce to taste
6 ounces lump crabmeat

① Position the rack in the center of the oven and preheat the oven to 425°F. Generously grease a large baking sheet with some olive oil dabbed on a paper towel.

② In a small saucepan, bring the water, olive oil, salt, and pepper to a boil over high heat. Reduce the heat to medium-low and whisk in the flour. Cook, whisking all the while, until the bottom and sides of the pan are coated with a white film. Scoop the mixture into a large bowl; cool for 3 minutes.

③ With an electric mixer on medium speed, beat the egg into the flour mixture until smooth. Beat in the egg white until smooth, then beat in the Parmigiano-Reggiano, sage, and hot red pepper sauce until well combined, about 1 minute. Remove the beaters and stir in the crabmeat.

④ Drop by tablespoonfuls onto the prepared baking sheet, spacing the mounds about 1 inch apart. Set the sheet aside for 10 minutes to air-dry the mounds.

⑤ Bake until golden brown and puffed, about 30 minutes. Cool on the baking sheet for 2 minutes, then cool on a wire rack for at least 10 minutes or until room temperature.

Shrimp Sage Puffs: Substitute 6 ounces medium shrimp, peeled, deveined, and cooked, for the crabmeat. For the easiest substitution, just buy cooked cocktail shrimp at your supermarket. Mince the cooked shrimp very finely before adding them to the batter.

Herb Puffs: Omit the crabmeat and increase the sage to 1 1/2 tablespoons—or substitute any minced herb you prefer.

Potato Cups

Transform small, red-skinned potatoes into cups to hold herbed crème fraîche and a dollop of caviar, whether salmon, osetra, or beluga. Admittedly, this appetizer is only as good as the caviar you use—so consider it a treat and go for broke. You'll need a very sharp knife to slice the cooked potatoes without tearing the skin. *Makes 24 potato cups*

Twenty-four 1½-inch-diameter round red-skinned potatoes
1 cup crème fraîche or sour cream
2 tablespoons minced dill fronds
¼ cup salmon, osetra, or beluga caviar

❶ Bring about 2 inches of water to a boil over high heat in a large saucepan. Place the potatoes in a vegetable steamer, set it over the boiling water, and cover. Reduce the heat to medium and steam the potatoes until just tender when pierced with a fork, with a little give, about 15 minutes. Pour the potatoes into a colander set in the sink and refresh under cool, running water until room temperature.

❷ Cut a thin slice off the bottom of each potato (so it will stand up), then use a small melon-baller or a grapefruit spoon to scoop out a rounded hole on the side of the potato opposite the cut bottom. Set aside for 10 minutes, just to make sure the centers are at room temperature.

❸ Mix the crème fraîche or sour cream with the dill in a small bowl. Spoon 2 teaspoons into each potato. Top each with about ¼ teaspoon caviar and serve.

Variations: Substitute parsley, thyme, or chervil for the dill.

Omit the dill and stir either 2 teaspoons curry powder or 1 teaspoon wasabi powder into the crème fraîche or sour cream.

Substitute Aïoli (page 45) for the crème fraîche or sour cream.

Omit the caviar and top each filled potato with a small slice of Gravlax (page 75) or smoked salmon. Or top each with a smoked oyster.

Prosciutto Nibbles

Prosciutto is unsmoked, air-dried, salt-cured, pressed ham, originally from Parma, but now made in many places in Italy as well as in the United States. If you want to find the real deal, look for "Prosciutto di Parma" or "Prosciutto di San Daniele" stamped on the rind—and expect to pay commensurately. When buying other versions, ask to taste first. The taste should be salty but bright; the meat should be a little chewy. If it tastes metallic or dull, it's been for sale too long.

Have the butcher cut the ham into paper-thin strips, which he or she will lay between pieces of waxed butcher paper and seal in a plastic bag. Do not unwrap the bag until you're ready to use the prosciutto; the slices are so thin and dry, they will turn leathery if exposed too long to the air.

Cut the slices into manageable strips, then wrap them around fresh fig halves, prunes soaked in Armagnac, honeydew or cantaloupe chunks, apple wedges that have been rinsed with lemon juice, pineapple spears, steamed asparagus spears, or Brie slices dabbed with fruit chutney.

Spiced Nuts

A little oil and some dried spices—there's nothing to making spiced nuts. *Makes 2 cups*

Start by lightly toasting 2 cups nuts in a preheated 350°F oven on a large baking sheet for 5 minutes. Cool the nuts on the baking sheet, then follow one of these formulas.

To Make	Heat 1 tablespoon fat in a large skillet over medium heat.	Add the toasted nuts and cook until aromatic, about 2 minutes.	Add the liquid and cook until the nuts are sticky and coated.	Toss in the spice and stir over the heat until coated, about 20 seconds.
Butter Pecans	Unsalted butter	Toasted pecan halves	1 tablespoon brandy or Cognac	1 teaspoon salt
Chili Pecans	Walnut oil	Toasted pecan halves	2 teaspoons Worcestershire sauce	1½ tablespoons chili powder
Smoky Pecans	Canola oil	Toasted pecan halves	1 teaspoon Worcestershire sauce and 1 teaspoon liquid smoke	1¾ teaspoons paprika, ½ teaspoon ground cumin, ½ teaspoon sugar, ½ teaspoon salt, and ¼ teaspoon cayenne
Cinnamon Almonds	Almond oil	Toasted whole almonds	1 tablespoon white rum	2 teaspoons ground cinnamon, 2 teaspoons sugar
Curried Pistachios	Mustard oil or canola oil	Unsalted pistachios	1 tablespoon lemon juice	1 tablespoon curry powder
Honey Walnuts	Walnut oil	Walnut halves	1 tablespoon honey and 1 teaspoon water	½ teaspoon salt
Szechuan Peanuts	Peanut oil	Unsalted roasted peanuts	2 teaspoons Asian chili sauce	1 teaspoon five-spice powder, 1 teaspoon crushed Szechuan peppercorns, 1 teaspoon salt

Once the nuts are coated in the spices, pour them onto a large baking sheet and cool to room temperature, stirring occasionally, about 1 hour. Store in a ziplock plastic bag at room temperature for up to 2 weeks.

❋ Cheesy Bits ❋

We love cheese as a savory alternative to dessert, but we usually don't put it out unadorned with other nibbles. Perhaps it's a little too heavy? Or naked? But no doubt about it: dressed up, crunchy or gooey, cheesy appetizers are always gone in a flash.

Asiago Shortbread Rounds

These are a crunchy, cheesy version of refrigerator cookies: the dough can be stored in the refrigerator, tightly wrapped, for up to one month. Slice off as many rounds as you need, bake them as directed, and return the log to the fridge to await another party. *Makes about 40 appetizers*

> 12 tablespoons (1½ sticks) cool unsalted butter, cut into ½-inch pieces
> 8 ounces aged Asiago, finely grated
> 1½ cups all-purpose flour
> 1 teaspoon dry mustard
> ½ teaspoon freshly ground black pepper
> ¼ teaspoon salt
> 6 tablespoons heavy cream

① **If you're working with a food processor:** Place the butter and cheese in the processor fitted with the chopping blade; pulse until a homogenous if still crumbly mixture forms, about like dry Play-Doh. Add the flour, dry mustard, pepper, and salt; process until crumbly, like a piecrust dough before you add the water. With the machine running, add the cream through the feed tube and process until a dry dough forms—it will not fully cohere at this stage.

If you're working by hand: Place the butter and cheese in a large bowl and use a pastry cutter or a potato masher to cut the butter into small pieces with the cheese mixed into them. Add the flour, dry mustard, pepper, and salt; continue working the pastry cutter through the ingredients. The mixture will be very stiff, but keep working until it looks like dampened but coarse sand. Stir in the cream with a fork until a dry dough forms.

② Turn the dough out onto a clean, dry work surface. Knead until it holds together as a ball. Shape into a fairly compact log about 12 inches long. Wrap tightly in plastic wrap and refrigerate for at least 2 hours.

③ Position a rack in the center of the oven and preheat the oven to 375°F. Line a large baking sheet with a silicone baking mat or parchment paper.

④ Unwrap the log and slice off as many ¼-inch rounds as desired. Place on the prepared baking sheet 2 inches apart. Bake until golden and slightly firm to the touch, about 20 minutes. Cool on the baking sheet for 2 minutes, then transfer to a wire rack to cool completely.

To store: The wrapped log can be refrigerated for up to 1 month; the baked biscuits, once cooled, can be stored in an airtight container at room temperature for up to 3 days.

Variations: Substitute Parmigiano-Reggiano or Pecorino Romano for the Asiago.

Increase the black pepper to as much as 1 tablespoon.

Add caraway seeds, celery seeds, or fennel seeds with the flour.

Add up to 1 teaspoon hot red pepper sauce with the cream.

Gougères

These balls of crunchy, puffed dough are best hot from the oven; plan on baking them off as your guests arrive. Our only sure tip: make these on a dry, clear day. *Makes 36 gougères*

> 1 cup water
> 4 tablespoons (½ stick) unsalted butter, cut into chunks
> 1 cup all-purpose flour
> 1 teaspoon salt
> 4 large eggs, at room temperature
> 8 ounces Gruyère or Emmentaler, grated with a microplane or the smallest holes of a box grater

1 Line a large baking sheet with a silicone baking mat or parchment paper; set aside.

2 Place the water and butter in a medium saucepan set over medium-high heat. Bring the mixture to a boil, melting the butter and stirring occasionally.

3 Reduce the heat to medium-low; stir in the flour and salt with a wooden spoon. Keep stirring over the heat until the dough coheres, dries out, and coats the sides of the pan with a milky film, forming a thin crust across its bottom, about 3 minutes or maybe up to 6 minutes. Remove the pan from the heat and let stand for 5 minutes.

4 Using an electric mixer at medium speed, beat in the eggs, one at a time. (You can also transfer the dough to a stand mixer and beat in the eggs with the paddle attachment.) Once the eggs have been thoroughly incorporated, beat in the cheese.

5 Drop by heaping teaspoonfuls onto the prepared baking sheet, spacing the mounds 2 inches apart. Alternatively, place the dough in a pastry bag fitted with a #9 plain tip or in a ziplock plastic bag from which you've snipped off one corner; pipe onto the baking sheet in 1-inch mounds.

6 Set the baking sheet aside to let the mounds dry out for 15 minutes.

7 Meanwhile, position the rack in the center of the oven and preheat the oven to 425°F.

8 Bake until puffed and golden, about 15 minutes. Cool on the sheet for 2 minutes before removing and serving. To make additional batches, cool the baking sheet for 10 minutes before making extra mounds and letting them dry out (change the parchment paper if it's browned, spotty, or frizzled) or use a second prepared baking sheet on which you've put a second set of mounds as the first set bakes.

Variations: Add 1 teaspoon freshly ground black pepper with the cheese.

Add 2 teaspoons chopped stemmed thyme or chopped fresh dill with the cheese.

Substitute Parmigiano-Reggiano or hard, aged, white Cheddar for the Gruyère or Emmentaler.

Brie and Mango Quesadillas

Quesadillas often suffer from a certain dullness, so we jazz them up with bolder flavors. Serve with a fiery salsa on the side (see page 47). *Makes 4 servings*

2 fresh poblano chiles, Italian frying peppers, or New Mexican green or red chiles
1 ripe mango, peeled, pitted, and thinly sliced
4 ounces Brie, rind removed, cut into long strips
Four 12-inch flour tortillas

❶ To char the peppers, preheat the broiler. Place the chiles on a baking sheet lined with aluminum foil set 4 inches from the heat source. Roast until charred on all sides, turning often with tongs, about 6 minutes. Alternatively, hold the chiles with metal tongs over an open gas flame to char them on all sides.

❷ Place the chiles in a bowl and seal with plastic wrap or place them in a paper bag and seal. Set aside for 10 minutes, then peel off the blackened skins before stemming and seeding the chiles. Cut the chiles into long strips.

❸ Again, preheat the broiler. Divide the chile strips, mango slices, and Brie slices between 2 tortillas. Top each with one of the remaining tortillas; press gently to close.

❹ Place the quesadillas on a large baking sheet and set under the broiler, about 4 inches from the heat, until lightly browned. Turn with a large metal spatula and continue cooking until lightly browned, about 1 minute. Cool for 2 minutes, then cut into wedges before serving.

Parmesan and Pear Quesadillas: Substitute a ripe, cored, thinly sliced pear and shaved Parmigiano-Reggiano for the mango and Brie.

Peach and Goat Cheese Quesadillas: Substitute 2 ripe, pitted, thinly sliced peaches and 4 ounces soft goat cheese for the mango and Brie.

Baked Feta

Use only high-quality feta, sold immersed in brine in plastic containers. Spoon the dip onto crackers or use it as a decadent topping for baked potatoes. *Makes 6 servings*

1 pound feta, drained
¼ teaspoon red pepper flakes
4 sun-dried tomatoes, packed in oil

❶ Position the rack in the center of the oven and preheat the oven to 375°F.

❷ Crumble the cheese into a small casserole or other oven-safe crock that holds about 2 cups. Press down to compact the cheese without mashing it. Sprinkle the red pepper flakes over the cheese, then line the tomatoes on top.

❸ Cover tightly with aluminum foil or cover the crock with its tight-fitting lid. Bake until soft and runny, about 20 minutes. Let stand for 5 minutes at room temperature before serving.

Variation: Substitute crumbly goat cheese for the feta; or place Brie, Camembert, or cambozola in the freezer for 15 minutes, then slice off the rind and slice the firmed-up cheese into small, irregular pieces.

For Chile con Queso, the traditional Tex-Mex dip, see the sauce for Migas (page 16).

Ham and Cheese Phyllo Cups

These look as if they take more time than they actually do. Use a mini muffin tin to form the little bundles of phyllo and filling. They're good hot or at room temperature. *Makes 24 tartlets*

6 sheets frozen phyllo dough, thawed in the
    package in the refrigerator
About 3 tablespoons unsalted butter, melted
    and cooled, for greasing and brushing
8 ounces prosciutto or smoked deli ham,
    finely chopped
4 ounces Gruyère, shredded
2 tablespoons mango chutney
1 teaspoon stemmed thyme
¼ teaspoon salt
¼ teaspoon freshly ground black pepper

❶ Position the rack in the center of the oven and preheat the oven to 375°F. Lightly brush a 24-indentation mini muffin tin or two 12-indentation mini-muffin tins with melted butter, then set aside.

❷ Lay the phyllo sheets out on your work surface and cover them loosely with a layer of plastic wrap and then a clean, dry kitchen towel.

❸ Remove one phyllo sheet from the stack and brush it with melted butter. Fold the sheet in half, shorter side to shorter side. Brush it again with melted butter, then fold it in half, again shorter side to shorter side. Brush with melted butter, then cut it into four 3-inch squares.

❹ Push the squares down into the indentations of the prepared muffin tin so the phyllo is in the tin, but its edges form a frilly edge sticking up out of the top of the indentation. Repeat with the remaining phyllo sheets, filling all the indentations.

❺ Bake for 5 minutes. Meanwhile, mix the prosciutto or ham, cheese, chutney, thyme, salt, and pepper together in a medium bowl.

❻ Remove the pan from the oven, cool for a minute or so, then fill the little shells with the prepared ham mixture. You may have to press the filling into any cups that have puffed up.

❼ Return the pan to the oven and bake until the phyllo is browned and crispy and the filling bubbles slightly, about 8 minutes. Cool the tin on a wire rack for 10 minutes, then unmold the tartlets and either serve or continue cooling on a wire rack to room temperature.

Variations: Use Asiago, Parmigiano-Reggiano, Emmentaler, aged Cheddar, or aged Gouda as the cheese.

Add a few dashes of hot red pepper sauce or Asian chili sauce with the ham.

Use any flavor fruit chutney you prefer, including a homemade variety (see page 388).

A Cheese Tray

If you do want to put out a selection of cheeses before dinner, remember these tips:

• Have a range of cheeses, hard to soft, strong to mild.

• Remember that stronger flavors overpower those more delicate. Pair a soft goat cheese with an aged Gouda, a blue with hard Parmigiano-Reggiano, or a mild sheep's milk like Manchego with a slightly more assertive Borenkaas.

• Cheese tastes better at room temperature. Prepare the tray an hour before you serve it, but cover it with plastic wrap so the cheese doesn't dry out.

• Match the cheese to fruit and berries, but avoid citrus and bananas.

• Have a range of crackers and bread on hand. Also consider chutneys and other savory spreads that will match well with the cheeses you've selected.

Nothing warms up the appetite like a good crunch. And several of these—the fried scallops, for example—would even be fine fare for dinner on their own. These recipes were developed with standard stovetop cookware in mind; use an electric deep-fryer at will (after consulting the manufacturer's instructions, of course).

Onion Rings with a Buttermilk Crust

Although many people like Vidalias and other sweet onions here, we prefer the stronger-tasting, thick-cut, standard yellow onions. They're a better match to this tangy batter. *Makes 8 servings*

    4 to 7 cups peanut oil
    1 cup all-purpose flour
    1 cup regular or low-fat buttermilk
    ¼ cup canola oil
    2 large yellow onions, cut into ½-inch slices,
       then divided into rings
    Salt to taste

❶ Pour enough peanut oil into a large saucepan to come about halfway up the sides. Clip a deep-frying thermometer to the inside of the pan and set it over medium heat until the thermometer registers 350°F.

❷ Meanwhile, whisk the flour, buttermilk, and canola oil in a large bowl until smooth.

❸ Dip a few onion rings in the batter, shake off the excess, then slip them into the hot oil. Adjust the heat so the oil stays a constant 350°F. Fry until golden, turning once or twice with a metal meat fork or a metal spoon, 3 to 4 minutes. Transfer to a wire rack with a slotted spoon, sprinkle with a little salt, and continue frying more rings.

Garnishes: ketchup, malt vinegar, Mayonnaise (page 121), or Sesame Dipping Sauce (page 74).

Variations: Omit the onions and cut bell peppers into ½-inch-thick rings, removing the seeds and white inner membranes. Dip these rings in the batter and fry until crispy, about 3 minutes, turning once or twice.

This tangy batter is also excellent on shrimp. Lightly dip peeled, deveined medium shrimp into the batter, and fry until crispy, about 4 minutes, turning once or twice. It's also good on chicken wings or drumsticks—coat with flour, dip in the batter, and fry until crispy, about 10 minutes, turning once or twice.

Mix and Match

In truth, most of these crusts—with the exception of the cornmeal crust on the Fried Cheese with a Spiced Crust (page 70) and the ginger crust on the Fried Calamari (page 72)—are interchangeable. We offer suggestions after some recipes, but you can experiment, too.

Just remember this: foods must be fried quickly once they're coated. The flour's glutens can turn sticky, the coating can slip off, and the food itself can interact in strange (and even unhealthy) ways with the coating.

Fried Olives in a Bread-Crumb Crust

A coating of plain bread crumbs makes simple olives a fabulous cocktail snack. Although pitted olives are not our first choice in most cases, they make these appetizers easy, one-bite wonders. *Makes 8 appetizer servings*

> 4 to 5 cups canola oil
> ½ cup all-purpose flour
> 1 large egg
> 2 tablespoons milk (regular, low-fat, or fat-free)
> 2 cups plain dried bread crumbs
> 24 large pitted green olives

1 Pour the canola oil into a large saucepan until it comes about a third of the way up the sides. Set the pan over medium heat and clip a deep-frying thermometer to the inside of the pan. Heat until the temperature registers 350°F.

2 Meanwhile, place the flour in one shallow bowl or soup plate. Beat the egg and milk in a small bowl with a fork until foamy. Place the bread crumbs in a third bowl or plate.

3 Roll an olive in the flour, just to coat it lightly, then dip it in the egg mixture. Allow the excess to drip back off, then roll it in the bread crumbs just before slipping it into the hot oil. Repeat with about a third of the olives. Fry until lightly brown, about 2 minutes, turning once or twice with a slotted metal spoon. Transfer to a fine-mesh wire rack and continue making more fried olives. Serve warm.

Variations: Substitute any stuffed pitted green olive you like—such as those stuffed with garlic, pimientos, almonds, or anchovies.

Fried Cheese with a Spiced Crust

Cheese threatens to liquefy under the slightest heat, so cheese strips need a thin dusting of flour before they're battered and fried: the flour barrier seals in the gooey goodness. Panfrying these sticks lets the coating get deeply browned and extra crunchy. *Makes 6 servings (or 12 pieces)*

> ½ cup all-purpose flour
> 2 large eggs
> 2 cups plain dried bread crumbs
> 1 tablespoon paprika
> 1 teaspoon onion powder
> 1 teaspoon dried thyme
> ½ teaspoon salt, plus additional to taste
> ¼ teaspoon cayenne
> 3 tablespoons olive oil
> ½ pound frozen mozzarella, Jarlsberg, Cheddar, Emmentaler, or Gouda, cut into thin spears about 3 inches long, 1 inch wide, and ½ inch thick (see Note)

1 Place the flour in a shallow soup bowl and set it on your work surface, the first in a lineup. Crack the eggs in a second soup bowl; lightly beat them with a fork. Finally, mix the bread crumbs, paprika, onion powder, thyme, ½ teaspoon salt, and the cayenne in a third soup plate.

2 Dip all the cheese sticks in the flour, just enough to give them a light coating. Set aside on a wire rack.

3 Heat a skillet over medium heat, then add the olive oil. Dip a coated cheese stick in the eggs, let the excess drip off, then roll it in the bread-crumb mixture to coat lightly. Slip it into the skillet, then quickly make a few more coated cheese sticks and get them into the skillet.

④ Fry undisturbed until lightly browned, about 2 minutes. Watch carefully so the sticks don't burn, lowering the heat if they brown too quickly. Flip and continue cooking until browned on both sides, about 2 more minutes. Transfer to a wire rack, then continue making more cheese sticks. Season with additional salt, if desired, and serve at once.

Note: Freezing helps cheese hold its shape as you cut and coat it. Place any of these cheeses in the freezer for about 20 minutes before you slice them.

Variations: You can also use soft cheeses like Brie, Camembert, or cambozola. Freeze for 1 hour, then remove the rind and cut the firmed-up cheese into spears as indicated. Work quickly so they don't defrost before they get into the hot oil.

This crust is also good on zucchini strips or summer squash rounds. Cut either into strips about the same size as the cheese strips before coating, dredging, and frying.

The Art of Frying

Deep-frying is dehydration: all those pops and splatters are moisture being boiled off by the hot oil, leaving food crisp. But the process is unpredictable. Anyone who's forgotten to water a garden for a few days knows exactly how relentless yet imprecise the trouble can be. That's why most deep-fried things are coated: the batter dehydrates (and gets crunchy) while protecting the food within.

Remember these tips:

• Keep the oil's temperature constant. With electric deep-fryers, this is no trick, since the thermostat regulates the heat. With a saucepan, monitor the temperature with a deep-frying thermometer clipped to the inside of the pan. The whole process is a matter of balance: adjust the heat so the oil's temperature remains constant.

• Don't crowd the pan. If you put too many things in at once, the oil's temperature will drop and the crust won't dehydrate. Instead, it will absorb oil without displacing moisture and end up gummy.

• Use a wire rack to drain food once it comes out of the oil. A deep-fried tidbit sitting on a paper towel will be a soggy deep-fried tidbit sitting on a wet paper towel. A fine-weave wire rack is preferable: the food drains without sinking through the slats.

Oil for Frying

Our preference is usually for peanut oil with its fairly high smoke point (that is, the point at which oil starts to volatilize and can catch fire); it also imparts a faint, aromatic taste that doesn't compete with other flavors. Asian peanut oils are not refined like American bottlings; they have a distinct taste and a much lower smoke point—and so are not recommended here. Rapeseed, grape seed, canola, and safflower oil would also be good choices.

Fried Calamari with a Ginger Crust

A thick batter ruins calamari; a better choice is a light, crunchy crust made from ground gingersnaps. The oil here is slightly hotter to get the calamari cooked quickly; do not let the rings brown deeply or they will be tough. *Makes 6 servings*

> 4 to 7 cups peanut oil
> 1 cup all-purpose flour
> ½ cup yellow cornmeal
> ½ cup gingersnap cookies, finely ground to a powder in a food processor or in a sealed plastic bag with the bottom of a heavy saucepan
> 1 pound calamari, cleaned and cut into ¼-inch rings (see Note)
> Salt to taste

❶ Add enough peanut oil to come about halfway up the sides of a large saucepan. Clip a deep-frying thermometer to the inside of the pan and set it over medium-high heat until the temperature registers 375°F.

❷ Meanwhile, mix the flour, cornmeal, and ground gingersnaps in a small bowl. Place the calamari rings in a large colander set in the sink, then shake the flour mixture over them. Shake the colander repeatedly until some of the flour mixture has adhered to the rings and the excess has been shaken off.

❸ Slip about a quarter of the coated rings into the hot oil and fry until golden blond, about 2 minutes, turning once or twice with a slotted spoon. Transfer to a wire rack and season lightly with salt. Continue making more of the coated rings, working in batches.

Garnishes: Classic Cocktail Sauce (page 61), Simple Asian Dipping Sauce (page 74), or Wasabi Mayonnaise (page 121).

Note: What stops most home cooks from making this restaurant favorite is the problem of cleaning the squid. Fortunately, many markets sell already prepared calamari rings; if not, most fishmongers will do the cleaning for you.

If you want to tackle it, first remember that there's a spiny quill inside the squid's body. Armed with that knowledge and working over the sink (the ink sac may rupture), run your finger into the tubelike body and pull everything out (but not off), including that sharp quill. Slice off the tentacles just below the eyes, removing the innards as well. Slice the tentacles into a little "bouquet" if you want to fry them and discard everything else from inside as well as the "hard beak." Rinse the body with water, then pull the gray, blue, or mottled laminate-like sheath off the outside of the body. If it will not come free, scrape it off with a sharp paring knife. Finally, cut the body into ¼-inch-wide rings.

Fried Scallops with a Beer-Batter Crust

Frothy beer gives these scallops a light coating, yeasty and a little salty. *Makes 8 appetizer servings or 4 main-course servings*

> 4 to 7 cups peanut oil
> 1¼ cups all-purpose flour
> ½ teaspoon baking powder
> About 2 teaspoons salt
> ¼ teaspoon freshly ground black pepper
> 1 large egg, lightly beaten
> 1 cup beer, at room temperature but not flat
> 2 pounds bay or diver scallops, trimmed, each cut in half into two disks

❶ Pour enough oil into a large saucepan so that it comes halfway up the sides. Clip a deep-frying thermometer to the inside of the pan and place the pan over medium heat. Heat to 350°F.

❷ Meanwhile, whisk 1 cup flour, baking powder, 1 teaspoon salt, and pepper in a large mixing bowl. Whisk in the egg and beer until smooth.

❸ Place the halved scallops in a sieve set in the sink; dust the remaining ¼ cup flour over them. Shake the sieve until they are lightly coated but the excess flour has fallen off.

❹ Dip a coated scallop into the prepared batter; gently slide it into the hot oil. Repeat with the remaining scallop halves, dipping and frying only as many as will fit in the pan in one layer without crowding. Fry until golden, 2 to 3 minutes, turning once or twice with metal tongs. Transfer to a wire rack. While they're hot, sprinkle with salt, as desired. Continue making more fried scallops with the remaining batter.

Garnishes: Basic Pizza Sauce (page 183), jarred pizza sauce, or Dijon mustard.

Variations: You can use this classic batter for just about any flour-coated, fried tidbit: seeded bell pepper strips, onion rings, broccoli florets, cauliflower florets, peeled and deveined shrimp, or chicken drumlets. You can also fry bone-in chicken pieces with this batter; they will take up to 20 minutes to be fully cooked.

If you want to make a meal out of these fried wonders, consider pairing them with a green salad dressed with a classic vinaigrette (see page 100). They're also nice alongside simple sides like sliced tomatoes with salt and rice vinegar or sliced cucumbers with salt and sesame oil. For the most part, avoid grilled sides; the smoky taste easily overpowers the delicate, fried coatings. For a wintry treat, try floating fried bits in a Creamy Vegetable Soup (page 131).

Fried Oysters with a Panko Crust

Panko bread crumbs, a Japanese specialty (see page 659), give these briny oysters an exceptionally lacy coating. *Makes 8 appetizer servings or 4 main-course servings*

> 4 to 7 cups peanut oil
> 1 tablespoon paprika
> 1 teaspoon onion powder
> ½ teaspoon freshly ground black pepper
> ¼ cup regular or low-fat buttermilk
> 24 large shucked oysters
> 2 cups panko bread crumbs
> 1 teaspoon salt, or more to taste

❶ Pour enough peanut oil into a large saucepan to come about halfway up the sides. Clip a deep-frying thermometer to the inside of the pan, set it over medium-high heat, and heat until the temperature registers 375°F.

❷ Meanwhile, whisk the paprika, onion powder, and pepper into the buttermilk in a large bowl. Add the oysters, stir gently, and set aside.

❸ Place the bread crumbs on a large plate; pick up an oyster and dredge it in the bread crumbs, coating thoroughly. Slip it into the oil and repeat with about 5 more of the oysters. Fry until lightly brown, about 2 minutes, turning once or twice with a metal slotted spoon. Transfer to a wire rack, sprinkle with salt to taste, and continue making more fried oysters, working in batches. Season with salt before serving.

Garnishes: Wasabi Mayonnaise (page 121) or Classic Cocktail Sauce (page 61), or Simple Asian Dipping Sauce (page 74).

Vegetable Tempura

For the laciest tempura, use finely crushed ice in the batter: the crystals will explode when they hit the very hot oil. Rice flour is a very low-gluten flour made from ground rice; look for it in the Asian food section of many supermarkets or at health food stores. *Makes 6 to 8 appetizer servings*

    4 to 7 cups vegetable oil
    ½ cup all-purpose flour
    ¼ cup rice flour
    1 teaspoon baking powder
    1 large egg white, beaten until frothy
    ½ cup water
    ½ cup pulverized ice (see Note)
    2 pounds mixed vegetables, such as baby
        carrots, seeded bell peppers, zucchini, or
        scallions, cut into long, thin strips
    Salt to taste

1 Pour enough vegetable oil into a large saucepan that it comes about halfway up the sides. Clip a deep-frying thermometer to the inside of the pan and place the pan over medium heat. Heat the oil to 375°F.

2 Whisk the all-purpose flour, rice flour, and baking powder in a large mixing bowl. Whisk in the egg white until combined, then whisk in the water and ice. Tiny ice particles should be left in the batter, but no chunks of ice.

3 Dip a vegetable strip into the batter, then slip it into the hot oil. Stand back—the batter will pop. Dip and fry only as many vegetable strips as will fit into the pan without crowding. Fry until crisp and blond, not browned, about 2 minutes; avoid turning the tempura more than once so as not to dislodge the coating. Remove with a slotted metal spoon and drain on a fine-mesh wire rack. Sprinkle with a pinch of salt. Repeat with the remaining vegetables, working in batches.

Garnishes: Simple Asian Dipping Sauce (below), Sesame Dipping Sauce (below), plain soy sauce, or soy sauce mixed with a little prepared wasabi paste.

Note: To pulverize ice, seal it in a plastic bag and go at it with the bottom of a heavy saucepan or a meat mallet. Drain off any excess water that develops.

Variation: Use this same batter to make shrimp, scallop, or fish fillet tempura. Fry until lacy and crisp, about 3 minutes.

Vinegary Dips for Fried Things

While flavored mayonnaises (page 121), Aïoli (page 45), or Classic Cocktail Sauce (page 61) are traditional condiments for fried tidbits, we like the tangy zip of vinegary sauces. For any of these, whisk the ingredients in a small bowl.

Simple Asian Dipping Sauce

    ¼ cup soy sauce
    1 tablespoon rice vinegar
    1 teaspoon sugar

Sesame Dipping Sauce

    3 tablespoons soy sauce
    3 tablespoons rice vinegar
    1 teaspoon toasted sesame oil

Malty Sauce

    ⅓ cup malt vinegar
    1½ teaspoons prepared horseradish

Mignonette

    ½ cup white wine or champagne vinegar
    2 small shallots, minced
    2 teaspoons freshly ground black pepper

These ride the line between a starter and a meal; just add a tossed salad or some side veggies and you can call many of them dinner. Many can also be plated as a more formal first course.

Gravlax

A Swedish specialty, gravlax is cured salmon. Buy only fresh salmon, not previously frozen fillets. Serve it with any or all of these: sliced pumpernickel bread, table crackers, cornichons or small dill pickles, drained capers, chopped hard-cooked egg yolks, chopped hard-cooked egg whites, chopped red onion, sour cream, crème fraîche, or Dijon mustard mixed with chopped herbs. *Makes about 12 small servings*

One 2-pound salmon fillet, skinned
　(see Note)
¼ cup kosher salt
3 tablespoons sugar
1 teaspoon freshly ground black pepper
2 cups dill fronds, cut into 2-inch sections

❶ Gently run your hand over the salmon's flesh to ensure there are no bones remaining. Be careful—the bones can pierce your skin. Should you find any, remove them with a sterilized pair of tweezers.

❷ Mix the salt, sugar, and pepper together in a small bowl. Rub this mixture into both sides of the fillet, taking care to get the seasonings into the flesh without mashing or tearing it.

❸ Place half the dill fronds in a glass 13 × 9-inch baking dish, then lay the fillet on top. Cover with the remaining fronds, pushing them down so they adhere to the flesh. Cover tightly and refrigerate for at least 24 hours or up to 2 days.

❹ Remove the dill and wipe off any salt mixture adhering to the fillet. Place it on a cutting board or a wooden serving tray. Slice into paper-thin pieces with a long, thin knife, angling the blade through the flesh for slightly wider pieces.

Note: Your fishmonger can skin the salmon for you. If you'd like to do it yourself, place the fillet skin side down on a large cutting board. Pick up the narrowest tip of the fillet and run a long, thin, very sharp slicing knife between the flesh and the skin, angling the blade down toward the skin without cutting through to the cutting board. Draw the blade back and forth, cutting between the flesh and skin. Once you have some of the skin detached, hold the loose skin down against the cutting board with one hand and continue to work the knife between the flesh and skin, thereby taking the flesh off the skin (rather than sawing the skin off the flesh). You may have to stop several times and reposition the blade; keep the tension constant and firm on the loosened skin.

Variations: In all of these, omit the dill.

Lightly toast 2 tablespoons cumin seeds in a dry skillet over medium heat until aromatic, about 2 minutes. Cool completely, then place half of these cumin seeds in the baking dish, top with the rubbed salmon, then press the remaining cumin seeds gently into the flesh.

Reduce the sugar to 1½ tablespoons. Add 2 teaspoons wasabi powder and 2 teaspoons ground ginger with the remaining sugar.

Substitute 1 cup packed, shredded sage, tarragon, or basil leaves for the dill fronds.

Add 1 teaspoon ground cinnamon to the salt and sugar mixture.

Add 2 teaspoons crushed juniper berries to the salt and sugar mixture.

Add 2 tablespoons chopped fresh rosemary to the salt and sugar mixture.

Ten Things to Do with Gravlax

1. Roll thinly sliced gravlax in flour tortillas that have been spread with softened cream cheese and sprinkled with chopped parsley or dill.

2. Add chopped gravlax to a green salad, preferably one with a creamy vinaigrette (pages 102–103).

3. Fold chopped gravlax into scrambled eggs just before you remove them from the pan (see page 14).

4. Place thinly sliced gravlax on purchased blinis, crumpets, or toasted English muffins, then top with crème fraîche and caviar.

5. Make appetizer sandwiches by placing thinly sliced gravlax in between pumpernickel slices that have been spread with unsalted butter; cut into quarters.

6. Wrap thinly sliced gravlax around pickled okra spears, pickled green beans, or cornichons.

7. Spread mayonnaise on toast, top with thinly sliced gravlax and shredded Cheddar—broil until the cheese melts.

8. Lay thin slices of gravlax over deviled eggs (see page 59).

9. Thinly slice the gravlax, roll the slices into balls, and pierce with bamboo skewers; serve with your favorite mayonnaise salad dressing as a dip (see pages 104–105).

10. Serve thinly sliced gravlax on top of Lentil-Nut Patties (page 504), then top with sour cream or crème fraîche.

Squid Salad with Saffron, Chickpeas, and Sherry Vinegar

This light salad is refreshing and tart, a good match for sweet cocktails or beer. *Makes 4 to 6 servings*

2 tablespoons sherry vinegar
¼ teaspoon saffron, crumbled
3 tablespoons olive oil
2 garlic cloves, minced
1 pound cleaned squid (see page 72), cut into thin rings and the tentacles quartered
¾ cup canned chickpeas, drained and rinsed
1 jarred whole roasted red bell pepper or pimiento, sliced into thin strips
1 teaspoon chopped oregano leaves or ½ teaspoon dried oregano
¼ teaspoon salt
¼ teaspoon freshly ground black pepper

1. Mix the vinegar and saffron in a small bowl or teacup; set aside for 10 minutes.

2. Place the olive oil and garlic in a large skillet, then set it over low heat. Cook, stirring often, until the garlic frizzles at the edges, about 2 minutes.

3. Raise the heat to medium and stir in the squid. Cook, stirring constantly, for 30 seconds.

4. Add the vinegar and saffron; cook, tossing all the while, until the squid is opaque and a little firm but not hard, about 1 minute.

5. Remove the skillet from the heat and stir in the chickpeas, red bell pepper or pimiento, oregano, salt, and pepper. Mix well; then pour into a large, nonreactive bowl. Cover and refrigerate for at least 4 hours or up to 3 days.

Variations: Substitute thyme, rosemary, or marjoram for the oregano. Also add up to ½ teaspoon red pepper flakes with the chickpeas.

Tuna Tartare on Gaufrettes

Tartare is usually a raw-beef preparation, but tuna has a similar texture and a milder flavor. Gaufrettes are waffle-cut potato chips. You'll need a mandoline—or you can simplify the whole process, forgo making your own Gaufrettes, and use purchased, wavy- or waffle-cut potato chips.

Makes 8 appetizer servings or 4 lunch servings

¼ cup canola oil
1 tablespoon lemon juice
1 tablespoon ginger juice
1 teaspoon toasted sesame seeds
1 teaspoon finely diced seeded fresh jalapeño chile
1 small scallion, minced
1½ pounds sushi-quality tuna
¼ cup chopped cilantro leaves
1 teaspoon salt
Freshly ground black pepper to taste
Gaufrettes (recipe follows)

1 Mix the canola oil, lemon juice, ginger juice, sesame seeds, jalapeño, and scallion in a small bowl; set aside for 10 minutes.

2 Trim off any tough white nerve fibers in the tuna, then slice it into ¼-inch strips. Cut each of these strips into ¼-inch dice. Draw the knife through the fish, rather than sawing.

3 Gather the tuna pieces together—be careful, they are fragile and can turn to mush quickly—and place in a large bowl. Stir in the oil mixture and the cilantro, salt, and pepper. To serve, mound the Tuna Tartare on a serving platter or onto individual plates, and serve with the Gaufrettes on the side as a scoop to pick up the tuna.

Variations: Add 2 teaspoons grated lemon zest to the oil dressing.

Add 1 teaspoon wasabi powder to the oil dressing.

Add 1 garlic clove, pressed through a garlic press, to the oil dressing.

Substitute lime juice for the lemon juice.

Gaufrettes
Makes about 50 waffle-cut potato chips

2 to 3 large Russet potatoes, peeled, cut in half the short way, and soaked in cool water for 15 minutes
4 to 6 cups peanut oil
Salt to taste

1 Fit a mandoline with the waffle blade. Grip a potato half with the food guard and run the cut side of the potato over the blade. Rotate 90 degrees and run it again over the blade. A waffle-cut slice should fall out of the bottom of the machine. Check the slice to make sure the holes are visible and that the slice holds together when picked up—otherwise, adjust the blade. Continue making more slices, rotating the potato and grip by 90 degrees after each cut. Lay the slices on paper towels.

2 Pour the peanut oil into a large saucepan until it comes about halfway up the sides, clip a deep-frying thermometer to the inside of the pan, and set over medium-high heat. Bring the oil to 375°F.

3 Slip several slices into the oil; fry until lightly browned, about 2 minutes, turning once or twice. Adjust the heat so the oil's temperature remains constant. Transfer the gaufrettes to a fine-mesh wire rack and continue frying more. Season with salt, as desired, within seconds of their coming out of the oil. (The gaufrettes can be made in advance; once cooled, store them in a sealed container at room temperature for up to 1 day.)

Seared Foie Gras with Apricot Relish

This fatty, creamy goose or duck liver may have fancy restaurant overtones, but nothing could be easier to fix—with a well-seasoned cast-iron skillet (page 20) and good ventilation. Look for smooth, pinkish, compact, small lobes. *Makes 8 servings*

One 2-pound lobe foie gras, well chilled
Apricot Relish (recipe follows)

❶ Run very hot water over a sharp chef's knife until the blade is quite hot. Slice the foie gras into ¾-inch-thick slices, making 2 or 3 slices before reheating the knife under hot water. Place the slices on a platter, cover with plastic wrap, and refrigerate for at least 1 hour or up to 24 hours.

❷ Heat a large, well-seasoned cast-iron skillet over high heat until smoking, about 5 minutes. Slip several strips of foie gras into the skillet; keep the others in the refrigerator. Cook until browned and crisp on the outside (but soft to the touch), no more than 1 minute. Turn with a metal spatula and cook until browned, about 1 additional minute. The strips will have rendered a great deal of fat. Transfer to serving plates, pour off the fat in the pan, and continue frying more. Serve with the Apricot Relish.

Variations: Forgo the Apricot Relish and drizzle the seared strips of foie gras with aged, syrupy balsamic vinegar or pomegranate molasses. Or serve the seared foie gras over pineapple rounds that have been coated with canola oil and then grilled over high heat until lightly browned, about 3 minutes, turning once—or with the Grilled Pineapple Salsa (page 356).

Apricot Relish Makes about *3 cups*

1 medium onion, chopped
1 garlic clove, minced
2 cups chopped pitted fresh apricots
   (8 to 10 whole apricots)
1 cup packed light brown sugar
½ cup cider vinegar
¼ cup dried cranberries, chopped
2 tablespoons lemon juice
1 tablespoon minced peeled fresh ginger
½ tablespoon mustard seeds
½ teaspoon red pepper flakes
½ teaspoon ground cinnamon
½ teaspoon salt

Place the onion, garlic, apricots, brown sugar, cider vinegar, dried cranberries, lemon juice, ginger, mustard seeds, red pepper flakes, cinnamon, and salt in a medium saucepan set over medium heat. Stir until the mixture comes to a simmer, then reduce the heat and simmer slowly until thickened, about 40 minutes. Cover and set aside off the heat while you prepare the foie gras—or cool somewhat, transfer to a plastic container, cover, and refrigerate for up to 3 days; bring back to room temperature before serving.

Savory Tarts

Call it make-ahead elegance: a walnut crust, prebaked in a 10-inch tart pan, and filled with a savory filling. *Makes 8 servings (one 10-inch tart)*

½ cup toasted walnut halves
1 cup all-purpose flour, plus additional for
   dusting and rolling
½ teaspoon salt
½ stick (4 tablespoons) cold unsalted butter,
   cut into small chunks
3 to 4 tablespoons very cold water
One of the five fillings (recipes follow)

① First make the crust. Position the rack in the center of the oven and preheat the oven to 375°F.

② Grind the walnuts in a food processor fitted with a chopping blade until coarsely ground—not powdered but also in no way chunky. Add the flour and salt; pulse once or twice to combine.

③ Drop in the butter and pulse until incorporated and cut into small pieces. Add the water and pulse until a dough forms.

④ Lay a piece of wax paper on the work surface and lightly dust it with flour. Turn the dough out onto it; dust the dough lightly with flour. Roll it until 11 inches in diameter and about ¼ inch thick—you can tell if it's the right circumference by holding the 10-inch tart pan over it and checking that it's about 1 inch larger than the circumference of the pan.

⑤ Gently lift the wax paper and crust off the work surface, invert it over a 10-inch tart pan with a removable bottom, and press the crust down into the pan. Peel off the wax paper and continue pressing the crust into the pan, pushing it up the sides about 1 inch and making sure it gets into any fluted edges. Prick the crust many times across the bottom and sides with a fork.

⑥ Bake until lightly browned and firm to the touch, about 35 minutes. Transfer to a wire rack and cool at least 30 minutes or up to 4 hours. (Once baked and cooled, the crust can be stored, covered, at room temperature for up to 24 hours.)

⑦ Next, prepare one of these five fillings in the tart shell:

Stilton, Peaches, and Basil

Arrange 3 peaches, pitted and thinly sliced, across the bottom of the crust. Lay 6 basil leaves over the slices, then sprinkle with 3 ounces crumbled Stilton.

Crab and Pesto

Sprinkle 15 ounces lump crabmeat, picked over for shell and cartilage, across the tart crust. Dot with ½ cup Pecan Pesto (page 179) or Sage Pesto (page 293) in 1-tablespoon increments, spreading them a bit with a rubber spatula.

Pears and Parmesan

Arrange 2 ripe pears, cored and thinly sliced, across the crust, then top with 3 ounces thinly shaved Parmigiano-Reggiano. Drizzle 1 tablespoon honey over the cheese.

Plums and Asiago

Brush 2 teaspoons Dijon mustard over the tart bottom with a pastry brush. Top with 4 ripe plums, seeded and thinly sliced. Sprinkle 2 tablespoons pine nuts over the tart, then top with 2 ounces grated Asiago.

Caramelized Onions and Bacon

Heat 2 tablespoons olive oil in a large skillet set over low heat. Add 2 medium onions, thinly sliced, and 1 tablespoon caraway or fennel seeds. Reduce the heat to very low and cook, stirring frequently, until golden and soft, about 30 minutes. Do not let the onions brown. At the same time, fry 4 strips bacon in a nonstick skillet set over medium heat until crispy, about 5 minutes, turning two or three times. Transfer the bacon to a plate lined with paper towels to drain, then crumble into small bits. Mix the crumbled bacon into the onions when they're finished cooking. Spoon this mixture into the tart shell.

8 Finally, bake the tart. Position the rack in the center of the oven and preheat the oven to 400°F.

9 Bake the filled tart until the cheese melts and/or the filling starts to bubble, about 12 minutes. Cool on a wire rack for at least 10 minutes or up to 3 hours before slipping the tart out of its removable ring to slice and serve.

One Crust, Three Classics: Focaccia, Pissaladière, and Pizza

Focaccia is an Italian flatbread, topped simply with aromatics and salt. Pissaladière is a thin-crust pizza from Nice, topped with slow-cooked onions, anchovies, and olives. And pizza? It's high time it got put in its rightful place: as an appetizer, served with a summery fruit punch or an aperitif. *Makes 12 appetizer servings or 6 main-course servings; makes one large 17 × 11-inch crust*

The Crust

1¼ cups warm water (between 105°F
   and 115°F)

½ teaspoon sugar

½ ounce (2 standard packages or
   5 teaspoons) active dry yeast

⅓ cup olive oil, plus additional for greasing
   the bowl

1 teaspoon salt

4 cups or more all-purpose flour

1 Pour the water into the bowl of a stand mixer or into a large bowl, add the sugar, and sprinkle the yeast over the top. Set aside for 5 minutes until bubbling. (If the yeast does not get fizzy, start over.) Stir in the oil and salt.

2 **If you're using a stand mixer:** Attach the bowl, snap on the dough hook, and begin adding the flour in ½-cup increments, mixing at medium speed all the while, until a pliable but firm dough forms, not sticky but soft and smooth. You may use a little more than 4 cups of flour, depending on the day's humidity and the flour's glutens. Continue kneading at medium speed for 10 minutes, adding splashes of flour if the dough starts to stick or crawl up the hook. Don't use all the flour unless you need to—you simply want a smooth dough that's not tacky or gummy.

If you're working by hand: Stir about 3 cups of the flour into the yeast mixture with a wooden spoon. Once the dough begins to form and becomes difficult to stir, turn it out onto a clean, floured work surface and begin kneading in more flour in small increments until a pliable, firm dough forms; continue dusting the work surface and your hands with flour to prevent sticking. Knead for 10 minutes, grinding the heel of one hand into the dough while pulling it with the fingers of the other, until the dough is smooth, somewhat elastic, and quite soft.

3 Grease a large bowl with some olive oil dabbed on a paper towel. Gather the dough into a ball, place it in the bowl, and turn it over so that it's lightly coated with oil. Cover loosely with plastic wrap or a clean kitchen towel and set aside in a warm, draft-free place until doubled in bulk, about 1 hour.

Once the dough has doubled in bulk, turn it into one of the three classics.

1. Focaccia

2 tablespoons tomato paste

2 tablespoons olive oil, plus additional for
   greasing the pan

4 garlic cloves, minced

1 tablespoon chopped rosemary leaves or
   2 teaspoons crushed dried rosemary

1 to 2 teaspoons coarse-grained salt

❶ Position the rack in the center of the oven and preheat the oven to 450°F. Lightly oil a 17 × 11-inch lipped baking pan.

❷ Punch the dough down, then turn it into the prepared pan. Press it evenly to the corners, stretching and pulling as necessary. Cover with plastic wrap and set aside again in a warm, dry place to rise until doubled in bulk, about 1 hour. Use your fingers to dimple the top of the dough by pressing into it without pressing all the way through to the pan.

❸ Remove the plastic wrap.

❹ Paint the top of the dough with the tomato paste, using a pastry brush or the back of a small flatware spoon dipped in a little water. Drizzle the top of the dough with the olive oil, then sprinkle on the garlic, rosemary, and salt.

❺ Bake until puffed, golden, and brown, about 25 minutes. Cool for 5 minutes before cutting and serving, or cool completely and serve at room temperature.

2. Pissaladière
    ¼ cup olive oil, plus additional for greasing
        the pan
    3 large onions, sliced into thin rings
    1 bay leaf
    1 tablespoon stemmed thyme
    7 ounces anchovy fillets packed in olive oil,
        drained and rinsed
    24 pitted black olives, halved
    ½ teaspoon freshly ground black pepper

❶ Punch the dough down and turn it over in the bowl, cover again with plastic wrap or a clean kitchen towel, and set aside in a warm, draft-free place a second time until doubled in bulk, about 1 more hour.

❷ Meanwhile, place the olive oil in a large skillet and set it over very low heat. Add the onions and bay leaf, stir well, cover, and cook for 15 minutes, stirring once or twice. Do not let the onions brown; they should simply soften and give off quite a bit of liquid.

❸ Uncover the skillet and continue cooking very slowly until the onions are golden and sugary sweet, about 40 minutes. If the onions start to brown, reduce the heat even further or remove the pan from the heat for a few minutes until it cools down a bit.

❹ Position the rack in the center of the oven and preheat the oven to 450°F. Lightly oil a 17 × 11-inch lipped baking sheet.

❺ Once the dough has risen a second time, punch it down and turn it out onto the prepared baking sheet. Press it evenly to the corners, stretching and pulling as necessary.

❻ Remove and discard the bay leaf from the onions; stir in the thyme. Spread the onions evenly across the dough, then make a grid or diagonal pattern across them with the anchovy fillets, laying them tip to tail. Dot the olives in a decorative pattern across the dough, then sprinkle on some pepper.

❼ Bake until puffed and golden, about 20 minutes. Cool in the pan for 5 minutes before cutting and serving.

Variations: Add ¼ teaspoon ground cloves to the onions with the thyme.

Dot 1 tablespoon capers, drained and rinsed, over the onions with the olives.

Sprinkle the onions with 1 teaspoon coarse-grained salt before adding the anchovies.

Lightly paint the crust with Dijon mustard before spreading on the onions.

Grate Parmigiano-Reggiano over the top the moment it comes out of the oven.

3. Pizza

2 cups Basic Pizza Sauce (page 183), jarred
pizza sauce, Sun-Dried Tomato and
Roasted Garlic Pesto (page 48), or Sage
Pesto (page 293)

1 pound mozzarella, shredded

1 Punch the dough down and turn it over in
the bowl, cover again loosely with plastic wrap
or a clean kitchen towel, and set aside in a warm,
draft-free place a second time until doubled in
bulk, about 1 more hour.

2 As the dough finishes rising, position the rack in
the center of the oven and preheat the oven to 450°F.
Lightly oil a 17 × 11-inch lipped baking sheet.

3 Once the dough has risen a second time, punch
it down and turn it out onto the prepared baking
sheet. Press it evenly to the corners, stretching and
pulling as necessary. Spread the pizza sauce or pesto across the dough, then sprinkle on the cheese.

4 Bake until golden and gooey, about 20 minutes. Cool for 5 minutes before cutting.

Other Pizza Toppings: Before you add the
cheese, you can also sprinkle any of these over
the pizza:

8 ounces pepperoni, thinly sliced

8 ounces Italian sausage meat, fried with
1 tablespoon olive oil in a skillet over
medium heat until browned, about
3 minutes

8 ounces sliced mushrooms, cooked with
2 teaspoons olive oil in a skillet over
medium heat until they give off their
liquid and it evaporates, about 5 minutes

8 canned artichoke hearts, drained and cut
into quarters

2 red or green bell peppers, cored,
seeded, and thinly sliced

1 medium onion, thinly sliced

3 to 4 garlic cloves, minced

Although the name "pâté" may call up images of a fussy, '50s appetizer, not all pâtés are created equal—or are equally hard to create. Here are five that run the gamut from a chunky French pâté to a creamy vegetarian chopped liver.

Classic Country Pâté

This is a traditional pâté with an important change: to protect the mélange from the heat, we line the pan with pancetta, rather than caul fat or butter. Beef liver is too strong and will overpower the flavors, so search out calf's liver or pork liver at meat counters. Serve with minced hard-cooked eggs (see page 59), Dijon mustard, cornichons or other small pickles, drained capers or larger caper berries, as well as toasted baguette rounds, melba toast, or plain crackers. *Makes about 20 servings*

½ pound pancetta, sliced paper thin
¼ pound fatback or pork fat
1 pound ground pork
¾ pound ground veal (see Note)
½ pound calf's or pork liver, finely
   chopped
1 large shallot, minced
1 garlic clove, minced
2 large egg yolks
⅔ cup Cognac or brandy
2 teaspoons finely grated orange zest
1 teaspoon salt
1 teaspoon stemmed thyme or ½ teaspoon
   dried thyme
½ teaspoon grated nutmeg
½ teaspoon ground allspice
½ teaspoon freshly ground black pepper
¼ teaspoon ground cloves
4 bay leaves

❶ Position the rack in the center of the oven and preheat the oven to 375°F. Line the bottom and sides of a 6-cup pâté pan or a 9 × 5 × 3-inch loaf pan with the pancetta slices.

❷ Grind the fatback or pork fat through a meat grinder, or puree it with 1 tablespoon water in a food processor fitted with the chopping blade until smooth, scraping down the sides of the canister as necessary.

❸ Transfer the ground fatback or pork fat to a large bowl. Gently stir in the ground pork, ground veal, liver, shallot, garlic, egg yolks, Cognac or brandy, orange zest, salt, thyme, nutmeg, allspice, pepper, and cloves, taking care not to break up the meat's fibers.

❹ Spoon into the prepared pan. Smooth the top, then lay the bay leaves across it in a decorative pattern. Cover tightly with aluminum foil. Place in a larger baking pan and fill with very hot tap water until it comes halfway up the outside of the pâté or loaf pan.

❺ Bake until an instant-read meat thermometer inserted into the middle of the pâté registers 160°F, 1½ to 2 hours. Take the pan out of the water bath and carefully drain off any fat. Cover again with foil, then weight it down with cans or bricks, laying them right on the covered pâté. Refrigerate for at least 1 day, preferably 2 days, or up to 4 days. Remove the weights, foil, and bay leaves to serve. If you've baked the terrine in a traditional pan, serve it directly from there; if not, then invert it onto a cutting board, shake vigorously, and wipe with hot, damp paper towels to release the mold, then reinvert it onto a serving plate.

Note: If you can't find ground veal, use an additional ½ pound ground pork and ¼ pound ground beef, preferably ground chuck.

Variations: Substitute a hearty red wine such as a Zinfandel or Merlot for the Cognac.

Substitute 2 teaspoons chopped tarragon leaves for the thyme; omit the nutmeg and allspice.

Mousse Pâté

This velvety pâté begs for champagne. It's best made with mild duck livers, but chicken livers are a fine stand-in. Serve with toasted Italian bread or sesame crackers and with pickled onions, pickled green beans, or thinly sliced red onions. You can also sprinkle a few drops of aged balsamic vinegar on each serving. *Makes 20 servings*

2 tablespoons unsalted butter
4 medium shallots, minced
2 pounds duck or chicken livers
¾ cup Cognac or brandy
2 teaspoons unflavored powdered gelatin
¼ cup dry white wine
Vegetable or canola oil, for greasing the pan
⅔ cup heavy cream
1 teaspoon salt
½ teaspoon ground allspice
½ teaspoon ground mace
½ teaspoon freshly ground pepper,
    preferably white pepper

1 Melt the butter in a large skillet over medium heat. Add the shallots and cook until soft, about 5 minutes. Add the livers and sauté until brown, stirring frequently, about 5 minutes.

2 Add the Cognac or brandy and bring the mixture to a simmer, scraping up any browned bits on the bottom of the skillet. (Should the alcohol ignite, cover the skillet immediately and remove it from the heat for 20 seconds, or until the fire is out.) Cook, stirring often, until the Cognac has reduced to a glaze and the livers are cooked through, about 10 minutes.

3 Meanwhile, sprinkle the gelatin over the wine in a small bowl and set aside to soften for 5 minutes. Lightly oil a 1-quart loaf pan or a 1-quart terrine.

4 Stir the cream and the softened gelatin mixture into the skillet. Reduce the heat to very low and stir just until the gelatin dissolves, about 5 seconds. Do not let the sauce return to a boil. Remove the skillet from the heat and stir in the salt, allspice, mace, and pepper.

5 Pour the entire contents of the pan into a large food processor fitted with a chopping blade (work in batches if you need to). Process until silky, then pour and smooth into the prepared loaf pan or terrine.

6 Place in the refrigerator to cool, then cover with plastic wrap and continue chilling until set, at least 6 hours or overnight. To serve, turn the pan or terrine upside down onto a serving platter and unmold the terrine. You may need to wipe the outside of the mold with paper towels doused in hot water to loosen the pâté.

Variations: Substitute dry vermouth for the wine.

Substitute ground cinnamon for the allspice.

Substitute grated nutmeg for the mace.

Add 2 minced garlic cloves with the shallots.

Three-Layer Vegetable Pâté

Here's a creamy, layered, vegetarian pâté, a silkier version of those sold at deli counters. *Makes about 16 servings*

- 12 tablespoons (1½ sticks) unsalted butter, cut into chunks, plus additional for greasing the pan
- 3 large onions, chopped
- 6 garlic cloves, minced
- 1 teaspoon stemmed thyme
- ½ teaspoon grated nutmeg
- ½ teaspoon salt
- ½ teaspoon freshly ground black pepper
- 2 large carrots, peeled and thinly sliced into rings (about 1½ cups)
- 2 cups packed broccoli florets
- 1 tablespoon tomato paste, preferably reduced-sodium tomato paste
- 3 large eggs plus 3 large egg yolks
- 1⅔ cups canned white beans, drained and rinsed

1 Melt the butter in a large skillet set over medium-low heat. Add the onions, stir well, and reduce the heat to very low. Cook, stirring frequently, until golden and very soft, about 20 minutes; do not let the onions brown—keep the heat very low and stir often.

2 Add the garlic and continue cooking for 5 minutes, then stir in the thyme, nutmeg, salt, and pepper. Set the mixture aside for 10 minutes.

3 Meanwhile, place the sliced carrots in a vegetable steamer set over simmering water. Cover and steam until quite soft, about 8 minutes. Place the carrots in the bowl of a food processor or the canister of a large blender.

4 Fill the steamer basket with the broccoli florets (add more water to the pan, if necessary).

Cover and steam until very soft, about 6 minutes. Drain the florets in a colander set in the sink, then rinse with cool water to spike the bright green color.

5 Position the rack in the center of the oven and preheat the oven to 350°F. Butter a 9 × 5 × 3-inch loaf pan and set it aside.

6 Pour a third of the onion mixture in the skillet into the food processor or blender canister with the carrots. Add the tomato paste, 1 egg, and 1 egg yolk. Process or blend until smooth.

7 Pour this carrot mixture into the prepared loaf pan, smoothing it to the sides and creating as flat a surface as possible with a rubber spatula. Clean and dry the food processor or blender canister.

8 Place the white beans in the food processor or blender canister, then add half the remaining onion mixture along with 1 egg and 1 egg yolk. Process or blend until smooth, scraping down the sides of the bowl or canister as necessary.

9 Gently spoon this mixture evenly over the top of the carrot mixture. Smooth it flat, then gently rap the pan against your work surface to release any trapped bubbles and to condense the mixture slightly. Clean and dry the food processor or blender canister.

10 Place the broccoli florets in the food processor or blender canister. Add the remaining onion mixture, as well as the remaining egg and egg yolk. Process or blend until smooth.

11 Gently spoon this green mixture into the prepared loaf pan, taking care not to get the white bean mixture mixed into it, but also to create a smooth, flat top without any air pockets. Again, gently rap the pan against your work surface.

12 Butter a piece of aluminum foil and cover the pan with it, buttered side down. Place the loaf pan in a larger baking dish or roasting pan. Fill the baking dish or roasting pan with hot tap water until it comes halfway up the loaf pan.

13 Bake until set, about 2 hours. The pâté will rise up slightly and be firm, not jiggly; a flatware knife inserted into the center should come out clean. Remove the pan from the water bath and cool at room temperature for 10 minutes.

14 With the foil cover still in place, weight the top of the terrine with a brick covered in plastic wrap or a couple of heavy cans, laying them on their sides. Place these weights directly onto the foil-covered pâté.

15 Refrigerate for at least 8 hours, until chilled and firm, or for up to 3 days. To serve, unmold onto a serving platter—a paper towel damp with warm water can help loosen the pâté from the pan when you turn it upside down on the platter.

Variations: Substitute cubed golden beets for the carrots; steam them until tender when pierced with a fork, about 15 minutes.
Substitute ½ pound thin, peeled asparagus spears, cut into 2-inch sections, for the broccoli.
Substitute 2 cups frozen spinach, thawed and squeezed dry of all excess moisture, for the broccoli; omit steaming the spinach.
Substitute tarragon for the thyme.
Substitute ground cloves for the nutmeg.

Chopped Liver

We prefer a combination of calf's liver and chicken livers for this Jewish deli favorite. Serve with Challah (page 222), rice cakes, bagels, or crackers; with coarse sea salt to sprinkle on each serving; and with sliced radishes, thinly sliced red onions, and/or thinly sliced tomatoes. *Makes about 12 servings*

1½ pounds chicken livers, cut in half
½ pound calf's liver, cut into 2-inch pieces
3 tablespoons olive oil (see Note)
2 large onions, chopped
3 hard-cooked eggs (see page 59), peeled
1 teaspoon salt
½ teaspoon freshly ground black pepper

1 Line a broiler tray with aluminum foil; preheat the broiler.

2 Place both kinds of liver on the lined broiler pan and set them 4 to 6 inches from the heat source. Broil until cooked through, about 8 minutes, turning once. Set aside.

3 Heat a large skillet over medium heat. Add the olive oil, then the onions, and cook, stirring frequently, until softened and sweet, about 8 minutes.

4 Once the livers are cool enough to handle, cut them into 2-inch chunks and add them along with any accumulated juices to the skillet. Stir well, cover, reduce the heat to low, and continue cooking for 5 minutes. Set aside to cool for 5 minutes.

5 Grind the livers, onions, and eggs through a meat grinder set at a coarse setting. You'll need to work in batches; be careful of your fingers near the blades. Alternatively, put the contents of the skillet and the eggs in the bowl of a large food processor fitted with the chopping blade; pulse a few times, then process quickly, just until velvety, not until mushy. Be careful: the food processor quickly turns it into baby food. Stir in the salt and pepper, then smooth the mixture into a serving dish.

To store: Cover and refrigerate for up to 2 days.

Note: For a more authentic taste, substitute schmaltz (or rendered chicken fat), available in kosher or kosher-style delis and some high-end supermarkets. But we've left out this traditional heart-stopper—and broiled the chicken livers, too—for a lighter take on this rather heavy starter.

Variations: Add ½ teaspoon grated nutmeg, ground cumin, or ground allspice with the salt.

Vegetarian Chopped Liver

We don't like vegetarian fakes, especially since there are so many good vegetarian dishes to be made. But we're partial to this walnut and lentil "pâté" because it goes so well with a slice of crunchy baguette and some Dijon mustard. *Makes about 8 servings*

⅔ cup French or green lentils, picked over
    for stones
½ cup walnut pieces
3 tablespoons walnut oil
2 medium onions, chopped
1 celery rib, chopped
4 hard-cooked eggs (see page 59), peeled
    and cut into quarters
1 teaspoon salt
½ teaspoon freshly ground black pepper

1 Bring a large pot of water to a boil over high heat. Add the lentils, stir well, reduce the heat to medium, cover partially, and cook until very tender, until the lentils begin to break apart, about 20 minutes.

2 Meanwhile, place the walnut pieces in a large skillet and toast them over medium heat until they are browned and aromatic, tossing frequently, about 4 minutes. Transfer to the bowl of a food processor fitted with the chopping blade.

3 Return the skillet to the heat. Add the walnut oil, then the onions and celery. Reduce the heat to low and cook, stirring frequently, until the onions are soft and golden, about 10 minutes. Pour the contents of the skillet into the food processor.

4 Drain the lentils in a colander set in the sink; then add to the food processor along with the eggs, salt, and pepper. Process until chunky-smooth, scraping down the sides of the bowl as necessary. The texture is a matter of personal taste: if you prefer a smoother pâté, run the processor a while longer.

To store: Transfer to a serving bowl, cover with plastic wrap, and refrigerate for up to 2 days; return to room temperature before serving.

Variations: Substitute pecan halves, pine nuts, or skinned hazelnut halves for the walnuts.

Substitute 6 shallots for the onions.

Add one of the following with the salt and pepper: 2 teaspoons stemmed thyme, ½ teaspoon ground cardamom, ½ teaspoon ground mace, ¼ teaspoon grated nutmeg, ¼ teaspoon ground cloves, or ¼ teaspoon cayenne pepper.

All these appetizers are filled—then rolled, fried, baked, or steamed. They're not for weekdays; most take a little time but are great for weekends or holiday parties.

Summer Rolls

Here's a no-cook affair of translucent wrappers holding fresh ingredients. A staple in Southeast Asian cooking, rice paper wrappers are made from rice flour, water, and salt; rolled to thin sheets, they're dried on bamboo mats (thus, their crosshatch designs). Found in the Asian food section of most markets and in all Asian grocery stores, they can be stored in a cool, dark, dry place for up to 3 months. *Makes 12 summer rolls*

Canola or vegetable oil, for greasing the
    baking sheet
12 rice paper wrappers
One of the five summer roll fillings that
    follow
For dipping: Salsa (page 47), Wasabi
    Mayonnaise (page 121), Simple Asian
    Dipping Sauce (page 74), Sesame Dipping
    Sauce (page 74), Mignonette (page 74),
    Peanut-Ginger Sauce (page 508), seasoned
    rice vinegar, and/or your favorite
    vinaigrette (see pages 100–104)

❶ Dab a little oil on a paper towel and lightly grease a large baking sheet; cover it loosely with plastic wrap and set aside.

❷ Fill a large, shallow bowl or a small baking pan with warm water. Pick up one brittle, dried wrapper and make sure it isn't cracked or broken. Slip it into the water and soak just until pliable, usually less than 25 seconds. Remove it from the water and place it on your work surface.

❸ Place the filling in a horizontal line in the bottom quarter of the wrapper. Fold two sides of the circle over the filling, then roll the wrapper up, rolling it away from you. Don't push down, but make sure the filling is compact inside the wrapper. Slip the filled wrapper under the plastic wrap covering the baking sheet. Continue making more of the summer rolls, slipping them under the plastic wrap so they don't dry out. Store at room temperature for about 1 hour or in the refrigerator for up to 4 hours. Serve with a dipping sauce on the side.

The Five Fillings for Summer Rolls

Don't mix the ingredients together; simply divide them among the 12 summer rolls and place them on top of each other in the wrapper before rolling it up (as directed in step 3).

1. 1 pound tempeh, cut into very thin strips
   4 ounces radish sprouts
   ½ cup Peanut-Ginger Sauce (about
       2 teaspoons per roll, page 508)

2. 36 purchased cooked medium shrimp, peeled
   and deveined
   4 scallions, cut into 1-inch pieces
   2 red bell peppers, cored, seeded, and diced
   ½ cup hoisin sauce (2 teaspoons per roll)

3. 8 ounces cooked chicken, chopped
   1 medium cucumber, peeled and shredded
       through the large holes of a box grater

½ cup mango or other fruit chutney
(2 teaspoons per roll)

4. About 4 ounces smoked salmon or Gravlax
(page 75), cut into long strips
6 radishes, cut into thin rings
½ cup crème fraîche (2 teaspoons per roll)

5. 12 cherry tomatoes, roughly chopped
2 celery ribs, finely chopped
1 large ripe mango, peeled, pitted, and
chopped
A few dashes of hot red pepper sauce to taste

Tips for Success

• The water must be warm to soften the
wrappers; replace it often.

• Wipe your counter often or the wrappers will
get water-logged.

• The rolls will stick together if they touch on
the baking sheet.

• The rolls are best within an hour of their being
made.

Chinese Dumplings

Shanghai-style wrappers are thinner but stay firmer, less slippery after they're steamed (and crisper
after they're fried). Make these dumplings up to 8
hours before you steam them; once stuffed, store
them, covered with plastic wrap, on a cornstarch-
dusted baking sheet in the refrigerator. *Makes about
40 dumplings*

¾ pound ground pork
¼ pound medium shrimp (about 35 per
pound), peeled and deveined
¼ cup canned preserved Szechuan
cabbage, turnip, or mixed vegetables
(see page 660)
4 scallions, thinly sliced

2 tablespoons minced peeled fresh ginger
1 tablespoon soy sauce
1 tablespoon rice vinegar
½ teaspoon sugar
40 or more circular Shanghai-style dumpling
wrappers
Cornstarch, for dusting the baking sheet
Nonstick spray or canola oil, for greasing the
steamer baskets
Simple Asian Dipping Sauce (page 74),
Sesame Dipping Sauce (page 74), Chinese
prepared mustard, or purchased sweet-
and-sour dipping sauce as a garnish

1 Place the pork, shrimp, preserved vegetable, and
scallions in a food processor fitted with a chopping blade; pulse until well mixed. Add the ginger, soy sauce, vinegar, and sugar. Pulse until finely
chopped, about like a coarse meat loaf mixture.
(The filling can be made up to 1 day in advance;
cover it tightly and store it in the refrigerator.)

2 Place one of the wrappers on your work surface. Place about 1 teaspoon filling in the center
of the wrapper. Wet your finger and run it along
half the circumference of the circle. Fold the circle closed into a half-moon, then pinch the edges
together to seal.

3 Pick up the dumpling and dab a little water
on the crescent edge. Begin crimping this curved
edge closed, starting at one end and folding a little
piece of the seam over itself, like crimping fabric
or paper, and then again, and again until you've
created a small, tight clutch or purse. Set aside
on a cornstarch-dusted baking sheet and continue
making more dumplings.

4 Bring about 2 inches of water to a simmer in a
large pot. Meanwhile, spray several bamboo baskets
with nonstick spray or lightly oil them. Place the
dumplings in one layer in each, then stack them
over the simmering water. Cover and steam until somewhat translucent and quite tender, about

10 minutes. Alternatively, steam the dumplings in batches in a metal vegetable steamer set over simmering water; spray the steamer with nonstick spray or line it with cabbage leaves to keep the wrappers from sticking. Serve with one or more dipping sauces on the side.

To turn the dumplings into potstickers:
Complete the dumpling recipe through step 3. Heat a 10- or 12-inch nonstick skillet over medium heat. Add 1 tablespoon sesame oil and 10 to 15 dumplings to the skillet, giving them some breathing room because they will expand. Fry undisturbed until the bottoms are brown and crispy, about 3 minutes. Add about ½ cup water to the pan, cover, and raise the heat to medium-high. Boil until the water has been all absorbed or evaporated and the filling is cooked through, about 8 minutes. Uncover, shake the pan to release the dumplings, and continue cooking until the bottoms crisp a second time, about 1 more minute. Transfer to a serving plate and continue frying more dumplings.

❋ Stuffed Half-Moons: Empanaditas, Samosas, and Pierogi ❋

Here's a mix-and-match affair. Some of the six fillings that follow are traditional for empanaditas (small, baked empanadas), samosas (fried East Indian dumplings), or pierogi (boiled Polish dumplings), but you can pair just about any filling with any dough, thereby creating the appetizer you want.

Empanaditas

These Latin American half-moons get brown and crunchy in the oven. Make sure you seal them well so that the filling doesn't leak. If you want an authentic taste, substitute lard for the solid vegetable shortening. *Makes about 32*

3 cups all-purpose flour, plus additional for dusting
2 teaspoons salt
½ cup plus 2 tablespoons solid vegetable shortening
3 large eggs
½ cup very cold water plus 2 tablespoons water
One of the six fillings that follow, preferably Herbed Turkey, South American Picadillo, or Vietnamese Picadillo

❶ Mix the flour and salt in a large bowl. Cut in the shortening with a pastry cutter or a fork until the mixture resembles coarse meal.

❷ Whisk 2 of the eggs and ½ cup cold water in a small bowl, then pour this into the flour mixture. Stir with a fork until a soft dough forms—but do not overwork: it should cohere into a ball but still be crumbly. Gather together, wrap in plastic, and set aside at room temperature for 1 hour. Meanwhile, make one of the six fillings on page 92.

❸ Position the rack in the center of the oven and preheat the oven to 350°F. Line a large baking sheet with parchment paper or a silicone baking mat.

❹ Divide the dough in half. Lightly dust your work surface with flour and roll out half the dough until it's a large sheet about ⅛ inch thick. Cut into sixteen 3½-inch circles, using a thick-rimmed water glass or a cookie cutter.

⑤ Place 1½ teaspoons of the filling in the center of each circle. Wet your finger with a little water, then run it around the rim of one of the circles. Fold in half, creating a half-moon; press the wet edges together to seal completely, even to the corners. Place on the prepared baking sheet and continue making the empanaditas, spacing them about 1 inch apart.

⑥ Repeat the process with the second half of the dough, making 32 empanaditas in all.

⑦ Beat the remaining egg and the remaining 2 tablespoons water in a small bowl. Brush the empanaditas with the egg wash, then bake until golden, about 25 minutes. Cool on the baking sheet for 2 minutes, then serve or transfer to a wire rack to cool completely.

Samosas

Serve these deep-fried Indian pockets as soon as they're made; accompany them with plain yogurt mixed with chopped mint or parsley. *Makes about 32*

    4 cups all-purpose flour
    1 teaspoon salt
    8 tablespoons (1 stick) cool unsalted butter,
        cut into chunks
    ½ cup plus 2 tablespoons plain yogurt
        (regular or low-fat but not fat-free)
    ¼ cup very cold water
    One of the six fillings that follow, preferably
        Cheese, Potato, Curried Squash and Pea,
        or Herbed Turkey
    3 to 5 cups canola oil

① Mix the flour and salt in a large bowl. Cut in the butter using a pastry cutter or a fork until the mixture resembles coarse meal.

② Stir in the yogurt, then the water, just until a loose dough forms and holds together. Gather it into a ball and wrap in plastic. Set aside at room temperature for 1 hour. Meanwhile, make one of the six fillings that begin on page 92.

③ Divide the dough in half; lightly dust your work surface with flour. Roll out one of the dough halves until it's about ⅛ inch thick. Cut it into sixteen 3½-inch circles, using a thick-rimmed water glass or a cookie cutter.

④ Place 1½ teaspoons of the filling in the center of each of the circles. Wet your finger, then run it around the rim of one of the circles. Fold the circle in half, enclosing the filling in a half-moon. Press the edges together to seal. Set aside and continue making the half-moon samosas with the remaining circles, then repeat the process with the second half of the dough.

⑤ Place the canola oil in a large, high-sided skillet or sauté pan so that it comes about 2 inches up the sides of the pan. Clip a deep-frying thermometer to the inside of the pan and heat over medium-high heat until the temperature reaches 350°F.

⑥ Slip a few of the samosas into the pan, taking care not to crowd them. Adjust the heat so the oil's temperature remains constant. Fry until golden, turning once or twice with a slotted metal spoon, about 4 minutes. Transfer to a wire rack and continue frying the samosas until all are done.

Pierogi

These boiled Polish dumplings are a little slippery but still very luscious. Serve them the classic way: drizzled with melted butter and sprinkled with poppy seeds. *Makes about 36*

- 1 cup warm water
- 3 large eggs
- 2 tablespoons canola oil
- 2 teaspoons salt
- 4 cups all-purpose flour, or more as necessary
- One of the six fillings that follow, preferably Cheese or Potato

1 Whisk the water, eggs, canola oil, and salt in a large bowl until fairly uniform. Stir in the flour until a dough forms, adding more in 2-tablespoon increments if the dough is still too sticky.

2 Knead the dough in the bowl a few times until smooth, then dust the work surface with flour and turn the dough onto it. Knead about 10 minutes, digging into the dough with one palm while pulling with the other hand, adding more flour should the dough become sticky. Once it is smooth and soft, wrap the dough in plastic wrap and set aside at room temperature for 1 hour. Meanwhile, make one of the six fillings.

3 Unwrap the dough and divide it in half. Dust the work surface again lightly with flour, then roll one of the pieces out until it's 1/8 inch thick. Cut it into sixteen 3½-inch circles, using a cookie cutter or a thick-rimmed drinking glass.

4 Place 1¼ teaspoons filling in the center of each circle. Wet your finger and run it around the edge of one of the circles. Fold the circle over the filling, creating a half-moon. Seal the edges tightly, then repeat with the remaining circles—and then with the other half of the dough, making all the pierogi.

5 Bring a large stockpot of salted water to a boil over high heat. Drop the pierogi into the water. Reduce the heat to medium and simmer slowly for 10 minutes. Drain in a colander set in the sink.

The Six Fillings for Empanaditas, Samosas, or Pierogi

1. Cheese Filling

Makes about 1 cup

- ½ pound soft goat cheese such as Montrachet or low-fat farmer cheese, crumbled
- 1 large egg yolk
- 1 teaspoon canola oil or melted unsalted butter
- 1½ teaspoons all-purpose flour
- 1 teaspoon sugar, minced parsley, thyme, or oregano leaves, optional

Mix all the ingredients in a large bowl with a wooden spoon until smooth. Use at once or cover and refrigerate for up to 24 hours.

2. Potato Filling

Makes about 1 cup

- 1 medium baking potato, peeled and cut into cubes
- 2 tablespoons unsalted butter, melted and cooled
- ¼ teaspoon paprika
- ¼ teaspoon onion powder
- ¼ teaspoon salt
- ¼ teaspoon freshly ground black pepper
- ⅛ teaspoon garlic powder

① Bring a large pot of water to a boil over high heat. Add the potato and cook until tender when pierced with a fork, about 15 minutes. Drain in a colander set in the sink and cool for 5 minutes, then press through a potato ricer into a large bowl or place in a sieve and press through the mesh with the back of a wooden spoon.

② Stir in the butter, paprika, onion powder, salt, pepper, and garlic powder until smooth. Use at once; do not refrigerate.

3. Curried Squash and Pea Filling

Makes a little more than 1 cup

   1 cup frozen pureed winter squash, thawed,
      or 1 cup butternut squash puree
      (see Note, page 173)
   ¼ cup frozen peas
   2 teaspoons curry powder
   2 teaspoons potato or cornstarch

Stir all the ingredients together in a large bowl until smooth. Use at once or cover and refrigerate for up to 24 hours.

4. Herbed Turkey Filling

Makes about 1 cup

   2 teaspoons olive oil
   1 medium shallot, minced
   1 garlic clove, minced
   6 ounces ground turkey
   ½ teaspoon salt
   ¼ teaspoon ground cinnamon
   ¼ teaspoon turmeric
   ⅛ teaspoon ground cloves

   ⅛ teaspoon freshly ground black
      pepper
   1 tablespoon tomato paste
   2 teaspoons dry vermouth or dry white
      wine

① Heat a large skillet over medium heat. Swirl in the olive oil, then add the shallot and cook until softened, stirring frequently, about 3 minutes. Add the garlic; cook for 20 seconds.

② Crumble in the ground turkey. Cook, stirring frequently, until browned, about 4 minutes.

③ Stir in the salt, cinnamon, turmeric, cloves, and pepper. Cook for 15 seconds, then stir in the tomato paste and vermouth or wine.

④ Bring the mixture to a simmer, then set aside off the heat for 30 minutes; or place in a bowl, cover with plastic wrap, and store in the refrigerator for up to 2 days.

5. South American Picadillo

Makes about 1 cup

   2 teaspoons olive oil
   2 garlic cloves, minced
   4 ounces lean ground beef
   1 hard-cooked egg (see page 59), finely
      chopped
   1½ tablespoons chopped pitted green
      olives
   1 tablespoon chopped golden raisins
   1 tablespoon minced cilantro
      leaves
   2 teaspoons tomato paste
   ¼ teaspoon salt
   ⅛ teaspoon freshly ground black
      pepper

1 Heat a large skillet over medium heat, then swirl in the olive oil and add the garlic. Cook, stirring frequently, until aromatic, about 20 seconds. Crumble in the ground beef and cook, stirring frequently, until browned and cooked through, about 4 minutes.

2 Remove the pan from the heat and cool for 5 minutes. Then stir in the egg, olives, raisins, cilantro, tomato paste, salt, and pepper. Continue cooling for at least 20 more minutes, or place in a large bowl, cover, and refrigerate for up to 2 days.

Picadillo

A picadillo is a spicy meat mélange, much favored in South American countries. In Cuba, warm picadillo is served with rice and beans as a main course. The Vietnamese version here is our flight of fancy. You can serve either of these two on its own—but double the recipe, making at least 2 cups. Serve with warm flour tortillas, lettuce leaves, or crackers.

6. Vietnamese Picadillo

Makes about 1 cup

1 teaspoon peanut oil
2 medium scallions, white and green parts minced separately and set aside
1 teaspoon minced peeled fresh ginger
1 garlic clove, minced
6 ounces lean ground beef
1 tablespoon creamy peanut butter or tahini
1 tablespoon lime juice
2 teaspoons fish sauce
¼ to ½ teaspoon chili paste
1 medium radish, minced
1 tablespoon chopped cilantro leaves
1 tablespoon chopped mint leaves

1 Heat a large wok or skillet over medium-high heat. Pour in the peanut oil, wait for a few seconds, then add the white parts of the scallion. Stir-fry for 30 seconds, just to soften, and then add the ginger and garlic. Stir-fry for 15 seconds before crumbling in the ground beef. Continue cooking, stirring constantly, until the meat is browned and cooked through, about 5 minutes. Transfer to a large bowl and cool for 10 minutes.

2 Whisk the peanut butter, lime juice, fish sauce, and chili paste in a small bowl until smooth. Stir into the ground beef mixture along with the radish, cilantro, mint, and the green parts of the scallions. Set aside for 20 minutes or cover and refrigerate for up to 2 days.

Salads

Dressed salads are western fare. they began their culinary life in the early years of the Roman empire as a digestive aid. By the Renaissance, a salad, like revenge, was a dish best served cold; salted meats and greens were tossed with citrus, raisins, and nuts, dressed with oil and vinegar, and sprinkled with paprika or sugar. In the nineteenth century, tossed greens were such a European obsession that one Frenchman, the Chevalier d'Albignac, is said to have made a living in London by going house to house and dressing his patrons' salads.

But surely the exact moment when salads came of age is when they passed into cliché—via Shakespeare, of course. In *Antony and Cleopatra*, to be exact. Toward the end of the first act, the Nile Queen laments her youthful dalliance with Caesar: "My salad days, when I was green in judgment . . ."

She may have grieved for hers; we welcome ours. In the spring and summer, the markets burst with produce: lettuce, tomatoes, radishes, cucumbers, the whole fare.

Unfortunately, all salads are here today, gone tomorrow. Tuna salad can't last more than a day or two; potato salad simply won't. Summer's heat puts the spike to tender greens and winter inevitably careens around the corner, smashing the market to bits. Even vinegar, the longtime and perfect mate of lettuce, is actually its enemy: one splash and those water-doped cells start to break down.

Perhaps their transitory nature gives salads such a lasting pleasure. For a little while, salad days are the best days you can have, whether you're dating Caesar or not.

❀ *The Ultimate Salad Bar* ❀

Doesn't everyone know how to make a salad? A recipe for one is about like a recipe for cheese and crackers. Here, we've just tried to clarify the choices. We start with the greens themselves, then move on to the important sparks and spikes like fruit, nuts, croutons, and even grilled chicken that make a salad more than just lettuce in a bowl. Finally, we offer thirty dressings that can make a salad stand on its own, whether you serve it before or after the main course.

A Greens Primer

Our markets overflow with greens. There's a wide variety to this leafy fare, but the best salads are made with a combination of greens, no one predominant. Here, we map out the territory so you can develop a signature mix that reflects your taste.

Lettuces

Long the centerpiece of a salad, these floppy, flappy greens are divided into four categories.

Butterhead Lettuce

Common Varietal(s): Boston, Bibb

Exotic Varietal(s): Red Butter, Green Butter, Tennis Ball, Grosse Blonde Paresseuse

What It Looks Like: Big-eared, concave leaves curling up into a loose ball

What You Look For: An earthy smell, a tight root, and no rust spots on the leaves

What You Get: A mild, slightly tangy/sweet taste

Pros: A match for simple dressings, stone fruits, toasted nuts, corn, and mild vegetables

Cons: Turns depressingly gooey if long-dressed

Crisphead Lettuce

Common Varietal: Iceberg

Exotic Varietal(s): Great Lakes, Vanguard, Western, Imperial, Reine de Glace

What It Looks Like: A compact, tight, cabbage-like ball

What You Look For: Heavy to the hand, a rust-free stem, and no brown spots on the leaves

What You Get: A mildly acidic but clean canvas for other flavors; crunch without bitterness

Pros: For muscular, well-stocked salads and creamy dressings; can be served in wedges

Cons: Watery and insipid if grown improperly; turns bitter in the heat

Loose-Leaf Lettuce

Common Varietal(s): Red Leaf, Green Leaf

Exotic Varietal(s): Lolla Rossa, Red Oak Leaf, Green Oak Leaf

What It Looks Like: Flappy, wide, soft leaves that gently lift off a base

What You Look For: A conical head, tight at the bottom but looser at the top

What You Get: A mild, grassy, sweet taste

Pros: An excellent second fiddle to other greens

Cons: Can glom onto the roof of your mouth; wrong for burgers and sandwiches

Long-Leaf Lettuce

Common Varietal: Romaine

Exotic Varietal: Cos

What It Looks Like: Broad, stiff, crunchy spear that skyrockets off a tight base

What You Look For: A compact core, spot-free stem, leaves that shade from pale green to dark, each with a firm, pale spine

What You Get: Crisp leaves with a slightly bitter, almost tart flavor

Pros: A crunch against creamy dressings and with softer lettuces

Cons: The darker, the more astringent

Chicories and Endives

These originally separate categories are now fused because of their common trait: a refreshing pepperiness. The name-game gets complicated because of French, British, and American traditions. Be forewarned: these "greens" (not all of them are green) can be astringent and tough. To avoid the problem? Choose young, small heads.

Chicory

Common Varietal: Sugarloaf

Exotic Varietal(s): Grumolo, Catalogna

What It Looks Like: A curly, loose-leaf head with moderately stiff leaves that may or may not frizz at the edges

What You Look For: Fleshy leaves with firm (but not rigid or fibrous) stems

What You Get: A toothy, somewhat acidic bite

Pros: Its sophisticated taste and chewy texture pairs well with creamy and sweet dressings

Cons: Easily overwhelms mild greens; mature, dark leaves can be tough

Red Chicory

Common Varietal(s): Radicchio, Chioggia Radicchio, Verona Radicchio (round heads)

Exotic Varietal(s): Treviso (spear head), Castelfranco (yellow-tinged)

What It Looks Like: A waxy, firm head with pronounced white veins

What You Look For: A tight head that is heavy to the hand

What You Get: A pleasant bitterness that in moderation will not overwhelm milder lettuces

Pros: Its substantial texture and bite (even roasted or grilled)

Cons: Leaves long exposed to the light can be tough and shockingly bitter

Dandelion Greens

Common Varietal: (same)

Exotic Varietal: (same)

What It Looks Like: Long, spiky, jagged leaves with a tubular stem

What You Look For: Pliable, resilient leaves

What You Get: An aggressive bitterness that cries out for balsamic or creamy dressings

Pros: A combative edge against citrus and sliced onions; can be chopped and stirred into soups for a sour spark

Cons: Can be a bully in the salad bowl

Belgian Endive

Common Varietal: Belgian Endive

Exotic Varietal(s): California (or Red Leaf) Endive

What It Looks Like: A waxy, spearlike head fringed in yellow or red

What You Look For: A pale, tight head with color only at the edges; should be wrapped in tissue paper to protect it from the light

What You Get: A crunchy, tender spike in salads; ironically, these are actually chicories, not endives, grown in the dark off a root base

Pros: Pairs well with tomatoes, cheese, basil, smoked salmon, or creamy dressings

Cons: Turns increasingly pungent when exposed to light

Curly Endive

Common Varietal: Curly Chicory

Exotic Varietal: Frisée

What It Looks Like: A frizzy, lacy, floppy green with leaves that end in spidery tendrils; the color yellows toward a pale base

What You Look For: A pale head (the more green, the more bitter)

What You Get: A bitter, pungent taste and a chewy texture

Pros: Makes a great foil for eggs, bacon, creamy dressings, and strong flavors

Cons: Not only aggressive but also expensive

Escarole

Common Varietal(s): Broad-Leaf Endive, Escarole

Exotic Varietal(s): Scarole, Batavian

What It Looks Like: Wide, flat, dark green leaves that open off a yellow core

What You Look For: A compact head with moderate yellowing at its center

What You Get: A succulent, bittersweet green

Pros: Perks up moderately flavored salads; even better simmered in soups

Cons: Pugnacious, tough dark leaves

Microgreens, Mild to Bold

Not technically a botanical or agricultural category, these are small-leaf greens: some baby versions of their adult kin; others, small even in their mature phase. Most are familiar from packaged salad mixes, but markets now routinely sell them on their own, often in small wicker baskets. Perfect for mixing with other greens, most are too subtle or soft to create a satisfying salad on their own. They mostly lack varietals and exotic names since they themselves are often an exotic varietal of other larger greens.

Baby Oak Leaf Lettuce

What It Looks Like: An immature version of red or green oak leaf lettuce (see page 96); the small leaves do indeed look like tiny oak leaves

What You Look For: Springy leaves that have not wilted or gone rusty

What You Get: A mild taste without the cloying softness often attributed to the adult kin

Pros: A delicate, refreshing green with a smooth, sweet finish

Cons: Knocked senseless by anything more assertive than a cucumber

Mâche

Also Known As: Corn Salad, Cow Salad, Lamb's Lettuce, Rampon, or Doucette

What It Looks Like: A small, delicate green with thin, rounding leaves that sometimes end in an almost heart-shaped tip

What You Look For: If possible, buy this delicate green with its root ball or planting packet still attached

What You Get: A sweet, delicate, mildly grassy taste

Pros: Pairs well with radishes, corn, tomatoes, and cucumber

Cons: Extremely perishable—use it the day you buy it

Baby Spinach

What It Looks Like: Small, round, or oval spinach leaves, often with a slightly waxy finish

What You Look For: Tender, pliable greens without any tough stems or curly edges

What You Get: A salad-mix staple, thanks to its mild taste and tender bite

Pros: Stands up fairly well to bigger tastes and pairs well with protein and croutons

Cons: Overwhelmed by bitter greens and spicy dressings

Watercress

What It Looks Like: Small, rounded leaves off tender stems

What You Look For: Small stems and tender leaves; avoid large stems which are fibrous and must be removed

What You Get: A mustardy bite

Pros: Excellent on hamburgers or sandwiches, best with citrus vinaigrettes

Cons: Can be tough and chewy if the leaves are too mature or improperly stored

Mizuna

Also Known As: Japanese Mustard Greens

What It Looks Like: Tiny, spiky, pale green leaves

What You Look For: Smaller leaves with tender, pliable stems

What You Get: An acidic, almost lemony bite

Pros: Will perk up most salads but best against crunchy, light greens like a crisphead lettuce

Cons: Packs a wallop; should be worked into a salad in the same way radicchio is

Arugula

Also Known As: Rocket, Rugola, or Roquette (actually, now considered a larger category of cultivated, broad-leaf, non-head-forming greens, all from a wild, feathery plant little seen anymore)

What It Looks Like: Thin, jagged leaves, often like a spiky oval

What You Look For: Smaller leaves without waxiness or thick stems

What You Get: A hearty dose of bitter pepper

Pros: A good match for spicy salads, Asian foods, or citrus—and terrific on a pizza

Cons: Larger leaves can be tough and should be stemmed to avoid the fibrous core

Sorrel

What It Looks Like: Pale green, oblong leaves that become arrow-like at the stem

What You Look For: Pliable leaves, preferably less than 4 inches long

What You Get: A sour, very strong taste

Pros: In moderation, intensifies other tastes and stands up well to creamy dressings; often used directly in soups and stews like cabbage or kale

Cons: Because of its high oxalic acid content, large doses can cause stomach upset

❊ *How to Mix-and-Match Greens* ❊

Now that we've nailed down the categories of greens, this chart should help you make your own salad mix. Mix greens from adjacent categories for a balance of taste and texture. For example, iceberg goes well with romaine or Bibb—or both. But Bibb will be beaten senseless by dandelion greens. You needn't settle on a pair; try three from three adjacent categories, or choose two from one and a third that's more assertive to its left.

Delicate	Mild	Tangy	Bitter	Belligerent
Bibb, Boston, and most Butterhead varietals	Iceberg and most Crisphead varietals	Romaine	Belgian Endive	Round-head varietals of Radicchio
Grosse Blonde Paresseuse, Reine de Glace, and some Crisphead exotics	Red Leaf Lettuce	Green Leaf lettuce	Sugarloaf Endive	Dandelion Greens
Baby Oak Leaf lettuces	Lolla Rossa	Mature Red or Green Oak Leaf Lettuce	Frisée	Sorrel
Mâche	Baby Spinach	Batavian and younger heads of Escarole	Escarole and most of its varietals	Curly Endive
		Mizuna	Arugula	
		Watercress	Spearlike varietals of Radicchio	

The Five Steps for Working with Greens

❶ Trim. If there's a base knot or root base to the head, trim it off to let the leaves flop free; remove and discard any discolored or tough outer leaves. Cut out any long, fibrous stems.

❷ Wash. Fill a cleaned sink with cool water, then plunge the trimmed greens into it. Soak for 3 to 5 minutes, stirring once or twice, to let any sand or grit fall to the bottom of the sink. Remove carefully without draining the water, washing off individual leaves if still dirty. Once all the greens are out of the sink, drain the water and wash away the grit.

❸ Dry. Take them for a whirl in a salad spinner or gently dab them dry between generous layers of paper towels.

❹ Store. Roll the leaves between dry paper towels and store in a sealed plastic bag with a few holes poked in it at room temperature for up to 6 hours or in the crisper for up to 4 days.

❺ Chop. Tear leafy greens by hand; chop others with a chef's knife into bite-sized chunks.

Composed vs. Tossed

A composed salad has its ingredients artfully layered and arranged on individual plates, the dressing drizzled over the top. A tossed salad has, well, its ingredients and their dressing tossed together in a bowl, ready to be served. The choice is yours: elegance vs. efficiency.

Thirty Salad Dressings

Here's a list of thirty dressings, simple to complex, spiky to creamy. It's a mix-and-match affair with the greens you choose, but we offer suggestions. Each recipe makes enough for a four-serving salad. Double, triple, or quadruple at will. Keep the extra dressing sealed in a glass jar in the refrigerator for up to 2 weeks; the clotted oil will reliquefy as the dressing comes back to room temperature.

To make any of these vinaigrettes: Whisk everything except the oil in a small bowl, then slowly whisk in the oil until opaque and emulsified.

Classic Vinaigrettes

All made with olive oil, these are good for light salads, bitter greens, fresh fruit, sliced tomatoes, or steamed vegetables. You can also toss them on a light, crisp potato salad.

Balsamic Vinaigrette

1½ tablespoons balsamic vinegar
¼ teaspoon salt
¼ teaspoon freshly ground black pepper
⅓ cup extra virgin olive oil

Sherry Vinaigrette

1 garlic clove, crushed
1½ tablespoons sherry vinegar
¼ teaspoon salt
¼ teaspoon freshly ground black pepper
¼ teaspoon stemmed thyme or ⅛ teaspoon dried thyme
⅓ cup extra virgin olive oil

Poppy Seed Vinaigrette

2 tablespoons white wine vinegar
1 tablespoon toasted poppy seeds
½ teaspoon sugar
¼ teaspoon salt
⅓ cup extra virgin olive oil

Fruit Vinaigrettes

These are sweeter, a better foil to more assertive flavors. Avoid sweet fruit accents and go for sugar snap peas, green beans, asparagus, nuts, or croutons with these dressings.

Orange Vinaigrette

1 tablespoon frozen orange juice
   concentrate, thawed
1 tablespoon rice vinegar
¼ teaspoon salt
¼ teaspoon freshly ground black pepper
¼ cup canola oil

Apple Caraway Vinaigrette

1½ tablespoons frozen apple juice
   concentrate, thawed
1 tablespoon apple cider vinegar
½ teaspoon crushed caraway seeds
¼ teaspoon salt
⅛ teaspoon freshly ground black pepper
¼ cup canola oil

Raspberry Vinaigrette

2 tablespoons raspberry vinegar
¼ teaspoon salt
¼ teaspoon freshly ground black pepper
⅓ cup grapeseed or walnut oil

Cranberry Vinaigrette

1 tablespoon frozen cranberry juice
   concentrate, thawed
1 tablespoon red wine vinegar
¼ teaspoon salt
¼ teaspoon freshly ground black pepper
¼ cup olive oil

Pomegranate Vinaigrette

1 tablespoon red wine vinegar
2 teaspoons pomegranate molasses
¼ teaspoon salt
¼ teaspoon freshly ground black pepper
⅛ teaspoon salt
⅓ cup walnut oil

What's Mesclun?

From a Provençal word for "mixed," mesclun is not any one lettuce but a mix. Although European mixes tend to be crisp and bitter, American versions move toward the sweet and soft.

Croutons

For 4 servings, heat 2 tablespoons oil (walnut, grape seed, olive, canola, etc.) in a large skillet set over medium heat; or melt 2 tablespoons unsalted butter in the skillet. Add 2 minced garlic cloves and/or 2 teaspoons minced fresh rosemary, oregano, parsley, or thyme. Cook until aromatic, about 1 minute; then add 2 cups cubed day-old bread (sourdough, white, whole wheat, rye, etc.). Reduce the heat to low and cook, stirring constantly, until crunchy and lightly browned. Season with ¼ teaspoon salt and ¼ teaspoon freshly ground black pepper.

Herb Vinaigrettes

These work on summery green salads, accented with fruits and toasted nuts. They are also good with pasta and vegetable salads.

Basil Vinaigrette

1½ tablespoons white wine or champagne vinegar
1 tablespoon minced basil leaves
¼ teaspoon salt
¼ teaspoon freshly ground black pepper
⅛ teaspoon sugar
⅓ cup olive oil

Lemon Tarragon Vinaigrette

1 small shallot, minced
2 tablespoons lemon juice
1 teaspoon Dijon mustard
1 teaspoon minced tarragon leaves or
  ½ teaspoon dried tarragon
¼ teaspoon salt
¼ teaspoon freshly ground black
  pepper
⅓ cup olive oil

Mint Vinaigrette

1 small shallot, minced
¼ cup chopped mint leaves
2 tablespoons white wine vinegar
¼ teaspoon sugar
¼ teaspoon salt
¼ cup olive oil

Creamy Vinaigrettes

These dressings are good drizzled on iceberg wedges or tossed in fairly assertive salads with endive or radicchio in the mix. The dressings also work exceptionally well with main-course salads, since the creaminess complements any protein in the salad.

Mustard Vinaigrette

1 small shallot, minced
½ tablespoon Dijon mustard
1 tablespoon white wine vinegar
⅓ cup olive oil

Honey Mustard Vinaigrette

1 garlic clove, minced
1 tablespoon white wine vinegar
1½ teaspoons Dijon mustard
1 teaspoon honey
¼ teaspoon salt
¼ teaspoon freshly ground black pepper
⅓ cup olive or mustard seed oil

Classic French Bistro Vinaigrette

1 garlic clove, crushed
1 large egg yolk, preferably a pasteurized
    yolk, at room temperature
1½ tablespoons white wine vinegar
½ teaspoon Dijon mustard
¼ teaspoon salt
¼ teaspoon freshly ground black pepper
½ cup olive oil

Lemon Tahini Vinaigrette

1 tablespoon lemon juice
½ tablespoon tahini
½ tablespoon white balsamic vinegar
½ tablespoon Dijon mustard
¼ teaspoon salt
¼ cup olive oil

Neutral Salad Oils

Canola oil, corn oil, safflower oil, sunflower oil, soy bean oil, cottonseed salad oil, grapeseed oil—in truth, these oils have such a faint taste that they are practically interchangeable in salad dressings. Refined peanut oil is also neutral, although some bottlings, particularly Asian ones, can have a pronounced taste. If you want to add a little flavor without pitching over into walnut, sesame, or extra virgin olive oil territory, try almond oil.

Asian Vinaigrettes

These pair well with strong greens and sweet vegetables like a mix of shredded carrot and chopped endive or cubed apple and chopped romaine. They're also good drizzled on grilled fish or steamed Brussels sprouts as a "finishing sauce."

Ponzu Vinaigrette

2½ tablespoons lemon juice
2 tablespoons soy sauce
1 teaspoon sugar
3 tablespoons peanut oil

Sesame Vinaigrette

1½ tablespoons rice vinegar
1 tablespoon toasted sesame oil
½ teaspoon soy sauce
¼ cup peanut oil

Lime Ginger Vinaigrette

1½ tablespoons lime juice
½ tablespoon white wine vinegar
1 teaspoon minced peeled fresh ginger
¼ teaspoon salt
¼ teaspoon freshly ground black pepper
¼ cup olive oil

Spicy Asian Vinaigrette

2 tablespoons rice vinegar
1 teaspoon minced peeled fresh ginger
½ teaspoon soy sauce
½ teaspoon chili oil
¼ cup peanut oil

Unusual Vinaigrettes

These easily overpower delicate, summery greens, sweet fruits, or ripe tomatoes. Try them with very assertive salad mixes as well as drizzled on wilted spinach, turnip greens, or roasted root vegetables. Toasted walnut oil, used in the first dressing, has a much more pronounced taste than regular walnut oil and should be used sparingly.

Toasted Walnut Vinaigrette

1½ tablespoons cider vinegar
½ teaspoon finely grated lemon zest
¼ teaspoon salt
¼ teaspoon freshly ground black pepper
1½ tablespoons toasted walnut oil
¼ cup canola oil

Coffee Vinaigrette

2 tablespoons balsamic vinegar
½ teaspoon instant espresso
  powder
¼ teaspoon salt
⅓ cup walnut oil

Saffron Vinaigrette

1½ tablespoons red wine vinegar
1 teaspoon finely grated orange zest
⅛ teaspoon saffron threads, dissolved in
  2 teaspoons hot water for 5 minutes
¼ teaspoon salt
⅓ cup olive oil

Chipotle Vinaigrette

1 chipotle in adobo, seeded and minced
1 tablespoon lime juice
½ teaspoon ground cumin
¼ teaspoon salt
¼ cup peanut oil

Creamy Dressings

To make any of these more substantial dressings, whisk all the ingredients together in a small bowl; they can be stored, covered, in the refrigerator for up to 2 days. For those dressings that use mayonnaise, consider making your own (see page 121).

Butter Dressing

Best on light, summery greens mixed with raw or steamed vegetables

4 tablespoons (½ stick) unsalted butter,
  melted and cooled
1 tablespoon lemon juice
1 teaspoon stemmed thyme
½ teaspoon sugar
¼ teaspoon salt
¼ teaspoon freshly ground black pepper
¼ teaspoon grated nutmeg

Mayonnaise Dill Dressing

Best on crunchy greens as well as in potato salads, pasta salads, and on poached salmon

½ cup mayonnaise (regular, low-fat, or
  fat-free)
2 tablespoons white wine vinegar
1 tablespoon chopped dill fronds
1 teaspoon dry mustard
½ teaspoon sugar
¼ teaspoon salt
¼ teaspoon freshly ground black pepper

Thousand Island Dressing

Best as the classic: on iceberg wedges—or as a dip for vegetables

1 small scallion, minced
¼ cup mayonnaise (regular, low-fat, or
  fat-free)

1 tablespoon ketchup
1 tablespoon heavy cream
1 tablespoon pickle relish
½ tablespoon white wine vinegar
1 teaspoon Dijon mustard
¼ teaspoon salt
¼ teaspoon freshly ground black pepper
Hot red pepper sauce to taste

Green Goddess Dressing

Best on chopped, crunchy salads with strong, slightly bitter greens

2 anchovy fillets, minced
1 small scallion, minced
6 tablespoons mayonnaise (regular, low-fat, or fat-free)
2 tablespoons sour cream (regular, low-fat, or fat-free)
1 tablespoon minced parsley leaves
1 tablespoon minced dill fronds
1 tablespoon minced basil leaves
1 teaspoon red wine vinegar
A few dashes of hot red pepper sauce to taste

Creamy Curry Dressing

Best with a well-stocked green salad with lots of raw or steamed vegetables among the greens

1 garlic clove, crushed
½ cup mayonnaise (regular, low-fat, or fat-free)
2 tablespoons sour cream
1 tablespoon curry powder
2 teaspoons lemon juice
½ teaspoon garlic powder
¼ teaspoon salt

Buttermilk Dressing

Best on summery, light greens, such as Bibb lettuce, mixed with some chopped fresh herbs and fresh fruit

1 garlic clove, crushed
3 tablespoons buttermilk (regular, low-fat, or fat-free)
3 tablespoons sour cream (regular, low-fat, or fat-free)
2 teaspoons stemmed thyme or 1 teaspoon dried thyme
¼ teaspoon salt
¼ teaspoon freshly ground black pepper
A few dashes of hot red pepper sauce to taste

Blue Cheese Dressing

Excellent with almost any match of greens—and great on pasta or potato salads

1 small shallot, minced
½ cup mayonnaise (regular, low-fat, or fat-free)
¼ cup crumbled blue cheese
2 tablespoons sour cream (regular, low-fat, or fat-free)
1 tablespoon white wine vinegar
1 teaspoon Worcestershire sauce

Extra Virgin Olive Oil

Extra virgin olive oil wasn't created for sautés; most of its flavor volatilizes and is lost. It was made for salads and as a finishing splash on roasted or steamed vegetables. Buy a cold-pressed olive oil for sautéing; save the extra virgin stuff for when it counts.

❋ *Salad Accents* ❋

A good salad is more than just lettuce and dressing. Balance the greens with accents that match their flavors. Frankly, it's a matter of preference: some people like sweet accents such as peaches with bitter greens like arugula; others like strong, assertive tastes such as blue cheese or toasted nuts. In fact, either will work. For a full, flavorful, salad that serves four, choose one accent from at least each of two categories and pair them with 4 to 6 cups shredded greens. See page 102 for some of our favorite combinations. Main-course salads usually include protein of some sort—but remember: the point of a main-course salad is the greens. Don't overload them with extras.

Crisp-savory (1½ cups of any or any combination)	Juicy-sweet (choose one)	Crunchy (½ cup of any or any combination)	Protein (choose one)
Sugar snap peas	1 pitted ripe peach, sliced	Toasted walnut pieces	½ pound bacon, fried and chopped
Quick-steamed broccoli florets	1 pitted ripe nectarine, sliced	Toasted pecan pieces	2 cups cubed chicken meat
Sliced scallions	1 medium tomato, chopped (see page 111)	Toasted skinned chopped hazelnuts	¾ pound cooked medium cocktail shrimp (see page 61 for a technique for cooking shrimp)
Sliced red onion or minced shallot	1 medium apple, cored and chopped	Roasted unsalted cashews	¾ pound firm tofu, cubed
Thinly sliced celery ribs	1 medium jicama, peeled and chopped	Roasted unsalted peanuts	12 ounces lump crabmeat, picked over for shell and cartilage
Sliced water chestnuts	1 medium cucumber, peeled, seeded, and thinly sliced	Roasted unsalted sunflower seeds	2 cups canned red or white beans, drained and rinsed
Thinly sliced radishes	½ cup dried raisins, cherries, or cranberries	Croutons (page 101)	2 to 4 ounces grated, crumbled, or cubed cheese, including Asiago, Parmigiano-Reggiano, Gorgonzola, Cheddar, or aged Gouda
Thinly sliced or diced, seeded, and cored bell pepper			

Building the Ultimate Green Salad

Now that you have all the pieces, create your favorite salad. One tip: serve salads with creamy dressings and strong flavors as first courses; serve those with milder flavors and tamer vinaigrettes after the main course to clear the palate and aid digestion. *Makes 4 servings*

1 Start with a large, cool salad bowl. Better too much room than dressed leaves flopping onto the counter.

2 Add a mix of greens (see pages 96–99). They can be difficult to measure. Who wants to jam tender leaves into measuring cups? Figure on a little more than a large handful per person—thus, about five handfuls for four people. If possible, keep the greens at room temperature and serve them the day you buy them.

3 Add a couple of salad accents (see page 106).

4 Finally, choose a salad dressing, mild to bold (pages 100–105). Drizzle it on the salad or serve on the side. Your clean hands actually make the best tool for tossing a salad. Never dress the greens before you're ready to serve the salad; acid breaks them down and renders them mushy.

❋ *Side Salads* ❋

The common thread here? These salads aren't first courses per se, nor are they stand-alones. Instead, they're designed to go with other things: roasts, casseroles, sautés, but primarily, of course, a piece of bread.

A Bowl of Vinegary Cucumbers

Every summer, we keep a bowl of this salad in the fridge, replenishing it as it runs low. *Makes 8 servings*

    3 to 4 large cucumbers, peeled and thinly
        sliced
    1 medium red onion, sliced into very thin
        rounds and broken into rings
    ¾ cup white wine vinegar
    2 tablespoons sugar
    2 teaspoons salt

1 Place the cucumbers and onion in a large bowl; pour in the vinegar, then fill the bowl with cool water until the vegetables are submerged. Stir in the sugar and salt until dissolved.

2 Cover with plastic wrap and refrigerate for at least 24 hours or up to 2 weeks. Drain the cucumbers and onions with a slotted spoon when serving.

Variations: Add 1 seeded and chopped pickled or fresh jalapeño chile with the onion.

Add 1 tablespoon dried dill, 1 tablespoon chopped chives, or 1 teaspoon red pepper flakes with the sugar.

Add 6 whole cloves, 6 crushed juniper berries, or 4 crushed allspice berries with the sugar. (Do not eat these with the cucumbers and onions.)

Sweet Corn and Onion Salad

Many local farmers' markets sell roasted corn on the cob all summer, making this summery, Southwestern-spiked side even easier to make. *Makes 6 servings*

6 ears corn
Vegetable oil, for greasing the grill rack
1 large red onion, cut into thick slices
2 tablespoons lime juice
½ teaspoon ground cumin
½ teaspoon salt
Several dashes of hot red pepper sauce to
    taste
2 tablespoons walnut oil

❶ Peel open the corn husks, remove the silk from the ears, and pat the husks back in place. Fill your sink with cool water, add the ears in their husks, and soak for 20 minutes.

❷ Meanwhile, heat a gas grill to medium heat or build a medium-heat coal bed in a charcoal grill. Lightly oil the grill rack. (For a method using the broiler, see the *Variations*.)

❸ Remove the corn from the water and drain. Place the ears in their wet husks directly over the heated grill or the coal bed. Cover and grill for 5 minutes, turning a couple of times. Transfer to a cutting board and cool for 5 minutes.

❹ Meanwhile, place the onion slices directly over the heat; grill until lightly browned, about 3 minutes, turning two or three times. Transfer to the cutting board to cool.

❺ Remove the husks from the corn and cut off one end of the cobs so they will stand upright on a cutting board. Holding the ears carefully, slice the kernels off the cobs with a large knife, cutting down between the kernels and the cob. Discard the cobs. Chop the onion slices into kernel-sized pieces.

❻ Whisk the lime juice, cumin, salt, and hot red pepper sauce in a medium serving bowl. Slowly whisk in the walnut oil. Add the corn kernels and onion; toss well to serve.

Variations: To forgo the grill, preheat the broiler and place the soaked corn in its husks and the onions on an aluminum foil–lined broiler pan 4 to 6 inches from the heat, turning several times, until lightly browned.

For a creamier salad, omit the walnut oil and stir in ¼ cup mayonnaise with the lime juice and seasonings.

Grilled Salad

We've been unabashed fans of grilled lettuce ever since we lived off this salad one summer in north-eastern Vermont. There's no need for a formal dressing: the lettuce picks up the smoky flavor of the grill and keeps plenty of olive oil in the leaves. If you don't have access to a grill, you can use a grill pan (see step 3). *Makes 6 servings*

½ cup olive oil
1 large head romaine lettuce, cut in half,
    outer leaves removed
2 small heads radicchio, cut in quarters,
    outer leaves removed
2 small heads Belgian endive, cut in half,
    outer leaves removed
3 tablespoons balsamic vinegar, preferably
    aged balsamic vinegar
½ teaspoon salt
½ teaspoon freshly ground black pepper

❶ Heat a gas grill to high heat for direct cooking or prepare a high-heat, well-ashed coal bed in a charcoal grill. Set the grate about 5 inches from the heat.

2 Pour the olive oil in a large baking dish; dip the lettuce sections into the oil on all sides, then place them cut side down on the grate directly over the heat. Cook, covered, until lightly browned and a little wilted, about 4 minutes, turning once. Transfer to a cutting board; cool for a few minutes.

3 Core the romaine and radicchio. Shred all the lettuces with a large knife into 1-inch slices. Place in a large serving bowl; toss with the vinegar, salt, and pepper.

Using a grill pan: Heat it to medium-high heat and then add the oil-dipped lettuce. Cook just until slightly wilted and browned, about 3 minutes, turning once.

Variations: Soak 2 long rosemary spears in water for 10 minutes, then lay these in a drip pan over the heat source or directly on top of the coals before grilling the lettuces to infuse them with some of the rosemary flavor.

Toss one 6-ounce jar marinated artichoke hearts, drained and roughly chopped, and/or one 6-ounce jar pimientos, sliced, with the sliced grilled lettuce.

Roasted Radicchio and Shallots

Roasting radicchio mellows its edge, leaving it with just enough spike to complement the sweet, caramelized shallots. *Makes 6 servings*

> 3 medium shallots, peeled
> 5 tablespoons olive oil
> 2 medium heads radicchio, outer leaves
>   removed (see Note)
> 2 tablespoons balsamic vinegar
> ¼ to ½ teaspoon salt

1 Position the rack in the center of the oven and preheat the oven to 350°F.

2 Place the shallots in a large baking dish, pour 2 tablespoons olive oil over them, and toss to coat. Cover with aluminum foil and roast for 30 minutes.

3 Cut the radicchio heads into quarters through the base so the leaves stay intact in the quarters. Rub the remaining 3 tablespoons oil on the radicchio quarters.

4 Uncover the baking dish and add the radicchio. Roast, uncovered, until the radicchio is lightly browned and the shallots are quite soft, about 20 more minutes. Transfer all to a cutting board; let stand for 10 minutes.

5 Roughly chop the radicchio and shallots; scrape them and any residual oil into a large serving bowl. Toss with the balsamic vinegar and salt to serve.

Note: Some markets are tricky: they often remove the outer leaves of radicchio heads to keep them looking fresh and bright. Check the stem and make sure there are no layers missing from the tight-pack head.

Variations: Substitute Belgian endive heads for the radicchio; cut them in half lengthwise before roasting.

Add 4 to 6 unpeeled garlic cloves with the shallots. Once roasted, squeeze the soft pulp into the salad with the vinegar.

Add 2 teaspoons chopped herbs—thyme, rosemary, oregano, and/or parsley, for example—with the salt.

For a spikier salad, substitute white wine vinegar for the balsamic vinegar—or try lemon juice for a bright spark.

Tomato Basil Salad

The trick to this simple salad is to leach the excess water out of the tomatoes while infusing them with vinegar—all before tossing them with the olive oil. Since the tomatoes will break down under the vinegar's acid, there's no need to use fancy heirloom tomatoes here—unless, of course, you want to go for broke. Even slightly hard beefsteak tomatoes will soften up nicely. *Makes 8 servings*

2 pounds medium tomatoes, cut into eighths
2 tablespoons red wine vinegar
1 teaspoon salt, preferably kosher salt or coarse sea salt
½ teaspoon freshly ground black pepper
3 tablespoons olive oil, preferably extra virgin olive oil
¼ cup chopped basil leaves

1 Toss the tomatoes, vinegar, salt, and pepper in a large bowl; cover and set aside at room temperature for at least 2 hours or up to 12 hours, stirring occasionally.

2 Carefully remove the tomatoes from the marinade, using a slotted spoon. Place them in a serving bowl and toss with the olive oil and basil. Serve at once.

Variations: Add up to 4 garlic cloves, quartered, with the salt and pepper. Leave them behind when you transfer the tomatoes to the serving bowl.

Substitute chives, oregano, marjoram, parsley, or tarragon for the basil—or substitute a mixture equal to ¼ cup.

Substitute 2 tablespoons stemmed thyme for the basil.

Panzanella (Tomato Bread Salad)

This Italian salad of tomatoes and cubed bread is a hearty side, good for summer barbecues and winter roasts. *Makes 6 servings*

4 cups cubed day-old baguette, crunchy French bread, or any crusty bread (about 1-inch cubes), toasted
1½ pounds medium tomatoes, cut into eighths
1 medium cucumber, peeled, cut in half lengthwise, seeded, and diced
1 small red onion, finely chopped
1 garlic clove, crushed
1½ tablespoons red wine vinegar
½ teaspoon salt, preferably sea salt
½ teaspoon freshly ground black pepper
¼ cup olive oil, preferably extra virgin olive oil

1 Mix the bread, tomatoes, cucumber, and red onion in a large serving bowl.

2 Whisk the garlic, vinegar, salt, and pepper in a small bowl; whisk in the olive oil.

3 Pour the dressing over the vegetables and bread, toss well, and serve at once.

Variations: Substitute ½ pound trimmed green beans, blanched, or 1 cup canned chickpeas, drained and rinsed, for the cucumber.

Add 1 pound fresh mozzarella, cut into 1-inch cubes, with the bread.

Add 2 or 3 chopped anchovy fillets with the bread.

Add 1 tablespoon chopped oregano leaves or chopped parsley leaves with the bread.

Substitute balsamic vinegar for the red wine vinegar.

Serve with shaved Parmigiano-Reggiano over the top.

Tomatoes

Most tomatoes are picked green and ripened with ethylene gas, an unsatisfactory practice at best. If possible, buy vine-ripened tomatoes. They should be deeply colored and firm but with some give; they should also have a mildly acrid smell at the stem. If you buy tomatoes with the stem still attached, don't be fooled: woody, hard stems still most likely mean the tomatoes were picked green and allowed to ripen off the vine. Store fresh tomatoes in a dark, cool place; use within a day or two of purchase. Never refrigerate tomatoes—the cold will turn off the flavor esters, which will never turn back on.

Tomato Name	Benefits	Use(s)
Cherry, Pear, Teardrop	Juicy, mildly acidic, sweet	Raw in salads and as appetizers
Rome, Roma, or Plum	More flesh than juice, sturdy, mild taste	In stews, braises, roasts; perfect for pasta sauces; raw in salads (in a pinch)
Slicing, Marmande, Early Boy, Early Girl	Juicy, acidic, sweet/sour	Raw with coarse salt and balsamic vinegar, in fresh tomato sauces and simple sautés
Beefsteak and many heirloom varietals	Sweet, fruity, delicate	For slicing and in sandwiches or with burgers
Yellow	Low acidity, fragrant, very sweet	Raw in salads and sandwiches; as appetizers; great paired with soft or blue cheese
Zebra, Green Grape, and other green varietals	Moderate acidity, a little tart	Raw in salads, also good for slicing
Green (unripe)	Bitter, chewy, firm	Sliced, dipped in beer batter (see page 72), and fried

Seeding Tomatoes

We don't seed tomatoes—except in the most fussy preparations. First, the better your tomatoes, the fewer the seeds. Second, there's a lot of flavor in those seeds and the juice around them.

However, some people have trouble digesting the seeds or insist on pitch-perfect aesthetics. If you want to seed tomatoes, cut them in half at the equator and gently squeeze them, cut side down, over a bowl, thereby pushing out the seeds and the pulp. You may also have to run your finger with some chambers to dislodge stubborn seeds.

Tomato, Wax Bean, and Olive Salad

For this salad, the best balsamic is a syrupy one, aged at least three years. *Makes 6 servings*

¾ pound wax beans, cut into 1-inch lengths
1¼ pounds tomatoes, seeded and cut into a 1-inch dice
6 tablespoons green olives, preferably fat, juicy Spanish olives, pitted and sliced
2 medium shallots, sliced into thin rings
1½ tablespoons balsamic vinegar
½ teaspoon salt
½ teaspoon sugar
½ teaspoon freshly ground black pepper
3 tablespoons extra virgin olive oil

❶ Bring a large pot of water to a boil over high heat. Add the beans, cook for 1 minute, then drain in a colander set in the sink and refresh with cool water until room temperature. Drain well and transfer to a large serving bowl.

❷ Add the tomatoes, olives, and shallots; toss well.

❸ Whisk the vinegar, salt, sugar, and pepper in a small bowl; slowly whisk in the olive oil. Pour the dressing over the salad and toss gently to serve.

Variations: Substitute green beans for the wax beans.

Substitute peeled asparagus for the wax beans; blanch for 2 minutes.

Substitute 3 scallions, thinly sliced, for the shallots.

Can't get enough tomatoes? Check out the Roasted Tomato Soup (page 133) and the various chilled tomato soups (see pages 157–159) in the soup chapter. Or, of course, peruse the chapter on Pasta and Noodles, starting on page 169.

Chopped Summer Salad

The fresh taste of summer is enhanced by the spark of a bar staple: Angostura bitters. Look for it in the drink aisle at your supermarket. For the best presentation, make sure the vegetables are all cut to the same overall size. *Makes 6 servings*

3 tablespoons white wine vinegar
2 teaspoons chopped dill fronds or 1 teaspoon dried dill
1 teaspoon sugar
1 teaspoon salt
½ teaspoon freshly ground black pepper
6 tablespoons olive oil, preferably extra virgin olive oil
2 to 6 dashes of Angostura bitters (see Note)
8 large radishes, cut into a ¾-inch dice
2 medium cucumbers, peeled, halved lengthwise, seeded, and cut into a ¾-inch dice
1 large yellow summer squash, cut into a ¾-inch dice

❶ Whisk the vinegar, dill, sugar, salt, and pepper in a large serving bowl. Whisk in the olive oil in a slow, steady stream, then whisk in the bitters.

❷ Add the radishes, cucumbers, and squash. Toss well before serving.

Note: Add only a couple of drops of the bitters the first time to see if you like its edge.

Variations: Substitute sherry vinegar or champagne vinegar for the white wine vinegar.

Substitute stemmed thyme for the dill.

Reduce the radishes to 4 and add 3 medium scallions, thinly sliced.

Asian Sugar Snap Salad

Sugar snaps have a tough vein running along the concave edge. To remove it, hold the stem and zip the thread off the casing. *Makes 8 servings*

2 pounds sugar snap peas, fibrous stems zipped off
1½ tablespoons toasted sesame oil
1½ tablespoons rice vinegar
1 tablespoon minced peeled fresh ginger
1 teaspoon soy sauce

① Bring a large saucepan of water to a boil over high heat. Add the sugar snaps and cook until snap-tender, 1 to 2 minutes. Drain in a colander set in the sink, then refresh with cool water until room temperature. Drain well.

② Whisk the sesame oil, rice vinegar, ginger, and soy sauce in a serving bowl. Add the sugar snaps and toss to serve.

Green Bean Salad with Boiled Lemon, Pecans, and Parmigiano-Reggiano

This is a reinvented classic from Puglia in southern Italy; it owes much of its flavor to the boiled lemon skin, incredibly mellow and refreshing. *Makes 6 servings*

1 large lemon
1½ pounds green beans, trimmed and cut into 1-inch lengths
1 tablespoon white wine vinegar
½ teaspoon salt
½ teaspoon freshly ground black pepper
6 tablespoons extra virgin olive oil
½ cup toasted pecans
3 ounces Parmigiano-Reggiano, shaved

① Place the lemon in a small saucepan, cover with water, and bring to a boil over high heat. Cover, reduce the heat to medium, and simmer until tender when pierced with a fork, about 20 minutes. Drain in a colander set in the sink and cool to room temperature (do not run cool water over the lemon).

② Cut the lemon in half. Gently scoop out the pulpy insides, placing them in a fine-mesh sieve set over a small bowl. Squeeze the pulp a little to extract some of the juice without letting any of the fibrous bits through the mesh, then set aside over the bowl to drain. Slice the lemon rind into ¼-inch strips, then chop these strips.

③ Bring a large pot of water to a boil over high heat. Add the beans and cook for 2 minutes. Drain in a colander set in the sink and refresh with cool water until room temperature. Drain well.

④ Discard the lemon pulp. Whisk the vinegar, salt, and pepper into the bowl with the lemon juice in the bowl. Slowly whisk in the olive oil.

⑤ Place the green beans, chopped lemon rind, pecans, and Parmigiano-Reggiano in a large serving bowl. Add the dressing and toss to coat.

Variations: Substitute sugar snap peas, chopped asparagus spears, or broccoli florets for the green beans.

Substitute Asiago or Pecorino Romano for the Parmigiano-Reggiano.

Fennel and Pear Salad

An easy way to prepare this Italian-inspired salad is to slice the fennel and pear with a mandoline, the blade set just under 1/8 inch. Make sure you use the food guard to protect your fingers as the fruit and vegetable pass over the very sharp blades. Or use a food processor fitted with the 1mm slicing blade, although it will juice the ingredients, rendering them a little soggy. Failing all that, a sharp chef's knife will do the trick. *Makes 4 servings*

1 large fennel bulb

2 ripe pears

3 ounces Parmigiano-Reggiano, shaved

1/3 cup lemon juice

3 tablespoons olive oil, preferably extra virgin olive oil

1/2 teaspoon salt

1/2 teaspoon freshly ground black pepper

1 Trim the bottom off the fennel bulb; trim off the stalks and fronds. Remove and discard the outer layer. Slice the bulb into 1/8-inch-thick slices. Separate these, then cut any intact sections into very thin spears. Place in a large serving bowl.

2 Peel the pears, then core them by inserting a melon baller into their thick end and coring out the seeds with a rotating motion. Slice into 1/8-inch-thick slices. Place in the bowl with the fennel.

3 Add the Parmigiano-Reggiano, lemon juice, olive oil, salt, and pepper; toss to serve.

Variations: Substitute 1 large apple for the pears.

Substitute Asiago or Pecorino Romano for the Parmigiano-Reggiano.

Substitute white balsamic vinegar for the lemon juice.

Jicama and Arugula Salad with Blood Orange Vinaigrette

Jicama is a root vegetable, sort of like a huge water chestnut with a thin, brown skin. It's sometimes considered the celery of Latin America. Once peeled, it's so crisp and nutty, it makes an excellent salad alongside sandwiches. *Makes 8 servings*

Two 1-pound jicamas, peeled and quartered (see Note)

2 blood oranges

3 tablespoons red wine vinegar

1 tablespoon chili powder

1/2 teaspoon salt

1/3 cup olive oil, preferably extra virgin olive oil

2 cups chopped arugula leaves (remove the stems if fibrous or tough)

1 Shred the jicama through the large holes of a box grater or with the shredding blade of a food processor.

2 Squeeze the juice from the oranges into a serving bowl, taking care to remove any seeds. Whisk in the vinegar, chili powder, and salt. Slowly whisk in the olive oil.

3 Add the shredded jicama and arugula; toss well to serve.

Note: It's easiest to peel the jicamas with a paring knife, rather than a vegetable peeler.

Variations: Substitute regular oranges plus 1/2 teaspoon sugar for the blood oranges.

Sprinkle 1/4 cup toasted sliced almonds over the salad.

Sprinkle 1 tablespoon toasted sesame seeds over the salad.

Marinated Shiitake Salad

Although the stems of shiitakes are too fibrous to be digestible, they can be frozen and added to vegetable stock when you make it (see page 166). Mung bean sprouts should be small and crisp-tender, with no brown or rusty spots and very tight heads. *Makes 6 servings*

¼ cup white wine vinegar
2 tablespoons minced peeled fresh ginger
1 teaspoon sugar
½ teaspoon salt
½ teaspoon freshly ground black pepper
3 tablespoons canola oil
1 tablespoon toasted sesame oil
1 pound shiitake mushrooms, stemmed and thinly sliced
1 red bell pepper, cored, seeded, and diced
4 medium scallions, thinly sliced
2 cups mung bean sprouts, roughly chopped

❶ Whisk the vinegar, ginger, sugar, salt and pepper in a large bowl; slowly whisk in the canola oil and sesame oil.

❷ Add the sliced mushrooms, bell pepper, scallions, and sprouts. Toss to coat, then cover and set aside at room temperature for 1 hour before serving.

Variations: Substitute stemmed cremini mushrooms for the shiitakes.
  Substitute white balsamic vinegar for the white wine vinegar; omit the sugar.
  Substitute 2 medium shallots, thinly sliced, for the scallions.

Southwestern Fruit, Melon, and Berry Salad

Toasted cumin seeds set off the taste of fresh fruit in this easy summer pleaser. *Makes 6 servings*

1 teaspoon cumin seeds
1 small ruby-red grapefruit
1 medium cantaloupe, peeled, seeded, and chopped
1 ripe mango, peeled, pitted, and chopped
1 small shallot, minced
1 cup blueberries
1 tablespoon lime juice
1 tablespoon almond oil
¼ teaspoon salt

❶ Toast the cumin seeds in a small skillet over low heat until lightly browned and quite aromatic, shaking the pan often, about 3 minutes. Set aside to cool for 10 minutes.

❷ Cut off about ¼ inch of the stem end of the grapefruit, just so it will sit flat on the cutting board. Set it down so, then slice off about ⅛ inch of the top. Slice down along the natural curve of the fruit, taking off the skin and the pith. Hold the grapefruit over your serving bowl and use a small paring knife to free the individual sections from the membrane that encases them, letting the segments and any extra juice fall into the bowl. (Take care not to cut your hand!)

❸ Add the cantaloupe, mango, shallot, and blueberries. Toss in the toasted cumin seeds, lime juice, almond oil, and salt.

Variations: Substitute 1 large orange for the grapefruit.
  Substitute a small honeydew melon for the cantaloupe.
  Substitute ½ pint raspberries or blackberries for the blueberries.

Although coleslaw has come a long way from its Dutch roots (*koolsla,* or cold cabbage), there's still no reason to stand on ceremony: a slaw can use any shredded vegetables.

Creamy Coleslaw

We credit James Peterson with this technique to get rid of the cabbage's natural wateriness. *Makes 10 servings*

One 3-pound head white cabbage, outer
    leaves removed, quartered, and then cored
1 tablespoon salt, preferably kosher salt
⅔ cup mayonnaise, homemade (see page
    121) or purchased (regular, low-fat, or
    fat-free)
⅓ cup sour cream (regular, low-fat, or
    fat-free)
2 tablespoons Dijon mustard
1 tablespoon white wine vinegar
1 teaspoon sugar
2 celery ribs, thinly sliced
1 large shallot, finely diced

1 Slice the cabbage as thinly as possible on a cutting board, then place it in a large bowl. Add the salt and rub the cabbage between your hands, working the salt into it until you can't feel any more salt granules in the mix. Place the salted cabbage in a large colander and drain in the sink for 1 hour.

2 Whisk the mayonnaise, sour cream, mustard, vinegar, and sugar in a large serving bowl.

3 Rinse the cabbage to get rid of the excess salt; squeeze it dry in batches between paper towels. Add it to the dressing.

4 Add the celery and shallot. Toss well, cover, and refrigerate for at least 1 hour or up to 2 days.

Variations: Add 1 tablespoon chopped parsley leaves and/or 2 teaspoons stemmed thyme with the celery.

Add ¼ cup golden raisins with the celery.

Add 1 tablespoon capers, drained and rinsed, with the celery.

Substitute 1 large carrot, shredded through the large holes of a box grater, for the celery.

Substitute 1 small red onion, thinly sliced, for the shallot.

Substitute 1 pickled jalapeño chile, seeded and finely chopped, for the capers.

Vinegary Slaw

Long a staple in New York delis (where it's known as "health salad"), this easy slaw gets better as it sits in the fridge. *Makes 8 servings*

¾ cup white vinegar
⅓ cup sugar
2 teaspoons salt
½ teaspoon freshly ground black pepper
1 small head white cabbage (about
    1½ pounds)
2 large carrots
1 medium green bell pepper, cored, seeded,
    and finely diced
1 medium red bell pepper, cored, seeded,
    and finely diced

❶ Whisk the vinegar, sugar, salt, and pepper in a large bowl.

❷ Shred the cabbage and carrots through the large holes of a box grater or with the shredding blade of a food processor.

❸ Toss the shredded cabbage and carrots along with the green and red bell peppers into the dressing. Cover and refrigerate for at least 12 hours or up to 1 week, stirring occasionally to coat all the vegetables. Serve by scooping up the vegetables with a slotted spoon, letting any excess dressing drain off.

Variations: Add 2 teaspoons chopped dill fronds, 1 teaspoon red pepper flakes, or 1 teaspoon stemmed thyme with the sugar.

Substitute white wine vinegar for the white vinegar.

Substitute 4 celery ribs, thinly sliced, for the bell peppers.

Radish Slaw

Shredded radishes make a crisp, peppery side salad, great with sandwiches or burgers. *Makes 8 servings*

6 tablespoons champagne or white wine
　　vinegar
1 tablespoon sugar
1 tablespoon chopped parsley leaves
½ teaspoon salt
½ teaspoon freshly ground black pepper
3 tablespoons canola, sunflower, or
　　grapeseed oil
24 large red radishes
2 medium cucumbers, peeled, sliced in half
　　lengthwise, and the seeds scooped out
2 large carrots

❶ Whisk the vinegar, sugar, parsley, salt, and pepper in a large serving bowl; slowly whisk in the oil.

❷ Shred the radishes, cucumbers, and carrots through the large holes of a box grater or with the shredding blade of a food processor. Toss with the dressing in the bowl. Cover and refrigerate for at least 4 hours or up to 3 days.

Variations: Substitute stemmed thyme or minced tarragon for the parsley.

Substitute 2 medium apples, peeled and cored, for the cucumbers.

Asian Carrot Slaw

Here, we pair carrots with Asian flavors for a mellow take on the picnic classic. *Makes 6 servings*

¾ pound pearl onions
1 pound large carrots
½ cup dried cranberries
½ cup coarsely chopped toasted unsalted
　　cashews
2 tablespoons rice vinegar
1 tablespoon soy sauce
1 tablespoon finely grated peeled fresh
　　ginger

❶ Bring a large pot of water to a boil over high heat. Add the onions and cook for 3 minutes. Drain in a colander set in the sink, then rinse with cool water.

❷ Peel the onions, then gently squeeze them to separate the soft, inner layers. Roughly chop these layers and place them in a large serving bowl.

❸ Using the large holes of a box grater, shred the carrots into the onions. Stir in the dried cranberries and cashews.

❹ Whisk the vinegar, soy sauce, and ginger in a small bowl. Pour this over the carrot mixture and toss gently to serve.

Variations: Substitute sunflower seeds or toasted sliced almonds for the cashews; increase the soy sauce to 1½ tablespoons.

Substitute dried cherries or dried currants for the dried cranberries.

Add ½ teaspoon Asian red chili sauce or chili oil with the ginger.

Add 1 teaspoon toasted sesame oil with the ginger.

Central American Slaw

This is a fanciful creation: a creamy slaw that has the bright flavors of Latin America. *Makes 10 servings*

½ cup mayonnaise, homemade (see page 121) or purchased (regular, low-fat, or fat-free)
¼ cup sour cream (regular, low-fat, or fat-free)
3 tablespoons lime juice
1 teaspoon ground cumin
1 teaspoon salt
½ teaspoon freshly ground black pepper
Several dashes of hot red pepper sauce to taste
One 2-pound head green cabbage, cored
1 medium green bell pepper, cored and seeded
2 medium mangoes, peeled, pitted, and chopped
1 medium jicama, peeled, quartered, and then cut into matchsticks
2 tablespoons packed chopped cilantro leaves

1 Whisk the mayonnaise, sour cream, lime juice, cumin, salt, pepper, and hot red pepper sauce in a large serving bowl.

2 Shred the cabbage and bell pepper through the large holes of a box grater or with the shredding blade of a food processor.

3 Toss the shredded vegetables, mangoes, jicama, and cilantro with the dressing. The salad can be covered and refrigerated for up to 2 days.

Variations: Add ½ teaspoon ground cinnamon with the cumin.

Add 1 or 2 seeded and chopped pickled jalapeño chiles with the mangoes.

Shiitake Slaw

Bok choy should have large, dark green leaves and small white stems; Napa cabbage heads should be tight, without any browned leaves. *Makes 8 servings*

1 tablespoon toasted sesame oil
6 ounces shiitake mushrooms, stems removed, caps thinly sliced
5 tablespoons soy sauce
3 tablespoons canola or peanut oil
3 tablespoons lime juice
1 teaspoon sugar
2 garlic cloves, crushed
One 1-pound head Napa cabbage, cored
8 ounces bok choy
¼ cup chopped unsalted roasted peanuts
2 tablespoons packed minced cilantro leaves

1 Heat a large skillet over medium heat. Swirl in the sesame oil, then add the mushrooms and cook until they give off their liquid and it evaporates to a glaze, about 4 minutes, stirring frequently. Set aside to cool for 15 minutes.

2 Whisk the soy sauce, oil, lime juice, sugar, and garlic in a large serving bowl.

3 Shred the cabbage and bok choy with the large holes of a box grater or with the shredding blade of a food processor. Alternatively, thinly slice the cabbage and bok choy.

4 Add the cabbage and bok choy to the dressing. Stir in the mushrooms and any oil in the pan as well as the peanuts and cilantro; toss well. The salad can be covered and stored in the refrigerator for up to 3 days.

Here are the salads that come out of the fridge for a quick meal or the cooler for a picnic. Keep them well chilled until you serve them.

(More Than Just) Tuna Salad

We like to dress up the usual fare with chutney, cashews, and grapes. Makes 4 servings (can be halved, doubled, or tripled)

> ¼ cup mayonnaise, homemade (see page 121) or purchased (regular, low-fat, or fat-free)
>
> 2 tablespoons mango chutney
>
> 2 teaspoons lime juice
>
> ½ teaspoon salt
>
> ¼ teaspoon freshly ground black pepper
>
> A few dashes of hot red pepper sauce to taste
>
> Two 6-ounce cans white tuna packed in water, drained
>
> ½ cup chopped toasted unsalted cashews
>
> 24 seedless red grapes, halved
>
> 2 celery ribs, thinly sliced

1 Whisk the mayonnaise, mango chutney, lime juice, salt, pepper, and hot red pepper sauce in a large bowl.

2 Stir in the tuna, cashews, grapes, and celery with a wooden spoon.

To store: Cover and refrigerate for up to 2 days.

Variations: Add 1 teaspoon celery seeds.

Add 1 teaspoon curry powder with the chutney; substitute lemon juice for the lime juice.

Substitute any flavor chutney you like for the mango chutney, including your own homemade (see page 388).

Substitute chopped roasted unsalted peanuts, chopped toasted walnut pieces, or chopped toasted pecan pieces for the cashews.

Substitute 1 small green bell pepper, cored, seeded, and finely diced, for the celery.

Fresh Tuna Salad

This light, flavorful salad can stand in as a main course. Choose high-quality tuna that smells fresh and clean, preferably sushi-grade tuna. *Makes 4 servings (can be halved, doubled, or tripled)*

> 1 pound green beans, trimmed and halved (about 4 cups)
>
> 7 tablespoons olive oil, 6 tablespoons of it extra virgin olive oil
>
> One 12- to 16-ounce tuna steak (about ½ inch thick)
>
> 2 tablespoons sherry vinegar
>
> 2 teaspoons Dijon mustard
>
> 2 teaspoons chopped tarragon leaves
>
> ½ teaspoon salt
>
> ½ teaspoon freshly ground black pepper
>
> ½ cup pitted halved black olives
>
> 1 medium tomato, preferably a yellow tomato, seeded (see page 111) and diced

1 Bring a large pot of water to a boil over high heat. Add the beans and cook for 2 minutes.

Drain in a colander set in the sink, then refresh under cool, running water until room temperature. Set aside.

2 Heat a large skillet over medium heat. Swirl in 1 tablespoon standard olive oil, then add the tuna steak. Cook until medium-rare (a dark pink center), 3 to 4 minutes, turning once. Transfer to a cutting board and cool for 5 minutes.

3 Move your fingers across the tuna to find out which way the grain lies, then slice the steak against the grain into ½-inch-thick slices. If some of the strips are long, slice them in half or in thirds.

4 Whisk the vinegar, mustard, tarragon, salt, and pepper in a small bowl. Slowly whisk in the 6 tablespoons extra virgin olive oil.

5 Place the beans, tuna, olives, and tomato in a large bowl. Add the dressing and toss gently to serve. (Not recommended for storing.)

Variations: Substitute halved broccoli florets, trimmed and halved wax beans, sliced asparagus spears, or stemmed and halved sugar snap peas for the green beans.

Substitute a flavored olive oil, such as rosemary or basil oil, for the 6 tablespoons extra virgin olive oil in the dressing.

Substitute ¼ cup toasted sliced almonds and ¼ cup raisins for the olives.

For a main-course presentation, leave the tuna slices long. Dress the beans, olives, and tomatoes as indicated, spoon them over lettuce leaves on serving plates, and lay the tuna slices on top.

Poached Salmon Salad

Have lots of crunchy bread on hand for open-faced sandwiches. *Makes 4 servings (can be halved, doubled, or tripled)*

1½ cups dry vermouth or dry white wine
1½ cups water
2 bay leaves
1 pound skin-on salmon fillet, cut in half widthwise
2 tablespoons mayonnaise, homemade (see page 121) or purchased (regular, low-fat, or fat-free)
2 tablespoons sour cream (regular, low-fat, or fat-free)
2 tablespoons minced cornichons (about 5) or dill pickles
2 teaspoons capers, drained and chopped
2 teaspoons minced dill fronds or 1 teaspoon dried dill
2 teaspoons lemon juice
½ teaspoon salt
½ teaspoon freshly ground black pepper

1 Bring the vermouth or wine, the water, and bay leaves to a boil in a large skillet set over high heat. Add the salmon skin side down, cover, reduce the heat to low, and cook for 1 minute.

2 Remove the pan from the heat and set aside, covered, for 10 minutes. Transfer the salmon to a cutting board and continue cooling until easily handled.

3 Whisk the mayonnaise, sour cream, cornichons, capers, dill, lemon juice, salt, and pepper in a large bowl until creamy. Peel off the salmon skin, then crumble the fish into the dressing. Toss gently to serve.

To store: Cover and refrigerate for up to 2 days.

Variations: Substitute 3 tablespoons pickle relish or chowchow for the cornichons and capers.

Substitute stemmed thyme, minced oregano leaves, or parsley leaves for the dill.

Substitute lime juice for the lemon juice.

Omit the ground pepper and add a few dashes of hot red pepper sauce or chili oil with the salt.

Mayonnaise and Its Progeny

There's nothing like homemade mayonnaise, a classic French sauce that's an emulsion of egg yolks, oil, acid, and seasonings. We cook the eggs first so there are no issues with eating raw eggs.

Basic Mayonnaise
Makes about 1¼ cups

2 large egg yolks
2 tablespoons water
1½ tablespoons lemon juice
½ teaspoon dry mustard
½ teaspoon salt
A couple of dashes hot red pepper sauce to taste
1 cup canola, corn, or vegetable oil

① Whisk the egg yolks, water, lemon juice, dry mustard, salt, and hot red pepper sauce in a small saucepan until smooth. Set the pan over low heat and cook, whisking constantly, until the first bubble appears. The moment it does, remove from the heat and whisk constantly for 1 minute.

② Pour the contents of the pan into a food processor fitted with the chopping blade or a large blender. Process or blend until smooth, about 30 seconds.

③ Scrape down the sides of the bowl or canister; with the machine running, dribble in the oil a drop at a time through the feed tube or the hole in the blender's lid; once about half of the oil has been added, add more in a slow, thin, steady stream. When all the oil has been added, continue processing or blending until thick, about 1 minute, scraping down the sides of the bowl or canister occasionally. Transfer to a medium bowl; cover and refrigerate for up to 1 week.

Flavored Mayonnaises

For these, stir the ingredients together in a small bowl. Covered, they can be kept in the refrigerator for up to 1 week.

Classic Tartar Sauce
Makes about 1¼ cups
1 cup mayonnaise
2 tablespoons purchased pickle relish or finely chopped bread-and-butter pickles
2 tablespoons minced red onion
2 tablespoons minced parsley leaves

Mango Mayonnaise
Makes about 1½ cups
1 cup mayonnaise
½ cup mango chutney
2 teaspoons Worcestershire sauce

Wasabi Mayonnaise
Makes a little over
1 cup
1 cup mayonnaise
1 tablespoon prepared wasabi paste
1 tablespoon rice vinegar

Shrimp Salad

The celery should be very crisp to complement the shrimp. *Makes 4 servings (can be doubled or tripled)*

1¼ pounds medium shrimp (about 35 per pound), peeled and deveined
2 small radishes, finely diced
1 celery rib, finely diced
3 small sweet pickles, finely chopped, or 2 tablespoons sweet pickle relish
½ cup mayonnaise, homemade (see page 121) or purchased (regular, low-fat, or fat-free)
3 tablespoons sour cream (regular, low-fat, or fat-free)
1 tablespoon lemon juice
2 teaspoons minced tarragon leaves or 1 teaspoon dried tarragon
¼ teaspoon salt
¼ teaspoon freshly ground black pepper
Several dashes of hot red pepper sauce, or to taste

❶ Fill a large bowl halfway with ice water and set it aside. Bring a large pot of water to a boil over high heat. Add the shrimp and cook until pink and firm, about 3 minutes.

❷ Remove the shrimp with a slotted spoon or strainer; place them in the ice water to chill. Drain and blot dry with paper towels. Coarsely chop the cooked shrimp and set aside.

❸ Combine the radishes, celery, pickles, mayonnaise, sour cream, lemon juice, and tarragon in a large bowl.

❹ Add the shrimp and stir until all the ingredients are well combined; stir in the salt, pepper, and hot red pepper sauce.

To store: Cover and refrigerate for up to 2 days.

For an easier take on this salad: Use 1 pound frozen, precooked cold-water ("baby" or "salad") shrimp, thawed. Because they are so small, do not chop them.

Chicken Salad

We've cut down the mayo in traditional chicken salad, but livened up the flavors with tahini, Worcestershire sauce, and Dijon mustard. *Makes 6 servings (can be doubled)*

1 tablespoon olive oil
1¼ pounds boneless skinless chicken breasts
6 tablespoons mayonnaise, homemade (see page 121) or purchased (regular, low-fat, or fat-free)
1 tablespoon lemon juice
1 tablespoon tahini
2 teaspoons Worcestershire sauce
1½ teaspoons Dijon mustard
½ teaspoon salt
½ teaspoon freshly ground black pepper
3 jarred whole roasted red peppers or pimientos, chopped (about ½ cup)
1 medium shallot, minced
1 celery rib, minced

❶ Preheat the broiler and line the broiler rack with aluminum foil. Rub the oil into the chicken breasts, place them 4 to 6 inches under the heat source, and broil until lightly browned, until an instant-read meat thermometer inserted into the thickest part of the breast registers 160°F (our preference) or 170°F (the USDA recommendation), about 15 minutes, turning occasionally. Transfer to a cutting board and cool for 10 minutes.

2 Whisk the mayonnaise, lemon juice, tahini, Worcestershire sauce, mustard, salt, and pepper in a small bowl; set aside.

3 Slice the chicken into thin strips, then cut these into bite-sized pieces. Place them in a large bowl along with the roasted red peppers or pimientos, shallot, and celery.

4 Pour the dressing over the chicken mixture, then toss gently to serve.

To store: Cover and refrigerate for up to 2 days.

Variations: Reduce the mayonnaise to ¼ cup and add 2 tablespoons sour cream (regular, low-fat, or fat-free) with it.

Substitute ½ small red onion, thinly sliced, for the shallot.

Add ¼ cup toasted sliced almonds or chopped toasted walnut pieces with the celery.

For an easier salad, substitute a purchased rotisserie chicken for the boneless skinless breasts. Take the breast meat off the bones, remove the skin, chop the meat, and add it to the salad. For a whole rotisserie chicken, you'll need to double the dressing in step 2 and the vegetables in step 3.

Serving Suggestions

Try any of these salads in pita pockets or on toasted rye bread, split baguettes, toasted French bread, bagels, burger buns, or toasted English muffins. Mound them on toasted baguette rounds as an appetizer. Or try them in celery ribs, lettuce cups, Belgian endive spears, seeded melon halves, or hollowed-out tomato halves for a fancier dish.

Egg Salad

June Cleaver may have made it a staple and Lisa Lubner's mother may have made it kitsch but neither spiked it with horseradish. *Makes 4 servings (can be halved, doubled, or tripled)*

½ cup mayonnaise, homemade (see page 121) or purchased (regular, low-fat, or fat-free)
2 tablespoons prepared white horseradish
2 tablespoons Dijon mustard
1 tablespoon chopped dill fronds or 1½ teaspoons dried dill
1 medium shallot, minced
1 celery rib, minced
1 small dill pickle, minced
½ teaspoon freshly ground black pepper
¼ teaspoon salt
8 cooled, hard-cooked large eggs (see page 59 for instructions on how to hard-cook eggs)

1 Whisk the mayonnaise, horseradish, mustard, dill, shallot, celery, pickle, pepper, and salt in a medium bowl.

2 Peel the eggs, roughly chop them, and stir gently into the mayonnaise mixture.

To store: Cover and refrigerate for up to 2 days.

Variations: Substitute tarragon leaves for the dill.

Substitute 2 tablespoons corn relish or 1 tablespoon hot chowchow for the dill pickle.

Mayonnaise Salad Safety

All salads made with mayonnaise must be kept chilled, at or below 40°F. If you're taking them to a picnic, make sure their sealed container is buried in the ice in the cooler. That said, no mayonnaise salad freezes well.

You can turn any green salad into a main course with some protein and crunchy vegetables (see page 106), but here are some specialized salads for dinner.

Poached Egg, Bacon, and Frisée Salad

Although the bistro classic (in French, *Salade aux Lardons*) doesn't usually have honey and mustard in it, we've given it an American twist that works well with the salty bacon. For another version of this salad with lentils, see French Lentils with Bacon (page 505). *Makes 4 servings*

1 pound slab bacon, cut into ½-inch pieces
2 medium shallots, thinly sliced into rings
3 tablespoons plus ½ teaspoon white wine vinegar
2 teaspoons Dijon mustard
2 teaspoons honey
½ teaspoon freshly ground black pepper
4 large eggs, at room temperature
2 large heads frisée or curly endive (see page 97), torn into bite-sized pieces

❶ To render the fat, place the bacon in a cold skillet set over low heat. When the bacon starts to sizzle, stir well, then cook slowly until crispy and well browned, about 15 minutes, stirring occasionally. Use a slotted spoon to transfer the bacon to a plate lined with paper towels, keeping the rendered fat in the pan.

❷ Raise the heat to medium. Add the shallots and cook, stirring frequently, until softened, about 2 minutes.

❸ Remove the skillet from the heat and whisk in the 3 tablespoons vinegar, the mustard, honey,

and pepper until creamy. Cover and set aside to keep warm.

❹ Bring a large saucepan filled halfway with water to a boil over high heat. Add the remaining ½ teaspoon vinegar and reduce the heat so the water simmers very slowly.

❺ Crack each of the eggs into small bowls or teacups, then slip the eggs into the water. Reduce the heat even further and cook at a very gentle simmer until the whites are set and the yolks are filmed over, 2 to 3 minutes. (For tips on poaching eggs, see page 18.)

❻ Meanwhile, divide the frisée among four plates. Top with the bacon bits.

❼ Transfer a poached egg to each salad, using a slotted spoon to drain it well before setting it on the greens. Rewhisk the dressing in the pan, then drizzle it among the salads before serving.

For a lower-fat alternative: Use roughly chopped Canadian bacon. Cook it with 1 tablespoon canola oil until lightly browned, about 5 minutes. It won't render much fat, so add another 1 teaspoon canola oil to the pan to cook the shallots.

You can also cut down on the salt by parboiling the bacon in a large saucepan of water for 1 minute before draining in a colander set in the sink and then frying.

BLT Salad

Here's a salad made with the inner workings of our favorite sandwich. *Makes 4 servings*

½ pound sliced bacon
¼ cup homemade mayonnaise (page 121) or purchased mayonnaise (regular, low-fat, or fat-free)
1 tablespoon lemon juice
½ tablespoon Dijon mustard
2 teaspoons Worcestershire sauce
½ teaspoon freshly ground black pepper
1 large head romaine lettuce, cored and chopped (about 8 cups)
2 large beefsteak tomatoes, cut into 1-inch pieces

1 Heat a large skillet over medium heat. Add the bacon and fry until crisp, about 5 minutes, turning often. Transfer to a wire rack and drain for 5 minutes, then roughly chop the bacon.

2 Meanwhile, whisk the mayonnaise, lemon juice, mustard, Worcestershire sauce, and pepper in a large bowl.

3 Add the romaine, tomatoes, and chopped bacon; toss gently but well.

Variations: Reduce the bacon to ¼ pound. After it has fried for 2 minutes, add ½ pound medium shrimp, peeled and deveined, and continue cooking until pink and firm, about 3 minutes.

Add 1 ounce shredded Parmigiano-Reggiano or Cheddar with the romaine.

Check out the main-course potato salads in the vegetable chapter (see pages 482–484).

Margarita Shrimp Salad

Here, shrimp are steeped in a margarita-style marinade, then quickly cooked and served on a summery, composed green salad with avocado, orange, and red onion. *Makes 6 servings*

¼ cup tequila
2 teaspoons finely grated orange zest
1 teaspoon finely grated lime zest
½ teaspoon salt
1½ pounds medium shrimp (about 35 per pound), peeled and deveined
¼ cup homemade mayonnaise (see page 121) or purchased mayonnaise (regular, low-fat, or fat-free)
¼ cup sour cream (regular, low-fat, or fat-free)
¼ cup lime juice
2 teaspoons chili powder
1 teaspoon ground cumin
1 teaspoon sugar
1 tablespoon canola oil
6 cups mixed salad greens (see page 99)
1 ripe Hass avocado, peeled, pitted, and cut into ½-inch cubes
1 small red onion, thinly sliced into rings
1 orange, peeled and cut into segments

1 Whisk the tequila, orange zest, lime zest, and salt in a large bowl. Add the shrimp, toss well, cover, and refrigerate for 1 hour, stirring occasionally.

2 Meanwhile, whisk the mayonnaise, sour cream, lime juice, chili powder, cumin, and sugar in a small bowl; set aside.

3 Drain the shrimp, reserving the marinade. Heat a large skillet over medium heat. Swirl in the canola oil, then add the shrimp and cook, stirring constantly, until pink and firm, about 3 minutes. Transfer the shrimp to a small bowl.

4 Take the skillet off the heat and pour in the reserved marinade. Set the skillet back over the heat and bring to a boil. Should the alcohol catch fire, quickly cover the skillet and set it off the heat until the fire stops, about 20 seconds. Boil until reduced to a glaze, pour over the shrimp, and stir well.

5 Divide the salad greens among six plates. Top with the avocado, red onion, and orange. Spoon the shrimp and any glaze onto the salads. Dot the mayonnaise dressing onto the salad before serving.

Variations: Divide any of the following among the plates: 1/2 cup toasted sliced almonds, 1/2 cup toasted pecan pieces, Croutons (page 101), or 1 to 2 pickled jalapeño chiles, seeded and chopped.

South American Pork Salad

This salad is a streamlined version of salpiçon, a popular Chilean potato salad. *Makes 6 servings*

  2 garlic cloves, crushed
  2 tablespoons chili powder
  1/4 cup plus 2 tablespoons lime juice
  1 teaspoon dried oregano
  1 teaspoon ground cumin
  1/2 teaspoon freshly ground black pepper
  Two 1-pound pork tenderloins, trimmed
  3 pounds small purple-fleshed or red-
    skinned potatoes
  6 cups purchased mesclun salad mix or
    mixed salad greens (see page 99)
  12 radishes, thinly sliced
  6 scallions, thinly sliced
  1/2 teaspoon salt
  1/2 cup olive oil, preferably extra virgin
    olive oil
  Several dashes of hot red pepper sauce to
    taste
  1/2 cup chopped cilantro leaves

1 Mix the garlic, chili powder, 2 tablespoons lime juice, oregano, cumin, and pepper in a small bowl. Rub this mixture into the tenderloins; cover and refrigerate for at least 2 hours or overnight.

2 Bring a large saucepan of water to a boil over high heat. Drop in the potatoes and boil until tender when pierced with a fork, about 25 minutes. Drain in a colander set in the sink. When cool enough to handle, quarter each potato.

3 Preheat the broiler; line the broiler pan with aluminum foil. Broil the tenderloins 4 to 6 inches from the heat source until an instant-read meat thermometer inserted into the thickest part of the tenderloin registers 155°F (our preference) or 170°F (the USDA recommendation), about 15 to 18 minutes, turning occasionally. Transfer to a cutting board for 5 minutes, then slice into thin rounds.

4 Divide the greens among six serving plates. Top with the sliced tenderloin, quartered potatoes, radishes, and scallions.

5 Place the remaining 1/4 cup lime juice and salt in a small bowl. Slowly whisk in the olive oil. Whisk in the hot red pepper sauce.

6 Spoon the dressing over the composed salads, then top with the cilantro before serving.

Variations: Add any of the following to the salad: 12 black or green olives, pitted and halved; 1 ripe mango, peeled, pitted, and thinly sliced; 1 ripe avocado, peeled, pitted, and thinly sliced; or 1/4 cup roasted unsalted peanuts.

Thai-Inspired Beef Salad

Most Southeast Asian salads are chopped salads eaten in lettuce cups; here, we've Americanized the presentation by creating a composed salad on greens. *Makes 4 servings*

1 pound London broil, trimmed
½ cup bottled chili sauce, such as Heinz
2 tablespoons honey
1 teaspoon ground cumin
2 small shallots, minced
2 tablespoons lime juice
2 tablespoons fish sauce
1 teaspoon packed light brown sugar
½ to 1 teaspoon Asian red chili paste
2 tablespoons peanut oil, preferably an Asian
   bottling
8 cups purchased mesclun salad mix or
   mixed salad greens (see page 99)
24 basil leaves, torn into shreds
12 mint leaves, torn into shreds

❶ Place the London broil in a baking dish that will just hold it. Whisk the chili sauce, honey, and cumin in a small bowl; pour over the steak. Turn it to coat it well, then cover and refrigerate for 30 minutes or up to 4 hours.

❷ Preheat the broiler; line the broiler rack with aluminum foil. Remove the London broil from the marinade; discard the marinade.

❸ Broil 4 to 6 inches from the heat until medium rare, turning once, until an instant-read meat thermometer inserted into the thickest part of the steak registers 125°F (our preference) or 145°F (the USDA recommendation), 12 to 14 minutes. Transfer to a cutting board and let stand for 5 minutes.

❹ Run your fingers over the steak to see which way the grain runs, then slice the steak against the grain into 1-inch strips. (To determine a steak's grain, see page 394.) If desired, cut each into bite-sized pieces.

❺ Whisk the shallots, lime juice, fish sauce, brown sugar, and chili paste in a small bowl. Slowly whisk in the peanut oil.

❻ Toss the greens, basil, and mint in a large bowl. Add the lime juice dressing and toss to coat.

❼ Divide the dressed greens among four serving plates. Lay the beef slices over the top before serving.

Variations: Add 4 large radishes, thinly sliced; 1 large carrot, shredded through the holes of a box grater; or 1 small cucumber, peeled, halved, seeded, and thinly sliced to the greens.

Soups

ALMOST EVERY CULTURE HAS ITS SOUP-AS-PENICILLIN MYTH: CHICKEN IN Jewish and Chinese homes, potato or lamb among Irish families, peanut in sub-Saharan enclaves. That's because soup is immediately and identifiably comforting. It's not a fancy braise or sauté; there's no complicated technique. Yes, you can make your own stock, but you don't have to.

Vegetable soups are the easiest because the taste of the vegetables must come through—the soup therefore must remain uncomplicated. Soups made with grains and legumes are by and large more time-consuming but also heartier—as are those that include some kind of protein, from chicken to cheese. These latter are all stand-alones, perfect for a meal on their own. Finally, cold soups, a shock to some, are a brilliant way to set off a barbecue or bring a little light to winter doldrums.

Hearty stocks round out this chapter. They're made two ways: with the long-simmered method and the much faster pressure cooker method. Consider making a batch and freezing it in small portions; even substituting 1 cup of homemade stock for packaged broth will make a world of difference in any recipe.

So here's to the cures: creamy soups for the winter blues, hearty soups after a hard day's work, and even cold soups for summertime bliss. Some are traditional; some fanciful; none fancy. The point is to get a bowl of comfort on the table.

These are the simplest soups—in smaller portions, they're starters; with salad and bread, they make a light main course. Most can be made in advance and stored in the refrigerator for a couple of days—or frozen in individual servings for microwave lunches or dinners later on.

Spring or Fall Vegetable Soup

Here's a basic vegetable soup in two versions. Choose either the spring or autumn vegetables in the recipe list. The parsley should be cooked slowly at first to infuse the oil. *Makes 6 servings*

2 tablespoons olive oil
1 large yellow onion, finely chopped
¼ cup chopped parsley leaves
2 garlic cloves, minced
1 large beefsteak tomato, cored and finely chopped
8 cups (2 quarts) chicken broth
1 bay leaf

Spring Vegetables
2 medium zucchini, roughly chopped
2 medium yellow summer squash, roughly chopped
1 medium fennel bulb, trimmed and roughly chopped
½ pound green beans, ends trimmed and cut into 1-inch pieces
½ pound asparagus spears, ends trimmed and cut into 1-inch pieces
½ pound sugar snap peas, stems and fibrous veins removed, roughly chopped

Winter Vegetables
4 medium carrots, peeled and thinly sliced
1 medium acorn squash, peeled, halved, seeded, and roughly chopped
¾ pound yellow-fleshed potatoes, such as Yukon golds, peeled and diced

½ pound Brussels sprouts, quartered
½ pound cremini or white button mushrooms, thinly sliced

1 teaspoon salt
½ teaspoon freshly ground black pepper

❶ Heat a large Dutch oven or soup pot over low heat. Swirl in the olive oil, then add the onion and parsley. Cook slowly, stirring often, until the onion is golden, about 7 minutes.

❷ Add the garlic, cook for 15 seconds, then add the tomato. Stir well, raise the heat to medium-high, and pour in the broth, scraping up any browned bits on the pan's bottom as the broth comes to a simmer.

❸ Stir in the bay leaf and all the spring vegetables (the zucchini, yellow squash, fennel, green beans, asparagus, and sugar snaps) or winter vegetables (the carrots, acorn squash, potatoes, Brussels sprouts, and mushrooms).

❹ Cover, reduce the heat to low, and simmer slowly until the vegetables are tender, about 30 minutes for the spring vegetables, 45 minutes for the winter ones. Remove the bay leaf; stir in the salt and pepper before serving.

Variations: Stir in 2 cups cooked and drained shaped pasta (ziti, rigatoni, farfalle) during the last 5 minutes of cooking.

For a brighter taste, stir in 2 teaspoons cider or white wine vinegar with the salt.

For a deeper taste, use beef broth instead of chicken.

For a richer soup, add the rind from a wedge of Parmigiano-Reggiano with the vegetables. Shave off the wax and any ink with a vegetable peeler before adding. The cheese will melt as the vegetables cook; discard the remnant after cooking.

A road map for
Creamy Vegetable Soup

Here's a rich, thick, yet light cream soup. Use any of the vegetables called for, but remember that the cooking times will be different (firmer vegetables, of course, require longer cooking). *Makes 6 servings*

1 First, make the creamy base. Melt

3 tablespoons unsalted butter

in a large saucepan or soup pot set over medium heat.

2 The moment the foaming subsides, sprinkle

2 tablespoons all-purpose flour

over the butter. Whisk over the heat until the mixture is a thin paste, not browned at all but also not grainy, about 1 minute.

3 Whisking constantly, slowly pour in

either 4 cups chicken broth or 4 cups vegetable broth

Continue whisking until the mixture comes to a low simmer and thickens.

4 Now stir in 4 cups of any one of the following:

Asparagus spears, trimmed and cut into 1-inch pieces
Baby artichokes, trimmed and quartered
Broccoli florets, chopped
Brussels sprouts, trimmed and quartered
Carrots, thinly sliced
Cauliflower florets, chopped
Celery ribs, stringy veins removed from each rib, then thinly sliced
Chard, center veins removed, the leaves washed and roughly chopped
Corn kernels
Fennel, trimmed of all fronds and the thick base, then thinly sliced
Green beans, trimmed and cut into 1-inch pieces
Baby spinach leaves, chopped
Winter squash, seeded, peeled, and cut into 1-inch pieces

5 Cover, reduce the heat to low, and cook, stirring once in a while, until the vegetables are tender, 15 to 40 minutes, depending on which vegetables you've chosen.

6 Working in batches if necessary, pour or ladle the soup into a food processor fitted with the chopping blade or into a large blender; process or blend until smooth, scraping down the sides of the bowl as necessary. Return the puree to the pan or pot. Alternatively, use an immersion blender to puree the soup right in the pot.

7 Stir in 1 cup of any of the following:

Heavy cream
Light cream
Half-and-half
Whole milk
Fat-free evaporated milk

Also add one of the following:

2 tablespoons chopped parsley leaves
2 tablespoons chopped tarragon leaves
1 tablespoon chopped marjoram leaves
1 tablespoon chopped chives
1 tablespoon chopped rosemary leaves
2 teaspoons stemmed thyme

8 Bring the soup to a simmer over medium heat, stirring frequently. Reduce the heat and simmer very slowly, just a bubble or two at a time, uncovered, for 10 minutes.

9 Before serving, stir in

1 teaspoon salt, or to taste

10 Garnish each bowl with a sprinkling of one of the following:

Freshly ground white or black pepper
Grated nutmeg
Grated or ground mace
Ground allspice

Tips for Success

• Use a whisk in steps 1 and 2, a wooden spoon thereafter.

• For the freshest, most delicate taste, do not sauté or sweat the vegetables; instead, add them directly to the simmering broth.

• Do not be tempted to add more cream; less is more in this simple soup.

Roasted Garlic Soup

Here's a garlicky version of French onion soup: all the onions are replaced by garlic and shallots. Double or triple the recipe for larger meals or servings. *Makes 4 servings*

4 garlic heads
8 medium shallots, peeled
3 tablespoons olive oil
4 cups (1 quart) beef broth
¼ cup brandy or Cognac
2 teaspoons stemmed thyme
1 teaspoon salt
½ teaspoon freshly ground black pepper
4 ounces Gruyère or Emmentaler

1 Position the rack in the center of the oven and preheat the oven to 400°F.

2 Slice ½ inch or so off the top of the garlic heads so that all the cloves are exposed. Place them on a sheet of aluminum foil, drizzle with 1½ tablespoons olive oil, and seal the packet closed. Roast in the oven until the cloves are as soft as room-temperature butter, about 40 minutes.

3 At the same time, place the shallots in a small, shallow baking dish; drizzle with the remaining 1½ tablespoons olive oil; and roast until browned, caramelized, and softened, stirring occasionally, about 30 minutes.

4 Remove both the garlic and shallots from the oven; cool at room temperature for 15 minutes.

5 Squeeze the soft pulp out of the garlic heads and into a large saucepan. Roughly chop the shallots and add them to the pan. Stir in the broth, brandy or Cognac, thyme, salt, and pepper. Set the pan over the heat and bring to a simmer.

⑥ Cover, reduce the heat to low, and simmer slowly for 45 minutes to blend and soften the flavors. To serve, grate about an ounce of cheese into each of the bowls. Ladle the soup over the cheese.

Variations: Substitute dry sherry, dry vermouth, dry Madeira, dry Marsala, or red wine for the brandy.

Rub several baguette rounds with olive oil, then toast them until crunchy. Place in the bowls, then grate the cheese over them; ladle the soup around and over the rounds.

Garlic Broth: Simmer the soup as directed, then strain it through a fine-mesh sieve lined with cheesecloth or a large coffee filter into a medium pot. Reheat over low heat, then serve with or without the cheese.

Roasted Tomato Soup

Simplicity defined, this soup is best with garden-fresh tomatoes. Slow-roasting concentrates their flavor. *Makes 4 servings*

2 pounds Roma or plum tomatoes, halved lengthwise
1 medium onion, quartered
2 tablespoons olive oil
2 cups chicken or vegetable broth
1 bay leaf
Coarse-grained or kosher salt for garnish
Basil leaves, sliced into thin strips, for garnish

① Position the rack in the center of the oven and preheat the oven to 325°F.

② Toss the tomatoes and onion with the olive oil on a large lipped baking sheet. Roast slowly, stirring occasionally, until the tomatoes have shriveled and the onion has softened and turned golden at the edges, about 45 minutes. Set aside to cool at room temperature for 10 minutes.

③ If there are browned bits in the baking sheet (and if it's flameproof), set it over medium heat, add a tablespoon or two of water, and scrape up those browned bits. Place the tomatoes, onion, and any of this juice from the pan in a large food processor or blender; process or blend until chunky-smooth. Alternatively, dice the tomatoes and onions on a chopping board, but make sure you catch and save every drop of juice.

④ Pour the chopped vegetables and all their juice into a large saucepan or a small Dutch oven. Add the broth and bay leaf; bring to a simmer over medium-high heat. Cover, reduce the heat to low, and simmer for 5 minutes to blend the flavors.

⑤ To serve, remove and discard the bay leaf. Ladle the soup into bowls; sprinkle the salt and basil over each serving.

Variations: Add up to 6 garlic cloves, peeled, with the tomatoes and onion.

Add ¼ cup dry sherry, dry vermouth, or dry white wine with the broth.

Add 2 teaspoons stemmed thyme with the bay leaf.

Stir 1 cup heavy cream into the soup with the broth.

Drizzle aged, syrupy balsamic vinegar over the soup in the bowls.

Set a small dollop of sour cream or crème fraîche in the center of each bowl.

Charred Tomato Soup: Prepare a gas barbecue for medium-heat cooking or make a medium-heat coal bed in a charcoal grill. Cut the onion into ½-inch slices; brush these and the tomato halves generously with olive oil. Place them on the grate about 4 inches from the heat. Cover and grill until charred, about 5 minutes. Turn and roast until charred on the other side, about 4 minutes. Process or blend as directed and continue with the recipe at step 4.

Pear and Leek Soup

This light soup is sweet yet rich, thanks to creamy Bartlett pears. Remember the rule for fruit: if it doesn't smell like anything, it probably won't taste like anything. To ripen pears, place them in a brown paper bag, seal, and set on the counter for 1 to 2 days. *Makes 6 servings*

1 tablespoon unsalted butter
1 large leek, white and pale green parts only, halved lengthwise, washed carefully between the layers of any grit and sand, and thinly sliced
3 pounds ripe Bartlett pears, peeled, cored, and sliced
¾ cup dry white wine or dry vermouth
5 cups chicken or vegetable broth
One 2-inch piece of fresh ginger, peeled and cut into thin matchsticks
1 teaspoon salt
Freshly ground pepper, preferably white pepper, for garnish
Chopped parsley leaves for garnish

1 Melt the butter in a large pot or Dutch oven set over low heat. Add the leek and cook, stirring frequently, for 5 minutes. Add the pears; cook, stirring often, until quite soft and the pears are almost pureed, about 15 minutes.

2 Use the back of a wooden spoon to mash the pears against the side of the pan. Stir in the wine or vermouth. Cook, stirring often, until the wine or vermouth is reduced by half, about 3 minutes.

3 Stir in the broth and ginger. Raise the heat to medium-high and bring to a simmer. Cover, reduce the heat to low, and simmer slowly until thickened and creamy, about 30 minutes. Stir in

the salt; garnish individual servings with ground pepper and chopped parsley.

Apple and Leek Soup: Substitute apples for the pears. Add 1 teaspoon finely grated lemon zest with the ginger.

Pea Soup

Fresh peas may well be the essence of spring, but you don't have to wait until May to enjoy this easy soup since frozen peas are a good alternative. If you use fresh peas, buy about 4 pounds in their shells to yield the correct amount of shelled peas. *Makes 6 servings*

3 tablespoons unsalted butter
2 large leeks, white and pale green parts only, halved lengthwise, washed carefully of any grit and sand in the layers, and thinly sliced
2 tablespoons all-purpose flour
3 cups chicken broth
1½ pounds fresh peas, shelled, or 4 cups frozen peas (about 1¼ pounds)
1 bay leaf
½ teaspoon salt, plus additional to taste
½ teaspoon freshly ground pepper, preferably white pepper
¼ cup water
1 cup milk (regular, low-fat, or fat-free)
Grated nutmeg for garnish

1 Melt 2 tablespoons butter in a large saucepan over low heat. Add the leeks, reduce the heat even further, and cook very slowly, stirring occasionally, until quite soft but not at all browned, about 10 minutes. Should the leeks begin to brown, remove the pan from the heat; let it cool off, stirring constantly; then reduce the heat even further before continuing.

2 Add the remaining 1 tablespoon butter and stir until melted. Sprinkle the flour over the leeks, count to ten, then whisk over the heat for 1 minute, taking care not to let the flour brown.

3 Raise the heat to medium and whisk in the broth in a slow, steady steam. Continue whisking constantly until the mixture thickens and comes to a simmer.

4 Set ½ cup peas aside. Reduce the heat to low and add the remaining peas to the soup along with the bay leaf, salt, and pepper. Simmer very slowly, stirring occasionally, until the peas are quite tender, about 12 minutes.

5 Meanwhile, bring the water to a boil in a small saucepan set over high heat. Add the reserved peas, reduce the heat to low, and cook for 30 seconds. Drain in a colander set in the sink.

6 Remove the bay leaf from the large saucepan. Pour the mixture into a large food processor fitted with the chopping blade or into the canister of a large blender. Process or blend until smooth, scraping down the bowl or canister as need be to make sure everything is incorporated. Pour the puree back into the saucepan. Alternatively, use an immersion blender right in the pan to puree the soup.

7 Working over low heat, slowly whisk in the milk and bring the soup to the first bubble, just warmed through; then remove it from the heat to avoid a "cooked milk" taste. Check to see if the soup needs more salt. Ladle into bowls, dot the fresh peas over each serving, and sprinkle with a little grated nutmeg.

Variations: Substitute almond oil or canola oil for the butter.

For a richer soup, substitute half-and-half or evaporated milk for the milk.

Fry up 3 or 4 slices of bacon, turkey bacon, or soy bacon until crisp; crumble over the soup in the bowls. (In this case, add no extra salt because of the bacon.)

Crab and Pea Soup: Mound a little lump crabmeat, picked over for shell and cartilage, in the middle of each bowl before ladling in the soup.

Herbed Pea Soup: Add 3 parsley sprigs, 2 oregano sprigs, and 2 thyme sprigs with the bay leaf; remove them with the bay leaf before you puree the soup.

Creamless Creamy Asparagus Soup

Thick asparagus spears can be stringy; make sure the ones you buy are only about as wide as a pencil. If not, pare them down with a vegetable peeler. There's no cream in this soup; the potato does the job. *Makes 4 servings (can easily be doubled)*

Nonstick spray
2 ounces prosciutto, thinly sliced
1 tablespoon plus 1 teaspoon canola oil
1 medium onion, chopped
2 garlic cloves, slivered
12 ounces Yukon gold or other yellow-
    fleshed potatoes, peeled and cut into
    ½-inch dice
2 teaspoons chopped parsley leaves or
    1 teaspoon dried parsley
1 teaspoon stemmed thyme or ½ teaspoon
    dried thyme
4 cups (1 quart) chicken broth
1 pound plus 4 ounces (20 ounces) thin
    asparagus spears, peeled and cut into
    1-inch segments
½ teaspoon salt, plus additional to taste
¼ teaspoon freshly ground pepper, preferably
    white pepper
1 small scallion, green part only, thinly
    sliced

1 Spray a large chef's knife with nonstick spray, then chop the prosciutto into small pieces. Heat a large skillet over medium heat, add 1 teaspoon canola oil, then the prosciutto. Fry until crispy, stirring often, about 2 minutes. Transfer to a plate and set aside.

2 Heat a large saucepan or small Dutch oven over medium heat. Swirl in the remaining 1 tablespoon oil, then add the onion. Cook, stirring often, until translucent, about 3 minutes. Add the garlic and cook for 20 seconds.

3 Add the potatoes, parsley, and thyme; cook, stirring constantly, for 1 minute. Pour in the broth, scrape up any browned bits on the pan's bottom, and bring to a simmer. Cover, reduce the heat to low, and simmer slowly for 15 minutes.

4 Add the asparagus, cover, and continue simmering until the potatoes and asparagus are quite soft when pierced with a fork, about 10 minutes. Stir in the salt and pepper.

5 Transfer the soup to a large food processor fitted with a chopping blade or into a large blender. You may have to work in batches if your appliances are small. Process or blend until smooth, scraping down the sides of the bowl once or twice to make sure everything is pureed. Return the soup to the saucepan. Alternatively, use an immersion blender to puree the soup right in the pot.

6 Bring back to a low simmer over low heat. Check to see if the soup needs any additional salt. To serve, ladle into bowls; top with fried prosciutto bits and sliced scallions.

Variations: Substitute savory, chervil, oregano, or marjoram for the parsley.

Stir 2 teaspoons lemon juice into the soup after it's been pureed.

Grate a little Parmigiano-Reggiano or Gruyère over the soup in the bowls.

Drizzle a little aged, syrupy balsamic vinegar over the soup in the bowls.

Steam several thin asparagus spears until crisp-tender, cut them into small pieces, and use them to garnish the top of each serving bowl.

Pumpkin Bisque

A bisque is traditionally a creamy soup of vegetables and shellfish; these days, it's any rich cream soup. For a quicker version, see the squash variation. *Makes 6 servings*

> One 3-pound pumpkin, peeled, seeded, and
> the flesh cut into 3-inch cubes (see page
> 466)
> 1 tablespoon canola oil
> 4 tablespoons (½ stick) unsalted butter
> 2 tablespoons all-purpose flour
> 1 cup heavy cream
> 3 cups vegetable broth
> 1 teaspoon salt
> ½ teaspoon ground cinnamon
> ½ teaspoon grated nutmeg
> ½ teaspoon freshly ground black pepper

1 Position the rack in the center of the oven and preheat the oven to 400°F. Spread the pumpkin pieces on a large lipped baking sheet and toss with the canola oil.

2 Bake, tossing a few times, until very soft and lightly browned in spots, about 45 minutes. Cool on the baking sheet for 10 minutes, then transfer to a large food processor fitted with the chopping blade. Process until smooth, then set aside.

3 Melt the butter in a large saucepan set over medium-low heat. Once the foaming subsides, sprinkle the flour over the butter. Whisk over the heat for 30 seconds, just to get rid of the flour's raw taste.

④ Whisk in the cream in a slow, steady steam; bring to a simmer, whisking all the while. Simmer for 1 minute, whisking constantly.

⑤ Whisk in the broth and the pumpkin puree until smooth; whisk in the salt, cinnamon, nutmeg, and pepper. Simmer uncovered, whisking often, until creamy and thick, about 10 minutes.

Variations: Substitute ½ teaspoon rubbed sage for the cinnamon and nutmeg.

Add 2 teaspoons minced peeled fresh ginger with the pumpkin puree.

Omit the cinnamon and nutmeg; add ¼ teaspoon cayenne pepper in their place.

Place cooked shrimp, jumbo lump crabmeat, or cooked chopped lobster meat in the serving bowls before ladling in the soup.

Squash Bisque: Substitute three 10-ounce packages frozen winter squash puree, thawed, for the pumpkin. Start the recipe at step 3; whisk in the squash puree as you would the pumpkin puree.

Storing Soup

Omit any garnishes; store, covered, in the refrigerator for 2 or 3 days. Soups with flour, bread crumbs, or potato will thicken in storage: add a little broth to thin them out before reheating. Once chilled, soups can be frozen, covered, for up to 2 months (although the vegetables will not be as vibrant after thawing). Perk up the taste of previously frozen soups with a teaspoon or two of lemon juice.

Ginger and Cauliflower Soup

The highlight here is the ginger—in three forms, fresh, ground, and crystallized. The cauliflower gives the soup body and creaminess without adding any actual cream. *Makes 8 servings*

2 tablespoons canola oil
1 large yellow onion, chopped
One 2½-pound cauliflower head, trimmed and broken into small florets
¼ cup minced peeled fresh ginger
⅓ cup chopped crystallized ginger
2 tablespoons finely grated orange zest, plus additional for garnish
1 teaspoon ground ginger
1 teaspoon salt
½ teaspoon freshly ground pepper, preferably white pepper
4 cups (1 quart) vegetable broth
2 cups plain yogurt (regular, low-fat, or fatfree)
2 tablespoons honey

① Heat a large saucepan or soup pot over medium heat. Add the canola oil, then the onion. Cook, stirring often, until softened, about 4 minutes.

② Stir in the cauliflower florets and minced fresh ginger; cook, stirring often, until very aromatic, about 2 minutes.

③ Stir in the crystallized ginger, orange zest, ground ginger, salt, and pepper. Cook for 30 seconds, then stir in the broth, scraping up the browned bits on the pan's bottom.

④ Bring to a simmer; then cover, reduce the heat to low, and simmer slowly until the cauliflower is very tender, about 30 minutes.

⑤ Working in batches as needed, pour the contents of the pan into a large food processor fitted with the chopping blade or into a large blender. Process or blend until smooth; turn off the machine to occasionally scrape down the sides of the bowl to make sure everything is incorporated. Pour the puree back into the saucepan. Alternatively, use an immersion blender to puree the soup in the pan.

6 Whisk in the yogurt and honey; bring to a simmer over medium heat, whisking constantly. Ladle into bowls; if desired, grate a little orange zest over each serving.

Variations: Substitute unsalted butter for the canola oil.

Add up to ¼ teaspoon cayenne pepper with the ground ginger.

For a brighter taste, substitute 1 tablespoon finely grated lemon zest for the orange zest.

Curried Ginger Soup: Add 2 teaspoons ground coriander, 1 teaspoon dry mustard, 1 teaspoon ground cinnamon, 1 teaspoon ground cumin, ½ teaspoon freshly ground black pepper, and ½ teaspoon garlic powder with the ground ginger.

Pureeing in a Blender

When you blend hot liquids in a blender, the heat can cause increased air pressure under the lid, blowing it off and spraying the soup everywhere, causing a mess at the very least or a nasty burn at the worst. To avoid this volatile reaction, remove the center cap from the blender's lid, thereby allowing better air flow; cover the hole in the lid loosely with a kitchen towel. Hold the towel in place while you puree the hot ingredients. If the blender's lid doesn't have a removable center cap, remove the lid entirely and cover the blender with a clean kitchen towel—but beware: you can still burn yourself if the hot liquids soak the towel.

Thai-Inspired Squash and Mushroom Soup

Here's a spicy Thai curry soup with Western vegetables. *Makes 6 servings*

1 medium shallot, peeled and quartered
One 1½-inch piece lemongrass, white part only, tough outer leaves removed, the remainder thinly sliced
1 garlic clove, quartered
1 cardamom pod
½ teaspoon ground coriander
½ teaspoon ground cumin
½ teaspoon ground cinnamon
¼ teaspoon ground mace
¼ teaspoon turmeric
¼ teaspoon cayenne
Two medium 1½-pound acorn squashes
2 tablespoons peanut oil
1 pound cremini or white button mushrooms, cleaned and cut into quarters
3 cups vegetable broth
1⅔ cups canned regular coconut milk or light coconut milk
¼ cup fish sauce
2 tablespoons packed light brown sugar
2 red bell peppers, cored, seeded, and cut into ½-inch strips
5 scallions, cut into ½-inch pieces
12 basil leaves

1 Place the shallot, lemongrass, garlic, cardamom, coriander, cumin, cinnamon, mace, turmeric, and cayenne in a mini food processor; process until pastelike and fairly smooth. Alternatively, thinly slice the shallot, mince the lemongrass, and crush the garlic; place these and the remaining spices in a mortar and grind them with the pestle until pastelike.

2 Cut the two squashes in half, scoop out the seeds, then lay the halves cut side down on a

---

cutting board. Use a sharp knife to peel off the skin in long arcs, following the natural curve of the squash. Any small bits remaining can then be shaved off. Chop the flesh into ½-inch pieces and set aside.

3 Heat a large saucepan or pot over medium heat. Swirl in the peanut oil, then stir in the prepared spice mixture. Cook, stirring constantly, for 1 minute.

4 Add the mushrooms and cook until they give off their liquid and it's bubbling, stirring frequently, about 3 minutes.

5 Stir in the broth, coconut milk, fish sauce, and brown sugar, scraping up any browned bits on the bottom of the pan.

6 Bring the soup to a simmer, then stir in the squash and bell peppers. Cover, reduce the heat to very low, and simmer slowly, stirring occasionally, until the squash is fork-tender, about 25 minutes. Stir in the scallions and basil, cover, and set aside off the heat for 5 minutes.

Variations: For a quicker dish, substitute 1 tablespoon yellow Thai curry paste for all the aromatics in the ingredients list (from the shallots to the cayenne). Add the curry paste in step 3.

For a hotter dish, add 2 or 3 small hot Thai red chiles (often called "Thai hots"), sliced into thin rings, to the soup with the spice paste.

For a more authentic taste, add 1 teaspoon fermented shrimp paste with the spices.

Use only 1 squash; add 1 pound yellow- or red-fleshed fingerling potatoes, cut into ½-inch pieces, with the squash.

Use only 1 squash; stir 1 pound medium shrimp, peeled and deveined, into the soup during the last 5 minutes of cooking, before you add the scallions and basil.

Three-Mushroom Soup with Lemongrass

The bright, aromatic taste of lemongrass is a perfect match with mushrooms, given here in heaping quantities. If enoki are not available, you can do without them. If you can't find both the other two mushrooms, forgo the shiitake and use 1 pound cremini or white mushrooms in the soup. *Makes 6 servings*

> 2 tablespoons olive oil
> 2 medium yellow onions, halved and
>   thinly sliced
> 8 ounces cremini or white button
>   mushrooms, cleaned and thinly sliced
> 8 ounces shiitake mushrooms, stems
>   removed and discarded, caps cleaned
>   and thinly sliced
> ½ cup dry sherry or dry vermouth
> 1 lemongrass stalk, cut into 2-inch sections,
>   each bruised with a mallet or the bottom
>   of a heavy pot
> 6 cups (1½ quarts) vegetable broth
> 1 small bunch enoki mushrooms, cleaned
>   and separated
> ½ teaspoon salt
> ¼ teaspoon freshly ground black
>   pepper

1 Heat a large saucepan over medium heat. Swirl in the olive oil, then add the onions and cook, stirring often, until soft, about 4 minutes.

2 Add the cremini and shiitake; cook, stirring often, until they brown slightly and begin to give off their liquid, about 3 minutes.

3 Add the sherry or vermouth and the lemongrass. Raise the heat to medium-high and boil until the liquid in the pan has reduced by half, about 3 minutes.

4 Pour in the broth; bring to a simmer over medium-high heat. Cover, reduce the heat, and

simmer slowly until the mushrooms are quite tender, about 8 minutes.

5 Stir in the enoki, salt, and pepper. Cover and set aside off the heat for 5 minutes. Remove and discard the lemongrass pieces before serving.

Variations: Slice 6 ounces pencil-thin asparagus spears into 1-inch segments and add them with the enoki.

Add 8 ounces small broccoli florets (or large florets cut into slices) with the enoki.

Omit the lemongrass; add 1 teaspoon finely grated lemon zest, 3 parsley sprigs, and 2 bay leaves in its place; remove the parsley and bay leaves before serving.

Omit the lemongrass; add 2 tablespoons chopped lemon balm in its place.

For a thicker soup, whisk 3 tablespoons tomato paste into the sauce before adding the broth.

Root Vegetable Soup

There's a supermarket of root vegetables in this soup. The recipe makes a lot, but you can have individual frozen servings as a welcome lunch (omit the sour cream for freezing). If you can't find all these roots at your market, use any combination of 2½ pounds root vegetables with the carrots and potatoes. *Makes 8 servings*

2 tablespoons unsalted butter
1 large onion, chopped
2 large carrots, peeled and thinly sliced
2 medium turnips, peeled and chopped
2 medium parsnips, peeled and thinly sliced
1 large rutabaga, peeled and chopped
1 large Russet or baking potato, peeled and chopped
8 cups (2 quarts) chicken broth
1 bay leaf
1½ teaspoons salt, plus additional to taste
½ teaspoon freshly ground black pepper
½ cup sour cream (regular, low-fat, or fat-free)
½ cup chopped parsley leaves

1 Melt the butter in a soup pot or Dutch oven over medium heat; add the onion. Cook, stirring occasionally, until translucent, about 4 minutes.

2 Add the carrots, turnips, parsnips, rutabaga, and potato; cook, stirring almost constantly, until they start to turn golden and even translucent, 5 to 7 minutes.

3 Pour in the broth; add the bay leaf, salt, and pepper; and scrape up any browned bits on the pan's bottom. Bring to a simmer; then cover, reduce the heat to low, and simmer until the vegetables are quite soft when pricked with a fork, about 45 minutes.

4 Remove and discard the bay leaf. Take the pot off the heat. Ladle about half the soup into a food processor or a large blender; process or blend until smooth. Stir this puree back into the pot. Check to see if the soup needs any salt; stir in the sour cream and parsley until smooth.

Variations: Increase the butter to 3 tablespoons and add 4 ounces chopped pancetta with the onion; fry until frizzled and crisp, then continue with the recipe, omitting the salt.

After the onion has softened, cook 2 minced garlic cloves in the butter for 20 seconds before adding the root vegetables.

Add 1 tablespoon stemmed thyme; 1 tablespoon packed oregano leaves, chopped; or 2 teaspoons packed tarragon leaves, chopped, with the bay leaf.

Add 1 teaspoon dry mustard with the root vegetables.

Add up to ¼ teaspoon cayenne pepper with the root vegetables.

For a less tangy soup, substitute 1 cup heavy cream for the sour cream; let the soup simmer slowly over the heat for 2 minutes to take the raw taste off the cream before serving.

Potato and Roasted Chile Soup

Here's a great early-spring or late-autumn soup. Although not traditional, it would even work as a start to the Thanksgiving meal. *Makes 6 servings*

    2 poblano chiles
    2 tablespoons unsalted butter
    1 large yellow onion, chopped
    2 celery ribs, thinly sliced
    2 pounds white boiling potatoes, peeled and
        cut into ½-inch cubes
    2 teaspoons stemmed thyme or 1 teaspoon
        dried thyme
    1½ teaspoons ground cumin
    ½ teaspoon salt
    ½ teaspoon freshly ground black pepper
    4 cups (1 quart) chicken broth
    1½ cups sour cream (regular, low-fat,
        or fat-free)
    ¼ cup chopped cilantro leaves

1 Using a pair of metal tongs, hold the chiles over an open gas flame until charred on all sides. Alternatively, set them on an aluminum foil–lined baking sheet or broiler pan 4 to 6 inches from a preheated broiler and broil, turning often, until charred on all sides. In either case, place the chiles in a medium bowl, cover with plastic wrap, and set aside for 10 minutes.

2 Peel off the blackened skin, then stem and seed the chiles. Chop into ½-inch pieces and set aside. Wash your hands thoroughly to remove the chili oils. Do not touch your eyes.

3 Melt the butter in a large saucepan set over medium heat. Add the onion and celery; cook, stirring often, until translucent, about 4 minutes. Add the potatoes and cook until slightly softened at the edges, about 3 minutes.

4 Stir in the chopped poblanos, thyme, cumin, salt, and pepper; cook until aromatic, about 20 seconds. Pour in the broth and bring to a simmer, scraping up any browned bits on the pan's bottom. Cover, reduce the heat to low, and simmer slowly until the potatoes are quite soft, about 45 minutes.

5 Ladle half the liquid and vegetables into a large food processor fitted with the chopping blade or into a large blender; process or blend until smooth.

6 Pour the puree back into the soup and bring to a simmer over medium heat, stirring constantly. Stir in the sour cream and cilantro, cover, and set aside off the heat for 5 minutes before serving.

Variations: Fry 2 ounces pancetta, chopped, in the butter with the onion and celery until crisp.

Stir 1½ cups fresh corn kernels or frozen corn, thawed, into the soup with the potatoes.

Stir 2 ounces shredded Cheddar into the soup with the sour cream.

An Immersion Blender

This thin, handheld blender has blades on one end; it can be immersed directly in a soup or sauce to puree it right in the pan. When the blender is on, move it up and down, stirring the sauce to get all the solids in contact with the blades. Keep the blades off the pan's bottom to avoid nicking nonstick surfaces; keep the electrical cord away from the heat.

These soups begin to cross the line into full-fledged main courses. They're hearty and rich—some are pureed; others are left chunky for texture and tooth.

Southwestern Corn Chowder

Cumin and corn are a savory/sweet contrast at the heart of some of the best cooking in the American Southwest. Pureeing half the soup gives it a creamy texture but leaves a lot of the vegetables intact. In the end, it's strictly optional—you could puree none of the soup. Cream is optional, too, because the potato thickens the soup quite a bit.

Makes 4 servings

2 tablespoons olive oil
1 large onion, chopped
1 celery rib, chopped
2 garlic cloves, minced
4 ears corn, husked, the kernels cut off
1 large Russet or baking potato, peeled and
    cut into ½-inch cubes
2 teaspoons stemmed thyme or 1 teaspoon
    dried thyme
1 teaspoon ground cumin
1 teaspoon dry mustard
½ cup dry white wine
4 cups (1 quart) chicken broth
½ cup heavy cream, optional
½ teaspoon salt, or to taste
½ teaspoon freshly ground black pepper

❶ Heat a large saucepan or soup pot over medium heat. Swirl in the olive oil, then add the onion and celery. Cook, stirring often, until translucent, about 3 minutes. Add the garlic and cook for 30 seconds.

❷ Add the corn and potato; cook, stirring often, until the potato pieces begin to brown slightly and soften at the corners, about 3 minutes.

❸ Stir in the thyme, cumin, and dry mustard. Cook, stirring constantly, until aromatic, about 20 seconds. Add the wine, bring to a simmer, and cook until reduced to a thick glaze, scraping up any browned bits on the pan's bottom, about 3 minutes.

❹ Pour in the broth and bring to a simmer. Reduce the heat and simmer slowly, uncovered, until the potatoes are quite tender when pierced with a fork, about 20 minutes.

❺ If desired, ladle or pour half the soup into a large food processor fitted with a chopping blade or into a large blender; process or blend until smooth, scraping down the sides of the bowl or canister once or twice. Pour the puree back into the soup.

❻ Stir in the cream, if desired, and heat until just bubbling. Season with salt and pepper.

Variations: Garnish with seeded diced red and green bell peppers.

Add up to 1 teaspoon red pepper flakes with the thyme.

Substitute dry sherry, dry vermouth, dry Madeira, Cognac, or brandy for the wine.

Stir in ½ pound lump crabmeat, picked over for shell and cartilage, either with the cream or after you have returned the pureed soup to the pan.

After the puree has gone back into the pot:

Slip ½ pound boneless skinless chicken breasts, cut into cubes, into the soup; simmer, stirring often, until cooked through, about 8 minutes; then add the cream, if desired.

Stir in ½ pound medium shrimp (about 35 per pound), peeled and deveined; simmer, stirring often, until pink and firm, about 4 minutes; then add the cream, if desired.

Or drop ¾ pound mussels, scrubbed and debearded, into the soup; simmer, stirring frequently, until opened, about 4 minutes; then add the cream, if desired.

Mushroom, Barley, and Lentil Soup

Lentils give this American diner favorite a light but earthy flavor. Use any mixture of fresh mushrooms you want, even hen of the wood, black trumpets, or porcini. *Makes 6 servings*

3 tablespoons olive oil
2 medium yellow onions, finely chopped
3 medium carrots, peeled and finely chopped
3 medium celery ribs, finely chopped
18 ounces (1 pound plus 4 ounces) cremini or white button mushrooms, cleaned and thinly sliced
6 cups (1½ quarts) beef broth
3 cups water
3 medium Roma or plum tomatoes, roughly chopped
½ cup pearl barley (do not use quick-cooking)
½ cup French (or green) lentils
2 bay leaves
2 tablespoons chopped fresh rosemary or 1 tablespoon dried rosemary, crumbled
1 teaspoon salt, or to taste
½ teaspoon freshly ground black pepper

1 Heat a Dutch oven or soup pot over medium heat. Swirl in the olive oil, then stir in the onions, carrots, and celery. Cook stirring frequently, until the carrots have softened and the onions are fragrant, about 4 minutes.

2 Stir in the mushrooms and cook, stirring frequently, for 2 minutes, just until their juices begin to make a sauce in the pan.

3 Stir in the broth, water, tomatoes, barley, lentils, bay leaves, and rosemary; bring to a simmer. Cover, reduce the heat to low, and simmer until the barley and lentils are quite tender, stirring occasionally to prevent the barley from sticking to the pan's bottom, about 1 hour. Discard the bay leaves; stir in the salt and pepper before serving.

Variations: Add a smoked ham hock or bone or beef soup bone with the broth; remove either at the end of the cooking, slice the meat off, and return the meat to the pot. If you're using a ham bone, forgo any additional salt.

For a deeper taste, add 1 ounce dried mushrooms, such as chanterelles, porcini, or black trumpets, with the other mushrooms.

For a lighter soup, substitute chicken or vegetable broth for the beef broth.

Reduce the water to 2 cups and add 1 cup dry white wine with the remaining water.

Greek-Inspired Red Lentil Soup with Oregano, Dill, and Lemon Zest

Red lentils, familiar from East Indian dals, break down as they cook, creating a very thick soup. *Makes 6 servings*

2 tablespoons olive oil
1 large yellow onion, finely chopped
1 medium yellow bell pepper, cored, seeded, and finely chopped
2 garlic cloves, minced
2 canned anchovy fillets, chopped
2 cups red lentils, picked over for stones and rinsed
1 tablespoon minced oregano leaves
1 tablespoon capers, drained, rinsed, and minced

1 teaspoon finely grated lemon zest
6 cups (1½ quarts) chicken broth
1 tablespoon minced dill fronds
Tzatziki (page 46) for garnish, optional

1 Heat a large saucepan or soup pot over medium heat. Swirl in the olive oil, then add the onion and bell pepper. Cook, stirring often, until softened, about 3 minutes. Add the garlic and anchovies; cook for 30 seconds.

2 Stir in the lentils, oregano, capers, and lemon zest; cook, stirring constantly, until very aromatic, about 30 seconds.

3 Pour in the broth; bring to a simmer, stirring almost constantly to scrape up any browned bits on the pot's bottom and to make sure the lentils don't stick.

4 Cover, reduce the heat to low, and simmer very slowly, stirring fairly often, until the lentils are quite tender and have begun to break down, about 40 minutes. If desired, garnish each serving with a generous dollop of Tzatziki (page 46).

Lima Bean and Kale Soup

Lima beans are full of complex sugars, so they can create quite a lot of foam as they cook. Make sure you change the soaking water once and also leave the lid ajar during parts of the cooking so the foam doesn't become an annoyance. Use either large or small lima beans for this recipe—or substitute dried butter beans. For a quicker version with frozen lima beans, see the variation. *Makes 6 servings*

1 cup dried lima beans
8 cups (2 quarts) chicken broth
3 tablespoons olive oil
2 large yellow onions, quartered, then thinly sliced

2 cups canned diced tomatoes with their juice
1½ pounds kale, center stems cut out, leaves washed and chopped
½ teaspoon salt, or to taste
¼ teaspoon red pepper flakes

1 Place the lima beans in a large bowl, cover them with cool water to the depth of 2 inches, and set aside to soak for at least 8 hours or overnight, changing the water once.

2 Drain the beans in a colander set in the sink. Place them in a soup pot or Dutch oven and stir in the broth. Bring to a simmer over medium-high heat, stirring occasionally.

3 Skim off any foam from the broth as well as any bean skins or beans that bob on the surface. Cover with the lid ajar, reduce the heat a little, and simmer for 15 minutes.

4 Meanwhile, heat a large skillet over low heat. Add the olive oil, then the onions. Cook, stirring often, until golden and quite soft, about 10 minutes.

5 Pour the entire contents of the skillet into the pot with the beans; cover again with the lid ajar, reduce the heat even further, and simmer very slowly for 30 minutes.

6 Stir in the tomatoes. Now cover the pot tightly and simmer slowly for 15 minutes.

7 Add the kale to the soup. You'll probably have to work in batches, adding a couple of handfuls, then stirring until they wilt enough that you can add some more. Once all the kale has been added, stir in the salt and red pepper flakes. Return the soup to a simmer, cover, and continue cooking until the lima beans are tender and the kale is wilted, about 30 minutes.

Lima Bean, Sausage, and Kale Soup: Add 1 pound sweet or hot Italian sausage, cut into small rings, with the onions; cook until browned, about 5 minutes.

Lima Bean, Clam, and Kale Soup: Reduce the broth to 6 cups and add 2 cups fish broth or clam juice with the remaining broth; stir 1½ pounds clams, scrubbed of any sand, into the soup during the last 5 minutes of its cooking—simmer until the clams open (discard any that do not).

Quick Lima Bean and Kale Soup: Substitute 2 cups frozen lima beans, thawed, for the dried beans. Omit steps 1 through 3; cook the onions right in the soup pot. Add the lima beans and 7 cups chicken broth, simmer for only 10 minutes, and continue with the recipe. In step 7, you'll only need to simmer the soup until the kale is tender, about 10 minutes.

Kasha Varnishkes Soup

Kasha varnishkes are a New York deli favorite: toasted buckwheat groats (kasha) and bow-tie egg noodles (varnishkes) with lots of sautéed onions. Here, we've turned this classic into a hearty soup.
Makes 6 servings

    2 tablespoons canola oil
    2 large yellow onions, chopped
    2 medium carrots, peeled and diced
    2 cups medium or coarse kasha (aka toasted buckwheat groats)
    2 teaspoons stemmed thyme or 1 teaspoon dried thyme
    1 teaspoon minced sage leaves or ½ teaspoon dried sage
    3 garlic cloves, minced
    8 cups (2 quarts) beef broth
    5 ounces fresh or 3 ounces dried bow-tie (or farfalle) pasta

1 Heat a large saucepan or Dutch oven over low heat. Swirl in the canola oil, then add the onions and carrots. Immediately reduce the heat to very low and cook, stirring frequently, at the lowest simmer until the onions are golden, almost brown, and very sweet, about 40 minutes.

2 Stir in the kasha, thyme, sage, and garlic; cook for 30 seconds, stirring all the while. Pour in the broth and bring the soup to a simmer over medium-high heat, scraping up any browned bits on the pot's bottom. Cover, reduce the heat to low, and simmer for 30 minutes.

3 Add the pasta, stir well, cover again, and continue cooking until tender, about 2 minutes for fresh pasta and 5 minutes for dried.

Variations: Add ¼ teaspoon crumbled saffron threads with the kasha.

Add ½ cup dry sherry or dry white wine with the broth.

African Peanut Soup

This fiery stew can be cooled down considerably by a dollop of yogurt, sour cream, or crème fraîche *Makes 6 servings*

    2 tablespoons canola oil
    1 large yellow onion, finely chopped
    1 large red bell pepper, cored, seeded, and chopped
    3 garlic cloves, minced
    1½ cups chopped roasted unsalted peanuts
    1 teaspoon salt
    ½ teaspoon cayenne pepper
    1½ pounds sweet potatoes, peeled and cut into 1-inch cubes
    1 pound small red-skinned potatoes, quartered

One 28-ounce can diced tomatoes (3½ cups)
3 cups vegetable broth
Plain yogurt, sour cream, or crème fraîche
for garnish

1 Heat a large saucepan over medium heat. Swirl in the canola oil, then add the onion and bell pepper. Cook, stirring often, until softened, about 3 minutes. Add the garlic; cook for 20 seconds.

2 Stir in the peanuts, salt, and cayenne; cook, stirring constantly, until aromatic, about 1 minute.

3 Stir in the sweet potatoes, red-skinned potatoes, tomatoes, and broth; bring to a simmer.

4 Cover, reduce the heat to low, and simmer until the potatoes are tender when pierced with a fork, about 1 hour. To serve, top individual bowls with yogurt, sour cream, or crème fraîche.

Variations: Substitute turnips, peeled and cubed, for the red-skinned potatoes.

Increase the broth to 3½ cups and add 2 cups chopped, stemmed chard or chopped, stemmed kale with the potatoes.

Stir ½ pound boneless skinless chicken breasts, cut into cubes, into the stew just as the potatoes become tender; simmer until the chicken is firm and cooked through, about 8 minutes.

Stir ½ pound medium shrimp (about 35 per pound), peeled and deveined, into the stew at the end; cook until pink and firm, about 5 minutes.

For another bean soup, check out the Black-Eyed Pea and Ham Hock Stew (page 500).

White Bean Soup with Leeks, Tarragon, and Thyme

Here, some white beans are pureed to thicken the light, lemony broth. Egg yolks are stirred in just at the very end for a rich, silky finish. *Makes 6 servings*

1½ cups dried white beans, preferably
    cannellini beans
4 tablespoons (½ stick) unsalted butter
2 medium leeks, white and pale green parts
    only, halved, washed carefully for sand
    and grit in the inner chambers, and thinly
    sliced
2 celery ribs, thinly sliced
2 garlic cloves, minced
8 cups (2 quarts) chicken broth
2 teaspoons finely grated lemon zest
2 tarragon sprigs
2 thyme sprigs
1 bay leaf
1 teaspoon salt
½ teaspoon freshly ground black pepper
2 large egg yolks
2 tablespoons lemon juice
Grated nutmeg for garnish

1 Place the beans in a large bowl, cover them to a depth of 2 inches with cool water, and set aside to soak for 12 hours or overnight, changing the water once. Alternatively, place the beans in a large pot, fill with water to a depth of 2 inches, and bring to a boil over medium-high heat; cook for 2 minutes, drain, place in a large bowl, cover with cool water to a depth of 2 inches, and set aside to soak for 2 hours.

2 Melt the butter in a large saucepan or soup pot set over low heat. Add the leeks, celery, and garlic; cook very slowly, stirring often, until soft, golden, and sweet, but not brown, about 10 minutes.

③ Pour in the broth; stir in the lemon zest, tarragon, thyme, and bay leaf. While the soup comes to a simmer, drain the beans in a colander set in the sink and rinse under cool water. When the soup comes to a simmer, add the beans to the pot.

④ Cover, reduce the heat to low, and cook slowly, stirring once in a while, until the beans are tender, about 1½ hours.

⑤ Discard the bay leaf, tarragon, and thyme sprigs. Remove 2 cups beans from the pot and place them in a large bowl.

⑥ Working in batches, pour the rest of the soup into a large food processor fitted with the chopping blade or into a large blender; process or blend until smooth, scraping down the sides of the bowl or canister as necessary to make sure everything is pureed. Return the puree to the pan or pot. Alternatively, use an immersion blender to puree the soup directly in the pan or pot.

⑦ Stir the reserved beans, salt, and pepper into the soup; bring to a simmer over medium-high heat, stirring almost constantly. Cook for 5 minutes to thicken slightly.

⑧ Whisk the egg yolks in a small bowl. Whisking constantly, add 1 cup soup to the yolks in a thin, steady stream. Once smooth, whisk this mixture into the pot until smooth; then whisk in the lemon juice, cover, and set off the heat for 5 minutes. Do not let the soup boil once the egg yolks have been added to it. For garnish, grate a little nutmeg over each serving.

Variations: Substitute olive oil for the butter; omit the nutmeg and drizzle some extra virgin olive oil over each serving as garnish.

Add ½ to 1 teaspoon red pepper flakes with the lemon zest.

Add 1 medium turnip, peeled and diced, or 2 medium parsnips, peeled and thinly sliced, with the leeks.

Reduce the broth to 5 cups; add 1 cup dry white wine with the remaining broth.

For a little crunch, float Croutons (page 101) in the soup for garnish or add 2 additional celery ribs, thinly sliced, to the soup once the puree is back in the pot.

For a quicker version, cut the broth to 5 cups and use 4 cups canned white beans, drained and rinsed, adding them in step 3; simmer for only 20 minutes.

Broth in Soups

These recipes use a range of broths: chicken, vegetable, beef, and even fish. You can substitute vegetable broth, say, for chicken broth in a recipe, but you will end up with a lighter soup. In some cases—say, Chilled Tomato Soup with Cucumber-Apple Salsa (page 157)—you might also run a taste competition between the tomatoes and the vegetables in the broth. In many cases, substitute beef broth for a heartier soup, a better fit for a winter afternoon. For the best taste, make your own stock (see pages 164-167).

If you use canned or packaged broths, buy a few varieties, do a test, and decide which is best. No amount of fresh ingredients will overcome the taste of insipid broth. You want a rich taste—not overpowering, watery, dull, or sharp.

Also, we recommend using reduced-sodium or even no-sodium canned broth. You'll be better able to control the saltiness of the final dish—and to create a soup to your taste.

❋ Hearty Soups ❋

These soups cross the line from first courses into main courses. Of course, you can still offer them as starters but serve smaller portions. All include some form of protein, even if it be cheese or eggs.

Classic Chicken Soup

Ask a hundred grandmothers how to make chicken soup and you'll get a hundred recipes that all come down to this process for extracting the most flavor out of the chicken. *Makes 6 servings*

One 1½-pound whole bone-in chicken breast
2 pounds bony chicken parts (wings, backs, necks, feet, or legs)
2 medium onions, quartered
12 cups (3 quarts) water
4 medium carrots, peeled and cut into 2-inch pieces
4 celery ribs, cut into 4-inch pieces
1 medium parsnip, peeled and cut into 2-inch pieces
4 whole garlic cloves, peeled
¼ cup roughly chopped dill fronds
1½ teaspoons salt, plus more as needed
1 teaspoon whole black peppercorns
1 bay leaf

❶ Place all the chicken and onions in a large soup pot or Dutch oven. Pour in the water and set the pot over high heat. Bring to a full simmer; cook for 5 minutes.

❷ Use a large spoon to skim any foam or scum off the top of the soup. Add the carrots, celery, parsnip, garlic, dill, salt, peppercorns, and bay leaf. Reduce the heat to low and cook, uncovered, for 25 minutes.

❸ If necessary, skim the soup a second time. Remove the chicken breast and half the carrots from the pot. Cover the pot, reduce the heat even more, and simmer very slowly over very low heat for 1½ hours.

❹ Meanwhile, when the chicken breast is cool enough to handle, remove the skin and take the meat off the bone; chop the meat into bite-sized pieces. Thinly slice the carrots. Place both in a bowl, cover with plastic wrap, and refrigerate.

❺ Set a large, fine-mesh sieve, chinois, or strainer over a large bowl in the sink. Ladle the soup into the sieve (or other device), straining it into the bowl and emptying the sieve as it fills with solid materials. The soup can be made up to this point ahead of time; cover the strained soup and refrigerate separately from the chicken and carrots for up to 2 days.

❻ To serve, skim any fat from the top of the soup and pour it back into a pot. Bring to a simmer over medium-high heat. Add the sliced carrots and chopped breast meat; reduce the heat to low and simmer slowly to heat through, about 5 minutes. Check for salt before serving.

Chicken and Rice Soup: Stir 2 to 3 cups cooked white or brown rice into the soup with the cooked carrots and breast meat.

Chicken Noodle Soup: Cook 3 ounces small, thin egg noodles or rice noodles in the soup when it's been put back on the stove to be reheated after straining.

Conja de Galinha (Brazilian Chicken Soup): Increase the garlic to 8 cloves, omit the dill and parsnip, and add 2 thyme sprigs and ½ teaspoon red pepper flakes with the garlic. Cook and strain as directed. Once the strained soup is back in the pan, add 2 cups cooked white rice and 1 tablespoon lime juice with the sliced carrots and chicken meat.

Egg Drop Soup: Omit the carrot and parsnip; add four 1-inch-thick pieces of peeled ginger in their place. After the chicken meat has been added to the strained soup and it is simmering slowly, lightly beat 2 large eggs in a small bowl, then drizzle them slowly into the soup, stirring all the while; the moment all the eggs have been added, take the soup off the heat.

Matzo Ball Soup: Make matzo balls by whisking 2 large eggs, 2 tablespoons canola oil, and 2 tablespoons water in a large bowl; stir in ⅔ cup matzo meal, 1½ teaspoons baking powder, 1 teaspoon salt, 1 teaspoon onion powder, ½ teaspoon mild paprika, and ¼ teaspoon garlic powder until pastelike. Refrigerate while you bring 3 quarts (12 cups) of water to a boil in a large saucepan set over high heat. With wet hands, form the matzo mixture into 1-inch balls, about the size of golf balls. Gently drop them into the boiling water; once they've all been added, cover, reduce the heat to low, and simmer for 25 minutes. (They can be made up to this point 2 days in advance; transfer them to a large baking dish, cover with plastic wrap, and refrigerate.) Add the boiled matzo balls to the soup with the cooked chicken meat.

Easy Chicken Soup

When you don't have time to make long-simmered chicken soup, try this 30-minute version. *Makes 6 servings*

1 pound boneless skinless chicken breasts, cut into bite-sized pieces
2 medium shallots, thinly sliced
2 medium carrots, peeled and thinly sliced
1 celery rib, thinly sliced
6 cups (1½ quarts) chicken broth
1 tablespoon chopped parsley leaves or 1½ teaspoons dried parsley
2 teaspoons chopped dill fronds or 1 teaspoon dried dill
1 teaspoon salt
½ teaspoon freshly ground black pepper

Place all the ingredients in a large saucepan or soup pot. Bring to a simmer over high heat. Cover, reduce the heat to low, and simmer very slowly until the chicken is cooked through, about 15 minutes.

Cheese Soup

Here is a soup version of cheese fondue. *Makes 6 servings*

4 tablespoons (½ stick) unsalted butter
1 garlic clove, peeled and mashed with the side of a knife
3 tablespoons all-purpose flour
3 cups whole milk
2 cups vegetable broth
1 cup dry white wine or dry vermouth
2 tablespoons Worcestershire sauce
2 teaspoons paprika
½ teaspoon celery seeds
12 ounces aged cheese, such as Gruyère, Emmentaler, Gouda, Asiago, or Parmigiano-Reggiano, finely grated

1 Melt the butter in a large saucepan or soup pot set over medium-low heat. Add the garlic and cook, stirring often, until golden, about 30 seconds.

2 Sprinkle the flour over the butter, count to ten, then whisk over the heat until the mixture forms a thick paste. Continue whisking for 20 seconds, but do not let the flour brown.

3 Whisk in the milk in a thin, steady stream; continue whisking over the heat until the mixture comes to a low simmer and thickens, about 1 minute.

4 Whisk in the broth, wine or vermouth, Worcestershire sauce, paprika, and celery seeds until smooth, then bring the mixture back to a low simmer, whisking constantly.

5 Reduce the heat to low and simmer slowly, uncovered, whisking once in a while, for 10 minutes.

6 Reduce the heat even further, add the cheese, and whisk until smooth. Whatever you do, do not let the soup return to a boil or the fat of the cheese will fall out of suspension. To be very cautious, remove the pot from the heat just after you've added the cheese.

Variations: Add ½ teaspoon red pepper flakes with the broth.

Substitute hot paprika or even smoked paprika for the mild paprika.

Substitute fennel or caraway seeds for the celery seeds.

Use a mixture of grated cheeses: Asiago, Parmigiano-Reggiano, and Grana Padano; Gouda and a hard goat cheese; Emmentaler and Gruyère; or any combination you prefer.

Escarole Soup with White Beans and Roasted Garlic

This Italian soup of greens and pancetta is made richer by poaching eggs in it at the end. Make sure the yolks are runny so they'll melt into the individual servings when broken. *Makes 6 servings*

3 tablespoons olive oil
6 ounces pancetta, finely chopped
2 medium onions, finely chopped
2 medium heads escarole (about 1 pound
    each—see page 98), cored, shredded,
    and washed, but not dried
6 cups (1½ quarts) chicken broth
1 tablespoon chopped sage leaves or
    1 teaspoon rubbed sage
3 cups canned cannellini or other small
    white beans, drained and rinsed
1 garlic head, roasted (see page 460)
3 ounces Parmigiano-Reggiano, finely grated
1 teaspoon salt, or to taste
½ teaspoon freshly ground black pepper
6 large eggs

1 Heat a large saucepan or soup pot over medium heat. Swirl in the olive oil, add the pancetta, and sauté until browned and frizzled at the edges, stirring frequently, about 2 minutes.

2 Add the onions and cook until pale but very fragrant, stirring often, about 2 minutes.

3 Add the escarole and cook just until the greens begin to wilt, tossing constantly, about 1 minute. Stir in the broth and sage, raise the heat to high, and bring to a simmer.

4 Reserve 1 cup of the beans in a small bowl; stir the remainder into the soup. Cover the saucepan, reduce the heat to low, and simmer for 20 minutes.

⑤ Meanwhile, squeeze the roasted garlic pulp from its hulls into the bowl with the reserved beans. Mash with a fork until smooth.

⑥ After the soup has cooked for 20 minutes, whisk a small amount of the soup broth into the garlic-bean puree, just to dissolve it; then stir this combined mixture back into the soup. Stir in the cheese, salt, and pepper until the cheese melts.

⑦ Reduce the heat to very low so the soup stays hot without bubbling. Crack the eggs, one at a time, into a small custard cup or other small bowl, slip them into the soup, and cook until soft-set, about 3 minutes.

⑧ Use a large ladle to gather up the eggs one by one from the soup, place them in individual serving bowls, and ladle the soup around them.

Variations: Top each bowl with 1 tablespoon chopped pitted black olives or a small amount of purchased caponata (a Sicilian eggplant salad). Since either olives or caponata can be quite salty, reduce the amount of salt in the soup to 1/8 teaspoon or none at all.

Place a toasted round of bread in each bowl before adding the soup. For a richer soup, drizzle each toasted round with extra virgin olive oil before placing it in the bowl.

Soup vs. Stew

The difference is one of degree. A soup is thinner, more broth per spoonful. A stew is actually a type of braise: a meat or vegetable dish that's long-cooked, the liquid reduced until the whole thing is quite thick. All sorts of stews can be found in the chicken, fish, and meat chapters.

Cabbage, Potatoes, and Bacon Soup

Hearty, filling, and wintry. *Makes 4 servings*

> 2 tablespoons unsalted butter
> 6 ounces bacon strips, chopped
> 1 large onion, chopped
> 1 small head white cabbage, cored and shredded (about 8 cups)
> 1 pound yellow-fleshed potatoes, such as Yukon golds, peeled and cut into 1/2-inch pieces
> 1¾ cups canned cannellini beans, drained and rinsed
> 1½ teaspoons stemmed thyme or ¾ teaspoon dried thyme
> 1 teaspoon caraway seeds
> ½ teaspoon freshly ground black pepper
> 4 cups (1 quart) chicken broth
> 1 tablespoon cider vinegar
> Salt to taste

① Melt the butter in a large saucepan or soup pot set over medium heat. Add the bacon and fry until crisp, turning a couple of times, about 3 minutes. Use a slotted spoon to transfer the bacon to a plate lined with paper towels.

② Add the onion; cook, stirring often, for 1 minute. Add the cabbage and continue cooking, stirring often, until wilted, about 3 minutes.

③ Add the potatoes; cook, stirring often, for 2 minutes. Then add the beans, thyme, caraway seeds, pepper, and crispy bacon bits; cook until fragrant, about 20 seconds.

④ Pour in the broth; bring to a simmer, scraping up any browned bits on the pan's bottom. Cover, reduce the heat to low, and simmer slowly until the cabbage and potatoes are tender, about 45 minutes. Before serving, stir in the vinegar; season with salt (just remember that the bacon is quite salty).

Variations: Substitute olive or canola oil for the butter.

Substitute turkey or soy bacon for the pork bacon.

Substitute 2 large shallots, chopped, for the onion.

Substitute any variety of small canned beans for the cannellini—red kidney, Great Northern, or even pinto beans.

Substitute minced sage for the caraway seeds.

Sweet-and-Sour Meatball Soup

This soup is like a deconstructed version of stuffed cabbage; pears and vinegar provide the sweet-and-sour contrast. *Makes 6 servings*

1 pound lean ground beef
3 tablespoons dry couscous
1 large egg, lightly beaten
2 teaspoons stemmed thyme or 1 teaspoon
    dried thyme
½ teaspoon salt, or more to taste
¼ teaspoon grated nutmeg
1 tablespoon canola oil
1 medium onion, chopped
4 cups packed shredded Savoy cabbage
    (about half a medium head, cored)
One 28-ounce can diced tomatoes (3½ cups)
2 medium pears, peeled, halved, and cored
4 cups (1 quart) chicken broth
3 tablespoons white wine vinegar
2 teaspoons packed light brown sugar
1 tablespoon chopped sage leaves or
    1 teaspoon rubbed sage
½ teaspoon freshly ground black pepper

❶ Combine the ground beef, couscous, egg, thyme, ¼ teaspoon of the salt, and the nutmeg in a large bowl. Form into 18 meatballs; set aside.

❷ Heat a soup pot or Dutch oven over medium heat. Swirl in the canola oil, then add the onion.

Cook, stirring often, until translucent, about 3 minutes.

❸ Add the cabbage; cook, stirring often, until wilted, about 3 minutes. Then add the tomatoes and bring to a simmer, stirring occasionally.

❹ Shred the pears into the stew through the large holes of a box grater. Stir well, then pour in the broth. Bring the mixture to a simmer, then cover, reduce the heat to low, and simmer for 5 minutes.

❺ Drop the meatballs into the soup, cover again, and simmer slowly, stirring once in a while, for 1 hour. Stir in the vinegar, brown sugar, sage, pepper, and the remaining ¼ teaspoon salt (or more to taste) and simmer for 10 more minutes.

Masaman Beef Soup with Chiles, Garlic, and Ginger

Masaman is a traditional Thai curry; the word actually means "Muslim" in Thai and refers to fiery curry blends that include cinnamon and cardamom, both brought to Thailand by Persian merchants via India. *Makes 6 servings*

2 tablespoons peanut oil
4 large dried red New Mexican chiles,
    stemmed, seeded, and cut into large
    pieces
2 medium shallots, peeled and quartered
3 garlic cloves, halved
3 cardamom pods
1 teaspoon cumin seeds
2 tablespoons minced peeled fresh ginger
1 teaspoon ground cinnamon
¼ teaspoon grated nutmeg
2 medium onions, halved and thinly sliced
1 pound sirloin, trimmed and cut against the
    grain into thin strips

6 cups (1½ quarts) beef broth

1 cup coconut milk (regular or low-fat)

1 lemongrass stalk, trimmed, cut into 4-inch pieces, each crushed somewhat with the side of a knife or the bottom of a heavy saucepan

1 pound green beans, trimmed and cut into 1-inch sections

1 tablespoon tamarind paste, pomegranate molasses, or red currant jelly

❶ Heat a medium skillet over medium heat, swirl in 1 tablespoon peanut oil, and add the chiles, shallots, garlic, cardamom pods, and cumin seeds. Cook until very aromatic, shaking the pan repeatedly and vigorously so nothing burns, about 2 minutes. Set aside off the heat for 10 minutes.

❷ Pour the entire contents of the skillet into a large food processor; add the ginger, cinnamon, and nutmeg. Process until coarsely ground and pastelike. Set aside.

❸ Heat a Dutch oven or soup pot over medium heat. Swirl in the remaining tablespoon oil, then add the onions. Cook, stirring often, until translucent, about 3 minutes. Stir in the spice mixture; cook until fragrant, stirring constantly, about 30 seconds.

❹ Add the beef; cook until browned, turning once or twice, about 2 minutes.

❺ Pour in the broth and coconut milk; bring to a simmer, scraping up the browned bits on the pan's bottom. Add the lemongrass, cover, reduce the heat to low, and simmer until the beef is very tender, about 20 minutes.

❻ Remove and discard the lemongrass. Stir in the green beans and the tamarind paste, pomegranate molasses, or red currant jelly until smooth. Cover and set aside off the heat for 5 minutes.

Variations: Add 2 cups cooked white or brown rice or 8 ounces rice noodles, cooked and drained, with the tamarind paste.

Garnish the soup with chopped, peeled, pitted mango, yogurt, or crème fraîche.

For a quicker dish, omit all the spices and aromatics (even the lemongrass); substitute up to 1 tablespoon masaman curry paste or hot red Thai curry paste, often available in East Indian markets, adding it in step 3.

Vietnamese-Inspired Spiced Pork Soup

Here's a simplified approach to a traditional Vietnamese soup. *Makes 6 servings*

8 cups (2 quarts) chicken broth

8 scallions, halved lengthwise

Four ¼-inch-thick disks peeled fresh ginger

One 4-inch cinnamon stick

4 whole cloves

4 allspice berries

1 star anise pod

8 ounces pork loin, quartered lengthwise and thinly sliced

¼ cup fish sauce

1 tablespoon soy sauce

1 teaspoon packed light brown sugar

½ teaspoon freshly ground black pepper, plus more for garnish

3 cups mung bean sprouts

½ cup chopped mint leaves

¼ cup chopped cilantro leaves

1 tablespoon lime juice

❶ Bring the broth, scallions, ginger, cinnamon stick, cloves, allspice, and star anise to a simmer in a large pot set over high heat. Cover, reduce the heat to very low, and simmer slowly for 1 hour.

❷ Remove and discard the aromatics, using a small strainer or a slotted spoon. Add the pork, fish sauce, soy sauce, brown sugar, and pepper; bring back to a simmer over high heat. Cover, reduce the heat to low, and simmer slowly until the pork is tender, about 30 minutes.

3 Stir in the bean sprouts, mint, cilantro, and lime juice just before serving. Sprinkle each serving with ground black pepper for garnish.

Variations: Add 3 dried red Asian chiles with the ginger; remove and discard them with the other aromatics.

Substitute boneless skinless chicken breasts, cut into thin strips, for the pork; simmer for only 15 minutes.

Substitute firm or silken-firm tofu for the pork; simmer for only 5 minutes.

Lamb and Wild Rice Soup

In traditional Irish soups, the lamb is not browned before being added to the soup. Without a caramelized crust, the lamb becomes velvety and luxurious. If you can't find lamb shoulder, use lamb stew meat. Wild rice adds an earthy, grassy taste, a fine foil for the lamb and little more sophisticated than white rice. *Makes 8 servings*

10 cups (2½ quarts) beef, chicken, or
    vegetable broth
2 pounds lamb shoulder meat, trimmed of
    excess fat and cut into 2-inch cubes
1½ cups wild rice
2 medium onions, halved and thinly sliced
4 medium carrots, peeled and thinly sliced
2 celery ribs, thinly sliced
2 teaspoons stemmed thyme or 1 teaspoon
    dried thyme
1 teaspoon salt, plus additional to taste
½ teaspoon freshly ground black pepper

1 Place the broth and lamb in a large saucepan or soup pot, set over high heat, and bring to a full

simmer. Cover, reduce the heat to low, and simmer slowly until the lamb is nearly tender, skimming any fat or impurities from the top of the soup as necessary, about 1 hour.

2 Add the wild rice, return to a simmer, and cook, covered, for 20 minutes.

3 Add the onions, carrots, celery, thyme, salt, and pepper. Continue cooking, covered, until the carrots are tender, about 30 minutes.

Variations: Substitute any of the following for the carrots: 3 medium parsnips, peeled and cut into ½-inch-thick rounds; ¾ pound green beans, trimmed and cut into 2-inch sections; ¾ pound rutabaga, peeled and cut into 1-inch cubes; or ¾ pound turnip, peeled and cut into 1-inch cubes

Mexican Lime Soup

In the Yucatán, lime soup is something of a passion: tart, refreshing, and satisfying. Have lots of tortillas on hand (see page 241). *Makes 6 servings*

6 cups (1½ quarts) chicken broth
8 garlic cloves, peeled and lightly smashed
    with the side of a knife
2 medium onions, cut into quarters
2 fresh jalapeño chiles, stemmed, quartered,
    cored, and seeded
4 whole cloves
1½ pounds medium shrimp (about 35 per
    pound), peeled and deveined
¼ cup chopped cilantro leaves
¼ cup lime juice
Kosher or coarse-grained salt for garnish

1 Bring the broth, garlic, onions, jalapeños, and cloves to a boil in a large saucepan or soup pot set over high heat. Cover, reduce the heat to very low, and simmer slowly for 20 minutes.

② Place a colander, sieve, or other larger strainer over a large bowl set in the sink. Working in batches as necessary, ladle and/or pour the soup through the mesh, discarding the vegetables and aromatics as the basket fills up. Return the soup to the pan or pot; bring to a low simmer over medium-high heat.

③ Stir in the shrimp, cilantro, and lime juice. Cook until the shrimp are pink and firm, about 3 minutes. Sprinkle a little salt over each serving.

Variations: Substitute sea scallops, cleaned and thinly sliced into 2 disks, for the shrimp.

Substitute cubed firm or silken-firm tofu for the shrimp; do not simmer—simply cook to heat through, about 2 minutes.

Omit the shrimp; add 2 pounds mussels, scrubbed and debearded, with the cilantro and lime juice. Simmer, covered, for 5 minutes, until the mussels open. Discard any that do not.

Omit the shrimp; add the cilantro and lime juice as directed. Place ⅔ cup cubed cooked skinless chicken or turkey meat in each bowl; ladle the soup over the meat.

Shrimp and Scallop Chowder

Roasting the corn gives this soup extra flavor; the grated potato thickens it to give it an earthy taste without a lot of added cream. *Makes 6 servings*

4 ears corn
½ pound medium shrimp (about 35 per pound) in their shells
3 large onions, quartered
3 garlic cloves
5 cups (1 quart plus 1 cup) vegetable broth
½ tablespoon whole black peppercorns
2 bay leaves
2 tablespoons unsalted butter

1 medium baking potato (about 8 ounces), peeled
1 cup heavy cream
1 pound bay scallops, cleaned
¼ cup packed parsley leaves, chopped
½ teaspoon salt

① Peel the husks back about two-thirds of the way down each corn ear. Remove the silks, then pull the husks back up and into place around the ears. Soak in cool water for 20 minutes.

② Preheat a grill pan or a griddle over medium-high heat or heat a stovetop grill to medium-high heat. Alternatively, prepare a gas barbecue for high-heat cooking or build a high-heat, ashed coal bed in a charcoal grill. Place the ears in their husks in the pan or on the grill grate; cook until the husks steam and have definite char marks, turning several times, about 8 minutes. Remove from the heat and cool for 10 minutes.

③ Meanwhile, peel and devein the shrimp, reserving the shells separately. Peel and quarter 2 onions; set them aside.

④ Peel the husks off the corn, then cut each ear in half. Stand them on a cutting board, cut side down, and slice off the corn by running a large knife along the cob, thereby shaving off the individual kernels. Set the kernels aside.

⑤ Place the cobs, shrimp shells, quartered onions, garlic, broth, peppercorns, and bay leaves in a large saucepan or soup pot. Set it over high heat and bring to a boil. Cover, reduce the heat to low, and simmer slowly for 30 minutes. Skim any foam or impurities off the top of the soup.

⑥ Working in batches as necessary, strain the soup through a sieve or colander set over a large bowl in the sink; discard the solids.

7 Place the soup and half the prepared corn kernels in a large food processor fitted with the chopping blade or in a large blender; process or blend until smooth. Set aside.

8 Chop the remaining onion, then melt the butter in a large, clean saucepan or soup pot set over medium heat. Shred the potato through the large holes of a box grater and into the pot. Stir well, add the chopped onion, and cook, stirring often, until the onion is translucent, about 4 minutes.

9 Add the remaining corn kernels; cook, stirring constantly, for 1 minute. Pour in the cream, bring to a simmer, and cook for 2 minutes, stirring once in a while.

10 Stir in the soup puree. Bring to a simmer again and cook, stirring quite often, until the shredded potatoes are almost tender, about 5 minutes.

11 Add the scallops and peeled shrimp; continue cooking just until the shrimp are pink and firm, about 3 minutes. Stir in the parsley and salt, cover, and set aside off the heat for 5 minutes.

Vatapa with Tomatoes and Snapper

This rich Brazilian coconut stew is thickened with a mixture of beer and ground peanuts. *Makes 6 to 8 servings*

    3 tablespoons peanut oil
    1 large yellow onion, coarsely chopped
    4 garlic cloves, minced
    2 to 4 fresh jalapeño chiles, seeded and minced
    2 tablespoons minced peeled fresh ginger
    One 28-ounce can diced tomatoes (3½ cups)
    3 cups vegetable broth
    One 12-ounce bottle beer, preferably an
        amber or lager
    ½ cup unsalted roasted peanuts

    1 cup coconut milk
    1½ pounds skinless snapper fillets, cut into
        1-inch chunks
    ½ cup finely chopped parsley leaves
    ½ cup finely chopped cilantro leaves
    1 teaspoon salt
    ½ teaspoon freshly ground black pepper
    1 or 2 quartered limes for garnish

1 Heat a large pot or Dutch oven over medium heat. Swirl in the peanut oil, then add the onion and cook, stirring often, until translucent, about 3 minutes. Add the garlic, jalapeños, and ginger; cook, stirring constantly, for 30 seconds.

2 Pour in the tomatoes; break them up with a wooden spoon. Pour in the broth and beer. Raise the heat and bring to a boil. Cover, reduce the heat to low, and simmer for 20 minutes.

3 Meanwhile, place the peanuts in a food processor and process until finely ground, like coarse meal. Be careful not to turn them to peanut butter. Transfer the ground nuts to a medium bowl, add the coconut milk, and stir well. Set aside.

4 Add the snapper to the soup. Cover and cook for 3 minutes.

5 Add the peanut mixture to the soup. Cook, stirring constantly but gently so as not to break up the fish, until the soup returns to a simmer and thickens slightly, about 2 minutes.

6 Stir in the parsley, cilantro, salt, and pepper. Serve with lime wedges on the side for squeezing over individual servings.

Variations: Substitute medium shrimp, peeled and deveined; cooked, chopped lobster meat; or other skinless fish fillets for the snapper—or use a combination of them.

❋ Cold Soups ❋

An oxymoron? Not exactly. Cold soups are a refreshing way to start a meal in the summer or a delightful lunch with some bread and a salad any time of year. Best of all, they can be made in advance and stored in the refrigerator for several days. However, stone-cold is as bad as lukewarm: all taste best if you let them stand at room temperature for 10 or 15 minutes before serving.

Chilled Tomato Soup with Cucumber-Apple Salsa

No amount of herbs can overcome mealy tomatoes. Without the salsa, this fresh soup can be served in shot glasses. *Makes 8 servings*

1 tablespoon olive oil
4 medium shallots, chopped
3 pounds fresh beefsteak, Roma, plum, or heirloom tomatoes, cored and chopped
6 basil leaves, chopped
1 teaspoon stemmed thyme or ½ teaspoon dried thyme
4 cups (1 quart) chicken broth
2 tablespoons Worcestershire sauce (see Note)
½ teaspoon freshly ground black pepper
1 large cucumber
1 small sweet apple, such as a Gala or Rome, peeled, cored, and chopped
¼ cup chopped dill fronds
2 tablespoons white balsamic vinegar
½ teaspoon sugar
Several dashes of hot red pepper sauce to taste
½ teaspoon salt, or to taste

1 Heat a large saucepan over medium heat. Swirl in the olive oil, then add the shallots. Cook, stirring often, until translucent, about 4 minutes.

2 Add the tomatoes, stir well, then add the basil and thyme. Cook just until aromatic, about 20 seconds, then pour in the broth and Worcestershire sauce.

3 Bring to a simmer, scraping up any browned bits on the pan's bottom. Cover, reduce the heat to low, and simmer until the tomatoes are very soft, about 20 minutes. (It should still look like a soup, not a tomato sauce.) Season with pepper, then set off the heat to cool for 5 minutes.

4 Pour the contents of the pan into a large food processor fitted with a chopping blade or into a large, wide-bottomed blender. (Work in batches, if necessary.) Process or blend until pureed, scraping down the sides of the bowl or canister as necessary. Alternatively, use an immersion blender to puree the soup right in the pan.

5 Pour the pureed soup into a large pitcher, container, or bowl; cover and refrigerate until chilled, at least 4 hours or up to 2 days.

6 Peel the cucumber with a vegetable peeler, then slice it in half lengthwise. Scrape out the seeds with a small spoon, then dice the flesh and place in a medium bowl. Stir in the apple, dill, vinegar, sugar, and hot red pepper sauce. Season with salt.

7 To serve, mound a little cucumber salsa in the middle of each bowl, then ladle the soup around the salsa.

Note: Check the label on the chicken broth can; if it contains a lot of sodium, cut the Worcestershire sauce to 1½ tablespoons.

Variations: For a heartier soup, substitute beef broth for the chicken broth.

For a lower-acid soup, use yellow tomatoes; reduce the Worcestershire sauce to 1 tablespoon.

Substitute 1 tablespoon lime juice for the white balsamic vinegar.

Add 1 chopped seeded fresh jalapeño chile to the salsa with the apple.

Set the salsa on top of a small dollop of sour cream, crème fraîche, or plain yogurt.

For a Moroccan flavor, cook 2 minced garlic cloves with the shallots; omit the basil and thyme, and add 2 teaspoons ground cumin, 1 teaspoon ground cinnamon, and 1 teaspoon ground coriander in their stead. Also substitute mint for the dill in the salsa.

For an East Indian flavor, cook 2 minced garlic cloves and 2 tablespoons minced peeled fresh ginger with the shallots; omit the basil and thyme, and add 1½ tablespoons curry powder in their stead. Also, substitute chopped fresh cilantro for the dill and stir ½ cup plain yogurt into the salsa.

Top each serving with ¼ cup lump crabmeat, picked over for shell and cartilage; baby cooked shrimp (also known as "salad shrimp"); or chopped cooked lobster meat.

Gazpacho

Hand-chopping the vegetables preserves their individual tastes and textures—the secret to classic gazpacho. *Makes 8 servings*

6 cups no-salt tomato juice
2 cups beef broth
¼ cup red wine vinegar
¼ cup lemon juice
¼ cup extra virgin olive oil
2 teaspoons Worcestershire sauce
1 teaspoon salt, or to taste
½ teaspoon freshly ground black
     pepper
Several dashes of hot red pepper sauce to
     taste
2 large beefsteak tomatoes, minced
     (see Note)
3 celery ribs, thinly sliced
1 small onion, minced
2 garlic cloves, crushed
2 medium green bell peppers, cored, seeded,
     and finely chopped
2 medium cucumbers, peeled, halved
     lengthwise, seeded, and finely chopped

1 Whisk the tomato juice, broth, vinegar, lemon juice, olive oil, Worcestershire sauce, salt, pepper, and hot red pepper sauce in a large bowl, pitcher, or resealable container.

2 Stir in the tomatoes, celery, onion, and garlic. Cover and refrigerate for at least 6 hours or up to 2 days.

3 Four hours before serving, stir in the bell peppers and cucumber. Cover and refrigerate.

4 Check to see if the soup needs any more salt. Serve ice cold in soup bowls, shot glasses, or wineglasses.

Note: We don't seed the tomatoes but we do cut them to save every bit of juice. If you want to seed them for aesthetics, see page 111.

Variations: Add 1 tablespoon minced oregano leaves or 2 teaspoons stemmed thyme with the tomatoes.

Substitute 2 medium scallions, thinly sliced, for the small onion.

Substitute one large fennel bulb, trimmed and finely chopped, for either the bell peppers or the cucumbers.

Drizzle each serving with additional extra virgin olive oil.

Float a small toast round, drizzled with extra virgin olive oil, in each bowl of soup.

Stir ½ teaspoon ground cumin into 1 cup sour cream; spoon dollops on top of each serving.

Steam and then chill ½ pound mussels, debearded and cleaned, or clams, cleaned; place the mussel or clam meat in the bowl before spooning in the soup.

Serve shucked raw oysters on the side (see page 364), using them and their scrubbed shells to scoop up the soup.

Chilled Tomato Wheat Berry Soup

We first learned about this classic Italian soup from Michele Scicolone. She serves it hot; we love it cold. *Makes 6 servings*

1 pound wheat berries (see page 487)
1 tablespoon olive oil
1 large onion, finely chopped
3 celery ribs, thinly sliced
1¼ pounds plum or Roma tomatoes, finely chopped
2 garlic cloves, minced
6 cups (1½ quarts) beef broth
1 cup dry red wine

1⅔ cups canned white beans, drained and rinsed
2 ounces Parmigiano-Reggiano, grated
¼ cup finely chopped parsley leaves
¼ cup packed basil leaves, finely chopped
Extra virgin olive oil for garnish

❶ Place the wheat berries in a large bowl, cover with cool water, and set aside for at least 8 hours or overnight.

❷ Drain the berries in a fine-mesh sieve or colander set in the sink, then rinse them well under cool running water. Set aside.

❸ Heat a large saucepan or soup pot over medium heat. Swirl in the olive oil, then add the onion and celery; cook just until crisp-tender, about 2 minutes, stirring often. Stir in the tomatoes, garlic, and the drained wheat berries; cook, stirring constantly, for 1 minute.

❹ Pour in the broth and wine. Bring to a simmer; then cover, reduce the heat to low, and simmer until the wheat berries are tender but toothsome, about 50 minutes.

❺ Stir in the beans and cook, covered, for 10 minutes. Pour the soup into a large container, cover, and refrigerate until chilled, at least 6 hours or up to 2 days.

❻ Mix the cheese, parsley, and basil in a small bowl. Ladle the soup into bowls, then mound a little of the parsley mixture in each. Drizzle some extra virgin olive oil over each serving.

Variations: Add ½ teaspoon red pepper flakes with the tomatoes.

Substitute red wine for the white wine.

Drizzle a little lemon juice or white balsamic vinegar over each serving with the olive oil.

Cold Cucumber Spinach Soup

Creamy and luscious, this cold soup uses baby spinach leaves for their delicate bite. *Makes 8 servings*

1 tablespoon unsalted butter
1 large leek, white and pale green parts only, halved lengthwise, washed carefully of any sand and grit, and thinly sliced
1 large Russet or baking potato, peeled and chopped
2 medium cucumbers, peeled, halved lengthwise, seeded with a small spoon, and chopped
4 cups (1 quart) vegetable broth
1 cup packed baby spinach leaves
¼ cup chopped dill fronds
1½ teaspoons dry mustard
½ teaspoon salt, or to taste
½ teaspoon freshly ground black pepper
1 cup heavy cream

1 Melt the butter in a large saucepan over medium heat. Add the leek; cook, stirring often, until soft, about 3 minutes. Add the potato and cucumbers; cook for 1 minute.

2 Pour in the broth, then add the spinach, dill, dry mustard, salt, and pepper. Bring to a simmer, scraping up any browned bits on the pan's bottom.

3 Cover, reduce the heat to low, and simmer slowly until the potatoes are extremely tender when pierced with a fork, about 30 minutes. Set aside to cool for 10 minutes.

4 Pour the contents of the pan into a large food processor fitted with the chopping blade or into a wide-canister blender. (Work in batches, if need be.) Process or blend until smooth, scraping down the sides of the bowl or canister once in a while. Pour into a large resealable container, pitcher, or bowl; cover and refrigerate for 6 hours.

5 Stir in the cream; check to see if the soup needs more salt. Cover and refrigerate for at least 2 more hours until well chilled or for up to 2 days.

Variations: Add 2 bay leaves with the spinach; discard the bay leaves before processing or blending.

Add one 4-inch cinnamon stick with the spinach; discard the stick before processing or blending.

Substitute stemmed watercress, stemmed arugula, or chopped escarole leaves for the baby spinach.

Substitute 2 tablespoons chopped cilantro leaves for the dill.

Substitute sour cream for the heavy cream.

Cold Carrot Ginger Soup

Ginger can become quite spicy in larger quantities, so this soup is cooled off with a little orange marmalade, added off the heat to preserve its bitter edge. *Makes 6 servings*

2 tablespoons olive oil
2 large onions, chopped
2 garlic cloves, minced
1 or 2 serrano chiles, stemmed, seeded, and minced
3 tablespoons minced peeled fresh ginger
2 pounds carrots, peeled and chopped
2 large tart apples, such as Granny Smith, Empire, Pippin, or Northern Spy, peeled, cored, and chopped
1 cup dry vermouth or dry white wine
6 cups vegetable broth
1 to 2 tablespoons orange marmalade (see Note)
1 teaspoon salt, or to taste
½ teaspoon freshly ground pepper, preferably white pepper
Plain yogurt (regular, low-fat, or fat-free) for garnish
6 small fresh cilantro sprigs for garnish

1 Heat a large saucepan or pot over medium heat. Swirl in the olive oil, then add the onions and cook, stirring often, until translucent, about 4 minutes. Add the garlic, chiles, and ginger; cook for 30 seconds.

2 Add the carrots and apples; cook, stirring often, until the apples begin to soften at their edges, about 5 minutes.

3 Pour in the vermouth or wine; cook, stirring almost constantly, until reduced to a thick glaze, scraping up any browned bits on the pan's bottom, about 4 minutes.

4 Pour in the broth and bring to a simmer. Cover, reduce the heat to low, and simmer slowly until the carrots are soft and very tender, about 35 minutes.

5 Working in batches as necessary, pour the soup into a large food processor fitted with a chopping blade or into the canister of a large blender. Process or blend until smooth, scraping down the bowl or canister once or twice to make sure everything has been pureed. Alternatively, use an immersion blender to puree the soup right in the pot.

6 Add 1 tablespoon orange marmalade, the salt, and pepper; continue blending until combined. Taste the soup; add up to 1 tablespoon more marmalade as desired for sweetness and a little spiky bitterness, blending the marmalade thoroughly into the soup.

7 Transfer to a large bowl, pitcher, or container; cover and refrigerate for at least 6 hours or up to 3 days.

8 Check the soup for salt and add a little more, if desired. Spoon into bowls, top with a generous dollop of yogurt and a sprig of cilantro.

Note: Look for a marmalade with distinct bits of orange rind floating in the jam—or better yet, one made from whole, thin orange slices that you will have to chop.

Variations: For a sweeter soup, substitute pears for the apples.

For a tart soup, add 1 tablespoon lemon juice with the orange marmalade.

Use more exotic flavors of marmalade, including pear/lemon or grapefruit.

Drizzle the top of the soup with toasted pumpkinseed oil or toasted sesame oil.

Spicy Watermelon Soup

Here's a simple, no-cook, summer cooler, refreshing and tart. *Makes 4 servings*

One small 6-pound red watermelon or a 6-pound chunk of red watermelon (see Note)
4 teaspoons superfine sugar, or to taste
2 teaspoons lime juice
½ teaspoon salt, or to taste
Several dashes of hot red pepper sauce to taste
1 bay leaf
1 teaspoon whole black peppercorns

1 Cut the rind off the melon; working over a bowl to catch any juice, remove and discard all the black seeds and as many of the white seeds as you can. Cut the flesh into chunks; add these and any collected juice to a large food processor fitted with the chopping blade. Process until smooth.

2 Pour the soup through a fine-mesh sieve into a large bowl; do not push any solids through the mesh. If any foam passes through the mesh and into the bowl, skim it off with a spoon.

③ Stir in the sugar, lime juice, salt, and hot red pepper sauce, up to ½ teaspoon. Taste for sweetness; add more sugar, if desired. Submerge the bay leaf and peppercorns in the soup, cover, and refrigerate until chilled, at least 4 hours or up to 2 days.

④ Before serving, remove the bay leaf and peppercorns. Check the soup for salt and sugar, adding a little more of either or both if need be.

Note: Seedless watermelon will make the job so much easier.

Variations: Omit the bay leaf and submerge any of the following into the soup before chilling: 6 thyme sprigs, lightly crushed; 4 dried red Asian chiles; 3 mint sprigs, crushed; one or two 4-inch cinnamon sticks; or 1 star anise pod. Remove before serving.

To garnish, make cantaloupe or honeydew balls with a melon baller; float these in the soup. Or place a small mound of fruit salsa (see page 47) in the bowl with the soup.

Chilled Honeydew Soup with Figs and Prosciutto

Since melon, figs, and prosciutto are a classic appetizer combination, we crafted a very simple melon soup that brings them all together in the bowl. *Makes 4 servings*

One 2- to 2½-pound ripe honeydew
   melon
1 cup Chardonnay or white grape juice
1 tablespoon lime juice
2 to 3 tablespoons superfine sugar (see Note)
Coarse-grained salt or kosher salt for
   garnish
6 ripe fresh figs, preferably black Mission
   figs
1 ounce prosciutto, thinly sliced

① Cut the melon in half and scoop out the seeds. Working over a bowl to catch any juice, use a large flatware tablespoon to scoop out the flesh.

② Place the chunks of honeydew and any accumulated juice in a large food processor fitted with the chopping blade or into the canister of a large blender. Add ¾ cup Chardonnay or white grape juice, the lime juice, 2 tablespoons sugar, and the salt. Process or blend until smooth, scraping down the sides of the bowl as necessary. Taste for sweetness and add up to 1 tablespoon more sugar as desired.

③ Transfer the puree to a large bowl, pitcher, or container; cover and refrigerate for at least 4 hours or up to 3 days, stirring occasionally.

④ Stem the figs and thinly slice them. Use a sharp chef's knife to cut the prosciutto into small strips.

⑤ Stir the remaining ¼ cup Chardonnay or white grape juice into the soup until smooth. Pour into four bowls. Arrange the figs and prosciutto strips over the soup. Sprinkle each bowl with some coarse-grained or kosher salt, just 6 or 7 grains per bowl.

Note: Superfine sugar is simply sugar ground more finely, better to dissolve in liquids. Look for it either with the sugar or in the bar or drink section of your supermarket.

Variations: Substitute any kind of melon you desire: cantaloupe, Charentais, Crenshaw, Christmas, Galia, or Sharlyn.

Add several dashes of hot red pepper sauce to the melon puree before chilling.

Chilled Blueberry Chipotle Soup

We made this no-cook, hot-and-sweet soup for a Thanksgiving dinner one year when everything was Southwestern inspired. *Makes 6 servings*

2 medium cucumbers, peeled, halved lengthwise, seeded, and chopped

2 garlic cloves, crushed

1 canned chipotle chile in adobo sauce, stemmed, seeded, and chopped

2 cups fresh blueberries

1 cup plain yogurt (regular, low-fat, or fat-free)

2 tablespoons honey

1½ tablespoons lime juice

½ teaspoon ground cumin

½ teaspoon salt, or more to taste

❶ Place all the ingredients in a large food processor fitted with the chopping blade or in a large blender. Process or blend until fairly smooth, scraping down the sides of the bowl or canister occasionally to make sure everything is blended.

❷ Pour into a large bowl, pitcher, or container; cover and refrigerate until chilled, at least 4 hours or up to 2 days.

❸ Before serving, stir well and check the soup to make sure it doesn't need any additional salt. If the soup has gotten thick, thin it out with a little water, no more than a tablespoon or two to loosen it up. It may also be foamy; simply stir it down.

Variations: Omit the garlic; add 1 medium shallot, quartered, with the cucumber.

Substitute ground ginger for the cumin.

Garnish the soup with minced scallions or some thin avocado wedges.

Cold Pear Soup with Parmigiano-Reggiano and Honey

Since the honey is a garnish for the dish, use a full-flavored, aromatic variety. *Makes 6 servings*

3 pounds ripe Bartlett pears

1 tablespoon lemon juice

1 pound Russet or baking potatoes

2 tablespoons unsalted butter

1 large yellow onion, thinly sliced

¼ cup dry vermouth or dry white wine

4 cups (1 quart) chicken or vegetable broth

1 cup milk (regular, low-fat, or fat-free)

½ teaspoon salt, or more to taste

½ teaspoon freshly ground pepper, preferably white pepper

4 ounces Parmigiano-Reggiano, finely grated (about 1 cup)

¼ cup chopped parsley leaves

¼ cup honey

❶ Peel, core, and slice the pears. Place them in a large bowl, add the lemon juice, and cover with cool water.

❷ Peel the potatoes and cut into ½-inch pieces. Add to the water with the pears. Set aside.

❸ Melt the butter in a large saucepan or medium pot set over low heat. Add the onion and cook very slowly, stirring once in a while, until golden, about 12 minutes.

❹ Drain the pears and potatoes. Add them to the pot and continue cooking, stirring often, until the pears have begun to soften at the edges, about 10 minutes.

❺ Add the vermouth or wine, raise the heat to medium-high, and bring to a simmer. Cook, stirring once or twice, for 2 minutes. Pour in the broth and milk; bring back to a simmer. Cover, reduce the heat to low, and simmer slowly until the potatoes are extremely tender, about 45 minutes.

⑥ Pour the soup into a large food processor; process until smooth. Alternatively, use an immersion blender in the pot to puree the soup. Stir in the salt and pepper. Pour the soup into a large bowl, pitcher, or container; cover and refrigerate until chilled, about 4 hours or up to 3 days.

⑦ Before serving, check to see if the soup needs any more salt. Ladle into bowls; top each with cheese (about 2½ tablespoons), parsley (about 2 teaspoons), and honey (about 2 teaspoons).

Variations: Substitute sweet apples like Golden Delicious or Macoun for the pears.

Substitute 2 tablespoons stemmed thyme for the parsley (about 1 teaspoon per serving).

Substitute crumbled blue cheese for the Parmigiano-Reggiano.

❈ *Stock* ❈

Nothing beats homemade stock; it will make even mundane recipes special. These recipes offer two techniques: the traditional method of long-simmering and the fast-cooked, pressure-cooker method (which we actually prefer because it squeezes more flavor from the bones and vegetables).

Chicken Stock

Makes about 2½ quarts

3 pounds chicken parts (wings, necks, backs,
    or bones with some meat adhering to them)
1 large onion, coarsely chopped
2 carrots, peeled and sliced
2 celery ribs, sliced
3 or 4 dried mushrooms
3 parsley sprigs
3 thyme sprigs
1 bay leaf
1 teaspoon salt
¼ teaspoon whole black peppercorns
11 cups water, or as needed

❶ **Traditional method:** Place all the ingredients in a large soup pot or Dutch oven and bring to a

simmer over high heat. Reduce the heat to very low, cover partially, and simmer very slowly, just the merest bubble, for 2 hours.

Pressure cooker method: Place all the ingredients in a large pressure cooker; add enough water so that everything is submerged but the water is not above the maximum fill line. Lock on the lid and bring to high pressure over medium-high heat (follow the manufacturer's instructions). Reduce the heat to medium and cook at high pressure for 25 minutes. Set aside off the heat and let the pressure return to normal (again, follow the manufacturer's instructions), about 15 minutes.

❷ Strain the soup through a sieve or colander set over a large bowl in the sink. Cover and refrigerate overnight so the fat will congeal on top of the soup.

3 Skim off the fat, then divide the soup into individual containers and refrigerate for up to 3 days or freeze for up to 3 months.

Turkey Stock: Substitute 1 turkey carcass with some meat adhering to the bones, cut into 6 or 8 pieces, for the chicken.

Beef Stock

Makes about 2½ quarts

2½ to 3 pounds beef bones, such as short
    rib bones or the bones from a standing
    rib roast with some of the meat still
    adhering
1 large onion, chopped
2 carrots, peeled and sliced
2 celery ribs, sliced
6 parsley sprigs
4 thyme sprigs
2 bay leaves
1 teaspoon salt
½ teaspoon whole black peppercorns
11 cups water, or as needed

1 Position the rack in the center of the oven and preheat the oven to 425°F. Lay the bones on a large rimmed baking sheet; bake until browned and caramelized, about 20 minutes.

2 **Traditional method:** Pour all the bones and any liquid on the baking sheet into a large soup pot or a Dutch oven. Add the remaining ingredients and enough cool water to cover everything to a depth of 2 inches. Bring to a boil over high heat. Reduce the heat to very low, cover partially, and simmer very slowly for 3 hours.

Pressure cooker method: Pour the bones and liquid on the baking sheet into a large pressure cooker. Add the remaining ingredients and enough water to cover everything but do not go above the maximum fill line. Lock on the lid and bring to high pressure over high heat (read the manufacturer's instructions). Reduce the heat to medium and cook at high pressure for 1 hour. Set the cooker off the heat and let the pressure return to normal, about 30 minutes (again, read the manufacturer's instructions to discover the pressure indicators of your model).

3 Strain through a sieve or colander into a large bowl set in the sink. Cover and refrigerate overnight so the fat solidifies on top of the stock.

4 Skim off the fat, then spoon into individual containers, cover, and store in the refrigerator for up to 2 days or in the freezer for up to 3 months.

Tips for Success with Homemade Stock

• If you use the traditional method for making stock, make sure the lid is slightly askew over the pot so the soup reduces very slowly without boiling away.
• When you pour or ladle the soup into the strainer, let the solids rest there so they drip their liquid into the bowl. Don't press them against the mesh; the attendant collagens and fat can cloud the stock.
• Ladle the stock into 1- or 2-cup containers so you can use discrete amounts in recipes without any waste.

Fish Stock

Makes about 2 quarts

    3 pounds fish heads and bones, gills
        removed, bones rinsed of blood
    1 large onion, chopped
    2 carrots, peeled and sliced
    2 celery ribs, sliced
    6 parsley sprigs
    3 thyme sprigs
    1 bay leaf
    1 teaspoon salt
    ¼ teaspoon whole black peppercorns
    7 cups water, or as needed
    1 cup dry white wine or dry vermouth

① **Traditional method:** Combine everything in a large soup pot or Dutch oven and bring to a boil over high heat. Cover partially, reduce the heat to very low, and simmer very slowly, just the slightest bubble, for 1 hour.

Pressure cooker method: Combine everything in a large pressure cooker, adding enough water that everything is covered but the water does not rise above the maximum fill line. Lock on the lid and bring to high pressure over high heat (read the manufacturer's instructions for various indicators and safety methods). Reduce the heat to medium and cook at high pressure for 18 minutes. Set aside off the heat and let the cooker return to normal pressure, about 15 minutes.

② Strain through a sieve or colander set over a large bowl in the sink. Ladle into small containers, seal, and store in the refrigerator for 2 days or in the freezer for 3 months.

Shrimp Stock: Substitute the shells from 3 pounds shrimp for the fish heads and bones.

Vegetable Stock

Makes about 2 quarts

    2 large onions, quartered
    2 medium turnips, peeled and quartered
    4 carrots, peeled and cut into 1-inch
        sections
    3 celery ribs, cut into 1-inch sections
    2 parsnips, peeled and cut into 1-inch
        sections
    2 tablespoons olive oil
    ½ cup dry vermouth or dry white wine
    1 small head cabbage, quartered
    6 parsley sprigs
    6 thyme sprigs
    2 bay leaves
    1 teaspoon salt
    ¼ teaspoon whole black peppercorns
    8 cups (2 quarts) water

① Position the rack in the center of the oven and preheat the oven to 400°F. Place the onions, turnips, carrots, celery, and parsnips in a large roasting pan or on a large, lipped, flameproof baking sheet; toss with the olive oil.

② Bake, tossing occasionally, until browned and soft, about 40 minutes. Scoop the vegetables into a large soup pot, Dutch oven, or large pressure cooker.

③ Set the roasting pan or baking sheet over the burners on your stove (it will probably cover two). Pour in the vermouth or wine, then turn the heat to medium-high. Scraping all the while, bring the liquid to a simmer, getting up as much of the browned bits as you can. (If you've used a nonstick pan, use only cookware designated for use on nonstick surfaces.) Pour the contents of the baking sheet into the pot, oven, or cooker.

4 **Traditional method:** Add the cabbage, parsley, thyme, bay leaves, salt, peppercorns, and water; bring to a boil over high heat. Cover partially, reduce the heat to low, and simmer slowly for 45 minutes.

Pressure cooker method: Add the cabbage, parsley, thyme, bay leaves, salt, peppercorns, and the water (or as much of it needed to reach the fill line—do not use more than 8 cups. Lock on the lid and bring to high pressure over high heat (check the manufacturer's instructions). Reduce the heat to medium and cook at high pressure for 10 minutes. Set aside off the heat and let the cooker return to normal pressure according to the manufacturer's instructions, about 10 minutes.

5 Strain through a sieve or colander set over a large bowl in the sink. Discard the vegetable solids. Ladle into small containers, seal, and store in the refrigerator for 2 days or in the freezer for up to 2 months.

Pasta and Noodles

PASTA IS THE MOST VERSATILE FOOD: IT CAN GO FROM AN ELEGANT FIRST course to a down-home dinner with nary a change. It's a terrific weeknight dinner and a stunning weekender. So carb-phobes, beware. We're passionate about pasta.

We divided this chapter into the segments of a pasta production line. We start with homemade noodles, egg to whole wheat, beet to spinach: techniques to make the dough, ways to shape it, and tips to cook pasta. Esoteric, yes—but getting your hands in the dough is just out-and-out fun.

Then we move on to sauces and fillings: from a no-cook tomato sauce to a beat-the-winter-doldrums lamb ragù. Along the way, look for the two basic Italian sauces (marinara and cream sauce), with their variations and uses, and a year's worth of lasagne. We round out the chapter with a set of Asian noodle dishes.

We offer suggestions of what goes with what—but again, it's the versatility of pasta that amazes us. The same dough can be shaped in ravioli, cut into noodles, frozen, or dried; it can be put on the side of the plate or at the center; it can be baked in a cheesy casserole or served with a fresh tomato sauce. No wonder we're passionate about pasta.

Here are instructions for how to make pasta dough and shape it into noodles—as well as recipes for three pasta imitators (gnocchi and the like). There are no sauces here; those start on page 179. This is all about the foundation of a noodle dish: the pasta itself.

Basic Pasta Dough

Although it's not traditional, we add a little olive oil to pasta dough. Some chefs add milk, but a fragrant oil is a better foil for the eggs. Once you've made the dough, see page 175 to find out how to shape it into noodles. *Makes about 1 pound fresh pasta*

Dry Ingredients
2 cups all-purpose flour, plus more for dusting and to keep the dough from sticking
½ teaspoon salt

Wet Ingredients
3 large eggs, at room temperature, lightly beaten (see Note)
2 tablespoons olive oil

To make pasta by hand:

1. Whisk the dry ingredients in a large bowl. Make a small well, piling the dry ingredients up the sides; or dump the mixture out onto a clean, flat work surface and make a well in the center of the pile.

2. Place the wet ingredients in the well. Using a fork, begin beating the wet ingredients, adding a little of the dry mixture from the well's walls.

3. Whisking with the fork, incorporate more and more of the dry ingredients into the wet. Once the mixture in the center turns pasty, start collapsing the well's walls into the wet ingredients, whisking in more and more of the flour mixture until a wet dough forms. If you're working in a bowl, when the dry ingredients have been almost all incorporated into the wet, turn the contents of the bowl out onto a clean, dry work surface.

4. Knead the dough just until it holds its shape, incorporating as much of the dry ingredients into the wet as possible. Use the heel of one hand to press gently into the dough, twisting without tearing as you incorporate the dry ingredients. Add a few drops of water if the dough is brittle, a little more flour if it's sticky. (On any given day, flour and eggs have varying moisture contents; pasta can end up slightly drier in one batch than another.)

5. Divide the dough into 4 lemon-sized balls. Cover with a clean kitchen towel and let rest at room temperature for 10 or 15 minutes to relax the glutens before continuing on page 175.

To make pasta in a food processor:

1. Place the dry ingredients in a food processor fitted with a chopping blade. Pulse a couple of times to combine.

2. Add the wet ingredients all at once. Process just until a dough begins to form.

3. Turn the barely cohering dough out onto a clean, dry, lightly floured work surface. You will now undoubtedly need to add more flour than

you would to the handmade pasta dough because of the way the food processor disassembles the proteins and glutens in the dough. Follow the remainder of the kneading instructions from step 4 on the preceding page.

Note: If you're curious about why we add eggs to our pasta dough, see "The History of Durum Wheat" on page 178.

Tips for Success

• In order for the eggs to absorb the flour properly, they must be at room temperature. Set them out on the counter in their shells for 15 minutes or place them in a bowl of warm—not hot—water for 5 minutes.

• Overkneading or overprocessing produces tough, slippery pasta. Feel the dough—it should be smooth and supple, like a baby's skin, and neither brittle nor sticky.

• Double or triple any of these pasta dough recipes for crowds.

Serving Size

In most of this section, we've gone by volume or weight measures (2 cups, 1 pound, etc.), rather than by the number of servings, since pasta's versatility means it'll be served at various times, from starter to main course, depending on the meal. If the noodles are a first course, a single batch of noodles and sauce will be enough to get 4 to 6 people ready for what's to come. If the sauced pasta is for the main course, you'll want a salad, vegetables, and bread to go along with it—or you can double the recipe.

Seven Pasta Variations

Following one of the two techniques on page 170, you can create endless variations. Here are the dry and wet ingredients for seven other pastas.

1. No-Yolk Pasta

Makes about 1 pound fresh pasta

Dry Ingredients
2 cups all-purpose flour, plus more for dusting and to keep the dough from sticking
½ cup whole wheat flour
½ teaspoon salt

Wet Ingredients
4 large egg whites, at room temperature, lightly beaten
½ tablespoon water

Note: Once it is formed in lemon-sized balls, let this pasta rest 1 hour before rolling it out.

Sauce Suggestions: For almost any sauce.

2. Whole Wheat Pasta

Makes about 1 pound fresh pasta

Dry Ingredients
1½ cups all-purpose flour, plus more for dusting and to keep the dough from sticking
1 cup whole wheat flour
½ teaspoon salt
½ teaspoon freshly ground black pepper

Wet Ingredients
4 large eggs, at room temperature, lightly beaten
¼ cup olive oil

Sauce Suggestions: Try this pasta with earthy sauces like the simple Walnut Sauce (page 181) or the creamy Mushrooms and Sage Sauce (page 189).

Pasta Shapes

For flat noodles, here's the basic range:

capellini (the thinnest, around 1/8 inch wide)
linguine (about 1/4 inch wide)
fettuccine (about 3/8 inch wide)
tagliatelle (about 1/2 inch wide)
pappardelle (over 5/8 inch wide, even up to 1 inch)

Tubular noodles are mostly available as dried pasta—unless you have an electric pasta extruder or live near a high-end supermarket that offers fresh pasta in the refrigerator case. They also come in a thin-to-thick continuum: from capelli d'angelo (angel hair) to spaghettini to the familiar spaghetti, and then on up through various hollow tubes like bucatini and perciatelli.

In general, thinner noodles are better for fresh tomato sauces and other simple sauces. The chunkier the sauce, the wider the noodle—although we're partial to a butter sauce on wide pappardelle.

Finally, there are shaped pastas: ziti (hollow tubes), penne (larger hollow tubes), rigatoni (ribbed hollow tubes), rigate (larger ribbed hollow tubes), rotelle (spirals or wagon wheels, depending on the manufacturer), farfalle (bow ties), and the like.

There are ways to make some of them at home. For example, for curly fusilli, snip fettuccine noodles into 6-inch lengths, twist them into corkscrews, and let them dry on a clean kitchen towel. But going to all this trouble isn't terribly practical, given the range available at the supermarket. By and large, we save shaped pastas for baked dishes and salads.

---

3. Chestnut Pasta

Makes about 1 pound fresh pasta

Dry Ingredients
1 cup all-purpose flour, plus more for dusting and to keep the dough from sticking
1 cup chestnut flour
1/2 teaspoon salt

Wet Ingredients
3 large eggs, at room temperature, lightly beaten
2 tablespoons walnut oil

Sauce Suggestions: Try this pasta with rich sauces such as the Rabbit Ragù (page 191) or one of the variations to the Cream Sauce (pages 185–186)—or, best of all, to go with the wide noodles in the Winter Lasagna (page 207).

4. Beet Pasta

Makes about 1 pound fresh pasta

Dry Ingredients
2 cups all-purpose flour, plus more for dusting and to keep the dough from sticking
1/2 teaspoon salt

Wet Ingredients
1 large egg plus 1 large egg yolk, at room temperature
1/2 cup beet puree (see Note)
1 tablespoon olive oil

Note: To make beet puree, cook 2 peeled and halved medium beets in a large pot of boiling water set over high heat until tender when pierced with a fork, about 15 minutes. Drain, reserving about 2 tablespoons of the cooking water. Cool, then cut into chunks and puree in a food processor fitted with the chopping blade with just as much cooking water as you need to make a puree. Or puree two medium canned beets in a food processor.

Sauce Suggestions: We like these noodles with light olive oil sauces such as Sautéed Garlic Sauce (page 180).

5. Butternut Squash Pasta

Makes about 1 pound fresh pasta

Dry Ingredients
2 cups all-purpose flour, plus more for dusting and to keep the dough from sticking
½ teaspoon salt

Wet Ingredients
2 large eggs, at room temperature
½ cup mashed cooked butternut squash puree (see Note)

Note: To make a butternut squash puree, cut a small 1-pound butternut squash in half, scoop out the seeds, and roast it on a lipped baking sheet, cut side down, in a preheated 400°F oven until soft, about 30 minutes. Cool, then scoop out the soft, inner flesh; you'll have more puree than you need, but what's left over makes a great side dish, mashed like potatoes.

Sauce Suggestions: These noodles go well with any simple cream or butter sauce.

You needn't make your own noodles for a great pasta dish. In fact, you often shouldn't. Some dishes are better with dried pasta. By and large, fresh pasta is softer, more luxurious, and more fragile; dried pasta is heartier, more toothsome, and far less subtle, a better complement to thicker sauces.

6. Red Pepper Pasta

Makes about 1 pound fresh pasta

Dry Ingredients
2 cups plus 2 tablespoons all-purpose flour, plus more for dusting and to keep the dough from sticking
½ teaspoon salt

Wet Ingredients
1 large egg plus 1 large egg yolk, lightly beaten, at room temperature
1 cup red pepper puree (see Note)

Note: Four jarred pimientos, drained and rinsed, should yield about 1 cup puree when processed in a food processor or a large blender.

Sauce Suggestions: We prefer these with the Walnut Sauce (page 181) or Clams and Cherry Tomatoes (page 188).

7. Spinach Pasta

Makes about 1 pound fresh pasta

Dry Ingredients
2 cups all-purpose flour, plus more for dusting and to keep the dough from sticking
½ teaspoon salt

Wet Ingredients
1 large egg plus 1 large egg white, at room temperature
1 tablespoon olive oil
One 10-ounce package frozen chopped spinach, thawed, squeezed of all excess moisture, and pureed in a food processor or large blender

Sauce Suggestions: Spinach noodles are very versatile and work well with about any light sauce—just steer clear of ragùs.

Turning the Dough into Noodles

Once you have made a dough in lemon-sized balls, use one of these two methods to make noodles. (See pages 199–200 for instructions on turning the dough into shapes for stuffing.)

To make noodles with a rolling pin:

1 Lightly flour your work surface, place one of the pasta balls on it, and flour a wooden rolling pin. Flatten the ball slightly, then begin rolling it out with quick, short, but smooth movements, pushing the dough away from you rather than down against the work surface. Rotate the dough and repeat the process at different angles until you have a circle about 9 inches in diameter.

2 To stretch the dough, dust it with a little flour, then roll it about a quarter of the way onto the pin, like the music over a player-piano reel. Holding the dough onto the pin with one hand, use the other hand to stretch the part that still lies on the work surface, pulling the dough toward you and rolling the pin away from you at the same time. Keep a firm pressure, but be gentle—don't tear the pasta. Unroll the dough, rotate it about a quarter turn, and stretch again. Work quickly: you're trying to overcome the glutens and the dough has a tendency to snap back to its original state.

3 Unroll the dough, give it a light dusting of flour, and again roll about a quarter of it onto your pin. Gently roll the pin back and forth against the work surface, moving your hands over the pin itself, from the center to the outside, thereby rolling and stretching the dough as you rock it back and forth on the pin. Work quickly here, too—you're trying to beat the clock because the dough is drying and could start cracking. Unroll the sheet, rotate it several degrees, roll about a quarter of it back onto the pin, and repeat. You'll need to do this several times, at several different angles on the sheet.

4 Once the dough is less than ⅛ inch thick, unroll it from the pin, lay it flat against the work surface, then gently fold it up, turning over 6-inch segments of the dough until it looks like a sheet of paper that's been folded (but not creased). Slice the folded dough into strips anywhere from ¼ inch to over ½ inch wide (see page 172); unfold the noodles. Open a cabinet door, lay a clean kitchen towel over it, and drape the noodles over the towel to dry while you shape the other balls.

To make noodles in a pasta machine:

1 Lightly dust one of the pasta balls with flour, then run it through the machine on the widest setting. Fold the dough in half and run it through again. Do this about eight or nine times until the dough is fairly smooth. Add a small dusting of flour any time the dough starts to stick.

2 Decrease the thickness setting of the rollers by one notch, lightly flour the dough again, and run it through. As it comes out the other end, catch it with your hand and pull it gently away from the machine, cranking all the while with your other hand.

3 Keep reducing the thickness setting by one notch, running the pasta sheet through the machine each time and catching it as it comes out. (We like slightly thicker noodles and rarely go to the narrowest setting; instead, we prefer the next-to-thinnest setting—#6 on most modern machines.)

4 Once the sheet has come out of the machine for the last time, switch the crank mechanism and run the sheet through the cutting blades, thereby making noodles the width you desire. Open a cabinet door, lay a clean kitchen towel over the door, and drape the noodles over it to dry while you shape the other balls.

Cooking Pasta

1 Bring a large pot of unsalted water to a boil. Use about 6 quarts water for a pound of fresh pasta or ½ pound dried pasta, with an extra quart for every succeeding ½ pound fresh or dried pasta. You needn't really measure; just have enough water so the pasta moves freely in the pot.

2 Salt the water once it's boiling. Use about 1 tablespoon salt per ½ pound fresh or dried pasta. Of course, you can begin with salted water, but it'll take longer to come to a boil. Never add oil. It will result in slippery noodles that won't catch the sauce.

3 Add the noodles. If you're using dried pasta, don't break dried noodles in half. Let them sit in the water, their ends exposed, until they soften enough that you can bend them with a wooden spoon and submerge them in the boiling water.

4 Stir well and often but gently. If you don't stir them, the noodles will drop to the bottom and stick.

5 Cook until supple but still firm to the bite. For fresh noodles, that's the moment they float to the surface, plus about 10 seconds. For dried noodles, they may never float and it can take anywhere from 5 to 9 minutes. It's all balance: you don't want to crunch the noodles between your molars but you also don't want to mush them against your soft palate. The only way to know if they're done? No, don't throw a noodle against a wall. Scoop one out and taste it.

6 Drain the noodles in a colander set in the sink. If the sauce is ready, don't rinse the noodles; the sticky glutens will catch the sauce. Always reserve a little of the pasta cooking liquid; use this to thin out a sauce that's too thick. If the sauce is not ready, rinse the noodles with warm water so they won't glue together.

7 Serve at once. Don't let warm pasta sit around. Ideally, the sauce should come off the flame just as you're draining the noodles. But in the forgiving world of pasta, a near miss is as good as perfection.

Storing Fresh Pasta

While dried pasta has an indefinite shelf life, fresh pasta is perishable. Plan on cooking noodles within 30 minutes of making them.

If you want more lag time, toss the noodles with a little all-purpose flour or finely ground cornmeal to keep them from sticking and store in a tightly closed ziplock plastic bag in the refrigerator for up to 24 hours.

Beyond that, freeze fresh pasta. Wind the flour or cornmeal-dusted noodles into little nests and lay them out in one layer on a large baking sheet. Freeze until firm, then seal in plastic bags and store in the freezer for up to 3 months. Drop them directly from the freezer into boiling water, but treat them like dried pasta—that is, they'll need a little longer cooking time, perhaps 4 or 5 minutes.

Here are our favorite pretenders: they act like pasta, are made from a pastalike dough, are extremely versatile (can be a side dish, main course, or first course), and yet are not pasta. Still and all, they go perfectly with most of our pasta sauces (starting on page 179).

Spaetzle

In German, the name means "little sparrows"; less prosaically, they're malformed strips of dough. As a side dish, spaetzle are best with the Butter and Fresh Herbs Sauce (page 181). Once boiled, they can also be dropped right into a pot of soup during the last 3 minutes of cooking. *Makes about 4 servings (about 4 cups cooked spaetzle)*

> 1½ cups all-purpose flour
> ½ teaspoon salt
> ¼ teaspoon baking powder
> ¼ teaspoon grated nutmeg
> 2 large eggs, lightly beaten, at room temperature
> ½ cup plus 2 tablespoons milk (regular, low-fat, or fat-free)

❶ While you prepare the dough, bring a large pot of water to a boil over high heat. Use at least 6 quarts of water, but leave a generous amount of headspace in the pot.

❷ Whisk the flour, salt, baking powder, and nutmeg in a large bowl, then whisk in the eggs and milk until a sticky, wet batter forms. There should be no grains of flour visible, but stop whisking the moment they disappear to avoid setting up the glutens and rendering the spaetzle tough.

❸ Create the spaetzle using one of these three methods. Do not use all the batter at once. Since spaetzle cook fast, make the dumplings in batches to keep the first rounds from getting waterlogged and overcooked.

With a spaetzle maker: Pour a small amount of the dough into the machine, set it over the pot, and turn the crank to force small nodules of dough into the boiling water.

With a grater: Lay a flat, wide-hole grater over the pot of boiling water like a bridge. Pour some of the batter onto the grater, then wipe it across the holes with a wooden spoon or a rubber spatula so that the dough falls into the water in little round bits. Wipe in the direction of least resistance, not against the sharp edges.

With a cutting board and a knife: Pour a little of the batter onto a small, stiff cutting board. Hold this over the boiling water, then use a knife to cut off tiny pieces of the batter, separating them from the larger mass and wiping them off the board's side and into the boiling water with a clean, swift swipe.

❹ Stir well, then cook the spaetzle just until they float to the top of the water plus about 5 seconds. Scoop them out with a slotted spoon, drain over the pot, then place them in a colander in the sink to await the full batch. Repeat this whole process from step 3 with the remaining dough, working in batches.

Spinach and Cheese Dumplings

These dumplings are formed into little ovals, like mini quenelles. Toss them with the Cream Sauce (page 185), the Alfredo Sauce (page 186), or the Gorgonzola Sauce (page 186). Or make a simple tomato sauce like the Marinara Sauce (page 182), toss in the dumplings, pour the mixture into a baking dish, and bake in a preheated 350°F oven until bubbling, about 25 minutes. *Makes 6 servings*

One 10-ounce package frozen chopped spinach, thawed and squeezed of all moisture

¾ cup ricotta, regular or low-fat (do not use fat-free)

3 ounces Parmigiano-Reggiano, grated

3 large egg yolks, at room temperature

6 tablespoons all-purpose flour, or more as needed

½ teaspoon freshly ground black pepper

¼ teaspoon grated nutmeg

1 Mix all the ingredients in a large bowl until fairly smooth, like a thick paste. Add a little more flour if necessary—but do not add enough that the mixture turns into a dough. Cover the bowl with plastic wrap and refrigerate for at least 1 hour or up to 2 days.

2 Bring a large pot of water to a boil over high heat. Scoop out rounded teaspoonfuls of the cold spinach mixture; use a second teaspoon to make an egg-shaped dumpling, passing it between the teaspoons until it's correctly formed. Drop the dumpling into the simmering water. Make about 8 more dumplings using this method; stir well in the pot. Cook until they float and are puffed, turning them in the water with a wooden spoon a few times, about 10 minutes.

3 Remove the dumplings from the water with a slotted spoon and place them on a paper towel–lined plate. Repeat the process with the remaining batter until all the dumplings are made.

To store: The dumplings can be tossed with a little fine-ground cornmeal, sealed in a plastic bag, and stored in the freezer for up to 2 months.

Gnocchi

Open a bottle of wine and get your friends rolling these traditional potato dumplings. Serve with the Marinara Sauce (page 182), the Alfredo Sauce (page 186), or the Gorgonzola Sauce (page 186), or with Clams and Cherry Tomatoes Sauce (page 188). In fact, they'll go with just about any of the cooked sauces except the heavy ragùs. *Makes 4 servings*

2 pounds Russet potatoes, scrubbed (see Note)

2 large egg yolks, at room temperature, lightly beaten

2 teaspoons salt

1 to 1½ cups all-purpose flour, plus additional for dusting

1 Position the rack in the center of the oven, then preheat the oven to 400°F. Place the potatoes in the center of the rack and bake until soft, about 1 hour and 15 minutes. Transfer to a cooling rack just until they can be handled easily, about 10 minutes.

2 Cut the potatoes in half lengthwise and scoop the white insides into a potato ricer. Press the flesh into a large bowl. Alternatively, scoop the insides into a large bowl and lightly mash them with a fork, just until broken up into small bits, not until smooth.

③ Stir in the egg yolks and salt with a fork. Add 1 cup flour and stir just until a dough begins to form.

④ Lightly flour a clean work surface, dump the contents of the bowl onto it, and knead until smooth but still slightly sticky, about 4 minutes, adding additional flour as needed in 1-tablespoon increments to make a workable but soft dough. The day's humidity and the flour's moisture content will make all the difference. You're looking for a silky, soft, pliable texture.

⑤ Bring a large pot of water to a boil over high heat. For best results, use about 6 quarts of water in an 8-quart stockpot.

⑥ Meanwhile, pull off a section of dough about the size of a lemon. Dust your hands and the work surface lightly with flour, then roll the piece of dough between your palms to form a cylinder about 1 inch thick and 10 inches long.

⑦ Slice the cylinder into 1-inch segments. Place the tines of a clean fork against the work surface, back side up. Gently roll the dough pieces up the fork, barely pressing down, to give them an indented pattern that will hold the sauce; they will be slightly squished. Place the finished gnocchi on the prepared baking sheet and continue with the remaining dough. Cover these pieces on your work surface with a clean kitchen towel, then repeat steps 6 and 7 with the remaining dough.

⑧ Gather the gnocchi loosely in your hands and drop them into the boiling water. Stir well, then cook undisturbed until they float to the surface, about 2 minutes. Drain but do not rinse. Toss with a sauce while they're still warm.

Note: Gnocchi must only be made with Russet potatoes because of their unique starch/moisture balance.

The History of Durum Wheat—or Why We Make Pasta with Eggs

Italian pasta was once made solely from water and durum, a wheat with amazingly strong proteins and glutens (thus, known as a "hard" wheat). Back then, Italy was the global producer.

When pasta's popularity flashed across Europe in the late 1800s, wheat farmers came into boom times—so much so that other nations got in on the act. Italian farmers soon lost out to those on the more fertile Ukrainian steppes. Unfortunately, the Russian Revolution followed by two world wars brought about the near collapse of the Russian wheat industry. American entrepreneurs jumped into the gap. Today, most of the world's durum comes from North Dakota.

And almost all of it goes into commercial production. Milled durum (aka "semolina flour") occasionally shows up as "pasta flour" in high-end supermarkets, but even there it's hard to find. To complicate matters, what's marketed as semolina is sometimes not durum at all; any finely ground flour can be semolina, even rice flour.

For convenience' sake, we make pasta with all-purpose flour, the baking standard. Because it's a softer flour, it won't make a dough with water. Remember kindergarten? All-purpose flour and water make paste. So protein-rich eggs are added to make up for all-purpose flour's slacker structure.

Although this may appear at first blush to be just a list of pasta sauces, it's actually a section of sauced dishes: each sauce is offered as a complete pasta dish, noodles and all. You can, of course, pick and choose with wide latitude, although we've given our preference for the type of noodles with each sauce. We've divided the section into three parts: sauces that need minimal preparation, ones that require a little more, and ragùs, long simmered but worth the effort.

Sauced Pasta Dishes with Little Preparation

Pasta con Salsa Cruda (Pasta with a No-Cook Tomato Sauce)

This no-cook sauce is best when tomatoes are at their ripest. Prepare the sauce first so it can be tossed with the still-warm pasta. *Makes enough sauce for 1 pound fresh or 12 ounces dried pasta*

6 tablespoons extra virgin olive oil
½ teaspoon white wine vinegar
½ teaspoon sugar
¼ teaspoon salt
¼ teaspoon freshly ground black pepper
2 pounds ripe Italian plum tomatoes (about 8 tomatoes)
¼ cup chopped basil leaves
1 pound fresh or 12 ounces dried pasta, cooked and drained

❶ Whisk the olive oil, vinegar, sugar, salt, and pepper in a large bowl.

❷ Cut the tomatoes into several sections, then hold these over the sink or a trash can and scoop out the seeds and their membranes with a small spoon or your finger, thereby preserving the flesh. Roughly chop the flesh, then add it and the basil to the olive oil dressing. Stir well, then set aside for 5 to 10 minutes to marinate while you cook the pasta.

❸ Toss the drained, still-warm pasta with the fresh tomato sauce.

Pasta Recommendations
   Fresh: linguine, fettuccine, No-Yolk Pasta (page 171), and Gnocchi (page 177)
   Dried: any flat noodle; with macaroni, this sauce makes an easy pasta salad

Pasta with Pecan Pesto

This light, untraditional pesto matches well with fresh pasta. *Makes enough sauce for 1 pound fresh or 12 ounces dried pasta*

For the Pecan Pesto:
¼ cup pecan pieces
2 cups tightly packed basil leaves
¼ cup extra virgin olive oil
2 tablespoons water
½ teaspoon freshly ground black pepper
¼ teaspoon salt
1½ ounces Parmigiano-Reggiano, grated
2 garlic cloves, quartered

For the Noodles:
1 pound fresh or 12 ounces dried pasta, cooked and drained

① To make the Pecan Pesto, toast the pecans in a dry skillet set over medium-low heat until lightly browned and aromatic, about 4 minutes, stirring often. Pour into the bowl of a food processor fitted with the chopping blade and cool for 5 minutes.

② Add the basil, olive oil, water, pepper, salt, cheese, and garlic to the food processor. Close the lid and pulse a few times to break up the chunks. Scrape down the sides of the bowl with a rubber spatula and process until fairly smooth. Alternatively, grind the toasted pecans, basil, pepper, salt, and garlic in a mortar with a pestle; once finely ground, about like cornmeal, grind in the olive oil and water in small splashes, then stir in the cheese.

③ Pour the pesto over the still-warm noodles.

To store the pesto: Spoon it into a glass jar or a small plastic container, cover with a light film of olive oil, and refrigerate for up to 4 days.

Pasta Recommendations
   Fresh: almost any noodle, although wider-cut noodles give more tooth
   Dried: almost any shaped pasta like ziti or farfalle

Of all the culinary myths, the one about Marco Polo's bringing pasta back to Italy from the East may be the most persistent. But consider this: in 1279, among the catalog of effects from the estate of a Genoese gentleman, there's a reference to a basket of dried pasta. Marco Polo didn't make it back to Venice until 1298. Enough said.

Pasta with a Sautéed Garlic Sauce

All this simple, traditional Italian dish needs is a glass of red wine, some crunchy bread, and a vinegary salad. *Makes enough sauce for 1 pound fresh or 12 ounces dried pasta*

   6 garlic cloves, minced
   ⅓ cup olive oil
   ¼ teaspoon red pepper flakes
   1 pound fresh or 12 ounces dried pasta, cooked and drained
   ½ teaspoon salt
   ¼ cup chopped parsley leaves

① So that the garlic begins to infuse the oil even before it starts to cook, put the garlic and the oil in a large skillet, then set the skillet over very low heat. Cook, stirring occasionally, until the garlic softens and turns golden, about 7 minutes.

② Add the red pepper flakes, then the cooked pasta. Toss, then remove the skillet from the heat, and sprinkle on the salt and parsley.

Pasta Recommendations
   Fresh: thin pasta like cappellini or linguine, Beet Pasta (page 172)
   Dried: any flat or round noodle, preferably a thin noodle like linguine or spaghetti

Pasta with a Roasted Garlic Sauce

The sweetness of roasted garlic melts into the oil to create a luscious sauce. Use only fresh rosemary—dried rosemary won't have time to soften. *Makes enough sauce for 1 pound fresh or 12 ounces dried pasta*

   2 garlic heads, roasted (see page 460)
   ½ teaspoon salt
   ¼ teaspoon freshly ground black pepper
   3 tablespoons unsalted butter

2 tablespoons olive oil
1 tablespoon chopped rosemary leaves
1 pound fresh or 12 ounces dried pasta,
cooked and drained

1 Squeeze the roasted garlic out of the hulls and into a small bowl. Add the salt and pepper; mash with a fork until creamy.

2 Heat a large skillet over medium heat. Add the butter and olive oil. Once the butter has melted, stir in the mashed garlic puree and let it melt somewhat, stirring constantly. Add the rosemary and cook until fragrant, about 10 seconds. Add the pasta and toss to coat.

Pasta Recommendations
   Fresh: fettuccine, Whole Wheat Pasta (page 171), Beet Pasta (page 172)
   Dried: any flat or round noodle, particularly thicker noodles

Pasta with Butter and Fresh Herbs

Simple and rich, this is a great first course. Just don't pair it with a creamy main course. *Makes enough sauce for 1 pound fresh or 12 ounces dried pasta*

8 tablespoons (1 stick) unsalted butter
1 medium shallot, minced
2 tablespoons chopped rosemary leaves
1 tablespoon chopped oregano leaves
1 tablespoon stemmed thyme
1 pound fresh or 12 ounces dried pasta,
cooked and drained
2 tablespoons chopped parsley leaves
¼ to ½ teaspoon salt

1 Melt the butter in a large skillet over medium-low heat. Continue cooking just until the foam subsides. Do not let the butter brown; if it does, immediately remove the skillet from the heat.

2 Add the shallot and cook, stirring often, until softened, about 2 minutes. Add the rosemary, oregano, and thyme; cook just until wilted, about 5 seconds.

3 Toss in the pasta, parsley, and salt. Stir well and serve.

Pasta Recommendations
   Fresh: fettuccine, Spinach and Cheese Dumplings (page 177), or Gnocchi (page 177)
   Dried: flat, thin noodles such as linguine or tubular shapes like ziti

Pasta with Butter and Poppy Seeds: Omit the rosemary, oregano, and thyme; use 3 tablespoons poppy seeds in their stead.

Pasta with a Walnut Sauce

We're quite partial to this crunchy sauce. Double or even triple the garlic, if you like. *Makes enough sauce for 1 pound fresh or 12 ounces dried pasta*

½ cup walnut pieces
¼ cup plain dried bread crumbs
½ teaspoon salt
¼ teaspoon freshly ground black pepper
3 tablespoons walnut oil
3 tablespoons unsalted butter
2 garlic cloves, minced
1 pound fresh or 12 ounces dried pasta,
cooked and drained

1 Heat a large nonstick skillet over medium heat. Add the walnuts and toast until lightly browned and aromatic, about 4 minutes, tossing frequently. Empty into the bowl of a food processor; cool for 10 minutes. Add the bread crumbs, salt, and pepper; process until finely ground. Set aside.

2 Return the skillet to medium heat and add the walnut oil and butter. When the butter has melted, add the garlic. Sauté just until softened, about 2 minutes. Add the cooked pasta, toss, and transfer to a serving bowl. Sprinkle the ground walnut mixture over the top before serving.

Pasta Recommendations
  Fresh: linguine or even thinner-cut pasta, Whole Wheat Pasta (page 171)
  Dried: any flat or round dried pasta, particularly thinner shapes like spaghetti

Pasta Dishes with Moderate Preparation

Pasta Marinara

Look no further for the most versatile pasta sauce.
Makes about 2 cups

  2 tablespoons olive oil
  1 medium onion, finely chopped
  2 garlic cloves, minced
  1 tablespoon minced oregano or 2 teaspoons dried oregano
  1 tablespoon stemmed thyme or 2 teaspoons dried thyme
  One 28-ounce can whole tomatoes (3½ cups)
  1 bay leaf
  ¼ teaspoon grated nutmeg
  ¼ teaspoon salt
  ¼ teaspoon freshly ground black pepper
  1 pound fresh or 12 ounces dried pasta, cooked and drained

1 Heat a medium saucepan over medium heat. Pour in the olive oil, then add the onion and sauté until soft, about 2 minutes, stirring frequently. Add the garlic, oregano, and thyme; sauté just until you can really smell the herbs, about 10 seconds.

2 Pour in the tomatoes and crush them with a wooden spoon or a pastry cutter. The sauce should be chunky, but with no large pieces. Add the bay leaf and nutmeg; bring the sauce to a simmer.

3 Reduce the heat to low and simmer, uncovered, until thickened, about 20 minutes. You want a wet sauce, not too thick, but also not soupy. Season with salt and pepper. To serve, place about 1 cup of the sauce in a serving bowl or platter. Top with the warm noodles, then pour on the rest of the sauce.

To store: Omit the pasta and spoon the sauce into a plastic container or a ziplock freezer bag; store in the refrigerator for up to 3 days or in the freezer for up to 1 month.

Pasta Recommendations: Any fresh or dried pasta

Four Adaptations of Marinara Sauce

Pasta Fra Diavolo: Omit the thyme and nutmeg, increase the garlic to 4 cloves, and add 1 to 2 teaspoons red pepper flakes with the oregano.

Pasta à la Vodka: Drain the tomatoes before you add them to the sauce; add ¾ cup vodka with them (be careful of alcohol around an open flame). Once the sauce has simmered and thickened, stir in 1 cup heavy cream, bring the sauce to a full boil, and cook for an additional 3 minutes at high heat, just to let the cream condense. Although we prefer a chunky vodka sauce, you can use an immersion blender off the heat to turn this into a smooth sauce, or you can cool the sauce for a few minutes, then pour it into a large blender or food processor and puree the sauce.

Pasta Puttanesca: Omit the nutmeg and salt. Add ¼ cup chopped pitted black olives, 2 tablespoons rinsed capers, and 4 chopped anchovy fillets with the oregano and thyme.

Basic Pizza Sauce: Omit the pasta. Cool the sauce, then place it in a food processor fitted with the chopping blade. Add 1 teaspoon sugar; pulse just until any big chunks are blended, but not until the sauce is smooth. Use this as a topping to your favorite pizza; store whatever's left over in a plastic bag or container in the freezer for up to 1 month.

Four Easy Marinara Dishes

Pasta Marinara with Clams: Stir 2 pounds clams, cleaned of any sand, into the pot during the last few minutes of cooking. Cover the pot and cook until the clams open, about 3 minutes. Discard any clams that do not open.

Pasta Marinara with Shrimp: Stir in 1½ pounds cleaned and deveined medium shrimp (about 35 per pound) during the last few minutes of cooking. Cover the pan and cook until the shrimp are pink and firm, about 2 minutes.

Pasta Marinara with Squid: Sauté 1 pound cleaned squid, cut into rings, in a large skillet set over medium heat with 1 tablespoon olive oil until cooked through, about 3 minutes (see page 72 for tips on how to clean squid). Add the contents of the skillet to the marinara during the last 2 or 3 minutes of cooking.

Mussels Marinara: Forget the pasta altogether. During the last few minutes of cooking, add 2 pounds mussels, cleaned and debearded (see page 360), to the sauce. Cover and simmer about 2 minutes, just until the mussels open. Discard any that do not open.

Three More Substantial Marinara Dishes

I. Marinara and Meatballs

Make these simple meatballs, fry them up, and set them aside—then make the marinara in another pan. The meatballs are best if they're browned, then simmered in the sauce. *Makes 4 servings, about 16 meatballs*

½ pound ground veal or ground beef, preferably 80% lean
½ pound sweet Italian sausage, casings removed
½ cup plain dried bread crumbs
1 large egg, at room temperature, lightly beaten
¼ cup milk (regular, low-fat, or fat-free)
2 tablespoons chopped parsley leaves
¼ teaspoon ground allspice
¼ teaspoon salt
¼ teaspoon freshly ground black pepper
2 tablespoons olive oil
4 cups (that is, a double batch) Marinara Sauce (page 182) without the pasta or 4 cups purchased marinara sauce
1 pound fresh or 12 ounces dried noodles (do not use shaped pasta), cooked and drained
2 ounces Parmigiano-Reggiano, grated, for garnish, optional

1 Mix the veal or beef, sausage, bread crumbs, egg, milk, parsley, allspice, salt, and pepper in a large bowl with a wooden spoon, taking care not to mush the meat's fibers but making sure everything is well combined.

2 Wet your hands, then shape 2 tablespoons of the mixture into a ball. Continue making balls this size, lining them on a plate.

3 Heat a large skillet over medium heat. Pour in 1 tablespoon olive oil, then place about half the meatballs in the skillet. Brown on all sides, turning often, about 6 minutes. Transfer to a plate lined with paper towels. Add the remaining oil and fry the second batch of meatballs. (The meatballs can be made in advance; cover and refrigerate for up to 48 hours.)

4 Make or heat up the Marinara Sauce. Once it's simmering, add the meatballs and cook them in the sauce as it reduces, about 20 minutes.

5 Place the pasta in a serving bowl or platter. Add the sauce and meatballs on top. If desired, sprinkle the grated cheese over the dish.

II. No-Fry Eggplant Marinara Casserole

We've taken some of the weight out of this Italian-American favorite to give brighter, fresher flavors. *Makes 6 servings*

 2 medium eggplants, sliced into ½-inch
   rings
 2 teaspoons salt
 Nonstick spray
 6 ounces Parmigiano-Reggiano, shaved into
   thin strips
 4 cups (that is, a double recipe) Marinara
   Sauce (page 182) without the pasta or
   4 cups purchased marinara sauce

1 Lightly salt the eggplant slices and stand them up in a colander or lay them out on paper towels on the counter to sweat for 15 minutes. Meanwhile, position the racks in the top and bottom thirds of the oven and preheat the oven to 375°F.

2 Blot the eggplant dry with paper towels. Spray two lipped baking sheets with nonstick spray and lay the eggplant slices evenly and in one layer across them.

3 Place one tray on each rack and bake for 10 minutes. Turn the slices over, then reverse the trays top to bottom. Continue baking until the slices are a little dried out and firm, about 10 more minutes. After you remove them from the oven, lower the top rack so that it's in the middle of the oven (be careful—it's hot) and maintain the oven's temperature.

4 Spoon about 1 cup Marinara Sauce into a 13 × 9-inch baking dish. Lay half the eggplant slices in the dish, making a layer. Top them with half the shaved cheese. Spoon and spread about 1½ cups Marinara Sauce over the cheese. Place the remaining eggplant slices in the pan as a single layer, then place the remaining cheese on top of them. Spoon the remaining Marinara Sauce over the casserole.

5 Bake in the middle of the oven until bubbling, about 25 minutes. Let stand at room temperature for 5 minutes before serving.

III. Baked Pasta Marinara Casserole with Blue Cheese, Peas, and Artichoke Hearts

Here's comfort food with pancetta, peas, and artichoke hearts—and three kinds of cheese. *Makes 8 servings*

 2 tablespoons unsalted butter
 6 ounces pancetta, diced
 1 teaspoon red pepper flakes
 4 cups (that is, a double batch) Marinara
   Sauce (page 182) without the pasta
   or 4 cups purchased marinara
   sauce

1 pound dried, shaped pasta, such as fusilli, farfalle, ziti, penne, or rigate, cooked and drained

One 10-ounce bag frozen peas, thawed

One 10-ounce package frozen artichoke hearts, thawed and quartered

8 ounces provolone, mozzarella, Swiss, Emmentaler, Gruyère, shredded or diced

6 ounces Parmigiano-Reggiano, Asiago, or ricotta salata, grated

4 ounces Gorgonzola, cambozola, or Danish blue, crumbled

1 Position the rack in the center of the oven and preheat the oven to 350°F.

2 Melt the butter in a large skillet over medium heat. Add the pancetta and cook until frizzled and crispy, about 3 minutes. Stir in the red pepper flakes, then pour the contents of the pan into a large bowl. Mix in the Marinara Sauce, cooked pasta, peas, and artichoke hearts.

3 Combine the cheeses in a second bowl.

4 In a 13 × 9-inch baking pan or a 3-quart, high-sided, round casserole, layer the ingredients in this order: a third of the pasta mixture, a third of the cheese, half the remaining pasta mixture, half the remaining cheese, the remaining pasta mixture, and the remaining cheese (see Note).

5 Bake, uncovered, until bubbling and gooey, about 30 minutes for a 13 × 9-inch pan or 45 minutes for the round casserole. Let stand at room temperature for 10 minutes before serving.

Note: A 13 × 9-inch baking pan makes a crunchier casserole; a high-sided round one makes a creamier casserole.

Pasta with Cream Sauce

Along with the Marinara Sauce (page 182), Cream Sauce is the other pasta topper that can be varied endlessly; it is the basis for Pasta Alfredo and a host of other dishes. *Makes about 2 cups sauce*

3 tablespoons unsalted butter

1½ tablespoons all-purpose flour

1 cup whole milk

1 cup heavy cream

2 ounces Parmigiano-Reggiano or Grana Padano, grated

Freshly ground white pepper to taste (see Note)

1 pound fresh or 12 ounces dried pasta, cooked and drained

1 Melt the butter in a large saucepan over low heat. Sprinkle the flour over the melted butter, wait for 5 seconds, then whisk until smooth. Do not brown the flour, but do let it cook about 15 seconds, whisking all the while, just so it loses its raw taste.

2 Whisk in the milk in a slow, steady stream. Whisking all the while, let the mixture come to a simmer and cook slowly for 1 minute. (Be careful: the sauce can clump if you're not paying close attention. If it does, you'll have to start over.)

3 Whisk in the cream. Cook, whisking constantly, until the sauce bubbles.

4 Remove the pan from the heat and whisk in the cheese until it melts. Season with pepper, add the pasta, and toss.

Note: White pepper is for aesthetics. If you use black pepper, you'll simply have dark specks in the sauce.

Fresh: fettuccine, tagliatelle, pappardelle
Dried: any round noodle

Variations: Add any of these herbs to the sauce with the cheese: 2 tablespoons chopped parsley leaves, 2 tablespoons chopped tarragon leaves, 2 tablespoons stemmed thyme, or 1 tablespoon chopped rosemary leaves.

To make a garlicky cream sauce, mince 3 garlic cloves and soften them in the melted butter for 1 minute before whisking in the flour.

To make a roasted garlic cream sauce, roast 2 garlic heads, following the instructions on page 460. Cool, then squeeze the roasted garlic into the oil before you add the flour, stirring it up so that it melts somewhat into the oil.

Six Sauces from Cream Sauce

Pasta Alfredo: Double the cheese, adding either 4 ounces grated Parmigiano-Reggiano or 2 ounces grated Parmigiano-Reggiano and 2 ounces grated Pecorino Romano.

Pasta Primavera: Add one 10-ounce bag frozen peas and carrots, thawed, or frozen mixed vegetables, thawed, with the cheese.

Pasta and Asparagus: Cut 1 pound pencil-thin asparagus spears into 1-inch pieces. Add these to the cream sauce with the cheese; let the pan stand off the heat for 3 minutes before adding the pasta.

Pasta, Ham, and Peas: Sauté 1 cup chopped ham in the butter before you add the flour. Stir one 10-ounce bag frozen peas into the sauce with the cream.

Pasta, Prosciutto, and Cream Sauce: Roughly chop 1/4 pound thinly sliced prosciutto; briefly sauté this in the butter before you add the flour.

Pasta with Gorgonzola Sauce: Stir 2 ounces crumbled Gorgonzola into the sauce with the Parmigiano-Reggiano.

Pasta Carbonara

Although a traditional carbonara is not made with cream, its addition keeps the yolks from breaking and makes this classic easier to make at home.

Makes enough sauce for 1 pound fresh or 12 ounces dried pasta

6 ounces bacon slices, chopped

4 garlic cloves, minced

1/3 cup heavy cream

1 pound fresh or 12 ounces dried pasta, cooked and drained

2 ounces Parmigiano-Reggiano, grated

2 ounces Asiago or Pecorino Romano, grated

2 large eggs, at room temperature, lightly beaten

1/4 teaspoon freshly ground black pepper

1 Heat a large skillet over medium-high heat. Add the bacon and cook, stirring occasionally, until browned and frizzled, about 3 minutes. Use a slotted spoon to transfer the bacon bits to a plate lined with paper towels; drain all but 1 tablespoon bacon fat from the skillet.

2 Place the skillet over medium heat. Add the garlic and sauté just until softened, about 30 seconds, stirring constantly. Stir in the bacon bits and cream; remove the pan from the heat.

3 Add the cooked pasta, toss quickly, then add both kinds of cheese and the eggs all at once. Stir quickly and steadily with a wooden spoon—the eggs should emulsify into the cream and cheese without scrambling. Season with pepper.

Pasta Recommendations
Fresh: fettuccine, tagliatelle, Whole Wheat Pasta (page 171)
Dried: any flat noodle

Pasta Arrabbiata

Here's an Italian classic, but with less fat and a lot more spike. Clam juice gives it a richness that matches well with the heat. *Makes enough sauce for 1 pound fresh or 12 ounces dried pasta*

1 tablespoon olive oil
1 tablespoon unsalted butter
3 garlic cloves, minced
1½ to 2½ teaspoons red pepper flakes, or
    more to taste
One 28-ounce can diced tomatoes (3½ cups)
One 8-ounce bottle clam juice or ½ cup Fish
    Stock (page 166)
¼ teaspoon salt
1 pound fresh or 12 ounces dried pasta,
    cooked and drained
¼ cup chopped parsley leaves

1 Heat a large saucepan over medium heat. Add the olive oil and butter. The moment the butter melts, add the garlic and sauté just until aromatic, about 15 seconds. Stir in the red pepper flakes and sauté for 5 seconds.

2 Pour in the tomatoes and the clam juice or fish stock. Bring the mixture to a simmer, then reduce the heat to low and simmer at the merest bubble until thick, about 20 minutes. Season with salt.

3 Place the cooked pasta in a serving bowl, add the sauce, and top with the parsley.

Pasta Recommendations
    Fresh: not advisable because the spicy sauce can overpower delicate, soft, fresh pasta
    Dried: any noodle, particularly thin noodles, even capelli d'angelo (angel hair); Spinach Pasta (page 173).

Variations: Add 1 pound peeled and deveined medium shrimp (about 35 per pound), 1½ pounds clams, cleaned of any sand, or 1½ pounds mussels, cleaned of any sand and debearded, during the last few minutes of cooking. Stir them in, cover the pan, and cook until the shrimp turn pink and firm or until the clams and mussels open (discard any that don't).

Pasta Pomodoro

This is a buttery tomato sauce that holds up to almost any noodle. *Makes enough sauce for 1 pound fresh or 12 ounces dried pasta*

6 tablespoons unsalted butter, cut into
    chunks
1 large onion, chopped
2 pounds Italian plum tomatoes (about 8),
    chopped
½ teaspoon salt
¼ teaspoon freshly ground black
    pepper
1 pound fresh or 12 ounces dried pasta,
    cooked and drained
2 ounces Parmigiano-Reggiano, grated

1 Place 4 tablespoons butter and the onion in a medium saucepan and then set it over very low heat. As the butter melts, stir the onions frequently so they're coated in it. Cook, stirring often, until the onions soften and turn golden, about 10 minutes.

2 Raise the heat to medium and add the tomatoes. Stir well and continue cooking until they break down and form a thickened sauce, about 10 minutes.

3 Swirl in the remaining 2 tablespoons butter until it melts. Season with salt and pepper, then add the pasta and cheese.

Pasta Recommendations
    Fresh: tagliatelle, pappardelle, Beet Pasta (page 172), Chestnut Pasta (page 172)
    Dried: any wide round or flat noodle such as bucatini or fettuccine

Pasta with Clams and Cherry Tomatoes

Clams are a gorgeous match to cherry tomatoes.
Makes enough sauce for 1 pound fresh or 12 ounces dried pasta

¼ cup olive oil
4 garlic cloves, minced
¼ cup dry vermouth
1¾ pounds small clams, such as littlenecks, their shells scrubbed of any sand
16 cherry tomatoes, quartered
12 basil leaves, shredded
1 pound fresh or 12 ounces dried pasta, cooked and drained
2 ounces Parmigiano-Reggiano, grated
Freshly ground black pepper to taste

❶ Heat a large saucepan over medium heat. Add the olive oil, then the garlic. Sauté until golden, about 2 minutes, stirring often.

❷ Pour in the vermouth, then add the clams. Cover the pan and cook until the clams open, about 3 minutes. Discard any that do not open.

❸ Stir in the cherry tomatoes and basil. Cook just until the tomatoes soften, about 1 minute, stirring occasionally.

❹ Stir in the pasta. Remove the pan from the heat. Stir in the cheese, then transfer to a serving bowl. Give the dish a few grinds of pepper before serving.

Pasta Recommendations
    Fresh: thinner noodles like cappellini
    Dried: any medium-flat noodle like fettuccine

Pasta with Cockles and Cherry Tomatoes: Substitute cockles for the clams. Clean them of any sand; discard any that do not open during cooking. Use a very thin noodle to catch the little cockles.

Pasta with Sausage and Broccoli Raab

If you have homemade stock on hand, use 1 cup without boiling it down. *Makes enough sauce for 1 pound fresh or 12 ounces dried pasta*

2 cups canned chicken or beef broth
2 tablespoons olive oil
1 pound Italian sausage, chicken, turkey, or pork, hot or mild, thinly sliced
2 garlic cloves, thinly sliced
¼ cup dry vermouth
½ teaspoon grated nutmeg
12 ounces broccoli raab (about 2 packed cups), chopped into 1-inch pieces
1 pound fresh or 12 ounces dried pasta, cooked and drained
2 ounces Parmigiano-Reggiano cheese, grated

❶ To concentrate its flavors, place the broth in a medium saucepan set over high heat. Bring it to a boil and cook until reduced to 1 cup, about 4 minutes. Set aside.

❷ Heat a large skillet over medium heat. Add the olive oil, then the sausage. Cook until golden and somewhat firm, about 3 minutes. Drain all but 2 tablespoons of fat from the skillet.

③ Return the skillet to medium heat and add the vermouth, scraping up any browned bits on the bottom of the pan. When the sauce comes to a boil, pour in the reduced broth, then add the broccoli raab. Cover and simmer until softened, about 2 minutes.

④ Uncover the skillet, add the pasta and cheese, and toss well.

Pasta Recommendations
 Fresh: any wide noodle, from fettuccine to pappardelle, Spinach Pasta (page 173)
 Dried: thicker round or flat noodles, or shaped spirals like fusilli

Pasta with Mushrooms and Sage

This simple sauce adheres to our rule for all cream sauces: a little cream goes a long way. *Makes enough sauce for 1 pound fresh or 12 ounces dried pasta*

 3 tablespoons unsalted butter
 4 garlic cloves, minced
 ½ pound cremini or white button mushrooms, cleaned of any dirt and sliced
 ¼ cup heavy cream
 ¼ cup dry white wine
 2 tablespoons minced sage leaves
 1 pound fresh or 12 ounces dried pasta, cooked and drained
 2 ounces Asiago, Pecorino Romano, or Grana Padano, grated
 ½ teaspoon freshly ground black pepper
 ¼ teaspoon salt

① Heat the butter in a large skillet set over medium heat. The moment the foam subsides, and well before the butter browns, add the garlic and cook until softened, about 2 minutes, stirring often.

② Add the mushrooms and continue cooking until they give off their moisture and it mostly evaporates, about 3 minutes, stirring frequently.

③ Add the cream, wine, and sage; bring the mixture to a simmer.

④ Add the pasta, cheese, pepper, and salt. Toss well over the heat and serve at once.

Pasta Recommendations
 Fresh: pappardelle, Whole Wheat Pasta (page 171), Butternut Squash Pasta (page 173)
 Dried: almost any shaped pasta or very thick-cut noodles

Variations: Substitute brandy or Cognac for the vermouth. If the sauce flames, cover the pan immediately and remove it from the heat.

Pasta Melanzane

Eggplant and olive oil are a luxurious combination. Make sure you use a high-quality oil, one with lots of flavor. For an easy variation, susbstitute lemon- or rosemary-flavored oil. *Makes enough sauce for 1 pound fresh or 12 ounces dried pasta*

 1 large eggplant (about 1½ pounds), cut into ½-inch-thick slices
 2 teaspoons salt
 ¼ cup olive oil
 1¾ cups canned or fresh diced tomatoes with their juice
 ½ cup dry red wine
 1 tablespoon minced oregano leaves
 ¼ teaspoon red pepper flakes
 ¼ teaspoon freshly ground black pepper
 1 pound fresh or 12 ounces dried pasta, cooked and drained

1 Sprinkle the eggplant slices with the salt, then stand them up in a colander to drain in the sink or spread them out on paper towels on the counter. After 15 minutes, blot the slices dry, then cut into strips about ½ inch wide.

2 Heat a large, high-sided skillet over medium heat. Add about 2 tablespoons of the oil, then slip as many eggplant strips as will fit comfortably in the pan. Fry until soft and tender, about 3 minutes. Transfer the strips to a large plate lined with paper towels, add the remaining oil to the skillet, and cook the remaining eggplant strips as you did the first batch. Transfer these to a second plate lined with paper towels. Blot all the slices dry.

3 Return the strips to the skillet, set it over medium heat, and add the tomatoes, wine, oregano, red pepper flakes, and pepper. Bring the sauce to a simmer, then cover the pan with the lid askew, and reduce the heat to very low, just so the sauce bubbles slowly. Cook until somewhat thickened, about 10 minutes.

4 Stir in the pasta and toss to coat.

Pasta Recommendations
   Fresh: not advisable because the soft texture of the sauce needs the firmer texture of dried pasta
   Dried: any noodle or shaped pasta, particularly tubes like ziti, penne, or rigatoni

Ragù

Ragùs are thick, rich sauces, many of them long-simmered and all of them time-consuming in their own way. No, they're probably not weeknight fare; but any of them will make the most memorable Saturday evening dinner with friends.

Ragù Bolognese

This is the classic, the one you'll make again and again. You can double or triple it at will. It also stores well: freeze it in a resealable plastic container for up to 3 months. *Makes enough sauce for 1 pound fresh or 12 ounces dried pasta*

   2 tablespoons olive oil
   2 tablespoons unsalted butter
   1 medium onion, chopped
   2 celery ribs, thinly sliced into crescents
   1 carrot, peeled and thinly sliced
   2 garlic cloves, minced
   ½ pound ground beef, preferably 80% lean
   ¼ pound ground pork
   ⅔ cup milk, regular or low-fat
   ¼ teaspoon grated nutmeg
   1 cup white wine, preferably an Italian white
   One 28-ounce can whole tomatoes, preferably Italian plum tomatoes, crushed or cut up in the can with kitchen shears (3½ cups)
   2 teaspoons minced oregano leaves or 1 teaspoon dried oregano
   ½ teaspoon salt
   Beef broth, as needed
   1 pound fresh or 12 ounces dried pasta, cooked and drained
   1 ounce Parmigiano-Reggiano, grated
   ¼ teaspoon freshly ground black pepper

1 Heat a large saucepan over medium heat. Add the olive oil and butter. When the butter melts, add the onion and cook just until translucent, about 2 minutes.

② Add the celery and carrot; cook until glistening and slightly softened, about 1 minute. Add the garlic and cook until fragrant, about 20 seconds, stirring constantly.

③ Crumble in the beef and pork with a fork, taking care to keep the meat's fibers intact but not to leave any large clumps. Stir a few times; the moment the meat loses its pink raw color, stir in the milk and nutmeg. Raise the heat to medium-high and cook, stirring once in a while, until the milk has almost evaporated, about 4 minutes.

④ Stir in the wine, scraping up any browned bits on the pan's bottom. Keep the heat fairly high and continue simmering until the wine has reduced by half.

⑤ Stir in the tomatoes, oregano, and salt. When the mixture comes to a simmer, turn the heat to very low. Simmer, uncovered, at the slightest bubble, just a pop or two, for about 1 hour. You want the sauce to thicken considerably but you must not let it dry out. If it does, add beef broth in ¼-cup increments—but do not allow it to get soupy. It's a delicate balance; just remember: this is a meat sauce, not a tomato sauce.

⑥ To serve, spoon about ½ cup of the sauce in the bottom of a large bowl or serving platter. Top with the hot pasta, then the remainder of the ragù. Sprinkle the grated cheese and pepper over the top.

Pasta Recommendations
Fresh: tagliatelle, No-Yolk Pasta (page 171), Whole Wheat Pasta (page 171)
Dried: any flat noodle

Rabbit Ragù

This is a simpler version of ragù, more complex than a simple pasta sauce, but not as time-consuming as a standard ragù. The rabbit meat is moist and quite luxurious. *Makes enough sauce for 1 pound fresh or 12 ounces dried pasta*

> 2 tablespoons olive oil
> 1 small rabbit (about 1½ pounds), cut into large pieces (see Note)
> 1 medium onion, chopped
> 2 carrots, chopped
> 1 cup chicken broth
> ¼ cup dry white wine, preferably an oaky wine like a Chardonnay
> 1 bay leaf
> 1 pound Roma or plum tomatoes (about 4 large tomatoes), chopped
> 1 tablespoon stemmed thyme
> ½ teaspoon salt
> ½ teaspoon freshly ground black pepper
> ⅛ teaspoon ground cloves
> 1 pound fresh or 12 ounces dried pasta, cooked and drained

① Heat a large, high-sided sauté pan or a Dutch oven over medium heat. Add the olive oil, then the rabbit pieces. You may need to work in batches, depending on the size of your pan. Brown the rabbit on all sides, about 3 minutes, turning occasionally.

② Once all the rabbit pieces are browned, place them all in the pan, in one layer if possible, and add the onion and carrots. Cook just until the vegetables start to soften, about 1 minute; then pour in the broth and wine. Scrape up any browned bits on the bottom of the pan and tuck in the bay leaf.

③ Cover the pan, reduce the heat to low, and simmer until the rabbit meat is tender enough to fall off the bones, about 40 minutes.

4 Use a slotted spoon to transfer the rabbit pieces to a colander set in the sink. Remove the pan from the heat; discard the bay leaf.

5 Once the rabbit is cool enough to handle, take the meat off the bones, taking care to discard any cartilage but also to keep the meat in strips or pieces. Discard the bones and joints. Chop any large pieces into chunks.

6 Skim any fat in the sauce, then return the pan to medium heat. Add the tomatoes and bring the mixture to a simmer. Cook until the tomatoes break down and the sauce thickens somewhat, about 5 minutes.

7 Stir in the prepared rabbit meat, thyme, salt, pepper, and cloves. Toss with the cooked pasta to serve.

Note: If you're squeamish about cutting up a rabbit, or if you're unsure of its anatomy, ask your butcher to do this for you.

Pasta Recommendations
   Fresh: pappardelle, Chestnut Pasta (page 172), Spinach Pasta (page 173)
   Dried: any wide, flat noodle

For a lighter ragù that needs no pasta, try the monkfish version, page 342.

Lamb Ragù

Here's an unusual ragù, silky and intense. The deep flavors will mask any delicate pasta, so forgo grated cheese and pair it with plain egg noodles. *Makes enough sauce for 1 pound fresh or 12 ounces dried pasta*

   3 tablespoons olive oil
   1 large onion, chopped
   2 medium carrots, peeled and sliced into
      thin rings
   4 garlic cloves, minced
   1 pound boneless leg of lamb, cut into
      ¼-inch pieces (see Note)
   1 tablespoon all-purpose flour
   2 tablespoons packed chopped sage leaves
   2 tablespoons chopped rosemary leaves
   ¼ teaspoon freshly ground black pepper
   2 cups chicken or beef broth
   1½ cups dry white wine, preferably an oaky
      wine like a California Chardonnay
   ¼ cup tomato paste
   ¼ teaspoon salt
   1 pound fresh or 12 ounces dried pasta,
      cooked and drained

1 Heat a large saucepan over medium heat. Swirl in the olive oil, then add the onion and carrots. Sauté until soft, about 3 minutes. Add the garlic and sauté just until aromatic, about 20 seconds.

2 Add the lamb and brown it fairly well, stirring often, for about 3 minutes.

3 Sprinkle the flour over the lamb, stir well, and cook for 20 seconds, stirring constantly, just to get rid of the flour's raw taste. Do not brown the flour.

4 Add the sage, rosemary, and pepper. Cook for 15 seconds, then stir in the broth and wine, scraping up any browned bits on the pan's bottom. Raise the heat to medium-high and bring the mixture to a simmer, stirring all the while.

5 Stir in the tomato paste until it has melted. Reduce the heat to very low and simmer at the merest bubble for 30 minutes with the lid partially askew, stirring well and often to prevent sticking.

6 Cover the pot and continue simmering until the lamb is quite tender, about 30 minutes, stirring every once in a while. Season with salt before serving.

7 To serve, place about ¼ cup in the bottom of a large serving bowl or platter. Mound the pasta on top, then pour the rest of the ragù over it.

Note: These are tiny pieces, like a small dice. As you work with the meat, remove any tendons, fat, or leathery silverskin (a translucent, tough membrane that runs along the muscle). You'll need a sharp, heavy knife for this task.

To store: The lamb ragù can be cooled completely and then stored in a resealable plastic or glass container in the refrigerator for up to 3 days or in the freezer for up to 1 month.

Pasta Recommendations
    Fresh: not advisable because the sauce's strong flavors easily overpower soft noodles
    Dried: any round, tubular noodle

Chicken Liver Ragù

We first learned about this Italian classic from Marcella Hazan. We've simplified her recipe and taken out some of the fat, but it'll still take the chill off a winter day. *Makes enough sauce for 1 pound fresh or 12 ounces dried pasta*

    2 tablespoons olive oil
    1 tablespoon unsalted butter
    1 medium onion, roughly chopped
    3 garlic cloves, minced

½ pound chicken livers, any discolored spots
    and all fat removed, roughly chopped
⅓ pound ground pork or veal
¼ cup dry white wine or dry vermouth
1 cup chicken broth
2 teaspoons stemmed thyme or 1 teaspoon
    dried thyme
¼ cup heavy cream
1 tablespoon tomato paste
¼ teaspoon salt
¼ teaspoon freshly ground black pepper
1 pound fresh or 12 ounces dried pasta,
    cooked and drained
1 ounce Parmigiano-Reggiano, grated
¼ teaspoon grated nutmeg

1 Heat a large saucepan over medium heat. Add the olive oil and butter. When the butter has melted, add the onion. Sauté, stirring frequently, until softened, about 2 minutes. Add the garlic and cook for just 15 seconds.

2 Add the chicken livers and the ground pork or veal, breaking the latter apart with a fork. Cook, stirring constantly, just until the livers lose their raw color, about 2 minutes.

3 Stir in the wine or vermouth, scraping up any browned bits on the bottom of the pan. When the wine or vermouth comes to a full simmer, stir in the broth and thyme. Reduce the heat to very low and simmer, partially covered, at a very slow bubble until the livers are tender, about 10 minutes, stirring often.

4 Stir in the cream and tomato paste. Raise the heat and let the sauce come to a full boil, then remove from the heat and season with salt and pepper.

5 Spoon some of the warm sauce in the bottom of a large bowl or platter. Add the pasta, then pour the remaining sauce over the top. Sprinkle with the cheese and nutmeg.

To store: Place in a resealable container in the refrigerator for up to 3 days or in the freezer for up to 1 month.

Pasta Recommendations
   Fresh: thick, wide noodles, Spinach Pasta (page 173), Whole Wheat Pasta (page 171)
   Dried: any wide, flat noodle

Dan Dan Ragù

Our last, very spicy ragù is a world away from the others—from China, to be exact. *Makes enough sauce for 1 pound fresh or 12 ounces dried pasta*

   3 tablespoons sesame oil
   3 tablespoons Shaoxing or dry sherry
   2 tablespoons soy sauce
   2 tablespoons minced peeled fresh ginger
   ¾ pound ground pork or ground beef, preferably 80% lean
   1 tablespoon peanut oil
   4 scallions, thinly sliced
   4 garlic cloves, thinly sliced
   1 medium carrot, peeled and sliced into thin rings
   1 teaspoon sugar
   1¾ cups chicken broth
   2 teaspoons Asian red chile paste
   1 tablespoon natural-style peanut butter or tahini
   1 tablespoon rice vinegar
   1 pound fresh or 12 ounces dried egg noodles, cooked and drained
   ¼ cup chopped roasted unsalted peanuts

❶ Whisk the sesame oil, Shaoxing or sherry, soy sauce, and ginger in a medium bowl. Crumble in the beef or pork, stir to coat thoroughly, cover, and refrigerate for at least 4 hours or overnight.

Let the mixture sit at room temperature for 15 minutes before proceeding with the recipe.

❷ Heat a large saucepan over medium heat. Swirl in the peanut oil, then add the scallions, garlic, and carrot. Sauté just until the scallions turn translucent, about 2 minutes. Do not let the garlic brown.

❸ Crumble the pork or beef into the pan with a fork; add any remaining marinade in the bowl. Cook just until the meat loses its raw, pink color, about 1 minute.

❹ Sprinkle the sugar over the meat, then stir in the broth, scraping up any browned bits on the bottom of the pan. Bring the mixture to a simmer, then stir in the chili paste and peanut butter or tahini.

❺ Reduce the heat to very low, so the sauce bubbles at just the slightest simmer. Set a lid askew over the pan and cook until the pork or beef is very tender and the sauce has thickened somewhat, about 15 minutes, stirring occasionally.

❻ Stir in the vinegar. To serve, mound the noodles on a serving platter or in a deep bowl. Top with the sauce, then sprinkle the peanuts over the dish.

To store: Keep in a resealable plastic or glass container in the refrigerator for up to 4 days or in the freezer for up to 1 month.

Pasta Recommendations
   Fresh: not advisable since the sauce needs a pasta with more tooth
   Dried: Any Asian egg noodle (see page 213), dried udon noodles, or dried soba noodles

❋ *Stuffed Pasta: Shells, Manicotti, Ravioli, and Cappelletti* ❋

It's a four-step process: (1) make the filling, (2) make the dough, (3) shape and stuff it, and (4) sauce or bake it. Naturally, choose the filling, dough, and sauce before you start to make a dish. Stuffed pastas are great to make at parties—get your guests in on the act: open a bottle of Pinot Gris and soon everyone's making ravioli.

Step 1: Make the filling.

Each of the following fillings was designed to make 1 pound fresh ravioli or cappelletti. If you're making manicotti or stuffed shells, double the filling recipe.

While the fillings were designed to work with almost any stuffed pasta, we recommend filling shells and manicotti with Basic Cheese, Lemon Ricotta, Squash and Goat Cheese, Artichoke, Bacon and Potato, or Ground Veal (the latter three will not work with a pastry bag; use a small spoon—see pages 199–200 for stuffing instructions).

As a rule, ravioli and cappelletti can be stuffed with any of the fillings, although Artichoke, Ground Veal, and Crab may prove a bit too chunky for cappelletti and can pierce the small shapes.

If you want to sauce stuffed pasta with Cream Sauce or one of its variations (pages 185–186), use a noncheese filling like Chestnut. If you're going to use a thicker sauce like one of the ragùs, use a simple filling like Cheese or Caramelized Leek.

The Ten Fillings

1. Cheese Filling

Makes a little more than 1½ cups

1 cup ricotta, regular or low-fat (do not use fat-free)
4 ounces mozzarella, preferably fresh mozzarella, shredded
4 ounces Parmigiano-Reggiano, grated
1 large egg yolk
¼ teaspoon grated nutmeg
¼ teaspoon salt
¼ teaspoon freshly ground black pepper

Use a wooden spoon to combine all the ingredients in a medium bowl. (Do not whisk—the ricotta will liquefy.) Use at once or cover and refrigerate for up to 2 days.

2. Lemon Ricotta Filling

Makes a little more than 1½ cups

1½ cups ricotta, regular or low-fat (do not use fat-free)
2 ounces Parmigiano-Reggiano, grated
1 teaspoon finely grated lemon zest
¼ teaspoon salt
¼ teaspoon freshly ground black pepper

Use a wooden spoon to combine all the ingredients in a medium bowl. Use at once or cover and refrigerate for up to 1 day.

3. Squash and Goat Cheese Filling

Makes about 1½ cups

One 1-pound butternut squash, halved,
   the seeds scooped out
¼ cup soft goat cheese, such as
   Montrachet
1 large egg yolk, at room
   temperature
½ teaspoon stemmed thyme
¼ teaspoon grated nutmeg
¼ teaspoon salt

1 Position the rack in the center of the oven and preheat the oven to 400°F. Place the squash cut side down on a lipped nonstick baking sheet. Bake until soft, about 40 minutes. Cool on the sheet, then scoop out the flesh. You should have about 1¼ cups.

2 Place the squash, goat cheese, egg yolk, thyme, nutmeg, and salt in a medium bowl; stir until smooth. Use at once or cover and store in the refrigerator for up to 2 days.

Broccoli and Goat Cheese Filling: Substitute 1¼ cups frozen chopped broccoli, thawed and squeezed of all excess moisture, for the squash. Place the ingredients in a blender or a food processor fitted with the chopping blade; blend or process until smooth.

4. Caramelized Leek Filling

Makes about 1½ cups

4 tablespoons (½ stick) unsalted butter, cut
   into chunks
4 large leeks, white and pale
   green parts only, halved lengthwise
   and washed carefully of any grit and
   sand between the layers, then thinly
   sliced (about 6 cups)
1½ ounces Parmigiano-Reggiano,
   grated
1 teaspoon balsamic vinegar

1 Place the butter and leeks in a skillet and then set it over low heat. As the butter melts, continually stir the leeks until they're coated with it.

2 Once the butter has fully melted, cook, stirring often, until the leeks soften, about 5 minutes. Do not let the leeks brown—if they do, remove the skillet from the heat and let them cool before proceeding.

3 Reduce the heat to very low, cover the skillet, and cook stirring often, until the leeks are golden and caramelized, about 10 minutes. Cool in the skillet, then stir in the cheese and vinegar. Use at once or transfer to a resealable plastic container and refrigerate for up to 3 days.

5. Artichoke Filling

Makes about 1½ cups

One 9-ounce box frozen artichoke hearts,
    thawed
1 large egg yolk
1 small shallot, quartered
2 ounces Asiago, grated
¼ cup finely chopped parsley leaves
½ teaspoon stemmed thyme
¼ teaspoon salt

1 Place the artichoke hearts in a food processor fitted with a chopping blade; pulse until finely chopped. Alternatively, place the hearts on a cutting board and rock a chef's knife through them, back and forth in all directions, until they're finely chopped.

2 Place the chopped artichokes in a medium bowl and stir in the remaining ingredients. Use at once or store in the refrigerator for up to 3 days in a resealable container.

Freezing Ravioli and Cappelletti

Make and stuff them, then lay them on a large baking sheet and freeze until the pieces are stiff; drop into ziplock plastic bags and freeze for up to 3 months. Drop directly from the freezer into the lightly simmering water, letting them boil gently (don't let them knock around in the pot) for 1 to 2 minutes, until thawed, cooked through, and hot.

6. Bacon and Potato Filling

Makes about 1½ cups

2 teaspoons vegetable oil
3 bacon strips
1 medium shallot, sliced into rings
½ pound red-skinned, waxy potatoes, peeled
    and cubed
1 cup water
¼ teaspoon grated nutmeg

1 Heat a large skillet over medium heat. Add the vegetable oil, then the bacon and fry for 2 minutes. Turn, add the shallot, and continue cooking until the bacon is crispy and the shallot has softened, about 2 more minutes.

2 Use a slotted spoon to transfer the bacon and shallot to a paper towel–lined plate. Drain off all but 1 tablespoon fat in the skillet. Return the pan to medium heat and add the potatoes. Fry until browned, about 3 minutes, turning occasionally.

3 Pour the water into the skillet, cover, and cook until the potatoes are tender, about 5 minutes.

4 Drain and place the potatoes in a medium bowl. Cool about 5 minutes, then mash with a fork or potato masher. You can also put them through a potato ricer. Crumble in the bacon, then add the shallot and nutmeg. Stir well, then use at once.

Consider making a party out of stuffing pasta. Get several of your friends to make two or three fillings—or have them prepared in advance. Roll out the dough, open a bottle of wine, and have a blast.

7. White Bean and Sage Filling

Makes about 1½ cups

1⅔ cups canned white beans, drained and rinsed
2 ounces Asiago, grated
2 garlic cloves, minced
1 tablespoon minced sage leaves
¼ teaspoon salt
¼ teaspoon freshly ground black pepper

❶ Place the beans in a large bowl and mash them with a potato masher, a pastry cutter, or a fork. You want a creamy if still slightly chunky puree.

❷ Stir in the cheese, garlic, sage, salt, and pepper and use at once—or store in a resealable plastic container in the refrigerator for up to 3 days.

8. Chestnut Filling

Makes about 1½ cups

2 cups canned steamed chestnuts
6 tablespoons heavy cream
2 teaspoons finely grated orange zest
¼ teaspoon grated nutmeg
¼ teaspoon salt
¼ teaspoon freshly ground black pepper

Place the chestnuts in a food processor fitted with a chopping blade; pulse until roughly chopped. Add the remaining ingredients and process until smooth. Use at once or store in a resealable plastic container in the refrigerator for up to 3 days.

9. Ground Veal Filling

Makes about 1½ cups

1 tablespoon unsalted butter
3 garlic cloves, minced
¾ pound ground veal
½ cup beef broth
2 teaspoons minced oregano leaves
1 large egg yolk
3 ounces Parmigiano-Reggiano, grated
2 teaspoons raisins, finely chopped
¼ teaspoon salt
¼ teaspoon freshly ground black pepper
¼ teaspoon ground cloves

❶ Melt the butter in a large skillet over low heat. Add the garlic and cook just until aromatic, about 15 seconds. Crumble in the ground veal, raise the heat to medium, and continue cooking until browned, about 5 minutes, stirring often.

❷ Pour in the broth, raise the heat to medium-high, and cook stirring often, until most of the liquid in the pan has evaporated, about 5 minutes. Stir in the oregano and set aside to cool.

❸ Once the mixture has cooled, transfer it to a medium bowl and stir in the egg yolk, cheese, raisins, salt, pepper, and cloves. Use at once or store in the refrigerator for up to 24 hours.

For an interesting filling for precooked shells, try one of the two Picadillos (pages 93-94). Sauce them simply with melted butter, extra virgin olive oil, lemon juice, one of the simple vinegary dips (page 74), or even fresh salsa (page 47).

10. Crab Filling

Makes about 1½ cups

1 tablespoon unsalted butter
1 medium shallot, minced
½ pound crabmeat, picked over for shell and
    cartilage
¼ cup plain dried bread crumbs
2 teaspoons Dijon mustard
1 teaspoon lemon juice
¼ teaspoon salt
¼ teaspoon freshly ground black pepper

1 Melt the butter in a medium skillet set over medium heat. Add the shallot and cook, stirring often, until softened, about 1 minute. Add the crab, stir well, and remove from the heat.

2 Stir in the bread crumbs, mustard, lemon juice, salt, and pepper. Set aside for 5 minutes to cool, then use at once.

Step 2: Make the dough.
You only need to do this if you're using fresh pasta; dried pasta is already shaped so you can skip to step 3. For fresh pasta, follow steps 1 through 3 in the instructions for making fresh pasta from a pasta machine (see page 174). Once you get to step 3, continue stretching and flattening the pasta sheet to the thinnest possible setting on the machine to create a very long, paper-thin sheet of pasta. Place this sheet on a clean kitchen towel spread out on your work surface, then continue with more pasta balls until you have several of these long sheets.

For fresh manicotti: Cut the prepared pasta sheets (see page 174) into 6-inch sections. Bring a large pot of water to a boil, drop the sections in, and boil for 30 seconds. Remove from the pot with a slotted spoon and place in a colander in the sink. Rinse with cool water, then lay the sections on your work surface. Spoon 2 to 3 tablespoons of filling about ½ inch from the side borders along one side of each section. Roll them up like cigars (not tightly, but together). Place them seam side down in a lightly oiled 13 × 9-inch baking sheet.

For fresh ravioli: Place a scant tablespoon of filling in small balls down the prepared pasta sheet, spacing them about 2 inches apart. Fold the sheet in half lengthwise so it covers the filling, keeping each dot in a distinct pile. Use a ravioli cutter (with a crimped edge), a pizza cutter, or a paring knife to cut between the fillings and make the ravioli. Working with floured fingers, pick up the ravioli and press the edges closed—a ravioli cutter is supposed to seal them, but often it doesn't. Set aside to dry for 10 minutes, then cook, following the instructions for cooked pasta on page 175. Do not let the water come to a full boil. Instead, drop the ravioli in when it's lightly simmering, then reduce the heat so it doesn't roll too much and break open the pasta. Use a slotted spoon to transfer the ravioli to a colander set in the sink.

For fresh cappelletti: These little rounded "hats" with pointy tips are often called tortellini in the United States. Cut the prepared pasta sheets into 2-inch squares, using a pizza cutter or a sharp paring knife; you may be able to get double rows of squares out of the sheets if they're wide enough. Separate the squares. Place about ½ teaspoon filling in the center of each. Fold closed, opposite corner to opposite corner, so that it makes a triangle. Flour your fingers, pick up the triangle, and seal the edges. Turn the triangle so the point farthest from the filling is at the top, then bend the other two points gently around your finger so that they meet. Pinch the two points together, then gently slide the cappelletto off your finger. The top point should be sticking up like the point of a Renaissance cap (thus, the name). Once made, set the cappelletti aside to dry for 10 minutes. Cook according to the directions for cooking pasta on page 175, but do not let the water come to a full boil. When lightly simmering, drop them in, then reduce the heat so they cook gently without knocking around in the pot. Use a slotted spoon to transfer them to a colander in the sink.

Step 3: Shape and stuff the pasta.

For dried shells: Because you need a specialized mold or a very deft hand technique to shape these, and because they will be long-baked in a casserole, we recommend using only dried pasta shells. Medium ones are preferable; they're more elegant and the filling bakes evenly. (Small shells are not made for stuffing.) Cook them first according to the package instructions, then spoon the filling into the shells, stuffing them about two-thirds full; the filling should not overlap the edges. Place the shells, stuffing side up, in a lightly oiled large baking dish.

For dried manicotti: If you're working with dried tubes, they must be cooked first, following the directions on the package and on page 175. Once cooked, they should be rinsed and cooled somewhat. Either fill them using a small flatware spoon or place the filling in a pastry bag fitted with a ½-inch round tip and squeeze the filling into the tubes. In either case, get the filling into the middle of the tube, stuffing the center but tapering down to about half-filled at each end. Set the tubes as you fill them in a lightly oiled 13 × 9-inch baking dish.

Step 4: Sauce or bake the stuffed pasta.

For ravioli and cappelletti: Toss them with the sauce you've chosen, or lay them on individual serving plates and nap a little sauce over the top. Choose a simple oil or butter sauce, such as Sautéed Garlic (page 180), Walnut Sauce (page 181), or Butter and Fresh Herbs (page 181)— or choose a simple tomato sauce like Marinara (page 182). You can also top them with Ragù Bolognese (page 190), Lamb Ragù (page 192), or Chicken Liver Ragù (page 193).

For shells and manicotti: By and large, choose a cooked tomato sauce, such as Pomodoro (page 187), Marinara (page 182), Fra Diavolo (page 182), or Puttanesca (page 182). Steer clear of chunky sauces, cream sauces, or ragùs. To bake them, preheat the oven to 350°F. Pour the sauce over the stuffed shapes in the baking dish, taking care to get it between them and onto the bottom of the pan. If desired, grate Parmigiano-Reggiano or mozzarella over the dish. Cover with aluminum foil and bake for 20 minutes. Uncover the dish and continue baking until bubbling and hot (any cheese should be starting to melt), about 10 more minutes. Let stand for 5 minutes at room temperature before serving.

Pasta Casseroles

Crowd-pleasers all, here are our revamps of the classics made with bigger flavors and unexpected twists.

Macaroni and Four-Cheese Casserole with Asparagus and Prosciutto

This is a layered mac-and-cheese. *Makes 8 servings*

4 ounces Asiago, shredded

4 ounces Parmigiano-Reggiano, shredded

4 ounces Pecorino Romano, shredded

4 ounces mozzarella, shredded

5 tablespoons unsalted butter, plus additional for the baking dish

½ pound thinly sliced prosciutto, chopped

12 ounces pencil-thin asparagus spears, peeled and cut into sections to match the length of the dried pasta you've selected (see Note)

1 large onion, chopped

¼ cup all-purpose flour

4 cups (1 quart) whole or low-fat milk (do not use fat-free), at room temperature

12 ounces dried ziti, rigatoni, or fusilli, cooked and drained

2 teaspoons dry mustard

¼ teaspoon ground allspice

1 Mix the cheeses in a large bowl and set aside.

2 Position the rack in the center of the oven and preheat the oven to 350°F. Lightly butter a 3-quart, high-sided, round baking dish; set it aside.

3 Melt 1 tablespoon butter in a large skillet. Add the prosciutto and cook, stirring often, until brown and crispy, about 3 minutes. Stir in the asparagus and set aside.

4 Melt the remaining 4 tablespoons butter in a large saucepan over medium-low heat. Add the onion and cook until softened, about 3 minutes, stirring frequently.

5 Sprinkle the flour over the onion, wait for 5 seconds, and cook, stirring constantly so the flour loses its raw taste, about 15 seconds. Do not brown.

6 Whisk in the milk in a slow, steady stream. Continue cooking, whisking all the while, until the mixture thickens and begins to bubble, about 3 minutes. Stir in the cooked pasta, dry mustard, and allspice, as well as the prosciutto and asparagus mixture.

7 Place one-quarter of the pasta and cream sauce in the baking dish; top with a quarter of the cheese. Spoon a third of the remaining pasta and cream sauce in the dish, coating it to the sides of the dish; top with a third of the remaining cheese. Spoon half the remaining pasta sauce into the dish; top with half the remaining cheese. Finally, add the remaining pasta sauce to the dish and then the remaining cheese.

8 Bake until gooey and lightly browned, about 30 minutes. Let stand at room temperature for 5 minutes before serving.

Note: Shave asparagus with a vegetable peeler, taking off the tough, outer skin. If the spears are too thick, simply continue shaving them down until they become pencil width.

Pastitsio

Although most versions of this Greek classic are made to cut into neat squares, our version has a creamy pasta layer on top of a traditional ground lamb concoction. *Makes 8 servings*

Canola oil for greasing the pan
½ cup pitted green olives, preferably Greek olives
2 anchovy fillets
2 medium shallots, halved
2 garlic cloves, quartered
¼ cup chopped dill fronds
3 tablespoons olive oil
1 teaspoon finely grated lemon zest
½ teaspoon freshly ground black pepper
1 pound ground lamb
1 cup dry white wine
2 ripe Italian plum tomatoes, finely chopped
3 tablespoons unsalted butter
3 tablespoons all-purpose flour
2½ cups whole milk
½ cup heavy cream
6 ounces Asiago, grated
½ teaspoon ground cinnamon
2 large eggs plus 1 large egg yolk, at room temperature
8 ounces dried penne, ziti, or rigatoni, cooked and drained

1 Position the rack in the center of the oven and preheat the oven to 350°F. Lightly grease the inside of a 2-quart, high-sided, round casserole dish or a 13 × 9-inch baking dish with some canola oil dabbed on a paper towel; set aside.

2 Place the olives, anchovy fillets, shallots, garlic, dill, 2 tablespoons olive oil, lemon zest, and pepper in a food processor fitted with the chopping blade. Pulse until finely chopped, not quite a paste. Alternatively, grind these ingredients in a mortar with a pestle. Set aside.

3 Heat a large skillet over medium heat. Swirl in the remaining 1 tablespoon olive oil, then crumble in the ground lamb. Cook, stirring often, until browned, about 5 minutes. Add the olive mixture; cook, stirring constantly, until the mixture begins to stick to the bottom of the pan, about 3 more minutes.

4 Pour in the wine and scrape up any browned bits in the bottom of the pan. When the wine comes to a simmer, add the tomatoes. Reduce the heat somewhat and simmer until thickened and ragùlike, stirring often, perhaps about 10 minutes. Pour the contents of the pan into the prepared casserole and set aside.

5 Melt the butter in a large saucepan over medium-low heat. As soon as it's melted, sprinkle the flour over it, wait for 5 seconds, then whisk and cook just until the flour's fully combined in the butter and bubbling a bit, about 15 seconds. Do not brown.

6 Whisk in the milk in a slow, steady stream until smooth; whisk in the cream. Reduce the heat to low and cook, whisking constantly, until thickened and bubbling, about 2 minutes. Whisk in the cheese and cinnamon just until the cheese melts. Do not return to a simmer. Remove the pan from the heat.

7 Whisk the eggs and egg yolk in a large bowl. Very slowly whisk the hot cream sauce into the beaten eggs. Stir in the cooked pasta and pour this mixture over the meat mixture in the casserole.

8 Bake, uncovered, until the top is lightly browned and the custard is set and bubbling lightly, about 40 minutes for the round casserole and 30 minutes for the 13 × 9-inch baking dish. Let stand at room temperature for 5 minutes before serving.

9 To serve, make sure you scoop up both layers— or scoop out servings of the cheese layer and top them with some of the meat layer below.

Noodle Kugel with Fresh and Dried Fruit

A deli favorite, this sweet side is often served with brisket (see page 393). We've reinterpreted the dish with modern flavors so that it'll pair well with roast beef, turkey, or chicken. It's sweet enough to make an interesting dessert with strong coffee. *Makes 8 servings*

6 large eggs, at room temperature
½ cup sugar
½ cup water
¼ cup walnut oil, plus additional for greasing the baking dish
½ cup golden raisins, chopped
½ cup chopped fresh pineapple
½ cup chopped peeled cored apple
2 tablespoons lemon juice
1 teaspoon finely grated lemon zest
1 teaspoon vanilla extract
½ teaspoon salt
2 pounds (a double recipe) fresh Chestnut Pasta (page 172) or 1½ pounds dried egg noodles, cooked and drained

1 Position the rack in the center of the oven and preheat the oven to 350°F. Lightly oil a 13 × 9-inch baking dish.

2 Whisk the eggs, sugar, water, and walnut oil in a large bowl until the sugar dissolves. Stir in the raisins, pineapple, apple, lemon juice, lemon zest, vanilla, and salt, then stir in the noodles.

3 Pour into the prepared pan and bake until the top is browned, about 1 hour. Let stand at room temperature at least 5 minutes before serving.

A Year of Lasagne

Spring Lasagna with Carrots, Peas, and Asparagus

This lasagna is like baked pasta primavera—lots of veggies in a light tomato sauce, lemon-scented creamy cheese layers, and fresh asparagus spears on the noodles. *Makes 8 servings*

For the Tomato and Vegetable Sauce:
3 tablespoons unsalted butter
2 tablespoons olive oil
2 medium onions, chopped
4 garlic cloves, minced
One 28-ounce can whole tomatoes, crushed or snipped to pieces in the can with kitchen shears (3½ cups)
3½ cups mixed diced carrots and shelled peas, or one 1-pound bag frozen peas and carrots, thawed
2 tablespoons stemmed thyme
1 teaspoon salt
½ teaspoon freshly ground black pepper
½ teaspoon grated nutmeg

For the Cheese Filling:
32 ounces regular or low-fat ricotta cheese (do not use fat-free)
2 large eggs, at room temperature
½ teaspoon finely grated lemon zest

For the Noodles:
Six 12 × 5-inch sheets homemade fresh Spinach Pasta (page 173), 9 no-boil lasagna noodles, or 12 to 15 dried lasagna noodles
1 pound pencil-thin asparagus spears

1 Position the rack in the center of the oven and preheat the oven to 350°F.

② To make the tomato and vegetable sauce, heat a large saucepan over medium heat; add the butter and olive oil. When the butter has almost melted, add the onions and cook, stirring often, until translucent, about 3 minutes. Add the garlic and cook, stirring constantly, until aromatic, about 15 seconds.

③ Pour in the tomatoes and their juice along with the peas and carrots. Stir well and bring the mixture to a simmer.

④ Stir in the thyme, salt, pepper, and nutmeg. Simmer just to blend the flavors and boil off a lot of the liquid, about 10 minutes. You certainly don't want sauce as thick as a ragù—more like a loose tomato sauce but beware of a watery sauce. Remove the pan from the heat and set aside.

⑤ To make the cheese filling, whisk the ricotta, eggs, and lemon zest in a large bowl. Do not beat—the ricotta should not turn watery.

⑥ If you're using fresh pasta sheets: Cook them as directed on page 208. It's easiest to cook them one at a time. Do not cook them all the way—leave them a little firm since they'll cook as the lasagna bakes. Drain the fresh pasta sheets in a colander in the sink—be careful: they're fragile.

If you're using dried lasagna noodles: Cook as directed on page 208 and drain in a colander set in the sink—but again do not cook them all the way; leave them a little crunchy so they'll continue to soften in the casserole.

⑦ The last step before assembling the casserole is to prepare the asparagus. Trim off any beige or woody ends; shave off the outer skin to ensure that the spears will be tender after they're baked. If your asparagus is not pencil thin, shave down the spears with a vegetable peeler.

⑧ Assemble the lasagna in a 13 × 9-inch baking pan: 1 cup tomato sauce spread across the bottom of the pan; 2 homemade pasta sheets, 3 no-boil noodles, or 4 to 5 cooked dried lasagna noodles; 1½ cups tomato sauce; half the cheese filling (use a rubber spatula to spread it evenly); half the asparagus spears (lay them tip to foot in alternating directions); 2 more homemade pasta sheets, 3 no-boil noodles, or 4 to 5 cooked drained dried lasagna noodles; 1½ cups tomato sauce; the remaining cheese filling; the remaining asparagus spears; the remaining noodles; and finally the remaining tomato sauce.

⑨ Cover the pan with a layer of parchment paper, then a layer of aluminum foil. Bake for 35 minutes, then uncover the pan and continue baking until bubbling and gooey, about 10 more minutes. Let the pan stand at room temperature for 5 minutes.

Summer Lasagna with Fresh Mozzarella, Sausage, and Basil

This lasagna starts with a basic tomato sauce. But there's no cheese filling, just strips of mozzarella and fresh basil leaves layered with sausage. *Makes 8 servings*

For the Tomato Sauce:
¼ cup olive oil
2 medium onions, chopped
6 garlic cloves, minced
4 pounds Roma or plum tomatoes (16 to 18 tomatoes), roughly chopped
2 tablespoons chopped oregano leaves
1 teaspoon sugar
1 teaspoon salt
1 teaspoon freshly ground black pepper
2 tablespoons tomato paste

For the Casserole:

1 tablespoon olive oil

¾ pound sweet Italian pork, chicken, or turkey sausage

Six 12 × 5-inch sheets fresh homemade pasta (page 170), 9 no-boil lasagna noodles, or 12 to 15 dried lasagna noodles

24 basil leaves, cut into thin strips

1 pound fresh mozzarella, thinly sliced

① Position the rack in the center of the oven and preheat the oven to 350°F.

② To make the tomato sauce, heat a large saucepan over medium heat. Swirl in ¼ cup olive oil, then add the onions and cook until softened, about 2 minutes, stirring constantly. Add the garlic and cook just until aromatic, about 20 seconds.

③ Add the tomatoes, oregano, sugar, salt, and pepper. Bring the sauce to a simmer. Reduce the heat to low and simmer until the tomatoes break down and the sauce thickens, 30 to 40 minutes. Stir in the tomato paste.

④ Meanwhile, heat a large skillet over medium-high heat. Swirl in 1 tablespoon olive oil, then add the sausage. The moment the sausage starts to frizzle, reduce the heat somewhat and continue cooking until the sausages are browned on all sides, about 8 minutes, turning every so often. Transfer the sausages to a cutting board and let them stand for a few minutes until you can easily cut them into thin rings.

⑤ **If you're using fresh pasta:** Cook it following the instructions on page 208 just until it's pliable, no more than 1 minute, then drain the noodles in a colander in the sink. Don't overcook the pasta—it needs to absorb moisture in the casserole (a task that no-boil noodles will do well).

If you're using dried noodles: Cook as directed on page 208, but do not cook them all the way; leave them a little firm since they'll continue to cook in the casserole.

⑥ To build the casserole in a 13 × 9-inch pan, follow this method: 1 cup tomato sauce across the pan's bottom; 2 sheets of homemade pasta, 3 no-boil noodles, or 4 to 5 cooked, drained dried lasagna noodles; 1½ cups tomato sauce; half the sausage rings; half the basil leaves; half the cheese slices; 2 more sheets of homemade pasta, 3 no-boil noodles, or 4 to 5 cooked, drained dried lasagna noodles; 1½ cups tomato sauce; the remaining sausage rings; the remaining basil; the remaining cheese; the remaining noodles; and finally the remaining tomato sauce.

⑦ Cover the pan with parchment paper, then aluminum foil. Bake for 35 minutes, then uncover the pan and continue baking until hot, bubbling, and set, about 15 more minutes. Let stand at room temperature for 10 minutes before serving.

Autumn Lasagna with Chicken Ragù, Pine Nuts, and Raisins

This modern take on a medieval casserole is made with a chicken ragù and layered with shaved Parmigiano-Reggiano, golden raisins, pine nuts, and chestnut noodles (or no-boil noodles, if you want a short cut). *Makes 8 servings*

For the Chicken Ragù:

2 tablespoons olive oil

1 tablespoon unsalted butter

1 medium onion, diced

1 medium carrot, peeled and diced

3 garlic cloves, minced

8 ounces pancetta, finely chopped

1½ pounds boneless skinless chicken thighs, diced into ½-inch pieces

¼ pound chicken gizzards, finely chopped

½ cup dry white wine or dry vermouth

12 minced sage leaves

2 bay leaves

½ teaspoon grated nutmeg

½ teaspoon ground cloves

2 cups chicken broth

¼ cup tomato paste

For the Casserole:

6 tablespoons pine nuts

Six 12 × 5-inch sheets fresh Chestnut Pasta (page 172), 9 no-boil lasagna noodles, or 12 to 15 dried lasagna noodles

6 ounces Parmigiano-Reggiano, thinly shaved

6 tablespoons dry white wine

6 tablespoons golden raisins

❶ To make the chicken ragù, heat a large saucepan over medium heat. Add the olive oil and butter—the moment the butter melts, add the onion and carrot. Cook, stirring often, until softened, about 3 minutes. Add the garlic and cook until aromatic, about 15 seconds.

❷ Add the chopped pancetta and cook until frizzled and browned, about 3 minutes, stirring often.

❸ Stir in the chopped thighs and gizzards. Reduce the heat to medium-low and cook until they're well browned, stirring often, about 8 minutes.

❹ Pour in the wine or vermouth; use a wooden spoon to scrape up any browned bits on the bottom of the pan. Stir in the sage, bay leaves, nutmeg, and cloves. Pour in the broth; stir in the tomato paste until it dissolves. Reduce the heat to low, set the cover askew, and simmer very

slowly for 30 minutes. Then cover the pan and continue cooking until the gizzard pieces are tender, about 30 more minutes. Remove the pan from the heat and set aside. Remove and discard the bay leaves.

❺ Position the rack in the center of the oven and preheat the oven to 375°F.

❻ Place a small skillet over medium heat and add the pine nuts. Toast just until golden, about 4 minutes, tossing frequently. Pour into a small bowl and cool for 5 minutes.

❼ **If you're using fresh pasta:** Cook it first (see page 208). Once you add the pasta sheets to the water, cook for just 1 minute, just to set the noodles; they will cook more in the casserole. The noodles tear easily, so drain them gently in a colander set in the sink. (If some tear, reassemble them in the casserole as you layer it.)

If you're using dried lasagna noodles: Cook them in the same way, but a little longer, perhaps 4 minutes, just until they start to get a little tender; drain in a colander set in the sink.

❽ Layer the lasagna in a 13 × 9-inch pan this way: ½ cup chicken ragù, spread in the bottom of the pan; 2 sheets of homemade pasta, 3 no-boil noodles, or 4 to 5 cooked, drained dried lasagna noodles; 1½ cups chicken ragù; half the cheese, placed evenly on the ragù; 3 tablespoons white wine sprinkled over the cheese; half the toasted pine nuts and half the raisins; 2 more sheets of homemade pasta, 3 no-boil noodles, or 4 to 5 cooked, drained dried lasagna noodles; 1½ cups chicken ragù; the remaining cheese; 3 tablespoons white wine, again sprinkled over them; the remaining pine nuts and raisins; the remaining pasta; and finally the remaining chicken ragù, making sure it covers the casserole thoroughly.

❾ Cover the pan with a layer of parchment paper, then a layer of aluminum foil. Bake for 40 minutes, then uncover and continue baking until dense, compact, and bubbling, about 5 more minutes. Let stand at room temperature for 10 minutes.

Winter Lasagna with Mushrooms, Spinach, and Tarragon

Here, a rich velouté (a flour-and-butter-thickened stock) is layered with a mushroom ragù and grated cheese. *Makes 8 servings*

For the Mushroom Ragù:
2 tablespoons unsalted butter
1½ pounds white button or cremini mushrooms, brushed of all visible dirt and thinly sliced
One 16-ounce package frozen chopped spinach, thawed and squeezed dry
4 teaspoons minced tarragon leaves or 2 teaspoons dried tarragon
½ teaspoon grated nutmeg

For the White Wine Velouté:
8 tablespoons (1 stick) unsalted butter, cut into small pieces
1 large onion, minced
6 tablespoons all-purpose flour
2 cups chicken broth
2 cups whole or low-fat milk (do not use fat-free)
1 cup white wine, preferably a smooth white Burgundy or a fruity Pinot Gris

For the Casserole:
Six 12 × 5-inch sheets homemade Whole Wheat Pasta (pages 171), 9 no-boil lasagna noodles, or 12 to 15 dried lasagna noodles, preferably whole wheat noodles
12 ounces Emmentaler, Gruyère, or Appenzeller, grated

❶ To make the mushroom ragù, melt the 2 tablespoons butter in a large skillet set over medium heat. Add the mushrooms and sauté until they give off their liquid and it reduces to a glaze, about 4 minutes.

❷ Stir in the chopped spinach, tarragon, and nutmeg. Cook for 1 minute, stirring constantly, then set the skillet off the heat. Cover and set aside.

❸ To make the white wine velouté, place the cut-up 8 tablespoons butter and the onion in a large, cool saucepan and set it over medium-low heat. As the butter melts, stir often so that the onion is coated.

❹ Reduce the heat to low and cook until the onion is very soft, almost caramelized, and golden, stirring often, about 12 minutes.

❺ Cover, reduce the heat even further, and cook for another 5 minutes, stirring once or twice. Meanwhile, position the rack in the center of the oven and preheat the oven to 400°F.

❻ Take the lid off the pan and sprinkle the flour evenly over the onion. Whisking constantly, cook just so the flour loses its raw taste and forms a paste with the liquid in the pan, about 20 seconds. Do not brown.

❼ Whisk in the broth and milk in a slow, steady stream. Raise the heat to medium-low and continue cooking, whisking constantly, until the sauce starts to bubble and gets noticeably thicker, about 2 minutes.

8 Whisk in the wine and continue simmering, whisking all the while, until thickened like a heavy cream sauce, about 2 minutes. Set the pan aside off the heat and give the mixture one more good whisking.

9 **If you're using fresh pasta:** Cook the sheets, as per the directions below. Cook them only a minute or two, just until they're set. Drain in a colander set in the sink.

If you're using dried noodles: Cook them the same way but for about 4 minutes, just until they start to get tender; drain them in a colander set in the sink.

10 Assemble the casserole in a 13 × 9-inch baking dish this way: ½ cup white wine velouté, spread across the bottom of the dish; 2 sheets of home-made pasta, 3 no-boil noodles, or 4 to 5 cooked, drained dried lasagna noodles; 2 cups white wine velouté, spread over the noodles with a rubber spatula; half the mushroom ragù, spread gently over the casserole; a third of the grated cheese; 2 more sheets of homemade pasta, 3 no-boil noodles, or 4 to 5 cooked, drained dried noodles; 2 cups white wine velouté; the remaining mushroom ragù; half the remaining grated cheese; the remaining pasta; the rest of the white wine velouté; and finally the rest of the grated cheese.

11 Bake, uncovered, until bubbly and set, about 40 minutes. Let stand at room temperature for 5 minutes before serving.

Lasagna Noodles

If you're making lasagna noodles from fresh pasta, follow steps 1 through 3 on page 174. Once you have long sheets, cut them so they're 11 or 12 inches long; trim their edges so they're about 5 inches wide. Save the shorter sheets for lasagna noodles, too; you'll need to patch these together in the pan as you build the lasagna. Drape the sheets over a kitchen towel placed over a cupboard door; dry for 30 minutes before boiling. Only boil them until they float to the surface, less than 1 minute—they will cook more in the casserole. Drain in a colander set in the sink. Be forewarned: the noodles are easily torn.

Or use no-boil lasagna noodles, a newfangled convenience. They're wider and shorter than the standard noodles; they must be placed in the pan parallel to the 9-inch side. They don't really fit (they're too short), but they expand as they soak up the sauce in the oven. Indeed, we used the no-boil noodles extensively in testing these lasagna. They're brilliant for soaking up extra moisture and correcting a watery sauce.

Or substitute the standard, dried lasagna noodles. You'll need about 12, maybe 15 noodles. Boil and drain according to the package instructions, then slice to fit and patch together in the pan, laying them parallel to the 13-inch side.

Noodles have a long history in Asia. Although there's a specific provenance for every recipe here, most of these dishes now escape nationalist origins. They're found across the continent—and ours, too.

Cold Sesame Noodles

This dish is often served first in New York Chinese restaurants—and is gobbled up in a flash (we love it so). *Makes 4 servings*

6 tablespoons toasted sesame oil

3 tablespoons Chinese toasted sesame paste, tahini, or natural-style creamy peanut butter

2 tablespoons soy sauce

2 tablespoons Chinese black vinegar or 1½ tablespoons Worcestershire sauce plus ½ tablespoon white wine vinegar

2 teaspoons chili oil or Asian red chili paste

2 teaspoons sugar

2 teaspoons minced peeled fresh ginger

1 pound fresh or 12 ounces dried Chinese egg noodles, cooked and drained

1 large cucumber, peeled, seeded, and diced

❶ Whisk the sesame oil; sesame paste, tahini, or peanut butter; soy sauce; black vinegar or its substitute; chili oil or chili paste; sugar; and ginger in a large bowl.

❷ Add the noodles and cucumber. Toss to coat and serve at once, or cover and refrigerate for up to 24 hours. If the noodles absorb too much sauce, refresh them with a splash of nice vinegar.

Lo Mein

This sauce is a combination of a Chinese stir-fry sauce and a Vietnamese black pepper sauce. By cooking the noodles in the sauce, they absorb the flavor and become irresistible. *Makes 4 servings*

1 tablespoon peanut oil

6 ounces medium shrimp (about 35 per pound), peeled and deveined

3 garlic cloves, minced

1½ cups chicken broth

3 tablespoons soy sauce

2 tablespoons Shaoxing or dry sherry

1 teaspoon sugar

½ teaspoon freshly ground black pepper or 1 teaspoon cracked black peppercorns, or more to taste

1 pound fresh round egg noodles or 12 ounces dried Chinese egg noodles, cooked and drained

1 cup mung bean sprouts

6 ounces smoked ham, shredded, or 6 ounces firm tofu, cubed

¼ cup chopped cilantro leaves

2 teaspoons toasted sesame oil

❶ Heat a large nonstick wok over medium-high heat. Swirl in the peanut oil, then add the shrimp and garlic. Stir-fry just until the shrimp turns pink, about 1 minute.

2 Stir in the broth, soy sauce, Shaoxing or sherry, sugar, and black pepper. Bring to a simmer.

3 Add the noodles. Raise the heat to high and cook, tossing constantly, until the noodles absorb much of the sauce and what remains is a glaze, about 3 minutes.

4 Add the bean sprouts, ham or tofu, and the cilantro; cook, stirring gently but constantly, until heated through, about 30 seconds. Remove from the heat, add the sesame oil, and toss gently.

Crispy Noodles with Pork and Snow Peas

Here, a crunchy bed of noodles becomes a bed for an aromatic pork stir-fry. Of course, you could put any of the stir-fries in this book on top of this noodle bed—try the Orange Chicken Stir-Fry (page 274), the Fiery Shrimp or Scallop Cashew Stir-Fry (page 371), or the Vietnamese-Inspired Black Pepper Pork Stir-Fry (page 432). *Makes 4 servings*

12 dry mushrooms, preferably Chinese black
    mushrooms
Boiling water
1½ cups chicken broth
¼ cup oyster sauce
4 teaspoons Shaoxing or dry sherry
2 teaspoons soy sauce
2 teaspoons sugar
4 teaspoons cornstarch
2 teaspoons water
12 ounces fresh egg noodles or 8 ounces dried
    Chinese egg noodles, cooked and drained
2 teaspoons toasted sesame oil
2 cups snow peas (about 8 ounces)
3 tablespoons peanut oil
3 scallions, cut into 1-inch segments
2 garlic cloves, minced
2 tablespoons peeled minced fresh ginger
6 ounces pork loin, cut into matchsticks

1 Place the mushrooms in a large bowl and cover with boiling water. Set aside to soak until softened, about 15 minutes. Drain and slice.

2 Whisk the broth, oyster sauce, Shaoxing or sherry, soy sauce, and sugar in a small bowl; set aside. Whisk the cornstarch and water in another small bowl; set aside as well. Finally, toss the cooked egg noodles with the toasted sesame oil in a medium bowl.

3 Bring a medium pot of water to a boil over high heat. Add the snow peas and blanch for 20 seconds. Drain in a colander set in the sink and refresh under cold water.

4 Heat a large nonstick wok over medium-high heat. Swirl in 2 tablespoons peanut oil, then add the noodles. Spread across the bottom of the wok and press into a cake; cook until brown, about 2 minutes. Flip and cook until brown on the other side, about 1 minute. Transfer the cake to a heat-safe serving platter and place it in the oven, turned to 225°F.

5 Swirl the remaining 1 tablespoon peanut oil into the wok. Add the scallions, garlic, and ginger; stir-fry until aromatic, about 20 seconds. Add the pork and continue stir-frying until cooked through, about 3 minutes.

6 Add the blanched snow peas and sliced mushrooms. Cook, stirring constantly, until heated through, about 20 seconds.

7 Pour in the broth mixture. Bring to a simmer, stir well, then cook undisturbed until the sauce reduces slightly, about 30 seconds.

8 Finally, stir in the cornstarch mixture. Cook just until the mixture thickens and starts to boil, about 20 seconds. Remove from the heat and pour this mixture onto the bed of crispy noodles.

Hot-and-Sour Lobster with Noodles

We crossed the classic Chinese soup with a stir-fry noodle dish. The only sweetness here comes from the lobster itself. *Makes 4 servings*

Two 8-ounce raw lobster tails, meat removed and thinly sliced, or two 8-ounce frozen lobster tails, thawed and thinly sliced
2 garlic cloves, minced
2 tablespoons peeled minced fresh ginger
2 teaspoons cornstarch
1 teaspoon toasted sesame oil
2 tablespoons peanut oil
2 medium shallots, thinly sliced
2 teaspoons Asian red chili paste
½ pound chopped Chinese broccoli, chopped broccoli raab, or broccoli florets
½ cup chicken broth
¼ cup soy sauce
2 tablespoons Shaoxing or dry sherry
2 tablespoons rice vinegar
1 pound fresh round egg noodles or 12 ounces dried Chinese noodles, cooked and drained

1 Toss the lobster meat, garlic, ginger, cornstarch, and sesame oil in a medium bowl until the lobster is coated and the cornstarch has dissolved. Set aside for 10 minutes.

2 Heat a large nonstick wok or high-sided sauté pan over medium-high heat. Add the peanut oil, then the shallots. Stir-fry for 30 seconds, then add the chili paste. Stir to coat.

3 Add the Chinese broccoli, broccoli raab, or broccoli florets. Stir-fry just until slightly wilted, about 1 minute.

4 Add the lobster and all its marinade. Cook, stirring constantly, just until the lobster loses its transparency, less than 1 minute.

5 Stir in the broth, soy sauce, Shaoxing or sherry, and rice vinegar. Bring the sauce to a simmer and add the noodles. Toss gently to coat and serve at once.

Variations: Substitute 1 pound medium shrimp (about 35 per pound), peeled and deveined, or 1 pound sea scallops, sliced into disks, for the lobster.

Singapore Mai Fun

Here's a take-out favorite: a curry dish made with rice vermicelli. For the most authentic taste, use an Asian curry powder, like one of the Madras-style bottlings from Singapore or Thailand. Buy barbecued pork from your local Chinese restaurant, make your own (page 427), or substitute smoked ham. *Makes 4 servings*

8 ounces rice vermicelli
3 tablespoons peanut oil
1 large egg, lightly beaten
4 ounces purchased Chinese-style barbecued pork, Char Siu (page 427), or smoked ham, thinly sliced
4 ounces medium shrimp (about 35 per pound), cleaned, deveined, and cut in half
4 ounces boneless skinless chicken breast, thinly sliced
1 tablespoon curry powder
2 scallions, cut into 1-inch pieces
3 tablespoons soy sauce
3 tablespoons chicken broth

① Place the vermicelli in a large bowl and cover them with very hot water, the hottest your tap can produce. Set aside to soften for 10 minutes, then drain.

② Heat a large nonstick wok or sauté pan over medium-high heat. Swirl in 1 tablespoon peanut oil, then add the egg. Scramble quickly over the heat, taking care to get the egg off the sides of the pan. The moment it sets, transfer to a small bowl.

③ Add the remaining 2 tablespoons peanut oil to the wok. Stir in the pork, shrimp, and chicken. Cook, tossing constantly, until the chicken is cooked through, about 3 minutes. Add the curry powder; cook, stirring constantly, just until aromatic, about 20 seconds.

④ Add the noodles; stir-fry until coated in the sauce, about 30 seconds.

⑤ Add the scallions, soy sauce, and broth; return the scrambled egg to the wok. Toss and stir over the heat until the noodles are coated with the sauce, about 1 minute.

Pad Thai

A Thai classic, this quick stir-fry exemplifies Asian noodle dishes with its incredible adaptability. It can be varied endlessly to move it away from strict banality and into a new dish you can enjoy each time. *Makes 4 servings*

8 ounces dried rice noodles
3 tablespoons fish sauce
3 tablespoons ketchup
2 tablespoons honey
2 tablespoons dry vermouth
2 tablespoons peanut oil
1 large shallot, minced
2 garlic cloves, minced
½ teaspoon red pepper flakes
½ pound medium shrimp (about 35 per pound), cleaned and deveined

1½ cups mung bean sprouts
2 medium scallions, sliced into 1-inch pieces
2 tablespoons chopped roasted unsalted peanuts
Lime wedges for garnish

① Place the rice noodles in a large bowl and cover them with hot water, the hottest your tap can produce. Set aside to soften for 10 minutes, then drain.

② Whisk the fish sauce, ketchup, honey, and vermouth in a small bowl; set aside.

③ Heat a large nonstick wok over medium-high heat. Swirl in the peanut oil; add the shallot, garlic, and red pepper flakes; and stir-fry for 30 seconds.

④ Add the shrimp; stir-fry until pink and firm, about 2 minutes. Pour the prepared sauce into the pan and bring the mixture to a simmer.

⑤ Add the noodles; cook, tossing and stirring constantly, until they've absorbed the sauce, about 2 minutes.

⑥ Toss in the bean sprouts, scallions, and peanuts; stir-fry just until heated through, about 30 seconds. Serve with lime wedges on the side, which should be squeezed over the dish before eating.

Variations: Substitute ½ pound boneless skinless chicken breast, cut into thin strips, or ½ pound pork loin, cut into bite-sized pieces, for the shrimp.

Substitute 1 pound baby bok choy, thinly sliced, for the bean sprouts.

Add 1 red bell pepper, cored, seeded, and sliced into thin strips, with the shallot.

Shred 2 large carrots and add them with the shrimp.

Add ½ cup frozen corn kernels, thawed, with the bean sprouts.

Add ¼ cup chopped cilantro leaves with the bean sprouts.

Add ¼ cup dried currants with the bean sprouts.

Add 8 shredded basil leaves with the bean sprouts.

Scramble an egg in the wok before you begin the stir-fry. Swirl in 1 tablespoon peanut oil into the hot wok, then add 1 lightly beaten large egg; cook just until set, stirring almost constantly, about 1 minute. Transfer the scrambled egg to a small bowl, then continue with the stir-fry as directed. Add the scrambled egg to the dish with the bean sprouts.

An Asian Noodle Primer

Chinese Egg Noodles. These come in as many widths and styles as Italian noodles. Fresh versions are found in the refrigerator case; check the package to avoid preservatives and colorings. Dried egg noodles are often wound into little nests before being packaged. In either case, the wheat used makes all the difference—egg noodles are slightly gummier and more slippery than Italian egg pasta. Cook them as you would dried Italian pasta (page 174), but stir carefully to uncoil the nests in the boiling water.

Dried Rice Noodles. Sometimes called rice sticks, these pale white noodles are often sold in clear bags. They come in a variety of widths; for these recipes, the choice is yours. Rice noodles must be soaked in hot water to soften them and to remove some of the starch, which can cloud the final dish.

Dried Rice Vermicelli. These are the Asian, rice-based equivalent of angel hair pasta, transparent and sold in long, wound skeins. They, too, must be soaked in hot water before use; once softened, stir well to uncoil.

Fresh Rice Noodles. These sheets of rolled rice pasta are sold on the street in Chinatown or at most Chinese markets. Highly perishable, they should be used the day of purchase. Slice the rolled sheets into 1-inch sections and toss them into a stir-fry.

Beef Chow Fun

While this Chinese classic should only be made with fresh noodles, you can use dried—just make sure you buy the widest ones available. There's no need to mix the sauce ingredients in advance, provided you're aggressive about tossing the stir-fry as it cooks. *Makes 4 servings*

½ pound sirloin, thinly sliced against the grain (see page 394)
2 garlic cloves, minced
1 tablespoon plus 2 teaspoons soy sauce
1 teaspoon sugar
1 teaspoon cornstarch
½ teaspoon sesame oil
2 tablespoons peanut oil
1 large onion, sliced in half, then into ½-inch-thick semicircles
¾ pound baby bok choy, washed of all sand, the water still adhering to the leaves
3 tablespoons hoisin sauce
2 tablespoons rice vinegar
½ teaspoon chili paste
1 pound fresh rice noodles, cut into 1-inch segments, or 12 ounces wide dried rice noodles, soaked in very hot water for 10 minutes

❶ Mix the sirloin strips, garlic, 2 teaspoons soy sauce, sugar, cornstarch, and sesame oil in a large bowl until the cornstarch dissolves and the steak is coated in the marinade. Cover and refrigerate for at least 30 minutes or up to 24 hours.

❷ Heat a large nonstick wok or a high-sided sauté pan over medium-high heat until smoking. Swirl in the peanut oil, then add the onion. Toss and stir constantly until the onion turns translucent, about 1 minute.

3 Stir in the beef strips and any remaining marinade in the bowl. Toss and stir until the beef browns, about 3 minutes.

4 Dump in all the bok choy at once. Using two wooden spoons, pick up the vegetables and steak; toss them until the bok choy is slightly wilted, about 2 minutes.

5 Pour in the hoisin, rice vinegar, chili paste, and the remaining 1 tablespoon soy sauce. Cook, tossing constantly, for 30 seconds.

6 Stir in the noodles. Toss to coat and cook for about 30 seconds, just until they're heated through and coated with the sauce.

Variations: Substitute 1/2 pound pork loin, cut into bite-sized pieces, or 1/2 pound boneless skinless chicken breasts, cut into thin strips, for the sirloin. Cook the pork or chicken about 2 minutes before adding the bok choy.

Substitute 1/2 pound firm tofu for the beef—in this case, stir it and its marinade into the pan after the bok choy.

Substitute 1/2 pound thinly sliced Char Siu (page 427) or purchased Chinese barbecued pork for the beef; omit the marinade and add the barbecued pork after the bok choy.

Asian stir-fries and noodle dishes move fast. Make sure you have all your ingredients prepped in advance.

Pad See Ew

Made with fresh rice noodles, this dish is sold in Thailand as grab-and-go street food. The sauce is spicy/sweet, thanks to sweet soy sauce, an Indonesian product. *Makes 4 servings*

2 tablespoons peanut oil
1 large onion, halved and sliced into
    semicircles
1 red or green bell pepper, cored, seeded,
    and thinly sliced
6 garlic cloves, minced
1/2 pound boneless skinless chicken breasts,
    thinly sliced
2 tablespoons sweet soy sauce (see page 661)
2 tablespoons soy sauce
1 tablespoon rice vinegar
2 teaspoons Asian red chili paste, preferably
    a Thai bottling such as Sriracha
1 pound fresh rice noodles, cut into 1-inch
    segments, or 12 ounces wide dried rice
    noodles, soaked in very hot water for
    10 minutes
1/3 cup packed basil leaves, shredded

1 Heat a large nonstick wok or sauté pan over medium heat. Swirl in the peanut oil, then add the onion, bell pepper, and garlic. Stir-fry just until softened, about 1 minute.

2 Add the chicken. Continue stir-frying until cooked through, about 3 minutes.

3 Stir in the sweet soy sauce, soy sauce, rice vinegar, and chili paste. Bring the sauce to a simmer.

4 Stir in the noodles and basil. Cook, tossing constantly, until heated through, about 30 seconds. Serve at once.

Bread

DESPITE DIRE WARNINGS FROM CULINARY SCOLDS, BREAD MAKING IS NOT A dying art. One stroll down the bread aisle of the modern supermarket puts to rest that end-of-Western-civilization scenario. Time was, white bread was all most of us could get; crunchy loaves were specialty items, brought back by some uncle or aunt who had visited a major city with an ethnic enclave. Today, good bread is available in abundance.

Bread making is not just a professional affair. Yeast sales have recently increased and bread books do a brisk business. Yeast breads, while time-consuming, are hardly laborious because the yeast does most of the work for you. Provided you nail down a few techniques, you just set the dough to rise and go about your life.

Of course, not all breads need yeast. Quick breads, a distinctly American invention, can give you a carb fix in a flash, breakfast to dinner. Popovers, muffins, biscuits, sweet and savory loaves—with baking powder or soda, these are in easy reach of a weekday schedule.

So here's a set of the basics—nothing fancy, all everyday, and all fairly straightforward.

All these require yeast, although not all of them take time to rise. Breadsticks (page 227) and Yeast Biscuits (page 229) use yeast as an oven leavener, sidestepping the process of letting the dough first double in bulk.

White Bread

Here's the standard, the loaves for sandwiches and toast. Since all-purpose flour is softer than bread flour, it better replicates the texture of American white bread. Because this bread's such a classic, we've doubled the recipe. Stick a loaf in the freezer for later. *Makes 2 loaves*

> 3 tablespoons sugar
> Two ¼-ounce packages active dry yeast or 5 teaspoons active dry yeast
> 1 cup warm milk (regular, low-fat, or fat-free), between 105°F and 115°F
> 1¼ cups plus 2 tablespoons warm water, between 105°F and 115°F
> 3 tablespoons unsalted butter or solid vegetable shortening, melted and cooled, plus additional for greasing the bowl and the pans
> 1 tablespoon salt
> About 7½ cups all-purpose flour

❶ Sprinkle the sugar and yeast over the milk in the bowl of a stand mixer or a large mixing bowl. Stir gently and set aside until foamy, about 3 minutes. (If the mixture does not foam, start again—the yeast was bad or the water was not the right temperature.)

❷ Stir in the water, the melted butter or shortening, and the salt. Stir in 2 cups flour until dis-

solved, and then stir in 2 more cups flour just until barely moistened.

❸ **If you're using a stand mixer:** Attach the dough hook, add another 2 cups flour, and begin mixing the dough at medium speed until the flour is incorporated. Add more flour in ½-cup increments until a soft, smooth dough forms, not sticky and quite pliable. Stop adding flour the moment the dough reaches this consistency; continue kneading at medium speed for 10 minutes.

If you're working by hand: Stir in about 1 to 2 additional cups flour with a wooden spoon, just until a dough starts to cohere; then turn the dough onto a clean, well-floured work surface and begin kneading in more flour in ⅓-cup increments until a soft, smooth dough forms. Dust the work surface again with flour and continue kneading the dough for 10 minutes, digging into it with the heel of one hand while pulling it with the fingers of the other. Add a little flour if the dough gets sticky—but no more flour than necessary.

❹ Place a small amount of butter or shortening on a piece of wax paper and grease a large bowl. Gather the dough into a ball, put it in the bowl, turn it over so that it's coated, and cover the bowl loosely with plastic wrap or a clean kitchen towel. Set aside in a warm, dry, draft-free place until doubled in bulk, until you can make a permanent indentation with your finger, about 40 minutes.

5 Use a little butter or shortening on a piece of wax paper to grease two 9 × 5 × 3-inch loaf pans. Gently punch the dough down by slowly plunging your fist into it. Turn it out onto a clean, well-floured work surface. Divide in half.

6 Roll one half between your palms and the work surface to form a 12-inch log. Fold both ends over to meet in the middle of the log, press down, rotate the mass 90 degrees, and roll again to a 12-inch log. Finally, fold the ends over again and roll under your palms to a 9-inch log. Place it in one of the prepared pans, then repeat with the other half of the dough and the other pan. Cover loosely with plastic wrap or a kitchen towel; return to that warm, draft-free place to rise until doubled in bulk, about 35 minutes.

7 Meanwhile, position the rack in the center of the oven; preheat the oven to 400°F.

8 Bake until golden and hollow-sounding when tapped, 25 to 30 minutes. Cool in the pans on a wire rack for 10 minutes, then turn the loaves out and continue cooling on the wire rack for at least 15 minutes, or to room temperature.

To store: Cool to room temperature, then wrap in plastic and keep at room temperature for up to 2 days or freeze for up to 3 months; thaw by unwrapping and placing on a wire rack until room temperature.

Honey White Bread: Substitute honey for the sugar. (You'll probably have to add a little more flour to the dough, perhaps 1/4 cup.)

Herbed White Bread: In step 5, grease the pans and punch down the dough as directed. Divide the dough in half and roll each half into a rectangle about 18 inches long, 9 inches wide, and 1/2 inch thick. (Width here is more important than length.) Brush the top of each with 2 tablespoons melted butter; sprinkle 1/2 cup chopped chives, parsley leaves, cilantro leaves, or basil leaves, or a combination of any of these; or 2 tablespoons stemmed thyme; or 2 teaspoons curry powder. Beginning at one of the short ends, roll the rectangle into a spiral loaf that's 9 inches wide. Place in the loaf pans (if the loaves are a little too long, tuck the ends underneath). Cover loosely with a clean kitchen towel and set aside to rise in a warm, draft-free place until doubled in bulk, about 40 minutes. Bake as directed.

Baguettes

The best thing about these long, thin loaves is that they're more crust than bread. *Makes 2 baguettes*

One 1/4-ounce package active dry yeast or
   2 1/2 teaspoons active dry yeast
2 teaspoons sugar
1 cup warm water, between 105°F and
   115°F
About 2 3/4 cups bread flour, plus additional
   for dusting
1 teaspoon salt
1/2 teaspoon white wine vinegar
Nonstick spray or canola oil for greasing
4 small ice cubes

1 Sprinkle the yeast and sugar over the water in the bowl of a stand mixer or in a large mixing bowl; set aside until foamy, about 3 minutes. (If the yeast does not bubble up, start over—the water was not at the right temperature or the yeast went bad with age.)

2 Stir in 2 cups flour, the salt, and vinegar.

3 **If you're working with a stand mixer:** Attach the bowl and the dough hook to the mixer and begin beating at medium speed to combine the ingredients. Add the flour in ¼-cup increments, beating fully after each, until a soft, pliable, smooth dough forms. Continue beating the dough with the hook for 8 minutes.

If you're working by hand: Stir in another ¼ cup flour, then dust a clean, dry work surface with flour and turn the dough out onto it. Kneading all the while, add more flour in ¼-cup increments, working it in by pressing into the dough with the heel of one hand while twisting the mass with the other, constantly moving and repositioning the mass until a smooth, pliable, soft dough forms. Continue kneading for 10 minutes.

4 Spray a large bowl with nonstick spray or grease it with a little canola oil dabbed on a paper towel. Gather the dough into a ball, place it in the bowl, and turn it over so the top is coated with some oil. Cover and set aside in a warm, dry, draft-free place until doubled in bulk, until an indentation from your finger will not pop back, about 1 hour.

5 Gently push your fist into the dough to deflate it, destroying its structure without smashing it flat. Lightly dust a clean, dry work surface with flour and turn the dough out onto it. Divide in half, then roll each underneath your palms into a baguette about 14 inches long, tapered at the ends.

6 Spray a large baking sheet with nonstick spray or oil it lightly with canola oil. Transfer the loaves to the baking sheet, cover with a clean kitchen towel, and set aside in a warm, dry, draft-free place until puffed and about doubled in circumference, about 40 minutes.

7 Meanwhile, position the rack in the center of the oven; preheat the oven to 450°F.

8 Once the bread has risen a second time, use a clean razor blade or a very sharp paring knife to make three or four diagonal slashes in each loaf, each cut about ½ inch deep. Cut the bread; don't deflate it.

9 Place the pan with the loaves in the oven, then throw the ice cubes onto the oven floor and shut the door. The steam will turn the bread crisp but keep it moist inside. Bake until lightly browned and hollow-sounding when tapped, about 20 minutes. Cool on the baking sheet for 5 minutes, then transfer to a wire rack to cool completely.

To store: Cool to room temperature, then keep at room temperature, unwrapped, for 6 hours, or wrap in plastic wrap and store at room temperature for 1 day or freeze for up to 3 months.

Bread and Flour

Bread flour is a high-gluten flour, made from milled hard wheat (as opposed to the softer, lower-gluten all-purpose flour). It also contains malted barley flour (to help yeast produce lots of carbon dioxide), and potassium bromate or vitamin C (which strengthens the flour's glutens). Look for bread flour in the baking aisle; store for up to 6 months in a well-sealed plastic bag in a cool (about 70°F), dry place.

Each bread recipe has been developed using specific flours: whole wheat, bread, all-purpose, and rye. We have steered clear of esoteric flours found in specialty markets. Flour substitutions can result in gummy, flat, or tough bread.

Yeast

Yeast is a living microorganism that produces carbon dioxide as it grows and multiplies—for which it needs food (sugar or other starches), moisture, and warmth. Although there are hundreds of kinds of yeast floating in the air around us, two are used in food preparation, baker's yeast and brewer's yeast.

Brewer's yeast has little place in the modern kitchen, but baker's yeast is available as either active dry or quick-rising. Our recipes are made with active dry yeast. It can be found in the baking aisle or the refrigerator case in ¼-ounce packets. Should you buy it in bulk at a health-food store or baking-supply store, use 2½ teaspoons in place of the familiar packet. If you do use quick-rising yeast, the rising time may be cut in half.

Baker's yeast is also sold in cakes. These have a higher moisture content, are quite perishable, and must be refrigerated. They should be broken apart and stirred into the warm liquids. One .06-ounce cake is the same as one ¼-ounce packet of dry yeast.

Finally, instant yeast, a convenience product, need not be proofed (that is, turned foamy) in a warm liquid. Instead, it's mixed directly into the dry ingredients. Use 2½ teaspoons in place of every ¼-ounce packet. You must also include whatever liquid was designated to proof the yeast; add it—still warm—with the other wet ingredients.

All baker's yeast has a shelf life. Check the expiration date on the packet. Cake yeast lasts only a week or so; dry yeast lasts longer, but not indefinitely. Dry yeast of any variety can be stored in the freezer (which can extend its shelf life by up to 6 months), but it should be at room temperature when you use it in a recipe.

Brioche

This may be the ultimate French bread: buttery, light, a little cakey, and very good with jam. The eggs must be at room temperature; leave them on the counter for 15 minutes. *Makes 1 loaf or 8 rolls*

One ¼-ounce package active dry yeast or
  2½ teaspoons active dry yeast
1 tablespoon sugar
½ cup warm whole milk, between 105°F and
  115°F
2 large eggs, at room temperature
1 stick (8 tablespoons) unsalted butter,
  melted and cooled, plus additional for
  greasing the pan
1 teaspoon salt
2¾ to 3¼ cups bread flour, plus additional
  for dusting
1 large egg yolk, whisked with 1 tablespoon
  water in a small bowl

❶ Sprinkle the yeast and sugar over the milk in a small bowl. Set aside until bubbling and frothy, about 4 minutes. (If the mixture does not froth, start over—the milk's temperature was off or the yeast was bad.)

❷ Meanwhile, whisk the whole eggs, melted butter, and salt in the bowl of a stand mixer or in a large bowl until fairly smooth and creamy.

❸ Stir the yeast mixture into the egg mixture, then stir in 1½ cups flour.

❹ **If you're working with a stand mixer:** Attach the bowl and dough hook to the mixer, then begin beating at medium speed, first adding ½ cup flour and then more in ¼-cup increments, letting each be incorporated before adding the next, until a smooth, soft dough forms. Continue kneading for 10 minutes, adding more flour in

1-tablespoon increments if the dough sticks or starts to climb up the hook.

If you're working by hand: First, stir in another ½ cup flour. Then generously dust a clean, dry work surface with flour and turn the dough out onto it. Begin kneading in more flour in ¼-cup increments, working it into the dough with a firm but nonetheless gentle pressure as you pull and twist the mass. Use the heel of your hand, twisting it slightly as you press into the dough. Continue working the mass and adding more flour until a soft, pliable, smooth dough forms; then knead until as soft and smooth as an infant's skin, about 10 minutes.

⑤ Lightly butter a large bowl, then gather the dough into a ball and place in the bowl. Turn the dough over so that the top is lightly greased, cover the bowl with a clean towel, and set aside in a warm, dry, draft-free place until the dough has risen to twice its volume, until an indentation made by your finger will not pop back out, about 1 hour.

⑥ Gently push your fist into the dough, deflating it and steadily squashing it. Lightly flour a clean, dry work surface again with flour and turn the dough out onto it.

To make a loaf: Form the dough into an oblong loaf and place it in a lightly buttered 9 × 5 × 3-inch loaf pan. Cover with a clean kitchen towel and set aside in a warm, dry place until doubled in bulk, about 45 minutes.

To make a braid: Divide the dough into thirds and roll each on a lightly floured work surface into a 12-inch log. Lay the logs on the work surface, parallel to each other and quite close together. Pinch one end of all three logs together and braid the strands as you would

hair: take the outside log nearest the end that is joined together and move it between the other two, then take the opposite outside log and move it between the other two, and so on, pushing down slightly to compact, until the loaf is braided. Tuck the ends under the loaf, then place in a lightly buttered 9 × 5 × 3-inch loaf pan. Cover with a kitchen towel and set aside in a warm, dry place until doubled in volume, about 1 hour.

To make a round brioche: Turn the dough out onto a lightly floured work surface, then cut off about a sixth of the dough and set it aside. Shape the remainder into a large, slightly flattened ball, then gently punch a hole in the middle with your fist. Roll the small piece of dough into a ball and wedge it into this indentation. Lightly butter a large baking sheet and transfer the loaf to it. Cover with a kitchen towel and set aside until doubled in bulk, about 1 hour.

To make brioche rolls: Butter small, fluted brioche tins, then divide the dough into 8 equal parts. Pinch a small bit of dough off each, about 1 rounded tablespoon of dough. Roll each of the larger pieces on a lightly floured work surface into balls, then place them in the tins. Push an indentation in the middle of each with your thumb. Roll the small bits of dough into balls and place in the indentations. Set the individual tins on a large baking sheet, cover with a kitchen towel, and set aside until doubled in bulk, about 40 minutes.

⑦ Position the rack in the center of the oven and preheat the oven to 400°F.

⑧ When the dough has doubled in bulk a second time, brush the loaves or rolls lightly with the egg yolk wash, coating them without letting excess wash run down and collect around them.

9 Bake until well browned, until the rolls or loaves sound hollow when tapped, about 18 minutes for rolls or 25 to 30 minutes for loaves. Cool on the baking sheet for a minute or so, then transfer the rolls in their tins or the loaves to a wire rack to continue cooling. Turn the rolls out of their tins after 10 minutes.

To store: Cool completely to room temperature and place in a resealable plastic bag to keep at room temperature for up to 2 days—or freeze for up to 2 months.

Three Refrigerator Jams

Nothing beats homemade jam, but there's no reason to get out the canning kettle. In less than an hour, you can make jam that will keep in your refrigerator for up to a month. Run the containers you'll use through an empty, no-soap, heated-dry cycle of the dishwasher so you can spoon the jam into them while they're hot.

Berry Jam Makes about 3 cups
5 cups raspberries, blackberries,
    blueberries, or sliced strawberries,
    or any combination
2 cups sugar
1 tablespoon lemon or lime juice
1/4 teaspoon salt

1 Place all the ingredients in a large pot, set it over medium-high heat, and stir constantly until simmering.

2 Reduce the heat to low and simmer until thickened, 15 to 18 minutes, stirring often, especially during the last few minutes as the berries break down.

3 Spoon into glass canning jars or other nonreactive heatproof containers. Seal and store in the refrigerator for up to 1 month.

Fig Jam Makes about 4 cups
15 large fresh figs, stemmed
    and chopped
2 1/2 cups sugar
1/3 cup water
3 tablespoons lemon juice
1/4 teaspoon almond extract
1/4 teaspoon salt

1 Place all the ingredients in a large pot, set over medium-high heat, and stir until simmering.

2 Reduce the heat to low and simmer until thick and jamlike, 10 to 12 minutes, stirring almost constantly.

3 Spoon the jam into glass canning jars or other nonreactive heatproof containers. Seal and store in the refrigerator for up to 1 month.

Quince Jam Makes about 4 cups
About 4 cups water
2 tablespoons lemon juice
3 ripe quince (about 2 pounds), peeled, cored,
    and placed in acidulated water
3 cups sugar

1 Bring the water and lemon juice to a simmer in a large pot over high heat. Shred the quince into the pot through the large holes of a box grater. Reduce the heat to medium-low and simmer for 10 minutes, stirring occasionally.

2 Stir in the sugar. Reduce the heat to low and simmer slowly, uncovered, until pink, thick, and jamlike, about 40 minutes, stirring often to avoid scorching, particularly toward the end. (Reduce the heat further if the liquid evaporates too quickly—or stir in another 1/2 cup water if the pot starts to dry out.)

3 Spoon into glass canning jars or other nonreactive heatproof containers. Seal and store in the refrigerator for up to 1 month.

Challah

Although this egg bread is traditionally made on the Sabbath or certain holidays in Jewish homes, it makes an excellent dinner loaf or exceptional French toast the next morning. *Makes 1 loaf*

> One ¼-ounce package active dry yeast or 2½ teaspoons active dry yeast
> ¾ cup plus 1 tablespoon warm water, between 105°F and 115°F
> 1 tablespoon honey
> ¼ cup canola oil, plus additional for greasing
> 1 large egg plus 1 large egg yolk, at room temperature
> 1 teaspoon salt
> 3 to 3½ cups bread flour, plus additional for dusting
> 1 large egg yolk, whisked with 2 tablespoons water in a small bowl

❶ Sprinkle the yeast over the water in the bowl of a stand mixer or in a large mixing bowl. Stir in the honey and set aside until bubbling and foamy, about 3 minutes. (If the mixture does not become quite foamy, start over—either the yeast was bad or the water's temperature was off.)

❷ Stir in the canola oil, whole egg, 1 egg yolk, and salt until fairly smooth.

❸ **If you're working with a stand mixer:** Attach the bowl and dough hook. Add about 2 cups flour and then beat at medium speed until incorporated. Begin adding more flour in ¼-cup increments, adding another only after the previous one has been incorporated, until a soft, pliable, smooth dough forms. Toward the end of the process, you may need to add the flour in smaller amounts, no more than a rounded tablespoonful, to make sure you get just enough flour into the dough so that it isn't sticky but also doesn't turn dry. Continue kneading for 10 minutes.

If you're working by hand: Stir 2½ cups flour into the yeast mixture, then turn it out onto a floured work surface. Flour your hands, then begin to knead the bread, pressing down and twisting with the heel of one hand while gently pulling with the other hand. Add more flour in ¼-cup increments until a soft, pliable, smooth dough forms, about as soft as supple potter's clay; the process should take about 5 minutes. Continue kneading until very smooth and soft, about 10 minutes, adding more flour in 1-tablespoon increments if the dough starts to turn sticky.

❹ Lightly grease a large bowl, gather the dough together, place it in the bowl, and turn it over so the top is now lightly oiled. Cover with a clean kitchen towel and set aside in a warm, dry place until doubled in volume, until you can make a finger-sized indentation that won't pop back out, about 1 hour.

❺ Lightly flour a cleaned work surface. Gently push your fist into the dough to deflate it and lightly squash it, then turn it out onto the work surface. Divide the dough into 3 equal pieces. Roll each of these into a 12-inch log. Place the three logs together parallel on the work surface, then pinch one end together to hold all three in place.

❻ Braid by taking the outer log and pulling the section nearest the joined end over the log next to it and into the space between the other two logs. Repeat with the other side, again pulling it over the adjacent log and toward the space on the other side. The logs should remain attached at one end; make sure that the loaf doesn't mound too high at its center. Once the strands have been braided, tuck the ends underneath and shimmy the loaf between your hands into a compact shape; place on a lightly oiled, baking sheet. Cover with a kitchen towel and set aside in a warm, dry place until doubled in volume, about 45 minutes.

7 Position the rack in the center of the oven and preheat the oven to 375°F.

8 Brush the loaf with the prepared egg-yolk wash, covering the braids without soaking them too much and without getting lots of egg runoff onto the baking sheet.

9 Bake until lightly browned, until the loaf sounds hollow when tapped, about 40 minutes. Cool on the baking sheet for a minute or so, then transfer to a wire rack to cool completely.

To store: Once the loaf's at room temperature, seal it in a large plastic bag and store at room temperature for up to 2 days or in the freezer for up to 2 months; allow the unwrapped loaf to thaw on a wire rack for 1 hour.

Whole Wheat Bread

Whole wheat flour gives bread a chewy, toothsome texture, perfect for sandwiches. *Makes 1 loaf*

> One ¼-ounce package active dry yeast or
>   2½ teaspoons active dry yeast
> 2 cups warm water, between 105°F and
>   115°F
> 1½ tablespoons unsulfured molasses
> 2 tablespoons canola oil, plus additional for
>   greasing
> 2 teaspoons salt
> 2½ cups whole wheat flour
> 1¼ to 1½ cups all-purpose flour, plus
>   additional for dusting

1 Sprinkle the yeast over the water in the bowl of a stand mixer or in a large mixing bowl. Stir in the molasses and set aside until foamy and bubbling, about 3 minutes. (If the mixture does not bubble up into foam, start over—the yeast was bad or the water temperature wasn't right.)

2 Stir in the canola oil and salt, then stir in the whole wheat flour plus ½ cup all-purpose flour.

3 **If you're working with a stand mixer**: Attach the bowl and dough hook to the mixer, add ¼ cup all-purpose flour, and begin beating at medium speed until incorporated. Add more flour in ¼-cup increments until a soft, smooth, even dough forms. Continue kneading for 10 minutes until the dough is very soft and airy, adding more flour in 1-tablespoon increments if the dough starts to stick or climb up the hook.

If you're working by hand: Stir in another ¼ cup all-purpose flour, then turn the dough out onto a clean, dry, well-floured work surface. Flour your hands and knead the dough by gently twisting the heel of one hand into it while pulling and twisting with the other hand. Add more all-purpose flour in ¼-cup increments until a smooth, soft, pliable dough forms. Continue kneading for 10 minutes, turning and repositioning the dough repeatedly so it's evenly worked.

4 Dab a little oil on a paper towel and grease a large, clean bowl. Gather the dough into a ball, place it in the bowl, and turn it over so the top is lightly greased. Cover the bowl with a clean kitchen towel or plastic wrap and set aside in a warm, dry, draft-free place until doubled in bulk, until an indentation made with your finger stays put and doesn't spring back, about 1 hour.

5 Lightly flour a clean, dry work surface. Punch the dough down by plunging your fist into it without completely flattening it. Turn the dough out onto the work surface, knead once or twice, then shape into a single loaf.

6 Lightly oil a 9 × 5 × 3-inch loaf pan, place the loaf in it, cover loosely with a kitchen towel, and return it to the warm, dry, draft-free place until again doubled in bulk, about 45 minutes.

7 Meanwhile, position the rack in the center of the oven; preheat the oven to 400°F.

8 Bake until lightly browned, until the loaf sounds hollow when tapped, about 30 minutes. Cool in the pan on a wire rack for 5 minutes, then turn the loaf out of the pan and continue cooling on the wire rack to room temperature.

To store: Seal in a large plastic bag and keep at room temperature for up to 2 days or in the freezer for up to 2 months.

Honey Wheat Bread: Substitute 2 tablespoons honey for the molasses. (You may need to add up to ¼ cup more all-purpose flour.)

The amount of flour used for a yeast bread depends on the amount of moisture in the flour and ambient factors in your kitchen (temperature, humidity, and even altitude). Add just enough flour to the batter to make a pliable dough. Start with the minimal amount; you can always add more.

Yeast develops in a fairly strict temperature range. Thus, the water or milk must be heated between 105°F and 115°F. This range is slightly lower than the hot water out of many taps and certainly well below boiling or even simmering, but there's no way to be sure of the exact temperature without a thermometer. Always err on the high side if you're going to heat the liquid in one container, and then pour it into another (pouring cools a liquid considerably). Heating a liquid in a microwave on high for 10 to 20 seconds may do the trick, but again, you'll need a thermometer to be sure.

Rye Bread

A little sugar makes rye bread softer without your having to resort to esoteric flours. *Makes 1 loaf*

One ¼-ounce package active dry yeast plus
    1 teaspoon active dry yeast, or
    3½ teaspoons active dry yeast
1 tablespoon sugar
1½ cups warm water, between 105°F and
    115°F
1 tablespoon canola oil, plus additional for
    greasing
1 tablespoon caraway seeds
2 teaspoons salt
1½ cups all-purpose flour, plus additional
    for dusting
About 1½ cups rye flour

1 Sprinkle the yeast and sugar over the water in the bowl of a stand mixer or in a large mixing bowl. Set aside until foamy, about 3 minutes. (If the mixture does not foam, start again.)

2 Stir in the canola oil, caraway seeds, and salt, then stir in the all-purpose flour until a smooth batter forms. Stir in ½ cup rye flour.

3 **If you're working with a stand mixer:** Attach the bowl and dough hook to the mixer, add ½ cup rye flour, and begin beating at medium speed. Add more rye flour in 2-tablespoon increments until a soft, smooth, even but slightly sticky dough forms, about 5 minutes. Continue kneading for 10 more minutes, adding more rye flour in 1-tablespoon increments if the dough starts to stick or climb up the hook.

If you're working by hand: Stir in another ¼ cup rye flour, then turn the dough out onto a clean, dry, well-floured work surface. Dust your hands with all-purpose flour and knead the dough by gently twisting the heel of one hand into it while pulling and twisting with the other. Add more rye flour in ¼-cup increments until a smooth, soft, pliable, but slightly sticky dough forms. Continue kneading for 10 minutes, turning and repositioning the dough repeatedly so it's evenly worked.

4 Grease a large bowl, gather the dough into a ball, and place it in the bowl. Turn the dough over so the top is lightly greased, then cover the bowl with plastic wrap or a clean kitchen towel and set aside in a warm, dry place until doubled in bulk, until an indentation made with your finger doesn't pop back out, about 1½ hours.

5 Gently push your fist into the dough to deflate it, then turn it out onto a clean, dry work surface that you've dusted with some all-purpose flour. Knead a couple of times, then shape the loaf into a half-flattened football.

6 Lightly grease a large baking sheet and place the loaf on it. Cover loosely with a kitchen towel and set aside in a warm, dry place until doubled in bulk, about 1 hour.

7 Position the rack in the center of the oven and preheat the oven to 400°F.

8 Once the dough has risen again, slash its top in three diagonal, parallel lines with a clean razor blade or a sharp knife, spacing the cuts about 3 inches apart. Cut down only about ½ inch, just until the dough pulls back a little.

9 Bake until browned, until the loaf sounds hollow when tapped, about 40 minutes. Cool on the baking sheet for 5 minutes, then transfer to a wire rack to continue cooling.

To store: Cool to room temperature, then seal in a plastic bag and keep at room temperature for 2 days or in the freezer for up to 2 months.

Onion Rye Bread: Cook ¼ cup finely minced yellow onion in 1 tablespoon canola oil in a skillet set over medium heat, just until softened. Cook, then add the onion and any oil in the skillet with the canola oil called for in the recipe.

Dinner Rolls

These are simple dinner rolls, but you can shape them into Parker House, crescent, or monkey-bread rolls. If you like more crust, throw two or three ice cubes onto the floor of the oven when you put the bread in. *Makes about 3 dozen rolls*

> One ¼-ounce package active dry yeast or
>   2½ teaspoons active dry yeast
> 1½ tablespoons sugar
> 1 cup warm whole milk, between 105°F
>   and 115°F
> 3 tablespoons unsalted butter, melted and
>   cooled somewhat but still warm, plus
>   additional solid butter for greasing
> 1 tablespoon salt
> 3 to 3½ cups all-purpose flour, plus
>   additional for dusting

1 Sprinkle the yeast and sugar over the warm milk in the bowl of a stand mixer or in a large bowl. Set aside until foamy, about 3 minutes. (If the mixture does not froth and bubble, start again.)

2 Stir in the melted butter and salt, then stir in 1 cup flour. Cover the bowl with plastic wrap and set aside until enlarged like a sponge-type dough (that is, as if you made a muffin batter and then set it aside at room temperature until it became airy, thick, and foamy), 15 to 20 minutes.

3 **If you're working with a stand mixer:** Attach the bowl and dough hook to the mixer, add 2 cups flour, and beat at medium speed until a smooth, soft, pliable dough forms, about 8 minutes, adding

more flour in 1-tablespoon increments if the dough starts to stick or climbs up the hook toward the mixer.

If you're working by hand: Stir in 2 cups flour, then lightly dust a clean, dry work surface with flour and turn the dough out onto it. Dust your hands with flour, then knead the dough for 10 minutes, adding more flour should it become tacky, until the dough is quite soft and smooth, about like a newborn's skin.

④ Lightly butter a large bowl, gather the dough into a ball, and place it in the bowl. Turn the dough over so the top is lightly buttered, then cover the bowl with plastic wrap or a kitchen towel and set aside in a warm, dry, draft-free place until doubled in bulk, until you can make a permanent indentation with two fingers in the dough, about 1 hour.

⑤ **To make Parker House rolls:** Turn the dough out onto a lightly floured work surface. Do not flour the top of the dough, but roll it out until it's a large circle about ¼ inch thick. Cut the dough into 2½-inch circles with a round cookie cutter or a thick-rimmed drinking glass. Fold a little more than a third of the circle over onto itself (sticky topside to sticky topside), press lightly to adhere, and set aside (each roll should look about like a pair of lips with the bottom lip stuck out). Lightly butter a large baking sheet, place the rolls on it, cover loosely with a kitchen towel, and return to the warm, dry, draft-free place until again doubled in bulk, about 40 minutes.

To make crescents: Turn the dough out onto a lightly floured work surface and divide it into 6 equal balls. Lightly flour each, then roll into circles about ¼ inch thick. Cut each into 6 pie-shaped wedges. Starting at the edge of the wedge that used to be circumference of the circle, roll up toward their points, thereby making elongated crescents. Bend them slightly for the classic crescent look. Place on a lightly buttered baking sheet, cover with a clean kitchen towel, and return to a warm, dry place until doubled in bulk, about 40 minutes.

To make monkey bread rolls: Turn the dough out onto a lightly floured work surface. Pinch off almond-sized sections and roll these into balls. Lightly butter the indentations of at least two standard 12-cup muffin tins. Drop 3, 4, or 5 of the little balls into each indentation; cover with a clean kitchen towel; and return to the warm, dry, draft-free place until again doubled in bulk, about 40 minutes.

⑥ Meanwhile, position the rack in the center of the oven; preheat the oven to 375°F.

⑦ Bake until lightly browned, until the rolls sound hollow when tapped, about 20 minutes. Cool in the tins on a large wire rack for 5 minutes, then turn out the rolls and let them cool on the rack.

To store: Cool to room temperature, then place in large, resealable plastic bags at room temperature for up to 3 days or in the freezer for up to 3 months.

Hot Chocolate

Good bread needs hot chocolate; here's one inspired by Mexican chocolate. For two servings, place 2½ cups whole milk, 1 tablespoon sugar, ¼ teaspoon almond extract, ¼ teaspoon ground cinnamon, ⅛ teaspoon salt, and 2 ounces finely chopped bittersweet or semisweet chocolate in a medium saucepan set over medium-low heat; whisk constantly until smooth, with tiny bubbles along the inner rim of the pan, about 3 minutes.

Breadsticks

The crispest breadsticks are made with yeast, but they shouldn't be left to rise. Note that you don't use a full ¼-ounce packet of yeast. *Makes 24 breadsticks*

1½ teaspoons active dry yeast
1 teaspoon sugar
¾ cup warm water, between 105°F and 115°F
2 tablespoons olive oil
1 teaspoon salt
About 2 cups all-purpose flour, plus
    additional for dusting
1 large egg white, whisked with
    1 tablespoon water in a small bowl

❶ Sprinkle the yeast and sugar over ¼ cup warm water in a large bowl; set aside until foamy, about 3 minutes. (If the mixture does not bubble and foam, start over.)

❷ Meanwhile, position the rack in the center of the oven and preheat the oven to 325°F. Line a large baking sheet with parchment paper.

❸ Stir the remaining ½ cup warm water, olive oil, and salt into the yeast mixture, then stir in the flour.

❹ Lightly dust a clean, dry work surface with flour, then turn the dough out onto it. Dust your hands with flour and knead the dough, pushing it with one hand while gently grinding the heel of your other hand into it. Add more flour if the dough becomes sticky; continue kneading until the dough is smooth, pliable, and soft, about 5 minutes.

❺ Divide the dough into 24 pieces, each about the size of a whole walnut. Lightly dust the work surface with flour, then roll these pieces under your palms into 8-inch sticks, about the thickness of a drinking straw. Pick each one up with one end in each hand and swing it like a mini-jump rope to thin it out to about 10 inches long.

❻ Place the sticks on the prepared baking sheet, spacing them about 1½ inches apart. Brush very lightly with the egg-white wash; the wash should not puddle alongside the sticks.

❼ Bake until lightly browned and quite firm to the touch, about 45 minutes. Cool on the baking sheet for 3 minutes, then gently transfer to a wire rack to continue cooling.

To store: Cool to room temperature and then seal in a large plastic bag at room temperature for up to 3 days. Not recommended for freezing.

Variations: Once you've brushed the sticks with the egg-white wash, sprinkle them with caraway seeds, coarsely ground black pepper, fennel seeds, kosher salt, or sesame seeds.

English Muffins

Make your own? Sure. They're better than the ones you buy in the grocery store. Don't split these open with a fork; use a knife to cut them into disks. *Makes 16 English muffins*

One ¼-ounce package active dry yeast or
    2½ teaspoons active dry yeast
½ teaspoon sugar
¼ cup warm water, between 105°F and 115°F
1¼ cups warm milk (regular, low-fat, or
    fat-free), between 105°F and 115°F
¼ cup solid vegetable shortening, melted
    and cooled, plus additional for greasing
    the bowl and the griddle
2 tablespoons honey
1 teaspoon salt
1 large egg, lightly beaten, at room
    temperature
4½ cups all-purpose flour, or a little more
About 1 cup yellow cornmeal

❶ Sprinkle the yeast and sugar over the water in a small bowl. Set aside until foamy, about 5 minutes. (If the yeast does not fizz, either it has gone bad or the water wasn't the right temperature—throw the mixture out and start again.)

❷ Pour the milk into the bowl of a stand mixer or a large bowl. Stir in the yeast mixture, the shortening, honey, and salt, then stir in the egg.

❸ **If you're working with a stand mixer:** Attach the dough hook and beat in 3 cups of flour, first at low speed, then at medium speed. Continue adding flour in ½-cup increments, beating all the while, until all the flour has been added. Continue beating until a soft, smooth, pliable dough forms, about 5 minutes. If the dough starts to crawl up the hook or sticks to the bowl, add a little more flour, less than ¼ cup, to get it smooth and soft. Knead at medium speed for 5 minutes.

If you're working by hand: Stir in about 2½ cups flour with a wooden spoon, then continue stirring in flour in ¼-cup increments until the total amount of flour is about 3½ cups. Lightly flour a clean, dry work surface; turn the dough out onto it; and begin kneading in more flour in ¼-cup increments, pulling and twisting the dough with one hand while pushing down onto it with the heel of the other. Continue adding flour until a smooth, soft dough forms. Knead the dough for 5 minutes, adding as little flour as possible to make a smooth, soft, pliable dough.

❹ Once all the flour has been added and the dough is as smooth as a baby's skin, grease a clean, large bowl with a little shortening on a paper towel, then add the dough. Turn it over to coat it with the shortening, cover loosely with a kitchen towel or plastic wrap, and set aside in a warm, dry place until doubled in bulk, about 1½ hours.

❺ Deflate the dough by plunging your fist gently but firmly into it. Lightly dust a work surface with cornmeal, then turn the dough out onto it. Lightly dust the dough with cornmeal and roll with a rolling pin until about ⅜ inch thick. Cut into 3-inch circles, using a round cookie cutter or a thick-rimmed drinking glass. Dust a large baking sheet with cornmeal and place the cutout circles on it. Cover loosely with a clean kitchen towel and set aside to rise in a warm, dry place for 20 minutes.

❻ Grease a flat griddle with a little shortening on a paper towel, then heat it over medium-low heat. Add a few of the English muffins, as many as will fit comfortably, reduce the heat to low, and cook until lightly browned, about 16 minutes, turning once. The heat should be so low that the muffins "bake" on the griddle. Transfer to a wire rack and continue griddle-baking the muffins until all are done.

To store: Cooled to room temperature, the English muffins can be kept in a ziplock bag for up to 3 days or in the freezer for up to 2 months.

Things To Do with English Muffins

❶ Use them in streamlined Eggs Benedict (page 20).

❷ Make a scrambled egg sandwich.

❸ Use them as buns for Salmon Burgers (page 355), Inside-Out Cheeseburgers (page 404), or Lentil-Nut Patties (page 504).

❹ Use them for just about any sandwich—but particularly one with leftover Italian-Inspired Basil and Pancetta Meat Loaf (page 406).

❺ Split them and make English muffin pizzas by topping with jarred or homemade pizza sauce (page 183) and shredded mozzarella cheese, then broiling until bubbling.

Yeast Biscuits

These light, traditional, Southern biscuits are not set aside to double in bulk like bread; rather, the yeast is just one of three leaveners. For Baking Powder Biscuits, page 231. *Makes about 16 biscuits*

2 tablespoons plus 1 teaspoon sugar

One ¼-ounce package active dry yeast or 2½ teaspoons active dry yeast

¼ cup warm water, between 105°F and 115°F

1½ cups cake flour (see page 655)

1 cup all-purpose flour, plus additional for dusting and more as necessary

1 teaspoon baking powder

1 teaspoon baking soda

½ teaspoon salt

½ cup solid vegetable shortening

¾ cup plus 2 tablespoons regular or low-fat buttermilk (do not use fat-free)

1. Sprinkle 1 teaspoon sugar and the yeast over the water in a medium bowl. Set aside until frothy, about 5 minutes. Meanwhile, position the rack in the center of the oven and preheat the oven to 400°F.

2. Mix both flours, the baking powder, baking soda, salt, and the remaining 2 tablespoons sugar in a large bowl. Cut in the shortening with a fork or a pastry cutter, pressing the shortening through the tines and into the flour mixture until the whole thing resembles coarse meal.

3. Use a fork to stir in the buttermilk and the foamy yeast mixture until a soft dough forms, adding any additional all-purpose flour as necessary to keep the dough pliable.

4. Dust a clean, dry work surface with flour and dump the dough onto it. Knead lightly just until smooth, about 1 minute.

5. Lightly flour the work surface again; lightly flour the dough and a rolling pin. Roll to about ½ inch thick; cut into 2-inch circles using a biscuit cutter, cookie cutter, or a thick-rimmed drinking glass.

6. Place the rounds on a large baking sheet at least 2 inches apart and bake until puffed and lightly browned, about 12 minutes.

Make-Ahead Tip: Make the dough through step 4, then seal in plastic wrap in the refrigerator for up to 1 week. Take out as little or as much as you need for any given morning, let the ball of dough come somewhat to room temperature (about 20 minutes on the counter), and then roll and bake as directed.

Herbed Yeast Biscuits: Stir any of the following into the batter with the buttermilk: 2 tablespoons finely chopped basil leaves, 2 tablespoons finely chopped chives, 1 tablespoon stemmed thyme, 1 tablespoon chopped parsley leaves, or 1 tablespoon finely chopped rosemary leaves.

Sticky Buns with Four Fillings

Gooey and wonderful. *Makes 12 sticky buns*

¾ cup plus 2 tablespoons warm whole milk, between 105°F and 115°F

One ¼-ounce package active dry yeast or 2½ teaspoons active dry yeast

⅓ cup plus 1 teaspoon granulated sugar

2 large egg yolks, at room temperature, lightly beaten

¼ teaspoon salt

About 3¼ cups all-purpose flour, plus additional for dusting

One of the four fillings that follow

3 tablespoons unsalted butter, melted and cooled, plus additional for greasing the bowl and the pan

Sticky Bun Icing (page 231)

1 Place the milk in the bowl of a stand mixer or a large bowl. Sprinkle on the yeast and 1 teaspoon sugar. Set aside until frothy, about 5 minutes. (If the yeast doesn't turn bubbly, throw it out and start again.)

2 Stir in the egg yolks, salt, and the remaining ⅓ cup sugar, then stir in about 2 cups flour.

3 **If you're working with a stand mixer:** Attach the dough hook and begin mixing the dough, first on low speed, then on medium speed. Continue beating, adding flour in ¼-cup increments until a soft, pliable dough forms, not sticky at all. After you've added a total of 3 cups flour, continue kneading the dough at medium speed for 10 minutes. If the dough starts to crawl up the hook or sticks to the bowl, add more flour, but no more than ¼ cup, just to keep it smooth.

If you're working by hand: Stir in 1 more cup flour, dust your work surface with flour, and turn the dough out onto it. Knead in additional flour until the dough is soft, smooth, but a little firm—dig into it with the heel of one hand, then grab it with the other hand and pull it forward, twisting as you do so. Knead about 10 minutes until the dough is as soft as a baby's skin.

4 Lightly butter a large, clean bowl, then put the dough in it. Turn it over to coat it with butter, cover the bowl loosely with a kitchen towel or plastic wrap, and set aside in a warm, dry place until doubled in bulk, about 1 hour.

5 Meanwhile, make the filling of your choice. Set aside.

6 Lightly dust the work surface with flour, then deflate the dough by pressing your fist gently but firmly into it. Turn the dough out onto the work surface, dust it and a rolling pin with flour, and roll to a 16 × 8-inch rectangle, about ¼ inch thick. Brush the top of the dough with the melted butter, then top with the filling, spreading it across the rectangle, but leaving a ½-inch border all around.

7 Starting at one of the long sides of the rectangle, roll it up, pressing gently to compact the spiral but not so firmly as to force any of the filling out of it. You should end up with a 16-inch-long tube. Slice into 12 rolls, each about 1¼ inches thick.

8 Lightly butter a 13 × 9-inch baking dish. Place the rolls in it so they're flat, one of the cut sides down; space them out evenly in the pan (they will rise and grow together). Cover loosely with a clean kitchen towel or plastic wrap and set aside in a warm, dry place until doubled in bulk, about 1 hour.

9 Position the rack in the center of the oven and preheat the oven to 350°F.

10 Once the rolls have doubled in bulk, bake until browned with bubbling centers, about 25 minutes. Cool in the pan for 10 minutes, then invert the pan onto a cutting board and cool for at least another 20 minutes before icing with the Sticky Bun Icing.

Four Sticky Bun Fillings

1. Simple Brown Sugar Filling
1¼ cups packed dark brown sugar
2 teaspoons ground cinnamon

2. Raisin and Cinnamon Filling
¾ cup dried currants or chopped raisins
½ cup packed dark brown sugar
1 teaspoon ground cinnamon
1 teaspoon grated orange zest

3. Honey, Pistachio, and Apricot Filling

½ cup finely chopped dried apricots

½ cup finely chopped pistachios

¼ cup honey

4. Marmalade Filling

1¼ cups orange marmalade or homemade Quince Jam (page 221)

¼ cup finely chopped walnuts or pecans

Sticky Bun Icing

Makes about ½ cup

1 cup confectioners' sugar

1 tablespoon milk (regular, low-fat, or fat-free)

½ teaspoon vanilla extract

Mix the ingredients in a medium bowl until smooth. Drizzle over the sticky buns once cooled.

❄ Quick Breads ❄

Even if you don't have time for yeast, you still have time for bread. When baking soda or baking powder replaces yeast, bread still rises—perhaps not as high, but certainly in less time. So here's a set of biscuits, scones, and the like, followed by lots of quick-bread loaves, sweet and savory, and all rounded out with tortillas.

Baking Powder Biscuits

Biscuits need not just be for breakfast; they're great dinnertime fare, particularly with a hearty soup or stew. *Makes about a dozen biscuits*

2¼ cups all-purpose flour, plus additional for dusting

4 teaspoons baking powder

½ teaspoon salt

5 tablespoons cool unsalted butter, cut into chunks, or 5 tablespoons solid vegetable shortening

¾ cup plus 1 tablespoon cold milk (regular, low-fat, or fat-free)

❶ Position the rack in the center of the oven and preheat the oven to 425°F.

❷ Whisk the flour, baking powder, and salt in a large bowl. Cut in the butter or shortening, using a pastry cutter or a fork, until the mixture looks like coarse meal. Alternatively, place the dry ingredients in a food processor fitted with the chopping blade, pulse a couple of times to combine, then add the butter or shortening and process to the desired consistency; turn the mixture out into a large bowl.

❸ Stir in the milk with a fork, just until a soft dough forms. Do not overmix.

❹ Lightly dust a clean, dry work surface with flour, gather the dough into a ball, and turn it out onto the work surface. Dust the dough with flour and knead two or three times, just until it starts to adhere. It will be a little sticky—as long as it's not clumping between your fingers, you needn't add any more flour.

5 Press—do not roll—the dough into a round-ish shape a little less than 1 inch thick. Cut into 2½-inch rounds, using a cookie cutter or a thick-rimmed glass. Try to cut out the rounds so that there's very little dough left over; you can pat out the scraps a second time with a little more flour, but they will be tougher. Transfer the rounds to a large baking sheet.

6 Bake until golden brown and puffed but dry to the touch on top, 13 to 15 minutes. Serve at once.

Buttermilk Biscuits: Reduce the baking powder to 2 teaspoons. Add 2 teaspoons baking soda with the remainder; substitute cold regular or low-fat buttermilk for the milk.

Cheese Biscuits: Add 2 ounces grated cheese with the flour. Harder, aged cheeses work best—an aged Gouda, Gruyère, Parmigiano-Reggiano, Asiago, etc.

These two recipes will yield one or two extra biscuits.

Cream Scones with Orange Glaze

Scones should be a cake and a biscuit all in one. Cream, although traditional, makes for a gummy scone, so we prefer half-and-half for a lighter—and better—crumb. For the best results, use cake flour. *Makes 8 scones*

> 3¼ cups cake flour (see page 655), plus additional for dusting
> 2 tablespoons sugar
> 1 tablespoon baking powder
> ½ teaspoon salt
> 6 tablespoons cold unsalted butter, cut into chunks
> 2 large eggs, at room temperature
> ¾ cup half-and-half
> ½ cup dried currants or golden raisins
> Orange Glaze (recipe follows)

1 Position the rack in the center of the oven and preheat the oven to 425°F.

2 Mix the flour, sugar, baking powder, and salt in a large bowl. Cut in the butter with a fork or a pastry cutter until the mixture resembles coarse meal, pressing the butter through the tines and into the flour until uniformly textured like very coarse sand.

3 Whisk the eggs and half-and-half in a medium bowl. Pour into the flour mixture; stir a few times with a wooden spoon, just until moistened. Stir in the currants or raisins, just until a batter starts to pull together but still lies in bits and pieces in the bowl.

4 Dust a clean, dry work surface with flour, then turn the batter onto it. Knead a few times until the dough holds its shape. Should it be sticky, lightly dust your hands with flour. Be careful: for tender scones, you want to add the smallest amount of flour possible at this stage. Gently pat—do not roll—the dough into a circle about 9 inches wide. Cut it into 8 pie-shaped wedges and transfer these to a large baking sheet.

5 Bake until lightly browned and somewhat firm to the touch, about 18 minutes. Cool on the baking sheet for 2 minutes, then transfer to a wire rack to cool for at least 5 minutes before serving. Cool completely and top with Orange Glaze.

To store: Once fully cooled, do not top with the glaze; instead, store in a ziplock plastic bag for up to 2 days at room temperature or for up to 2 months in the freezer.

Variations: Add ½ teaspoon ground cinnamon and/or ¼ teaspoon grated nutmeg with the sugar.

Substitute chopped dried apples; chopped dried figs; chopped dried pineapple; chopped dried strawberries, dried blueberries, dried cranberries; or mini-chocolate chips for the dried currants or raisins.

Orange Glaze *Makes about ⅓ cup*

1 tablespoon orange juice
1 teaspoon grated orange zest
1 teaspoon unsalted butter, melted and cooled
½ to ¾ cup confectioners' sugar

Mix the juice, zest, and melted butter in a small bowl; stir in just enough confectioners' sugar so that a smooth glaze forms. Drizzle over the cooled scones before serving.

Maple Walnut Scones

Walnuts and maple syrup—is there a better combination? *Makes 8 scones*

1¾ cups all-purpose flour, plus additional for dusting
½ cup cake flour (see page 655), plus additional if necessary
2 teaspoons baking powder
½ teaspoon salt
6 tablespoons cool unsalted butter, cut into chunks
½ cup finely chopped toasted walnut pieces
1 large egg, at room temperature
½ cup yogurt (regular, low-fat, or fat-free)
¼ cup plus 1 teaspoon maple syrup
1 large egg yolk
2 tablespoons milk (regular, low-fat, or fat-free)

① Position the rack in the center of the oven and preheat the oven to 375°F. Line a large baking sheet with parchment paper or a silicone baking mat; set aside.

② Mix both flours, the baking powder, and salt in a large bowl. Cut in the butter with a pastry cutter or a fork, pressing the flour and butter together through the tines until the mixture resembles coarse meal.

③ Stir in the walnut pieces, the whole egg, the yogurt, and ¼ cup maple syrup. Stir just until a batter comes together into a moist dough.

④ Lightly dust a clean, dry work surface with flour, then turn the dough out onto it. Knead a few times, just until the dough begins to hold its shape. If it's sticky, add a touch more cake flour, just to keep it moist but stable. Gently press—do not roll—into a circle about 8 inches in diameter.

⑤ Slice the circle into 8 wedges, like a pie. Transfer these to the prepared baking sheet.

⑥ Whisk the egg yolk, the remaining 1 teaspoon maple syrup, and the milk in a small bowl. Brush this mixture over the scones.

⑦ Bake until brown and firm, about 20 minutes. Cool on the baking sheet for a couple of minutes, then transfer to a wire rack to continue cooling for at least 10 minutes before serving.

To store: Once cooled, seal in ziplock plastic bags and keep at room temperature for up to 2 days or in the freezer for up to 2 months.

Honey Walnut Scones: Substitute honey for the maple syrup.

Almond or Pecan Scones: Substitute finely chopped toasted sliced almonds or pecan pieces for the walnuts.

Try them iced with the Sticky Bun Icing (page 231).

Buttermilk Muffins

Plain and simple, these are great with eggs or a thick, creamy soup. *Makes 12 muffins*

> 1 cup all-purpose flour
> 1 cup cake flour (see page 655)
> 3 tablespoons sugar
> 2 teaspoons baking powder
> ½ teaspoon baking soda
> ½ teaspoon salt
> 1 cup buttermilk (regular, low-fat, or fat-free)
> 4 tablespoons (½ stick) unsalted butter, melted and cooled, plus additional for greasing the muffin tins
> 1 large egg

1 Position the rack in the center of the oven and preheat the oven to 400°F. Lightly butter the indentations of a 12-cup muffin tin (see Note); set it aside.

2 Whisk both flours, the sugar, baking powder, baking soda, and salt in a large bowl.

3 Whisk the buttermilk, melted butter, and egg in a medium bowl. Stir into the flour mixture with a wooden spoon just until a grainy batter forms. There should be little grains of flour still visible; do not stir until smooth.

4 Fill the muffin tin's indentations about two-thirds full. Bake until puffed, brown, and slightly firm to the touch, about 25 minutes. Cool in the tin for 5 minutes, then unmold and continue cooling on a wire rack.

To store: Once cooled, place in a ziplock plastic bag and keep at room temperature for up to 4 days or in the freezer for up to 3 months.

Note: There are no standard-sized muffin tins. These muffins work best in tins the indentations of which hold about ½ cup water. If yours are larger, divide the batter among as many indentations as you can, then fill the others halfway with water.

Variations: Add ⅔ cup chopped toasted nuts—such as unsalted peanuts, pecan pieces, walnut pieces, or skinned hazelnuts—with the sugar.

Reduce the sugar to 1 tablespoon and add ⅔ cup shredded cheese—such as Cheddar, Gruyère, or Emmentaler—with the remaining sugar.

Add ¾ cup mini-chocolate chips or fresh berries—such as blueberries, raspberries, or sliced strawberries—to the batter just as you stir the wet ingredients into the dry.

Popovers

Popovers may be the consummate jam vehicles, but that's not all. Break them open and fill them with scrambled eggs. Or use them instead of English muffins for Eggs Benedict (page 20) or as a bed for Baked Huevos Rancheros (page 26). You must make them in a popover pan or 1-cup glass custard cups. *Makes 6 popovers*

> Nonstick spray or unsalted butter for greasing the pan or cups
> 2 large eggs
> 1 cup milk (regular, low-fat, or fat-free)
> 1 tablespoon solid vegetable shortening or unsalted butter, melted and cooled
> 1 cup all-purpose flour
> ½ teaspoon salt

1 Spray a popover pan with nonstick spray or lightly butter the indentations. Position the rack in the center of the oven, place the popover pan on it, and preheat the oven to 425°F. Alternatively, spray or butter six glass 1-cup custard cups, set on a lipped baking sheet, and place in the oven while they preheat. Heat the pan or cups for 10 minutes.

② Place the eggs, milk, and melted fat in a food processor fitted with the chopping blade or in a large blender. Pulse a couple of times or blend a few seconds to combine. Add the flour and salt; process or blend until smooth.

③ Remove the pan or the cups from the oven. Be careful: they're hot. Divide the batter among them, filling each about two-thirds full.

④ Bake until puffed, brown, and crunchy on top, about 40 minutes. Do not open the oven during the first 30 minutes of baking. Serve at once; popovers are unsuitable for storage.

Banana Bread

We make our banana bread with walnut oil for a nutty taste without any nuts. Of course, you can always add them—see the variations. For a deeper taste, use toasted walnut oil, found in specialty or gourmet markets. *Makes 1 loaf*

> 1½ cups all-purpose flour, plus additional for dusting the pan
> 1 teaspoon baking soda
> ½ teaspoon ground cinnamon
> ½ teaspoon salt
> ½ cup packed light brown sugar
> ½ cup granulated sugar
> 5 tablespoons walnut oil, plus additional for greasing the pan.
> 2 large eggs, at room temperature
> 3 large, very ripe bananas, peeled and mashed in a small bowl
> 2 teaspoons vanilla extract

① Position the rack in the center of the oven; preheat the oven to 350°F. Dab a little oil on a paper towel; lightly grease a 9 × 5 × 3-inch loaf pan. Add a little flour and coat the interior evenly but lightly by turning and tilting the pan; tap out any excess.

② Whisk the flour, baking soda, cinnamon, and salt in a medium bowl until uniform.

③ Beat both sugars and the walnut oil in a large bowl, using an electric mixer at medium speed, until smooth and creamy, about 4 minutes. Scrape down the sides of the bowl and beat in the eggs one at a time. Beat in the bananas and vanilla until smooth.

④ Scrape down and remove the beaters. Fold in the flour mixture with a rubber spatula, just until there are no white streaks or patches in the dough but not until smooth—there may be some floury graininess visible. Scrape the batter into the prepared pan, smoothing it evenly to the corners.

⑤ Bake until lightly browned, until a toothpick inserted into the center of the loaf comes out with a few moist crumbs attached, about 1 hour and 5 minutes. Cool in the pan on a wire rack for 5 minutes, then unmold and continue cooling on the rack for at least 10 minutes before slicing.

To store: Cool to room temperature, then seal in a large plastic bag for up to 3 days at room temperature or freeze for up to 3 months.

Variations: Add ½ cup walnut pieces, pecan pieces, or chopped cashews with the baking soda.

Add ⅔ cup bittersweet or semisweet chocolate chips with the baking soda.

Substitute 5 tablespoons cool unsalted butter, cut into chunks, for the walnut oil.

Substitute almond oil for the walnut oil; add ¼ teaspoon almond extract with the vanilla.

Add ½ teaspoon maple or rum extract with the vanilla.

Add 1 teaspoon finely grated orange or lemon zest with the vanilla.

Lemonade Bread

Frozen lemonade concentrate makes this quick bread quicker. You'll need a blender to emulsify the concentrate. *Makes 1 loaf*

- 2 cups all-purpose flour, plus additional for dusting the pan
- ⅓ cup sugar
- 2 teaspoons baking powder
- ½ teaspoon salt
- 4 tablespoons unsalted butter (½ stick), melted and cooled, plus additional solid butter for greasing the pan
- ½ cup frozen lemonade concentrate, thawed (do not use low-calorie or diet concentrate)
- ¼ cup regular or low-fat buttermilk (do not use fat-free)
- 1 large egg
- 1 tablespoon finely grated lemon zest
- 1 teaspoon vanilla extract

1 Position the rack in the center of the oven and preheat the oven to 350°F. Lightly butter and flour a 9 × 5 × 3-inch loaf pan, making sure the corners are coated. Whisk the flour, sugar, baking powder, and salt in a large bowl.

2 Place the lemonade concentrate, melted butter, buttermilk, egg, zest, and vanilla in a large blender or food processor; cover and blend or process until smooth. Pour over the flour mixture; stir with a wooden spoon until a corn bread–like batter forms. Spread into the prepared pan.

3 Bake until lightly browned, until a toothpick inserted into the middle of the loaf comes out clean, about 40 minutes. Cool in the pan on a wire rack for 10 minutes, then unmold and continue cooling on the rack for at least 10 minutes before slicing.

To store: Cool completely, then place in a sealable plastic bag and store at room temperature for up to 3 days or in the freezer for up to 3 months.

Lemonade Blueberry Bread: Fold 1 cup fresh blueberries into the batter along with the flour mixture.

Lemonade Poppy Seed Bread: Add 3 tablespoons poppy seeds into the dry ingredients with the flour.

Limeade Bread: Substitute frozen limeade concentrate, thawed, for the lemonade concentrate; also substitute lime zest for the lemon zest.

Gingerbread

Make sure your ground ginger is fresh, no more than 6 months old. *Makes 8 servings*

- 1½ cups all-purpose flour, plus additional for dusting the pan
- 1 cup cake flour (see page 655)
- 1 tablespoon ground ginger
- 2 teaspoons ground cinnamon
- 2 teaspoons baking soda
- ½ teaspoon ground cloves
- ¼ teaspoon salt
- ½ cup solid vegetable shortening, plus additional for greasing the pan
- ½ cup sugar
- ¾ cup unsulfured molasses
- 1 large egg, at room temperature
- 1 teaspoon vanilla extract
- ¾ cup regular or low-fat buttermilk (do not use fat-free) or ¾ cup plus 1 tablespoon regular or low-fat plain yogurt

1 Position the rack in the center of the oven and preheat the oven to 350°F. Lightly grease and flour a 9-inch baking pan; set aside. Whisk both flours, the ginger, cinnamon, baking soda, cloves, and salt in a medium bowl; set aside as well.

2 Using an electric mixer, beat the shortening and sugar at medium speed in a large bowl until creamy and smooth, about 3 minutes. Beat in the molasses for 2 minutes.

3 Scrape down the sides of the bowl with a rubber spatula and beat in the egg and vanilla. Then beat in the buttermilk or yogurt until smooth.

4 Scrape off and remove the beaters. Fold in the flour mixture with a rubber spatula, working in even arcs so as not to set the flour's glutens, just until there are no white patches left in the batter. Scrape and spread the batter into the prepared pan.

5 Bake until well browned, until a toothpick inserted into the center of the cake comes out clean, about 45 minutes. Cool in the pan on a wire rack for 15 minutes before cutting into squares.

To store: Cool to room temperature, then cover with plastic wrap and keep at room temperature for up to 3 days.

Variations: For a spicier bread, add ½ teaspoon ground black pepper with the salt and 2 tablespoons finely minced crystallized ginger with the vanilla.
   Add ¾ cup bittersweet or semisweet chocolate chips with the cake flour.

Cheddar Bread

Some sugar is necessary to build a good structure in a savory quick bread—but less than you might expect. This bread is exceptional when spread with Tapenade (page 42). *Makes 1 loaf*

   1 large egg, at room temperature
   1 cup milk (regular, low-fat, or fat-free)
   6 tablespoons unsalted butter, melted and
      cooled
   1 cup all-purpose flour
   1 cup whole wheat flour
   1 tablespoon sugar
   1 tablespoon baking powder
   2 teaspoons dry mustard
   ½ teaspoon salt
   6 ounces Cheddar, shredded (about 1½ cups)
   ¼ cup chopped chives or the finely chopped
      green parts of 2 scallions

1 Position the rack in the center of the oven and preheat the oven to 350°F. Lightly butter and flour a 9 × 5 × 3-inch loaf pan.

2 Whisk the egg in a medium bowl until lightly beaten, then whisk in the milk and melted butter until fairly smooth. Set aside.

3 Whisk both flours, the sugar, baking powder, dry mustard, and salt in a large bowl. Stir in the Cheddar and chives with a wooden spoon.

4 Stir in the milk mixture all at once; keep stirring just until a dry, sticky, doughlike batter forms. Spread into the prepared pan, taking care to get it evenly to the corners.

5 Bake until golden, until a toothpick inserted into the center of the bread comes out clean, about 1 hour. Cool on a wire rack for at least 15 minutes before unmolding and cutting into slices.

To store: Cool to room temperature, then seal in a large plastic bag and keep at room temperature for up to 2 days or freeze for up to 3 months.

Variations: Substitute Gruyère, Emmentaler, Asiago, Pecorino Romano, aged Gouda, white Cheddar, or Parmigiano-Reggiano for the Cheddar.

Pizza Bread

No kid could turn down this quick bread. It's also a great appetizer for adults with Classic Cocktails (pages 54–55). Make two loaves and you don't even need dinner. *Makes 1 loaf*

⅓ cup olive oil, plus additional for greasing the pan
1 small onion, finely chopped
1 small green bell pepper, cored, seeded, and finely chopped
4 ounces white button or cremini mushrooms, cleaned and finely chopped
1 cup all-purpose flour, plus additional for dusting the pan
½ cup yellow cornmeal
1 tablespoon sugar
1 tablespoon baking powder
½ teaspoon salt
2 large eggs, lightly beaten in a small bowl
3 tablespoons tomato paste
2 ounces Parmigiano-Reggiano, shredded
¼ cup water
1 tablespoon minced rosemary leaves or 2 teaspoons dried rosemary
1 tablespoon stemmed thyme or 2 teaspoons dried thyme
½ teaspoon garlic powder

❶ Heat a large skillet over medium heat. Pour in the olive oil, then add the onion and bell pepper. Cook, stirring often, until softened, about 3 minutes.

❷ Add the mushrooms and continue cooking, stirring frequently, until they give off their liquid and it mostly evaporates, about 5 minutes. Pour the contents of the skillet into a large bowl; set aside to cool at room temperature for 15 minutes.

❸ Meanwhile, position the rack in the center of the oven and preheat the oven to 350°F. Dab a little olive oil on a paper towel and grease a 9 × 5 × 3-inch loaf pan. Add a little flour and coat the interior evenly, tapping out the excess. Finally, whisk the flour, cornmeal, sugar, baking powder, and salt in a medium bowl.

❹ Stir the eggs and tomato paste into the mushroom mixture, then stir in the cheese until uniform. Stir in the water, rosemary, thyme, and garlic powder. Add the flour mixture and stir until a fairly smooth, pink-red, thick batter forms. Spoon, scrape, and spread into the prepared pan.

❺ Bake until puffed and firm to the touch, until a toothpick inserted into the center of the loaf comes out clean, about 45 minutes. Cool on a wire rack for 15 minutes before unmolding and slicing.

To store: Cool completely on the rack, then seal in a plastic bag and store at room temperature for up to 2 days.

Pepperoni Pizza Bread: Omit the mushrooms; reduce the oil to ¼ cup. Add 4 ounces chopped pepperoni with the cheese.

Quiche Lorraine Bread

Quiche Lorraine is the classic: eggs, bacon, and Gruyère. Here's a quick bread that replicates the taste and is best for breakfast or on the coffee table with cocktails. *Makes 1 loaf*

    4 ounces thick-cut bacon, thinly sliced
    4 medium scallions, diced
    4 tablespoons (½ stick) unsalted butter,
        melted and cooled, plus additional butter
        for greasing the pan
    1¾ cups plus 2 tablespoons all-purpose flour,
        plus additional for dusting the pan
    1 tablespoon sugar
    2 teaspoons baking soda
    ½ teaspoon salt
    2 large eggs, lightly beaten in a small bowl
    ½ cup regular or low-fat buttermilk (do not
        use fat-free)
    4 ounces Gruyère, shredded

1 Heat a large skillet over medium heat. Add the bacon and cook until crisp, stirring often, about 4 minutes.

2 Add the scallions; cook until wilted, stirring constantly, about 1 minute. Pour the contents of the pan into a large bowl; set aside to cool for 15 minutes.

3 Meanwhile, position the rack in the center of the oven and preheat the oven to 350°F. Lightly butter and flour a 9 × 5 × 3-inch loaf pan; set aside.

4 Whisk the flour, sugar, baking soda, and salt in a medium bowl; set aside as well.

5 Stir the melted butter into the bacon and scallions, then stir in the eggs, buttermilk, and cheese until uniform. Add the flour mixture and stir until a creamy, rich batter forms. Scrape and spread into the prepared pan.

6 Bake until puffed and fairly firm to the touch, until a toothpick inserted into the center of the loaf comes out clean, about 50 minutes. Cool on a wire rack for at least 15 minutes before unmolding and slicing.

To store: Cool to room temperature on the rack, then seal in a plastic bag and keep at room temperature for up to 3 days.

Variations: Add 1 minced garlic clove with the scallions.

Substitute 1 large shallot, thinly sliced into rings, for the scallions.

Substitute Emmentaler or Swiss for the Gruyère.

Add a few dashes of hot red pepper sauce with the cheese.

Irish Soda Bread

Here's a streamlined version of this bakery favorite. *Makes 1 small round loaf*

    2 cups all-purpose flour, plus additional for
        dusting
    ½ cup raisins, chopped
    2 tablespoons sugar
    1 tablespoon caraway seeds, crushed in a
        mortar with a pestle or on a sheet of wax
        paper, under a heavy saucepan
    1 tablespoon baking soda
    ½ teaspoon salt
    1 cup whole or low-fat buttermilk (do not
        use fat-free)

1 Position the rack in the center of the oven and preheat the oven to 375°F.

2 Mix the flour, raisins, sugar, caraway seeds, baking soda, and salt in a large bowl. Stir in the buttermilk until a fairly thick but still crumbly batter starts to form.

3 Lightly dust the work surface and your hands with flour. Turn the dough out onto it and gather it into a ball, working the dough just a little to form the shape without its getting sticky. Press down gently so that you have a rounded loaf, as if a third of the ball has sunk into the work surface.

4 Use a sharp knife or a clean razor blade to make an "X" in the top of the dough, cutting down about ½ inch into the dough. Transfer the loaf to a baking sheet.

5 Bake until hollow when tapped, until golden but firm, 30 to 35 minutes. Cool on the baking sheet for 5 minutes, then transfer to a wire rack and cool for at least 20 minutes before slicing.

To store: Cool to room temperature and seal in a plastic bag for up to 1 day. Not recommended for freezing.

Variations: Substitute fennel seeds or sesame seeds for the caraway seeds.

Substitute dried currants, dried blueberries, or chopped dried strawberries for the raisins.

Sprinkle the top of the loaf with 1 teaspoon kosher salt before baking.

Place about a teaspoon of unsalted butter on each quarter of the bread's top before baking.

Corn Bread

The debate may rage on about whether or how much sugar should go in corn bread, but we prefer the taste of honey. *Makes about 6 servings*

¾ cup yellow cornmeal
⅔ cup all-purpose flour, plus additional for dusting the pan
½ teaspoon baking powder
½ teaspoon baking soda
¼ teaspoon salt
1 large egg, at room temperature
3 tablespoons unsalted butter, melted and cooled, plus additional butter for greasing the pan
¾ cup regular or low-fat buttermilk (do not use fat-free)
2 tablespoons honey

1 Position the rack in the center of the oven and preheat the oven to 350°F. Lightly butter and flour an 8-inch square pan; set aside. Whisk the cornmeal, flour, baking powder, baking soda, and salt in a large bowl; set aside as well.

2 Lightly whisk the egg in a medium bowl, then whisk in the buttermilk, melted butter, and honey until fairly smooth.

3 Use a wooden spoon or rubber spatula to fold the egg mixture into the cornmeal mixture, just until the dry ingredients are thoroughly moistened. Spoon out and spread into the prepared pan.

4 Bake until golden at the edges and a little puffed, until a toothpick inserted into the center of the corn bread comes out clean, about 30 minutes. Cool on a wire rack before slicing into squares to serve.

To store: Cool completely, slice into squares, and store in a sealable bag for up to 2 days.

Variations: Add any or all of the following with the buttermilk: 2 ounces finely grated Parmigiano-Reggiano or Cheddar; ½ cup corn kernels; 1 or 2 fresh jalapeño chiles, seeded and chopped; 2 teaspoons chili powder; or 1 teaspoon chopped oregano leaves.

Corn Tortillas

Corn tortillas are amazingly simple to make: just three ingredients. *Makes 12 tortillas*

2 cups masa harina (see page 659)
1 teaspoon salt
About 1 cup water

❶ Mix the masa harina and salt in a medium bowl; stir in ½ cup water, then continue stirring in more water in 1-tablespoon increments until a soft dough forms (you'll probably use a little less than 1 cup water in all, but the amount actually used depends entirely on the day's humidity and the moisture content of the masa harina). Divide the dough into 12 balls, each about 2 inches in diameter.

❷ Roll the balls between sheets of plastic wrap into circles 6 inches in diameter and ⅛ inch thick. Alternatively, use a tortilla press, following the manufacturer's instructions, to press the balls into tortillas. In either case, place the flattened disk between sheets of wax paper or plastic wrap as you make them.

❸ Set a medium skillet, preferably nonstick, over medium heat until a drop of water sizzles in the pan. Slip in a flattened disk and cook until speckled brown and slightly puffed, about 1 minute. Turn and cook until mottled on the other side, a little less than 1 minute. Transfer to a plate lined with a clean kitchen towel; fold the towel closed. Continue making the tortillas, stacking them in

the towel one on top of the other. Corn tortillas are fragile and not suitable for storage.

Flour Tortillas

Try these light tortillas with Migas (page 16) or alongside an omelet. *Makes 16 tortillas*

2½ cups plus 2 tablespoons all-purpose flour
1 teaspoon baking powder
1 teaspoon salt
½ teaspoon sugar
3 tablespoons solid vegetable shortening or lard
1 cup warm water

❶ Put the flour, baking powder, salt, and sugar in a food processor; pulse to whisk. Add the shortening or lard in chunks and pulse until an even, fine-grain mixture. With the machine running, add the water through the feed tube; process until a soft dough forms. Alternatively, whisk the flour, baking powder, salt, and sugar in a large bowl; cut in the shortening or lard with a pastry cutter or a fork until a fine-grain dough forms. Stir in the water with a fork until a pliable, cohesive, Silly Putty–like dough forms.

❷ Turn the dough out onto a dry, clean work surface and knead for 30 seconds. Gather into a ball, cover with plastic wrap, and set aside for 15 minutes.

❸ Divide the dough into 16 balls, each about the size of a Ping-Pong ball. Roll between sheets of plastic wrap into circles about 6 inches in diameter and ⅛ inch thick. (The thickness is more important than the diameter; they needn't be perfectly round, just roundish.)

❹ Set a skillet, preferably nonstick, over medium heat until a drop of water skitters around the pan.

Reduce the heat to medium-low and add 1 tortilla; cook until blistered with brown speckles and slightly puffed, about 1 minute. Turn and continue cooking until the other side is speckled, about 1 more minute. Keep the cooked tortillas warm as you make more by wrapping the ones that are in a clean kitchen towel or a cloth napkin.

To store: Wrap the tortillas in a clean kitchen towel and store at room temperature for up to 12 hours. To reheat, warm the entire stack, wrapped in the towel, in a microwave oven on high for 15 to 20 seconds.

Chicken, Turkey, and Other Birds

ALL THESE BIRDS FLOCK TOGETHER—NOT IN THE WILD, BUT AT THE MARKET and in our kitchens. In the end, they form one culinary category because of that sweet, subcutaneous layer of fat that protects the meat and caramelizes the skin as it roasts.

There's also their common dark side: ironically, the white meat, the bane of many home cooks. Simply put, all birds resist even cooking; the breast dries out long before the thigh has cooked—unless (as you'll see) you take a few easy precautions.

All difficulties aside, most of us return to chicken again and again, our default dinner. No wonder: it takes less time than beef, is less temperamental than fish, and suffers fewer cultural no-nos than some other meats. If our being at the top of the food chain has its many conundrums, eating birds is one of its better pleasures. We've taken the airborne and rendered them table-locked. It's a carnivore's paradise: bone, skin, and meat. Flightless, we soar.

Chicken

Chicken is the American table's most versatile staple: high in protein, relatively low in fat, with a mild taste that picks up and intensifies a host of preparations, from the simplest butter-and-herb combos to those many-condiment stir-fry concoctions.

Perfect-Every-Time Roast Chicken

A two-step process—starting the bird out breast side down and then turning it once during roasting—ensures that the skin gets crispy, the bird browns evenly, and the more delicate white meat is fully basted before it meets the heat on its own. *Makes 4 to 6 servings*

> One 4- to 5-pound chicken, giblets and neck removed
> 6 tarragon sprigs
> 2 tablespoons olive oil or 2 tablespoons unsalted butter, at room temperature
> 1 teaspoon kosher salt
> Butcher's twine

1 Position the rack in the middle of the oven (or so that there's at least 2 inches between the top of the bird and the top of the oven); preheat the oven to 400°F.

2 Slip one finger between the skin and the meat on one side of the breast just above the large cavity opening. Gently work your fingers into the growing pocket between the skin and meat. Take care not to stretch the skin to a dowager's elasticity. Once you have a pocket, do the same on the other side of the breast.

3 Slip 3 tarragon spears under the skin on each side of the breast, smoothing them evenly over the meat. Pat the skin on both sides back into place.

4 Rub all the outer skin of the bird with the olive oil or softened butter, then gently massage the salt into the skin. Truss the bird with butcher's twine (see page 249).

5 Place a rack in a large roasting pan, then place the bird on the rack breast side down. Roast for 20 minutes.

6 Reduce the oven temperature to 350°F. Turn the bird breast side up, taking care not to let any of the hot grease inside the body scald you. Baste the bird with any pan drippings, then continue roasting until very brown, basting every 20 minutes or so with pan drippings, until a meat thermometer inserted into the thickest part of the thigh registers 165°F (our preference) or 180°F (the USDA recommendation), about 50 to 70 more minutes. The juices from the thigh, when pierced, should run clear. If the skin starts to brown too deeply, lightly tent the bird with aluminum foil to prevent scorching. Transfer to a cutting or carving board; let stand for 10 minutes at room temperature before carving (see page 247 for carving tips).

Variations: Insert different herbs under the skin. Try 10 thyme sprigs (5 on each side of the breast), 8 oregano sprigs (4 on each side), 2 tablespoons rosemary leaves (1 tablespoon on each side), or a combination of oregano and rosemary. For a milder, grassier taste, add a couple of sprigs of parsley to any herb you choose.

For a more aromatic bird, place 1 small onion, quartered; 2 celery ribs, cut into 3-inch pieces;

and 2 bay leaves inside the large body cavity before you truss the legs. Discard these aromatics before serving.

For a more velvety taste, double the amount of oil or butter; put half directly on the meat under the skin of both breast halves before you slip in the herbs, then put the rest of the fat over the skin as directed.

For crisper skin, unwrap the chicken from its store packaging, remove the giblets and neck, and set the chicken on a large plate, uncovered, in the refrigerator for 24 hours.

For a 3- to 4-pound broiler or fryer chicken, cook it breast side down for 15 minutes, then roast it breast side up at 350°F for about 45 minutes, to the desired internal temperature.

❊ Shopping for Chicken ❊

The USDA recognizes three types of chicken: "fryers" or "broilers" (under 7 weeks old with a cleaned weight of 2½ to 4 pounds), "roasters" (about 4 months old and 5 to 7 pounds), and "stewers" (a large laying hen up to 1½ years old).

Although stewing hens are tougher, better for braises, there's little difference between a fryer and a roaster (besides weight and age), given modern feeding practices. In the end, follow these four rules when you're at the market:

1. Choose chicken by weight, buying what the recipe requires.

2. Look for supple skin with a pale pink cast, neither leathery nor spongy.

3. Check the expiration date and note whether it is a "sell by" or a "use by" date. There is no government standard or requirement for dating poultry. All dating is voluntary, done without third-party supervision.

4. Rely on your sense of smell. A fresh chicken should have almost no odor—if any, it should be bright, a little bracing and fresh, not sulfurous or metallic.

Some processed chickens are injected with a saline solution in a chicken broth base. Read all labels carefully. While juiced birds are more succulent for the grill, they have a higher sodium content and are prebrined, like kosher birds. Reduce the salt in the recipe—you can add more at the table.

One final note. Contrary to common lore, the pink liquid in the package is not blood. It's water absorbed during the initial chilling process, tinted by residual hemoglobin in the meat. All blood is removed during processing; only a little remains at the joints. Blood in the meat renders a processed chicken unfit for human consumption by U.S. law.

Cooking Poultry to the Right Temperature

The USDA recommends that most poultry (with the exception of oddities like pheasant) be cooked to an internal temperature of 180°F at the thigh and 170°F at the breast. Pop-up timers, a modern convenience, are usually placed in the breast; but truth is, the roasted internal temperature is more accurate at the thigh. The breast's varying thickness makes it a fairly unreliable gauge.

We prefer a lower temperature at the thigh, around 165°F. Frankly, almost all bacterial growth stops at 140°F and most bacteria are eliminated by 160°F. Plus, we like the meat slightly pink at the bone. (By contrast, most Continental chefs take the bird out of the oven at 150°F or lower—that is, bloody at the bone.)

If you choose to cook a bird to a temperature below the USDA guideline, you should understand both the benefits (juicier, more tender meat) and the complications (some pathogens may remain). If you're in doubt or if you prefer absolutely no pink bits in the meat, hold out for the higher temperature.

The only reliable way to determine the roasted temperature is with a meat thermometer. By and large, you have two choices: an instant-read thermometer, inserted at the moment you want to know the temperature; or the traditional, leave-it-in-while-roasting probe, inserted before the bird goes into the oven. Don't confuse the two; an instant-read thermometer's dial will melt in the oven.

Insert the thermometer's needlelike shaft into the thigh at its thickest part, the part that juts out toward the smaller opening at the back of the bird (that is, the neck opening). Make sure the shaft gets to the center of the thigh but doesn't touch the bone. If it will not stay stationary, try again on the other thigh.

Some recipes in older cookbooks recommend you take a bird out of the oven when it's 10 degrees below the required temperature. While this trick works with cuts of beef and pork, it doesn't work as well with poultry. Yes, a turkey will continue to gain as much as 7 or 8 degrees as it sits; a whole chicken, perhaps 4 or 5 degrees. But a boneless skinless chicken breast? No more than a degree or two. For safety's sake, cook the meat to the required temperature, rather than relying on the slipshod method of letting the temperature rise by atmospherics.

Chicken Roasted in a Salt Crust

Under the salt dome, chicken steams and roasts all at once, resulting in an impossibly juicy bird, not well browned but quite tasty—and not nearly as salty as you might expect. The grape leaves impart a delicate, earthy taste and make desalting the bird much easier. Use kosher salt, a coarse-grained salt that, paradoxically, adheres to a compact dough. *Makes 4 to 6 servings*

6 pounds kosher salt
3 cups water
One 16-ounce jar grape leaves, drained and
    rinsed
2 lemons, cut into quarters
2 bay leaves
1 tablespoon cracked black peppercorns
One 4- to 5-pound chicken, giblets and neck
    removed
Butcher's twine

1 Position the rack in the lower third of the oven; preheat the oven to 350°F.

2 Stir the salt and water in a large bowl to form a thick, doughlike paste. Place 3 cups in the bottom of a large roasting pan, patting it out to about 5 inches larger than the chicken. Pack down, then cover completely with a double layer of overlap-

ping grape leaves (perhaps 15 in total), leaving a 1-inch border of salt at the edges.

❸ Place the lemon quarters, bay leaves, and peppercorns inside the chicken, then truss the bird with butcher's twine (see page 249).

❹ Place the chicken on the grape-leaf bed, then cover the chicken with the remaining grape leaves, leaving no exposed holes. Fold up any exposed leaves on the grape-leaf bed to meet those already on the chicken.

❺ Gently mound the remaining salt dough onto the leaves, thereby covering the chicken but taking care not to disturb the leaves. Mold the salt mixture to the bird's shape. Seal any and all cracks by wetting your hands and patting the salt in place.

❻ Roast until a meat thermometer inserted in the thigh registers 160°F (our preference) or 175°F (the USDA recommendation), about 1 hour and 30 minutes to 1 hour and 45 minutes (see Note). Let stand at room temperature for 10 minutes. (In this case, the internal temperature will rise in the salt dome as the chicken sits.)

❼ Whack the crust a couple of times with a meat mallet to break it. Carefully remove the pieces, making sure they don't crumble into the meat. Remove and discard the grape leaves, lemon wedges, bay leaves, and peppercorns; transfer the chicken to a board for carving.

Note: To test for doneness, push an instant-read thermometer into the chicken through the salt crust, eyeing where the thigh is through the crust itself. If you're unsure of placement, make a little finger indention in the crust as you're shaping it to show you where to guide the thermometer in. Or use an old-fashioned, oven-safe probe. Once the chicken is covered in the leaves, insert the probe into the thickest section of the thigh through the leaves, then build the salt crust over the bird and around the probe, leaving its display sticking outside the crust, which should hold it in place while the chicken roasts.

Carving a Whole Chicken

It's really just a matter of finding the joints which have been loosened significantly by the heat. You can usually wiggle them apart, cutting through the skin and any remaining meat with a sharp knife.

Start by removing the thigh/leg quarters. Pull one whole quarter back from the body until you hear the joint pop, then insert the tip of your knife into the now-loosened joint and slice down. Do the same with the smaller joint between each thigh and leg.

Place the body breast side up on a large cutting board. Insert a large knife into the main cavity, position the blade to one side of the spine, and slice down through the ribs. Repeat on the other side of the spine before removing it.

Now turn the chicken breast side down and cut straight down through the breastbone and its cartilage, dividing the breast in half. This takes work, especially in larger birds. Cut the breast/wing sections into three pieces the short way, leaving the wing attached to one as its serving piece.

Alternatively, pull the wings back until the joint pops, insert the knife at an angle into this joint's center, and slice off the wing without taking off too much breast meat. Follow the contour of the breastbone and slice down to remove the breast meat on each side as a fillet. Lay these skin side up on your carving board and cut into slices against the grain (that is, the short way, or at a diagonal the short way for slightly longer slices).

Stewed Chicken

Time was, we were addicted to this dish at New York's Second Avenue Deli. The restaurant's gone now, but we continue to make this simple comfort food at home: a whole chicken, stewed with vegetables, served with noodles and the broth.
Makes 4 to 6 servings

1 tablespoon olive oil
One 4- to 5-pound whole chicken, giblets
    and neck removed, trussed with butcher's
    twine (see page 249)
3 carrots, peeled and cut into
    2-inch pieces
2 medium leeks, white and pale green parts
    only, split lengthwise, the inner layers
    washed carefully of any sand, then sliced
    into 2-inch pieces
2 celery ribs, cut into 2-inch pieces
1 parsnip, peeled, cut into 2-inch sections,
    and each cut into lengthwise quarters
1 bay leaf
About 6 cups chicken broth, or enough just
    to cover the bird in the pot
1 teaspoon salt
½ teaspoon freshly ground black pepper
4 ounces dried egg noodles
1 tablespoon chopped dill fronds

① Heat a large skillet over medium heat. Add the olive oil, then the trussed chicken breast side down. Brown well for about 2 minutes, shaking and nudging to make sure the skin isn't sticking. Turn the chicken breast side up and continue cooking until golden, turning on all sides and basting often with the pan juices, about 8 more minutes.

② Transfer to a Dutch oven that will hold the bird snugly; it must not swim around. Add the carrots, leeks, celery, parsnip, and bay leaf, sticking the vegetables down around the chicken. Pour in the broth; add the salt and pepper. Set over medium-high heat and bring to a simmer.

③ Cover, reduce the heat to low, and cook at a very slow bubble until the vegetables are tender and a meat thermometer inserted into the thickest part of the thigh without touching bone registers 165°F (our preference) or 180°F (the USDA recommendation), 50 to 65 minutes. Using large tongs to pick up the chicken and a spatula to support it from underneath, transfer to a cutting or carving board for 10 minutes before carving. If desired, skim the fat off the broth.

④ Raise the heat to high and bring the liquid in the pot to a full simmer. Add the noodles and dill, stir well, reduce the heat to medium, and cook until the noodles are tender, about 5 minutes. Serve in large bowls with the broth, noodles, and vegetables ladled over the cut-up pieces of chicken.

Slow cooker method:
Follow step 1. Once the chicken has been browned, place it and the remaining ingredients except for the noodles and dill in a slow cooker. Cook on high for 3½ to 4 hours. Remove the chicken from the slow cooker (the bird may fall apart), pour the cooking liquid and vegetables into a large saucepan, then bring to a simmer over high heat. Add the noodles and dill, reduce the heat to medium, and cook until the noodles are tender, about 5 minutes.

If you use a larger stewer (7 to 8 pounds), truss it and brown as directed in steps 1 and 2 in a very large skillet. Transfer it to a very large Dutch oven and then add the broth (without the vegetables); you may need to use up to 10 cups broth. Bring the broth to a simmer over medium-high heat, cover, reduce the heat to low, and cook for 30 minutes. Then add the vegetables, salt, and pepper and continue with the recipe from step 4.

Variations: Omit the celery and parsnip and add 2 large turnips, peeled and diced, or 1 large rutabaga, peeled and diced, in their stead.

Substitute 1 tablespoon chopped sage leaves for the dill.

Finish the cooking broth with 2 teaspoons rice vinegar or lemon juice just before serving.

Chicken Halves Roasted over Squash

Here, whole chicken halves are roasted on a bed of cubed squash. If you don't have a cleaver heavy enough to split a whole bird, ask the butcher to do it for you. *Makes 4 to 6 servings*

2 tablespoons unsalted butter
1 medium onion, chopped
1 red bell pepper, cored, seeded, and chopped
1 large acorn squash (about 2 pounds), peeled, seeded, and cut into very small ½-inch cubes
1 tablespoon stemmed thyme or 2 teaspoons dried thyme
½ teaspoon salt
½ teaspoon freshly ground black pepper
One 4- to 5-pound chicken, giblets and neck removed, then split in half from tip to tail
2 tablespoons Dijon mustard
1 tablespoon maple syrup

1 Position the rack in the center of the oven and preheat the oven to 350°F.

2 Melt 1 tablespoon butter in a large skillet set over medium heat. Add the onion and bell pepper; cook, stirring frequently, until soft and aromatic, about 3 minutes.

3 Add the remaining tablespoon of butter, stir in the squash, and cook, stirring once in a while, until slightly softened at the edges, about 4 minutes.

4 Stir in the thyme, salt, and pepper; cook until aromatic, about 15 seconds. Mound the mixture in the center of a 13 × 9-inch baking pan.

5 Use the two halves of the chicken to form a teepee skin side up over the vegetables. Make sure no vegetable is uncovered.

6 Whisk the mustard and maple syrup in a small bowl. Brush over the skin.

7 Bake until golden until a meat thermometer inserted in the thigh registers 165°F (our preference) or 180°F (the USDA recommendation), between 1 hour and 1 hour 20 minutes. Transfer the chicken halves to a cutting board; let stand at room temperature for 10 minutes before carving and serving with the vegetables.

Variations: Substitute 2 medium leeks, halved lengthwise, cleaned, and thinly sliced, for the onion.

Add one 10-ounce package frozen chopped spinach, thawed and squeezed dry, with the squash.

Substitute any hard winter squash such as blue hubbard, butternut, or kabocha for the acorn squash.

Trussing a Bird

Roasting flattens meat because the fibers collapse. To preserve a bird's appearance for presentation and to ensure even cooking, you often have to truss the bird—that is, tie it together to hold its shape. You'll need dye-free, food-safe butcher's twine, available in kitchenware stores, online outlets, and sometimes hardware stores.

To truss a bird, pull the wings up close to the breast to protect the white meat, then tie them in place by wrapping the twine around the bird a couple of times before knotting it. Tie the legs together over the large opening, crossing them over each other and winding the twine around them before knotting it, thereby mostly closing the large opening.

Ten Things to Do with Leftover Roast Chicken—or a Purchased Rotisserie Chicken

First, skin the chicken, take the meat off the bones, and coarsely chop the meat. Then . . .

1 Chicken Caesar Salad. Shred a head of romaine lettuce, tossing it with the chicken meat and some anchovy fillets. Toss with Classic French Bistro Vinaigrette or Lemon Tahini Vinaigrette (page 103), and lots of freshly grated Parmigiano-Reggiano.

2 Chicken Greek Salad. Toss the cut-up chicken meat with mixed salad greens, pitted black olives, chopped red onion, chopped cucumber, crumbled feta, anchovy fillets, and some chopped oregano leaves; dress the salad with Sherry Vinaigrette (page 100).

3 Quick Chicken Soup. Bring 1 quart (4 cups) chicken broth, a couple of thinly sliced celery ribs, a thinly sliced carrot, and some fresh dill to a simmer in a large saucepan over medium-high heat. Simmer for 10 minutes, add the chicken meat, and simmer for another 5 minutes. If desired, add a few ounces of fresh egg noodles and cook until tender.

4 Curried Chicken Salad. Toss chopped chicken meat, raisins, chopped cashews, chopped celery, and chopped red onion with equal parts mayonnaise and yogurt, seasoned with a little curry powder and a splash of lemon juice.

5 Chicken Burritos. Heat the chopped chicken meat in a large skillet with some red tomato or tomatillo salsa (just enough to moisten it, not to make it runny). Divide this among large flour tortillas with chopped tomato, shredded lettuce, and grated cheese before folding the tortillas closed.

6 Chicken Pasta Casserole. Toss the chopped chicken with your favorite jarred pasta sauce; add cooked elbow macaroni or ziti, chopped oregano leaves, chopped parsley leaves, and some shredded mozzarella. Pour into a casserole dish and bake, covered, in a preheated 350°F oven until bubbling, 25 minutes or so.

7 Waldorf-Inspired Chicken Salad. Toss the chooped chicken meat with mayonnaise, sliced green grapes, chopped walnuts, chopped celery, diced red onions, and a splash of lemon juice. Serve it in hollowed-out tomato shells.

8 Barbecue Chicken Pizza. Spread a large frozen pizza crust with barbecue sauce; top with the chicken as well as bell pepper strips and thinly sliced mushrooms. Top with shredded smoked mozzarella or smoked Gouda before baking as directed by the pizza crust instructions. Or make your own pizza dough and bake as directed (see pages 80 and 82).

9 Easy Vietnamese Summer Rolls. Mix the chopped chicken, minced scallions, shredded carrots, bean sprouts, and hoisin sauce. Soak rice-paper wrappers one at a time for no more than 30 seconds in warm water, place them on the work surface, then fill with a little of the chicken mixture and roll closed like egg rolls.

10 Chicken Reuben. Place the chopped chicken, Russian dressing, drained and squeezed-dry sauerkraut, and a slice of Swiss cheese between slices of rye bread. Panfry in a little melted butter until the bread is crisp and the cheese melts.

What to Do with a Cut-Up Chicken

Grilled Chicken with Sweet-and-Spicy Barbecue Sauce

You can make barbecued chicken with any individual parts you like (breasts, thighs, drumsticks, or wings), but a whole bird gives everyone the most choices. *Makes 6 to 8 servings*

> Canola oil for greasing the grill grate
> One 4- to 5-pound chicken, giblets and neck removed, cut into 9 pieces (page 254)
> Sweet-and-Spicy Barbecue Sauce (recipe follows)

1 Set up a grill for direct cooking over medium heat—that is, heat a gas grill to medium heat or build a medium-hot, well-ashed coal bed in a charcoal grill.

2 Lightly oil the grill grate. Place the chicken, skin side down, 4 to 6 inches directly over the heat source or coals. Mop with the Sweet-and-Spicy Barbecue Sauce. Cover the grill and cook, turning occasionally and mopping generously with the sauce, until the sauce has caramelized and the juices from the meat run clear, and until a meat thermometer inserted into the thickest part of the breast without touching bone registers 160°F (our preference) or 170°F (the USDA recommendation), 16 to 18 minutes.

3 Since the breasts, wings, and back will be done first, move them to a cooler part of the grate, cover the grill, and continue to cook the thighs and legs for about 5 more minutes, until a meat thermometer inserted into the thickest part of the thigh without touching the bone registers 165°F (our preference) or 180°F (the USDA recommendation). Mop generously with any remaining sauce, transfer to a carving board, and let stand for 5 minutes.

To make "grilled" chicken in a broiler, preheat the broiler and cover a broiler pan with aluminum foil, spraying it lightly with nonstick spray to prevent sticking. Place the chicken pieces skin side down on the foil and broil 4 to 6 inches from the heat source for 10 minutes (without mopping with the sauce). Turn and continue broiling for 5 more minutes. Turn again and mop generously with the Sweet-and-Spicy Barbecue Sauce. Continue broiling, mopping often and turning, until the chicken reaches the desired internal temperature, 3 to 5 more minutes. Again, the breast, wings, and back will be done first.

Sweet-and-Spicy Barbecue Sauce

Consider making a double batch of this sauce, freezing half, and saving it for your next backyard barbecue. *Makes about 2¼ cups*

> ⅔ cup tomato paste
> ⅔ cup water
> ½ cup packed dark brown sugar
> ¼ cup unsulfured molasses
> ¼ cup cider vinegar
> 2 tablespoons chili powder
> 2 tablespoons light corn syrup
> 1 tablespoon Worcestershire sauce
> 1 teaspoon onion powder
> 1 teaspoon salt
> 1 teaspoon freshly ground black pepper
> ½ teaspoon garlic powder
> ½ teaspoon cayenne, or less to taste

1 Whisk the tomato paste, water, brown sugar, molasses, vinegar, chili powder, corn syrup, Worcestershire sauce, onion powder, salt, ground pepper, garlic powder, and cayenne in a medium saucepan set over medium heat until the sugar dissolves.

2 Bring the mixture to a simmer; then reduce the heat to low and simmer, uncovered, until slightly thickened, whisking fairly often to make sure it's not sticking, about 10 minutes.

Variations: Add any of the following to the sauce: 1 tablespoon smoked paprika, 2 teaspoons dried oregano, 1 teaspoon ground cumin, 1 teaspoon celery seed, and/or ¼ teaspoon ground cloves.

For a more savory sauce, reduce the brown sugar to ¼ cup; or omit the brown sugar altogether and add ¼ cup maple syrup.

While the threat of salmonella need not be sensationalized, a good cook takes a few precautions. Never rinse raw poultry. Doing so can cause cross-contamination of surface bacteria in your kitchen through random splashes or runoff in the sink. Besides, bacteria are killed by heat, not running water.

After working with raw poultry, wash your hands with soap under very warm water for 20 seconds (about the amount of time it takes you to sing a chorus of "Jingle Bells"). Wash all cutting boards and utensils with hot, soapy water, preferably in the dishwasher. Also wash all kitchen surfaces with a bleach-based cleaner when you're finished.

If you hold off carving or serving a bird for a few minutes after it's out of the oven, it will be juicier and more tender every time. During long roasting, the natural juices have been squeezed to the edges by the collapsing muscle fibers; as the fibers relax, the juices have a chance to slip back between the layers.

Tandoori Chicken

In this East Indian classic, chicken is marinated in a yogurt sauce, then cooked at high heat until golden. Because of bacterial concerns, never marinate the chicken for more than 6 hours. Here are two ways to make it: in the oven and on the grill. *Makes 6 to 8 servings*

2 cups regular or low-fat yogurt (do not use fat-free)
2 tablespoons lemon juice
2 teaspoons chili powder
2 teaspoons ground coriander
2 teaspoons ground ginger
1 teaspoon salt
½ teaspoon garlic powder
½ teaspoon freshly ground black pepper
¼ teaspoon cayenne pepper, optional
One 4- to 5-pound chicken, giblets and neck removed, cut into 9 pieces, skin removed (see page 254)
Canola oil or nonstick spray for greasing the rack
1 large onion, sliced into ½-inch-thick rings
2 lemons, cut into wedges
Garnishes and condiments: Apple-Cucumber Raita (page 409), mango chutney, diced tomatoes, shredded lettuce, and/or a flat bread such as East Indian na'an, lefse, lavash, or even flour tortillas

To make it in the oven:
1 Whisk the yogurt, lemon juice, chili powder, coriander, ginger, salt, garlic powder, black pepper, and cayenne, if using, in a large mixing bowl until smooth.

2 Cut each chicken breast in half (thereby making 4 pieces of breast meat). Toss all the pieces in the yogurt mixture. Cover and refrigerate for at least 2 hours but for no more than 6 hours.

③ Position the rack in the center of the oven; preheat the oven to 425°F. Line a large baking sheet with aluminum foil and place a broiler rack or metal cooling rack with feet (not rubberized ones) on the sheet. Lightly oil the rack or spray it with nonstick spray.

④ Remove the chicken from the marinade, shaking off any excess but leaving a thin coating. Discard the marinade. Set the chicken pieces bone side down on the prepared rack and bake for 20 minutes.

⑤ Add the onion slices and lemon wedges and continue cooking until the chicken is well browned and a meat thermometer inserted into the thickest part of the thigh registers 165°F (our preference) or 180°F (the USDA recommendation), 10 to 15 more minutes. Let stand at room temperature for 5 minutes before serving with the garnishes, condiments, and bread, squeezing the roasted lemon wedges over the chicken and onions.

To make it on the grill:
① Do steps 1 and 2.

② Oil the grill grate and heat a gas grill to high heat or build a high-heat red-hot-ashed coal bed in a charcoal grill.

③ Remove the chicken from the marinade, shaking off any excess but leaving a thin coating. Discard the marinade. Place the chicken legs and thighs bone side down directly over the heat. Cover and grill for 3 minutes.

④ Add the breast pieces bone side down, the wings, and the back. Cover and grill, turning all the pieces once, until the juices run clear and the desired internal temperature has been reached, about 17 minutes. Transfer to a platter; tent with aluminum foil to keep warm.

⑤ Oil a wadded paper towel, grasp it with long kitchen tongs, and again oil the grate. Add the onion slices and grill for 1 minute. Turn, then add the lemon wedges rind side down. Cover and cook until the onions are brown, about 2 additional minutes. Serve the chicken and grilled onions with the flat bread and condiments, squeezing the grilled lemon wedges over the chicken and onions.

Sweet-and-Sour Chicken: Follow the technique for the Tandoori Chicken, but omit the yogurt marinade with all its spices. Instead, in a large bowl, whisk 1/2 cup crushed pineapple in juice, 3 tablespoons soy sauce, 3 tablespoons honey, 3 tablespoons lemon juice, 1 1/2 tablespoons grated peeled fresh ginger, 1/2 teaspoon red pepper flakes, and 2 minced garlic cloves. Add the chicken pieces, cover, and refrigerate for at least 4 hours or up to 12 hours, tossing occasionally. Discard the marinade and roast or grill as directed above.

Kosher Chickens

Kosher chickens are raised and processed differently than nonkosher chickens. But without delving into kosher law, we can safely say that the main difference for home cooks is that the birds are salted during processing. Because of water absorbed during chilling, they are in effect prebrined. If you're using a kosher chicken, cut down on the salt in the recipe—or cut it out altogether—because of the meat's high sodium content. Never brine a Kosher chicken at home.

How to Cut Up a Whole Chicken

Why pay extra for a cut-up chicken when you can do the job yourself?

❶ Place the bird breast side up on the work surface and gently stretch one wing out from the body. Press your finger between the wing and the breast until you can tell where the two join, where the bone forms a knucklelike structure. Place your knife right over the joint in the bird's "armpit" and slice down, cutting through the center of the joint. If you meet hard resistance, you've hit bone; adjust the angle of your blade to slice directly through the center of the joint, severing the wing from the body but taking a little breast meat with it. Repeat with the other wing. Cut away any hanging skin around the joints.

❷ Do this same operation with the thigh quarters. Position the bird so that the large cavity opening is facing you. Hold the breast in one hand and the whole thigh-leg quarter in the other; gently pry them apart until you hear a pop, thereby disjointing the hip. Feel down into the meat for the ball-and-socket joint, which is now either loose or completely separated. Place your knife over the center of that joint and slice down, taking off the whole thigh quarter. Repeat with the other side of the bird.

❸ Lay the thigh quarter skin side down. Wiggle the leg and look for the inside of the knee joint, again feeling it with your fingers. Place the knife right over that wiggle point and slice down, severing the drumstick from the thigh. Repeat with the other leg quarter. Trim off any excess skin.

❹ What's left is a whole breast with the back attached. Set it breast side up; it will tip slightly to one side. Insert the knife directly in the large cavity opening so the tip of the knife extends almost all the way through the body. Cut down through all the ribs and bones about 2 inches to the side of the backbone. Repeat this action on the other side of the backbone, thereby removing the back.

❺ Lay the remaining breast skin side down on the work surface. Spread the two sides open flat, pushing them down toward the work surface until the breastbone cracks. Cut down through the middle of the breastbone. The breastbone of older or larger chickens will not crack easily. In this case, you'll need to eye the breastbone and slice down one side of it, thereby leaving one side of the breast with the bone and the other without. Slice off any extraneous bits of rib and skin hanging off the bottom of the breast halves. The chicken now lies in 9 pieces.

Finally, there's the question of what to do with all those giblets. Consider these four ideas:
• Freeze them and use them cut into tiny bits to enrich most wine-based braises and stews (remember that the liver has a much stronger taste than the other parts).
• Make Giblet Gravy (page 287) for just about any roasted bird.
• Make a Corsican fressure, a dish of stewed innards. Follow the recipe for Civet de Poulet (page 279), but use 3 pounds cut-up giblets, rather than the thighs and gizzards the recipe calls for. This stew will be quite rich and will easily feed 12 when served over rice, noodles, or couscous.
• Use any and all poultry livers for Chopped Liver (page 86).

Broiled Lemon Chicken

With an aromatic and slightly sticky glaze, this easy chicken dish is good party fare. *Makes 6 to 8 servings*

>   1 cup lemon juice
>   ¼ cup olive oil
>   ¼ cup white wine vinegar
>   3 tablespoons chopped rosemary leaves or 2 tablespoons dried rosemary, crumbled
>   2 tablespoons chopped oregano leaves or 1 tablespoon dried oregano, crumbled
>   1 teaspoon salt
>   ½ teaspoon freshly ground black pepper
>   3 garlic cloves, minced
>   One 4- to 5-pound chicken, giblets and neck removed, cut into 9 pieces (see page 254)

❶ Whisk the lemon juice, olive oil, vinegar, rosemary, oregano, salt, pepper, and garlic in a large bowl.

❷ Slice the chicken breasts in half the short way. Toss all the chicken pieces in the lemon marinade. Cover and refrigerate for at least 4 hours or up to 24 hours.

❸ Line a broiler pan with aluminum foil. Preheat the broiler. Drain the chicken, reserving the marinade.

❹ Place the chicken pieces skin side down on the prepared pan and broil 4 to 6 inches from the heat source, turning once, for 20 minutes.

❺ Pour the marinade over the chicken, turn the pieces, and continue broiling until the marinade has thickened to a glaze and a meat thermometer inserted into the thickest part of the thigh without touching bone registers 165°F (our preference) or 180°F (the USDA recommendation), basting several times with the marinade in the pan and turning once or twice more, 3 to 6 more minutes. Let stand at room temperature for 5 minutes before serving.

Variations: Substitute parsley for the rosemary and thyme for the oregano.

Add ½ teaspoon red pepper flakes to the marinade before adding the chicken.

For a sweet-and-sour version, whisk 1 tablespoon sugar or 2 teaspoons light corn syrup into the marinade before adding the chicken.

For a healthier dish, use skinless chicken parts. Reduce the cooking time by 4 minutes under the broiler before pouring the marinade over the pieces.

Grilled Lemon Chicken: Complete steps 1 and 2 of the recipe. Then oil the grill grate and preheat a gas grill to high heat or build a high-heat, red-hot-ashed coal bed in the center of a charcoal grill. Place the drained chicken pieces skin side up directly over the heat, cover the grill, and cook for 8 minutes, turning once. Baste the chicken generously with the marinade, turn again, and continue cooking for 8 to 10 more minutes, turning occasionally and mopping frequently with the marinade until golden brown and the desired internal temperature has been reached.

Baked Lemon Chicken: Complete steps 1 and 2 of the recipe. Preheat the oven to 350°F. Pour the chicken pieces and all the marinade into a 13 × 9-inch baking pan. Bake, basting occasionally with the pan juices, until they reduce to a glaze and the chicken is quite golden, about 1 hour. An instant-read meat thermometer inserted into the thickest part of the breast should read about 170°F or maybe even higher. However, the salty marinade will protect the meat.

Enchilada Chicken

No, not chicken enchiladas. Instead, this oven-bake replicates their taste without the time-consuming task of building a chili sauce and stuffing tortillas. Remove the skin from the chicken because it will leach too much fat into the dish. To make the dish in advance, complete the recipe through step 3, then cover and refrigerate the casserole for 1 day or freeze it for 1 month (never refreeze thawed chicken and let the casserole thaw overnight in the refrigerator before baking). *Makes 6 to 8 servings*

  2 cups homemade salsa (page 47) or
      purchased salsa, preferably a chunky,
      garden-vegetable variety that's not too
      sweet
  5 tablespoons chili powder
  One 4- to 5-pound chicken, giblets and neck
      removed, cut into 9 pieces and the skin
      removed (see page 254)
  1⅔ cups canned kidney beans, drained and
      rinsed
  8 ounces Cheddar, shredded through the
      large holes of a box grater

① Position the rack in the center of the oven and preheat the oven to 350°F.

② Place the salsa and chili powder in a large blender or a food processor fitted with the chopping blade; blend or process until smooth.

③ Lay the skinless pieces of chicken bone side down in a 13 x 9-inch baking pan. Sprinkle the beans among the pieces, then pour the salsa mixture over the chicken, coating everything.

④ Bake uncovered for 35 minutes.

⑤ Baste the chicken with the sauce, then sprinkle the cheese over the dish. Continue bak-

ing until the sauce is bubbling, the cheese has melted, and an instant-read meat thermometer inserted into the thickest part of a thigh without touching the bone registers 165°F (our preference) or 180°F (the USDA recommendation), about 15 more minutes.

Variations: Customize this dish to your heart's content by simply varying the salsa you use.

Use 4 to 5 pounds skinless chicken thighs and legs, rather than a whole chicken.

Or use 4 to 5 pounds skinless chicken breasts, but cook the dish only 30 minutes before adding the cheese. Do not use boneless chicken pieces.

Organic Poultry

In the best case scenario, look for birds labeled "certified organic." The unadorned term "organic" can mean a range of things; "certified organic" means some agency has overseen some or all stages of the meat's production.

Organic cooperatives and agencies vary state to state. Check with your government's Web site to ascertain the standards in your locale—and make your voice heard if the issue matters to you.

Some organic boards and cooperatives insist on total control, often called "egg to market oversight." Each egg is numbered and the chicken is watched through growth and processing to the market. Other agencies are less exacting, with the least aggressive insisting on only production terms.

In the end, the best answer is to become an informed consumer. Certified by whom? How?

Panfried Chicken

We prefer a simple, "country" method for frying skin-on chicken: seasoned flour and lots of hot oil. We recommend a 14-inch skillet for frying it all in one batch; if you don't have a skillet that large, work in two batches, the dark meat before the white. *Makes 6 to 8 servings*

2 cups all-purpose flour
1 tablespoon mild paprika
2 teaspoons freshly ground black pepper
4 to 6 cups canola oil
One 4- to 5-pound chicken, giblets and neck removed, cut into 9 pieces (see page 254)
Salt to taste

1 Place the flour, paprika, and pepper in a large bag, preferably a supermarket paper bag. Seal the top and shake well.

2 Clip a deep-frying thermometer to the inside of a large, high-sided sauté pan or a very large 14-inch skillet, set it over medium-high heat, and pour in enough oil to come about 2 inches up the sides of the pan. Heat until the temperature registers 350°F.

3 Drop the chicken pieces into the bag with the seasoned flour, close the bag by rolling the top down, and shake well, thereby coating the chicken.

4 Remove the chicken pieces from the bag and slip them into the hot oil. Fry until browned, about 10 minutes, adjusting the heat so the temperature remains constant.

5 Turn the pieces with metal tongs and continue cooking until crisp all over, until an instant-read meat thermometer inserted into the thigh at its thickest part without touching bone registers 165°F (our preference) or 180°F (the USDA rec-

ommendation), 6 to 8 more minutes. Transfer the chicken pieces to a wire rack and immediately season with salt. Let stand for a couple of minutes before serving.

Variations: Add any of the following to the flour with the paprika and pepper: 2 teaspoons onion powder, 1 teaspoon garlic powder, 1/2 teaspoon grated nutmeg, 1/4 teaspoon ground cloves, or up to 1/4 teaspoon cayenne.

For a more authentically Southern dish, substitute peanut oil for the canola oil.

Tips for Success

• The chicken should go straight from the flour to the fat. If it sits, the coating will turn gummy.

• Watch the oil's temperature; adjust the heat so it stays at a constant 350°F.

• If you're using a deep-fryer, you still have to turn the chicken once; check to make sure it hasn't stuck to the fryer basket.

Skinless Fried Chicken

Taking the skin off the chicken doesn't mean you have to lose a crunchy crust. Because this crust insulates so well, the chicken cooks more quickly. *Makes 6 servings*

2 cups all-purpose flour
2 teaspoons mild paprika
1 teaspoon freshly ground black pepper
1⅓ cups buttermilk (regular, low-fat, or fat-free)
1 large egg
4 to 6 cups canola oil
One 4- to 5-pound chicken, giblets and neck removed, cut into 9 pieces, skin removed
Salt to taste

① Whisk the flour, paprika, and pepper in a medium bowl, then pour this mixture onto a large plate or a large sheet of wax paper.

② Whisk the buttermilk and egg in a shallow baking dish or a pie plate.

③ Clip a deep-frying thermometer to the inside of a large, high-sided sauté pan or a large skillet, set it over medium-high heat, and pour in enough oil to come about 2 inches up the sides of the pan. Heat until the temperature registers 350°F. During the rest of the cooking, be on the lookout to adjust the heat so the oil's temperature remains constant.

④ Roll the chicken pieces in the seasoned flour, then dip them in the buttermilk mixture. Shake off the excess and roll them a second time in the seasoned flour.

⑤ Slip the pieces bone side up into the hot oil. Fry until golden brown, about 6 minutes.

⑥ Turn the pieces with metal tongs and continue frying until crisp and golden on all sides, about 6 more minutes. Transfer to a wire rack and sprinkle with salt. Let stand for a couple of minutes before serving.

Variations: Add any of the following to the flour mixture: 2 teaspoons dried parsley, 2 teaspoons dried oregano, 1 teaspoon onion powder, ½ teaspoon garlic powder, or ¼ teaspoon grated nutmeg.

Remember that salt in an ingredient list is mostly a matter of suggestion, particularly if it's added at the end of the cooking. Always adjust the amount to your taste.

Pecan-Crusted Oven-Fried Chicken

This crunchy crust was inspired by the Texas combination of pecans and cumin. *Makes 6 to 8 servings*

3 tablespoons chopped pecan pieces
2 teaspoons celery seeds
6 tablespoons plain dried bread crumbs
2 teaspoons paprika
½ teaspoon ground cumin
½ teaspoon onion powder
¼ teaspoon grated nutmeg
¼ teaspoon freshly ground black pepper
1½ cups milk (regular, low-fat, or fat-free)
One 4- to 5-pound chicken, giblets and neck removed, cut into 9 pieces
Salt to taste

① Position the rack in the lower third of the oven and preheat the oven to 400°F. Line a baking sheet with parchment paper or a silicone baking mat.

② Grind the pecan pieces and celery seeds in a spice grinder, mini-food processor, or clean coffee grinder until finely ground but not a paste.

③ Whisk the pecan mixture in a medium bowl with the bread crumbs, paprika, cumin, onion powder, nutmeg, and pepper. Pour onto a large plate or a large sheet of wax paper. Pour the milk into a baking dish or a shallow pie plate.

④ Slip the chicken pieces into the milk, coating them well. Then immediately press them in the bread-crumb mixture and turn to coat, making sure the spices stick. Place the pieces skin side up on the prepared baking sheet.

⑤ Bake until golden brown, until a meat thermometer inserted into the thickest part of the breast and the thigh without touching the bone registers 165°F (our preference) or 180°F (the USDA recommendation), 35 to 45 minutes. Season with salt the moment the chicken is out of the oven, then let the pieces stand at room temperature on the baking sheet for 5 minutes (do not move so the crust can set).

Variations: If you want extra-crispy oven-fried chicken, spray each piece with a light coating of nonstick spray after it's been dipped into the bread-crumb mixture.

You can also make skinless oven-fried chicken. The crust will be thicker if you use buttermilk, rather than regular milk.

Coconut Chicken Curry

Serve this fiery farrago with bowls of jasmine rice and diced peeled mango for garnish. *Makes 8 servings*

2 tablespoons unsalted butter
3 large onions, chopped
2 garlic cloves, minced
2 tablespoons minced peeled fresh ginger
1 tablespoon turmeric
2 teaspoons ground coriander
2 teaspoons dry mustard
1 teaspoon ground cinnamon
1 teaspoon ground cumin
1 teaspoon ground ginger
½ teaspoon freshly ground black pepper
Up to ½ teaspoon cayenne pepper
1½ cups regular or reduced-fat coconut milk
½ cup water
One 4- to 5-pound chicken, giblets and neck removed, cut into 9 pieces (see page 254, skin removed
¼ cup cilantro leaves, chopped

1. Melt the butter in a large saucepan, Dutch oven, or medium stockpot over low heat. The moment it's melted, while there's still some foam, add the onions. Raise the heat to very low and cook, stirring frequently, until golden and soft, about 15 minutes. Add the garlic and fresh ginger; cook, stirring constantly, for 1 minute.

2. Stir in the turmeric, coriander, dry mustard, cinnamon, cumin, ground ginger, black pepper, and cayenne to taste. Raise the heat to medium and cook, stirring constantly, until aromatic, about 20 seconds.

3. Stir in the coconut milk and water, then add the chicken pieces, submerging them in the liquid. Raise the heat to medium-high and bring to a simmer.

4. Cover, reduce the heat to low, and simmer quite slowly for 40 minutes until the chicken is very tender, almost falling off the bone.

5. Skim any visible fat off the surface of the sauce; stir in the cilantro just before serving.

Variations: Omit all the dried herbs and spices, from the turmeric through the cayenne in the ingredient list, and stir in 2 to 3 tablespoons bottled yellow curry paste. Or substitute up to 1½ tablespoons Thai curry paste—but beware, it's absurdly hot!

Add 1 green tart apple, such as a Granny Smith, peeled, cored, and roughly chopped, with the onion.

Add 2 carrots, thinly sliced, with the onion.

Add 2 scallions, thinly sliced, with the garlic and fresh ginger.

Stir in ½ cup golden raisins, ½ cup slivered almonds, and/or ¼ cup chopped unsalted roasted cashews with the cilantro.

Southwestern-Inspired Arroz con Pollo with Chiles, Chorizo, and Beer

Here's our untraditional, Southwestern version of the Spanish casserole—no whole tomatoes, just a heady broth thickened with tomato paste and spiked with fresh poblanos. *Makes 8 servings*

2 poblano chiles
12 ounces dried Spanish chorizo, cut into
    ½-inch pieces (see Note)
One 4- to 5-pound chicken, giblets and neck
    removed, cut into 9 pieces (see page 254)
½ teaspoon freshly ground black
    pepper
1 large onion, chopped
2 garlic cloves, minced
1 cup dry sherry
One 12-ounce bottle dark or
    amber beer
1½ cups chicken broth
1 tablespoon tomato paste
2 teaspoons chopped oregano leaves or
    1 teaspoon dried oregano
2 teaspoons stemmed thyme or 1 teaspoon
    dried thyme
1 teaspoon saffron, crumbled and soaked in
    1 tablespoon water for 5 minutes
1 teaspoon salt
2 bay leaves
1 cup long-grain white rice

1 Char the chiles over an open gas flame, holding them over it with metal tongs; or broil them until blackened on all sides on a large baking sheet about 5 inches from a preheated broiler, turning occasionally, about 8 minutes. Place the chiles in a paper bag and seal tightly, or place them in a bowl and cover tightly with plastic wrap. Set aside for 10 minutes.

2 Peel the blackened skin off the chiles. Stem, seed, and roughly chop the chiles, then set aside.

3 Position the rack in the center of the oven and preheat the oven to 350°F.

4 Set a large, heat-safe Dutch oven or a very large, heavy oven casserole over medium heat. Add the chorizo and brown lightly, turning occasionally, about 4 minutes. Transfer to a plate; set aside.

5 Cut each breast in half the short way. Season all the chicken pieces with the pepper, add them to the pot, and brown in the rendered chorizo fat, turning occasionally, about 10 minutes. Transfer to a second plate and set aside as well.

6 Drain off all but 1 tablespoon fat from the pot. Return the pot to medium heat and add the onion. Cook, stirring constantly, until translucent, about 3 minutes. Add the garlic and cook for 20 seconds.

7 Pour in the sherry and scrape up any browned bits on the pot's bottom while the sherry comes to a simmer. Cook for 1 minute to reduce the sherry a bit.

8 Pour in the beer and chicken broth, then stir in the tomato paste until it dissolves. Stir in the chopped poblanos, oregano, thyme, saffron with its soaking water, salt, and bay leaves. Bring back to a simmer.

9 Stir in the rice, chorizo, chicken pieces, and any accumulated juices, submerging the meat somewhat in the liquid. Bring to a simmer, making sure no grains of rice stand outside the liquid on the chicken pieces.

10 Cover and bake until almost all the liquid has been absorbed, the rice is tender, and the chicken has cooked through, about 1 hour. If the seal on your pot is not perfect, the casserole may dry out as it bakes. If so, sprinkle more water over the dish

in ½-cup increments as it bakes. Discard the bay leaves before serving.

Note: You can use Mexican chorizo, but since it's raw, fry it in 1 tablespoon canola oil until well browned, about 5 minutes.

Variations: Add up to 1 teaspoon red pepper flakes with the bay leaves.

Sprinkle 1 cup fresh or frozen peas, thawed, over the dish during the last 10 minutes of cooking.

Stir 1 to 2 pounds scrubbed clams, 1 to 2 pounds cleaned and debearded mussels, or 1 pound peeled and deveined medium shrimp (about 30 per pound) into the casserole during the last 10 minutes of cooking.

Sprinkle ¼ cup chopped parsley leaves over the casserole during the final 5 minutes of cooking.

Greek-Inspired Chicken Casserole with Leeks, Pine Nuts, and Raisins

Instead of having a phyllo top, this aromatic main course is baked in a phyllo-lined casserole. *Makes 8 servings*

One 4- to 5-pound chicken, giblets and neck removed, cut into 9 pieces (see page 254)
2 lemons, cut into quarters
10 cracked black peppercorns
3 bay leaves
2 tablespoons olive oil, plus additional for greasing the pan and brushing the phyllo
2 leeks, dark green parts removed, white and light green parts halved and thoroughly rinsed for sand, then thinly sliced
¼ cup pine nuts
⅓ cup golden raisins
2 tablespoons retsina, dry vermouth, or dry white wine

2 tablespoons chopped fresh dill or 1 tablespoon dried dill
1 tablespoon ground cinnamon
2 teaspoons finely grated lemon zest
1 teaspoon salt
½ teaspoon freshly ground black pepper
12 frozen phyllo sheets, laid on the work surface under plastic wrap and a dry kitchen towel
⅓ cup toasted walnut pieces, finely chopped
3 large eggs, lightly beaten

1 Place the chicken pieces in a large stockpot; add the lemon wedges, peppercorns, and bay leaves. Fill the pot with water until it covers the chicken by 1 inch. Set over high heat and bring the water to a boil. Reduce the heat to medium, cover partially, and simmer until the chicken is cooked through and almost falling off the bones, about 40 minutes.

2 Drain the chicken in a colander set in the sink; discard the lemon wedges, peppercorns, and bay leaves. When the chicken is cool enough to handle, skin and bone it, shredding the meat somewhat. Set aside.

3 Heat a large skillet or sauté pan over medium-low heat. Add 2 tablespoons olive oil, then the leeks. Reduce the heat to low and cook slowly, stirring often, until quite soft and golden, about 7 minutes.

4 Stir in the pine nuts; continue cooking, stirring frequently, until quite fragrant, about 2 minutes.

5 Stir in the shredded chicken as well as the raisins, wine, dill, cinnamon, lemon zest, salt, and pepper. Remove the pan from the heat and set aside to cool for 10 minutes. (The casserole can be made up to this point in advance; cover the

chicken mixture in a large container or bowl and refrigerate for up to 2 days, then microwave it to room temperature before proceeding.)

6 Position the rack in the center of the oven and preheat the oven to 375°F.

7 Lightly oil a 13 × 9-inch baking dish. Lay four of the phyllo sheets in each of the four quadrants of the baking dish, making sure they all come up the sides of the pan and hang over the edges by about 2 inches (they will also overlap in the center of the dish). Brush the sheets with olive oil, then sprinkle about half the chopped walnuts over them.

8 Do the same with a second layer of four phyllo sheets, brushing them again with olive oil and sprinkling on the remaining nuts.

9 Make a final layer of phyllo sheets. This time, brush only the parts of these sheets that lie along the top of the casserole's sides with oil but take care to get down in the layers.

10 Stir the beaten eggs into the chicken mixture, then pour into the phyllo-lined pan. Fold the overhanging edges over the filling, just so they make a decorative border around the casserole, covering the filling at the edges.

11 Bake until the phyllo has browned and the filling is bubbling, about 35 minutes. Let the casserole cool on a wire rack for 10 minutes before serving.

For an easier casserole: Use an unflavored rotisserie chicken. Skip steps 1 and 2 (thereby omitting the lemons, peppercorns, and bay leaves); skin, bone, and shred the meat, adding it to the sauce in step 5.

What to Do with Chicken Breasts

Glazed Chicken Breasts

Any honey will work here, but these baked breasts would be enhanced by a strong-flavored variety.
Makes 4 servings

1 cup orange juice
⅓ cup honey
⅓ cup white wine vinegar
2 teaspoons stemmed thyme plus 15 thyme
   sprigs soaked in water for 15 minutes
1 teaspoon finely grated orange zest
1 tablespoon unsalted butter
½ teaspoon salt
¼ teaspoon freshly ground black pepper
Canola oil for greasing the baking sheet
Four 10- to 12-ounce bone-in skin-on or
   skinless chicken breasts

1 Whisk the orange juice, honey, vinegar, stemmed thyme, and orange zest in a small saucepan set over medium-high heat until the honey dissolves. Bring the mixture to a boil.

2 Reduce the heat to low and simmer, uncovered, whisking occasionally, until syrupy, about 8 minutes. Whisk in the butter, salt, and pepper; remove the pan from the heat and cool for 10 minutes. (This glaze can be made up to 2 days in advance. Store, covered, in the refrigerator; reheat it in a small saucepan, thinned with a little extra orange juice, until bubbling.)

3 Position the rack in the center of the oven and preheat to 400°F. Oil a large baking sheet. Drain the thyme sprigs and place them on the sheet.

4 Place the chicken breasts, bone side down, on the sprigs. Pour the sauce over the breasts and bake for 15 minutes.

5 Baste with the glaze and pan juices, then continue baking, mopping every 5 minutes or so, until the glaze has turned syrupy and caramelized and a meat thermometer inserted into the thickest part of a breast without touching the bone registers 165°F (our preference) or 170°F (the USDA recommendation), 20 to 35 more minutes.

6 Transfer the chicken breasts to a cutting board or a carving platter; let stand for 5 minutes before serving with any remaining orange glaze on the side.

Variations: Add any of the following to the orange glaze before bringing it to a simmer: 2 crushed garlic cloves, 1/4 teaspoon red pepper flakes, 1/4 teaspoon ground cinnamon, or 1/8 teaspoon ground cloves.

Substitute rosemary for the thyme; use about 8 rosemary sprigs as the bed for the breasts.

Brining Chicken Breasts

While it's not necessary, chicken breasts are juicier if you brine them first. Make a solution of 3 cups water and 1/4 cup salt, preferably kosher salt, in a very large bowl, whisking until the salt has dissolved. Add the breasts, then add enough cool water to cover by 1 inch. Stir well, then cover and refrigerate for 1 hour or up to 4 hours. Drain and pat the breasts dry before you use them. Because of the higher sodium content of brined breasts, omit the salt from any marinade. Do not use a kosher chicken or other prebrined breasts.

Looking for wings? Try Lemon Wings, Sesame Wings, or Buffalo Wings (page 58).

Herbed Chicken Breasts

The flavors here mimic those that have made Tuscan cooking a North American favorite: lemon zest, rosemary, and olive oil. Although expensive extra virgin olive oil isn't necessary, a good bottle of syrupy balsamic vinegar will work wonders.
Makes 6 servings

Six 10- to 12-ounce bone-in skin-on or
    skinless chicken breasts, cut in half the
    short way
4 garlic cloves, slivered
3 tablespoons olive oil, plus additional for
    oiling the baking sheet
3 tablespoons finely chopped rosemary
    leaves
1½ tablespoons finely grated lemon zest
½ teaspoon red pepper flakes
1 teaspoon salt
3 tablespoons aged balsamic vinegar

1 Toss the breasts, garlic, olive oil, rosemary, lemon zest, red pepper flakes, and salt in a large bowl until the chicken is coated in the spices. Alternatively, place all these ingredients in a ziplock plastic bag, seal it, and shake until the chicken has been well coated. Refrigerate for 1 hour, tossing occasionally.

2 Position the rack in the center of the oven. Preheat the oven to 400°F. Lightly oil a large baking sheet.

3 Remove the breasts from the marinade with all the spices adhering. Place bone side down on the prepared baking sheet. Bake for 30 minutes.

4 Increase the oven temperature to 450°F. Brush the vinegar evenly over the breasts without knocking off the spices. Continue baking until well browned, until a meat thermometer inserted into the thickest part of a breast registers 165°F (our preference) or 170°F (the USDA recommendation), 8 to 10 more minutes. Let stand at room temperature for 5 minutes. If desired, skim and discard any visible fat from the pan juices and spoon the juices over the chicken when serving.

Variations: Either add with or substitute for the rosemary: 3 tablespoons finely chopped parsley leaves, 3 tablespoons finely chopped oregano leaves, or 2 tablespoons stemmed thyme.

Rubbed and Roasted Breasts

Begin with a half-recipe of the Cajun Dry Rub, Jerk Dry Rub, or Pepper Dry Rub for the Roast Turkey Breast (pages 290–291). Rub the bone-in breasts (skin on or off) with a little canola oil, then pat this spice mixture onto the breasts. Cover and refrigerate for at least 6 hours or overnight. Bake in a preheated 400°F oven on a lightly oiled baking sheet for 30 to 40 minutes, until a meat thermometer inserted into the thickest part of the breast registers 165°F (our preference) or 170°F (the USDA recommendation). Brined chicken breasts (see page 263) would make even more succulent fare, but omit the salt from the rub mixture.

Bone-In, Boneless, Skin-On, Skinless

In truth, bone-in and boneless breasts make all the difference in a recipe—do not substitute one for the other. But skin-on or skinless? It makes a much smaller difference, especially if the meat has been marinated or rubbed, mostly just a difference in terms of the higher fat content of skin-on breasts. Bone-in breasts are sometimes sold with a little flab of ribs hanging off one side; slice this off for aesthetics, if you wish.

Couscous-Stuffed Chicken Breasts

The natural pocket in a chicken breast between the thicker section of meat and the so-called "tender" cries out for an aromatic stuffing—like the one here, with a Moroccan-inspired mixture of scallions, thyme, raisins, and couscous. *Makes 6 servings*

1½ cups chicken broth
1 cup couscous
1 large shallot, thinly sliced
½ cup raisins, chopped
2 teaspoons olive oil, plus additional for greasing the pan
1 teaspoon ground cumin
1 teaspoon salt
½ teaspoon ground cinnamon
½ teaspoon ground coriander
½ teaspoon freshly ground black pepper
Six 10- to 12-ounce bone-in skin-on or skinless chicken breasts
6 tablespoons warm water
¼ cup Fig Jam, homemade (page 221) or purchased; orange marmalade; or a purchased shallot-onion marmalade
1 teaspoon ground ginger

1 Bring the broth to a boil in a medium saucepan set over high heat. Stir in the couscous, cover, and set aside off the heat for 5 minutes.

2 Mix the shallot, raisins, olive oil, cumin, ½ teaspoon salt, cinnamon, coriander, and the pepper into the couscous. Cool for 10 minutes.

3 Cut the breasts in half the short way, cutting a bit on the diagonal through the thickest part of the meat so that both halves end up about the same size. Run your thumb along the cut meat—you'll

discover a natural pocket where the fibers separate into the firmer breast meat and the so-called "tender." Insert a sharp paring knife into this natural rift and slice open a small pocket without cutting all the way through the breast in any direction. Gently pry the pocket open with your fingers, then pack it with ¼ cup of the couscous stuffing.

④ Position the rack in the center of the oven; preheat the oven to 375°F. Lightly oil a large baking sheet. Place the breasts slit side down on it (with the visible stuffing in the pocket against the bottom of the pan).

⑤ Whisk the warm water, jam or marmalade, ginger, and the remaining ½ teaspoon salt in a small bowl. Brush half this mixture over the chicken breasts. Bake for 25 minutes.

⑥ Baste generously with the fig glaze, using all of it. Continue baking until deeply browned, until a meat thermometer inserted into the thickest part of a breast registers 160°F (our preference) or 170°F (the USDA recommendation), about 20 additional minutes. Transfer the breasts to a serving platter or a cutting board for 5 minutes.

To make a pan gravy, skim and discard any visible fat from the pan juices, pour the juices into a small saucepan, and set it over high heat. Whisk in about ½ cup chicken broth until the mixture comes to a simmer. Reduce the heat to medium and boil, whisking occasionally, until reduced by half, about 2 minutes.

Variations: Substitute 1⅓ cups cooked wild rice for the couscous.

Substitute 2 teaspoons stemmed thyme or chopped rosemary leaves for the cumin, cinnamon, and coriander.

Omit the jam or marmalade and ginger; instead, make a glaze with 3 tablespoons soy sauce, 3 tablespoons water, 3 tablespoons thawed unsweetened apple juice concentrate, 2 teaspoons sesame oil, and 1 teaspoon ground coriander. (Do not make a pan gravy with these drippings.)

Chicken Breasts in Wine Cream Sauce

This easy cream sauce would be welcome alongside steamed asparagus and buttered noodles.
Makes 4 servings (can be doubled)

> 1 tablespoon olive oil
> 1 tablespoon unsalted butter
> Four 10- to 12-ounce bone-in skin-on chicken breasts
> ½ teaspoon freshly ground black pepper
> 1 small onion, chopped
> 4 ounces white button mushrooms, cleaned and thinly sliced
> 2 tablespoons brandy
> 1½ tablespoons all-purpose flour
> 1½ cups dry white wine
> 6 tablespoons heavy cream
> ½ teaspoon salt
> ½ teaspoon grated nutmeg

① Position the rack in the center of the oven (or nearest the center so that your Dutch oven will fit) and preheat the oven to 325°F.

② Heat a small, oven-safe Dutch oven or casserole over medium heat. Add the olive oil, then melt the butter. Season the chicken breasts with the pepper, then add to the pot skin side down just as the butter's foaming abates.

③ Cook until browned, shaking the pot a few times so they don't stick, about 3 minutes. Turn and cook until browned on the other side, about 2 minutes. Transfer to a large plate.

④ Add the onion; cook, stirring frequently, until translucent, about 3 minutes. Add the mushrooms; cook, stirring occasionally, until they begin to give off their liquid, about 2 minutes.

⑤ Pour in the brandy. Should the sauce flame, cover the pot and set it aside off the heat for 20 seconds. Stir well, raise the heat to medium-high, and cook until the liquid has reduced to a thin glaze, about 2 minutes.

⑥ Sprinkle the flour over the mushroom mixture and cook undisturbed for 15 seconds. Stir well and cook for 10 seconds (do not let the flour brown).

⑦ Slowly pour in the wine, whisking all the while and scraping up any browned bits on the pot's bottom. Reduce the heat to low and cook, stirring constantly, until bubbling and thickened, 1 to 2 minutes.

⑧ Pour in the cream, then stir in the salt and nutmeg. Return the chicken and any accumulated juices to the pot. Raise the heat and bring the sauce to a full simmer.

⑨ Cover, place in the oven, and bake until a meat thermometer inserted into the thickest part of a breast registers 165°F (our preference) or 170°F (the USDA recommendation), 30 to 35 minutes, stirring a couple of times. Let stand, covered, at room temperature for 5 minutes before serving.

Variations: Substitute ¼ teaspoon ground allspice for the nutmeg.

Omit the nutmeg altogether and add 2 teaspoons stemmed thyme or 2 teaspoons chopped tarragon leaves.

South African–Inspired Chicken Curry with Apricots and Peppers

Curries from South Africa show the cultural intersection of that region: British, Dutch, African, and Indonesian. This is a very unusual dish, a sweet-sour mélange that's somehow both summery and wintry. The buttermilk is a traditional, tangy finish. Serve with bowls of brown rice or Root Vegetable Mash (page 473). *Makes 6 servings*

2 tablespoons canola oil
Six 10- to 12-ounce bone-in skin-on or skinless chicken breasts, cut in half the short way
2 medium onions, chopped
2 tablespoons minced peeled fresh ginger
2 garlic cloves, minced
2 bay leaves
2 teaspoons turmeric
2 teaspoons ground cumin
2 teaspoons ground coriander
2 teaspoons chili powder
1 teaspoon ground cinnamon
1 teaspoon salt
¼ teaspoon cayenne pepper
2 cups chicken broth
¼ cup all-fruit apricot spread
½ cup chopped dried apricots
1 red or green bell pepper, cored, seeded, and chopped
1 tablespoon red wine vinegar
¼ cup buttermilk (regular, low-fat, or fat-free)

① Heat a very large skillet or a large Dutch oven over medium heat. Swirl in the canola oil, then add the breasts bone side up. Cook until browned, about 3 minutes, shaking the pan occasionally to make sure they're not sticking. Turn and continue cooking until browned on both sides, about 3 more minutes. Transfer to a plate and set aside.

❷ Drain off all but 1 tablespoon fat in the pan and add the onions. Cook, stirring often, until softened, about 2 minutes.

❸ Add the ginger, garlic, and bay leaves; cook for 15 seconds. Stir in the turmeric, cumin, coriander, chili powder, cinnamon, salt, and cayenne. Cook until aromatic, stirring constantly, about 10 seconds.

❹ Pour in the broth, scraping up any browned bits on the bottom of the pan with a wooden spoon. Add the all-fruit spread and stir until simmering.

❺ Return the chicken breasts to the pan along with the dried apricots, bell pepper, and vinegar. Cover, reduce the heat to low, and simmer slowly, stirring once in a while, until the chicken is cooked through, until a meat thermometer inserted into the thickest part of a breast registers 160°F (our preference) or 170°F (the USDA recommendation), 25 to 35 minutes.

❻ Stir in the buttermilk and simmer for 1 minute. Remove the pan from the heat and set aside, covered, for 5 minutes to blend the flavors.

Looking for other chicken curries? Try the South African-Inspired Chicken Curry (page 266), the Cambodian-Inspired Chicken Curry (page 269), or the Burmese-Inspired Chicken and Yellow Lentil Curry (page 283).

Sautéed Boneless Skinless Chicken Breasts with Mushrooms and Thyme

One-pan simplicity: just sear the breasts, build the sauce, and finish the two together. Avoid using a high-sided Dutch oven for a boneless skinless chicken breast sauté because the pan can inadvertently steam the meat, turning it mushy. *Makes 4 servings*

3 tablespoons unsalted butter
Four 5- to 6-ounce boneless skinless
   chicken breasts
½ teaspoon freshly ground black pepper
2 medium shallots, minced
8 ounces cremini or white button
   mushrooms, cleaned and sliced
½ cup chicken broth
1 tablespoon stemmed thyme or
   1½ teaspoons dried thyme
2 teaspoons Dijon mustard
½ teaspoon salt

❶ Melt 2 tablespoons butter in a large skillet or sauté pan set over medium heat. Meanwhile, season the breasts with the pepper.

❷ The moment the butter's foaming subsides, slip the breasts into the pan and cook, partially covered or covered with a splatter shield, until browned, about 8 minutes, turning once but making sure several times that the breasts are not sticking. Transfer to a plate and set aside.

❸ Melt the remaining tablespoon of butter in the skillet, then add the shallots. Cook, stirring often, until softened, about 2 minutes.

❹ Add the mushrooms and cook, stirring once in a while, just until they start to give off their liquid, about 2 minutes. Stir in the broth, thyme, and mustard, then return the breasts to the pan with any accumulated juices.

5 Cover and cook until a meat thermometer inserted into the center of a breast registers 165°F (our preference) or 170°F (the USDA recommendation), about 10 minutes. Season with salt to taste before serving.

Variations: Substitute fennel seeds, chopped oregano leaves, or chopped rosemary leaves for the thyme.

Increase the mustard to 1 tablespoon and add 2 tablespoons raisins, dried currants, or dried blueberries with it.

Sautéed Boneless Skinless Chicken Breasts with Shallots and Radishes

Radishes get incredibly sweet and mellow when sautéed. *Makes 4 servings*

Four 5- to 6-ounce boneless skinless chicken
    breasts
½ teaspoon freshly ground black pepper
2 tablespoons olive oil
6 large radishes, thinly sliced
2 medium shallots, thinly sliced into rings
½ cup dry vermouth or dry white wine
½ cup chicken broth
1 tablespoon white wine vinegar
1 tablespoon unsalted butter
½ teaspoon salt

1 Season the breasts with the pepper. Heat a large skillet or sauté pan over medium heat. Swirl in the olive oil, then add the breasts to the skillet. Cook, partially covered or covered with a splatter shield, until browned, about 5 minutes, turning once but making sure several times that the breasts are not sticking. Transfer to a plate and set aside.

2 Add the radishes and shallots to the skillet. Cook, stirring frequently, until softened, about 2 minutes. Pour in the vermouth or wine and the broth; scrape up any browned bits on the bottom of the pan with a wooden spoon as the sauce comes to a simmer.

3 Return the breasts and any accumulated juices to the pan. Cover and cook until a meat thermometer inserted into the center of a breast registers 165°F (our preference) or 170°F (the USDA recommendation), about 10 minutes.

4 Transfer the breasts to a serving platter. Swirl the vinegar into the liquid in the pan, then whisk in the butter until it melts. Season with salt and pour the sauce and the vegetables over the breasts to serve.

Variations: Add 1 tart green apple, such as a Granny Smith, peeled, cored, and diced, with the radishes.

Add 2 teaspoons stemmed thyme or chopped parsley leaves with the vinegar.

Add ¼ cup toasted walnut pieces with the vinegar.

A Breast Is a Breast Is a Breast—or Is It?

Chickens have one "breast"—the large, meaty, chestlike area above their legs. But in culinary parlance, we divide the breast into two sections or lobes—left and right—and refer to each of these as a "breast." In other words, a chicken has one breast in the barnyard but two in the kitchen. To complicate matters, you can indeed find "whole breasts" at your market—that is, both halves kept together.

The same goes for boneless skinless breasts. It would be more accurate to say "boneless skinless breast halves," but the construction is awkward and its misplaced accuracy can lead to confusion (as someone starts hacking in half the breasts they buy at the store).

Braised Boneless Skinless Chicken Breasts with Tomatoes and Artichoke Hearts

These stewed breasts can be made and refrigerated up to 2 days in advance; reheat, covered, in a 325°F oven for about 15 minutes. *Makes 4 servings*

2 tablespoons olive oil
1 tablespoon unsalted butter
Four 5- to 6-ounce boneless skinless chicken breasts
1 small onion, chopped
2 garlic cloves, minced
1 tablespoon all-purpose flour
¼ cup dry white wine or dry vermouth
1¾ cups canned diced tomatoes
One 12-ounce package frozen artichoke hearts, thawed
2 teaspoons chopped tarragon leaves or 1 teaspoon dried tarragon
½ teaspoon freshly ground black pepper
½ teaspoon salt

1 Heat a small Dutch oven or a high-sided sauté pan over medium heat. Add the olive oil, then melt the butter. Add the chicken breasts and brown them on both sides, about 6 minutes, turning once but shaking the pan a few times to make sure they don't stick. Transfer to a large plate.

2 Add the onion to the pan; cook, stirring often, until softened, about 2 minutes. Add the garlic and cook for 20 seconds.

3 Sprinkle the flour into the pan, stir well, and cook undisturbed for 15 seconds. Whisk in the wine or vermouth in a slow, steady stream, all the while scraping up any browned bits on the pan's bottom. Continue cooking, whisking constantly, until thick and bubbling, about 1 minute.

4 Stir in the diced tomatoes, artichoke hearts, tarragon, and pepper. Return the chicken breasts and any accumulated juices to the pan, nestling the breasts into the liquid.

5 Bring the sauce to a simmer, reduce the heat to low, cover, and simmer slowly until the sauce thickens slightly and a meat thermometer inserted into the center of a breast registers 165°F (our preference) or 170°F (the USDA recommendation). Set off the heat, covered, for 5 minutes; season with salt before serving.

Variations: Substitute red wine for the white wine.

Substitute frozen okra or lima beans, thawed, for the artichoke hearts.

Substitute stemmed thyme or chopped oregano leaves for the tarragon.

Remove the chicken breasts once they're cooked through, then stir ¼ cup heavy cream into the sauce. Bring the sauce to a boil and reduce slightly, just to get rid of the raw cream taste and to thicken somewhat, about 2 minutes.

Cambodian-Inspired Chicken Curry with Lemongrass and Coconut Milk

Cambodian curries are more subtle and aromatic than others from Southeast Asia. This dish is not terribly hot, even a little tart, and actually quite comforting. It's best served alongside jasmine rice or over Ginger Squash Puree (page 474). *Makes 6 servings*

4 garlic cloves, halved
One 4-inch piece of peeled fresh ginger, cut into quarters
2 large shallots, quartered
¼ cup chopped peeled fresh lemongrass (about 4 large stalks)
1½ tablespoons rice vinegar
1 teaspoon turmeric

1 teaspoon freshly grated lime zest

1 teaspoon salt

½ teaspoon red pepper flakes

2 tablespoons peanut or canola oil

Six 5- to 6-ounce boneless skinless chicken breasts, each cut into 4 pieces

1 cup chicken broth

1 cup coconut milk (regular or low-fat)

1 tablespoon fish sauce

1 teaspoon packed light brown sugar

1 tablespoon lime juice

1 Place the garlic, ginger, shallots, lemongrass, vinegar, turmeric, lime zest, salt, and red pepper flakes in a large spice grinder, a large cleaned coffee grinder, or a mini-food processor. Grind or process just until finely pulverized, on the verge of turning into a paste. Alternatively (and more authentically), pulverize all the ingredients in a mortar with a pestle; start by dicing the shallots, garlic, ginger, and lemongrass, then working them against the salt in the mortar before adding the vinegar, turmeric, lime zest, and red pepper flakes.

2 Heat a large nonstick skillet over medium heat. Swirl in the oil, then add the spice mixture. Cook, stirring constantly, until very aromatic, about 1 minute.

3 Add the chicken; cook, turning often, until lightly browned, about 4 minutes.

4 Stir in the broth, coconut milk, fish sauce, and brown sugar, scraping up any browned bits on the bottom of the pan. Bring to a simmer, cover, reduce the heat to low, and cook for 10 minutes.

5 Skim the sauce for any visible fat and stir in the lime juice just before serving.

Bacon-Wrapped Stuffed Boneless Skinless Chicken Breasts

Dried fruit and bacon are a perfect combination for chicken breasts. *Makes 4 servings*

¾ cup finely chopped dried apricots

½ cup finely chopped dried cranberries

1 tablespoon chopped rosemary leaves

2 teaspoons olive oil

½ teaspoon ground black pepper

Four 5- to 6-ounce boneless skinless chicken breasts

8 bacon slices

1 Position the rack in the middle of the oven. Preheat the oven to 400°F. Mix the apricots, cranberries, rosemary, olive oil, and pepper in a small bowl.

2 To create a pocket in one of the breasts, put it on the work surface, smooth side up. Eye the thickest part of one of its long sides and insert a paring knife there with the blade parallel to the work surface. Slip the knife from side to side, thereby making small cuts back and forth in the meat without cutting through to the other side or out the ends. Take your time—don't be impatient. Once you have created a slitlike pocket, repeat with the remaining breasts.

3 Gently pry the pockets open with your fingers, then stuff about one-quarter of the dried fruit filling into each. Wrap 2 slices of bacon completely around each breast so that the strips pass over the openings with the filling and their ends meet on the "bottom" of the breast. Place the chicken breasts seam side down in one layer in a 9-inch square baking dish or a medium shallow casserole.

4 Bake, basting occasionally with pan drippings, until the bacon is brown and crisp, about 40 minutes. Because of the stuffing, it's very difficult to take the temperature of the breasts—you should do this, but make sure you're only taking the temperature of the meat (not the stuffing) and that it's either 165°F (our preference) or 170°F (the USDA recommendation). Let the breasts stand at room temperature for 5 minutes before serving.

Variations: You can use any combination of dried fruit you wish; just make sure you end up with about 1¼ cups finely chopped dried fruit. Try dried apples, dried strawberries, dried pitted dates, or pitted prunes. The best combinations are sweet and tart: prunes and cherries, for example.

For a deep glaze, drizzle 1 teaspoon aged balsamic vinegar or 1 teaspoon maple syrup over each breast during the last 5 minutes of cooking.

Best-Ever Grilled Chicken Sandwiches

Without access to a grill, make these sandwiches in a well-oiled grill pan set over medium-high heat. *Makes 4 servings*

> 2 small onions, sliced paper thin
> 4 bay leaves
> Four 5- to 6-ounce boneless skinless chicken breasts
> 3 cups water
> ¼ cup kosher salt
> 2 tablespoons honey
> 10 black peppercorns, crushed in a mortar with a pestle, a spice grinder, or a mini-food processor
> Canola oil for the grill grate
> 1 beefsteak tomato, cut into 4 thick slices
> 1 small red onion, cut into 4 thick slices
> 8 large thick-cut slices white or country white bread
> Mayonnaise, mustard, or Classic French Bistro Vinaigrette (page 103) for garnish

❶ Layer the onion rings and bay leaves in a 13 × 9-inch baking dish; place the breasts on top.

❷ Whisk the water, salt, and honey in a medium bowl until the salt and honey dissolve; stir in the peppercorns. Pour over the chicken breasts, then add enough cool water so that the breasts are submerged. Cover and refrigerate for at least 4 hours or up to 12 hours, turning the breasts occasionally without disturbing the onions.

❸ Oil the grill grate and heat a gas grill to high heat or build a high-heat, red-hot-ashed coal bed in a charcoal grill.

❹ Remove the breasts from the marinade; discard the marinade. Pat the breasts dry with paper towels.

❺ Place the breasts 4 to 6 inches over the heat source on the gas grill or over the coals in the charcoal grill. Grill, turning once, until browned, until a meat thermometer inserted into thickest part of a breast registers 165°F (our preference) or 170°F (the USDA recommendation), 10 to 13 minutes. Transfer the breasts to a carving board and let rest for 5 minutes. Maintain the grill's temperature.

❻ If possible, oil the grill grate again. Place the tomato and red onion slices over high heat; grill just until browned, maybe even a little charred, about 2 minutes, turning once. Transfer to the carving board and set aside.

❼ Place the bread slices on the grill over high heat. Toast 1 minute, turning once, until brown. Build the sandwiches on the toasted bread with the chicken, tomato slices, grilled red onion, and the condiment of your choice for garnish.

Variations: Add any of the following to the sandwiches: 1 large ripe avocado, peeled, pitted, and thinly sliced; 1 cup bean, garlic, or radish sprouts; 1 large cucumber, peeled and shaved into long strips with a vegetable peeler; grilled zucchini slices; grilled cored and seeded yellow bell pepper strips; or slices of fried bacon.

Chicken Pastrami

You can make a pastrami out of almost anything; it's just spice-cured, cooked meat. Here, boneless skinless chicken breasts are transformed into the deli favorite, just right for sandwiches. *Makes 6 to 8 servings*

3 cups warm water
3 tablespoons kosher salt
2 tablespoons cracked coriander seeds
2 tablespoons cracked black peppercorns
6 garlic cloves, crushed
6 cracked allspice berries
2 bay leaves
Six 5- to 6-ounce boneless skinless chicken breasts
3 tablespoons canola oil
1 tablespoon packed light brown sugar
1 teaspoon freshly ground black pepper
2 teaspoons ground coriander
1½ teaspoons dry mustard
1½ teaspoons ground ginger
½ teaspoon garlic powder

❶ Whisk the warm water and salt in a large bowl until the salt dissolves. Add the coriander, peppercorns, garlic, allspice berries, and bay leaves. Set aside to cool to room temperature, about 30 minutes.

❷ Place the breasts in a large roasting pan or baking dish. Pour the spiced salt water over them. If the breasts are not submerged, add just enough cool water to do so. Cover and refrigerate for at least 12 hours or up to 24 hours, turning the breasts occasionally.

❸ Position the rack in the center of the oven and preheat the oven to 325°F.

❹ Remove the breasts from the brine, rinse them, and pat dry with paper towels. Discard the brine and all spices; wash the pan or baking dish. Place a wire rack in it.

5 Mix the brown sugar, ground pepper, ground coriander, dry mustard, ground ginger, and garlic powder in a small bowl. Rub the canola oil all over the breasts, then rub a scant 2 teaspoons of this mixture into each of the breasts. Place them on the rack in the pan.

6 Bake until lightly browned and an instant-read meat thermometer inserted into the thickest part of a breast registers 160°F (our preference) or 170°F (the USDA recommendation), between 1 hour and 15 minutes and 1 hour and 40 minutes. Cool at least 10 minutes, then thinly slice before serving—or cool completely and store, wrapped in plastic, in the refrigerator for up to 4 days.

Stir-Fry Chicken Packets

A stir-fry without the mess of a stir-fry: strips of chicken breast and vegetables are baked in parchment packets with Asian spices. Serve them over rice or wilted greens. *Makes 4 servings*

Four 5- to 6-ounce boneless skinless chicken breasts, sliced into ¼-inch strips
4 scallions, thinly sliced
2 red bell peppers, cored, seeded, and thinly sliced
3 garlic cloves, minced
One 12-ounce can baby corn, drained, the ears halved
8 ounces snow peas (about 3 cups)
2 tablespoons minced peeled fresh ginger
2 tablespoons soy sauce
2 tablespoons rice vinegar
2 teaspoons Asian red chili sauce
2 teaspoons sesame oil, preferably toasted sesame oil

1 Position the rack in the center of the oven; preheat the oven to 400°F.

2 Mix all the ingredients together in a large bowl.

3 Lay two 16-inch sheets of parchment paper on your work surface, one on top of the other. Spoon a quarter of the chicken mixture with some sauce into the middle of the paper. Fold the two opposing short ends over the mixture, then seal the packet closed by bring the other two long sides together and crimping them to make a packet. Crimp the short ends as well. Be sure the seal is tight so no steam will leak. Place this packet on a large, lipped baking sheet; then make three more of these packets, using the same amount of chicken mixture in each (that is, a third of what's left for the second one, half of what's left for the third one, and the remainder for the last one).

4 Bake for 30 minutes. Leave the packets on the baking sheet for 10 minutes before serving. You can either transfer the packets themselves to plates using a large spatula, or you can open them up and spoon them into bowls or over any side dish you've chosen.

Variations: Substitute 12 ounces sliced water chestnuts or bamboo shoots for the baby corn.

Substitute 8 ounces small broccoli florets for the snow peas.

Substitute 2 tablespoons frozen orange juice concentrate, thawed, for the rice vinegar.

Omit the chile sauce and sesame oil; add 2 teaspoons lemon juice instead.

Omit only the chile sauce and add up to 2 teaspoons prepared Thai curry paste instead— but be careful; it's wickedly hot.

Orange Chicken Stir-Fry

In this renovated stir-fry, breast meat is first sautéed, then a flavorful orange sauce is built around it. *Makes 4 servings*

> 3 tablespoons frozen orange juice
>   concentrate, thawed
> 2 tablespoons soy sauce
> 2 tablespoons Chinese black vinegar, or
>   1 tablespoon plus 1 teaspoon balsamic
>   vinegar and 2 teaspoons Worcestershire
>   sauce
> 1 tablespoon Shaoxing or dry sherry
> 1 tablespoon Asian red chili sauce
> 2 teaspoons sugar
> 1 tablespoon peanut oil
> 3 garlic cloves, minced
> 2 tablespoons minced peeled fresh ginger
> ¾ pound boneless skinless chicken breast,
>   sliced into ¼-inch strips
> 2 cups broccoli florets
> 6 shiitake mushrooms, stems removed, caps
>   thinly sliced
> 3 scallions, cut into 1-inch pieces
> 2 teaspoons finely grated orange zest
> 1 teaspoon cornstarch or arrowroot,
>   whisked into 1 tablespoon water in a
>   small bowl

1 Whisk the orange juice concentrate, soy sauce, black vinegar or its substitutes, Shaoxing or sherry, chili sauce, and sugar in a small bowl until the sugar dissolves; set aside.

2 Heat a large wok or a large, high-sided sauté pan over medium-high heat until a drop of water skitters around the pan. Swirl in the peanut oil, then add the garlic and ginger. Stir-fry until aromatic, about 20 seconds (do not let the garlic brown). Add the chicken strips and stir-fry for 2 minutes until almost cooked through.

3 Add the broccoli and mushrooms; stir-fry until the mushrooms begin to give off their liquid to form a sauce, about 1 minute.

4 Pour in the orange juice concentrate mixture and bring the sauce to a simmer, stirring occasionally.

5 Add the scallions and orange zest; cook for 1 minute, stirring a few times. Then stir the cornstarch or arrowroot mixture into the sauce. Wait for it to come back to a boil, just until thickened, about 15 seconds. Remove from the heat and let stand for a couple of minutes before serving.

Variations: Substitute sugar snap peas, snow peas, cauliflower florets, sliced carrots, or seeded red bell pepper strips for the broccoli florets.

For an even hotter dish, add ½ teaspoon red pepper flakes to the orange juice concentrate mixture.

No-Fry Kung Pao Chicken

There's no reason to deep-fry chicken to make this take-out favorite. Walnuts offer a deep, nutty crunch. *Makes 4 servings*

> 2 tablespoons soy sauce
> 2 tablespoons rice vinegar
> 1 tablespoon Shaoxing or dry sherry
> ½ cup walnut pieces
> 1 tablespoon sesame oil, preferably toasted
>   sesame oil
> 16 dried red Asian chiles
> 1 carrot, peeled and finely diced
> 2 garlic cloves, minced
> 2 tablespoons minced peeled fresh ginger
> ¾ pound boneless skinless chicken breasts,
>   cut into ¼-inch strips
> 2 medium scallions, cut into 1-inch pieces
> 1 medium green bell pepper, cored, seeded,
>   and diced

¼ teaspoon crushed Szechuan peppercorns
or 1 teaspoon finely grated orange zest
1 teaspoon cornstarch or arrowroot, dissolved
in 1 tablespoon water in a small bowl

❶ Mix the soy sauce, rice vinegar, and Shaoxing or sherry in a small bowl; set aside.

❷ Toast the walnuts in a dry wok or high-sided sauté pan set over medium-high heat until aromatic and lightly browned, about 3 minutes, stirring almost constantly. Transfer to a small bowl.

❸ Swirl the sesame oil into the wok or pan. Add the chiles, carrot, garlic, and ginger; stir-fry for 1 minute.

❹ Add the chicken strips; stir-fry, tossing constantly, until lightly browned and almost cooked through, about 2 minutes.

❺ Add the scallions, bell pepper, and Szechuan peppercorns or orange zest; stir-fry until aromatic, about 1 minute.

❻ Return the walnuts to the pan, then pour in the soy sauce mixture. Bring the sauce to a simmer. Cook, stirring occasionally, for 1 minute.

❼ Stir in the cornstarch or arrowroot mixture. Simmer until just thickened, probably less than 20 seconds. Immediately remove from the heat and let rest for a couple of minutes before serving.

Variations: Add one 8-ounce can sliced water chestnuts, drained, or one 8-ounce can sliced bamboo shoots, drained, with the scallions.

Add 1 cup preserved Asian vegetables, such as turnips or radishes, with the scallions. (Be careful: some of these preparations are fiery hot.)

Substitute 1 cup broccoli florets, cauliflower florets, or snow peas for the bell pepper.

What to Do with Chicken Legs and Thighs

Pan-Roasted Chicken Quarters with Herb Butter

Air-drying the chicken in the refrigerator ensures the crispest skin; adding the herb butter, the best taste. *Makes 6 servings*

Six 8- to 10-ounce skin-on drumstick-
and-thigh quarters, visible excess fat
removed
½ teaspoon salt
½ teaspoon freshly ground black
pepper
1 tablespoon olive oil
One of the three herb butters that
follow (page 276)

❶ Blot the chicken quarters dry, place them on a large baking sheet, and season with salt and pepper. Refrigerate, uncovered, for 24 hours.

❷ Position the rack in the center of the oven and preheat the oven to 325°F.

❸ Heat a large grill pan, cast-iron skillet, or oven-safe skillet over medium-high heat. Brush or swirl in the olive oil, then add the quarters, skin side down. Cook until well browned, turning once, 12 to 15 minutes.

❹ Place the pan or skillet in the oven and cook until the juices run clear, 15 to 20 minutes, until a meat thermometer inserted into the thickest part of the thigh without touching bone registers 165°F (our preference) or 180°F (the USDA recommendation). Let stand at room temperature for 2 minutes, transfer to serving plates, and top with a scant tablespoon of one of the herb butters.

Three Herb Butters

To make any of these, mash the butter and olive oil in a small bowl with a fork. Add the remaining ingredients and press them into the butter through the tines of the fork. Make them up to a week in advance; store, covered, in the refrigerator; and use them straight from the refrigerator (they'll melt on the hot chicken).

1. Parsley and Thyme Butter

Makes about 6 tablespoons

  3 tablespoons unsalted butter, at room temperature
  1 tablespoon olive oil
  2 tablespoons chopped parsley leaves
  2 teaspoons stemmed thyme
  ¼ teaspoon salt

2. Garlic Lemon Butter

Makes about 6 tablespoons

  3 tablespoons unsalted butter, at room temperature
  1 tablespoon olive oil
  2 teaspoons finely grated lemon zest
  1 teaspoon lemon juice
  ¼ teaspoon salt
  2 finely minced garlic cloves

Dark Meat Chicken

If you were able to find a chicken in the wild, you'd discover that it had only dark meat—the breast muscles darker from flight and use, from being consistently oxygenated. Dark meat tends to be fattier and better able to stand up to more substantial cooking techniques like stewing and braising.

3. Smoked Paprika Butter

Makes a little less than 6 tablespoons

  4 tablespoons unsalted butter, at room temperature
  1½ tablespoons olive oil
  2 teaspoons smoked paprika
  ¼ teaspoon salt

Outdoor/Indoor Chicken Quarters with Blueberry Ginger Barbecue Sauce

Whether you cook the quarters indoors or out, marinating them in buttermilk offers a tart backtaste to match this sweet and aromatic sauce. The Blueberry Ginger Barbecue Sauce gives a sweet, aromatic pop to the meat. *Makes 6 servings*

  1¼ cups buttermilk (regular, low-fat, or fat-free)
  3 tablespoons minced sage leaves or 1 tablespoon rubbed sage
  1½ tablespoons paprika
  1 tablespoon maple syrup
  1 tablespoon dry mustard
  1 teaspoon salt
  Six 8- to 10-ounce skin-on drumstick-and-thigh quarters, all visible fat trimmed
  6 teaspoons canola oil, plus additional for the grate or the pan
  Blueberry Ginger Barbecue Sauce (recipe follows)

To make the quarters outdoors:

1 Place the buttermilk, sage, paprika, maple syrup, dry mustard, and salt in a large ziplock plastic bag; seal the bag and shake to combine. Add the chicken quarters, seal again, and shake to coat. Refrigerate for 30 minutes, shaking occasionally.

2 Oil the cooking grate, then heat a gas grill to high heat or build a high-heat, red-hot-ashed coal

bed in a charcoal grill. Remove the chicken quarters from the marinade; pat dry with paper towels. Discard the marinade and the plastic bag. Rub 1 teaspoon oil into each quarter.

3 Place the quarters skin side down on the grate directly over the heat source or the coals. Cover the grill and cook for 10 minutes.

4 Pour about half of the warm Blueberry Ginger Barbecue Sauce into a small bowl (reserving half that won't touch the partially cooked poultry). Baste the quarters generously with some of the sauce, turn, and baste the other side.

5 Cover and continue grilling, basting once more, until browned and the juices run clear, until a meat thermometer inserted into thickest part of thigh without touching bone registers 165°F (our preference) or 180°F (the USDA recommendation), 7 to 10 more minutes. Transfer the quarters to a carving board and let rest for 5 minutes. Serve with the reserved Blueberry Ginger Barbecue Sauce on the side.

To make the quarters indoors:
1 Complete step 1 on page 276.

2 Position the rack in the center of the oven and preheat the oven to 325°F. Remove the quarters from the marinade; pat dry with paper towels. Discard the marinade and the bag.

3 Heat a large grill pan, cast-iron skillet, or ovenproof skillet over medium-high heat. Brush or swirl in 1 tablespoon canola oil; add the quarters skin side down. Cook until nicely browned but not cooked through, 12 to 15 minutes, turning once.

4 Pour about half of the Blueberry Ginger Barbecue Sauce into a small bowl, reserving half that won't touch the partially cooked poultry. Gener-

ously brush the quarters with some of the sauce; turn them skin side up and brush again.

5 Place the pan or skillet in the oven, uncovered, and bake until lacquered, until a meat thermometer inserted into the thickest part of the thigh without touching the bone registers 165°F (our preference) or 180°F (the USDA recommendation), 15 to 20 minutes. Transfer the quarters to a carving board and let rest for 5 minutes. Serve with the reserved Blueberry Ginger Barbecue Sauce as a garnish.

Blueberry Ginger Barbecue Sauce
This sauce would also be welcome with almost any chicken, sausage, or pork barbecue. *Makes about 1½ cups*

2 cups blueberries
1 cup sugar
¼ cup red wine vinegar
2 tablespoons minced peeled fresh ginger
1 teaspoon lemon juice
1 scallion, minced
1 garlic clove, minced
½ teaspoon salt

1 Place all the ingredients in a large saucepan set over medium-high heat. Stir until the sugar dissolves and the mixture comes to a light simmer.

2 Reduce the heat to low and continue simmering, stirring often, until as thick as ketchup, about 20 minutes. This sauce can be made ahead and stored, covered, in the refrigerator for up to 1 week.

Variations: Add 2 teaspoons stemmed thyme, 1 teaspoon red pepper flakes, ½ teaspoon freshly ground black pepper, or ½ teaspoon grated nutmeg with the blueberries.

Other chicken dishes: Chicken Salad (page 122); Classic Chicken Soup (page 148); Autumn Lasagna (page 205); Pad Thai (page 212); Pad See Ew (page 214); Potato, Chicken, and Green Bean Salad with Champagne Tarragon Vinaigrette (page 482); and Asian-Inspired Dirty Rice with Chicken, Edamame, and Walnuts (page 491).

Stovetop Chicken and Rice

A workday dish, this has become a favorite in our cooking classes. It's rich and homey—and ever so easy, thanks to dried mushrooms and no-fuss thigh quarters. *Makes 4 servings (can be doubled)*

1 ounce dried mushrooms, such as shiitakes, morels, porcini, chanterelles, or a mixture
2½ cups boiling water
1 tablespoon olive oil
1 tablespoon unsalted butter
Four 8- to 10-ounce skin-on drumstick-and-thigh quarters, visible excess fat removed
½ teaspoon freshly ground black pepper
2 medium shallots, finely chopped
2 garlic cloves, minced
⅔ cup dry white wine or dry vermouth, or more as necessary
¾ cup white rice
2 bay leaves
½ teaspoon salt

❶ Place the mushrooms in a medium bowl, add the boiling water, and set aside until fragrant and pliable, about 20 minutes.

❷ Heat a deep 12-inch skillet or a medium Dutch oven over medium heat. Add the olive oil, then melt the butter. Season the chicken quarters with pepper and slip them into the pan skin side down. Cook until golden, about 5 minutes, checking occasionally to make sure they haven't stuck.

❸ Turn the quarters. Sprinkle the shallots and garlic among them. Cook for 2 minutes, shaking the pan occasionally.

❹ Pour in the wine or vermouth. Use a wooden spoon to scrape up any browned bits under the chicken pieces. Simmer until the vermouth or wine has been reduced to a glaze, 3 to 4 minutes.

❺ Add the rice, making sure that no grains are stuck on top of the chicken but that they're evenly distributed in the pan. Take the mushrooms out of their liquid and sprinkle them in the pan, pressing them down among the chicken pieces. Strain the mushroom liquid into the pan through a fine-mesh sieve (to catch any sand or grit), pouring the liquid over the chicken to catch any rice grains and wash them to the bottom. Tuck in the bay leaves.

❻ Shake the pan to distribute everything evenly and bring the sauce to a simmer. Cover, reduce the heat to low, and simmer slowly until the rice is tender and a meat thermometer inserted into the thickest part of the thigh without touching bone registers 165°F (our preference) or 180°F (the USDA recommendation), 15 to 20 minutes. If you find that the pan is drying out during the last few minutes of cooking, add more wine in ¼-cup increments and lower the heat further; if there's too much liquid in the pan, uncover it during the last few minutes of cooking so that there's just a light sauce with the rice in the pan. Season with salt before serving.

Variations: Add 2 teaspoons chopped tarragon leaves or 2 teaspoons stemmed thyme with the wine or vermouth.

Substitute red wine for the white wine; if you do, use 2 tablespoons unsalted butter, omitting the olive oil.

For an Italian taste, use dry Marsala instead of the white wine.

For a Spanish-influenced dish, substitute dry sherry for the white wine. Also add ¼ teaspoon saffron to the dried mushrooms before adding the boiling water. Top the dish with 1 cup fresh or frozen peas before covering and cooking the rice.

Persian-Inspired Chicken and Walnuts

This classic is made with tart pomegranate molasses and earthy walnuts. Serve with basmati, Texmati, or red rice on the side (see page 495). *Makes 6 to 8 servings*

3 tablespoons unsalted butter
3 pounds bone-in skin-on or skinless chicken thighs
½ teaspoon ground cinnamon
½ teaspoon freshly ground black pepper
1 large onion, chopped
1¼ cups finely chopped walnut pieces
2 cups chicken broth
3 tablespoons pomegranate molasses
2 tablespoons tomato paste
1½ tablespoons lemon juice
1 teaspoon salt

1 Position the rack in the oven so a large pot or a Dutch oven can fit comfortably in it. Preheat the oven to 350°F.

2 Melt the butter in a Dutch oven, large pot, or oven casserole. Season the chicken with cinnamon and pepper; slip the thighs into the pan. Cook until browned on both sides, turning occasionally, about 10 minutes, Transfer to a plate and set aside.

3 Add the onion and cook, stirring frequently, until soft and translucent, about 3 minutes.

4 Stir in the walnuts and cook, stirring often, until lightly toasted, about 2 minutes.

5 Pour in the broth, scrape up any browned bits on the bottom of the pan with a wooden spoon, and then stir in the pomegranate molasses, tomato paste, and lemon juice. Bring the sauce to a simmer, then return the thighs and any accumulated juices to the pan.

6 Cover and bake until the meat is quite tender and the sauce is bubbling, stirring once in a while, about 1 hour and 15 minutes. Season with salt and let stand at room temperature, covered, for 5 minutes before serving.

Variations: Substitute 3 medium shallots, chopped, for the onion.
Add 3 garlic cloves, minced, with the walnuts.
For a curried variation, add 2 teaspoons curry powder with the broth, then substitute 2 tablespoons tamarind paste for the pomegranate molasses.

Civet de Poulet

This is a French stew (pronounced see-VAY duh poo-LAY) of thighs and gizzards. The trick is to cut the bacon, gizzards, onions, carrots, and prunes to exactly the same size—about ½-inch pieces. *Makes 6 to 8 servings*

4 ounces thick-cut bacon, chopped
12 ounces chicken gizzards, trimmed of all visible fat and chopped
3 pounds bone-in skinless chicken thighs
2 medium onions, chopped
2 large carrots, peeled and chopped
2 teaspoons stemmed thyme or 1 teaspoon dried thyme
1 teaspoon salt
½ teaspoon ground allspice
½ teaspoon freshly ground black pepper
1 tablespoon all-purpose flour
3 cups red wine
8 pitted prunes, chopped
2 bay leaves

1 Position the rack nearest the middle of the oven so that a Dutch oven or oven-safe pot can fit inside; preheat the oven to 350°F.

2 Fry the bacon in a large Dutch oven or oven-safe pot over medium heat until the fat renders from it, about 2 minutes.

3 Add the gizzards and continue cooking, stirring often, until browned and the bacon is quite crisp, about 6 more minutes. Transfer the bacon and gizzards to a large plate lined with paper towels and set aside.

4 Add the chicken thighs to the pot; brown on both sides, turning occasionally, about 8 minutes. Transfer them to the plate with the bacon and gizzards; set aside.

5 Pour off all but 2 tablespoons fat from the pot. Return it to medium heat; add the onions and carrots. Cook, stirring often, until aromatic and softened, about 4 minutes.

6 Sprinkle the thyme, salt, allspice, and pepper over the vegetables; cook until quite aromatic, about 15 seconds. Sprinkle the flour over everything, cook undisturbed for 15 seconds, then stir well and continue cooking for 15 more seconds.

7 Pour in the wine and bring the sauce to a simmer, stirring constantly and scraping up any browned bits on the bottom of the pot. Cook just until the sauce thickens, less than 1 minute.

8 Return the bacon, gizzards, and thighs to the pot. Stir in the prunes and tuck in the bay leaves. Bring the sauce to a simmer.

9 Cover and bake until the thighs are quite tender and the meat is almost falling off the bone, stirring once in a while, about 1½ hours. Discard the bay leaves before serving.

Variations: Add 8 ounces sliced mushrooms to the stew after you've cooked the onions and carrots; cook, stirring constantly, for 2 minutes.

For a lighter dish, substitute white wine for the red wine. Even lighter still? Omit the bacon.

For a heartier stew, add 2 turnips, peeled and chopped, and/or 3 parsnips, peeled and chopped, with the carrots. In this case, increase the wine to 3½ cups.

Chicken Fricassee with Leeks, Mushrooms, and Tarragon

Do not use paper-thin pancetta; ask your butcher for a 4-ounce chunk and chop it yourself at home.
Makes 6 to 8 servings

2 tablespoons unsalted butter
3 pounds bone-in skinless chicken thighs
4 ounces pancetta, chopped
2 leeks, trimmed, white and pale green parts only, cut in half, washed carefully between the layers for dirt, then thinly sliced in half-moons
8 ounces white button or cremini mushrooms, cleaned of any dirt and thinly sliced
2 teaspoons chopped tarragon leaves or 1 teaspoon dried tarragon
1 teaspoon salt
½ teaspoon ground cloves
½ teaspoon freshly ground black pepper
1 tablespoon all-purpose flour
3 cups white wine

1 Position the rack so that a Dutch oven or oven-safe pot can fit safely inside the oven and preheat the oven to 350°F.

2 Melt the butter in a Dutch oven or a large oven-safe pot. Add the chicken thighs and brown on both sides, turning occasionally, about 8 minutes. Transfer to a plate and set aside.

3 Add the pancetta and cook until frizzled and lightly browned, stirring often, about 3 minutes. Add the leeks and cook, stirring often, until soft, about 5 minutes.

4 Add the mushrooms and cook, stirring frequently, until they give off their liquid and it evaporates into a glaze, about 5 more minutes.

5 Sprinkle the tarragon, salt, ground cloves, and pepper over the vegetables, stir well, and cook until aromatic, about 15 seconds. Then sprinkle in the flour. Cook undisturbed for 15 seconds, then stir well and continue cooking for about 20 seconds (do not brown the flour).

6 Slowly pour the wine into the pot, stirring all the while. Bring to a simmer, stirring constantly to get any browned bits off the pot's bottom and to keep the flour from sticking. Once simmering, return the thighs and any accumulated juices to the pot.

7 Cover and bake until the chicken is very tender, almost falling off the bone, stirring once in a while, about 1½ hours.

Variations: Add 2 celery ribs, thinly sliced, and/or 2 carrots, thinly sliced with the leeks. Increase the wine to 3½ cups.

Add 2 or 3 minced garlic cloves with the mushrooms.

Tuck a couple of bay leaves into the sauce before you return the thighs to the pot. Discard the bay leaves before serving.

Creamy Chicken Fricassee: After the casserole has baked, remove the thighs to a large serving platter or serving bowl and tent with aluminum foil to keep warm. Set the pot over medium heat and stir in ½ cup heavy cream. Bring the sauce to a simmer; cook for 1 minute, stirring constantly. Pour the cream sauce over the thighs.

Jerk Chicken Thighs and Plantains

"Jerk" is Jamaican for spicy, but you can control the bang in this oven-bake. Use very ripe plantains, ones with almost black skins. *Makes 6 servings*

1 tablespoon chili powder
1 tablespoon dried thyme
1½ teaspoons ground cinnamon
1 teaspoon ground ginger
1 teaspoon salt
½ teaspoon ground allspice
¼ teaspoon garlic powder
⅛ to ½ teaspoon cayenne to taste
3 pounds bone-in skinless chicken thighs
Canola oil for greasing the baking dish
2 medium onions, chopped
1 large green bell pepper, cored, seeded, and chopped
2 ripe medium plantains, peeled, halved lengthwise, and cut into ½-inch sections
1¼ cups canned drained diced tomatoes
1 cup chicken broth

1 Grind the chili powder, thyme, cinnamon, ginger, salt, allspice, garlic powder, and cayenne in a spice grinder, cleaned coffee grinder, or mini-food processor until powdery. Massage this mixture into the chicken thighs and set them aside at room temperature for 5 minutes.

2 Position the rack in the center of the oven; preheat the oven to 350°F. Lightly oil a 13 × 9-inch baking pan.

3 Mix the onions, bell pepper, plantains, tomatoes, and broth in a large bowl, then spread them into the prepared pan. Place the thighs on top.

4 Cover and bake until the plantains are soft and the chicken is quite tender, almost falling off the bone, about 1 hour and 15 minutes. Let stand for 5 minutes at room temperature before serving.

Chicken Pot Pie with a Sour Cream Biscuit Topping

Here's the ultimate winter warmer. Work quickly to make the biscuit topping once the chicken stew has been prepared. *Makes 6 servings*

3 tablespoons unsalted butter
1 large onion, finely chopped
2 celery ribs, finely chopped
2 medium carrots, peeled and finely chopped
1½ pounds boneless skinless chicken thighs, cut into ½-inch pieces
1½ cups plus 2 tablespoons all-purpose flour
1 cup chicken broth
⅓ cup dry vermouth or dry white wine
⅓ cup heavy cream
1 tablespoon Dijon mustard
2 teaspoons stemmed thyme or 1 teaspoon dried thyme
1 teaspoon salt
½ teaspoon freshly ground black pepper
2 teaspoons baking soda
1 teaspoon dry mustard
½ cup milk (regular, low-fat, or fat-free)
¼ cup regular or low-fat sour cream (do not use fat-free)
2 tablespoons unsalted butter, melted and cooled
2 tablespoons chopped chives or the chopped green portion of a small scallion

1 Position the rack in the center of the oven and preheat the oven to 400°F.

2 Melt 3 tablespoons butter in a large, oven-safe, high-sided skillet or sauté pan. Add the onion, celery, and carrots; cook, stirring frequently, until soft and aromatic, about 3 minutes.

3 Add the chicken and cook, stirring frequently, until a little browned, about 4 minutes.

4 Sprinkle 2 tablespoons flour over the chicken and vegetables, cook undisturbed for 15 seconds,

then stir well and cook for another 15 seconds, just so the flour loses its raw taste but before it starts to brown.

5 Slowly pour in the broth, vermouth or wine, and cream, stirring constantly so the flour doesn't clump. Stir in the Dijon mustard, thyme, ½ teaspoon salt, and pepper. Bring to a simmer, stirring constantly and scraping up any browned bits on the pan's bottom with a wooden spoon. Once simmering, cover and set aside while you prepare the topping.

6 Whisk the remaining 1½ cups flour in a large bowl with the baking soda, dry mustard, and the remaining ½ teaspoon salt. In a medium bowl, whisk the milk, sour cream, melted butter, and chopped chives.

7 Stir the milk mixture into the flour mixture with a wooden spoon until a sticky dough forms. Spoon this dough in heaping tablespoonfuls into mounds on top of the hot chicken mixture in the pan.

8 Bake, uncovered, until the biscuit topping browns and the chicken filling is bubbling, about 30 minutes. Let stand at room temperature for 5 minutes before serving.

Variations: Substitute 1 medium potato, peeled and cut into small cubes, or 1 medium turnip, peeled and cut into small cubes, for the celery.

Reduce the boneless skinless thighs to ½ pound and add ¾ pound boneless skinless chicken breasts, cut into ½-inch cubes, with the remaining thigh meat.

Omit the cream and increase the broth to 1⅓ cups. Also reduce the Dijon mustard to 1½ teaspoons.

Burmese-Inspired Chicken and Yellow Lentil Curry

Burmese curries are often made with yellow lentils, related to chickpeas and sold as "chana dal" in East Asian markets and high-end markets. Serve with flat breads like na'an, lefse, lavash, or flour tortillas, as well as with chopped seeded cucumber, chopped peeled mango, and Apple-Cucumber Raita (page 409) or even Tzatziki (page 46) for condiments. *Makes 6 servings*

1½ cups chana dal, or yellow lentils, picked
    over for stones and rinsed
1 tablespoon ground cumin
1 tablespoon paprika
2 teaspoons turmeric
1 teaspoon freshly grated lemon zest
1 teaspoon salt
½ teaspoon grated nutmeg
½ teaspoon freshly ground black pepper
¼ teaspoon ground cloves
1½ pounds boneless skinless chicken thighs,
    trimmed of any visible fat
1 tablespoon canola oil
1 large onion, chopped
3 cups chicken broth, or more as necessary
Chopped parsley or cilantro leaves as garnish

1 Place the lentils in a large pot, cover them with cool water to a depth of 2 inches, and set the pot over high heat. Bring to a slow boil, cover, reduce the heat to low, and simmer slowly, stirring once in a while, until tender, about 25 minutes. Drain in a fine-mesh colander set in the sink; set aside.

2 Whisk the cumin, paprika, turmeric, lemon zest, salt, nutmeg, pepper, and cloves in a small bowl. Add the chicken thighs and toss to coat.

3 Heat a large nonstick skillet over medium heat. Add the canola oil, then the onion. Cook, stirring often, until soft and translucent, about 3 minutes.

4 Add the chicken and any spice mixture remaining in the bowl. Cook until lightly browned, stirring almost constantly so the spices don't burn, about 2 minutes.

5 Pour in the broth and use a wooden spoon to scrape up any browned bits on the bottom of the pan.

6 Stir in the cooked lentils and bring the mixture to a simmer. Cover, reduce the heat to low, and simmer until the chicken is quite tender and the lentils are a little soft, stirring once in a while to make sure the lentils are not scorching, about 30 minutes. (If they do begin to stick, add more broth to the pan.) Garnish with parsley or cilantro.

Garlic-Roasted Drumsticks

To serve, spoon the drumsticks into individual bowls, then ladle the soupy vegetables and garlic cloves around them. As you eat the dish, squeeze the garlic cloves out of their husks onto crusty bread, spreading the garlic like butter. The drumsticks' skin should be removed because it will never get crispy in this covered casserole. *Makes 6 servings*

2 medium onions, chopped
4 celery ribs, cut into ½-inch pieces
1 large sweet potato, peeled and dried into
    very small, ½-inch pieces
2 medium garlic heads, broken into
    individual cloves but not peeled
1 tablespoon unsalted butter, melted and
    cooled
2 tablespoons minced parsley leaves
2 teaspoons stemmed thyme or 1 teaspoon
    dried thyme
2 bay leaves
1 teaspoon salt
½ teaspoon freshly ground black pepper
12 skinless chicken drumsticks

❶ Position the rack in the center of the oven and preheat the oven to 350°F.

❷ Mix the onions, celery, sweet potato, garlic cloves, melted butter, parsley, and thyme in a large bowl; spread this mixture into a 13 × 9-inch baking pan or a large roasting pan, making a bed for the drumsticks. Wedge in the bay leaves, then season the mixture with salt and pepper. Lay the drumsticks on top.

❸ Cover and bake until the vegetables are soft and the drumsticks are cooked through, about 1 hour and 30 minutes. Let stand for 5 minutes at room temperature. Discard the bay leaves before serving.

Variations: Substitute olive oil or walnut oil for the butter.

Substitute 1 tablespoon minced tarragon leaves for the parsley.

Substitute 1 teaspoon smoked paprika for the thyme.

❈ *Turkey* ❈

Annually, each American ate over 17 pounds of turkey! Yes, that's more than a single Thanksgiving dinner, but most is made up of luncheon meats and deli sandwiches. And that's too bad. A roast turkey is one of the better dishes for a party.

No-Fail Roast Turkey with Four Wet Rubs

Why wait for Thanksgiving to enjoy this American staple? Brining the bird protects it during long roasting, ensuring a crisp-outside, moist-inside turkey every time. *Makes 10 to 12 servings*

6 cups water
1 cup salt
One 12- to 14-pound whole turkey, giblets and neck removed, excess skin and fat from both openings trimmed (see Note)
2 medium onions, quartered
3 bay leaves
One of the four wet rubs that follow
Butcher's twine

❶ Whisk the water and salt in a bowl or pot large enough to hold both the bird and about 8 more cups water. Place the turkey in the bowl or pot, then pour in enough cold water to cover fully. Place in the refrigerator, covered, for at least 4 hours but no more than 12 hours.

❷ Position the rack in the lower third of the oven and preheat the oven to 350°F. Remove the turkey from the brine and pat dry. Place the onions and bay leaves in the large cavity.

❸ Insert a finger between the skin and meat on one side of the breast over the large cavity opening; gently work more fingers into the space without stretching the skin too much as it comes free of the meat, thereby creating a pocket between the skin and the meat. Do the same on the other side of the breast.

④ Massage a quarter of the chosen spice rub over the meat exposed under the skin on each side of the breast, again taking care not to stretch the skin too much. Rub the rest of the spice mixture over the exterior skin, patting the breast skin back into place. Truss the bird with butcher's twine (see page 249), then set it on a roasting rack in a roasting pan.

⑤ Roast until well browned, basting occasionally with the pan juices (but taking care not to dislodge the rub), until a meat thermometer inserted into the thickest part of the thigh without touching bone registers 165°F (our preference) or 180°F (the USDA recommendation), 3 to 3½ hours. When pierced, the juices in the thigh should run clear. Let the turkey stand at room temperature for 15 minutes before carving; discard the bay leaves before carving (see page 286).

Note: A 12-pound hard-frozen turkey will take 2 to 3 days to thaw in the refrigerator. You can speed up the process by wrapping the frozen bird tightly in plastic wrap so there are no leaks and fully submerging it in a huge pot of cold water set in the refrigerator; a 12-pounder will take 6 to 7 hours to thaw.

Skipping the brine:
Kosher turkeys should not be brined; those already injected with a saline solution (read the label) should also forgo this process. To omit the saltwater brine, skip step 1 in the above recipe and cover the spice-rubbed turkey for the first hour in the oven with aluminum foil. Remove the foil and baste lightly with 3 tablespoons olive oil or unsalted butter, melted. Baste every 30 minutes thereafter with pan drippings, taking care to keep the herb crust intact.

Four Wet Rubs

These rubs contain no salt since the turkey has been brined. If you skip the brine, add ½ to 1 tablespoon kosher salt to any of these rubs. Simply mix them in a small bowl.

1. Italian Wet Rub

3 tablespoons olive oil
1 tablespoon rubbed sage
1 tablespoon dried rosemary, crushed
1 tablespoon dried thyme
1 teaspoon onion powder
1 teaspoon garlic powder
½ teaspoon freshly ground black pepper

2. Herb Butter Wet Rub

4 tablespoons unsalted butter, melted and cooled
1 tablespoon dried basil
1 tablespoon dried oregano
1 tablespoon dried rosemary, crushed
2 teaspoons dried thyme
½ teaspoon garlic powder
½ teaspoon freshly ground black pepper

3. Southwestern Wet Rub

3 tablespoons canola oil
2 tablespoons chili powder
1 tablespoon ground cumin
2 teaspoons dried oregano
1 teaspoon garlic powder
½ teaspoon ground cinnamon
½ teaspoon freshly ground black pepper

4. Szechuan Wet Rub

2 tablespoons canola oil
2 tablespoons sesame oil
1 tablespoon ground Szechuan peppercorns
1 tablespoon ground coriander
1 tablespoon five-spice powder
1 teaspoon garlic powder
1 teaspoon ground dried orange zest
½ teaspoon freshly ground black pepper

Four Things to Go with Roast Turkey

I. Onion Gravy

Using a long-handled spoon, remove the hot, roasted onions from the body cavity; place them on a cutting board. Cool a few minutes, then roughly chop them. Strain the liquid in the roasting pan and skim off any visible fat. Add enough water so that the total liquid equals 1½ cups; bring this mixture along with the chopped onions to a simmer in a small saucepan set over medium-high heat. Meanwhile, whisk 2 teaspoons arrowroot in 1 tablespoon cool water in a small bowl. Whisk this mixture into the simmering gravy just until thickened, about 10 seconds. Remove at once from the heat; season with salt and pepper to taste.

How to Carve a Turkey

Use a meat fork and a thin carving knife, the better to get down inside the joints; but be judicious in your use of the fork. No random stabbing. Every hole causes the bird to lose essential juices.

1. Begin by cutting the skin and some of the meat that lies between the breast and the thigh quarter, running your knife closer to the breast side as you cut down. Once the thigh has been loosened from the bird, wiggle it a bit to find the ball-and-socket joint that joins it to the body. Slice straight down through this joint. Set this thigh-and-drumstick quarter aside and repeat on the other side.

2. Next, wiggle the drumstick where it joins the thigh, again revealing the joint. Slice down through the joint, removing the drumstick. Repeat with the other thigh side.

3. Once the thigh is on its own, slice the meat off the bone at a diagonal to yield the largest chunks.

4. Now do that same wiggling operation in order to find the wing joints, taking the wings off the bird by slicing through the joints that hold them to the body. If desired (particularly for a large bird), crack the wing into the drumlet and the winglet by bending them open at the opposite position from their natural angle until you hear the joint pop. Once revealed, slice through the joint.

5. Finally, hold the breast with the meat fork at the top of the concave-curving breastbone ridge. Begin at the outside of the breast (farthest from the breastbone) and draw the knife slowly through the meat in long, controlled cuts to produce thin slices. Alternatively, you can cut down on one side of the breastbone, following its natural curve, and take off the whole side of the breast, thereafter slicing it separately.

II. Giblet Gravy

While the turkey is roasting, place the heart, gizzard, and neck as well as 2 cut-up celery ribs, ½ tablespoon cracked black peppercorns, and 1 bay leaf in a small saucepan with 2 cups chicken broth and 2 cups water. Set the pan over medium-high heat and bring to a simmer. Cover, reduce the heat, and simmer slowly until the gizzard is tender, about 1 hour. Add the liver and continue simmering for 20 minutes. Drain the mixture in a colander, reserving 2 cups of the broth. Discard the celery, bay leaves, and peppercorns; dice the heart, gizzard, and liver as well as any available meat from the neck, set on a plate, and refrigerate.

After the turkey comes out of the oven, skim the pan drippings; you should have about ½ cup liquid.

Melt 3 tablespoons unsalted butter in a large skillet, then sprinkle 3 tablespoons all-purpose flour over it. Wait for 10 seconds, then stir well and cook until beige, about 1 minute. Whisk in a small amount of the reserved giblet broth, just a couple of tablespoons at a time, slowly dissolving the flour mixture into the broth. Take your time here—you don't want lumps. Continue whisking in the broth, then stir in the reserved pan liquid. The moment the mixture comes to a low simmer, remove it from the heat and stir in the diced giblet meat. Season with salt and pepper.

What's the difference between a fresh and a frozen turkey? In truth, not a lot. First off, the USDA permits so-called fresh turkeys to be stored at 26°F (in effect, frozen), thereby improving their shelf life. Second, modern flash-freezing is so effective that frozen turkeys taste almost as fresh as those so-called fresh ones.

III. Corn Bread Sausage Dressing

This is a traditional Southern dressing. If you don't want to make your own corn bread, buy unsweetened corn muffins and leave them out overnight on the counter. Also take the crust off the white bread, cube it, and leave it uncovered on the counter overnight. To turn this dressing into a stuffing for the bird, see page 289. *Makes 10 to 12 servings*

> 4 cups day-old cubed Corn Bread (page 240)
> 4 cups day-old cubed white bread, crusts removed and discarded
> 1 tablespoon canola oil, plus additional for greasing the pan
> ¾ pound sweet Italian sausage, casings removed
> 1 large onion, chopped
> 2 celery ribs, thinly sliced
> 1 cup dry white wine or dry vermouth
> ¼ cup chopped parsley leaves
> 2 teaspoons chopped marjoram leaves or 1 teaspoon dried marjoram
> 2 teaspoons stemmed thyme or 1 teaspoon dried thyme
> 1 teaspoon fennel seeds
> 1 teaspoon salt
> ½ teaspoon freshly ground black pepper
> 1 cup chicken broth
> ½ cup brandy
> 1 large egg, lightly beaten in a small bowl

1 Position a rack in the center of the oven; preheat the oven to 350°F. Lightly grease a 13 × 9-inch baking pan; set aside. Place the corn bread and bread cubes in a large bowl; set aside as well.

2 Heat a large skillet over medium heat, swirl in the canola oil, then crumble in the sausage meat. Cook, stirring frequently, until browned, about 6 minutes. Transfer the sausage to the bowl with the bread, using a slotted spoon; drain off all but 3 tablespoons fat.

③ Return the skillet to medium heat; add the onion and celery. Cook, stirring often, until aromatic and somewhat softened, about 3 minutes. Transfer this mixture to the bowl with the sausage and bread.

④ Set the skillet over medium-high heat and pour in the wine or vermouth. Bring the mixture to a simmer, scraping up any browned bits on the skillet's bottom. Boil until the mixture reduces by half, about 2 minutes.

⑤ Pour the liquid in the skillet over the contents of the bowl. Stir in the parsley, marjoram, thyme, fennel seeds, salt, and pepper; then stir in the broth, brandy, and egg until everything is moistened. Pour into the prepared pan, spreading gently to the corners. Cover with aluminum foil.

⑥ Bake for 30 minutes, then remove the foil and continue baking until lightly browned, about 15 minutes.

Variations: Add 2 diced carrots or 1 cored, seeded, and diced red bell pepper with the celery.

Add 1 cup frozen corn or fresh corn kernels cut off the ear with the eggs.

Omit the marjoram and fennel seeds; add 2 teaspoons rubbed sage with the thyme.

IV. Sourdough Sweet Potato Dressing

This easy dressing would be a welcome side for a turkey coated with the Southwestern Wet Rub.
Makes 10 to 12 servings

　1 tablespoon almond or canola oil
　2 tablespoons unsalted butter, plus additional for greasing the pan
　1 large onion, finely chopped
　2 celery ribs, finely sliced

1½ pounds sweet potatoes, peeled and diced into ½-inch cubes
6 tablespoons slivered almonds
4 ounces cremini or white button mushrooms, cleaned and thinly sliced
1 tart green apple, such as Granny Smith, peeled, cored, and chopped
½ cup dry white wine or dry vermouth
One 1-pound day-old sourdough loaf, crust removed and discarded, cut into 1-inch cubes
2 teaspoons rubbed sage
2 teaspoons dried thyme
1 teaspoon salt
½ teaspoon freshly ground black pepper
1½ cups chicken broth

① Position the rack in the center of the oven and preheat the oven to 375°F. Lightly butter a 13 × 9-inch baking dish and set it aside.

② Heat a large skillet over medium heat. Add the almond or canola oil, then 1 tablespoon butter. Once the butter's melted, add the onion, celery, sweet potatoes, and almonds; cook, stirring often, until the onion softens, about 4 minutes. Transfer to a large bowl.

③ Return the skillet to medium heat; add the remaining 1 tablespoon butter. Once the butter's melted, add the mushrooms and apple. Cook, stirring frequently, until the mushrooms give off their liquid, about 3 minutes.

④ Stir in the wine or vermouth, raise the heat to medium-high, and continue cooking until the liquid in the pan has reduced to a thin glaze, about 4 minutes.

⑤ Stir the contents of the skillet into the bowl with the onion mixture. Also stir in the bread cubes, sage, thyme, salt, and pepper. Add the broth and stir just until moistened, not until the bread starts to break down. Spread into the prepared pan and cover with aluminum foil.

6 Bake for 25 minutes. Remove the foil and continue baking until firm and lightly browned, about 20 more minutes.

Variations: Substitute chopped walnut or pecan pieces for the almonds. Also substitute walnut oil for the almond oil, if using.

Substitute shiitake mushrooms, stems discarded and caps thinly sliced, for the cremini.

Omit the apple; add 1 large zucchini, shredded through the large holes of a box grater, with the broth.

Dressing into Stuffing

Dressing (cooked separately) gives you more crunch per bite than stuffing (cooked in the bird). However, either of the above dressings can be turned into a stuffing. Make it up to the point in which you spread it in the pan, but use only half the broth called for. Place the mixture in a large bowl, cover, and refrigerate until cool, about 1 hour or up to 24 hours.

Rub the turkey with the Italian Wet Rub, or Southwestern Wet Rub (pages 285–286). Do not stuff the turkey's large cavity with onion and bay leaves as directed; instead, stuff the cooled dressing into the large cavity. The mixture will expand as it bakes, so leave about a ½-inch headspace in the cavity and don't pack the dressing down. Any additional dressing should be moistened with ¼ cup broth and baked in a small baking dish alongside the bird until lightly browned, about 20 minutes or so.

Truss the bird as directed, then roast, allowing at least 30 additional minutes, maybe as much as 1 hour, for the stuffed bird to come to the desired temperature. A meat thermometer inserted into the center of the stuffing in the cavity should read 160°F. Remove the stuffing from the bird before carving.

Barbecued Turkey with Three Dry Rubs

For the barbecue, cook the bird over indirect heat—that is, not directly over the heat source or the coals, but to the side. Because of this slow-roasting method, you needn't brine the turkey. Dry rubs get the skin extra-crispy. *Makes 10 to 12 servings*

1 tablespoon canola oil, plus additional for the grill grate
One 12- to 14-pound turkey, giblets and neck removed
One of the three dry rubs that follow
2 medium onions, cut into quarters
2 celery ribs, cut into 3-inch segments
Butcher's twine

1 Massage the canola oil into the turkey's skin, then gently lift the breast skin off the meat, following the procedure in step 3 of the No-Fail Roast Turkey recipe (page 284).

2 Massage 1 tablespoon dry rub under the skin of one half of the breast, taking care not to stretch the skin. Repeat with the other side of the breast. Pat the skin into place, then massage the remaining rub all over the turkey, from the breast to the legs.

3 Stuff the cavity with the onions and celery. Truss the bird with butcher's twine (see page 249). Set aside at room temperature while the grill preheats.

4 Preheat the grill for indirect cooking—that is, place a drip pan on one half of the bottom grate or coal grate; heat the other side of the gas grill to medium heat or build a medium-heat, well-ashed coal bed on the other side of the grate. Alternatively, build the coal bed in the center of the grill, then use a grill rake to push the coals to the perimeter, setting the drip pan in the now vacant center of the coal grate. If using a charcoal grill, have more charcoal briquettes on hand to keep the heat at a medium level while cooking.

⑤ Place the turkey over the drip pan, indirectly over medium heat. Cover and barbecue until the skin is crispy and a meat thermometer inserted into the thickest part of the thigh registers 165°F (our preference) or 180°F (the USDA recommendation), 2½ to 3 hours. Transfer to a large carving or cutting board for 10 minutes before carving (see page 286).

To barbecue a turkey on the rotisserie:
Skewer the bird on the spit, threading it through the twine tying the legs together, running it through the body cavity, piercing some of the vegetables inside, and piercing the flesh of the breast nearest the neck opening, close to the breastbone; use the spit hooks to fix the bird in place. Set up the rotisserie according to the manufacturer's instructions, then cover the grill and roast for about 2½ hours over medium heat, or until the internal temperature reaches the desired degree.

Tips for Success

• Measure the distance from the grill grate to the lid before you start this recipe. Some older gas grills may not be large enough to handle a whole turkey. If you have hanging baskets in the lid, remove them before barbecuing the bird.

• Don't stuff a barbecued turkey; the stuffing will not cook as fast as the bird, resulting in undercooked stuffing or a dried-out bird.

• If you're using a kosher turkey or one that's been injected with a saline solution, cut the salt in the dry rub by half.

Three Dry Rubs

Mix any of these together in a small bowl.

1. Cajun Dry Rub

2 tablespoons coarse-grained salt, preferably kosher salt
1 tablespoon sweet paprika
1 tablespoon dried parsley
2 teaspoons sugar
1 teaspoon ground cumin
1 teaspoon rubbed sage
1 teaspoon celery seed
½ teaspoon freshly ground black pepper
¼ teaspoon garlic powder
¼ teaspoon cayenne pepper

2. Jerk Dry Rub

1½ tablespoons coarse salt, preferably kosher salt
1 tablespoon dehydrated onion
1 tablespoon dried thyme
1 tablespoon sugar
2 teaspoons garlic powder
2 teaspoons ground allspice
1 teaspoon ground cinnamon
1 teaspoon cayenne pepper
½ teaspoon grated nutmeg
½ teaspoon freshly ground black pepper

3. Pepper Dry Rub

1½ tablespoons cracked black peppercorns
1 tablespoon mustard seeds, crushed
1 tablespoon coarse-grained salt, preferably kosher salt
2 teaspoons packed light brown sugar
1 tablespoon sweet paprika
1 teaspoon garlic powder

Roast Turkey Breast with Fresh Herb Rub

A turkey breast is the best way to have a roast turkey dinner in less time. This spice mixture is reminiscent of that stirred into osso buco in northern Italy. Since the breast cooks more quickly, fresh herbs won't singe or turn bitter. We prefer turkey breast on its own cooked to USDA standards; the texture is not as soft and cloying as at lower temperatures. *Makes 8 servings*

3 tablespoons olive oil
2 tablespoons chopped parsley leaves
2 tablespoons chopped oregano leaves
2 tablespoons chopped rosemary leaves
1 tablespoon grated lemon zest
1 teaspoon chopped mint leaves
1 teaspoon salt, preferably kosher salt
½ teaspoon freshly ground black pepper
One 5- to 5½-pound bone-in
    turkey breast

1 Position the rack in the center of the oven and preheat the oven to 375°F.

2 Mix the olive oil, parsley, oregano, rosemary, lemon zest, mint, salt, and pepper in a small bowl; set aside.

3 Gently pry the skin away from the breast meat by inserting one finger into one side of the breast, nearest the top "point," and then working more fingers into the opening until the skin comes loose; take care not to stretch the skin out. Repeat this technique on the other side of the breast.

4 Massage about a quarter of the spice mixture onto the meat under the skin on one half of the breast. Repeat with a third of the remaining spice mixture on the other half of the breast.

5 Pat the skin back in place. Sprinkle the remaining herb mixture all over the turkey breast. Place the breast skin side up on a rack in a roasting pan.

6 Roast until browned and a meat thermometer inserted into the thickest part of the meat registers 170°F (both our preference and the USDA recommendation for turkey breast), about 1 hour and 30 minutes, basting every 15 minutes with the pan juices after the first 45 minutes but taking care not to dislodge the herbs. Transfer to a cutting or carving board and let rest for 10 minutes before carving.

Variations: Substitute marjoram for the rosemary and orange zest for the lemon zest.

Wine-Braised Turkey Breast

This recipe can be made in either the slow cooker or the oven. If you do the former, don't remove the lid during cooking. If the latter, baste the bird fairly often. *Makes 8 servings*

1½ cups dry white wine or dry vermouth
½ cup chicken broth
¾ ounce dried porcini mushrooms
2 medium shallots, roughly chopped
1 bay leaf
1 teaspoon chopped sage leaves or
    ½ teaspoon rubbed sage
1 teaspoon stemmed thyme or ½ teaspoon
    dried thyme
½ teaspoon salt
¼ teaspoon freshly ground black pepper
One 5- to 5½-pound bone-in turkey breast
1 tablespoon canola oil
2 tablespoons brandy or water
1 tablespoon all-purpose flour

1 Mix the wine or vermouth, broth, mushrooms, shallots, bay leaf, sage, thyme, salt, and pepper in a large bowl; set aside.

2 If you're using the slow cooker, set it up on the counter. If you're using the oven, position the rack in the middle and preheat the oven to 325°F. Prick the turkey breast all over the skin with a fork to release some of the fat while you brown it.

3 Heat a large skillet over medium heat. Swirl in the canola oil, then add the turkey breast skin side down. Brown well, about 3 minutes, taking care that the skin doesn't stick; then turn and continue browning on all sides, turning occasionally, about 7 more minutes.

4 Remove the breast from the skillet and place in the slow cooker or in a large, oven-safe Dutch oven or covered casserole. Pour the wine mixture over the breast, making sure the mushrooms and bay leaf are submerged in the liquid.

5 **If using the slow cooker:** Cover and cook undisturbed until a meat thermometer inserted halfway into the center of the thickest part of the breast meat without touching bone registers 170°F (our preference and the USDA recommendation for turkey breast), about 4 hours on high or 6 to 7 hours on low.

If using the oven: Cover and bake, basting every 20 minutes or so, until a meat thermometer inserted halfway into the center of the thickest part of the breast meat without touching bone registers 170°F, about 2 hours and 15 minutes.

6 Transfer the breast to a carving board or platter. Tent with aluminum foil to keep warm.

7 Skim the fat off the pan juices, then transfer them to a small saucepan set over medium-high heat; bring to a simmer. Meanwhile, whisk the brandy or water and flour in a small bowl until the flour dissolves.

8 Reduce the heat to medium and whisk in the flour mixture in a slow, steady stream. Whisk constantly until the mixture thickens. Simmer, whisking constantly, for 1 minute. Serve on the side with the sliced breast (follow the instructions in step 5 for how to carve a turkey, page 286).

Variations: Substitute dried chanterelle mushrooms for the porcinis.

Substitute rosemary for the sage and oregano for the thyme.

Add up to ½ teaspoon red pepper flakes to the wine mixture.

Add 1 cup thinly shaved fennel to the wine mixture.

Oven-Barbecued Turkey Wings

A little sweet and very smoky, these wings make excellent picnic fare for a summer afternoon. Look for smoked paprika in specialty and gourmet markets. *Makes 6 servings*

2 tablespoons smoked paprika
1 tablespoon dried parsley
1 tablespoon kosher salt
2 teaspoons packed light brown sugar
1 teaspoon ground cumin
1 teaspoon rubbed sage
½ teaspoon celery seed
½ teaspoon freshly ground black
    pepper
¼ teaspoon garlic powder
¼ teaspoon cayenne pepper
6 turkey wings, tips removed, any excess
    skin and fat trimmed

1 Mix the smoked paprika, parsley, salt, brown sugar, cumin, sage, celery seed, black pepper, garlic powder, and cayenne in a small bowl. Rub this mixture into the skin on the wings, coating them evenly.

2 Place the wings on a metal wire rack, such as a cooling rack for cookies (so long as it doesn't have rubber feet). Set this rack in a roasting pan, a broiler pan, or on a lipped baking sheet. Cover lightly with plastic wrap and refrigerate for at least 1 hour or up to 24 hours.

3 Position the rack in the center of the oven; preheat the oven to 350°F. Take the wings out of the refrigerator for 15 minutes while the oven preheats.

4 Roast the wings on their wire rack in the pan until browned and crisp, about 2 hours. Cool for 5 minutes before serving.

Variations: Omit the smoked paprika rub given here and use the Cajun Dry Rub, Jerk Dry Rub, or Pepper Dry Rub (page 290) given for the Barbecued Turkey.

Sage Pesto–Rubbed Turkey London Broil

Here boneless turkey breast is sliced into thin strips, marinated in a sage pesto, then quickly cooked. The pesto is also great on its own, as a dip or a sauce, a sage reinterpretation of a classic. *Makes 6 servings*

The Sage Pesto:

    1 cup packed flat-leaf parsley leaves
    ¼ cup tightly packed sage leaves
    3 tablespoons pine nuts, toasted
    3 tablespoons freshly grated Parmigiano-
        Reggiano
    1 teaspoon salt
    ½ teaspoon freshly ground black pepper
    3 garlic cloves, quartered
    1 cup olive oil, plus additional for greasing
        the grill grate or the pan

One 2-pound boneless skinless turkey
    breast

1 Process the parsley, sage, pine nuts, Parmigiano-Reggiano, salt, pepper, and garlic in a food processor fitted with the chopping blade. Pour in the olive oil and pulse to blend, scraping down the sides of the bowl as necessary; then process until pureed, about 1 minute. Alternatively, make the pesto in a blender or even in a mortar, grinding the herbs and then slowly adding the oil in a thin drizzle as you work it in with the pestle.

2 Slice the turkey breast into 1-inch slices on the bias by placing a knife at a 45-degree angle to the cutting surface and making long, even strokes through the meat. Place the slices in a large bowl; toss with the sage pesto. Cover and refrigerate for at least 1 hour or overnight.

3 **To grill:** Oil the grill grate and heat a gas grill to medium heat or prepare a medium-hot, well-ashed coal bed in a charcoal grill. Place the turkey slices (with the pesto adhering to them) on a gas grill directly over the heat source or 4 to 6 inches directly over the coals. Grill until lightly browned, turning once, 7 to 8 minutes.

To cook on the stovetop: Lightly oil a seasoned grill pan or a large cast-iron pan and heat it over medium heat. Lay the turkey slices in the pan and cook until lightly browned, turning once, about 9 minutes.

Variations: You can coat the turkey strips with other pestos like the Sun-Dried Tomato and Roasted Garlic Pesto (page 48) or the Pecan Pesto (page 179).

Serving Ideas:
- Chop the meat and add it to some mustard and mayonnaise for turkey salad.
- Make sandwiches with the slices.
- Chop the meat and mix it with sour cream for a baked-potato topper.

Turkey Cutlets with Lemon Butter

This sauté uses a streamlined version of the lemon-and-butter "française" sauce. *Makes 4 servings*

½ cup all-purpose flour
½ teaspoon salt
¼ teaspoon freshly ground black pepper
3 tablespoons unsalted butter
1½ pounds turkey scaloppine or four 5- to 6-ounce turkey breast cutlets, pounded to ¼-inch thickness
½ cup dry white wine or dry vermouth
1 lemon, cut into 8 slices
¼ cup chopped parsley leaves

1 Mix the flour, salt, and pepper on a large plate or in a shallow baking dish or pie plate.

2 Melt the butter in a large skillet set over medium heat.

3 Dredge the turkey cutlets in the flour mixture to coat both sides. Shake off any excess and slip the cutlets into the skillet. Reduce the heat to medium-low; cook until browned on both sides, turning once, about 5 minutes. Transfer to a plate or cutting board.

4 Pour the wine or vermouth into the pan, add the lemon slices, raise the heat to medium-high, and bring to a boil, scraping up any browned bits. Boil until reduced by half, then reduce the heat to low and return the cutlets to the pan. Cook just until heated through, about 2 minutes, turning once. Sprinkle each cutlet with 1 tablespoon parsley before serving.

Variations: Add 1 teaspoon dried thyme, ½ teaspoon grated nutmeg, ¼ teaspoon ground cloves, or ¼ teaspoon cayenne pepper to the flour mixture.
Substitute basil leaves for the parsley.

Creamy Caraway Turkey Cutlets over Noodles

A hearty but quick meal for a cold night. Have everyone at the table get ready to eat the moment the dish is done. *Makes 4 servings*

½ cup all-purpose flour
2 teaspoons paprika
½ teaspoon salt
½ teaspoon freshly ground black pepper
2 large eggs, at room temperature
2 tablespoons milk (regular, low-fat, or nonfat)
1 cup plain dried bread crumbs
6 tablespoons unsalted butter
1½ pounds turkey scaloppine or four 5- to 6-ounce turkey breast cutlets, pounded to ¼-inch thickness
1 tablespoon caraway seeds
1 pound homemade noodles (see page 170), cooked and drained, or 12 ounces dried wide egg noodles, cooked and drained according to the package instructions
Chopped parsley leaves as garnish, optional

1 First, mix the flour, paprika, salt, and pepper together on a large dinner plate or in a pie plate. Next, lightly beat the eggs with the milk in a wide, shallow bowl. Finally, spread the bread crumbs onto a second large dinner plate. Set these three parts of the breading aside in a line in that order.

2 Melt 3 tablespoons butter in a medium skillet set over medium-high heat.

3 Meanwhile, dredge the turkey first in the flour mixture, shaking off any excess. Then dip in the beaten egg mixture, letting any excess drip off. Finally, dredge in the bread crumbs, coating both sides.

④ Place the prepared turkey in the skillet and cook until golden, turning once, about 5 minutes. Transfer to a serving platter and tent with aluminum foil.

⑤ Melt the remaining 3 tablespoons butter in the skillet; as it melts, scrape up any browned bits stuck to the bottom of the skillet. Add the caraway seeds and toast for 15 seconds, stirring constantly.

⑥ Add the cooked noodles, toss well, then cook for 30 seconds, or until heated through. Divide the noodles among four serving plates, top with the cutlets, and garnish with parsley, if desired.

Variations: Add ¼ teaspoon ground cinnamon with the caraway seeds.

Substitute poppy seeds or fennel seeds for the caraway seeds.

Pecan-Crusted Turkey Cutlets

This Southern-inspired recipe requires a triple dip for the cutlets, creating a slightly thicker crust that browns beautifully. *Makes 4 servings*

½ cup all-purpose flour
2 large egg whites
2 tablespoons water
Several dashes of hot red pepper sauce
¾ cup plain dried bread crumbs
½ cup finely chopped pecan pieces
2 teaspoons stemmed thyme or 1 teaspoon
   dried thyme
½ teaspoon salt
½ teaspoon freshly ground black
   pepper
2 tablespoons canola oil
2 tablespoons unsalted butter
1½ pounds turkey scaloppine or four
   5- to 6-ounce turkey breast cutlets,
   pounded to ¼-inch thickness

① First, place the flour on a large plate. Next, whisk the egg whites, water, and hot red pepper sauce in a shallow pie plate or baking dish. Finally, mix the bread crumbs, pecans, thyme, salt, and pepper in a second shallow pie plate or baking dish. Set these three things aside in a line in this order.

② Heat a large skillet over medium heat. Add the canola oil, then melt the butter. Working quickly, dip a turkey cutlet in the flour, coating lightly. Dip in the egg-white mixture on both sides, letting any excess drip off. Dredge in the seasoned bread-crumb mixture, coating both sides. Then slip the cutlet into the skillet and repeat with the other cutlets, making as many as will fit in the pan at once.

③ Cook until golden brown on both sides, turning once, about 5 minutes. If cooking the cutlets in batches, loosely tent those made with aluminum foil to keep them warm without making the crust soggy.

Variations: Substitute walnut pieces or skinned hazelnuts for the pecans.

Add 1 teaspoon ground cumin with the thyme.

Add 1 teaspoon smoked paprika with the thyme.

For these cutlet sautés, you can use either precut turkey scaloppine or turkey breast cutlets, which look something like boneless skinless chicken breasts. If possible, cut the latter into two thin fillets, then pound them to ¼-inch thickness between two sheets of wax paper or plastic wrap with the smooth side of a meat mallet or a heavy, large saucepan. Because the cutlets are larger, you may need to cook them in batches or use more than one skillet, dividing the ingredients between them.

Three Turkey Burgers

The trick to tasty turkey burgers is actually not to undercook them; for the best texture, let them get charred on the outside and well cooked throughout. *Makes 4 burgers (can be doubled or tripled)*

1. Ultimate Turkey Burgers

1 pound ground turkey, preferably a mix of white and dark meat
1 tablespoon Worcestershire sauce
1 tablespoon Dijon mustard
1 small shallot, minced
2 tablespoons chopped basil leaves

2. Herbed Turkey Burgers

1 pound ground turkey, preferably a mix of white and dark meat
1 tablespoon tahini
2 teaspoons chopped tarragon leaves or 1 teaspoon dried tarragon
2 teaspoons chopped oregano leaves or 1 teaspoon dried oregano
1 teaspoon onion salt
¼ teaspoon garlic powder
¼ teaspoon grated nutmeg

3. Asian Turkey Burgers

1 pound ground turkey, preferably a mix of white and dark meat
2 scallions, minced
1 tablespoon minced peeled fresh ginger
1 tablespoon soy sauce
½ tablespoon rice vinegar
1 teaspoon sesame oil, preferably toasted sesame oil
1 teaspoon honey

Canola oil for the grill grate, broiler pan, or skillet

1 Mix the ingredients for any one of the three burgers in a large bowl, preferably using your cleaned hands, taking care to work all the spices into the meat without damaging its fibers.

2 Form 4 patties, using a quarter of the mixture for each and patting them into compact but not dense rounds. Gently press your thumb into the center of one side, thereby creating a rounded depression that will help keep the patty from gathering into a ball as it cooks. (The patties can be made in advance to this point; place in a single layer on a plate, cover with plastic wrap, and refrigerate for up to 8 hours.)

3 If using a grill, preheat the grill for high-heat cooking or build a well-ashed, red-hot, high-heat coal bed in a charcoal grill; oil the grill grate with canola oil. Place the burgers directly over the heat and grill until charred, turning once, until an instant-read meat thermometer inserted into the centers of the burgers registers 165°F (our preference and the USDA recommendation), about 8 minutes.

If using a grill pan or skillet, heat it over high heat until a drop of water dances around the pan. Pour in a little canola oil, swirl it around the pan, and add the burgers. Reduce the heat to medium-high and cook until the burgers are well browned and firm, turning once, until an instant-read meat thermometer inserted in their centers registers 165°F, about 8 minutes.

If using a broiler, preheat the broiler and line a broiler pan with aluminum foil. Brush the foil lightly with canola oil, then lay the burgers on it and broil until browned and firm, turning once, until an instant-read meat thermometer inserted into the centers of the burgers registers 165°F, about 9 minutes.

Eight Things to Do with Leftover Turkey

1. Turkey Club. Layer sliced turkey, crispy bacon, sliced tomatoes, and lettuce on crunchy whole wheat toast—slather it with mayonnaise, mustard, or a combination of the two. Also add sliced avocado, thinly sliced red onion, and/or radish sprouts.

2. Turkey Salad. Mix chopped turkey, chopped celery, chopped gherkins, and a sliced radish or two with some mayonnaise, a touch of Dijon mustard, and a splash of lemon juice. Serve in lettuce cups.

3. Composed Turkey Salad. Toss shredded romaine lettuce and baby spinach leaves with chopped turkey, sprouts, a diced apple, a chopped tomato, and a sprinkle of salt. Spoon on 1/2 cup of any salad dressing (see pages 100–105).

4. Southwestern Turkey Scramble. Spray a large nonstick skillet with nonstick spray; set it over medium heat. Sauté chopped onion and a few chopped sun-dried tomatoes for 1 minute. Stir in chopped turkey, lightly beaten eggs, and a sprinkle of chili powder, ground cumin, and salt; cook, stirring, just until the eggs set and are fluffy, about 1 minute.

5. Italian Turkey Soup. Mix 2 cups canned, 4 cups (1 quart) white beans, drained and rinsed, with chicken broth, some chopped turkey, a little sliced fennel or a chopped small head of escarole in a large saucepan until simmering. Add a little dried rosemary, dried oregano, and dried thyme; cook for 5 minutes.

6. Turkey Enchiladas. Divide chopped turkey between 4 tortillas. Add 2 tablespoons refried beans and 1 tablespoon shredded Cheddar to each, then roll the enchiladas closed. Place them in an 8-inch square baking dish. Puree 1 cup mild salsa with a little chili powder and enough tomato juice to make a sauce, then pour it over the enchiladas. Bake, uncovered, at 350°F until bubbling, about 15 minutes.

7. Turkey Broccoli Stir-Fry. Spray a large nonstick wok with nonstick spray and stir-fry 2 or 3 sliced scallions, a few diced garlic cloves, and 1 tablespoon chopped peeled fresh ginger for 20 seconds over medium-high heat. Add several handfuls of broccoli florets and some chopped turkey; stir-fry for 1 minute. Pour in about 1/4 cup bottled teriyaki stir-fry sauce; bring to a simmer and serve.

8. Turkey Stuffed Baked Potatoes. Bake two large baked Russet potatoes (see page 464). When cool enough to handle, slice them in half and scoop the insides into a large bowl. Stir in some chopped turkey, a generous dollop of plain yogurt or sour cream, 1 chopped scallion, and 4 chopped asparagus spears. Pile back into the skins and top each with 1 tablespoon shredded cheese; bake at 400°F for 15 minutes.

Turkey Meat Loaf with Couscous and Dried Cranberries

Ground turkey, while good for your waistline, can take on a depressingly slippery texture when cooked; but you can avoid this problem by adding couscous and dried fruit. *Makes 6 to 8 servings*

¾ cup boiling water
½ cup couscous
3 tablespoons olive oil, plus additional for
    oiling the pan
1 medium onion, chopped
1 celery rib, chopped
6 tablespoons dried cranberries, chopped
2 tablespoons chopped parsley leaves
2 teaspoons stemmed thyme or 1 teaspoon
    dried thyme
2 teaspoons chopped sage leaves or
    1 teaspoon rubbed sage
1 teaspoon salt
¼ teaspoon freshly ground black pepper
1¼ pounds ground turkey, preferably a mix
    of white and dark meat
2 tablespoons mango chutney

1 Pour the boiling water over the couscous in a large bowl; set aside until the water has been absorbed, about 5 minutes.

2 Meanwhile, heat a large skillet over medium heat. Swirl in the olive oil, then add the onion and celery. Cook, stirring frequently, until soft and aromatic, about 3 minutes. Stir in the cranberries, parsley, thyme, sage, salt, and pepper. Remove from the heat.

3 Once the water has been fully absorbed into the couscous, stir the vegetable mixture into it. Set aside uncovered to cool for 15 minutes.

4 Meanwhile, position the rack in the center of the oven and preheat the oven to 350°F. Lightly oil a 13 × 9-inch baking pan and set aside.

5 Crumble the turkey into the couscous mixture. Use your cleaned hands to mix thoroughly, taking care not to break up the meat's fibers. Form in the prepared pan into an oval loaf about 8 inches long and 2 inches high, tapering toward the ends, like a football cut in half lengthwise. Stir the chutney in a small bowl until spreadable, then brush over the top of the loaf.

6 Bake until lightly browned, until a meat thermometer inserted into the thickest part of the loaf registers 165°F (our preference and the USDA recommendation), about 55 minutes. Let stand at room temperature in the baking dish for 5 minutes before removing and slicing.

Variations: Substitute chopped raisins, chopped dried currants, or chopped dried cherries for the cranberries.

Add ⅓ cup walnut pieces or unsalted shelled pistachios to the couscous with the vegetable mixture.

Omit the thyme and sage; add 2 teaspoons curry powder or garam masala in their stead.

Turkey Chili Verde

There's no added salt in this green chili because canned chiles and tomatillos often have quite a bit; you can adjust the final seasoning to taste, of course. Top the chili with sour cream, plain yogurt, chopped peeled cucumber, chopped peeled mango, or chopped seeded yellow tomatoes. *Makes 6 servings*

2 fresh poblano chiles
2 tablespoons canola oil
1 large onion, chopped
2 garlic cloves, minced
1¼ pounds ground turkey, preferably a mix
    of white and dark meat
One 4-ounce can chopped mild green chiles

Two 11-ounce cans tomatillos, drained and
    chopped, or 12 fresh tomatillos, chopped
1 tablespoon ground cumin
1½ tablespoons chopped oregano leaves or
    2 teaspoons dried oregano
½ teaspoon freshly ground black pepper
4 cups (1 quart) chicken broth
3 cups canned white beans, drained and rinsed
½ cup chopped cilantro leaves
2 tablespoons lime juice

1 Either toast the poblano chiles over an open gas flame by holding them a few inches above the fire with metal tongs, turning them until they're completely blackened; or broil them 4 inches from a preheated broiler on a lipped baking sheet or broiler tray, turning occasionally, until blackened on all sides. Place the chiles in a paper bag and seal well, or place them in a medium bowl and cover tightly with plastic wrap. Set aside for 10 minutes. Peel off the outer charred layer before seeding and chopping the chiles; set aside.

2 Heat a large saucepan or medium pot over medium heat, swirl in the canola oil, and add the onion. Cook, stirring often, until softened, about 3 minutes. Add the garlic and cook for 20 seconds.

3 Crumble in the turkey and cook, stirring frequently, until it loses its raw, pink color and browns somewhat, about 5 minutes. Add the canned chiles and the chopped poblanos; cook, stirring constantly, for 1 minute.

4 Add the tomatillos, cumin, oregano, and pepper. Stir well, then cook undisturbed for 30 seconds. Stir in the broth and beans and bring the mixture to a simmer.

5 Reduce the heat to low and simmer very slowly, uncovered and at the merest bubble, for 1½ hours, stirring occasionally.

6 Stir in the cilantro and lime juice, cover, and remove the pot from the heat to steep for 5 minutes before serving.

Variations: Substitute ground chicken, preferably a mix of white and dark meat, for the ground turkey.

For a red chili, substitute one 28-ounce can crushed tomatoes for the tomatillos.

Goat Cheese, Poblano, and Turkey Tortilla Casserole

This casserole is almost better the next day, once the flavors have melded. *Makes 8 to 10 servings*

1 tablespoon canola oil, plus additional for
    greasing the pan and brushing on the
    tortillas
1 medium onion, finely chopped
3 garlic cloves, minced
1 pound ground turkey, preferably a mix of
    white and dark meat
12 fresh tomatillos, papery hulls removed
    and the green fruit roughly chopped
2 cups regular or low-fat sour cream (do not
    use fat-free)
1 cup chopped cilantro leaves
3 poblano chiles, charred, peeled, seeded,
    and chopped (see step 1 in the preceding
    recipe)
Eighteen 8-inch corn tortillas
10 ounces soft goat cheese, such as
    Montrachet
4 ounces Parmigiano-Reggiano, finely
    grated

1 Heat a large skillet over medium heat, swirl in the canola oil, and add all but 2 tablespoons of the onion. Cook, stirring often, until translucent, about 3 minutes. Add the garlic and cook for 20 seconds.

2 Crumble in the turkey and cook, stirring frequently, until it loses its raw, pink color, about 5 minutes.

3 Add the tomatillos and continue cooking, stirring often, until they soften and the mixture resembles a thick salsa, about 10 minutes. Remove the pan from the heat, pour its contents into a large bowl, and set aside to cool for 10 minutes.

4 Stir in the sour cream, chopped cilantro, chopped chiles, and the reserved 2 tablespoons chopped onion; set aside.

5 Position the rack in the center of the oven and preheat the oven to 400°F. Brush the tortillas with a little oil on both sides and stack them into three piles. Wrap each stack in aluminum foil and place the packets in the oven for 15 minutes. Remove and unwrap, being careful of the heat.

6 Lower the oven temperature to 350°F. Lightly oil a 13 × 9-inch baking dish. Spread each of the tortillas on one side with an even coating of the goat cheese.

7 Build the casserole by placing 6 tortillas cheese side up across its bottom. Top with a third of the turkey mixture. Lay another 6 tortillas, cheese side up on top of the turkey mixture, then top with half the remaining turkey. Lay a final layer of the remaining tortillas over the dish, then top with the remaining turkey mixture. Top the entire dish with the Parmigiano-Reggiano.

8 Bake until lightly browned and bubbling, about 45 minutes. Let stand at room temperature for 10 minutes before serving.

Variations: For a less rich casserole, substitute thickened and drained low-fat or fat-free yogurt for the sour cream. Line a colander or fine-mesh sieve with cheesecloth, add 2½ cups yogurt, and place over a large bowl. Set aside in the refrigerator to drain for 6 hours, until the yogurt is moderately thick.

Substitute 2 ounces Monterey Jack, grated, and 2 ounces Asiago, grated, for the Parmigiano-Reggiano.

Turkeys Climbing a Tree

Here's a turkey rendition of Ants Climbing a Tree, a classic Szechuan stir-fry. Bean thread noodles, sometimes called "glass noodles," are available in the Asian aisle of almost all markets. *Makes 4 servings*

> 4 ounces bean-thread noodles
> Boiling water
> 8 ounces ground turkey
> 2 tablespoons plus 1 teaspoon soy sauce
> 1½ tablespoons plus 1 teaspoon Shaoxing or dry sherry
> 1½ teaspoons sesame oil, preferably toasted sesame oil
> ½ cup chicken broth
> ½ teaspoon sugar
> 1 tablespoon peanut oil
> 4 scallions, cut into 1-inch pieces
> 2 garlic cloves, minced
> 1 tablespoon minced peeled fresh ginger
> 1 teaspoon Asian red chili sauce

1 Place the bean-thread noodles in a medium bowl and cover with boiling water. Set aside to soak for 10 minutes.

2 Meanwhile, crumble the turkey into a medium bowl, then stir in 1 teaspoon soy sauce, 1 teaspoon Shaoxing or dry sherry, and 1 teaspoon sesame oil until the turkey is evenly coated. Set aside.

3 Whisk the broth and sugar with the remaining 2 tablespoons soy sauce, 1½ tablespoons Shaoxing or dry sherry, and ½ teaspoon sesame oil in a small bowl; set aside as well.

4 Heat a large wok, preferably nonstick, or a large, high-sided sauté pan over medium-high heat. Swirl in the peanut oil, then add the scallions, garlic, and ginger. Stir-fry for 1 minute, then add the chili sauce and stir-fry for 15 seconds.

5 Add the ground turkey and stir-fry until well browned, about 5 minutes.

6 Add the noodles and the reserved broth mixture. Stir well, then bring the entire mixture to a simmer, tossing constantly. Cook for 2 minutes, just until the sauce is mostly absorbed by the noodles.

Variations: Add any number of vegetables with the scallions: 10 ounces broccoli florets; 10 ounces cauliflower florets; 6 ounces fresh snow peas; 1 large zucchini or cucumber, peeled, halved lengthwise, and cut into thin half-moons.

Fried Rice with Ground Turkey

Here's a renovated take-out favorite, made with ground turkey and nutty brown rice. *Makes 4 servings*

2 tablespoons peanut oil
2 large eggs, lightly beaten
3 medium scallions, thinly sliced
2 garlic cloves, minced
2 tablespoons minced peeled fresh ginger
12 ounces ground turkey
1 large red bell pepper, cored, seeded, and diced
4 ounces snow peas, finely sliced
3 cups cooked brown rice
2 tablespoons soy sauce (regular or reduced-sodium)
2 tablespoons rice wine vinegar or white wine vinegar
1 teaspoon Asian red chili paste
2 teaspoons toasted sesame oil

1 Heat a large wok or high-sided sauté pan over medium heat, then swirl in 1 tablespoon peanut oil. Add the eggs and scramble lightly, just until set. Transfer to a small bowl.

2 Swirl in the remaining 1 tablespoon oil. Add the scallions, garlic, and ginger; stir-fry for 30 seconds.

3 Crumble in the ground turkey; stir-fry until it loses its raw, pink color, breaking up the large bits, about 4 minutes.

4 Add the bell pepper and snow peas; continue tossing and cooking for 30 seconds. Add the brown rice and stir-fry for 1 minute.

5 Pour in the soy sauce, vinegar, and chili paste; return the scrambled egg to the wok. Toss gently and cook, stirring constantly, for 30 seconds. Remove the wok from the heat and stir in the sesame oil just before serving.

Variations: Substitute one 8-ounce can sliced water chestnuts, drained, for the bell pepper.

Substitute 6 ounces Swiss chard, stemmed and roughly chopped, for the snow peas.

Add ½ cup chopped walnut pieces with the brown rice.

What's in Ground Turkey?

According to USDA guidelines, if the package says "ground turkey meat," it should contain only the meat without the fat or skin. If it says "ground turkey," it includes fat and skin. White meat alone is labeled as such; all other packaging should be assumed to be a combination of dark and white meat.

Treat these birds as you would any chicken: check expiration dates, make sure they don't smell sulfurous, thaw them in the refrigerator for 24 to 48 hours, and keep them only a day or two unfrozen.

Capon Stuffed with Potatoes, Bacon, and Sauerkraut

Capons start off tragically. They're unwanted roosters, castrated, fattened, and sold before they're 10 months old. But barnyard tragedy is a culinary miracle. A capon has moist, firm meat, like a cross between a chicken and a turkey, the best of both worlds. *Makes 6 to 8 servings*

1 pound small red-skinned potatoes
2 teaspoons canola oil
6 ounces bacon, cut into ½-inch pieces
1 pound fresh sauerkraut, rinsed and
    squeezed dry
½ teaspoon paprika
½ teaspoon freshly ground black pepper
One 6½- to 7½-pound capon, giblets and
    neck removed
Butcher's twine
½ teaspoon salt, optional (see Note)

❶ Peel the potatoes, cut them into ½-inch pieces, place in a medium bowl, and cover with cool water to a depth of 1 inch. Set aside to leach starch for 10 minutes.

❷ Meanwhile, heat a large skillet over medium heat. Swirl in the canola oil, add the bacon, and cook until crispy, stirring often, about 3 minutes.

❸ Using a slotted spoon, transfer the bacon to a large bowl. Drain off but reserve half the fat from the skillet; return the skillet with the remaining fat to medium heat.

❹ Drain the potatoes in a colander set in the sink. Add them to the skillet and cook until slightly browned, stirring often, about 5 minutes. Add to the bowl with the bacon.

❺ Rinse the sauerkraut in a colander set in the sink, then squeeze dry in batches. Add to the bacon and potatoes; stir in the paprika and pepper. Set the stuffing aside to cool for 30 minutes.

❻ Position the rack in the center of the oven and preheat the oven to 350°F.

❼ Stuff the sauerkraut mixture into the capon's large cavity, then truss the bird with butcher's twine (see page 249). If desired, gently rub the salt into the bird's skin.

❽ Set the capon on a rack in a large roasting pan. Baste it with half the reserved bacon fat from the skillet. Cover the bird with aluminum foil and roast for 1 hour.

❾ Uncover the bird, brush it with the remaining bacon fat, and continue roasting until the legs move freely, the capon is well browned, and a meat thermometer inserted into the stuffing registers 160°F and when inserted into the thickest part of the thigh without touching the bone registers 165°F (our preference) or 180°F (the USDA recommendation), 2 to 2½ hours. Let rest at room temperature for 5 minutes before removing the stuffing and carving the bird.

Note: The bacon and sauerkraut are quite salty; even the rendered bacon fat is loaded with sodium. Adding more salt is strictly optional.

Variations: Substitute turkey bacon, ground beef, or sausage meat (casings removed) for the bacon. If you still want a smoky taste, substitute smoked paprika for the mild paprika.

For a spinach and sweet potato stuffing, substitute 1 pound frozen spinach, thawed, drained, and squeezed of all moisture, for the sauerkraut; also substitute 1 pound sweet potato, peeled and diced into ½-inch cubes, for the red-skinned potatoes. Add 1 tablespoon balsamic vinegar with the bacon to this mixture before stuffing it into the bird.

Roast Poussins

A poussin is sometimes called a "squab chicken," but it's not to be confused with an actual squab (see page 315). It's a young chicken, 4 to 6 weeks old, and thus very small. Simpler cooking is better: roasting lets the sweet taste come through. However, you'll need several birds for a dinner party. *Makes 4 servings*

> Four 1¼- to 1½-pound poussins, giblets and
>   necks removed (see Note)
> 16 thyme sprigs
> 12 garlic cloves, unpeeled
> Butcher's twine
> 4 teaspoons salt
> 2 teaspoons freshly ground black pepper
> 1 teaspoon grated nutmeg
> 1 tablespoon peanut oil

❶ Position the rack in the center of the oven and preheat the oven to 375°F.

❷ Place a poussin on your work surface, then place 4 thyme sprigs and 3 garlic cloves inside the large body cavity. Truss the bird with butcher's twine (see page 249). Gently massage a quarter of the salt, pepper, and nutmeg into the skin. Set aside and repeat with the other birds.

❸ Heat a large 12- or 14-inch, oven-safe, heavy-duty skillet over medium heat. Swirl in the peanut oil, then add the poussins breast side up. Cook for 3 minutes, checking occasionally to make sure the skin's not sticking. Turn and continue cooking until browned on all sides, turning several times with metal tongs, about 7 more minutes.

❹ Place the skillet in the oven and bake, basting with pan juices about every 10 minutes until a meat thermometer inserted into the thickest part of the thigh registers 165°F (our preference) or 180°F (the USDA recommendation), 40 to 50 minutes. Let stand at room temperature for 5 minutes before carving; discard the thyme and garlic from inside the birds.

Note: Occasionally, you can find larger poussins, up to 2½ pounds. However, a four-person dinner party still needs three of these, mostly because of the higher bone-to-meat ratio.

Variations: Substitute butter, walnut oil, or olive oil for the peanut oil.

Substitute twelve 3-inch rosemary sprigs or 20 parsley sprigs for the thyme, dividing these evenly among the birds.

Cut 2 small oranges into 8 sections each and place 4 sections in the body cavity of each bird before trussing.

Flattened Cornish Game Hens

"Cornish game hen" is a misnomer. These aren't game birds; they're a cross between Cornish and White Rock chickens. The best way to sear the meat is to split them so they can be flattened against the hot surface of the skillet (see step 2 or have your butcher remove the backbone for you). You'll need a very large skillet—or two!—for these birds. You weight them down over the heat, either with another skillet or with a heavy saucepan. If yours isn't heavy enough to hold the bird against the hot surface, consider putting a couple of inches of warm water in it for weight. *Makes 4 servings*

Four ¾- to 1-pound Cornish game hens,
    giblets and necks removed
¼ cup olive oil
2 teaspoons salt, preferably kosher salt
1 teaspoon freshly ground black pepper
½ cup chicken broth
2 tablespoons lemon juice

1 Position the rack in the center of the oven and preheat the oven to 350°F.

2 Lay a hen on your work surface breast side up. Insert a sharp chef's knife into the large cavity opening, locate the backbone, and make a cut from tip to tail along one side of the bone. Make a second cut along the other side of the backbone, thereby removing it. Turn the bird over breast side down and spread it open by pressing the legs down toward the work surface. The breastbone may or may not crack. Once the bird is spread open, turn it over skin side up and flatten it against the work surface. Set aside and repeat with the other hens.

3 Rub the hens on both sides with olive oil, then gently massage salt and pepper into the meat and skin (about 1 tablespoon oil, ½ teaspoon salt, and ¼ teaspoon pepper for each bird).

4 Heat a very large, heavy skillet, preferably cast iron, or even two skillets, over medium-high heat until a drop of water skitters across the surface. Place the hens skin side down in the skillet(s), then use a heavy saucepan or other pot to press them down against the skillet, weighting them down against the hot surface. Immediately reduce the heat to medium. Cook undisturbed for 5 minutes with the heavier pan resting on the birds.

5 Remove the saucepan and turn the birds over. Place the skillet(s) in the oven and roast until golden, until a meat thermometer inserted into the meat without touching the bone registers 165°F (our preference) or 180°F (the USDA recommendation), 20 to 25 minutes.

6 Remove the skillet(s) from the oven. Transfer the birds to a serving platter; tent with foil.

7 Pour off the oil from one skillet and set it over medium-high heat. Swirl in the broth and lemon juice, scraping up any browned bits in the bottom of the skillet. Simmer the mixture until it reduces to a glaze, about 2 minutes. Pour this sauce over the birds before serving.

Variations: Marinate the birds in the refrigerator for up to 24 hours, first coating them in Tapenade (page 42), Pecan Pesto (page 179), or the Fresh Herb Rub for the turkey breast (page 291). If you use any of these marinades or rubs, omit oiling, salting, and peppering the birds, but do add at least 1 tablespoon olive oil to the skillet to prevent the birds from sticking as they sear.

Wild Rice–Stuffed Guinea Hens

Also called a *pintade*, a guinea hen has dark meat throughout but a very mild taste. *Makes 4 to 6 servings*

1 small shallot, chopped
2 cups cooked wild rice (see step 1 for Wild Rice Croquettes, page 490)
⅓ cup dried cranberries
1 teaspoon salt
1 teaspoon freshly ground black pepper
Two 3-pound guinea hens, giblets and necks removed
8 thick-cut bacon slices
Butcher's twine
¼ cup beef broth
¼ cup red wine
1 tablespoon unsalted butter

1 Position the rack in the center of the oven and preheat the oven to 350°F.

2 Mix the shallot, cooked wild rice, cranberries, salt, and pepper in a medium bowl. Divide this mixture in half and stuff each half into the large cavities of the hens.

3 Lay 4 bacon slices over one bird's breast so that the ends hang down to the wing areas, overlapping the slices a bit. Truss the bird (see page 249); you may also want to wrap the bird once or twice tip to tail to make sure the bacon stays in place. Repeat with the remaining bacon and the other bird.

4 Set the birds on a wire rack in a large roasting pan and roast until well browned, until a meat thermometer inserted into the center of the thighs without touching the bone registers 165°F (our preference) or 180°F (the USDA recommendation), and until the thermometer inserted into the center of the stuffing registers 160°F. Remove the birds from the oven and set them on a carving board or platter.

5 Skim the fat off the liquid in the roasting pan. If the roasting pan is not heat-safe (if, for example, you've used an aluminum baking sheet), transfer the pan drippings to a small saucepan, scraping up any browned bits as well. Set either the flameproof roasting pan or the saucepan over high heat; mix in the broth and wine. Bring to a boil, reduce the heat to medium, and simmer until reduced by half, about 2 minutes. Whisk in the butter and serve with the carved hens. (Carve them as you would a chicken— page 247—but do not divide the legs from the thighs and only cut the breast sections in half.)

Variations: Substitute chopped pitted prunes, chopped dried apricots, dried blueberries, or dried cherries for the dried cranberries.

Add ½ cup chopped walnuts or pine nuts to the wild-rice mixture.

Substitute port for the red wine.

Guinea Hens

These ground-nesting, seed- and insect-eating birds came to Western cooking as a result of colonialism in western Africa; they are now raised extensively in southern France. The meat has not been domesticated—meaning that it's all dark, all exercised, and ready for flight. The birds are also called "guinea fowl"— and indeed, it's sometimes hard to determine whether you've bought a hen or fowl, despite the gendered name. They taste quite close to old-fashioned, minimally processed chicken, moist and flavorful, and a real treat for a dinner party. If you can't find them at your market, look up suppliers on the web or in the Source Guide (page 663) who can drop-ship them frozen to you.

Guinea Hen Roasted with Oranges, Rosemary, and Red Wine

Roasting the bird over this aromatic mélange gives it a deep, sophisticated taste. Use a big, chewy red wine like a Côtes-du-Rhône or a California Cabernet. Use a very sharp chef's knife to make even slices of the oranges, cutting them at a 90-degree angle from the stem end. A mandoline, set at a ¼-inch cut, will also do the trick, but make sure you use the food guard. *Makes 4 small servings (can be doubled)*

> One 3-pound guinea hen, giblets and neck removed
> 1 teaspoon salt
> ½ teaspoon freshly ground black pepper
> 2 tablespoons olive oil
> 2 oranges, cut into thin, ¼-inch slices
> Four 5-inch rosemary spears
> ½ cup red wine

1 Lay the guinea hen breast side up on your work surface. Insert a sharp chef's knife into the large cavity opening, locate the backbone, and make a cut from tip to tail along one side of the bone. Make a second cut along the other side of the backbone, thereby removing it. You can also clean up the breast section by removing the wing tips and cutting off excess rib sections that dangle free.

2 Now find the main joint between the thigh and the main part of the body. Feel for the ball-and-socket joint with your fingers. Wedge the knife in there, then cut down, slicing the thigh and leg quarter off the body. Do the same on the other side of the bird. (If you're squeamish about these first two steps, ask your butcher to quarter the hen.)

3 Position the rack in the center of the oven and preheat the oven to 350°F. Gently massage the salt and pepper into both sides of all the bird's pieces.

4 Heat a large, oven-safe skillet, preferably cast iron, over medium-high heat until a drop of water dances across the hot surface. Swirl in the olive oil, then slip the sections of the bird into the pan skin side down. Cook until well browned, about 5 minutes, shaking the pan occasionally to make sure the skin doesn't stick.

5 Remove the guinea hen quarters from the skillet. Pour off all the fat. Lay the orange slices across the bottom of the skillet, placing them so that the quarters can sit on top of them. Lay the rosemary sprigs over the orange slices.

6 Return the guinea hen quarters to the pan skin side up, laying the pieces on the rosemary and oranges. Pour the wine over the birds, wetting them; slip the pan in the oven.

7 Roast, basting occasionally with the pan juices, until very brown, until an instant-read thermometer inserted into the meat without touching bone registers 165°F (our preference) or 180°F (the USDA recommendation), 40 to 50 minutes. Let stand at room temperature for 5 minutes before serving with the orange slices.

Variations: Substitute 15 thyme sprigs or 8 tarragon sprigs for the rosemary.

You can actually use this technique for chicken thigh-and-leg quarters, bone-in chicken breasts, or any small bird, even quail. The in-the-oven roasting times will vary dramatically—from 40 minutes for those chicken quarters to 10 minutes for quail. An instant-read meat thermometer will be your true guide.

Water Fowl: Ducks and Geese

Most people think of these as fatty meats. Yes, they both have a thick layer of fat along the breast; it aids their buoyancy (contrary to popular belief, it does not insulate them from the cold). But the meat below the fat is not well marbled. If the fat is rendered, you're left with luscious, succulent meat.

Roast Duck with Five Wet Rubs

Steaming the duck before roasting it renders out a lot of the fat, leaving you with a moist but less fatty dinner. *Makes 4 to 6 servings*

One 5- to 6-pound duck, giblets and neck
    removed
One of the five spice rubs that follow

1 Split the duck in half, tip to tail. (If you like, have your butcher do this for you.) Cut off any excess skin at either end, removing any extra fat as well. Prick the skin and fat all over with a fork, taking care not to prick down to the meat.

2 Place about an inch of water in a large Dutch oven or a large roasting pan with a cover. Place a roasting rack in the pan (with feet high enough so that the rack's mesh or slats do not sit in the water). Place the duck halves skin side down on the rack, then set the pan over high heat and bring the water to a simmer. Cover, reduce the heat to medium, and steam for 15 minutes. Meanwhile, preheat the oven to 375°F.

3 Remove the duck from the Dutch oven or roaster; discard any fat and liquid in the pan. Brush the spice mixture over the skin on both halves.

4 Place a wire rack over a large lipped baking sheet. (You can use a wire rack for cooling cookies, provided it has feet to lift it up a bit and those feet are not covered in plastic or rubber.) Place the ducks on the rack skin side up. Roast, uncovered, until brown and tender, until the wing joints move freely and a meat thermometer inserted into the center of the thigh without touching the bone registers 165°F (our preference) or 180°F (the USDA recommendation), 2 to 2½ hours. Cool on the rack for 5 minutes before transferring to a carving board.

Most ducks sold to North American consumers are Long Island ducks, a breed of mallards. Also known as Peking ducks, these white-feathered, big-breasted fowl all trace their heritage from four mallards imported from China in 1873. Long Island has long since been eaten up by residential real estate; almost all Long Island ducks are now raised in Wisconsin and Indiana.

By contract, muscovy ducks come from Latin and South America. They have been crossbred with mallards and are sometimes found at high-end markets. The meat is less fatty, gamier, more like wild ducks. Muscovies are smaller than Long Islands or mallards; if you substitute one, cut the cooking time by about one third.

Despite the fat under the skin, there's good news about ducks. The USDA recognizes no hormones suitable for farm-raised duck and allows no chemical additives. What's more, the agency has instituted fairly stringent requirements for antibiotic regimens, legalizing only a few and requiring that ducks be off them long before slaughter.

Five Wet Rubs for Duck

Mix any of these together in a small bowl.

1. Provençal Rub

2 tablespoons dry vermouth or dry white wine
1 tablespoon olive oil
2 teaspoons stemmed thyme or 1 teaspoon
    dried thyme
1 teaspoon minced oregano leaves or
    ½ teaspoon dried oregano
1 teaspoon salt

2. New England Rub

2 tablespoons frozen cranberry juice
    concentrate, thawed
1 tablespoon walnut oil
2½ teaspoons minced sage leaves or
    1 teaspoon rubbed sage
1 teaspoon salt

3. Chinese Rub

1 tablespoon rice vinegar
1 tablespoon sesame oil, preferably toasted
    sesame oil
1 tablespoon soy sauce
1 teaspoon five-spice powder

4. East Indian Rub

2 tablespoons frozen unsweetened apple
    juice concentrate, thawed
1 tablespoon mustard oil
1 teaspoon curry powder
1 teaspoon salt

5. Fennel Rub

2 tablespoons olive oil
2 tablespoons fennel seeds
2 teaspoons ground coriander
1 teaspoon salt
½ teaspoon freshly ground black pepper

Braised Duck with Shallots, Ginger, and Orange Juice

Braising a duck yields an incredibly tender bird, just as good the next day for picnic fare. *Makes 4 to 6 servings*

One 5- to 6-pound duck, giblets and neck
    removed and reserved, cut into 9 pieces
    like a chicken (see page 254), all excess
    fat and skin removed
2 medium shallots, chopped
6 garlic cloves, slivered
2 tablespoons minced peeled fresh
    ginger
2 teaspoons stemmed thyme or 1 teaspoon
    dried thyme
1 cup dry vermouth or dry white wine
2 cups orange juice

❶ Heat a medium oven casserole or a large, oven-safe pot over medium heat. Add the duck pieces, working in stages if you need to. Brown on all sides until crisp and most of the fat has been rendered, about 20 minutes, turning frequently. Transfer the pieces to a plate.

❷ Brown the neck, heart, and gizzard in the pot as well; they will be added to the braise for flavor but discarded when the duck is served. Meanwhile, preheat the oven to 375°F.

❸ Transfer the neck and giblets to a plate. Drain off all but 1 tablespoon fat in the pot. Return it to medium heat and add the shallots, garlic, ginger, and thyme. Cook, stirring frequently, just until tender, about 2 minutes.

❹ Add the vermouth; bring the mixture to a simmer, scraping up any browned bits on the bottom of the pot. Simmer until the vermouth has been reduced by half.

⑤ Stir in the orange juice, then return the duck and all its parts to the pot. Bring the liquid to a simmer, cover, and place in the oven. Cook until tender and the liquid has been reduced to a glaze, until a meat thermometer inserted into the thickest part of the thigh without touching bone registers 165°F (our preference) or 180°F (the USDA recommendation), 1¼ to 1¾ hours. Set aside at room temperature for 10 minutes; remove and discard the neck and giblets before serving.

Variations: Substitute cranberry juice for the orange juice.

Add one 4-inch cinnamon stick, 6 whole cloves, or 1 star anise pod to the pot with the orange juice. Remove before serving.

Shopping Tips for Duck

The ideal duck should be between 8 and 16 weeks of age, marked as a "broiler duckling" or "fryer duckling." As in chickens, a "roaster duckling" is larger, older, and sometimes tougher.

Because of the relatively large chest cavity and higher bone-to-meat ratio, a 5- to 6-pound duck will not serve as many people as a chicken of the same weight. If you have six big eaters or a dinner party for eight, consider doubling the recipe.

There are almost no fresh ducks available in our markets; even those marked "fresh" have most likely been previously frozen (they were fresh when slaughtered). Our best advice: know your supplier.

A thawed duck can be stored in the coldest part of the refrigerator for 2 days with the giblets and neck removed and stored separately. A frozen duck should take about 1½ days to thaw in the refrigerator.

Seared Duck Breasts with Peaches and Thyme

Duck breasts make a surprisingly simple dinner. Reduce the fat considerably by placing them in a cool pan and slowly heating them until most of the fat renders off. *Makes 4 servings*

4 medium boneless duck breast fillets
   (8 to 10 ounces each)
1 teaspoon salt
½ teaspoon freshly ground black
   pepper
2 medium shallots, minced
2 garlic cloves, minced
¾ cup dry white wine or dry
   vermouth
1 tablespoon white wine vinegar
1 tablespoon honey
2 large peaches, peeled, pitted, and
   sliced
1 tablespoon stemmed thyme

① Position the rack in the middle of the oven and preheat the oven to 350°F. Place the breasts skin side down on a cutting board and trim off all excess skin that hangs over the sides. Turn the breasts over; make three parallel diagonal cuts in the skin of each, cutting through the fat but not into the meat. Make three more diagonal cuts the other way, thereby making a crosshatch pattern in the skin.

② Place the breasts skin side down in a large, cool, oven-safe skillet. Set the skillet over medium-low heat and cook until browned, about 10 minutes.

③ Pour off all the rendered fat in the pan, turn the breasts skin side up, place the skillet in the oven, and roast until a meat thermometer inserted halfway into the thickest part of the breast registers 160°F (our preference) or 170°F (the USDA recommendation for duck breast), 12 to 17 minutes (see Note). Transfer the breasts to a plate, season with salt and pepper, and tent with aluminum foil to keep warm.

4 Pour off all but 1 tablespoon fat in the skillet. (Remember: the skillet's hot!) Place the skillet over medium-low heat, add the shallots, and cook until soft and fragrant, about 2 minutes, stirring constantly. Add the garlic, cook for 20 seconds, then pour in the wine or vermouth and the vinegar.

5 Raise the heat to high and bring the mixture to a boil, scraping up any browned bits on the bottom of the pan. Boil until reduced by half, about 2 minutes, stirring constantly. Swirl in the honey and cook just until the honey melts, about 5 seconds, stirring constantly.

6 Add the peaches and thyme; cook just until heated through, about 1 minute. Remove from the heat. To serve, slice the breasts into ¼-inch slices on the diagonal, arrange these on plates, and divide the sauce among them.

Note: Some people prefer much rarer breasts, around 130°F (medium-rare) or 140°F. If you're willing to go that low, understand the risks—you'll also end up with reddish meat.

Seared Duck Breasts with Apricots and Rosemary: Substitute 4 pitted and sliced apricots for the peaches; also substitute 2 teaspoons chopped fresh rosemary for the thyme.

Seared Duck Breasts with Plums and Cinnamon: Substitute 3 pitted and sliced plums for the peaches; also substitute 1 teaspoon ground cinnamon for the thyme.

Duck Confit Tzimmes

Tzimmes is usually eaten on Rosh Hashanah, the Jewish New Year. It's sweet, said to symbolize the wish for a sweet new year. Here, we've transformed it into the ultimate party dish. A French extravagance, duck confit is a duck leg preserved in duck fat. The legs are plump and juicy with an almost smoky flavor. Look for duck confit legs at the butcher counter or in the poultry case of almost all gourmet markets. *Makes 8 servings*

> 4 duck confit legs
> 1¼ pounds sweet potatoes, peeled and cut into 1-inch pieces
> 4 large carrots, peeled and cut into 1-inch pieces
> 8 ounces pitted prunes, quartered (about 1 cup)
> ⅓ cup chicken broth
> 3 tablespoons honey
> ½ teaspoon ground cinnamon
> ½ teaspoon salt
> ¼ teaspoon garlic powder
> ¼ teaspoon ground cloves

1 Position the rack in the bottom third of the oven and preheat the oven to 350°F.

2 Remove some of the white fat from the duck confit legs and smear it around a 13 × 9-inch baking pan to grease it. Remove and discard the remainder of the skin and fat from the legs. Shred the meat off the bones with a fork.

3 Place the meat in a large bowl and mix in the sweet potatoes, carrots, and prunes.

4 Whisk the broth, honey, cinnamon, salt, garlic powder, and ground cloves in a small bowl. Pour over the duck and vegetables; toss to coat. Turn this mixture and any juices into the prepared pan.

⑤ Cover and bake in the lower third of the oven for 1 hour, tossing every 15 minutes. Then uncover, toss well, and continue baking until the vegetables are tender, about 15 more minutes. Let stand, uncovered, for 5 minutes at room temperature before serving.

Steam-Roasted Goose

A goose is even fattier than a duck (more buoyancy for that big body), but the meat is mildly gamy and quite luxurious. Although it's graced many a holiday table, it's a good bit of exotic fare for your next dinner party. This two-step technique, similar to that used for duck, will give you the most tender meat every time. *Makes 6 to 8 servings*

> One 10- to 12-pound goose, giblets and
>   neck removed
> 1½ teaspoons salt
> 1 teaspoon freshly ground black
>   pepper
> Butcher's twine

❶ Trim off all excess fat and skin at both openings for the goose. Cut off the wing tips and discard them. Season the inside of the body with ½ teaspoon salt and the pepper. Truss the goose with butcher's twine (see page 249).

❷ Add about 1 inch of water to a large roasting pan and place it over medium-high heat. Place a footed roasting rack in the roasting pan and set the goose on the rack breast side up. Bring the water to a boil. Cover, reduce the heat to medium, and steam for 1 hour, adding more water if the pan starts to run dry.

❸ Position the rack in the center of the oven and preheat the oven to 375°F.

❹ Carefully remove the goose from the rack and drain the very hot fat from inside the body cavity. Set the goose on a rack over a broiler pan (or in a heavy-duty aluminum roasting pan set on a large baking sheet). Sprinkle the remaining 1 teaspoon salt over the outside of the goose.

❺ Roast, uncovered, until browned, basting occasionally with any fat that accumulates in the pan, until the legs move up and down easily, and until an instant-read thermometer inserted into the thickest part of the thigh without touching the bone registers 165°F (our preference) or 180°F (the USDA recommendation), 1½ to 2 hours. Let stand for 10 minutes at room temperature before carving.

Fruit-Stuffed Goose

A bread stuffing will get too soggy in a goose, so a dried fruit stuffing works best. This technique leaves you with a slightly chewier bird than steaming does, but with also the finest stuffing in the world, thanks to all that goose fat. This is the ultimate Christmas dish. *Makes 6 to 8 servings*

> 12 ounces pitted prunes (about 2 cups),
>   chopped
> 6 ounces dried cherries (about 1 cup),
>   chopped
> 2 cups dry vermouth or dry
>   white wine
> 2 tablespoons unsalted butter
> 1 large onion, chopped
> 2 celery ribs, chopped
> 4 tart green apples, such as Granny Smiths,
>   peeled, cored, and chopped
> 2 tablespoons stemmed thyme or
>   1 tablespoon dried thyme
> 1 teaspoon salt
> ½ teaspoon grated nutmeg
> ½ teaspoon freshly ground black pepper

One 10- to 12-pound goose, giblets and
    neck removed
Butcher's twine
Several bamboo skewers, soaked in water for
    10 minutes

1 Bring the prunes, dried cherries, and vermouth
or wine to a simmer in a large saucepan set over
medium heat. Cover, reduce the heat to low, and
simmer slowly until the dried fruit is soft and the
liquid has been almost all absorbed, stirring occasionally, about 20 minutes.

2 Transfer the fruit to a large bowl with a slotted
spoon. Raise the heat to high and reduce the remaining liquid to a glaze. Pour this over the fruit
and set aside.

3 Melt the butter in a large skillet set over medium heat, then add the onion and celery. Cook,
stirring occasionally, until softened, about 3 minutes. Pour into the bowl with the fruit.

4 Stir in the apples, thyme, salt, nutmeg, and pepper. Cool for 10 minutes. Meanwhile, position
the rack in the lower third of the oven; preheat
the oven to 325°F.

5 Trim off all excess fat and skin at both openings for the goose. Cut off the wing tips and
discard them. Pull the wings up so that they angle up onto the breast and tie them in place by
wrapping butcher's twine around the body a few
times. Also tie the legs together over the large
opening.

6 Gently pack the stuffing into the bird, taking
care not to press down. Any additional stuffing
can be placed in a small baking dish and baked
alongside the bird, dousing it occasionally with
rendered goose fat from the pan. Pull the skin
over the large opening and skewer it shut with

the bamboo skewers, threading them through
the skin on both sides and closing the opening.
Truss the goose with butcher's twine (see page
249). Set the goose on a rack in a heavy-duty
roasting pan set on a large baking sheet.

7 Roast until browned, until a meat thermometer inserted into the center of the stuffing through the large opening registers 165°F
(our preference) or 180°F (the USDA recommendation), about 3 hours. Remove from the
oven, carefully cut the twine over the legs, and
remove the skewers. Transfer the stuffing to a
bowl; tent with aluminum foil to keep warm.
Let the goose stand at room temperature for 10
minutes before carving. (See page 247 for tips
on carving a bird.)

Variations: Substitute chopped dried apricots
for the dried cherries; also add 1 teaspoon sugar
with the thyme.

Substitute pears for the apples; also add 2 teaspoons grated lemon zest with the thyme.

Goose Tips

While a gosling may sound tender, the meat
often lacks punch, about like fatty roast chicken.
Instead, we recommend a 10- to 12-pound adult
goose. Frozen, it will take about 2½ days to
thaw in the refrigerator. Be aware that there's
an even greater bone-to-meat ratio than in
ducks; this goose will only feed 6 to 8 people.
If the goose has any feathers or sharp quills still
embedded in the skin, remove these with a pair
of cleaned tweezers.

✤ Game Birds: Pheasant, Squab, and Quail ✤

Although these were once game birds, few still are. Of course, there are hunters who regularly track down their quota; but for the most part, these birds have now been domesticated—which is actually the good news. They're increasingly available in our markets and from suppliers on the Web.

Roast Pheasant with Brandy Cream Sauce

Because of the delicate cream sauce, this recipe is better for a domesticated pheasant, not a wild one. *Makes 4 servings*

One 3- to 3½-pound pheasant, giblets and
    neck removed
1 teaspoon salt
½ teaspoon freshly ground black pepper
Butcher's twine
2 tablespoons unsalted butter
8 thyme sprigs
1 medium shallot, minced
½ cup chicken broth
¼ cup brandy or Cognac
¼ cup heavy cream

❶ Position the rack in the center of the oven and preheat the oven to 350°F. Season the pheasant's skin and interior with salt and pepper; truss the bird with butcher's twine (see page 249).

❷ Melt the butter in a heavy-duty, oven-safe skillet set over medium heat. Add the bird breast side down. Cook until well browned, about 4 minutes, shaking the pan, moving the bird occasionally to make sure it doesn't stick, and basting it often with the pan juices. Turn and continue basting until brown on all sides, about 4 more minutes.

❸ Remove the pan from the heat and lift the bird up with metal tongs. Place the thyme sprigs in the pan, making a little bed. Put the bird over them, then place the skillet in the oven.

❹ Roast until well browned and crispy, until a meat thermometer inserted halfway into the thickest part of the breast registers 160°F (our preference and the USDA recommendation), basting occasionally with the pan juices, about 1¼ hours. Transfer to a carving platter or board.

❺ Remove the thyme from the very hot skillet and skim the pan drippings of any fat. Place the skillet over medium-high heat and add the shallot. Cook, stirring often, until soft, about 2 minutes. Stir in the broth, scraping up any browned bits on the pan's bottom.

❻ Once the broth comes to a simmer, stir in the brandy. (If the sauce flames, quickly cover the skillet and remove it from the heat for at least 20 seconds or until the fire is out.) Simmer, stirring occasionally, until reduced by two thirds. Stir in the cream, cook for 1 minute, and serve alongside the carved bird (see page 247 for carving tips).

Variation: Substitute 4 tarragon, chervil, or marjoram sprigs for the thyme.

Stewed Pheasant with Potatoes, Mushrooms, and Bacon

In French, this preparation is called *grand-mère* because it's said to be the kind of stew your grandmother would make (if she made pheasant). *Makes 4 servings*

1 tablespoon olive oil

4 ounces thick-cut bacon, roughly chopped

One 3- to 3½-pound pheasant, giblets removed, cut into 9 pieces like a chicken (see page 254)

1 large leek, white and pale green parts only, split down the middle, the inner leaves washed carefully of sand, and thinly sliced into half-moons

1 large baking potato, peeled and diced

10 ounces white button or cremini mushrooms, cleaned and thinly sliced

2 teaspoons stemmed thyme or 1 teaspoon dried thyme

½ cup dry white wine or dry vermouth

1 cup chicken broth

½ teaspoon grated nutmeg

½ teaspoon salt

½ teaspoon freshly ground black pepper

❶ Heat a large, oven-safe casserole or Dutch oven over medium heat. Add the olive oil, then the bacon. Fry until crisp, stirring often, about 3 minutes. Transfer to a plate lined with paper towels.

❷ Add the pheasant and cook in the fat, turning often, until the pieces are well browned on both sides, about 8 minutes. Transfer the pheasant pieces to a second plate.

❸ Pour off about half the fat in the pot, then set it back over medium heat and add the leek. Cook, stirring often, until softened, about 3 minutes.

❹ Add the potato; cook, stirring frequently, until browned, about 2 minutes.

❺ Add the mushrooms and thyme. Cook, stirring once in a while, just until the mushrooms have begun to give off their liquid, about 2 minutes.

❻ Pour in the wine or vermouth and scrape up any browned bits with a wooden spoon as the sauce comes to a simmer. Stir in the broth, nutmeg, salt, and pepper; bring back to a simmer.

❼ Return the bacon to the pot, then the pheasant and any accumulated juices. Place the pot in the oven and cook, uncovered, stirring a couple of times, until the pheasant is tender, until an instant-read meat thermometer inserted into the thickest part of the thigh without touching bone registers 160°F (our preference and the USDA recommendation), about 40 minutes.

Variations: Marinate the pheasant overnight with a bottle of red wine, a tablespoon of cracked black peppercorns, 2 bay leaves, and 2 whole cloves. Discard the marinade; substitute red wine for the white wine in the sauce.

Pheasant

Pheasants were introduced to North America by the idle rich who fancied themselves hunters. But the delicious meat won out over pretension; pheasants are now found both in the wild and at most specialty markets.

Wild pheasants are often sold partially cleaned. The kidneys and liver may still be attached and must be removed. There may also be some quills; remove these with tweezers.

Oddly, the USDA recommends cooking pheasants to a lower temperature than other fowl: 160°F, exactly our preference.

Seared Squabs with Sour Cherries and Port

Squabs are young domesticated pigeons, not like the kind in a city park, but like the wild bird preferred in France. Although the birds are not allowed to fly before slaughter, the meat is dark throughout with a pleasant if gamy taste that stands up well to rich sauces. *Makes 4 servings*

Four 1-pound squabs, giblets removed
2 tablespoons walnut oil
2 medium shallots, minced
2 cups pitted fresh or jarred sour
    cherries
1½ cups port

1 Slice the squabs in half by placing them breast side down on your work surface and cutting through on one side of the backbone with a heavy, sharp knife. Also slice through the skin under the wings by the thigh, making a long slit in the skin that will keep the birds from curling up as the skin shrinks in the oven.

2 Heat a very large skillet or two large skillets over medium heat. Add the walnut oil, then the birds skin side down. Cook for 5 minutes, then turn and continue cooking until well browned on both sides, about 5 more minutes. Transfer the birds to a plate; set aside.

3 Add the shallots to one or both of the skillets. Cook, stirring frequently, until soft, about 1 minute. Add the cherries and cook for 1 more minute.

4 Pour in the port (dividing it in half if you're using two skillets) and bring the mixture to a boil, scraping up any browned bits on the pan's bottom. Simmer until reduced by half, about 4 minutes.

5 Return the squabs and any accumulated juices to the skillet(s). Baste well with the sauce, simmering until the leg joints move freely and an instant-read meat thermometer inserted into the thigh registers 165°F (our preference) or 180°F (the USDA recommendation), 3 to 7 minutes. Serve with the cherry sauce mopped over the birds.

Variations: Substitute unsalted butter for the walnut oil.

Substitute fresh or jarred pitted plums, roughly chopped, for the cherries. Also add 2 teaspoons lemon juice with the port.

Add one 4-inch cinnamon stick, 3 whole cloves, or 1 star anise pod with the port.

Substitute a sweet Madeira or cream sherry for the port.

Pomegranate Quail

Quail is so sweet, it's a natural pairing with tart pomegranate molasses. *Makes 4 appetizer servings or 2 main-course servings (can be doubled or tripled)*

Four 4- to 4½-ounce quail, any giblets or
    innards removed
½ cup pomegranate molasses
¼ cup walnut oil, plus additional for the
    grill grate or pan
¼ cup chicken broth
1 tablespoon minced fresh mint
1 tablespoon packed light brown sugar
1 teaspoon salt
½ teaspoon freshly ground black pepper

1 Place the quail breast side up on your work surface. Insert a sharp knife into the body cavity and slice down on either side of the backbone, thereby cutting it out and allowing you to press the quail open flat. Turn it over and press it open flat again.

② Whisk the pomegranate molasses, walnut oil, broth, mint, brown sugar, salt, and pepper in a large baking dish. Add the quail and turn a few times to coat. Cover and refrigerate for at least 4 hours or overnight, turning the quail occasionally in the marinade.

③ **If using a grill:** Oil the grill grate and prepare the grill for direct cooking by either heating a gas grill to high heat or creating a hot, well-ashed coal bed in a charcoal grill. Take the quail out of the marinade and place them on the grill grate directly over the heat source or the coals. Cover and grill for 5 minutes, brushing occasionally with the marinade until lightly browned. Turn the quail, then move them to a cooler section of the grate. Mop with the marinade, cover, and continue cooking until well browned and the leg joints move freely, about 3 more minutes.

If using a grill pan or a skillet: Heat the pan over medium-high heat, swirl in about 2 teaspoons walnut oil, then slip the quail in skin side down. Baste immediately with the marinade, cover, and cook for 4 minutes. Baste them again, then turn them and continue cooking, uncovered, basting every once in a while, until browned on both sides and the leg joints move quite freely, about 4 more minutes.

Variations: Substitute frozen cranberry juice concentrate, thawed, for the pomegranate molasses.

Substitute almond oil or olive oil for the walnut oil.

Fish and Shellfish

QUICK, EASY, FRESH, LOW IN FAT, HIGH IN ESSENTIAL MINERALS AND PRO-
tein: we've all heard the good news about fish. Even fresh shellfish has come
up from the deep for their culinary kudos recently. Yet the bulk sold is canned or
made into fish sticks.

Fresh fish? It looks good, sounds good, is good; but people still sidle up to it warily.
Maybe it's that whole-fish dilemma: lying on the ice, eyeing you. We inhabit a sanitized
world; there's something strange about buying food in its original (or almost original)
state. "Food with face," as one friend puts it. Most of us never see a head-on chicken,
much less any recognizable part of a cow.

And perhaps seafood's much-touted quickness also gives some of us pause: prepare
it now, don't delay. Many people market once a week; fresh fish doesn't fit that strat-
egy.

Yet despite all that, fish and shellfish sales have ticked up in the last few years, thanks
in large part to better fish counters at supermarkets, but also to the ongoing popularity
of sushi and to our modern, fast-paced lives. What's more, fish sales are up the most
among the under-thirty-five crowd. Maybe the kids *were* paying attention in school. If
fish is the future, it's a fresh and fast one.

Rather than giving you a few preparations for red snapper, some for roughy, and then a handful for tilapia, we've grouped the recipes in this chapter in large subheadings based on the kind of fish or shellfish called for—and we've left a range of possibilities within each. That's partly because of the versatility of fish; snapper, roughy, and tilapia; all can be substituted for each other in these dishes. And it's partly because of market dynamics; with modern shipping and distribution, it may be hard to find any one kind of fish at any one time. So here are sautés, parchment packets, and escabeches, appropriate for a wide range of thin fish fillets.

Five Easy, One-Skillet Sautés for Thin White-Fleshed Fish Fillets

Simplicity in minutes. All these preparations work the same way: quickly sauté the floured fillets, take them out of the pan, and build a simple sauce. There's a range of fats used to sauté the fillets; if possible, use the same one that you will use in the sauce. *Makes 4 servings*

½ cup all-purpose flour
1 teaspoon salt, plus additional as desired
1 teaspoon freshly ground black pepper
1 tablespoon unsalted butter, olive oil, or canola oil
Four 4- to 6-ounce thin white-fleshed fish fillets
One of the five sauces that follow

❶ Whisk the flour, salt, and pepper on a dinner plate.

❷ Melt the butter in a large skillet over medium heat; or heat the skillet, then swirl in the oil.

❸ Pat the fillets dry with paper towels; then dredge them in the flour mixture, coating both sides well and shaking off the excess flour. Slip them into the pan.

❹ Cook until lightly browned, 2 to 3 minutes. Flip and cook until lightly browned on the other side, until the thin part of the fillet flakes when gently scraped with a fork, 1 to 2 minutes. Transfer to four serving plates or a serving platter; tent with aluminum foil to keep warm, if desired; and make the sauce in the same skillet.

1. *With Pistachios, Red Wine, and Cherries*

2 tablespoons shelled pistachios (see Note)
1 tablespoon unsalted butter
1 small red onion, chopped
2 garlic cloves, minced
¼ cup dry red wine
1 cup pitted halved sweet cherries, such as Bing or Rainier cherries, or jarred, pitted sweet cherries
¼ cup vegetable or fish broth
¼ teaspoon salt, or to taste
2 teaspoons stemmed thyme

❶ Toast the pistachios in the skillet over medium heat until lightly browned. Pour into a small bowl.

2 Melt the butter in the skillet. Add the onion and garlic; cook, stirring often, until soft, about 2 minutes.

3 Pour in the wine, scraping up any browned bits on the pan's bottom. Raise the heat to medium-high, bring the wine to a simmer, and cook until reduced by half, about 1 minute.

4 Add the cherries and broth. Bring to a simmer and cook until reduced by half, about 1 minute.

5 Stir in the pistachios, remove from the heat, and check the sauce to see if it needs any salt. Spoon over the fillets; sprinkle each fillet with ½ teaspoon thyme.

Note: If you can only find salted pistachios in their shells, omit the salt from the recipe.

Variations: Substitute pecan pieces, walnut pieces, or sliced almonds for the pistachios.

Add ¼ teaspoon cayenne pepper to the flour mixture.

Substitute olive oil for the butter; also substitute dry vermouth or white wine for the red wine.

Substitute oregano or marjoram for the thyme.

Skin On or Off?

Most fillets are sold skinless. That said, you can sometimes find them with their skin on; preparing them that way is largely a matter of taste. The skin can add a lot of briny taste, but it won't crisp in some sautés. To cook, score the skin with a knife, making two or three shallow, diagonal cuts, slicing only the skin and the white film underneath, never the meat itself. Start these fillets in the pan skin side down, cooking them a minute or so longer than required in the recipe; then turn and continue cooking skin side up for about 1 minute.

2. *With Oranges and Rosemary*

2 medium navel oranges (see Note)
1 tablespoon olive oil
1 medium yellow onion, chopped
2 tablespoons chopped rosemary leaves
⅓ cup dry white wine or dry vermouth
¼ teaspoon salt, or to taste

1 Slice ½ inch off the bottom of each orange, just so they will stand flat on your work surface. Use a sharp knife to cut around the natural curve of the oranges, thereby slicing off the orange peel and white pith underneath, exposing the orange flesh. Slice off any extraneous bits of rind or pith.

2 Hold the skinned orange over a medium bowl. Use a paring knife to cut down between the membranes, releasing the sections into the bowl and catching any juice. Once all the sections have been removed, squeeze the membranes over the bowl to extract any last drops of juice. Pick out any seeds and set the orange supremes and their juice aside.

3 Swirl the olive oil into the skillet. Add the onion and cook, stirring often, until soft, about 2 minutes.

4 Add the rosemary, wine or vermouth, orange, and any juice in the bowl. Raise the heat to medium-high and bring to a simmer. Cook until reduced by half, stirring often, about 2 minutes. Season with salt and spoon over the fillets.

Note: It's best to do the first two steps of this sauce (segmenting and juicing the orange) before you sauté the fillets.

Variations: Substitute 1 large pink grapefruit for the oranges.

Substitute chopped parsley leaves or 1 tablespoon stemmed thyme for the rosemary.

Add ¼ cup toasted sliced almonds with the orange sections.

Whisk 1 tablespoon unsalted butter into the warm sauce before spooning over the fillets.

3. With Zucchini and Olives
1 tablespoon olive oil
1 medium shallot, halved and thinly sliced
1 large zucchini, shredded through the large holes of a box grater
1 teaspoon finely grated lemon zest
¼ cup small pitted black olives
1 tablespoon chopped dill fronds or 2 teaspoons dried dill
¼ cup vegetable broth
1 tablespoon lemon juice
¼ teaspoon salt, or to taste

❶ Add the olive oil to the skillet. Toss in the shallot and cook, stirring constantly, for 1 minute. Add the zucchini and lemon zest; cook, stirring often, until softened, about 2 minutes.

❷ Stir in the olives and dill; cook for 1 minute. Pour in the broth and lemon juice. Bring to a simmer and boil until reduced by half, about 30 seconds. Season with salt and spoon the sauce over the fillets.

Variations: Substitute rosemary or oregano for the dill.

Add up to ½ teaspoon red pepper flakes with the lemon zest.

4. With Marsala Cream Sauce
1 tablespoon unsalted butter
8 ounces white button or cremini mushrooms, cleaned and thinly sliced
¼ cup dry Marsala
⅔ cup heavy cream
1 teaspoon stemmed thyme
¼ teaspoon salt, or to taste

❶ Melt the butter in the skillet. Add the mushrooms and cook until they give off their liquid and it reduces to a glaze, about 3 minutes.

❷ Pour in the Marsala, raise the heat to medium-high, and bring the mixture to a simmer, scraping up any browned bits on the bottom of the pan. Cook for 1 minute, then pour in the cream. Continue simmering until slightly thickened and reduced by about half, 1 to 2 more minutes.

❸ Remove the pan from the heat, stir in the thyme and salt, as desired. Spoon over the fillets.

Variations: Substitute Madeira or dry sherry for the Marsala.

Stir 1 ounce Parmigiano-Reggiano, finely grated, into the sauce with the thyme until smooth.

Substitute 8 shiitake mushroom caps, thinly sliced, for the button mushrooms.

Omit the cream entirely; simple sauté the mushrooms, deglaze the pan with the Marsala, and spoon the mixture over the fillets.

5. With Tomatoes, Shallots, and Cream
1 tablespoon unsalted butter
1 large shallot, chopped
6 tablespoons dry white wine or dry vermouth
1½ cups canned diced tomatoes with their juice
2 tablespoons chopped parsley leaves
2 tablespoons chopped dill fronds
½ cup heavy cream
¼ teaspoon salt, or to taste

❶ Melt the butter in the skillet; then add the shallot and cook, stirring frequently, until softened, about 3 minutes.

❷ Pour in the wine or vermouth; bring to a simmer, scraping up any bits on the pan's bottom. Boil until reduced to a glaze, about 2 minutes.

❸ Add the tomatoes, parsley, and dill. Continue simmering, stirring occasionally, until thickened slightly, until the tomatoes have broken down into a sauce.

④ Pour in the cream, bring back to a boil, and cook for 1 minute. Remove from the heat and season with salt. Spoon the sauce over the fillets.

Variations: Substitute oregano for the dill.

For a vodka sauce, reduce the cream to ¼ cup and add ¼ cup vodka with it.

Thai Curry Thin White-Fleshed Fish Fillets

We prefer to build our own curry blend, getting the heat just right—that is, sizzling. *Makes 4 servings*

Unsalted butter for greasing the pan
Four 4- to 6-ounce thin white-fleshed fish fillets
½ cup dry white wine or dry vermouth
4 garlic cloves, quartered
1 lemongrass stalk, cut into 4-inch segments, each bruised with the bottom of a heavy pot or the flat side of a meat mallet
One 4-inch cinnamon stick
¾ cup regular or low-fat coconut milk
2 tablespoons fish sauce
3 small green Thai chiles, seeded and finely minced
1 medium shallot, sliced into thin rings
1 tablespoon minced peeled fresh ginger
1 teaspoon coriander seeds
1 teaspoon finely grated lime zest
½ teaspoon salt
2 tablespoons shredded basil leaves

① Position the rack in the center of the oven and preheat the oven to 400°F. Lightly butter a 13 × 9-inch baking pan. Lay the fillets in the pan, overlapping as necessary.

② Bring the wine or vermouth, garlic, lemongrass, and cinnamon stick to a simmer in a small saucepan set over high heat.

③ Pour the sauce over the fillets, cover the pan with aluminum foil, and bake until the thin parts of the fish flake when gently scraped with a fork, about 12 minutes.

④ Carefully remove the fillets from the pan and transfer them to four serving plates. Tent with foil to keep warm, if desired.

⑤ Pour the contents of the baking pan into a large saucepan set over medium-high heat. Stir in the coconut milk and fish sauce, then stir in the chiles, shallot, ginger, coriander seeds, and zest. Bring to a simmer, then cover, reduce the heat to low, and simmer slowly for 3 minutes.

⑥ Strain the coconut mixture into a medium bowl, then spoon over the fish fillets. Season with salt, then sprinkle ½ tablespoon shredded basil over each fillet.

Variations: Add 4 kaffir lime leaves with the chiles.

For a more authentic taste, substitute galangal for the ginger.

For a milder dish, use only 1 chile.

Cooking Tips for Thin Fish Fillets

• Thin fillets are overcooked as quickly as they're cooked. When the thinnest part of the fillet can be flaked with a fork, the thickest part is done.
• Slip the fillets into the pan with the whiter or curved side down. You'll then flip them once and get them onto the plate right side up.
• Use a wide, slotted metal or nonstick-safe spatula. Fillets fall apart easily—the wider the utensil, the less likely they'll break.
• Consider warming your dinner plates as you make the dish. Place them in a preheated 250°F oven for 5 to 10 minutes, just long enough to knock off the chill.

Baked Buttery Thin White-Fleshed Fish Fillets with Wine and Chives

Here's an easy baked casserole. *Makes 6 servings*

> 2 pounds thin white-fleshed fish fillets
> 8 tablespoons (1 stick) unsalted butter, very soft, at room temperature
> ¼ cup chopped chives or the green parts of scallions (see Note)
> ½ teaspoon salt, preferably kosher or coarse-grained sea salt
> 1½ cups dry white wine (do not use dry vermouth)
> 1 tablespoon lemon juice
> ½ teaspoon freshly ground black pepper

❶ Position the rack in the center of the oven and preheat the oven to 400°F.

❷ Blot the fillets dry, then spread the soft butter evenly over both sides. Lay into a 13 × 9-inch flame-safe roasting or baking pan, overlapping as need be. Sprinkle the chives evenly over, among, and even under the fillets. Sprinkle with salt.

❸ Pour the wine over the fillets. Place the dish in the oven and bake until the fillets are firm to the touch, until they begin to flake when gently scraped with a fork at the thinnest parts, about 20 minutes.

❹ Carefully transfer the fillets to individual serving plates or a large serving platter; tent with aluminum foil to keep warm.

❺ Set the roasting pan or heat-safe baking pan over medium heat. (If you've used a baking pan that's not safe on a burner or over a flame, transfer its contents to a large skillet.) Bring the cooking liquid to a simmer, then stir in the lemon juice and pepper. Cook, stirring often, until reduced to a glaze, about 5 minutes. Spoon over the fillets.

Note: Scallions are stronger than chives. Compensate by using a big-flavored white wine like a Chardonnay.

Variations: Sprinkle ½ teaspoon red pepper flakes over the fillets before baking.

Lay 8 to 10 thyme sprigs in the baking dish, then lay the fillets on top of them. Remove the sprigs from the sauce just before serving.

Cornmeal-and-Maple–Crusted Thin White-Fleshed Fish Fillets

We've upped the servings here because frying fish fillets seems a task for bigger crowds—or for larger portions among four people. Work in batches if you need to—or divide the ingredients between two skillets. Be ready to serve these easy fillets the moment they come out of the pan. *Makes 6 servings*

> 2 large eggs
> 2 tablespoons maple syrup
> ½ cup finely ground yellow cornmeal
> ½ cup all-purpose flour
> 1 tablespoon chili powder
> ½ teaspoon freshly ground black pepper
> ¼ cup peanut oil
> Six 4- to 6-ounce thin white-fleshed fish fillets
> 1 teaspoon salt

❶ Whisk the eggs and maple syrup in a shallow soup bowl. Mix the cornmeal, flour, chili powder, and pepper on a serving plate with a fork until uniform.

❷ Heat the peanut oil in a large, deep-sided skillet or sauté pan over medium heat until the oil ripples.

❸ Meanwhile, pat the fillets dry with paper towels, then dredge them in the egg mixture on both sides, shaking off any excess. Gently press them into the cornmeal mixture, lightly coating both sides thoroughly and evenly. Shake off any excess and slide into the skillet. (With 6 fillets, you may need to work in batches.)

❹ Cook until brown and crisp, about 3 minutes. Turn and continue frying until brown on the other side, 2 to 3 minutes. Remove from the pan and season with salt.

Variations: Substitute curry powder or smoked paprika for the chili powder.

Fried Catfish Sandwiches: Use catfish fillets, then place them on hamburger buns with chopped lettuce, mayonnaise, and salsa.

Looking for other ways to fry fish? Cut thin white-fleshed fillets into 2-inch pieces, then substitute them for the scallops in the Fried Scallops, using the beer-batter crust and technique for frying (see page 72), or for the oysters in the Fried Oysters and using the Panko Crust and the technique called for in that recipe (see page 73).

Fish Broth

If there's a wide range of quality among varieties of canned chicken broth, there's an even wider one among fish broths. Look for frozen fish "demi-glace" at high-end markets; if you can't find it, substitute a good-quality vegetable broth. You can use clam juice, sold in bottles at most markets, but its taste will be less subtle and may overwhelm all but the strongest sauces.

Sweet-and-Sour Thin White-Fleshed Fish Fillets

Crispy but surprisingly light, these fillets are put in a thick, rich sauce, then topped with shredded vegetables. *Makes 4 servings*

> Four 4- to 6-ounce thin white-fleshed fish fillets
> 5 tablespoons Shaoxing or dry sherry
> 3 cups plus 1 tablespoon peanut oil
> 1 tablespoon plus 2 teaspoons cornstarch
> 1 tablespoon water
> 2 scallions, thinly sliced
> 1 garlic clove, minced
> 1 tablespoon minced peeled fresh ginger
> 3 tablespoons rice vinegar
> 3 tablespoons sugar
> 2 tablespoons soy sauce
> ½ cup chicken, vegetable, or fish broth
> 1 carrot, peeled and cut into matchsticks
> 1 celery rib, thinly sliced

❶ Pat the fillets dry with paper towels. Cut them into 2-inch pieces, place in a large baking dish, and sprinkle with 3 tablespoons Shaoxing or sherry. Cover and refrigerate for at least 30 minutes or up to 2 hours.

❷ Place 3 cups peanut oil in a large saucepan, clip a deep-frying thermometer to the inside of the pan, and set it over medium-high heat. Heat until the temperature registers 360°F.

❸ Drain off any excess Shaoxing or sherry in the dish, then sprinkle ½ tablespoon cornstarch over the fillets. Turn them over and sprinkle with another ½ tablespoon cornstarch. Make sure the fillets are lightly coated.

❹ Slip them into the hot oil. Fry until lightly browned, turning once, about 4 minutes, adjusting the heat so the temperature remains constant.

Transfer the fish to a wire rack. Set the oil aside to cool and save for another purpose or discard.

⑤ Whisk the remaining 2 teaspoons cornstarch with the water in a small bowl; set aside.

⑥ Heat a large wok or skillet over medium-high heat. Add the remaining 1 tablespoon peanut oil, then toss in the scallions, garlic, and ginger. Stir-fry until very aromatic, about 30 seconds.

⑦ Stir in the vinegar, sugar, soy sauce, and the remaining 2 tablespoons Shaoxing or sherry. Bring this mixture to a simmer, then stir in the broth.

⑧ Once the mixture comes back to a full boil, whisk in the cornstarch mixture and cook, stirring constantly, until thickened, about 20 seconds.

⑨ Mound the fish pieces on a serving platter; pour the thickened sauce over them. Top with the carrots and celery.

Variation: Add up to 1 teaspoon red pepper flakes or up to 12 Chinese dried red chiles with the vinegar. (Be careful: the volatilized chili oils can burn your eyes.)

For an authentic dish, serve the fillets and sauce over steamed snow peas or sautéed greens.

Tips for Buying Fish and Shellfish

• Ask questions before you buy; there are few government standards for labeling or advertising. If your fishmonger seems uninformed, find another.

• Most of the fish and shellfish sold are flash-frozen on the trawler, a step that actually improves the quality. "Fresh" fish is usually labeled as such (although "fresh" can mean "freshly thawed"). A reputable fishmonger will know exactly when and where the fish was caught.

• Sometimes the whole fish is defrosted at a processing plant, cut into fillets, and then refrozen for the trip to your market. This double-dip in the freezer leads to microscopic ice crystals in the fish—and thus, mushy fish when cooked. If possible, ask for "once-frozen" fish.

• Fresh fish shimmers; it is never opaque. If the fish has any opalescence—that is, a rainbow-colored, oil-like slick—it has most likely been stored improperly.

• Smell fish or shellfish before you buy it. It should smell like high tide on a spring morning, never like the tidal flats on an August afternoon.

• If possible, don't buy fresh fish or shellfish in a sealed package. If your market only carries fresh fish this way, never purchase a package with water or liquid in it (a sign of ice crystals in the fish and perhaps of bacterial breakdown at thawing).

• The scales of a whole fish should be slightly sharp; they should hold together, not flake off. In most cases, the eyes should be clear and rounded; the gills, red and bright with no milky film.

• Keep fish and shellfish cold. Consider keeping an ice-pack or cooler in your car. And put fish in the refrigerator the moment you get it home. Fresh fish stores best below 40°F, a temperature most likely below that of your refrigerator. For the best results, store fish in the refrigerator in its paper wrapper on top of a colander filled halfway with ice, set over a bowl or baking pan to catch the drips.

• In most cases, cook fresh fish and shellfish the day you buy it.

Seven Ways to Bake Thin White-Fleshed Fish Fillets in Packets

By baking thin fillets in parchment packets, the fish gently poaches in its natural juices, which meld into a sauce. Here's a list of flavor combinations with the technique to follow. *Makes 4 servings (each ingredient list is divisible by four; place a quarter of each in each packet—see the technique on page 326).*

1. With Zucchini and Tomatoes

Four 4- to 6-ounce thin white-fleshed fish fillets

2 tablespoons olive oil

1 large zucchini, thinly sliced

12 cherry tomatoes, quartered

8 sun-dried tomatoes, slivered

2 teaspoons fennel seeds

½ teaspoon salt

¼ cup dry white wine or dry vermouth

2. With Artichokes and Olives

Four 4- to 6-ounce thin white-fleshed fish fillets

2 tablespoons olive oil

8 artichoke hearts canned in water, drained, rinsed, and halved

8 pitted black olives

2 garlic cloves, minced

¼ cup sliced almonds

2 teaspoons finely grated lemon zest

½ teaspoon salt

½ teaspoon freshly ground black pepper

¼ cup vegetable or fish broth

3. With Fennel, Tomatoes, and Rosemary

Four 4- to 6-ounce thin white-fleshed fish fillets

8 cherry tomatoes, quartered

1 medium fennel bulb, fronds and stalks removed, bulb trimmed and thinly sliced

2 tablespoons olive oil

4 garlic cloves, minced

Four 4-inch rosemary sprigs

1 teaspoon salt

½ teaspoon freshly ground black pepper

¼ cup vegetable or fish broth

4. With Deconstructed Pesto

Four 4- to 6-ounce thin white-fleshed fish fillets

2 tablespoons olive oil

24 basil leaves

8 sun-dried tomatoes, finely chopped

4 garlic cloves, minced

¼ cup pine nuts

1 ounce Parmigiano-Reggiano, finely grated

½ teaspoon salt

½ teaspoon freshly ground black pepper

5. With Fresh Corn Relish

Four 4- to 6-ounce thin white-fleshed fish fillets

2 ears corn, kernels removed

1 red bell pepper, cored, seeded, and thinly sliced

1 small red onion, thinly sliced

¼ cup chopped parsley leaves

½ teaspoon salt

¼ teaspoon freshly ground black pepper

¼ teaspoon red pepper flakes

2 tablespoons unsalted butter

¼ cup dry white wine

6. Japanese Style

Four 4- to 6-ounce thin white-fleshed fish fillets

1 carrot, peeled and finely shredded

6 ounces enoki mushrooms, cleaned

2 tablespoons minced peeled fresh ginger

1 teaspoon wasabi powder

2 tablespoons mirin

2 tablespoons dry sake

2 tablespoons soy sauce

7. Stir-Fry Style

Four 4- to 6-ounce thin white-fleshed fish fillets

4 ounces snow peas

8 scallions, cut into 2-inch sections

1 red bell pepper, cored, seeded, and thinly sliced

2 tablespoons minced peeled fresh ginger

2 tablespoons soy sauce

2 tablespoons rice vinegar

2 teaspoons toasted sesame oil

1 Position the rack in the center of the oven; preheat the oven to 450°F.

2 Lay four 12-inch pieces of parchment paper on the work surface. If you'd like extra security in holding the packets together, double the parchment paper, using two sheets for each.

3 Place a fish fillet in the middle of each parchment sheet. Divide the remaining ingredients on top of the fillets, sprinkling or adding them in the order listed.

4 Bring the two long sides of one sheet of parchment paper together; fold and crinkle to seal. Crinkle the ends closed and fold underneath. Make sure the packet is completely sealed; any gaps will result in steam leaks and dried-out fish fillets. Transfer the packet to a large lipped baking sheet and repeat with the other three.

5 Bake until hot and steaming, until the thin end of a fillet flakes with a fork, 15 to 20 minutes. (Unfortunately, there's no way to tell if the fish is done, short of opening one of the packets; be careful: the steam is very hot.) Remove the baking sheet from the oven and let the packets stand at room temperature for 5 minutes. Transfer directly to plates with a large metal spatula. Or serve the fish right from the packets on the plates. If you have children, unwrap theirs for them.

Packets on the Grill

Because the parchment paper can ignite, lay a 12-inch piece of aluminum foil under each parchment paper sheet, add the ingredients as indicated, and fold the foil and parchment together, making sure no bits of parchment are sticking up outside the foil seal. (Fold the two together; if you first fold the parchment closed and then the foil, the sauce will leak into the foil packet, rather than stay with the fish.) Set the foil packets directly over high heat or 4 to 6 inches from a high heat coal bed, cover the grill, and bake for 12 minutes. Let stand for 5 minutes before serving.

Four Escabeches

These cold, vinegary dishes ride the line between a first course and a main one. All follow a similar technique: sear the fish, make the sauce, and refrigerate together. As a first course, serve on toasted bread or crackers with cocktails (for the classics, see pages 54–55). As a main course, serve in lettuce cups, tortilla wraps, or alongside a platter of steamed asparagus or boiled potatoes. Escabeches are truly international, found in many countries across the globe; we've replicated the tastes with the modern supermarket in mind. For an explanation of nonreactive bowls, see page 42.

I. Spanish-Inspired Escabeche with Red Peppers and Saffron

Makes 4 main-course servings

1 cup all-purpose flour

¼ cup olive oil

2 pounds thin white-fleshed fish fillets

1 medium yellow onion, chopped

2 garlic cloves, minced

2 jarred roasted red bell peppers or jarred whole pimientos, shredded into thin strips

2 teaspoons stemmed thyme or 1 teaspoon
   dried thyme

¼ teaspoon saffron

1 cup sherry vinegar

2 bay leaves

1 teaspoon sugar

½ teaspoon salt

½ teaspoon freshly ground black pepper

❶ Place the flour in a shallow soup bowl. Heat 2 tablespoons olive oil in a large skillet set over medium heat. Pat the fillets dry with paper towels; then dredge them in the flour, shake off the excess, and slip them into the pan. Cook until well browned, about 3 minutes. Flip and continue cooking until lightly browned on the other side, about 1 more minute. Transfer the fillets to a cutting board and let stand for 5 minutes.

❷ Slice the fillets into ½-inch pieces and place these in a large nonreactive bowl or a glass baking dish. Set aside.

❸ Clean and dry the skillet, then return it to medium heat. Add the remaining 2 tablespoons olive oil, then toss in the onion. Cook, stirring often, until soft, about 2 minutes. Add the garlic and cook for 20 seconds.

❹ Stir in the shredded bell peppers or pimientos, thyme, and saffron. Cook, stirring constantly, for 1 minute. Pour in the vinegar and bring to a simmer, scraping up any browned bits off the pan's bottom. Add the bay leaves, sugar, salt, and pepper; simmer for 1 minute.

❺ Pour over the fish. Cover and refrigerate for at least 4 hours or up to 48 hours. To serve, discard the bay leaves and scoop up pieces of the fish along with the marinade and vegetables.

II. Southwestern Escabeche with Poblanos, Corn, and Cumin

Makes 4 main-course servings

1 cup all-purpose flour

¼ cup canola oil

2 pounds thin white-fleshed fish fillets

1 medium yellow onion, chopped

2 garlic cloves, minced

2 poblano chiles, seeded and chopped

2 ears corn, husked and the kernels cut off
   the cobs, or 1¾ cups frozen corn, thawed

¼ cup chopped dried cherries, blueberries,
   or cranberries

2 teaspoons chopped oregano leaves or
   1 teaspoon dried oregano

½ teaspoon cumin seeds

½ teaspoon salt

½ teaspoon freshly ground black pepper

1 cup cider vinegar

❶ Place the flour in a shallow soup bowl. Heat 2 tablespoons canola oil in a large skillet set over medium heat. Pat the fillets dry with paper towels; then dredge in the flour, shake off the excess, and slip into the pan. Cook until well browned, about 3 minutes. Flip and continue cooking until lightly browned on the other side, about 1 more minute. Transfer to a cutting board and let stand for 5 minutes.

❷ Slice the fillets into ½-inch pieces and place in a large nonreactive bowl or a glass baking dish. Set aside.

❸ Clean and dry the skillet; return it to medium heat. Add the remaining 2 tablespoons oil and then the onion. Cook, stirring often, until soft, about 2 minutes. Add the garlic and chiles; cook for 20 seconds.

❹ Stir in the corn and dried fruit or berries; then stir in the oregano, cumin seeds, salt, and pepper.

Cook, stirring constantly, for 15 seconds, then pour in the vinegar. Bring the mixture to a simmer and cook for 1 minute.

⑤ Pour over the fish. Cover and refrigerate for at least 4 hours or up to 48 hours. To serve, scoop up pieces of the fish along with the marinade and vegetables.

III. Filipino-Inspired Escabeche with Potatoes and Ginger

Makes 4 main-course servings

1 cup all-purpose flour
¼ cup peanut oil
2 pounds thin white-fleshed fish fillets
1 medium yellow onion, chopped
4 garlic cloves, minced
4 teaspoons minced peeled fresh ginger
2 medium yellow-fleshed potatoes, such as Yukon golds, peeled and cut into very small cubes, less than ½ inch
1 cup rice vinegar
3 tablespoons soy sauce

① Place the flour in a shallow soup bowl. Heat 2 tablespoons peanut oil in a large skillet set over medium heat. Pat the fillets dry with paper towels; then dredge in the flour, shake off the excess, and slip into the pan. Cook until well browned, about 3 minutes. Flip and continue cooking until lightly browned on the other side, about 1 more minute. Transfer to a cutting board and let stand for 5 minutes.

② Slice the fillets into ½-inch pieces and place in a large nonreactive bowl or a glass baking dish. Set aside.

③ Clean and dry the skillet; return it to medium heat. Add the remaining 2 tablespoons oil and toss in the onion. Cook, stirring often, until soft, about 2 minutes. Add the garlic and ginger; cook for 20 seconds.

④ Add the potatoes and cook, stirring very often, until lightly browned, about 5 minutes.

⑤ Pour in the rice vinegar and soy sauce. Bring the mixture to a simmer and cook for 1 minute, scraping up any browned bits on the bottom of the pan.

⑥ Pour over the fish. Cover and refrigerate for at least 4 hours or up to 48 hours. To serve, scoop up pieces of the fish along with the marinade and vegetables.

IV. Sweet-and-Sour Escabeche

Makes 4 main-course servings

1 cup all-purpose flour
¼ cup canola oil
2 pounds thin white-fleshed fish fillets
1 medium yellow onion, thinly sliced
8 dried figs, stemmed and thinly sliced
2 tablespoons pine nuts
1 teaspoon fennel seeds
½ teaspoon salt
¼ teaspoon grated nutmeg
1 cup white balsamic vinegar

① Place the flour in a shallow soup bowl. Heat 2 tablespoons canola oil in a large skillet set over medium heat. Pat the fillets dry with paper towels; then dredge in the flour, shake off the excess, and slip into the pan. Cook until well browned, about 3 minutes. Flip and continue cooking until lightly browned on the other side, about 1 more minute. Transfer to a cutting board and let stand for 5 minutes.

2 Slice the fillets into ½-inch pieces and place in a large nonreactive bowl or a glass baking dish. Set aside.

3 Clean and dry the skillet; return it to medium heat. Swirl in the remaining 2 tablespoons oil, then add the onion and figs. Cook, stirring often, until soft, about 2 minutes.

4 Stir in the pine nuts, fennel seeds, salt, and nutmeg. Cook, stirring constantly, for 15 seconds, then pour in the vinegar. Bring the mixture to a simmer and cook for 1 minute.

5 Pour over the fish. Cover and refrigerate for at least 4 hours or up to 48 hours. To serve, scoop up pieces of the fish along with the marinade and vegetables.

❋ *Thick White-Fleshed Fish Fillets:* *Cod, Scrod, Haddock, Grouper, Sturgeon, Pollock, and Halibut* ❋

Since thicker fish fillets can endure more substantial cooking, they're good for complex sauces, braises, and roasts. These fillets are remarkably similar, with a few caveats: cod has a strong taste, halibut is quite meaty, and grouper can be overcooked as quickly as any thin fish fillet. Scrod, by the way, is simply a small cod or haddock, weighing under 2½ pounds. There's an even wider range of cooking times here because the fillets come in different thicknesses. In all cases, watch carefully and go by the visual cues rather than the timing.

Thick White-Fleshed Fish Fillets Poached with Tomatoes and Cinnamon

This scented tomato stew is the perfect sauce for a meaty, thick-fleshed fish. Use a high-quality extra virgin olive oil since it's the finishing "sauce" on the fish. To serve, lay the fillets over Perfect Mashed Potatoes (page 473) or cooked rice, then ladle the sauce on top. *Makes 4 servings*

> 1 tablespoon unsalted butter
> 4 medium shallots, peeled and quartered
> 2 garlic cloves, slivered
> 1½ pounds fresh tomatoes, preferably Roma or plum tomatoes, chopped
> One 4-inch cinnamon stick
> ¼ teaspoon fennel seeds
> ¼ teaspoon salt
> ¼ teaspoon freshly ground black pepper
> Six 4- to 6-ounce thick white-fleshed fish fillets, skinned
> 2 tablespoons extra virgin olive oil

1 Melt the butter in a large, deep skillet over medium heat. Add the shallots and cook until soft and golden, stirring often, about 5 minutes. Add the garlic and cook for 30 seconds.

2 Add the tomatoes; tuck in the cinnamon stick. Stir in the fennel seeds, salt, and pepper. Bring the sauce to a simmer; then cover, reduce the heat to low, and simmer; until the tomatoes break down and create a sauce, stirring once in a while, about 20 minutes.

3 Remove the cinnamon stick and discard it. Nestle the fish into the tomatoes, drizzle it with olive oil, cover, and poach until the thick, opaque layers split evenly when pulled with a fork, 10 to 15 minutes.

Variations: Add 2 celery ribs, thinly sliced, or 1 carrot, diced, with the tomatoes.

Reduce the tomatoes to 1 pound and add 1 medium eggplant, peeled and diced, with them. For a taste like ratatouille, substitute 2 teaspoons chopped oregano leaves and 2 teaspoons stemmed thyme for the fennel seeds.

Add ½ teaspoon red pepper flakes with the fennel seeds.

Substitute 3 cups canned diced tomatoes with their juice for the fresh tomatoes; simmer only about 10 minutes with the herbs.

Substitute 1 star anise pod for the cinnamon stick.

Thick White-Fleshed Fish Fillets Poached in Artichoke Stew

This Mediterranean-inspired stew couldn't be easier, thanks to canned artichoke hearts. Serve it with rice or couscous on the side. *Makes 4 servings*

2 tablespoons olive oil
1 large onion, finely chopped
2 garlic cloves, minced
6 canned artichoke hearts packed in water, rinsed and halved
3 tablespoons chopped pitted black olives
1 tablespoon capers, drained, rinsed, and chopped
1 teaspoon chopped oregano leaves or ½ teaspoon dried oregano

1 teaspoon stemmed thyme or ½ teaspoon dried thyme
¼ teaspoon freshly ground black pepper
⅛ teaspoon saffron
1 cup dry white wine (do not use dry vermouth)
Two large 8- to 10-ounce thick white-fleshed fish fillets
¼ teaspoon salt, or to taste

1 Heat a large, high-sided sauté pan or a small Dutch oven over medium heat. Swirl in the olive oil, then add the onion and cook, stirring often, until translucent, about 3 minutes. Add the garlic and cook for 15 seconds.

2 Stir in the artichoke hearts, olives, capers, oregano, thyme, pepper, and saffron. Cook, stirring constantly, for 1 minute; then pour in the wine. Bring the sauce to a simmer, cover, reduce the heat to low, and cook for 5 minutes.

3 Nestle the fish into the sauce, cover again, and cook until the thick, opaque layers can be separated when pulled with a fork, 10 to 15 minutes. Taste the stew for salt, season if necessary, and cut the fillets in half before serving.

Variations: Substitute fresh baby artichokes, trimmed and halved, for the canned artichokes; cook, covered, in the sauce until tender, about 30 minutes.

Add the supremes from 1 orange and ½ teaspoon sugar with the artichoke hearts (see page 319, right column, steps 1 and 2, for directions on how to take the supremes from an orange). Also substitute red wine for the white wine.

For a roasted garlic taste, omit the individual garlic cloves and roast a whole garlic head (see page 460). Cool, then squeeze the garlic pulp into the sauce when you add the artichoke hearts.

Mushroom-Coated Thick White-Fleshed Fish Fillets with Wine and Olives

Finely ground dried mushrooms make an excellent crust; toasting them enhances their flavor. Halibut makes a nice, mild-tasting choice for this dish. If you use larger, 8- to 10-ounce cod or grouper fillets, cut them in half the short way for even cooking. *Makes 4 servings*

¾ ounce dried porcini mushrooms
1½ teaspoons flour
Four 4- to 6-ounce thick white-fleshed fish
    fillets
1 tablespoon olive oil
½ cup dry white wine
24 pitted green olives, halved
1 teaspoon stemmed thyme or ½ teaspoon
    dried thyme
1 tablespoon unsalted butter
¼ teaspoon salt, or to taste
Freshly ground black pepper to taste

❶ Place the dried mushrooms in a skillet, then set the pan over medium heat. Cook, stirring often, until quite aromatic, about 2 minutes. Transfer the mushrooms to a food processor fitted with the chopping blade and cool for 10 minutes. Add the flour; process until finely ground.

❷ Pat the fillets dry with paper towels, then massage the mushroom mixture evenly into the flesh.

❸ Heat a large skillet over medium heat. Swirl in the olive oil, then add the fish fillets. Shake the pan several times within the first few seconds to make sure the fillets aren't sticking, then cook until lightly browned, about 2 minutes. Flip and cook for 2 more minutes.

❹ Pour the wine into the pan without getting it on the fish. Sprinkle the olives around the pan and add the thyme. Bring the sauce to a simmer; then reduce the heat to low, cover, and simmer until the fish is firm to the touch and flakes when scraped lightly with a fork, 8 to 12 minutes.

❺ Transfer the fillets to four serving plates. Raise the heat to high and bring the sauce to a simmer. Cook until reduced to a glaze, about 2 minutes. Remove the pan from the heat, swirl in the butter until it melts, check the sauce to see if it needs any salt, and spoon it over the fish. Sprinkle each with a little ground pepper just before serving.

Variations: Use any variety of dried mushroom you want: chanterelles, shiitakes, morels, or a mixture. Substitute 3 tablespoons drained and rinsed capers for the olives.

Grilled Thick White-Fleshed Fish Fillets with Sesame Barbecue Glaze

We've adapted a traditional Chinese dumpling dip to become a sauce for grilled fish. See below for instructions on making this dish under a broiler. *Makes 4 servings*

Canola oil for the grill grate
Four 4- to 6-ounce thick white-fleshed fish
    fillets
Sesame Barbecue Glaze (recipe follows)

❶ Preheat a gas grill to high heat or prepare a high-heat, well-ashed coal bed in a charcoal grill.

❷ Generously oil the grill grate and set it 4 to 6 inches over the heat source or coal bed. Alternatively, generously oil a grilling basket.

③ Place the fish directly over the heat and brush generously with the Sesame Barbecue Glaze. Cover and grill until the thick, opaque layers can be separated evenly with a fork, 10 to 15 minutes, turning once with a wide spatula and mopping generously several times with the sauce.

To prepare this dish in the broiler: Place the fillets about 6 inches from a preheated broiler, mop with the Sesame Barbecue Glaze, then cook until the thick, opaque layers can be separated evenly with a fork, 11 to 14 minutes, turning once and mopping several times with the sauce.

Sesame Barbecue Glaze

You can also use this sauce for sea bass fillets; score the skin in several places with a sharp knife, then cook the fish as directed. It could also be used on marlin, swordfish, or mahimahi steaks. Or try it with chicken breasts on the grill. *Makes about ¾ cup*

  ¼ cup soy sauce
  ¼ cup rice vinegar
  2 scallions, minced
  2 garlic cloves, minced
  2 tablespoons minced peeled fresh ginger
  2 tablespoons sesame oil, preferably toasted sesame oil
  1 teaspoon chili oil
  1 teaspoon packed dark brown sugar

Place all the ingredients in a food processor fitted with the chopping blade; process until smooth. Or finely mince the vegetables and aromatics and stir all the ingredients in a medium bowl.

Thick White-Fleshed Fish Fillets Roasted over Caramelized Onions

Work carefully to get the onions golden and sweet, tending them over a low flame. *Makes 4 servings*

  ½ cup all-purpose flour
  1 teaspoon salt
  ½ teaspoon freshly ground black pepper
  3 tablespoons olive oil
  1 tablespoon unsalted butter
  3 large yellow onions, halved and very thinly sliced
  1 jarred roasted red pepper or jarred pimiento, cut into thin slices
  2 tablespoons chopped parsley leaves
  2 teaspoons chopped rosemary leaves or 1 teaspoon dried rosemary
  Four 4- to 6-ounce thick white-fleshed fish fillets, such as halibut or cod
  Aged balsamic vinegar or pomegranate molasses as garnish, optional

① Position the rack in the center of the oven and preheat the oven to 350°F. Whisk the flour, salt, and pepper on a serving plate or in a shallow soup bowl; set aside.

② Heat a large, deep, oven-safe skillet or sauté pan over medium-low heat. Add 2 tablespoons olive oil and the butter. The moment the butter's melted, add the onions, stir well, and reduce the heat to very low. Cook, stirring often, until golden and very soft, about 20 minutes. Do not let the onions brown; if they do, lower the heat further or remove the pan from the heat for a minute to stop the cooking.

③ Stir in the roasted pepper or pimiento, parsley, and rosemary; cook for 1 minute, stirring constantly.

④ Blot the fish fillets dry with paper towels. Dredge them in the flour mixture on all sides, coating evenly and shaking off the excess. Set them on top of the onions and drizzle the fillets with the remaining 1 tablespoon olive oil.

⑤ Place the pan in the oven and bake until the fish is lightly browned and firm to the touch, and until the thick, opaque layers can be pulled apart with a fork, 10 to 15 minutes. Drizzle individual servings with aged balsamic vinegar or pomegranate molasses, if desired.

Variations: For a stronger taste, substitute 8 medium shallots, peeled and thinly sliced, for the onions.

Omit the rosemary and add 1 teaspoon caraway seeds with the parsley.

Thick White-Fleshed Fish Fillets Roasted over Chard and Garlic

Place the garlic in the oil before you set the pan over the heat so that the slivers do not brown and turn bitter. *Makes 4 servings*

> Four 4- to 6-ounce thick white-fleshed fish fillets
> 5 tablespoons olive oil
> ½ teaspoon salt
> ½ teaspoon freshly ground black pepper
> 5 garlic cloves, slivered
> 1½ pounds Swiss chard, stems removed, leaves washed but not dried and then chopped
> 2 tablespoons white wine
> 2 tablespoons balsamic vinegar

① Position the rack in the center of the oven and preheat the oven to 450°F. Pat the fillets dry with paper towels, then rub them with 2 tablespoons olive oil. Sprinkle with salt and pepper; set aside.

② Place the remaining 3 tablespoons olive oil and the garlic in a large, oven-safe sauté pan or skillet. Set the pan over low heat and cook for 2 minutes, stirring often, taking care not to brown the garlic.

③ Raise the heat to medium and lay the wet greens in the pan. Count to ten, then toss with tongs to get the garlic strewn throughout the leaves. Sprinkle the wine over the greens, cover, and steam until wilted but not limp, tossing once or twice, about 3 minutes.

④ Uncover the pan and place the prepared fillets on top of the greens. Set the pan in the oven and roast until the opaque layers can be separated evenly when pulled with a fork, 10 to 15 minutes.

⑤ Remove the pan from the oven; drizzle the vinegar over the fillets and greens before serving.

Variation: Substitute other greens for the chard, like beet greens, escarole, or dandelion greens.

Thick White-Fleshed Fish Fillets Roasted over Potato Gratin

Slice the onions and potatoes thinly, less than ⅛ inch. A mandoline is admittedly the best tool for the job. Here, use a large fish fillet, which you will slice into pieces after baking. *Makes 4 servings*

> 4 tablespoons (½ stick) unsalted butter
> 1 large onion, very thinly sliced
> 1 pound large yellow-fleshed potatoes, such as Yukon golds, peeled and very thinly sliced
> 1 teaspoon stemmed thyme or ½ teaspoon dried thyme
> ½ teaspoon grated nutmeg
> ½ teaspoon freshly ground black pepper
> 1½ pounds large, thick white-fleshed fish fillets, such as halibut or cod
> ½ pound thinly sliced bacon
> 1½ cups half-and-half

1 Position the rack in the center of the oven and preheat the oven to 350°F.

2 Melt 2 tablespoons butter in a large skillet set over medium heat. Add the onion and cook, stirring often, until soft, about 5 minutes.

3 Meanwhile, melt the remaining 2 tablespoons butter in a small saucepan over low heat or in a small bowl in the microwave.

4 Spread the onions into the bottom of a 13 × 9-inch baking dish. Lay the potato slices over them, overlapping as necessary. Drizzle the melted butter over the potato slices. Sprinkle the thyme, nutmeg, and pepper over them.

5 Set the fish fillet on top of the potatoes. Cover the fish with the bacon, overlapping the strips as necessary and tucking them under the fillet. Place in the oven and bake for 10 minutes.

6 Pour the half-and-half around the fish in the dish, taking care not to get it on the bacon, but to get it all over the exposed potatoes.

7 Return to the oven and continue baking until the bacon is crisp, the potatoes are tender, and the fish is firm to the touch, 35 to 40 minutes. Let stand at room temperature for 5 minutes, then transfer the fish to a cutting board and slice into four servings. Divide the potatoes and onions among four plates and top with the bacon-wrapped fish.

Thick White-Fleshed Fish Fillets with Roasted Parsnips and Garlic

The oven-caramelized vegetables are used for a stew to poach the fish. If you can only find larger fillets—say, 10 ounces each—cut them in half the short way for even cooking here. Warm the dinner plates before you add the fish and vegetables to the sauce so the dish stays hot at the table. *Makes 4 servings*

> 4 large parsnips, peeled and cut into ½-inch-thick rounds
> 1 garlic head
> 2 tablespoons olive oil
> 1 cup dry white wine (do not use dry vermouth)
> 1 tablespoon chopped sage leaves or 1½ teaspoons rubbed sage
> ½ teaspoon salt
> ½ teaspoon freshly ground black pepper
> Four 4- to 6-ounce thick white-fleshed fish fillets, such as grouper, cod, or halibut

1 Position the rack in the center of the oven and preheat the oven to 375°F.

2 Place the parsnips in a small, shallow roasting pan. Break the garlic head into its separate cloves (do not peel); scatter among the parsnips. Drizzle with the olive oil, toss, and roast until the parsnips are tender and the garlic is soft, stirring occasionally, about 45 minutes. Cool on a wire rack for 10 minutes.

3 Squeeze the garlic cloves out of their husks and into a large skillet or sauté pan. Whisk in the wine until fairly smooth, then scoop the parsnips out of the roasting pan and into the sauce. Stir in the sage, salt, and pepper.

4 Set the skillet or sauté pan over medium-high heat and bring the sauce to a simmer. Add the fillets, cover, reduce the heat to low, and simmer slowly until tender, until the fish can be flaked with a fork, 10 to 15 minutes.

⑤ Transfer the fish fillets and parsnips to four serving plates. Raise the heat under the sauce and bring it to a boil. Cook until reduced to a glaze, about 2 minutes. Pour over the fish and parsnips.

Variations: Substitute carrots for the parsnips.

Substitute vegetable broth for the white wine— or use a combination of ½ cup wine and ½ cup broth.

For a richer sauce, whisk 1 or 2 tablespoons unsalted butter into the reducing sauce in step 5.

Thick White-Fleshed Fish Fillets with Avocado Salad and Warm Mustard Vinaigrette

This is the fanciest dish in this section, worthy of dinner-party fare. Don't salt the avocado salad; it will weep too much. Instead, let the vinaigrette carry the salt. You can also use bass fillets for this dish—if so, roast them skin side down. *Makes 4 servings*

½ cup all-purpose flour
½ teaspoon freshly ground black pepper
Four 4- to 6-ounce thick white-fleshed fish fillets, such as grouper or halibut
¼ cup olive oil
20 cherry tomatoes, quartered
The supremes from 2 large navel oranges (see instructions on page 319)
1 ripe Hass avocado, peeled, pitted, and diced
2 teaspoons finely chopped rosemary leaves
2 tablespoons white wine vinegar
2 teaspoons grainy or coarse-ground mustard
½ teaspoon salt

① Position the rack in the center of the oven and preheat the oven to 400°F. Whisk the flour and pepper on a serving plate or in a shallow soup bowl.

② Pat the fillets dry with paper towels; dredge them in the flour mixture, coating evenly but shaking off the excess.

③ Heat a large, oven-safe skillet over medium-high heat. Add 2 tablespoons olive oil, then slip the fillets into the pan. Shake the pan several times to make sure they haven't stuck, then place it in the oven and roast until the thick, opaque layers can be easily pulled apart with a fork, about 12 minutes.

④ Meanwhile, mix the tomatoes, orange supremes, avocado, and rosemary in a medium bowl. Divide among four serving plates, mounding to the center.

⑤ When the fillets are done, transfer them to the plates, setting them atop the avocado salad.

⑥ Set the same skillet over medium heat and add the remaining 2 tablespoons olive oil. Scrape up any browned bits in the pan, then whisk in the vinegar, mustard, and salt. Bring to a simmer, then spoon over the fillets.

These all require special preparation: some must be roasted with the skin on, some are easily overpowered by complex sauces, and some are just unique.

Trout Fillets with a Pecan-Mustard Crust

Trout is more fragile and sweeter than other fish. The skin is almost always left on, partly to keep the meat from falling apart and partly to impart flavor. Here, the skin crisps nicely, thanks to the ground nuts and this double technique: first on the stove, then in the oven. Grind the nuts to the same consistency as the bread crumbs. For a grilled or roasted whole trout, see page 354. *Makes 4 servings*

½ cup toasted pecan pieces, finely ground
¼ cup plain dried bread crumbs
1 teaspoon stemmed thyme or ½ teaspoon dried thyme
¼ teaspoon salt
¼ teaspoon freshly ground black pepper
Four 6- to 8-ounce skin-on gold, red, river, brook, or rainbow trout fillets
2 tablespoons Dijon mustard
2 tablespoons canola oil

1 Position the rack in the center of the oven and preheat the oven to 375°F. Mix the ground pecans, bread crumbs, thyme, salt, and pepper on a serving plate or in a shallow soup bowl.

2 Pat the fillets dry with paper towels, then smear the mustard over the flesh of each fillet.

3 Heat a large, oven-safe skillet over medium-high heat. Swirl in the canola oil. Dip the fillets into the bread-crumb mixture mustard side down, patting to make sure the coating adheres evenly. Slip them into the pan mustard side up (that is, skin side down). Cook for 1 minute.

4 Slide the skillet into the oven and cook until the crust is brown and the flesh underneath the crust flakes when gently scraped with a fork at its thinnest part, about 12 minutes. Let stand at room temperature for 5 minutes before transferring to serving plates.

Variation: Use any kind of mustard you prefer: coarse-grained, stone-ground, or even a flavored mustard (if you use the latter, omit the thyme from the bread-crumb mixture).

Bacon-Wrapped Trout Fillets Sandwiched with Spinach

The bacon strips will hold these trout fillets and their spinach filling together. *Makes 4 servings*

2 tablespoons olive oil
2 garlic cloves, minced
8 ounces spinach, stemmed (if necessary), washed, and chopped (the water still adhering to the leaves)
½ teaspoon salt
½ teaspoon freshly ground black pepper

¼ teaspoon grated nutmeg

1½ tablespoons plain dried bread crumbs

Four 6- to 8-ounce trout fillets

16 slices (about 12 ounces) thin-cut pork bacon, turkey bacon, or soy bacon

2 teaspoons white wine vinegar

1 Place the olive oil and garlic in a large skillet, then set the pan over low heat. Heat the oil slowly, stirring often, until the garlic is golden, about 2 minutes.

2 Raise the heat to medium, count slowly to five, and add the spinach. Toss well, cover, and reduce the heat to low. Cook until wilted, tossing once or twice, about 5 minutes. Season with salt, pepper, and nutmeg; then remove the pan from the heat and stir in the bread crumbs. Set aside to cool for 5 minutes.

3 Position the rack in the center of the oven and preheat the oven to 400°F.

4 Blot the fillets dry with paper towels, then cut each in half the short way. Lay 8 fillet halves skin side down on your work surface, then top each with a quarter of the stuffing (about 2 heaping tablespoons). Lay the other half of each fillet on top skin side up, thereby creating a trout sandwich.

5 Wrap 2 strips of bacon around each little sandwich, winding the strips around the short way so as to seal the sandwich closed, overlapping the strips as need be.

6 Set a large, oven-safe skillet over medium heat. Once it's hot, add the trout fillets with the bacon seams down. Brown the bacon on one side, turn the fillet sandwiches over, and brown on the other side, about 7 minutes in all.

7 Place the skillet in the oven and roast until the bacon is crispy and the trout flakes when picked with a fork, about 5 minutes. Let stand at room temperature for 5 minutes. Drizzle ½ teaspoon vinegar over each fillet before serving.

Variations: Substitute chard, escarole, or finely chopped kale for the spinach. (The kale will need to cook a little longer, perhaps 4 minutes or so; add a little wine or vegetable broth to the pan if it dries out.)

Stir 1 ounce finely grated Parmigiano-Reggiano or hard, aged Gouda into the spinach after it wilts.

Add up to ½ teaspoon red pepper flakes with the nutmeg.

Salmon Roast

Related to trout, wild salmon live in both salt and fresh water. Today, most of us buy farm-raised salmon; these live entirely in salt water. While more economical, they do not have the delicate taste of their wild kin. They're also fattier, and the fat is the place where toxins are mostly found. If you are going to eat farm-raised salmon, cut off the skin and any visible fat. For this elegant, dinner-party dish, 2 salmon fillets are tied around a creamy filling. *Makes 6 servings*

One 2-pound king (or chinook), coho (or silver), sockeye (or red), or Atlantic salmon fillet, skinned

One of the two fillings that follow

Butcher's twine

3 tablespoons olive oil

1 Position the rack in the center of the oven; preheat the oven to 400°F. Cut the salmon fillet in half the short way.

2 Place one half of the fillet on your work surface with the side down that would have had the skin on it. Spread one of the two fillings evenly over the fillet, mounding it toward a strip in the center; also leave a 1-inch border at each end. Top with the second half of the fillet, this time with the side that would have had the skin facing up. Tie together in four places with butcher's twine, pulling the sides together as well as you can to cover the filling. Make sure the ends are closed as well. Rub the outside with the olive oil. Set in a medium roasting pan.

③ Bake until the filling bubbles and the meat flakes at its thin ends when gently scraped with a fork, about 30 minutes. Let stand at room temperature for 10 minutes before slicing off the twine and carving the roast into thick, round slices.

Feta Filling

> One 10-ounce package frozen chopped spinach, thawed and squeezed dry of all moisture
> 8 ounces feta, crumbled
> 2 tablespoons chopped dill fronds or 1 tablespoon dried dill
> 1 tablespoon lemon juice
> ½ teaspoon salt
> ½ teaspoon freshly ground black pepper
> ½ teaspoon grated nutmeg

Mash the cheese in a medium bowl with a fork, then stir in the dill, lemon juice, salt, pepper, and nutmeg to create a gooey mixture.

Crab Filling

> 8 ounces lump crabmeat, picked over for shell and cartilage
> 1 ounce Asiago or Parmigiano-Reggiano, grated
> ¼ cup olive oil
> ¼ cup plain dried bread crumbs
> 1 medium shallot, minced
> 2 garlic cloves, minced
> 2 teaspoons chopped oregano leaves or 1 teaspoon dried oregano
> ½ teaspoon salt
> ¼ teaspoon freshly ground black pepper

Mix all the ingredients in a large bowl, taking care not to break up the crabmeat but getting the bread crumbs thoroughly moistened and distributed in the mixture.

Salmon Roast for Crowds
Double this roast by purchasing two 2-pound fillets; do not slice them in half. Rather, double the amount of filling and top one with the other, so the sides that would have had the skin are both facing out. Roast about 45 minutes.

Salsa Salmon

Salmon is best when it's slightly underdone, with a pink, warm center. One way to tell is to use a fork to flake the meat. Another is to insert a flatware knife into the meat at the thickest part, hold the knife there for 5 seconds, then touch the side of the blade to your lips: it should feel warm, not cool or hot. In this recipe, roasting salmon under fresh salsa keeps the meat incredibly moist. *Makes 4 servings*

> Canola oil for the baking sheet
> One 2-pound king (or chinook), coho (or silver), sockeye (or red), or Atlantic salmon fillet, skin on or off, left whole or cut the short way into 4 equal pieces
> 2 medium tomatoes, quartered
> 1 medium shallot, quartered
> 1 serrano chile, halved and seeded
> 1 garlic clove, halved
> 2 teaspoons lime juice
> 1 teaspoon chili powder
> 1 teaspoon ground cumin
> ½ teaspoon salt
> ½ teaspoon freshly ground black pepper
> Several dashes of hot red pepper sauce to taste

① Lightly oil a large baking sheet or roasting pan. Place the salmon fillet or fillets skin side down (or former skin side down) in the pan. Set aside.

2 Place the tomatoes, shallot, serrano chile, garlic, lime juice, chili powder, cumin, salt, pepper, and hot red pepper sauce in a food processor fitted with the chopping blade. Pulse until coarsely ground, like a chunky salsa. If you prefer an even chunkier salsa, chop all these vegetables by hand; some will remain crunchy after baking.

3 Spoon over the exposed salmon flesh, spreading it to the sides. Cover the pan loosely with plastic wrap and refrigerate for at least 15 minutes or up to 1 hour.

4 Position the rack in the center of the oven and preheat the oven to 400°F. Take the salmon out of the refrigerator while the oven preheats.

5 Uncover and bake until hot, until the meat can be pulled into opaque, moist layers with a fork, about 12 minutes for individual pieces or 25 minutes if the fillet has been left whole. Let stand at room temperature for 5 minutes before serving.

Variation: Use about 1¹/₂ cups of any salsa you like, purchased or homemade (see page 47).

Other salmon recipes are those for salmon steaks (pages 345–349), Gravlax (page 75), Poached Salmon Salad (page 120), or Salmon Burgers (page 355).

Skinning and Deboning Salmon

For tips on skinning a salmon fillet, see the Note on page 75. Often, small, quill-like bones are left in a fillet. Run your hand gently over the meat to see if there are any—but be careful: the bones can pierce your fingers. When you find some, pull them out with a pair of sterilized tweezers or kitchen pliers.

Bass in a Fennel Broth

Here, you cook the bass in an aromatic onion broth but serve it in a much more delicate fennel broth. *Makes 6 servings*

8 cups (2 quarts) vegetable broth
4 fennel bulbs, trimmed, with the small
    feathery fronds minced and reserved
3 cups water
¼ cup dry white wine or dry vermouth
1 large onion, quartered
1 celery rib, cut into chunks
10 black peppercorns
4 parsley sprigs
Six 4- to 6-ounce skin-on black, striped,
    spotted, or sea bass fillets (see Note)
½ teaspoon kosher or sea salt, or to taste

1 Pour the broth into a large saucepan and set it over high heat. Thinly slice the fennel and add it to the broth once it comes to a boil. Cover tightly, reduce the heat to very low, and simmer very slowly for 1 hour. Strain over a large bowl, then pour back into the large saucepan. Set aside, covered, off the heat. Discard the sliced fennel.

2 Combine the water, wine or vermouth, onion, celery, peppercorns, parsley, and salt in a medium saucepan set over high heat. Bring the mixture to a boil, cover, reduce the heat to low, and simmer very slowly for 30 minutes.

3 Strain the onion mixture through a fine-mesh sieve and into a large sauté pan or high-sided skillet; set over medium-high heat and bring to a simmer. Also place the fennel infusion in its saucepan over medium-low heat.

4 Score the skin on the bass fillets in three or four places with a sharp knife. Slip them into the strained onion broth, cover, and poach until the fillets are opaque and can be flaked at their thinnest part with a fork, about 5 minutes.

⑤ Gently transfer the fillets to four large soup bowls. Ladle the hot fennel broth over them. Sprinkle a few feathery fennel fronds over each bowl and garnish with salt.

Note: The name "bass" is tossed onto a variety of fish, from fresh and saltwater, many of them not true bass. Sea bass, for example, is actually a member of the grouper family. Do not use Chilean sea bass (aka Patagonian toothfish), a deep-water predator now almost fished to extinction.

Variations: Substitute 2 large peeled sweet potatoes, cut into 1/2-inch-thick wheels, for the fennel.

Substitute 1 large turnip, peeled and cut into 1/2-inch wheels, 1 large parsnip, peeled and cut into 1/2-inch rounds; and 1 large carrot, peeled and cut into 1/2-inch rounds for three of the fennel bulbs. Add these vegetables with the remaining fennel bulb.

Substitute salmon for the bass (score the skin as well).

Bass with Apples, Cabbage, and Warm Cumin Vinaigrette

This elegant dish is made in three parts: the vegetable mixture, the fish with its crisped skin, and the vinaigrette. *Makes 4 servings*

> 2 tablespoons unsalted butter
> 1 small yellow onion, thinly sliced
> 1 medium tart apple, such as a Granny Smith or a Pippin, peeled, cored, and diced
> 2 garlic cloves, minced
> One 1-pound head Savoy cabbage, cored and shredded
> 1 2/3 cups canned chickpeas, drained and rinsed

> 2 cups dry white wine or dry vermouth
> 1 teaspoon salt
> 1/2 teaspoon freshly ground black pepper
> Four 4- to 6-ounce skin-on black, striped, spotted, or sea bass fillets (see Note of previous recipe)
> 1/4 cup olive oil
> 1 small red onion, minced
> 1 teaspoon crushed cumin seeds
> 1 1/2 tablespoons white wine vinegar
> 2 teaspoons lime juice

① Melt the butter in a large saucepan set over medium heat. Add the yellow onion; cook, stirring often, until translucent, about 3 minutes. Add the apple and 1 minced garlic clove; cook until softened, about 1 minute.

② Add the cabbage and chickpeas; stir over the heat until the cabbage begins to wilt, about 1 minute.

③ Pour in the wine or vermouth; add 1/2 teaspoon salt and 1/4 teaspoon pepper. Raise the heat to high and bring the mixture to a simmer. Reduce the heat and simmer slowly, uncovered, until the cabbage is soft and the wine has mostly evaporated, about 20 minutes.

④ Meanwhile, position the rack in the center of the oven and preheat the oven to 400°F.

⑤ Once the cabbage mixture is done, cover the pan and set aside off the heat to keep warm. Score the bass skin in three or four places on each fillet, then blot dry with paper towels.

⑥ Heat 2 tablespoons olive oil in a large, oven-safe skillet. Season the fillets with the remaining 1/2 teaspoon salt and 1/4 teaspoon pepper. Place them skin side down in the skillet and cook for 1 minute, shaking the skillet repeatedly so they don't stick.

7 Place the skillet in the oven and roast until the thin part of a fillet flakes when gently scraped with a fork, about 12 minutes. Meanwhile, mound the warm cabbage mixture on four serving plates.

8 Remove the skillet from the oven and place the fillets on top of the vegetables skin side up. Tent very loosely with aluminum foil to keep warm.

9 Place the skillet over medium-high heat and add the remaining 2 tablespoons olive oil. Add the red onion and cook, stirring often, until softened, about 2 minutes.

10 Add the remaining minced garlic clove and the cumin seeds. Cook, stirring all the while, until aromatic, about 20 seconds. Pour in the vinegar and lime juice. Bring to a simmer and immediately spoon this dressing over the fish on the plates.

Variations: Add 1 tablespoon minced peeled fresh ginger with the cabbage.

Substitute 2 cups jarred roasted chestnuts, quartered, for the chickpeas.

Monkfish Braised in White Wine with Leeks and Pancetta

More properly called "angler fish," this hideously ugly creature traps lobster, crab, and smaller fish in its cavernous mouth by twitching a wormlike lure from its head. The only part of the fish that we can eat is the tail, which makes for a silken, gelatinous fillet that tastes like spiny or Pacific lobster. *Makes 4 servings*

3 tablespoons unsalted butter
8 ounces pancetta, diced
1 large leek, dark green part removed, the
   rest halved, washed of any internal grit,
   and thinly sliced
2 cups dry white wine

2 teaspoons chopped rosemary leaves
1 bay leaf
1½ to 2 pounds monkfish fillet, cut into
   4 pieces
1 tablespoon chopped parsley leaves

1 Position the rack in the center of the oven and preheat the oven to 450°F.

2 Melt 1 tablespoon butter in a large ovenproof skillet set over medium heat. Add the pancetta; cook, stirring often, until crisp, about 4 minutes.

3 Add the leek and cook until soft, stirring often, about 3 minutes.

4 Pour in the wine and scrape up any browned bits on the pan's bottom. Add the rosemary and bay leaf, bring the sauce to a simmer over medium-high heat, and cook until reduced by half, about 4 minutes.

5 Place the fish in the skillet, then place the skillet in the oven. Bake for 5 minutes, then turn the pieces over and continue baking until firm and opaque, until a flatware knife inserted into the thickest part of the fillet and held there for 5 seconds feels warm to your lips (a gelatinous center) or hot (a firm center), about 5 to 10 minutes.

6 Transfer the monkfish pieces to four serving plates. Return the skillet to medium-high heat and bring the sauce to a boil. Swirl in the remaining 2 tablespoons butter in two additions, then add the parsley and spoon the sauce over the fish.

Variation: For a more classic French dish, substitute red wine for the white wine.

Italian-Inspired Monkfish Ragù

This is a streamlined version of a traditional Trieste stew. It's great over pasta, polenta, or Perfect Mashed Potatoes (page 473) or Root Vegetable Mash (page 473). *Makes 6 servings*

2 tablespoons olive oil
1 large yellow onion, chopped
2 celery ribs, thinly sliced
1 fennel bulb, trimmed of its fronds, thinly sliced, and chopped
1 Italian frying pepper or green bell pepper, seeded and chopped
3 garlic cloves, minced
3 cups canned diced tomatoes with their juice
1½ cups vegetable broth
3 tablespoons tomato paste
2 teaspoons stemmed thyme or 1 teaspoon dried thyme
1 teaspoon fennel seeds
½ teaspoon salt, plus additional to taste
½ teaspoon freshly ground black pepper
¼ teaspoon red pepper flakes
2 pounds monkfish fillet, cut into 1-inch chunks
1 tablespoon red wine vinegar

❶ Heat a large saucepan over medium heat, then swirl in the olive oil. Add the onion and celery; cook, stirring often, until softened and aromatic, about 3 minutes.

❷ Add the fennel and continue cooking for 1 minute, stirring often.

❸ Add the frying or green pepper and garlic; cook for 20 seconds.

❹ Pour in the tomatoes and broth, scrape up any browned bits on the pan's bottom, and bring the mixture to a simmer over medium-high heat.

❺ Whisk in the tomato paste until dissolved; then stir in the thyme, fennel seeds, salt, pepper, and red pepper flakes. Cover, reduce the heat to low, and simmer slowly until the vegetables are very tender and the sauce has thickened, about 1 hour, stirring occasionally.

❻ Stir in the monkfish, cover, and cook just until the chunks are opaque, about 5 minutes. Stir in the vinegar and season with salt before serving.

Variation: Add 1 pound Swiss chard, spinach, or escarole, stemmed or cored, washed, and the leaves roughly chopped, with the monkfish.

Seared Mackerel Fillets with Radicchio, Cranberries, and Port

Any variety of mackerel will do in this recipe but smell the fillets to make sure the aroma is not too strong. They need a preparation with bold flavors—here, a combination of bitter, sour, and sweet. *Makes 4 servings*

½ cup all-purpose flour
1 teaspoon salt, plus more as desired
½ teaspoon freshly ground black pepper
2 tablespoons olive oil
Four 4- to 6-ounce skin-on or skinless mackerel fillets
1 medium shallot, minced
½ cup chopped fresh cranberries
3 cups shredded radicchio (see page 97)
¼ cup vegetable or fish broth
¼ cup port

1 Mix the flour, salt, and pepper on a serving plate. Heat a large skillet over medium heat, then swirl in the olive oil. Dredge the fillets in the flour mixture, coating both sides and shaking off any excess, then slip them into the pan.

2 Cook until lightly browned, about 3 minutes. Flip and continue cooking until the thin part of the fillet flakes when gently scraped with a fork, about 3 more minutes. Use a large metal spatula to gently transfer the fillets to four serving plates or a serving platter; tent loosely with aluminum foil to keep warm.

3 Add the shallot to the skillet; cook, stirring constantly, just until barely softened, about 30 seconds. Add the cranberries; cook, stirring often, for 1 minute.

4 Add the radicchio; cook, tossing with two wooden spoons or tongs, until wilted, about 3 minutes.

5 Pour in the broth and port, raise the heat to medium-high, and bring to a simmer, scraping up the browned bits on the pan's bottom. Simmer until the radicchio is tender, less than 1 minute. Check to see if the sauce needs more salt, then spoon over the fillets.

Variations: Add 2 garlic cloves, minced, with the cranberries.

Substitute sweet vermouth or cream sherry for the port.

Drizzle a little balsamic vinegar or red wine vinegar over the dish just before you serve it.

Black Cod with Coconut and Ginger

Black cod—also known as sable—is an oily fish, rich enough to pair with this sweet, spicy coconut rub. *Makes 4 servings*

Canola oil for greasing the baking dish
½ cup shredded unsweetened desiccated coconut (see page 656)
1 teaspoon ground ginger
¼ teaspoon cayenne pepper
Two 10-ounce black cod fillets, skinned
2 tablespoons lime juice
½ teaspoon salt

1 Position the rack in the center of the oven and preheat the oven to 400°F. Lightly oil a 13 × 9-inch baking dish; set aside.

2 Place the coconut, ginger, and cayenne in a mini food processor, a regular food processor fitted with the chopping blade, or a large spice grinder. Grind until the consistency of cornmeal.

3 Pat the fillets dry with paper towels, then rub them with the lime juice and salt. Pat the coconut mixture all over the fillets, coating them evenly. Place in the prepared baking dish.

4 Bake until lightly browned, until a flatware knife inserted into the thick part of a fillet and held there for 5 seconds feels warm to your lips (for a gelatinous fillet) or hot (for a firmer fillet), 10 to 13 minutes.

Variations: For a sweeter crust, add 1 teaspoon packed light brown sugar with the coconut.

Substitute lemon juice for the lime juice.

Reduce the lime juice to 1 tablespoon and add 1 tablespoon gold or white rum with the remaining lime juice on the fillets.

Fried Sardines

Fresh sardines are nothing like canned ones. Fried with a semolina coating, they make a light main course. *Makes 4 servings*

¼ cup olive oil
¾ cup all-purpose flour
¼ cup semolina or finely ground yellow
　　cornmeal
12 whole sardines, scaled and cleaned
1 teaspoon kosher or coarse-grained sea salt
½ teaspoon freshly ground black pepper
2 lemons, halved

❶ Heat the olive oil in a large, deep skillet, sauté pan, or wok set over medium-high heat until there are a few ripples across its surface.

❷ Meanwhile, mix the flour and semolina on a large plate. Pat the sardines dry with paper towels, then dredge them in this flour mixture, coating both sides evenly and thoroughly. Shake off any excess.

❸ Slip the sardines one at a time into the oil, holding them by the tails and lowering them slowly into the oil. Work in batches, if the skillet or wok is not big enough to hold them all comfortably in one layer.

❹ Fry until golden on both sides, turning once or twice with a metal spatula, about 6 minutes. Transfer to a wire rack. Season with salt and pepper. Let stand at room temperature for 5 minutes, then serve each with a lemon half to be squeezed over the fish.

To eat the sardines, use a fork to pull the meat down off the spine, pulling it off the tiny bones as you rake it onto your plate. Always check for bones before eating.

Variations: Season the flour with 2 teaspoons dried oregano and/or 1 teaspoon dried thyme.

Serve the sardines with red pepper flakes on the side for garnishing.

Omit the salt and pepper. Instead, mix 2 tablespoons kosher or coarse-grained sea salt with 1 teaspoon freshly ground black pepper. Place in a small bowl and set this in the middle of the table as a "dip" for the sardines as everyone debones and eats them.

Skate with Potatoes and Garlic

Skate wing is traditionally browned in butter, then served with a simple sauce. We prefer a meat-and-potatoes approach that doesn't mask the delicate taste. *Makes 4 servings*

¼ cup olive oil
3 pounds yellow-fleshed potatoes, such as
　　Yukon golds, cut into very small, ½-inch
　　pieces
6 garlic cloves, minced
2 teaspoons chopped oregano leaves or
　　1 teaspoon dried oregano
1 tablespoon white wine vinegar
2 cups vegetable or fish broth
Two 1-pound skate wings, each cut in half
　　into separate, fanlike "wings"
½ teaspoon salt, or to taste

❶ Heat a large, deep skillet or sauté pan over medium heat. Pour in the olive oil, then add the potatoes. Cooking, stirring often, until the potatoes have started to brown and are getting a crunchy crust, about 12 minutes.

❷ Add the garlic; cook, stirring constantly, for 1 minute. Add the oregano and vinegar; stir well over the heat for 10 seconds. Pour in the broth and scrape up any browned bits on the pan's bottom. Bring the mixture to a full simmer.

③ Lay the skate-wing pieces over the potatoes. Cover, reduce the heat to medium-low, and steam until the thin parts of the wings flake when gently scraped with a fork and until the potatoes are tender, about 5 minutes. Season with salt before serving. Scoop up the wings and potato stew with a large ladle or spatula and serve in bowls.

Variations: Add 1 carrot, finely diced, with the garlic.

Substitute 2 teaspoons chopped rosemary leaves or 1 teaspoon dried rosemary, crushed, for the oregano.

Reduce the broth to 1 cup and add 1 cup dry white wine with the remaining broth.

❋ Fish Steaks: Marlin, Tuna, Mahimahi, Swordfish, Halibut, Opah, or Salmon Steaks ❋

Not all fish flakes. Some deepwater fish is so meaty, it can be sliced into steaks. And salmon can be sliced through the body, rather than along the spine, thereby creating steaklike cuts. Any of these fish steaks will work in most of the recipes; a few recipes at the end of this section were designed for a specific type of fish.

Asian-Inspired Fish Steaks with Ginger Butter

Marinate the fish steaks first with ginger, soy sauce, and a few other Asian ingredients; once they are cooked, top them with this spicy butter. *Makes 4 servings*

- 4 tablespoons (½ stick) unsalted butter, cut into several pieces, at room temperature
- 2 tablespoons minced peeled fresh ginger
- 2 tablespoons minced chives or the green part of a scallion
- Four 6- to 8-ounce marlin, tuna, mahimahi, swordfish, halibut, opah, or salmon steaks, about 1 inch thick
- 2 tablespoons Shaoxing or dry sherry
- 2 tablespoons soy sauce
- 2 teaspoons rice vinegar
- 2 teaspoons sugar
- 1 tablespoon canola oil

① Use a fork to mash the butter, ginger, and chives or scallion in a small bowl until the herbs are well mixed into the softening butter. Cover and refrigerate for at least 2 hours or up to 2 days.

② Place the fish steaks in a baking dish just large enough to hold them compactly without overlapping. Whisk the Shaoxing or sherry, soy sauce, rice vinegar, and sugar in a small bowl until the sugar dissolves. Pour over the steaks; turn to coat. Cover and refrigerator for 2 to 3 hours.

③ Heat a large grill pan or skillet over medium-high heat (see Note). Add the canola oil, tilt the skillet to coat, and slip the steaks into the pan. Shake the pan several times during the first 30 seconds of cooking to make sure they don't stick. Cook until lightly browned, 3 to 4 minutes. Flip and continue cooking until somewhat firm to the touch and lightly browned, 3 to 4 more minutes.

④ Transfer the steaks to four individual serving plates or a serving platter. Top each with a quarter of the butter mixture (about 1½ tablespoons per steak).

Note: If the steaks won't fit in one skillet, use two skillets—but double the oil, putting 1 tablespoon in each. Or work in batches in one skillet, adding another tablespoon of oil after you remove the first batch of steaks.

Four More Butter Combinations for Fish Steaks

Flavored butters are wonderful on fish steaks. Keep one or two on hand in the freezer, tightly wrapped in plastic, for 2 months so they're ready for fish steaks. Omit the Asian marinade above in step 2 and simply pan-sear the steaks, using the technique in step 3. Substitute any of these compound butters for the ginger butter.

1. *Lemon Parsley Butter*

- 4 tablespoons (½ stick) unsalted butter, cut into several pieces
- 2 tablespoons minced parsley leaves
- 1 tablespoon lemon juice

2. *Mushroom Butter*

- 4 tablespoons (½ stick) unsalted butter, cut into several pieces
- ¼ ounce dried porcini, shiitake, chanterelle, or morel mushrooms, toasted in a dry skillet over medium heat, then ground to a fine powder in a mini-food processor
- ½ teaspoon freshly ground black pepper

3. *Walnut Butter*

- 4 tablespoons (½ stick) unsalted butter, cut into several pieces
- ¼ cup toasted walnut pieces, ground to a powder in a mini-food processor

4. *Wasabi Butter*

- 4 tablespoons (½ stick) unsalted butter, cut into several pieces
- 2 teaspoons prepared wasabi paste

Pepper-Crusted Fish Steaks with Sweet-and-Sour Barbecue Glaze

Peppercorns lose their zing over time; make sure yours are fresh, within six months of purchase.
Makes 4 servings

- 1 tablespoon black peppercorns
- Four 6- to 8-ounce marlin, tuna, mahimahi, swordfish, halibut, opah, or salmon steaks, about 1 inch thick
- Canola oil for the grill grate or the grill pan
- Sweet-and-Sour Barbecue Glaze (recipe follows)

① Crush the peppercorns to a fairly fine powder in a mortar using a pestle, or in a sealed plastic bag using the bottom of a heavy saucepan or the smooth side of a meat mallet. Press the peppercorns into the fish steaks; set aside.

② Preheat a gas grill for high-heat cooking or prepare a high-heat well-ashed coal bed in a charcoal grill. Alternatively, heat a grill pan over medium-high heat.

③ Generously oil the grill grate and set it 4 to 6 inches over the heat, or swirl a little oil into the grill pan. Place the steaks directly over the heat source on the grill or in the grill pan. Mop with the Sweet-and-Sour Barbecue Glaze; grill or cook for 3 to 4 minutes, basting the top of the steaks one more time with the glaze as they cook.

④ Flip the steaks, baste again with the glaze, and grill or cook until lightly browned and marked, mopping one more time, about 3 minutes (see Note).

Note: The timing here will produce medium-rare steaks: ones with a warm center, pink or milky depending on the fish. If you prefer a steak to be more done, leave it on the grill about 1 additional minute per side. For a less done steak—particularly good for tuna, but resulting in a cool red center—shave 1 minute off the cooking time after you flip the steaks. If you prefer rare fish steaks, make sure they are fresh; ask if they are "sushi-quality."

Sweet-and-Sour Barbecue Glaze

Great with tuna on the grill, this glaze can match a range, from marlin to mahimahi, and can also be used for chicken, turkey, or pork on the grill. *Makes ¾ cup*

> ¼ cup soy sauce
> ¼ cup lemon juice
> ¼ cup honey

Whisk the ingredients in a small bowl until the honey is dissolved. (The sauce can be made ahead and stored, covered, in the refrigerator for up to 1 week.)

Blackened Fish Steaks

Culinary guru James Peterson has an excellent technique for this Cajun classic: he coats only one side of the steaks in the spice rub, allowing you better control so the spices won't burn and become bitter. You'll need two skillets: one to get smoking hot and the other to finish the steaks at a lower temperature. Use only dried herbs in this rub; fresh herbs will burn and turn bitter. *Makes 4 servings*

> Four 6- to 8-ounce marlin, tuna, mahimahi, swordfish, halibut, opah, or salmon steaks, about 1 inch thick
> 5 tablespoons peanut oil
> 1 teaspoon dried oregano
> 1 teaspoon dried thyme
> 1 teaspoon dried marjoram
> ½ teaspoon sugar
> ¼ teaspoon cayenne pepper
> ¼ teaspoon celery seed
> ¼ teaspoon salt

① Pat the fish steaks dry with paper towels, then rub 1 tablespoon canola oil into them.

② Mix the oregano, thyme, marjoram, sugar, cayenne, celery seed, and salt in a small bowl. Rub each steak on one side only with a quarter of the spice mixture. Set aside spiced side up.

③ Heat a large skillet, preferably cast iron, over medium-high heat until smoking, about 5 minutes. Add 2 tablespoons oil, then the fish spiced side down. Cook for 90 seconds. Meanwhile, heat another skillet over medium-low heat.

④ Swirl the remaining 2 tablespoons oil into the second skillet. Transfer the steaks from the very hot skillet into the second one, flipping them spiced side up (but gently so as to preserve the crust). Cook until aromatic and somewhat firm to the touch, about 5 minutes for a medium-rare center, 6 minutes for a medium center, and 8 minutes for a well-done center.

Variations: Substitute dried parsley for the marjoram.

Substitute fennel seeds for the celery seeds.

Increase the cayenne to ½ teaspoon—but make sure the stove vent is running at full speed: the chili oils will volatilize and can burn your eyes.

Venetian-Style Tuna Steaks with Sweet, Vinegary Onions

Here's a seared tuna steak topped with a sweet-and-sour Venetian mélange. *Makes 4 servings*

Four 6- to 8-ounce tuna steaks, about 1 inch thick
1 teaspoon kosher or coarse-grained sea salt
¼ cup olive oil
1 large yellow onion, chopped
½ cup red wine vinegar
2 tablespoons sugar
2 teaspoons chopped oregano leaves or 1 teaspoon dried oregano
1 teaspoon freshly ground black pepper

❶ Rub the tuna steaks with the salt and set aside.

❷ Heat a large grill pan, a deep skillet, or a high-sided sauté pan over medium heat. Add the olive oil, then slip the tuna steaks into the pan. Cook until lightly browned, about 3 minutes. Flip and cook for 1 more minute for a rare center, 2 minutes for a medium-rare center, and 4 minutes for a well-done center. Transfer the steaks to a plate and tent with aluminum foil to keep warm.

❸ Reduce the heat to low and add the onion to the pan. Cook, stirring often, until golden, caramelized, and soft, about 8 minutes.

❹ Whisk in the vinegar and sugar, stirring until the sugar dissolves. Raise the heat to medium-high and bring the sauce to a simmer. Toss in the oregano and pepper; cook, stirring once in a while, until reduced to a glaze, about 3 minutes.

❺ Slip the steaks back into the pan; cover and set aside off the heat for 1 minute to reheat.

Coconut-Crusted Salmon Steaks

The East Indian–influenced spice paste caramelizes over the rich steaks, creating a luxurious dish. *Makes 4 servings*

2 serrano chiles, halved and seeded
2 medium shallots, roughly chopped
One 2-inch section peeled fresh ginger, cut into 4 pieces
3 tablespoons coconut milk
2 tablespoons lemon juice
1 tablespoon tomato paste
1 teaspoon dry mustard
1 teaspoon packed light brown sugar
½ teaspoon salt
⅛ teaspoon ground cloves
Four 1½- to 2-inch-thick salmon steaks (see Note)

❶ Place the chiles, shallots, ginger, coconut milk, lemon juice, tomato paste, dry mustard, brown sugar, salt, and cloves in a mini-food processor, a regular food processor fitted with the chopping blade, or a blender. Process or blend until paste-like, scraping down the sides of the canister as necessary. Alternatively, grind the spices and aromatics in a mortar with a pestle, adding the liquids slowly to incorporate as you grind.

2 Spread the mixture evenly over the salmon steaks. Cover and refrigerate for at least 30 minutes or up to 2 hours.

3 Preheat the broiler. Line the broiler pan or a large baking sheet with aluminum foil to make cleanup easier. Transfer the salmon steaks to the prepared pan or sheet, taking care not to knock off the paste.

4 Broil about 6 inches from the heat source until very aromatic and somewhat firm, about 5 minutes. Turn and continue broiling until very browned, about 4 minutes for rare steaks, 6 minutes for medium, and 8 minutes for well done. You can also check the doneness by flaking the side of one steak with a fork. Let stand at room temperature for a couple of minutes before serving.

To grill the salmon steaks: Generously oil the grill grate, then set it 4 to 6 inches over a high heat or a high-heat, well-ashed coal bed. Add the coated steaks directly over the heat, cover, and grill for 10 to 14 minutes.

Note: Some markets now sell salmon steaks made from boneless, skinless salmon fillets, wrapped in netting so they look like more traditional salmon steaks. These should be cooked about 1 minute less per side.

For other tuna ideas, consider Tuna Tartare on Gaufrettes (page 77), a Fresh Tuna Salad (page 119), or Tuna Burgers (page 355).

Swordfish Kabobs with Walnut Paprika Barbecue Sauce

Swordfish is meaty enough to be skewered and topped with a barbecue sauce of walnuts, paprika, and beer. *Makes 4 servings*

1½ pounds swordfish steaks, skin removed,
    cut into sixteen 2-inch cubes
Walnut Paprika Barbecue Sauce
    (recipe follows)
Canola oil for the grill grate or broiler pan
12 white button or cremini mushrooms,
    cleaned
4 zucchini, cut into 2-inch sections
4 long metal skewers; or four 12-inch
    bamboo skewers, soaked in water
    20 minutes, then drained

1 Place the swordfish cubes in a large baking dish. Pour Walnut Paprika Barbecue Sauce over them; toss gently to coat. Cover and refrigerate for at least 30 minutes but no more than 3 hours, tossing occasionally.

2 Preheat a gas grill for high-heat cooking or prepare a high-heat, well-ashed coal bed in a charcoal grill. Generously oil the grill grate. Alternatively, line a broiler pan with aluminum foil and preheat the broiler; generously oil the foil.

3 Remove the swordfish cubes from the barbecue sauce, reserving the sauce. Skewer 4 cubes, 3 mushrooms, and 4 pieces of zucchini onto each metal skewer, alternating vegetables and fish. If using bamboo skewers, place 2 pieces of fish, 2 pieces of zucchini, and 1 or 2 mushrooms on each skewer; wrap the exposed ends of bamboo skewers in aluminum foil to prevent burning.

4 **To grill:** Place the kabobs on the grate directly over the heat. Cover and grill until the fish is firm,

8 to 10 minutes, turning once and mopping frequently with the reserved barbecue sauce. Let stand at room temperature for 5 minutes before serving.

To broil: Place the kabobs 4 to 6 inches from the heat and cook until the fish is firm, 8 to 10 minutes, turning once and basting several times with the reserved barbecue sauce. Let stand at room temperature for 5 minutes before serving.

Walnut Paprika Barbecue Sauce

Makes a little more than 1 cup

¾ cup beer, preferably a wheat or amber beer
¼ cup chopped walnut pieces
2 tablespoons walnut oil
2 tablespoons paprika
1½ teaspoons sugar
½ teaspoon salt
½ teaspoon finely ground black pepper

Place the beer, walnuts, walnut oil, paprika, sugar, salt, and pepper in a blender or a food processor fitted with the chopping blade; blend or process until smooth.

Variations: Substitute sliced almonds for the walnut pieces and almond oil for the walnut oil.

Reduce the paprika to 1½ tablespoons and add ½ tablespoon hot paprika, or substitute smoked paprika for all the paprika.

Pulled Halibut Cheeks

Enormous halibut cheeks are slightly stringy and can be pulled like classic pulled pork or chicken dishes. Have hamburger buns at the ready. *Makes 4 servings*

¼ cup hoisin sauce
¼ cup Shaoxing or dry sherry
¼ cup vegetable or fish broth
¼ cup ketchup
1 tablespoon rice vinegar
1 tablespoon minced peeled fresh ginger
2 teaspoons packed brown sugar
1 teaspoon five-spice powder
½ teaspoon Asian red chili sauce
2 garlic cloves, crushed
8 large halibut cheeks
2 tablespoons peanut oil

1 Stir the hoisin sauce, Shaoxing or sherry, broth, ketchup, vinegar, ginger, brown sugar, five-spice powder, chili sauce, and garlic in a medium saucepan over medium heat until simmering. Cook for 5 minutes, stirring often; then cool to room temperature, about 1 hour.

2 Lay the cheeks in a large baking dish; pour the sauce over them. Cover and refrigerate for at least 1 hour or up to 24 hours.

3 Remove the cheeks from the marinade; let stand at room temperature for 5 minutes. Meanwhile, pour the marinade into a medium saucepan and bring to a low simmer over medium heat.

4 Heat a large skillet over medium heat. Pat the cheeks dry, add 1 tablespoon oil to the pan, then add the cheeks. Cook until browned, about 4 minutes, shaking the pan almost constantly during the first 30 seconds of cooking to prevent sticking.

5 Add the remaining oil to the pan, turn the cheeks, and continue cooking until well browned and firm to the touch, about 4 more minutes. Transfer to a cutting board and let stand for 5 minutes.

6 Shred the cheeks along the natural lines of the meat, using two forks. Add to the barbecue sauce, heat to simmering, and serve at once.

☀ *Whole Fish* ☀

A whole fish presented at the table may conjure up images of fine dining, but in truth it's easy to prepare. Check the ingredient list of individual recipes for the specific fish that are appropriate. Always have your fishmonger clean and scale the fish for you.

Whole Fish Wrapped in Grape Leaves

Jarred grape leaves protect a whole fish from the heat; they also lend the meat a slightly herbaceous flavor. *Makes 4 servings*

One 8-ounce jar grape leaves, drained and rinsed
1 small lemon, sliced into paper-thin rings, preferably with a mandoline
One 2½- to 3-pound snapper of any variety: black, striped, or spotted bass; whole large-mouth bass or freshwater bass; any variety of whole drum; or whole parrotfish, orange roughy, ocean perch, tilapia, or sea trout, scaled and cleaned
1 tablespoon olive oil, plus additional for the grill grate
½ teaspoon salt
½ teaspoon freshly ground black pepper
8 parsley sprigs
Butcher's twine

❶ Lay three quarters of the grape leaves on your work surface, overlapping them to form a compact bed that you will later fold up onto the fish; reserve the other leaves to lay over the fish. Lay 4 lemon slices down the center of the leaves.

❷ Score the fish's skin three times in parallel, diagonal cuts on each side of the body, cutting down only about ½ inch, not through to the bones. Oil the fish on both sides with 1 tablespoon olive oil; salt and pepper each side. Place the parsley sprigs and another 3 or 4 lemon slices inside the fish's body cavity. Set the stuffed fish over the lemon slices on the grape leaves.

❸ Arrange the remaining lemon slices over the top of the fish, then lay the reserved grape leaves over the body. Fold the bottom leaves up to cover the sides of the fish, tucking them under the top leaves to seal the fish in a grape-leaf packet. Pat to adhere, then tie in several places with butcher's twine to close the fish and the leaves in one packet.

To oven-roast:
❹ Position the rack in the center of the oven and preheat the oven to 375°F. Place a metal rack in a large baking sheet or roasting pan. Set the wrapped fish on the rack.

❺ Roast until the leaves are crispy and a metal skewer inserted through the leaves and into the flesh comes out hot, about 25 minutes. Untie the fish; discard the grape leaves and lemon slices before serving.

To grill:
❹ Preheat the gas grill for medium-heat cooking or build a medium-heat, well-ashed, wide coal bed in the center of a charcoal grill.

❺ Generously oil the grill grate and set it 4 to 6 inches over the heat source or coal bed. Place the wrapped fish directly over medium heat.

6 Cover and grill until the leaves are crispy, until a metal skewer inserted through the leaves and into the flesh comes out pretty warm, 20 to 25 minutes. Untie the fish; discard the grape leaves and lemon slices before serving.

Variation: Sprinkle ¼ cup chopped dill fronds over the grape leaves before adding the lemon slices; then sprinkle another ¼ cup chopped dill fronds over the fish before closing it in the leaves.

Cambodian-Style Oven-Steamed Fish

Called "ah mawk" in Cambodia, this whole fish is traditionally steamed in banana leaves. Since these are hard to find in our markets, parchment paper makes a good workaday (if less aromatic) substitute. We've upped the spices to compensate. *Makes 4 servings*

> ⅔ cup regular or low-fat coconut milk
> ⅓ cup vegetable broth
> ½ cup chopped cilantro leaves
> 2 tablespoons fish sauce
> 2 tablespoons lime juice
> 1 tablespoon packed light brown sugar
> One 2½- to 3-pound whole snapper of
>   any variety; black, striped, or spotted
>   bass; large-mouth or freshwater bass;
>   any variety of drum; parrotfish; orange
>   roughy; ocean perch; tilapia; or sea trout,
>   scaled, cleaned, and gutted
> 10 dried Chinese red chiles
> 5 scallions, cut into thirds
> 1 piece lemongrass, cut into 2-inch segments
>   and bruised with the bottom of a heavy
>   pot
> One 4-inch cinnamon stick
> 1 star anise pod

1 Whisk the coconut milk, broth, cilantro, fish sauce, lime juice, and brown sugar in a medium bowl.

2 Score the fish's skin three times in parallel, diagonal cuts on each side of the body, cutting down only about ½ inch, but not through to the bones.

3 Place the fish in a large baking dish, pour the coconut mixture over it, and turn to coat. Cover and refrigerate for 1 hour, turning occasionally in the marinade. Meanwhile, position the rack in the center of the oven and preheat the oven to 450°F.

4 Lay a large piece of parchment paper on your work surface, a sheet large enough that it will fully enwrap the whole fish. Lay a second sheet on top of it.

5 Remove the fish from the marinade and place it in the middle of the parchment sheets. Spoon about ¼ cup of the marinade over the fish. Place the chiles, scallions, lemongrass, cinnamon stick, and star anise on the paper with the fish.

6 Seal the packet closed, folding up the long ends and crimping them closed, then crimping the short ends closed. Place the packet on a large, clean baking sheet.

7 Bake until the fish flakes when pricked with a fork (you'll have to pull open the packet), about 20 to 25 minutes. Cool on the baking sheet for 5 minutes before opening the packet and transferring the whole fish to a serving plate.

Variations: Add three 1-inch pieces of peeled fresh ginger or galangal to the coconut marinade.

Rub the inside of the fish with 1 teaspoon Thai yellow curry paste before roasting.

Whole Fried Fish with Two Asian Sauces

Nothing beats a whole fish in a Chinese restaurant—or at home. Actually, it's an easy dish: slip the fish in the hot oil and it's nearly done. Use a splatter shield over the wok or skillet to prevent a greasy mess on the stove and counters. *Makes 4 servings*

About 6 cups peanut oil
One 2½- to 3-pound whole snapper of any variety, striped bass, spotted bass, tilapia, orange roughy, or parrotfish, scaled, cleaned, and gutted, the fins and tail trimmed off
½ cup cornstarch, placed on a large serving plate
One of the two sauces that follow

❶ Pour the peanut oil into a large wok or a very deep skillet and set it over medium-high heat. Clip a deep-frying thermometer to the edge of the pan and heat until the temperature registers 350°F.

❷ Meanwhile, score the fish's skin on each side with a sharp knife, making three parallel, diagonal, 4-inch cuts in the skin, each ½ inch deep. Pat the fish dry with paper towels, then dredge it in the cornstarch, coating both sides evenly. Shake off the excess.

❸ Holding the fish by the tail, slowly lower its head into the hot oil. Hold it there while you count to ten, then lower about half of the body into the oil. Again, count to ten before slipping the whole fish into the hot oil. This technique will keep the oil's temperature more steady and will minimize splatter.

❹ Fry until golden brown and quite crispy, about 12 minutes, turning once and spooning the hot oil over the fish. Transfer the fish to a wire rack and set aside at room temperature for 5 minutes. Then place it on a serving platter and pour one of the two sauces over the fish before serving.

Sweet-and-Sour Sauce
Makes about ½ cup

1 garlic clove, minced
½ cup vegetable, chicken, or fish broth
2 tablespoons rice vinegar
1 tablespoon minced peeled fresh ginger
1 tablespoon sugar
½ tablespoon soy sauce
½ teaspoon toasted sesame oil
½ teaspoon Asian red chili sauce
2 teaspoons cornstarch, whisked with 1 tablespoon water until smooth in a small bowl
2 scallions, thinly sliced

❶ Combine the garlic, broth, rice vinegar, ginger, sugar, and soy sauce in a medium saucepan set over medium heat. Bring the mixture to a simmer, stirring until the sugar has dissolved. Reduce the heat and simmer slowly for 5 minutes.

❷ Whisk in the sesame oil and chili sauce; whisk in the cornstarch mixture. Cook until thickened, about 20 seconds. Stir in the scallions and serve warm over the fish.

Chinese Black Bean Sauce
Makes about ½ cup

1 tablespoon peanut oil
2 medium shallots, minced
3 garlic cloves, minced
2 tablespoons minced salted (or preserved) Chinese black beans
1 tablespoon minced peeled fresh ginger
½ cup vegetable, chicken, or fish broth
3 tablespoons soy sauce
2 tablespoons Shaoxing or dry sherry

1 teaspoon sugar

½ teaspoon Asian red chili sauce

2 teaspoons cornstarch, whisked with
   1 tablespoon water until smooth in a
   small bowl

2 scallions, thinly sliced

❶ Heat a medium saucepan over medium heat. Swirl in the peanut oil, then the shallots, garlic, Chinese black beans, and ginger. Cook, stirring constantly, until aromatic, about 30 seconds.

❷ Whisk in the broth, soy sauce, Shaoxing or sherry, sugar, and chili sauce. Bring to a simmer, whisking constantly; then reduce the heat and simmer slowly, whisking occasionally, for 5 minutes.

❸ Stir in the cornstarch mixture and simmer until thickened, about 20 seconds. Stir in the scallions and serve warm with the fish.

Herb-Stuffed Whole Trout

Always elegant, always simple: there's not a lot better than a whole trout stuffed with fresh herbs. Plan on one trout per person. *Makes 4 servings*

Four 12- to 14-ounce whole brook, rainbow, river, red, or gold trout, scaled and cleaned

2 teaspoons salt, preferably kosher or coarse-grained salt

2 teaspoons freshly ground black pepper

8 parsley sprigs

8 thyme sprigs

Four 5-inch rosemary sprigs

2 tablespoons olive oil, plus additional for the grill grate or the frying pan

❶ Blot the trout dry with paper towels. Season the inside of each trout with ½ teaspoon

salt and ½ teaspoon pepper. Lay 2 parsley sprigs, 2 thyme sprigs, and 1 rosemary sprig in each trout's body cavity, then close the cavity over the herbs. Rub 2 tablespoons olive oil over the skin of each trout.

To grill:

❷ Lightly grease the grill rack with olive oil. Preheat a gas grill for medium heat or build a medium-heat coal bed in the center of a charcoal grill's coal grate.

❸ Place the grate 4 to 6 inches from the heat source or coal bed. Place the trout on the rack directly over the heat source or the coal bed. Alternatively, oil a grill basket and place the trout in it.

❹ Cover and grill until browned and firm, about 5 minutes. Turn with a large metal spatula, cover, and continue cooking until the meat flakes with a fork at its thinnest part, 4 to 6 more minutes. Let stand off the heat for 5 minutes before serving.

To oven-roast:

❷ Position the rack in the center of the oven and preheat the oven to 425°F. Heat 1 tablespoon olive oil in a large, oven-safe skillet or two skillets.

❸ Slip the trout into the skillet or skillets; cook for 3 minutes. Flip, then place the pan(s) in the oven and roast until the meat at the thin end of the trout flakes when gently pulled with a fork, 8 to 10 minutes. Let the trout stand in the skillets at room temperature for 5 minutes before serving.

Variations: Substitute chives for the parsley or thyme; or substitute tarragon for the rosemary.

Sprinkle a few dashes of hot red pepper sauce over the herbs before you close the trout.

❊ *Fish Burgers and Cakes* ❊

The trick is neither to lard them with fat nor to weigh them down with bread crumbs. Instead, bind them with just enough spices and herbs to let the fresh taste of the fish or shellfish come through. They're delicate, so take care when flipping them or transferring from the pan or grill to the plate.

Tuna Burgers

To heighten these delicate, Asian flavors, dice the tuna into even cubes, each one no more than ¼ inch. Serve these burgers on buns with a little Wasabi Mayonnaise (page 121). *Makes 4 burgers (can be doubled or tripled)*

> 1½ pounds tuna steak
> 3 tablespoons chopped chives or the finely minced green part of a scallion
> 1 tablespoon plus 1 teaspoon minced peeled fresh ginger
> 1 tablespoon plus 1 teaspoon Worcestershire sauce
> ½ teaspoon freshly ground black pepper
> 1 tablespoon canola or peanut oil

❶ Pat the tuna steak dry with paper towels, then cut the steak into ¼-inch-thick slices. Dice these into small ¼-inch cubes. Remove any tough, white nerve fibers.

❷ Place the tuna in a bowl and gently stir in the chives, ginger, Worcestershire sauce, and pepper. (The dish can be made ahead up to this point; cover and refrigerate for up to 8 hours.)

❸ Form the mixture into 4 patties; pat until firm.

❹ **To fry:** Heat a large skillet over medium-high heat. Swirl in the oil, then slip the burgers into the pan. Cook until well browned, about 2 minutes, pressing down lightly with a metal spatula to compact once or twice. Gently flip the burgers and continue cooking until the outside of the burgers is no longer translucent and browned, about 2 minutes.

To grill: Preheat a gas grill to high heat or build a high-heat, well-ashed coal bed in a charcoal grill. Generously oil the grill grate, then place it 4 to 6 inches from the heat source. Add the burgers and grill until browned and a little firm to the touch, about 4 minutes, turning once.

Salmon Burgers

Fresh salmon makes a much better burger than canned salmon. Pulse the salmon in the food processor only until it looks like ground turkey, not a paste. Have your fishmonger skin the salmon for you, or see page 75 for tips on how to do it yourself. Serve these patties on hamburger buns with the standard burger condiments, or in pita pockets with a creamy dressing, shredded lettuce, and diced tomato. *Makes 4 burgers (can be doubled or tripled)*

> 1 pound boneless skinless salmon fillet, cut into 3 pieces
> 1 large egg white, lightly beaten in a small bowl
> ⅓ cup plain dried bread crumbs
> 1 medium scallion, green part only, minced

2 tablespoons homemade mayonnaise
   (see page 121) or purchased regular
   or low-fat mayonnaise
   (do not use fat-free)
2 teaspoons chopped dill fronds or
   1 teaspoon dried dill
1 teaspoon celery seeds
1 teaspoon lemon juice
½ teaspoon salt
½ teaspoon freshly ground
   black pepper
1 tablespoon olive oil

1. Place the fillet pieces in a food processor fitted with the chopping blade; pulse until coarsely chopped. Add the egg white; pulse a couple of times, just to incorporate.

2. Transfer the mixture to a large bowl; stir in the bread crumbs, scallion, mayonnaise, dill, celery seeds, lemon juice, salt, and pepper. (The burgers can be made ahead up to this point; cover and refrigerate for up to 2 hours.)

3. Form the salmon mixture into 4 patties; pat gently until firm.

4. **To fry:** Heat a large skillet over medium heat. Swirl in the olive oil, then add the salmon patties. Shake the pan several times during the first 30 seconds of cooking to make sure the patties aren't sticking. Cook until lightly browned, about 2 minutes, then turn and continue cooking until golden and a little firm to the touch, about 3 more minutes.

To grill: Preheat a gas grill to high heat or prepare a high-heat, well-ashed coal bed in a charcoal grill. Generously oil the grill grate and place it 4 to 6 inches from the heat. Place the patties directly over the heat and grill 5 minutes, turning once with a metal spatula, until golden.

Grilled Pineapple Salsa

Every good burger or fish cake needs a great condiment. *Makes about 6 cups*

1 large, ripe pineapple, skinned, cored, and cut
   into 3-inch chunks
1 tablespoon canola oil, plus additional for the
   grate
1 large cucumber, peeled, seeded, and
   chopped
1 fresh jalapeño chile, seeded and minced
½ cup lime juice
2 tablespoons soy sauce
2 tablespoons honey
2 tablespoons minced peeled fresh ginger

1. Toss the pineapple chunks with the canola oil in a large bowl.

2. Preheat a gas grill to medium heat or prepare a medium-heat, well-ashed coal bed in a charcoal grill. Alternatively, heat a grill pan over medium heat.

3. Lightly oil the grill grate. (If using a grill pan, do not add extra oil to the pan.) Place the pineapple chunks directly over the heat or in the pan; grill or cook until lightly browned and warm, about 2 minutes, turning once.

4. Transfer the pineapple to a cutting board and cool for a couple of minutes. Chop into 1-inch chunks, then toss in a large bowl with the cucumber, jalapeño chile, lime juice, soy sauce, honey, and ginger.

To store: Cool to room temperature, then cover and refrigerate for up to 3 days.

Halibut Burgers

A few finely ground shrimp bind these burgers without any bread crumbs. *Makes 4 burgers (can be doubled or tripled)*

    20 ounces halibut steaks, cut into 4 or 5
        large pieces
    4 ounces medium shrimp (about 35 per
        pound), peeled and deveined
    2 tablespoons chopped dill fronds or
        1 tablespoon dried dill
    1 tablespoon Dijon mustard
    ½ teaspoon salt
    ½ teaspoon freshly ground black pepper
    1 tablespoon canola oil

1 Place the halibut and shrimp in a food processor fitted with the chopping blade; process until finely ground but not pastelike.

2 Add the dill, mustard, salt, and pepper. Pulse just a few times until well mixed. (The burgers can be made in advance up to this point; transfer to a medium bowl, cover, and refrigerate for up to 8 hours.)

3 Pat the mixture into 4 patties, compacting them somewhat so they'll cohere when cooked.

4 **To fry:** Heat a large skillet over medium-high heat. Add the canola oil, then slip the burgers into the pan. Cook until lightly browned, pressing down a couple of times with a metal spatula to compact, about 4 minutes. Flip and continue cooking until firm and lightly browned on the other side, about 5 minutes.

To grill: Preheat a gas grill to high heat or prepare a high-heat, well-ashed coal bed in a charcoal grill. Use the oil to grease the grill grate; place it 4 to 6 inches from the heat. Place the patties directly over the heat and grill 6 minutes, turning once with a metal spatula, until golden.

Almond-Crusted Cod Cakes

Fresh cod makes tender, light cakes; these are bound with mashed potatoes. Be gentle when flipping so their crusts stay intact. Serve them with a simple vinegary dipping sauce (page 74), a creamy salad dressing (pages 104–105), or Classic Tartar Sauce (page 121). *Makes 8 cod cakes (can be doubled)*

    1 pound white-fleshed boiling potatoes,
        peeled and cut into 1-inch cubes
    12 ounces skinless cod fillets
    2 tablespoons olive oil
    1 medium red onion, minced
    1 celery rib, minced
    1 garlic clove, minced
    2 tablespoons chopped chives or the green
        part of a scallion
    1 tablespoon chopped tarragon leaves or
        1½ teaspoons dried tarragon
    1 teaspoon salt
    ½ teaspoon freshly ground black pepper
    Several dashes of hot red pepper sauce to taste
    1 large egg, lightly beaten in a small bowl
    ½ cup toasted sliced almonds, coarsely
        ground in a food processor

1 Bring a large pot of water to a boil over high heat. Add the potatoes and cook until tender when pierced with a fork, about 15 minutes. Use a slotted spoon to lift them out of the water in batches, draining off most of the water; transfer to a large bowl. Keep their cooking water at a boil. Coarsely mash the potatoes with a potato masher, a slotted spoon, or a large fork; set aside.

2 Lower the heat so the water boils slowly and drop in the cod. Simmer for 5 minutes. Transfer with the slotted spoon to a cutting board, letting the water first drain off. Roughly chop the cod, then add it to the potatoes. Set aside to cool for 10 minutes.

③ Meanwhile, heat a large skillet over medium heat. Swirl in the olive oil, then add the onion and celery. Cook, stirring often, until soft and translucent, about 2 minutes. Add the garlic, cook for 20 seconds, then set the skillet off the heat for 5 minutes.

④ Add the entire contents of the skillet to the bowl with the cod and potatoes. Stir in the chives, tarragon, salt, pepper, and hot red pepper sauce, then stir in the egg until fairly smooth. There may still be some small potato lumps in the batter. You can crush these with a fork or leave them be—your choice.

⑤ Sprinkle the ground almonds on a large plate. Form the batter into 8 patties, using about ⅓ cup in each, dipping each on both sides into the ground nuts. (You may have to rinse your hands while making the patties because the mixture is sticky.) Set aside.

⑥ Clean and dry the large skillet. Set it over medium heat for a minute or so, then add the butter. The moment the foaming stops, tilt the pan every which way to coat its bottom, then slip the cakes in. Fry until golden, about 3 minutes, then flip gently with a large spatula and continue frying until crisp, about 2 minutes.

Variations: Substitute pecan pieces, walnut pieces, or skinned, toasted halved hazelnuts for the almonds.

Add 4 black pitted olives, finely chopped, with the herbs.

For a more Mediterranean taste, substitute olive oil for the butter; also substitute 2 teaspoons chopped rosemary leaves and 1 teaspoon stemmed thyme for the tarragon.

Crab Cakes

Panko bread crumbs, a Japanese specialty, make these cakes very light. *Makes 6 crab cakes (can be doubled or tripled)*

1 tablespoon unsalted butter
1 small onion, minced
1 celery rib, minced
12 ounces crabmeat, picked over for shell and cartilage
2 large egg yolks, lightly beaten in a small bowl
½ cup panko bread crumbs
⅓ cup homemade mayonnaise (see page 121) or purchased regular or low-fat mayonnaise (do not use fat-free)
2 tablespoons Dijon mustard
1 tablespoon lemon juice
½ teaspoon freshly ground black pepper
A few dashes of hot red pepper sauce
2 to 4 tablespoons olive oil
Salt to taste

① Melt the butter in a medium skillet set over medium heat. Add the onion and celery; cook, stirring constantly, until softened and aromatic, about 3 minutes. Transfer to a bowl and set aside to cool for 5 minutes.

② Stir in the crabmeat, egg yolks, bread crumbs, mayonnaise, mustard, lemon juice, pepper, and hot red pepper sauce.

③ Scoop up ½ cup of the mixture and gently form it into a patty between your hands. Continue making patties until you have 6 of them. (The recipe may be made ahead to this point—cover the cakes on a plate and refrigerate for up to 12 hours.)

④ Heat a large skillet over medium heat. Swirl in 2 tablespoons of the olive oil, then add as many cakes to the skillet as possible without crowding. Shake the pan to make sure the cakes don't stick.

⑤ Fry until brown, about 3 minutes, then turn and continue cooking until browned on the other side, about 3 more minutes. Transfer to a wire rack to drain; if you need to make additional cakes, add more olive oil to the pan before frying them. Salt to taste before serving, remembering that the crab and mustard are salty.

❋ Mussels, Clams, Cockles, and Oysters ❋

These are bivalves—that is, mollusks with a two-part shell held together by a tiny, strong muscle. Scallops, although a bivalve, are most often cooked outside their shells and thus fall into a different culinary category (see pages 366–375). For an appetizer, check out the Cold Sake-and-Ginger Mussels (page 60).

Ten One-Pot Preparations for Mussels, Clams, or Cockles

A big pot of mussels, clams, or cockles, a few bottles of beer, and some crunchy bread—that's dinner. While there are differences among these bivalves, they cook up in similar ways; so we've developed recipes that can be used with any of them. Follow the technique below, then plug the ingredients into the steps. One warning: do not mix bivalves—since they open at different times, some will turn tough from long exposure to the cooking liquid. *Makes 4 main-course or 6 to 8 first-course servings (see Note)*

Basic Technique

① Heat the fat in a large pot over medium-high heat.

② Add the vegetables and aromatics; cook, stirring frequently, until softened, about 4 minutes.

③ Add the seasonings; cook for 20 seconds.

④ Pour in the liquids; bring to a full simmer.

⑤ Add the bivalves—the mussels, clams, or cockles. Cover the pot, reduce the heat to medium-low, and simmer until opened, about 3 minutes for cockles, 6 minutes for mussels, and 8 minutes for clams. The larger the bivalve, the longer it will take to open. But do not let them cook beyond their opening or they will get tough.

Note: You can double any of these recipes, provided you have a very large stockpot; but you'll need to lengthen the cooking times a bit to let the extra sauce come to a simmer and to cook the additional vegetables. You can also halve the yield, making a two-serving dish.

Tips for Success

• Most of the recipes have no salt because the bivalves themselves are salty. However, tastes vary, so always check for salt before serving.

• These dishes come together very quickly. Have everyone and everything at the ready.

• Only use fresh herbs; dried will not have enough time to soften.

1. Mussels, Clams, or Cockles with Brandy, Apples, and Sage

Fat
2 tablespoons unsalted butter

Vegetables and aromatics
1 medium yellow onion, chopped
2 celery ribs, thinly sliced
2 tart apples, such as Granny Smiths
   or Macouns, peeled, cored,
   and chopped

Seasoning
1 tablespoon minced sage leaves
½ teaspoon salt
½ teaspoon freshly ground black pepper
¼ teaspoon grated nutmeg

Liquids
Two 8-ounce bottles clam juice or 2 cups
   vegetable broth
½ cup brandy
¼ cup heavy cream

Bivalves
4 pounds mussels, scrubbed and debearded;
   4 pounds clams, scrubbed; or 4 pounds
   cockles, scrubbed

2. Mussels, Clams, or Cockles with White Wine and Fennel

Fat
2 tablespoons olive oil

Vegetables and aromatics
1 large yellow onion, chopped
2 medium fennel bulbs, fronds trimmed,
   bulbs trimmed and very thinly sliced
2 garlic cloves, minced

Seasonings
1 tablespoon stemmed thyme
2 teaspoons finely grated orange zest

Liquids
1½ cups dry white wine
1 cup vegetable broth

Bivalves
4 pounds mussels, scrubbed and debearded;
   4 pounds clams, scrubbed; or 4 pounds
   cockles, scrubbed

Selecting and Handling Bivalves

Always look over mussels, clams, cockles, and oysters before you buy them. The shells should be intact, without any cracks or chips. When you get them home, look through them carefully to see if any are open. They should close when tapped or gently squeezed. If there are any that don't, discard them.

Line a large bowl with several damp paper towels, pour the bivalves into it, and top with several more wet paper towels. Store in the refrigerator for up to 12 hours.

To help clams expel any sand, fill a large bowl with water, add the clams plus 1 or 2 tablespoons cornmeal, and refrigerate for 1 hour. They'll spit out any grit in favor of the food.

All bivalve shells should be scrubbed with a plastic brush to get rid of any grit.

Mussels often have wiry hairs protruding from the shells—the so-called beard by which they attach themselves to rocks, posts, and other mussels. Farm-raised mussels, the bulk of the market, have few to none of these beards. Beards must be removed before cooking. Yank off those wiry hairs and cook within 5 minutes.

Once cooked, discard any bivalves that do not open.

3. Mussels, Clams, or Cockles in Red Wine

Fat
2 tablespoons unsalted butter

Vegetables and aromatics
8 ounces mushrooms, cleaned and very thinly sliced
1 large yellow onion, chopped
1 medium carrot, peeled and very thinly sliced
2 garlic cloves, minced

Seasonings
1 tablespoon chopped parsley leaves
2 teaspoons stemmed thyme
2 bay leaves
¼ teaspoon freshly ground black pepper

Liquids
2 cups red wine
2 tablespoons brandy, Cognac, or Armagnac, optional

Bivalves
4 pounds mussels, scrubbed and debearded; 4 pounds clams, scrubbed; or 4 pounds cockles, scrubbed

4. Chowder-Style Mussels, Clams, or Cockles

Fat
2 tablespoons unsalted butter

Vegetables and aromatics
1 large yellow onion, chopped
1 celery rib, thinly sliced
6 ounces thin-cut bacon, chopped
2 garlic cloves, minced

Seasoning
2 teaspoons stemmed thyme

Liquids
2 cups heavy cream
½ cup vegetable broth

Bivalves
4 pounds mussels, scrubbed and debearded; 4 pounds clams, scrubbed; or 4 pounds cockles, scrubbed

5. Provençal-Style Mussels, Clams, or Cockles

Fat
1 tablespoon olive oil
1 tablespoon unsalted butter

Vegetables and aromatics
1 medium onion, chopped
1 medium leek, white and green parts only, halved, washed for any grit, then thinly sliced
1 medium fennel bulb, fronds trimmed, bulb trimmed and very thinly sliced
8 Roma or plum tomatoes, diced
1 garlic clove, minced

Seasonings
2 teaspoons stemmed thyme
⅛ teaspoon saffron

Liquids
2 cups vegetable broth
¼ cup Pastis, Pernod, or Ricard

Bivalves
4 pounds mussels, scrubbed and debearded; 4 pounds clams, scrubbed; or 4 pounds cockles, scrubbed

6. Japanese-Style Mussels, Clams, or Cockles

Fat
1 tablespoon canola oil

Vegetables and aromatics
3 scallions, thinly sliced

Seasonings
½ cup chopped pickled "sushi" ginger

Liquids
2 cups dry sake
¼ cup soy sauce
1 tablespoon prepared wasabi paste

Bivalves
4 pounds mussels, scrubbed and debearded; 4 pounds clams, scrubbed; or 4 pounds cockles, scrubbed

7. Spanish-Style Mussels, Clams, or Cockles

Fat
2 tablespoons olive oil

Vegetables and aromatics
1⅔ cups canned chickpeas, drained and rinsed
12 cherry tomatoes, halved
1 medium yellow onion, chopped
1 medium red bell pepper, cored, seeded, and thinly sliced
3 garlic cloves, crushed

Seasonings
1 tablespoon chopped fresh oregano
½ teaspoon freshly ground black pepper
¼ teaspoon crumbled saffron

Liquids
1¾ cups vegetable broth
½ cup dry sherry

Bivalves
4 pounds mussels, scrubbed and debearded; 4 pounds clams, scrubbed; or 4 pounds cockles, scrubbed

8. Indonesian-Style Mussels, Clams, or Cockles

Fat
1 tablespoon unsalted butter
1 tablespoon canola oil

Vegetables and aromatics
3 medium shallots, thinly sliced into rings
3 garlic cloves, minced
3 Thai or serrano chiles, halved, seeded, and minced
1 lemongrass stalk, cut into 1-inch segments, each crushed
2 tablespoons minced peeled fresh ginger

Seasonings
2 tablespoons chopped cilantro leaves
1 teaspoon turmeric
¼ teaspoon ground cloves
One 4-inch cinnamon stick

Liquids
1 cup regular or low-fat coconut milk
1 cup vegetable broth
½ cup Shaoxing or dry sherry
2 tablespoons fish sauce

Bivalves
4 pounds mussels, scrubbed and debearded; 4 pounds clams, scrubbed; or 4 pounds cockles, scrubbed

9. Mussels, Clams, or Cockles in a Thai Coconut Curry

Fat
2 tablespoons canola oil

Vegetables and aromatics
5 medium scallions, thinly sliced
1 large green bell pepper, cored, seeded, and thinly sliced
3 garlic cloves, crushed
2 tablespoons minced peeled fresh ginger

Seasonings
¼ cup chopped cilantro leaves
Up to 1 tablespoon red Thai curry paste or yellow Thai curry paste
1 tablespoon packed light brown sugar

Liquids
1½ cups vegetable broth
1 cup regular or low-fat coconut milk

Bivalves
4 pounds mussels, scrubbed and debearded; 4 pounds clams, scrubbed; or 4 pounds cockles, scrubbed

10. "Barbecued" Mussels, Clams, or Cockles

Fat
1 tablespoon peanut oil

Vegetables and aromatics
1 large red onion, thinly sliced
4 celery ribs, thinly sliced
3 garlic cloves, minced

Seasonings
2 tablespoons chili powder
1 tablespoon paprika
2 teaspoons dry mustard
½ teaspoon freshly ground black pepper
¼ teaspoon cayenne pepper

Liquids
1 cup tomato sauce
1 cup chicken broth
2 tablespoons cider vinegar
1 tablespoon Worcestershire sauce
1 tablespoon honey
1 teaspoon liquid smoke

Bivalves
4 pounds mussels, scrubbed and debearded; 4 pounds clams, scrubbed; or 4 pounds cockles, scrubbed

Grilled Oysters Rockefeller

A light bread crumb topping matches well with the briny, seared oysters in this cocktail classic. After you've shucked the oysters, sit them in the larger half of their shells, the halves to which they were originally attached. Cook the oysters within minutes of shucking them. *Makes 4 servings*

3 tablespoons unsalted butter, melted and cooled
½ cup plain dried bread crumbs
2 scallions, minced
1 garlic clove, minced
2 tablespoons minced parsley leaves
2 tablespoons Pernod, Pastis, or other licorice-flavored liqueur
1 teaspoon salt
1 teaspoon freshly ground black pepper
Several dashes of hot red pepper sauce, or more to taste
2 dozen large, fresh raw oysters in their shells, shucked (see page 364)
1 ounce Parmigiano-Reggiano, finely grated

❶ Mix the butter, bread crumbs, scallions, garlic, parsley, liqueur, salt, pepper, and hot red pepper sauce in a medium bowl. Set aside.

❷ Divide the bread-crumb topping among the oysters; sprinkle each with some of the cheese.

❸ **To grill:** Preheat a gas grill for medium heat or build a medium-heat, wide, well-ashed coal bed in a charcoal grill. Place the grate on the grill about 4 inches over the heat. Place the oysters shell side down directly over the heat. Cover and grill until the cheese melts and the topping browns, about 5 minutes.

To broil: Preheat the broiler, then lay the prepared oysters in their shells on the broiler rack. Set them about 6 inches from the heat and broil until the cheese melts and the bread crumbs brown a bit, about 4 minutes. Let stand at room temperature for 5 minutes before serving.

How to Shuck Oysters

Hold the oyster in its shell in one hand and insert an oyster shucker or small, heavy-duty, flat-head, well-cleaned screwdriver into the joint between the two shells, the tiny pivot point at the small, tapering ends of the shell (where the oyster would be hanging off a tree if it were a pear). Be careful not to chip the shell; pry it open by twisting the shucker into the pivot point and wrenching the shell's two halves apart. Clean out any fractured shell bits, then run the shucker under the oyster meat to cut off the inside of the shell. Place the meat and any accumulated juices in the larger half of the shell; discard the smaller half.

Beef and Oyster Casserole

Oysters give the beef a salty, subtle flavor. The buttery top crust makes this dish old-fashioned comfort food. *Makes 6 servings*

7 tablespoons unsalted butter
1 large onion, chopped
4 ounces cremini mushrooms, thinly sliced
1½ pounds 93% lean ground beef
1¼ cups all-purpose flour, plus additional for dusting
1 cup beef broth
12 oysters, shucked, with their juices, or one 8-ounce container shucked oysters
2 teaspoons stemmed thyme or 1 teaspoon thyme
2 teaspoons minced sage leaves or 1 teaspoon rubbed sage
1 teaspoon salt
½ teaspoon freshly ground black pepper
3 tablespoons solid vegetable shortening
1 to 2 tablespoons ice water

❶ Position the rack in the center of the oven and preheat the oven to 375°F.

❷ Melt 4 tablespoons (½ stick) unsalted butter in a large saucepan. Add the onion and cook, stirring often, until softened, about 3 minutes.

❸ Add the mushrooms; continue cooking until they give off their liquid and it almost all evaporates, about 5 minutes, stirring often.

❹ Crumble in the ground beef. Cook, stirring often, until browned, about 5 minutes.

❺ Sprinkle ¼ cup flour over the mixture in the pan and cook, stirring all the while, for 1 minute.

❻ Stirring constantly, slowly pour in the broth; continue cooking and stirring until the sauce comes to a boil and thickens slightly, about 1 minute.

7 Stir in the oysters, thyme, sage, ½ teaspoon salt, and the pepper; cook, stirring often, for 2 minutes. Pour into a 10-inch, 2-quart, round, high-sided casserole and set aside.

8 Place the remaining 1 cup flour in a medium bowl; stir in the remaining ½ teaspoon salt. Cut in the shortening and the remaining 3 tablespoons butter with a pastry cutter or a fork until the mixture resembles coarse meal. Add 1 tablespoon ice water; stir with a fork just until a dough begins to form, adding more ice water as necessary.

9 Sprinkle the work surface with a little water, then lay a large piece of wax paper over it. Lightly flour the wax paper, then turn the dough out onto it. Knead once or twice to get the dough to adhere, then dust it with flour and pat it into a flattened ball. Roll into a circle that is 1 inch wider than the diameter of the casserole.

10 Pick up the wax paper (and the dough circle on it) and flip it over on top of the casserole. Peel off the wax paper, leaving the dough on top of the casserole. Seal it to the edges.

11 Bake until the topping is lightly browned and the filling is bubbling underneath, about 40 minutes. Let stand at room temperature for 5 minutes before serving.

Variations: Omit the pastry top; buy frozen puff pastry, thaw according to the package directions, and cut a sheet to fit the top of the casserole.

For a richer casserole, use 1 pound lean ground beef and ½ pound ground veal.

Add ½ teaspoon red pepper flakes or several dashes of hot red pepper sauce with the thyme.

Creamy Oyster Étouffée

Although crawfish are customary in this Louisiana specialty, oysters make a briny and richer dish. Have lots of white rice to make a bed for this rich stew. *Makes 6 servings*

4 tablespoons (½ stick) unsalted butter
1 large yellow onion, diced
2 celery ribs, thinly sliced
1 medium green bell pepper, cored, seeded, and diced
3 garlic cloves, minced
2 teaspoons stemmed thyme or 1 teaspoon dried thyme
¼ to ½ teaspoon cayenne pepper
¼ cup all-purpose flour
3 cups fish, vegetable, or chicken broth
1 cup dry white wine or dry vermouth
1½ pounds shucked oysters
½ cup heavy cream
Salt to taste

1 Melt the butter in a large saucepan set over low heat. Add the onion, celery, and bell pepper. Cook, stirring often, until softened, about 3 minutes. Add the garlic, thyme, and cayenne; cook for 20 seconds.

2 Sprinkle the flour evenly over the mixture, count to ten, then cook, whisking constantly, until the flour has incorporated and turned golden, about 3 minutes.

3 Whisking constantly, add the broth in a slow, thin stream. Whisk in the wine until smooth. Raise the heat to medium and bring to a low simmer.

4 Add the oysters (and any juice) along with the cream. Stir well, cover, reduce the heat to very low, and cook just until the oysters are opaque and the sauce is thick, about 3 minutes. Let stand off the heat for 5 minutes and check the dish to see if it needs any salt.

❈ Shrimp and Scallops ❈

Although barely related biologically, shrimp and scallops are interchangeable in most of these recipes because we don't eat the whole animal; rather, we eat its largest muscle—in shrimp, the one that runs along the tail; and in scallops, the one that opens and closes the shell. The one rule in all these preparations? Don't overcook. Shrimp and scallops are done within minutes of being added to a dish. Longer cooking toughens them considerably.

A road map for
Oven-Roasted Shrimp or Scallops

This may be the quickest way to cook these favorites. The oil is slowly infused with the herbs, then a simple dressinglike sauce is made after the shrimp or scallops have cooked. *Makes 4 servings*

1 Place

 ¼ **cup olive oil**

in a 13 × 9-inch baking dish or a 10-inch square baking dish.

2 Add one or two of the following to the baking dish:

 12 thyme sprigs
 8 parsley sprigs
 8 dried red Asian chiles
 6 oregano sprigs
 6 dill fronds
 Four 4-inch rosemary sprigs
 4 garlic cloves, slivered
 A handful of chives

3 Position the rack in the center of the oven and place the baking dish on the rack. Now set the oven to 450°F and let it preheat for 15 minutes with the dish in the oven so the aromatics slowly infuse the oil.

4 Remembering that the dish is very hot, stir in *one* of the following:

 1½ **pounds medium shrimp (about 35 per pound), peeled and deveined**
 1½ **pounds cleaned sea scallops, each cut into 2 disks**
 1½ **pounds cleaned bay scallops**

5 Cook until the shrimp are pink and firm or the scallops are opaque, about 4 minutes for bay scallops, 5 minutes for the halved sea scallops, and 7 minutes for shrimp, tossing a couple of times.

6 Remove the hot baking dish from the oven and stir in:

 1 teaspoon kosher or coarse-grained
  sea salt
 ½ teaspoon freshly ground black pepper

Also stir in one of the following:

 2 tablespoons red wine vinegar
 2 tablespoons sherry vinegar
 2 tablespoons balsamic vinegar
 3 tablespoons lemon juice
 3 tablespoons rice vinegar
 ¼ **cup orange juice**
 ¼ **cup dry white wine**

7 Toss well, scraping up any browned bits and allowing the liquid to evaporate a little from the pan's heat; then serve at once.

Shrimp or Scallops in Spicy Tomato Sauce

Have lots of bread on hand to slurp up every drop of this sauce. Serve the dish over Perfect Mashed Potatoes (page 473), Root Vegetable Mash (page 473), polenta, or spaghetti. *Makes 4 servings*

3 tablespoons olive oil
1 medium shallot, thinly sliced
4 garlic cloves, minced
2 to 4 small fresh chiles, such as serranos or Thai hots, seeded and thinly sliced
1 teaspoon stemmed thyme or ½ teaspoon dried thyme
1 teaspoon fennel seeds
3½ cups canned diced tomatoes with their juice
2 pounds medium shrimp (about 35 per pound), peeled and deveined; 2 pounds cleaned sea scallops, each cut into two disks; or 2 pounds cleaned bay scallops
½ teaspoon salt, or to taste
½ teaspoon freshly ground black pepper

1 Heat a large saucepan over medium heat. Add the olive oil, then the shallot. Cook, stirring often, until soft, about 2 minutes. Add the garlic and cook for 20 seconds (do not let the garlic brown).

2 Add the chiles, thyme, and fennel seeds. Stir well, cook for 10 seconds, then pour in the tomatoes and all their juice. Bring the mixture to a simmer; then reduce the heat to low and cook, uncovered, until the tomatoes have broken down and the sauce has started to thicken, about 10 minutes.

3 Raise the heat to medium and add the shrimp or scallops. Stir well and cook until the shrimp are pink and firm or the scallops are opaque, about 2 minutes for scallops and 4 minutes for shrimp. Season with salt and pepper.

Variations: For a smoother sauce, use crushed tomatoes.

For a thicker sauce, add 1 tablespoon tomato paste with the canned tomatoes.

For a more complex taste, add 1 teaspoon anchovy paste with the chiles.

For a tangier sauce, add 1½ tablespoons balsamic vinegar with the shrimp or scallops.

Shrimp or Scallop Rogan Josh

This Kashmir curry is usually made with lamb, but sweet shrimp or scallops make a nice contrast to the spicy heat. Pure chili powder is made only from ground chiles—look for it in Southwestern markets or make your own by grinding a seeded and stemmed dried New Mexican red chile in a spice grinder. *Makes 4 servings*

2 teaspoons ground cumin
2 teaspoons ground coriander
1 teaspoon pure chili powder
1 teaspoon ground cinnamon
1 teaspoon ground ginger
½ teaspoon turmeric
¼ teaspoon ground cloves
¼ teaspoon saffron, crumbled
1 pound yellow-fleshed potatoes, such as Yukon golds, cut into 1-inch cubes
2 tablespoons canola oil
2 cups beef broth
1½ pounds medium shrimp (about 35 per pound), peeled and deveined; 1½ pounds cleaned sea scallops, each cut into 2 disks; or 1½ pounds cleaned bay scallops; or a combination of all three to weigh 1½ pounds

1 cup regular or low-fat yogurt (do not use fat-free)

¼ cup packed chopped cilantro leaves

½ teaspoon salt, or to taste

❶ Mix the cumin, coriander, chili powder, cinnamon, ginger, turmeric, cloves, and saffron in a large bowl. Add the potatoes and 1 tablespoon canola oil; toss well to coat. Set aside at room temperature for 10 minutes.

❷ Heat a large pot or a Dutch oven over medium heat. Swirl in the remaining 1 tablespoon oil, then add the potatoes and all their spices, making sure you scrape the bowl clean. Cook, stirring frequently, until the potatoes start to brown a little and the spices are quite aromatic, about 2 minutes.

❸ Pour in the broth and bring to a simmer, scraping up any browned bits on the pan's bottom. Reduce the heat to very low and simmer slowly, uncovered, until the potatoes are tender, about 20 minutes.

❹ Stir in the shrimp or scallops, raise the heat to medium-high, and bring back to a full simmer. Cook, stirring frequently, until the shrimp are pink and firm or the scallops are opaque, about 3 minutes.

❺ Remove the pan from the heat and stir in the yogurt until smooth. Season with cilantro and salt before serving.

Variations: For a sweeter stew, add 1 large carrot, shredded through the large holes of a box grater, with the potatoes in the spice mixture.

For a lighter stew, substitute vegetable broth for the beef broth.

Reduce the shrimp or scallops to ¾ pound and add 1 pound mussels, scrubbed and debearded (see page 360), with the remainder. Simmer the soup until the mussels open.

Add 2 cups baby spinach leaves with the shrimp or scallops.

Shrimp: Packaging, Peeling, and Deveining

Although the shrimp lying on the ice at your market may look fresh, they were almost certainly frozen at harvest. In the end, you're better off doing what the market does: buying them in frozen packs and defrosting them yourself. Look for packages labeled "IQF" or "individual quick-frozen," meaning that each shrimp has been frozen separately, rather than in a tangled mess in a block of ice. Thaw overnight in a covered bowl in the refrigerator.

All labels for shrimp—"jumbo," "colossal"—are mere window dressing. The only way to tell the size is knowing how many make a pound. By and large, we call for those that take about 35 to make a pound—they are large but not gigantic. So-called U-10s (under 10 per pound) are huge; U-5s, gigantic.

In most cases, shrimp must be peeled and deveined. To peel a shrimp, turn it over so that its legs face you, take the shrimp in both hands, and use your thumbs to pull the legs gently away from each other, thereby tearing the shell down the middle of its thinner underside. Peel back the shell, then grasp the very end of the tail, just at the feathery flippers, and pull the meat free.

To devein a shrimp, place it on your work surface so the convex (or curved out) side faces you. Run a paring knife along the curve, slitting the meat only until the dark vein is revealed. Use the end of the knife to pull up the vein (which, of course, you discard). That unsavory vein, by the way, is actually the shrimp's digestive track.

Shrimp or Scallops with Lemon Dill Cream Sauce

Adding an egg yolk keeps the cream sauce from curdling in the face of the lemon juice—and makes the dish even more luxurious. *Makes 4 servings*

2 tablespoons unsalted butter
1 medium yellow onion, finely chopped
1½ pounds large shrimp (about 20 per pound), peeled and deveined; 1½ pounds cleaned sea scallops; or 1½ pounds cleaned bay scallops
2 tablespoons chopped dill fronds or 1 tablespoon dried dill
1 cup heavy cream
1 large egg yolk, lightly beaten in a small bowl, at room temperature
2 tablespoons lemon juice
½ teaspoon salt
¼ teaspoon freshly ground pepper, preferably white pepper

1 Melt the butter in a large skillet or sauté pan set over low heat. Add the onion, reduce the heat even further, and cook slowly, stirring often, until translucent and golden, about 10 minutes.

2 Add the shrimp or scallops and the dill. Cook, stirring constantly, for 20 seconds, just several good turns in the pot; then pour in the cream.

3 Raise the heat to medium-high and bring the sauce to a simmer, stirring constantly. Cook until reduced by half, about 2 minutes.

4 Remove the shrimp or scallops from the sauce with a slotted spoon and place them on a plate.

5 Continue to boil the cream sauce for 1 minute. Whisk about ½ cup of the cream sauce into the egg yolk until smooth. Remove the pan from the heat and whisk this combined mixture back into the remaining cream sauce in the pan.

6 Whisk in the lemon juice, salt, and pepper; then return the shellfish and any accumulated juices to the pan. Stir well, cover, and set aside off the heat for a few minutes, until the shrimp are pink and firm or the scallops are opaque.

Shrimp or Scallops with Orange Rosemary Cream Sauce: Substitute rosemary for the dill and 2 tablespoons frozen orange juice concentrate, thawed, for the lemon juice.

Shrimp or Scallops with a Grapefruit Tarragon Cream Sauce: Substitute tarragon for the dill; add 1 teaspoon finely grated grapefruit zest with the tarragon. Substitute freshly squeezed grapefruit juice for the lemon juice.

Easy Shrimp Substitutions

For shrimp bakes, substitute medium shrimp (about 35 per pound) for any of the fish fillets baked in packets (see pages 325–326); place about 6 ounces peeled and deveined shrimp in each packet, seal, and bake until pink and firm, about 15 minutes.

Or for shrimp stews, substitute 1 to 1½ pounds deveined medium shrimp for the mussels, clams, or cockles in any of their preparations (see pages 359–363). Stir in the shrimp as you would the bivalves, cover, and simmer until pink and firm, about 4 minutes. In-shell shrimp have more flavor; shelled shrimp are easier to eat.

Shrimp or Scallop Walnut Stir-Fry

This is a basic stir-fry: not too hot, not too sticky, not too vinegary. Serve it over rice or steamed greens. *Makes 4 servings*

3 tablespoons soy sauce
3 tablespoons rice vinegar
1 teaspoon sugar
3 tablespoons peanut oil
¾ cup walnut halves
4 medium scallions, thinly
    sliced
2 garlic cloves, minced
3 tablespoons minced peeled fresh
    ginger
6 ounces snow peas, trimmed
2 celery ribs, thinly sliced
1 pound medium shrimp (about 30 per
    pound), peeled and deveined;
    1 pound cleaned sea scallops, each cut
    into two disks; or 1 pound cleaned bay
    scallops
1 teaspoon toasted sesame oil

❶ Whisk the soy sauce, rice vinegar, and sugar in a small bowl; set aside.

❷ Heat a large wok or high-sided sauté pan over medium-high heat. Add 1 tablespoon peanut oil, then the walnuts. Cook, stirring constantly, until fragrant and golden, about 2 minutes. Transfer the walnuts to a plate and set aside.

❸ Add the remaining 2 tablespoons oil, then add the scallions, garlic, and ginger; stir-fry for 1 minute. Toss in the snow peas and celery; cook, stirring frequently, 1 minute.

❹ Add the shrimp or scallops; cook, stirring constantly, until the shrimp are pink and firm or the scallops are opaque, 2 to 3 minutes.

❺ Pour in the soy sauce mixture and bring to a simmer. Continue cooking, stirring frequently, until the sauce is reduced to a glaze, about 2 minutes.

❻ Toss the walnuts back into the pan and stir-fry for 10 seconds. Turn off the heat and drizzle the sesame oil over the dish.

Variations: Substitute broccoli or cauliflower florets for the snow peas.

Add up to 1 teaspoon red pepper flakes with the shrimp.

Looking for more shrimp dishes? Check out Filled Omelets (page 23), Seafood and Cheese Fondue Casserole (page 27), Steamed Shrimp with Classic Cocktail Sauce (page 61), Shrimp Yakitori (page 61), the shrimp filling for Summer Rolls (page 88), Shrimp Salad (page 122), Margarita Shrimp Salad (page 125), Mexican Lime Soup (page 154), Shrimp and Scallop Chowder (page 155), Pasta Marinara with Shrimp (page 183), Lo Mein (page 209), Singapore Mai Fun (page 211), Pad Thai (page 212), the shrimp variation to Southwestern-Inspired Arroz con Pollo (page 260), Crab, Shrimp, and Scallop Bread Pudding (page 379), or Autumn Paella with Chicken, Sausage, Shrimp, and Olives (page 498). Or use the Beer Batter (page 72) or Tempura Batter (page 74) to make crispy fried shrimp.

Fiery Shrimp or Scallop Cashew Stir-Fry

Japanese mirin adds a sweet contrast to the vinegar and red pepper flakes in this stir-fry. Make sure you use unsalted cashews. *Makes 4 servings*

3 tablespoons soy sauce

3 tablespoons mirin

1 tablespoon sesame oil

1 tablespoon rice vinegar

½ teaspoon red pepper flakes

2 tablespoons peanut oil

4 medium scallions, thinly sliced

4 garlic cloves, minced

2 tablespoons minced peeled fresh ginger

1 pound medium shrimp (about 30 per pound), peeled and deveined; 1 pound cleaned sea scallops, each cut into 2 disks; or 1 pound cleaned bay scallops

5 celery ribs, thinly sliced

½ cup roasted unsalted cashews

2 teaspoons cornstarch dissolved in 2 tablespoons water

❶ Whisk the soy sauce, mirin, sesame oil, rice vinegar, and red pepper flakes in a small bowl; set aside.

❷ Heat a large wok or high-sided sauté pan over medium-high heat. Swirl in the peanut oil, then add the scallions, garlic, and ginger; stir-fry for 1 minute.

❸ Add the shrimp; cook, stirring constantly, just until vaguely pink, about 1 minute. Add the celery and cashews; stir-fry for 2 minutes.

❹ Pour in the soy sauce mixture, bring to a simmer, and cook for 1 minute. Swirl in the cornstarch and water mixture; continue cooking until thickened and bubbling, stirring constantly, for less than 1 minute.

Variations: Substitute 4 cups small broccoli or cauliflower florets for the celery.

Add up to 1 teaspoon red Chinese chili sauce with the red pepper flakes.

Scallops

Although almost all of a scallop is edible, we only have access to the round muscle that connects the halves of the shell. (The roe is highly prized in many other cultures.)

Scallops are extraordinarily perishable, so they are most often sold out of their shells, cleaned and ready to cook. If yours have a small, tubular muscle still attached to the round disk, remove that muscle and either add it to the dish or discard it; it's slightly tougher than the disk but fully edible.

There are many scallop species, but they are all collapsed into two at our markets: bay and sea. Bay scallops are found mostly on the East Coast of the United States and Canada. They are small (it takes about 100 to make a pound) and sweet. They cook fast, about half as long as the more standard sea scallops, which are larger (about 30 per pound) and a little more briny.

When purchasing scallops, look for firm, pale beige to pink meat. If starkly white, they have been soaked in water to increase their weight. Use raw scallops within a day of purchase. Since all are sold already cleaned, it's more economical to buy them individually quick-frozen in large bags and thaw them yourself—exactly as your fishmonger did.

If the recipe calls for the larger sea scallop to be cut in half, cut it through the middle so it forms two disks (not down from the top to form two half-moons).

Szechuan Shrimp or Scallop Pumpkin Stir-Fry

In this autumnal dish, the pumpkin sweetens the vinegary sauce. *Makes 4 servings*

3 tablespoons Chinese black vinegar or 1½ tablespoons Worcestershire sauce and 1½ tablespoons white wine vinegar
2 tablespoons soy sauce
1½ tablespoons packed light brown sugar
½ teaspoon Asian red chili sauce
One 2-pound pumpkin, peeled, halved, seeded, and cut into ½-inch cubes (see page 466)
3 tablespoons peanut oil
12 whole dry Asian red chiles
1 orange, zest only, shaved off in long strips with a vegetable peeler
One 4-inch cinnamon stick, broken into 3 pieces
1 star anise pod
3 medium scallions, chopped
1½ pounds medium shrimp (about 30 per pound), peeled and deveined; 1½ pounds cleaned sea scallops, each cut into 2 disks; or 1½ pounds cleaned bay scallops

❶ Whisk the black vinegar (or its substitutes), soy sauce, brown sugar, and chili sauce in a small bowl until the sugar dissolves; set aside.

❷ Place the pumpkin cubes in a large saucepan, cover them with water to a depth of 1 inch, set the pan over medium heat, and bring to a simmer. Cover, reduce the heat to medium-low, and simmer until tender, 15 to 20 minutes. Drain in a colander set in the sink.

❸ Place the peanut oil, chiles, orange zest strips, cinnamon stick, and star anise in a large wok or high-sided sauté pan, then set the pan over low heat. Cook, stirring frequently, until the aromatics begin to brown, about 6 minutes. Remove and discard the aromatics with a slotted spoon, leaving the scented oil behind.

❹ Raise the heat to medium-high. Add the scallions; stir-fry for 1 minute.

❺ Add the shrimp or scallops; stir-fry until the shrimp become pink and fairly firm or the scallops are opaque, about 3 minutes.

❻ Add the prepared pumpkin and soy sauce mixture; and bring to a simmer. Cook until the shrimp and pumpkin are coated with the slightly thickened sauce, about 1 minute.

Variations: Substitute butternut or acorn squash for the pumpkin.

Add ½ pound broccoli florets with the scallions.

Rosemary-Skewered Shrimp

Consider serving these with a light green salad of lettuce, tomatoes, crumbled feta, and a classic vinaigrette (see pages 100–101). *Makes 4 servings (can be doubled)*

½ cup olive oil
1 tablespoon finely grated lemon zest
1 tablespoon finely grated orange zest
½ teaspoon chopped mint leaves
½ teaspoon salt
1 pound large shrimp, about 15 per pound, peeled and deveined
4 to 8 fresh rosemary sprigs

❶ Stir the olive oil, both zests, mint, and salt in a large bowl. Cover and set aside at room temperature for at least 4 hours or up to 3 days.

2 Add the shrimp. Cover and set aside at room temperature for 15 minutes.

3 Remove the shrimp from the marinade, keeping them covered lightly with the zest and mint. Skewer onto the rosemary sprigs, threading them on each sprig by first using a paring knife to cut a guide hole in the thick center of each shrimp. Don't thread them onto the sprigs against the direction of the leaves.

4 **To grill:** Preheat a gas grill for medium-heat cooking or prepare a wide, medium-heat, well-ashed coal bed in a charcoal grill. Use some of the oil from the marinade to oil the grill grate; place the grate 4 to 6 inches from the heat. Set the skewers directly over the heat; cook for 3 minutes. Turn and continue cooking until the shrimp are firm and pink, about 3 more minutes.

To broil: Preheat the broiler; line the broiler pan with aluminum foil to make cleanup easier. Place the skewers in the broiler pan 4 to 6 inches from the heat. Broil for 2 minutes, baste generously with the marinade, turn, and continue cooking until the shrimp are firm and pink, about 3 more minutes.

Looking for more scallop recipes? Check out Fried Scallops with a Beer-Batter Crust (page 72), Shrimp and Scallop Chowder (page 155), Crab, Shrimp, and Scallop Bread Pudding (page 379), or Summer Paella with Lobster, Mussels, Scallops, and Rosé Wine (page 497).

Shrimp in Their Shells with Garlic Cream Sauce

Warning: this is a messy dish. But it's worth every napkin used. Eat them by slurping the cream off the shells, then peeling the shrimp. *Makes 4 servings*

2 tablespoons unsalted butter
8 garlic cloves, minced
1 medium shallot, minced
1 tablespoon chopped oregano leaves or
    1½ teaspoons dried oregano
½ teaspoon salt
¼ teaspoon freshly ground black pepper
1½ pounds large shrimp in their shells
    (about 15 per pound)
¼ cup vegetable or fish broth
1 cup heavy cream

1 Melt the butter in a very large skillet over low heat. Add the garlic and shallot, lower the heat even further, and cook slowly until softened and golden, about 5 minutes. Should the butter start to brown, remove the pan from the heat and let it cool down before continuing.

2 Add the oregano, salt, and pepper; cook, stirring often, for 20 seconds.

3 Raise the heat to medium and add the shrimp. Toss with wooden spoons or tongs until they start to turn pink, about 2 minutes.

4 Pour in the broth; scrape up any browned bits on the bottom of the pan. Bring to a simmer and cook until reduced to a glaze, about 1 minute.

5 Pour in the cream; bring the sauce back to a simmer. Cook until the cream has been reduced to a thick sauce that coats the shrimp, about 3 minutes.

Variations: For a wine cream sauce, substitute ½ cup white wine for the broth; boil until reduced to a glaze, about 3 minutes.

For an even richer dish, stir ¼ cup finely grated Parmigiano-Reggiano, Asiago, or Grana Padano into the cream sauce just before serving.

Basil-Seared Scallops with Yellow Pepper Relish

For this dish, a seasoned cast-iron skillet can get smoking hot, but the scallops won't stick. If you don't have a cast-iron skillet, add an additional 2 tablespoons oil to the pan before you add the scallops. If you're using a grill, make sure the grate is well oiled. *Makes 4 servings*

> 20 large sea scallops
> 3 tablespoons olive oil
> 1 teaspoon salt
> ½ teaspoon freshly ground black pepper
> 20 basil leaves
> Yellow Pepper Relish (recipe follows)

❶ Place the scallops in a large resealable plastic bag; add the olive oil, salt, and pepper. Seal and gently toss. Set aside at room temperature for 10 minutes.

On the stove:
❷ Heat a large skillet, preferably cast iron, over high heat until smoking, about 5 minutes.

❸ Add the scallops one flat side down and do not touch them for 2 minutes. (Once they caramelize, you'll be able to get them off the pan without their sticking.)

❹ Reduce the heat to medium and gently turn the scallops. Lay a basil leaf over each. Reduce the heat to low, cover, and continue cooking until the basil has wilted and the scallops are opaque and

firm to the touch, about 3 more minutes. Serve on a bed of Yellow Pepper Relish.

On the grill:
❷ Heat a gas grill to medium heat or build a medium-heat, well-ashed coal bed in a charcoal grill. Oil the grate with some of the oil from the marinade in the bag.

❸ Place the scallops on the grate about 4 inches from the heat. Grill for 2 minutes.

❹ Turn the scallops and lay a basil leaf over each. Cover the grill and continue cooking until opaque and somewhat firm to the touch, about 2 more minutes. Serve on a bed of Yellow Pepper Relish.

Yellow Pepper Relish

This sweet-and-sour relish is also good with roast chicken, grilled fish, or burgers. *Makes 1½ cups*

> 2 medium yellow bell peppers, cored, seeded, and cut into quarters
> 1 small onion
> Boiling water
> ½ cup plus 2 tablespoons white vinegar
> 3 tablespoons sugar
> ¼ teaspoon salt
> ¼ teaspoon red pepper flakes

❶ Bring a large teakettle of water to a boil over high heat. Shred the bell peppers and onion through the large holes of a box grater or in a food processor fitted with the shredding blade. Place in a large bowl, cover with the boiling water to a depth of 1 inch, and set aside for 5 minutes. Drain in a colander set in the sink.

❷ Place the bell peppers and onion in a medium saucepan. Stir in ½ cup cool water and ½ cup vinegar; bring to a simmer over high heat. Remove from the heat, cover, and let stand for 10 minutes. Drain in a colander set in the sink.

③ Return the bell peppers and onion to the saucepan. Stir in the remaining 2 tablespoons vinegar, the sugar, salt, and red pepper flakes. Bring to a simmer over medium-high heat. Reduce the heat to low and simmer for 10 minutes, or until thickened like marmalade, stirring often.

To store: Cover and refrigerate for up to 1 week.

❊ *Lobster and Crab* ❊

These big crustaceans are perfect home fare. Just have lots of napkins on hand—you can't eat them without getting messy.

Lobster with Vanilla Butter

Nothing could be simpler—or more elegant—than lobster. Here are three ways to cook this delicacy with a buttery accompaniment. *Makes 4 servings*

> Four 1¼- to 2-pound live lobsters, rinsed
>   under cold water
> Canola oil for the grate if grilling
> Vanilla Butter (recipe follows, page 377)

To boil:
① Select a pot large enough to hold all the lobsters and plenty of water. Bring 2 to 3 gallons of water to a boil over high heat. There must be enough water to cover the lobsters once they're in the pot.

② Slide the lobsters into the pot headfirst. Cover and simmer until they turn completely red, 8 to 10 minutes for 1¼-pound lobsters, 10 to 12 minutes for 1½-pound lobsters, and 14 to 16 minutes for 2-pounders. If you're concerned about undercooking the lobster, you can snap off the tail and see if the meat inside is opaque (that is, no longer translucent). Drain and let stand at room temperature for 5 minutes before serving with the Vanilla Butter on the side.

To grill:
① Stopper the sink and fill it halfway with ice water. Preheat a gas grill to high heat or build a high-heat, well-ashed coal bed in a charcoal grill.

② While the grill's heating, select a pot large enough to hold all the lobsters and plenty of water. Bring 2 to 3 gallons of water to a boil in the pot over high heat.

③ Slip the lobsters in headfirst; cook just until they stop moving, about 2 minutes. Remove them with tongs and plunge them into the ice water. Cool for 5 minutes, then drain on paper towels.

④ Place a lobster belly side down on a large cutting board. With the sharp edge facing the lobster's eyes, pierce the shell behind the head with a heavy knife. Pull the knife back and slice through the head. Remove the knife, turn the lobster around, and slice back from the same point to the end of the tail. Repeat with the other 3 lobsters.

⑤ Generously oil the grill grate with canola oil and set it 4 to 6 inches over the heat. Place the lobster halves cut side down directly over the heat. Cover and cook for 2 minutes. Use tongs to turn them all cut side up; brush the meat generously with about half the Vanilla Butter. Cover and continue grilling until the meat is opaque and somewhat firm, about 5 minutes for 1¼-pound lobsters, 6 minutes for 1½-pound lobsters, and 8 minutes for 2-pounders. Serve with additional Vanilla Butter on the side.

To bake:

① Position the rack in the center of the oven and preheat the oven to 425°F.

② Complete steps 2–4 for grilling lobsters.

③ Snap off the large claws just where they join the body. Repeat with the other 3 lobsters.

④ Take a large sheet of aluminum foil and gently crumple it into ridges; its ridges will help the uneven lobster halves sit flat on the baking sheet. Place the foil on the baking sheet; set the claws on it, toward the edges. Bake for 6 minutes. Meanwhile, clean some of the brown material out of the thorax, or body cavity. Brush the exposed meat in the tail with a little of the Vanilla Butter.

⑤ Place the lobster bodies cut side down on the aluminum sheet, spacing them apart and setting them among the hillocks until they sit flat. Continue roasting until the meat is opaque and somewhat firm, about 7 minutes for 1¼-pound lobsters, 9 minutes for 1½-pound lobsters, and 12 minutes for 2-pounders. Serve with the remaining Vanilla Butter on the side.

Lobsters

Lobsters must be alive when they're cooked. Buy them only at markets where they're kept in a visible tank. When a lobster is picked up, the tail should flap. Do not buy the lobster if it falls limp or if the thorax (the body cavity) has foam coming out of the cracks.

When you get the lobsters home, store them in the packs provided by the market or unwrap the packaging and wrap them loosely but individually in several sheets of dampened newspaper.

Some people prefer to kill a lobster before boiling it. To do so, plunge a knife into a lobster's head, right between the eyes, thereby slicing its brain in half and killing the animal instantly. However, it will leak some juices as it's cooked and the meat can end up waterlogged.

How to Eat a Lobster

If the body is whole, twist the tail off the thorax (the main part of the body). Set the tail aside and turn the thorax belly side up. Twist off the large claws, leaving the knuckle joints attached to the claws. Crack open the knuckle joints one by one with a nutcracker, lobster cracker, or heavy mallet; remove the meat from each knuckle. Crack open the claws; wiggle the small part of the pincher free and pull out the meat in the claw. Slit the tail along the soft underside, then remove the meat inside. Slice the tail meat into chunks. Depending on the size of the lobster, the back tail fins may or may not have meat in them. Pull off each of the smaller legs and chew the shoulder meat out of their ends. If desired, tear open the smaller legs and pull out the thin meat inside.

Vanilla Butter

Makes about ½ cup

8 tablespoons unsalted butter
1 vanilla bean
1 teaspoon salt
¼ teaspoon sugar

❶ Melt the butter in a small saucepan set over medium heat. Remove it from the heat and let it stand at room temperature for 5 minutes.

❷ Skim the foam off the top of the butter with a small spoon. Slowly pour the butter into a small bowl, leaving the whitish milk solids in the pan. Discard the solids.

❸ Split the vanilla bean in half lengthwise; scrape the tiny seeds out of the bean with a sharp paring knife, then scrape them into the butter in the bowl. Stir in the salt and sugar. Set aside on the back of the stove to keep warm while you prepare the lobsters.

How to Eat a Crab

Take a mallet and bash the crab's face a couple of times, just at the eyestalks. Doing so should loosen the top and bottom parts of the shell. Pry off the top part of the shell and discard. Scrape out any green matter and the spongy, frondlike gills. If possible, snap the body in half. Snap off the legs one by one, cracking each to remove the meat inside and clearing off any shell at the shoulder joint to get at the crabmeat inside. Give the claws a couple of hard knocks to crack them, then remove the meat by peeling away the shell and wiggling the small part of the pincher free. Finally, dig into the chambers in the body to reveal the large bits of lump crabmeat, taking care to break the cartilage gently so as not to get any in the meat.

Crab Boil

You'll need an enormous pot for this simple dish. Look for blue or rock crabs in specialty markets or in Asian markets. Handle them with tongs and remember: if they're not fighting, they're probably dead and should be discarded.

Makes 6 servings

¼ cup kosher salt
2 tablespoons celery seeds
2 tablespoons finely cracked black
    peppercorns
1 tablespoon dry mustard
1 tablespoon paprika
1 teaspoon red pepper flakes
½ teaspoon ground allspice
½ teaspoon ground ginger
½ teaspoon ground cloves
6 quarts water
2 small onions, quartered
1 lemon, cut into eighths
4 bay leaves
1½ pounds very small red-skinned potatoes
    (if larger, cut in half)
Twelve 6-inch-diameter blue or rock crabs
6 ears corn, husked and halved

❶ Mix the kosher salt, celery seeds, peppercorns, dry mustard, paprika, red pepper flakes, allspice, ginger, and cloves in a small bowl; set aside.

❷ Bring the water, onions, lemon, and bay leaves to a boil in a very large pot set over high heat. Add all but 2 tablespoons of the salt mixture (reserving those 2 tablespoons for garnish).

❸ Add the potatoes and cook until fairly tender when pierced with a fork, about 15 minutes.

❹ Use tongs to get the crabs into the pot. Add the corn, cover, and bring back to a boil. Cook until the corn and potatoes are tender, about 5 minutes from the moment the crabs hit the water. To tell if

---

the crab is done, snap off one of the legs and make sure the meat inside is opaque, not translucent.

5 Drain everything in the sink. Discard the onions, lemon, bay leaves, and spices. Place the crabs, potatoes, and corn on an enormous platter. Sprinkle the remaining spice mixture over everything. Serve with mallets on the side for cracking open the crabs.

Crab Claws in Chili Sauce

Stone crabs are harvested by catching them, removing one claw, and throwing them back so that the claw can grow back and the crab can live another day. You can find the cooked claws frozen in tubs at the fish counter or thawed at the counter; here, they're stir-fried in a scorching, ketchuplike sauce. *Makes 4 servings*

2 tablespoons soy sauce
2 tablespoons rice vinegar
2 tablespoons packed light brown sugar
3 tablespoons peanut oil
3 medium shallots, minced
6 garlic cloves, minced
3 tablespoons minced peeled fresh ginger
4 pounds cooked medium stone crab claws
   (about 7 per pound)
4 Roma or plum tomatoes, chopped
2 to 4 teaspoons red Asian chili paste
   to taste
2 teaspoons cornstarch whisked with
   1½ tablespoons water until smooth
   in a small bowl

1 Whisk the soy sauce, rice vinegar, and brown sugar in a small bowl until the sugar dissolves.

2 Heat a large wok or high-sided sauté pan over medium-high heat. Swirl in the peanut oil, then add the shallots, garlic, and ginger. Stir-fry until aromatic, about 1 minute.

3 Add the crab claws; stir-fry for 1 minute. Then add the tomatoes and chili paste; cook, stirring constantly, until the tomatoes start to break down, about 2 minutes.

4 Pour in the soy sauce mixture; bring to a simmer. Stir in the cornstarch mixture; bring back to a simmer and cook, stirring constantly, until thickened, about 10 seconds.

Variations: Substitute 4 pounds cooked Jonah crab claws.

Substitute 4 pounds in-shell crayfish or 2 pounds medium or large deveined shrimp in their shells. Stir-fry these an extra minute before adding the tomatoes, just until they begin to turn red or pink.

Pan-Seared Soft-Shell Crabs with Brown Garlic Butter

So-called soft-shell blue or rock crabs are crabs that have just molted and therefore lack a hard shell, so you can eat them whole, provided your fishmonger has cleaned them for you. *Makes 6 servings*

8 tablespoons (1 stick) unsalted butter,
   cut into chunks
2 garlic cloves, minced
1½ cups all-purpose flour
1 tablespoon salt, plus additional
   to taste
1 teaspoon freshly ground black pepper
1 teaspoon mild paprika
1 teaspoon dried thyme
¼ teaspoon cayenne pepper
2 tablespoons canola oil
12 cleaned soft-shell crabs

❶ Place the butter and garlic in a large skillet; set it over low heat until the butter melts. Raise the heat to medium-low and cook until the foaming stops, the milk solids fall out of suspension, and the butter starts to turn golden, about 3 minutes. Immediately remove the pan from the heat, cover, and set aside.

❷ Whisk the flour, 1 tablespoon salt, pepper, paprika, thyme, and cayenne on a large plate.

❸ Heat a large skillet over medium heat. Swirl in the canola oil. Dip several of the crabs in the flour mixture, coating them evenly and thoroughly and then shaking off the excess. Slip as many crabs as will fit into the skillet and cook until browned, about 4 minutes. Turn and continue cooking until browned on the other side, about 4 minutes.

❹ Transfer to a serving platter and continue making more crabs. Serve by spooning a little of the garlic butter over each crab.

Variation: Forgo the brown garlic butter (step 1). Fry the crabs using the technique in steps 2 through 4; serve with lemon wedges or malt vinegar as a garnish.

Crab, Shrimp, and Scallop Bread Pudding

Here's a true seafood indulgence: a creamy, delicious casserole based on a Chilean dish, Chupa. Make sure the bread is stale so it doesn't fall apart instantly when soaked in the broth mixture.
Makes 10 to 12 servings

3 cups vegetable broth
1 cup dry white wine
1 pound medium shrimp (about 35 per pound), cleaned and deveined
1 pound bay scallops
2 cups whole or low-fat milk (do not use fat-free)
1 large day-old and very stale Italian bread loaf, cut into 1-inch cubes (6 cups)
2 large eggs
3 tablespoons unsalted butter, melted and cooled, plus additional for greasing the pan
1 tablespoon paprika
4 teaspoons chopped oregano leaves or 2 teaspoons dried oregano
Many dashes of hot red pepper sauce to taste, up to 1 teaspoon
12 ounces lump crabmeat, picked over for shell and cartilage
8 ounces Gruyère, shredded
½ teaspoon salt
½ teaspoon freshly ground black pepper

❶ Bring the broth and wine to a simmer in a large saucepan set over high heat. Add the shrimp and cook for 1 minute. Add the scallops and cook until they are opaque and the shrimp are pink but not yet firm, about 2 more minutes.

❷ Transfer the shellfish to a colander set in the sink with a slotted spoon. Remove the broth mixture from the heat. Refresh the shellfish under cool running water. Roughly chop the shrimp and scallops. Place on a plate; cover and refrigerate.

③ Skim off any foam from the broth mixture; bring back to a boil on high heat. Boil vigorously until reduced to 2 cups. Stir in the milk.

④ Place the bread in a large bowl. Pour the broth mixture over it; set aside to soak for 1 hour.

⑤ Meanwhile, position the rack in the center of the oven and preheat the oven to 375°F. Lightly butter a 13 × 9-inch casserole.

⑥ Lightly whisk the eggs in a large bowl with the cooled, melted butter, paprika, oregano, and hot red pepper sauce. Stir this mixture into the bread mixture along with the chopped shrimp and scallops. Stir in the crabmeat, half the grated cheese, the salt, and pepper.

⑦ Pour this mixture into the prepared baking dish. Sprinkle the top with the remaining cheese.

⑧ Bake until bubbling and golden brown, 25 to 30 minutes. Let stand at room temperature for 10 minutes before serving.

Can't get enough crab? Check out Filled Omelets (page 23), Crab and Scallion Filling for a frittata (page 24), Crab Sage Puffs (page 62), Crab and Pesto Savory Tart (page 79), and the Crab Filling for ravioli (page 199).

For squid recipes, check out Fried Calamari with a Ginger Crust (page 72) or Squid Salad (page 76).

Beef, Pork, and Other Meats

THIS CHAPTER TAKES ON THE ESSENTIAL PROBLEM OF MEAT: TOO MUCH FANdango ruins a good cut. Roasting, grilling, even no-fuss braising—simpler techniques bring out the best flavors.

Of course, there are a few complicated dishes here—some stews, for example, that require extra time. These are a result of less expensive cuts that require long cooking to get tender.

Frankly, most of the work needs to be done at the market. Buy good-quality meat from a reputable supplier. If your market has butchers on site, get to know them. (If there never seems to be anyone back there, find another market.) The butchers are your best bet for making the right choices. They'll know what's fresh, what looked good when it came in, and what cut up well without too much tendon or fat. Unfortunately, we've moved into a faceless marketplace where we've lost sight of the relationships across the counter. Buck the trend! Even at big-box warehouse stores, someone's probably cutting meat back there.

And once you do your work at the store, you can make the best meat dishes imaginable at home—because then it's only a matter of keeping it simple.

❊ Beef ❊

If you're not cooking steaks, roasts, or even ground beef within 6 hours of getting them into your refrigerator, remove the store packaging, place the beef on a plate, cover loosely with wax paper, and set in the coldest part of your refrigerator for no more than 2 days. (The store's plastic wrap aids bacterial production in your refrigerator's humid environment.) Our other tip? Forgo inner marbling for a leaner cut. You'll barely miss it if you cook the meat to the proper temperature.

Strip, Shell, or Club Steaks

These steaks are taken from the top loin, a part of the larger short loin. It lies in the upper half of the cow right about at the midway point, between the ribs up front and the larger sirloin behind. The whole top loin is a very tender piece; the muscle does little during the cow's life to toughen it. If a steak cut from it has a piece of the bone, it's a "club steak"; if not, it's a "strip" or "shell steak." Here are two cooking techniques, indoors and outdoors. (See page 385 for an explanation of a steak's doneness.) *Makes 4 servings*

¼ cup olive oil
Four 8- to 10-ounce, ¾- to 1-inch-thick
  strip, shell, or club steaks, trimmed
2 teaspoons kosher salt
2 teaspoons finely crushed black peppercorns

❶ Begin by rubbing ½ tablespoon olive oil into each side of each steak. Coat each side with ¼ teaspoon salt and ¼ teaspoon pepper, gently massaging them into the steak. Alternatively, sprinkle the salt and pepper on a sheet of wax paper and press the oiled steaks into the mixture. Set aside at room temperature while you heat the oven or grill, then follow one of these two methods.

If you're cooking the steaks indoors:

❷ Position the rack in the center of the oven and preheat the oven to 450°F.

❸ Heat one or two large skillets, preferably well-seasoned cast iron, over high heat until smoking, about 5 minutes. Turn on the overhead ventilation, if you have it; or open a window and door to create a draft to blow out the smoke.

❹ Place the steaks in the pan(s) and cook undisturbed for 3 minutes. (The steaks will stick at first, but the intense caramelization should loosen them up from a well-seasoned pan.)

❺ Flip the steaks with tongs or a large spatula (never poke them with a meat fork—this allows the juices to leak out). Put the skillet(s) in the oven. Roast without disturbing until an instant-read meat thermometer inserted diagonally into the central, thickest part of a steak registers

120°F (our definition of rare; the USDA does
  not recommend rare beef), 4 to 5 minutes
125°F (our definition of medium-rare—and
  our preference for these cuts), 5 to 6 minutes
145°F (the USDA's definition of medium-rare),
  7 to 8 minutes
160°F (the USDA's definition of medium), 9 to
  10 minutes

or 170°F (the USDA's definition of well done), about 12 minutes

⑥ Remove the skillet(s) from the oven, transfer the steaks to a cutting board, and let them stand at room temperature for 5 minutes. (See page 20 for hints on the care of cast iron.)

If you're cooking the steaks on the grill:
② Heat a gas grill to high heat or build a well-ashed, high-heat coal bed in a charcoal grill.

③ Place the steaks on the grill directly over the heat, 4 to 6 inches above it. Cover and grill undisturbed for 4 minutes.

④ Flip the steaks (as indicated in step 5 on page 382), cover, and continue grilling until an instant-read meat thermometer inserted diagonally into the thick center of a steak registers

120°F (our definition of rare; the USDA does not recommend rare beef), 2 to 3 minutes
125°F (our definition of medium-rare and our recommendation), 3 to 4 minutes
145°F (the USDA's definition of medium-rare), about 6 minutes
160°F (the USDA's definition of medium), about 8 minutes
or 170°F (the USDA's definition of well done), about 9 minutes

⑤ Transfer the steaks to a carving board and let them stand at room temperature for 5 minutes before serving.

Tips for Success

• Coarse salt and crushed peppercorns make a crunchy crust. Crush peppercorns in a mortar with a pestle or in a sealed plastic bag with a rolling pin or the bottom of a heavy saucepan.

• Untrimmed strip steaks have a fatty "tail" that curls around one end. Trim this off for a more classic look—and a leaner steak. Also trim off the fatty, outer rind; you don't need it for this high-temperature, fast-cook method.

• Use a cast-iron or other heavy-duty skillet. Nonstick coatings may not be safe at these temperatures.

• While larger cuts of meat should be removed from the oven when they're a few degrees below the recommended temperature, these steaks are really too thin to worry about the degree or two they'll rise off the heat.

• Keep in mind that thinner steaks cook more quickly; shave several minutes off the cooking time.

• Let the steaks rest at room temperature so that the juices have time to reincorporate into the meat's fibers.

Six Tips for Safety When Working with Meat

① Wash your hands and all cutting surfaces with hot, soapy water before and after handling meat.
② Chop meat and vegetables on separate boards with separate knives.
③ Do not return cooked meat to a dirty cutting board or platter.
④ Use an instant-read meat thermometer to tell if the meat's cooked to the proper temperature.
⑤ If working with a barbecue sauce, wash the mop or other utensils between uses; keep any barbecue sauce hot over low heat. At the end, bring the sauce to a simmer for 3 minutes before using any additional for dipping at the table.
⑥ Refrigerate leftovers promptly.

Rib-Eye Steaks

A rib eye is the boneless round eye of meat attached to the ribs. Although you could call the round eyes of meat on a standing rib roast "rib eyes," these popular steaks are usually taken from the bones farther along the rib cage than those chosen for the best roasts. Use the same cooking technique as for strip steaks, but cook the rib eyes a minute or two less. The extra honeycombs of fat cook the meat more quickly.

Delmonico Steak

In the Midwest, a Delmonico is usually a boneless sirloin steak, a fairly chewy cut that benefits from a little added flavor like a rub or a flavored butter (see pages 385–386). In some parts of the country, particularly Texas and California, Delmonico is just another name for a rib eye. And in New York, the erstwhile home of Delmonico's restaurant, it's a strip or club steak, with or without the bone. In all cases, cook these steaks as you would strip steaks.

T-Bone or Porterhouse Steaks

Many people consider these the Cadillacs of steaks because they include the best of both worlds, found on each side of the middle bone in the short loin (shaped roughly like a "T"). On one side, there's a strip steak; on the other, a piece of the tenderloin (or fillet). In general, a T-bone has less of the tenderloin than a porterhouse. We don't recommend pan-searing these steaks. As the meat cooks, it contracts slightly from the bone, pulling up off the surface of the pan as the bone rests against the metal, thus negating all that searing and browning. *Makes 4 servings*

Two 1¼-pound, ¾- to 1-inch-thick porterhouse or T-bone steaks (see Note)
3 tablespoons olive oil

1 teaspoon salt
1 teaspoon freshly ground black pepper

1 Preheat the broiler; line the broiler pan with aluminum foil.

2 Rub the steaks on both sides with the olive oil (about ¾ tablespoon per side). Season one side of the steaks with half the salt and pepper.

3 Set the steaks in the broiler pan and place them 4 inches from the heat source salted side up. Broil for 4 minutes.

4 Turn the steaks over, season the other side with the remaining salt and pepper, and continue broiling until an instant-read thermometer inserted diagonally into the thickest part of the larger side of the steaks registers

120°F (our definition of rare; the USDA does not recommend rare beef), 4 to 5 minutes
125°F (our definition of medium-rare and our preference for these steaks), 5 to 6 minutes
145°F (the USDA's definition of medium-rare), about 8 minutes
160°F (the USDA's definition of medium), about 10 minutes
or 170°F (the USDA's definition of well done), about 12 minutes

5 Transfer the steaks to a carving board and let them stand at room temperature for 5 minutes before serving. Porterhouse steaks and T-bones are usually sliced before they're served; cut the two sides off the bone by tracing a knife along the natural inside curve of the bone, then slice each piece into strips against the grain (see page 394 for an explanation of a meat's grain).

To carve T-bones and Porterhouses, lay the steak on a carving board so that it looks rather like a heart, the tapered end nearest you. Starting at the top, run a sharp knife around the inside perimeter of the bone on each side, cutting away each side's meat in one piece. Leave about ¼-inch meat along the bone for the biggest carnivore at the table to gnaw. Slice the meat into long, ½-inch-thick strips against the grain (see page 394).

Note: Do not trim these steaks. The perimeter of fat will keep them juicy under the broiler's heat.

Variations: Use a seasoned olive oil such as one flavored with lemon or roasted red peppers.

Mash 3 peeled garlic cloves into the oil before adding it to the steaks.

Omit the salt and pepper; use 1 tablespoon lemon pepper seasoning. When you flip the steaks, squeeze 1 tablespoon lemon juice over them.

Spice Rubs and Flavored Butters for Steaks

To add more flavor, try one of these spice rubs or flavored butter. Mix any of the rubs in a small bowl, oil the steaks as directed, and gently massage the rub into the meat. Forgo the salt and pepper in the recipes (the rubs already have them). Each rub mixture makes enough for 4 steaks; double or triple the quantity as needed. For the best taste, set the coated steaks on a platter, cover with wax paper, and refrigerate for at least 4 hours or up to 24 hours.

Chili Rub
2 tablespoons chili powder
2 teaspoons dried oregano
1½ teaspoons salt
1 teaspoon ground cumin
1 teaspoon packed light brown sugar
1 teaspoon freshly ground black pepper
½ teaspoon garlic powder

When Is the Beef Done?

Although we give cooking times for beef, we debated doing so at first. There are so many factors involved: how cold your refrigerator is, how cold the meat is, how marbled the meat is, how accurate your oven is, how consistent the heat is, how often you open the door, what the composition of your roasting pan is, etc. In the end, the only reliable test is done with an instant-read meat thermometer, inserted diagonally into the center of the meat for 5 seconds to get an accurate reading.

What that temperature actually means is a matter of debate. For example, we prefer beef rarer than the USDA guidelines. Theirs have been established for safety; ours, for safety and taste. Should you choose to follow our recommendations, realize what you're doing, buy certified organic beef from a reputable butcher, and cook it within a day of purchase. Rare meat should not be consumed by anyone with immune deficiencies, expectant mothers, or the infirm.

Our definitions are rare, 120°F; medium-rare, 125°F; medium, 140°F; and well done, 160°F.

The USDA's are rare, not recommended; medium-rare, 145°F; medium, 160°F; and well done, 170°F.

However, you'll notice that we don't strictly adhere to these temperatures inside some recipes. We sometimes suggest you take the beef off the heat at a slightly lower temperature than those given. Larger cuts of beef continue to cook off the heat, the fat still hot in the meat. Also note that there are no temperatures given for fattier, tougher cuts that are stewed, braised, or roasted—brisket, for example—because these are cooked to temperatures well beyond medium, even well done, until the meat falls apart.

Rosemary-Garlic Rub

3 tablespoons minced rosemary leaves

2 garlic cloves, crushed

2 teaspoons salt, preferably kosher salt

2 teaspoons freshly ground black pepper

Singapore-Inspired Rub

2 tablespoons lemon pepper seasoning

1 teaspoon ground coriander

1 teaspoon ground cumin

1 teaspoon ground ginger

1 teaspoon onion powder

1 teaspoon salt

½ teaspoon garlic powder

½ teaspoon grated nutmeg

½ teaspoon ground cinnamon

½ teaspoon ground cardamom

¼ teaspoon ground cloves

¼ teaspoon cayenne pepper

For flavored butters, see the herb butters for chicken quarters (see page 276) or the butter combinations for fish steaks (see page 346). Add a pat of butter to the top of the hot steak *after* it's out of the pan or off the grill.

Grading Beef

The USDA names eight categories of beef, "prime" to "canner." Prime is fattier, more marbled, and thus more resistant to turning tough or taking on a liverlike tang. Rarely seen in supermarkets, prime is usually reserved for restaurants and high-end butcher shops. The three gradations routinely found in supermarkets are "choice," "select," and sometimes "standard." In the end, we actually prefer choice, even over prime. It's leaner, a little chewier, with a bolder flavor; it does, however, require greater accuracy in its internal roasted temperature to ensure tenderness. Select beef is best reserved for stewing.

Tenderloin

A tenderloin is the other part of the short loin, the luxurious, little-used (and thus very tender) muscle that runs on the other side of the bone that carries the part from which strip steaks are cut. It's also the smaller side of a porterhouse or T-bone steak. When sliced, the rounds are called "filets mignons." Never roast a tenderloin to any degree of doneness higher than medium; the extra heat will toughen this lean cut into leather. The recommended internal temperatures given here are a little lower than the ones advised because this cut will indeed gain in degrees as it rests at room temperature. *Makes 6 servings*

Butcher's twine

One 3-pound center-cut tenderloin, trimmed (see Note)

6 tablespoons unsalted butter, melted and cooled, or 6 tablespoons olive oil

3 garlic cloves, crushed

2 tablespoons coarse salt, such as kosher or coarse-grained sea salt

1 tablespoon crushed black peppercorns (see tip for success, page 383)

❶ Wrap and knot butcher's twine securely but not tightly around the tenderloin in three places to keep the meat cylindrical.

❷ Mix the melted butter or olive oil and garlic in a small bowl. Brush about 2 tablespoons of the mixture onto the tenderloin, then gently massage the salt and pepper into the meat. Place in a large roasting pan and set aside at room temperature while you preheat the oven or prepare the grill, before you follow one of these two methods.

To roast in the oven:

❸ Position the rack in the center of the oven and preheat the oven to 375°F.

④ Roast, basting three or four times with the additional garlic mixture, until an instant-read meat thermometer inserted diagonally into the thickest part of the tenderloin registers

118°F (our definition of rare), 18 to 20
    minutes
122°F (our definition of medium-rare), about
    22 minutes
128°F (our definition of medium), about 25
    minutes
140°F (the USDA's definition of medium-rare),
    about 30 minutes
or 155°F (the USDA's definition of medium),
    about 40 minutes

⑤ Transfer to a carving board; let stand for 5 minutes. Slice off the twine, then carve the roast into ½-inch rounds.

To grill:
③ Heat a gas grill to high heat or build a well-ashed, high-heat coal bed in a charcoal grill.

④ Place the tenderloin on the grate directly over the heat, 4 to 6 inches above it. Cover and grill, turning occasionally and basting three or four times with the butter or oil mixture, until an instant-read meat thermometer inserted diagonally into the thickest part of the tenderloin registers

118°F (our definition of rare), 16 to 18
    minutes
122°F (our definition of medium-rare), 20 to
    22 minutes
128°F (our definition of medium), about 25
    minutes
140°F (the USDA's definition of medium-rare),
    about 30 minutes
or 155°F (the USDA's definition of medium),
    about 38 minutes

⑤ Transfer to a carving board; let stand for 5 minutes. Slice off the twine and carve the roast into ½-inch rounds.

Note: A center-cut tenderloin is the long tube of meat minus the chateaubriand (the thick end) and the thinner tail, as well as the small rope of meat that runs underneath the tenderloin. Trim off any visible fat, then slice off the silver skin, a paper-thin, translucent, indigestible membrane that runs over the surface of the meat. (Or have your butcher trim the tenderloin for you.)

An herb-mustard crust for a tenderloin:
Use only olive oil for the basting mixture; roast or grill as directed. While the tenderloin stands at room temperature for 5 minutes, mix ½ cup chopped mixed herbs on a plate (for example, chives, tarragon, and parsley; parsley, rosemary, and oregano; or parsley and thyme). Spread 2 tablespoons Dijon mustard over the hot roast, then roll it in the fresh herbs before slicing.

Two Refrigerator Chutneys

A chutney is a savory, vinegary jam, excellent with roasted or grilled meat, particularly beef. It's usually processed and canned, but you can simplify the process by putting either of these in the refrigerator to set up, where they will keep for 2 months.

Blackberry-Rhubarb Chutney

Makes about 5 cups

4 cups blackberries

3 rhubarb stalks, peeled of stringy excess and then thinly sliced

2 celery ribs, thinly sliced

1 medium red onion, chopped

One 3-inch piece of fresh ginger, peeled and minced

3 garlic cloves, minced

3 dried Chinese red chiles

1¼ cups packed dark brown sugar

½ cup granulated sugar

½ cup dry red wine

½ cup red wine vinegar

1 teaspoon ground cinnamon

1 teaspoon salt

¼ teaspoon ground cloves

1 Combine the ingredients in a large pot and bring to a simmer over medium-high heat, stirring often.

2 Reduce the heat to medium-low and simmer until dense and jamlike, about 40 minutes, stirring almost constantly once the blackberries break down and the mixture starts to thicken.

3 Remove the chiles. Spoon into cleaned glass canning jars. Seal and refrigerate for up to 1 month.

Tomato-Cranberry Chutney

Makes about 7 cups

8 large red tomatoes

2 large red bell peppers, cored, seeded, and chopped

1 large red onion, chopped

1 orange, peeled and cut into segments, plus 1 tablespoon grated orange zest

One 4-inch piece of fresh ginger, peeled and minced

1 cup dried cranberries

1 cup red wine vinegar

1 cup granulated sugar

½ cup packed dark brown sugar

1 teaspoon ground cinnamon

1 teaspoon mustard seeds

1 teaspoon freshly ground black pepper

1 teaspoon salt

½ teaspoon red pepper flakes

1 Bring a large pot of water to a boil over high heat. Meanwhile, place a large bowl of ice water in the sink.

2 Once the water boils, drop in the tomatoes and cook for 30 seconds, just to loosen their skins. Transfer with a slotted spoon to the ice water bath. Cool completely, then slip off the skins and discard them. Roughly chop the tomatoes.

3 Place the chopped tomatoes and the rest of the ingredients in a large saucepan; bring to a simmer over medium-high heat, stirring often.

4 Reduce the heat to low and simmer uncovered, stirring often, until thickened, about 45 minutes.

5 Continue cooking, stirring constantly to prevent scorching, until ketchuplike, about 15 more minutes.

6 Spoon into clean glass canning jars, seal, and store in the refrigerator for up to 1 month.

Standing Rib Roast

Sometimes erroneously called a "prime rib" (the cut may or may not be graded prime—see page 386), a rib roast is made of the cow's ribs plus the eye of meat under them. We do not recommend boneless rib roasts; the point here is to char the bone taste into the meat. Otherwise, you might as well enjoy a rib-eye steak (see page 384). Again, the temperatures are a little lower than those recommended for beef (see page 385) because this large roast will gain degrees as it rests. *Makes 6 hefty servings*

1 three-bone 6½- to 7½-pound standing
   rib roast (see Notes)
Butcher's twine
2 tablespoons coarse salt, such as kosher salt
2 teaspoons freshly ground black pepper
   (see Notes)

Cooking the roast in the oven:
❶ Position the rack in the center of the oven and preheat the oven to 375°F.

❷ To help the roast keep its shape while roasting, wrap and knot butcher's twine securely but not too tightly around it, circling the twine in a single loop between each bone and over the eye meat. Coat the roast in salt and pepper, getting the seasonings all over the meat.

❸ Place the roast in a large, heavy roasting pan bone side down (so that the bones arc underneath the meat, holding the roast up). Roast until an instant-read meat thermometer inserted diagonally into the center of the roast without touching bone registers

118°F (our definition of rare), about 1 hour and
   45 minutes
122°F (our definition of medium-rare), about
   1 hour and 55 minutes

128°F (our definition of medium), about 2 hours
140°F (the USDA definition of medium-rare),
   about 2 hours and 10 minutes
or 155°F (the USDA's definition of medium),
   about 2 hours and 20 minutes

❹ Remove the roast from the oven, set on a carving board, and tent with aluminum foil for 10 to 15 minutes before carving (see page 390).

Cooking the roast on the grill:
❶ Wrap and knot butcher's twine around the roast as in step 2 above; coat with salt and pepper. Seal the roast in aluminum foil; place it bone side down in a disposable roasting pan.

❷ Preheat a gas grill for high-heat cooking or build a high-heat, well-ashed coal bed in a charcoal grill.

❸ Set the roasting pan with the beef on the grill grate directly over the heat, 4 to 6 inches above it. Cover and roast until an instant-read meat thermometer inserted diagonally into the roast's center without the probe touching bone registers 115°F, about 1 hour and 20 minutes.

❹ Remove the pan and roast from the grill. Unwrap the roast—be careful: the juices in the packet are hot. Discard the pan, foil, and all rendered "juices" (they're mostly fat).

❺ Return the roast bone side down to the grill grate. If using a gas grill, reduce the heat to medium; if using a charcoal grill, partially close the vents and do not feed the fire. Cover and grill for 5 minutes, then turn the roast onto its side and grill, covered, for 2 minutes. Repeat on the other side of the roast to char.

❻ Return the roast to its original position of bone side down and continue roasting until an instant-read meat thermometer inserted into the center of the roast without the probe touching bone registers

118°F (our definition of rare), about 3 more
   minutes
122°F (our definition of medium-rare), about
   7 more minutes
128°F (our definition of medium), about
   10 more minutes
140°F (the USDA definition of medium-rare),
   about 15 more minutes
or 155°F (the USDA definition of medium),
   about 20 more minutes

7 Transfer to a carving board, tent with foil, and let stand for 10 minutes at room temperature before carving (see right).

Note: You can cook smaller or larger roasts: two-bone, four-bone, or even five-bone roasts. Plan on two healthy appetites per bone. The timing will be dramatically changed; figure on about 16 minutes per pound for medium-rare and adjust the timing accordingly, relying on your instant-read meat thermometer. For big parties, we prefer to roast two 3-bone rib roasts, rather than one colossal one.

Cracked black peppercorns are not recommended. They don't impart enough flavor as they mingle with the juices. But remember that black pepper is indeed perishable—it loses much of its zip in long storage. Plan on replacing black pepper every six months or so.

Selecting a Rib Roast

In butcher parlance, a cow's rib bones are numbered, starting with the bone farthest from the shoulder (and nearest the hip). Bones 1 through 4 are the meatiest: the least gristle and fat. Bones 2 and above have a separate arc of meat above the center eye with a honeycomb of fat running between the two. Above bone 4, the center eye starts to break up and include large pockets of fat. For the best standing rib roast, choose bones 1 through 3.

Ask the butcher to slice off the backbone if it's still attached. (Save this for beef stock; see page 165).

Do not let the butcher slice the center eye of the meat off the bones and tie it back on. You want the bones to cradle the meat and infuse it with flavor as it roasts.

For a more aesthetic presentation, ask for the roast to be "frenched"—that is, the fat and meat cleaned from the ends of the bones, leaving the eye of meat exposed below.

Carving a Rib Roast

Stand the roast so its bones are pointing up. Hold the roast in place with a meat fork inserted into the center eye. Use a long, thin carving knife to slice along and around the inside arc of the bones, thereby removing the entire center eye in one piece. Do not carve too close to the bones; leave some meat for those who like to gnaw. Stand the now-boneless eye cut side down on the carving board, hold it in place with a meat fork, and slice down, starting with one of the ends to create a thin slice and then carving off more as you move along the roast. We prefer steaklike, 1/2-inch-thick slices. Finally, slice between the bones to separate them.

Lemon Pepper London Broil

There's no cut named "London broil." Rather, it's a way to cook and slice a less expensive cut—but not always the same cut. In days past, a London broil was made from flank steak; today, most of that cut goes to restaurants, so London broil is most often made at home with top round, the back end of the cow. It's not a terribly flavorful cut, so it needs a good dose of zippy marinade. Tenderize this lean cut by marinating it in a lemony vinaigrette before giving it a peppery crust.

Makes about 4 servings

½ cup olive oil
6 tablespoons lemon juice
1½ tablespoons minced peeled fresh
   ginger
1 tablespoon soy sauce
2 teaspoons finely grated lemon zest
2 teaspoons sugar
2 pounds top round, trimmed of any
   peripheral fat
2 teaspoons whole black peppercorns,
   cracked in a plastic bag with a meat
   mallet or the bottom of a large
   saucepan
Canola oil for the grill grate, if using

1 Whisk the olive oil, lemon juice, ginger, soy sauce, lemon zest, and sugar in a baking dish.

2 Add the beef; turn to coat. Cover and refrigerate for at least 2 hours but no more than 8 hours, turning occasionally.

3 Remove the meat from the marinade. Pat the cracked peppercorns over the top, bottom, and sides of the steak.

4 **To cook under the broiler:** Preheat the broiler. Line the broiler pan with aluminum foil to make cleanup easier. Broil 5 inches from the heat source, turning once, until an instant-read meat thermometer inserted diagonally into the center, the thickest part of the meat, registers

120°F (our definition of rare), about 14 minutes
125°F (our definition of medium-rare), about
   18 minutes
130°F (our definition of medium), about
   21 minutes
145°F (the USDA's definition of medium-rare),
   about 27 minutes
or 160°F (the USDA's definition of medium),
   about 32 minutes

To cook on the grill: Heat a gas grill for high-heat cooking or prepare a well-ashed, high-heat coal bed in a charcoal grill. Remove the beef from the marinade. Oil the grill grate. Place the beef 4 to 6 inches directly over high-heat coals. Cover and grill, turning once, until an instant-read meat thermometer inserted diagonally into the center of the thickest part of the steak registers

120°F (our definition of rare), about 9 minutes
125°F (our definition of medium-rare), about
   11 minutes
130°F (our definition of medium), about
   14 minutes
145°F (the USDA's definition of medium-rare),
   about 18 minutes
or 160°F (the USDA's definition of medium),
   about 20 minutes

5 Transfer the steak to a carving board, tent with foil, and let stand at room temperature for 10 minutes. Slice into ⅛-inch-thick slices against the grain and on the bias (see page 394).

Flank Steak Negimaki

This is an American take on a Japanese classic, scallion-stuffed steak rolls, flavored with a Chinese-inspired marinade. Instead of individual rolls, we stuff a flank steak with the vegetables, then cook it and slice it into stuffed strips. If you don't want to go to the trouble of making a pocket in the steak, ask your butcher to do it for you. *Makes 4 main-course servings*

One 1¾-pound flank steak
8 asparagus spears, shaved with a vegetable peeler to the width of a pencil
8 medium scallions
Butcher's twine
¼ cup dry vermouth or dry white wine
¼ cup soy sauce
3 tablespoons hoisin sauce
2 tablespoons orange juice
2 tablespoons minced peeled fresh ginger
1 tablespoon rice vinegar
½ teaspoon chili oil or Asian red chili sauce
1 garlic clove, crushed
Canola oil for the grill grate, if using

❶ To cut a pocket in the flank steak, make a long, narrow incision in the thicker, longer side of the steak with a sharp chef's knife. Flip the steak over and deepen the incision by slicing farther into the meat at the same place. Keep flipping and slicing gently (to prevent tearing) until a pocket is formed—do not cut through to the opposite side but leave ½ inch of meat on the three remaining sides to hold the pocket together.

❷ Trim the asparagus spears and scallions to fit and place in the pocket lengthwise (parallel to the incision), placing each spear and scallion so they alternate directions.

❸ Tie closed by wrapping and knotting butcher's twine around the steak at 3-inch increments, perpendicular to the asparagus and scallions. Place in a large loaf pan or a medium baking dish.

❹ Whisk the vermouth or wine, soy sauce, hoisin sauce, orange juice, ginger, vinegar, chili oil or sauce, and garlic in a small bowl. Pour over the stuffed steak; turn to coat. Cover and refrigerate for at least 2 hours or up to 6 hours, turning occasionally.

❺ Remove the meat from the marinade; reserve the marinade. Bring the meat to room temperature as the broiler or grill heats.

❻ To broil: Preheat the broiler and line the broiler pan with aluminum foil. Place the stuffed steak in the pan about 5 inches from the heat source. Broil, turning occasionally and basting often with the reserved marinade, until an instant-read meat thermometer inserted into the meat (but not the vegetables) registers 125°F for our definition of medium-rare, about 20 minutes, or 145°F for the USDA's definition of medium-rare, about 25 minutes.

To grill: Heat a gas grill to medium heat or build a well-ashed, medium-heat coal bed in a charcoal grill. Oil the grate. Place the stuffed steak on the grate directly over medium heat or on the charcoal grill 4 to 6 inches directly over medium-heat coals. Cover and grill, turning occasionally and basting often with the reserved marinade, until an instant-read meat thermometer inserted into the meat (but not the vegetables) registers 125°F for our definition of medium-rare, about 18 minutes, or 145°F for the USDA's definition of medium-rare, about 22 minutes.

❼ Transfer to a carving board, tent with foil, and let stand at room temperature for 5 minutes. Slice off one piece of twine, then carve by making long slices perpendicular to the vegetables in the pocket (against the meat's grain). Cut off the remaining pieces of twine only as you reach them while slicing.

Horseradish-Braised Brisket with Root Vegetables

A brisket comes from the cow's breast; the cut is rather stringy but tenderizes beautifully during long cooking. The leanest section—and our preference—is the first cut, also known as the flat cut. Less marbled, it does have a layer of fat on top which you can leave in place if you want a richer meal. Oven-braised, the meat turns sweet and luscious. The horseradish, too—it mellows beautifully in this braise. *Makes 8 servings*

2 tablespoons canola oil

One 4-pound first-cut brisket, trimmed of most visible surface fat

2 medium onions, halved and thinly sliced

2 medium carrots, peeled and cut into 1-inch pieces

2 medium parsnips, peeled and cut into 1-inch pieces

1 medium turnip, peeled and cut into 1-inch pieces

1 cup red wine

3 cups beef broth

2 teaspoons Dijon mustard

2 teaspoons stemmed thyme or 1 teaspoon dried thyme

½ teaspoon salt, or more to taste

½ teaspoon freshly ground black pepper

2 bay leaves

3 tablespoons bottled white horseradish

1 tablespoon potato starch whisked into 1 tablespoon water in a small bowl, optional

1 Heat a large pot or Dutch oven over medium heat. Swirl in the canola oil, then add the brisket. Brown on both sides, turning once, about 8 minutes. Transfer to a large cutting board; set aside.

2 Add the onions, carrots, parsnips, and turnip to the pot; cook, stirring often, until lightly browned, about 5 minutes.

3 Pour in the wine and bring to a simmer, scraping up any browned bits on the pot's bottom.

4 Pour in the broth; swirl in the mustard until smooth. Add the thyme, salt, pepper, and bay leaves. Bring to a full simmer. Nestle the brisket into the sauce. Spread the horseradish on any exposed portion of the meat.

5 Cover and place in the oven. Bake until the meat is fork-tender, 3 to 3½ hours (or even 4 hours, depending on the cow's size, health, and diet).

6 Remove the meat and vegetables from the pot. The brisket is quite tender, so hold it up with a large spatula to keep it from breaking apart. Place all on a large, clean cutting board. Place the vegetables on a serving platter.

7 If you want to thicken the sauce, set the pot over medium heat and bring the sauce to a simmer. Whisk in the potato starch mixture; cook, whisking constantly, until slightly thickened, about 1 minute.

8 Slice the brisket against the grain. Place it on the serving platter. Discard the bay leaves, check the sauce to see if it needs salt, and pour the sauce over the meat and vegetables.

Variations: Substitute a large potato, peeled and cut into 1-inch cubes, for the turnip.

Reduce the broth to 2 cups and add 1½ cups canned diced tomatoes with the broth.

Add one 4-inch cinnamon stick with the bay leaves.

Slow Cooker Variation: Brown the meat in a large skillet as in step 1. Add all the vegetables, aromatics, and mustard to a 6-cup slow cooker; pour in ½ cup red wine and 1 cup beef broth. Coat the brisket with the horseradish. Nestle the meat in the cooker, cover, and cook on low until fork-tender, about 8 hours.

Oven-Barbecued Brisket

If you can't find a brisket this large, use two smaller ones of equal weight. You can always forgo the tomato puree barbecue sauce here and use about 4 cups of your favorite bottled barbecue sauce.

Makes 12 servings

2 large onions, cut into ½-inch rings
2 celery ribs, thinly sliced
6 garlic cloves, quartered
1 tablespoon whole black peppercorns
4 allspice berries
1 bay leaf
One 6-pound first-cut brisket, trimmed of most visible surface fat
Boiling water
1 medium shallot, minced
3½ cups canned tomato puree
½ cup packed dark brown sugar
½ cup cider vinegar
2 tablespoons smoked paprika (see Note)
1 tablespoon Worcestershire sauce
1 tablespoon ground coriander
1 teaspoon ground allspice
1 teaspoon ground cloves
1 teaspoon dry mustard
½ teaspoon celery seeds

❶ Position the rack in the center of the oven and preheat the oven to 350°F.

❷ Place the onions, celery, garlic, peppercorns, allspice berries, and bay leaf in a deep roasting pan. Set the brisket on top, then pour in boiling water until the brisket is covered.

❸ Cover the pan with aluminum foil and bake until nearly tender, about 2½ hours.

❹ Transfer the meat to a large cutting board; discard all the liquid, vegetables, and aromatics in the pan.

❺ Whisk the shallot, tomato puree, brown sugar, vinegar, smoked paprika, Worcestershire sauce, coriander, ground allspice, cloves, dry mustard, and celery seeds in a large bowl until the sugar has dissolved.

❻ Return the meat to the roasting pan; slather with the tomato sauce mixture.

❼ Bake, uncovered, until the meat is fork-tender and the sauce is bubbling, about 1 hour. Let stand at room temperature for 5 minutes before removing the brisket from the pan and slicing against the grain (see below).

Note: If you can't find smoked paprika, substitute 1 tablespoon regular paprika and 1 teaspoon liquid smoke.

Variations: Substitute honey for the brown sugar.

Add 1 teaspoon red pepper flakes with the tomato puree.

Slicing Beef against the Grain

Meat should be sliced so that the most fibers are exposed in each cut. In American butchering techniques, the fibers run through the cuts, not along their surface planes. Sometimes you can see the fibers on the outside of the cut. If so, slice 90 degrees to their direction. At other times, run your fingers along the surface of the meat to tell which way the fibers are running. Once in a while, it's just trial and error: slice a small piece off the end of the meat and look at the fibers.

Thinner cuts like steaks should also be sliced "on the bias"—that is, into wider strips. To get the most width out of the strips, tilt your knife so that the blade angles slightly and is thereby held on a diagonal to the meat itself. Slice across the meat, removing a wider cut than you would have if you'd sliced straight down.

Beef Ribs with Plum-and-Rum Barbecue Sauce

A barbecue favorite, beef ribs are the decadent treats found under a standing rib roast. They can be difficult to track down outside of Texas, but most butcher counters will have them in the back. *Makes 6 servings*

Two 3-pound racks beef ribs
Plum-and-Rum Barbecue Sauce
    (recipe follows)

1 **To make the ribs in the oven:** Position the rack in the center of the oven and preheat the oven to 400°F. Fill a large, lipped baking pan with ½ inch water; place a footed large wire rack in the pan. Set the ribs on the rack, then cover the pan tightly with aluminum foil. Bake for 1 hour. Remove the pan and the foil; pour off any hot liquid in the pan. Reduce the oven's temperature to 350°F. Baste the ribs with the prepared barbecue sauce, then roast, uncovered, until the ribs are tender, until the meat is pulling away from the bones, 1 to 1½ hours.

To make the ribs on the grill: Set up the grill for indirect cooking by heating half of a gas grill to high heat or building a high-heat, well-ashed coal bed on one side of a charcoal grill. Place a drip pan underneath the portion of the grate that's not heated; set the ribs over the pan. Baste with the prepared sauce and cover the grill. Barbecue until the ribs are mahogany colored and the meat pulls back from the bones, mopping frequently with more sauce, 1½ to 2 hours.

2 In either case, transfer the ribs to a carving board; let stand for 5 minutes. Carve between the bones and serve with additional barbecue sauce on the side.

Five Other Uses for the Plum-and-Rum Barbecue Sauce

1 Make a double batch; place it in a slow cooker with a 4-pound pork loin. Cover and cook on high for 8 hours. Shred the meat into the sauce and serve on buns as an easy version of pulled pork.

2 Use it as a mop for chicken breasts or thighs on the grill.

3 Continue cooking the sauce until it thickens to a ketchuplike consistency, about 15 additional minutes. Use it as a dip for chips, French fries, or crackers; or as a spread for sandwiches, burritos, or wraps.

4 Increase the beef broth to 1 cup; after the sauce has cooked for 10 minutes, add 2 or 3 pounds clams, scrubbed of dirt, or mussels, scrubbed and debearded. Cover the pot and cook until they open, about 5 minutes. Discard any that do not open before serving.

5 Use the sauce as you would a salsa—or in combination with a salsa—to make "barbecued" nachos.

Plum-and-Rum Barbecue Sauce
1 medium onion, finely chopped
2 tablespoons minced peeled fresh ginger
1½ cups canned tomato sauce
½ cup plum preserves or jam
½ cup beef broth
¼ cup dark rum, such as Myers's
2 tablespoons Dijon mustard
2 tablespoons Worcestershire sauce
¼ teaspoon ground cloves
¼ teaspoon finely ground black pepper
Several dashes of hot red pepper sauce to
    taste

1 Bring the onion, ginger, tomato sauce, plum preserves or jam, broth, rum, mustard, Worcestershire sauce, cloves, pepper, and hot red pepper sauce to a simmer in a medium saucepan over medium heat, stirring until fairly smooth.

2 Reduce the heat and simmer slowly until slightly thickened, stirring occasionally, about 20 minutes; keep the sauce warm over low heat while you make the ribs. (The sauce can be made ahead; store it, tightly covered, in the refrigerator for up to 5 days—reheat over medium heat until barely simmering.)

Braised Beef Short Ribs with Cabbage, Port, and Vanilla

These juicy, moist bits of rib, about 3 inches long, are taken from the chuck, the part of the beef between the neck and shoulder. They need long, slow, moist cooking to tenderize them. This is a rich, complex dish; follow it with a simple, vinegary salad. *Makes 6 servings*

1 tablespoon unsalted butter
6 ounces pancetta, chopped
4½ pounds bone-in or 2½ pounds boneless beef short ribs
1 large onion, chopped
4 garlic cloves, minced
1 small head red cabbage, shredded through the large holes of a box grater (about 4 cups)
1 tablespoon juniper berries
1 teaspoon fennel seeds
½ teaspoon ground allspice
1½ cups port
1 cup beef broth
2 tablespoons tomato paste
One 5-inch rosemary sprig or 1 tablespoon dried rosemary, crushed
One 4-inch cinnamon stick
1 vanilla bean
1 bay leaf
½ teaspoon salt, or more to taste
¼ teaspoon freshly ground black pepper

1 Position the rack in the center of the oven and preheat the oven to 350°F.

2 Melt the butter in a large Dutch oven or soup pot set over medium heat. Add the pancetta and fry until crisp, stirring often, about 4 minutes. Transfer the pancetta to a plate lined with paper towels and set aside.

3 Working in batches as necessary, add the ribs to the pot and brown on all sides, turning occasionally, about 4 minutes per batch. Transfer to a large plate and set aside.

4 Drain all but 2 tablespoons fat from the pot. Add the onion and garlic; cook, stirring often, until softened, about 4 minutes.

5 Add the cabbage, juniper berries, fennel seeds, and allspice. Cook, stirring often, until the cabbage wilts a bit, about 4 minutes.

6 Pour in the port; bring the sauce to a simmer. Cook for 2 minutes to reduce it somewhat, then stir in the beef broth and tomato paste until smooth.

7 Add the rosemary, cinnamon stick, vanilla bean, bay leaf, salt, and pepper. Return all the short ribs, any accumulated juice, and the pancetta to the pot. Bring to a full simmer, cover, and place in the oven.

8 Bake until the rib meat is fork-tender, about 2½ hours. Discard the rosemary sprig, cinnamon stick, vanilla bean, and bay leaf before serving. The juniper berries are difficult to find, but they should be removed from individual servings.

Variations: Substitute 4 cups shredded Brussels sprouts for the cabbage.

To make a stew, take the meat out of the pot, remove it from the bones, discard the bones, roughly chop the meat, and stir it back into the sauce. If you think it is too watery, transfer to a large saucepan and simmer over medium-high heat until slightly thickened.

Polynesian Short Ribs

This is a sweet, sticky, salty, oven-broiled version of short ribs. For an even more luxurious dish, use veal short ribs. In any event, do not use canned pineapple chunks—the canning process will have destroyed most of the enzyme that tenderizes the meat. The rule for fresh pineapple is the same as that for almost any fruit: if it doesn't smell like anything at the store, it won't taste like anything at home. *Makes 4 main-course servings or 8 first-course servings*

    2 cups peeled, cored, fresh pineapple
        chunks
    ½ cup soy sauce
    ½ cup packed light brown sugar
    ¼ cup dry sherry, Shaoxing, or sake
    2 tablespoons minced peeled fresh ginger
    4 teaspoons toasted sesame oil
    ½ teaspoon freshly ground black pepper
    4 garlic cloves, quartered
    5 pounds bone-in beef short ribs

① Place the pineapple chunks, soy sauce, brown sugar, sherry or its substitute, ginger, sesame oil, pepper, and garlic in a food processor fitted with the chopping blade or in a large blender. Process or blend until smooth.

② Pour the sauce into a large bowl. Prick the meat on the ribs all over with a fork to allow the marinade to penetrate, add the ribs to the bowl, and toss to coat. Cover and refrigerate overnight or up to 48 hours, tossing occasionally.

③ Preheat the broiler. Line the broiler pan with aluminum foil to make cleanup easier. Meanwhile,

drain the marinade from the ribs and bring it to a low simmer in a small saucepan.

④ Place the ribs on the prepared broiler pan; broil 4 to 5 inches from the heat source until browned and sizzling, about 8 minutes for each of the four sides (that is, a little over 30 minutes in total), mopping occasionally with the marinade. Let stand at room temperature for 5 minutes before serving.

Variations: Substitute 1 large shallot, peeled and quartered, for the garlic.

For a smokier taste, add ½ teaspoon liquid smoke or 1 teaspoon smoked paprika to the marinade.

Pot Roast with Cranberries, Carrots, and Horseradish

Shoulder or chuck are relatively inexpensive cuts, honeycombed with fat and in need of long stewing to make them tender. If you'd like a less fatty pot roast, use bottom round, still a rich cut of meat. *Makes 6 servings*

    2 pounds beef shoulder or chuck roast
        (1 or 2 pieces)
    1½ teaspoons salt
    ½ teaspoon freshly ground black
        pepper
    3 tablespoons olive oil
    ⅓ cup bottled white horseradish
    1 large onion, halved and thinly sliced
    2 garlic cloves, quartered
    4 large carrots, peeled and cut into 1-inch
        pieces
    1½ cups whole fresh cranberries
    1½ cups beef broth
    2 bay leaves

① Position the rack in the lower third of the oven and preheat the oven to 325°F. Season the beef with salt and pepper on all sides.

2 Heat a large, oven-safe Dutch oven or casserole over medium heat. Swirl in the olive oil, then add the seasoned beef and brown it on all sides, turning occasionally, about 8 minutes. Transfer to a plate. Coat the top side of the beef with the horseradish; set aside.

3 Add the onion and garlic to the pot; cook for 1 minute, stirring all the while. Add the carrots and cranberries; cook, stirring constantly, for 1 minute.

4 Pour in the broth, scrape up any browned bits on the pot's bottom, and bring to a simmer. Once the sauce is bubbling, nestle the beef into the pan. Tuck in both bay leaves.

5 Cover and bake until the meat is so tender, it can be shredded with a fork, about 2 hours. To serve, discard the bay leaves; place chunks or slices of the beef in deep bowls; and ladle the broth and vegetables around them.

Variations: Substitute 2 parsnips for 2 of the carrots.

Use only 2 carrots and add 1 pound small red-skinned potatoes with the remaining carrots; increase the broth to 2½ cups.

Substitute pitted sour cherries for the cranberries; stir in 1 teaspoon sugar with the broth.

Substitute pitted Bing cherries for the cranberries; stir in 2 teaspoons lemon juice with the broth.

For a meat and potatoes variation, increase the broth to 2½ cups and tuck in 1 pound small white potatoes, scrubbed, with the bay leaves.

Burgundian Beef Stew with Brandy and Mushrooms

This is our simplified technique for boeuf Bourguignon, the French classic. Chuck will give you a fattier, richer stew; bottom round, a healthier but slightly chewier alternative. Buy a good but inexpensive wine for marinating the beef—a bottle you might bring to an office party. Serve the stew over Perfect Mashed Potatoes (page 473), Root Vegetable Mash (page 473), or purchased cooked egg noodles. *Makes 8 servings*

4 pounds beef chuck or bottom round, trimmed and cut into 1½-inch pieces
2 medium yellow onions, thinly sliced
2 carrots, peeled and thinly sliced
2 celery ribs, thinly sliced
4 garlic cloves, minced
6 thyme sprigs
2 rosemary sprigs
10 whole black peppercorns
1 bay leaf
One 750ml bottle red wine
¾ pound thick-cut bacon, roughly chopped
⅓ cup all-purpose flour
1 tablespoon unsalted butter
1½ pounds cremini or white button mushrooms, sliced
8 ounces pearl onions, trimmed; or 8 ounces frozen pearl onions, thawed
¼ cup brandy or Cognac
1 tablespoon black or red currant jelly
1 teaspoon salt, or more as desired
½ teaspoon freshly ground black pepper

1 Place the beef, onions, carrots, celery, garlic, thyme, rosemary, peppercorns, and bay leaf in a very large plastic container, enameled pot, or other nonreactive bowl (see page 42 for an explanation of nonreactive cookware). Pour in the red wine; toss well. Cover and refrigerate for at least 8 hours or up to 48 hours, tossing occasionally. The longer you let the beef marinate, the deeper the taste.

2 Position a rack in the lower third of the oven and preheat the oven to 350°F.

3 Remove the meat from the bowl; pat dry with paper towels. Set a large strainer or colander over a bowl in the sink and strain the vegetables and aromatics from the wine, reserving the solids and liquid separately.

4 Set a large, oven-safe casserole or Dutch oven over medium heat. Add the bacon and fry until crisp and irresistible, about 4 minutes. Transfer the bacon to a paper towel–lined plate and set aside.

5 Pour off and discard half the fat from the pot. Add the meat, working in batches if necessary. Brown well on all sides, about 15 minutes in total, turning often and removing some pieces so others will fit. You want a deep, dark crust.

6 Once all the pieces of meat have been browned, return all of them to the pot; add all the vegetables and aromatics from the marinade. Cook, stirring often, until the vegetables begin to soften, about 10 minutes.

7 Sprinkle the flour over the vegetables and meat. Stir well to coat, then place the pot in the oven and bake, uncovered, for 20 minutes to brown the flour, stirring once or twice.

8 Return the pot to medium heat on top of the stove. Pour in the wine from the marinade. Bring to a boil, then scrape up any browned bits on the pan's bottom.

9 Cover and return to the oven. Bake for 1½ hours.

10 Meanwhile, melt the butter in a large skillet. Add the mushrooms and pearl onions; cook until the mushrooms give off their liquid and it evaporates to a glaze, about 8 minutes, stirring often but gently so as not to break up the onions.

11 Remove the pan with the mushrooms and onions from the heat; pour in the brandy or Cognac. If the liquor should flame, cover the pan immediately and wait 20 seconds for the fire to go out. Use a wooden spoon to scrape up any browned bits on the bottom into the sauce in the skillet. Set aside.

12 Remove the casserole or pot from the oven. Transfer the pieces of meat with metal tongs or a slotted spoon to a large plate. Set aside.

13 Set a very large colander over a large bowl in the sink. Taking care because the pan is hot, strain the sauce through the colander. Discard everything in the strainer.

14 Return the meat to the pot; pour in the strained cooking liquid. Add the mushrooms, pearl onions, and any juice in the skillet. Stir well, cover, and return to the oven. Bake until the meat is fork-tender, about 40 more minutes.

15 Stir in the jelly until dissolved. Season with salt and pepper, adding more salt as desired. Ladle into bowls to serve.

Variation: Omit the jelly. Add 12 halved pitted prunes or halved dried figs to the pot when you pour in the mushrooms and onions.

Spanish-Inspired Beef Stew with White Wine and Hazelnuts

Here, you ladle this rich stew over a thickening mixture of seasoned hazelnuts and bread crumbs in individual bowls. *Makes 6 servings*

¼ cup olive oil
3 pounds beef chuck or stew meat, cut into
    1½-inch pieces
2 large onions, thinly sliced
2 teaspoons stemmed thyme or
    1 teaspoon dried thyme
2 teaspoons minced sage leaves or
    1 teaspoon dried sage
1 teaspoon fennel seeds
1 teaspoon salt
½ teaspoon ground allspice
½ teaspoon freshly ground black pepper
2 bay leaves
One 750ml bottle floral, fruity white wine,
    such as a Spanish white or a Pinot Gris
½ cup hazelnuts
½ cup packed parsley leaves
⅓ cup pitted green olives
1 tablespoon capers, drained and rinsed
2 thick slices stale bread, broken into pieces
2 garlic cloves, quartered
6 Roma or plum tomatoes, chopped

1 Position the rack in the lower third of the oven and preheat the oven to 350°F.

2 Heat an oven-safe casserole or a large Dutch oven over medium heat. Swirl in the olive oil, then add the beef pieces and brown well, working in batches if need be. Don't crowd the pot; you want the pieces to get a dark, caramelized crust. Transfer to a large plate and set aside.

3 Add the onions to the pot; cook, stirring often, until softened, about 4 minutes.

4 Return the beef to the pot. Stir in the thyme, sage, fennel seeds, salt, allspice, pepper, and bay leaves. Cook, stirring constantly, for 1 minute.

5 Pour in the wine; bring to a simmer, scraping up any browned bits on the pan's bottom.

6 Cover and bake until the meat is fork-tender and the wine has reduced to a thick sauce, about 1½ hours.

7 Meanwhile, toast the hazelnuts in a large skillet over medium-low heat until browned and aromatic, about 4 minutes, shaking the pan often. Pour the hot hazelnuts into a clean kitchen towel and cool for a few minutes. Gather together and rub the hazelnuts against each other inside the towel to remove most of their papery skins.

8 Pick the hazelnuts out of the towel and transfer them to a large food processor fitted with a chopping blade, leaving the skins behind. Add the parsley, olives, capers, bread, and garlic; process until finely ground but not powdery, like coarse bread crumbs. Set aside.

9 Once the beef is tender and the sauce has reduced, take the pan out of the oven, discard the bay leaves, and stir in the tomatoes. Cover and set aside off the heat for 15 minutes to allow the flavors to soften. To serve, place about ⅓ cup of the hazelnut mixture in the bottom of deep bowls, then ladle the beef stew on top.

Variations: Add ⅛ teaspoon saffron threads with the thyme; omit the allspice.
Substitute oregano for the sage.
Substitute red wine for the white wine and almonds for the hazelnuts. Toast the almonds as you would the hazelnuts in step 7—but remember, there are no skins to rub off.

Flemish-Inspired Beef Stew with Beer, Bacon, and Root Vegetables

This is a simplified waterzooi, a thick, beer-based stew served in Belgium. For the best taste, use a dark Belgian beer. *Makes 8 servings*

6 ounces thick-cut bacon, roughly chopped

2 pounds beef bottom round, cut into 1-inch cubes

2 tablespoons unsalted butter

1 large onion, finely chopped

12 ounces cremini or white button mushrooms, thinly sliced

2 garlic cloves, minced

3 tablespoons all-purpose flour

1 cup beef broth, or more as needed

One 12-ounce bottle dark Belgian beer

1½ tablespoons Dijon mustard

2 large carrots, peeled and cut into 1-inch pieces

1 large parsnip, peeled and cut into 1-inch pieces

1 small turnip, peeled and cubed

1 teaspoon caraway seeds

1 bay leaf

½ teaspoon salt, or to taste

½ teaspoon freshly ground black pepper

1 Heat a large Dutch oven or soup pot over medium heat. Add the bacon and fry until crisp, stirring often, about 5 minutes. Transfer to a plate lined with paper towels.

2 Add the beef to the pot, working in batches if necessary to prevent crowding. Brown in the bacon fat until each piece has a dark, caramelized crust, turning often, about 6 minutes per batch. Transfer to the plate with the bacon.

3 Pour off all the fat in the pot. Add the butter, melt just until the foaming subsides, then add the onion. Cook, stirring often, until softened, about 2 minutes.

4 Add the mushrooms. Cook until they release their liquid and soften, stirring often, about 3 minutes.

5 Add the garlic, cook for 20 seconds, then sprinkle the flour into the pot. Count to ten, then stir well and cook just until everything's well coated and the flour starts to brown.

6 Stirring constantly, slowly pour in the broth—the constant stirring will help the flour dissolve into the sauce. Stir in the beer and mustard until the foaming subsides. Bring to a simmer, scraping up any browned bits on the pot's bottom.

7 Return the beef and bacon to the pot. Add the carrots, parsnip, turnip, caraway seeds, and bay leaf. Cover, reduce the heat to very low, and simmer very slowly, stirring once in a while, until the beef is fork-tender, about 2 hours. Especially during the last 30 minutes of cooking, stir often to make sure the sauce doesn't stick. If the sauce gets too thick, add more beef broth in ½-cup increments. Set aside, covered, for 10 minutes. Season with salt and pepper; discard the bay leaf before serving.

Variations: When you take the stew off the heat, stir in ¼ cup chopped pitted green olives.

Omit the parsnip and turnip; use 1 medium celeriac or rutabaga, peeled and cut into 1-inch cubes.

Slow Cooker Variation: Cook the dish up to step 6 as directed. Pour the contents of the pot into a 6-quart slow cooker; add the browned beef, bacon, and the remaining ingredients. Cover and cook on low until the meat is fork-tender, about 7 hours.

Indonesian-Inspired Beef Curry

Mince the aromatics finely so they almost dissolve into the coconut sauce. Serve over white, jasmine, brown, or red rice (see page 495). *Makes 6 servings*

3 tablespoons canola oil
1½ pounds beef bottom round, thinly sliced
2 medium shallots, minced
2 tablespoons minced peeled fresh ginger
5 garlic cloves, minced
2 to 3 Thai hot chiles, seeded and thinly sliced
3 cardamom pods, finely crushed
One 4-inch cinnamon stick
2 teaspoons ground coriander
2 teaspoons ground cumin
½ teaspoon ground cloves
½ teaspoon salt
½ teaspoon freshly ground black pepper
1 cup beef broth
1 cup regular or low-fat coconut milk
1 tablespoon lime juice

1 Heat a large, high-sided skillet or Dutch oven over medium heat. Swirl in 1 tablespoon canola oil, then add the beef, working in batches to prevent overcrowding. Lightly brown the strips on both sides, about 2 minutes. Transfer to a large plate; pour off any fat in the pot.

2 Swirl in the remaining 2 tablespoons oil. Add the shallots, ginger, and garlic; cook until softened, stirring often, about 2 minutes.

3 Stir in the chiles; cook, stirring often, until aromatic, about 1 minute. Add the cardamom pods, cinnamon stick, coriander, cumin, cloves, salt, and pepper; cook for 30 seconds.

4 Pour in the broth and bring to a simmer, scraping up any browned bits on the pan's bottom. Stir in the coconut milk.

5 Return the beef to the pan. Cover, reduce the heat to very low, and simmer slowly until the beef is tender, about 45 minutes. Discard the cinnamon stick and stir in the lime juice just before serving.

Variations: For a milder dish, substitute serrano chiles for the Thai hots.

Add 3 allspice berries with the cinnamon stick; discard them at the end as well.

Grilled Chili

Chili doesn't have to be made just with ground beef; it only needs to be a chili-laced stew or braise. The best chili is a chunky stew—*and* includes the charred taste from the grill. If you don't have a grill, use a well-seasoned grill pan. There's quite a bit of chili powder in this recipe. Bottlings vary tremendously—if yours is extremely hot, you may want to reduce the amount by half. *Makes 4 servings*

1 pound sirloin steak, cut against the grain into thin strips (see page 394)
2 garlic cloves, minced
¼ cup chili powder
1 tablespoon lime juice
½ teaspoon ground cumin
Canola oil for the grate or grill pan
2 medium onions, sliced into ½-inch rings
2 medium green bell peppers, cored, seeded, and quartered
8 Roma or plum tomatoes, halved
2 ears corn, husks removed
One 12-ounce bottle amber or lager beer
½ cup beef broth
1 tablespoon paprika, preferably smoked paprika
1 teaspoon salt, or more to taste

1 Toss the steak, garlic, 2 tablespoons chili powder, lime juice, and cumin in a large bowl; cover and refrigerate for 20 minutes, tossing once or twice.

2 Prepare a gas grill for high-heat cooking or build a well-ashed, high-heat coal bed in a barbecue grill. Lightly oil the grill grate and set it 4 to 6 inches over the fire. Alternatively, lightly oil a large grill pan and heat it over medium-high heat until a drop of water sizzles across its surface.

3 Place the onion rings, bell peppers, tomato halves, and corn on the grill or in the pan; cook until well marked with grill lines, turning occasionally, about 4 minutes. Transfer the vegetables to a cutting board; set aside.

4 Remove the steak from the marinade, keeping the slices coated. Grill until medium-rare, turning once, about 2 minutes per side. Transfer to the cutting board (see Note).

5 Roughly chop the onions, bell peppers, and tomatoes. Slice the kernels off the corn cobs. Chop the steak slices into bite-sized chunks. Put all of this in a large saucepan.

6 Pour in the beer and broth, add the paprika and the remaining 2 tablespoons chili powder, and bring to a simmer over medium-high heat, stirring occasionally. (You can, of course, cook with the pan directly on the grill.) Partially cover, reduce the heat to low, and cook until thickened, about 20 minutes. Season with salt before serving.

Note: If you want to keep the steak medium-rare, leave it out of the saucepan in step 5, cook the chili as directed, and then stir the chopped steak into the chili for the last 2 or 3 minutes of cooking, just to heat through.

Deconstructed Chili

This is a way to please everyone: a beef and pork stew with all the other aromatic elements of chili kept separate. Everyone builds what they like in their bowls. We give you the recipe for the stew; the rest is up to your imagination (see serving instructions on page 404). *Makes 6 servings*

> 6 dried New Mexican or Californian red chiles, seeded, deveined, and torn into large chunks
> 2 dried ancho chiles, seeded, deveined, and torn into large chunks
> Boiling water
> 2 garlic cloves, minced
> 1 tablespoon packed chopped oregano leaves or 2 teaspoons dried oregano
> 1 teaspoon ground cumin
> ½ teaspoon salt, plus more if needed
> 2 cups chicken broth
> 1 pound beef bottom round, cut into ½-inch cubes
> 1 pound pork loin, cut into ½-inch cubes

1 Place the chile chunks in a large skillet and set it over medium heat. Cook until lightly toasted, about 1 minute, turning once.

2 Set the chiles in a large bowl and cover with boiling water. Set aside until softened, about 15 minutes. Drain in a colander set in the sink.

3 Set the chiles in a large food processor fitted with the chopping blade or in a large blender. Add the garlic, oregano, cumin, and salt; pulse a couple of times to blend. Pour in the broth; process or blend until smooth.

4 Pour the sauce into a large saucepan; stir in the beef and pork. Set the pan over medium heat and bring to a low simmer.

⑤ Cover, reduce the heat to low, and simmer slowly, stirring occasionally, until the meat is fork-tender, about 2½ to 3 hours. Season with additional salt if desired.

To serve, place the pot of chili on the table and surround it with bowls of black beans, chopped avocado tossed with a splash of lime juice, chopped red onion, seeded and chopped bell pepper, chopped tomatoes, chopped cilantro, chopped parsley, chopped and seeded jalapeño chiles, sour cream, grated cheese, corn chips, and/ or tortilla chips. Everyone chooses whatever they want, piling it into the bowls and mixing it up as desired.

Inside-Out Cheeseburgers

The best burgers are made from 80% lean ground beef. Most of the fat is rendered during cooking, leaving a burger not appreciably fattier but definitely more tasty than those made with leaner ground beef. Putting the cheese inside the burgers keeps it from melting onto the grill or griddle. Let these burgers rest for a couple of minutes before you serve them because the cheese gets very hot inside. *Makes 4 burgers*

> ¼ cup grated Cheddar, at room
>   temperature
> ¼ cup grated Brie, rind removed, at room
>   temperature (see Note)
> 1½ pounds 80% lean ground beef
> 1 tablespoon Worcestershire sauce
> 1 teaspoon paprika
> ½ teaspoon freshly ground black pepper
> Canola oil

① Mix both cheeses in a small bowl; set aside.

② Use a fork to stir the beef, Worcestershire sauce, paprika, and pepper in a medium bowl. Divide this mixture into 8 portions; roll each into a ball and flatten into patties about 4 inches in diameter.

③ Mound about 2 tablespoons of the cheese mixture in the center of 4 patties, leaving a ½-inch border around the perimeter of each. Top each with one of the 4 remaining patties. Pat and pinch the edges to seal tightly.

④ Prepare the grill for direct, high-heat cooking; lightly oil the grill grate. Alternatively, lightly oil a large grill pan, griddle, or skillet; heat it over medium heat. Place the patties on the grate 4 to 6 inches directly over the heat or into the grill pan, griddle, or skillet. Cook, turning once, until well browned, until an instant-read thermometer inserted into the top portion of a patty without touching the cheese filling registers 160°F (for medium) or 170°F (for medium well), 7 to 10 minutes. Do not press down on the burgers while they cook; the seams can split and the fillings leak. Transfer to a cutting board and let stand for 5 minutes.

Note: The Brie is easier to grate if it's frozen for 20 minutes.

Variations: Add any of the following to the cheese mixture: ¼ cup cooked crumbled bacon, 1 tablespoon minced red onion, 1 tablespoon stemmed thyme, 1 tablespoon chopped pine nuts, 2 teaspoons chopped walnuts, ½ teaspoon garlic powder, or several dashes of hot red pepper sauce.

Also, use any combination of cheeses you prefer: Asiago and Provolone, Parmigiano-Reggiano and mozzarella, or buffalo mozzarella and Boursin. Or slather half the patties with softened goat cheese, plain or herbed, then top and seal as directed.

Plain Hamburgers: Omit the cheese filling; divide the seasoned beef mixture into 4 balls and press into 4 patties. Make a thumb-sized indentation in one side of the patties to keep them from drawing up into a ball on the grill. Because the resulting burgers will be solid beef (rather than two layers of it), cook a minute or two longer, using the temperature guidelines given in step 4.

Beef and Mushroom Burgers

Fresh and dried mushrooms add moisture to burgers; more important, they add a deep, rich flavor.
Makes 4 burgers

6 large cremini mushrooms, cleaned and
    sliced
1 ounce dried porcini mushrooms
1 small shallot, quartered
1 tablespoon chopped parsley leaves or
    2 teaspoons dried parsley
2 teaspoons chopped tarragon leaves or
    1 teaspoon dried tarragon
1 teaspoon salt
½ teaspoon freshly ground black pepper
Canola or vegetable oil for oiling the grill
    grate
1½ pounds 80% lean ground beef

➊ Place the creminis, dried mushrooms, shallot, parsley, tarragon, salt, and pepper in a food processor; pulse until finely ground.

➋ Preheat a grill for direct high heat; lightly oil the grill grate. Alternatively, oil a large griddle, grill pan, or skillet and heat over medium-high heat.

➌ Transfer the mushroom mixture to a large bowl; use a fork to stir in the ground beef. Form into 4 patties, compressing slightly and creating a thumb-sized indentation on one side of each to keep them from compacting to a ball over the heat.

➍ Place the patties 4 to 6 inches directly over the heat or in the pan. Cook, turning once, until well browned, until an instant-read meat thermometer inserted into the center of one of the patties registers 160°F (for medium) or 170°F (for medium

well), 7 to 10 minutes. Transfer to a cutting board and let stand for 5 minutes.

Variations: Substitute any variety of dried mushroom you want: chanterelles, morels, black trumpets, or a combination.

Substitute almost any herb for the tarragon: marjoram, oregano, rosemary, thyme, rosemary, chervil, or chives.

Buns

Lightly butter or oil the cut side of hamburger buns, English muffins, potato rolls, or challah rolls; place them, cut side down, onto the grate or in the pan after you've removed the burgers. Toast until lightly browned, about 2 minutes. Brushing them first with walnut oil gives them a nutty taste that nicely complements the beef.

Here's the whole set of burgers in the book: Ultimate Turkey Burgers (page 296), Herbed Turkey Burgers (page 296), Asian Turkey Burgers (page 296), Tuna Burgers (page 355), Salmon Burgers (page 355), Halibut Burgers (page 357), and Lentil-Nut Patties (page 504).

Substitute ground buffalo for the ground beef in any of these recipes. Because buffalo is so lean, add slightly more broth or wine.

Spiced Ketchup

Spice up bottled ketchup by mixing 1 teaspoon ground allspice, ½ teaspoon ground cloves, and ¼ teaspoon garlic powder into 1 cup ketchup.

Italian-Inspired Basil and Pancetta Meat Loaf

There are two kinds of meat loaf: smooth or chunky. We're unabashed fans of the latter because there's more tooth per bite. (We're mostly opposed to meat you can eat with a spoon.) Laying pancetta over the meat loaf keeps it moist and flavorful. Ask your butcher slice the pancetta paper thin. *Makes 6 servings*

Olive oil for greasing the loaf pan
1 day-old Kaiser roll or other white roll, torn into bits
2 garlic cloves, quartered
1 cup packed basil leaves
¼ cup grated Parmigiano-Reggiano (about 1 ounce)
1 teaspoon salt
1½ pounds 90% to 93% lean ground beef (see Note)
¼ cup pine nuts
1 large egg, lightly beaten in a small bowl
3 ounces pancetta, thinly sliced

1 Position the rack in the center of the oven and preheat the oven to 350°F. Lightly oil a 9 × 5 × 3-inch loaf pan with olive oil; set it aside.

2 Place the roll, garlic, basil, Parmigiano-Reggiano, and salt in a food processor fitted with a chopping blade; process until finely ground. Transfer to a large bowl.

3 Make sure your hands are clean and dry, then mix in the ground beef, pine nuts, and egg by hand, working the basil mixture into the meat without destroying its fibers.

4 When the mixture is uniform, mound it into the prepared loaf pan, about like a 10-inch football cut in half lengthwise. Lay the pancetta slices over the top of the meat loaf, overlapping the slices so that they all fit.

5 Bake until the pancetta is sizzling, until an instant-read thermometer inserted into the center registers 155°F (our preference) or 165°F (the USDA recommendation), 1 hour to 1 hour and 15 minutes. (The temperature will rise by about 5 degrees as it rests.) Let stand at room temperature for 5 minutes before unmolding and slicing.

Note: Leaner ground beef is preferred because it produces a more roastlike texture. The fat is also not rendered off as effectively as it is with burgers, given the bread crumbs.

Variations: Substitute ½ cup oregano leaves and ½ cup parsley leaves for the basil.

Substitute Asiago, Pecorino Romano, or a hard, aged Gouda for the Parmigiano-Reggiano.

Substitute chopped walnut pieces for the pine nuts.

Beef and Vegetable Meat Loaf

Portobello mushroom caps give this meat loaf an earthy taste. Make sure you mince the mushroom caps finely; do it in a food processor, if desired. *Makes 6 servings*

3 tablespoons canola oil, plus additional for the baking sheet
1 small onion, finely chopped
1 celery rib, finely chopped
1 pound portobello mushroom caps, finely minced
1½ pounds 90% to 93% lean ground beef
1 large egg, lightly beaten in a small bowl
½ cup fresh bread crumbs, such as from a day-old roll or 2 bread slices
2 tablespoons tomato paste
1 tablespoon Dijon mustard
1 tablespoon Worcestershire sauce

2 teaspoons stemmed thyme or 1 teaspoon
   dried thyme
1 teaspoon minced rosemary leaves or
   ½ teaspoon crushed dried rosemary
½ teaspoon salt
½ teaspoon freshly ground black pepper

1 Heat a large skillet over medium heat. Swirl in the canola oil, then add the onion and celery. Cook, stirring often, until softened, about 3 minutes.

2 Add the minced mushrooms; continue cooking, stirring often, until they release their liquid, it evaporates, and the pan is almost dry, about 6 minutes. Set the pan aside to cool for 10 minutes.

3 Position the rack in the center of the oven and preheat the oven to 350°F. Lightly oil a large lipped baking sheet; set aside.

4 Pour the mushroom mixture into a large bowl. Crumble in the beef; then add the egg, bread crumbs, tomato paste, mustard, Worcestershire sauce, thyme, rosemary, salt, and pepper.

5 Make sure your hands are clean and work the meat into the spices, bread crumbs, and other ingredients, taking care not to destroy the meat's fibers but to get the mixture uniform. Form into a 10-inch loaf shaped about like a football cut in half the long way.

6 Set on the prepared baking sheet and bake until golden brown, until an instant-read meat thermometer inserted into the middle of the loaf registers 155°F (our preference) or 165°F (the USDA recommendation), about 1 hour to 1 hour and 15 minutes. Let stand at room temperature for 5 minutes, as the internal temperature rises 5 degrees or so before slicing.

Variations: Substitute any variety or combination of mushrooms you desire, such as shiitake mushroom caps, cremini, or even the luxurious porcini.

Southwestern Ground Beef Stew with Pumpkin and Almonds

Pumpkin dissolves into this aromatic stew without thickening it; the body instead comes from the ground chiles. *Makes 6 servings*

¼ cup almonds, finely chopped
4 Californian or New Mexican dried red
   chiles, seeded, deveined, and torn into
   large pieces
2 dried ancho chiles, seeded, deveined, and
   torn into large pieces
2½ cups chicken broth
6 ounces bacon, chopped
1 large onion, chopped
2 garlic cloves, minced
1 pound 90% to 93% lean ground beef
1 small pumpkin, about 1½ pounds, peeled,
   halved, seeded, and cut into 1½-inch
   pieces (see page 466 for tips on preparing
   a pumpkin)
3 plum or Roma tomatoes, chopped
2 teaspoons ground cinnamon
1 teaspoon ground allspice
1 teaspoon ground cloves
1 teaspoon salt, or more as needed
½ teaspoon freshly ground black pepper

1 Heat a large, high-sided skillet over medium heat. Add the almonds and cook, stirring almost constantly, until lightly browned and aromatic, about 3 minutes. Pour into a small bowl and set aside.

2 Return the skillet to medium heat. Add the chiles and cook, stirring often, until lightly toasted and aromatic, about 2 minutes.

③ Pour in the broth, raise the heat to high, and bring to a simmer. Cover, reduce the heat to low, and simmer for 10 minutes. Set aside to cool for 5 minutes.

④ Pour the contents of the skillet into a food processor fitted with the chopping blade or into a large blender; process or blend until smooth. Set aside.

⑤ Heat a large saucepan or soup pot over medium heat. Add the bacon; cook, stirring often, until frizzled, about 5 minutes.

⑥ Add the onion and garlic; cook, stirring often, until softened, about 4 minutes.

⑦ Crumble in the ground beef; cook, stirring every so often, until lightly browned, about 5 minutes.

⑧ Stir in the pureed chili mixture, then stir in the reserved toasted almonds, pumpkin, tomatoes, cinnamon, allspice, cloves, salt, and pepper. Bring to a simmer, stirring frequently.

⑨ Cover, reduce the heat to low, and simmer slowly, stirring once in a while, until the pumpkin is tender, about 25 minutes. Check for salt before serving.

Variations: Substitute butternut squash, peeled, halved, seeded, and chopped, for the pumpkin.

Substitute pecan pieces for the almonds.

For a more-inspired stew, add ½ ounce semisweet chocolate, finely grated, with the pumpkin.

For a spicier dish, puree one chipotle in adobo sauce, seeded, with the softened chiles.

Swedish-Inspired Creamy Ground Beef Stew

In this stovetop dish, the cabbage and onion melt into the sauce, sweetening it considerably. *Makes 6 servings*

3 tablespoons unsalted butter
1 large onion, halved and thinly sliced
1 small head green cabbage, cored and shredded through the large holes of a box grater (about 6 packed cups)
1½ pounds 90% to 93% lean ground beef
3 tablespoons all-purpose flour
1½ cups beef broth
1 teaspoon grated nutmeg
½ teaspoon caraway seeds
½ teaspoon ground allspice
½ teaspoon freshly ground black pepper
¼ teaspoon ground cloves
1 cup sour cream (regular, low-fat, or fat-free)
½ teaspoon salt, or to taste

① Melt the butter in a large saucepan set over medium heat. Add the onion and cook, stirring often, until translucent, about 4 minutes.

② Add 4 cups cabbage (reserve the remainder until step 5). Cook, stirring often, until softened, about 4 minutes.

③ Crumble in the ground beef; cook, stirring frequently, until lightly browned, about 5 minutes.

④ Sprinkle the flour over the mixture in the pan. Stir well, then slowly stir in the broth. Stirring all the while, bring to a simmer; cook until thickened, about 1 minute.

⑤ Stir in the nutmeg, caraway seeds, allspice, pepper, cloves, and the remaining 2 cups cabbage.

Cover and simmer until the cabbage is tender, about 25 minutes.

6 Take the pan off the heat and stir in the sour cream until smooth. Season with salt before serving.

Variations: Substitute 2 leeks, white and green parts only, halved, washed thoroughly for sand, and thinly sliced, for the onions.

For a lighter dish, substitute vegetable broth for the beef broth.

Stir 1 to 2 tablespoons cider vinegar into the sauce before adding the sour cream.

Curried Ground Beef and Potato Stew with Apple-Cucumber Raita

This is a fairly traditional curry, made with a spice blend. Serve it in lettuce cups with the cooling yogurt sauce on the side. *Makes 8 servings*

¼ cup canola oil
2 medium onions, finely chopped
3 serrano chiles, seeded and thinly sliced
4 garlic cloves, minced
2 tablespoons minced peeled fresh ginger
2 pounds 90% to 93% lean ground beef
2 tablespoons ground cumin
1½ tablespoons ground coriander
1 tablespoon paprika
1 teaspoon ground cardamom or finely ground cardamom pods
½ teaspoon cayenne
2 cups vegetable broth
1½ pounds red-skinned potatoes, cut into 2-inch pieces
½ teaspoon salt, or more to taste
1 head Bibb, Boston, or romaine lettuce, leaves separated
Apple-Cucumber Raita (recipe follows)

1 Heat a large saucepan over medium heat. Swirl in the canola oil, then add the onions, chiles, garlic, and ginger. Cook, stirring all the while, until aromatic, about 2 minutes.

2 Crumble in the beef; cook, stirring often, until browned, about 5 minutes. Stir in the cumin, coriander, paprika, cardamom, and cayenne.

3 Pour in the broth and bring the sauce to a simmer. Stir in the potatoes. Cover, reduce the heat to low, and simmer slowly until the potatoes are quite tender when pierced with a fork, about 1 hour. Season with salt as desired. To serve, spoon into the lettuce leaves as if they were cups set on plates and top with Apple-Cucumber Raita.

Apple-Cucumber Raita
Makes about 2½ cups

1½ cups plain yogurt
1 cup chopped peeled apple
½ cup chopped peeled seeded cucumber
2 tablespoons minced red onion
1 teaspoon garam masala
¼ teaspoon salt

Mix all the ingredients in a medium bowl; cover and chill for up to 2 days.

Stuffed Cabbage

This deli favorite is a great make-ahead dish. Choose a dark green, loose-leaf head of Savoy cabbage and use the outer leaves. *Makes 6 servings*

12 large Savoy cabbage leaves
1 pound 90% to 93% lean ground beef
1 large shallot, minced
1 garlic clove, minced
1 cup cooked white rice (see page 495)

¼ cup chopped golden raisins

1 teaspoon salt

1 teaspoon stemmed thyme or ½ teaspoon
   dried thyme

½ teaspoon caraway seeds

½ teaspoon freshly ground black pepper

1 cup canned tomato sauce

1 cup chicken broth

3 tablespoons lemon juice

1½ tablespoons sugar

2 Roma or plum tomatoes, finely chopped

❶ Bring a large pot of water to a boil over high heat. Add the cabbage leaves and submerge them with a wooden spoon. Reduce the heat to medium-low and cook until tender and pliable, about 8 minutes. Drain in a colander set in the sink; set aside.

❷ Position the rack in the center of the oven; preheat the oven to 400°F.

❸ Mix the ground beef, shallot, garlic, rice, raisins, salt, thyme, caraway seeds, and pepper in a large bowl.

❹ Lay one of the cabbage leaves on the work surface; mound ¼ cup ground beef filling in the center of the leaf. Fold the sides over the filling, then roll the leaf closed. Place it seam side down in a 13 × 9-inch baking pan; continue making additional rolls.

❺ Mix the tomato sauce, broth, lemon juice, sugar, and chopped tomatoes in a large bowl; pour into the baking pan over the stuffed rolls. (The casserole can be made ahead up to this point; cover and refrigerate for up to 2 days, but allow the dish to come back to room temperature before baking.)

❻ Cover first with parchment paper, then with aluminum foil; bake until bubbling, until the filling has cooked completely, and until an instant-read meat thermometer inserted into the center of one of the rolls registers 160°F (our preference for medium) or 170°F (the USDA recommendation for well done), about 1 hour and 15 minutes. Let stand at room temperature for 5 minutes.

Portuguese-Inspired Ground Beef Stew with Clams and Hazelnuts

This hearty stew is made with red wine, a savory contrast to the ground beef. Serve over white or brown rice—or over steamed greens such as kale, collard greens, or spinach (see pages 460 and 465). Also serve a bottled Portuguese red chili sauce on the side, if desired. *Makes 8 servings*

1 cup hazelnuts

¼ cup olive oil

1 large onion, halved, then thinly sliced

1 large red bell pepper, cored, seeded, and
   thinly sliced

1 large yellow bell pepper, cored, seeded,
   and thinly sliced

6 garlic cloves, slivered

2 pounds 90% to 93% lean ground beef

1 cup dry red wine

1 tablespoon paprika

2 teaspoons stemmed thyme or 1 teaspoon
   dried thyme

½ teaspoon salt, plus more if needed

½ teaspoon freshly ground black pepper

¼ teaspoon saffron threads, crumbled

2 pounds mahogany or other small clams,
   scrubbed (see page 360)

¼ cup chopped parsley leaves

❶ Position the rack in the center of the oven; preheat the oven to 350°F. Place the hazelnuts on a large lipped baking sheet; toast until lightly browned and aromatic, tossing occasionally, about 5 minutes.

❷ Cool the hazelnuts on the baking sheet for 5 minutes, then pour them into a clean kitchen towel. Fold the towel closed and rub the hazelnuts together, thereby taking off their papery outer skins. However, some stubborn bits will remain on the nuts.

③ Pour the hazelnuts into a food processor or a mini-food processor; process until finely ground, about like cornmeal. Set aside.

④ Heat a large saucepan or pot over medium heat. Swirl in the olive oil, then add the onion. Cook, stirring often, until translucent, about 4 minutes.

⑤ Add both bell peppers and the garlic; cook, stirring frequently, until softened, about 3 minutes.

⑥ Crumble in the ground beef; cook, stirring often, until browned, about 5 minutes.

⑦ Pour in the wine; bring to a simmer, scraping up any browned bits on the pan's bottom.

⑧ Stir in the paprika, thyme, salt, pepper, saffron, and the ground hazelnuts. Bring to a simmer, reduce the heat to low, and cook until slightly reduced, about 15 minutes.

⑨ Add the clams, stir well, and bring to a full simmer over medium heat. Cover and simmer just until the clams open, about 10 minutes, stirring once or twice—but gently so as not to dislodge the clam meat from the shells. Before serving, stir in the parsley and check to see if the stew needs any more salt (remember that the clams are quite salty).

Variations: Substitute mussels, cleaned and debearded (see page 360), for the clams; simmer only until they open, about 5 minutes.

For a smoky taste, substitute 1 teaspoon smoked paprika for the regular paprika.

For a much hotter stew, substitute hot Hungarian paprika for the regular paprika—use anywhere from 1 teaspoon to 1 tablespoon, depending on your tolerance for heat.

Ground Beef

Most ground beef is marked by the percentage of fat in the beef once it's been ground. By U.S. law, no ground beef can have more than 30% fat. (Such a product would thus be labeled "70% ground beef.") Most ground beef is labeled 80%, 90%, and 93%.

Be forewarned that there is a vast difference between products labeled "ground beef" and those labeled "hamburger." Ground beef must not have any added fat, other than what is present in the meat that's ground. Hamburger, by contrast, may have additional fat ground into the meat and may have a fat content far higher than 30%.

That said, there are some teeth in the ground-beef monikers. According to the USDA, 100 grams of "lean" ground beef must have less than 10 grams of fat, 4.5 grams of saturated fat, and 95 milligrams of cholesterol; 100 grams of "extra lean" must have less than 5 grams of fat, 2 grams of saturated fat, and 95 grams of cholesterol.

When purchasing ground beef, remember that the sell-by date on the package has no governmental authorization; you must trust your local market and butcher. Do not buy meat that has turned fully brown; do not use meat with a funky smell or shimmery sheen. Also remember that most beef is ground at local supermarkets, not at plants under USDA supervision.

If you're not going to use ground beef within a day of purchase, remove it from its packaging, seal it in a ziplock bag, and freeze it for up to 2 months. Thaw ground beef in the refrigerator, never on the counter. A pound should take about 24 hours to thaw.

Veal

Because of somewhat verifiable if still aggrandized news reports, the veal industry in North America has collapsed. Or to be more accurate, its mass-production end has. Although many people lost their jobs, the industry is coming back in important and sustainable ways. Sweet, tender veal is now a specialty meat, raised mostly on family farms.

Veal Chops

Perhaps the best way to enjoy veal is in this simple preparation for a veal chop. Grilling can mask the delicate taste; roasting can toughen the meat. Most veal chops are cut like steaks. A loin chop is the veal equivalent of a porterhouse steak; a rib chop, about the equivalent of a bone-in rib eye. Either of these chops is great for this simple preparation. Veal shoulder chops, however, have more tendons and cartilage; they must be long cooked to become tender and so are not recommended here. *Makes as many servings as you have chops*

> As many 12-ounce, 1½-inch-thick rib or
>   loin veal chops as you need
> 1 tablespoon olive oil per chop
> ½ minced garlic clove per chop
> ½ teaspoon minced rosemary leaves per
>   chop
> ¼ teaspoon finely grated lemon zest per
>   chop

❶ Trim the perimeter fat off the chops, then rub each with olive oil.

❷ Mix the garlic, rosemary, and lemon zest in a small bowl; gently massage this mixture into both sides of each chop (about ½ teaspoon mixture on each side of each chop). Set the chops on a plate, cover with plastic wrap, and set aside at room temperature for 20 minutes.

❸ Line the broiler pan with aluminum foil to make cleanup easier. Preheat the broiler.

❹ Set the chops in the broiler pan and broil 5 inches from the heat, turning once, until browned and medium-rare, until an instant-read meat thermometer inserted into the thick center of one chop registers 135°F (our preference) or 160°F (the USDA recommendation), 10 to 15 minutes.

Veal Rib Roast

This is the veal version of a standing rib roast—a showstopper at any dinner table. Do not use a veal shoulder roast; the meat will be too tough. *Makes 8 servings*

> One 4-bone standing veal rib roast
>   (see Note)
> 4 garlic cloves, quartered
> 1 tablespoon coarse-grained salt, preferably
>   kosher salt
> 1 teaspoon freshly ground black pepper
> 3 rosemary sprigs
> 3 thyme sprigs
> Butcher's twine

❶ Position the rack in the center of the oven and preheat the oven to 375°F.

2 Use a sharp paring knife to make sixteen slits all over the roast; slip a sliver of garlic into each slit. Sprinkle the salt and pepper all over the roast. Lay the rosemary and thyme sprigs over the center eye of meat; tie them in place by wrapping butcher's twine around the roast between the bones, thereby also tying the meat itself to hold its shape while roasting.

3 Set the roast in a large, heavy-duty roasting pan or a disposable aluminum roasting pan. Roast until an instant-read meat thermometer inserted into the center of the roast without touching bone registers 135°F (our definition of medium-rare) or 160°F (the USDA definition for medium-rare), 1 hour and 15 minutes to 1 hour and 45 minutes. Transfer the roast to a carving board and let stand for 10 minutes before carving (see page 390 for tips on carving a standing rib roast).

Note: Do not trim off the outer layer of fat as you do for veal chops (see page 412). This outer layer will protect the meat in the oven.

Variations: For a French taste, substitute 3 parsley sprigs and 3 tarragon sprigs for the rosemary and thyme.

For a deeper Italian taste, keep the rosemary and substitute 3 oregano sprigs for the thyme.

Or keep the thyme and substitute about a dozen chives for the rosemary.

Cooking Veal

Veal should be cooked to a pink, warm center—a little higher in temperature than medium-rare for beef. In no circumstance should it be cooked to higher temperatures; it will dry out and become tasteless. That said, the internal temperatures are higher for veal than beef. At 120°F, veal would be raw, not rare.

Veal Scaloppine, Five Ways

Scaloppine are generally sliced from the round. They are usually pounded thin by the butcher—between ⅛ and ¼ inch thick. If yours are more than ¼ inch thick, place them between sheets of plastic wrap and pound them thinner with the smooth side of a meat mallet or the bottom of a saucepan. These easy preparations all begin with lightly sautéing the scaloppine, then making a simple sauce. Do not overcook or they will turn leathery. *Makes 4 light servings (can be doubled)*

> 1 pound thin veal scaloppine
>   (see headnote)
> 1 teaspoon salt
> ½ teaspoon freshly ground black
>   pepper
> ½ cup all-purpose flour
> 2 tablespoons unsalted butter
> 2 tablespoons olive oil
> One of the five sauce preparations that
>   follow

1 Season the veal strips with salt and pepper. Place the flour on a large plate.

2 Melt the butter with the olive oil in a large skillet or high-sided sauté pan set over medium heat.

3 Dip the strips in the flour, coating both sides. Shake off any excess and slip into the pan, working in batches if need be. If you can't fit all the scaloppine in the pan at once, use only half the butter and oil for the first batch, then use the rest for the second batch. Cook until very lightly browned, turning once, about 4 minutes.

4 Transfer to a large clean plate, tent with aluminum foil, and set aside while you make one of the following sauces in the same pan you used for the veal.

1. Peppers and Pancetta

4 ounces pancetta, chopped

1 small red onion, chopped

4 Italian frying peppers or cubanelles, seeded and thinly sliced, or 2 medium green bell peppers, cored, seeded, and thinly sliced

2 garlic cloves, minced

1 teaspoon fennel seeds

2 tablespoons white wine vinegar

1 cup chicken broth

1 Add the pancetta to the skillet; cook, stirring frequently, until lightly browned, about 2 minutes.

2 Add the onion; cook, stirring all the while, until softened, about 2 minutes.

3 Add the peppers, garlic, and fennel seeds; cook for 1 minute to soften.

4 Pour in the vinegar and bring to a full simmer; cook until the vinegar has been reduced to a glaze, scraping up any browned bits on the pan's bottom.

5 Pour in the broth, raise the heat to medium-high, and simmer until reduced by half, about 3 minutes.

6 Slip the scaloppine back into the pan along with any accumulated juices on the plate. Reduce the heat to medium-low and cook until rewarmed, about 1 minute.

2. Lemon, Garlic, and Artichoke Hearts

2 medium shallots, thinly sliced

6 to 8 canned artichoke hearts packed in water, drained and roughly chopped

5 garlic cloves, slivered

2 teaspoons finely grated lemon zest

1 tablespoon capers, drained and rinsed

¼ cup lemon juice

1 cup chicken broth

1 Add the shallots to the pan; cook, stirring often, until softened, about 1 minute.

2 Add the artichoke hearts and garlic; cook, stirring constantly, for 1 minute.

3 Add the lemon zest and capers, cook for 20 seconds, then pour in the lemon juice. Bring the sauce to a simmer, scraping up any browned bits on the pan's bottom. Cook, stirring once or twice, until reduced by half, about 1 minute.

4 Pour in the broth, raise the heat to medium-high, and simmer until reduced by half, about 3 minutes.

5 Slip the scaloppine back into the pan along with any accumulated juices on the plate. Reduce the heat to medium-low and cook until rewarmed, about 1 minute.

3. Tomatoes and Olives

1 medium onion, finely chopped

2 garlic cloves, minced

2 teaspoons minced oregano leaves or 1 teaspoon dried oregano

1 teaspoon stemmed thyme or ½ teaspoon dried thyme

¼ teaspoon red pepper flakes

½ cup dry red wine, dry Marsala, or dry Madeira

8 Roma or plum tomatoes, chopped

⅔ cup chopped pitted black olives

1 tablespoon balsamic vinegar

1 Add the onion to the pan; cook, stirring frequently, until translucent, about 2 minutes.

2 Add the garlic; cook for 30 seconds.

3 Stir in the oregano, thyme, and red pepper flakes; cook for 20 seconds until aromatic, then pour in the wine. Bring to a simmer, scraping up any browned bits on the pan's bottom.

❹ Add the tomatoes and olives. Cook, stirring occasionally, until the wine in the sauce has reduced by half and the tomatoes have started to break down, about 5 minutes.

❺ Stir in the vinegar, then slip the scaloppine back into the pan along with any accumulated juices on the plate. Reduce the heat to medium-low and cook until rewarmed, about 1 minute.

4. Prunes, Brandy, and Shallots

2 medium shallots, thinly sliced
16 pitted prunes, quartered, soaked in ½ cup brandy for 10 minutes
1 teaspoon ground allspice
½ teaspoon grated nutmeg
1 cup chicken broth
½ cup heavy cream

❶ Add the shallots to the pan; cook, stirring often, until softened, about 1 minute.

❷ Pour in the prunes with their soaking liquid. Should the brandy catch fire, cover the pan and remove it from the heat until the fire is out, about 20 seconds. Cook, stirring constantly, until the brandy has reduced by half, about 3 minutes.

❸ Add the allspice and nutmeg, stir well, then pour in the broth. Raise the heat to medium-high and bring to a full simmer, scraping up any browned bits on the pan's bottom. Cook, stirring frequently, until reduced by half, about 3 minutes.

❹ Pour in the cream, stir well, and cook until reduced by a third, about 1 minute.

❺ Slip the scaloppine back into the pan along with any accumulated juices on the plate. Re-

duce the heat to medium-low and cook until rewarmed, about 1 minute.

5. Apples and Cream

1 medium shallot, minced
1 large tart apple, such as a Granny Smith or a Pippin, cored, peeled, and thinly sliced
4 ounces cremini mushrooms, thinly sliced
1 teaspoon stemmed thyme or ½ teaspoon dried thyme
1 teaspoon minced sage leaves or ½ teaspoon dried sage
½ cup chicken broth
¼ cup brandy or Cognac
6 tablespoons heavy cream

❶ Add the shallot to the pan; cook, stirring often, until translucent, about 1 minute.

❷ Add the apple and mushrooms; cook, stirring almost constantly, until the apple has softened, about 2 minutes.

❸ Add the thyme and sage, then pour in the broth. Stir well and pour in the brandy or Cognac. Should the sauce flame, cover the pan and remove it from the heat until the fire is out, about 20 seconds. Raise the heat to medium-high and cook until reduced by half, about 2 minutes.

❹ Stir in the cream and cook until reduced by a third, about 1 minute.

❺ Slip the scaloppine back into the pan along with any accumulated juices on the plate. Reduce the heat to medium-low and cook until rewarmed, about 1 minute.

Spanish-Inspired Osso Buco with Chickpeas, Olives, and Saffron

Here's an Iberian interpretation of the Italian classic: round, bone-in cuts of veal shin are stewed in a smoky, fiery tomato sauce. Serve over cooked white or brown rice, Perfect Mashed Potatoes (page 473), Root Vegetable Mash (page 473), cooked and drained pappardelle (see page 172), or corn bread squares (see page 240). *Makes 8 servings*

6 ounces thick-cut bacon, sliced into ½-inch pieces

Eight 1-pound pieces of veal osso buco

2 teaspoons salt

1 teaspoon freshly ground black pepper

1 large onion, chopped

4 garlic cloves, minced

1 cup canned chickpeas, drained and rinsed

½ cup sliced pitted green olives

1 tablespoon smoked paprika

1 tablespoon stemmed thyme or 2 teaspoons dried thyme

1 teaspoon hot Hungarian paprika

¼ teaspoon saffron threads, crumbled

2 bay leaves

1½ cups dry sherry

3½ cups canned diced tomatoes with their juice (a 28-ounce can)

¼ cup chopped cilantro leaves

1 tablespoon sherry vinegar

1 Position the rack in the lower third of the oven and preheat the oven to 350°F.

2 Heat a very large oven-safe Dutch oven or a very large oven casserole over medium heat. Add the bacon and fry until crisp, stirring often, about 5 minutes. Transfer to a plate and set aside.

3 Season the osso buco pieces with salt and pepper, then add them to the pot, working in batches to brown them evenly as necessary. Cook until well browned, about 4 minutes; then turn and continue cooking until well browned on the other side, about 4 more minutes. Transfer the osso buco pieces to a large plate and set aside.

4 Add the onion to the pot; cook, stirring often, until translucent, about 3 minutes. Add the garlic and cook for 20 seconds.

5 Stir in the chickpeas and olives; cook for 1 minute, stirring constantly.

6 Add the smoked paprika, thyme, hot paprika, saffron, and bay leaves; cook, stirring constantly, until quite aromatic, about 30 seconds.

7 Raise the heat to medium-high and pour in the sherry. Bring the sauce to a boil, scraping up any browned bits on the pot's bottom. Continue boiling until reduced by half, about 2 minutes.

8 Stir in the tomatoes and their juice, then stir in the cooked bacon. Nestle the pieces of osso buco into the pot, leaving them flat (not standing on their sides) and as submerged in the sauce as possible. Bring to a simmer.

9 Cover and place the pot in the oven. Bake until the meat is fork-tender, changing the positions of the pieces occasionally so they have all spent time in the sauce, about 2½ hours.

10 Using a large slotted spoon, transfer the pieces of osso buco to serving bowls or plates. Place the hot pot or casserole over high heat, bring the sauce to a full boil, and stir in the cilantro and vinegar. Ladle the sauce over the osso buco and serve at once.

Variations: Substitute venison or goat osso buco for the veal.

Add 1 green bell pepper, cored, seeded, and chopped, with the onion.

For a somewhat sweeter dish, add 2 carrots, finely chopped, with the onion.

Substitute 2 medium baking potatoes, peeled and cubed, for the chickpeas.

For a milder dish, substitute mild paprika for the hot Hungarian variety.

If you can't find hot Hungarian paprika, substitute up to ½ teaspoon cayenne pepper.

Southwestern Veal Stew with Chiles, Cinnamon, and Honey

Mince the vegetables quite small so they almost dissolve into this cinnamon-spiked sauce. Cornmeal thickens the stew. *Makes 6 servings*

1 large onion, minced
2 garlic cloves, minced
1 pickled jalapeño chile, seeded and minced
2 tablespoons ancho chili powder or finely ground seeded and stemmed dried New Mexican red chiles
2 tablespoons canola oil
2½ pounds veal shoulder or leg meat, trimmed of all fat and cut into 1-inch chunks
1 tablespoon honey
1½ teaspoons ground cinnamon
1½ teaspoons ground cumin
½ teaspoon salt, plus more as necessary
2 cups chicken broth
1½ tablespoons yellow cornmeal

1 Position the rack in the center of the oven and preheat the oven to 350°F. Mix the onion, garlic, jalapeño chile, and chili powder in a medium bowl; set aside.

2 Heat a large, oven-safe Dutch oven or other large casserole over medium heat. Swirl in the canola oil, then add the chunks of veal. Cook, turning frequently, until well browned, about 10 minutes.

3 Stir in the onion mixture; cook, stirring often, until very fragrant and the onion pieces are quite soft, about 3 minutes. (Be careful: the chile oils will volatilize and can burn your eyes—don't stand directly over the pot.)

4 Stir in the honey, cinnamon, cumin, and salt; cook, stirring constantly, for 30 seconds.

5 Stir in the broth and bring to a simmer, scraping up any browned bits on the pan's bottom.

6 Stir in the cornmeal, then cover the casserole and place in the oven. Bake, stirring occasionally, until the meat is fork-tender and the sauce has thickened, about 2 hours. Check to see if the sauce needs salt before serving.

Variations: Add 1 medium turnip, peeled and diced, and 2 parsnips, peeled and thinly sliced, with the veal.

Add 2 teaspoons chopped oregano leaves or 1 teaspoon dried oregano with the cinnamon.

Reduce the broth to 1½ cups; add ½ cup red wine with the remaining broth.

Use beef broth for a heartier stew.

Creamy Veal and Onion Stew

The veal almost melts into the cream in this decadent stovetop stew, perfect over cooked and drained egg noodles. The stew must cook very slowly, just the barest simmer, so the veal gets impossibly tender. For an easier prep, use peeled frozen pearl onions right out of the freezer. *Makes 6 servings*

5 tablespoons unsalted butter
2½ pounds veal shoulder or leg meat, trimmed of all fat and cut into 1-inch cubes
2 tablespoons all-purpose flour
1½ cups chicken broth
1 cup dry white wine

1½ teaspoons stemmed thyme or 1 teaspoon
   dried thyme

½ teaspoon ground allspice

½ teaspoon salt, or more to taste

¼ teaspoon freshly ground pepper, preferably
   white pepper

1 pound pearl onions, peeled

1 cup heavy cream

1 Melt 2 tablespoons butter in a large Dutch oven or very large saucepan. Add the veal cubes and cook, stirring often, just until they have a hint of brown but are very light in color, about 3 minutes. Transfer to a large plate and set aside.

2 Melt 2 additional tablespoons butter in the pan. Sprinkle the flour over the melted butter, then whisk until smooth. Do not let the flour brown. The moment it's smooth, slowly pour in the broth, whisking all the while.

3 Whisk in the wine in a slow stream, making sure there are no lumps. Bring the sauce to a simmer and cook, whisking all the while, until thickened, about 1 minute.

4 Whisk in the thyme, allspice, salt, and pepper. Return the pieces of veal and any accumulated juices to the pan. Bring to a simmer; then cover, reduce the heat to very low, and simmer slowly, stirring occasionally, for 1 hour.

5 Meanwhile, melt the remaining 1 tablespoon butter in a large skillet over low heat. Add the onions and cook, stirring often, until lightly golden, about 5 minutes.

6 Pour the cream among the onions, stir well, raise the heat to medium, and bring to a full simmer. Cook, stirring once in a while, until reduced by half, about 3 minutes. Pour into the pan with the veal.

7 Stir well, set the lid askew, and simmer very slowly, stirring once in a while, until the meat is fork-tender and the sauce has thickened, about 1½ hours.

Variations: Substitute 2½ pounds boneless skinless chicken thighs, cut into 1-inch pieces, for the veal; reduce the broth to 1 cup and the wine to ½ cup. Simmer only 20 minutes before adding the cream and onions then only about 1 hour after adding it.

Substitute oregano or rosemary for the thyme.

Use beef broth for a heartier stew, vegetable broth for a lighter one.

Add 1 pound sliced cremini or white button mushrooms with the onions.

Stir in 1 tablespoon Dijon mustard with the cream.

Add 2 cups fresh shelled peas or frozen peas for the last 3 minutes of cooking.

Veal Meat Loaf Braised in a Tomato, Herb, and Wine Broth

This recipe requires that you move the meat loaf around after it's been formed, so make sure you pat together a cohesive, sturdy loaf. If you can't find ground veal, use a total of 1 pound lean ground beef and ½ pound ground pork. You can also buy a veal shoulder roast and ask your butcher to grind it for you—but do not grind the leg or chops because that would be simply too wasteful. *Makes 6 servings*

½ cup all-purpose flour

1 pound ground veal

½ pound 90% to 93% lean ground beef

½ cup fresh bread crumbs, such as from a
   day-old roll or 2 bread slices

1 tablespoon Dijon mustard

1 teaspoon minced oregano leaves or
   ½ teaspoon dried oregano

1½ teaspoons salt

½ teaspoon grated nutmeg

½ teaspoon fennel seeds

1 teaspoon freshly ground black pepper

1 large egg, lightly beaten in a small bowl

2 tablespoons olive oil

½ pound white button or cremini mushrooms, thinly sliced

2 garlic cloves, minced

½ cup dry vermouth or dry white wine

1⅔ cups canned diced tomatoes with their juice

1 cup beef broth

1 teaspoon stemmed thyme

1 bay leaf

1 Position the rack in the center of the oven; preheat the oven to 325°F. Sprinkle the flour on a large plate and set aside.

2 Make sure your hands are clean and dry. Mix the ground veal, ground beef, bread crumbs, mustard, oregano, 1 teaspoon salt, nutmeg, fennel seeds, ½ teaspoon pepper, and the egg in a large bowl until uniform. Don't mush the meat's fibers into a paste; instead, get the ingredients evenly distributed in a still slightly coarse mixture.

3 Form into a loaf about 10 inches long but flat on the bottom. Roll in the flour to coat and set aside.

4 Heat a large, deep, oven-safe skillet over medium heat. Swirl in the olive oil, then gently slip the meat loaf into the pan. Brown on all sides, turning occasionally with two large spatulas, about 6 minutes. As the meat browns, its gets firmer—and easier to turn.

5 Sprinkle the mushrooms around the meat loaf. Continue cooking until they give off their liquid, stirring them as you can around the meat, about 3 minutes.

6 Sprinkle the garlic in the pan; continue cooking until the mushroom liquid evaporates, about 3 minutes.

7 Pour in the vermouth or wine; continue cooking until it has reduced to a glaze, about 3 minutes, carefully turning the meat loaf once if it browns and continuing to stir the mushrooms in the pan as you can.

8 Add the tomatoes, broth, thyme, bay leaf, the remaining ½ teaspoon salt, and the remaining ½ teaspoon pepper to the pan. Bring the sauce to a simmer.

9 Cover the pan, place in the oven, and bake, basting occasionally with the pan juices and sauce, until the meat loaf is lightly browned and an instant-read thermometer inserted into the thickest part of the loaf registers 155°F (our preference) or 165°F (the USDA recommendation), 1 hour and 15 minutes to 1 hour and 30 minutes. Let stand at room temperature for 5 minutes before slicing; discard the bay leaf before serving.

Variations: Add 1 small onion, finely chopped, with the mushrooms.

Substitute a dry red wine for the vermouth or white wine.

Omit the fennel seeds; add ½ teaspoon caraway seeds to the sauce with the beef stock.

After you remove the meat loaf, pour the sauce into a medium saucepan, stir in ½ cup heavy cream, and bring to a simmer for 5 minutes to thicken somewhat.

The quality of pork has improved dramatically with great studies in its safety, its taste, and even its fat content (it's about 30% leaner than in the 1980s). For culinary purposes, a pig is divided into four sections: loin (tenderloin, loin, and all chops), leg (ham), side (ribs and American-style bacon), and shoulder (hocks and most ground pork, as well as the cuts for pulled pork). The order of these recipes follows those demarcations.

From the Loin

Boneless Pork Cutlets with Apples and Leeks

It's hard to find a faster, easier, or more flavorful dinner than boneless pork chops. They're simply the loin sliced into rounds. Look for center-cut chops—also sometimes called "center-cut pork cutlets." The loin is actually divided into three sections with its center being the leanest and tastiest. We prefer thicker, meatier chops, a good foil to bold sauces. *Makes 4 servings*

> Four thick 6- to 8-ounce boneless center-cut
>   pork loin chops
> 1 teaspoon salt, plus more if needed
> ½ teaspoon freshly ground black pepper
> 1 tablespoon canola oil
> 1 tablespoon unsalted butter
> 2 large leeks, white and pale green parts
>   only, split lengthwise, washed carefully of
>   any grit between the layers, then thinly
>   sliced into half-moons
> 2 large tart apples, such as Granny Smith
>   or Pippin, peeled, cored, and thinly
>   sliced
> 1½ teaspoons caraway seeds
> ¼ teaspoon grated nutmeg
> ½ cup chicken broth
> 1 teaspoon cider vinegar

❶ Season the pork chops with salt and pepper.

❷ Heat a large skillet over medium heat. Add the canola oil, then slip the chops into the pan. Brown on both sides, about 3 minutes, turning once. Transfer to a plate; set aside.

❸ Add the butter, let it melt, then add the leeks and apples. Cook, stirring often, until softened, about 4 minutes.

❹ Stir in the caraway seeds and nutmeg; cook until aromatic, about 20 seconds. Pour in the broth; bring to a simmer, scraping up any browned bits on the skillet's bottom.

❺ Return the chops and any juices on the plate to the skillet. Cover, reduce the heat to low, and simmer until an instant-read meat thermometer inserted into the chops registers 155°F (our preference) or 160°F (the USDA recommendation), about 10 minutes. Stir in the vinegar just before serving; check the sauce for salt seasoning.

Variations: Substitute 1 large red onion, halved and thinly sliced, for the leeks.

Substitute 2 pears, peeled, cored, and thinly sliced, for the apples.

Substitute wine for the broth; in this case, omit the vinegar.

Boneless Pork Cutlets and Brussels Sprouts Sauté

For the best taste, buy small Brussels sprouts, the heads tight and green. Trim off the woody stems, then slice the heads into very thin strips, almost shredding them. *Makes 4 servings*

Four ½- to 1-inch-thick 6- to 8-ounce
    boneless center-cut pork loin chops
½ teaspoon salt, or more to taste
½ teaspoon freshly ground black pepper
1 tablespoon canola oil
1 pound Brussels sprouts, trimmed and
    thinly sliced, almost shredded
1 cup chicken broth
1 tablespoon white Worcestershire sauce or
    Worcestershire sauce for chicken
1 tablespoon Dijon mustard
1 teaspoon honey
½ teaspoon ground allspice

❶ Season the chops with salt and pepper; set aside.

❷ Heat a large, deep skillet or a sauté pan over medium heat. Swirl in the canola oil, then add the chops. Cook until lightly browned, about 3 minutes, turning once. Transfer to a plate and set aside.

❸ Add the Brussels sprouts to the pan; cook, stirring constantly, until slightly wilted, about 1 minute.

❹ Pour in the broth and bring to a simmer, scraping up any browned bits on the skillet's bottom.

❺ Stir in the white Worcestershire sauce, mustard, honey, and allspice until smooth. Return the chops and any accumulated juices to the pan.

❻ Cover, reduce the heat to low, and cook until an instant-read meat thermometer inserted into one of the chops registers 155°F (our preference) or 160°F (the USDA recommendation), about 10 minutes.

❼ Place the chops on a serving platter or four serving plates; tent with aluminum foil to keep warm. Raise the heat to high, bring the sauce to a boil, and cook, stirring often, until reduced by half, about 2 minutes. Check for salt, then pour over the chops.

Variations: Substitute Savoy cabbage or red cabbage, cored and shredded; or leeks, white and pale green parts only, halved, washed carefully for sand, and thinly sliced, for the Brussels sprouts.

Substitute boneless skinless chicken breasts for the pork chops; cook the breasts an additional 5 minutes, or until an instant-read meat thermometer inserted into the thickest part of 1 breast registers 160°F (our preference) or 170°F (the USDA recommendation).

Cooking Pork to the Right Temperature

Time was, people overcooked pork; older cookbooks recommend an internal temperature somewhere around 180°F. This scorching was for fear of trichinosis. However, if present at all, the pests are killed at 137°F. Still, the USDA, in a bid for safety, suggests an internal temperature of 160°F for medium. Unfortunately, pork loses a great deal of internal moisture at such temperatures; we recommend an internal temperature of 155°F, well within safety limits and the range of error for modern thermometers. As with beef, treat temperature as the gold standard for testing a cut's doneness; time values are just rough guides.

Boneless Pork Cutlets with Peppers and Vinegar

This bracing pork sauté is inspired by a simple dish often served in Italian trattoria. Because the chops are pounded thin, there's little need to take their internal temperature: they're cooked through in minutes. The mildly hot-and-sour combination calls out for a glass of hearty Sicilian red wine. *Makes 4 servings*

Four 6- to 8-ounce boneless center-cut pork
  loin chops
1 teaspoon salt
½ teaspoon freshly ground black pepper
3 tablespoons olive oil
1 small onion, halved and thinly sliced
1 red bell pepper, cored, seeded, and thinly
  sliced
1 green cubanelle or Italian frying pepper,
  cored, seeded, and thinly sliced
2 teaspoons minced oregano leaves or
  1 teaspoon dried oregano
1 teaspoon sugar
1 cup dry white wine or dry vermouth
2 tablespoons white balsamic vinegar or
  white wine vinegar

❶ Season the pork chops with salt and pepper. Place them between two sheets of plastic wrap and pound to ¼-inch thickness using the smooth side of a meat mallet or the bottom of a heavy saucepan—or have your butcher do this for you. Set aside.

❷ Heat a large, high-sided skillet or sauté pan over medium heat. Swirl in 1 tablespoon olive oil, then add the chops and brown on both sides, turning once, about 3 minutes. Transfer to a plate and set aside.

❸ Swirl in the remaining 2 tablespoons oil, then add the onion and both peppers. Cook, stirring often, until softened, about 4 minutes.

❹ Add the oregano and sugar; cook for 30 seconds. Pour in the wine or vermouth, bring to a boil, and scrape up any browned bits on the pan's bottom. Boil until reduced by half, about 3 minutes.

❺ Return the chops and any accumulated juices to the pan. Stir in the vinegar; then cover, reduce the heat to low, and cook, basting occasionally, for 2 minutes.

Variation: If you can't find a cubanelle or Italian frying pepper, substitute 1 green bell pepper, cored, seeded, and chopped, and add ½ teaspoon red pepper flakes with the oregano.

Boneless Pork Cutlets with a Mustard Maple Cream Sauce

A light cream sauce gently enhances the sweetness of both the maple syrup and the pork, all balanced by a touch of mustard. *Makes 4 servings*

Four 6- to 8-ounce boneless center-cut pork
  loin chops
1 teaspoon salt
½ teaspoon freshly ground black pepper
2 tablespoons unsalted butter
2 medium shallots, halved and thinly sliced
2 tablespoons coarse-grained mustard
1½ tablespoons maple syrup
½ cup dry white wine
½ cup heavy cream

❶ Season the chops with the salt and pepper. Set them between sheets of plastic wrap and pound to ¼-inch thickness using the smooth side of a meat mallet or the bottom of a heavy saucepan. Set aside.

❷ Melt the butter in a large, high-sided skillet or sauté pan set over medium heat. Slip the chops into the pan and brown evenly on both sides, about 3 minutes, turning once. Transfer to a plate and set aside.

③ Add the shallots; cook, stirring often, until softened, about 2 minutes.

④ Stir in the mustard and maple syrup until smooth, then stir in the wine. Bring to a boil, scraping up any browned bits on the pan's bottom. Boil for 30 seconds, then pour in the cream.

⑤ Return the chops and any accumulated juices to the pan. Baste with the sauce and cook for 1 minute at a full boil. Serve at once.

Variations: Add 2 garlic cloves, minced, with the shallots.

Substitute Dijon mustard for the coarse-grained mustard.

Grate nutmeg over the dish before serving.

Panfried Bone-In Pork Chops

Although they require slightly more preparation than boneless chops, bone-in pork chops offer more flavor because the bone infuses the meat. Look for either rib chops (an eye of meat under a rib bone) or loin chops (the pork equivalent of a T-bone steak). Trim off the outer periphery of fat.

Makes 4 servings (see Note)

¼ cup canola oil
1 cup all-purpose flour
1 teaspoon salt
1 teaspoon dried thyme
½ teaspoon freshly ground black pepper
2 large egg whites, at room temperature
1½ cups dried bread crumbs
Four 6- or 7-ounce, ½-inch-thick bone-in rib or loin pork chops, all peripheral fat trimmed

① Pour the canola oil into a large, high-sided skillet, then set it over medium-high heat until the oil has ripples across its surface.

② Meanwhile, mix the flour, salt, thyme, and pepper on a plate. Whisk the egg whites in a shallow soup plate or a pie plate until foamy. Finally, spread the bread crumbs on another plate.

③ Dip a pork chop into the flour, coating it on both sides; then dip it into the egg white to moisten both sides thoroughly. Finally, dredge both sides in the bread crumbs and slip into the hot oil. Repeat with the remaining pork chops.

④ Fry until lightly browned, about 5 minutes. Gently turn the chops over with a large spatula so as not to dislodge the crust and fry on the other side until lightly browned, about 5 more minutes. It's hard to use an instant-read meat thermometer with these chops since the surrounding oil is so hot; you should take their internal temperature, however, when they're out of the oil and it should be 155°F (our preference) or 160°F (the USDA recommendation).

Note: You can double or triple the recipe, but don't double or triple the oil. Instead, fry the chops in batches, adding more oil as need be.

Variations: Substitute any dried herb you like for the thyme: equivalent amounts of oregano, rosemary, paprika, marjoram, parsley, or tarragon.

Spice up any flour mixture with ¼ teaspoon cayenne pepper.

Omit the bread crumbs and place 1½ cups chopped pecan pieces, walnut pieces, or skinned hazelnut pieces on the plate. Lower the heat to medium once the chops go in the skillet so the nuts don't burn, but cook the chops a minute or two longer.

Oven-Fried Bone-In Pork Chops

This aromatic bread-crumb coating can be made in larger batches; store it in a sealed plastic bag for up to 1 month, using it when you want to oven-fry more chops. *Makes 4 servings*

> Canola oil or nonstick spray for the baking
>   sheet
> 1 cup regular or low-fat buttermilk (do not
>   use fat-free)
> 1 cup plain dried bread crumbs
> 1 tablespoon mild paprika
> 1 tablespoon fennel seeds
> 1 teaspoon celery seeds
> 1 teaspoon onion powder
> 1 teaspoon salt
> ½ teaspoon freshly ground black pepper
> ¼ teaspoon garlic powder
> Four 6- or 7-ounce, ½-inch-thick bone-in
>   loin or rib pork chops, trimmed of any
>   peripheral fat

1 Position the rack in the middle of the oven and preheat the oven to 375°F. Lightly oil or spray a large lipped baking sheet and set it aside.

2 Pour the buttermilk into a wide shallow bowl or a pie plate. Mix the bread crumbs, paprika, fennel seeds, celery seeds, onion powder, salt, pepper, and garlic powder on a large plate until uniform.

3 Dip a pork chop into the buttermilk, coating both sides but letting the excess drain off. Dip it into the bread crumb mixture, coating both sides and shaking off the excess. Lay it on the prepared baking sheet and continue with the other pork chops.

4 Bake for 20 minutes, then gently turn the chops with a wide spatula so as not to knock off the crust. Continue baking until browned, until an instant-read meat thermometer inserted diag-onally into one of the chops registers 155°F (our preference) or 160°F (the USDA recommendation), about 10 minutes. Let stand at room temperature for 5 minutes before serving.

Variations: Substitute smoked paprika for the regular paprika.

Add 1 teaspoon dried thyme or 1 teaspoon dried oregano with the other herbs.

Omit the celery seeds and substitute 1½ teaspoons caraway seeds for the fennel seeds.

Tequila-Brined Bone-In Pork Chops

A salt brine plumps pork chops; the tequila will give them a slightly aromatic, sweet taste. There's no need to use the best tequila here, but certainly use one you would drink on its own. *Makes 4 servings*

> 1½ cups tequila
> 1 cup water
> ¼ cup salt, preferably kosher salt
> 1 tablespoon sugar
> 4 garlic cloves, thinly sliced
> 2 tablespoons cumin seeds, crushed
> 1 tablespoon mustard seeds, crushed
> ½ teaspoon red pepper flakes
> Four 6- or 7-ounce, ½-inch-thick bone-in
>   loin or rib pork chops, trimmed
> 2 bay leaves

1 Whisk the tequila, water, salt, sugar, garlic, cumin seeds, mustard seeds, and red pepper flakes in a large bowl until the salt and sugar dissolve. Pour into a large resealable plastic bag.

2 Add the pork chops and the bay leaves. Seal closed, shake well, and refrigerate for at least 8 hours or up to 48 hours. Shake and turn the bag occasionally to make sure the chops are coated in the marinade.

3 **To broil:** Preheat the broiler and line the broiler pan with aluminum foil. Remove the chops from the marinade; do not blot dry but discard the marinade. Place them in the pan 5 inches from the heat source; broil, turning once, until well browned, until an instant-read meat thermometer inserted diagonally into the center of the chops registers 155°F (our preference) or 160°F (the USDA recommendation), about 18 minutes. Let stand at room temperature for 5 minutes before serving.

To grill: Heat one half of a gas grill to medium heat while putting a drip pan under the unheated section of the grate; or build a medium-heat, well-ashed coal bed in a charcoal grill before raking the coals to the perimeter and placing a drip pan in the center of the grate. Remove the chops from the marinade; do not blot dry but discard the marinade. Place over the drip pan, cover, and cook for 20 minutes, turning once. If you're using a charcoal grill, you may need to add more briquettes to maintain the fire. Move the chops directly over the heat and continue cooking, turning once, until browned, until an instant-read meat thermometer inserted into the chops registers 155°F (our preference) or 160°F (the USDA recommendation), about 6 more minutes. Let stand on a carving board for 5 minutes before serving.

Variations: For a no-buzz marinade, omit the sugar and substitute white cranberry juice, apple juice, or white grape juice for the tequila. If you don't want the added sugar, substitute a fruit-herbal brewed tea, cooled.

For a margarita marinade, omit the garlic, cumin seeds, and mustard seeds; reduce the water to ½ cup; add ½ cup Cointreau or other orange-flavored liqueur plus 1 tablespoon finely grated lime zest to the marinade.

Apricot-Braised Bone-In Pork Chops

This slightly sour tomato-and-apricot braise turns simple pork chops into elegant fare. *Makes 4 servings*

Four 6- or 7-ounce, ½-inch-thick bone-in loin or rib pork chops, trimmed of fat
1 teaspoon salt
½ teaspoon freshly ground black pepper
1 tablespoon canola oil
1 medium shallot, minced
2 teaspoons minced peeled fresh ginger
3 ounces dried apricots, thinly sliced (about ½ cup)
2 teaspoons stemmed thyme or 1 teaspoon dried thyme
Two 4-inch cinnamon sticks
½ cup chicken broth
1⅔ cups canned diced tomatoes with their juice
2 teaspoons lemon juice

1 Season the chops with salt and pepper.

2 Heat a large, deep skillet over medium heat. Add the canola oil, then slip in the chops. Brown on both sides, about 4 minutes, turning once. Transfer to a plate; set aside.

3 Add the shallot and ginger; cook, stirring often, until softened, about 1 minute. Stir in the apricots, thyme, and cinnamon sticks. Cook, stirring often, until aromatic, about 20 seconds.

4 Pour in the broth; scrape up any browned bits on the pan's bottom. Pour in the tomatoes and bring to a simmer. Nestle the chops in the sauce.

5 Cover, reduce the heat to low, and simmer until an instant-read meat thermometer inserted into a chop registers 155°F (our preference) or

160°F (the USDA recommendation), about 15 minutes. Discard the cinnamon sticks and swirl in the lemon juice before serving.

Variations: Substitute unsalted butter for the canola oil.

Substitute dried plums or chopped dried cherries for the apricots.

Add ¼ teaspoon red pepper flakes with the thyme.

Pork Tenderloin

A tenderloin is the leanest cut of pork: the little-used muscle by the loin, starting at about its center and running toward the haunches. Because of the lack of fat, it's best marinated before cooking. Watch the temperature carefully; pork tenderloins are easily overcooked. Roast them to a slightly lower temperature than other cuts since they toughen at higher temperatures. *Makes 6 servings*

Two 1-pound pork tenderloins, trimmed of any silverskin (see Note)
One of the four marinades that follow
2 teaspoons olive oil or canola oil

❶ Place the tenderloins and all the ingredients for the marinade you've chosen in a large resealable plastic bag; zip closed, then rub the marinade all over the meat through the plastic. Refrigerate for at least 4 hours or up to 24 hours, massaging the marinade occasionally into the meat.

❷ **To bake:** Position the rack in the center of the oven and preheat the oven to 400°F. Remove the tenderloins from the marinade; blot dry. Heat a large, oven-safe skillet over medium-high heat, then swirl in the olive oil or canola oil (use olive oil if it's also found in the marinade). Add the tenderloins and brown on all sides, turning a few times, about 5 minutes. Place the skillet in the oven and

bake until an instant-read meat thermometer inserted diagonally into the thickest part of the tenderloins registers 150°F (our preference) or 160°F (the USDA recommendation), 10 to 14 minutes. Let stand for 5 minutes on a carving board before slicing into rounds and serving.

To grill: Heat a gas grill to high heat or prepare a well-ashed, high-heat coal bed in a charcoal grill. Lightly oil the grill grate and set it 4 to 6 inches over the heat. Remove the tenderloins from the bag and place them directly over the heat. Grill, turning often, until an instant-read meat thermometer inserted diagonally into the thickest part of the meat registers 150°F (our preference) or 160°F (the USDA recommendation), 12 to 16 minutes. Let stand on a carving board for 5 minutes before slicing into rounds.

Note: Most tenderloins have a thin, translucent membrane arcing over the meat; slice it off before marinating. Do not confuse it with the more opaque, milky white fat which should be left on to keep the meat moist as it roasts.

Four Marinades for Pork Tenderloin

1. *Lemon Pepper Marinade*
⅓ cup olive oil
2 tablespoons finely grated lemon zest
1½ teaspoons salt
1½ teaspoons freshly ground black pepper

2. *Teriyaki Marinade*
½ cup canned crushed pineapple
6 tablespoons soy sauce
3 tablespoons dry sake or dry white wine
2 tablespoons packed light brown sugar
1 tablespoon minced peeled fresh ginger
2 garlic cloves, crushed

3. Spiced Apple Marinade

½ cup frozen unsweetened apple juice
  concentrate, thawed
½ cup water
½ teaspoon ground cinnamon
½ teaspoon ground cumin
½ teaspoon salt
½ teaspoon freshly ground black pepper
¼ teaspoon ground cloves
⅛ teaspoon cayenne pepper

4. Honey-Orange Marinade

½ cup frozen orange juice concentrate,
  thawed
¼ cup soy sauce
2 tablespoons honey
2 tablespoons apple cider vinegar
1 tablespoon minced peeled fresh ginger
2 garlic cloves, crushed

Char Siu

This is the classic Chinese barbecued pork but made leaner by using pork tenderloin. Roasting the meat directly on the oven rack permits the best air circulation—thus giving the best jerkylike texture to the meat's exterior. Use three smaller or two larger tenderloins for this recipe. Char Siu is great in composed salads, as an appetizer, as part of a buffet, or as a substitute for the meat in almost any spicy stir-fry that doesn't include long simmering. *Makes 8 to 10 servings*

3 pounds pork tenderloin, trimmed of
  any silverskin (see Note on
  page 426)
1 cup peeled, cored, and chopped fresh
  pineapple
2 garlic cloves, crushed
¼ cup soy sauce
¼ cup honey
¼ cup packed light brown sugar
2 tablespoons Shaoxing or dry sherry

2 tablespoons hoisin sauce
6 drops red food coloring, optional but
  traditional
Nonstick spray or canola oil
¼ cup chicken broth

1 Butterfly the tenderloins by laying them on your work surface and splitting them lengthwise, running the knife along the tenderloin parallel to the work surface without cutting through—thus, they can be opened up and pressed flat.

2 Whisk the pineapple, garlic, soy sauce, honey, brown sugar, Shaoxing or sherry, hoisin sauce, and food coloring, if using, in a medium bowl until the sugar dissolves.

3 Place the tenderloins in a large resealable plastic bag, add the pineapple marinade, seal, and shake well to coat the meat. Refrigerate for at least 6 hours or up to 24 hours, occasionally shaking the bag and rubbing the marinade into the meat through the plastic.

4 Clean the oven rack; spray it with nonstick spray or rub a little canola oil on it. Position it in the middle of the oven, then preheat the oven to 350°F. Place the broiler pan or a disposable aluminum pan under the rack to catch any drips.

5 Remove the tenderloins from the marinade and let them sit at room temperature while the oven heats. Also, pour all the marinade into a small saucepan, add the broth, and bring to a simmer over high heat; cook, stirring often, for 2 minutes. Adjust the heat so that the marinade stays at the barest simmer.

6 Place the tenderloins directly on the oven rack over the drip pan; roast for 1½ hours, turning about once every 20 minutes and basting frequently with the hot marinade. The meat will get

well done, but the marinade will preserve its juiciness. Remove the tenderloins from the oven and let them stand on a carving board for 5 minutes before slicing thinly.

Tuscan-Inspired Roasted Pork Loin with Potatoes and Garlic

In this dish, the potatoes and garlic slowly roast in the pork's juices. For a more intense taste, seal the coated loin in a plastic bag and marinate in the refrigerator for up to 2 days. *Makes 6 servings*

2 large baking potatoes
1 garlic head plus 3 garlic cloves, minced
4 tablespoons (¼ cup) chopped fresh rosemary
5 tablespoons olive oil
2 teaspoons finely grated lemon zest
1 teaspoon coarse-grained or kosher salt
One 2- to 2½-pound boneless center-cut
  pork loin, trimmed of all surface fat and
  tied in three places (see Note)
Freshly ground black pepper to taste

1 Cut the potatoes into 2-inch pieces. (You can peel them, but the skin will get crunchy as they roast.) Place in a large bowl and cover with water by 2 inches. Set aside at room temperature for 20 minutes so the potatoes lose some starch.

2 Meanwhile, position the rack in the center of the oven and preheat the oven to 375°F. Mix the 3 minced garlic cloves, 2 tablespoons chopped rosemary, 2 tablespoons olive oil, lemon zest, and salt in a large bowl; rub this mixture all over the tied pork loin.

3 Drain the potatoes and blot dry with paper towels. Place in a 12- to 14-inch oven-safe skillet or sauté pan. Pour the remaining 3 tablespoons oil over the potatoes and set over medium heat.

4 Once the potatoes start to sizzle, cook, stirring occasionally, until they begin to turn translucent at their edges and brown a bit, about 5 minutes.

5 Break up the garlic cloves from the whole head (do not peel) and sprinkle them among the potatoes; add the remaining rosemary, sprinkling it among the potatoes.

6 Nestle the pork loin in the middle of the skillet. Place in the oven and roast until the meat has browned, until an instant-read meat thermometer inserted into the center of the loin registers 155°F (our preference) or 160°F (the USDA recommendation), about 1 hour and 10 minutes, turning the loin once or twice and tossing the potatoes occasionally. Grind some black pepper over the roast just before serving.

Note: Sometimes the loin includes part of the backbone; this will indeed improve the taste when roasted, but it makes the loin very difficult to carve. Instead, look for boneless center-cut pork loins or have your butcher slice off the backbone for you. With the bone removed, the roast should be tied to hold its shape; wrap butcher's twine around the roast in three places, securing its cylindrical shape.

Variations: Add 2 tablespoons minced oregano leaves or minced parsley leaves and/or ½ teaspoon red pepper flakes to the rub for the pork.

Substitute 1½ pounds small red-skinned or yellow-fleshed potatoes, cut in half, for the baking potatoes.

Remove the pork from the roasting pan when done and toss the potatoes and garlic cloves with 1 tablespoon balsamic vinegar before serving.

You can create a gravy for the loin. Place the

heavy-duty flame-safe roasting pan over medium heat, pour in ¼ cup chicken broth or white wine, and bring to a simmer, scraping up any browned bits in the pan. Skim the sauce for any fat, then reduce by half, about 1 minute.

German-Inspired Pork Loin Stuffed with Sauerkraut

Stuffed with sauerkraut, covered in bacon—all you need is the beer. This roast uses a very large loin roast. Have the butcher butterfly it for you—that is, spread it open so it will lie flat on your work surface. *Makes 10 servings*

> One 1-pound package fresh sauerkraut, drained and squeezed of all excess moisture
> 2 tablespoons Dijon mustard
> 2 tablespoons gin
> 1 tablespoon caraway seeds
> One 4- to 4½-pound boneless pork loin roast, trimmed of all surface fat and butterflied
> 1 pound sliced bacon
> Butcher's twine
> Canola oil for the grill grate, if using

❶ Mix the sauerkraut, mustard, gin, and caraway seeds in a medium bowl.

❷ Lay the loin rough side up on your work surface. Spread the sauerkraut mixture down the center, leaving a ½-inch edge at each end. Fold the loin closed.

❸ Lay the bacon over the top of the meat, overlapping each strip by ½ inch. Tie the bacon in place with butcher's twine, wrapping the twine around the roast to close it and hold its round shape but also wrapping it the long way over the roast. (You can stuff the pork up to 24 hours in advance; cover and refrigerate, but let stand at room temperature for 10 minutes before proceeding.)

❹ **To roast:** Position the rack in the center of the oven and preheat the oven to 325°F. Place the loin bacon side up in a large roasting pan or broiler pan. Roast until an instant-read meat thermometer inserted into the thickest part of the loin without its touching the stuffing registers 155°F (our preference) or 160°F (the USDA recommendation), about 1 hour and 45 minutes. Let the loin stand on a carving board at room temperature for 5 minutes before serving.

To barbecue: Heat half a gas grill to medium heat while placing a drip pan or disposable aluminum roasting pan under the unheated section of the grate; or build a medium-heat, well-ashed coal bed in a charcoal grill, then rake the coals to the perimeter and place a drip pan or disposable aluminum pan in the center of the grill. Dab canola oil on some paper towels, then lightly oil the section of the grate over the drip pan. Place the loin bacon side up over the drip pan, cover the grill, and barbecue for 3 hours, adding extra charcoal briquettes as the fire dies down, until an instant-read meat thermometer inserted into the thickest part of the loin registers 155°F (our preference) or 160°F (the USDA recommendation). Move the loin directly over the fire and cook, turning onto all sides, until the bacon gets crispy, about 5 minutes. Let the loin stand on a carving board for 5 minutes before serving.

Cold Sliced Pork Loin in Szechuan Garlic Sauce

Here's a make-ahead party dish: the pork cooks and then marinates overnight in a garlic sauce. Slice it up and serve it cold. *Makes 10 servings*

One 3-pound boneless center-cut pork loin, trimmed of all surface fat
Butcher's twine
10 medium scallions
One 4-inch piece of peeled fresh ginger, cut into 8 rounds
2 teaspoons salt
6 tablespoons soy sauce
6 tablespoons minced garlic
3 tablespoons toasted sesame oil
3 tablespoons water
2 tablespoons black Chinese vinegar or 1½ tablespoons balsamic vinegar and ½ tablespoon Worcestershire sauce
2 tablespoons rice vinegar
2 tablespoons sugar
1 to 2 tablespoons chili oil
3 medium cucumbers

❶ Cut the pork loin into 3 pieces; tie each piece once around its middle with a piece of butcher's twine (see page 249).

❷ Place the loin pieces in a large pot or Dutch oven. Cover with water to a depth of 1 inch. Slice 8 scallions lengthwise; add them to the pot. Also add the ginger and salt. Cover and bring to a boil over medium-high heat. Reduce the heat and simmer for 40 minutes. Remove the pot from the stove and place in the refrigerator to chill for at least 12 hours or up to 24 hours. (Set a doubled kitchen towel under the pot to protect your refrigerator shelf from the heat.)

❸ Mince the green parts of the remaining 2 scallions. Mix these with the soy sauce, garlic, sesame oil, water, black vinegar or its substitutes, rice vinegar, sugar, and chili oil in a medium bowl. Cover and refrigerate for up to 24 hours.

❹ Peel the cucumbers, slice them into thin rounds, and make a bed on a serving platter. Remove the loin pieces from the cooking liquid, cut off the twine, and slice into thin rounds. (Discard the cooking liquid.) Place over the cucumbers and pour the sauce on top.

Variations: Add 4 dried red Chinese chiles to the pot with the ginger.
Add 1 star anise pod or two 4-inch cinnamon sticks to the pot with the ginger.

Pork and Peanut Stir-Fry

Mirin, the sweetened Japanese rice wine, balances the red pepper flakes and vinegar. *Makes 4 servings*

1 pound boneless center-cut pork loin, trimmed of surface fat
3 tablespoons soy sauce
3 tablespoons mirin
2 teaspoons sesame oil
2 teaspoons rice vinegar
½ teaspoon red pepper flakes (see Note)
2 tablespoons peanut oil
1 large onion, halved and thinly sliced
6 garlic cloves, minced
2 tablespoons minced peeled fresh ginger
3 celery ribs, thinly sliced
3 ounces snow peas, trimmed and thinly sliced
½ cup roasted unsalted peanuts
2 teaspoons cornstarch whisked in a small bowl with 2 tablespoons water

❶ Cut the loin into ¼-inch-thick rounds, then cut these into thin strips. Set aside.

❷ Whisk the soy sauce, mirin, sesame oil, rice vinegar, and red pepper flakes in a small bowl; set aside as well.

3 Heat a large nonstick wok or high-sided sauté pan over medium-high heat. Swirl in the peanut oil; then add the onion, garlic, and ginger. Stir-fry until aromatic, until the onion has started to turn translucent, about 1 minute.

4 Add the pork; cook, tossing constantly, until lightly browned, about 2 minutes.

5 Add the celery, snow peas, and peanuts. Stir-fry until glistening, about 2 minutes.

6 Pour in the soy sauce mixture, bring to a simmer, and cook for 1 minute.

7 Swirl in the cornstarch mixture, bring to a simmer, and cook until thickened and bubbling, stirring frequently, about 30 seconds.

Note: Remember that chili oils interact over time, rendering various spices less subtle and aromatic. Replace red pepper flakes at least once a year.

Variations: Substitute any number of vegetables for the celery and snow peas: broccoli florets, cauliflower florets, peeled and sliced water chestnuts, peeled and sliced bamboo shoots, green beans cut into 1-inch segments, and/or thinly sliced carrots.

Hunan Pork Stir-Fry

Hunan cooking often uses lamb, but pork is a flavorful—and quicker-cooking—alternative. The sauce replicates a spicy and sweet Hunan barbecue sauce. It'll only be as hot as the red chili sauce you use. Go for broke and double the amount—or pass extra on the side. *Makes 4 servings*

1 pound boneless center-cut pork loin, trimmed of surface fat
1 tablespoon peanut oil
6 medium scallions, thinly sliced

2 garlic cloves, minced
2 tablespoons minced peeled fresh ginger
2 medium bell peppers, preferably 1 red and 1 yellow, cored, seeded, and thinly sliced
1 medium onion, thinly sliced
2 tablespoons hoisin sauce
2 tablespoons soy sauce
2 tablespoons rice vinegar
2 teaspoons Asian red chili sauce
2 teaspoons toasted sesame oil
2 teaspoons cornstarch whisked with 1½ tablespoons water in a small bowl

1 Cut the loin into ¼-inch-thick rounds, then cut these into thin strips. Set aside.

2 Heat a large nonstick wok or high-sided skillet over medium-high heat. Swirl in the peanut oil; add the scallions, garlic, and ginger. Cook, tossing constantly, until fragrant, about 20 seconds.

3 Add the bell pepper strips and onion slices; cook, stirring constantly, for 1 minute. Then add the pork; cook, stirring and tossing all the while, until lightly browned, about 2 minutes.

4 Stir in the hoisin sauce, soy sauce, rice vinegar, chili sauce, and toasted sesame oil. Bring to a full simmer.

5 Stir in the cornstarch mixture; cook, stirring often, until thickened, about 20 seconds. Remove from the heat, cover, and set aside for 2 minutes before serving.

Variations: You can substitute any protein in this dish so long as you use about 1 pound and you cut it into matchstick strips: boneless skinless chicken breasts, lamb loin, sirloin steak, or turkey cutlets. You can also substitute small shrimp, cleaned and deveined, or small bay scallops.

Vietnamese-Inspired Black Pepper Pork Stir-Fry

Traditional Vietnamese black pepper sauces are tamed by caramelized sugar to create a sweet/fiery combination that cries out for rice or potatoes. Make sure your black pepper is quite fresh; the heat of the peppercorns dulls over time. *Makes 4 servings*

1 pound boneless center-cut pork loin, trimmed of all surface fat
2 tablespoons peanut oil
1 teaspoon salt
6 garlic cloves, halved
2 tablespoons sugar
2 to 3 teaspoons freshly ground black pepper
¼ cup vegetable broth
1 tablespoon fish sauce
2 cups mung or soy bean sprouts

❶ Cut the loin into ¼-inch-thick rounds, then cut these into thin strips. Season with salt.

❷ Heat a large, high-sided skillet over medium heat. Swirl in 1 tablespoon peanut oil, then add the pork and brown well, about 2 minutes, stirring often. Transfer to a large plate.

❸ Add the remaining 1 tablespoon peanut oil, then the garlic. Cook, stirring constantly, until aromatic, about 1 minute.

❹ Add the sugar. Cook, stirring frequently, until the sugar melts, turns golden, and begins to caramelize, about 3 minutes.

❺ Add the pepper, stir for 5 seconds, then pour in the broth and fish sauce. Stir until boiling and smooth, about 1 minute. Add the pork and any accumulated juices; cook for 30 seconds.

❻ Add the sprouts, toss, cover, and remove from the heat for 5 minutes before serving.

From the Leg

Fresh Ham

A ham comes from a pig's back leg, usually from the middle of the "thigh" to the hip. Hams are available "fresh" (meaning raw) or "cured" (that is, partially cooked). For this recipe, use either a bone-in or boneless fresh ham. If the former, choose the shank-end, a ham from closer to the shin. If the latter, choose one from the butt end; this cut should be butterflied by your butcher so that it will lie flat. *Makes 12 to 14 servings*

2 cups apple cider
1 cup dry white wine
1 tablespoon honey mustard
2 teaspoons salt
1 teaspoon stemmed thyme or ½ teaspoon dried thyme
1 teaspoon minced sage leaves or ½ teaspoon dried sage
1 teaspoon freshly ground black pepper
½ teaspoon ground cloves
2 garlic cloves, crushed
One 8- to 10-pound bone-in or boneless fresh ham
Butcher's twine, if using a boneless ham

❶ Whisk the cider, wine, mustard, salt, thyme, sage, pepper, cloves, and garlic in a large bowl.

❷ Place the ham in a large roasting pan; pour the cider marinade over it. Turn to coat, then cover and refrigerate for 48 hours, turning the meat occasionally so that it is well coated with the marinade.

❸ Position the rack in the center of the oven and preheat the oven to 325°F. While the oven heats, set the roasting pan with the ham and marinade out on the counter. If you're using a butterflied, boneless ham, roll it closed and secure it in at least three places with butcher's twine.

4. Place the pan in the oven and roast the ham, basting it frequently with the marinade, until an instant-read meat thermometer inserted into the thickest part of the meat registers 155°F (our preference) or 160°F (the USDA recommendation), 2 hours and 40 minutes to 3 hours and 20 minutes, depending on the size of the ham, its fat content, and the desired degree of doneness.

5. Transfer to a carving board, tent with aluminum foil, and let stand at room temperature for 15 minutes. Meanwhile, skim any visible fat from the pan juices, strain them into a small saucepan, and bring to a boil over high heat. Cook until slightly reduced, about 2 minutes; then serve with the carved ham.

Baked Cured Ham with Two Glazes

Choose a cured—or smoked—ham that is either partially cooked (brought to an internal temperature of 137°F to kill bacteria) or fully cooked (brought to about 148°F). Both must still be cooked at home. Ready-to-eat hams are cooked to a much higher temperature and are not recommended for this recipe. *Makes 12 to 14 servings*

One 12-pound smoked ham (can be spiral-cut)
One of the two glazes that follow

1. Position the rack in the center of the oven and preheat the oven to 325°F. Place the ham in a large roasting pan and cover with aluminum foil.

2. Bake until an instant-read meat thermometer inserted into the thickest part of the meat without touching bone registers 130°F, 1½ to 2 hours.

3. Meanwhile, whisk either of the two glazes in a small bowl.

4. Remove the foil and baste the ham with some of the marinade. Continue baking, open to the heat and basting frequently, until an instant-read meat thermometer inserted into the center of the ham registers 155°F (our preference) or 160°F (the USDA recommendation), about 40 minutes. Make sure you thoroughly wash the basting utensil after each use so you're not carrying bacteria back and forth between the marinade and the ham. Once done, remove the ham from the roasting pan, transfer to a carving board, tent with foil, and let stand at room temperature for 10 to 15 minutes before carving.

Two Glazes for Ham

1. *Orange Marmalade Glaze*
1 cup orange marmalade
1 cup dry white wine or dry
    vermouth
¼ cup brandy
¼ cup light or gold rum
1 teaspoon dry mustard
1 teaspoon ground ginger

2. *Spiced Molasses Glaze*
1 cup chicken broth
¼ cup molasses
¼ cup Dijon mustard
1 teaspoon ground cinnamon
½ teaspoon grated nutmeg
¼ teaspoon ground allspice
¼ teaspoon cayenne pepper

Ham Steak with Raisins and Wine Sauce

Ham steaks are usually taken from the hind end of the pig; they most often contain a slice of the bone. *Makes 4 servings*

¾ cup sweet white wine, such as a Riesling
½ cup golden raisins
2 tablespoons unsalted butter
One 2-pound cured or smoked ham steak
    (about ½ inch thick)
2 shallots, halved and thinly sliced
1 garlic clove, minced
1 tablespoon chopped rosemary leaves
½ teaspoon freshly ground black pepper
2½ tablespoons white wine vinegar
1 cup chicken broth

1 Bring the wine and raisins to a simmer in a small saucepan set over high heat. Cover, remove the pan from the heat, and set aside for 30 minutes.

2 Melt 1 tablespoon butter in a large skillet set over medium heat, add the ham steak, and fry until nicely browned on both sides, 8 to 10 minutes, turning once. Transfer the ham to a large plate; set aside.

3 Melt the remaining tablespoon butter in the skillet, add the shallots, and cook, stirring often, until softened, about 2 minutes. Add the garlic and cook for 30 seconds.

4 Pour the wine and raisins into the skillet. Raise the heat to high and bring to a boil. Cook until the liquid has been reduced to a thick glaze, about 1 minute.

5 Stir in the rosemary, pepper, and vinegar; cook, stirring constantly, for 20 seconds.

6 Pour in the broth, bring to a boil, and cook, stirring often, until reduced by half, about 2 minutes.

7 Add the ham back to the skillet, baste with the sauce, reduce the heat to low, and cook for 1 minute to heat through.

Variations: Substitute any dried fruit you like for the raisins: dried cherries, dried cranberries, chopped dried apricots, chopped dried apples, or chopped pitted prunes.

Pork Ribs

Oven-Barbecued Pork Ribs

Cooking ribs is a balancing act. Is the meat done? Is it tender? Does it still barely adhere to the bone? You may perfect your technique over time, but the first taste will hook you. Look for meaty, heavy rib racks with minimal fat clumps at the ends of the bones. *Makes 2 racks, 4 to 6 servings*

1½ tablespoons packed light brown sugar
1½ tablespoons chili powder
1 tablespoon mild or smoked paprika
2 teaspoons salt
1 teaspoon dry mustard
1 teaspoon ground cumin
1 teaspoon dried thyme
1 teaspoon freshly ground black pepper
Two 2-pound racks pork ribs

1 Mix the brown sugar, chili powder, paprika, salt, mustard, cumin, thyme, and pepper in a small bowl.

2 Peel any thin, translucent membrane off the back of the racks, then make an incision between each of the ribs, starting at the leaner ends and cutting 2 inches down between them. (You can also have your butcher do this for you.) Rub the dry spice mixture over both sides of the meat, taking care to massage it in gently. Wrap the ribs in aluminum foil or plastic wrap and refrigerate at least overnight or up to 2 days.

3 Position the rack in the center of the oven and preheat the oven to 275°F. Unwrap the ribs and set them out on the counter for 15 minutes while the oven heats.

4 Set a metal rack in a broiler pan, roasting pan, or disposable aluminum pan. Set the ribs meat side down onto the rack. Bake for 30 minutes.

5 Turn and continue baking until the meat has pulled back from the bones and is falling-apart tender in between the ribs, about 3 hours. Let stand at room temperature on a carving board for 10 minutes before slicing between the ribs and serving.

Variation: Substitute 6 tablespoons of your favorite barbecue seasoning rub for the spice mixture in this recipe.

Barbecued Baby Back Ribs with Maple Bourbon Barbecue Sauce

Baby back ribs are the small ribs at the upper end of the rib cage. Once a Danish specialty, they were ground for feed in the United States—until the savvy marketing campaigns of many restaurants made them the most popular version of pork ribs. There's no need to use a single-batch, high-end bottle of bourbon here, just one with a good caramel taste. *Makes 4 hearty main-course servings*

Four 1-pound racks baby back ribs
One 750ml bottle bourbon
2 cups chicken broth
1 teaspoon liquid smoke
2 tablespoons canola oil, plus additional for
    the grill grate
2 large onions, chopped
1 cup plus 2 tablespoons cider
    vinegar
1 cup ketchup
½ cup bottled chili sauce, such as Heinz

½ cup lemon juice
½ cup maple syrup
2 tablespoons Worcestershire sauce
2 tablespoons dry mustard
¼ teaspoon ground cloves
Several dashes of hot red pepper sauce
    to taste

1 Lay the racks meat side down on your work surface. Look to see if they have a translucent membrane running over the meat and bones. Starting at the smallest bones, gently lift up the membrane with a knife, then pull it off with your hands, much like pulling a sheet of glued paper off something. Discard the membrane; set the ribs aside.

2 Reserve ½ cup bourbon. Pour the remainder of the bourbon, the broth, and liquid smoke into a very large roasting pan or a disposable aluminum pan. If you don't have a pan that's large enough, divide the ingredients between two pans. Place the meat in the marinade, turn, cover, and refrigerate at least overnight or up to 2 days.

3 Heat a large saucepan over medium heat. Swirl in the canola oil, then add the onions. Cook, stirring often, until translucent, about 4 minutes.

4 Add the vinegar, ketchup, chili sauce, lemon juice, maple syrup, Worcestershire sauce, dry mustard, cloves, and hot red pepper sauce; then stir in the remaining ½ cup bourbon. Bring to a simmer, stirring constantly.

5 Reduce the heat to low and simmer until the sauce is slightly thickened, about 25 minutes, stirring once in a while. Cover and set aside while you prepare the grill. (The sauce can be made in advance; cover and refrigerate for up to 2 days, but bring it back to a low simmer over medium heat before continuing.)

6 Preheat half of a gas grill to medium heat and set a drip pan under the unheated section of the grate, or build a medium-heat, well-ashed coal bed in a charcoal grill, rake the coals to one side, and place a drip pan under the section of the grate not directly above the heat. Dab some oil on a paper towel and lightly oil the unheated section of the grate, setting it about 5 inches above the heat.

7 Place the ribs meat side down on the unheated section of the grill over the drip pan; brush them generously with the barbecue sauce. Cover and barbecue for 40 minutes, basting the ribs with more sauce every 10 minutes.

8 Turn the ribs meat side up; cover again; and continue barbecuing over the unheated grill section until the meat pulls back from the bones and is very tender, about 1 hour, basting with sauce every 10 minutes. If using a charcoal grill, add more briquettes occasionally to keep the medium-heat fire burning. If you want crispy ribs, transfer them to the part of the grate directly over the heat for the last 5 minutes of cooking, searing the outside of the meat on both sides. Transfer to a carving board and let stand for 5 minutes before slicing between the ribs to serve.

To prepare baby back ribs in the oven: Position the rack in the center of the oven and preheat the oven to 250°F. Lay the prepared ribs bone side down on a baking sheet; roast for 1½ hours. Bathe the ribs in barbecue sauce and continue roasting, basting occasionally, until the meat has pulled away from the bones and is fork-tender, about 1 more hour.

You can also use this sauce on the Oven-Barbecued Pork Ribs (page 434). Mop it onto the ribs during their final 30 minutes in the oven.

Other Cuts of Pork

Pulled Pork with Beer Barbecue Sauce

Pulled pork is a Southern religion. Serve on hamburger or hot dog buns, on toasted English muffins, with pickle relish, with pickled jalapeño rings, with sliced red onions, or with hot red pepper sauce on the side, or with A Bowl of Vinegary Cucumbers (page 107). *Makes 8 servings*

One 3½- to 4-pound boneless pork shoulder roast
Butcher's twine
1 tablespoon packed light brown sugar
1 tablespoon chili powder
1 tablespoon salt, preferably kosher salt
1 teaspoon dry mustard
1 teaspoon ground cumin
1 teaspoon ground cinnamon
½ teaspoon freshly ground black pepper
¼ teaspoon cayenne pepper
4 cups grilling wood chips, soaked in water at least 3 hours, then drained, if grilling
Beer Barbecue Sauce (recipe follows)

1 Tie the pork shoulder with butcher's twine so that it resembles a football. (Some pork shoulders are sold with a twine netting already in place.)

2 Mix the brown sugar, chili powder, salt, dry mustard, cumin, cinnamon, pepper, and cayenne in a small bowl. Massage this mixture into the pork. (Wash your hands carefully afterward to avoid getting cayenne in your eyes.) Cover with plastic wrap and refrigerate at least overnight or up to 48 hours.

3 **To grill:** Heat half a gas grill to medium heat and place a drip pan under the unheated section of the grate; or build a well-ashed, medium-heat coal bed in a charcoal grill, rake the coals to one side, and place a drip pan or other disposable aluminum

pan on the unheated side of the grill. Place the wood chips in the drip pan. Set the pork on the unheated section of the grill grate over the drip pan. Cover and barbecue until the meat is charred and falls apart when pulled with a fork, until an instant-read meat thermometer inserted into the center of the meat registers 175°F, about 3 hours.

To bake: Position the rack in the center of the oven and preheat the oven to 300°F. Set the pork in a roasting pan and bake until the meat can be pulled apart with a fork and an instant-read meat thermometer inserted into the thickest part of the meat registers 175°F, 3½ to 4 hours.

4 Transfer the pork to a carving board and let rest for 10 minutes. Slice off the twine, then cut the meat into chunks. Pull these chunks into threads with two forks, saving all the juice on the cutting board.

5 Place the shredded pork and all juice in a large saucepan. Stir in the Beer Barbecue Sauce. Heat over medium heat or place the pot directly over the heat on the grill until simmering. Cook, stirring often, until heated through, about 10 minutes.

Beer Barbecue Sauce
Makes a little less than 3 cups

> One 12-ounce bottle beer, preferably a
>   wheat beer or a summer ale
> 1¾ cups canned tomato sauce
> 6 tablespoons ketchup
> 6 tablespoons cider vinegar
> ¼ cup bottled chili sauce, such as Heinz
> 3 tablespoons packed dark brown sugar
> ½ teaspoon red pepper flakes
> ¼ teaspoon garlic powder
> 1 dried ancho chile, cored and seeded, then
>   ground in a spice grinder or mini-food
>   processor, or 2 tablespoons ancho chile
>   powder

Whisk all the ingredients in a medium saucepan set over medium heat. Bring to a simmer, then reduce the heat and simmer slowly until thickened, about 20 minutes. Keep warm on the stove or cover and refrigerate for up to 3 days.

Filipino-Inspired Pork Butt in Vinegar

This is a wonderful way to cook a luxurious cut: first braising it, then frying it crispy. *Makes 6 servings*

> 3 pounds boneless pork butt, cut into 2-inch
>   pieces
> ½ cup rice vinegar
> ¼ cup soy sauce
> 1 teaspoon freshly ground black pepper
> 1 garlic head, cloves separated and peeled
> 2 bay leaves
> 2 cups vegetable broth
> 1 tablespoon fish sauce
> 1 tablespoon lime juice
> 2 tablespoons solid vegetable shortening
>   or lard

1 Place the pork, rice vinegar, soy sauce, pepper, garlic, and bay leaves in a large nonreactive bowl (see page 42); stir well, cover, and refrigerate for at least 8 hours or up to 48 hours.

2 Transfer the entire contents of the bowl to a large saucepan. Stir in the broth, set over medium-high heat, and bring to a simmer, stirring often.

3 Skim off any impurities or foam that rises to the surface, cover, reduce the heat to low, and simmer slowly until tender, about 1½ hours.

4 Transfer the meat to a large bowl with a slotted spoon. Scoop out the garlic cloves and place them in a separate bowl. Set both aside.

⑤ Strain the hot broth, discarding all the solids, and return it to the large saucepan. Stir in the fish sauce and lime juice; bring to a boil over high heat. Boil until reduced by two thirds, about 8 minutes.

⑥ Meanwhile, melt the shortening or lard in a large skillet set over medium-high heat. Add the pork pieces; fry until crispy on two sides, turning once, about 6 minutes. Work in batches if you need to.

⑦ Stir the pork into the simmering sauce. Squeeze all the garlic out of the hulls and into the sauce. Bring back to a simmer, stirring all the while to melt the garlic into the sauce before serving.

❈ *Lamb* ❈

Lamb is a mildly gamy but very sweet meat. Technically, a lamb is under one year of age, usually around 8 months. So-called spring lamb is a moniker like "jumbo shrimp"—a label with no enforced value.

Lamb Chops

Lamb chops are found in three varieties: shoulder, loin, and rib. Shoulder chops are fattier, more fibrous, and better for stewing. Loin or rib chops can be a little bland but either will work here; both marinades will improve their natural qualities. Loin chops are sometimes sold as "double chops": two bones per chop. Cook these perhaps half again as long, paying close attention to the internal temperature. *Makes 4 servings*

Eight 6-ounce, 1-inch-thick lamb
    shoulder or loin or rib chops, trimmed of
    peripheral fat
One of the two marinades that follow
Canola oil for the grate, if grilling

① Place the chops and one of the marinades in a large plastic bag. Seal, massage the marinade into the chops through the plastic, and refrigerate for at least 8 hours or up to 24 hours, occasionally massaging the chops in the marinade through the plastic.

② Remove the chops from the marinade and blot dry with paper towels. Set aside at room temperature while you prepare the broiler or grill.

③ **To broil:** Line the broiler pan with aluminum foil and preheat the broiler. Place the chops in the pan and broil, turning once, until browned and sizzling, until an instant-read meat thermometer inserted diagonally into the center of the meat without the probe touching bone registers 135°F (our preference for medium-rare) or 145°F (the USDA recommendation), 8 to 10 minutes for loin chops and 15 minutes for shoulder chops.

To grill: Preheat the charcoal grill for high-heat cooking or build a well-ashed, high-heat coal bed in a charcoal grill. Lightly oil the grate, set it 4 to 6 inches over the heat, and place the chops directly over the heat or coal bed. Grill, turning once, until browned and sizzling, until an instant-read meat thermometer inserted into one of the chops registers 135°F (our preference for medium-rare) or 145°F (the USDA recommendation), 7 to 8 minutes for loin chops and 11 to 12 minutes for shoulder chops.

4 Let the chops stand on a cutting board or serving plates for 5 minutes before serving.

Note: Cooking the chops to medium-rare allows you to preserve both the meat's taste and texture. You can cook lamb to medium—an internal temperature of 155°F—but the meat will toughen considerably. Medium-well or well done are not recommended.

Two Marinades for Lamb Chops

1. Gin Marinade
1 cup gin
2 tablespoons juniper berries, crushed
2 teaspoons freshly grated lemon zest
½ teaspoon salt
½ teaspoon freshly ground black pepper
2 garlic cloves, crushed
1 bay leaf

2. Apple Pomegranate Marinade
1 small onion, minced
½ cup apple juice
3 tablespoons pomegranate molasses
2 teaspoons minced dill fronds or 1 teaspoon dried dill
½ teaspoon salt
½ teaspoon freshly ground black pepper

Lamb Sirloin

This delicately flavored if unusual cut cooks up just like a beef sirloin; it should be served thinly sliced, perhaps over a composed salad. Omit the bacon and try it over the BLT salad (page 125). Marinate two or three 8-ounce lamb sirloin cutlets about 1½ inches thick, trimmed of fat, in one of the two marinades for the chops; then broil or grill, turning once, until an instant-read meat thermometer inserted into the thickest part registers 135°F (our preference for medium-rare) or 145°F (the USDA recommendation), about 15 minutes. Let the sirloin stand on a cutting board for 5 minutes, then carve at an angle into thin, wide, long strips.

Rack of Lamb

There's hardly anything more elegant than a rack of lamb, the tender eye of meat just below the exposed bones. Make sure that the rack is "frenched"—that the tendons and fat have been scraped from between the bones, leaving only the round eye of lamb loin visible. Leave the thin layer of fat on the round eye; it protects the meat as it cooks. *Makes 6 servings*

One of the four rubs that follow
Two 1¼- to 1½-pound, 8-bone racks of
   lamb, frenched
1 tablespoon olive oil

1 Mix one of the four rubs in a small bowl.

2 Coat the racks with the rub, massaging it into the eye of the meat and making a "crust." Set the racks in a large baking dish, cover, and refrigerate for at least 2 hours or up to 24 hours.

3 Position the rack in the center of the oven and preheat the oven to 400°F.

④ If you've used the Mustard and Walnut Crust, proceed to step 4, place the rack in a roasting pan, and add 3 minutes to the roasting time. For the other three crusts, heat a large skillet, preferably cast iron, over medium-high heat. Swirl in the olive oil, then add the lamb racks bone side up. Cook until well browned, about 5 minutes, shaking the pan occasionally so the meat doesn't stick.

⑤ Turn the racks over so that the bones arc against the pan and lift the meat up slightly. Place the skillet in the oven and bake until well browned, until an instant-read meat thermometer inserted into the center of the loin without the probe's touching bone registers 135°F (our preference for medium-rare) or 145°F (the USDA recommendation), about 20 minutes.

⑥ Transfer the rack from the skillet to a carving board and let rest at room temperature for 5 minutes. To serve, use a large knife to slice between the bones, thereby separating the chops.

To grill a rack of lamb: Place a drip pan on one side of a gas grill; preheat the other side to high heat. Or build a high-heat, well-ashed coal bed in a charcoal grill, then use a grill rake or a cleaned garden trowel to push the coals to the perimeter of the grill so you can set a drip pan in the center under the grate. Lightly oil the grill grate with canola or olive oil, then place it 4 to 6 inches over the heat source. Place the racks herbed side up over the drip pan (indirectly over the heat). Cover and barbecue until an instant-read meat thermometer inserted halfway into the meat (but missing the bones) registers 135°F (our preference for medium-rare) or 145°F (the USDA recommendation), about 25 minutes. During prolonged grilling, the bones, especially if frenched, may burn; to help prevent this, place a thin sheet of aluminum foil between them and the grate. Transfer the racks to a carving board; let stand at room temperature for 5 minutes before carving between the chops to serve.

Four Rubs for Rack of Lamb

1. Garlic and Rosemary Rub
3 tablespoons olive oil
3 tablespoons minced rosemary leaves
2 teaspoons finely grated lemon zest
1 teaspoon salt
½ teaspoon freshly ground black pepper
4 garlic cloves, crushed

2. Green Tea Rub
3 tablespoons canola oil
2 tablespoons green tea leaves, ground to a powder in a spice grinder, or 1 tablespoon powdered green tea (do not use instant green tea)
4 teaspoons ground coriander
1 teaspoon salt

3. Fresh Herb Rub
3 tablespoons olive oil
2 tablespoons minced parsley leaves
2 tablespoons minced oregano leaves
2 tablespoons minced rosemary leaves
1 tablespoon finely grated lemon zest
1 teaspoon minced mint leaves
1 teaspoon salt
½ teaspoon freshly ground black pepper

4. Mustard and Walnut Crust
¼ cup Dijon mustard
½ cup fresh bread crumbs
½ cup finely ground walnut pieces
2 tablespoons minced rosemary leaves
1 teaspoon salt
½ teaspoon freshly ground black pepper

Note: This crust mixture makes an actual crust on the meat; pat it into place and work gently with the rack to keep the crust in place while it cooks.

Bone-in Roasted Leg of Lamb with Garlic and Allspice

Leg of lamb has a stronger taste than the rack or chops—more musky, somehow more elemental, less sweet, and beefier. *Makes 8 to 10 servings*

10 garlic cloves, peeled and halved lengthwise

1½ tablespoons ground allspice

One 6- to 7-pound bone-in leg of lamb

1 tablespoon salt, preferably coarse-grained or kosher salt

½ tablespoon freshly ground black pepper

2 large onions, sliced into ¼-inch rings

3 tablespoons olive oil

❶ Position the rack in the center of the oven and preheat the oven to 375°F. Mix the garlic and ½ tablespoon allspice in a small bowl until the halved cloves are well coated.

❷ Slip the tip of a paring knife into the meat at random but equidistant spacings, creating twenty small slits, some only ½ inch deep and some up to 2 inches deep.

❸ Push the coated garlic cloves into the slits, using the smaller cloves for shallower slits. Rub the remaining 1 tablespoon ground allspice all over the outside of the leg of lamb, then gently massage in the salt and pepper.

❹ Toss the onion rings and the olive oil in a large, heavy, deep roasting pan or broiler pan. Set the prepared leg of lamb on top.

❺ Roast until browned, until an instant-read meat thermometer inserted diagonally into the thickest part of the meat without the probe touching bone registers

125°F (our definition of rare), about 1½ hours

135°F (our definition of—and preference for—medium-rare), about 1 hour and 45 minutes

145°F (the USDA recommendation for medium-rare), about 2 hours

or 160°F (the USDA recommendation for medium), about 2 hours and 10 minutes

In all cases, check the roast after 1 hour to see where things stand.

❻ Use silicone oven mitts or large spatulas to transfer the leg of lamb to a cutting board so you can avoid pricking the meat and losing juice. Let stand at room temperature for 10 minutes.

❼ Set the roasting pan or broiler pan over medium-high heat and scrape up any browned bits with the onions in the pan, using the accumulated juices. If the pan is exceptionally dry, add 1 or 2 tablespoons water. Bring the sauce to a simmer, then turn off the heat.

❽ To carve the leg of lamb, set it bone side down on the carving board. Cut thin slices by starting at the top and slicing off a piece at a diagonal down toward the exposed bone (never cut parallel to the bone). When you've cut off several slices, turn the leg over and slice off more pieces, always cutting horizontally from the thickest part down to the exposed bone.

Variations: Substitute minced fresh rosemary or oregano for the allspice.

Substitute 8 medium shallots, sliced into thick rings, for the onions.

Deglaze the pan with 2 tablespoons white wine.

Braised Boneless Leg of Lamb with Almonds, Apricots, and Dates

In this dish, the leg is braised in an aromatic tomato broth, which is then ladled over the slices. Have your butcher butterfly the leg open for you.

Makes 8 servings

One 3½- to 4-pound boneless butterflied leg
    of lamb, all surface fat trimmed
6 ounces dried apricots
2 tablespoons sliced almonds
1 teaspoon cumin seeds
½ teaspoon salt
½ teaspoon freshly ground black pepper
Butcher's twine
2 tablespoons canola oil
1 large onion, halved and thinly sliced
8 garlic cloves, halved lengthwise
4 pitted dates, finely chopped
1½ teaspoons ground cumin
1 teaspoon ground coriander
¼ teaspoon saffron threads, crumbled
1 tablespoon tomato paste
2 teaspoons finely grated lemon zest
2 cups beef broth
Two 4-inch cinnamon sticks

1 Lay the leg of lamb rough side up on your work surface so that it's an oblong with the ends pointing away from you left and right. Lay the dried apricots over the meat, starting at the left side and working three quarters of the way across the meat. Sprinkle the almonds, cumin seeds, salt, and pepper over the apricots.

2 Starting at one long side of the oblong, the end without any dried apricots, roll the leg of lamb closed, sealing everything inside. Tie the butcher's twine in four places around the leg to hold it closed, with one tie at each end.

3 Position the rack in the center of the oven and preheat the oven to 350°F.

4 Heat a large casserole or Dutch oven over medium heat. Swirl in the canola oil, then add the tied leg of lamb. Brown it on all sides, about 8 minutes, turning occasionally. Transfer to a large plate and set aside.

5 Add the onion, garlic, and dates to the pot. Cook, stirring constantly, until softened, about 2 minutes.

6 Stir in the cumin, coriander, and saffron; cook for 20 seconds, then stir in the tomato paste and lemon zest until the paste dissolves and coats the vegetables. Pour in the broth, add the cinnamon sticks, and bring the sauce to a simmer, stirring constantly.

7 Return the leg of lamb and any accumulated juices to the pan, cover, and place in the oven. Roast, basting occasionally, until an instant-read meat thermometer inserted into the thickest part of the leg registers

125°F (our definition of rare), about 1 hour and
    20 minutes
135°F (our definition of—and preference for—
    medium-rare), about 1 hour and 30 minutes
145°F (the USDA recommendation for
    medium-rare), about 1 hour and 40 minutes
or 160°F (the USDA recommendation for
    medium), about 2 hours

In any case, take the meat's temperature after 1 hour to see how it's cooking.

8 Transfer the leg of lamb to a carving board; let stand at room temperature for 5 minutes—the temperature will go up by about 5 degrees. Discard the cinnamon sticks, skim any fat off the juices in the pan, and bring them to a boil over medium-high heat. Slice the meat into rounds before serving and serve with the pan juices on the side.

Variations: Substitute chopped dried cherries or chopped dried cranberries for the apricots.

Add 2 bay leaves with the cinnamon sticks; discard them along with the sticks.

Reduce the broth to 1 cup; add 1 cup white wine with the remaining broth.

Roasted Boneless Leg of Lamb with Mint Pesto

This easy pesto is smeared on the butterflied leg. The slices are great the next day for sandwiches. *Makes 8 servings*

One 3½- to 4-pound butterflied boneless leg of lamb, trimmed of all surface fat
Mint Pesto (recipe follows)
Butcher's twine

1 Position the rack in the center of the oven and preheat the oven to 350°F.

2 Lay the meat rough side up on your work surface. Spread all but 3 tablespoons Mint Pesto over the inside of the meat, leaving a ½-inch border around the perimeter. Starting at one narrow end, roll the meat closed, compacting it somewhat but not too tightly so that the pesto stays inside the roll.

3 Tie the meat in four places, securing rounds of butcher's twine around each end and then also at about a third of the way in from each side. Don't tie the meat so tightly that the pesto oozes out, but do make sure the roll is held together. Rub the outside of the meat with the remaining Mint Pesto.

4 Place the meat in a large, heavy roasting pan or the broiler pan. Place in the oven and roast until an instant-read meat thermometer inserted diagonally into the thickest part of the meat registers

125°F (our definition of rare), about 1 hour and 25 minutes
135°F (our definition of—and preference for—medium-rare), about 1 hour and 30 minutes

145°F (the USDA recommendation for medium-rare), about 1 hour and 45 minutes
or 160°F (the USDA recommendation for medium), about 1 hour and 55 minutes

In any case, take the roast's temperature after 1 hour to see where things stand.

5 Let the meat stand on a carving board at room temperature for 5 minutes before slicing it into rounds.

Variations: Substitute the Sun-Dried Tomato and Roasted Garlic Pesto (page 48) or the Pecan Pesto (page 179) for the pesto in this recipe.

Mint Pesto
This can also be a dip for vegetables or a sauce for pasta. *Makes a little more than 1 cup*

2 garlic cloves, quartered
½ cup packed basil leaves
¼ cup packed mint leaves
¼ cup packed parsley leaves
¼ cup toasted pine nuts
¼ cup freshly grated Parmigiano-Reggiano
3 tablespoons olive oil
1 teaspoon salt
½ teaspoon freshly ground black pepper

Place all the ingredients in a large food processor fitted with the chopping blade; pulse until chopped, then process until pasty but still a little coarse.

For more lamb dishes, check out Lamb and Wild Rice Soup (page 154), Lamb Ragù (page 192), Pastitsio (page 202), and Lamb Byriani (page 492).

Braised Lamb Shanks

Now we come to it, the ultimate braised dish. You sear the succulent meat in a fiery-hot oven, then build the sauce in the pan and let the meat's natural juices do the work in a lower-heat oven. Use a large ladle to get the shanks out of the pot so the meat doesn't fall off the bones. You'll also need a large oven casserole or Dutch oven—a heavy, huge pot that can go from oven to stovetop. *Makes 6 servings*

Six 1¼-pound lamb shanks

3 tablespoons olive oil

1 teaspoon salt

½ teaspoon freshly ground black pepper

1 cup white wine or dry vermouth

18 pearl onions, peeled

6 Roma or plum tomatoes, chopped

2 medium carrots, peeled and thinly sliced

1 celery rib, thinly sliced

2 garlic cloves, minced

3 cups chicken broth

2 teaspoons stemmed thyme or 1 teaspoon
    dried thyme

2 teaspoons chopped rosemary leaves or
    1 teaspoon dried rosemary, crushed

2 bay leaves

2 tablespoons all-purpose flour mashed with
    2 tablespoons room temperature unsalted
    butter in a small bowl until smooth

① Position the rack in the center of the oven and preheat the oven to 475°F.

② Toss the shanks, olive oil, salt, and pepper in a large bowl. Pour into a large Dutch oven or very large, heavy-duty oven casserole. Roast in the oven until the shanks are well browned, about 35 minutes, turning several times.

③ Remove the pot from the oven and decrease the oven's temperature to 350°F. Set the pot over medium heat. Pour in the wine and stir to scrape up all the browned bits in the pot, bringing the wine to a full simmer. Remember that the pot itself is very hot!

④ Stir in the onions, tomatoes, carrots, celery, garlic, broth, thyme, rosemary, and bay leaves. Bring the sauce to a simmer.

⑤ Cover and return the pot to the oven. Bake until the meat is falling off the bones, stirring gently once in a while to make sure each shank has been submerged in the sauce, about 1½ hours.

⑥ Whisk the flour-butter mixture into the pot until fully dissolved, cover again, and bake until the sauce has thickened, about 5 minutes. Discard the bay leaves. Serve the shanks in deep bowls with lots of the sauce ladled around them.

Variations: Substitute parsnips for the carrots.

Add 2 medium baking potatoes, peeled and cut into ½-inch pieces, with the onions and other ingredients.

Stir in 2 tablespoons tomato paste with the broth until the sauce is smooth before baking.

Lamb, Potato, and Greens Stew

We've crossed a Brazilian stew (caldo verde) with a traditional Irish preparation to come up with a winter warmer stocked with greens and potatoes. The secret to a great lamb stew? Never brown the meat; let it tenderize and soften in the soup at a gentle boil. *Makes 6 servings*

1½ pounds lamb stew meat

1 quart (4 cups) chicken broth

3 large leeks, white and pale green parts
    only, halved, carefully washed of
    any sand in the inner layers, and sliced
    into thin half-moons

1 tablespoon stemmed thyme or 2 teaspoons
    dried thyme

1 medium baking potato (about
　　8 ounces), peeled
1 large bunch collard greens (6 to 8 leaves),
　　washed, stemmed, and chopped
1 teaspoon salt
1 teaspoon freshly ground black pepper

❶ Place the lamb in a medium saucepan, cover with cold water to a depth of 2 inches, and bring to a boil over high heat. Cook for 10 minutes, skimming the fat and foam off the pot once or twice. Drain and rinse the meat under cold water.

❷ Pour the broth into a large saucepan or pot; bring to a simmer over high heat. Add the leeks and thyme. Simmer for 10 minutes, then add the lamb. Partially cover the pot, reduce the heat to low, and simmer slowly for 35 minutes, skimming off any fat and foam.

❸ Grate the potato into the pot using the large holes of a box grater. Stir well, cover, and simmer for 5 minutes, stirring once or twice.

❹ Stir in the collards, salt, and pepper. Cover and continue simmering until the greens and lamb are quite tender, about 12 minutes, stirring occasionally.

Variation: Use any bitter, leafy green, such as kale, mustard greens, spinach, or escarole.

Stewed Greek Meatballs with Artichokes, Dill, and Lemon

Mince the red onion so that there are no bits of onion visible in the meatballs. This stew can be made the day before; reheat it over medium heat until bubbling. *Makes 6 servings*

1½ pounds ground lamb
1 large egg
¼ cup fresh bread crumbs (see Note)
1 small red onion, minced
2 teaspoons minced oregano leaves or
　　1 teaspoon dried oregano
2 teaspoons minced dill fronds or
　　1 teaspoon dried dill
1 teaspoon freshly ground black pepper
½ cup plus 2 tablespoons all-purpose flour
¼ cup olive oil
1 small yellow onion, chopped
1 tablespoon capers, drained and chopped
1 teaspoon ground cinnamon
2 chopped anchovy fillets or 2 teaspoons
　　anchovy paste
2 cups vegetable broth
1 large tomato, chopped
One 12-ounce package frozen artichoke
　　hearts, thawed and halved; or one
　　14-ounce can artichoke hearts packed in
　　water, drained, rinsed,
　　and halved
1 tablespoon tomato paste
1 tablespoon lemon juice
1 teaspoon salt
1 bay leaf

❶ Position the rack in the center of the oven and preheat the oven to 325°F.

❷ Mix the ground lamb, egg, fresh bread crumbs, red onion, oregano, dill, and ½ teaspoon pepper in a large bowl until well combined. Form into 16 golf ball–sized balls.

3 Place ½ cup flour on a large plate. Heat a large saucepan or casserole over medium heat. Swirl in 2 tablespoons olive oil. Dip several of the meatballs in the flour, coating them completely; add them to the pan. Fry until browned on all sides, about 5 minutes, turning occasionally. Transfer to a plate and repeat with more of the meatballs.

4 Once all the meatballs have been browned, pour off any grease or rendered fat in the pan, set it back over medium heat, and add the remaining 2 tablespoons oil.

5 Add the yellow onion and cook, stirring often, until translucent, about 5 minutes.

6 Stir in the capers, cinnamon, and anchovies or anchovy paste. Cook, stirring constantly, for 30 seconds; then stir in the remaining 2 tablespoons flour until the vegetables are well coated.

7 Add the broth in a slow, steady stream, whisking all the while to keep the sauce from clumping. Bring the sauce to a light simmer, whisking all the while.

8 Stir in the tomato, artichoke hearts, tomato paste, lemon juice, salt, bay leaf, and the remaining ½ teaspoon pepper. Return the meatballs and any accumulated juices on the plate to the pot, submerging the balls somewhat in the sauce. Bring to a simmer.

9 Cover and place in the oven. Bake until the sauce is reduced somewhat, about 1 hour, stirring occasionally. Discard the bay leaf before serving.

Note: Make fresh bread crumbs by removing the crust from a day-old slice of bread and chopping it coarsely in the food processor. You can also mince the crustless bread on a cutting board, then continue to rock the knife through the pieces until they look like coarse snowflakes.

Variations: Reduce the ground lamb to 1 pound and use ½ pound lean ground beef with the remaining lamb.

Add ½ teaspoon red pepper flakes with the capers.

For a heartier dish, substitute beef broth for the vegetable broth.

Stir ½ pound medium shrimp, peeled and deveined, into the stew during the final 5 minutes of cooking; continue baking until the shrimp are pink and firm.

❀ Venison and Rabbit ❀

Here are two game meats—although they're hardly game anymore. Wild venison and rabbit are not available for sale—and in fact illegal to sell—in almost all commercial markets. Instead, high-quality purveyors are now selling farm-raised venison and rabbit. These meats are also available in overnight drop shipments from suppliers on the Web.

Venison Stew with White Wine and Pumpkin

Although venison shoulder makes the lightest stew, you can substitute cubed leg meat for a heartier concoction. Serve this stew over Whole Wheat Pasta (page 171), Chestnut Pasta (page 172), Perfect Mashed Potatoes (page 473), or brown rice. *Makes 6 servings*

1 tablespoon unsalted butter
6 ounces pancetta, chopped
2½ pounds boneless venison shoulder, trimmed of surface fat and cut into 2-inch pieces
1 teaspoon salt, plus more to taste
½ teaspoon freshly ground black pepper
1 large onion, halved and thinly sliced
6 garlic cloves, minced
2 teaspoons cumin seeds
2 teaspoons minced oregano leaves or 1 teaspoon dried oregano
Two 4-inch cinnamon sticks
2 cups fruity white wine, such as a Riesling
One 3-pound pumpkin, peeled, seeded, and cut into 2-inch pieces (see page 466), about 6 cups

❶ Position the rack in the center of the oven and preheat the oven to 350°F.

❷ Melt the butter in a large, oven-safe pot, Dutch oven, or casserole set over medium heat. Add the pancetta and cook, stirring often, until frizzled at the edges and browned, about 5 minutes. Transfer to a plate and set aside.

❸ Place the meat in the pot; season with salt and pepper. Cook, stirring often, until well browned, about 7 minutes. Transfer to a large bowl and set aside.

❹ Add the onion to the pot; cook, stirring often, until softened and sweet, about 3 minutes. Add the garlic and cook for 20 seconds.

❺ Add the cumin seeds, oregano, and cinnamon sticks; cook, stirring often, until aromatic, about 30 seconds. Pour in the white wine and bring to a simmer, scraping up any browned bits on the pot's bottom.

❻ Return the meat and any accumulated juices to the pot. Stir in the pumpkin pieces. Bring to a full simmer.

❼ Cover and place in the oven. Bake until the venison is fork-tender, stirring occasionally, about 2 hours. Check the sauce for salt and discard the cinnamon sticks.

Variations: Just about any hard squash will work in place of the pumpkin; try acorn, butternut, or blue Hubbard. Cut 2-inch pieces so they soften without dissolving into the stew.

Cider-Marinated Venison Loin

A venison loin has a deeper, richer taste: more gamy but also more indulgent. Trim the loin of its silverskin, the translucent membrane that lies along the curve of the meat; otherwise, the meat will curl as it cooks. To remove the silver skin, slice underneath and along the meat's surface plane. *Makes 6 servings*

2 cups apple cider

¼ cup orange juice

¼ cup maple syrup

3 tablespoons walnut oil

1 tablespoon Dijon mustard

1 teaspoon ground cinnamon

¼ teaspoon grated nutmeg

¼ teaspoon ground cloves

One 2½-pound venison loin, trimmed, silver skin removed

Butcher's twine

1 teaspoon salt

½ teaspoon freshly ground black pepper

8 whole cloves

Canola oil for the grill grate

❶ Whisk the cider, orange juice, maple syrup, walnut oil, mustard, cinnamon, nutmeg, and cloves in a medium bowl until smooth. Set aside.

❷ Tie the loin in three places, wrapping butcher's twine around the meat each time and tying it off so the loin will stay cylindrical as it cooks. Place the loin in a large roasting pan or large baking dish; gently massage the salt and pepper into the meat. Use the pointed ends of the cloves to push them in like tacks at various places on the loin.

❸ Pour the apple cider marinade over the loin, cover, and refrigerate for at least 8 hours or up to 24 hours, turning occasionally so the loin is coated.

❹ To roast: Position the rack in the center of the oven and preheat the oven to 400°F. Place the loin in a large, deep roasting pan and roast for 15 minutes, basting generously three times with the marinade. Continue roasting undisturbed until an instant-read meat thermometer inserted into the thickest part of the loin registers 130°F (our preference for medium-rare), 145°F (the USDA recommendation for medium-rare), or 160°F (the USDA recommendation for medium), 10 to 18 more minutes, depending on the temperature chosen.

To grill: Preheat a gas grill to high heat or prepare a high-heat, well-ashed coal bed in a charcoal grill. Lightly oil the grate with canola oil, then set it 4 to 6 inches over the heat source. Remove the loin from the marinade and place it directly over the heat. Cover and grill for 15 minutes, turning twice and mopping generously with the marinade each time. Continue grilling until an instant-read meat thermometer inserted into the thickest part of the loin registers 130°F (our preference for medium-rare), 145°F (the USDA recommendation for medium-rare), or 160°F (the USDA recommendation for medium), 7 to 15 more minutes, depending on the temperature chosen.

❺ Transfer the meat to a cutting board and let it stand at room temperature for 5 minutes before slicing into ½-inch-thick rounds.

Roasted Rabbit and Fennel

Rabbit is a good alternative to chicken. The anatomy can be tricky, so have the butcher cut the rabbit into pieces for you if you're unsure. This is a simple Italian way to roast rabbit, letting the meat's juices slowly soften the fennel underneath. *Makes 6 servings*

- 3 medium fennel bulbs, trimmed and thinly sliced
- 3 tablespoons olive oil
- 2 teaspoons salt
- ¼ cup dry white wine
- 1 teaspoon freshly ground black pepper
- 2 tablespoons crushed fennel seeds
- Two 3-pound rabbits, each cut into 6 pieces (2 hind legs, 2 front legs, and 3 pieces of back/loin)

❶ Position the rack in the center of the oven and preheat the oven to 400°F.

❷ Toss the fennel slices, 1 tablespoon olive oil, and 1 teaspoon salt in a large roasting pan. Flatten out the fennel until it covers the pan, then place in the oven and roast for 10 minutes.

❸ Remove the pan from the oven. Decrease the oven's temperature to 350°F. Pour the wine over the fennel pieces.

❹ Rub the remaining 2 tablespoons olive oil over the rabbit pieces, then gently massage the remaining 1 teaspoon salt, the pepper, and fennel seeds into the pieces.

❺ Lay the rabbit pieces over the fennel, return to the oven, and bake for 30 minutes.

❻ Use tongs or a wide spatula to turn the rabbit pieces over without tearing the meat. Continue roasting until the rabbit is cooked through, until an instant-read meat thermometer inserted into the breast registers 160°F (our preference and the USDA recommendation), 10 to 15 minutes longer. Let stand at room temperature for 5 minutes before serving the rabbit and fennel slices.

Variations: Sprinkle 2 garlic cloves, minced, or 1 garlic head, broken into cloves but not peeled, over the fennel slices just before you add the rabbit. If using whole garlic cloves, squeeze them out when roasted and spread on bread like butter.

Omit the olive oil; rub 3 tablespoons softened unsalted butter into the meat before adding the spices.

Rabbit Stewed with Red Wine, Mushrooms, and Pearl Onions

This is the best of country French cooking: a deep braise with complex layered flavors. *Makes 6 servings*

- Two 3-pound rabbits, each cut into 6 pieces (2 hind legs, 2 front legs, and 3 pieces of back/loin)
- One 750ml bottle red wine, preferably a French Burgundy or an Oregon Pinot Noir
- 1 large onion, thickly sliced
- 2 large carrots, peeled and thickly sliced
- 2 celery ribs, cut into thick chunks
- 2 garlic cloves, quartered
- 2 bay leaves
- 6 thyme sprigs
- 1 teaspoon cracked black peppercorns
- 6 ounces thick-cut bacon, roughly chopped
- 2 tablespoons all-purpose flour
- 2 tablespoons olive oil
- ¾ pound cremini or white button mushrooms, sliced
- ¾ pound pearl onions, peeled

① Mix the rabbit pieces, wine, sliced onion, carrots, celery, garlic, bay leaves, thyme, and peppercorns in a very large bowl, making sure all the meat is submerged in the liquid. Cover and refrigerate for at least 24 hours or up to 48 hours, stirring occasionally.

② Position the rack in the center of the oven and preheat the oven to 350°F.

③ Fry the bacon in a large Dutch oven or large casserole set over medium heat until crispy, stirring occasionally, about 4 minutes. Transfer to a plate and set aside.

④ Remove some of the rabbit pieces from the marinade, blot them dry with paper towels, and place them in the hot bacon fat. Brown on both sides, shaking or moving occasionally so they don't stick, about 3 minutes per side. Transfer the pieces to a large, clean bowl and continue working until all the rabbit has been browned.

⑤ Drain the marinade through a colander or sieve into another large bowl; set the solids and marinade aside separately.

⑥ Sprinkle the flour over the fat in the pot, wait 5 seconds, then whisk constantly until pastelike and lightly browned, about 2 minutes.

⑦ Whisking all the while, slowly add the strained marinade to the pot; continue whisking until you have a slightly thick, smooth sauce. Return the rabbit and any juices to the pan, then add the vegetables and aromatics from the marinade.

⑧ Bring to a simmer, stirring well. Cover and place in the oven. Bake for 1 hour.

⑨ Meanwhile, heat a large skillet over medium heat. Swirl in 1 tablespoon olive oil and add the mushrooms. Cook, stirring often, until they have given off most of their liquid and it has been reduced to a glaze, about 5 minutes. Transfer to a large bowl.

⑩ Return the skillet to medium heat. Add the remaining 1 tablespoon olive oil, then the pearl onions. Cook, stirring often, until lightly browned, about 5 minutes. Pour into the bowl with the mushrooms.

⑪ Remove the pot from the oven. Transfer the rabbit pieces to a clean, large bowl. Remembering that the pot is very hot, strain the cooking liquid through a sieve or colander into a large bowl set in the sink. Discard all the solids, then return the strained liquid to the pot. Set it over medium-high heat and add the rabbit, mushrooms, onions, and fried bacon. Stir well and bring to a simmer.

⑫ Cover, place the pot back in the oven, and cook until the rabbit meat is falling off the bones, about 1 more hour. Check the sauce for salt before serving.

Variations: Substitute unsalted butter for the olive oil.

Add 8 pitted prunes, halved, or 6 dried apricots, quartered, with the mushrooms.

Add 1 medium turnip, peeled and cut into 1-inch cubes, or 3 parsnips, peeled and sliced into ½-inch rings, with the mushrooms, onions, and bacon.

Other rabbit dishes include the Rabbit Ragù (page 191) and the Winter Paella with Rabbit, Quail, and Duck Confit (page 499).

Vegetables

IN A BALANCED MEAL, A VEGETABLE DISH SHOULD FUNCTION AS A COUNTER-weight, the other half of a plate, not an afterthought, but complimentary and complementary. Pair sweeter vegetables with more earthy main courses, blander vegetables with stronger-tasting meats, and find a side dish with a little acid (lemon juice, vinegar, etc.) to set against a simple, no-cream fish or pork sauté. Call it a balancing act, the same as for any good duo. There's no Laurel without Hardy, no Steve without Eydie, no Massachusetts without Mississippi.

That said, for an average weeknight, there's no need to get bound up in complicated decisions. Just consider texture and taste: crunchy with moist (asparagus with roast chicken, say) or creamy with chewy (mashed potatoes with steak). That forethought already assures you that your dinner is beyond the ordinary.

Still and all, some of these dishes are beyond being mere sides: the vegetable casseroles (see pages 477–481) and the potato salads (see pages 482–484), for example. While these could be a vegetable anchor on a larger buffet, most will be the center-piece to a meal.

With vegetables, fresh is everything. While we do call for some frozen convenience products (corn, peas, and pearl onions, for example), we assume that the vegetables you use are fresh from the market.

Here are the fundamentals of cooking vegetables—what to look for, how to store them, how to prepare them, all contained in narrative recipes rather than the more familiar formulas. We do not, for example, tell you how much olive oil to drizzle on asparagus spears. If you bear in mind that to drizzle is less than to dollop and to dash, less than to drench, you'll be fine.

Artichokes—Baby Artichokes

Look for small heads about the size of a votive candle. These are not immature artichokes, but rather the smaller blooms that grow toward the bottom of the stalk. They should have no bruising or browning. The leaves should be tight against the head. Four baby artichokes per person is a generous serving.

To store: Seal in a plastic bag and refrigerate for up to 4 days.

To prepare: Wash to get rid of any dirt between the leaves. Snip off the tough outer leaves, cut off the top quarter, and trim back the stem. Cut each in half. As you finish trimming, drop in a large bowl of cool water with the juice of half a lemon.

To braise: Heat a little olive oil in a large skillet over medium heat, add the baby artichokes, and cook for 1 minute, stirring constantly. Add equal parts water and white wine or dry vermouth to a depth of about ½ inch; also add a slight sprinkling of any chopped herb you choose (parsley, thyme, rosemary, tarragon, oregano, marjoram, etc.). Bring to a simmer, cover, reduce the heat to low, and cook until tender, about 15 minutes.

To grill: Toss the halved baby artichokes with some olive oil and a little kosher salt. Prepare the grill for high-heat cooking, place the artichokes cut side down directly over the heat, and cook, turning once or twice, until tender, about 8 minutes.

To steam: Place a steamer basket over 2 inches of boiling water in a large pot set over high heat. Cover, reduce the heat to medium, and steam until tender, about 15 minutes.

To serve: Season with salt, then toss with finely grated lemon or grapefruit zest, a pat of unsalted butter, some sesame oil, or toasted pumpkin seed oil.

Artichokes—Globe Artichokes

Look for large, tight, round heads with the stems attached, verdant to forest green leaves, and no discolored or bruised leaves. In general, smaller artichokes are more tender. Buy 1 per person.

To store: Refrigerate in a plastic bag for up to 3 days.

To prepare: Fill a large bowl halfway with cool water and add the juice of half a lemon. Remove the smaller leaves around the base of the artichoke as well as the first ring or two of large leaves. Slice off the top quarter of the artichoke; use kitchen shears to snip the sharp tips off the remaining leaves. The stem can be removed or left on (it is edible); if left on, trim ½ inch off the bottom and peel off the outer layer with a vegetable peeler. Wash well to remove any grit between the leaves, then place the artichoke in the lemon water and repeat with the other artichokes.

To steam: Place the artichokes stem side up in a large vegetable steamer over 2 inches of simmering water in a large pot set over high heat. Cover, reduce the heat to medium-low, and steam until the stem ends are tender when pierced with a fork, 40 to 60 minutes.

To boil: Bring a large pot of water to a boil over high heat; add 1 tablespoon salt. Add the artichokes and bring back to a boil. Cover, reduce the heat to medium-low, and simmer until the bottoms are tender when pierced with a sharp knife, 35 to 40 minutes. Drain and cool, then remove the prickly inner leaves with a spoon.

To cook in a pressure cooker: Place the artichokes and 2 cups water, vegetable broth, or chicken broth in the cooker; lock on the lid and bring to high pressure over high heat. Reduce the heat to medium and cook at high pressure for 12 minutes. Follow the manufacturer's instructions for quick-releasing the lid.

To serve: Salt while still warm and offer melted butter, extra virgin olive oil, or a vinaigrette (see page 100) for dipping the leaves and heart. To eat, scrape the meat off the leaves by pulling their concave side against your front upper teeth; the hairy choke should be removed and the tender, firm heart should also be served with a dipping sauce. Once cooked, globe artichokes can be kept, uncovered, for up to 5 hours and served at room temperature.

Asparagus

Asparagus is available in white, green, or purple spears. Choose thin, sturdy, evenly sized spears without bruising or discoloration. The spearlike heads should be firm and tight; the cut ends should not be desiccated, fibrous, or woody. The general rule: the thinner, the more tender. Plan on 5 to 6 ounces per serving.

To store: Unfasten any ties or remove the rubber band; slice about ½ inch off the bottom of each spear. Stand the spears straight up in a glass with about 1 inch of water, cover the tops with a plastic bag, and refrigerate for no more than 2 days.

To prepare: Rinse well. If the green or purple spears are thicker than a pencil, shave off the tough outer skin with a vegetable peeler. White asparagus, grown without sunlight, must be stripped with a vegetable peeler to remove the fibrous outer casing.

To braise: Bring about 1 inch of water, vegetable broth, white wine, or a combination of any two, plus a couple of lemon slices, to a boil in a large skillet over high heat. Add the spears, cover, reduce the heat to low, and simmer until tender when pierced with a fork, about 15 minutes for white, 6 minutes for green, and 4 minutes for purple.

To grill: Prepare the grill for medium-heat cooking; lightly oil the rack. Place the green or purple spears directly over the heat; cook until lightly browned, turning occasionally, about 6 minutes. (White asparagus does not lend itself to grilling.)

To microwave: Place the spears in a glass pie plate; add about ½ inch water, drizzle with a little olive oil, and cover tightly. Microwave on high until tender, about 9 minutes for white, 4 minutes for green, and 3 minutes for purple.

To serve: Toss with coarse-grained sea salt or kosher salt and freshly ground black or white pepper as well as toasted sliced almonds, finely grated lemon zest, a dab of chutney, a dollop of Dijon mustard, a spoonful of crème fraîche, a splash of a sweet vinegar like balsamic or sherry, or a drizzle of extra virgin olive oil.

Beets

Look for dark ruby, bright orange, or creamy white skins without obvious bruising or scales. The somewhat exotic American "candy cane" varietal has ruby and white rings. The thin, tail-like top root should be firm, not limp. If possible, buy similarly sized bunches with the greens still attached. Although the greens slowly leach moisture from the beets, their presence usually indicates freshness at the market. In general, larger beets can be tough, even woody. Plan on 2 medium beets per person.

To store: Snip off the greens, leaving about 1 inch of stem attached. Seal the beets in a plastic bag perforated with a few small holes and refrigerate for up to 3 weeks. (The greens can be prepared within 1 or 2 days—see page 460.)

To prepare: Cut off the remnants of the stems and the root. Rinse gently but well. Peeling beets removes essential nutrients; however, if you cook them with their skins on, they must be cooked whole and you must then let them cool slightly before slipping off the now-loose skins. If you prefer, you can, of course, peel the beets first. Remove any red stains on your hands by rubbing them with kosher salt under warm running water.

To roast: Wrap in aluminum foil, seal tightly, and bake in a preheated 400°F oven until tender when pierced with a fork, 45 to 55 minutes. Let rest at room temperature for 10 minutes before removing the foil and slipping off the skins. Alternatively, peel the beets and cut them into 1-inch pieces, toss with a generous splash of olive oil in a 13 × 9-inch baking pan, and bake, stirring occasionally, in a preheated 400°F oven until browned and tender, 35 to 45 minutes.

To sauté: Heat a little olive oil and a pat of unsalted butter in a large skillet over medium heat. Peel the beets and grate them through the large holes of a box grater into the pan. Stir in one or more minced garlic cloves, a splash of lemon juice, and a pinch of sugar. Cook, stirring constantly, for 1 minute. Add water to a depth of about ¼ inch and bring to a simmer. Cover, reduce the heat to low, and cook until tender, about 8 minutes.

To steam: Cut in half. Place in a steamer basket over 2 inches of boiling water in a large pot set over high heat. Cover, reduce the heat to medium, and steam until tender, about 15 minutes.

Let stand at room temperature for 10 minutes before slipping off the skins.

To microwave: Cut in half; place in a large glass baking dish or pie plate. Add ¼ cup water or broth and a splash of white wine. Cover and microwave on high for 10 to 12 minutes. Let stand at room temperature, covered, for 10 minutes before slipping off their skins.

To serve: Toss with salt and pepper as well as either unsalted butter, olive oil, walnut oil, almond oil, toasted sesame oil, mustard oil, or lemon juice; or a chopped herb and some crème fraîche, sour cream, or plain yogurt.

Belgian Endive

See guidelines in the salad chapter, page 97.

To store: Wrap in paper towels and seal in a plastic bag for no more than 2 days.

To prepare: Cut the spearlike heads in half through the stem, but keep the root end intact to hold the head together.

To roast: Place cut side down on an oiled baking sheet; drizzle another 1 tablespoon olive oil over each head. Roast in a preheated 400°F oven without turning until lightly browned and crisp around the edges, about 20 minutes.

To grill: See page 108.

To serve: Toss with coarse-grained sea salt or kosher salt and drizzle with more olive oil, as desired; or top with a creamy vinaigrette (see page 102).

Bok Choy

This cabbage-style vegetable comes in a variety of shapes and colors, from large Savoy cabbage–like heads with stark white center veins and dark green leafy tips to thin, dark green stalks with flowering buds, as well as tiny heads made up of 3 or 4 leaves that shade tip to stem from forest green to white. Bok choy sprouts—2-inch, leafy shoots available in late winter—have a mild, nutty taste. In any case, plan on ½ pound per person.

To store: Line a plastic bag with paper towels, add the bok choy, seal well, and refrigerate for up to 3 days.

To prepare: Soak in a cleaned sink full of cool water, stirring once or twice, then rinse to dislodge any sand from between the leaves before unstoppering the sink and washing away the grit. Trim off the stems. Leave small heads intact, but cut larger ones in halves, quarters, or 2-inch pieces.

To braise and serve: Place in a pan with ¼ inch of water. Bring to a boil over high heat, cover, reduce the heat to low, and cook until wilted and tender, about 4 minutes. Drain well. If desired, now add a little unsalted butter, olive oil or dark sesame oil, and some salt to the pan; return the bok choy to the heat and toss until coated.

To stir-fry and serve: Heat a little peanut oil in a large wok over medium-high heat. Add some chopped garlic cloves and minced peeled fresh ginger. Toss over the heat for 30 seconds. Add the bok choy; stir-fry until it begins to wilt, about 2 minutes. Add a little soy sauce and rice vinegar in a 2-to-1 ratio. Continue cooking, stirring constantly, until tender but crunchy, about 2 more minutes.

To roast and serve: Use only large heads; slice them in quarters through the root ball. Generously oil a large lipped baking sheet, place the bok choy on the pan, and rub them around to coat all sides. Bake, turning once, in a preheated 375°F oven until the thick stalks are tender and the leaves are just beginning to frizzle at the ends, about 25 minutes. Cut the thick stalk off each quarter and season with kosher or coarse-grained sea salt.

Broccoli and Broccolini

Look for sturdy dark green spears with tight buds, no yellowing, and a high floret-to-stem ratio. Some varietals have purple tints or accents. Broccolini is a cross between broccoli and a Chinese green; it should be prepared just as broccoli. In either case, plan on 5 to 6 ounces per serving.

To store: Trim about ½ inch off the bottom of each stem. Stand up in large drinking glasses with about 1 inch of water, cover the heads with a plastic bag, and refrigerate for up to 4 days.

To prepare: Wash well. Cut into small florets; thick stalks should be shaved with a vegetable peeler.

To roast: Slice the stalks into long, spearlike quarters. Place these spears and the florets on a lightly oiled lipped baking sheet; sprinkle with olive oil. Roast in a preheated 400°F oven until lightly browned and crunchy-tender, tossing once or twice, about 40 minutes.

To steam: Slice the stalks into 1-inch segments; also cut these in half through a cut side. Place in a steamer basket set over 2 inches of water and the juice of half a lemon in a large pot set over high heat. Cover, reduce the heat to medium, and steam for 2 minutes. Add the florets, cover again, and continue steaming until tender, about 5 minutes.

To microwave: Slice the stems into 1-inch segments. Place the stems and florets in a large glass baking dish. Add a splash of broth, wine, dry vermouth, or water, as well as a small pat of unsalted butter or a drizzle of olive oil. Cover and microwave on high until tender, about 4 minutes.

To serve: Toss with salt and pepper; if desired, add chopped parsley, finely grated lemon zest, or minced peeled fresh ginger.

Broccoli Raab

A classic Italian green, broccoli raab (or rabe, but pronounced "rahb") is a leafy green with hearty, edible stems. It should be dark green from top to bottom; the small stalks should be firm and have no cabbage smell, a sign of age. Since it's bitter and a little sharp, plan on 3 to 4 ounces per person.

To store: Place in a plastic bag, poke a couple of small holes in the bag, seal, and refrigerate for up to 3 days.

To prepare: Wash thoroughly to remove any grit or dirt. Trim ½ inch off each stem.

To braise: Cut into 3-inch chunks. Heat a couple of tablespoons of olive oil in a large skillet; add several minced garlic cloves and a few red pepper flakes. Cook for 30 seconds. Add the broccoli raab, stir well, and pour in dry vermouth, white wine, vegetable broth, or unsweetened apple juice to a depth of less than ¼ inch. Cover and cook until tender, stirring occasionally, about 6 minutes.

To roast: Place whole on a lightly oiled baking sheet and drizzle with some olive oil. Bake in a preheated 400°F oven, turning once, until tender and browned, about 15 minutes.

To serve: Season with salt and a little sugar, if desired, as well as with finely grated lemon zest, aged balsamic vinegar, white balsamic vinegar, rice vinegar, or more red pepper flakes.

Brussels Sprouts

If possible, buy Brussels sprouts still attached to their stalks. Look for tight, firm, small deep green heads without yellowed leaves or insect holes. In general, the smaller the head, the less bitter the taste. Excluding the stalk, plan on about 4 ounces (¼ pound) per person.

To store: Stand the stalk with the heads attached in a cool, dry part of the house and store at room temperature for up to 2 days. If you have loose heads, seal them in a plastic bag and refrigerate for up to 3 days. (The longer the refrigeration, the more bitter the taste.)

To prepare: Slice the heads off the stalk; discard it. Cut the tiny stem off each head: remove the outermost leaves. Wash under cool water in a colander in the sink.

To braise: Place in a large skillet with about ½ inch dry white wine, dry vermouth, or vegetable

or chicken broth; bring to a simmer over medium-high heat. Cover, reduce the heat to low, and cook until tender, about 7 minutes. Remove the sprouts with a slotted spoon, raise the heat to high, add a big pat of unsalted butter, and boil the liquid down to a glaze to pour over the cooked sprouts.

To steam: Place in a steamer basket over 2 inches of boiling water in a large pot set over high heat. Cover, reduce the heat to medium, and steam until tender when pierced with a fork, 6 to 8 minutes.

To microwave: Place in a large glass baking dish. Add some broth or water to a depth of perhaps ¼ inch and a drizzle of olive oil. Cover tightly and microwave on high until tender, about 6 minutes.

To roast: Toss with some olive oil in a 13 × 9-inch baking pan. Roast in a preheated 350°F oven, tossing often, until lightly browned and tender, about 40 minutes.

To serve: Toss with salt and freshly ground black pepper as well as with Dijon mustard, balsamic vinegar, white balsamic vinegar, lemon juice, melted unsalted butter, walnut oil, olive oil, or a splash of Cointreau.

Cabbage

Look for tight, compact, unblemished heads that are heavy in the hand. A medium head will make 4 servings.

To store: Seal in a plastic bag with a few holes poked in it and refrigerate for up to 1 week.

To prepare: Cut in half through the root end, then make a *V* cut to remove the tough, fibrous core that moves up from the stem. Remove and discard the outer layer of leaves, then wash the remainder well for grit and sand. Cut into thin, ribbonlike shreds. (That distinct cabbage smell—hydrogen sulfide—occurs at about 6 minutes over the heat; thinner strips cook more quickly.)

To sauté: Heat a little canola oil, olive oil, or unsalted butter in a large skillet over medium heat. Add the cabbage and toss until wilted, about 2 minutes. Add some caraway seeds, curry powder, chili powder, lemon pepper seasoning, or minced peeled fresh ginger. Also pour in a splash of white wine, white wine vinegar, balsamic vinegar, or broth. Continue cooking, stirring often, until crunchy-tender, about 2 more minutes.

For other cabbage recipes, see pages 116–118, 396, and 469.

Carrots

Although commonly orange, carrots can also be white, yellow, maroon, or purple. Look for firm, long, straight, crack-free roots without any gray, white, or desiccated residue on the skin. If the greens are attached, they should be fresh, even perky, never wilted or slimy. Bagged "baby" carrots are actually full-grown carrots peeled and cut to a uniform size and shape. A serving is 4 to 5 ounces.

To store: Place in a plastic bag, seal, poke a hole or two through the bag, and refrigerate for up to 2 weeks.

To prepare: If limp, refresh in ice water for 30 minutes. Unless the skin looks thick or desiccated, carrots need not be peeled, just washed. However, for a sweeter taste (if fewer nutrients), peel with a vegetable peeler. If using full-sized carrots, cut in half lengthwise and then into ½-inch pieces.

To sauté: Melt a big pat of unsalted butter in a large skillet over medium-low heat. Add the carrots and cook, stirring often, until tender, about 15 minutes. Add a pinch of sugar or half a spoonful of honey or maple syrup, raise the heat to medium-high, and stir until the sauce forms a glaze.

To roast: Toss in a large baking dish with some olive oil; bake in a preheated 350°F oven, tossing often, until lightly browned but still crisp, 30 to 45 minutes.

To steam: Place the carrots in a steamer basket over 1 inch of water in a large pot set over high heat. Bring to a boil, cover, reduce the heat to low, and steam for 10 to 15 minutes.

To microwave: Place the carrots in a large glass baking dish or pie plate. Add broth or white wine to a depth of ½ inch. Cover and microwave on high until tender, about 5 minutes.

To serve: Season with salt and pepper, then add additional unsalted butter or olive oil, if desired, before tossing with lemon juice, mango chutney, bottled white horseradish, cayenne pepper, stemmed thyme, chopped mint leaves, or chopped parsley leaves.

Cauliflower

White, green, or purple, a cauliflower head should be tight and clear of brown or yellow spots; the green leaves at the stem should still be firmly attached, not limp or withered. Plan on 6 ounces per person.

To store: Take off the store packaging, wrap the head in plastic wrap, and store in the hydrator for up to 1 week.

To prepare: Trim off all leaves; cut the head in half through the stem. Cut out the thick stalk and core; cut the remainder into bite-sized florets. Wash in a colander in the sink.

To roast: Toss the florets with some olive oil on a large lipped baking sheet. Bake in a preheated 375°F oven until browned and tender, tossing occasionally, about 30 minutes.

To roast the entire head: Do not cut into florets. Toss the florets Trim off the leaves and stem; also hollow out the core as it extends up into the head. Rub the head with olive oil and place it stem side up on a lipped baking sheet. Bake in a preheated 375°F oven for 30 minutes, then turn stem side down and continue roasting until the head is tender in the center when pierced with a knife, about 15 more minutes.

To sauté: Melt a couple of pats of unsalted butter in a large skillet set over medium heat; add a little olive oil. Add the florets and cook, stirring often, until the butter has browned and the florets are tender, about 10 minutes.

To braise: Place the florets in a large skillet with a sprinkle of caraway seeds and equal parts broth and milk to a depth of 1 inch. Bring to a simmer, reduce the heat to low, cover, and cook until tender, about 4 minutes.

To steam: Place the florets in a steamer basket over 2 inches of simmering water and the juice of a lemon in a large pot set over high heat. Cover, reduce the heat to medium, and steam until tender, 6 to 8 minutes.

To microwave: Place the florets in a large glass baking dish. Add equal parts broth and milk to a depth of ½ inch. Cover tightly and microwave on high until tender, about 4 minutes.

To serve: First season with salt and pepper while warm, then sprinkle with freshly grated Parmigiano-Reggiano, Pecorino Romano, or Asiago; finely grated lemon zest; toasted sesame oil; or toasted pumpkin seed oil.

Celery Root (or Celeriac)

Look for small, firm, bruise-free, knob-free bulbs that are heavy to the hand. If the tail-like taproot is still attached, it should be firm, not limp.

To store: Wrap in plastic and place in the hydrator for up to 1 week.

To prepare: Cut off any knobs and all hairy roots as well as the taproot and any green leaves. Peel with a vegetable peeler, then cut into 1-inch chunks and drop these in a large bowl of cool water with the juice of half a lemon.

To braise: Melt a couple of pats of unsalted butter in a large saucepan set over medium heat. Add the drained celery root pieces; cook, stirring often, until browned, about 2 minutes. Add some broth, white wine, or a combination of both, and a generous pinch of sugar; cover and simmer until tender, about 15 minutes. Uncover, raise the heat to medium–high, and boil until the liquid is reduced to a glaze. If desired, mash with a potato masher or a hand mixer.

To roast: Toss the chunks with olive oil and bake in a preheated 400°F oven, tossing frequently, until tender and lightly browned, about 35 minutes.

To serve: While warm, season with salt and pepper before tossing with unsalted butter.

Corn

Run your fingers along the husk to feel the kernels; they should be apparent, distinct, full, and without gaps. The silk should be soft; the husk, supple; the ear, heavy. A large ear of corn is a serving.

To store: Do not refrigerate; place in a cool, dark, dry storage place for up to 2 days.

To grill: Pull back the husks without removing them; remove the silk. Replace the husks and soak in cool water for 20 minutes. Meanwhile, prepare the grill for high-heat cooking. Place the corn in the husks directly over the heat and grill until lightly browned, turning occasionally, about 8 minutes. Remove the husks before serving.

To boil: Bring a large pot of water to a boil over high heat. Remove the husks and silk. Add the corn, the juice of a small lemon, and a generous pinch of sugar (salt toughens corn). Cover and boil for 3 minutes. Remove from the heat and let the corn stand in the hot water, covered, until tender, 7 to 10 minutes.

To steam: Remove the husks and silk. If necessary, break or cut the cobs in half so they fit in a steamer. Set over 2 inches of water combined with a spoonful of sugar in a large pot over high heat. Bring to a boil, cover, and steam until tender, about 4 minutes.

To microwave: Remove the husks and silk. Place the ears in a large glass baking dish or microwave-safe container, snapping in half to fit if necessary. Add a splash of water, cover tightly, and microwave on high until tender, about 4 minutes.

To sauté: Remove the husks and silk, cut off one end so the ear will stand up on your work surface, and slice the kernels from the cob by running a knife along the ear. Melt some unsalted butter in a large skillet over medium heat; add the kernels and ½ teaspoon sugar; and cook, stirring constantly, until tender, about 3 minutes. Stir in ½ teaspoon cider vinegar.

To serve: Season with salt just before eating; also add unsalted butter, chutney, ground cumin, ground cinnamon, or grated nutmeg while warm.

Eggplant, Italian or Japanese

Look for smooth, glossy skins without wrinkles or spongy spots. If the eggplant is small and young, the peel is edible without any bitter tang. Eggplants are sexed: males have fewer seeds and are less bitter. Male eggplants have a smooth, round blossom end without any indentations. Plan on ⅓ pound per serving.

To store: Store in a cool, dry place at room temperature for up to 2 days or refrigerate on a shelf (not in the hydrator) for up to 3 days.

To prepare: Wash well. If the skin is rubbery or thick, peel off with a vegetable peeler. Cut off the stem and slice into ½-inch-thick circles. Eggplants are watery; large ones can become soggy when cooked. To reduce their water content, lightly salt the slices, stand them up in a colander in the sink, and allow them to weep for 30 minutes; wipe off the salt and any surface water with a paper towel before proceeding.

To fry: Heat a generous pour of olive or canola oil in a large skillet over medium-high heat. Dip the slices of eggplant first into a mixture of beaten eggs and a splash of water, then into all-purpose flour, crushed saltines, or plain dried bread crumbs. Slip into the skillet and cook, turning once, until browned and tender, about 5 minutes.

To grill: Prepare the grill for high-heat cooking; brush the rounds generously with olive oil. Place directly over the heat and grill until browned, about 6 minutes, turning once.

To roast: Smear olive oil generously over the rounds; place them on a large, lipped oiled baking sheet; and bake, turning once, until soft and lightly browned, about 30 minutes.

To serve: Season with salt and accessorize with a creamy dressing (see page 104), a vinaigrette (see page 100), or a mayonnaise (see page 121).

Escarole

For a description, see page 98.

To store: Line a large plastic bag with paper towels, set the escarole head inside, seal, and refrigerate for up to 3 days.

To prepare: Cut into quarters through the root, leaving some of the root on each quarter so the leaves will stay together. Wash thoroughly to remove all grit. Do not dry.

To roast: Place on a lightly oiled lipped baking sheet, drizzle with more olive oil, and bake in a preheated 400°F oven until tender and lightly browned, turning once, 10 to 12 minutes.

To serve: Season with salt and pepper before drizzling with white or aged balsamic vinegar.

Fennel

Fennel bulbs should be tight and white, with bright green stalks and feathery fronds. Avoid browned or bruised bulbs. A serving is between 4 and 6 ounces.

To store: Wrap in plastic and refrigerate for up to 1 week.

To prepare: Remove the outermost segments and trim the green stalks down to the top of the white bulb. Trim a thin slice from the bottom to remove any dried-out root section. Slice the remaining bulb into 1-inch pieces.

To braise: Heat a little olive oil in a large skillet over medium heat. Add the fennel and cook for 1 minute, stirring constantly. Add a generous splash of white wine or dry vermouth. Cover, reduce the heat to medium-low, and cook until tender, about 15 minutes.

To steam: Fill a pan with 2 inches of water, add about 2 tablespoons jarred pickling spices, and bring to a simmer over high heat. Place the fennel in a steamer basket and set over the simmering water. Cover, reduce the heat to medium, and steam until tender, about 15 minutes.

To roast: Toss with olive oil on a lightly oiled baking sheet. Bake in a preheated 400°F oven, turning once, until lightly browned, about 25 minutes.

To serve: Season with salt and pepper; if desired, drizzle with balsamic vinegar, Chinese black vinegar, red wine vinegar, or lemon juice.

Garlic

Choose tight, plump, firm heads with papery skins that are not peeling away or desiccated. Avoid any heads with sprouts. Purple garlic (also called "Mexican" or "Italian" garlic) is milder than the familiar American white variety. So-called elephant garlic is actually a relative of the leek family; if used, increase the cooking time by 50 percent.

To store: Store in an open container at room temperature in a cool, dark place away from potatoes or other vegetables for up to 60 days. Once the cloves are separated from the head, they can be stored in their papery hulls at room temperature for about 5 days.

To prepare: If peeling, give the individual cloves a good whack with the side of a chef's knife to loosen the hulls from the meat. You can also blanche the whole head in boiling water for 30 seconds to help you remove the hulls.

To roast: Cut off the top quarter of the head. Wrap the unpeeled head in aluminum foil and bake in a preheated 400°F oven until tender and soft, 50 to 70 minutes. Squeeze out the pulp to spread on bread as a butter substitute or stir into soups as a mild thickener.

To candy (an excellent condiment with any green vegetable): see page 52.

Green, Wax, or Purple Beans

Look for firm beans with even coloration and no brown spots. Purple beans will turn green when cooked. A fresh bean will snap in half when bent. Buy 4 to 6 ounces per serving.

To store: Seal in a plastic bag and refrigerate for up to 3 days.

To prepare: Snap off the stems and wash well in a colander set in the sink.

To sauté: Cut into 2-inch lengths. Heat 1 or 2 tablespoons walnut or olive oil in a large skillet over medium heat. Add the beans and cook until crisp-tender, stirring constantly, about 3 minutes.

To steam: Set in a steamer basket over 1 inch of simmering water in a large pot over high heat. Cover, reduce the heat to medium, and steam until crisp-tender, about 5 minutes.

To microwave: Place in a large glass baking dish; add water or broth to a depth of ½ inch. Cover tightly and microwave on high for 4 minutes.

To serve: Season with salt and pepper, then toss with toasted sliced almonds, toasted pecan pieces, poppy seeds, freshly grated lemon zest, a splash of vinegar, a pat of unsalted butter, or a light grating of Parmigiano-Reggiano.

Greens (Swiss Chard, Mustard Greens, Turnip Greens, Beet Greens, or Kale)

Bitter greens should have deep intense colors; the leaves should be perky, neither wilted nor soft. Plan on 7 to 8 ounces uncooked greens per person.

To store: Line a plastic bag with paper towels, poke a few holes in the bag, add the greens, seal, and store in the refrigerator for up to 3 days.

To prepare: Soak in a cleaned sink of cool water, agitating two or three times to thoroughly remove any sand or grit. Remove from the water; do not dry. Cut off the thick stems, even if they run up into the leaves. Slice the leaves into 2-inch pieces.

To sauté and serve: Heat a generous splash of olive or canola oil in a large skillet over medium heat. Add several minced garlic cloves and cook for 30 seconds. Rinse the greens one more time, do not dry, add to the skillet, and toss over the heat until wilted. Also add chili powder or smoked paprika, if desired. Cover, reduce the heat to low, and cook, stirring occasionally, until tender, about 7 minutes. Uncover, reduce the liquid to a glaze, and sprinkle with salt and a little balsamic vinegar. (Note: if desired, first fry a few slices of bacon in the skillet, remove, and crumble; cook the greens in the rendered bacon fat, as directed, then toss with the bacon before serving.)

For spinach, see page 465.

Jerusalem Artichokes (aka Sunchokes)

Look for large, smooth-skinned if otherwise gnarled chokes (actually a member of the sunflower family). Avoid any that are soft or have sprouts. Plan on about 5 to 6 ounces per serving. (They can be substituted for half the potatoes in Perfect Mashed Potatoes—boil with the potatoes as directed on page 473.)

To store: Keep in a plastic bag in the refrigerator for up to 5 days.

To prepare: Peel with a vegetable peeler; cut into quarters or 1-inch pieces, whichever is smaller.

To roast: Toss with olive oil in a 13 × 9-inch baking dish and bake in a preheated 350°F oven, stirring once or twice, until browned and tender, about 25 minutes.

To boil: Place in a large pot of boiling salted water over high heat and cook until tender, about 10 minutes.

To steam: Place in a steamer basket over 1 inch of boiling water in a large pot set over high heat; cover, reduce the heat to medium, and steam until tender, about 12 minutes.

To serve: Season with salt and ground pepper, preferably white pepper, before tossing with unsalted butter, olive oil, toasted sesame oil, or toasted pumpkinseed oil.

Mushrooms

While there are great differences among mushroom varietals, most will sauté in the same way for a side dish. Look for closed caps with few gills showing.

The caps should be evenly colored without gashes or bruises; the stems should not be shriveled. None should be soft. Portobello mushrooms do have visible gills and should be cooked differently (see below).

To store: Refrigerate in a paper bag (not plastic) for up to 3 days.

To prepare: If they are to be cooked at once, you can wash mushrooms; either rinse them or submerge them in water to remove dirt. Trim about ¼ inch off each stem. For shiitakes, remove and discard the fibrous stems.

To sauté and serve all mushrooms except portobello caps: Heat unsalted butter or olive oil in a skillet over medium heat; add the mushrooms and cook, stirring occasionally, until they give off their liquid, about 3 minutes. Add any chopped herb or red pepper flakes; continue cooking, stirring occasionally, until the mushroom liquid has been reduced to a glaze, 2 to 5 minutes, depending on the varietal. Season with salt and serve; or add a big splash of white wine, red wine, dry vermouth, port, or brandy and continue cooking until the sauce is again a glaze, about 1 minute.

To grill and serve portobello caps: Prepare a grill for high-heat cooking. Brush the caps lightly with olive oil and set directly over the heat; grill, turning once, until softened and juicy, about 6 minutes. Season with salt and pepper before serving.

To broil portobello caps: Preheat the broiler; line a broiler pan with aluminum foil and spray it with nonstick spray or brush with olive oil. Brush the caps with olive oil and broil 4 to 6 inches from the heat, turning once, until softened and juicy, about 6 minutes. Season with salt and pepper.

Okra

Look for short, oblong, bruise-free spears with distinct tips. Plan on 5 to 6 ounces per serving.

To store: Seal in a plastic bag and refrigerate for up to 3 days.

To prepare: Wash well. The caps of larger spears can be tough and should be removed.

To stew and serve: Slice the spears in half the short way. Place in a pan with canned diced tomatoes, chopped onion, minced garlic cloves, stemmed thyme, red pepper flakes, and salt. Bring to a simmer over medium-high heat; cover, reduce the heat to low, and simmer, stirring occasionally, until tender, about 15 minutes.

To grill and serve: Toss the whole spears with a generous amount of olive oil and a good splash of vinegar in a large bowl; refrigerate overnight. Prepare the grill for high-heat cooking; generously oil the grill grate. Salt the okra and place directly over the heat, cover, and grill until lightly browned and marked by the grate, turning occasionally, about 5 minutes.

To fry and serve: Cut the spears into ½-inch-thick rounds. Toss in a large bowl with yellow cornmeal until thoroughly coated. Heat about ½ inch melted solid vegetable shortening, lard, or canola oil in a large skillet until waggly over medium-high heat. Add the okra, reduce the heat to medium, and cook about 2 minutes, until the pieces on the bottom are browned. Turn gently with a metal spatula, placing the browned pieces on top and the less-done ones underneath; continue cooking until uniformly browned. Transfer to a plate lined with paper towels to drain; salt well while hot.

To pickle and serve: Place about 1½ pounds okra spears in a large nonreactive bowl. Bring 1 quart (4 cups) white wine vinegar, 2 cups water, ¼ cup salt, and ¼ cup jarred pickling spice to a boil in a large saucepan. Pour over the okra, cool to room temperature, cover, and refrigerate for at least 48 hours or up to 1 week.

Parsnips

Look for firm, straight, fairly smooth roots without blemishes or soft spots. The skin should not be leathery. A serving is about 5 ounces.

To store: Seal in a plastic bag in the coldest part of the refrigerator for up to 5 days.

To prepare: Trim off both ends and peel with a vegetable peeler.

To steam: Cut into 2-inch sections; halve the thick ends lengthwise to promote even cooking. Place in a vegetable steamer over about 1 inch of simmering water in a large pot set over high heat. Cover, reduce the heat to medium, and steam until tender when pierced with a fork, about 6 minutes. If desired, steam a couple of small, white-fleshed potatoes with them, then mash with an electric mixer in a medium bowl with additional unsalted butter and some milk, cream, or buttermilk.

To sauté: Cut into ½-inch-thick rounds. Melt a couple pats of unsalted butter in a large skillet set over medium-low heat. Add the parsnips and cook, stirring often, until lightly browned, about 5 minutes. Stir in some chopped parsley leaves, stemmed thyme, poppy seeds, or fennel seeds; cook for 1 additional minute.

To roast: Cut into 2-inch chunks. Toss with olive or canola oil on a lipped baking sheet and bake in a preheated 400°F oven until lightly browned, tossing occasionally, about 30 minutes.

To serve: Season with salt and pepper, preferably white pepper, and toss with unsalted butter, olive oil, or chili powder.

Peas

Look for bright green firm pods. Smaller pods have sweeter, more tender peas. If using preshelled peas, taste one if possible; it should be sweet, not starchy. If using frozen peas, do not thaw. A serving is 9 to 10 ounces in-shell peas or 4 ounces shelled peas. For sugar snap peas, see the recipe on page 113.

To store: Refrigerate in their pods in a plastic bag for up to 2 days; if using fresh shelled peas, cook them the day you buy them.

To prepare: Shell peas by zipping the stem and its fibrous string down the inside concave curve of the shell; pry open the shell and slip the peas out and into a bowl with your finger or thumb.

To sauté: Melt a couple pats of unsalted butter in a large skillet over medium heat. Add the peas and, if desired, a couple of minced garlic cloves and/or some minced fresh herb. Cook, stirring often, until the peas are bright green, about 3 minutes.

To microwave: Place the peas in a glass baking dish or microwave-safe bowl with a generous splash of water, broth, white wine, or dry vermouth and perhaps a small drizzle of olive oil. Cover tightly and microwave on high for 2 minutes.

To serve: Season with salt and pepper and add a little olive oil, unsalted butter, or toasted sesame oil while hot; also garnish with roasted shallots (see page 464), Candied Garlic (page 52), or chopped chives, if desired.

Plantains

They should be a deep, lustrous yellow with many black spots or streaks and even one or two soft spots. A serving is about half a large plantain.

To store: Set in a cool, dry place at room temperature for up to 3 days; use them before they turn mushy.

To prepare: Cut off the ends and use a small knife to help remove the peel. Cut the inner flesh into 1½-inch slices.

To sauté and serve: Heat some canola oil in a large skillet over medium heat. Add the slices cut side down and fry until browned, about 2 minutes. Flip and press down lightly with the back of the spatula. Fry until browned and tender, about 3 more minutes. Season with salt and freshly ground black pepper.

Potatoes (Red-Skinned, Yellow-Fleshed, or Purple-Fleshed)

Choose small to medium potatoes with firm, evenly colored skins. Peeling only slightly changes

their nutrient value since most of the important vitamins and minerals are clustered about ¼ inch below the skin. A serving is about 6 ounces.

To store: Potatoes should never be refrigerated (the cold turns off important flavor esters). Store in a cool, dark place for up to 1 week; if stored in a very cool place (around 50°F), they will keep for up to a month.

To prepare: Scrub under cool water to remove any dirt or grime.

To boil: Place in a large pot, cover with water to a depth of 2 inches, and bring to a boil over high heat. Reduce the heat to low, cover partially, and simmer until tender when pierced with a fork, 12 to 18 minutes, depending on the potatoes' size.

To steam: Place in a steamer basket over 2 inches of simmering water in a large pot set over high heat. Cover, reduce the heat to medium, and steam until tender when pierced with a fork, 10 to 20 minutes.

To roast: Cut in half or quarters and toss with olive oil, salt, and pepper—and some chopped rosemary or oregano, if desired. Place in a large roasting pan and bake in a preheated 400°F oven until browned, crisp, and tender, tossing occasionally, 40 minutes to 1 hour.

To serve: Salt and pepper while warm; coarse-grained sea salt or kosher salt works best against the creamy texture. Also toss with melted unsalted butter or olive oil and/or any chopped herb, poppy seeds, or crème fraîche, if desired.

Potatoes (Russet or Baking)

Look for dark-skinned large potatoes that are firm and evenly shaped. The skin should not be soft, mushy, or scaly. Plan on 1 baking potato per person.

To store: See tips for storing potatoes above.

To prepare: Scrub well under cool running water to remove any dirt.

To bake: Place directly on the oven rack in a preheated 375°F oven; bake until tender when pressed, 1 hour to 1 hour and 30 minutes.

To microwave: Start the potatoes in the oven to give the skins the appropriate crunchy texture. First, bake directly on the oven rack in a preheated 375°F oven for 30 minutes, then transfer to the microwave and cook on high until tender when pressed, 5 to 10 minutes.

To serve: Season with salt and pepper while warm; also add unsalted butter, chopped scallions, salsa, barbecue sauce, Chile con Queso (page 16), sour cream, plain yogurt, or crème fraîche.

For Oven Fries, see page 472.

For Perfect Mashed Potatoes, see page 473.

Radishes

Look for firm, brightly colored radishes, preferably with the greens still attached. Plan on 3 to 4 ounces per person. Black radishes, a Chinese vegetable, should be grated raw into salads or stir-fries.

To store: Slice off the greens and refrigerate in a plastic bag for up to 1 week. (The greens are edible although sandy; wash well and sauté with a little olive oil or unsalted butter in a skillet over medium heat until wilted, then season with salt and pepper.)

To prepare: Slice off the taproot and any stems left from the greens. Wash well to remove any sandy residue. Halve larger radishes. To firm up limp radishes, place them in ice water for 20 minutes.

To sauté and serve: Melt a couple of pats of unsalted butter in a large skillet over medium heat. Add the radishes, stir well over the heat for 1 minute, then add enough red wine to cover them halfway. Bring to a simmer, cover, and cook until just tender, about 4 minutes. Transfer the radishes to a serving dish; bring the liquid in the pan to a full boil, add some salt and pepper, and cook until reduced to a glaze.

Shallots

Look for medium bulbs with distinct lobes; the papery skins should be shiny and rosy-rust in color. The bulbs should feel firm, not spongy, and there should be no green shoots coming from the tops. Plan on about 4 ounces per serving.

To store: Place in a cool, dark, dry place for up to 3 weeks.

To prepare: Peel off the papery hulls; if there are 2 or more lobes, pry them apart.

To roast and serve: Toss with olive oil and bake in a roasting pan in a preheated 350°F oven, tossing occasionally, until softened and golden, about 45 minutes to 1 hour. Season with salt while warm.

Spaghetti Squash

Choose a squash that is pale yellow and firm with no brown soft spots. Untrimmed, a serving is about 4 ounces.

To store: Keep in a cool, dark place for up to 1 week.

To prepare: Split the squash in half and scoop out the seeds with a grapefruit spoon without removing too much of the stringy flesh.

To steam: Place cut side down in a steam basket over 2 inches of water. Bring to a boil over high heat, cover, reduce the heat to medium, and steam until tender when pierced with a fork, about 30 minutes. Cool, then scrape out the flesh with a fork to create the spaghetti-like texture.

To roast: Place cut side down on an oiled baking sheet and bake in a preheated 350°F oven until tender when pierced with a fork, about 45 minutes. Cool and shred as above.

To serve: Once shredded, season with salt and pepper; then toss with unsalted butter, olive oil, walnut oil, a fruit chutney, or an Asian chili paste, plus perhaps a minced herb, chili powder, or curry powder.

Spinach

Tender baby spinach is often available in bags, prewashed and ready to eat; figure on 4 ounces per serving. Larger leaf spinach, often sold in bulk, can be curly or smooth, depending on the variety; buy about 6 ounces per person (you will remove the stems). In either case, avoid leaves that are yellowed, soft, or flimsy.

To store: Line a large plastic bag with paper towels, place the spinach inside, poke a few holes in the bag, seal, and refrigerate for up to 4 days.

To prepare: Fill a cleaned sink basin with cool water, add the leaves, stir a few times, then let stand for 5 minutes so the sand and grit sink to the bottom. If using baby spinach leaves, take them for a spin afterward in a salad spinner or dry them well between paper towels. If using larger leaves, remove them from the water, do not dry, cut out the fibrous stems, and roughly chop the leaves.

To braise: Heat some canola oil, olive oil, or bacon fat in a large, deep skillet over medium heat. Add some minced garlic; cook for 15 seconds. Add the spinach, then a large splash of water, broth, or white wine, or a combination of any two. Cover and cook, stirring occasionally, until tender, about 4 minutes.

To steam: Do not dry the leaves; place them in a skillet heated over medium heat, grate a little nutmeg over the top, cover, and steam for 2 minutes, tossing occasionally.

To serve: Season with salt and pepper and toss with balsamic vinegar, white wine vinegar, or finely grated Parmigiano-Reggiano.

Summer Squash (Zucchini and Yellow Crookneck)

Smaller zucchini and yellow squash (under 8 inches) are sweeter and have fewer seeds. The skins should be smooth and firm without brown spots. A serving is about 5 ounces.

To store: Refrigerate in a plastic bag for up to 4 days.

To prepare: Do not peel but wash well. Cut off ¼ inch at both ends.

To steam: Slice into ½-inch rings. Place in a steamer basket with a thinly sliced red onion. Place over 1 inch of simmering water in a large pot set over high heat. Cover, reduce the heat to medium, and cook until tender, about 5 minutes.

To sauté: Shred through the large holes of a box grater. Heat some olive oil in a large skillet over medium heat. Add a minced garlic clove and the shredded squash. Cook, stirring frequently, until tender, about 7 minutes.

To grill: Slice into ½-inch rings. Prepare the grill for medium-heat cooking. Brush the rings generously with olive oil. Place directly over the heat and cook until marked and tender, turning once, 3 to 4 minutes.

To serve: Season with salt and pepper, then toss with toasted sliced almonds, grated lemon or orange zest, walnut oil, unsalted butter, or olive oil.

Sweet Potatoes or Yams

Look for long, evenly shaped sweet potatoes with taut if papery skins. Figure on one 8-ounce sweet potato per person; buy similarly sized potatoes so they cook at the same rate.

To store: Set in a cool, dry place for up to 1 week; never refrigerate.

To prepare: Scrub well of any dirt.

To bake: Set the potatoes on a baking sheet to protect the oven from the sugar that will drip out. Bake in a preheated 375°F oven until tender when pressed, between 1 hour and 1 hour and 30 minutes, depending on the size of the potatoes.

To braise: Peel and cut into 1-inch pieces. Place in a large skillet with enough vegetable broth to come about ½ inch up the pan and a spoonful of honey; bring to a simmer over high heat. Cover, reduce the heat to low, and cook until almost tender, about 15 minutes. Uncover, raise the heat to medium-high, and reduce the liquid in the pan to a glaze, about 2 minutes.

To steam: Peel and cut into 2-inch pieces. Place in a steamer basket in a pot with 2 inches of simmering water set over high heat. Cover, reduce the heat to medium, and steam until tender, about 20 minutes.

To serve: Season with salt and pepper while warm; also add ground cinnamon, grated nutmeg, and/or ground mace, if desired; and top with unsalted butter, chutney, or finely grated Asiago.

Turnips

They should be firm with smooth skins that have a light violet or pink tinge near the top. If possible, buy turnips with the perky, firm greens still attached. A serving is 5 to 6 ounces.

To store: Remove the greens, leaving an inch of stem attached to each turnip (see page 460 for ways to use the greens); set the turnips in a cool, dark place for up to 4 days.

To prepare: Cut off the taproots and the greens' stems. Wash well to remove any dirt. Larger turnips should be peeled and quartered; baby turnips can be used "as is." Either can replace half the potatoes in Perfect Mashed Potatoes (page 473).

To boil: Place in a large pot and cover with cold water to a depth of 2 inches. Bring to a boil over high heat. Cover, reduce the heat to low, and cook until they are tender when pierced with a fork, about 20 minutes. Drain in a colander set in the sink.

To steam: Place in a steamer basket over 2 inches of simmering water in a large pot set over high heat. Cover, reduce the heat to medium, and cook until tender when pierced with a fork, about 15 minutes.

To serve: Season with salt and pepper, then toss with unsalted butter, balsamic vinegar, or sour cream.

Winter Squash (Acorn Blue Hubbard, Buttercup, Butternut, Calabaza, Carnival, Delicata, Hubbard, Kabocha, Kuri, or Pumpkin)

Look for firm skin with no soft or mushy spots; some squashes may have a few rough, barnaclelike patches. The skins of smaller winter squashes like acorn and delicata are edible after cooking. Plan on 6 ounces uncooked, untrimmed squash per serving.

To store: Place in a cool, dark spot for up to 5 days.

To prepare: If the skin is edible, scrub the skin for dirt; remove the stem or its remnants. Cut the squash in half through the stem; scrape out seeds and attendant fibers with a grapefruit spoon.

If the skin is not edible, the hard squash must be peeled. Cut it in half and set it cut side down on your cutting board. Use a chef's knife to follow the natural curve of the skin, thereby removing it and leaving the meat behind. Scrape out the seeds and all strings with a grapefruit spoon, then chop the meat into the desired cubes.

To roast: Do not peel. Place the halves cut side down on an oiled or sprayed baking sheet and bake in a preheated 400°F oven until tender when pierced with a sharp knife, 25 minutes to 1 hour, depending on the varietal. Scoop out the flesh to mash, if desired.

To braise: Slice the halves into long wedges, 2 to 4 wedges per half, depending on the size. Place in a pot large enough to hold all the squash; add water, unsweetened apple juice, orange juice, white wine, chicken broth, or vegetable broth to a depth of about 1 inch. Bring to a simmer over medium-high heat. Cover, reduce the heat to low, and simmer until tender when pierced with a fork, 20 to 30 minutes, depending on the varietal.

To microwave: Slice the halves into wedges, as above. Place in a large glass baking dish; add water, unsweetened apple juice, white wine, or vegetable broth to a depth of about ½ inch. Cover and microwave on high for 15 minutes; let rest, covered, at room temperature for 10 minutes.

To serve: Season with salt and pepper—then dot with unsalted butter and drizzle with maple syrup; or scrape out the soft flesh and mix with a fork with unsalted butter or walnut oil and, if desired, some chutney. If you've used fruit juice, remove the squash and boil the juice down to a syrup to drizzle on top.

❁ *Vegetable Side Dishes* ❁

These preparations are a little more hearty, hefty, or sophisticated than simple, one-vegetable side dishes, made from the narrative recipes on pages 452–467. Rather, these that follow will work alongside deep-flavored fish dishes like the Thick White-Fleshed Fish Fillets Poached with Tomatoes and Cinnamon (page 329), or as a side to steaks (see page 382) or roast turkey (see page 284). Along with a green salad, some of them are substantial enough for a light meal.

Zucchini and Lemon Sauté

In this summery side dish, the oil used to soften the zucchini becomes a simple sauce. *Makes 4 servings*

The zest from 4 lemons, removed with the
  large holes of a box grater (see Note)
3 tablespoons olive oil
2 large zucchini, shredded through the large
  holes of a box grater
1½ tablespoons cider vinegar
½ teaspoon salt
½ teaspoon freshly ground black
  pepper

❶ Bring a small pot of water to a boil over high heat. Add the lemon zest and boil until tender and lacking its bitter edge, about 10 minutes. Drain in a fine-mesh sieve or small-holed colander set in the sink, then refresh under cool running water.

❷ Heat a large skillet over medium heat. Add the olive oil, then the shredded zucchini. Cook, stirring often, until wilted and warmed but not until the zucchini begins to break down and give off its water, about 2 minutes. Transfer the contents of the skillet to a large serving bowl.

❸ Stir in the boiled lemon zest, vinegar, salt, and pepper. Serve at once while warm.

Note: Take care not to press the lemons hard against the grater; you'll end up with too much of the bitter white pith along with the zest.

Variations: Add 2 tablespoons pine nuts, chopped pecan halves, or chopped walnut pieces to the skillet with the zucchini.

Add a few dashes of hot red pepper sauce with the vinegar.

Shave a large strip of Parmigiano-Reggiano or Asiago over each warm serving, letting it melt slightly over the zucchini's heat.

Yellow Squash Noodles with Butter, Peas, and Cream

Look for fairly straight, long summer squash, ones you can easily run a vegetable peeler over to create these "noodles." *Makes 4 servings*

2 pounds yellow squash
2 tablespoons unsalted butter
1 tablespoon olive oil
1 medium red onion, halved and thinly sliced
2 garlic cloves, minced
1 cup shelled fresh peas or thawed frozen peas
¼ cup heavy cream
½ teaspoon freshly ground black pepper
¼ teaspoon salt
¼ teaspoon red pepper flakes
2 ounces Parmigiano-Reggiano, finely grated (about ½ cup)

1 Use a vegetable peeler to make long, thin noodles from the squash, running it along their flat surfaces, turning the squash after each strip. Don't shave them into their seedy cores—which you should discard.

2 Melt the butter in the olive oil in a large skillet over medium-low heat. Add the onion, reduce the heat to low, and cook, stirring often, until softened, about 6 minutes. Add the garlic, raise the heat to medium, and cook for 20 seconds.

3 Add the prepared squash noodles and cook until tender, tossing often, about 3 minutes. (Kitchen tongs work best.) Add the peas; cook for 1 minute.

4 Stir in the cream and bring to a boil. Stir in the pepper, salt, and red pepper flakes; then remove from the heat and stir in the cheese until melted.

Variations: For a stronger taste, substitute Asiago for the Parmigiano-Reggiano.

Substitute ½ cup pine nuts for the peas.

For an even creamier dish, omit the Parmigiano-Reggiano and stir in 2 ounces soft goat cheese such as Montrachet into the sauce until melted.

Sautéed Baby Artichokes and Shiitake Mushrooms

Here's an easy sauté that goes well with roast chicken or beef. *Makes 6 servings*

4 teaspoons lemon juice
12 baby artichokes
2 tablespoons olive oil
2 medium shallots, finely chopped
12 ounces shiitake mushrooms, stems removed and discarded, caps thinly sliced
1 teaspoon finely grated lemon zest
1 teaspoon stemmed thyme or ½ teaspoon dried thyme
½ teaspoon salt
½ teaspoon freshly ground black pepper
¼ cup chicken broth
1 tablespoon unsalted butter

1 Bring a large pot of water plus 2 teaspoons lemon juice to a boil over high heat.

2 Cut the stems off the artichokes and remove any tough dark green outer leaves. Quarter the artichokes, then add them to the boiling water. Blanch the outer leaves until just tender, about 5 minutes; drain in a colander set in the sink.

3 Heat a large skillet over medium heat. Swirl in the olive oil, then add the shallots. Cook, stirring often, until softened, about 5 minutes.

4 Add the mushrooms and continue cooking, stirring often, until they give off their liquid, about 4 minutes.

⑤ Add the artichoke quarters; cook for 3 minutes, stirring frequently. Stir in the lemon zest, thyme, salt, and pepper; cook for 20 seconds.

⑥ Pour in the broth and raise the heat to medium-high. Scrape up any browned bits on the pan's bottom and continue cooking, stirring every so often, until the liquid in the pan has reduced to a glaze, about 2 minutes. Stir gently at this stage to keep the artichoke quarters together.

⑦ Remove the pan from the heat and stir in the remaining 2 teaspoons lemon juice and the butter until melted. Serve warm.

Variations: Add 2 ounces chopped prosciutto with the shallots.

Substitute white wine for the broth.

Substitute 2 teaspoons packed chopped tarragon leaves or packed chopped oregano for the thyme.

Broccoli in Garlic Sauce

Although often served as a main course with rice, this dish can also go alongside a roast turkey coated with the Szechuan rub (see page 286) or alongside Dan Dan Ragù (page 194). *Makes 6 servings*

2 tablespoons oyster sauce
2 tablespoons soy sauce
1 tablespoon Shaoxing or dry sherry
1 teaspoon sugar
2 tablespoons peanut oil
2 medium scallions, thinly sliced
6 garlic cloves, slivered
2 tablespoons minced peeled fresh ginger
2 pounds broccoli, florets cut off, stalks cut into ½-inch pieces
¼ cup vegetable broth
1 teaspoon cornstarch dissolved in 1 tablespoon water in a small bowl or cup
2 teaspoons toasted sesame oil

① Whisk the oyster sauce, soy sauce, Shaoxing or sherry, and sugar in a small bowl; set aside.

② Heat a large wok or high-sided sauté pan over medium-high heat. Swirl in the peanut oil, then add the scallions, garlic, and ginger; stir-fry for 30 seconds.

③ Add the broccoli; cook, tossing constantly, for 2 minutes.

④ Pour in the prepared oyster sauce mixture, bring the sauce to a simmer, and cook for 1 minute, stirring constantly.

⑤ Add the dissolved cornstarch and water; toss until thickened, about 30 seconds. Remove the pan from the heat and drizzle the sesame oil over the top.

Asparagus in Garlic Sauce: Substitute thin green asparagus spears, cut into 2-inch segments.

Sautéed Cabbage and Bacon

Here's a wintry side, best served alongside sausages or roast turkey. Savoy cabbage is a leafy variety; look for tight heads that are heavy to the hand. Cook cabbage quickly to avoid that distinctive, sulphurous odor. *Makes 6 servings*

1 medium head Savoy cabbage (about 2½ pounds)
8 strips bacon (about 4 ounces), finely chopped
1 medium onion, finely chopped
½ teaspoon finely ground black pepper
¼ teaspoon grated nutmeg

① Bring a large pot of water to a boil over high heat.

2 Meanwhile, slice the core off the cabbage, separate the leaves, and wash them for any dirt. Remove any tough, thick stems.

3 Add the cabbage leaves to the water; blanch for 1 minute, making sure the leaves are thoroughly submerged in the water. Drain in a colander set in the sink, rinse with cool water, and chop the leaves into 2-inch pieces.

4 Heat a large skillet over medium heat. Add the bacon pieces; cook, stirring often, until browned and frizzled, about 4 minutes. Transfer the bacon to a plate and set aside.

5 Add the onion to the bacon grease; cook, stirring often, until soft and lightly browned, about 3 minutes.

6 Add the chopped cabbage; cook, tossing often, until wilted and hot, about 5 minutes. Stir in the bacon, pepper, and nutmeg; serve warm.

Variations: Add 1⅔ cups canned white beans, drained and rinsed, with the chopped cabbage.

Add ¼ cup heavy cream or ¼ cup white wine to the cabbage after it has cooked for 2 minutes in step 6. Cook until the cream or wine is reduced to a thick glaze before adding the bacon, pepper, and nutmeg.

For other side-dish ideas, look at some of the vegetable salads like Roasted Radicchio and Shallots (page 109), Asian Sugar Snap Salad (page 113), or Green Bean Salad with Boiled Lemon, Pecans, and Parmigiano-Reggiano (page 113).

Skillet Butternut Squash and Brandy

A little butter, a touch of brandy—it all brings out the natural sugars in butternut squash. The cooking time is quick, provided you cut the squash into very small cubes. For an even quicker dish, look for precut butternut squash in your market's produce section and then cut the cubes even smaller as directed here. *Makes 4 servings*

1 tablespoon unsalted butter
1 small onion, chopped
1 small butternut squash (about 1 pound), peeled, halved, seeded, and cut into ½-inch cubes
¼ cup vegetable broth
⅓ cup brandy
1 teaspoon honey
½ teaspoon salt
¼ teaspoon freshly ground black pepper

1 Melt the butter in a large skillet over medium heat. Add the onion; cook, stirring often, until softened, about 3 minutes.

2 Add the butternut squash; cook, stirring constantly, for 2 minutes.

3 Pour in the broth, then the brandy and honey. Stir well, cover, and reduce the heat to low. (Be careful of brandy around an open flame; pour it gently into the middle of the skillet.) Simmer until the squash is tender, stirring once in a while, about 12 minutes.

4 Uncover the pan, raise the heat to medium-high, add the salt and pepper, and cook, stirring frequently, until the liquid in the pan has reduced to a glaze, about 2 minutes.

Variations: Substitute Cognac or red wine for the brandy, or use all broth and no alcohol (½ cup plus 2 tablespoons broth).

Spaghetti Squash, Cannellini Beans, and Broccoli Raab

Once baked and removed from its shell, spaghetti squash turns into strings like pasta, as in this classic Italian combination. *Makes 6 servings*

One 3-pound spaghetti squash, halved
   lengthwise through the stem, seeded,
   roasted, and cooled (see page 464)
2 tablespoons olive oil
6 garlic cloves, slivered
1²⁄₃ cups canned cannellini beans, drained
   and rinsed
1 pound broccoli raab, chopped
   (about 6 cups)
1 teaspoon salt
½ teaspoon grated nutmeg
½ teaspoon red pepper flakes
½ cup vegetable broth
2 tablespoons unsalted butter

1 Scrape the cooked flesh out of the squash and into a large bowl with a fork so that it separates into little filaments or threads. Set aside.

2 Heat a large, high-sided skillet or sauté pan over medium heat. Add the olive oil, then the garlic. Cook until quite aromatic, stirring often, about 1 minute.

3 Toss in the beans, broccoli raab, salt, nutmeg, and red pepper flakes; stir well, then pour in the broth. Cover and steam for 5 minutes, stirring a couple of times. Add the butter and squash; toss well until heated through.

Variations: Omit the beans; increase the broccoli raab to 1½ pounds.
   For a sweeter dish, substitute broccoli florets or peas for the broccoli raab.

Roasted Brussels Sprouts and Roots

This is our default holiday side dish: a sheet pan of caramelized, irresistible parsnips, sprouts, and the rest. The trick is to cut everything the same size: about the size of a small Brussels sprout. *Makes 8 servings*

3 medium parsnips, peeled and sliced into
   ½-inch rings
2 medium acorn squash, peeled, seeded, and
   cubed
1 medium rutabaga, peeled and cubed
1 medium turnip, peeled and cubed
¼ cup olive oil
1 pound small Brussels sprouts, stems
   trimmed, tough outer leaves removed
1 tablespoon coarse-grained salt, such as
   kosher salt

1 Position the rack in the center of the oven; preheat the oven to 375°F.

2 Place the parsnips, squash, rutabaga, and turnip on a large lipped baking sheet; toss with 3 tablespoons olive oil. Roast, tossing occasionally, for 35 minutes.

3 Toss the Brussels sprouts with the remaining 1 tablespoon oil in a large bowl. Add them to the baking sheet, toss well, and continue roasting, tossing occasionally, until caramelized and lightly browned, about 25 more minutes. Season with salt and cool for 5 minutes before serving.

Variations: Substitute 1 pound sweet potatoes, peeled and cubed, for the acorn squash.
   Substitute carrots for the parsnips.

Oven-Roasted Ratatouille

Roasting the vegetables in this tomato and eggplant side caramelizes their sugars better than stewing them in a saucepan. *Makes 6 servings*

  2 medium tomatoes (about 1 pound total
    weight), chopped
  2 medium zucchini (about 1 pound total
    weight), halved lengthwise and cut into
    ½-inch slices
  2 small eggplants (about 1 pound total
    weight), quartered and cut into ½-inch
    slices
  1 large red onion, chopped
  3 garlic cloves, minced
  3 tablespoons olive oil
  1 teaspoon minced oregano leaves or
    ½ teaspoon dried oregano
  1 teaspoon stemmed thyme or ½ teaspoon
    dried thyme
  ½ teaspoon salt
  ½ teaspoon freshly ground black pepper

1 Position the rack in the center of the oven and preheat the oven to 375°F.

2 Toss all the ingredients in a large bowl, then pour them into a large, shallow roasting pan or casserole.

3 Cover and bake for 45 minutes, stirring a few times; then uncover and continue baking, stirring frequently, until the vegetables are soft, about 15 minutes. Serve warm.

Variations: Add any of the following to the vegetable mixture: ¼ cup sliced pitted black olives; 2 jarred roasted red bell peppers or pimientos, chopped; or up to ½ teaspoon red pepper flakes.

Top each serving with a little grated Parmigiano-Reggiano, Pecorino Romano, or Asiago.

Oven Fries

For best results, do not use an insulated baking sheet but do use a nonstick one. *Makes 8 servings*

  4 pounds large baking potatoes, preferably
    Russets, scrubbed clean
  ½ cup canola oil
  1 tablespoon coarse-grained salt, preferably
    kosher salt
  1 teaspoon freshly ground black pepper
  ½ teaspoon cayenne pepper

1 Position the rack in the center of the oven and preheat the oven to 400°F.

2 Cut the potatoes in half at their middle (that is, the short way). Cut each of these halves in half lengthwise. Cut each of these lengthwise into 3 long wedges or spears.

3 Place in a large bowl and toss with the canola oil, salt, and pepper. Spread onto a large lipped baking sheet. Sprinkle the cayenne over the potatoes.

4 Bake undisturbed for 40 minutes. Then toss and continue baking until crisp and well browned, tossing occasionally, about another 40 minutes.

Variations: For spiced fries, add 1 teaspoon onion powder and ½ teaspoon garlic powder with the cayenne.

Omit the cayenne; add 1½ teaspoons dried thyme and 1 teaspoon dried parsley in its place. Or substitute rosemary and oregano for an Italian-inspired taste.

Oven Sweet Potato Fries: Substitute sweet potatoes for the baking potatoes; roast about 35 minutes, tossing occasionally.

Perfect Mashed Potatoes

Ours are made (1) with skin-on, yellow-fleshed Yukon golds and (2) without cream. Instead, we give them body with milk, butter, broth, and a little mustard. *Makes 6 servings*

> 2 pounds yellow-fleshed potatoes, preferably Yukon golds, scrubbed (see Note)
> ¼ cup milk (regular, low-fat, or fat-free)
> ¼ cup chicken or vegetable broth
> 2 tablespoons unsalted butter
> 1½ teaspoons Dijon mustard
> 1 teaspoon salt
> ½ teaspoon freshly ground black pepper

1 Bring a large pot of water to a boil over high heat. Add the potatoes, reduce the heat to medium, set the lid ajar, and boil until the potatoes are tender when pierced with a fork, about 20 minutes.

2 Meanwhile, stir the milk and broth in a small saucepan and warm it gently over low heat. Do not simmer.

3 Drain the potatoes in a colander set in the sink. Place them in a large bowl—or back in the saucepan you just used. Mash with a potato masher or beat with an electric mixer at medium speed until fairly creamy. (Do not use an electric mixer in a nonstick saucepan.)

4 Pour in the warmed milk mixture, then add the butter, mustard, salt, and pepper. Mash or beat until fairly smooth but with chunks of skin visible, about 40 seconds. Serve warm.

Note: Of course, you can also use medium white-fleshed potatoes. You may need to add up to ¼ cup additional milk, depending on how dry the potatoes are after beating.

Variations: Add ¼ cup sour cream with the butter.

Omit the mustard; add ¼ teaspoon grated nutmeg with the salt.

For skinless mashed potatoes, peel the potatoes before boiling.

Root Vegetable Mash

Far from the ordinary, this flavorful mash is a good foil to fish and chicken sautés. *Makes 4 to 6 servings*

> 1 pound white turnips, peeled and cut into 2-inch chunks
> ½ pound parsnips, peeled and cut into 2-inch chunks
> ½ pound rutabaga, peeled and cut into 2-inch chunks
> 2 tablespoons unsalted butter
> 2 tablespoons sour cream (regular, low-fat, or fat-free)
> 1 tablespoon chopped tarragon leaves, chopped savory leaves, or chopped chives
> 1 teaspoon salt
> ½ teaspoon freshly ground black pepper

1 Set the turnips, parsnips, and rutabaga in a large vegetable steamer over 2 inches of simmering water in a pot set over high heat. Cover, reduce the heat to medium, and steam until everything is very tender when pierced with a fork, about 30 minutes.

2 Transfer the root vegetables while still warm to a large bowl; add the butter, sour cream, herb of your choice, salt, and pepper. Mash with a potato masher or an electric beater until smooth.

Variations: Substitute 1 pound celery root, peeled and cut into 2-inch cubes, for the turnips.

Substitute ½ pound white-fleshed potatoes, peeled and cut into 2-inch cubes, for the rutabaga.

Ginger Squash Puree

Here's a squash version of mashed potatoes—with ginger to give it an Asian accent. Serve it as you would mashed potatoes or use it as a bed for grilled meat or fish. *Makes 6 servings*

1 large kabocha squash (about 2¼ pounds), split in half through the stem and seeded
1 tablespoon canola oil
3 tablespoons grated peeled fresh ginger
2 tablespoons unsalted butter
1 tablespoon honey
½ teaspoon salt

❶ Position the rack in the center of the oven and preheat the oven to 400°F. Rub the canola oil over a large lipped baking sheet with a paper towel.

❷ Place the squash halves cut side down on the baking sheet and roast until quite tender, about 40 minutes. Cool on a wire rack for 10 minutes.

❸ Scrape the warm flesh out of the squash and place in a large food processor fitted with the chopping blade. Add the ginger, butter, honey, and salt. Process until smooth. Alternatively, mash the baked squash and the other ingredients in a large bowl with an electric mixer at medium speed.

Variations: You can use other squash, provided they are of the same weight. Blue Hubbard is quite creamy; pumpkin, while difficult to work with, is also good (see page 466).

Some winter squash, like butternut and acorn, can have fibrous threads, rendering the final mash a bit stringy. However, if this doesn't bother you, they make acceptable substitutes.

Curried Cauliflower, Pears, Chickpeas, and Peas

This is a new take on an East Indian classic, a hearty side dish to be paired with other bold flavors. The pears give the other vegetables a perfumed sweetness that stands up well to roasts or makes a savory main course over brown rice. *Makes 6 servings*

2 tablespoons mustard oil or canola oil
1 large onion, chopped
2 garlic cloves, minced
1 tablespoon minced peeled fresh ginger
1 teaspoon dry mustard
1 teaspoon turmeric
1 teaspoon ground cumin
1 teaspoon ground cinnamon
1 teaspoon dried thyme
1 teaspoon salt
¼ teaspoon saffron threads
⅛ teaspoon cayenne pepper
1 head cauliflower, cut into florets (about 8 cups) (see page 457)
2 ripe pears, peeled, cored, and chopped
1 cup canned chickpeas, drained and rinsed
2 cups vegetable broth
1 cup shelled fresh peas or thawed frozen peas
1 cup plain yogurt (regular, low-fat, or fat-free)

❶ Heat a large saucepan over medium heat. Swirl in the oil, then add the onion. Cook, stirring often, until translucent, about 3 minutes. Stir in the garlic and ginger; cook for 30 seconds.

② Stir in the dry mustard, turmeric, cumin, cinnamon, thyme, salt, saffron, and cayenne. Cook, stirring constantly, until aromatic, about 30 seconds.

③ Stir in the cauliflower florets. Cook, stirring often, for 1 minute. Then stir in the pears and chickpeas; cook, stirring often, for 1 minute.

④ Pour in the broth and bring to a simmer, scraping up any browned bits on the pan's bottom. Cover, reduce the heat to low, and simmer for 10 minutes.

⑤ Stir in the peas and yogurt until smooth. Simmer, uncovered, stirring often, until the cauliflower is quite tender, about 5 minutes.

Variations: Stir 2 cups chopped stemmed chard or beet greens into the stew with the peas.

Substitute 1 tablespoon yellow curry powder for the dry mustard, turmeric, cumin, cinnamon, and thyme. For a hotter dish, substitute up to 1 tablespoon Thai yellow curry paste for these spices.

Butternut Squash Soufflé with Ginger Cream

This airy, light, savory soufflé makes gorgeous dinner party fare—but does require good timing. You must serve it within a minute or two of its coming out of the oven. *Makes 4 servings*

1 tablespoon canola oil
1 small butternut squash (about 1 pound), split lengthwise and seeded
4 large eggs, at room temperature, separated
2 tablespoons unsalted butter, plus additional for greasing
2 tablespoons all-purpose flour
1 cup milk (regular, low-fat, or fat-free)
1 teaspoon Dijon mustard
1 teaspoon paprika
½ teaspoon grated nutmeg
½ teaspoon stemmed thyme or ¼ teaspoon dried thyme
½ teaspoon salt
½ teaspoon freshly ground black pepper
Ginger Cream (recipe follows)

① Position the rack in the center of the oven and preheat the oven to 400°F.

② Spread the canola oil around a large lipped baking sheet with a paper towel. Set the squash cut side down on it. Bake until the flesh is quite tender, about 45 minutes.

③ Cool on a baking rack, then scoop the flesh into a food processor fitted with the chopping blade. Process until pureed. You should have about 1½ cups; if you have more, reserve it for another use, such as the Ginger Squash Puree (page 474) or the squash filling for stuffed pasta (see page 196).

④ Decrease the oven temperature to 375°F. Lightly butter a 2-quart soufflé dish; set aside.

⑤ Place the egg yolks in a large bowl and whisk until smooth and creamy, about 1 minute. Set aside.

⑥ Melt the butter in a large saucepan set over medium heat. Add the flour and whisk constantly for 30 seconds, just until pastelike and sizzling.

⑦ Whisk in the milk in a slow, steady stream. Continue whisking over the heat until smooth, thickened, and bubbling, about 2 minutes. Whisk in the mustard, paprika, nutmeg, thyme, salt, and pepper until smooth.

⑧ Slowly whisk this hot milk mixture into the yolks; continue whisking until smooth. Whisk in the butternut squash puree. Set aside.

⑨ Beat the egg whites in a large bowl with an electric mixer at high speed until soft, droopy peaks can be formed with the tip of a rubber spatula.

⑩ Fold half the egg whites into the squash mixture with a rubber spatula until smooth. Mound the remaining egg whites onto the top and slowly fold them in, using long, gentle arcs, just until there's no more white visible in the mixture. Pour and mound this mixture in the prepared soufflé dish.

⑪ Bake until puffed and lightly browned, about 45 minutes. Serve without delay, pouring 1 tablespoon of the warm Ginger Cream over each helping.

Ginger Cream

This savory sauce is also great with roasts—or add 1 to 2 tablespoons sugar with the salt for a dessert sauce. *Makes about ¼ cup*

> ¼ cup heavy cream
> One 4-inch piece of ginger, peeled and cut
>   into 6 pieces
> ¼ teaspoon salt

Heat the cream, ginger, and salt over low heat in a small saucepan until bubbles fizz around the pan's inner edge. Remove from the heat, cover, and set aside on the stove to keep warm. Fish out the ginger pieces before serving.

Vegetable Casseroles

While these dishes require a bit of preparation, they're all make-ahead wonders. Prepare any of these casseroles without baking them, cover, and refrigerate for up to 24 hours. Or bake it off and refrigerate or freeze individual portions for warming up at another time.

Brussels Sprouts and Potato Gratin

A traditional, French gratin hasn't any cheese; the potato starch naturally thickens the cream, creating a luscious, creamy side dish. *Makes 8 servings*

6 tablespoons unsalted butter, plus additional
    for greasing the pan
1 large red onion, chopped
1 pound Brussels sprouts, stems and outer
    leaves removed, then thinly sliced, almost
    shredded
2½ pounds yellow-fleshed potatoes,
    preferably Yukon golds
1 tablespoon stemmed thyme or 2 teaspoons
    dried thyme
1 teaspoon salt
½ teaspoon freshly ground black pepper
¼ teaspoon grated nutmeg
2 cups heavy cream
1 cup vegetable broth

1 Position the rack in the center of the oven and preheat the oven to 350°F. Lightly butter a 13 × 9-inch baking dish; set aside.

2 Melt 3 tablespoons butter in a large skillet over medium heat. Add the onion, reduce the heat to low, and cook, stirring often, until golden, about 10 minutes.

3 Add the Brussels sprouts and raise the heat to medium. Cook, stirring often, until softened, about 6 minutes. Set aside off the heat.

4 Peel the potatoes, then thinly slice them the long way into strips no more than ¼ inch thick. It's best to use a mandoline, but you can use a knife if it's quite sharp.

5 Layer half the potatoes across the bottom of the buttered baking dish. Spread the Brussels sprouts mixture evenly over the potatoes. Sprinkle evenly with the thyme, ½ teaspoon salt, the pepper, and nutmeg; then top with the remaining potato slices. Sprinkle the remaining ½ teaspoon salt over the dish, then pour the cream and broth evenly over the dish. Dot with the remaining 3 tablespoons butter.

6 Bake until the potatoes are golden and tender and most of the liquid has been absorbed, about 1½ hours. During the last 30 minutes, use a large spoon to catch some of the juices and cream bubbling up between the potatoes; baste the potatoes two or three times to moisten them on top.

To cool: Let stand on a wire rack at room temperature for 10 minutes before serving.

Leek, Apple, and Potato Gratin: Substitute 3 large leeks for the onion. Use only the white and pale green parts; halve them lengthwise, wash carefully of grit, and slice thinly. Also substitute 2 large tart apples, such as Granny Smith apples, for the Brussels sprouts.

Mushroom, Shallot, and Potato Gratin: Substitute 6 medium shallots for the onion; also substitute 2 pounds cleaned and thinly sliced white button or cremini mushrooms for the Brussels sprouts. Cook the mushrooms until they have released their moisture and it has almost all evaporated, about 9 minutes.

Chard and Potato Gratin: Substitute 2 pounds Swiss chard, washed, stemmed, and roughly chopped, for the Brussels sprouts. Also add 2 minced garlic cloves with the chard. If desired, omit the thyme and nutmeg; use 2 teaspoons fennel seeds in their place.

Broccoli and Potato Gratin: Use a yellow onion instead of a red onion. Substitute 4 cups finely chopped broccoli florets for the Brussels sprouts.

Baked Zucchini Casserole

This rich casserole with ricotta and Parmigiano-Reggiano should be cooled at least 20 minutes so it can be cut into squares when served. *Makes 9 servings*

6 medium zucchini
1 teaspoon salt
1 tablespoon unsalted butter
1 medium onion, finely chopped
3 large eggs plus 1 large egg white, whisked until fairly smooth in a small bowl
¾ cup finely grated Parmigiano-Reggiano
½ cup regular or low-fat ricotta cheese (do not use fat-free)
½ cup plain dried bread crumbs
1 tablespoon chopped dill fronds or 2 teaspoons dried dill
2 tablespoons canola oil

❶ Shred the zucchini through the large holes of a box grater. Toss with the salt and place in a colander in the sink to drain for 15 minutes.

❷ Squeeze out as much of the moisture from the zucchini as you can, working in batches. Place the zucchini in a large bowl; set aside.

❸ Position the rack in the center of the oven and preheat the oven to 375°F.

❹ Melt the butter in a large skillet over medium heat. Add the onion, reduce the heat to low, and cook, stirring often, until soft and golden, about 7 minutes.

❺ Pour the contents of the skillet into the bowl with the zucchini. Cool for 5 minutes, then stir in the beaten eggs and egg white, the Parmigiano-Reggiano, ricotta, bread crumbs, and dill.

❻ Place the canola oil in a 9-inch square baking pan; tilt the pan so the oil covers its bottom and sides. Place the oiled pan in the oven for 5 minutes to heat it through.

❼ Pour in the zucchini mixture, spread it evenly to the sides, and bake until slightly mounded, a little browned, and set when tapped, about 50 minutes. Set the pan on a wire rack for at least 20 minutes. Once fully cooled, the casserole can be covered with plastic wrap and stored in the refrigerator for up to 3 days. Cut the casserole out of the pan in squares.

Vegetable Parmesan with Eggplant, Zucchini, and Mushrooms

Here's a no-fry vegetable casserole version of an Italian-American favorite. *Makes 8 servings*

2 small eggplants
2 medium zucchini
2 medium yellow summer squash
1 tablespoon salt
3 large portobello mushroom caps
½ cup olive oil
2 medium onions, minced
3 garlic cloves, minced
1 tablespoon chopped oregano leaves or 1½ teaspoons dried oregano

1 teaspoon stemmed thyme or ½ teaspoon
    dried thyme

½ teaspoon freshly ground black pepper

3½ cups canned diced tomatoes

¼ cup chopped basil leaves

6 ounces Parmigiano-Reggiano

½ teaspoon grated nutmeg

1 Peel the eggplants and slice them the long way into ½-inch-thick strips. Slice the zucchini and squash the long way into ½-inch strips (you may have to cut off the crooked necks and slice these separately).

2 Lay a double layer of paper towels on your work surface, place all the strips on the towels, and sprinkle 1½ teaspoons salt over them. Turn over and sprinkle on the remaining 1½ teaspoons salt.

3 Let stand for 30 minutes, turning once after 15 minutes. Meanwhile, divide the racks into the top and bottom thirds of the oven and preheat the oven to 400°F.

4 Blot all the vegetable strips dry with clean paper towels, then set the strips on two large lipped baking sheets; do not overlap any strips. Thinly slice the mushroom caps and place these on the trays as well. Drizzle 3 tablespoons oil over all the vegetables, then turn them over and drizzle 3 tablespoons on their other sides. (You can spread the oil around with a pastry brush for better coverage.)

5 Place in the top and bottom thirds of the oven and bake for 15 minutes. Reverse the sheets top to bottom and back to front, flip the vegetables over, and continue baking until soft, lightly browned, and a little shriveled, about 15 more minutes. Remove the sheets from the oven and place on wire cooling racks. Shift the racks in the oven so one

is in the middle and reduce the oven temperature to 350°F.

6 Heat a large skillet or sauté pan over medium heat. Swirl in the remaining 2 tablespoons oil and add the onions. Cook, stirring often, until translucent, about 3 minutes. Add the garlic, oregano, thyme, and pepper; cook for 30 seconds.

7 Pour in the tomatoes, stir well, and bring to a simmer. Cover, reduce the heat to low, and simmer slowly for 30 minutes, stirring occasionally. Uncover the pan, raise the heat to medium, and continue cooking until thickened slightly, about 5 minutes. Stir in the basil.

8 Use a cheese plane or a vegetable peeler to shave the Parmigiano-Reggiano into thin strips.

9 Layer these in the following order evenly in a 13 × 9-inch baking dish: a quarter of the tomato sauce, the eggplant slices, a quarter of the cheese strips, a third of the remaining tomato sauce, the zucchini slices, a third of the remaining cheese strips, half the remaining tomato sauce, the mushroom slices, half the remaining cheese, the yellow squash strips, all the remaining tomato sauce, and all the remaining cheese strips. Some of the vegetables may not entirely cover the pan in a single layer; you can make up for any deficits in the next layer of vegetables above. Sprinkle the top with nutmeg.

10 Bake until the cheese has melted and browned a bit on top and the sauce is bubbling, about 40 minutes. (You may want to lay a large piece of aluminum foil on the rack below the casserole after it has baked for 30 minutes to catch any drips.) Set on a wire rack for 10 minutes before cutting into squares to serve.

Moroccan Vegetable Casserole

These flavors were modeled on those in North African tagines—but here, they're incorporated into a casserole you can cut into squares to go alongside roasts, whole fish, or grilled steaks. *Makes 8 servings*

3 large plum or Roma tomatoes, chopped
8 large pitted dates, chopped
3 garlic cloves, minced
¼ cup packed chopped cilantro leaves
1 tablespoon packed chopped rosemary leaves
1 tablespoon paprika
2 teaspoons ground cumin
2 teaspoons salt
1 teaspoon ground cinnamon
1 teaspoon ground ginger
½ teaspoon freshly ground black pepper
½ cup vegetable broth
¼ cup olive oil
1 tablespoon honey
¼ teaspoon saffron threads, crumbled
3 large yellow-fleshed potatoes, such as
  Yukon golds, peeled and thinly sliced
3 large zucchini, thinly sliced into rings
3 large carrots, shredded through the holes
  of a box grater
1 medium red onion, cut into thin rings

❶ Position the rack in the center of the oven and preheat the oven to 350°F.

❷ Mix the tomatoes, dates, garlic, cilantro, and rosemary in a medium bowl; set aside. Mix the paprika, cumin, salt, cinnamon, ginger, and pepper in a separate small bowl; set aside as well.

❸ Mix the broth, olive oil, honey, and saffron in a small saucepan, set over low heat, and heat just until a few puffs of steam come off the top of the liquid.

❹ Meanwhile, layer these in the following order in a high-sided, 4-quart casserole, Dutch oven, or oval casserole: the potato slices, a third of the spice mixture, half the tomato mixture, the zucchini, half the remaining spice mixture, all of the remaining tomato mixture, the carrots and onion rings, and the remainder of the spices. Make sure you lay or sprinkle the ingredients in even layers in the pan. Pour the warmed broth mixture over the top.

❺ Cover and bake until bubbling, about 1 hour and 10 minutes. Uncover and continue baking to dry out the top slightly and thicken the casserole a bit, 10 to 20 minutes. Transfer to a wire rack and cool for 10 minutes before slicing into squares to serve.

Variations: Add up to ½ teaspoon red pepper flakes to the spice mixture.

Substitute 6 chopped pitted prunes or 6 dried apricots for the dates.

Add 1 teaspoon orange-flower water with the honey.

Vegetable Pot Pie with Fennel, Artichoke Hearts, and Tarragon

Pay attention to the ingredients here; many are divided and used in different sections of the recipe. *Makes 6 servings*

10 tablespoons unsalted butter
1 medium onion, chopped
2 celery ribs, thinly sliced
1 small fennel bulb, bottom sliced off,
  fronds removed, then chopped
1½ cups plus 2 tablespoons all-purpose
  flour
1 cup milk (regular, low-fat, or fat-free)
1 cup vegetable broth
⅓ cup plus ¼ cup heavy cream

One 12-ounce package frozen artichoke
hearts, thawed and quartered

1 cup shelled fresh peas or thawed frozen
peas

2 jarred roasted red peppers or pimientos,
chopped

1 teaspoon packed chopped tarragon leaves
or ½ teaspoon dried tarragon

1 teaspoon salt

½ teaspoon grated nutmeg

4 ounces Gruyère, finely grated

1 ounce Parmigiano-Reggiano, finely grated

2 teaspoons baking powder

2 tablespoons chopped chives or the minced
green part of a scallion

½ teaspoon stemmed thyme or ¼ teaspoon
dried thyme

① Melt 4 tablespoons (½ stick) butter in a large
saucepan set over medium heat. The moment the
foaming subsides, add the onion, celery, and fennel. Cook, stirring often, until softened, about 4
minutes.

② Sprinkle 2 tablespoons flour over the vegetables, wait for 10 seconds, then cook, stirring constantly, for 30 seconds.

③ To dissolve the flour, slowly whisk in the milk
in a thin, steady stream until the sauce is fairly
smooth. Whisk in the broth and ¼ cup cream.
Continue cooking, stirring constantly, until thickened and bubbling.

④ Stir in the artichoke hearts, peas, red peppers
or pimientos, tarragon, ¾ teaspoon salt, and nutmeg. Pour this mixture into an 8-cup gratin dish
or a 10-inch round oval casserole. Sprinkle the
Gruyère over the top and set aside.

⑤ Position the rack in the center of the oven and
preheat the oven to 400°F.

⑥ Melt the remaining 6 tablespoons butter in a
small saucepan or in a small bowl in the microwave. Set aside to cool for 5 minutes.

⑦ Meanwhile, whisk the Parmigiano-Reggiano,
baking powder, chives or scallion, thyme, and the
remaining 1½ cups flour and ¼ teaspoon salt in
a large bowl until uniform.

⑧ Pour the reserved melted butter and the remaining ⅓ cup cream into the flour mixture and
stir with a fork until a loose, wet dough forms.

⑨ Drop the dough in 2-tablespoon increments,
making a cobblestone pattern over the vegetable
and cheese mixture in the casserole dish, covering
most of the mixture but leaving a few air holes so
steam can escape.

⑩ Bake until bubbling, until the dough has turned
golden brown and is firm to the touch, about 25
minutes.

To cool: Set on a wire rack for 5 minutes before
serving.

Variations: Substitute ¾ pound parsnips,
peeled and cut into ½-inch-thick rings, for the
fennel.

Substitute ¾ pound butternut squash, peeled,
halved, seeded, and cut into ½-inch cubes, for
the artichoke hearts.

We've long felt that potato salad is too important to be left on the side of the plate, so here are three main-course versions.

Potato, Chicken, and Green Bean Salad with Champagne Tarragon Vinaigrette

If desired, arrange the items on a plate as in a composed salad, then drizzle the dressing on top. *Makes 6 servings*

> One 3- to 3½-pound chicken, quartered
> 1½ pounds yellow-fleshed or red-skinned fingerling potatoes, scrubbed
> ½ pound haricots verts or very thin green beans
> 1 medium shallot, minced
> 1 cup halved seedless green grapes
> ½ cup toasted walnut pieces, toasted pine nuts, or sun-dried tomatoes
> 3 tablespoons champagne or white wine vinegar
> 3 tablespoons chopped tarragon leaves
> 1 tablespoon Dijon mustard
> 1 teaspoon salt
> ½ teaspoon freshly ground black pepper
> ½ cup olive oil, preferably extra virgin olive oil

1 Bring a large pot of salted water to a boil over high heat. Add the chicken quarters. Reduce the heat to medium, cover, and cook for 20 minutes, or until the chicken is tender. Remove from the pot with two slotted spoons or a long-handled strainer. Set aside to cool but maintain the water's boil.

2 Add the potatoes to the pot and cook until tender when pierced with a fork, about 22 min-utes. Transfer to a colander set in the sink with a slotted spoon or strainer; set aside to cool slightly but maintain the water's boil.

3 Add the haricots verts or green beans to the pot, blanch for 2 minutes, then drain in a second colander set in the sink. Run cool water over the beans until they are room temperature.

4 When the chicken is cool enough to handle, remove the skin, take the meat off the bones, and slice it into bite-sized chunks. Slice the potatoes into 1-inch chunks and cut the beans into 1-inch strips. Place all three in a large bowl. Add the shallot, grapes, and the walnuts, pine nuts, or sun-dried tomatoes. Toss gently to combine.

5 In a small bowl, whisk the vinegar, tarragon, mustard, salt, and pepper until smooth. Continue whisking while you drizzle in the olive oil in a slow, steady stream until creamy.

6 Pour the dressing over the potato mixture. Toss to coat, taking care not to break up the po-tatoes.

To store: Cover with plastic wrap and refrigerate for up to 2 days; allow the salad to return to room temperature before serving.

For an easier salad, use a 3½-pound purchased rotisserie chicken; take the meat off the bones and roughly chop it before adding it to the other ingredients. If desired, chop the skin and add it, too.

Warm Potato, Bacon, and Vegetable Salad with Honey Mustard Dressing

Best served warm, this chunky potato salad is hearty enough to stand up to a glass of German dark beer. *Makes 6 servings*

1¾ pounds small red-skinned potatoes, scrubbed and cut into a ¼-inch dice

4 large carrots, cut into ½-inch rounds

1 teaspoon vegetable oil

1 pound thick-cut bacon, chopped into ½-inch pieces

2 medium red onions, thinly sliced

2 celery ribs, thinly sliced

1 cup shelled fresh or thawed frozen peas

3 tablespoons parsley leaves, chopped

1 tablespoon chopped dill fronds

¼ cup cider vinegar

1½ tablespoons Dijon mustard

2 teaspoons honey

½ teaspoon salt

½ teaspoon freshly ground black pepper

1 Bring a large pot of salted water to a boil. Add the potatoes and cook for 10 minutes. Then add the carrots and cook until the potatoes are tender when pierced with a fork, about 10 additional minutes. Drain in a colander set in the sink, cool for 10 minutes, then transfer to a large bowl.

2 Meanwhile, heat a large skillet over medium-high heat. Add the vegetable oil, then fry the bacon until crisp, stirring frequently, about 4 minutes. Use a slotted spoon to transfer the cooked bacon to the bowl with the potatoes and carrots; leave the rendered bacon grease in the pan.

3 Reduce the heat to medium and add the onions to the bacon drippings. Cook, stirring frequently, until soft and translucent, about 3 minutes. Pour the onions and any remaining bacon drippings into the bowl with the potatoes, then gently stir in the celery, peas, parsley, and dill.

4 In a small bowl, whisk the vinegar, mustard, honey, salt, and pepper until smooth; pour over the potatoes and gently toss until well combined. The salad is best served warm.

Spanish-Inspired Potato Salad with Chickpeas, Saffron, and Pine Nuts

This main course is reminiscent of dishes served with dry sherry in Madrid tapas bars. If you can only find Mexican-style chorizo, slice it into ½-inch sections and fry it in the oil until it is cooked through, about 5 minutes. *Makes 6 servings*

1¾ pounds small yellow-fleshed potatoes, scrubbed

½ cup plus 1 tablespoon olive oil

1 pound dried Spanish chorizo, cut in half lengthwise, then into ½-inch sections

1½ cups canned chickpeas, drained and rinsed

3 jarred pimientos, drained and cut into thin strips

1 small red onion, thinly sliced

3 celery ribs, chopped

½ cup toasted pine nuts

¼ cup chopped parsley leaves

3 tablespoons sherry vinegar or white wine vinegar

1½ teaspoons anchovy paste

½ teaspoon freshly ground black pepper

⅛ teaspoon saffron threads soaked in a small bowl with 1 tablespoon hot water for 5 minutes

½ cup olive oil, preferably extra virgin olive oil

1 Bring a medium pot of water to boil. Add the potatoes and boil until tender when pierced with a fork, about 14 minutes. Drain in a colander set in the sink and cool slightly, then cut the potatoes in half or into 1-inch chunks, whichever is smaller. Place in a large serving bowl.

2 Heat a medium skillet or sauté pan over medium heat. Swirl in 1 tablespoon olive oil, then add the chorizo. Cook, stirring frequently, until reddish brown and sizzling, about 2 minutes. Transfer with a slotted spoon to a plate lined with paper towels to drain.

3 Stir the chorizo into the potatoes along with the chickpeas, pimientos, onion, celery, pine nuts, and parsley.

4 Whisk in the vinegar, anchovy paste, pepper, and saffron (with its water) until smooth. Continue whisking as you drizzle in the olive oil in a slow, steady stream; whisk until emulsified, about 1 minute. Pour over the potato salad and gently toss to serve warm.

Grains, Beans, Lentils, and Tofu

BEHOLD THE POWER OF THE POTATO! IT HAS NUDGED GRAINS, BEANS, AND lentils off our plates to become America's favorite side. By the 1980s, the only time most of us saw a grain was the rice alongside Chinese takeout.

The potato's success—and we're unabashed fans—has actually been great news for grains and legumes. They've had to stand up for themselves to become more than just thoughtless additions. Besides, in most of the world, they're not side dishes anyway; they are main courses—or, like rice, absolutely integral to the main course. Most of these recipes are indeed for main courses; the power pack of nutrients that makes grain and legumes a global staple can be highlighted once they're moved to the center of the plate.

We've included tofu here because it's made from soybeans and functions in the same way as many main-course legumes—that is, as a meat substitute.

Mushroom Barley Salad

Barley is an ancient grain, now used primarily in beer and whiskey production. Pearl barley is made of hulled and polished barley grains. It's available in several varieties, depending on the thickness of the grain itself; coarse or medium pearl barley is best for this dish. Consider making this dish ahead and storing it, covered, in the refrigerator for up to 3 days, a good lunch to pull out when the days get hectic. *Makes 6 servings*

3½ cups water
1 cup coarse or medium pearl barley
1 tablespoon unsalted butter
8 ounces cremini or white button mushrooms, chopped
1 medium red bell pepper, cored, seeded, and chopped
1 small red onion, finely chopped
2 celery ribs, halved lengthwise and thinly sliced
¼ cup mayonnaise, regular, low-fat, or homemade (page 121)
¼ cup chopped parsley leaves
3 tablespoons white wine vinegar
2 tablespoons walnut oil or olive oil
1 tablespoon Dijon mustard
1 tablespoon stemmed thyme or 1½ teaspoons dried thyme
½ teaspoon salt
½ teaspoon freshly ground black pepper

1. Bring the water to a boil in a medium saucepan set over high heat. Stir in the barley; cover, reduce the heat to low, and simmer until tender, stirring occasionally, about 35 minutes. Drain in a fine-mesh colander set in the sink and transfer to a large serving bowl. Set aside.

2. Melt the butter in a large skillet over medium heat. Add the mushrooms and cook, stirring often, until they release their liquid and it reduces to a glaze, about 4 minutes.

3. Add the bell pepper, onion, and celery; cook, stirring often, until softened, about 2 minutes. Transfer the contents of the skillet to the bowl with the barley.

4. Stir in the mayonnaise, parsley, vinegar, oil, mustard, thyme, salt, and pepper. Set aside for 10 minutes to blend the flavors or cover and refrigerate for up to 3 days.

Variations: For a creamier salad, increase the mayonnaise to ½ cup.

For a more nutritious salad, use hulled or whole-grain barley; adjust its cooking times as indicated on the package.

For a quicker salad, bring only 2 cups water to a boil over high heat. Stir in 1 cup quick-cooking barley, reduce the heat to low, cover, and simmer until tender, about 10 minutes. Drain as directed and proceed with the recipe.

Wheat Berry Salad with Orange and Avocado

Wheat berries are whole unprocessed wheat kernels, a tight pack of fiber and protein with a nutty taste. One warning: they must be soaked overnight before cooking. *Makes 4 servings*

1 cup wheat berries
1 large orange
1 ripe avocado, cut in half, seeded, and diced
1 medium red bell pepper, cored, seeded, and diced
1 small red onion, diced
1 garlic clove, minced
¼ cup mayonnaise (regular, low-fat, or fat-free)
¼ cup plain yogurt (regular, low-fat, or fat-free)
3 tablespoons lemon juice
1 tablespoon chili powder
2 teaspoons Worcestershire sauce
1½ teaspoons ground cumin
Several dashes of hot red pepper sauce to taste

1 Place the wheat berries in a large skillet set over medium-low heat; toast, shaking the pan frequently, until they smell nutty and some pop from the heat, about 3 minutes. Pour into a large bowl and cover with cool water to a depth of 3 inches. Set aside for at least 12 hours or overnight.

2 Bring a quart (4 cups) of water to a boil in a medium saucepan over high heat. Drain the wheat berries and add them to the pot. Stir well, reduce the heat to low, and simmer until tender, about 50 minutes. Drain in a fine-mesh colander set in the sink.

3 Slice about ¼ inch off the top and bottom of the orange. Set it flat on your work surface. Slice off the skin and white pith, following the orange's curve with the blade of the knife. Hold the orange in your hand over a serving bowl; cut between the white membranes to release the sections one by one, letting them and any juice fall into the bowl. Watch your hand—do not slice through the orange. At the end, squeeze the remaining membranes to extract any additional juice.

4 Stir the avocado, bell pepper, onion, garlic, and drained wheat berries into the bowl with the orange sections and juice.

5 In a small bowl, whisk the mayonnaise, yogurt, lemon juice, chili powder, Worcestershire sauce, cumin, and hot red pepper sauce until smooth. Pour over the wheat berry mixture; toss well.

Variations: Omit the yogurt; use ½ cup mayonnaise.

Add 6 ounces cooked, peeled, and deveined medium shrimp, chopped, with the avocado.

Grain Anatomy

Grains have at least four parts: the hull, bran, germ, and endosperm. These are variously edible, depending on the grain. A "whole grain" has at least the bran along with the tender endosperm. Most of the nutrients are found in the hull, bran, and germ; the endosperm is a starchy core that would provide protein to the seed were it to germinate.

For another barley dish, see Mushroom, Barley, and Lentil Soup (page 143).

For another dish with wheat berries, see Chilled Tomato Wheat Berry Soup (page 159).

Looking for more dishes with wild rice? There's Lamb and Wild Rice Soup (page 154) and Wild Rice-Stuffed Guinea Hens (page 305).

Basil Tabbouleh with Pine Nuts and Cucumber

Tabbouleh is a salad made with bulgur wheat, a lightly processed form of the kernel that's been steamed, dried, and crushed. It's familiar as a Middle Eastern salad, but here's an Italian-inspired version. *Makes 6 servings*

1½ cups boiling water
1 cup bulgur wheat
¼ cup pine nuts
1 medium cucumber, peeled, halved
    lengthwise, seeded, and chopped
1 small red onion, finely chopped
16 cherry tomatoes, preferably yellow
    tomatoes, halved
1 cup packed finely chopped basil leaves
¼ cup olive oil
¼ cup lemon juice
1 teaspoon salt
½ teaspoon freshly ground black pepper

❶ Pour the boiling water over the bulgur in a large bowl. Cover loosely with a clean kitchen towel and set aside until the water is absorbed and the bulgur is cool, about 1 hour.

❷ Meanwhile, toast the pine nuts in a large skillet over medium heat until aromatic and lightly browned, stirring often, about 4 minutes. Set aside to cool to room temperature.

❸ Fluff the bulgur with a fork and place in a serving bowl. Stir in the toasted pine nuts, cucumber, onion, tomatoes, basil, olive oil, lemon juice, salt, and pepper. (The salad can be made ahead; cover and refrigerate for up to 3 days.)

Variations: Substitute 3 medium scallions, thinly sliced, for the red onion.

Substitute walnut or pecan pieces for the pine nuts; toast in the skillet as directed and then roughly chop the nuts.

Add ½ cup dried cranberries, dried blueberries, or dried cherries with the cucumber.

Add 1 pound medium shrimp, peeled, deveined, and cooked, with the cucumber.

Curried Buckwheat and Mushroom Loaf

Buckwheat is often classed with grains, although in fact it's an herb indigenous to the Russian steppes. Kasha is roasted hulled buckwheat kernels. Here's a vegetarian version of meat loaf, wrapped in cabbage leaves to keep it moist; it's great for dinner but also for sandwiches on toasted rye the next day. *Makes 8 servings*

1 cup coarse-medium or coarse kasha
    (toasted buckwheat groats)
1½ cups walnut pieces
3 tablespoons unsalted butter
1 large yellow onion, finely
    chopped
2 celery ribs, minced
1 medium carrot, shredded through
    the large holes of a box
    grater
6 ounces cremini or white button
    mushrooms, cleaned and thinly
    sliced
2 garlic cloves, minced
1 teaspoon curry powder
1 teaspoon ground ginger
1 teaspoon ground cumin
1 teaspoon salt
1 small head Savoy cabbage
Canola oil for greasing the
    loaf pan
3 large eggs, at room temperature
¼ cup chopped parsley leaves
Dijon mustard for garnish

1. Toast the kasha in a large skillet set over medium-low heat until nutty and lightly browned, stirring often, about 3 minutes.

2. Meanwhile, bring 2 cups water to a boil in a medium saucepan set over high heat.

3. Add the toasted buckwheat, cover, reduce the heat to medium-low, and simmer until all the water has been absorbed, about 12 minutes. Let stand at room temperature, covered, for 5 minutes before fluffing with a fork. Set aside.

4. Place the walnut pieces in the skillet, set it over medium heat, and toast until lightly browned and aromatic, about 3 minutes. Transfer to the bowl of a food processor fitted with the chopping blade and set aside.

5. Melt the butter in the skillet over medium heat. Add the onion and cook, stirring often, just until softened, about 2 minutes.

6. Add the celery and carrot; continue cooking, stirring frequently, until aromatic, about 2 minutes.

7. Add the mushrooms; continue cooking, stirring once or twice, until they give off their liquid and it reduces to a glaze, about 6 minutes.

8. Add the garlic, curry powder, ginger, cumin, and salt. Cook, stirring constantly, for 30 seconds. Transfer to a large bowl and cool for 15 minutes.

9. Process the walnut pieces until finely ground; stir them into the vegetable mixture. Also stir in the fluffed buckwheat. Set aside.

10. Bring a large pot of water to a boil over high heat. Tear off the cabbage leaves, add them to the pot, and boil until very pliable, about 3 minutes. Drain in a colander set in the sink and refresh under cool running water.

11. Position the rack in the center of the oven; preheat the oven to 350°F. Bring a large teakettle of water to a boil over high heat.

12. Lightly oil a 9 × 5 × 3-inch loaf pan. Line the bottom and sides of the pan with cabbage leaves; some of them should stick 3 or 4 inches over the top rim.

13. Lightly beat the eggs in a small bowl; stir them and the parsley into the buckwheat mixture. Mound the mixture into the prepared pan, spreading it evenly to the corners. Fold the overhanging leaves over the loaf, then cover with more cabbage leaves, sealing the loaf in the pan.

14. Take the teakettle off the heat and let the water stop boiling. Place the loaf pan in a large, deep roasting pan or baking dish. Pour the very hot water into the larger pan until the water level reaches halfway up the outside of the loaf pan.

15. Bake until a knife inserted into the center of the loaf comes out clean and the loaf itself feels set, about 1 hour.

16. Remove the hot pan from the hot water bath; cool on a wire rack for at least 15 minutes before unmolding and serving with Dijon mustard on the side—or cool completely in the refrigerator and serve chilled.

Quinoa and Shiitake Pilaf

Quinoa (pronounced KEEN-wah), a South American staple, is the only grain that can truly function as a meat substitute since it has all eight amino-acid chains found in meat. It's a soft, nutty grain, known for the halo the germ creates around each kernel when cooked. Mince the vegetables quite fine so their texture doesn't overwhelm the tiny grains. *Makes 6 servings*

2 tablespoons olive oil
1 medium shallot, minced
1 medium carrot, peeled and minced
1 celery rib, minced
4 ounces shiitake mushroom caps, thinly
    sliced
1 cup quinoa, rinsed in a fine-mesh
    colander set in the sink and drained
1 teaspoon stemmed thyme or ½ teaspoon
    dried thyme
2 cups vegetable broth
2 teaspoons finely grated lemon zest
½ teaspoon salt
½ teaspoon freshly ground black pepper
1 bay leaf

1 Heat a large saucepan over medium heat. Swirl in the olive oil, then add the shallot, carrot, and celery. Cook, stirring often, until softened and lightly browned, about 6 minutes.

2 Add the shiitakes; cook, stirring often, until softened, about 2 minutes.

3 Stir in the quinoa and thyme; cook, stirring constantly, for 1 minute. Then pour in the broth and bring to a simmer, scraping up any browned bits on the pan's bottom.

4 Stir in the lemon zest, salt, pepper, and bay leaf. Cover, reduce the heat to low, and simmer until all the liquid has been absorbed, about 18 minutes.

5 Set aside, covered, off the heat for 5 minutes; then fluff the mixture with a fork before serving.

Variations: Add 1 cup finely diced butternut or acorn squash with the shallot.

Stir in 1 cup shelled fresh or frozen peas before you set the pan aside off the heat.

Wild Rice Croquettes

Wild rice isn't rice at all; it's the seed from a grass indigenous to the marshlands of the upper Midwest (although now grown across the country). There are varietal blends on the market—or single-variety packs. Either will work for these fried-up patties, but don't use a blend that includes brown rice, white rice, or other grains. *Makes 6 croquettes*

1½ cups water
½ cup wild rice
2 tablespoons walnut oil
8 scallions, very thinly sliced
10 ounces white button or cremini
    mushrooms, cleaned and thinly sliced
¼ cup dried cranberries, chopped
1 tablespoon packed minced sage leaves
1 teaspoon salt
½ teaspoon freshly ground black pepper
2 large eggs, at room temperature
⅓ cup panko bread crumbs
2 tablespoons canola oil, plus more as
    necessary

1 Stir the water and wild rice in a medium saucepan, then bring to a boil over medium-high heat. Cover, reduce the heat to low, and simmer until the rice is tender, 40 to 50 minutes. Drain any remaining water from the pan and set aside.

2 Heat a large skillet over medium heat. Swirl in the walnut oil, then add the scallions. Cook, stirring constantly, for 1 minute.

3 Add the mushrooms and cook, stirring often, until they have given off their liquid and it has all evaporated, about 6 minutes.

4 Stir in the cranberries, sage, salt, and pepper. Cook for 20 seconds, then transfer to the bowl of a food processor fitted with the chopping blade. Process until finely chopped. Transfer to a large bowl and stir in the wild rice. Cool for 15 minutes.

5 Lightly beat the eggs in a small bowl, then stir them and the bread crumbs into the wild rice mixture.

6 Make 6 patties out of the mixture. Your hands will get a little messy; the patties must be compacted to adhere. Moistening your hands helps.

7 Heat a large skillet over medium heat. Swirl in the canola oil, then slip in as many patties as will easily fit. Fry for 3 minutes, then use two metal spatulas to turn them over: slip one under the patty and use the other to hold the patty in place as it's being flipped. Fry until lightly browned, about 3 more minutes. If you need to make a second batch, add up to 2 tablespoons more oil to the pan before adding the additional patties.

Variations: Substitute chopped golden raisins or chopped dried cherries for the cranberries.

Substitute any minced herb for the sage—thyme, marjoram, parsley, or tarragon. (Avoid dill which may not complement the other flavors.)

Substitute ground walnuts for the panko bread crumbs.

Asian-Inspired Dirty Rice with Chicken, Edamame, and Walnuts

Whole-grain brown rice and shelled soybeans (or *edamame* in Japanese) shift the flavors east for this Louisiana favorite. Look for shelled edamame in the freezer section of most markets. The secret is to chop the chicken meat to fairly small pieces; no one should have to cut them with a knife at the table. *Makes 6 servings*

3 tablespoons canola oil
1 large onion, finely chopped
½ pound boneless skinless chicken thighs, cut into ½-inch pieces
½ pound chicken gizzards, all fat removed, the rest chopped into ¼-inch pieces
1 cup brown rice
¼ cup soy sauce
3 scallions, thinly sliced
2 garlic cloves, minced
1 tablespoon minced peeled fresh ginger
2 cups chicken broth
2½ cups shelled unsalted soybeans, or edamame (see Note)
½ cup chopped toasted walnut pieces

1 Position the rack in the center of the oven and preheat the oven to 350°F.

2 Heat a large Dutch oven or oven-safe pot over medium heat. Swirl in the canola oil, then toss in the onion. Cook, stirring often, until softened, about 4 minutes.

3 Add the chicken thighs and gizzards; cook, stirring often, until the meat loses its pink, raw color, about 7 minutes.

4 Add the rice; stir well to coat in the oil and juices. Pour in the soy sauce, then add the scallions, garlic, and ginger. Cook for 30 seconds, stirring all the while, until the rice has absorbed the soy sauce.

⑤ Pour in the broth and add the soybeans. Bring the mixture to a simmer, stirring to get any browned bits up off the pan's bottom.

⑥ Cover, place in the oven, and bake until the liquid has been absorbed and the rice is tender, about 45 minutes. Fluff the rice and stir in the nuts before serving.

Note: Edamame are usually sold in their shells; you'll need to remove these fibrous husks, revealing the small beans inside.

For 2½ cups, you'll need 12 ounces shelled or about 24 ounces in the shells.

Variations: Increase the broth to 2½ cups and add 2 cups chopped leafy greens such as chard, collard greens, or beet greens; 1 cup cubed, seeded, and peeled winter squash; or 1 cup jarred peeled steamed chestnuts.

Substitute ½ pound turkey or pork sausage, cut into small rings, for the gizzards.

Lamb Byriani

This layered rice casserole from India usually includes some kind of protein—here, we've used lamb, reminiscent of what would be used in the Kashmir region. Serve it with chopped unsalted cashews, minced red onion, chopped cilantro leaves, chopped mint leaves, and bottled hot red pepper sauce as condiments. *Makes 8 servings*

    2 tablespoons canola oil
    1 large onion, chopped
    3 medium carrots, peeled, halved
        lengthwise, and thinly sliced
    1½ pounds trimmed boneless leg of lamb,
        cut into 1-inch pieces
    4 teaspoons mild curry powder
    6 garlic cloves, slivered
    4½ cups chicken broth

    2 tablespoons unsalted butter, plus
        additional for greasing the baking dish
    2 tablespoons minced peeled fresh
        ginger
    2 cups basmati rice (see Note)
    1½ teaspoons salt
    ¼ teaspoon saffron threads
    ¼ teaspoon ground cloves
    ¼ teaspoon cayenne pepper
    One 4-inch cinnamon stick
    ½ cup chopped dried apricots
    2 cups plain yogurt

① Heat a large saucepan over medium heat. Swirl in the canola oil, then add the onion and carrots. Cook, stirring often, until softened, about 4 minutes.

② Add the lamb; cook, stirring often, until browned, about 8 minutes.

③ Add the curry powder and half the garlic; cook, stirring often, until aromatic. Stir in 1 cup broth and bring to a simmer, scraping up any browned bits in the pan.

④ Cover, reduce the heat to low, and simmer slowly for 30 minutes.

⑤ In the meantime, position the rack in the center of the oven and preheat the oven to 350°F. Lightly butter a 13 × 9-inch baking dish and set aside.

⑥ While the lamb continues to cook, melt the butter in a second large saucepan over medium heat. Add the remainder of the garlic and the ginger; cook, stirring all the while, until slightly softened and very aromatic, about 1 minute.

⑦ Add the rice, salt, saffron, cloves, cayenne, and cinnamon stick; stir well to coat the rice in the fat and pour in the remaining 3½ cups broth. Bring to a simmer.

8 Cover, reduce the heat to low, and simmer until the rice is fairly tender but still with a little tooth to the bite, until almost all the liquid has been absorbed, about 14 minutes. Set aside off the heat.

9 After the lamb has cooked for 30 minutes, remove it from the broth with a slotted spoon, place in a medium bowl, and stir in the apricots and yogurt. (Reserve the broth in the pan.)

10 Remove the cinnamon stick from the rice. Spread half the rice evenly across the bottom of the baking dish. Top with the lamb mixture, spreading it to the sides; then spoon and spread the remainder of the rice over the top of the dish. Pour the cooking broth evenly over the dish.

11 Cover with aluminum foil and bake until the rice and lamb are tender, about 45 minutes. Set aside at room temperature for 10 minutes, covered, before serving.

Note: In Hindi, "basmati" mean aromatic. It's a long-grain rice from India now grown extensively in the U.S.

Variations: Substitute beef or veal stew meat for the lamb—or substitute chopped boneless skinless chicken thighs, but only cook them in the broth for 10 minutes.

This is a fairly complicated dish, so we only used bottled curry powder, doctored with saffron, cloves, and cayenne. If you want to make your own curry blend, omit the curry powder and its doctoring spices and use the spice blend in the Coconut Chicken Curry (page 259—do not use the coconut milk) or the Shrimp or Scallop Rogan Josh (page 367).

Porcini Risotto

Risotto is a creamy rice dish, usually served as a first course in larger Italian meals, but it can also be enjoyed on its own during the week. How do you get around all that stirring on a Wednesday evening? With a pressure cooker (see page 494)—but here the traditional technique is given first. *Makes 4 servings*

¾ ounce dried porcini mushrooms
1½ cups boiling water
1 quart (4 cups) chicken broth
2 tablespoons olive oil
1 tablespoon unsalted butter
1 large onion, thinly sliced
2 garlic cloves, minced
1 teaspoon stemmed thyme or ½ teaspoon dried thyme
1 teaspoon salt
½ teaspoon freshly ground black pepper
¼ teaspoon saffron threads, optional
1 cup Arborio rice (see box, page 494)
2 ounces Parmigiano-Reggiano, finely grated

1 Place the dried mushrooms in a large bowl, cover with the boiling water, and set aside to soften for 20 minutes.

2 Transfer the mushrooms to a cutting board with a slotted spoon, reserving their soaking liquid. Roughly chop the mushrooms. Strain the liquid through a colander lined with cheesecloth or a fine-mesh sieve like a chinoise to remove any sand. Set the mushrooms and liquid aside separately.

3 Bring the broth to the barest simmer (just a bubble or two) in a medium saucepan over low heat. Adjust the heat so the broth stays this warm without boiling. Continue with one of the two methods that follows.

Traditional method:

4 Heat the olive oil and butter in a kettle or a large saucepan over medium heat until the butter has melted. Add the onion; cook, stirring often, until softened, about 3 minutes.

5 Stir in the chopped mushrooms, garlic, thyme, salt, pepper, and saffron, if using. Cook, stirring all the while, for 30 seconds.

6 Pour in the rice; cook, stirring often, until slightly translucent, about 2 minutes.

7 Pour in the mushroom soaking liquid; cook, stirring constantly, until it has completely evaporated, about 1 minute.

8 Pour in ½ cup warmed broth. Reduce the heat to very low and stir constantly over the heat until the broth has been absorbed into the rice.

9 Add more broth in ¼-cup increments until the rice is tender but with just a little tooth to the bite, about 40 minutes, stirring all the while.

10 Remove the pan from the heat and stir in the cheese before serving.

Pressure cooker method:

4 Heat the olive oil and butter in the kettle of a large pressure cooker over medium heat until the butter has melted. Add the onion; cook, stirring often, until softened, about 3 minutes.

5 Stir in the chopped mushrooms, garlic, thyme, salt, pepper, and saffron, if using. Cook, stirring all the while, for 30 seconds.

6 Pour in the rice; cook, stirring often, until slightly translucent, about 2 minutes.

7 Raise the heat to high and add the mushroom soaking liquid and all the broth. Stir well, then lock the lid in place. Bring the cooker to high pressure, following the instructions given by the manufacturer.

8 Adjust the heat so that the pressure stays at high and cook for 7 minutes. Unlock the lid by the quick-release method, usually by running cold water over the cooker until the indicator tells you that the pressure is normal or by some other system designed by the manufacturer (check the instruction booklet).

9 Return the pot to medium heat and stir until creamy, about 1 minute. Stir in the cheese before serving.

Variations: Add 2 cups seeded and cubed butternut squash or pumpkin with the rice.

Stir in 4 cups chopped, stemmed, and washed chard, spinach, or beet greens with the stock.

Arborio Rice

Once this short-grained, fat-kerneled rice was grown only in the Po River region of Italy. Now it's grown commercially in many areas of North America. Its high starch content makes it perfect for long-simmered rice dishes, giving them a creaminess prized in Italian cooking. Spanish rice dishes, especially paella, traditionally use Valencia rice, like Arborio but slightly less chewy. Unfortunately, this varietal is hard to find in the United States, but Arborio makes an excellent if not exact substitute. Never use long-grain white rice in place of Arborio.

Rice

Rice is available in two basic forms: brown and white. Brown rice is a whole grain: it's hulled, but the bran, germ, and endosperm are intact. White rice is processed to remove the bran and germ as well as the hull, leaving only the starchy white endosperm. Red rice and some other varietals are simply types of brown rice.

To cook, bring the amount of water specified to a boil over high heat, stir in the rice, bring back to a boil, cover, reduce the heat to very low, and simmer slowly until the grains are tender.

Some types of rice should be salted before cooking; some should not (the salt toughens the bran so that the rice cannot absorb enough water to get tender). Any type, however, can have 1 tablespoon unsalted butter stirred in with the kernels.

Any of these amounts can be doubled; any white rice recipe can be tripled. Brown rice can be doubled but not tripled, as the heavy grains become glued to the bottom of the pan.

For 1 cup of raw rice . . .

Type	Characteristics	Amount of water	Salt the water?	Rinse the rice first?	Cooking time	Yield
White Long Grain	Firm, tender, bland, separate, white grains	2 cups	Yes	No	15 to 18 minutes	3¼ cups
Brown Long Grain	Chewy, nutty, thick, separate grains	2½ cups	Yes	No	30 to 45 minutes	3¼ cups
Basmati/Texmati	Firm, mildly aromatic, separate grains	1¾ cups	Yes	No	15 to 18 minutes	3½ cups
Brown Basmati	Tan, whole-grain, nutty, firm grains	2¼ cups	Yes	Yes	40 to 42 minutes	3½ cups
Jasmine	Soft, mildly perfumed, white, separate grains	1¾ cups	Yes	No	16 to 19 minutes	3¼ cups
Wehani	Dark brown to red, very nutty, chewy, and somewhat sticky grains	2½ cups	Yes	Yes—and several times	40 minutes	2¾ cups
Red	Russet-colored, thin-grained, chewy, nutty brown rice	2½ cups	No	Yes—and several times	45 minutes	3 cups
Thai Black	Whole-grain, grassy, slightly sticky, russet, black, or purple grains	1½ cups	No	Yes	25 minutes	2 cups
White Medium Grain	Sticky, chewy, somewhat glutinous grains	2 cups	Yes	Yes—and several times	20 to 22 minutes	3¼ cups
Brown Medium Grain	Less sticky, fat, chewy grains	2¼ cups	No	Yes—and several times	40 minutes	3¼ cups

A Year of Paella

Paella is a saffron-infused Spanish rice dish that includes fish and other meats. We're unabashed fans—this is our favorite dinner party dish. The rice is cooked uncovered, usually in a large paella pan: a concave, two-handled, shallow baking dish a little over a foot long. However, a 14-inch cast-iron skillet works just as well. Although the dish is traditionally cooked in a specially designed well over an open flame, an oven provides the radiant heat we can't reproduce with a top-of-the-range, flat-burner stove. At the end, the rice should be creamy but with a little bite, a good contrast to the meat and/or shellfish. So here's a year's worth of our favorite rice dish, one for every season.

Spring Paella with Lamb, Pancetta, Peas, and Artichokes

Makes 6 servings

- 5 cups (1 quart plus 1 cup) chicken broth
- ¼ teaspoon saffron threads
- 1½ pounds lamb loin, trimmed of any surface fat
- ½ teaspoon salt
- ½ teaspoon freshly ground black pepper
- 3 tablespoons olive oil
- 6 ounces thick-cut pancetta, diced
- 1 large leek, white and pale green parts only, sliced lengthwise, washed carefully of any sand in the inner rings, and thinly sliced
- 8 baby artichokes, halved, dark outer leaves removed, and stems trimmed
- 1 cup dry, light white wine, preferably a Spanish white
- 2 tablespoons chopped rosemary leaves
- 2½ cups Arborio or Valencia rice
- 1½ cups shelled fresh peas or thawed frozen peas

1. Heat the broth and saffron in a medium saucepan over low heat until steaming but not simmering. Reduce the heat to very low, cover, and keep warm.

2. Position the rack in the center of the oven and preheat the oven to 375°F. Season the lamb loin with salt and pepper.

3. Heat a 14-inch paella pan or cast-iron skillet over medium heat. Swirl in the olive oil, then add the loin. Brown on all sides, about 6 minutes. Transfer to a plate and set aside.

4. Add the pancetta; cook, stirring often, until lightly browned, about 4 minutes.

5. Add the leek; cook, stirring frequently, until softened, about 3 minutes. Add the baby artichoke halves; cook, stirring often, until aromatic, about 1 minute.

6. Add the wine and rosemary; bring the sauce to a simmer, scraping up any browned bits in the pan. Simmer until the wine has been reduced to a thick glaze, stirring once in a while, about 5 minutes.

7. Stir in the rice to coat well with the sauce; cook, stirring constantly, until translucent, about 1 minute.

8. Pour in the warmed broth mixture and bring to a simmer. Reduce the heat and simmer, uncovered, for 10 minutes, stirring occasionally.

9. Meanwhile, slice the lamb into 1-inch pieces. When the rice has cooked for 10 minutes, tuck the slices into the simmering sauce. Sprinkle the peas over the top.

10. Place in the oven and bake until the liquid has been mostly absorbed and the rice is fairly tender,

about 15 minutes. Remove from the oven, set on a wire rack, cover tightly with aluminum foil, and set aside at room temperature for 10 minutes before serving.

Summer Paella with Lobster, Mussels, Scallops, and Rosé Wine

Makes 6 servings

3 cups chicken broth
1 cup bottled clam juice
¼ teaspoon saffron threads
¼ cup olive oil
1 large yellow onion, chopped
4 garlic cloves, minced
4 plum or Roma tomatoes, chopped
1 cup rosé wine
2 teaspoons packed minced oregano leaves or 1 teaspoon dried oregano
2 teaspoons stemmed thyme or 1 teaspoon dried thyme
½ teaspoon salt
½ teaspoon freshly ground black pepper
2½ cups Arborio or Valencia rice
One 2-pound live lobster (see Note)
½ pound green beans, stems trimmed and cut into 1-inch pieces
1½ pounds mussels, debearded and scrubbed of any sand (see page 360)
1 pound sea scallops

❶ Heat the broth, clam juice, and saffron in a medium saucepan until steaming but not simmering. Reduce the heat to very low, cover, and keep warm without boiling.

❷ Position the rack in the center of the oven and preheat the oven to 375°F.

❸ Heat a 14-inch paella pan or cast-iron skillet over medium heat. Swirl in the olive oil, then add the onion. Cook, stirring often, until translucent, about 4 minutes. Add the garlic and cook for 30 seconds.

❹ Stir in the tomatoes; continue cooking, stirring often, until they begin to break down, about 3 minutes.

❺ Pour in the wine; bring to a simmer, scraping up any browned bits in the pan. Raise the heat and simmer until reduced by half, about 3 minutes.

❻ Stir in the oregano, thyme, salt, and pepper. Then stir in the rice and the warmed broth. Bring to a simmer, reduce the heat to medium, and simmer for 10 minutes.

❼ Meanwhile, set the lobster on a lipped cutting board to catch any internal juices. Plunge the tip of a sharp knife into its head about ½ inch behind its eye stalks, thereby piercing the brain and instantly killing it. Slice the lobster in half lengthwise.

❽ Stir the green beans into the simmering rice, then set the mussels around the perimeter of the pan, partially submerging them. Arrange the scallops in the pan in a circle inside the mussels, partially submerging them as well, and then lay the lobster halves in the center of the pan cut side down.

❾ Place in the oven and bake for 15 minutes, or until most of the liquid has been absorbed and the rice is fairly tender. Transfer to a wire rack, cover tightly with aluminum foil, and set aside for 10 minutes. If desired, remove the lobster meat from the shell and place on top of the paella before serving.

Note: If you don't want to work with a whole live lobster, substitute two frozen, in-shell, 12-ounce tails, thawed and split in half lengthwise.

Autumn Paella with Chicken, Sausage, Shrimp, and Olives

Makes 8 servings

1 quart (4 cups) chicken broth

¼ teaspoon salt

¼ teaspoon saffron threads

3 tablespoons olive oil

¾ pound sweet or hot Italian sausage, cut into 2-inch pieces

3 pounds chicken thighs (see Note)

1 large yellow onion, chopped

1 medium green bell pepper, cored, seeded, and thinly sliced

1¾ cups canned diced tomatoes

½ cup dry sherry, dry vermouth, or dry white wine

1 tablespoon smoked paprika

2 teaspoons stemmed thyme or 1 teaspoon dried thyme

2½ cups Arborio or Valencia rice

¼ pound medium shrimp (about 30 per pound), peeled and deveined

½ cup halved pitted green olives

1 Heat the broth, salt, and saffron over medium heat until steaming; do not boil. Cover, reduce the heat to very low, and keep warm without simmering.

2 Heat a 14-inch paella pan or cast-iron skillet over medium heat. Swirl in the olive oil, then add the sausage. Cook until browned, turning occasionally, about 8 minutes. Transfer to a large plate.

3 Add the chicken thighs; cook, turning a couple of times, until browned, about 8 minutes. Transfer to the plate as well.

4 Position the rack in the center of the oven and preheat the oven to 375°F.

5 Meanwhile, pour off all but 2 tablespoons fat from the pan. Add the onion and bell pepper; cook, stirring often, until softened, about 3 minutes.

6 Pour in the tomatoes and the sherry, vermouth, or wine. Stir in the smoked paprika and thyme; bring to a simmer. Continue cooking until almost all the liquid in the pan has been absorbed, about 10 minutes, stirring occasionally.

7 Stir in the rice; continue stirring over the heat until translucent, about 1 minute.

8 Pour in the warmed broth mixture and bring to a full simmer. Reduce the heat somewhat and simmer, uncovered, for 10 minutes.

9 Return the chicken thighs and sausage to the pan, tucking them into the simmering rice.

10 Arrange the shrimp over the top of the dish, pressing them down just slightly into the sauce. Sprinkle the olives over the dish.

11 Place in the oven and bake until an instant-read meat thermometer inserted into one of the chicken thighs without touching bone registers 165°F (our preference) or 180°F (the USDA recommendation), 15 to 20 minutes. Transfer to a wire rack, cover tightly with aluminum foil, and set aside at room temperature for 10 minutes before serving.

Note: You can use skin-on or skinless thighs. If you choose the lower-fat, skinless version, brown them in step 2 only about 5 minutes, turning once.

Winter Paella with Rabbit, Quail, and Duck Confit

Makes 6 servings

6 tablespoons olive oil

3 quails, quartered

¾ pound chorizo, preferably dried Spanish chorizo, cut into 1-inch pieces

1 small rabbit, quartered

1 quart (4 cups) beef or veal broth, plus additional as necessary (see Note)

1 cup red wine

¼ teaspoon saffron threads

2 duck confit legs

1 large yellow onion, chopped

6 garlic cloves, chopped

1¾ cups canned diced tomatoes

2 teaspoons stemmed thyme or 1 teaspoon dried thyme

1½ teaspoons smoked paprika

1 teaspoon salt

1 bay leaf

2½ cups Arborio or Valencia rice

1 Have a large platter standing by to hold all the meat that you'll brown. Heat a large skillet over medium heat. (If you're going to use a 14-inch cast-iron pan to make the paella, use it to brown the meat.) Swirl in 2 tablespoons olive oil, then slip in the quails and brown on both sides, about 8 minutes in total. Transfer to the platter.

2 Add the chorizo and cook, stirring often, until well browned, about 5 minutes. Transfer to the platter as well; cover and set in the refrigerator.

3 Drain all but 2 tablespoons fat from the pan and slip the rabbit quarters into the pan. Cook, turning once, until browned, about 8 minutes.

4 Pour in the broth, red wine, and saffron; bring to a simmer, scraping up any browned bits in the pan. Cover, reduce the heat to low, and simmer slowly until the rabbit is tender and cooked through, about 30 minutes. Remove the rabbit to the platter and cool until you can handle it, about 10 minutes. Keep the cooking liquid warm in the skillet over very low heat; you should have about 4 cups broth (add more if necessary).

5 Once the rabbit has cooled, so you can handle it, take the meat off the bones, discarding the bones and cutting the meat into bite-sized pieces. Also take the meat off the duck confit legs, shredding it with a fork. Set all the meat aside at room temperature.

6 Position the rack in the center of the oven and preheat the oven to 375°F.

7 Heat a 14-inch paella pan or cast-iron skillet over medium heat. Swirl in the remaining 4 tablespoons (¼ cup) oil and add the onion. Cook, stirring often, until translucent, about 4 minutes. Add the garlic and cook for 1 minute.

8 Stir in the tomatoes, thyme, smoked paprika, salt, and bay leaf. Cook, stirring often, until almost all the liquid has been absorbed, about 10 minutes.

9 Add the rice to the pan and stir over the heat until translucent, about 1 minute. Strain the warmed broth mixture into the pan (thereby removing any bits of bones and such) and bring to a simmer. Cook, uncovered, for 10 minutes.

10 Tuck all the meat into the simmering sauce, arranging it around the pan. Place in the oven and bake until almost all the liquid has been absorbed and the rice is fairly tender, about 15 minutes.

Transfer to a wire rack, cover tightly with aluminum foil, and set aside at room temperature for 10 minutes before serving.

Note: If you use standard canned beef broth, enrich it with 2 teaspoons beef or veal demi-glace, found in the freezer case of high-end markets.

❋ Beans and Lentils ❋

With their high protein content, dense pack of important minerals (like calcium, phosphorus, and iron), and portability when dried, these legumes have been a staple for at least four thousand years. Dried beans should be firm and tight with few cracks, wrinkles, or indentations (all signs of improper storage).

Black-Eyed Pea and Ham Hock Stew

Black-eyed peas are a popular American legume, originally from China but brought to the States via the slave trade. *Makes 6 servingss*

2 tablespoons peanut oil
1 large onion, chopped
2 celery ribs, thinly sliced
1 quart (4 cups) vegetable broth
3½ cups canned diced tomatoes, drained in
   a fine-mesh colander in the sink
1 cup dried black-eyed peas
2 teaspoons stemmed thyme or 1 teaspoon
   dried thyme
¼ teaspoon cayenne pepper
One 1-pound smoked ham hock, preferably
   nitrate-free
1 garlic head, roasted (see page 460)

❶ Heat a large saucepan or soup pot over medium heat. Swirl in the peanut oil, then add the onion and celery. Cook, stirring often, until softened, about 5 minutes.

❷ Stir in the broth, tomatoes, black-eyed peas, thyme, and cayenne; bring to a simmer, stirring frequently. Nestle the ham hock into the stew; then cover, reduce the heat to low, and simmer for 1 hour and 15 minutes.

❸ Remove the hock from the stew; cut the meat off the bone and shred it into small bits. Stir these back into the stew. Also, squeeze the roasted garlic out of the papery hulls and into the stew.

❹ Stir well, cover, and continue simmering, stirring occasionally, until the black-eyed peas are quite tender and the stew has thickened somewhat, about 30 minutes.

Variations: Add 1 carrot, peeled and thinly sliced, or 2 parsnips, peeled and thinly sliced, with the celery.

Omit the ham hock. Add 2 teaspoons smoked paprika with the thyme. After the stew has cooked for 1 hour and 15 minutes, stir in 8 ounces chopped boneless skinless chicken thighs or chopped boneless dark turkey meat.

Cuban Black Beans

Here's a pot of black beans that's great as a side for Southwestern or other spicy dishes. While the beans can cook pretty much unaided for the first part of the recipe, they need to be watched carefully during the last 20 minutes to make sure they don't stick and scorch. *Makes 8 servings*

1 pound dried black beans
2 tablespoons canola oil
2 medium yellow onions, chopped
1 medium green bell pepper, cored, seeded, and chopped
1 celery rib, minced
2 garlic cloves, minced
¼ cup chopped cilantro leaves
1 tablespoon minced oregano leaves
1 teaspoon salt
½ teaspoon freshly ground black pepper
Several dashes of hot red pepper sauce
2 bay leaves
One 4-inch cinnamon stick
6 cups vegetable broth
3 tablespoons sherry vinegar
2 teaspoons sugar

① Place the beans in a large bowl, cover with cool water to a depth of 2 inches, and set aside to soak for at least 8 hours or up to 12 hours. If desired, change the water once or twice to aid in the reduction of intestinal distress. Alternatively, bring the beans and enough water to cover them by 1 inch to a boil in a large saucepan; drain, place in a large bowl, cover with cool water to a depth of 2 inches, and set aside to soak for 2 hours.

② Heat a large pot over medium heat. Swirl in the canola oil, then add the onions, bell pepper, and celery. Cook, stirring often, until softened, about 4 minutes. Add the garlic and cook for 30 seconds.

③ Stir in the cilantro, oregano, salt, pepper, hot red pepper sauce, bay leaves, and cinnamon stick. Cook, stirring all the while, until aromatic, about 20 seconds.

④ Stir in the beans, then pour in the broth and enough additional water to cover them by a depth of 2 inches. Raise the heat to high and bring to a simmer.

⑤ Reduce the heat to low and simmer, uncovered, until the beans are tender and the whole thing is just a little soupier than baked beans, 2 to 2½ hours.

⑥ Mash some of the beans against the side of the pot with a wooden spoon, then stir well so they thicken the mixture somewhat. Stir in the vinegar and sugar; continue cooking, stirring frequently, until the beans are very tender and most of the liquid has been absorbed, about 20 minutes. Discard the bay leaves and cinnamon stick before serving.

Variations: Add 1 medium carrot, shredded through the large holes of a box grater, with the onion.

Add 1 ancho chile, stemmed and seeded, or 1 chipotle in adobo, seeded, with the garlic.

Cut a large orange into quarters, add to the pot with the broth, and simmer with the beans. Discard the orange before serving.

Take the skin off 2 duck confit legs; add them to the pot with the broth. Remove the legs when done, debone the meat, shred it, and stir it back into the beans.

Chop 1 pound boneless skinless chicken thighs into ½-inch pieces, then add them to the pot with the vinegar.

Cuban Black Beans and Rice: Serve this dish over cooked white rice, ladling the beans over the rice bed. You can also serve South American Picadillo (pages 93–94) on the side.

Black Bean Soup: After you've mashed some of the beans to the sides of the pot, add up to 4 cups (1 quart) additional broth to thin the mixture out into a soup; continue cooking until the beans are tender, about 20 minutes.

Persian-Inspired Beans with Preserved Lemon and Dates

These sweet beans would be a welcome alternative to baked beans at any barbecue. Look for preserved lemons in the Middle Eastern section of your market. They're quite salty, so there's no additional salt in this dish. *Makes 6 servings*

2 cups dried pinto beans
2 tablespoons olive oil
1 large red onion, chopped
2 large carrots peeled, halved lengthwise, and thinly sliced
2 teaspoons ground coriander
2 teaspoons ground cumin
½ teaspoon ground cinnamon
½ teaspoon ground cloves
1½ quarts (6 cups) vegetable broth
¼ cup chopped pitted dates (do not use sugared dates)
2 preserved lemons, chopped

1 Place the beans in a large bowl, cover with cool water to a depth of 2 inches, and set aside to soak for at least 8 hours or overnight. If desired, change the water once during soaking. For a quicker soak, bring the beans and enough water to cover them by 1 inch to a boil in a large saucepan, drain, place in a large bowl, cover with cool water to a depth of 2 inches, and set aside to soak for 2 hours.

2 Heat a large saucepan or soup pot over medium heat. Swirl in the olive oil, then add the onion and carrots. Cook, stirring often, until softened, about 5 minutes.

3 Stir in the coriander, cumin, cinnamon, and cloves. Cook, stirring constantly, until aromatic, about 20 seconds.

4 Pour in the broth; stir in the dates and preserved lemons. Drain the beans in a colander set in the sink and rinse well. Add to the pan and bring to a simmer, stirring frequently.

5 Cover, reduce the heat to low, and simmer for 1 hour, stirring once or twice.

6 Uncover and continue simmering, stirring occasionally, until the beans are tender and have just begun to break down, about 1 more hour.

Persian-Style Beans with Lamb: Add an additional 2 tablespoons oil to the pot after you've cooked the onions and celery; add 1 pound cubed and trimmed lamb stew meat, brown well (about 5 minutes), and then continue with the recipe.

Black Bean and Plantain Puree

This is a sort of Latin American equivalent of mashed potatoes. Use it as a bed for thin white-fleshed fish fillets (see pages 318–326) or Barbecued Turkey (page 289). *Makes 4 servings as a side*

2 tablespoons canola oil
1 small red onion, chopped
2 garlic cloves, minced
1 large ripe (almost black) yellow plantain, peeled and thinly sliced
2 teaspoons chili powder
1 teaspoon ground cumin
½ teaspoon salt
1¼ cups canned black beans, drained and rinsed
⅓ cup vegetable broth
1 tablespoon lime juice
Several dashes of hot red pepper sauce

1 Heat a large saucepan over medium heat. Swirl in the canola oil, then add the onion and cook, stirring often, until soft, about 2 minutes. Add the garlic and cook for 30 seconds.

2 Toss in the plantain slices; cook, turning often, until softened, about 3 minutes.

3 Add the chili powder, cumin, and salt; cook, stirring constantly, until aromatic, about 20 seconds.

4 Add the beans and broth; bring to a simmer. Cover, reduce the heat to low, and simmer until all the liquid has been absorbed, about 3 minutes.

5 Pour the contents of the pan into a large blender or a food processor fitted with the chopping blade; add the lime juice and hot red pepper sauce. Blend or process until chunky or smooth, your preference. Serve warm or at room temperature—or place in a container, cover, and store in the refrigerator for up to 3 days. (See page 138 for tips about pureeing hot liquids in a blender.)

Variations: Add 1 small green bell pepper, cored, seeded, and chopped, with the onion—or stir the pepper raw into the puree, thereby giving it a little crunch.

Add 1 seeded and chopped fresh jalapeño chile with the spices.

Can't get enough beans? Try Black Bean Dip (page 44), White Bean and Sun-Dried Tomato Dip (page 45), Lime Bean and Kale Soup (page 144), White Bean Soup with Leeks, Tarragon, and Thyme (page 146), Escarole Soup with White Beans and Roasted Garlic (page 150), Turkey Chili Verde (page 298), and Spaghetti Squash, Cannellini Beans, and Broccoli Raab (page 471).

Beer-Baked Beans

A combination of chili sauce, beer, molasses, and spices will make this an irresistible side at your next barbecue. And you don't have to tell a soul it's a vegetarian dish. *Makes 6 servings*

3½ cups canned pinto beans, drained and
    rinsed (two 15-ounce cans)
One 12-ounce bottle beer, preferably an
    American lager or a Mexican dark beer
1 medium yellow onion, chopped
1 medium green bell pepper, cored, seeded,
    and chopped
⅓ cup bottled chili sauce, such as Heinz
2 tablespoons cider vinegar
1½ tablespoons dry mustard
1 tablespoon unsulfured molasses
1 tablespoon Worcestershire sauce
1 tablespoon tomato paste
½ teaspoon freshly ground black pepper
Several dashes of hot red pepper sauce

1 Position the rack in the center of the oven and preheat the oven to 400°F.

2 Stir all the ingredients in an oven-safe pot or casserole over medium heat until simmering.

3 Place in the oven and bake until thick and bubbling, stirring occasionally, about 1 hour.

Variations: Add any of the following to the pot: ¼ cup chopped raisins, 1 tablespoon chili powder, 1 teaspoon dried oregano, 1 teaspoon dried thyme, 1 teaspoon ground cinnamon, or ¼ teaspoon grated nutmeg.

Lentil, Walnut, and Apple Salad

An excellent source of iron and phosphorus, a lentil is a legume's pulse—or its dried seed. Brown lentils, the most common, have their seed casings removed in processing. Lentils break down quite easily, so take care not to overcook them. Chop the apple, celery, and walnuts to about the size of the lentils. *Makes 4 main-course servings*

1½ cups dried brown lentils, rinsed and
   picked over for small stones
1 tart green apple such as Granny Smith,
   peeled, cored, and finely chopped
2 celery ribs, finely chopped
½ cup toasted walnut pieces, finely
   chopped
3 tablespoons cider vinegar
2 teaspoons stemmed thyme
½ teaspoon salt
½ teaspoon freshly ground black pepper
¼ cup walnut oil

1 Place the lentils in a large pot, cover with water to a depth of 2 inches, and bring to a boil over medium-high heat, stirring occasionally.

2 Reduce the heat to low and simmer, stirring occasionally, until tender but with still a little resistance when bitten, about 10 minutes. Drain in a colander set in the sink and rinse well.

3 Pour the lentils in a serving bowl and toss with the apple, celery, and walnuts.

4 Whisk the vinegar, thyme, salt, and pepper in a small bowl; slowly whisk in the walnut oil. Pour over the lentils and toss well.

Variations: Substitute pecan pieces or unsalted shelled pistachios for the walnuts.

Add ½ cup dried cranberries, dried cherries, or dried blueberries with the apple.

Add 1 small red onion or 1 medium shallot, finely chopped, with the apple.

For a much stronger taste, use toasted walnut oil or mustard oil.

Lentil-Nut Patties

These vegetarian "burgers" are a great vehicle for mango chutney, ketchup, bottled chili sauce, salsa (see page 47), or any mayonnaise (see page 121). *Makes about a dozen patties*

¾ cup dried brown lentils, rinsed and
   picked over for small stones
1 tablespoon unsalted butter
1 medium onion, chopped
2 garlic cloves, minced
1 teaspoon ground cumin
1 teaspoon ground ginger
1 teaspoon salt
½ teaspoon turmeric
½ teaspoon ground cinnamon
¼ teaspoon ground cloves
1½ cups toasted walnut pieces
2 large egg yolks
2 tablespoons whole wheat flour, plus
   additional for rolling the patties
2 to 3 tablespoons canola oil, or more as
   necessary

1 Bring a large saucepan of water to a boil over high heat. Stir in the lentils, reduce the heat, and simmer until the lentils are so tender you can mash them with a fork, about 40 minutes.

2 Meanwhile, melt the butter in a large skillet over low heat. Add the onion and cook slowly, stirring frequently, until golden, about 10 minutes. Add the garlic and continue cooking until aromatic, about 1 more minute.

3 Drain the lentils and place them in a food processor fitted with the chopping blade. Add the en-

tire contents of the skillet along with the cumin, ginger, salt, turmeric, cinnamon, and cloves. Pulse once or twice, just to combine.

4 Add the walnut pieces, egg yolks, and flour. Process until fairly smooth, scraping down the sides of the bowl as necessary. Scrape the mixture into a large bowl and set aside to cool and stabilize for 15 minutes.

5 Dust your hands with flour, then roll 3 full, rounded tablespoons of the mixture into a ball. Roll it lightly in some more flour placed on a plate, then flatten and compress slightly into a patty. Set aside and continue making more patties.

6 Heat a large skillet, preferably nonstick, over medium heat. Swirl in 1 tablespoon canola oil, then slip as many patties into the pan as will comfortably fit in one layer. Fry until lightly browned, about 3 minutes, pressing the patties down once or twice with a flat metal spatula. Flip and fry until the other side has browned somewhat, about 3 more minutes. Transfer to a wire rack to drain, then add another tablespoon of oil to the skillet and continue frying more patties.

Variations: Add ¼ teaspoon cayenne pepper with the dried spices.

Substitute 1 tablespoon garam masala and ½ teaspoon salt for the dried spices.

Substitute the following mixture for the dried spices: 2 teaspoons chili powder, 1 teaspoon dried oregano, 1 teaspoon salt, ½ teaspoon ground cinnamon, and ½ teaspoon ground cumin.

More lentil dishes include Vegetarian Chopped Liver (page 87); Mushroom, Barley, and Lentil Soup (page 143); Greek-Inspired Red Lentil Soup (page 143); and Burmese-Inspired Chicken and Yellow Lentil Curry (page 283).

French Lentils with Bacon

French lentils—also known as green lentils—have a distinctly nutty taste, partly because the outer coating of the seed has been left on after processing. Here's a dish that combines two French classics: an egg-and-bacon salad and French lentils. *Makes 6 servings*

1 quart (4 cups) water
1½ cups green French lentils, washed and picked over for small stones
½ pound slab bacon, chopped into ½-inch cubes
2 large shallots, peeled, lobes halved, and thinly sliced
2 hard-cooked eggs (see page 59), shelled and chopped
½ cup sliced pitted green olives
2 tablespoons red wine vinegar
1½ teaspoons coarse-grained mustard
1 teaspoon salt
½ teaspoon freshly ground black pepper
6 tablespoons olive oil

1 Bring the water to a simmer in a large saucepan set over high heat. Stir in the lentils, reduce the heat to medium-low, and simmer until tender but not until the lentils begin to break apart, about 15 minutes. Drain in a fine-mesh colander set in the sink. Transfer to a serving bowl.

2 Fry the bacon in a large skillet set over medium heat until crunchy, browned, and irresistible, stirring often, about 5 minutes. Use a slotted spoon to transfer the bacon to the bowl with the lentils.

3 Drain off all but about 3 tablespoons fat in the skillet and return it to medium heat. Add the

shallots and cook, stirring often, until golden, about 5 minutes.

4 Add the contents of the skillet to the bowl with the lentils and bacon. Also stir in the hard-cooked eggs and olives.

5 Whisk the vinegar, mustard, salt, and pepper in a small bowl; slowly whisk in the olive oil until emulsified. Pour over the lentil mixture and toss well. (The salad may be made up to 2 days in advance; cover and refrigerate but allow it to come back to room temperature before serving.)

❊ *Tofu* ❊

Tofu, often a meat substitute, is made from soymilk and either calcium sulfate or nigari, a coagulant derived from salt. (Brands of less quality are coagulated with vinegar or lemon juice; read the label carefully.) There are basically four kinds of tofu: soft, firm, extra-firm, and a special "silken" variety prized for its smooth texture. Recently, "silken extra-firm" tofu has shown up in high-end markets, a boon to those seeking to have a meaty but still smooth texture.

Marinated Tofu Salad

Tofu replaces the mozzarella in this no-cook antipasto platter. *Makes 8 servings*

One 12-ounce package of silken extra-firm tofu
2 garlic cloves, minced
¼ cup white balsamic or white wine vinegar
2 teaspoons capers, drained and rinsed
1 teaspoon Dijon mustard
1 teaspoon minced rosemary leaves
½ teaspoon salt
½ teaspoon freshly ground black pepper
½ cup extra virgin olive oil
One 14-ounce can artichoke hearts packed in water, drained, rinsed, and quartered
One 12-ounce jar roasted peppers or pimientos, drained and cut into thin strips
One 7-ounce can hearts of palm, drained, rinsed, and cut into 2-inch chunks
1 small fennel bulb, bottom sliced off, fronds trimmed and discarded, the remainder cut into thin strips
1½ cups cherry tomatoes
¼ cup chopped packed parsley leaves
Jarred peperoncini and stuffed olives for garnish

1 Drain the tofu and remove it intact from its container. Wrap in four paper towels and place on a plate in the sink. Set a second plate on top of the block, then weight it with a small can of vegetables or beans for 10 minutes.

2 Meanwhile, whisk the garlic, vinegar, capers, mustard, rosemary, salt, and pepper in a large bowl. Whisk in the olive oil in a slow stream.

3 Remove the weight and the plate over the tofu, carefully unwrap the block, and discard any water on the plate. Cut the tofu into ½-inch cubes.

Place them in the dressing and stir well. Cover and refrigerate for at least 2 hours or up to 24 hours.

④ Combine the artichoke hearts, roasted peppers, hearts of palm, fennel, cherry tomatoes, and parsley in a large serving bowl. Pour in the tofu and all the dressing; toss gently. Sprinkle some peperoncini and stuffed olives over the platter before serving.

Sweet-and-Spicy Tofu Steak

By pressing some of the liquid out of firm tofu, its texture becomes much meatier. *Makes 4 servings*

> Two 14-ounce blocks extra-firm tofu
> ¼ cup soy sauce
> ¼ cup oyster sauce
> 3 tablespoons packed dark brown sugar
> 2 tablespoons lime juice
> 2 tablespoons fish sauce
> 2 teaspoons Asian red chili sauce
> Canola oil for oiling the grill grate or a
>   grill pan

① Slice each tofu block "horizontally" into 2 thin rectangles. Place the halves on a cutting board lined with paper towels; lay paper towels over the top of the tofu as well. Top with a second cutting board. Weight the top with a few apples, a 12-ounce can, or a small container filled with water. Set on a towel (to catch drips) in the refrigerator for 1½ hours.

② Place the compressed tofu blocks in a shallow baking dish. Whisk the soy sauce, oyster sauce, brown sugar, lime juice, fish sauce, and chili sauce in a small bowl. Pour over the tofu, turn, and marinate for 10 minutes. Turn and marinate for 10 more minutes.

③ Lightly oil the grill grate; prepare a gas grill for high-heat cooking or build a high-heat, well-ashed coal bed in a charcoal grill. Alternatively, lightly oil a grill pan and heat it over medium-high heat.

④ Grill the tofu steaks for 2 minutes per side, turning once, until marked, lightly browned, and hot. (Turn them with a wide metal spatula to keep from tearing them.) Serve immediately.

Variations: Add any of the following to the marinade: 2 tablespoons chopped scallion, 2 tablespoons minced peeled fresh ginger, 1 teaspoon ground cinnamon, or 1 teaspoon freshly ground black pepper.

Stuffed Tofu

Make these tofu pockets ahead, storing them, covered, in the refrigerator for up to 2 days; then steam them when you're ready. Each of the three fillings is paired with a sauce. *Makes 4 servings*

> Two 14-ounce blocks extra-firm tofu
> One of the three filling and sauce
>   combinations that follow

① Cut the tofu blocks "horizontally" into 2 thin rectangles, then cut each of these in half the short way. Make a pocket in each block by taking a small paring knife and inserting its tip, parallel to your work surface, into the center of one cut side. Slice gently forward, then take the knife out and slice the other way; repeat several times, thereby increasing the size of the pocket without slicing through any side of the block.

② Stuff an eighth (about 2 tablespoons) of the prepared filling into each pocket, using a small flatware spoon. Once all the pockets are stuffed, cover the tofu and refrigerate for at least 1 hour or up to 2 days.

3 Depending on the kind of vegetable steamer you have, fill it with the stuffed tofu blocks and set it over or in a saucepan with about an inch of water in the bottom. Bring to a boil over high heat; then cover, reduce the heat to low, and steam for 10 minutes. Serve the pockets by napping the prepared vinaigrette, sauce, or salsa over them on the plate.

Three Stuffings and Sauces for Stuffed Tofu

1. Shiitake Stuffing and Lemon Tahini Vinaigrette

For the stuffing, process 8 ounces shiitake mushroom caps, 1 quartered medium shallot, ½ cup walnut pieces, 2 teaspoons Dijon mustard, 2 teaspoons stemmed thyme (or 1 teaspoon dried), 1 teaspoon cornstarch, 1 teaspoon salt, and ½ teaspoon freshly ground black pepper in a food processor fitted with the chopping blade until smooth and pastelike, scraping down the sides of the canister as necessary.

For the vinaigrette, see page 100.

2. Ground Pork and Shrimp Stuffing with a Peanut-Ginger Sauce

For the stuffing, process 8 ounces ground pork, 4 ounces peeled and deveined shrimp, 2 teaspoons minced peeled fresh ginger, 4 chopped scallions, and 2 garlic cloves in a food processor until uniform and fairly smooth if still a little chunky.

For the sauce, whisk 3 tablespoons soy sauce, 2 tablespoons rice vinegar, 1 tablespoon minced peeled fresh ginger, 1 tablespoon peanut butter, teaspoon sugar, and several dashes of hot red pepper sauce in a small bowl until creamy.

3. Latin American Pinto Bean Filling and Salsa

For the stuffing, process 2 cups drained and rinsed canned pinto beans, 2 tablespoons lime juice, 2 tablespoons olive oil, 2 teaspoons ground cumin, 2 teaspoons fresh oregano leaves, 1 teaspoon salt, ½ teaspoon freshly ground black pepper, and several dashes of hot red pepper sauce.

For the salsa, see page 47 or use a purchased salsa.

Cakes

ONCE THE PROVINCE OF THE ROYAL AND RICH, CAKES WERE EATEN BY those who could afford personal bakers and the requisite ovens to make these heavenly but hardly nutritious concoctions. But after World War II, ovens became standardized, the middle class got its purchasing power, and the great Age of Cake began.

It shows no sign of subsiding. While doing cooking demos, we've found nothing brings out the stories like a cake: "My mother made . . ." or "For my birthday we . . ." Fad diets may come and go; carbs may be vilified, tolerated, or chemically modified; but a cake remains one of the kitchen's best pleasures.

That's because it is, in some ways, the kitchen's ultimate dessert. Part quick bread, part confection, cakes are almost iconic. They mark time for us: celebrations, anniversaries, promotions, graduations, and birthdays. A cake's always there at the moment of change, the moment when we slow time down. Who ever heard of a birthday pie?

But cakes have suffered from both the quick-fix industry and from obtuse recipes that insist on a combination of eight flours and four fats. Neither could be further from the truth. As long as you follow a few easy rules, you can indeed have your cake and eat it, too. No wonder cake remains the real reason anyone has an oven.

Some of these are easy; others, showstoppers. None needs buttercream or esoteric techniques. What else do they have in common? They don't take much effort but give you maximum results.

One-Bowl Chocolate Buttermilk Loaf Cake

Use a metal or silicone loaf pan; a glass one can superheat the chocolate, rendering the cake bitter. *Makes one 9 × 5-inch loaf cake*

    ¼ cup canola oil, plus additional for greasing
        the loaf pan
    1½ cups all-purpose flour, plus additional for
        dusting the pan
    1 cup sugar
    ⅓ cup sifted unsweetened cocoa powder
    1 teaspoon baking soda
    ½ teaspoon salt
    1 cup regular or low-fat buttermilk
        (do not use fat-free)
    1 teaspoon vanilla extract

1 Position the rack in the center of the oven and preheat the oven to 350°F. Dab a little canola oil on a paper towel and lightly grease a 9 × 5 × 3-inch loaf pan. Dust the pan evenly with flour before shaking out the excess.

2 Whisk the flour, sugar, cocoa powder, baking soda, and salt in a large bowl. Then stir in the buttermilk, canola oil, and vanilla with a wooden spoon just until an even if slightly grainy batter forms. (Do not beat—the cake will be tough because of the stretched wheat glutens.)

3 Pour the batter into the prepared pan, smooth it to the corners, and bake until puffed and firm, until a toothpick inserted into the center of the cake comes out with a few moist crumbs attached, 60 to 70 minutes.

To cool and unmold: Set the pan on a wire rack for 10 minutes; then turn the cake out, remove the pan, and cool completely on a wire rack.

To store: Wrap in plastic and store at room temperature for up to 2 days or in the freezer for up to 2 months.

Variations: Substitute 3 tablespoons unsalted butter, melted and cooled, for the canola oil. Grease the pan with unsalted butter as well.

Add 1 cup of any of the following or any combination of the following to the flour mixture before adding the buttermilk: semisweet chocolate chips, white chocolate chips, chopped raisins, dried currants, dried cherries, dried blueberries, walnut pieces, pecan pieces, or chopped skinned hazelnuts.

Add any of the following with the vanilla: 1½ teaspoons ground cinnamon, 1 teaspoon maple extract, 1 teaspoon rum extract, or ¼ teaspoon grated nutmeg.

Pay attention to the pan size. Some cakes are made in 8-inch round pans; some, in 9-inch pans. Switching pans will result in flattened or overflowing layers.

Pound Cake

We've cut down the butter for a light cake with a delicate crumb. *Makes one 9 × 5-inch loaf cake*

> 16 tablespoons (2 sticks) cool unsalted butter, cut into chunks, plus additional for greasing the pan
> 2 cups cake flour, plus additional for dusting the pan (see page 655)
> 5 large eggs, separated (see page 19), at room temperature
> ½ teaspoon salt
> ½ teaspoon cream of tartar
> 1 cup sugar
> 2 teaspoons vanilla extract

1 Position the rack in the center of the oven and preheat the oven to 350°F. Lightly butter a 9 × 5 × 3-inch loaf pan; dust it with flour, making sure the joints and corners are well coated before tapping out any excess.

2 If you're working with a stand mixer, attach the whisk. Place the egg whites and salt in a large bowl and beat with an electric mixer at medium speed until frothy, about 1 minute. Add the cream of tartar, increase the speed to high, and continue beating until soft peaks form in the spot where the beaters are turned off and lifted out of the mixture, about 3 minutes.

3 With the beaters running at high speed, add ⅔ cup sugar in 1-tablespoon increments until glossy, firm, moist peaks can be formed in the same way, about 2 more minutes, scraping down the bowl as necessary with a rubber spatula. Set aside.

4 If you're working with a hand mixer, clean and dry the beaters; if using a stand mixer, attach the paddle. Beat the chunks of butter and the remaining ⅓ cup sugar at medium speed in a second large bowl until creamy and silky, about 5 minutes. Beat in the egg yolks one at a time, making sure each is thoroughly incorporated before adding the next and scraping down the sides of the bowl as necessary. Beat in the vanilla.

5 Turn off the beaters, add half the flour, and beat at low speed just until moistened. Add the remainder of the flour and beat at low speed just until there are no streaks of flour visible.

6 Scrape down the beaters and remove them. Fold in half the beaten egg whites with a rubber spatula until dissolved in the batter (making sure there are no hidden pockets of flour as well). Then fold in the remainder of the egg whites very slowly and gently, just until even throughout the batter but still light and fluffy.

7 Pour and scrape the batter into the prepared pan, smoothing it to the corners. Bake until puffed, firm to the touch, and golden, until a toothpick inserted into the center of the cake comes out clean, about 1 hour.

To cool and unmold: Set the pan on a wire rack for 10 minutes, then turn the cake out of the pan and continue cooling on the rack to room temperature.

To store: Once cooled, wrap in plastic and keep at room temperature for up to 3 days or in the freezer for up to 3 months.

Lopsided Cakes?

If a cake rises more on one side than the other, your oven is probably tipped slightly, even by a fraction of an inch. Level the oven if you can, following the manufacturer's instructions. Or compensate by gently turning the pans a half-rotation while baking. Be careful: a jostle can deflate a cake before it's set.

Five Things to Do with a Pound Cake

I. Make Pound Cake Toast

Lay slices of pound cake on the broiler pan 4 to 6 inches under a preheated broiler and toast until lightly browned, turning once, about 3 minutes; brush the slices with butter or jam before serving.

II. Make a Pound Cake Berry Basket

Cut the top off the pound cake, hollow out the middle, and fill with berries that have been tossed with a little sugar. Top with Sweetened Whipped Cream (page 522), if desired.

III. Make Pound Cake Dessert Sandwiches

Spread pound cake slices with peanut butter, almond butter, walnut butter, or Nutella; spread the same number of pieces with the jam of your choice. Sandwich the two together and serve at once. Use Pound Cake Toast (see above), if desired.

IV. Make Pound Cake Ice Cream Sandwiches

Spread a few slices of pound cake each with 1/4 cup softened ice cream or gelato, top each with another slice of pound cake, then wrap in plastic, and freeze until the ice cream is hard again, about 3 hours.

V. Make Pound Cake Fudge Sundaes

Make Pound Cake Toast (see left); transfer the slices to a wire rack to cool. Place the toasted pound cake slices in serving bowls, then top with Vanilla Frozen Custard (page 644) and Hot Fudge Sauce (page 645), or purchased ice cream and hot fudge sauce, as well as Sweetened Whipped Cream (page 522) and toasted pecan pieces.

Check Your Oven's Calibration

Like pianos, ovens can go out of whack over time. Buy a small oven thermometer, hang it from the rack, and check the reading against your oven's dial or digital gauge. If the temperature you choose doesn't match the one on the thermometer, call a professional to reset the thermostat or compensate with the dial to get the correct temperature.

Cocoa powder should always be sifted through a fine-mesh strainer or sieve. The powder picks up environmental humidity and forms tight little balls that do not readily dissolve. You can force these through the mesh with the back of a wooden spoon, but you may still end up with a grainy batter or a cake with granules of undissolved cocoa.

Lemon Cake

A little almond extract brings out and balances the bright zing of lemon juice. *Makes one 9-inch round cake*

> 1½ tablespoons unsalted butter, melted and cooled, plus additional for greasing the pan
> ¼ cup all-purpose flour, plus additional for dusting the pan
> 3 large eggs, separated (see page 19), plus 3 large egg whites, all at room temperature
> ¼ teaspoon salt
> ¾ cup cake flour
> ½ cup sugar
> 1 teaspoon baking powder
> ¼ cup lemon juice
> 2 tablespoons finely grated lemon zest
> ¼ teaspoon almond extract
> 1 tablespoon confectioners' sugar

1. Position the rack in the center of the oven and preheat the oven to 350°F. Lightly butter a 9-inch round springform pan, then dust it with flour, shaking out any excess.

2. Beat the 6 egg whites and salt in a large bowl with an electric mixer at medium speed until frothy. Raise the speed to high and beat until you can make droopy peaks in the mixture by dabbing it with the turned-off beaters, about 3 minutes. Set aside.

3. Whisk both flours, the sugar, and baking powder in a medium bowl; set aside as well.

4. If you're working with a hand-held mixer, clean and dry the beaters; if you're working with a stand mixer, attach the paddle. Beat the egg yolks, lemon juice, lemon zest, butter, and almond extract at medium speed in a large bowl until fluffy and lemony yellow, about 2 minutes.

5 Turn the beaters off and scrape down the sides of the bowl. Add the prepared flour mixture and beat at low speed until a soft, moist, but slightly grainy batter forms, no more than 45 seconds. There should be no white grains of flour visible.

6 Remove the beaters and fold in the beaten egg whites with a rubber spatula, using long, even arcs, just until incorporated.

7 Pour the batter into the prepared pan and bake until puffed and springy, until a toothpick or cake tester inserted into the cake's center comes out with a few moist crumbs attached, about 40 minutes. Dust with confectioners' sugar when cooled by sifting the sugar through a fine-mesh strainer over the top of the cake.

To cool: Set the pan on a wire rack for 20 minutes, then release the springform ring and remove the cake to continue cooling to room temperature.

To store: Omit dusting the cake with confectioners' sugar. Keep the cake on the metal bottom of the springform pan; when completely cooled, wrap in plastic and store at room temperature for 2 days or freeze for up to 3 months. Dust with confectioners' sugar just before serving.

Variations: Substitute any of the following for the almond extract: 2 teaspoons finely minced basil leaves, 1/2 teaspoon mint extract, or 1/4 teaspoon ground cloves.

Lime Cake: Substitute lime juice and finely grated lime zest for the lemon juice and lemon zest. Omit the almond extract. You might also want to add 1 or 2 drops green food coloring with the lime juice.

Honey Cake

A slow oven keeps the honey from caramelizing too quickly. A mix of flours assures a tender cake.
Makes one 9-inch round cake

> 1/4 cup canola oil, plus additional for greasing the pan
> 1 cup all-purpose flour, plus additional for dusting the pan
> 1 cup whole wheat pastry flour (see page 657)
> 1 teaspoon baking soda
> 1 teaspoon ground cinnamon
> 1/2 teaspoon salt
> 1/4 teaspoon ground allspice
> 1/4 teaspoon grated nutmeg
> 3/4 cup honey
> 1/4 cup sugar
> 2 large eggs, at room temperature
> 2 teaspoons vanilla extract
> 1/4 cup milk (regular, low-fat, or fat-free)

1 Position the rack in the center of the oven and preheat the oven to 300°F. Dab a little oil on a paper towel and grease a 9-inch round springform pan. Lightly dust the inside of the pan with flour, shaking out any excess.

2 Whisk both flours, the baking soda, cinnamon, salt, allspice, and nutmeg in a medium bowl; set aside.

3 Beat the honey and sugar in a large bowl with an electric mixer at medium speed until creamy and light, about 1 minute. Beat in the eggs one at a time, waiting about 1 minute after adding the first before adding the second. Scrape down the sides of the bowl and beat in the canola oil and vanilla just until smooth.

4 Turn off the beaters, add half the prepared flour mixture, and beat at low speed until combined. Beat in the milk, then turn off the beaters and add the rest of the flour mixture. Beat at very low speed just until combined, until there are no white rifts of flour visible.

⑤ Pour into the prepared pan and bake until puffed and lightly browned, until a toothpick inserted into the center of the cake comes out clean, about 1 hour.

To cool: Set the cake in its pan on a wire rack for 10 minutes, then release the rim of the springform pan and continue cooling on the rack until room temperature.

To store: Keep the cake on the pan's bottom, wrap in plastic or place on a cake plate under a dome when completely cooled; store at room temperature up to 2 days. Wrapped, the cake can be stored in the freezer for up to 3 months.

Variations: Different varieties of honey will produce a range of flavors; try tree varietals like pine or chestnut or perfumy ones like orange blossom or star thistle.

Four Tips for Springform Pans

❶ Snap the pan's collar on tightly so there are no gaps that will result in leaks.

❷ When buttering and flouring the pan, coat the joint between the sides and the bottom.

❸ After unlatching the collar, slip the cake (still on the pan's bottom) out from the ring, then cool on a wire rack until room temperature, perhaps 1 hour.

❹ To remove the bottom, run a thin knife under the cake, the blade parallel to the pan's bottom, slicing off the merest fraction of the cake; gently remove the cake with the help of a wide spatula and transfer to a serving platter. If you're using a nonstick pan, remember that a knife can nick the pan's bottom, so use only approved nonstick-safe utensils.

Semolina Cake with Ginger and Pine Nuts

An Italian tradition, semolina cakes can range from savory to sweet; this one, leavened with beaten egg whites, is a light and easy dessert for any night of the week. *Makes one 8-inch cake*

> Unsalted butter for greasing the pan
> ½ cup plus 2 tablespoons semolina flour, plus additional for dusting
> ⅓ cup crystallized ginger
> ¼ cup plus 2 tablespoons pine nuts
> 4 large eggs, separated (see page 19), at room temperature
> ¼ teaspoon salt
> ¾ cup sugar
> 1 teaspoon ground ginger

❶ Position the rack in the center of the oven and preheat the oven to 350°F. Lightly butter an 8-inch springform cake pan (preferably) or an 8-inch, high-sided, round cake pan; dust the interior with semolina flour, coating the sides and bottom thoroughly and evenly before tapping out the excess.

❷ Place the crystallized ginger in a food processor fitted with the chopping blade; pulse until chopped. Add the pine nuts and process until pastelike.

❸ Place the egg whites and salt in a large bowl and beat until frothy, using an electric mixer at medium speed. Raise the speed to high and continue beating until soft peaks form in the place where the beaters are turned off and raised up out of the whites, about 3 minutes. Set aside.

❹ Clean and dry the beaters. Beat the egg yolks and sugar in a second large bowl until pale yellow, doubled in volume, and very velvety, about 4 minutes. The beaters, when turned off and lifted up, should drizzle thick ribbons back onto the top of the batter, ribbons that do not immediately dissolve. Beat in the ground ginger.

⑤ Scrape down the sides of the bowl and beat in the pine nut paste until fairly smooth. Scrape down the beaters and remove them. Fold in the semolina flour with a rubber spatula, working slowly and carefully until the semolina is moistened and evenly distributed in the grainy batter.

⑥ Fold in a quarter of the beaten egg whites with a rubber spatula; work evenly but not carefully, dissolving the whites into the thick batter. Then fold in the remaining beaten whites slowly and gently, turning them through the batter to get them evenly distributed without deflating them. There may be a few small white streaks visible in the batter (but no large white streaks).

⑦ Pour and scrape the batter into the prepared pan and bake until quite spongy but nonetheless firm to the touch, about 30 minutes.

To cool: Set on a wire rack for 20 minutes, then run a knife around the inside of the pan to loosen the cake from the edges. Invert the cake pan onto a cutting board, remove the pan, and then reinvert the cake onto a serving platter or cake plate. Or unlatch the springform collar and remove it, then run a knife under the bottom and gently slip the cake onto a serving platter or cake plate.

To store: Cover loosely with plastic wrap and set aside at room temperature for up to 3 days.

Ginger Macadamia Semolina Cake: Substitute unsalted roasted macadamia nuts for the pine nuts.

Spiced Pecan Semolina Cake: Substitute pecans for the pine nuts and ground cinnamon for the ground ginger.

Spiced Semolina Cake: Substitute ground cinnamon for the ground ginger; also add 1/4 teaspoon grated nutmeg and 1/8 teaspoon ground cloves with it.

Nut Cake

Split open and filled with jam, with a grainy, almost crunchy crumb, this cake is the perfect finish after a stew or soup. The cake is easily customized to your taste: use any jam you prefer.
Makes one 9-inch round cake

1 cup walnut pieces
3/4 cup whole almonds
3/4 cup pecan pieces
6 large eggs, separated (see page 19), plus 6 large egg whites, all at room temperature
1/2 teaspoon salt
1 cup granulated sugar
1/2 cup packed light brown sugar
1 teaspoon ground cinnamon
2 teaspoons vanilla extract
2 tablespoons walnut oil, plus additional for oiling the pan
1/2 cup all-purpose flour
3/4 cup jam or marmalade of any flavor you choose: raspberry, blueberry, blackberry, fig, orange marmalade
2 tablespoons confectioners' sugar

① Position the rack in the center of the oven and preheat the oven to 325°F. Spread all the nuts out onto a large baking sheet and toast until lightly browned and aromatic, about 8 minutes, tossing frequently. Set aside to cool for 20 minutes, but maintain the oven temperature.

② Place the nuts in a large food processor fitted with the chopping blade and process until finely ground like meal, not a paste. Set aside as well.

③ Beat the 12 egg whites and salt in a large bowl with an electric mixer at medium speed until frothy, about 1 minute. Raise the speed to high and continue beating until soft peaks form in the place where the beaters are turned off and raised up out of the whites, 3 to 4 minutes. Set aside.

4 Clean and dry the beaters. Beat the 6 egg yolks, granulated sugar, brown sugar, and cinnamon in a second large bowl until light, smooth, and creamy, about 5 minutes. Beat in the vanilla.

5 Beat in the walnut oil until smooth. Turn off the beaters, add the flour, and beat at low speed just until moistened, less than 1 minute.

6 Scrape down the beaters and remove them. Using a rubber spatula, fold in the ground nuts until evenly distributed.

7 Fold in a third of the beaten egg whites until smooth. Then fold in half the remaining egg whites just until they are distributed throughout the batter. Finally, fold in the remaining egg whites very slowly, in gentle arcs, just until they are even throughout the batter but not fully dissolved.

8 Dab a little walnut oil onto a paper towel and oil the interior sides and bottom of a 9-inch springform pan. Pour and scrape the batter into this pan, smoothing it gently but evenly to the corners without pressing down.

9 Bake until puffed and set, until the cake will not jiggle when shaken, 45 to 50 minutes. Cool on a wire rack for 15 minutes, then unlatch the sides of the pan and remove them. Continue cooling until room temperature, about 1 hour.

10 Run a long, thin knife between the cake and the pan's bottom, thereby releasing the cake. Gently slip the cake from the bottom and onto a cake plate or serving platter. Wipe off the knife, then cut the cake into 2 even disks, gently slicing through the cake without tearing it. You may have to remove the knife to clean and dry it while cutting; be patient and gentle.

11 Remove the top layer of the cake and set it aside. Spread the jam on the cut surface of the bottom layer. Return the top layer to the cake cut side down. Dust the top of the cake with confectioners' sugar just before serving.

To store: Set under a cake dome at room temperature for up to 2 days.

Chocolate Marble Bundt Cake

Some marble cakes have a single rift of chocolate; we prefer far more. *Makes one 10-inch cake*

- 10 tablespoons (1 stick plus 2 tablespoons) cool unsalted butter, cut into chunks, plus additional for greasing the pan
- 2 cups all-purpose flour, plus additional for dusting
- 1½ teaspoons baking powder
- ¼ teaspoon salt
- 1 cup sugar
- 1 large egg plus 2 large egg yolks, at room temperature
- 1 teaspoon vanilla extract
- ¾ cup milk (regular, low-fat, or fat-free)
- 1 ounce unsweetened chocolate, chopped, melted, and cooled

1 Position the rack in the center of the oven and preheat the oven to 350°F. Lightly butter a 10-inch Bundt pan; dust it with flour, shaking out the excess but making sure the creases are coated.

2 Whisk the flour, baking powder, and salt in a medium bowl; set aside.

3 Beat the butter and sugar in a large bowl with an electric mixer at low speed until the butter begins to soften, then beat at medium speed until light, fluffy, and lemony yellow, about 4 minutes.

4 Scrape down the sides of the bowl and beat in the egg for about 30 seconds. Beat in the egg yolks, then the vanilla until smooth.

5 Turn off the beaters, add half the flour mixture, and beat at low speed until incorporated. Add the milk and beat at low speed until smooth. Scrape down the beaters and remove them. Stir in the remaining flour mixture with a wooden spoon just until all the flour is moistened.

6 Transfer half the batter to a second bowl. Stir the melted chocolate into one of the batters.

7 Spoon some of the vanilla batter into the prepared pan, then pour on some of the chocolate batter, then more of the vanilla, then more of the chocolate, layering them in the pan in several additions. Once both batters are in the pan, stick a flatware knife into it without touching bottom and lightly swirl it a couple of times around the pan, thereby creating patterns in the batter but taking care not to blend them into one.

8 Bake until springy and lightly browned, until a toothpick inserted into the center of the cake comes out with a few moist crumbs attached, about 35 minutes.

To cool: Set the cake in the pan on a wire rack for 15 minutes; then turn it out, remove the pan, and continue cooling on a wire rack to room temperature.

To store: When completely cooled, cover in plastic wrap or place on a platter under a cake dome and set aside at room temperature for up to 2 days. Wrapped, it can be kept in the freezer for up to 3 months.

Variations: Add ½ teaspoon almond extract or ½ teaspoon mint extract to the white batter before swirling the two batters in the pan.

Mocha Marble Cake: Dissolve 2 teaspoons instant espresso powder into the melted chocolate before adding it to half the batter.

Coconut Pineapple Upside-Down Cake

Our version of this classic is as much a tropical fantasy as an American dessert. *Makes one 8-inch round cake*

11 tablespoons (1 stick plus 3 tablespoons)
    unsalted butter, plus additional for
    greasing the pan
6 tablespoons packed light brown sugar
One 20-ounce can pineapple slices in juice,
    drained
About 12 maraschino
    cherries
1 cup all-purpose flour
½ teaspoon baking powder
¼ teaspoon salt
¾ cup granulated sugar
2 large eggs plus 2 large egg yolks, at room
    temperature
1 cup shredded sweetened coconut
2 tablespoons gold rum
1 teaspoon vanilla extract

1 Position the rack in the center of the oven and preheat the oven to 350°F. Lightly butter the interior sides and bottom of an 8-inch cheesecake pan (see page 549) or an 8-inch round soufflé dish.

2 Melt 3 tablespoons butter in a small saucepan set over medium-low heat. Add the brown sugar and stir over the heat until dissolved. Pour this mixture into the bottom of the prepared pan, tipping the pan a bit to coat the bottom evenly.

3 Lay the pineapple rings on the pan's bottom, cutting them to fit. Place a cherry or two in the center of each ring.

④ Whisk the flour, baking powder, and salt in a medium bowl; set aside.

⑤ Beat the remaining 8 tablespoons (1 stick) butter and the granulated sugar in a large bowl with an electric mixer at medium speed until light and fluffy, about 5 minutes.

⑥ Beat in the eggs one at a time, then beat in the 2 egg yolks. Beat in the coconut, rum, and vanilla until you have a smooth batter laced with coconut.

⑦ Scrape down the beaters and remove them. Fold in the flour mixture with a rubber spatula just until moistened, until there's no more dry flour in the batter. Pour and scrape this batter into the prepared pan, taking care not to dislodge the pineapple or the cherries.

⑧ Bake until puffed and lightly browned, until a toothpick inserted into the center of the cake comes out clean, about 1 hour.

To cool and unmold: Set on a wire rack for 15 minutes, then turn the pan upside down onto a cake platter or serving plate. Tap the sides and bottom of the pan a few times with a flatware knife, then lift off the pan. Should any of the pineapple rings stay in the pan, peel them off and replace them on top of the cake along with any remaining sugar syrup in the pan.

To store: Lightly wrap with plastic or set under a cake dome and keep at room temperature for up to 2 days. (Not recommended for freezing.)

Variations: Substitute any drained, canned fruit in juice for the pineapples and cherries. Try 1½ cups canned blueberries (not blueberry pie filling); a 20-ounce can pitted plums, halved; or a 20-ounce can pears, thinly sliced. In all cases, omit the rum and reserve 2 tablespoons of the juice in the can to add to the cake batter.

Angel Food Cake

This light-as-air egg white cake has to be cooled upside down; the crusty top will cause the light cake to collapse if cooled upright. You'll need a small bottle to fit into the cake pan's tubular center to hold the cake upside down—or buy an angel food cake pan with feet around the rim. *Makes one 10-inch round tube cake*

Canola oil or nonstick spray for greasing
    the pan
1 cup cake flour
½ cup confectioners' sugar
12 large egg whites,
    at room temperature
½ teaspoon salt
1½ teaspoons cream of tartar
1 cup granulated sugar
2 teaspoons vanilla extract
Lemon Drizzle (recipe follows), optional

① Position the rack in the center of the oven and preheat the oven to 350°F. Lightly grease the bottom of a 10-inch round tube cake pan or angel food cake pan with a removable bottom. (Do not grease the sides or the inner tube; the cake will rise up and attach to them to build structure in the oven's heat.) Whisk the flour and confectioners' sugar in a small bowl; set aside.

② Beat the egg whites and salt in a large bowl, using an electric mixer at medium speed, until quite foamy, about 1 minute. Add the cream of tartar, increase the speed to high, and beat, scraping down the sides of the bowl occasionally with a rubber spatula, until soft peaks form in the place when the beaters are turned off and lifted out of the mixture, about 4 minutes.

③ Reduce the speed to medium and beat in the granulated sugar in 1-tablespoon increments. Once all the sugar has been added, continue beating until you cannot feel any sugar between your fingers, until soft, glossy peaks can be formed when the turned-off beaters are dipped quickly back in the mixture, about 4 minutes. Beat in the vanilla.

④ Scrape down the beaters and remove them. Fold in the flour mixture with a rubber spatula, using long, slow, even arcs that do not deflate the meringue. Fold just until the flour is evenly distributed; the flour should not be visible but the meringue may be grainy. Pour and scrape into the prepared pan.

⑤ Bake until puffed and lightly browned, about 45 minutes. The cake should feel set when touched.

To cool and unmold: If the pan has feet, turn it upside down and set aside for 1 hour. If not, invert the cake pan onto a small bottle, sticking the bottle through the center hole and tipping the cake pan to one side to balance it. Set aside for 1 hour, then remove the bottle and lift the cake, still attached to the pan's bottom, out of the removable sides. (You may need to run a knife around the sides to loosen the cake—be careful of nonstick surfaces.) Slice it off the bottom and the inner tube by running a long, thin knife between the cake and the pan; transfer the cake to a cake plate or serving platter and cool completely. Ice with Lemon Drizzle, if desired.

To store: Forgo the icing until you serve the cake; store it under a cake dome for up to 2 days.

Chocolate Angel Food Cake: Omit the confectioners' sugar; reduce the egg whites to 10. Beat in the granulated sugar as directed, but also beat in one additional tablespoon sugar. Fold in 8 ounces semisweet or bittersweet chocolate, finely grated through the small holes of a box grater or a microplane, with the flour.

Lemon Drizzle

The lemon juice keeps the sugar in a semiliquid form, perfect for drizzling over cakes. *Makes about ¼ cup*

¾ cup confectioners' sugar
1 tablespoon lemon juice
1 teaspoon finely grated lemon zest

Stir the confectioners' sugar, lemon juice, and lemon zest in a small bowl until smooth. Set aside for 10 minutes, then drizzle over the cooled cake.

Orange Sponge Cake

The addition of egg yolks gives this cake a texture that's a cross between an angel food cake and a traditional cake. Because the cake's slightly heavier, the pan needs to be lightly greased. Once cooled, fill the center with fresh berries and serve the slices with Sweetened Whipped Cream (page 522). *Makes one 10-inch round tube cake*

Unsalted butter or nonstick spray for greasing the pan
1 cup cake flour, plus additional for dusting the pan
6 large eggs, separated (see page 19), at room temperature
¼ teaspoon salt
½ teaspoon cream of tartar
1 cup sugar
2 tablespoons finely grated orange zest
1 tablespoon frozen orange juice concentrate, thawed

① Position the rack in the center of the oven; preheat the oven to 350°F. Lightly butter or spray the bottom, sides, and inner tube of a 10-inch round tube cake pan or angel food cake pan with a removable bottom; dust it with flour, shaking out the excess but making sure everything's well coated.

② Beat the egg whites and salt in a large bowl with an electric mixer at medium speed until foamy. Add the cream of tartar, increase the speed to high, and beat until you can create droopy peaks in the mixture by dabbing it with the turned-off beaters, about 3 minutes. Set aside.

③ Clean and dry the beaters. In a second large bowl, beat the egg yolks and sugar at medium speed until thick ribbons form when the beaters are turned off and lifted out of the mixture (the ribbons will drizzle onto the batter without immediately dissolving back into it), about 5 minutes. Beat in the orange zest and the orange juice concentrate.

④ Scrape down the beaters and remove them. Gently fold in the cake flour with a rubber spatula just until moistened.

⑤ Add the beaten egg whites with a rubber spatula in two additions, folding in half until fully incorporated, then folding in the remainder gently and slowly just until the egg whites are evenly distributed throughout the batter, if still a tad visible.

⑥ Pour the batter into the prepared pan and bake until a toothpick inserted into the center of the cake comes out clean, about 35 minutes.

To cool: Set the pan on a wire rack for 15 minutes, then run a long, thin knife around the inside rim of the cake and remove the sides. Set aside on the rack to continue cooling to room temperature.

To unmold: Run a knife along the bottom of the pan, slicing the cake off the tube pan. Also run the knife around the inner tube to release the cake there. Invert, then remove the tube pan's bottom. Reinvert the cake onto a serving plate.

To store: Cool completely, then set under a cake dome for up to 3 days at room temperature.

Lemon Sponge Cake: Substitute lemon zest and lemon juice for the orange zest and orange juice.

Lime Sponge Cake: Substitute lime zest and lime juice for the orange zest and orange juice.

Orange Coconut Sponge Cake: Fold in 1 cup shredded sweetened coconut with the first half of the egg whites.

Strawberry Shortcake

Here's simplicity itself: tender, yogurt-leavened biscuit cakes and fresh strawberries with Sweetened Whipped Cream. *Makes 8 strawberry shortcakes*

2¼ cups cake flour, plus additional for dusting
¼ cup sugar plus 3 tablespoons sugar
1 tablespoon baking powder
1 teaspoon baking soda
1 teaspoon salt
6 tablespoons cool unsalted butter, cut into chunks
⅔ cup plain regular or low-fat yogurt (do not use fat-free)
1 quart strawberries, hulled and sliced
1 tablespoon gold rum, brandy, Cognac, or bourbon
Sweetened Whipped Cream (recipe follows)

① Position the rack in the center of the oven and preheat the oven to 350°F. Line a large baking sheet with parchment paper or a silicone baking mat.

② Whisk the flour, ¼ cup sugar, the baking powder, baking soda, and salt in a medium bowl.

③ Cut the butter into the flour mixture, using a pastry cutter or a fork, working the butter through the tines until the whole thing resembles coarse meal. Stir in the yogurt with a wooden spoon until a soft dough forms.

④ Lightly flour a clean, dry work surface and turn the dough out onto it. Lightly flour the dough and press it into a circle about ½ inch thick (do not roll the dough—it will become too tough). Cut into 4-inch circles, using a 4-inch round cookie cutter or a thick-rimmed drinking glass. Gather the scraps together and gently press into another sheet to make more circles.

⑤ Place the rounds on the prepared baking sheet and bake until lightly browned, puffed, but dry to the touch, about 20 minutes. Cool on the baking sheet for a couple of minutes, then transfer to a wire rack to cool for at least 20 minutes. (The cakes can be made ahead of time and stored in an airtight container at room temperature for up to 3 days or in the freezer for up to 3 months.)

⑥ Meanwhile, toss the strawberries, 3 tablespoons sugar, and the rum in a large bowl; set aside to macerate for 20 minutes, tossing occasionally.

⑦ Slice open the shortcakes. Place the bottoms in soup bowls or other shallow bowls. Spoon on some sliced strawberries and Sweetened Whipped Cream, then add the tops and spoon more strawberries on top and around the bowl.

Variations: To spice the cakes, stir 1 teaspoon ground cinnamon, 1 teaspoon ground ginger, or ¼ teaspoon grated nutmeg into the flour mixture with the salt.

Substitute any berry for the strawberries: blackberries, raspberries, or blueberries. If using blueberries, also add 1 teaspoon finely grated lemon zest.

Sweetened Whipped Cream
Makes about 3 cups

> 1½ cups heavy cream
> 1½ tablespoons superfine sugar (see Note)
> 1 teaspoon vanilla extract, optional

Chill the bowl and beaters for 10 minutes in the refrigerator. Beat the cream in a chilled bowl, using an electric mixer at medium speed, until foamy. Raise the speed to high and continue beating, while adding the sugar in a thin, steady stream, until soft, luscious peaks can be formed off the turned-off beaters. Beat in the vanilla, if desired.

Note: This whipped cream should be used within minutes of its being made. If you want to set it aside, covered, in the refrigerator for up to 6 hours, substitute confectioners' sugar for the superfine sugar.

Non-Frightening Fruitcake

Fear not: ours is made with dried fruit, not unrecognizable glacéed fruit cubes. We use one-quart loaf pans, smaller than the 9 × 5-inch variety; the fruit bakes more evenly without too much dough around it. Allow yourself at least a 2-week lag so you can ripen the cakes in the refrigerator. *Makes 2 fruitcake loaves*

> 6 tablespoons unsalted butter, at room temperature, plus additional for greasing the pans
> 1¼ cups all-purpose flour, plus additional for dusting the pans
> 1½ cups chopped candied orange peel (about 8 ounces)
> 1 cup chopped dried cranberries (about 6 ounces)

1 cup chopped dried California apricots
   (about 6 ounces)

1 cup chopped dried pineapple
   (about 6 ounces)

¾ cup chopped dried cherries
   (about 4 ounces)

½ cup whole wheat pastry flour

1 teaspoon ground cinnamon

½ teaspoon baking powder

½ teaspoon salt

¼ teaspoon grated nutmeg

⅛ teaspoon ground cloves

¼ cup walnut oil

¼ cup granulated sugar

¼ cup packed dark brown sugar

2 tablespoons unsulfured molasses

2 teaspoons vanilla extract

2 large egg whites

12 pecan halves

6 tablespoons bourbon, whiskey, brandy,
   Cognac, or rum

1 Position the rack in the center of the oven and preheat the oven to 275°F. Lightly butter and flour the insides of two 1-quart, 9 × 4 × 2½-inch loaf pans.

2 In a large bowl, toss the candied orange peel, the dried cranberries, apricots, pineapple, cherries, and ½ cup all-purpose flour until well coated. Set aside.

3 Mix the remaining ¾ cup flour, the whole wheat pastry flour, cinnamon, baking powder, salt, nutmeg, and cloves in a medium bowl until uniform; set aside as well.

4 Using an electric mixer at medium speed, beat the butter, walnut oil, granulated sugar, and brown sugar in a large bowl until smooth and silky, about 3 minutes.

5 Beat in the molasses and vanilla, then beat in the egg whites one at a time, scraping down the sides of the bowl as necessary.

6 Scrape down and remove the beaters. Fold in the flour mixture with a rubber spatula just until moistened.

7 Stir this batter into the dried fruit. Pour and scrape the batter evenly into the two loaf pans. Decorate the tops of the cakes with 6 pecan halves each.

8 Bake until lightly browned and firm to the touch, until a toothpick or cake tester inserted into the center of the cakes comes out with a few moist crumbs attached, about 1 hour and 40 minutes. (For what to do with the liquor, see below.)

To cool: Set on a wire rack for 15 minutes. Invert the pans onto a cutting board, remove them, reinvert the cakes onto the wire rack, and cool to room temperature, about 1 hour.

To ripen and store: Drizzle 3 tablespoons liquor over each of two clean kitchen towels. Wrap one towel around each fruitcake, then seal tightly with plastic wrap. Place the loaves in the refrigerator for at least 2 weeks or up to 2 months, provided you peel off the towels and replace them with more liquor-soaked towels every 3 weeks or so. If you want to freeze the cakes, do so after ripening them with the liquor. Wrap the loaves simply in plastic wrap and freeze for up to 2 months.

Cake flour? Whole wheat pastry flour? Bittersweet chocolate? Unfamiliar ingredients? See the Glossary, pages 654–662.

❋ *Sheet Cakes* ❋

A single-layer sheet cake is ideal for office parties, birthdays, or other celebrations because it's easily transported in the pan and its large surface area is ideal for decorating. We've paired these sheet cakes with straightforward frostings: minimal fuss, maximum pizzazz.

Vanilla Sheet Cake with Vanilla Frosting

Perfect for birthdays, this simple sheet cake needs a level oven to keep it even in the pan (see page 511). Don't try baking this cake in any other size pan than the one called for, often designated a "half hotel sheet pan" in cookware stores. *Makes one 17 × 11-inch sheet cake*

> 1 pound (4 sticks) cool unsalted butter, cut into chunks, plus additional for greasing the pan
> 3½ cups cake flour, plus additional for dusting the pan
> 1 teaspoon baking powder
> ½ teaspoon salt
> 2 cups sugar
> 10 large eggs, at room temperature
> 1 tablespoon vanilla extract
> Vanilla Frosting (recipe follows)

❶ Position the rack in the center of the oven and preheat the oven to 350°F. Lightly butter a 17 × 11-inch sheet pan; dust it with flour, particularly in the crease between the bottom and the edges, before shaking out any excess flour.

❷ Whisk the flour, baking powder, and salt in a medium bowl; set aside.

❸ Use an electric mixer at low speed to beat the butter in a large bowl until slightly softened. Add the sugar, raise the speed to medium, and continue beating until light, creamy, and pale yellow, about 5 minutes.

❹ Beat in the eggs two at a time, scraping down the sides of the bowl as necessary and ensuring that each addition has been incorporated before adding the next. The whole process should take about 4 minutes. Beat in the vanilla.

❺ Turn off the beaters, add the half the flour mixture, and beat at low speed until a light, smooth batter forms. Add the rest of the flour mixture and beat just until moistened, no more than several turns.

❻ Scrape down the beaters and remove them. Give the batter a few turns with a rubber spatula to ensure that all the flour has been incorporated from the bottom. Pour and scrape evenly into the prepared pan. Rap the pan a couple of times against your work surface to get rid of any air bubbles.

❼ Bake until lightly browned but springy to the touch, until a toothpick inserted into the middle of the cake comes out clean, about 30 minutes. When fully cooled, ice with the Vanilla Frosting.

To cool: Set on a wire rack until room temperature, a little over 1 hour, before icing.

To store: Do not ice. Cover with plastic wrap and refrigerate for up to 3 days; let the cake stand at room temperature for 20 minutes before icing.

Vanilla Frosting

Makes about 3 cups

> 8 tablespoons (1 stick) unsalted butter,
>   at room temperature
> 6 tablespoons heavy cream
> ¼ cup light corn syrup
> 2 tablespoons vanilla extract
> ½ teaspoon salt
> 7 to 8 cups confectioners' sugar

❶ Beat the butter, cream, corn syrup, vanilla, and salt in a large bowl with an electric mixer at medium speed until creamy and smooth.

❷ Add about 6½ cups confectioners' sugar and beat at low speed until smooth.

❸ Add more confectioners' sugar in ¼-cup increments and beat at medium speed until a smooth, creamy frosting forms (usually about 1 additional cup confectioners' sugar).

You can also frost the Vanilla Sheet Cake with:

> Chocolate Frosting (page 526)
> Maple Cream Cheese
>   Frosting (page 539)
> a half recipe of the Chocolate Mousse
>   Frosting (page 535)
> a half recipe of the Chocolate Sour Cream
>   Frosting (page 535)
> or a double recipe of Lemon
>   Curd Filling (page 547)

Devil's Food Sheet Cake with Chocolate Frosting

This chocolate classic is paired with a dark, rich frosting. *Makes one 17 × 11-inch sheet cake*

> ⅔ cup sifted unsweetened cocoa powder
> 1 cup boiling water
> 12 tablespoons (1½ sticks) cool unsalted
>   butter, cut into chunks, plus additional for
>   greasing the pan
> 2 cups plus 2 tablespoons cake flour, plus
>   additional for dusting the pan
> 1 teaspoon baking soda
> ½ teaspoon salt
> 1¾ cups sugar
> 3 large eggs, at room temperature
> ½ cup regular or low-fat sour cream (do not
>   use fat-free)
> 2 teaspoons vanilla extract
> Chocolate Frosting (recipe follows)

❶ Place the cocoa powder in a small bowl, whisk in the boiling water until smooth, and set aside for 10 minutes.

❷ Position the rack in the center of the oven; preheat the oven to 350°F. Lightly butter a 17 × 11-inch baking pan (also known as a half hotel sheet pan). Dust it with flour, making sure it's evenly coated before shaking out the excess.

❸ Whisk the flour, baking soda, and salt in a medium bowl; set aside.

❹ Using an electric mixer at medium speed, beat the sugar and butter in a large bowl until smooth, creamy, and velvety, about 5 minutes.

❺ Beat in the eggs one at a time, scraping down the bowl after each addition and making sure each has been thoroughly incorporated before adding the next. Beat in the sour cream, vanilla, and cocoa mixture until smooth.

6 Turn off the beaters, add the flour mixture, and beat at low speed just until moistened, probably less than 1 minute. Scrape down the beaters and remove them.

7 Use a rubber spatula to turn the batter a few times just to make sure that there are no streaks of undissolved flour. Pour and scrape the batter evenly into the prepared pan; rap it against the counter a couple of times to knock out any air pockets.

8 Bake until springy to the touch, until a toothpick or cake tester inserted into the center of the cake comes out clean, about 25 minutes. When cooled, ice with the Chocolate Frosting.

To cool: Set on a wire rack until room temperature, at least 1 hour, before icing.

To store: Do not ice. Wrap in plastic and refrigerate for up to 3 days; allow it to sit out at room temperature for 20 minutes before icing.

Chocolate Frosting

18 tablespoons (2 sticks plus 2 tablespoons) unsalted butter, at room temperature
6 ounces bittersweet or semisweet chocolate, chopped, melted in the microwave or a double boiler over simmering water, and cooled
1½ tablespoons heavy cream
2 teaspoons vanilla extract
½ teaspoon salt
3½ to 4½ cups confectioners' sugar

1 Beat the butter, melted chocolate, cream, vanilla, and salt in a large bowl with an electric mixer at medium speed until soft and creamy, about 2 minutes.

2 Beat in the confectioners' sugar in ½-cup increments at low speed until a soft, spreadable, and

smooth frosting forms. Spread evenly over the top of the cake with an offset or rubber spatula.

You can also frost the Devil's Food Sheet Cake with:

Vanilla Frosting (page 525)
Cream Cheese Sour Cream Frosting
(page 527)
Italian Meringue Icing (page 543)
or Chocolate Whipped Cream
(page 546)

Carrot Sheet Cake with Cream Cheese Sour Cream Frosting

We prefer to make this cake in a 13 × 9-inch pan, deeper than a sheet pan. The cake then has a denser texture that stands up to this rich frosting, a tangy contrast to the sweet cake. *Makes one 13 × 9-inch sheet cake*

8 tablespoons (1 stick) cool unsalted butter, cut into chunks, plus additional for greasing the pan
2 cups all-purpose flour, plus additional for dusting the pan
½ cup cake flour
1½ teaspoons baking powder
1½ teaspoons ground cinnamon
½ teaspoon baking soda
½ teaspoon grated nutmeg
½ teaspoon salt
¾ cup packed dark brown sugar
¾ cup granulated sugar
½ cup walnut oil
5 large eggs, at room temperature
3 cups grated carrots (through the large holes of a box grater or with the grating blade in a food processor)
2 tablespoons finely grated orange zest
1 cup finely chopped toasted pecans, walnuts, or pine nuts
Cream Cheese Sour Cream Frosting
(recipe follows)

1 Position the rack in the center of the oven and preheat the oven to 350°F. Lightly butter and flour a 13 × 9-inch baking pan, making sure all the corners and edges are evenly coated and tapping out any excess.

2 Whisk both flours, the baking powder, cinnamon, baking soda, nutmeg, and salt in a medium bowl; set aside.

3 Using an electric mixer at medium speed, beat the butter, sugars, and walnut oil in a large bowl until creamy and light, about 4 minutes.

4 Beat in the eggs one at a time, making sure each is fully incorporated before adding the next. Beat in the grated carrots and orange zest until the batter itself is fairly smooth (although there will of course be threads of carrot and zest throughout).

5 Turn off the beaters, add half the prepared flour mixture, and beat at low speed just until moistened. Add the remaining flour mixture; beat just until evenly distributed.

6 Scrape down the beaters and remove them. Use a rubber spatula to fold in the nuts, taking care to turn the batter thoroughly to check for any pockets of flour or lumps. Pour and scrape into the prepared pan.

7 Bake until lightly puffed and springy to the touch, until a toothpick or cake tester inserted into the cake's center comes out with a few crumbs attached, about 55 minutes. Cool completely before icing.

To cool: Set on a wire rack until room temperature, at least 1½ hours, before topping with the Cream Cheese Sour Cream Frosting.

To store: Do not ice. Lightly cover with plastic wrap and refrigerate for up to 2 days; allow the cake to come back to room temperature before icing.

Cream Cheese Sour Cream Frosting

- 8 tablespoons (1 stick) unsalted butter, at room temperature
- 8 ounces regular or low-fat cream cheese (do not use fat-free)
- ½ cup packed dark brown sugar
- ½ cup regular sour cream (do not use low-fat or fat-free)
- 2 teaspoons vanilla extract
- 6 to 7 cups confectioners' sugar

1 Use an electric mixer to beat the butter, cream cheese, and brown sugar in a large bowl until creamy and smooth, about 3 minutes.

2 Add the sour cream and vanilla; continue beating until velvety, about 1 minute.

3 Turn off the beaters, add 5 cups confectioners' sugar, and beat on low until smooth.

4 Scrape down and remove the beaters. Stir in the remaining confectioners' sugar in ¼-cup increments with a rubber spatula until a smooth, rich frosting forms—it will be a little silkier than some icings, but will hold its shape when mounded on the spatula. Spread evenly over the cooled cake with an offset or rubber spatula.

Room Temperature Cakes

As tempting as a warm cake is, it's better eaten at room temperature. The cake has a chance to condense slightly, which improves the texture; it will definitely cut more easily; and it will taste better, the flavors having worked their way through the crumb.

Apple Sheet Cake

Make sure you leave plenty of time to let the apples and sugar macerate; the resulting liquid will create a dense, rich, but very moist cake. *Makes one 13 × 9-inch sheet cake*

> 5 large tart apples, such as Granny Smith, peeled, cored, and cut into ½-inch dice (about 5 cups)
> 1½ cups sugar
> ⅔ cup walnut oil, plus additional for greasing the pan
> 3 cups all-purpose flour
> 2 teaspoons baking powder
> 1½ teaspoons ground cinnamon
> ½ teaspoon baking soda
> ½ teaspoon salt
> 2 large eggs, at room temperature

1 Stir the apples and sugar in a large bowl; set aside to macerate for 30 minutes, stirring occasionally.

2 Position the rack in the center of the oven and preheat the oven to 350°F. Dab a little oil on a paper towel and lightly grease a 13 × 9-inch baking pan.

3 Whisk the flour, baking powder, cinnamon, baking soda, and salt in a medium bowl; set aside.

4 Whisk the walnut oil and eggs in a large bowl until creamy and light, about 2 minutes.

5 Stir in the entire apple mixture with a wooden spoon. Then stir in the prepared flour mixture, turning the batter to make sure all the flour has been moistened. Pour and scrape the batter evenly into the prepared pan.

6 Bake until lightly browned, until a toothpick or cake tester inserted into the center of the cake comes out with a few moist crumbs attached, about 55 minutes.

To cool: Set on a wire rack for at least 20 minutes before cutting.

To store: Cool to room temperature, then cover with plastic wrap and set aside at room temperature for up to 3 days. (Not recommended for freezing.)

Apple Raisin Cake: Use only 4 apples and add ½ cup chopped raisins with the remaining apples.

Pear Cake: Substitute 4 large pears, peeled, cored, and diced, for the apples. Add ¼ teaspoon grated nutmeg with the cinnamon.

Spiced Apple Cake: Reduce the cinnamon to 1 teaspoon; add 1¼ teaspoons ground ginger, ¼ teaspoon grated nutmeg, and ¼ teaspoon ground cloves with the remaining cinnamon.

Pumpkin Spice Sheet Cake

Serve this autumnal cake with crème fraîche, clotted cream, or Sweetened Whipped Cream (page 522), or frost it with Cream Cheese Sour Cream Frosting (page 527). *Makes one 13 × 9-inch sheet cake*

> ½ cup canola oil, plus additional for greasing the pan
> 1½ cups cake flour
> 1 cup all-purpose flour
> 1 tablespoon baking powder
> 2 teaspoons baking soda
> 2 teaspoons ground cinnamon
> 1 teaspoon ground ginger
> ½ teaspoon ground cloves
> ½ teaspoon salt
> ¼ teaspoon grated nutmeg
> 1 cup packed dark brown sugar

1 cup granulated sugar

3 large eggs, at room temperature

1½ cups canned pumpkin puree (do not use canned pumpkin pie filling)

1 cup regular or low-fat buttermilk (do not use fat-free)

1 Position the rack in the center of the oven and preheat the oven to 350°F. Dab a little canola oil on a paper towel and lightly grease a 13 × 9-inch baking pan.

2 Whisk both flours, the baking powder, baking soda, cinnamon, ginger, cloves, salt, and nutmeg in a medium bowl; set aside.

3 Use an electric mixer to beat both sugars and the eggs in a large bowl until very thick, velvety, and almost doubled in volume, about 5 minutes.

4 Beat in the canola oil, then beat in the pumpkin puree until smooth. Scrape down the sides of the bowl and beat in ½ cup buttermilk.

5 Turn off the beaters, add half the flour mixture, and beat at low speed just until moistened. Add the remaining ½ cup buttermilk and beat until fairly smooth. Then add the remaining flour mixture and beat for just a few seconds, just until the flour has been incorporated. Remove the beaters.

Thawing a Cake

If you've frozen the cake or its layers, thaw them in the refrigerator for at least 8 hours without unwrapping them. Then let them come back to room temperature before unwrapping them.

Frozen cakes can have a slightly chewy texture. To bring them back to somewhere near their original state, place the unwrapped, uniced layer or layers on a baking sheet in a preheated 350°F oven for 4 to 5 minutes. Do not microwave.

Give the batter a few turns with a rubber spatula to make sure there's no undissolved flour, then pour and scrape it into the prepared pan, smoothing it gently but evenly to the corners.

6 Bake until lightly browned and springy to the touch, until a toothpick or cake tester inserted into the center of the cake comes out clean, about 40 minutes.

To cool: Set the pan on a wire rack for at least 20 minutes before cutting.

To store: Cool completely, then cover with plastic wrap and set aside at room temperature for up to 2 days or freeze for up to 2 weeks (long freezing dulls the flavor).

Variations: Add ½ cup of any of the following with the flour: semisweet chocolate chips, bittersweet chocolate chips, cocoa nibs, chopped raisins, chopped dried cranberries, or chopped dried cherries.

When's a Cake Done?

Keep these four tips in mind:

1 The top should be lightly browned. If yours browns too quickly, cover it loosely with a piece of lightly greased or buttered foil, but do not let the foil touch the top surface.

2 The cake may pull slightly away from the pan's edge, but not so far away that the cake's edges are themselves slanted.

3 The cake should be firm but also spring back when gently touched at its center.

4 Finally, insert either a metal cake tester (available at cookware stores) or a wooden toothpick into the center of the cake and then gently remove it, pulling it straight back out of the hole you've made. There should either be a few crumbs attached or none at all, depending on the recipe's instructions.

These are the showstoppers, the frosted behemoths. We've offered our best suggestions for cake-and-frosting combinations, but become your own ultimate baker: mix and match to your heart's content.

Genoise Layers

This buttery French classic (said to be from Genoa) is the basis for a lighter-than-air layer cake as well as many other desserts. Frost these layers with almost any icing or frosting in this chapter—or follow the instructions below to turn the layers into spectacular specialty cakes. *Makes two 8-inch round cake layers*

- 6 tablespoons unsalted butter, melted and cooled, plus additional for greasing the pans
- ¾ cup cake flour, plus additional for dusting the pans
- 5 large eggs, at room temperature
- ¾ cup sugar
- 2 teaspoons vanilla extract
- ¼ teaspoon salt

1 Position the rack in the center of the oven and preheat the oven to 350°F. Lightly butter two 8-inch round cake pans; then dust them with flour, making sure they're evenly coated at the corner between the sides and the bottom before tapping out the excess.

2 If you're using a stand mixer, use the whisk attachment. Place the eggs and sugar in a large bowl and beat with an electric mixer at medium-high speed until tripled in volume and velvety,

about 7 minutes. When the whisk attachment or beaters are turned off and lifted out of the batter, the batter should run off in thick ribbons that lie on top of the batter in the bowl without immediately dissolving back into it. In truth, you cannot overbeat at this stage. Beat in the vanilla and salt.

3 Scrape down and remove the beaters. Sift ¼ cup flour into the batter through a flour sifter or a fine-mesh sieve; then fold in with a rubber spatula, using slow, even arcs, just until moistened. Repeat two more times, each time with ¼ cup flour.

4 Pour in the melted butter and continue folding until a fairly smooth batter forms.

5 Pour and scrape the dough evenly into the two cake pans. Rap them against the counter a couple of times to get rid of any air pockets.

6 Bake until lightly browned, set but still soft, and a little spongy to the touch, until a toothpick or cake tester inserted into the center of the cakes comes out with a few moist crumbs attached, about 22 minutes.

To cool and unmold: Set the cakes in the pans on a wire rack for 15 minutes. Run a knife around the inner rim of the pan to loosen the cake. then turn upside down, remove the pans, set a second rack over the cakes, turn them right side up, remove the top rack, and continue cooling until room temperature.

To store: Wrap the cooled layers individually in plastic and store at room temperature for up to 2 days.

Walnut Genoise: Substitute 6 tablespoons walnut oil and 1/2 tablespoon water for the melted butter. Use walnut oil to grease the pans as well. For a deeper taste, use toasted walnut oil (but not for greasing the pans).

Five Things to Do with a Genoise

I. Make a Frosted Layer Cake

Frost with Chocolate Frosting (page 526), Banana Frosting (page 534), Chocolate Whipped Cream (page 546), Italian Meringue Icing (page 543), Lemon Buttercream (page 540), Vanilla Buttercream (page 542), or Chocolate Mousse Frosting (page 535).

II. Make a Classic French Layer Cake

If the tops of the layers are at all hard, slice them off with a long, thin knife; if there are hardened bits around the top's perimeter, snip them off with kitchen shears. Slice each layer into two equal disks with a long, thin knife. Line a cake plate with wax paper (see page 532 for frosting tips), then place one disk on the plate. Brush with rum, bourbon, or Cognac; gently spread 1/2 cup jam of your choice across the layer. Top with the other half of this original layer, then frost with Chocolate Frosting (page 526), Lemon Buttercream (page 540), Chocolate Sour Cream Frost-

ing (page 535), or any icing of your choice. Add a third layer; again brush it with liquor and spread jam over it. Add the top layer, then ice the entire cake with the remaining frosting.

III. Make Individual Genoise Cakes

Once the layers are completely cooled, use a cookie cutter, a thick-rimmed round glass, or other design cutter to cut the cakes into any shapes you desire; set aside on a wire rack to dry for 15 minutes. Place the individual cakes on a cutting board and brush them lightly with Kahlúa, Chambord, Frangelico, Amaretto di Saronno, Cognac, or brandy; return them to a wire rack set over wax paper. Drizzle with Lemon Drizzle (page 520) or ice with Vanilla Frosting (page 525), Chocolate Frosting (page 526), or Cream Cheese Sour Cream Frosting (page 527).

IV. Make Raspberry Petits Fours

If the tops of the layers are hard, slice them off with a long, thin knife; if there are hard bits around the perimeters, snip them off with kitchen shears. Slice each of the cake layers into two equal disks with the long, thin knife—but do not remove the disks from on top of each other. Turn the circular layers into squares, cutting off the rounded edges; then cut each of these squares into rectangular pieces, making two equidistant cuts one way and three equidistant cuts the other in the layer. Separate all these two-tiered rectangles from each other. Remove the top from one rectangle, brush the bottom with 1/2 teaspoon bourbon, rum, whiskey, or Cognac, then spread on 1 teaspoon raspberry jam; return the top of the rectangle to the piece and set aside on a wire rack set over wax paper. Repeat with the remaining rectangles (you'll need a total of about 3 tablespoons raspberry jam and perhaps 2 tablespoons liquor). Once all the rectangles are on the wire rack, make the vanilla icing used for the Black and White cookies (page 564) and drizzle it over all of them, letting it run down the sides while coating the tops. Set aside to dry for 1 hour. Decorate the top of each petit four with candied violets, candied orange peel, or candied lemon peel. Stack the petits fours between sheets of wax paper in a plastic container and store, covered, in the refrigerator for up to 1 week; return to room temperature for 10 minutes before serving.

V. Make a Lady Baltimore Cake

Cool the cakes in the pans for 15 minutes, then invert onto a cutting board and reinvert onto a second cutting board. If the tops of the layers are hard, slice them off with a long, thin knife; if there are hard bits around the perimeters, snip them off with kitchen shears. Line a cake plate with wax paper (see below for tips), then place one layer of the cake cut side up on top of them, pulling the wax paper layers out so that they will later be easy to remove but still protect the cake plate. Grind ½ cup walnut pieces, ¼ cup dried figs, and ¼ cup raisins in a food processor fitted with the chopping blade until finely ground, almost paste-like; transfer to a large bowl. Make Seven-Minute Frosting (page 537). Stir 1 cup of the still-soft Seven-Minute Frosting into the fig mixture until spreadable; spread over the cake layer on the stand. Top with the second layer and frost with the remainder of the Seven-Minute Frosting.

How to Frost a Layer Cake

❶ If the layers are domed (peaked at their centers), slice off the tops with a long, thin knife so they are flat. If the tops aren't domed but there are crunchy rims around the perimeters, snip these off with kitchen shears.

❷ To protect the serving plate, lay four small sheets of wax paper on it before laying one cake layer top side down on the wax paper; the sheets should extend out from the cake's circumference at all points. Pull the sheets so they're as close to coming out from under the cake as possible; they will be easier to remove later.

❸ Spoon out about a quarter to a third of the frosting into the center of the layer. Use an offset spatula or the back of a stainless-steel soup spoon to spread the frosting out to the perimeter, making an even layer. Don't be persnickety—some frosting can drip over the sides. Rather than loading the top with icing, put the thickest layer in the middle of a cake where it will be held in place by the next layer. If there's a third layer to the cake, add it and repeat this step.

❹ Add the upper layer, top side up. Fill in any gaps between the layers by grouting them with frosting. Again, don't worry about a little mess—better at this point to have blobs of icing sticking out than to flatten them and track crumbs through the icing.

❺ Spoon most of the remaining frosting into the center of the top of the cake. Spread the frosting evenly with an offset spatula or the back of a stainless-steel soup spoon, pushing most of the icing toward the perimeter.

❻ Using a straight, thin spatula or a flatware knife, bring the excess frosting down over the sides of the cake, sweeping it over the upper edge and then smoothing it along the side to create an even rim. Be sure you have enough icing on the spatula so that crumbs aren't picked up and dragged along. Smooth out the icing and remove the wax paper sheets.

Buttery Vanilla Layer Cake with Banana Frosting

This is the simplest layer cake, best for birthdays.
Makes an 8-inch two-layer cake

12 tablespoons (1½ sticks) cool unsalted butter, cut into chunks, plus additional for greasing the pans
 2 cups cake flour, plus additional for dusting the pans
½ teaspoon baking powder
¼ teaspoon baking soda
¼ teaspoon salt
1 cup sugar
4 large eggs, at room temperature
2 teaspoons vanilla extract
Banana Frosting (recipe follows)

1 Position the rack in the center of the oven and preheat the oven to 325°F. Lightly butter two 8-inch round cake pans; dust them with flour, shaking out the excess but making sure the pans are well coated.

2 Whisk the flour, baking powder, baking soda, and salt in a medium bowl; set aside.

3 Beat the butter and sugar in a large bowl with an electric mixer at medium speed until creamy and light, about 4 minutes. If you rub a small bit of the mixture between your fingers, you should feel almost no sugar granules.

4 Beat in the eggs one at a time, adding another only after the former has been incorporated. Beat in the vanilla until smooth.

5 Turn off the beaters, add the flour mixture, and beat at low speed only a few turns, just until the flour is moistened and evenly distributed throughout the batter.

6 Remove the beaters and turn the batter a few times with a rubber spatula to make sure all the flour has been incorporated off the bowl's bottom. Pour and scrape evenly into the prepared pans; rap them against the counter to knock out any air pockets.

7 Bake until lightly browned and a little puffed, until a toothpick or cake tester inserted into the center of the cakes comes out clean, about 25 minutes. Cool completely before icing with Banana Frosting.

To cool and unmold: Transfer to a wire rack and cool for 10 minutes, then unmold the cakes by running a knife around the inner edge of the layers, inverting them onto a cutting board, removing the pans, and reinverting them onto the wire rack.

To store: Do not ice. Wrap the cooled layers in plastic and set aside at room temperature for up to 2 days.

The Butter's Temperature

The biggest baking myth? That the butter should be at room temperature. While soft butter is easy to work with, it cannot create the necessary structure for good cakes and cookies; the fat is too liquid to trap air molecules. In truth, the butter must be below 68°F to create a good batter.

Here's what we recommend: take the butter out of the fridge and cut it into chunks as you prep the ingredients. By the time you've finished measuring things out, the butter will be cool, not stone cold, and just about perfect.

However, an icing, frosting, or buttercream is another thing entirely. Here, you want density, less air. Leave the butter out at room temperature until soft, about 1 hour.

To ice: See page 532. Frost up to 4 hours before serving; store at room temperature.

Banana Frosting

For the best taste, the banana should be well beyond the stage where you'd slice it into cereal. *Makes enough frosting for a two-layer cake or a 13 × 9-inch sheet cake (can be doubled for 3-layer cakes)*

    1 small, very ripe banana (with many brown
        spots on the skin)
    1 tablespoon dark rum
    ⅛ teaspoon salt
    6 tablespoons unsalted butter, at room
        temperature
    4 to 4½ cups confectioners' sugar

❶ Mash the banana, rum, and salt in a large bowl with a fork until pureed.

❷ Add the butter and beat with an electric mixer at medium speed until smooth and creamy, about 2 minutes.

❸ Add 3½ cups confectioners' sugar and beat well. Stir in the remaining confectioners' sugar in ¼-cup increments with a wooden spoon until a soft, spreadable frosting forms (usually about ½ cup additional confectioners' sugar).

You can also frost the Buttery Vanilla Layer Cake with:

    Lemon Buttercream (page 540)
    Spiced Buttercream (page 541)

Chocolate Layer Cake with Chocolate Sour Cream Frosting or Chocolate Mousse Frosting

For this dense chocolate layer cake, take your pick of our two most decadent frostings, the first loaded with chocolate and the second with a marshmallowy texture. *Makes one 9-inch, two-layer cake*

    14 tablespoons (1 stick plus 6 tablespoons)
        cool unsalted butter, cut into chunks, plus
        additional for greasing the pans
    2¼ cups cake flour, plus additional for
        dusting the pans
    1 cup boiling water
    ¾ cup sifted unsweetened cocoa powder
    2½ teaspoons baking powder
    ½ teaspoon baking soda
    ½ teaspoon salt
    1½ cups sugar
    3 large eggs, at room temperature
    1 tablespoon vanilla extract
    Chocolate Sour Cream Frosting or
        Chocolate Mousse Frosting
        (recipes follow)

❶ Position the rack in the center of the oven and preheat the oven to 350°F. Lightly butter two 9-inch cake pans; dust them evenly and thoroughly with flour, shaking out any excess.

❷ Pour the boiling water over the cocoa powder in a small bowl, whisk until smooth, and set aside for 10 minutes.

❸ Meanwhile, clean and dry the whisk. Whisk the flour, baking powder, baking soda, and salt in a medium bowl; set aside as well.

❹ Beat the butter and sugar in a large bowl with an electric mixer at medium speed until light, smooth, barely grainy, and lemony creamy, about 4 minutes.

5 Scrape down the sides of the bowl and beat in the eggs one at a time, adding another only after the former has been thoroughly incorporated. Beat in the vanilla, then beat in the dissolved cocoa and water until smooth.

6 Turn off the beaters, add the prepared flour mixture, and beat at low speed just until the flour is fully moistened.

7 Scrape down and remove the beaters. Turn the batter a few times with a rubber spatula to make sure the flour is evenly distributed, then scrape evenly into the two pans. Rap the pans against your work surface to get rid of air pockets.

8 Bake until slightly puffed and firm to the touch, until a toothpick comes out clean, about 25 minutes. Cool completely before icing.

To cool and unmold: Transfer the layers to a wire rack and cool for 10 minutes, then unmold the cakes by running a knife around the inside perimeter of the layers, inverting them onto a cutting board, removing the baking pans, and reinverting the cakes onto the wire rack.

To store: Do not ice. Wrap the cooled layers individually in plastic wrap and keep at room temperature for up to 2 days before icing.

To ice: See page 532; frost no more than 4 hours before serving.

Chocolate Sour Cream Frosting
Makes enough frosting for a two-layer cake

24 ounces bittersweet chocolate, chopped, melted in the microwave or in a double boiler over simmering water, and cooled
2 cups regular or low-fat sour cream (do not use fat-free)

16 tablespoons (2 sticks) unsalted butter, at room temperature
2 teaspoons vanilla extract
½ teaspoon salt
¾ cup confectioners' sugar

1 Place the melted chocolate in a large bowl. With the electric beaters running at low speed, beat in the sour cream until smooth, then beat in the butter in half-stick increments, scraping down the sides of the bowl as necessary. Beat in the vanilla and salt, then the confectioners' sugar until smooth.

2 Place the bowl in the refrigerator and chill until the mixture begins to set and holds its shape when mounded on a spatula, about 1 hour. Frost the cake, then set it back in the refrigerator to chill for at least 30 minutes until the icing sets up. Let stand for 20 minutes at room temperature before serving.

Chocolate Mousse Frosting
Makes enough frosting for a two-layer cake

4 large egg whites, at room temperature
¼ teaspoon salt
½ teaspoon cream of tartar
1 cup sugar
⅓ cup water
1 tablespoon light corn syrup
16 tablespoons (2 sticks) unsalted butter, at room temperature
6 ounces bittersweet or semisweet chocolate, melted in the microwave or in a double boiler over simmering water and cooled
1 teaspoon vanilla extract

1 Place the egg whites and salt in a large bowl; beat with an electric mixer at medium speed until foamy. Add the cream of tartar, raise the speed to high, and beat until soft peaks can be formed by dipping the turned-off beaters into the mixture. Set aside.

② Place the sugar, water, and corn syrup in a small saucepan and stir over medium heat until the sugar has dissolved. Clip a candy thermometer to the inside of the pan, raise the heat to high, and cook undisturbed until the temperature reaches 250°F. Immediately remove the pan from the heat.

③ Beat the egg whites again for 5 seconds at medium speed, then begin adding the hot sugar syrup at the slowest drizzle, beating all the while at medium speed. Once all the sugar syrup has been added, continue beating until room temperature, about 5 minutes.

④ Beat in the butter in 2-tablespoon increments, scraping down the sides of the pan as necessary.

⑤ Beat in the melted chocolate and vanilla, then continue beating until quite soft, almost like a mousse, about 5 more minutes. The frosting will not firm up like a traditional buttercream; rather, it will remain soft, spreadable, and airy. Once the cake's been frosted, refrigerate for at least 2 hours to set the icing, but let stand at room temperature for 20 minutes before serving.

You can also frost the Chocolate Layer Cake with:

> a double batch of Italian Meringue Icing (page 543)
> Chocolate Whipped Cream (page 546)

Mocha Mousse Frosting: Stir 1 tablespoon instant espresso powder into the melted chocolate before adding it to the beaten egg whites.

Mint Chocolate Frosting: Substitute ½ teaspoon mint extract for the vanilla extract.

White Chocolate Mousse Frosting: Substitute white chocolate, melted and cooled, for the bittersweet or semisweet chocolate; omit the vanilla extract.

White Chocolate Orange Mousse Frosting: Substitute white chocolate, melted and cooled, for the bittersweet or semisweet chocolate; substitute orange extract for the vanilla extract.

Coconut Layer Cake with Seven-Minute Frosting

Here's a Southern favorite—and no wonder: the marshmallowy frosting perfectly complements the rich, coconut-laced layers. Note the two kinds of coconut: sweetened and unsweetened. *Makes one 8-inch two-layer cake*

> 8 tablespoons (1 stick) cool unsalted butter, cut into chunks, plus additional for greasing the pans
> 2 cups cake flour, plus additional for dusting the pans
> 2 cups shredded unsweetened coconut
> 1½ teaspoons baking powder
> ¼ teaspoon salt
> 1¼ cups sugar
> 4 large eggs, at room temperature
> ½ teaspoon almond extract
> ¾ cup milk (regular, low-fat, or fat-free)
> ½ cup shredded sweetened coconut
> Seven-Minute Frosting (recipe follows)

① Position the rack in the center of the oven and preheat the oven to 350°F. Lightly butter two 8-inch round cake pans; dust them with flour, knocking out the excess but making sure they are evenly coated.

② Spread the unsweetened coconut onto a large baking sheet and toast in the oven until lightly browned, stirring frequently, about 8 minutes. Set aside to cool completely. This coconut will be used to decorate the frosting; once cooled, it can be stored in a sealed plastic bag for up to 3 days.

③ Whisk the flour, baking powder, and salt in a medium bowl; set aside.

④ Beat the chunks of butter and sugar in a large bowl with an electric mixer at medium speed until light and pale yellow with only few sugar granules detectable, about 3 minutes.

⑤ Beat in the eggs one at a time, scraping down the sides of the bowl as necessary. Beat in the almond extract.

⑥ Turn off the beaters, add half the flour mixture, then beat at a very low speed just until the flour has been moistened. Add the milk and beat at low speed until fairly smooth. Beat in the remainder of the flour for a few seconds until moistened.

⑦ Scrape down the beaters, remove them, then use a rubber spatula to fold in the sweetened coconut just until evenly distributed. Pour the batter evenly into the two prepared pans and rap them against the counter a couple of times to remove any inadvertent air pockets.

⑧ Bake until springy and very lightly browned, until a toothpick or cake tester inserted into the center of the cakes comes out clean, about 30 minutes.

To cool and unmold: Set the layers on a wire rack and cool for 10 minutes; then unmold by inverting them onto a cutting board, removing the pans, and reinverting them onto the wire rack. Cool completely before icing with Seven-Minute Frosting.

To store: Wrap the layers individually in plastic and keep at room temperature for up to 3 days.

To ice: Working quickly, spread the still-soft Seven-Minute Frosting over the cake. Once frosted, sprinkle the toasted coconut over the top and sides of the cake and set aside under a cake dome for up to 6 hours.

Seven-Minute Frosting

Seven-Minute Frosting is a cooked frosting, like a modified Italian meringue, so named because it takes about 7 minutes to form in the double boiler over the heat (provided you're at sea level on a low-humidity day).

Makes enough frosting for a two-layer cake

> 3 large egg whites
> 2¼ cups sugar
> ½ cup water
> 2 teaspoons light corn syrup
> 2 teaspoons vanilla extract
> ¼ teaspoon salt

① Place the egg whites, sugar, water, corn syrup, vanilla, and salt in the top half of a large double boiler set over about 1 inch of simmering water in the bottom half. Alternatively, place the ingredients in a large bowl that fits snugly over a large saucepan with a similar amount of simmering water.

② Lower the heat so the water simmers slowly. Beat with an electric mixer at medium speed until the sugar dissolves and the egg whites are foamy. Raise the speed to high and continue beating, scraping down the sides of the bowl with a rubber spatula, until the consistency is like marshmallow fluff (the mixer will begin to have a hard time working and the frosting will begin to mass onto the beaters), about 7 minutes. There should be no grains of sugar you can feel between your fingers. Use immediately to frost the cake.

Variations: Reduce the vanilla extract to 1 teaspoon and add ½ teaspoon almond extract, maple extract, orange extract, or rum extract with the remaining vanilla.

Substitute ½ teaspoon mint extract or lemon extract for the vanilla.

Seven-Minute Frosting is also great on Cupcakes (pages 555–556) or used as a filling for Vanilla Sandwich Creams (page 575).

Banana Layer Cake with Maple Cream Cheese Frosting

Bananas cut down some of the fat in this three-layer cake, so you can save the calories for the frosting. The bananas must be very ripe—somewhat soft and with many, many brown blotches on the skin. Buy them several days before you intend to make this cake and leave them out on the counter to ripen. *Makes one 8-inch three-layer cake*

10 tablespoons (1 stick plus 2 tablespoons) cool unsalted butter, cut into chunks, plus additional for greasing the pans
2 cups cake flour, plus additional for dusting the pans
1 teaspoon baking powder
½ teaspoon baking soda
½ teaspoon salt
1 cup sugar
3 large eggs, at room temperature
2 teaspoons vanilla extract
3 very ripe large bananas, mashed in a small bowl with a fork
½ cup milk (regular, low-fat, or fat-free)
Maple Cream Cheese Frosting (recipe follows)

1 Position the rack in the center of the oven and preheat the oven to 350°F. Lightly butter three 8-inch round cake pans; dust them with flour, shaking out the excess after ascertaining that they're well coated.

2 Whisk the flour, baking powder, baking soda, and salt in a medium bowl; set aside.

3 Beat the butter and sugar in a large bowl with an electric mixer at medium speed until light, pale yellow, and quite airy, about 4 minutes.

4 Scrape down the sides of the bowl with a rubber spatula and beat in the eggs one at a time,

making sure each is thoroughly incorporated into the batter before adding the next. Beat in the vanilla, then beat in the mashed bananas until smooth.

5 Turn off the beaters, add half the flour mixture, and beat at low speed just until moistened. Add the milk and beat until well combined. Beat in the remaining flour for just a few seconds at low speed, just until moistened.

6 Scrape down and remove the beaters. Turn the batter a few times with a rubber spatula to make sure the flour is all moistened, then scrape the batter evenly into the three pans. Rap the pans a few times against your work surface to get rid of any air pockets.

7 Bake until lightly browned at the edges and a little puffed, until a toothpick or a cake tester inserted into the center of the cakes comes out clean, about 28 minutes.

To cool and unmold: Transfer to a wire rack and cool for 10 minutes, then unmold the cakes by running a knife around the pans' inner edge, inverting them onto a cutting board, removing the baking pans, and reinverting the cakes onto the wire rack. Cool completely before icing.

To store: Do not ice. Wrap the cooled layers individually in plastic wrap and store at room temperature for up to 2 days before icing.

To ice: See page 532. Frost no more than 6 hours before serving.

Variations: Add ½ teaspoon ground cinnamon, ¼ teaspoon grated nutmeg, or ¼ teaspoon grated mace with the salt.

Maple Cream Cheese Frosting

Makes enough frosting for a three-layer cake

8 ounces regular or low-fat cream cheese
   (do not use fat-free), at room temperature
6 tablespoons unsalted butter, at room
   temperature
¾ cup chopped toasted pecan pieces
6 tablespoons maple syrup
1 teaspoon vanilla extract
4½ to 5 cups confectioners' sugar

1 Beat the cream cheese and butter in a large bowl until smooth and light, using an electric mixer at medium speed, about 2 minutes.

2 Scrape down the sides of the bowl and beat in the pecans, maple syrup, and vanilla extract.

3 Turn off the beaters, add 3 cups confectioners' sugar, and beat at low speed until fully moistened and combined.

4 Remove the beaters and stir in more confectioners' sugar in ¼-cup increments with a wooden spoon until a smooth frosting forms.

You can also frost the Banana Layer Cake with:

Cream Cheese Sour Cream Frosting
   (page 527)
Banana Frosting (page 534)
Vanilla Buttercream (page 542)
Italian Meringue Icing (page 543)

Honey Cream Cheese Frosting: Substitute 5 tablespoons honey for the maple syrup.

Poppy Seed Layer Cake with Lemon Buttercream

For sheer heaven, we've paired a light cake with a thick, rich buttercream. Poppy seeds have an amazingly high oil content—which means they toast beautifully but also go rancid quickly. Store them in the refrigerator for up to 6 months. *Makes one 8-inch two-layer cake*

8 tablespoons (1 stick) cool unsalted butter,
   cut into chunks, plus additional for
   greasing the pans
2 cups cake flour, plus additional for dusting
   the pans
3 tablespoons poppy seeds
2 teaspoons baking powder
½ teaspoon salt
1 cup sugar
2 large eggs, at room temperature
¾ cup milk (regular, low-fat, or
   fat-free)
1 teaspoon vanilla extract
Lemon Buttercream (recipe follows)

1 Position the rack in the center of the oven and preheat the oven to 375°F. Lightly butter two 8-inch round cake pans; dust them thoroughly with flour, shaking out any excess.

2 Sprinkle the poppy seeds on a large baking sheet and bake just until aromatic, stirring once or twice, about 3 minutes. Alternatively, build a small sheet pan with a piece of aluminum foil, folding the sides up to create the edges; if you toast the seeds on this contraption, they'll be easier to pour into the batter. In either case, cool for 10 minutes.

3 Whisk the flour, baking powder, salt, and the toasted poppy seeds in a medium bowl; set aside.

4 Beat the butter and sugar in a large bowl with an electric mixer at medium speed until light and very yellow, about 4 minutes.

5 Scrape down the sides of the bowl and beat in the eggs one at a time, making sure the first is thoroughly incorporated before adding the second. Beat in ¼ cup milk and the vanilla until smooth.

6 Turn off the beaters, add a third of the flour mixture, and beat at low speed just until combined. Beat in another ¼ cup milk until smooth, then beat in half the remaining flour mixture at low speed. Beat in the remaining ¼ cup milk until smooth. Finally, add the remaining flour mixture and beat for just a few seconds, just until moistened.

7 Scrape down and remove the beaters. Turn the batter a few times with a rubber spatula to make sure there are no white streaks or dry patches, then scrape the batter evenly into the two pans. Rap them a couple of times against your work surface to knock out any air pockets.

8 Bake until lightly browned at the edges and a little puffed but still fairly pale in the middle, until a toothpick or cake tester inserted into the center of the cakes comes out clean, about 20 minutes. Cool completely before icing.

To cool and unmold: Transfer to a wire rack and cool for 10 minutes, then unmold the cakes by inverting them onto a cutting board, removing the baking pans, and reinverting the cakes onto the wire rack.

To store: Do not ice. Wrap the cooled layers individually in plastic wrap and keep for up to 2 days at room temperature.

To ice: See page 532. Frost the cake within 4 hours of serving.

Lemon Buttercream

A buttercream is a cooked frosting, the sugar syrup slowly turning the eggs into a creamy mass in which butter (and tons of it) is slowly beaten. *Makes enough frosting for a two-layer cake*

> 5 large egg yolks
> ¾ cup sugar
> ⅓ cup lemon juice
> 2 tablespoons light corn syrup
> ¼ teaspoon salt
> 1 teaspoon lemon extract, optional
> 24 tablespoons (3 sticks) unsalted butter,
>   at room temperature

1 Beat the egg yolks in a large bowl with an electric mixer at medium speed until doubled in volume, light, and very pale yellow, about 3 minutes. Set aside.

2 Place the sugar, lemon juice, corn syrup, and salt in a medium saucepan, clip a candy thermometer to the inside of the pan, and set it over medium-high heat. Stir until the sugar has completely dissolved, then bring the mixture to a simmer without disturbing and cook until the temperature reaches 250°F.

3 Beat the eggs at medium speed one more time to make sure they're fluffy, then beat in the hot sugar syrup in the slowest drizzle. Once all the sugar syrup has been added, continue beating until room temperature, about 10 minutes.

4 Beat in the lemon extract, if using. Then beat in the butter 2 tablespoons at a time.

5 Once all the butter has been added, continue beating until you have a smooth, creamy frosting, quite light but fairly thick, one that will hold its shape when mounded with a rubber spatula, about 10 minutes.

Mexican Wedding Layer Cake with Spiced Buttercream

This cake is designed to be a rendition of Mexican wedding cookies: a walnut cake with a cinnamon-spiced buttercream. *Makes one 8-inch two-layer cake*

8 tablespoons (1 stick) unsalted butter, melted and cooled, plus additional for greasing the pans

½ cup all-purpose flour, plus additional for dusting the pans

¼ teaspoon baking soda

¼ teaspoon salt

4 large eggs, at room temperature

½ cup sugar

1 teaspoon vanilla extract

1 cup finely ground walnuts (see Note)

Spiced Buttercream (recipe follows)

1 Position the rack in the center of the oven and preheat the oven to 350°F. Lightly butter two 8-inch round cake pans; dust thoroughly with flour, then shake out the excess.

2 Whisk the flour, baking soda, and salt in a medium bowl; set aside.

3 Beat the eggs and sugar in a large bowl with an electric mixer at medium speed until thick and doubled in volume, about 4 minutes. Beat in the vanilla.

4 Scrape down and remove the beaters. First, fold in the flour mixture gently with a rubber spatula just until moistened. Then fold in the ground walnuts in slow, even arcs. Finally, fold in the melted butter.

5 Scrape the batter evenly into the two pans. Rap them a few times against your work surface to knock out any air pockets.

6 Bake until set but still a little soft and spongy, until a toothpick or cake tester inserted into the center of the cakes comes out clean, about 20 minutes. Cool completely before frosting with the Spiced Buttercream.

To cool and unmold: Transfer to a wire rack and cool for 10 minutes, then unmold the cakes by running a knife around the pan's inner edge, inverting them onto a cutting board, removing the baking pans, and reinverting the cakes onto the wire rack.

To store: Do not ice. Wrap the layers individually in plastic wrap and keep at room temperature for up to 2 days.

To ice: See page 532.

Note: Grind the walnuts in a food processor fitted with the chopping blade until they are the consistency of coarse, dried bread crumbs.

Spiced Buttercream
Makes enough frosting for a two-layer cake

1 large egg plus 2 large egg yolks, at room temperature

¼ teaspoon salt

1 cup sugar

¼ cup water

1 tablespoon light corn syrup

24 tablespoons (3 sticks) unsalted butter, at room temperature

2 teaspoons ground cinnamon

1 teaspoon vanilla extract

½ teaspoon grated nutmeg

⅛ teaspoon ground cloves

1 Beat the egg, egg yolks, and salt in a medium bowl with an electric mixer at medium speed un-

til very creamy and tripled in volume, about 5 minutes. Set aside.

2 Mix the sugar, water, and corn syrup in a medium saucepan, clip a candy thermometer to the inside of the pan, and set it over medium-high heat. Stir until the sugar has dissolved, then continue cooking without disturbing until the temperature reaches 250°F. Remove from the heat; remove the thermometer.

3 Beat the egg yolks a few turns to make sure they're very fluffy, then begin adding the sugar syrup in a very slow, steady drizzle, with the beaters running at medium speed. Once all the sugar syrup has been added, continue beating until cool, about 10 minutes.

4 Beat in the butter, about 2 tablespoons at a time.

5 Once all the butter has been added, continue beating until thick and frostinglike, about 10 minutes. Beat in the cinnamon, vanilla, nutmeg, and cloves.

You can also frost the Mexican Wedding Layer Cake:

Seven-Minute Frosting (page 537)
Chocolate Sour Cream Frosting (page 535)
Chocolate Mousse Frosting (page 535)

Vanilla Buttercream: Omit the cinnamon, nutmeg, and cloves; increase the vanilla to 1 tablespoon. If desired, also beat in the seeds scraped from 1 vanilla bean.

Mint Buttercream: Omit the cinnamon, vanilla, nutmeg, and cloves; beat in ½ teaspoon mint extract and a few drops of green food coloring in their stead.

Whoopie Pie Layer Cake with Italian Meringue Icing

Here's a reinvention of a Southern favorite: a chocolate layer cake with a fluffy, marshmallowy filling. *Makes one 9-inch two-layer cake*

½ cup solid vegetable shortening, plus additional for greasing the pans
3 ounces unsweetened chocolate, chopped
1¾ cups plus 2 tablespoons cake flour, plus additional for dusting the pans
2 tablespoons sifted unsweetened cocoa powder
1 teaspoon baking powder
½ teaspoon baking soda
½ teaspoon salt
1½ cups sugar
2 large eggs plus 1 large egg yolk, at room temperature
1 teaspoon vanilla extract
1 cup milk (regular, low-fat, or fat-free)
Italian Meringue Icing (page 543)
Confectioners' sugar for garnish

1 Place the shortening and chocolate in the top half of a double boiler set over about 1 inch of simmering water. Alternatively, place the shortening and chocolate in a medium bowl that will fit snugly over a medium saucepan with about the same amount of simmering water in it. Adjust the heat so the water simmers slowly and does not boil. Stir until half the chocolate has melted, then remove the top half of the double boiler or the bowl from the saucepan (be careful of escaping steam!) and continue stirring away from the heat until the chocolate has fully melted. Set aside to cool, stirring once in a while, for 15 minutes.

2 Position the rack in the center of the oven and preheat the oven to 325°F. Lightly grease two 9-inch cake pans; dust them with flour, coating the bottom and sides lightly but thoroughly, then shaking out any excess.

❸ Whisk the flour, cocoa powder, baking powder, baking soda, and salt in a medium bowl.

❹ Beat the sugar, eggs, and egg yolk in a large bowl, using an electric mixer at medium speed, until thick and creamy, until the turned-off beaters drizzle firm ribbons back on top of the mixture, ribbons that do not immediately dissolve, about 4 minutes. Beat in the melted chocolate mixture, then beat in the vanilla until smooth.

❺ Beat in ½ cup milk, then turn off the beaters and add half the flour mixture. Beat at low speed just until moistened, then beat in the remaining milk at low speed. Add the remaining flour mixture; beat at low speed just until moistened, just for a few seconds.

❻ Scrape down the beaters and remove them. Give the batter a few turns with a rubber spatula to make sure there are no white streaks, then scrape evenly into the two pans. Rap the pans a few times against your work surface to get rid of any air pockets.

❼ Bake until springy to the touch, until a toothpick or cake tester inserted into the center of the cakes comes out clean, about 35 minutes. Cool completely before filling.

To cool and unmold: Transfer to a wire rack and cool for 10 minutes, then unmold the cakes by inverting them onto a cutting board, removing the baking pans, and reinverting the cakes onto the wire rack before cooling completely, about 1 hour.

To store: Do not ice. Wrap the cooled layers separately in plastic wrap and keep at room temperature for up to 2 days.

To fill: Up to 6 hours before you serve the cake, top one layer with the Italian Meringue Icing. Lay the second layer on top. Dust with confectioners' sugar just before serving.

Variation: Add 1½ teaspoons cinnamon, ¼ teaspoon grated nutmeg, or ¼ teaspoon grated mace with the cocoa.

Italian Meringue Icing

An Italian meringue is made by cooking the egg whites with a hot sugar syrup (as opposed to a Swiss meringue, made with raw egg whites, often put on top of meringue pies).

Makes enough icing for a two-layer cake

> 4 large egg whites
> ¼ teaspoon salt
> 1½ cups sugar
> ¾ cup water
> ½ teaspoon cream of tartar

❶ Beat the egg whites and salt in a large bowl with an electric mixer at medium speed until frothy. Increase the speed to high and beat until soft, droopy, white peaks can be formed by dipping the turned-off beaters into the mixture. Set aside.

❷ Place the sugar, water, and cream of tartar in a medium saucepan and clip a candy-making thermometer to the inside of the pan. Set the pan over medium heat and stir with a wooden spoon until the sugar has fully dissolved. Then continue cooking undisturbed until the temperature reaches 250°F.

❸ Beat the egg whites for 5 seconds at high speed, then slowly pour in the hot syrup at the barest drizzle with the beaters running.

❹ Once all the syrup has been added, continue beating until thick, marshmallowy, and cool, 7 to 10 minutes. Fill the cake immediately.

Linzer Layer Cake

A Linzer tart is an almond crust topped with raspberry jam, but here's a cake version with two almond layer cakes sandwiching raspberry jam.

Makes one 9-inch two-layer cake

Unsalted butter or nonstick spray for
    greasing the cake pans
1 cup all-purpose flour, plus additional for
    dusting the pans
¾ teaspoon baking powder
½ teaspoon salt
6 large egg whites, at room temperature
1 cup sugar
5 large egg yolks, at room temperature
3 tablespoons milk (regular, low-fat, or
    fat-free)
½ teaspoon vanilla extract
½ teaspoon almond extract
1 cup finely ground sliced or slivered almonds
⅔ cup raspberry jam
1 tablespoon confectioners' sugar

1 Position the racks in the center of the oven and preheat the oven to 350°F. Lightly butter or spray two 9-inch round cake pans; dust with flour, shaking out the excess.

2 Whisk the flour, baking powder, and salt in a medium bowl; set aside.

3 Beat the egg whites in a large bowl until foamy with an electric mixer at high speed. Slowly pour in ⅓ cup sugar in a thin, steady stream, beating all the while. Continue beating until the turned-off beaters will make droopy, satiny, soft peaks in the mixture when they're dabbed into it, about 5 minutes. Set aside.

4 Clean and dry the beaters. Beat the egg yolks and the remaining ⅔ cup sugar in a second large bowl at medium speed until very thick and pale yellow, about 3 minutes. Beat in the milk, vanilla, and almond extract until smooth. Scrape down and remove the beaters.

5 Fold in the ground almonds with a rubber spatula, then fold in the flour mixture just until there are no more white streaks in the batter.

6 Fold in half the beaten egg whites, then gently fold in the remainder of the beaten egg whites, using long, slow strokes so as not to deflate them. There may be a few white streaks of egg white still in the mixture. Pour and scrape the mixture evenly between the two prepared pans.

7 Bake until a toothpick or cake tester inserted into the middle of the cakes comes out clean, about 22 minutes. Cool completely before filling.

To cool and unmold: Transfer to a wire rack and cool for 10 minutes. Unmold the cakes by running a knife around the pans' inner edge, inverting them onto a cutting board, removing the pan, and then reinverting the cakes onto the wire rack. Cool completely, at least 45 minutes.

To store: Wrap the cooled layers individually in plastic and set aside at room temperature for up to 2 days.

To fill: Place one cake layer top side down on a serving platter or cake stand. Spoon the jam into the center of the cake and then spread it out to the edges with an offset spatula or the back of a soup spoon occasionally dipped into hot water. Set the other cake layer top side up on the jam. Place the confectioners' sugar in a fine-mesh sieve and dust it over the cake.

Variation: Substitute any flavor of jam you like for the raspberry—or use orange marmalade or another citrus marmalade.

Inside-Out Black Forest Layer Cake

Here's an American take on a Bavarian classic: a cherry layer cake with a chocolate whipped cream frosting. *Makes one 9-inch two-layer cake*

> 10 tablespoons (1 stick plus 2 tablespoons) cool unsalted butter, cut into chunks, plus additional for greasing the pan
> 3 cups cake flour, plus additional for dusting the pans
> 4 teaspoons baking powder
> ½ teaspoon salt
> ½ cup sugar
> 1 cup sour cherry jam
> 3 large eggs, at room temperature
> 2 teaspoons vanilla extract
> ¾ cup milk (regular, low-fat, or fat-free)
> Chocolate Whipped Cream (recipe follows)
> 2 ounces bittersweet or semisweet chocolate

1. Position the rack in the center of the oven and preheat the oven to 350°F. Lightly butter two 9-inch cake pans; dust thoroughly with flour, shaking out the excess.

2. Whisk the flour, baking powder, and salt in a medium bowl; set aside.

3. Beat the butter and sugar in a large bowl with an electric mixer at medium speed until light, creamy, and smooth, about 4 minutes. Scrape down the sides of the bowl and beat in the sour cherry jam.

4. Beat in the eggs one at a time, making sure each has been thoroughly incorporated without any visible eggy bits. Beat in the vanilla until smooth, then beat in ¼ cup milk.

5. Turn the beaters off, add a third of the flour mixture, and beat at low speed just until moistened. Beat in another ¼ cup milk, then beat in half the remaining flour mixture, again just until moistened. Finally, beat in the remaining ¼ cup milk, then beat in the remaining flour for just a few seconds, just to pull the flour into the batter.

6. Scrape down the beaters and remove them. Turn the batter a few times with a rubber spatula to make sure that there are no white streaks of undissolved flour, then scrape the batter evenly into the two pans. Rap the pans a few times against your work surface to get rid of any air pockets.

7. Bake until pale brown, set, and a little puffed, until a toothpick or cake tester inserted into the center of the cakes comes out clean, about 30 minutes. Cool completely before frosting with the Chocolate Whipped Cream.

To cool and unmold: Transfer to a wire rack and cool for 10 minutes, then unmold the cakes by inverting them onto a cutting board, removing the baking pans, and reinverting the cakes onto the wire rack to cool completely, about 1 hour.

To store: Do not ice. Wrap the cooled layers individually in plastic wrap and store at room temperature for up to 2 days.

To ice: See page 532. Spread the Chocolate Whipped Cream between the layers, over the top, and down the sides. Shave the bittersweet or semisweet chocolate through the large holes of a box grater or with a chocolate shaver over the cake; shave some of the chocolate onto a sheet of wax paper, then gently press this against the sides of the cake to get the shavings to adhere to the whipped cream. Once frosted, refrigerate for up to 4 hours before serving.

Variations: Any jam will do, provided it's a little tart, like orange marmalade (so long as the chunks of orange are not too large). You can also use blackberry or apricot jam, but also add 1 teaspoon finely grated lemon zest.

Chocolate Whipped Cream
Makes about 6 cups

3½ cups heavy cream
½ cup confectioners' sugar
1 tablespoon cornstarch
7 tablespoons sifted unsweetened cocoa
    powder

1 Whisk 1 cup cream, the confectioners' sugar, and the cornstarch in a medium saucepan set over medium-high heat until the mixture comes to a simmer. Whisking constantly, simmer for 30 seconds, then remove from the heat and cool completely, about 15 minutes.

2 Beat the remaining 2½ cups cream and the cocoa in a large bowl with an electric mixer at medium speed until the cocoa has dissolved. Increase the speed to high and continue beating until the beaters begin to leave tracks in the thickening cream.

3 With the beaters running, slowly add the cornstarch mixture. Continue beating until stiff peaks form, the kind you can mound on a rubber spatula. Ice the cake at once.

All-Purpose v. Cake Flour

In truth, we tried every cake with all-purpose flour, more readily accessible; but some simply needed the higher starch of cake flour. If you simply can't find cake flour, a somewhat tricky variation is to substitute 14 tablespoons all-purpose flour plus 1 tablespoon cornstarch for every cup of cake flour. The results won't be as tender or light but they'll be less gummy than if you'd used all-purpose flour only.

Lemon Meringue Layer Cake with Lemon Curd Filling

This is a cake version of our favorite pie—a light, buttery cake, one layer with a meringue topping, and a lemony filling to go between the layers.
Makes one 9-inch two-layer cake

1½ cups plus 1 tablespoon all-purpose flour,
    plus additional for dusting the pans
4 large eggs plus 2 large egg whites, at room
    temperature
1 cup plus 7 tablespoons sugar
¾ teaspoon salt
1 tablespoon finely grated lemon zest
2 teaspoons vanilla extract
5 tablespoons unsalted butter, melted and
    cooled, plus additional for greasing the
    pans
Lemon Curd Filling (recipe follows)

1 Position the rack in the center of the oven and preheat the oven to 350°F. Butter and lightly flour two 9-inch round cake pans; set aside.

2 Beat the 4 large eggs, 1 cup sugar, and ½ teaspoon salt in a large bowl with an electric mixer at medium-high speed; beat until very pale and doubled in volume, 8 to 10 minutes. Beat in the zest and vanilla.

3 Scrape down and remove the beaters. Fold in the melted butter with a rubber spatula just until incorporated. Add the flour and fold just until dissolved, until you can see no white bits in the batter. Divide between the two prepared pans.

4 Bake until lightly browned and springy to the touch, until a toothpick or cake tester inserted into the center of one of the layers comes out clean, about 25 minutes. Transfer to a wire rack and cool for 10 minutes, then invert the layers onto the rack and remove the pans. Cool completely, about 1 hour.

⑤ Meanwhile, make the Lemon Curd Filling (see right) and allow to cool completely at room temperature, about 30 minutes.

⑥ Heat the oven to 400°F. Transfer one of the cake layers to a large baking sheet, using a large, flat, metal spatula, even one used for barbecuing.

⑦ Beat the 2 egg whites and the remaining ¼ teaspoon salt in a large dry bowl with an electric mixer at high speed until you can form soft, droopy peaks by dipping the turned-off beaters into the mixture. Beat in the remaining 7 tablespoons sugar 1 tablespoon at a time; continue beating until glossy, until you can make stiff peaks with the turned-off beaters.

⑧ Spread and mound the egg white meringue onto the cake layer sitting on the baking sheet. Use a rubber spatula to create peaks and valleys in the meringue, spreading it to the rim of the layer.

⑨ Bake until the meringue is lightly browned, about 8 minutes.

⑩ Remove the sheet from the oven and cool on a wire rack for 15 minutes.

⑪ Transfer the other layer to a cake plate and spread the Lemon Curd Filling evenly over its top surface. Use 1 or 2 large wide, metal spatulas to set the meringue-topped layer atop the bottom layer.

To store: Cover loosely and refrigerate for up to 3 days; return to room temperature before serving.

Lemon Curd Filling

4 large egg yolks, at room temperature
½ cup lemon juice
½ cup sugar
4 tablespoons (½ stick) unsalted butter, at room temperature

① Place all the ingredients in the top half of a double boiler set over a pan with about 1 inch of simmering water in it—or place them in a medium bowl that fits over a medium saucepan with the same amount of simmering water. Adjust the heat so the water simmers gently.

② Beat with an electric mixer at medium speed until smooth, glossy, and thick, about like mayonnaise, 5 to 7 minutes. (Be careful of the electric cord around simmering water and heating elements.)

Additional Ways to Use Lemon Curd

This cake filling is indeed no more than an easy version of traditional lemon curd. You can make it on its own and then use it any number of ways.

① Make a double batch and pour into a prebaked pie shell (see page 592 for a crust and page 602 for instructions on how to prebake it). Fill with the curd, then cool completely. Top with Sweetened Whipped Cream (page 522) just before serving.

② Double the recipe and mound the Lemon Curd in a serving bowl, then top with a plethora of fresh blackberries, raspberries, and strawberries. For a sweeter dessert, mix the berries with 2 tablespoons sugar and set them aside for 5 minutes before placing on the curd.

③ Use it as the filling for Vanilla Sandwich Creams (page 575). Or use it to sandwich Almond Macaroons together (page 570).

④ Make an ice cream topping: thin out a batch by whisking in some rum, probably about ¼ cup, depending on how thin you want the sauce.

⑤ Make a type of Lemon Mousse by folding a batch of Lemon Curd into a batch of Sweetened Whipped Cream (page 522) and then spooning the mixture into wineglasses or goblets.

❊ *Cheesecakes* ❊

Cheesecakes are best when they have a chance to ripen in the refrigerator for a day or two, their flavors becoming more intense and the whole cake settling a bit into a dense wonder.

The Ultimate Cheesecake

Fine on its own, this ultracreamy but slightly chewy cheesecake is a blank canvas for many different toppings (see page 549). *Makes one 8-inch cheesecake*

2 tablespoons unsalted butter, melted and cooled
¼ cup finely ground blanched almonds
1½ pounds regular cream cheese (do not use low-fat or fat-free), softened to room temperature (see Note)
¾ cup granulated sugar
¼ cup packed dark brown sugar
3 large eggs, at room temperature
½ cup heavy cream
1 tablespoon vanilla extract
¼ teaspoon salt

❶ Position the rack in the center of the oven and preheat the oven to 325°F. Brush the melted butter over the inside of an 8-inch cheesecake pan. Alternatively, you can use an 8-inch springform pan if you first wrap its exterior with aluminum foil to prevent any water or batter leakage. Bring a teakettle of water to a boil over high heat.

❷ Sprinkle the ground almonds into the pan; turn until the bottom is coated with the almonds, tapping the pan so the almonds move up the sides as well. Leave any extra almonds on the bottom of the pan.

❸ Use an electric mixer to beat the cream cheese and both sugars in a large bowl until creamy, until you can feel few sugar granules between your fingers, about 6 minutes.

❹ Beat in the eggs one at a time, adding the next only after the previous one has been fully incorporated. After scraping down the sides of the bowl, beat in the cream, vanilla, and salt until smooth. Pour and scrape the batter into the prepared pan, doing so slowly so as not to dislodge any of the almonds.

❺ Take the water off the heat so that it stops boiling. Place the cake pan in a large roasting pan; fill the roasting pan with the very hot water until it comes halfway up the sides of the cake pan.

❻ Bake until set when jiggled and a little browned on top, about 1½ hours.

To cool: Remove the cheesecake pan or springform pan from the water bath and cool on a wire rack until room temperature, about 2 hours.

To store: When completely cooled, wrap the pan in plastic wrap and store in the refrigerator for up to 3 days.

To unmold: Run a knife gently around the interior rim of the pan; invert the cheesecake onto a cutting board, then reinvert it onto a serving plate or cake plate; or slip off the outer springform ring, slice the cake off the bottom with a long, thin knife, and slip it onto a serving platter or cake stand.

Note: Low-fat cream cheese will result in a slippery texture; fat-free cream cheese will produce a watery cheesecake that may not set.

Toppings: Once the cheesecake has cooled completely, top it with ½ cup softened blackberry jam, blueberry jam, orange marmalade, raspberry jam, or strawberry preserves, heated slowly in a small saucepan over low heat for about 1 minute, stirring constantly, until soft, then cooled for 10 minutes before spreading on the cheesecake.

Or top with a half recipe of Chocolate Whipped Cream (page 546).

Or top with ⅓ cup chopped candied ginger, chopped toasted almonds, chopped toasted pecan pieces, or chopped toasted walnut pieces; sprinkle about ¼ teaspoon grated nutmeg over the nuts.

Or top with 1 cup fresh blackberries, blueberries, raspberries, or sliced strawberries macerated with 1 tablespoon sugar in a small bowl for 10 minutes.

Or top with 2 ounces shaved bittersweet or semisweet chocolate.

Spiced Cheesecake: Beat in 1 teaspoon ground cinnamon, ½ teaspoon ground ginger, and ¼ teaspoon grated nutmeg with the vanilla.

Chocolate Cheesecake: Omit the brown sugar; increase the granulated sugar to 1¼ cups. Add 1 additional large egg yolk with the eggs. Add 4 ounces chopped unsweetened chocolate, melted in a bowl in the microwave or in the top half of a double boiler over simmering water, then cooled, with the cream and vanilla.

A Cheesecake Pan

A cheesecake pan is a round, high-sided cake pan without a removable bottom. In a springform pan, the seams between the sides and bottom can allow little bits of the cake to leak out—and can let water leak into the cake (with disastrous results).

Baklava Cheesecake

A whimsical dessert, this combines two of our favorite treats by setting a honey cheesecake in a phyllo/walnut crust with a rich vein of walnuts running through the cake's center. Since you don't bake this cheesecake in a water bath (the phyllo would turn gummy), you can use a springform pan. *Makes one 9-inch cheesecake*

1½ pounds regular cream cheese (do not use low-fat or fat-free—see Note on the previous recipe, page 548) softened to room temperature

¾ cup plus 2 tablespoons honey

3 large eggs, at room temperature

1 tablespoon all-purpose flour

1 tablespoon vanilla extract

3 cups walnut pieces, toasted and cooled

3 tablespoons packed dark brown sugar

½ teaspoon ground cinnamon

About 3 tablespoons unsalted butter, melted and cooled

4 sheets phyllo dough, laid on the work surface and covered with plastic wrap and a dry kitchen towel

1 Position the rack in the center of the oven and preheat the oven to 325°F.

2 Beat the cream cheese and ¾ cup honey in a large bowl, using an electric mixer at medium speed, until smooth, about 2 minutes.

3 Beat in the eggs one at a time, scraping down the bowl and making sure there are no eggy bits visible before adding the next. Finally, beat in the flour and vanilla until smooth. Set aside.

4 Grind the walnuts, brown sugar, and cinnamon in a food processor fitted with the chopping blade until sandlike, not powdery.

⑤ Generously brush the inside and bottom of a 9-inch springform pan with about 1 tablespoon melted butter, making sure you coat the joint between the walls and the bottom.

⑥ Generously brush a sheet of phyllo dough with a little melted butter, then lay it in the pan, forming it into the pan and overlapping the sides. Sprinkle about 1 tablespoon of the ground walnut mixture evenly over the parts of the phyllo sheet that are below the pan's rim.

⑦ Repeat with the remaining 3 sheets of phyllo, brushing them with butter, laying the second at a 90-degree angle to the first, sprinkling this second sheet with 1 tablespoon walnut mixture, and then continuing with the others until the pan is covered with overlapping phyllo sheets, each one sprinkled with 1 tablespoon walnut mixture.

⑧ Pour about half the batter into the phyllo-lined pan. Mix the remaining 2 tablespoons honey with the remaining walnut mixture. Sprinkle evenly over the batter.

⑨ Gently pour the remaining batter into the pan, taking care not to dislodge the walnut mixture. Scrape any excess out of the bowl and into the pan. Rap the pan a couple of times against your work surface to even out the batter. Trim any phyllo hanging over the edges of the pan with kitchen shears.

⑩ Bake until lightly browned and a little puffed, until the cake is set when jiggled but not completely firm, about 1½ hours.

To cool: Set on a wire rack until room temperature, about 2 hours.

To store: Wrap tightly in plastic wrap and store in the refrigerator for up to 3 days.

To serve: Undo the metal ring from the springform pan and slip it off; serve the cake right off the bottom of the springform pan.

Apricot Cheesecake

Here's a surprise: you can make a creamy, rich cheesecake with dried apricots and fat-free cream cheese. What's more, the texture is smoother, even creamier than our ultimate cheesecake. *Makes one 9-inch cheesecake*

> 1 cup dried California apricots (see Note)
> ½ cup water
> ½ cup Grape-Nuts cereal
> Nonstick spray
> 1 pound fat-free cottage cheese
> 1 pound fat-free cream cheese
> ½ cup packed light brown sugar
> ¼ cup granulated sugar
> ½ teaspoon salt
> 2 large eggs plus 2 large egg yolks, at room temperature
> 2 teaspoons vanilla extract
> ⅓ cup all-purpose flour

① Place the apricots and water in a small saucepan and set it over medium-high heat. Bring the liquid to a simmer; then cover, reduce the heat to low, and simmer until all the liquid has been absorbed, about 4 minutes. Set aside to cool for 30 minutes.

② Meanwhile, grind the cereal in a mini-food processor or large food processor fitted with the chopping blade until about the texture of cornmeal.

③ Spray the inside of a 9-inch springform pan with nonstick spray, taking care to coat the sides and the joint against the bottom. Pour the cereal in the pan, then turn it to coat the bottom and sides with cereal.

4 Position the rack in the center of the oven and preheat the oven to 325°F.

5 Place the apricots in a food processor fitted with the chopping blade and process until almost pureed. Add the cottage cheese and process for 1 minute. Scrape down the sides of the bowl; add the cream cheese, both sugars, and salt. Process until smooth.

6 Add the eggs one a time, processing the first into the batter before adding the second. Add the egg yolks and vanilla; again, process until smooth. Finally, scrape down the bowl one last time, add the flour, pulse until dissolved, then process until smooth. Pour the batter into the prepared pan.

7 Bake until set, until the cake will not jiggle when shaken but is nonetheless still a little moist at its center, about 45 minutes. Turn off the oven, leave the door ajar by a couple of inches, and leave the cake in the oven for 1 hour.

To cool: Transfer to a wire rack and cool completely, about 1 hour.

To store: Once cooled, wrap the pan in plastic and refrigerate for up to 4 days.

To unmold: Unlatch the collar and remove before slicing the cake.

Note: Dried California apricots are halves, quite tart—as opposed to the brownish, whole, rather dull Turkish apricots.

Apricot Ginger Cheesecake: Add 2 tablespoons chopped crystallized ginger with the vanilla.

Apricot Rum Cheesecake: Substitute gold rum for the water.

Peach Cheesecake: Substitute dried peaches for the apricots.

Rum Raisin Cheesecake: Substitute raisins for the apricots and gold rum for the water.

Cream Cheese

Cream cheese is a high-fat (around 33% fat), dense (less than 55% moisture) cheese. It was the brainchild of a New York farmer who, in 1872, wanted to make a rich cheese to compete with French specialties. He substituted cream for a good percentage of the whole milk—and cream cheese was born. An inventor he was—but not much of a marketer. That job fell to another New Yorker, A. L. Reynolds, who in 1880 began distributing the cheese under the brand-name "Philadelphia." The city of brotherly love was known for its high-quality craftsmanship, so Reynolds simply stuck the city name on his product. And stick it did. Even today, in Spain and Latin American countries, the cheese is simply known as "Philadelphia."

Despite its popularity, cream cheese is quite difficult to produce. Without delving too deeply into the chemistry of milk, suffice it to say that cream cheese is always threatening to liquefy, mostly because of ion charges in the mix. Stabilizers like guar gum are often added to keep the cheese solid. In many lower fat cream cheeses, more and more of these stabilizers are added for body.

In the U.S., low-fat and even fat-free cream cheeses are sometimes called "Neufchâtel" cheese, a misnomer and a confusion with a high-fat, rich, French cheese.

No recipe in this book calls for whipped cream cheese, aerated for spreading. And no recipe calls for flavored cream cheese. Save both of these for bagels or toast.

These light cakes are made in a 10 × 15-inch jelly roll pan or baking sheet, then wrapped up in a towel and cooled. Later, they're unwound, filled with a variety of concoctions, and rolled back up to be sliced into spiral-filled rounds.

Vanilla Sponge Roll Cake

Makes one 15-inch-long roll cake

Unsalted butter for greasing
6 large eggs, separated (see page 19),
   at room temperature
¼ teaspoon salt
½ cup sugar
1 tablespoon vanilla extract
⅔ cup all-purpose flour

❶ Position the rack in the center of the oven and preheat the oven to 350°F. Lightly butter a 15 × 10-inch jelly roll pan, then line it with parchment paper; grease the paper and the pan's sides.

❷ Place the egg whites and salt in a large bowl and beat with an electric mixer at high speed until the beaters form soft peaks when they are turned off and dabbed into the mixture, about 3 minutes. Set aside.

❸ If you're using a handheld mixer, clean and dry the beaters; if you're using a stand mixer, remove the whisk and attach the paddle. Beat the egg yolks and sugar at medium speed in a second large bowl until this mixture is so thick, it will run off the turned-off beaters in wide ribbons that do not immediately dissolve back into the mixture, about 4 minutes. Beat in the vanilla.

❹ Scrape down and remove the beaters. Fold in the flour with a rubber spatula just until moistened. Then fold in the beaten egg whites in three batches, taking care not to deflate them, using long, even strokes.

❺ Pour and scrape the batter evenly into the prepared pan, spreading it to the corners. Rap it a couple of times against the counter to get rid of any air bubbles.

❻ Bake until spongy to the touch and lightly browned, about 15 minutes. You'll need to roll it the moment it's out of the oven. (See page 553.)

Chocolate Sponge Roll Cake

Makes one 15-inch-long roll cake

Unsalted butter for greasing
¾ cup sifted unsweetened cocoa powder
½ cup all-purpose flour
6 large eggs, separated (see page 19)
¼ teaspoon salt
¾ cup sugar
2 teaspoons vanilla extract

❶ Position the rack in the center of the oven and preheat the oven to 350°F. Lightly butter a 15 × 10-inch jelly roll pan, then line it with parchment paper; butter the paper and the pan's sides.

② Lay a large sheet of wax paper on the work surface. Sift the cocoa powder and flour together through a fine-mesh sieve and onto the paper. Gather together what you've sifted and do so again. Set the paper with the sifted mixture aside.

③ Place the egg whites and salt in a large bowl and beat with an electric mixer at high speed until soft peaks form under the beaters when they are turned off and lifted quickly out of the mixture, about 3 minutes. Set aside as well.

④ If you're using a handheld mixer, clean and dry the beaters; if you're using a stand mixer, remove the whisk and attach the paddle. Beat the egg yolks and sugar at medium speed in a second large bowl until this mixture is so thick, it will run off the beaters or paddle in wide ribbons that do not immediately dissolve back into the mixture, about 3 minutes. Beat in the vanilla until smooth.

⑤ Scrape down the beaters and remove them. Fold in the cocoa mixture with a rubber spatula just until moistened. Then fold in the beaten egg whites in three batches, taking care not to deflate them, using long, even strokes.

⑥ Pour and scrape the batter into the prepared pan, spreading it to the corners. Rap it a couple of times against the counter to get rid of any air bubbles.

⑦ Bake until spongy to the touch and lightly browned, about 15 minutes. You'll need to work with it the moment's it's out of the oven. See the instructions for how to roll it below.

How to Roll and Fill a Sponge Roll

What You'll Need

A large, clean kitchen towel

Confectioners' sugar

One Vanilla or Chocolate Sponge Roll Cake, just out of the oven

One of the seven fillings listed on page 554

What to Do

① Generously dust a clean kitchen towel with confectioners' sugar; the towel should be larger than the jelly roll pan.

② Within 1 minute of the cake's coming out of the oven, invert the still-hot pan onto the kitchen towel; then remove the pan, leaving the cake behind. Do not peel off the parchment paper. Starting at one of the long ends of the cake, roll it up in the towel, using the towel as a guide, getting the towel and the parchment paper inside the cake as you roll it up. Cool on a wire rack for 1 hour.

③ Gently unroll the cake. Peel off the parchment paper; the towel will be under the cake.

④ Spread the filling of your choice on the top side of the cake, then roll it up again, enclosing the filling but this time leaving the towel behind.

To store: The filled cake can be covered in plastic wrap and refrigerated for up to 3 days. If you've used an ice cream filling or other frozen dessert filling, wrap the roll in plastic and store it in the freezer for up to 2 months; allow it to stand at room temperature for 10 minutes before slicing and serving.

Seven Fillings for a Sponge Roll

I. Jam

Soften 1½ cups raspberry, blackberry, blueberry, or strawberry jam in a small saucepan over low heat for about 2 minutes, stirring constantly

II. Softened Ice Cream

Soften 1 pint ice cream, gelato, sherbet, or sorbet at room temperature until spreadable, about 10 minutes.

III. Chocolate Sour Cream Frosting (page 535)

IV. Chocolate Whipped Cream (page 546)

Make a half recipe.

V. Chocolate Mousse Frosting (page 535)

Make a half recipe.

VI. Lemon Filling

2 large eggs plus 6 large egg yolks, at room temperature
8 tablespoons (1 stick) unsalted butter, at room temperature, cut into chunks
Finely grated zest of 2 lemons
1¼ cups lemon juice

Whisk all the ingredients together in the top half of a double boiler set over about 2 inches of simmering water or in a large bowl that fits snugly over a large pot with about the same amount of simmering water. Adjust the heat so the water simmers slowly. Continue whisking until thick, like lemon curd, about 18 minutes. Cool for at least 15 minutes before filling the sponge roll.

VII. Marshmallow Filling

4 tablespoons (½ stick) unsalted butter, at room temperature
3 tablespoons solid vegetable shortening
1 tablespoon vanilla extract
¼ teaspoon salt
About 1 cup confectioners' sugar
⅓ cup Marshmallow Fluff or Marshmallow Crème (see Note)

Beat the butter, shortening, vanilla, and salt in a large bowl until creamy and light, using an electric mixer at medium speed, about 2 minutes. Add 1 cup confectioners' sugar and the Marshmallow Fluff or Crème. Continue beating until marshmallowy. You may need to add more confectioners' sugar; do so in 1-tablespoon increments for a thick, smooth texture, but take care: you do not want it to become runny.

Note: Marshmallow Fluff is an East Coast delight. West of the Mississippi, Fluff is replaced by Marshmallow Crème, similar but slightly runnier. Either will work in these recipes; but if you use Marshmallow Crème, you may need to add a little more confectioners' sugar to give it a little body.

❋ Cupcakes ❋

Here are two all-purpose cupcakes. None has a frosting in tow; each can take almost any of the frostings, icings, and buttercreams in this chapter (with the exception of the Lemon Drizzle, Lemon Curd, or most of the fillings for the sponge rolls).

Vanilla Cupcakes

Makes 24 cupcakes

24 paper cupcake liners
2 cups cake flour
2 teaspoons baking powder
½ teaspoon salt
8 tablespoons (1 stick) cool unsalted butter, cut into chunks
1 cup sugar
1 large egg plus 2 large egg yolks, at room temperature
2 teaspoons vanilla extract
⅔ cup milk (regular, low-fat, or fat-free)

❶ Position the rack in the center of the oven and preheat the oven to 375°F. Line a standard 24-cup muffin tin or two 12-cup tins with the cupcake liners. If using silicone muffin tins, set them on a large baking sheet.

❷ Whisk the flour, baking powder, and salt in a medium bowl; set aside.

❸ Use an electric mixer to beat the butter and sugar in a large bowl until creamy and pale yellow, about 4 minutes. Beat in the egg, then the 2 egg yolks and the vanilla until smooth.

❹ Beat in half the milk. Turn off the beaters, add half the flour mixture, and beat at low speed just until moistened. Scrape down the sides of the bowl, beat in the remainder of the milk, then beat in the remainder of the flour mixture just until incorporated.

❺ Scrape down and remove the beaters. Use a rubber spatula to give the batter a few stirs, just to make sure there are no pockets of undissolved flour. Spoon the batter into the cups, filling them about two-thirds full.

❻ Bake until puffed and slightly firm to the touch, until a toothpick or a cake tester inserted into the center of a muffin comes out clean, about 30 minutes. Cool for 5 minutes, then unmold and cool on a wire rack until room temperature before frosting.

Chocolate Cupcakes

Makes 24 cupcakes

24 paper cupcake liners
2 cups cake flour
1 teaspoon baking soda
¼ teaspoon salt
8 tablespoons (1 stick) cool unsalted butter, cut into chunks
¾ cup packed light brown sugar
¾ cup granulated sugar
2 large eggs plus 1 large egg yolk, at room temperature
4 ounces unsweetened chocolate, chopped, melted, and cooled
1 teaspoon vanilla extract
1 cup milk (regular, low-fat, or fat-free)

❶ Position the rack in the center of the oven and preheat the oven to 375°F. Line a standard 24-cup muffin tin or two 12-cup tins with the cupcake liners. If using silicone muffin tins, set them on a large baking sheet.

❷ Whisk the flour, baking soda, and salt in a medium bowl; set aside.

❸ Use an electric mixer to beat the butter and both kinds of sugar in a large bowl until light and fluffy, about 5 minutes. Beat in the eggs one at a time, then beat in the egg yolk, melted chocolate, and vanilla until smooth.

❹ Beat in half the milk. Turn off the beaters, add half the flour mixture, and beat at low speed just until moistened. Scrape down the sides of the bowl, beat in the remainder of the milk, then beat in the remainder of the flour mixture, just for a few seconds.

❺ Scrape down and remove the beaters. Use a rubber spatula to stir the batter a few times, just to make sure the flour has dissolved. Spoon into the cups, filling them two-thirds full.

❻ Bake until puffed and slightly firm to the touch, until a toothpick or a cake tester inserted into the center of a muffin comes out clean, about 30 minutes. Cool for 5 minutes, then unmold and cool on a wire rack to room temperature before frosting.

Sour Cream Cupcakes

Makes 24 cupcakes

24 paper cupcake liners
1¾ cups cake flour
1½ teaspoons baking powder
½ teaspoon baking soda
¼ teaspoon salt
1 cup sugar
6 tablespoons cool unsalted butter, cut into chunks
2 large eggs, at room temperature
2 teaspoons vanilla extract
1 cup regular sour cream (do not use low-fat or fat-free)

❶ Position the rack in the center of the oven and preheat the oven to 375°F. Line a standard 24-cup muffin tin or two 12-cup tins with 24 paper muffin cups. If using silicone muffin tins, set them on a large baking sheet.

❷ Whisk the flour, baking powder, baking soda, and salt in a medium bowl; set aside.

❸ Use an electric mixer to beat the sugar and butter in a large bowl until creamy, light, and pale yellow, about 4 minutes. Beat in the eggs one at a time, then beat in the vanilla until smooth.

❹ Beat in the sour cream. Turn off the beaters, add the flour mixture, and beat at low speed just until moistened. Scrape down and remove the beaters. Use a rubber spatula to give the batter a few stirs, just to make sure the flour is all dissolved and even in the batter. Spoon the batter into the cups, filling them about two-thirds of the way full.

❺ Bake until puffed and slightly firm to the touch, until a toothpick or a cake tester inserted into the center of a muffin comes out clean, about 30 minutes. Cool in the tin for 5 minutes, then transfer to a wire rack to cool completely before frosting.

Frosting Cupcakes

The easiest way to divide a frosting onto cupcakes is to use a flatware tablespoon. You can better tell you're getting about the same amount on each cupcake; when you use a spatula, your accuracy is often off.

Mound the frosting in the middle of the cupcake, then use the back of the tablespoon to pull the icing down toward the edges, swirling the spoon a bit to make a decorative wave as it pulls down off the top center.

• Coffee Cakes •

Coffee cakes are part breakfast, part midday snack, and part dessert. Some people would never eat them before noon; others, never after. It's all a matter of taste, but nothing beats a good cup of hot coffee or tea to melt the crumbs into pure bliss.

Blueberry Buckle

A buckle is an old-fashioned American treat—with so much topping, it buckles under the weight. *Makes 8 servings*

12 tablespoons (1½ sticks) cold unsalted
    butter, cut into small pieces, plus
    additional for greasing the pan
1⅓ cups cake flour
⅔ cup granulated sugar
1 teaspoon baking powder
½ teaspoon salt
2 large eggs, at room temperature
¼ cup heavy cream or half-and-half
1½ teaspoons vanilla extract
2 cups fresh blueberries (see Note)
½ cup packed light brown sugar
3 tablespoons all-purpose flour
¼ teaspoon ground cinnamon
¼ teaspoon grated nutmeg

❶ Position the rack in the center of the oven and preheat the oven to 350°F. Lightly butter a 10-inch round baking dish and set it aside.

❷ Melt 4 tablespoons (½ stick) butter in a small saucepan set over low heat or in a small bowl in the microwave; set aside to cool while you prepare the batter.

❸ Whisk the cake flour, granulated sugar, baking powder, and salt in a large bowl. Cut in 8 table-spoons (1 stick) butter with a fork or a pastry cutter until the mixture resembles coarse meal, pressing the butter against the flour mixture and through the tines to break it up into smaller and smaller pieces.

❹ Whisk the eggs, cream or half-and-half, and vanilla in a small bowl. Stir this mixture into the flour mixture with a wooden spoon just until a wet batter forms; then gently fold in the blueberries. Pour this mixture into the prepared baking dish.

❺ Stir the brown sugar, all-purpose flour, cinnamon, and nutmeg into the melted butter. Sprinkle this mixture over the batter in the pan.

❻ Bake until lightly browned, until a toothpick inserted into the center of the cake comes out with a few moist crumbs attached, about 50 minutes.

To cool: Set the pan on a wire rack for at least 15 minutes before serving.

To store: Fully cooled, the cake can be covered and kept at room temperature for up to 3 days.

Note: Do not use frozen blueberries; the cake will be too wet.

Variations: Substitute chopped fresh cranberries or chopped pitted peeled apricots for the blueberries.

Increase the cake flour to 1½ cups and substitute raspberries for the blueberries.

Cranberry Pineapple Rum Coffee Cake

This coffee cake has a baked-on "frosting": a sweet/tart layer of cranberries and pineapple.
Makes 8 servings

2 cups cranberries
1 cup canned crushed pineapple, drained
½ cup packed light brown sugar
6 tablespoons gold rum
1 tablespoon cornstarch
½ teaspoon ground cinnamon
4 tablespoons (½ stick) cool unsalted butter, cut into small chunks, plus additional for greasing the pan
1½ cups all-purpose flour, plus additional for dusting the pan
1½ teaspoons baking powder
½ teaspoon salt
¼ teaspoon baking soda
¾ cup granulated sugar
¼ cup solid vegetable shortening
1 large egg, at room temperature
1 tablespoon vanilla extract
½ cup regular or low-fat plain yogurt (do not use fat-free)
⅓ cup milk (whole, low-fat, or fat-free)

1 Place 1½ cups cranberries in a food processor fitted with the chopping blade; process until finely chopped but not mushy. Scrape into a medium saucepan; stir in the remaining whole cranberries, the crushed pineapple, brown sugar, gold rum, cornstarch, and cinnamon; and set the pan over medium heat.

2 Cook, stirring frequently, until the whole berries pop and the mixture bubbles and thickens, about 5 minutes. Remove from the heat, transfer to a medium bowl, and set aside to cool for 20 minutes.

3 Meanwhile, position the rack in the center of the oven and preheat the oven to 375°F. Butter and lightly flour a 9-inch springform pan or other 9-inch round pan (see Note). Whisk the flour, baking powder, salt, and baking soda in a second medium bowl.

4 Beat the granulated sugar, 4-tablespoons butter, and shortening in a large bowl, using an electric mixer at medium speed, until creamy and smooth, about 3 minutes. After scraping down the sides of the bowl with a rubber spatula, beat in the egg and vanilla until smooth, then beat in the yogurt and milk.

5 Scrape down and remove the beaters. Fold in the flour mixture with a rubber spatula just until a thick batter forms. There may be some graininess still visible, but there should be no white streaks or patches. Scrape the batter into the prepared pan.

6 Top the batter with the prepared cranberry mixture, spreading it to the sides of the pan and coating the batter evenly.

7 Bake until the cake seems set when shaken, until a toothpick inserted into one of the places where the cake sticks up above the fruit comes out with a few moist crumbs attached, about 1 hour.

To cool: Set on a wire rack for 1 hour before unlatching the sides of the springform pan and removing the cake.

To store: Continue cooling to room temperature, then wrap the cake in plastic and store at room temperature for up to 2 days.

Note: If you don't use a springform pan, you won't be able to free the cake and present it on a platter—not a problem, except for aesthetics.

Variations: Substitute apple schnapps or apricot brandy for the gold rum.

Substitute ground ginger for the cinnamon.

Add ¼ teaspoon grated nutmeg with the cinnamon.

Raised Raisin
Coffee Cake

This yeast-raised coffee cake is made in a 13 × 9-inch pan. *Makes about 10 servings*

For the Coffee Cake:
¼ cup warm water (between 105°F and 115°F)

¼ cup plus ½ teaspoon sugar

2½ teaspoons active dry yeast (one ¼-ounce package)

1¾ cups regular or low-fat milk (do not use fat-free)

12 tablespoons (1½ sticks) unsalted butter, melted and cooled to room temperature, plus additional for greasing the pan

1 large egg yolk

1 teaspoon salt

3½ cups all-purpose flour

1 cup raisins

For the Topping:
2 tablespoons unsalted butter, melted and cooled

2 tablespoons sugar

❶ Place the water in a small bowl, add ½ teaspoon sugar, and then the yeast. Set aside until bubbly, about 3 minutes. (If the yeast does not fizz and bubble, either it has gone bad or the water is not the right temperature—pour it all out and start over.)

❷ Meanwhile, warm the milk over low heat in a small saucepan just until it's between 110°F and 115°F.

❸ Pour the milk into the bowl of a stand mixer or a large bowl; stir in the yeast mixture until dissolved. Then stir in the 12 tablespoons melted and cooled butter, the egg yolk, the salt, and the remaining ¼ cup sugar.

❹ **If you're working with a stand mixer**: Add about 2 cups flour to the milk mixture, attach the dough hook, and begin mixing the dough at first at low speed, then at medium speed. Continue adding the remaining flour in ½-cup increments. The resulting dough will be wet and sticky, a cross between a batter and a dough. Once all the flour has been added, continue beating for 2 minutes. Remove the hook, scrape down the bowl, cover it, and set aside in a warm, dry place until it has doubled in bulk, about 1 hour.

If you're working by hand: Stir about 2 cups flour into the milk mixture with a wooden spoon, then continue stirring in the remaining flour in ¼-cup increments. The dough will be quite sticky, difficult to stir, but keep working in the flour. Once all the flour has been added, continue stirring until it has all been absorbed in the sticky, batterlike dough. Cover the bowl and set aside in a warm, dry place until it has doubled in bulk, about 1 hour.

❺ Once the dough has doubled in bulk, stir it down with a wooden spoon, then stir in the raisins. Pour the dough into the prepared pan; set aside for 15 minutes.

❻ Meanwhile, position the rack in the center of the oven and preheat the oven to 350°F. Lightly butter a 13 × 9-inch baking pan.

❼ Brush the top of the cake with the 2 tablespoons melted and cooled butter, then sprinkle the sugar over the top.

8 Bake until lightly browned, until a toothpick inserted into the middle of the cake comes out with a few moist crumbs attached, about 1 hour and 10 minutes.

To cool: Set the pan on a wire rack for 10 minutes before serving.

To store: Once cooled to room temperature, cover and keep at room temperature for up to 2 days or freeze for up to 3 months.

Variations: Stir 1 teaspoon ground cinnamon, 1 teaspoon ground ginger, or ½ teaspoon grated nutmeg into the batter with the egg yolk.

Soak the raisins in 2 tablespoons brandy or Cognac for 20 minutes before adding them to the cake.

Stir 1 cup chopped walnut pieces or pecan pieces into the dough with the raisins.

Stir in ¼ teaspoon almond extract with the egg yolk; substitute slivered almonds for the raisins.

Cookies

W<small>E'VE SEEN COOKIES BLITZ THROUGH PEOPLE'S WILL POWER, NUTRI-</small>tional convictions, and diets. Perhaps it's the perfect ratio of crunch to sweet, outside to inside. And something elemental, too. It's dessert stripped to the bones. Far enough stripped that it's good any time of day. A piece of cake in the middle of the afternoon? Too decadent, best saved for vacation or a breakup. But a cookie? Who can ever resist?

All that for what was probably a culinary throwaway. As the story goes, cookies sprang from cakes: Dutch bakers would throw a dollop of batter into the oven to test its heat. *Kookje* became "cookie."

A quaint story, if unprovable. So what is true? There's very little fancy footwork involved when you're making cookies. More homespun and fairly easy, they're make-ahead treats. They may often be sidekicks to ice cream, gelato, pudding, red wine, or coffee; but they quietly steal the spotlight every time.

Their popularity is also a modern pleasure, something that took off with standardized ovens. Add a little dough and you've got instant satisfaction. No wonder no one can turn them down.

These are the cookies we return to again and again, just right for every occasion. Almost every one can be made ahead and frozen in a tightly sealed container between sheets of wax paper. Thaw the cookies at room temperature. Do refresh them, set them on a baking sheet and warm in a preheated 300°F oven for 3 to 5 minutes.

The Ultimate Chocolate Chip Cookies

These cookies have a little bit of everything—and lots of chocolate chips, of course. Search out bittersweet chocolate chips for the best taste. If you're not one for nuts, leave them out and increase the chocolate chips to 2½ cups. *Makes about 60 cookies*

    2 cups all-purpose flour
    1 teaspoon baking soda
    1 teaspoon salt
    12 tablespoons (1½ sticks) cool unsalted
        butter, cut into small chunks
    1 cup packed light brown sugar
    ⅓ cup tahini
    ½ cup granulated sugar
    ¼ cup honey
    2 large eggs, at room temperature
    1 tablespoon vanilla extract
    1 cup shredded unsweetened coconut
    1 cup rolled oats (do not use instant or
        steel-cut)
    1 cup chopped walnuts or pecans
    2 cups bittersweet or semisweet
        chocolate chips

1 Position the racks in the top and bottom thirds of the oven. Preheat the oven to 350°F. Whisk the flour, baking soda, and salt in a medium bowl; set aside.

2 Beat the butter in a large bowl with an electric mixer at medium speed until slightly softened, about 2 minutes. Add the brown sugar and tahini; continue beating until creamy, pale brown, and very light, about 4 minutes.

3 Beat in the granulated sugar and honey until you can feel only the slightest graininess in the batter, about 2 minutes. Beat in the eggs one at a time, scrape down the sides of the bowl, and then beat in the vanilla until smooth.

4 Beat in the coconut, oats, and walnuts just until uniform. Turn off the beaters, add the prepared flour mixture, and beat at low speed just until a dough begins to form. Scrape down the beaters, remove them, and fold in the chocolate chips with a rubber spatula, making sure there are no dry patches of flour left.

5 Drop by rounded tablespoonfuls onto two large, ungreased baking sheets, spacing the mounds about 3 inches apart. Bake in the top and bottom thirds of the oven for 9 minutes.

6 Flatten the cookies with the back of a metal spatula just to spread them a bit. Reverse the trays top to bottom and back to front and continue baking until set, lightly browned, and a little firm to the touch, about 9 more minutes.

To cool: Leave the cookies on the sheets for 2 minutes, then transfer to wire racks to cool completely. Cool the baking sheets for at least 5 minutes before making more cookies.

To store: Place in a sealed container between sheets of wax paper at room temperature for up to 3 days or in the freezer for up to 3 months.

For chewier, flatter cookies, bang the baking sheets against the wire racks of the oven after the cookies have baked for 15 minutes, thereby causing them to fall a bit during the last few minutes of baking.

For very chewy cookies, reduce the granulated sugar to ¼ cup and add ¼ cup light corn syrup with the remaining granulated sugar.

Peanut Butter Chocolate Chip Cookies: Substitute peanut butter for the tahini.

Maple Chocolate Chip Cookies: Substitute maple syrup for the honey.

Everything Chocolate Chip Cookies: Reduce the chocolate chips to 1½ cups; add ¾ cup chopped raisins or dried cranberries with the remaining chips.

Baking Sheets vs. Cookie Sheets

Technically, a baking sheet has four lipped sides; a cookie sheet has fewer; sometimes even none. We prefer baking sheets, even for cookies; if the dough is rolled into balls, they can't roll off onto the floor.

These recipes do not call for insulated cookie sheets, specialty products that can dramatically affect baking times.

Big Soft Sugar Cookies

These are the bakeshop classics, best the day they're made. *Makes 12 to 14 large cookies*

> 2 cups all-purpose flour
> ½ teaspoon baking powder
> ½ teaspoon baking soda
> ¼ teaspoon salt
> 1 cup sugar
> ¾ cup solid vegetable shortening
> 1 large egg plus 1 large egg white, at room temperature
> 2 teaspoons vanilla extract
> ¼ cup milk (regular, low-fat, or fat-free)

❶ Position the rack in the center of the oven and preheat the oven to 350°F. Line a large baking sheet with parchment paper or a silicone baking mat and set aside.

❷ Whisk the flour, baking powder, baking soda, and salt in a medium bowl; set aside as well.

❸ Beat the sugar and shortening in a large bowl with an electric mixer at medium speed until light and fluffy, about 3 minutes.

❹ Beat in the egg and egg white, scrape down the sides of the bowl, and beat in the vanilla until smooth.

❺ Turn off the beaters, add half the prepared flour mixture, and beat at low speed just until combined. Beat in the milk until smooth, scrape down the bowl again, and beat in the remaining flour mixture at low speed just until a dough forms.

❻ Give the dough a few turns with a rubber spatula to make sure there are no dry pockets of flour, then scoop up ¼-cup measurements of dough and place them on the prepared baking sheet, spacing them 4 inches apart. Gently press the mounds into 3-inch circles.

7 Bake until set but not too brown, just beige, and still somewhat soft to the touch, about 18 minutes. Another couple of minutes will yield much crunchier cookies.

To cool: Leave the cookies on the baking sheet for 5 minutes, then use a metal spatula to transfer them to a wire rack to continue cooling.

To store: When fully cooled, the cookies can be kept in a sealed container at room temperature for up to 1 day; freezing dramatically alters their texture and is not recommended.

Variations: Add ½ teaspoon ground cinnamon, ¼ teaspoon grated nutmeg, or ¼ teaspoon ground mace with the salt.

Add 1 teaspoon finely grated lemon zest with the egg white.

Reduce the vanilla to 1 teaspoon and add 1 teaspoon maple or rum extract with the remaining vanilla.

Dust the cookies with granulated sugar (about ½ teaspoon per cookie) or with colored sugar before baking.

Press a blanched almond or a walnut half into the top of each cookie before baking.

Packing the Brown Sugar

Because brown sugar crystals are fairly large, having been coated with molasses, they can have more "air space" between them when poured or stored. They need to be packed into measuring spoons and cups to get an accurate measure.

Black and Whites

These New York icons are large, cakey cookies with the tops iced in halves: one side chocolate and the other vanilla. *Makes about 16 cookies*

2¼ cups all-purpose flour, plus additional for your fingers
1 teaspoon baking powder
½ teaspoon baking soda
¼ teaspoon salt
¾ cup sugar
½ cup solid vegetable shortening, plus additional for greasing the baking sheet
2 large eggs, at room temperature
½ cup milk (regular, low-fat, or fat-free)
4 teaspoons vanilla extract
1½ ounces unsweetened chocolate, finely chopped
6 tablespoons water
2 tablespoons light corn syrup
3¾ cups confectioners' sugar

1 Position the rack in the center of the oven and preheat the oven to 350°F. Lightly grease a large baking sheet and set aside. Whisk the flour, baking powder, baking soda, and salt in a medium bowl; set aside as well.

2 Beat the sugar and shortening in a large bowl with an electric mixer at medium speed until light and fluffy, about 3 minutes. Scrape down the sides of the bowl with a rubber spatula, then beat in the eggs one at a time until smooth.

3 Turn off the beaters, add half the prepared flour mixture, and beat at low speed until the flour has been incorporated but some graininess remains in the batter. Beat in the milk and 2 teaspoons vanilla until smooth, then beat in the remaining flour mixture at low speed just until incorporated, just until no rifts of white flour are visible.

4 Scoop up ¼ cup of the batter and place it on the prepared baking sheet. Dip your palm in a little flour, then gently press the dough into a 3-inch circle. Continue making more of these dough circles, spacing them about 3 inches apart on the sheet.

5 Bake until lightly browned at the edges, set on top, but springy in the middle, about 12 minutes. Cool on the baking sheet for a couple of minutes, then transfer to a wire rack to cool completely, about 1 hour.

6 Once the cookies have cooled completely, place the chopped chocolate in a medium bowl; set aside. Place the water and corn syrup in a medium saucepan set over medium heat, stirring constantly at first until the corn syrup dissolves and then not at all until the mixture comes to a boil. Boil for 1 minute.

7 Remove the pan from the heat and stir in the confectioners' sugar until fully dissolved. Pour half this mixture over the chopped chocolate and stir until the chocolate has dissolved and the mixture is smooth. Stir the remaining 2 teaspoons vanilla into the remaining sugar mixture in the saucepan.

8 Frost half of a cookie top with the vanilla icing and the other half with the chocolate icing, making a straight line right through the diameter of the cookies that divides the icings. For colorfast reasons, it's best to work with the vanilla before the chocolate. If possible, use two spoons or spatulas, one for each icing. Should either icing become too stiff while you're working with it, put it in a medium bowl that will fit securely over a saucepan with about 1 inch of water brought to a boil over medium-high heat; stir over the heat just until the icing softens.

Almond Sugar Cookies

Good for dunking, these buttery, eggless cookies ride the line between crisp and cakey. *Makes about 24 cookies*

> 1¼ cups all-purpose flour, plus additional for dusting
> ¼ teaspoon baking soda
> ¼ teaspoon salt
> 8 tablespoons (1 stick) cool unsalted butter, cut into chunks
> ¼ cup plus 2 tablespoons granulated sugar
> ¼ cup packed light brown sugar
> ½ cup finely ground blanched or slivered almonds
> ¼ teaspoon almond extract

1 Position the rack in the center of the oven and preheat the oven to 375°F. Whisk the flour, baking soda, and salt in a medium bowl; set aside.

2 Beat the butter, ¼ cup granulated sugar, and the brown sugar in a large bowl with an electric mixer at medium speed until light, fluffy, and creamy, about 3 minutes, scraping down the sides of the bowl with a rubber spatula as necessary. Beat in the ground almonds and the almond extract.

3 Turn off the beaters, add the prepared flour mixture, and beat at low speed until a soft dough forms with no dry pockets of unmoistened flour.

4 Lightly dust a clean, dry, smooth work surface with flour and turn the dough out onto it. Gently press the dough into the shape of a deflated tire, then lightly dust it with flour. Roll to ¼-inch thickness. Dust with the remaining 2 tablespoons sugar. (If your work surface isn't large, divide the dough in half and roll each half separately, sprinkling each half with 1 tablespoon sugar.)

⑤ Cut the cookies out with a 1½- or 2-inch round cookie cutter, keeping the circles close together because a second rolling of the scraps will yield tough cookies. Transfer the rounds to a large, ungreased baking sheet, spacing them 2 inches apart.

⑥ Bake until lightly browned, just until the tops are set, about 10 minutes.

To cool: Leave the cookies on the baking sheet for 2 or 3 minutes, then transfer them to a wire rack to cool completely.

To store: The cookies can be stored in a sealed container at room temperature for up to 4 days or in the freezer for up to 3 months.

Variations: Add ¼ teaspoon grated nutmeg with the salt.

Add 1 teaspoon vanilla extract or ½ teaspoon rum extract with the almond extract.

Mix ¼ teaspoon ground cinnamon with the remaining 1 tablespoon sugar before sprinkling it over the rolled-out dough.

Press a blanched almond into the top of each cookie before baking.

Greased, Ungreased, and Lined Baking Sheets

Pay close attention to how the baking sheets are prepared. Some cookies need to be baked on a lined sheet to protect them from the heat, but others will spread and become overbaked at the edges. Some cookies need a little barrier of fat between them and the heat to get crisp bottoms; others will simply burn.

For the recipes in this book, silicone baking mats and parchment paper are interchangeable.

Snickerdoodles

Shortening gives these classics a light crunch with a soft interior. Butter would turn them too flaky.
Makes about 36 cookies

> 2¾ cups all-purpose flour
> 2 teaspoons cream of tartar
> 1 teaspoon baking soda
> ¼ teaspoon salt
> 1 cup solid vegetable shortening, plus additional for greasing the baking sheet
> 1¾ cups sugar
> 2 large eggs, at room temperature
> 2 tablespoons milk (regular, low-fat, or fat-free)
> 2 teaspoons vanilla extract
> 1½ teaspoons ground cinnamon
> ¼ teaspoon grated nutmeg

① Position the rack in the center of the oven and preheat the oven to 375°F. Lightly grease a large baking sheet and set it aside. Whisk the flour, cream of tartar, baking soda, and salt in a medium bowl; set aside as well.

② Beat the shortening and 1½ cups sugar in a large bowl with an electric mixer at medium speed until most of the sugar has dissolved, until you feel only a slight graininess between your fingers, about 4 minutes. Beat in the eggs one at a time, then beat in the milk and vanilla until smooth.

③ Turn off the beaters, add the prepared flour mixture, and beat at low speed just until a dough comes together in the bowl. Cover the bowl with a clean kitchen towel and set aside at room temperature for 10 minutes to relax the glutens but dissolve the flour.

④ Meanwhile, whisk the remaining ¼ cup sugar, the cinnamon, and nutmeg in a small bowl.

5 Roll generous tablespoonfuls of the dough into balls between your palms, then roll them in the sugar mixture, pressing gently to get the sugar to adhere. Space them on the prepared baking sheet about 2 inches apart.

6 Bake until flattened, crispy, and lightly browned, about 10 minutes.

To cool: Let the cookies stand on the baking sheet for 2 to 3 minutes, then transfer them to a wire rack to cool completely. Cool the baking sheet for at least 5 more minutes before greasing it again and adding more.

To store: Once fully cooled, the cookies can be kept in a sealed container at room temperature for up to 4 days or in the freezer for up to 3 months.

Variations: Omit the cinnamon and nutmeg from the sugar mixture in which you roll the balls; instead, use 1 1/2 teaspoons ground ginger and 1/4 teaspoon grated mace or 1 1/2 teaspoons pure chili powder and 1/2 teaspoon ground cinnamon.

Solid Vegetable Shortening

Shortening is used when we want a neutral taste without the slightly sour edge of butter. It wasn't always so—many old recipes call for lard, a definite and somewhat unsavory taste. Shortening came into widespread use during World War II, thanks to dairy rationing. Search out trans-fat-free solid vegetable shortenings, now readily available. Or look for nonhydrogenated vegetable shortenings, available in sticks like butter in the dairy case of many gourmet markets.

Molasses Oatmeal Cranberry Cookies

For chewier cookies, cut down on the baking time by a minute or two. For crisper cookies, rap the baking sheet against the oven rack halfway through baking. *Makes about 48 cookies*

16 tablespoons (2 sticks) cool unsalted butter, cut into chunks, plus additional for greasing the baking sheet
2 1/4 cups all-purpose flour
1 1/2 teaspoons baking soda
1 teaspoon ground cinnamon
1/2 teaspoon salt
1 1/2 cups sugar
6 tablespoons unsulfured molasses
2 large eggs, at room temperature
2 teaspoons vanilla extract
3 cups rolled oats (do not use quick-cooking)
2 cups dried cranberries

1 Position the rack in the center of the oven and preheat the oven to 375°F. Lightly butter a large baking sheet; set it aside. Whisk the flour, baking soda, cinnamon, and salt in a medium bowl; set aside too.

2 Beat the butter in a large bowl with an electric mixer at medium speed until slightly softened, about 2 minutes. Add the sugar and beat until light, creamy, and pale yellow, about 3 more minutes.

3 Add the molasses and beat until well combined, then beat in the eggs one at a time. Finally, beat in the vanilla until smooth.

4 Turn off the beaters, add the prepared flour mixture, and beat at low speed just until a soft dough starts to form. There will be some dry patches of flour left.

⑤ Scrape down the beaters, remove them, and stir in the oats and dried cranberries with a wooden spoon, just until evenly distributed and the flour is fully moistened.

⑥ Mound by rounded tablespoonfuls onto the prepared baking sheet, spacing them about 3 inches apart. Gently flatten the mounds a little with your hand or a rubber spatula.

⑦ Bake until brown but still pliable and soft, 12 to 14 minutes.

To cool: Leave the cookies on the baking sheet for a couple of minutes, then transfer them to a wire rack to cool completely. Cool the baking sheet for at least 5 minutes and butter it again before baking another batch.

To store: The cookies can be stored in an airtight container at room temperature for up to 3 days or in the freezer for up to 3 months.

Variations: Add 1/4 teaspoon grated nutmeg or ground cloves with the cinnamon.

Substitute raisins, dried blueberries, dried cherries, dried currants, or chopped dried pitted dates for the dried cranberries.

Reduce the dried cranberries to 1 cup and add 1 cup semisweet chocolate chips with the remaining cranberries.

Cookies are actually quite fragile when first out of the oven; they should be cooled a bit on the baking sheet so the bottoms can harden for support. Lift them gently off the sheet with a thin, metal spatula and transfer them to a wire cooling rack, preferably one with a relatively small crosshatch for the best support. If you've used a nonstick baking sheet, make sure you use bakeware designed specifically for such surfaces.

Mocha Crinkles

Coffee and chocolate combine to create these crunchy-outside, taffy-inside wonders. The flour mixture needs to be sifted to ensure that the confectioners' sugar and cocoa powder are evenly distributed throughout. *Makes about 72 cookies*

2 cups all-purpose flour
2 cups confectioners' sugar
1/2 cup sifted unsweetened cocoa powder, preferably Dutch process cocoa powder
2 teaspoons baking powder
1/2 teaspoon salt
4 ounces unsweetened chocolate, chopped
4 tablespoons (1/2 stick) unsalted butter, cut into small pieces
1 1/2 cups packed light brown sugar
1/3 cup light corn syrup
1 tablespoon instant espresso powder
1 tablespoon vanilla extract
4 large egg whites, lightly whisked in a small bowl, at room temperature

① Spread a sheet of wax paper on your work surface. Sift the flour, 1 1/2 cups confectioners' sugar, the cocoa powder, baking powder, and salt together, using a flour sifter or a fine-mesh sieve, allowing the sifted mixture to fall onto the wax paper. Repeat, making sure the cocoa powder is evenly distributed. Set aside.

② Place the chocolate and butter in the top of a double boiler or in a medium bowl that fits securely over a medium saucepan. Bring about an inch of water to a boil in the bottom of the double boiler or in the saucepan; place the top of the double boiler or the bowl over the simmering water, reduce the heat but maintain a simmer, and stir until half the chocolate has melted.

③ Remove the top of the double boiler or the bowl from over the water—be careful of any escaping steam—and continue stirring off the heat until the chocolate and butter have fully melted and the mixture is smooth. Transfer to the bowl for a standing mixer or to a large, clean bowl if you're using a handheld mixer; cool for 5 minutes.

4 Beat the brown sugar into the chocolate mixture, using an electric mixer at medium speed, until light and silky, about 1 minute. Beat in the corn syrup, instant espresso powder, and vanilla.

5 Scrape down the sides of the bowl, then beat in the egg whites all at once until smooth, a little less than 1 minute.

6 Remove the beaters and use a wooden spoon to stir in the flour mixture just until any trace of flour has disappeared. Cover the bowl with a clean kitchen towel and set in the refrigerator until the mixture becomes firm, at least 1 hour but no more than 8 hours.

7 Position the rack in the center of the oven and preheat the oven to 350°F. Line a baking sheet with parchment paper or a silicone baking mat; set aside.

8 Place the remaining ½ cup confectioners' sugar in a small bowl. Roll a small piece of the firm dough into a small ball about the size of a large olive. Roll the ball in the confectioners' sugar, then place it on the prepared baking sheet. Continue making sugared balls, spacing them about 1½ inches apart, until the baking sheet is full. (It may be easier to make all the balls first, then roll them all in the confectioners' sugar—that way, you are less likely to transfer confectioners' sugar back into the chocolate dough.) Return any unused dough to the refrigerator.

9 Bake until the cookies have spread and cracked at the edges and are somewhat firm to the touch, about 16 minutes.

To cool: Leave the cookies on the baking sheet for 5 minutes, then carefully transfer them to a wire rack using a metal spatula (they are still fragile because they're so fudgy inside). Cool the baking sheet for 5 minutes before baking further batches; if using parchment paper, replace it if it is greasy, crinkled, or browned. Let the baked cookies cool completely on the wire rack.

To store: Place in a sealed container for up to 4 days at room temperature; because of their soft insides, freezing is not recommended.

Variations: Add 1 teaspoon ground cinnamon or ground ginger with the flour.

Chocolate Chip Meringue Kisses

Studded with chocolate chips, these crisp cookies are smaller than traditional meringues so they have more crunch per bite. *Makes about 48 small meringue cookies*

4 large egg whites, at room temperature
¼ teaspoon salt
¼ teaspoon cream of tartar
1 cup superfine sugar (see Note)
1 cup mini-semisweet chocolate chips

1 Preheat the oven to 225°F. Line a large baking sheet with parchment paper or a silicone baking mat.

2 Beat the egg whites and salt in a large bowl with a mixer at medium speed until frothy. Add the cream of tartar, raise the speed to high, and beat until you can create soft peaks in the mixture by dabbing the turned-off beaters into it, about 3 minutes.

3 With the mixer running, add the sugar in 1-tablespoon increments, scraping down the sides of the bowl occasionally to make sure the sugar grains are getting fully incorporated into the egg whites. Once all the sugar has been added, beat until stiff and shiny peaks can be formed in the mixture, about 1 minute. You should feel absolutely no graininess from undissolved sugar between your fingers; if you do, keep beating.

④ Add the chocolate chips and pulse the beaters a few times just to incorporate. Drop by rounded teaspoonfuls onto the prepared baking sheet.

⑤ Bake until dry, about 45 minutes.

To cool: Leave the kisses on the baking sheet 30 minutes before transferring them to wire racks to cool completely.

To store: Seal in an airtight container at room temperature for up to 2 days (do not refrigerate or freeze).

Peppermint Meringue Kisses: Substitute crushed peppermint candies or candy canes for the mini-chocolate chips.

Toffee Meringue Kisses: Substitute finely crushed toffee for the mini-chocolate chips.

Almond Macaroons

These—like all classics—are a little temperamental: you have to pipe them out onto the baking sheet. High humidity will definitely destroy the batter, so make them on a sunny, dry day. Despite all that, there's a big payoff: a moist, domed almond cookie that's perfect with a bowl of berries.

Makes about 30 cookies

One 7-ounce tube almond paste
1 cup sugar
2 large egg whites, whisked until foamy in a
    small bowl, at room temperature
¼ teaspoon salt, optional

① Position the rack in the center of the oven and preheat the oven to 375°F. Line a large baking sheet with parchment paper or a silicone baking mat.

② Place the almond paste and sugar in a large bowl and beat with an electric mixer at medium speed until well blended, in soft but dry pieces, somewhat like the feel of Play-Doh but not smooth or creamy, about 5 minutes.

③ Beat in the egg whites in 1-tablespoon increments, making sure each is fully incorporated before adding the next and scraping down the sides of the bowl as necessary. When all the egg whites have been added, beat until the batter is the consistency of caulk or grout, a little grainy but very smooth, and able to hold its shape.

④ Drop by rounded teaspoonfuls onto the prepared baking mat. Alternatively, fill a pastry bag fitted with a #8 (⅝-inch) tip with the batter and pipe out small kisses that have about 1½ teaspoons batter in each; swirl the bag at the end of each dollop to create a twisty topknot on each macaroon.

⑤ Bake until lightly browned and a little cracked but still soft to the touch, about 8 minutes.

To cool: Let the cookies stand on the baking sheet for 4 minutes before transferring with a metal spatula to a wire rack to cool completely. Cool the baking sheet for 5 minutes before making more macaroons; replace the parchment paper if it's frizzled or browned.

To store: The macaroons can be kept at room temperature in an airtight container for up to 3 days; freezing is not recommended.

Chocolate-Dipped Almond Macaroons: Melt 6 ounces semisweet or bittersweet chocolate in the microwave on high or in the top part of a double boiler over simmering water just until there are still some chunks left; remove the chocolate from the heat and continue stirring until fully melted. Lay a large sheet of wax paper on your work surface, then dip the bottoms of the cooled cookies into the melted chocolate. Let the excess drizzle back into the bowl, then set the cookies on the wax paper to firm up, about 1 hour.

Coconut Macaroons

We learned the untraditional technique of adding flour and egg yolks to coconut macaroons from Tish Boyle, the editor-in-chief of *Chocolatier* magazine. We've adapted her technique for these very moist cookies made with two kinds of coconut, sweetened *and* unsweetened. *Makes about 36 cookies*

    1 large egg, at room temperature
    2 large egg whites, at room temperature
    1 cup sugar
    2 teaspoons vanilla extract
    ¼ cup all-purpose flour
    ¼ teaspoon salt
    2⅔ cups shredded sweetened coconut
        (one 7-ounce bag)
    1½ cups shredded unsweetened coconut

1 Position the rack in the center of the oven and preheat the oven to 350°F. Line a large baking sheet with parchment paper or a silicone baking mat.

2 Beat the egg, egg whites, and sugar in a large bowl with an electric mixer at medium speed until well combined and a little pasty, about 2 minutes. Beat in the vanilla.

3 Turn off the beaters, add the flour and salt, and beat at low speed just until combined.

4 Turn off the beaters again, add both kinds of coconut, and beat at low speed just until combined, until the coconut is evenly distributed in the batter.

5 Drop by rounded tablespoons onto the lined sheets, spacing the mounds about 3 inches apart. Bake until firm, about 15 minutes.

To cool: Leave the cookies on the baking sheet for 5 minutes, then transfer them to a wire rack to cool completely. Cool the baking sheet for 5 more minutes before adding more macaroons; replace the parchment paper if it's browned or crinkled.

To store: The cookies can be kept in an airtight container at room temperature for up to 3 days; freezing is not recommended.

Brown Sugar Refrigerator Cookies

Refrigerator cookies were our grandmothers' secret: a moist dough formed into a log, stored in the fridge, then sliced off and baked as needed. *Makes about 40 cookies*

    3 cups all-purpose flour, plus additional for
        dusting
    ½ teaspoon baking powder
    ½ teaspoon ground cinnamon
    ¼ teaspoon baking soda
    ¼ teaspoon salt
    8 tablespoons (1 stick) unsalted butter
    1 cup packed dark brown sugar
    ⅓ cup granulated sugar
    3 large egg whites, whisked in a small bowl
        until foamy, at room temperature
    1 teaspoon vanilla extract

1 Whisk the flour, baking powder, cinnamon, baking soda, and salt in a medium bowl; set aside.

❷ Beat the butter and both sugars in a large bowl with an electric mixer at medium speed until light and fluffy, about 3 minutes. Beat in the egg whites and vanilla until smooth.

❸ Turn off the beaters, scrape down the sides of the bowl, and add the prepared flour mixture. Beat at low speed just until a moist dough forms with no visible graininess.

❹ Lightly dust a clean, dry work surface with flour and turn the dough out onto it. Divide in half, then roll each half under your palms into a log about 10 inches long. Wrap each log in plastic wrap and place in the refrigerator for at least 4 hours (or longer—see below, "to store").

❺ Position the rack in the center of the oven and preheat the oven to 350°F. Unwrap one of the logs and slice off as many ½-inch-thick disks as you desire. Place these on an ungreased baking sheet, spacing them about 2 inches apart. Rewrap the log and return it to the refrigerator.

❻ Bake until firm to the touch and lightly browned, 20 to 25 minutes.

To cool: Leave the cookies on the baking sheet for a couple of minutes before transferring them to a wire rack to cool completely.

To store: Keep the wrapped logs in the refrigerator for up to 2 weeks; store the baked cookies in an airtight container at room temperature for up to 3 days.

Variations: Add ⅔ cup mini-chocolate chips, M&M's Baking Bits, or Reese's Pieces with the salt.

Add ¾ cup chopped raisins, dried currants, or chopped dried pitted dates with the salt.

Lemon Poppy Seed Refrigerator Cookies

Lemon extract is available near the vanilla extract in the spice aisle of almost every market. If you prefer lemon oil, use only ¼ teaspoon. *Makes about 60 cookies*

> 2¼ cups all-purpose flour, plus additional
> for dusting
> ½ cup poppy seeds
> ¼ teaspoon salt
> 16 tablespoons (2 sticks) cool unsalted
> butter, cut into chunks
> ½ cup granulated sugar
> ¼ cup packed light brown sugar
> 1 large egg yolk, at room temperature
> 1 teaspoon lemon extract

❶ Whisk the flour, poppy seeds, and salt in a medium bowl; set aside.

❷ Soften the butter in a large bowl with an electric mixer at medium speed, working the chunks just until they start to lose their shape and become a mass without turning gooey. Add both sugars and continue beating until creamy and lemony light, about 3 minutes. Beat in the egg yolk and the lemon extract until smooth.

❸ Turn off the beaters, add the prepared flour mixture, and beat at low speed just until a smooth dough forms with no pockets of undissolved flour.

❹ Lightly dust a clean, dry work surface with flour. Turn the dough out onto it, then divide in half. Roll each half under your palms into an 8-inch-long log; wrap each log in plastic. Refrigerate for at least 4 hours (see right, "to store").

❺ Position the rack in the center of the oven and preheat the oven to 325°F. Unwrap a log and slice it into as many ¼-inch-thick disks as you desire. Lay these out, leaving 2-inch spaces in between, on a large ungreased baking sheet. Rewrap the unused portion of the log and return to the refrigerator.

⑥ Bake until lightly browned and fairly dry to the touch, about 22 minutes.

To cool: Keep the cookies on the baking sheet for 5 minutes, then transfer them to a cooling rack with a metal spatula. Cool the baking sheet for an additional 5 minutes before adding more disks, if desired.

To store: Keep the wrapped logs in the refrigerator for up to 2 weeks; store the baked cookies in a tightly sealed container for up to 2 days.

Pine Nut Biscotti

These are the ultimate dunking cookies: Italian wedges baked twice to become very hard, just waiting to be dipped into a sweet dessert wine like Vin Santo—although we've also seen them dunked in red wine in Italy. The sugar is added to the dry ingredients, not beaten with the wet, to create a drier, crisper cookie. Pine nuts are soft, so a little cornmeal in the dough gives these biscotti extra crunch. *Makes about 48 biscotti*

> ⅔ cup pine nuts
> 2 cups all-purpose flour, plus additional for dusting
> ¾ cup sugar
> ¼ cup yellow cornmeal
> 2 teaspoons baking powder
> ½ teaspoon salt
> 3 large eggs, at room temperature
> 2 tablespoons brandy

① Position the racks in the top and bottom thirds of the oven and preheat the oven to 325°F. Line two baking sheets with parchment paper or silicone baking mats.

② Place the pine nuts in a dry skillet set over medium-low heat; cook, stirring often, until lightly browned and aromatic, about 4 minutes. Set aside while you make the batter.

③ Whisk the flour, sugar, cornmeal, baking powder, and salt in a medium bowl; set aside.

④ Beat the eggs and brandy in a large bowl with an electric mixer at medium speed until well combined but not fluffy, about 2 minutes. Turn the beaters off, add the flour mixture, and beat at low speed until a soft but crumbly and dry dough forms.

⑤ Scrape down and remove the beaters. Work the toasted pine nuts into the batter with a wooden spoon.

⑥ Lightly dust a clean, dry work surface with flour, then turn the dough out onto it. Knead until smooth and the pine nuts are evenly distributed, about 2 minutes. Divide the dough in half and roll each half under your palms into a 12-inch-long log.

⑦ Place each log on a separate baking sheet and bake in the top and bottom thirds of the oven for 10 minutes. Reverse the sheets top to bottom and continue baking until firm, lightly browned, and a little puffed, about 15 more minutes.

⑧ Remove the sheets from the oven and cool the logs on them for 30 minutes. (Maintain the oven's temperature.)

⑨ Transfer the logs to your work surface and use a serrated knife to slice them into ½-inch-thick pieces, cutting on the diagonal to get long, oblong biscotti. Place these cut side down on the baking sheets.

10 Return them to the oven to bake for 5 minutes. Remove them from the oven, flip all the cookies over to the other cut side, reverse the sheets top to bottom, and continue baking until dry and crunchy, about 5 more minutes.

To cool: Leave the biscotti on the baking sheets for 10 minutes, then transfer them to a wire rack to cool completely.

To store: Once cooled, they can be kept in an airtight container at room temperature for up to 10 days or in the freezer for up to 3 months.

Chocolate Cranberry Almond Biscotti

Forget the wine and dunk these in coffee. They pack well and can be sent over the miles for the holidays. *Makes about 24 cookies*

> 2 cups all-purpose flour, plus additional for dusting
> 1 cup sugar
> ½ cup sifted unsweetened cocoa powder
> 1 teaspoon baking powder
> ½ teaspoon baking soda
> ¼ teaspoon salt
> 3 large eggs, lightly beaten in a small bowl, at room temperature
> 2 teaspoons vanilla extract
> ½ cup dried cranberries
> ⅓ cup whole almonds, roughly chopped

1 Position the rack in the center of the oven and preheat the oven to 350°F. Line a large baking sheet with parchment paper or a silicone baking mat.

2 Mix the flour, sugar, cocoa, baking powder, baking soda, and salt in a medium bowl; stir in the eggs and vanilla with a wooden spoon, then stir in the dried cranberries and almonds.

3 Dust a clean, dry work surface with flour; turn the dough out onto it and knead a few turns until fairly smooth.

4 Divide the dough in half; roll each half into 8-inch-long logs. Place these 3 inches apart on the prepared baking sheet and bake until dry to the touch and a little puffed, about 25 minutes. Transfer the baking sheets to a wire rack and cool the logs on the baking sheet at least 30 minutes.

5 Transfer the logs to your work surface and use a serrated knife to cut them into ¾-inch cookies, slicing on the diagonal to create long, oblong biscotti.

6 Place these cut side down on the baking sheet and bake for 7 minutes. Turn all the cookies over so the other cut side is now down against the sheet and continue baking until crisp and lightly browned, about another 7 minutes.

To cool: Leave the biscotti on the baking sheets for 10 minutes, then transfer them to a wire rack to cool completely.

To store: They can be kept in an airtight container at room temperature for up to 2 weeks or in the freezer for up to 3 months.

Variations: Substitute any dried berry (blackberries, raspberries) for the cranberries. Chop any larger pieces of dried fruit so the bits are more even in the batter.

For a heartier almond taste, add ¼ teaspoon almond extract with the vanilla.

◉ Filled Cookies ◉

Like little layer cakes, these too are showstoppers. Admittedly, they involve a little work, but the payoffs are filled, sweet, dense, chewy wonders. They are also the easiest to customize since you can switch out one filling for another in some cases, or simply change the jam used for one you prefer.

Vanilla Sandwich Creams

In this mix-and-match recipe, you can choose the filling you want. Better still, make the cookies ahead and store them in an airtight container in the freezer for up to 3 months; thaw at room temperature for 30 minutes, then fill them when you're ready. *Makes a little over 24 cookies*

> 2¼ cups all-purpose flour, plus additional
>   for dusting
> ¼ teaspoon baking soda
> ¼ teaspoon salt
> 8 tablespoons (1 stick) cool unsalted
>   butter, cut into chunks
> ¼ cup solid vegetable shortening
> ⅔ cup sugar
> 2 large egg whites, whisked lightly
>   in a small bowl, at room
>   temperature
> 1 teaspoon vanilla extract
> One of the seven fillings that follow

❶ Position the rack in the center of the oven and preheat the oven to 350°F. Line a large baking sheet with parchment paper or a silicone baking mat.

❷ Whisk the flour, baking soda, and salt in a medium bowl; set aside.

❸ Beat the butter, shortening, and sugar in a large bowl with an electric mixer at medium speed un-

til soft, light, and airy, scraping down the sides of the bowl as necessary, about 2 minutes. Beat in the egg whites and vanilla until fairly smooth.

❹ Turn off the beaters, add the flour mixture, and beat at low speed until a soft dough forms. Gather the dough into a ball.

❺ Lightly dust a clean, dry work surface with flour and place the dough on it. Gently flatten the dough and dust it lightly with flour. Roll it to ⅛-inch thickness with a lightly floured rolling pin.

❻ Cut the dough into 2-inch circles using a round cookie cutter or a thick-rimmed drinking glass; make the circles close to each other because gathering the scraps and rerolling them will result in tough cookies. Use a lightly floured metal spatula to transfer the rounds to the prepared baking sheet, spacing them 2 inches apart. Cover any remaining rounds on the work surface with a clean kitchen towel.

❼ Bake until firm to the touch but still pale, not browned, about 18 minutes.

To cool: Leave the cookies on the baking sheet for 2 to 3 minutes, then transfer them to a wire rack to cool completely, about 1 hour. Cool the baking sheet for 5 minutes before baking more rounds; replace the parchment paper if it's frizzled or browned.

To store: Place the unfilled cookies in an airtight container and freeze for up to 3 months. Once filled, the cookies can be stored between sheets of wax paper in an airtight container at room temperature for up to 2 days; at this point, freezing is not recommended.

To fill: Place about 2 teaspoons of prepared filling in the center of the flat side of one cookie, then top with another cookie flat side down, squeezing gently so that the filling evenly fills out the round. If the filling is thick, roll about 1½ teaspoons of it into a ball between your fingers and set the ball on the flat side of one cookie before gently pressing the other cookie on top.

The Seven Sandwich Cookie Fillings

1. Vanilla Cream Filling

1½ tablespoons unsalted butter
1 tablespoon solid vegetable shortening
1½ cups confectioners' sugar
1 tablespoon vanilla extract
¼ teaspoon salt

Place the butter and shortening in a mini-food processor; pulse a couple of times, then scrape down the sides of the bowl. Add the confectioners' sugar; process until creamy. Add the vanilla and salt; process until well combined. Alternatively, cut the butter and shortening into the confectioners' sugar in a medium bowl, using a pastry cutter or a fork, until a smooth icinglike filling has formed; add the vanilla and salt, then stir until a stiff filling forms. This filling is quite stiff and must be rolled into small rounds (see "to fill," above).

2. Lemon Cream Filling

2 tablespoons unsalted butter, softened to room remperature
1 teaspoon finely grated lemon zest
1 teaspoon lemon extract
½ teaspoon vanilla extract
⅛ teaspoon salt
1¼ cups confectioners' sugar
1 to 2 tablespoons heavy cream

Beat the butter, lemon zest, lemon extract, vanilla, and salt in a small bowl with an electric mixer at medium speed until light and creamy. Add the confectioners' sugar and continue beating until a thick icing forms. With the beaters running, add just enough cream so that the mixture thins out to a pastelike consistency, not at all like icing. If you go too far and add too much cream, you can correct the thin filling with a little additional confectioners' sugar, probably no more than a tablespoon or two.

3. Peanut Butter Cream Filling

⅔ cup creamy peanut butter (do not use natural peanut butter)
4 tablespoons (½ stick) unsalted butter
1⅓ cups confectioners' sugar
2 teaspoons vanilla extract

Beat the peanut butter and butter in a medium bowl with an electric mixer at medium speed until smooth and light. Add the confectioners' sugar and vanilla; continue beating until smooth and thick. If you find the filling is too thick, you can thin it out with a few drops of milk or cream, beaten until smooth.

4. Maple Coffee Cream Filling

1½ tablespoons unsalted butter
1⅓ cups confectioners' sugar
2 tablespoons maple syrup
2 teaspoons instant espresso powder,
    whisked with 1 teaspoon hot water until
    dissolved
1 teaspoon vanilla extract
⅛ teaspoon salt

Place the butter and confectioners' sugar in a mini-food processor; process until well combined. Add the maple syrup, espresso powder mixture, vanilla, and salt. Process until smooth and icinglike. Alternatively, cut the butter into the confectioners' sugar in a medium bowl using a pastry cutter or a fork until fairly smooth. Stir in the remaining ingredients until creamy.

5. Pine Nut Cream Filling

½ cup pine nuts
1½ tablespoons solid vegetable
    shortening
2 teaspoons vanilla extract
2¼ cups confectioners' sugar
¼ teaspoon salt
Up to 1 tablespoon brandy; Cognac;
    a hazelnut-flavored liqueur, such as
    Frangelico; or an almond-flavored
    liqueur, such as Amaretto di
    Saronno

Process the pine nuts in a mini-food processor or a large food processor fitted with the chopping blade until finely ground. Add the shortening; process until combined. Add the vanilla and pulse a few times. Finally, add the confectioners' sugar and salt; process until a creamy, icinglike filling forms. Finally, add the liquor in 1-teaspoon increments and process just until the mixture thins to a smooth cookie filling.

6. Chocolate Truffle Cream Filling

¼ cup heavy cream
5 ounces bittersweet or semisweet chocolate,
    chopped
1½ tablespoons unsalted butter, at room
    temperature

Heat the cream in a small saucepan set over medium-low heat until small bubbles appear around the pan's inner rim. Pour the heated cream over the chocolate in a medium bowl; stir until the chocolate melts and the mixture is smooth. Add the butter and beat with an electric mixer at low speed until the color lightens somewhat and the mixture thickens slightly. Be careful—overbeating will cause the chocolate to seize. If it does break into a lump and a watery liquid, you may be able to fix it by beating in a tablespoon or two of heavy cream. If the mixture becomes stiff as you're filling the cookies, roll it into balls between your fingers and press these between the two cookies to create the sandwich filling.

7. Chocolate Hazelnut Cream Filling

3 ounces bittersweet or semisweet chocolate,
    chopped
½ cup plus 2 tablespoons Nutella

Place the chocolate in a medium bowl in the top half of a double boiler set over about 1 inch of simmering water or in a medium bowl that fits snugly over a medium saucepan with the same amount of simmering water. Stir until half the chocolate has melted, then remove the top half of the double boiler or the bowl from over the water and continue stirring until the chocolate has completely melted. Cool for 5 minutes, then stir in the Nutella. For an even richer filling, also stir in 1 tablespoon unsalted butter, softened to room temperature.

Fig Cookies

These cookies are designed to taste like those fig cookies we all grew up eating. You make a filled log and bake it off before slicing it into cookies.

Makes 36 cookies

16 ounces dried figs, preferably
    Turkish figs
8 ounces raisins
1 cup packed light brown sugar
⅓ cup lemon juice
⅓ cup water
3 tablespoons brandy or orange juice
½ teaspoon ground cinnamon
2 cups whole wheat pastry flour
1 cup all-purpose flour, plus additional for
    dusting
½ teaspoon baking powder
½ teaspoon baking soda
½ teaspoon salt
¾ cup granulated sugar
½ cup solid vegetable shortening
3 large eggs, at room temperature

❶ Place the figs and raisins in a food processor fitted with the chopping blade. Process until finely chopped, then pulse a few more times until the mixture gathers together in a sticky ball.

❷ Scrape the fig mixture into a medium saucepan set over medium heat. Stir in ¾ cup brown sugar, the lemon juice, water, brandy or orange juice, and cinnamon.

❸ Cook, stirring almost constantly, until the sugar dissolves and the mixture begins to bubble, about 5 minutes. Remove from the heat and set aside to cool completely, about 1 hour (or cover and refrigerate for up to 24 hours).

❹ Position the rack in the center of the oven and preheat the oven to 400°F. Line a large baking sheet with parchment paper or a silicone baking mat.

❺ Whisk both flours, the baking powder, baking soda, and salt in a medium bowl; set aside.

❻ Beat the granulated sugar, shortening, and the remaining ¼ cup brown sugar in a large bowl, using an electric mixer at medium speed, until creamy and smooth, about 4 minutes. Beat in the eggs one at a time, scraping down the bowl after each addition.

❼ Turn off the beaters, add the flour mixture, and beat at low speed just until a smooth dough starts to form. Remove the beaters and divide the dough into thirds.

❽ Sprinkle a few drops of water on your work surface, then lay a large sheet of wax paper over them. Sprinkle the wax paper with a little flour, then place one part of the dough on it. Press down gently to flatten, dust with flour, and lay a second sheet of wax paper over the dough.

❾ Roll the dough between the sheets of wax paper until it forms a 12 x 5-inch rectangle. Peel off the top sheet of wax paper.

❿ Spread a third of the fig mixture (about 1 cup) the long way down the middle of the rectangle. Leave a ½-inch border at each end and about an inch down each of the long sides of the rectangle. Fold one long side over onto the other so that you create a tube. Seal the long ends well, then crimp the short ends closed. Transfer the log to the prepared baking sheet and repeat steps 7, 8, and 9 with the other two pieces of dough and the remaining filling, leaving about 2 inches of space between the logs on the baking sheet.

⑪ Bake until lightly browned, about 15 minutes.

To cool and slice: Leave the logs on the baking sheet for 10 minutes, then transfer them to a wire rack and cool completely (do not pick them up; transfer them with spatulas to keep them from breaking apart in the middle). Cool for 1 hour, then slice into 1-inch pieces (the very ends will be pretty worthless—not much filling; they should be cut off and discarded).

To store: They can be kept in a sealed container at room temperature for up to 4 days.

Variations: Reduce the dried figs to 8 ounces and add 8 ounces dried Turkish apricots.
   Add ¼ cup chopped slivered almonds with the brown sugar to the fig mixture.
   For a fun dessert, use all the dough and filling to create one huge filled log, then bend it into a ring before baking; bring to the table to slice off individual cookies or servings.

Rugelach

These cakey rolls are often made with jam, but we prefer them with a simpler filling of walnuts and raisins. *Makes about 36 rugelach*

   16 tablespoons cool unsalted butter, cut into chunks
   8 ounces cream cheese, cut into chunks
   3 tablespoons granulated sugar
   2 cups all-purpose flour, plus additional for dusting
   ½ teaspoon salt
   1 cup finely chopped walnut pieces
   ½ cup packed light brown sugar
   ½ cup chopped raisins
   1 teaspoon ground cinnamon

① Beat the butter and cream cheese in a large bowl with an electric mixer at medium speed until softened, about 3 minutes. Beat in the granulated sugar until smooth, about 3 minutes.

② Turn off the beaters, add the flour and salt, and beat at low speed until a soft dough forms. Gather the dough together, divide it into 3 pieces, and form each into a ball. Wrap the balls in plastic and refrigerate for 15 minutes.

③ Meanwhile, position the rack in the center of the oven and preheat the oven to 350°F. Mix the walnut pieces, brown sugar, raisins, and cinnamon in a small bowl.

④ Lightly dust a clean, dry work surface with flour. Unwrap one of the pieces of dough, lightly flour it, and roll it out to a 12 × 8-inch rectangle. Sprinkle a third of the walnut mixture evenly over the dough.

⑤ Roll the rectangle closed, like a jelly roll, starting with one of the long sides. Cut the roll into 1-inch pieces. Place these on a large, ungreased baking sheet exactly as you cut them, with the spirals to the sides, not down against the baking sheet.

⑥ Bake until lightly browned, about 30 minutes.

⑦ Continue making the rugelach, using half the remaining walnut mixture for the next batch and then all the remaining mixture for the last piece of dough.

To cool: Leave the cookies on the baking sheet for a couple of minutes, then transfer them to a wire rack to cool completely, about 1 hour.

To store: The rugelach can be stored in an airtight container at room temperature for up to 3 days or in the freezer for up to 3 months.

Variations: Spread any flavor jam over the dough before sprinkling on the walnut mixture. You'll need about 1 cup jam (about ⅓ cup for each roll).

Or paint the dough with about 6 ounces semi-sweet chocolate, melted and cooled, before adding the walnut mixture.

Apricot Hamantaschen

Traditionally made at Purim, the feast to celebrate the salvation of the Jews by Queen Esther, hamantaschen are said to resemble the unfashionable, clownish three-pointed hat worn by the man who was trying to eradicate the exiles in Babylon. *Makes 16 cookies*

2¼ cups all-purpose flour, plus additional
    for dusting
½ teaspoon baking powder
¼ teaspoon salt
1 cup solid vegetable shortening
½ cup sugar
1 large egg, at room temperature
1 teaspoon vanilla extract
2 ounces dried California
    apricots
¾ cup apricot jam
Boiling water

❶ Whisk the flour, baking powder, and salt in a medium bowl; set aside.

❷ Beat the shortening and sugar in a large bowl with an electric mixer at medium speed until light and airy, about 3 minutes. Scrape down the sides of the bowl, then beat in the egg and vanilla until smooth.

❸ Turn off the beaters, add the flour mixture, and beat at low speed until a soft dough forms. Gather it together, divide it in half, and shape each half into a ball. Wrap the balls individually in plastic and refrigerate for 2 hours.

❹ Meanwhile, place the dried apricots in a small bowl and cover them with boiling water. Set aside for 30 minutes.

❺ Drain the apricots, then place them in a mini-food processor or a large blender with the apricot jam. Process or blend until fairly smooth, then set aside to cool to room temperature before using, about 1 hour.

❻ Position the rack in the center of the oven and preheat the oven to 400°F. Line a large baking sheet with parchment paper or a silicone baking mat; set aside.

❼ Lightly dust a clean, dry work surface with flour. Unwrap one of the balls of dough (keep the other in the refrigerator). Pinch off about 2 tablespoons of dough, roll it into a ball between your hands, then set it on the floured work surface. Press the ball down slightly to flatten it a little and lightly dust it with flour.

❽ Roll to a 4-inch circle. Place a tablespoon of the apricot filling in the center of the circle. Imagine the rim of the circle in thirds, in three even arcs. Fold each of these thirds up over the jam, thereby creating a triangular cookie with a little, curved triangular window that exposes the jam. You can use a thin metal spatula to lift the pieces of dough up toward the center to cover the filling partially. Pinch the sides closed over the filling, then use a metal spatula to transfer the cookie to the prepared baking sheet. Continue making more cookies, spacing them about 2 inches apart on the baking sheet. Refrigerate any remaining dough until you're ready to bake another batch.

9 Bake until lightly browned, about 20 minutes.

To cool: Keep the cookies on the baking sheet a couple of minutes, then transfer them to a wire rack to cool completely. Cool the baking sheet for 5 minutes before adding more cookies to it.

To store: The hamantaschen can be kept between sheets of wax paper in a sealed container at room temperature for up to 4 days or in the freezer for up to 3 months.

Variations: Substitute dried figs and Fig Jam (page 221) for the dried apricots and the apricot jam.

Substitute pitted prunes and plum preserves for the dried apricots and the apricot jam.

Jam Thumbprints

These are often made by placing jam in their centers before baking, but the jam can melt and even burn. So it's better to add it just as the cookies come out of the oven. Although not necessary for success, a nonstick baking or cookie sheet can make cleanup easier since the egg white wash will not stick to it. *Makes about 30 cookies*

> 2 cups all-purpose flour
> ½ teaspoon baking powder
> ½ teaspoon salt
> 16 tablespoons (2 sticks) cool unsalted butter, cut into chunks
> ½ cup packed light brown sugar
> 2 large egg yolks
> 1 tablespoon vanilla extract
> 2 large egg whites, whisked in a small bowl until frothy, at room temperature
> 1½ cups very finely chopped walnut pieces
> ½ cup homemade jam (see page 221) or any flavor jam you prefer

1 Position the rack in the center of the oven and preheat the oven to 375°F.

2 Whisk the flour, baking powder, and salt in a medium bowl; set aside.

3 Soften the butter in a large bowl with an electric mixer at medium speed just until it barely begins to turn creamy. Add the brown sugar and continue beating at medium speed until smooth and very light, about 4 minutes.

4 Beat in the egg yolks and vanilla. Turn off the beaters, add the prepared flour mixture, and beat at low speed just until a soft dough forms.

5 Pinch off a heaping tablespoon of the dough and roll it into a ball between your palms. Dip it in the beaten egg whites, then roll it in the nuts, pressing gently so they adhere, dotting the surface of the ball. Set the ball on an ungreased baking sheet, then continue making more, spacing them about 3 inches apart.

6 Bake for 5 minutes. Remove the baking sheet from the oven and use your thumb (be careful: the dough is hot—you can use a cleaned sewing thimble or a wooden spoon handle) to make a deep indentation in the center of each cookie just until the edges crack. Return the cookies to the oven and bake until lightly browned at the edges and somewhat firm to the touch, about 10 more minutes.

7 Remove the cookies from the oven and immediately place a heaping ½ teaspoon jam in each indentation.

To cool: Leave the cookies on the baking sheet for a couple of minutes, then transfer them to a wire rack to cool completely. Cool the baking sheet for at least 5 more minutes before making more cookies.

To store: Once fully cooled, the cookies can be stored between sheets of wax paper in a sealed container at room temperature for up to 3 days.

Variations: Customize them to your heart's content just by changing the flavor of the jam, but don't use jelly (it melts too quickly) or preserves (which have uneven chunks of fruit).

Jam Rolls

These cakey cookies are a cross between Rugelach (page 579) and a jelly doughnut. You make a log, spiraled with jam, then slice it into thick, chewy cookies. *Makes about 36 cookies*

3 cups all-purpose flour, plus additional for dusting
½ teaspoon baking powder
½ teaspoon ground cinnamon
¼ teaspoon baking soda
¼ teaspoon salt
⅔ cup packed light brown sugar
⅔ cup granulated sugar
½ cup solid vegetable shortening
3 large egg whites, lightly whisked in a small bowl, at room temperature
2 teaspoons vanilla extract
¾ cup jam, either homemade (see page 221) or store-bought
1 cup chopped pecan pieces

❶ Whisk the flour, baking powder, cinnamon, baking soda, and salt in a medium bowl; set aside.

❷ Beat both sugars and the shortening in a large bowl with an electric mixer at medium speed until light and beige, about 3 minutes. Beat in the egg whites and vanilla until smooth.

❸ Turn off the beaters, scrape down the sides of the bowl, and add the flour mixture. Beat at a very low speed until a soft dough forms. Remove the beaters, cover the bowl with a clean kitchen towel, and set aside for 15 minutes.

❹ Meanwhile, position the rack in the center of the oven and preheat the oven to 350°F. Line a large baking sheet with parchment paper or a silicone baking mat; set aside.

❺ Divide the dough in half and form each into a ball. Sprinkle a few drops of water on your work surface, then lay a large piece of wax paper on top of them. Lightly dust the wax paper with flour; place the dough in the middle of the paper. Gently flatten the dough, then lay another piece of wax paper over the top. Roll to a 12 × 8-inch rectangle.

❻ Peel off the top layer of wax paper and spread the dough evenly with 6 tablespoons jam. Sprinkle ½ cup chopped nuts evenly over the dough. Roll the rectangle up fairly tightly, starting with one of the 12-inch sides. Slice into ¾-inch disks. Place on the prepared baking sheet cut side down.

❼ Bake until lightly browned, about 35 minutes. Meanwhile, roll out the second piece of dough, add the jam and nuts, roll up, and cut into more cookies.

To cool: Let the baked cookies stand on the baking sheet for a couple of minutes at room temperature, then transfer them to a wire rack to cool completely. Cool the baking sheet for at least 5 minutes before putting more cookies on it; replace the parchment paper if it's singed.

To store: The cookies can be stored in an airtight container at room temperature for up to 3 days.

❀ *Bar Cookies* ❀

These ride the line between a cake and a cookie: made in a baking pan, cut into squares, not as crisp as cookies, but more portable than cake.

Triple Chocolate Brownies

What's the point in doing something halfway? These brownies are so dense and fudgy, you need to cool them in the pan for at least an hour before slicing. *Makes 16 large brownies*

4 ounces unsweetened chocolate, chopped
16 tablespoons (2 sticks) cool unsalted
   butter, cut into small chunks, plus
   additional for greasing the pan
¾ cup plus 2 tablespoons (14 tablespoons)
   all-purpose flour, plus additional for
   dusting the pan
¼ cup sifted unsweetened cocoa powder
1 teaspoon baking powder
½ teaspoon salt
1 cup packed light brown sugar
1 cup granulated sugar
3 large eggs, at room temperature
1 tablespoon vanilla extract
2 cups semisweet or bittersweet chocolate
   chips

❶ Set the chocolate in the top half of a double boiler placed over 1 inch of simmering water in the bottom half over high heat, or set it in a medium bowl that fits snugly over a medium saucepan with about the same amount of simmering water. Lower the heat to medium-low so the water simmers slowly, and stir until half the chocolate has melted. Remove the top half of the double boiler or the bowl from the heat and continue stirring until the chocolate has fully melted. Set aside to cool at room temperature for 10 minutes.

❷ Meanwhile, position the rack in the center of the oven and preheat the oven to 350°F. Lightly butter a 13 × 9-inch baking pan; dust it lightly with flour. Whisk the flour, cocoa powder, baking powder, and salt in a medium bowl until uniform; set aside.

❸ Beat the butter and both sugars in a large bowl with an electric mixer at medium speed until light, fluffy, and creamy, about 4 minutes, scraping down the sides of the bowl occasionally to make sure all the sugar is being beaten into the mixture.

❹ Beat in the eggs one at a time, making sure each is thoroughly incorporated before adding the next. Beat in the melted chocolate and vanilla until smooth.

❺ Turn off the beaters, add the prepared flour mixture, and beat at a very low speed until all the flour has all dissolved but not until the batter is smooth, about 1 minute. Scrape down and re-move the beaters; stir in the chocolate chips with a rubber spatula.

❻ Pour and scrape the batter into the pre-pared pan, getting it evenly into the corners and throughout. Bake until softly set, until a tooth-pick or cake tester inserted into the center comes out with moist crumbs attached, about 55 min-utes.

To cool: Place the pan on a wire rack and cool completely, at least 1 hour.

To store: Cut the brownies into squares in the pan and wrap each individually in wax paper; store at room temperature in a sealed container for up to 3 days.

Variations: Substitute white chocolate chips for the semisweet chocolate chips.

Substitute one of the following for the vanilla: 1½ teaspoons maple extract, 1½ teaspoons rum extract, 1 teaspoon almond extract, or 1 teaspoon coconut extract.

Stir in ½ cup of any of the following mix-ins, or ½ cup total volume of any combination of mix-ins, with the flour mixture: chopped dried apples, chopped pecans, chopped toasted hazelnuts, chopped unsalted cashews, chopped walnuts, dried blueberries, dried cherries, dried cranberries, raisins, slivered almonds, toasted pepitas, unsalted peanuts.

Buttermilk Blondies

Blondies are the original brownies: a chocolate-studded, buttery cake that's turned into a bar cookie. Don't use a glass baking pan; the batter will superheat and turn hard at the edges. *Makes 16 blondies*

16 tablespoons (2 sticks) cool unsalted butter, cut into small chunks, plus additional for greasing the baking pan
2⅔ cups all-purpose flour, plus additional for dusting the baking pan
1 teaspoon baking powder
1 teaspoon baking soda
½ teaspoon salt
1¼ cups packed light brown sugar
1 cup granulated sugar
3 large eggs, at room temperature
½ cup regular or low-fat buttermilk (do not use fat-free)
1 tablespoon vanilla extract
2 cups semisweet or bittersweet chocolate chips

1 Position the rack in the center of the oven and preheat the oven to 325°F. Lightly butter a 13 x 9-inch baking pan; dust it lightly with flour, taking care to coat the corners and the seams. Whisk the flour, baking powder, baking soda, and salt in a medium bowl; set aside.

2 Beat the butter and both sugars in a large bowl with an electric mixer at medium speed until light, creamy, and very smooth, about 4 minutes, scraping down the sides of the bowl frequently.

3 Beat in the eggs one at a time, making sure each is mixed well into the batter before you add the next. Beat in the buttermilk and vanilla until smooth.

4 Turn off the beaters, add the prepared flour mixture, and beat at very low speed just until a wet batter forms, one without any pockets of dry flour.

5 Scrape down and remove the beaters. Fold in the chocolate chips with a rubber spatula until uniform; pour and scrape into the prepared pan, getting the batter to the corners and even across the top.

6 Bake until golden brown, until a toothpick or cake tester inserted into the center comes out with moist crumbs attached, about 1 hour.

To cool: Set the baking pan on a wire rack and cool to room temperature, about 1½ hours.

To store: Cut the blondies into individual squares, wrap each in wax paper, and store in a sealed container at room temperature for up to 3 days.

Variations: Add one or more of the following spices to the flour mixture: 2 teaspoons ground cinnamon, 2 teaspoons ground ginger, 1 teaspoon ground mace, ½ teaspoon grated nutmeg.

Add one of the following flavorings with the vanilla: 2 teaspoons banana extract, 2 teaspoons banana extract, 2 teaspoons maple extract, 2 teaspoons orange extract, 2 teaspoons rum extract, or 1½ teaspoons almond extract.

Substitute butterscotch, milk chocolate, mint chocolate, peanut butter, or white chocolate chips for the semisweet chocolate chips.

Stir in 1¼ cups of any of the following mix-ins, or 1¼ cups total volume of any combination of mix-ins, with the chocolate chips: chopped dried apricots, chopped pecans, chopped toasted hazelnuts, chopped walnuts, cocoa nibs, dried cherries, dried currants, honey-roasted almonds, pine nuts, raisins, or slivered almonds.

Peanut Chocolate Bar Cookies

Here, a light cookie batter is baked in a pan, then "iced" with chocolate and peanuts. For the best taste, use salted peanuts. *Makes 36 bar cookies*

> 1½ sticks (12 tablespoons) cool unsalted butter, cut into chunks, plus additional for greasing the pan
> ½ cup packed dark brown sugar
> 1¼ cups all-purpose flour
> 12 ounces semisweet chocolate, chopped; or semisweet chocolate chips
> ½ cup light corn syrup
> 2 teaspoons vanilla extract
> 2½ cups salted roasted peanuts

1 Position the rack in the center of the oven and preheat the oven to 350°F. Lightly butter a 13 x 9-inch baking pan; set aside.

2 Beat 1 stick (8 tablespoons) butter and the brown sugar in a large bowl until the sugar dissolves and the mixture becomes quite fluffy, about 3 minutes. Add the flour and beat just until a crumbly dough forms. Press this dough into the bottom of the prepared pan, making sure there

are no cracks or gaps without pressing down too hard.

3 Bake until lightly browned at the edges, about 15 minutes. Transfer to a wire rack while you make the filling. (Maintain the oven temperature.)

4 Melt the remaining ½ stick (4 tablespoons) butter, the chocolate, and corn syrup in a medium saucepan set over very low heat, stirring constantly, just until all the chocolate has melted and the mixture is smooth. Stir in the vanilla.

5 Pour the chocolate mixture over the crust in the pan, spreading it gently but evenly to the edges. Dot the top with peanuts; press them into the chocolate with a flat spatula, not to submerge them but to make sure they're held by the chocolate.

6 Bake until the topping is bubbling and almost set, about another 15 minutes.

To cool: Transfer the pan to a wire rack and cool completely, about 2 hours.

To unmold: When the chocolate on top has set and cooled, invert the pan over a large cutting board and gently knock the whole sheet of bar cookies out of the pan. Remove the pan, then reinvert the sheet of bar cookies, using a second large baking sheet. Cut into squares.

To store: These bars can be kept in a sealed container between sheets of wax paper for up to 3 days.

Variations: Substitute walnut pieces or pecan pieces for the peanuts. Toast either of these in a large skillet with 1 teaspoon canola oil over medium heat until lightly browned, about 4 minutes. Sprinkle on 1½ teaspoons salt and shake well to coat.

Shortbread Bars

We first learned about this technique for making shortbread from Gale Gand, one of the country's best pastry chefs. You make the dough, freeze it, then grate it into the pan. The variations are endless, depending on the type of jam you prefer.
Makes about 16 bars

> 2 cups all-purpose flour
> ½ teaspoon baking powder
> ¼ teaspoon salt
> 16 tablespoons (2 sticks) cool unsalted
>   butter, cut into chunks
> 1 cup sugar
> 2 large egg yolks, at room temperature
> 1 teaspoon vanilla extract
> ½ cup homemade jam (see page 221) or the
>   jam of your choice
> Confectioners' sugar for dusting

1 Whisk the flour, baking powder, and salt in a medium bowl; set aside.

2 Soften the butter in a large bowl with an electric mixer at medium speed just until it starts to get gooey at the edges. Add the sugar and continue beating until the sugar has mostly dissolved and the mixture is quite fluffy, about 4 minutes.

3 Beat in the egg yolks one at a time, then the vanilla. Turn off the beaters, add the flour mixture, and beat at low speed until a smooth dough forms.

4 Divide the dough in half and roll each into a ball. Wrap each in plastic and set in the freezer until well chilled but not frozen, about 1 hour.

5 Position the rack in the center of the oven and preheat the oven to 350°F.

6 Unwrap one ball of dough and grate it through the large holes of a box grater into an 8-inch baking pan. Spread the dough shards gently but evenly to the corners without pressing down. Dot the jam over the dough; spread gently with a rubber spatula. Unwrap the other ball of dough and grate it into the pan, covering the jam and spreading the shards to the corners.

7 Bake until lightly browned and set on the top, 30 to 35 minutes.

To cool: Transfer the pan to a wire rack and cool completely, about 2 hours. Dust the top of the shortbread bars with confectioners' sugar and cut into 16 pieces (making four cuts each way in the pan).

To store: The bars can be kept between sheets of wax paper in a sealed container at room temperature for up to 3 days.

Lemon Bars

Use a microplane to get the lemon zest grated as thinly as possible—or shave it off with the large holes of a box grater and then mince it on a cutting board until you have the smallest, thinnest threads. *Makes 16 bar cookies*

> 16 tablespoons (2 sticks) cool unsalted
>   butter, cut into small cubes, plus
>   additional for greasing the pan
> 1½ cups plus 2 tablespoons all-purpose flour
> ⅓ cup plus 1 tablespoon confectioners' sugar
> ¼ teaspoon salt
> 1½ cups granulated sugar
> 3 large eggs plus 1 large egg yolk, at room
>   temperature
> 6 tablespoons lemon juice
> 1 tablespoon finely grated lemon
>   zest

1 Position the rack in the center of the oven; preheat the oven to 350°F. Lightly butter a 9-inch baking pan; set it aside.

2 Mix 1½ cups flour, ⅓ cup confectioners' sugar, and the salt in a large bowl. Add the chunks of butter and cut them into the flour mixture with a pastry cutter or a fork until the mixture is a little coarser than dry oat bran.

3 Press this mixture evenly across the bottom of the prepared pan, making sure there are no holes and compacting the mixture somewhat to form a cookielike crust.

4 Bake until lightly browned at the edges, about 25 minutes. Remove from the oven and set aside on a wire rack.

5 Without delay, beat the granulated sugar, eggs, and egg yolk in a medium bowl with an electric mixer at medium speed until pale yellow and quite thick, like a thin sabayon, about 3 minutes. Beat in the lemon juice and lemon zest, scrape down the sides of the bowl with a rubber spatula, and beat in the remaining 2 tablespoons flour. Pour this mixture evenly over the hot crust.

6 Return the pan to the oven and bake until the filling is set (it should jiggle a bit when shaken, but there should be no liquid in the mixture), about 25 minutes.

To cool: Transfer to a wire rack and cool completely, about 1 hour. Sprinkle the remaining 1 tablespoon confectioners' sugar over the pan, then cut the cookies into 16 squares (making four cuts each way in the pan).

To store: The bars can be kept in a sealed container between sheets of wax paper for up to 3 days.

Lime Bars: Substitute lime juice for the lemon juice; substitute 2 teaspoons finely grated lime zest for the lemon zest.

Lime Coconut Bars: Substitute lime juice for the lemon juice; substitute 1 tablespoon finely ground sweetened coconut for the lemon zest. When they're fully cooled, dust the top of the bars with 1 tablespoon finely ground sweetened coconut.

Orange Bars: Substitute thawed orange juice concentrate for the lemon juice; substitute orange zest for the lemon zest but also add 1 teaspoon lemon juice.

Maple Cheesecake Bars

A rich, sweet cheesecake filling, a salty bar cookie base—is there a better combination? Grind the pecans in a food processor until they are the consistency of fine cornmeal. *Makes 16 bar cookies*

6 tablespoons cool unsalted butter, cut into chunks, plus additional for greasing the pan
½ cup packed light brown sugar
1 cup plus 2 tablespoons all-purpose flour
⅔ cup finely ground pecan pieces
⅓ cup rolled oats (do not use quick-cooking)
½ teaspoon ground cinnamon
½ teaspoon salt
10 ounces regular or low-fat cream cheese (do not use fat-free), softened to room temperature
¼ cup maple syrup
1 teaspoon vanilla extract
1 large egg, at room temperature

1 Position the rack in the center of the oven and preheat the oven to 350°F. Lightly butter a 9-inch square baking dish; set aside.

② Beat the brown sugar and butter in a large bowl with an electric mixer at medium speed until light, airy, and pale brown, about 3 minutes.

③ Turn off the beaters. Add 1 cup flour, pecans, oats, cinnamon, and salt; beat at low speed until a crumbly dough forms, somewhat like a cobbler topping, about 1 minute.

④ Pour this mixture into the prepared pan and gently press across the bottom to create an even crust with no gaps or holes. Bake for 15 minutes, then transfer to a wire rack.

⑤ While the crust is baking, clean and dry the bowl and beaters. Beat the cream cheese at medium speed until slightly softened. Add the maple syrup and vanilla; beat until smooth. Scrape down the sides of the bowl, then beat in the egg. Once it is fully incorporated, beat in the remaining 2 tablespoons flour just until combined, no more than 15 or 20 seconds.

⑥ Pour the cream cheese mixture over the hot crust and return to the oven. Bake until the top is set when jiggled and the cream cheese topping has just begun to turn beige at the edges, about 20 minutes.

To cool and unmold: Transfer to a wire rack and cool for 15 minutes. The cheesecake topping will begin to pull away from the sides of the pan; run a knife around the interior perimeter of the pan to aid this process. Cool completely, about another 45 minutes.

To store: Cut into 16 bars and store between sheets of wax paper in a sealed container at room temperature for up to 3 days.

Honey Cheesecake Bars: Substitute honey for the maple syrup.

Coffee Cheesecake Bars: Substitute 2 tablespoons coffee-flavored liqueur such as Kahlúa and 2 tablespoons packed dark brown sugar for the maple syrup.

Brown Sugar Cheesecake Bars: Substitute brown sugar for the maple syrup. Reduce the flour added to the cream cheese mixture to 1½ tablespoons.

Coconut Cream Bars

A light coconut topping, spiked with lime juice, makes these crunchy bar cookies a fabulous treat anytime. To get the most juice out of a lime, make sure it's at room temperature and roll it under your palm against your work surface before slicing. *Makes 12 bar cookies*

1 stick (8 tablespoons) cool unsalted
    butter, cut into chunks, plus additional
    for greasing the pan
¾ cup plus 2 tablespoons granulated
    sugar
¼ cup packed light brown sugar
1¼ cups all-purpose flour
¼ teaspoon salt
2 large eggs
2 tablespoons lime juice
¼ teaspoon baking powder
1 cup shredded sweetened coconut
    (do not use unsweetened
    coconut)

① Position the rack in the center of the oven and preheat the oven to 350°F. Lightly butter an 8-inch baking dish and set it aside.

② Beat the butter, 2 tablespoons granulated sugar, and the brown sugar in a large bowl with an electric mixer at medium speed until the sugar dissolves and the mixture turns pale brown and very fluffy, about 4 minutes.

3 Add 1 cup plus 2 tablespoons flour and the salt; beat at low speed just until combined. Press this mixture into the bottom of the prepared pan, compacting it slightly and making sure there are no gaps or holes in this cookielike crust.

4 Bake until lightly browned, about 18 minutes. Transfer to a wire rack.

5 Without delay, clean and dry the mixer beaters. Beat the eggs with the remaining ¾ cup granulated sugar in a second medium bowl with an electric mixer until smooth, until the sugar has mostly dissolved, about 2 minutes.

6 Beat in the lime juice, then the remaining 2 tablespoons flour and the baking powder. Scrape down the sides of the bowl and beat in the coconut just until combined. Pour this mixture over the still-warm crust.

7 Bake until the filling has set and is a little browned, about 22 minutes.

To cool: Transfer the pan to a wire rack and cool completely, about 1 hour.

To store: Cut into 12 squares. Keep in a sealed container between sheets of wax paper at room temperature for up to 2 days.

Variations: Add ¼ teaspoon almond extract with the butter and sugars.

Lightly grate nutmeg or mace over the top of the filling before baking it.

For a tropical taste, add ¼ teaspoon rum extract with the butter and sugars. For a lighter taste, substitute lemon juice for the lime juice.

Blackberry Oat Bars

These pecan bars are not terribly sweet—and quite easy, thanks to blackberry jam. *Makes 16 bar cookies*

1 cup solid vegetable shortening, plus
　　additional for greasing the pan
Parchment paper
1½ cups all-purpose flour
1½ cups rolled oats (do not use quick-
　　cooking)
1 cup finely chopped pecan pieces
½ teaspoon ground cinnamon
½ teaspoon salt
⅔ cup packed light brown sugar
½ cup granulated sugar
1 large egg white
½ cup blackberry jam

1 Position the rack in the center of the oven and preheat the oven to 350°F.

2 Grease the bottom and sides of a 9-inch square pan with a little vegetable shortening dabbed on a piece of wax paper. Cut a piece of parchment paper to fit the bottom of the pan, press it into place, then grease the parchment paper. Set aside.

3 Mix the flour, oats, pecan pieces, cinnamon, and salt in a medium bowl; set aside as well.

4 Beat the shortening and sugars in a large bowl with an electric mixer at medium speed until creamy, until the sugars have mostly dissolved, about 3 minutes.

5 Beat in the egg white, scrape down the sides of the bowl, and then beat in the flour mixture just until you have a dry, crumbly dough.

6 Press about two-thirds of this dough into the bottom of the prepared baking pan. Dot the blackberry jam over the dough and gently spread it to an even coating, taking care not to disturb the crumbly dough. Sprinkle the remaining dough over the blackberry jam; press down lightly with the palm of your hand or a flat spatula to mash the topping a little into the jam.

7 Bake until lightly browned and the jam is barely bubbling, about 45 minutes.

To cool: Set the pan on a wire rack for at least 20 minutes before slicing into 16 bar cookies (making four cuts each way in the pan).

To store: The bars can be stored in a sealed container between sheets of wax paper at room temperature for up to 3 days.

Variations: Add either $\frac{1}{4}$ teaspoon grated nutmeg or $\frac{1}{8}$ teaspoon ground cloves with the cinnamon.

Substitute finely chopped walnut pieces for the pecan pieces.

Substitute different kinds of jam: strawberry, blueberry, apricot, raspberry, fig, or any other flavor you prefer. Do not use jelly (which will be too thin) or preserves (which will have large chunks of fruit).

Pies, Tarts, and Fruit Desserts

P IES HAVE MIGRATED FROM THE MIDDLE OF A RENAISSANCE MEAL TO THE end of a modern one, as well as from the middle of the afternoon to the late-night refrigerator raid; yet these crusty concoctions remain the same: a bit of excess, a bit of comfort.

There's something unbeatably retro about pies and tarts as well as their close kin like cobblers and crisps. We've lumped them together in this chapter because of their familiar, peerless formula: a sweet filling and a crunchy crust. Fancy or homey, American or Continental, simple, elegant, and irresistible, they all manage to adhere to this two-part blueprint.

Over the years, we've taken pies, tarts, crisps, and the like to picnics, casual suppers, formal dinner parties, and chorale rehearsals. These desserts evoke smiles—even among the black-bedecked Manhattan set. Everyone's surprised, pleased—and caught off guard, as if these fabulous desserts were rarities and wonders, nostalgic, yet somehow still of the moment.

They shouldn't be. They're surprisingly easy—lots of pizzazz for the buck, made from the freshest ingredients. No wonder everyone loves pie.

The best are a balance of crust and filling. Too much of either and the game tips off center. So here's a road map to making good pies: start with the crust, build the filling (starting on page 594), and bake.

Piecrusts

The Basic Short Crust

The term "short" refers to the crust's crispness (that is, it is not leavened or raised). A dash of vinegar makes it incredibly flaky by cutting the flour's gluten chains. All our pies are designed for a 9-inch glass or metal pie plate. Be forewarned: you will overfill an 8-inch pie plate or shortchange a 10-inch one. *Makes a single crust for a 9-inch pie (can be doubled for a top and bottom crust—see Note)*

    1 cup all-purpose flour, plus additional for
      dusting
    ½ teaspoon salt
    ⅓ cup solid vegetable shortening
    1 tablespoon cold unsalted butter
    2 to 4 tablespoons ice water
    ½ teaspoon apple cider vinegar

❶ Mix the flour and salt in a medium bowl. Use a pastry cutter or fork to cut in the shortening and butter in two equal additions, pressing the fat into the flour through the tines and against the sides of the bowl. Keep scraping any dough off the cutter or fork. Continue pressing the mixture together until it resembles very coarse sand.

❷ Stir 2 tablespoons ice water and the vinegar in a small bowl or glass, then use a fork to stir this mixture into the flour mixture until well combined. Add more cold water, about 1 teaspoon at a time, until the mixture can be formed into a ball.

❸ Sprinkle a few drops of water over your work surface, then lay a large piece of wax paper on top (so the paper won't scoot around while you roll out the crust). Dust the paper lightly with flour. Gather the dough into a ball, turn it onto the paper, and dust lightly with flour. Lay a second sheet of wax paper over the top and press down slightly until the ball of dough looks like a partially deflated basketball.

❹ Roll the dough through the wax paper with a rolling pin, pressing down lightly and using an even, steady pressure until you have a circle 11 or 12 inches in diameter. To make an even circle, turn the pin in a new direction after each roll. If you're not using the dough right away, leave it under the wax paper to stay moist; it can rest this way for 30 minutes.

❺ Peel off the top layer of wax paper, then pick up the dough by peeling the bottom sheet of wax paper off the work surface with the crust still attached. Invert the paper and the crust together over a 9-inch pie plate, center the crust in the plate, and peel off the wax paper. Press the crust gently into the pie plate with the excess hanging over the rim. If you're making a single-crust pie (that is, a bottom crust only), run a knife around the plate's outer rim and cut off any excess dough.

If you're making a double-crust pie, leave the dough hanging over the edge and cover the pie with a clean, dry kitchen towel. Proceed with the filling you've chosen. (The recipes start on page 594.)

Note: A single-crust pie is a pie with the crust only on the bottom; a double-crust pie is one with a top and bottom crust.

Tips for Crust Success

- Clean off your counter so you've got space to move the rolling pin freely.
- The water must be very cold to bind the crust without melting the fat. Start by making a glass of ice water several minutes before you begin to make the crust. Do not use any of the ice in the dough, of course.
- The less you handle the dough, the better. Some old-school chefs suggest you use your hands to cut in the fat, rubbing it between your fingers and into the flour. Unfortunately, your skin's natural oils will toughen the pastry considerably and your body heat will liquefy the fat.
- Use a light rolling pin. A heavy pin is great if you're rolling out twenty pounds of croissant dough. Exert only as much pressure as will get the crust rolled out to the necessary diameter without smushing the fat and destroying the flaky layers.
- Roll a crust on the radius, not the diameter. Rolling edge to edge can result in poorly shaped crusts with jagged peaks and inlets. Start at the middle of the dough and roll toward the edge, rotating the pin by 10 degrees with each new roll.

Three Other Crusts

Follow the technique on page 592 to create any of these: start with the dry ingredients, cut in the fat, then stir in the liquids. But there are two important changes: (1) because some of the fats are liquid, you have to stir them in rather than cutting them in—cut in the solid fats first, then stir in the liquid ones; and (2) because butter melts more quickly than shortening and because some fats are in a liquid state, these crusts are easier to work with if you pop them in the refrigerator for 10 to 15 minutes before you roll them out.

1. *Butter Crust*

Makes a single crust for a 9-inch pie (can be doubled to make a top and bottom crust)

1 cup all-purpose flour, plus additional for dusting
1 teaspoon sugar
¼ teaspoon salt
4 tablespoons (½ stick) cold unsalted butter, cut into chunks
2 tablespoons solid vegetable shortening
2 to 3 tablespoons ice water
½ teaspoon lemon juice

2. *Walnut Crust*

Makes a single crust for a 9-inch pie (can be doubled to make a top and bottom crust)

1 cup all-purpose flour, plus additional for dusting
½ teaspoon salt
1 tablespoon cold unsalted butter
¼ cup walnut oil (see Note)
2 to 3 tablespoons ice water
¼ teaspoon white vinegar

Note: If you use toasted walnut oil, it will give the crust an even deeper taste, which may overpower some fillings.

---

3. Almond Crust

Makes a single crust for a 9-inch pie (can be doubled to make a top and bottom crust)

- 1 cup all-purpose flour, plus additional for dusting
- 1 tablespoon finely chopped slivered almonds
- ½ teaspoon salt
- 1 tablespoon cold unsalted butter
- ¼ cup almond oil (see Note)
- 2 to 3 tablespoons ice water
- ¼ teaspoon white vinegar
- ¼ teaspoon almond extract

Note: This crust is quite wet and sticky; add additional flour when dusting and rolling if it's too much so.

A road map for Fruit Pie

Nothing beats a fruit pie made with fresh ingredients and an age-old technique. Here's a road map for creating dozens—just mix and match fillings to crusts. *Makes one 9-inch fruit pie*

1 Position the rack in the center of the oven and preheat the oven to 425°F. If desired, place a single sheet of aluminum foil on a rack right below the center rack, a sheet just large enough to catch any inadvertent drips and thus make cleanup easier. (Do not place a baking sheet under the pie; the sheet will impede heat flow.)

2 Start making the fruit filling. Mix any of the following in a large bowl and set aside for 10 to 15 minutes at room temperature so that the tapioca dissolves and the sugar begins to break down the fruit.

Apple

- 2¼ pounds tart fresh apples, such as Granny Smith, Pippin, Rome Beauty, Cortland, or Northern Spy, peeled, cored, and thinly sliced
- ⅓ cup granulated sugar
- ¼ cup packed light brown sugar
- 2 tablespoons all-purpose flour
- 1½ tablespoons quick-cooking tapioca
- 2 tablespoons heavy cream or half-and-half, optional
- 1 tablespoon golden rum, optional
- 1 teaspoon ground cinnamon
- ¼ teaspoon grated nutmeg, optional
- ¼ teaspoon salt

Apple Cranberry

- 1¾ pounds tart fresh apples, such as Granny Smith, Pippin, Rome Beauty, Cortland, or Northern Spy, peeled, cored, and thinly sliced
- 2 cups roughly chopped fresh cranberries or one 8-ounce package frozen cranberries, roughly chopped
- ¾ cup plus 2 tablespoons sugar
- 2 tablespoons all-purpose flour
- 1½ tablespoons quick-cooking tapioca
- 2 teaspoons lemon juice
- ½ teaspoon ground mace or grated nutmeg
- ¼ teaspoon salt

Apple Ginger

- 2¼ pounds tart fresh apples, such as Granny Smith, Pippin, Rome Beauty, Cortland, or Northern Spy, peeled, cored, and thinly sliced
- ¼ cup granulated sugar
- ¼ cup packed light brown sugar
- 2 tablespoons finely chopped crystallized ginger
- 2 tablespoons all-purpose flour
- 1½ tablespoons quick-cooking tapioca
- 2 teaspoons ginger juice
- ¼ teaspoon salt

Apricot

2 pounds fresh apricots (18 to 26 small apricots), pitted and quartered, or 2 pounds sliced frozen pitted apricots, thawed

¾ cup sugar

2 tablespoons quick-cooking tapioca

1 tablespoon all-purpose flour

1 tablespoon heavy cream, half-and-half, or whole milk, optional

¼ teaspoon grated nutmeg

¼ teaspoon salt

Blackberry

2½ pints (5 cups) fresh blackberries or 2 pounds frozen blackberries (do not thaw)

¾ cup sugar

2 tablespoons all-purpose flour

1½ tablespoons quick-cooking tapioca

1 teaspoon finely grated lemon zest

½ teaspoon ground cinnamon, optional

¼ teaspoon salt

Blueberry

2½ pints (5 cups) fresh blueberries or 2 pounds frozen blueberries (do not thaw)

⅔ cup sugar

2 tablespoons all-purpose flour

1½ tablespoons quick-cooking tapioca

1 teaspoon finely grated orange zest

¼ teaspoon ground cinnamon, optional

¼ teaspoon salt

Peach

2 pounds fresh peaches (about 8 medium peaches), peeled, pitted, and thinly sliced, or 2 pounds sliced frozen pitted peaches, thawed

½ cup granulated sugar

¼ cup packed light brown sugar

2 tablespoons all-purpose flour

1½ tablespoons quick-cooking tapioca

1 teaspoon vanilla extract

½ teaspoon ground cinnamon

¼ teaspoon salt

Pear

2½ pounds ripe pears, such as Anjou, Bartlett, or Comice, peeled, cored, and thinly sliced

½ cup sugar

2 tablespoons all-purpose flour

2 tablespoons quick-cooking tapioca

1 teaspoon lemon juice

½ teaspoon ground cinnamon

¼ teaspoon salt

Raspberry

5 cups (2½ pints) fresh raspberries or 2 pounds frozen raspberries (do not thaw)

¾ cup sugar

2 tablespoons quick-cooking tapioca

1½ tablespoons all-purpose flour

1 teaspoon finely grated lemon zest

¼ teaspoon salt

Rhubarb

2 pounds fresh rhubarb, peeled and thinly sliced (about 6 large stalks), or 2¼ pounds sliced frozen rhubarb (three 12-ounce packages—do not thaw)

1½ cups sugar

3 tablespoons quick-cooking tapioca

2 tablespoons all-purpose flour

1 teaspoon vanilla extract

½ teaspoon finely grated orange zest

¼ teaspoon salt

Sour Cherry

2¼ pounds fresh sour cherries, pitted (about 5 cups), plus the juice from the pitting, or 2 pounds frozen pitted sour cherries (do not thaw)

1¼ cups sugar

2 tablespoons all-purpose flour

2 tablespoons quick-cooking tapioca

¼ teaspoon almond extract

¼ teaspoon salt

Strawberry

1½ quarts (1 quart plus 1 pint) fresh
    strawberries, hulled and sliced

½ cup sugar

3 tablespoons all-purpose flour

3 tablespoons quick-cooking tapioca

1 tablespoon bourbon or brandy, optional

1 teaspoon finely grated lemon zest

½ teaspoon ground cinnamon, optional

¼ teaspoon salt

Strawberry Rhubarb

1 quart fresh strawberries, hulled and sliced

One 12-ounce package sliced frozen rhubarb
    or ¾ pound fresh rhubarb, peeled and
    thinly sliced

1¼ cups sugar

3 tablespoons all-purpose flour

2 tablespoons quick-cooking tapioca

1 teaspoon finely grated lemon zest

½ teaspoon salt

Sweet Cherry

2 pounds fresh sweet cherries (preferably
    Bing or Tartarian), pitted, plus the juice
    from the pitting, or 2¼ pounds frozen
    pitted sweet cherries (three 12-ounce
    packages—do not thaw)

⅔ cup sugar

2 tablespoons all-purpose flour

2 tablespoons quick-cooking tapioca

2 teaspoons lemon juice

¼ teaspoon almond extract

¼ teaspoon salt

3 While the filling rests, make one of the four crusts (see pages 592–594). Here, you have a decision. **Make a single crust,** line it into a 9-inch pie plate, and trim and crimp it as you will. **Or make a double recipe** and use half to form the bottom crust, reserving the other half in a ball under a dry kitchen towel.

In the end, the pie must be topped to protect the fruit. If you make a single crust, you'll need to add a crumb topping (see page 597). If you make a double crust, roll out the other half of the crust once the filling is in the shell.

4 Pour the filling into the prepared crust, mounding it toward the center but making sure that the fruit is evenly distributed. For a richer filling, dot with

    2 tablespoons unsalted butter, cut into very small pieces.

5 Top the filling with a second crust or one of the crumb toppings.

To make a top crust, dot your work surface with a few drops of water and lay a large piece of wax paper on top. Dust the paper lightly with flour, then place the other half of the pastry dough on top. Flatten the dough slightly with your palm, dust lightly with flour, and place a second sheet of wax paper over the top. Roll the dough out to a 10-inch circle. Peel off the top sheet of wax paper. Pick up the dough and the bottom piece of wax paper; turn them upside down on top of the pie. Center the rolled-out piece of dough, then peel off the wax paper. Crimp the top crust to the bottom by pinching the two together at the plate's rim; work all the way around so there are no holes. Cut six or eight 2- or 3-inch slits in the top crust, working your way around the middle to create a starburst pattern.

Alternatively, do not place the dough on top of the pie; instead, roll it out, peel off the top layer of wax paper, and cut the top crust dough into strips with a pastry crimper or a pizza wheel. Lay these over the top of the pie, trimming to fit and pinching against the rim of the crust. Begin with 2 strips at the diameter of the pie, each placed 90 degrees from the other; then work down to smaller strips in each direction, spacing them about ½ inch apart and overlaying them this way and that, creating a lattice pattern. Make sure each strip is crimped to the crust's edge so it doesn't become dislodged and shrink while baking.

Or roll out the top crust as directed, peel off the top piece of wax paper, and cut into various shapes using cookie cutters. Lay these over the top of the pie, starting with one attached to the bottom crust's rim at some point and then overlapping the shapes slightly, working your way across the pie so that several of the shapes connect to the crust's rim in other places.

Or make a crumb topping. Mix either of the following two toppings together in a medium bowl until sandlike, then use your fingers to crumble over the filling, covering it evenly and completely.

Crumb Topping
8 tablespoons (1 stick) unsalted butter, melted and cooled
¾ cup all-purpose flour
½ cup granulated sugar
½ cup packed light brown sugar
½ teaspoon ground cinnamon
¼ teaspoon grated nutmeg
¼ teaspoon salt

Oat Crumb Topping
1 cup all-purpose flour
½ cup rolled oats (do not use steel-cut or quick-cooking)
⅓ cup walnut oil or ⅓ cup unsalted butter, melted and cooled
¼ cup maple syrup
¼ cup packed light brown sugar
¼ cup chopped walnut pieces
1 teaspoon ground cinnamon

Because of their natural juiciness, all fruit pies must have thickened fillings; flour and cornstarch are common aids. A more old-school answer is to use quick-cooking tapioca; it gives the filling an incredibly smooth texture. However, because it is so silky, it's best mixed with a little all-purpose flour to give the pie some tooth.

6 Bake the pie for 10 minutes. Reduce the heat to 350°F and continue baking until the filling is bubbling, 40 minutes to 1 hour, depending on the filling (berries take less time; apples, more time). If the crust's edges begin to burn, cover them with a thin strip of aluminum foil while baking.

To cool: Place on a wire rack for at least 20 minutes before slicing.

To store: Once cooled, the pie can be covered with plastic wrap and stored at room temperature for up to 2 days or in the refrigerator for up to 4 days.

Crimping the Edge

Beautiful pies have a decorative rim. Once the dough is in the plate, trim off any excess, making sure some crust lies along the plate's rim.

The easiest way to embellish that upper edge is to press a fork (for tine marks) or the back of a spoon (for concave waves) into the crust that lies along the plate's rim.

Or make a series of cuts 1 inch apart along the crust that lies along the plate's upper rim. Pick up the right edge of each cut and stretch it up and into the middle of the next cut.

Or flute the edge. Take one hand and make a U with your thumb and index finger; insert the index finger from your other hand into this U. Now use this technique to go around the edge of the crust, positioning your fingers parallel to the bottom of the pie plate and pushing the U from the outside of the crust and the single index finger from the inside of the plate, thereby creating little waved edges all the way around.

Raisin Pie

This pie mocks the taste of mincemeat without larding in unsavory bits of suet. *Makes one 9-inch pie*

> 2 large tart apples, such as Granny Smith, peeled, cored, and cubed
> 2 cups raisins
> 1 large egg plus 2 large egg yolks, at room temperature
> 6 tablespoons packed dark brown sugar
> ¼ cup granulated sugar
> 1 tablespoon finely grated orange zest
> 1 teaspoon ground cinnamon
> ¼ teaspoon grated nutmeg
> ¼ teaspoon ground cloves
> ¼ teaspoon salt
> 1 recipe Short Crust (page 592), Butter Crust (page 593), or Walnut Crust (page 593), lined into a 9-inch pie plate

1 Position the rack in the center of the oven and preheat the oven to 350°F.

2 Place the apples and raisins in a large food processor fitted with the chopping blade. Pulse a few times to chop, then process for about 20 seconds until finely chopped.

3 Add the egg, egg yolks, both sugars, orange zest, cinnamon, nutmeg, cloves, and salt. Process until thick and gooey; pour and scrape evenly into the prepared crust. (No top crust is required.)

4 Bake until puffed and browned, until the filling wobbles slightly at the center without any waves when the pie is tapped, about 45 minutes.

To cool: Place on a wire rack for at least 20 minutes before slicing.

To store: Once cooled, the pie can be covered and refrigerated for up to 3 days.

Dried Fruit Pie with Crème Anglaise

For the best taste in this rich, chewy pie, look for plump, soft, dried fruits. Try a slice with Crème Anglaise (right). *Makes one 9-inch pie*

> 2 cups pitted prunes (about 12 ounces)
> 1¼ cups dried apricots (about 6 ounces)
> 1 cup dried cranberries (about 5 ounces)
> 1 cup dried apples (about 2 ounces)
> A double recipe Short Crust (page 592), Butter Crust (page 593), or Almond Crust (page 594)
> 1 large egg plus 1 large egg yolk, at room temperature
> ¾ cup packed light brown sugar
> ½ cup sliced almonds
> 4 tablespoons (½ stick) unsalted butter, melted and cooled
> 2 teaspoons vanilla extract
> ½ teaspoon ground cinnamon
> ½ teaspoon salt
> Crème Anglaise (recipe follows)

1 Place the prunes, apricots, cranberries, and apples in a large saucepan. Cover them with cool water to a depth of 2 inches and bring to a boil over high heat. Reduce the heat to medium-low and simmer slowly for 5 minutes. Drain in a colander set in the sink and cool for 10 minutes.

2 Meanwhile, position the rack in the bottom third of the oven and preheat the oven to 400°F. Roll out half the crust dough and line a 9-inch pie plate with it (for a fuller explanation, see page 592). Set aside, covered loosely with a clean, dry kitchen towel.

3 Use a slotted spoon to transfer the cooked dried fruit to a large cutting board. Coarsely chop the pieces and transfer to a large bowl. Stir in the

egg, egg yolk, brown sugar, almonds, butter, vanilla, cinnamon, and salt until uniform.

④ Remove the towel from the crust; pour and scrape the filling evenly into the prepared crust. Roll out the remaining pastry dough to form a top crust, as directed on page 596.

⑤ Bake for 20 minutes. Reduce the temperature to 350°F and continue baking until lightly browned, 30 to 35 minutes. Once cooled, serve with Crème Anglaise (see below).

To cool: Set on a wire rack for at least 45 minutes before slicing.

To store: Once cooled, the pie can be tightly covered and refrigerated for up to 3 days.

Variations: Add 2 tablespoons dark or golden rum with the egg.

Substitute 1 teaspoon ground ginger or ¼ teaspoon grated nutmeg for the cinnamon.

Crème Anglaise

This traditional French sauce (pronounced "crehm ahn-GLAYZ") is like melted ice cream—only richer. *Makes about 2 cups*

> 1¾ cups whole or low-fat milk (do not use fat-free)
> 1 vanilla bean, split in half lengthwise but still attached at the stem
> 4 egg yolks, at room temperature
> ½ cup sugar

① Heat the milk in a medium saucepan over medium heat until tiny bubbles fizz around the pan's inner rim.

② Drop the vanilla bean into the pan, cover, and set aside off the heat for 10 minutes.

③ Fish the bean out of the hot milk. Run a small knife along the inside of the bean, scraping out the tiny black seeds. Return these to the milk and stir well.

④ Set the milk over low heat and heat until wisps of steam rise from the surface. Do not let the milk bubble, boil, or simmer; adjust the heat so it stays this temperature.

⑤ Beat the egg yolks in a medium bowl with an electric mixer for 1 minute. Add the sugar and continue beating, occasionally scraping down the sides of the bowl with a rubber spatula until thick ribbons form off the beaters when they are turned off and lifted out of the bowl, ribbons that do not immediately dissolve back into the mixture but lie on top of it for a moment, about 5 minutes.

⑥ Beat about half the warmed milk into the egg mixture in a slow stream, then beat this combined mixture back into the saucepan with the remaining warmed milk. Stir over very low heat until the mixture coats the back of a wooden spoon (see page 7).

⑦ Remove from the heat and strain through a fine-mesh sieve into a medium bowl. Cool at room temperature for 15 minutes or cover with plastic wrap and store in the refrigerator for up to 2 days.

Variations: Omit the vanilla bean (and steps 1 and 2); simply heat the milk to the proper temperature as in step 4. Once the combined egg-milk mixture has been beaten into the pan, beat in 1 tablespoon vanilla extract.

Flavor Crème Anglaise with any liqueur by omitting the vanilla bean (steps 1 and 2). Instead, stir in 1 tablespoon coffee-flavored liqueur, such as Kahlúa; hazelnut-flavored liqueur, such as Frangelico; almond-flavored liqueur, such as Amaretto di Saronno; or other flavored liqueur before straining the sauce.

Pecan Pie

A Texas classic, this pie has been our default Thanksgiving dessert for years. Because of their high oil content, pecans have a relatively short shelf life—makes sure yours are fresh. Store them, tightly sealed, in the freezer. Serve this pie with Crème Anglaise (page 599). *Makes one 9-inch pie*

- 3 large eggs, at room temperature
- ¾ cup dark corn syrup
- 6 tablespoons unsalted butter, melted and cooled
- ¼ cup maple syrup
- 2 teaspoons vanilla extract
- ⅓ cup granulated sugar
- ⅓ cup packed dark brown sugar
- ½ teaspoon salt
- 1½ cups pecan halves
- 1 recipe Short Crust (page 592) or Butter Crust (page 593), lined into a 9-inch pie plate

1 Position the rack in the center of the oven and preheat the oven to 375°F.

2 Whisk the eggs, dark corn syrup, melted butter, maple syrup, and vanilla in a large bowl until smooth. Whisk in both sugars and the salt until the sugars dissolve. Stir in the pecan halves; pour into the prepared pie crust.

3 Bake until the crust is light brown and the filling is almost set, just the slightest jiggle at the center when tapped (no waves across its surface), 40 to 50 minutes.

To cool: Set on a wire rack until room temperature, about 1½ hours.

To store: Once cooled, the pie can be refrigerated, tightly covered, for up to 3 days.

Variations: Add ½ teaspoon ground cinnamon, ½ teaspoon ground ginger, or ¼ teaspoon grated nutmeg with the sugars.

Substitute 2 teaspoons finely grated orange zest for the vanilla.

Add ¼ teaspoon rum extract with the vanilla.

For a pecan pie with a kick, add up to ½ teaspoon cayenne pepper with the salt.

Chocolate Pecan Pie

More like a fudge pie, this pecan pie is best cold, when it has the texture of a candy bar. Because the pie is stiff to cut, pecan pieces work better than halves. *Makes one 9-inch pie*

- 6 tablespoons unsalted butter
- 4 ounces unsweetened chocolate, chopped
- 4 large eggs, at room temperature
- 1 cup packed dark brown sugar
- 1 cup dark corn syrup
- 1 tablespoon vanilla extract
- ½ teaspoon salt
- 2 cups pecan pieces
- 1 recipe Short Crust (page 592) or Butter Crust (page 593), lined into a 9-inch pie plate

1 Position the rack in the center of the oven; preheat the oven to 350°F.

2 Place the butter and chocolate in the top half of a double boiler with about 1 inch of water simmering over medium heat in the bottom half. Alternatively, place the butter and chocolate in a medium bowl that fits snugly over a medium saucepan with about the same amount of simmering water. Stir until half the chocolate and butter has melted, then remove the top half of the boiler or the bowl from the heat (beware of any escaping steam) and continue stirring until smooth. Set aside to cool for 10 minutes.

③ Whisk in the eggs one at a time, working quickly so the eggs don't cook in the hot mixture. Once all the eggs have been added and the mixture is fairly smooth, whisk in the brown sugar, dark corn syrup, vanilla, and salt. Stir in the pecan pieces, then pour into the prepared piecrust.

④ Bake until the pastry has browned and the filling is puffed and set (there is only the slightest jiggle at the center when the pie is tapped), about 55 minutes.

To cool: Set on a wire rack until room temperature before slicing, about 1½ hours.

To store: Once cooled, the pie can be covered and refrigerated for up to 3 days. You can also freeze the pie, then set at room temperature for 10 minutes, and serve like a candy bar.

Variations: Substitute walnut pieces or unsalted peanuts for the pecan pieces.

Add ½ teaspoon rum extract or maple extract with the vanilla.

Add ½ teaspoon ground cinnamon with the salt.

Pie Sidekicks

Sweetened sour cream or crème fraîche (1 cup sour cream or crème fraîche combined with 1 tablespoon confectioners' sugar and 2 teaspoons vanilla extract)

Vanilla or maple yogurt

Crème Anglaise (page 599)

Vanilla Frozen Custard (page 644)

Caramel Custard Sauce (made for the Steamed British Pudding, page 627)

Sweetened Whipped Cream (page 522)

Chocolate Whipped Cream (page 546)

Maple Walnut Pie

This pie's very autumnal—and begs for a glass of aged rum on the side. Toasted walnut oil is found at most gourmet markets and health food stores.

Makes one 9-inch pie

3 large eggs, at room temperature
1 cup maple syrup
½ cup granulated sugar
½ cup packed light brown sugar
2 tablespoons toasted walnut oil (see Note)
1 tablespoon vanilla extract
½ teaspoon salt
2 cups walnut pieces
1 recipe Short Crust (page 592) or Walnut Crust (page 593), lined into a 9-inch pie plate

① Position the rack in the center of the oven and preheat the oven to 350°F.

② Whisk the eggs and maple syrup in a large bowl until smooth. Whisk in both sugars, the toasted walnut oil, vanilla, and salt until the sugars dissolve. Stir in the walnut pieces and pour into the prepared crust.

③ Bake until the pastry at the edges is lightly browned and the filling is puffed and almost set, with just the slightest jiggle at the center when tapped (but no waves across its surface), about 55 minutes.

To cool: Place on a wire rack at least 30 minutes before slicing.

To store: Once cooled, the pie can be covered and refrigerated for up to 3 days.

Note: If you can't find toasted walnut oil, substitute regular walnut oil.

Variations: Add ½ teaspoon rum extract with the vanilla.

Add ½ teaspoon ground cinnamon or ¼ teaspoon grated nutmeg with the salt.

Good nut pies start with good nuts: fresh, never rancid or crumbled. Store nuts in a sealed plastic bag in the freezer for up to 1 year, but always smell them before use to make sure they haven't gone rancid. Use directly from the freezer.

Prebaking a Crust

Called more formally "blind baking," this step prevents the depressingly soggy crusts that often occur with puddinglike fillings. First, check the recipe to see if the filling, once in the crust, will also be baked; this will determine how long you prebake the crust (see below).

Position the rack in the center of the oven and preheat the oven to 425°F. Roll out the crust, fit it into the pie plate, trim it, and flute the edges, as directed on pages 592 and 597. Prick the bottom and sides in multiple places with a fork. Cover the crust with aluminum foil, then pour in about 2 cups ceramic pie weights or uncooked dried beans (which will not be suitable for cooking afterward, but can be used again and again as pie weights). Bake for 10 minutes. Gently peel off the foil, taking the weights with it; continue baking for about 3 more minutes, or until set, if the added filling will also be baked in the crust; or for 8 to 10 more minutes, until lightly browned, if the filling will not be baked more than a few minutes (at most, just long enough to brown the meringue). Cool on a wire rack for at least 15 minutes before using.

Custard Pie

This rich, old-fashioned pie is best after a barbecue or a wintry stew. It's also best eaten when still slightly warm—or cold for breakfast the next morning. *Makes one 9-inch pie*

- 2 large eggs plus 3 large egg yolks, at room temperature
- ½ cup sugar
- 1 tablespoon cornstarch
- 2 cups whole or low-fat milk (do not use fat-free)
- ¼ cup powdered nonfat dry milk (see Note)
- 1 tablespoon vanilla extract
- ¼ teaspoon salt
- 1 recipe Short Crust (page 592), Butter Crust (page 593), or Almond Crust (page 594), lined into a 9-inch pie plate and prebaked (for instructions on prebaking, see box left)
- ¼ teaspoon grated nutmeg

1 Position the rack in the center of the oven and preheat the oven to 350°F.

2 Whisk the eggs, egg yolks, and sugar in a large bowl until thick and lemony yellow, about 2 minutes.

3 Whisk in the cornstarch, then whisk in the milk, powdered nonfat dry milk, vanilla, and salt until the powdered milk is fully dissolved. Pour this mixture into the prebaked crust; sprinkle the nutmeg over the top.

4 Bake until puffed and set, about 1 hour.

To cool: Set on a wire rack for at least 30 minutes before slicing.

To store: The cooled pie can be covered and refrigerated for up to 2 days.

Note: The powdered milk provides body and texture, thereby keeping the number of egg yolks in check so the pie doesn't taste like a sweet omelet.

Variations: Add ½ teaspoon ground ginger with the nutmeg.

Sprinkle 2 tablespoons chopped crystallized ginger over the crust before pouring in the egg mixture.

Buttermilk Pie

So tangy but sweet, you'll need a strong cup of coffee on the side. *Makes one 9-inch pie*

1½ cups sugar
6 tablespoons unsalted butter, at room temperature
3 large eggs, at room temperature
2 tablespoons all-purpose flour
¼ teaspoon salt
1 cup plus 2 tablespoons regular or low-fat buttermilk (do not use fat-free)
2 teaspoons vanilla extract
2 teaspoons finely grated lemon zest
1 recipe Short Crust (page 592) or Butter Crust (page 593), lined into a 9-inch pie plate and prebaked (for instructions on prebaking, see page 602)

❶ Position the rack in the center of the oven; preheat the oven to 350°F.

❷ Beat the sugar and butter in a large bowl with an electric mixer at medium speed until creamy, lemony yellow, and fluffy, about 3 minutes.

❸ Scrape down the sides of the bowl and beat in the eggs one at a time, making sure each is fully incorporated before adding the next.

❹ Beat in the flour and salt until no graininess is visible; then beat in the buttermilk, vanilla, and lemon zest until smooth. Pour the mixture into the prebaked crust.

❺ Bake until the filling has almost set, until there's just the slightest jiggle at the center, about 1 hour and 5 minutes. Should the edges of the crust start to brown too deeply, cover them with a thin strip of aluminum foil.

To cool: Set on a wire rack for at least 30 minutes before slicing.

To store: Once cooled, the pie can be covered and refrigerated for up to 3 days.

Variations: Cool the prebaked pie crust to room temperature on a wire rack, about 1 hour. Paint the crust with 3 ounces bittersweet or semisweet chocolate, melted in a bowl in the microwave or in the top half of a double boiler over simmering water and then cooled. Set aside to harden for 30 minutes before you pour in the filling.

Once the filling has been poured into the crust, sprinkle ¼ teaspoon grated nutmeg, grated mace, or ground cinnamon over the top.

How Do You Know When a Custard Pie Is Set?

There's no need to stick a knife in it. Instead, note how the filling moves when the pie is gently tapped or moved from side to side. It should shimmy and shake in one piece, rather than ripple or flow in waves. In no case, however, should the filling be stationary and motionless when the pie is tapped (a sign of an overbaked custard).

Lemon Chess Pie

This Southern tradition is a buttery lemon custard with a velvety finish. *Makes one 9-inch pie*

    8 tablespoons (1 stick) unsalted butter, at
        room temperature
    1 cup packed light brown sugar
    1/2 cup granulated sugar
    3 large eggs plus 1 large egg yolk, at room
        temperature
    3 tablespoons all-purpose flour
    1/4 teaspoon salt
    1/4 cup lemon juice
    2 teaspoons finely grated lemon
        zest
    1 teaspoon vanilla extract
    1 recipe Short Crust (page 592) or
        Butter Crust (page 593), lined into a
        9-inch pie plate and prebaked
        (for instructions on prebaking,
        see page 602)

1 Position the rack in the center of the oven and preheat the oven to 350°F.

2 Beat the butter and both sugars in a large bowl with an electric mixer at medium speed until light and fluffy, about 3 minutes. Beat in the eggs one at a time, then beat in the egg yolk until smooth.

3 Beat in the flour and salt until no graininess is visible, then beat in the lemon juice, lemon zest, and vanilla. Make sure there's no undissolved material on the bottom of the bowl, then pour this mixture into the prebaked pie crust.

4 Bake until lightly browned and puffed, until the filling is almost set, just the slightest wobble at the center when the rim of the pie plate is tapped, about 45 minutes.

To cool: Set on a wire rack for at least 1 hour before slicing.

To store: Once cooled, the pie can be covered with plastic wrap and kept in the refrigerator for up to 2 days.

Lemon Rum Chess Pie: Reduce the lemon juice to 2 tablespoons and add 2 tablespoons gold rum with the remaining lemon juice.
Lemon Coconut Chess Pie: Reduce the lemon juice to 3 tablespoons and add 1/4 cup unsweetened coconut with the vanilla.
Lemon Ginger Chess Pie: Reduce the lemon juice to 3 tablespoons and add 1 tablespoon ginger juice with the vanilla.
Lime Chess Pie: Substitute lime juice and lime zest for the lemon juice and lemon zest.

Coconut Custard Pie

Here's a combination of a custard pie and a coconut cream one. For the best taste, use shredded (or "desiccated") unsweetened coconut. *Makes one 9-inch pie*

    4 large eggs plus 1 large egg yolk, at room
        temperature
    1/2 cup sugar
    2 cups milk (regular, low-fat, or
        fat-free)
    2 teaspoons vanilla extract
    1/2 teaspoon salt
    1 cup shredded (or "desiccated")
        unsweetened coconut
    1 recipe Short Crust (page 592) or Butter
        Crust (page 593), lined into a 9-inch pie
        plate and prebaked (for instructions on
        prebaking, see page 602)

1 Position the rack in the center of the oven and preheat the oven to 350°F.

2 Beat the eggs, egg yolk, and sugar in a large bowl with an electric mixer until creamy and lemony yellow, about 4 minutes.

3 Beat in the milk, vanilla, and salt, scraping down the sides of the bowl to make sure everything gets well combined. Beat in the coconut for a few seconds just until incorporated. Pour into the prebaked crust.

4 Bake until lightly browned and set, until a knife inserted into the filling comes out clean, about 50 minutes.

To cool: Set on a wire rack for 20 minutes before slicing.

To store: Once cooled, the pie can be covered tightly and refrigerated for up to 3 days.

Double Coconut Custard Pie: Reduce the milk to 1 cup and add 1 cup coconut milk with the remaining milk.

Coconut Rum Custard Pie: Reduce the milk to 1 ¾ cups and add ¼ cup gold rum with it; also add 1 additional large egg yolk.

Tropical Coconut Custard Pie: Add 2 teaspoons finely grated lime zest and ¼ teaspoon rum extract with the vanilla.

Coconut Custard Pie Brûlée: Once the pie has cooled to room temperature, preheat the broiler. Mix ⅓ cup packed light brown sugar with ¼ cup shredded sweetened coconut in a small bowl; sprinkle this mixture evenly over the pie. Cover the edge of the crust with aluminum foil so it won't get burned. Place the pie 4 to 6 inches from the heat source and broil until lightly browned and bubbling, about 3 minutes. Alternatively, use a small kitchen blowtorch to caramelize the sugar and brown the coconut.

Squash Ginger Pie

Although most of us grew up loving pumpkin pie, we were actually loving something else. The USDA allows other kinds of winter squash to be labeled "pumpkin"—and since most of the canned pumpkin is actually winter squash, we grew up eating something very much like this pie, only without the adult spike of crystallized ginger. *Makes one 9-inch pie*

1 recipe Walnut Crust (page 593) or Butter Crust (page 593), lined into a 9-inch pie plate and prebaked (for instructions on prebaking, see page 602)
2 tablespoons finely chopped crystallized ginger
1 large egg plus 2 large egg yolks, at room temperature
⅓ cup sugar
¼ cup honey
2 cups frozen squash puree, thawed (see Note)
1 cup whole milk (do not use low-fat or fat-free)
½ cup half-and-half
2 teaspoons freshly grated lemon zest
¼ teaspoon grated nutmeg
¼ teaspoon salt

1 Position the rack in the center of the oven and preheat the oven to 350°F. Sprinkle the prebaked crust with the chopped ginger; set aside.

2 Beat the egg, egg yolks, sugar, and honey in a large bowl with an electric mixer at medium speed until smooth and creamy, about 2 minutes. Beat in the squash puree, milk, and half-and-half until smooth.

3 Scrape down the sides of the bowl and beat in the lemon zest, nutmeg, and salt. Pour this mixture gently into the prebaked crust, taking care not to scatter the ginger pieces.

4 Bake until puffed and almost set, until there's just the slightest jiggle at the center of the pie, about 1 hour and 20 minutes. Should the crust start to brown too deeply, cover the edge with a thin strip of aluminum foil to protect it.

To cool: Set on a wire rack for at least 1 hour before slicing.

To store: The cooled pie can be covered in plastic wrap and refrigerated for up to 2 days.

Note: Frozen squash puree is available in the freezer case of most supermarkets. To make your own, position the rack in the center of the oven and preheat the oven to 375°F. Cut 2 medium acorn squashes, 2 small sugar pumpkins, 1 large butternut squash, or 1 large blue Hubbard squash in half through the stem. Scrape out the seeds and their fibrous threads with a grapefruit spoon. Spray a large lipped baking sheet with nonstick spray and place the squash or pumpkin halves on it cut side down. Bake until soft, until a knife easily pierces the skin, 45 minutes to 1 hour and 30 minutes, depending on the size and freshness of the squash. Cool the baking sheet on a wire rack for at least 1 hour, then scrape out the inner flesh from the squash and pumpkin and use 2 cups as directed.

Variations: For a more traditional taste, omit the crystallized ginger; increase the sugar to 6 tablespoons.

Add 1 teaspoon ground cinnamon with the nutmeg.

Pumpkin Pie: Omit the ginger; substitute 2 cups canned pumpkin puree (not pumpkin pie filling) for the squash puree.

Vanilla Cream Pie

The distinctions among cream, meringue, and icebox pies have long since broken down. Most cream pies can become meringue pies by exchanging the whipped cream for a meringue. Because of its alcohol base, vanilla extract can leave a sharp aftertaste in this creamy standard. We prefer a real vanilla bean for its pure, simple taste. *Makes one 9-inch pie*

> 2 cups milk (regular, low-fat, or fat-free)
> 1 vanilla bean, split in half lengthwise but still attached at the stem
> 3 large egg yolks, at room temperature
> ½ teaspoon salt
> ¾ cup sugar
> ¼ cup all-purpose flour
> 2 tablespoons cornstarch
> 1 recipe Short Crust (page 592) or Butter Crust (page 593), lined into a 9-inch pie plate and prebaked (for instructions on prebaking, see page 602)
> 1¼ cups heavy cream

1 Heat the milk in a medium saucepan over medium heat until small bubbles fizz around the pan's inner rim. Once the milk is hot, drop the split vanilla bean into the saucepan, cover, and set off the heat for 15 minutes.

2 Whisk the egg yolks and salt in a large bowl until creamy and smooth; set aside.

3 Use a fork to fish the vanilla bean out of the still-hot milk; transfer the bean to a cutting board. Use a knife to scrape the inside of the bean, removing the tiny black seeds. Return the seeds to the milk.

4 Set the pan back over medium-low heat. Whisk in ½ cup sugar, the flour, and cornstarch until there are no lumps or undissolved bits. Cook, whisking constantly, until thickened and barely bubbling, about 3 minutes.

5 Slowly whisk this hot mixture into the whisked egg yolks; continue whisking until smooth. Pour into the prebaked crust; set aside at room temperature for 10 minutes.

6 Place a piece of plastic wrap against the surface of the pie filling and place the pie in the refrigerator until chilled, at least 4 hours or overnight.

7 Just before serving, place a large bowl and the electric mixer's beaters or whisk attachment in the refrigerator for 10 minutes. (See page 609 for an explanation.)

8 Remove them and add the cream to the bowl. Beat with the electric mixer at high speed until bubbly and thick, about 20 seconds. Slowly beat in the remaining ¼ cup sugar in a thin stream until thickened and silky, until the whipped cream holds its shape on a spatula in rounded, soft, gentle waves, about 1 minute.

9 Gently peel the plastic wrap off the pie filling. Spoon the whipped cream over the pie, sealing it to the edges. Shape it with the back of a rubber spatula into waves. Serve at once.

Banana Cream Pie: Before adding the filling, line the bottom of the crust with 2 ripe bananas, thinly sliced. If desired, stand vanilla wafer cookies in the whipped cream as garnish.

Cherry Cream Pie: Stir 1 cup pitted, chopped sweet cherries into the vanilla filling just before pouring it into the crust.

Coconut Cream Pie: Stir 1 cup sweetened coconut in the vanilla filling before pouring it into the crust.

Spiced Vanilla Cream Pie: Add ¼ teaspoon ground cinnamon, ¼ teaspoon grated nutmeg, and ⅛ teaspoon ground cloves with the flour.

Vanilla Orange Cream Pie: Sprinkle 1 cup well-drained, canned mandarin orange sections over the prebaked crust before pouring in the vanilla filling.

Chocolate Cream Pie

We use a lot of chocolate here, so much that the filling tastes like chocolate mousse. The whipped cream topping is stabilized by cornstarch and thus is slightly thicker, a better foil to the rich filling.
Makes one 9-inch pie

3 ounces unsweetened chocolate, chopped
4 ounces semisweet chocolate, 3 ounces of it chopped and 1 ounce reserved
3 large egg yolks, at room temperature
½ teaspoon salt
2½ cups milk (regular, low-fat, or fat-free)
1 cup plus 3 tablespoons sugar
¼ cup plus 1 tablespoon cornstarch
3 teaspoons vanilla extract
1 recipe Short Crust (page 592), Walnut Crust (page 593), or Almond Crust (page 594), lined into a 9-inch pie plate and prebaked (for instructions on prebaking, see page 602)
1½ cups heavy cream

1 Bring about 1 inch of water to a simmer in the bottom half of a double boiler set over medium-high heat; place the chopped unsweetened and 3 ounces chopped semisweet chocolate in the top half and set it over the simmering water. Alternatively, place the chocolate in a medium bowl that fits snugly over a medium saucepan with about the same amount of simmering water. Stir until half the chocolate has melted, adjusting the heat so the water simmers slowly. Remove the top half of the double boiler or the bowl from the pan underneath (be careful of escaping steam); stir off the heat until smooth. Set aside to cool for 10 minutes.

❷ Meanwhile, whisk the egg yolks and salt in a large bowl until creamy; set aside.

❸ Place the milk in a large saucepan and whisk in 1 cup sugar and ¼ cup cornstarch. Set the pan over medium heat and cook, whisking constantly, until thickened and bubbling, about 4 minutes.

❹ Whisk about half the hot milk mixture in a slow, steady stream into the beaten egg yolks; then whisk this combined mixture back into the saucepan with the remaining milk mixture.

❺ Reduce the heat to low and continue cooking until thickened, until the mixture coats the back of a wooden spoon (see page 7). Remove the pan from the heat and slowly whisk in the melted chocolate and 2 teaspoons vanilla.

❻ Strain the mixture through a fine-mesh sieve and into the prebaked crust. Press a large sheet of plastic wrap right onto the filling and refrigerate until chilled, about 4 hours or overnight.

❼ Just before serving, place a large, clean bowl and the electric mixer's beaters or whisk attachment in the refrigerator for 10 minutes.

❽ Remove the bowl from the freezer and pour in the heavy cream. Beat with the electric mixer at high speed until frothy, about 20 seconds.

❾ Beat in the remaining 3 tablespoons sugar and the remaining 1 tablespoon cornstarch in a slow, steady stream; continue beating at high speed, scraping down the sides of the bowl with a rubber spatula, until the mixture forms soft, wavy

peaks on the spatula. Beat in the remaining 1 teaspoon vanilla.

❿ Gently peel the plastic wrap off the pie filling. Spoon the sweetened whipped cream onto the pie, using the back of a flatware spoon or a rubber spatula to make little hillocks and waves. Shave the remaining 1 ounce semisweet chocolate over the top of the whipped cream, using a chocolate grater or the large holes of a box grater.

Chocolate Almond Cream Pie: Make the Almond Crust (page 594) for the pie. Line the prebaked piecrust with ½ cup toasted sliced almonds before gently pouring in the filling, taking care not to disturb the almonds as you do so.

Chocolate Heath Bar Pie: Add three 1.3-ounce Heath Bars, finely chopped, to the whipped cream in the final seconds of beating just until well combined.

Chocolate Mint Pie: Substitute ½ teaspoon mint extract for the 1 teaspoon vanilla in the whipped cream. Also add 3 or 4 drops green food coloring to the whipped cream.

Mexican Chocolate Pie: Add ¼ cup toasted sliced almonds, 1 teaspoon ground cinnamon, and ¼ teaspoon almond extract to the filling with the melted chocolate and vanilla. Dust the top of the whipped cream with a little ground cinnamon as well as the shaved chocolate.

Chocolate Meringue Pie: Omit steps 7 through 11, thereby omitting the whipped cream, its additives, and flavorings, as well as the cooling process for the filling. With the filling still warm, preheat the oven to 425°F. Beat 6 large room temperature egg whites and ¼ teaspoon cream of tartar in a bowl with an electric mixer at high speed until you can make soft, droopy peaks off the end of a rubber spatula, then beat in ¾ cup confectioners' sugar in 1-tablespoon increments. Continue beating until the mixture makes stiff, firm, glossy, but still wet peaks on the tip of the spatula. Beat in 1 teaspoon vanilla extract, then spoon this meringue onto the hot filling. Seal the meringue to the crust's edges by pressing down with the rubber spatula to adhere the two together; make decorative waves in the meringue with the back of the spatula. Bake until the meringue is golden brown, about 8 minutes. Cool completely at room temperature; don't refrigerate until cooled because the meringue will shrink (see page 611).

Cold Cream, Room Temperature Egg Whites

Whipped cream is actually a foam glued together with fat. If the cream is cold—as well as the beaters and the bowl—it aids those fat molecules in sticking close together. Remember your high school science lessons? The warmer something is, the farther apart its molecules are. So use cream right out of the refrigerator; if you've just brought it home from the market, chill it a couple of hours so it will whip thicker and more smoothly. Also chill the bowl and beaters in the refrigerator for 10 minutes.

By contrast, the highest meringues start with room temperature egg whites, bowls, and beaters. A meringue is a foam held with a lattice of protein chains from the egg whites. These chains need to be elongated to form the structure—thus, the egg whites should be at room temperature so the chains aren't knotted up.

Butterscotch Cream Pie

Traditionally, a butterscotch cream pie is simply a vanilla cream pie made with brown sugar. That method doesn't capture the taste of butterscotch, so we developed this one, a derivative of the candy-making process. *Makes one 9-inch pie*

2 cups regular or low-fat milk (do not use fat-free)
¼ cup cornstarch
2 tablespoons all-purpose flour
3 large egg yolks, at room temperature
½ teaspoon salt
6 tablespoons unsalted butter, cut into chunks
1 cup packed light brown sugar
2 cups heavy cream
1 recipe Short Crust (page 592) or Butter Crust (page 593), lined into a 9-inch pie plate and prebaked (for instructions on prebaking, see page 602)
3 tablespoons confectioners' sugar
1 ounce praline candy, peanut brittle, or almond brittle, crushed to a powder in a mortar with a pestle or in a food processor

❶ Whisk the milk, cornstarch, and flour in a medium bowl until smooth, until no lumps of undissolved flour are visible. Also whisk the egg yolks and salt in a large bowl until smooth. Set both aside.

❷ Place the butter and brown sugar in a large saucepan and set it over medium heat. Cook, stirring constantly, until smooth and bubbly. Simmer for 3 minutes, then whisk in ½ cup cream (the mixture will roil up); whisk constantly and quickly until smooth and creamy. Remove the pan from the heat.

❸ Slowly whisk in the milk mixture. Set the pan over medium-low heat and cook, whisking constantly, until thickened and barely bubbling, about 1 minute.

④ Slowly whisk about half this milk mixture into the beaten egg yolks, then whisk the combined mixture back into the pan with the remaining milk mixture. Return the pan to low heat (if you're using an electric stove, place the pan over a second unused burner) and whisk constantly until slightly thickened, about 30 seconds.

⑤ Strain the mixture through a fine-mesh sieve into the prebaked pie crust. Gently press a piece of plastic wrap onto the filling and refrigerate until chilled, about 4 hours or overnight.

⑥ Place a large bowl and the beater(s) or whisk attachment from your electric mixer in the refrigerator for 10 minutes.

⑦ Remove the bowl and beater(s) from the freezer. Add the remaining 1½ cups cream to the bowl and beat with the electric mixer at high speed until frothy, about 20 seconds.

⑧ Beat in the confectioners' sugar at high speed in a slow, thin stream, then continue beating until the cream makes soft, rounded, smooth waves on a rubber spatula. Scrape down the sides of the bowl and beat in the ground candy at medium speed just until combined, about 10 seconds.

⑨ Gently peel the plastic wrap off the pie's filling, then spoon the flavored whipping cream over the filling, sealing it to the crust's edge and making little waves and hillocks with a rubber spatula or flatware tablespoon.

Butterscotch Chocolate Pie: Stirring constantly, melt 1 ounce bittersweet or semisweet chocolate in the top half of a double boiler set over a little simmering water over medium heat, or melt it in a bowl in the microwave on high in 15-second increments, stirring after each. Cool for 10 minutes, then paint this melted chocolate over the cooled, prebaked pie crust. Set aside to harden for 30 minutes before adding the filling.

Butterscotch Meringue Pie: Skip steps 6 to 10, thereby omitting the 1½ cups cream, confectioners' sugar, and candy. Work with the pie while the filling is still warm. Follow the same procedure for placing the meringue over the Chocolate Meringue Pie (page 608).

Coconut Cream Pie

To keep this pie from becoming cloyingly sweet, use unsweetened coconut. *Makes one 9-inch pie*

- 3 large egg yolks, at room temperature
- ¼ teaspoon salt
- 2 cups milk (regular, low-fat, or fat-free)
- 1 cup granulated sugar
- 3 tablespoons cornstarch
- 1¼ cups shredded (or "desiccated") unsweetened coconut
- 2 teaspoons vanilla extract
- 1 recipe Short Crust (page 592) or Butter Crust (page 593), lined into a 9-inch pie plate and prebaked (for instructions on prebaking, see page 602)
- 1½ cups heavy cream
- 2 tablespoons confectioners' sugar
- ¼ cup shredded sweetened coconut

① Whisk the egg yolks and salt in a large bowl until smooth; set aside.

② Place the milk in a large saucepan over medium heat. Whisk in the granulated sugar and cornstarch until smooth. Continue cooking, whisking constantly, until thickened and just beginning to bubble, about 4 minutes.

③ Whisk about half this milk mixture into the beaten egg yolks, then whisk the combined mixture back into the remaining milk mixture in the pan.

④ Reduce the heat to low and cook, stirring constantly, until the mixture can coat the back of a wooden spoon (see page 7). Strain through a fine-mesh sieve into a clean, large bowl.

⑤ Stir in the unsweetened coconut and 1 teaspoon vanilla. Pour into the prebaked pie crust. Lay a large piece of plastic wrap over the filling and press down gently. Refrigerate until chilled, about 4 hours or overnight.

⑥ Just before serving, place a large, clean bowl and the electric mixer's beaters or whisk attachment in the refrigerator for 10 minutes.

⑦ Remove the bowl from the freezer and pour in the cream. Beat with the electric mixer at high speed until frothy, about 20 seconds.

⑧ Beating at high speed, add the confectioners' sugar in 1-tablespoon increments. Continue beating at high speed, scraping down the sides of the bowl with a rubber spatula, until the mixture forms soft, wavy, smooth peaks on the spatula. Beat in the shredded sweetened coconut and the remaining 1 teaspoon vanilla.

⑨ Gently peel the plastic wrap off the pie filling. Spoon the sweetened whipped cream over the pie, using the back of a flatware spoon or a rubber spatula to make little hillocks and waves in the cream.

Coconut Ginger Pie: Add 1 teaspoon ground ginger with the cornstarch. If desired, sprinkle 1 tablespoon finely chopped crystallized ginger over the whipped cream topping before serving.

Tropical Coconut Pie: Line the unbaked pie shell with 1 ripe banana, thinly sliced, before adding the filling. Stir 1 teaspoon grated lime zest into the filling with the unsweetened coconut. Substitute rum extract for the vanilla extract in the whipped cream topping.

Meringues

Egg whites will not rise when beaten in the presence of moisture (water condensation, for example, from an improperly dried bowl) or fat (even a speck of egg yolk). Either will cause the lattice of protein chains to break down.

A meringue should be placed directly over a hot filling. This way, the meringue will cook from both directions, top and bottom. If placed on a cold filling, the meringue will actually cook only from the top down and will end up undercooked—which will result in a layer of viscous liquid forming between the filling and the meringue.

Meringues should also be sealed to the crust. Once you've dolloped all of the beaten egg white mixture onto the top of the pie, spread it gently to the edge, and then dab and press it into place against the crust so that it will adhere to the crust and not shrink back. Make sure there are no gaps, tears, or weak spots.

Despite anyone's best intentions, any meringue will weep—that is, form tiny brown drops of sticky liquid on its surface. However, you can cut down on the weeping by adding cornstarch, which absorbs some of the natural moisture (thus, we recommend confectioners' sugar, which contains cornstarch).

Finally, a meringue will shrink over time as the protein chains collapse. You can lessen this natural process by (1) cooling the pie to room temperature before placing it in the refrigerator and (2) not overcooking the meringue, thereby tightening the proteins and squeezing out necessary moisture.

Lemon Meringue Pie

To get the most juice from lemons, have them at room temperature and roll them along the kitchen counter, pressing down lightly, before slicing and juicing. *Makes one 9-inch pie*

3 large egg yolks, at room temperature
½ teaspoon salt
1¾ cups water
1½ cups granulated sugar
¾ cup lemon juice
6 tablespoons cornstarch
2 tablespoons all-purpose flour
2 teaspoons finely grated lemon zest
1 tablespoon unsalted butter
1 recipe Short Crust (page 592) or Butter Crust (page 593), lined into a 9-inch pie plate and prebaked (for instructions on prebaking, see page 602)
6 large egg whites, at room temperature
¼ teaspoon cream of tartar
¾ cup confectioners' sugar
1 teaspoon vanilla extract

1 Position the rack in the center of the oven and preheat the oven to 425°F. Whisk the egg yolks and salt in a large bowl until smooth; set aside

2 Whisk the water, granulated sugar, lemon juice, cornstarch, flour, and lemon zest in a large saucepan until the sugar, cornstarch, and flour dissolve.

3 Set over medium heat and cook, whisking constantly, until thickened and just beginning to bubble (just 2 or 3 bubbles), about 4 minutes. Remove from the heat.

4 Whisk about half this lemon mixture into the yolks in a thin, steady stream; then whisk this combined mixture back into the lemon mixture in the saucepan.

5 Set the pan over low heat (if you're using an electric stove, place the pan on a second, unused burner just now turned to low) and cook, whisking constantly, until thickened and just barely bubbling, about 2 minutes. Strain through a fine-mesh sieve into the prebaked crust.

6 Beat the egg whites and cream of tartar in a large bowl with an electric mixer at high speed until you can make foamy, soft, droopy peaks on the tip of a rubber spatula.

7 Beating all the while, add the confectioners' sugar in 1-tablespoon increments. Scrape down the sides of the bowl and beat in the vanilla. Continue beating until you can form silky, glossy, and moderately firm peaks on the spatula's tip.

8 Spoon the meringue onto the top of the still-warm pie, spreading it gently to the edge and gently pressing it against the crust so that it will seal tightly.

9 Bake until the meringue is lightly browned, about 8 minutes.

To cool: Set on a wire rack at least 30 minutes, then refrigerate at least 1 hour before slicing.

To store: Once completely cooled, the pie can be loosely covered in plastic wrap and kept in the refrigerator for up to 3 days.

Lime Meringue Pie: Substitute lime juice for the lemon juice and finely grated lime zest for the lemon zest. For a greener color, stir in 3 drops of green food coloring before straining the filling.

Orange Meringue Pie: Substitute frozen orange juice concentrate, thawed, for the lemon juice and grated orange zest for the lemon zest.

Burnt Sugar Meringue Pie

Here, sugar is "burnt" until it's a dark caramel, then added to the creamy filling to create a sweet if slightly bitter pie that's topped with clouds of meringue. *Makes one 9-inch pie*

3 large egg yolks, lightly beaten, at room temperature

2⅔ cups whole or low-fat milk (do not use fat-free)

½ teaspoon salt

2 cups granulated sugar

3 tablespoons cornstarch

1½ tablespoons all-purpose flour

1 tablespoon unsalted butter

2 teaspoons vanilla extract

1 recipe Short Crust (page 592), Butter Crust (page 593), or Walnut Crust (page 593), lined into a 9-inch pie plate and prebaked (for instructions on prebaking, see page 602)

6 large egg whites, at room temperature

¼ teaspoon cream of tartar

¾ cup confectioners' sugar

1 Position the rack in the center of the oven and preheat the oven to 400°F.

2 Whisk the egg yolks, ⅓ cup milk, and the salt in a large bowl until smooth. Whisk in ½ cup granulated sugar, the cornstarch, and flour until dissolved. Set aside.

3 Place the remaining 2⅓ cups milk in a large saucepan and set it over medium-low heat until little bubbles dot the pan's inner rim. Adjust the heat so the milk stays this hot without coming to a simmer.

4 Cook the remaining 1½ cups sugar in a heavy, large skillet over medium-high heat until the sugar starts to melt, about 3 minutes; stir well and continue cooking, stirring occasionally, until fully melted and light brown. Should the sugar begin to brown too darkly, remove the pan from the heat and continue stirring; the residual heat will continue melting the sugar.

5 Increase the heat under the milk to medium-high and slowly add the superhot, caramelized sugar, whisking all the while. The mixture will froth and roil—be very careful. Reduce the heat and continue whisking until smooth, about 2 minutes. If any of the sugar relumps in the pan, continue cooking and stirring until it dissolves again—but do not let the milk come to a full boil again. Remove the pan from the heat.

6 Whisk about half of this milk mixture in a thin stream into the egg yolk mixture until smooth, then whisk the combined mixture back into the milk mixture in the pan. Set the pan over low heat (if you're using an electric stove, place the pan over an unused burner just now turned to low) and cook, stirring constantly, until thickened and just beginning to bubble, about 2 minutes.

7 Remove from the heat and stir in the butter and 1 teaspoon vanilla; strain through a fine-mesh sieve into the prebaked crust.

8 Beat the egg whites and cream of tartar in a large bowl with an electric mixer at high speed until you can make soft, airy, droopy peaks with the tip of a rubber spatula. With the mixer running, add the confectioners' sugar in 1-tablespoon increments. Scrape down the sides of the bowl and continue beating at high speed until the mixture forms glossy, silky, smooth, but droopy peaks on the spatula's tip.

9 Spoon the meringue onto the hot custard, sealing the meringue against the crust's edge by

pressing down with a rubber spatula or a flatware spoon. Make little waves, ridges, and peaks in the meringue with the spatula or spoon.

🔟 Bake until the meringue lightly browns, about 8 minutes.

To cool: Set on a wire rack for 20 minutes, then refrigerate 1 hour before slicing.

To store: Once fully cooled, the pie can be refrigerated, lightly covered, for up to 2 days.

Raspberry Chiffon Pie

A light, airy chiffon pie set over a chocolate cookie crust is a refreshing summer treat, especially after a spicy meal. If you're concerned about raw eggs, use pasteurized, in-shell eggs. *Makes one 9-inch pie*

6 ounces chocolate wafer cookies
6 tablespoons unsalted butter, melted and cooled
⅔ cup plus 4½ tablespoons sugar
2 cups (1 pint) fresh raspberries
One ¼-ounce envelope unflavored gelatin or 2½ teaspoons unflavored gelatin
¼ cup white grape juice
1 cup heavy cream
3 large eggs, separated (see page 19), at room temperature
1 tablespoon raspberry liqueur, such as Chambord
Fresh raspberries or shaved chocolate for garnish, optional

1 Position the rack in the center of the oven and preheat the oven to 375°F.

2 Grind the chocolate cookies to the consistency of cornmeal in a food processor fitted with the chopping blade. Alternatively, place the cookies in a ziplock bag, seal it, and pulverize them with a rolling pin or the bottom of a heavy saucepan.

3 Pour the cookie crumbs into a large bowl; stir in the melted butter and 1½ tablespoons sugar until moistened. Press into the bottom and sides of a 9-inch pie plate, making sure there are no cracks in the crust and that the crumbs are evenly spread across the plate.

4 Bake until firm, about 7 minutes. Cool on a wire rack to room temperature, about 1 hour.

5 Place 2 cups raspberries in a fine-mesh sieve and set it over a medium bowl. Use the back of a wooden spoon to press and wipe the berries against the mesh, thereby removing the seeds and letting the puree drip into the bowl. (You may need to wipe the puree off the bottom of the sieve a few times to aid its dripping.) Set aside.

6 Sprinkle the gelatin over the juice in a small bowl; set aside for 10 minutes. Meanwhile, heat the cream in a large saucepan over medium heat until a few puffs of steam come off the surface.

7 Beat the egg yolks and ⅔ cup sugar with an electric mixer at medium speed in a large bowl until quite thick, velvety, and pale yellow.

8 Beating all the while, slowly pour half the warmed cream into the beaten egg yolk mixture, then return this combined mixture to the saucepan with the remaining cream. Keeping the heat at low, stir constantly until the mixture coats the back of a wooden spoon, about 1 minute (see page 7).

9 Strain through a clean fine-mesh sieve into a large, clean bowl. Stir in the softened gelatin and

juice until smooth, then stir in the prepared raspberry puree and raspberry liqueur. Refrigerate until slightly thickened, about 30 minutes.

⑩ Beat the egg whites with an electric mixer at medium speed in large bowl until frothy. Beating all the while, add the remaining 3 tablespoons sugar in a slow stream; continue beating until you can make smooth, soft, silky waves with a rubber spatula.

⑪ Fold the beaten egg whites into the berry mixture with the rubber spatula until uniform. Return to the refrigerator until the mixture can hold its shape without flattening out on a spoon, about 30 minutes. Spread into the cooled pre-baked crust; garnish with fresh raspberries and shaved chocolate, if desired.

To store: The pie can be tightly covered and refrigerated for up to 3 days.

Raspberry Mint Chiffon Pie: Add $1/2$ teaspoon mint extract with the raspberry liqueur.

Blackberry Chiffon Pie: Substitute 3 cups ($1\frac{1}{2}$ pints) blackberries for the raspberries.

Raspberry Daiquiri Chiffon Pie: Substitute white rum for the white grape juice, substitute lime juice for the raspberry liqueur, and add 2 teaspoons finely grated lime zest with the white rum.

Raspberry Ginger Chiffon Pie: Substitute gingersnap cookies for the chocolate cookies in the crust; garnish the pie with Sweetened Whipped Cream (page 522) and chopped crystallized ginger instead of shaved chocolate.

Raspberry Rum Chiffon Pie: Substitute dark rum such as Myers's for the white grape juice.

Peach Melba Chiffon Pie: Line the piecrust with 2 peaches, pitted and thinly sliced; also substitute Peach Schnapps, Peach Brandy, or canned peach nectar for the white grape juice.

Linzer Torte Chiffon Pie: Substitute almond cookies for the chocolate cookies; also substitute an almond-flavored liqueur such as Amaretto for the white grape juice.

Frozen Mai Tai Pie

Here's a frozen cocktail in a cookie crust. *Makes one 9-inch frozen pie*

35 vanilla wafer cookies
$3/4$ cup plus 2 tablespoons sugar
5 tablespoons unsalted butter, melted and cooled
Two $1/4$-ounce packages unflavored gelatin or 5 teaspoons unflavored gelatin
$1/4$ cup lime juice
$1/4$ cup gold or white rum
$1/4$ cup almond syrup, such as Orgeat
Two 11-ounce cans mandarin orange segments, drained, segments chopped
2 large egg whites, at room temperature
$1/4$ teaspoon salt
$2/3$ cup cold heavy cream
$1/3$ cup shredded sweetened coconut, toasted until lightly browned

① Crumble the wafer cookies in a food processor fitted with the chopping blade, add 2 tablespoons sugar, and process until finely ground. With the machine running, pour the melted butter through the feeding tube; continue processing just until moistened and uniform. Alternatively, pulverize the cookies and sugar in a sealed, ziplock plastic bag with a rolling pin or the bottom of a heavy saucepan. Pour the mixture into a large bowl and stir in the melted butter until uniform.

2 Pour into a 9-inch pie plate and press across the bottom and up the sides to form an even crust, level with the rim. Place in the freezer while you prepare the filling.

3 Sprinkle the gelatin over the lime juice and rum in a large bowl; set aside to soften for 10 minutes.

4 Place the almond syrup in a medium saucepan and set it over medium heat until barely simmering. Set aside off the heat for 5 minutes, then stir the almond syrup into the gelatin mixture and any liquid left in the large bowl until dissolved. Stir in the orange segments and place in the refrigerator until the mixture starts to set, about 30 minutes.

5 Bring about 2 inches of water to a simmer in the bottom of a double boiler or in a medium saucepan set over high heat; reduce the heat so the water is simmering gently. Place the egg whites and the remaining ¾ cup sugar in the top half of a stainless steel double boiler or in a medium bowl that will fit snugly over the pan. Beat away from the heat with an electric mixer at medium speed until foamy.

6 Place over the simmering water and continue beating at medium speed, scraping down the bowl with a rubber spatula, until shiny, smooth, and thick, about 3 minutes. (Be very careful of electric cords around heating elements.)

7 Remove the top half of the double boiler or the bowl from the heat—be careful of escaping steam—add the salt and continue beating until room temperature, about 4 minutes.

8 Use a rubber spatula to fold this cooked meringue into the cool, thickening orange-segment mixture. Return the bowl to the refrigerator for 15 minutes.

9 Clean and dry the mixer's beaters. Beat the cream in a chilled bowl until doubled in volume and firm but not yet dry and buttery. Fold into the orange-almond mixture until no white streaks are visible, then mound into the prepared pie shell. Freeze until firm, for at least 4 hours, overnight, or up to 7 days. Once firm, sprinkle the coconut over the top of the pie.

To store: The pie can be covered and kept in the freezer for up to 2 weeks.

To serve: Let the pie stand at room temperature for 10 minutes, then slice as desired.

Premade Frozen Crusts

If you remain crust-reticent and prefer only to use purchased frozen crusts, here are a few recommendations. Buy frozen deep-dish crusts; others may be too skimpy for a 9-inch pie. Although the directions say to use them frozen, they bake better if you let them sit out on the counter for 10 minutes. And look for crusts that use butter or trans-fat-free shortening instead of lard or hydrogenated fats.

The Ragtag Ends of Crust

After you've made a piecrust, you often have leftover bits of trimmed ends. Flatten them against your work surface, dust them with granulated sugar and a little ground cinnamon, and place them on a baking sheet. Bake in a preheated 425°F oven until crispy, 8 to 10 minutes. Cool on a wire rack for a few minutes, then dole them out to little hands that may not be able to wait for the pie to be baked.

• Tarts •

American pies come from a long tradition of Continental tarts. Ours were developed for a 10-inch tart shell with a removable bottom; look for this specialty pan in bakeware stores and from suppliers on the Web.

Sweet Pastry Dough

All tarts start with this classic dough, also called pâte brisée (pronounced "PAHT bree-ZAY"). It's light, firm, crunchy, and very buttery. You'll need ceramic pie weights or dried beans to weight the crust as it bakes. *Makes one 10-inch pastry crust for tarts*

2 cups all-purpose flour, plus additional for dusting
¼ cup sugar
½ teaspoon salt
10 tablespoons cool unsalted butter, cut into chunks
1 large egg yolk, at room temperature
2 to 3 tablespoons ice water

❶ Position the rack in the center of the oven and preheat the oven to 400°F.

❷ Stir the flour, sugar, and salt in a large bowl until well combined. Cut the butter into the flour with a pastry cutter or a fork, pressing the flour against the butter and through the tines, repeating this process until the mixture resembles coarse cornmeal or sand, until there are no chunks of butter visible.

❸ Stir in the egg yolk with a fork, then stir in the ice water in two additions until a loose dough forms.

❹ Dribble a few drops of water on your work surface, then lay a piece of wax paper over them. Dust lightly with flour, then gather the dough into a ball and place it on the floured paper. Press down lightly until the dough looks like a partially deflated basketball, then dust lightly with flour. Lay a second sheet of wax paper over the dough and roll the dough into a 12-inch circle.

❺ Peel off the top sheet of wax paper. Pick up the dough and the bottom sheet of wax paper; invert both over a 10-inch tart pan with a removable bottom (the bottom is in place, of course). Center the dough over the pan and peel off the wax paper.

❻ Gently push the dough into the pan, getting it into the corners and up the sides without tearing it. Trim off any excess above the pan's rim. The natural fluting of the edge will crimp the dough decoratively; just make sure the dough itself is pressed against this edge and formed to it.

❼ Prick the dough in several places across the bottom and sides with a fork. Lay a piece of aluminum foil over the dough in the pan and fill the foil with 2 cups ceramic pie weights or dried beans. (The beans will be worthless for cooking later, but can be used again and again as pie weights.)

❽ Bake for 15 minutes, then peel off the foil, taking the weights or beans with it. Continue baking until lightly browned, 7 to 9 minutes.

To cool: Set on a wire rack for at least 1 hour before using. (Be careful when handling the pan: the sides can slip off the crust if you place your hand under the pan's bottom.)

To store: Once completely cooled, the pan and crust together can be wrapped tightly with plastic and kept at room temperature for 24 hours.

Berry Cream Tart

Here's the fruit tart that's always beckoning from pastry shop windows: a traditional pastry cream topped with fresh fruit and glazed with melted jam. For an even smoother pastry cream, see the variations. *Makes one 10-inch tart*

2 cups whole or low-fat milk (do not use fat-free)
4 large egg yolks, at room temperature
½ cup sugar
2 teaspoons vanilla extract
¼ teaspoon salt
⅓ cup all-purpose flour
1 prebaked, cooled tart crust made from Sweet Pastry Dough (page 617) in a 10-inch tart pan with a removable bottom
2 cups raspberries, blackberries, blueberries, sliced hulled strawberries, or a combination of any of these
¼ cup red currant, raspberry, or white grape jelly
½ tablespoon water

❶ Place the milk in a medium saucepan over medium-low heat until a few wisps of steam come off the surface; adjust the heat so that the milk does not come to a simmer but remains this hot.

❷ Beat the egg yolks and sugar in a large bowl with an electric mixer at medium speed until thick, satiny ribbons run off the turned-off beaters, ribbons that do not immediately dissolve back into the mixture, about 4 minutes.

❸ Beat in the vanilla and salt until smooth, then beat in the flour until fully dissolved, scraping down the sides of the bowl to make sure every grain is incorporated.

❹ Beat about half the hot milk into the egg yolk mixture, then beat this combined mixture back into the hot milk in the pan until smooth. Reduce the heat to low (if you're working with an electric stove, use a second burner just now turned to low) and cook, stirring constantly, until thick, smooth, and just beginning to bubble, about 3 minutes.

❺ Pour into a large, clean bowl. Press a sheet of plastic wrap onto the top of the pastry cream and refrigerate until chilled, at least 2 hours or overnight. (It can also be stored in the refrigerator for up to 2 days.)

❻ Gently peel off the plastic wrap and use a rubber spatula to spread the pastry cream into the prebaked, cooled tart crust.

❼ Arrange the berries and/or strawberries over the top of the tart, working in circles and standing the berries up on their larger flat ends.

❽ Place the jelly and water in a small saucepan over low heat and stir until the jelly melts. Use a pastry brush or feather to paint the berries or fruit on top of the cream with jelly until glistening.

Variations: Substitute 1 tablespoon gold or white rum for the water in the glaze.

Omit the jelly and water; dust the top of the tart with confectioners' sugar, sifted through a fine-mesh sieve.

For a smoother pastry cream, beat ½ cup cold heavy cream in a chilled bowl with an electric mixer at high speed until light, soft, fluffy, and moundable; fold this into the chilled pastry cream before spreading it into the pastry shell.

Banana Cream Tart: Thinly slice 2 ripe bananas and lay the slices over the bottom of the baked, cooled crust. Spoon and spread the cooled pastry cream over the bananas, then either shave semisweet chocolate over the cream or grate nutmeg lightly over it. (Omit the berries, jelly, and water.)

Easy Lemon Tart

Three steps and you're done!
Makes one 10-inch tart

Lemon Curd Filling (page 547)
1 prebaked, cooled tart crust made from
   Sweet Pastry Dough (page 617) in a 10-
   inch tart pan with a removable bottom
Sweetened Whipped Cream (page 522)

❶ Spread the warm Lemon Curd Filling into the tart crust.

❷ Set plastic wrap right onto the curd to seal it, then refrigerate for at least 4 hours or overnight.

❸ Gently peel off the plastic wrap, then spoon and spread Sweetened Whipped Cream over the tart just before serving.

Removing the Removable Bottom

Once the tart crust has been baked, filled, and chilled, slip the sides off the tart pan by placing one hand on the bottom of the tart pan and gently pushing up; the tart on the removable bottom should slip free of the shell's collar.

Place the tart with its bottom directly on a cake plate or serving platter—or go the extra step of taking the tart off the removable bottom. Run a long, very thin knife between the bottom of the crust and the pan, working all the way around to loosen the crust. Tip the tart and the bottom at a slight angle and slip the tart onto a serving platter.

Chocolate Silk Tart

This luscious chocolate filling is a cross between mousse and fudge. *Makes one 10-inch tart*

4 ounces unsweetened chocolate,
   chopped
13 tablespoons (1 stick plus 5 tablespoons)
   cool unsalted butter, cut into chunks
1 cup packed light brown sugar
2 tablespoons confectioners' sugar
4 large egg yolks, at room temperature
2 tablespoons gold or white rum
1 teaspoon vanilla extract
1 prebaked, cooled tart crust made from
   Sweet Pastry Dough (page 617) in a
   10-inch tart pan with a removable bottom
1 cup heavy cream
1 tablespoon superfine or granulated sugar

❶ Place the chocolate in the top half of a double boiler set over about 1 inch of simmering water. Alternatively, place it in a medium bowl that fits securely over a medium saucepan with a similar amount of simmering water in it. Adjust the heat so the water simmers gently; stir until half the chocolate has melted.

❷ Remove the top half of the double boiler or the bowl from the heat; continue stirring until the chocolate has fully melted. Transfer to a medium bowl; set aside to cool for 5 minutes.

❸ Meanwhile, beat the butter, brown sugar, and confectioners' sugar in a large bowl with an electric mixer at medium speed until light and fluffy, about 5 minutes.

❹ Beat in the egg yolks one at a time, scraping down the bowl after each addition and making sure it is thoroughly incorporated before adding the next. Beat in the rum and vanilla until smooth.

5 Beat in the melted chocolate; continue beating until very smooth and somewhat thick, about 5 minutes. Spoon and spread into the prebaked, cooled tart crust. Refrigerate until chilled, for at least 2 hours or overnight. (After 2 hours, cover the tart with plastic wrap to protect it from any refrigerator odors.)

6 To serve, beat the cream and the superfine or granulated sugar in a chilled bowl with an electric mixer at medium speed until smooth, glossy peaks can be formed on a rubber spatula, about 3 minutes. Spoon and spread onto the tart or serve on the side.

Strawberry Mascarpone Tart

Mascarpone is a soft, unripened Italian cheese, best with fruits or berries. For the best taste, let this tart stand at room temperature for 20 minutes before slicing. *Makes one 10-inch tart*

½ cup regular or low-fat ricotta (do not use fat-free)
½ cup mascarpone, at room temperature
2 tablespoons sugar
1 teaspoon vanilla extract
1 prebaked, cooled tart crust made from Sweet Pastry Dough (page 617) in a 10-inch tart pan with a removable bottom
1½ quarts strawberries, hulled
½ cup strawberry, raspberry, or red currant jelly
1 tablespoon water

1 Mix the ricotta, mascarpone, sugar, and vanilla in a medium bowl until smooth. Spread evenly in the bottom of the prebaked, cooled tart crust.

2 Cut a little bit off the large ends of the strawberries, just so they'll stand up flat. Arrange them in a decorative pattern on top of the cheese mixture, standing them, point up, with the largest at the center and the smaller strawberries toward the crust's edge.

3 Melt the jelly and water in a small saucepan over low heat until thick but the consistency of paint. Cool for a couple of minutes, then paint this mixture over the strawberries with a pastry brush or pastry feather, or spoon it lightly over each of the individual berries.

4 Set aside to cool for 20 minutes, then cover with plastic wrap and store in the refrigerator for up to 2 days. Bring back to room temperature for 20 minutes before serving.

Frangipane Tart

A rich plum tart with a chewy, almond paste filling. *Makes one 10-inch tart*

5 ounces almond paste
⅓ cup unsalted butter
⅓ cup sugar
2 large eggs, at room temperature
2 tablespoons all-purpose flour
1 teaspoon vanilla extract
¼ teaspoon salt
1 prebaked, cooled tart crust made from Sweet Pastry Dough (page 617) in a 10-inch tart pan with a removable bottom
8 plums, pitted and quartered

1 Position the rack in the center of the oven and preheat the oven to 350°F.

2 Beat the almond paste and butter in a large bowl with an electric mixer at medium speed until soft and creamy, about 2 minutes.

3 Beat in the sugar until almost fully dissolved, then beat in the eggs one at a time until the mixture loosens up and gets creamy. Beat in the flour, vanilla, and salt, making sure the flour has completely dissolved.

4 Pour the almond mixture into the prebaked, cooled tart crust, spreading it to the corners. Lay the plum quarters skin side down in the cream and gently press them into it until the plums' upper edges sit just above the cream. You can arrange them in a decorative pattern or go for a more rustic look.

5 Bake until puffed and lightly browned, about 45 minutes.

To cool: Set on a wire rack for at least 20 minutes before removing the sides of the pan and slicing.

To store: Once fully cooled, wrap in plastic and refrigerate for up to 3 days.

French-Inspired Apple Tart

This buttery apple tart ("tarte Tatin") is best the moment it's made. *Makes one 10-inch tart*

> 3 pounds large tart apples, such as Granny Smith, Rome Beauty, Cortland, or McIntosh
> 2 teaspoons lemon juice
> 8 tablespoons (1 stick) unsalted butter, melted and cooled
> ½ cup granulated sugar
> ½ cup packed light brown sugar
> 1 recipe Sweet Pastry Dough (page 617), the dough rolled out between sheets of wax paper to a circle 11 inches in diameter
> Crème Anglaise (page 599), Vanilla Frozen Custard (page 644), or Sweetened Whipped Cream (page 522), as a garnish

1 Position the rack in the bottom third of the oven and preheat the oven to 425°F.

2 Peel, core, and slice the apples into ½-inch-thick wedges. Place them in a large bowl; toss well with the lemon juice.

3 Pour half the melted butter in a heavy, 10-inch ovenproof skillet. Add all the granulated sugar and ¼ cup brown sugar to the skillet. Set over medium heat and cook, stirring frequently, until the sugar has melted and the mixture starts to bubble, about 3 minutes.

4 While the skillet is still over the heat, arrange the apple slices in the sugar in a circular pattern. Place any remaining apple wedges on top of the arranged ones (these will cook down and not form a decorative pattern when the skillet is later inverted).

5 Sprinkle the remaining brown sugar over the apples; pour on the remaining melted butter.

6 Remove the pan from the heat. Place the rolled-out pastry dough on top of the apples, tucking the edges around the inside of the pan. Cut four slits in the dough to allow steam to escape.

7 Place the skillet in the oven and bake until the pastry is browned and the filling is lightly bubbling inside, about 30 minutes.

8 Set the skillet over medium heat. Be very careful: the pan is hot! Cook until the juices inside have thickened and the filling at the edges looks like jam, 3 to 5 minutes.

9 Set aside for 5 minutes off the heat. Place a lipped heat-safe serving platter over the skillet. Invert the two together and remove the pan. If any apples have stuck to the pan, peel them off with a metal spatula and place them on the tart. Scrape any juices out of the pan and spoon them over the apples. Serve at once with the garnish of your choice.

Pear Galette

This free-form tart is not made in a pan. Instead, you roll out the crust, top it with the fruit, fold the edges over, and bake on a sheet pan.

Makes 1 free-form tart (about 6 servings)

1½ pounds ripe fresh pears, such as Anjou, Barlett, or Comice, peeled, cored, and thinly sliced
1 teaspoon lemon juice
½ teaspoon ground cinnamon
1 ½ cups all-purpose flour, plus additional for dusting
6 tablespoons sugar
¼ teaspoon salt
5 tablespoons cool unsalted butter, cut into chunks
¼ cup (4 tablespoons) solid vegetable shortening
2 to 3 tablespoons ice water
¼ teaspoon cider vinegar

1 Position the rack in the center of the oven and preheat the oven to 350°F. Line a large baking sheet with parchment paper or a silicone baking mat.

2 Toss the sliced pears, lemon juice, and cinnamon in a large bowl; set aside.

3 Mix the flour, 4 tablespoons (1/4 cup) sugar, and the salt in a second, large bowl. Cut in the 4 tablespoons butter and all the shortening with a pastry cutter or two forks, pressing the fat and flour together through the tines repeatedly until the mixture looks like coarse sand with no chunks of shortening or butter visible.

4 Stir in 1 tablespoon ice water and the vinegar with a fork. Then stir in the remaining ice water in two additions until a soft dough begins to form.

5 Sprinkle a few drops of water on your work surface and lay a piece of wax paper on top of them. Sprinkle the paper lightly with flour, gather the dough together into a ball, and place it on the wax paper. Press down gently to make the ball look like a deflated tire, then dust lightly with flour and top with a second sheet of wax paper.

6 Roll the dough into a circle about 14 inches in diameter, starting in the middle and always rolling on the radius (not the diameter), rotating the pin after each roll to create a fairly even circle.

7 Peel off the top sheet of wax paper. Pick up the dough by picking up the underlying sheet of wax paper; invert both onto the prepared baking sheet. Center the dough circle on the baking sheet and peel off the wax paper.

8 Spoon the pears and juice into the middle of the tart, fanning the slices in a decorative pattern, but leaving a 2-inch border all the way around the perimeter of the tart. Sprinkle the remaining 2 tablespoons sugar over the pear slices, then dot them with the remaining 1 tablespoon butter.

9 Fold up the sides of the dough over the pear slices, pressing and pinching the edges together so that they fold over the fruit and form an uneven circle with a cutout hole in the middle where the fruit is visible. Make sure there are no holes in the crust dough; if so, patch them with dampened fingers by pulling the dough over itself.

10 Bake until lightly browned and the filling is gently bubbling, about 45 minutes. Cool the baking sheet on a wire rack for 20 minutes, then transfer the galette to a serving platter to continue cooling. Once fully cooled, store, tightly covered, in the refrigerator for up to 2 days.

Cobblers, Crisps, British Puddings, Pandowdies, Slumps, and Brown Betties

Here's what happened to pies and tarts once they began to take on regional and local overtones—simplified, modified, and homey. These are all riffs on a theme: a baked fruit or berry filling with a crust on top.

A road map for Fruit Cobbler

There's no telling what the name means: cobbled together, a crust like cobblestones, a simple dessert a cobbler would eat? In any event, it's a two-step dessert—a fruit filling under a biscuit topping. Serve with Sweetened Whipped Cream (page 522), Vanilla Frozen Custard (page 644), or purchased frozen yogurt. *Makes 6 servings*

1 Start by positioning the rack in the center of the oven and preheating the oven to 375°F. Lightly grease a 9-inch square pan with a little unsalted butter or walnut oil.

2 Next, mix any of the following together in a large bowl, pour into the prepared pan, and set aside for 10 to 15 minutes.

Apple

2½ pounds tart apples, such as Granny Smith, Pippin, Rome Beauty, Cortland, or Northern Spy, peeled, cored, and thinly sliced
⅓ cup granulated sugar
⅓ cup packed dark brown sugar
1½ tablespoon all-purpose flour
1 tablespoons quick-cooking tapioca
1 teaspoon lemon juice
1 teaspoon ground cinnamon
¼ teaspoon salt

Apricot

2 pounds fresh apricots, pitted and sliced; or 2 pounds sliced frozen pitted apricots, thawed
½ cup sugar
2 tablespoons quick-cooking tapioca
¼ teaspoon almond extract
¼ teaspoon salt

Blackberry

3 pints fresh blackberries or 2½ pounds frozen blackberries (do not thaw)
½ cup sugar
2 tablespoons quick-cooking tapioca
2 teaspoons lemon juice
¼ teaspoon salt

Blueberry

3 pints fresh blueberries or 2½ pounds frozen blueberries (do not thaw)
⅓ cup sugar
2 tablespoons quick-cooking tapioca
1 tablespoon lemon juice
¼ teaspoon salt

Fig

3 pints large fresh figs (about 18), stemmed and quartered
⅓ cup sugar
1 tablespoon quick-cooking tapioca
1 teaspoon lemon juice
1 teaspoon finely grated orange zest
¼ teaspoon salt

Gooseberry

3 pints gooseberries, papery hulls removed
    and stemmed
1½ cups sugar
2½ tablespoons quick-cooking tapioca
1 teaspoon vanilla extract
¼ teaspoon salt

Nectarine

3 pounds fresh nectarines, peeled, pitted,
    and sliced; or 2½ pounds sliced frozen
    pitted nectarines, thawed
⅓ cup granulated sugar
1 tablespoon packed light brown sugar
1 tablespoon quick-cooking tapioca
1 tablespoon all-purpose flour
1 tablespoon gold rum, optional
¼ teaspoon grated nutmeg
¼ teaspoon salt

Peach

2½ pounds fresh peaches, peeled, pitted, and
    sliced; or 2½ pounds sliced frozen pitted
    peaches, thawed
⅓ cup packed light brown sugar
1½ tablespoons quick-cooking tapioca
1 tablespoon all-purpose flour
1 teaspoon vanilla extract
¼ teaspoon almond extract, optional
¼ teaspoon salt

Peach Melba

2 pounds fresh peaches, peeled, pitted, and
    sliced; or three 12-ounce bags sliced
    frozen pitted peaches, thawed
1 pint fresh raspberries
½ cup sugar
1½ tablespoons quick-cooking tapioca
1 teaspoon finely grated lemon zest, optional
¼ teaspoon almond extract
¼ teaspoon salt

Pear

3 pounds ripe sweet fresh pears, such as
    Anjou, Bartlett, or Comice, peeled, cored,
    and sliced
¼ cup sugar
2 tablespoons honey
2 tablespoons quick-cooking tapioca
1 tablespoon lemon juice
½ teaspoon ground cinnamon
¼ teaspoon grated nutmeg, optional
¼ teaspoon salt

Pear Cranberry

2½ pounds ripe sweet fresh pears, such as
    Anjou, Bartlett, or Comice, peeled, cored,
    and sliced
8 ounces fresh cranberries, roughly chopped
¾ cup sugar
2 tablespoons quick-cooking tapioca
1 tablespoon brandy, optional
1 teaspoon finely grated lemon zest
¼ teaspoon ground mace
¼ teaspoon salt

Plum

2½ pounds ripe fresh plums, pitted and
    sliced
⅓ cup sugar
2 tablespoons quick-cooking tapioca
1 teaspoon finely grated lemon zest, optional
¼ teaspoon grated nutmeg
¼ teaspoon salt

Raspberry

3 pints fresh raspberries or 2½ pounds frozen
    raspberries (do not thaw)
½ cup plus 1 tablespoon sugar
2 tablespoons quick-cooking tapioca
2 teaspoons finely grated lemon zest
¼ teaspoon salt

Sour Cherry

2½ pounds fresh sour cherries, pitted, plus the juice from the pitting; or 2¼ pounds frozen pitted sour cherries do not thaw)

⅔ cup sugar

1½ tablespoons quick-cooking tapioca

1 tablespoon all-purpose flour

¼ teaspoon salt

Strawberry

2 quarts fresh strawberries, hulled and quartered

6 tablespoons sugar

2 tablespoons quick-cooking tapioca

1½ tablespoons all-purpose flour

1 teaspoon finely grated lemon zest

¼ teaspoon salt

Strawberry Rhubarb

1 quart fresh strawberries, hulled and quartered

¾ pound fresh rhubarb, peeled and thinly sliced; or one 12-ounce package frozen sliced rhubarb

1¼ cups sugar

2 tablespoons quick-cooking tapioca

1 tablespoon all-purpose flour

¼ teaspoon salt

Sweet Cherry

2½ pounds fresh sweet cherries (preferably Bing or Tartarian), pitted; or 2 pounds frozen pitted sweet cherries (do not thaw)

½ cup sugar

1½ tablespoons quick-cooking tapioca

1 tablespoon all-purpose flour

1 teaspoon lemon juice

1 teaspoon vanilla extract

¼ teaspoon salt

③ While the filling rests, make the biscuit topping of your choice. In each case, mix the dry ingredients in a large bowl, then stir in the liquid ingredients until a loose batter forms.

Biscuit Cobbler Topping

Dry Ingredients

1 cup all-purpose flour

3 tablespoons sugar

1 teaspoon baking powder

¼ teaspoon salt

Wet Ingredients

6 tablespoons milk (regular, low-fat, or fat-free)

4 tablespoons (½ stick) unsalted butter, melted and cooled

Cake Cobbler Topping

Dry Ingredients

1 cup all-purpose flour

3 tablespoons sugar

1½ teaspoons baking powder

¼ teaspoon salt

Wet Ingredients

3 tablespoons heavy cream

3 tablespoons unsalted butter, melted and cooled

1 large egg plus 1 large egg yolk, lightly beaten, at room temperature

1 teaspoon vanilla extract

Almond Cobbler Topping

Dry Ingredients

¾ cup all-purpose flour

⅔ cup toasted sliced almonds, finely ground

3 tablespoons sugar

1½ teaspoons baking soda

¼ teaspoon salt

Wet Ingredients

½ cup buttermilk (regular, low-fat, or fat-free)

2 tablespoons unsalted butter, melted and cooled

⅛ teaspoon almond extract

Brown Sugar Pecan Cobbler Topping

Dry Ingredients
1¼ cups all-purpose flour
½ cup chopped pecan pieces
¼ cup packed dark brown sugar
2 teaspoons baking powder
¼ teaspoon salt

Wet Ingredients
½ cup half-and-half, whole milk, or low-fat milk
4 tablespoons (½ stick) unsalted butter, melted and cooled

Lemon Oat Cobbler Topping

Dry Ingredients
1 cup all-purpose flour
½ cup rolled oats (do not use quick-cooking or steel-cut)
¼ cup sugar
2 teaspoons baking powder
2 teaspoons finely grated lemon zest
¼ teaspoon salt

Wet Ingredients
6 tablespoons half-and-half or whole milk
4 tablespoons (½ stick) unsalted butter, melted and cooled
1½ tablespoons lemon juice

4 Drop the prepared topping by heaping tablespoons onto the filling in the pan.

5 Bake until the fruit starts to bubble and the topping is lightly browned, about 45 minutes.

To cool: Set on a wire rack for at least 10 minutes before serving up with a large spoon.

To store: The cooled cobbler can be covered and stored at room temperature for up to 1 day or in the refrigerator for up to 2 days (but the cold will dramatically compromise the topping).

A road map for Fruit Crisp

A crisp is a cobbler with a crunchy topping. The fruit filling's the same; only the toppings have been changed. *Makes about 8 servings*

1 Position the rack in the center of the oven and preheat the oven to 350°F. Lightly grease a 9-inch square pan with a little unsalted butter or walnut oil.

2 Prepare one of the fillings for cobblers (pages 623–625), pour it into the pan, and set aside for 10 to 15 minutes while you prepare the topping.

3 Mix any of the following together in a large bowl.

Walnut Maple Oat Crisp Topping
½ cup all-purpose flour
½ cup rolled oats (do not use quick-cooking or steel-cut)
6 tablespoons packed light brown sugar
⅓ cup finely chopped walnuts
4 tablespoons (½ stick) unsalted butter, melted and cooled
2 tablespoons maple syrup
½ teaspoon ground cinnamon (see Note)
¼ teaspoon salt

Pecan Crisp Topping
1 cup all-purpose flour
½ cup finely chopped pecan pieces
6 tablespoons sugar
6 tablespoons unsalted butter, melted and cooled
¼ teaspoon salt

Walnut Raisin Crisp Topping
¾ cup all-purpose flour
½ cup finely chopped walnut pieces
⅓ cup chopped raisins
⅓ cup sugar

¼ cup rolled oats (do not use quick-cooking or steel-cut)
¼ cup walnut oil
1 teaspoon vanilla extract
¼ teaspoon salt

Coconut Crisp Topping

1 cup all-purpose flour
6 tablespoons packed light brown sugar
6 tablespoons shredded (or "desiccated") unsweetened coconut
6 tablespoons unsalted butter, melted and cooled
½ teaspoon salt

Ginger Almond Crisp Topping

1¼ cups all-purpose flour
½ cup chopped sliced almonds
6 tablespoons unsalted butter, melted and cooled
¼ cup finely chopped crystallized ginger
¼ cup sugar
¼ teaspoon salt

4 Crumble the topping over the prepared filling.

5 Bake until the filling is bubbling and the topping is lightly browned, about 40 minutes. Cool on a wire rack for at least 10 minutes before serving.

Note: Be careful of a double hit of cinnamon. Omit the cinnamon from either the filling or the topping in any pairing that has it in both.

Another American fruit dessert classic is a buckle: berries stirred directly into a quick batter. Because of its coffee cakelike crumb, we've included one on page 557 in the coffee cake chapter.

Steamed British Pudding with Caramel Custard Sauce

The good news? You don't need a hunk of suet to make this classic. In fact, the bright taste of the brandy and fruit comes through better if you cut down on the fat. Serve with Caramel Custard Sauce (page 628), Zabaglione (page 642), or Sweetened Whipped Cream (page 522). *Makes 8 servings*

1 cup brandy
1 cup chopped packed figs, preferably Calimyrna figs (about 6 ounces)
1 cup chopped pitted dates (about 6 ounces)
½ cup dried cherries or cranberries, chopped (about 3 ounces)
Juice and zest from 1 large orange
3 large eggs, lightly beaten
1 cup plus 2 tablespoons plain dried bread crumbs
¼ cup packed dark brown sugar
¼ cup granulated sugar
¼ cup solid vegetable shortening, preferably nonhydrogenated shortening, melted and cooled, plus additional for greasing the baking dish
2 teaspoons vanilla extract
½ teaspoon ground cinnamon
¼ teaspoon ground cloves
¼ teaspoon ground allspice
¼ teaspoon salt
Butcher's twine
Caramel Custard Sauce (recipe follows)

1 Bring the brandy, figs, dates, cherries or cranberries, orange juice, and orange zest to a simmer in a large saucepan set over medium heat. Cover, reduce the heat to low, and cook until the liquid has been absorbed, about 7 minutes. Set aside to cool completely, about 1 hour.

2 Grease a 1½-quart round, high-sided soufflé dish; set aside.

3 Stir the eggs, bread crumbs, brown sugar, granulated sugar, melted shortening, vanilla, cinnamon, cloves, allspice, and salt into the saucepan with the dried fruit until uniform.

4 Pour the mixture into the prepared soufflé dish; smooth the top flat.

5 Tear off a sheet of aluminum foil that will cover the dish and lightly grease the center portion that will sit over the pudding. Position the foil with the greased part down; tie butcher's twine around the outside of the dish to secure the foil. (You can also use a large rubber band.)

6 Set a small baking rack in the center of a large Dutch oven or pot that will hold the baking dish. Fill the pot with water until it comes just below the rack. Set the baking dish on the rack, set the pot over high heat, and bring the water to a boil.

7 Cover, reduce the heat to very low, and steam the pudding until set, about 1 hour and 45 minutes, checking the water frequently and adding more as needed.

8 Remove the hot dish from the pot and set, covered, on a wire rack to cool for at least 20 minutes. Serve with Caramel Custard Sauce (see opposite). If not serving immediately, store, covered, in the refrigerator for up to 3 days.

Variations: You can use any combination of dried fruit you like, so long as you have 2½ cups. Try these two combinations: 1 cup chopped dried apples, 1 cup chopped dried apricots, and ½ cup chopped dried cranberries; or 1 cup chopped dried nectarines, 1 cup chopped dried pineapple, and ½ cup chopped dried strawberries.

Caramel Custard Sauce

Makes about ⅔ cup

> 2 large egg yolks
> 1 teaspoon cornstarch
> 6 tablespoons sugar
> ½ cup heavy cream
> 1 tablespoon brandy or rum

1 Whisk the egg yolks and cornstarch in a large bowl; set aside.

2 Melt the sugar in a large saucepan set over medium heat, stirring a few times, until golden brown. Meanwhile, whisk the cream in a medium bowl until quite foamy.

3 Whisk the cream in a slow stream into the hot sugar. Be careful: it will roil up in the pan. If you work slowly and deliberately, drizzling the cream in and whisking all the while, you'll keep the foaming to a minimum. Once all the cream has been added, continue whisking over the heat until the sugar melts again and the mixture is smooth.

4 Slowly whisk the cream mixture into the egg yolks, dribbling it in and whisking all the while. Once it has been thoroughly whisked into the yolks, place this combined mixture back in the saucepan.

5 Reduce the heat to very low (if you're working with an electric stove, use a second burner just now set to low). Set the pan over the heat and whisk constantly until slightly thickened, not quite bubbling, about 1 minute.

6 Pour through a fine-mesh sieve into a medium bowl to remove any inadvertent bits of scrambled egg, then stir in the brandy or rum. Set aside at room temperature to cool for 15 minutes or cover and refrigerate for up to 3 days.

Summer Pudding

A summer pudding is an unbaked concoction of berries and bread; the bread soaks up the liquid, the natural pectin holds the thing together, and it molds into a pudding. You can even use frozen blueberries and raspberries to good effect (but use fresh strawberries for the best taste). If you want to make sure the pudding unmolds, line the baking dish or bowl with plastic wrap—a precautionary but unnecessary step. Serve with Sweetened Whipped Cream (page 522). *Makes 8 servings*

4 cups strawberries, hulled and sliced

1½ cups sugar

2 tablespoons white or gold rum

2 cups raspberries

2 cups blueberries

¼ teaspoon salt

1½-pound loaf sliced white sandwich bread, preferably a country white without hydrogenated shortening, crusts removed

1 Mix the strawberries, sugar, and rum in a large saucepan set over medium heat. Bring to a simmer, stirring often, and cook just until the strawberries soften and just begin to break down, about 1 minute.

2 Stir in the raspberries and blueberries, return to a simmer, and cook, stirring often, until sauce-like but still with visible berries in the mix, about 4 minutes. Set aside.

3 Cover the bottom of a 2-quart soufflé dish with bread slices. Spoon in one-third of the berries and their sauce. Place another layer of bread on top, then spoon in half the remaining berries and sauce. Place yet another layer of bread on top, then spoon in the remaining berries and sauce.

Finally, top with another layer of bread slices. Alternatively, you can make this pudding in a 2-quart mixing bowl; the bread layers will get larger as the bowl widens toward the top so adjust the amount of berries accordingly, making three (or four) layers of berries with bread in between and then on top.

4 Cover with plastic wrap, gently pressing the wrap down against the surface of the bread. Set a small plate on top, then set a 16-ounce can or a ramekin filled with water on top of the plate. Place the whole thing in a large pan to catch any drips (most likely, there'll be none) and refrigerate for at least 8 hours or up to 24 hours.

5 To unmold, remove the weight and plate, then peel off the plastic wrap. Place a serving platter over the soufflé dish (or bowl), invert, and shake a few times to make the pudding come free. Remove the bowl and slice the pudding into wedges to serve.

Variations: Substitute gooseberries, blackberries, or pitted cherries for the raspberries.

Add ½ teaspoon finely grated lemon zest with the strawberries.

Add ½ teaspoon ground cinnamon with the blueberries.

Add ¼ cup chopped crystallized ginger to the pan with the raspberries.

Substitute oat bread or wheat bread for the country-style white. Oat bread will have a slightly more slippery texture; wheat bread, a slightly nuttier taste.

Stir ½ cup toasted sliced almonds into the berry mixture after it has simmered.

Stir ½ cup shredded sweetened coconut into the berry mixture after it has simmered.

Reduce the sugar to 1½ cups; add ½ cup orange marmalade with the strawberries.

Peach Pandowdy

A pandowdy is probably so named because of its "dowdy" appearance: a sweet fruit filling with a crust laid on top, the crust then is cracked while it bakes so that the fruit bubbles up and partially covers it. *Makes 8 servings*

  4 tablespoons (½ stick) cool unsalted butter, plus additional for greasing the pan
  2½ pounds fresh peaches, peeled, pitted, and thinly sliced; or 2¼ pounds sliced frozen pitted peaches, thawed
  1 cup plus 2 tablespoons all-purpose flour
  ⅔ cup packed light brown sugar
  1 teaspoon finely grated lemon zest
  ½ teaspoon salt
  ¼ teaspoon grated nutmeg
  2 teaspoons brandy or rum
  ¼ cup solid vegetable shortening
  3 to 4 tablespoons ice water
  ½ teaspoon cider vinegar
  1 large egg white beaten with 1 teaspoon water
  1½ tablespoons granulated sugar
  1 teaspoon ground cinnamon
  Warmed Cream (recipe follows)

1 Position the rack in the center of the oven and preheat the oven to 425°F. Lightly butter a 9-inch square baking pan; set aside.

2 Toss the peaches, 2 tablespoons flour, brown sugar, lemon zest, ¼ teaspoon salt, and the nutmeg in a large bowl. Pour into the prepared pan, spreading evenly to the corners. Drizzle with the brandy or rum. Set aside.

3 Mix the remaining 1 cup flour and ¼ teaspoon salt in a large bowl. Cut in the butter and shortening with a pastry cutter or a fork, pressing the fat and flour through the tines until the mixture resembles coarse sand without any butter or shortening visible.

4 Stir 2 tablespoons ice water and the vinegar in a small glass. Stir into the flour mixture with a fork, then add more ice water in 1-tablespoon increments just until the dough starts to adhere. Gather into a ball.

5 Sprinkle a few drops of water across the work surface, then lay down a large sheet of wax paper. Dust it lightly with flour and turn the dough out onto it. Press the dough with the heel of your hand into a compact, flattened ball, then dust it lightly with flour. Lay a second piece of wax paper over the top.

6 Roll the dough into a 9-inch square, exactly the size of the pan you're using. If you work in alternating directions, turning the rolling pin 90 degrees after each change, you can get a pretty accurate square from the dough.

7 Peel off the top sheet of wax paper, then pick up the dough by picking up the bottom sheet of wax paper. Transfer it to the pan, invert the paper and dough, center the dough over the filling, and peel off the wax paper. Tuck any sides under the dough; don't seal it to the edges. Make two 3-inch slits in the dough with a knife so that steam can escape.

8 Brush the dough with the egg white mixture, then sprinkle the granulated sugar and cinnamon over the crust.

9 Place the pan in the oven and immediately lower the temperature to 350°F. Bake until the crust is lightly browned, about 40 minutes.

10 Crack the crust into 6 or 7 pieces with a dinner knife, partially submerging the pieces' edges into the fruit by pushing down with the knife. Continue baking until the filling is bubbling through the cracks, about 7 more minutes.

To cool: Set on a wire rack for at least 15 minutes before serving.

To store: Once completely cooled, the pandowdy can be tightly wrapped and refrigerated for up to 3 days.

Variations: Substitute nectarines for the peaches.

Substitute 1 teaspoon ground ginger for the lemon zest.

Reduce the peaches to 1½ pounds fresh or 1¼ pounds frozen and add 2 cups (1 pint) raspberries with the remaining peaches. Add 2 tablespoons granulated sugar with the brown sugar.

Add ½ cup shredded (or "desiccated") unsweetened coconut with the peaches.

Add ¼ cup sliced almonds with the peaches.

Mixed Berry Pandowdy: In step 2, omit the peach filling. Instead, mix together 1 pint (2 cups) fresh blackberries, 1 pint (2 cups) fresh blueberries, ½ pint (1 cup) fresh raspberries, 6 tablespoons sugar, 1 tablespoon quick-cooking tapioca, 1 tablespoon all-purpose flour, 1 teaspoon lemon juice, 1 teaspoon vanilla, and ¼ teaspoon salt. Pour into the prepared pan and continue with the recipe.

Warmed Cream

Here's a great topping for almost any fresh fruit dessert.

Makes about 1 cup

> 1 cup heavy cream
> 2 teaspoons sugar
> 1 teaspoon vanilla extract

Warm the cream in a small saucepan set over low heat until a few puffs of steam rise from its surface. Stir in the sugar and vanilla, then pour over individual servings of the pandowdy (or other fresh fruit pies, cobblers, or crisps).

Apple Cranberry Slump

A slump has a heavy, wet topping that slumps into the filling as it bakes. *Makes 8 servings*

> 3 tablespoons unsalted butter, melted and cooled, plus additional for greasing the baking dish
> 2 pounds tart apples, such as Pippin, Rome Beauty, or Granny Smith, peeled, cored, and thinly sliced
> 8 ounces fresh cranberries, roughly chopped
> 1 cup plus 1 tablespoon all-purpose flour
> 1¼ cups sugar
> 1 teaspoon ground cinnamon
> ¼ teaspoon ground nutmeg
> ¼ teaspoon ground cloves
> 1½ teaspoons baking powder
> ½ teaspoon salt
> ¾ cup milk (regular, low-fat, or fat-free)

❶ Position the rack in the middle of the oven and preheat the oven to 375°F. Lightly butter a 9-inch square or 10-inch round baking dish; set aside.

❷ Mix the apples, cranberries, 1 tablespoon flour, 1 cup sugar, cinnamon, nutmeg, and cloves in a large bowl. Pour this mixture into the prepared baking dish, spreading it evenly in the pan.

❸ Whisk the remaining 1 cup flour, the remaining ¼ cup sugar, baking powder, and salt in a second large bowl. Whisk in the milk and melted butter until fairly smooth. Pour this mixture evenly over the apple filling in the pan without worrying about getting it exactly to the corners and the edges.

❹ Bake until the filling is bubbling and the crust is browned and puffed, about 45 minutes.

To cool: Set on a wire rack for 10 minutes before serving (dish it up with a large spoon).

To store: Once fully cooled, the dish can be covered with plastic wrap and stored in the refrigerator for up to 2 days.

Variations: Substitute pears for the apples.

Substitute 1 pound rhubarb, peeled and thinly sliced, for the cranberries; increase the sugar with the fruit to 1 cup.

Substitute blueberries for the cranberries; decrease the sugar with the fruit to ½ cup.

Pear Walnut Ginger Brown Betty

A betty is fruit layered with buttered bread crumbs. You must use fresh bread crumbs; dried crumbs will be inedible. Although apples are traditional for this dish, pears make a juicy and fragrant dessert, one waiting for frozen yogurt or ice cream on the side. *Makes about 10 servings*

> 10 tablespoons (1 stick plus 2 tablespoons) unsalted butter, melted and cooled, plus additional for greasing the baking dish
> 5 cups fresh bread crumbs (see Note)
> 1 cup finely ground walnut pieces
> ¼ cup packed light brown sugar
> 1 teaspoon ground ginger
> ¼ teaspoon salt
> 3 pounds ripe pears, peeled, cored, and thinly sliced
> ½ cup granulated sugar

1 Position the rack in the center of the oven and preheat the oven to 375°F. Lightly butter a 13 × 9-inch baking dish; set aside.

2 Toss the bread crumbs, ground walnuts, melted butter, brown sugar, ginger, and salt in a large bowl.

3 Spread a third of the bread crumb mixture evenly over the prepared pan. Top with half the pear slices, distributing them evenly. Sprinkle ¼ cup granulated sugar over the pear slices. Cover them with half the remaining bread crumb mixture. Lay the remaining pear slices evenly across the baking dish and sprinkle them with the remaining ¼ cup granulated sugar. Cover these slices again with the remaining bread crumb mixture.

4 Bake until the juices are bubbling and the bread crumbs on the top are golden brown, 35 to 40 minutes.

To cool: Set on a wire rack for at least 15 minutes before serving.

To store: Once completely cooled, the dish can be wrapped in plastic and refrigerated for up to 3 days.

Note: To make fresh bread crumbs, tear a large, fresh, soft baguette or other soft bread into 2-inch chunks (remove the crust if it's crunchy); place these chunks in a food processor fitted with the chopping blade and process until ground.

Apple Walnut Brown Betty: Substitute 2¾ pounds apples for the pears; substitute cinnamon for the ginger.

Puddings, Custards, Mousses, and Soufflés

EGGS BEGIN AND END THIS BOOK. IT'S NO WONDER BECAUSE EGGS ARE NATURE's wonder, a perfect food. For the purposes of these desserts, eggs have long protein chains that must slowly unwind so they can reattach in wiry loops. Unfortunately, heat is both their friend and their enemy: it helps them elongate, but it can also solidify the bonds and make custards "break"—that is, become an incoherent mixture of goo and an unincorporable liquid.

But that rarely happens if you're careful with eggs over the heat. While most puddings and custards are relatively quick desserts, they do need your attention while you're making them. They're not "walkaways" like a cake once it's in the oven. Instead, carve out a moment when you can pay attention to what you're doing and you'll soon have bowls of comfort food.

If only all of life were like eggs: simple, pure, uncomplicated. The best of cooking. An ultimate pleasure.

❋ Puddings and Custards ❋

There are two kinds of custards: those with starch (cornstarch and flour in our recipes) or those without. The former are stirred directly over the heat; the latter, baked in a humidity-rich water bath. Both keep the unwound egg proteins from forming rigid bonds and so create luscious, creamy, thick puddings, custards, crèmes, and the like.

Vanilla Bean Pudding

This pudding is a little loose set, creamier than our Chocolate Pudding that follows. A vanilla bean gives it an intense taste without the unwelcome hint of alcohol. *Makes 6 servings*

1 vanilla bean
3 cups milk (regular, low-fat, or fat-free)
1 large egg plus 3 large egg yolks, at room temperature
⅓ cup sugar
2 tablespoons cornstarch
¼ teaspoon salt

❶ Split the vanilla bean in half lengthwise; run a paring knife along the inside of the halves, thereby scraping out the tiny seeds. Stir these and the bean's pod into the milk in a medium saucepan set over medium-low heat; continue stirring until little bubbles pop up around the pan's inner rim. Cover and set aside off the heat for 15 minutes.

❷ Fish the pod halves out of the milk, discard them, and return the pan to low heat, warming the milk gently just until wisps of steam come off its surface. Do not simmer.

❸ Meanwhile, whisk the egg, egg yolks, and sugar in a medium bowl until creamy, pale yellow, and quite thick, about 3 minutes.

❹ Slowly whisk about half the hot milk mixture into the egg mixture until smooth, then whisk this combined mixture back into the pan. Whisk in the cornstarch and salt until smooth.

❺ Set the pan over low heat (if you're using electric heat, set the pan over an unused burner just now turned to low). Cook, stirring constantly, just until the first bubble appears, until thickened somewhat and glossy, 2 to 3 minutes. Divide among six ½- or ¾-cup ramekins or custard cups. Refrigerate until set, about 4 hours or up to 3 days (see page 635 for a discussion of pudding skin).

Rum and Vanilla Bean Pudding: Add 2 tablespoons gold or white rum or ½ teaspoon rum extract with the cornstarch.

No Cream?

There are two ways to make puddings and custards rich: cream or egg yolks. We prefer the latter; they give the mixture a gelato-like smoothness without coating the tongue. What's more, because the yolks intensify the flavors so well, you can craft a rich pudding even out of fat-free milk.

Chocolate Pudding

Don't skimp on the vanilla; use a high-grade pure extract that will balance the chocolate. And never stop whisking the pudding over the heat! *Makes 6 servings*

> 3 large egg yolks, at room temperature
> 3 cups milk (regular, low-fat, or fat-free)
> 3 ounces unsweetened chocolate, chopped
> ¾ cup sugar
> ¼ cup all-purpose flour
> ½ teaspoon salt
> 1 tablespoon vanilla extract

❶ Whisk the egg yolks in a large bowl until creamy and smooth. Set aside.

❷ Clean and dry your whisk. Whisk the milk, chocolate, sugar, flour, and salt in a large saucepan over medium heat until the chocolate melts, the flour dissolves, and the mixture is smooth, slightly thickened, and just comes to its first bubble, about 6 minutes. Whisking all the while, let it bubble for 30 seconds. It will look like chocolate pudding at this stage.

❸ Whisk half the chocolate mixture into the egg yolks in a small, steady stream until smooth; whisk this combined mixture back into the remaining chocolate mixture in the pan.

❹ Reduce the heat to low (if you're working with an electric stove, use a different burner just now turned to low). Return the pan to the heat and cook, whisking constantly, until bubbling, 1 to 2 minutes.

❺ Remove the pan from the heat, whisk in the vanilla, and pour into a large serving bowl or six ½- or ¾-cup individual custard cups or ramekins. Refrigerate until set, about 2 hours. Once set, cover with plastic wrap and refrigerate for up to 3 days.

Banana Chocolate Pudding: Finely chop 1 ripe banana, place the pieces in the bottom of the serving bowl or divide them among the ramekins, then spoon the warm pudding over them. If desired, add ¼ teaspoon banana flavoring with the vanilla.

Mexican Chocolate Pudding: Add 1 teaspoon ground cinnamon with the flour. Add ¼ cup toasted slivered almonds and ¼ teaspoon almond extract with the vanilla.

Chili Chocolate Pudding: Add ¼ teaspoon cayenne pepper with the flour.

Orange Chocolate Pudding: Decrease the vanilla to 1½ teaspoons and add 1 tablespoon finely grated orange zest with it.

Pudding Skin

If you like pudding with skin, set the ramekins or custard cups in the refrigerator and don't cover them. When they are chilled, you can stretch a piece of plastic wrap over the rims to protect the puddings' insides from refrigerator odors; but frankly, that skin is quite a deterrent.

If you don't like skin, lay plastic wrap right on top of the warm pudding, securing the wrap to the inside walls of the ramekin or cup, thereby sealing the pudding into the bowl and leaving no room for the dreaded skin.

There's also this old trick for warding off the skin that adds a little fat: either hold a stick of unsalted butter over the still-hot pudding, touching it to the top in a few places; or place a small piece of butter on a knife and rub it quickly over the surface. The small layer of fat will keep the casein, the naturally occurring egg protein, from coming to the surface, drying out, and thus forming a skin.

Butterscotch Pudding

A good butterscotch dessert is hard to beat—and fairly simple: some caramelized sugar, a touch of butter, and a little salt for contrast. *Makes 6 servings*

    5 large egg yolks, at room temperature
    1½ tablespoons cornstarch
    ¼ cup packed dark brown sugar
    ¼ cup granulated sugar
    3 cups milk (regular, low-fat, or fat-free)
    3 tablespoons unsalted butter
    2 teaspoons vanilla extract
    ¼ teaspoon salt

❶ Whisk the yolks in a medium bowl until smooth, creamy, and thick, about 2 minutes. Whisk in the cornstarch until smooth. Set aside.

❷ Cook both sugars in a large saucepan set over medium heat, stirring almost constantly, until melted and golden, about 5 minutes.

❸ Meanwhile, heat the milk in a medium saucepan over medium-low heat until little bubbles fizz around the pan's inner edge.

❹ Stirring all the while, slowly add the warmed milk to the caramelized sugar. The mixture will froth at first, then the sugar will clump in the milk. Keep stirring over the heat until the sugar has calmed down and then remelted.

❺ Whisk about half the hot milk mixture into the egg yolks in a slow stream, then whisk this combined mixture back into the pan until smooth. Reduce the heat to low and whisk constantly until the first bubble, about 1 minute.

❻ Remove the pan from the heat and whisk in the butter, vanilla, and salt until smooth. If desired, strain the pudding through a fine-mesh sieve or a colander lined with cheesecloth to get rid of any inadvertent egg bits. Divide between six ½- or ¾-cup ramekins or custard cups. Refrigerate until set, about 4 hours or up to 3 days.

Variations: For a spiced pudding, add 1 teaspoon ground cinnamon and ¼ teaspoon grated nutmeg with the cornstarch.

For an even darker butterscotch taste, reduce the brown sugar to 3 tablespoons; beat 1 tablespoon unsulfured molasses into the egg yolks before adding the cornstarch.

Rum Butterscotch Pudding: Substitute 1 tablespoon dark rum, such as Myers's, for the vanilla.

Cup Custards

These are eggy, old-fashioned custards. You need six oven-safe ramekins or Pyrex custard cups as well as a 13 × 9-inch baking dish for making a water bath. *Makes 6 custards*

    3 large eggs plus 1 large egg yolk, at room
        temperature
    2½ cups milk (regular, low-fat, or fat-free)
    6 tablespoons sugar
    2 teaspoons vanilla extract
    ½ teaspoon grated nutmeg

❶ Position the rack in the center of the oven; preheat the oven to 350°F. Bring a teakettle of water to a boil over high heat.

❷ Whisk the eggs, egg yolk, milk, sugar, and vanilla in a large bowl until the sugar has fully dissolved.

❸ Ladle the mixture into six ¾-cup heat-safe ramekins or custard cups; sprinkle the nutmeg on top.

❹ Take the teakettle off the heat so the water stops boiling. Pull out the oven rack, place a 13 × 9-inch baking dish on it, and set the custard cups in the dish. Slowly pour the hot water into the baking dish until it reaches halfway up the outsides of the cups or ramekins.

⑤ Gently slide the rack back into the oven and bake until the custard is set when jiggled, about 45 minutes (see page 639).

⑥ Remove the cups from the hot water bath, taking care not to dribble water into the other pudding cups; set the cups on a wire rack to cool for at least 30 minutes before serving. Or cool completely, cover with plastic wrap, and store in the refrigerator for up to 3 days.

Variations: For a richer pudding, use 2 cups milk and ½ cup half-and-half.

Reduce the sugar to 3 tablespoons; add 3 tablespoons honey with the remaining sugar.

Stir ½ cup shredded unsweetened coconut into the mixture with the eggs.

Add ½ teaspoon maple extract or rum extract with the vanilla.

Substitute ground cinnamon or ground mace for the nutmeg—or add them with the nutmeg.

Crème Brûlée

Nothing's more classic than this French concoction: a flourless custard with a golden hard sugar crust you must crack with a spoon to get at the pudding underneath. Make sure you use flameproof ramekins. *Makes 6 servings*

  2 cups heavy cream
  6 large egg yolks, at room temperature
  ½ cup sugar
  ¼ teaspoon salt
  1 tablespoon vanilla extract

❶ Position the rack in the center of the oven; preheat the oven to 350°F. Bring a teakettle of water to a boil over high heat.

❷ Slowly heat the cream in a small saucepan over low heat until a few puffs of steam rise off the surface.

❸ Meanwhile, beat the egg yolks, ¼ cup sugar, and salt in a large bowl with an electric mixer at medium speed until pale yellow and satiny, about 2 minutes. Don't beat until doubled in volume or too thick; you don't want to get too much air in this custard.

❹ Beat the hot cream into the egg yolk mixture in a slow, steady stream, scraping down the sides of the bowl with a rubber spatula. Beat in the vanilla until smooth.

❺ Ladle about ½ cup of the mixture into each of six ½- or ¾-cup heat-safe ramekins. Place these in a 13 × 9-inch baking dish or a similarly sized roasting pan. Turn off the heat under the teakettle and let the water stop boiling.

❻ Pull out the oven rack and set the baking dish with the ramekins on it. Slowly pour the very hot water into the pan at its corner until the water comes halfway up the outsides of the ramekins.

❼ Slide the rack back into the oven and bake until the custard is set when jiggled (see page 639), about 45 minutes.

❽ Carefully remove the ramekins from the scalding water, taking care not to drip water in the other custards along the way. Cool on a wire rack until room temperature, about 45 minutes. Once cooled, cover with plastic wrap and refrigerate for up to 2 days.

❾ Before serving, sprinkle 2 teaspoons sugar over each chilled custard. Use a kitchen blowtorch to melt and brown the sugar, turning it into a liquid crust that will harden as it cools. Alternatively, preheat the broiler, set the ramekins on a baking sheet, and broil 4 inches from the heat until the sugar on the top is bubbling and brown. In either case, set aside to cool for at least 10 minutes to harden the crust on top and cool the heated dishes; or refrigerate for up to 2 hours, uncovered.

Variations: You can flavor the crème brûlée with just about any alcohol or liqueur, adding 2 tablespoons to the egg yolks before you beat them. However, be forewarned: because the fat content is rather high, the taste will be quite pronounced.

For a more classic look, omit the vanilla extract and stir in the seeds stripped from 1 vanilla bean, split lengthwise, in its stead.

Baked Chocolate Cream

This decadent dessert is a chocolate pudding with the texture of crème brûlée. Underbake the custards a tad so that they'll be soft and luscious. You can also use this pudding as a filling between the layers of a cake (but not as the frosting on top—see the variations). *Makes 6 servings*

> 1½ cups heavy cream
> 4 ounces semisweet chocolate, chopped
> 4 large egg yolks, at room
>   temperature
> 1½ tablespoons sugar
> ⅛ teaspoon salt
> 1 teaspoon vanilla extract

❶ Position the rack in the center of the oven and preheat the oven to 325°F. Bring a teakettle of water to a boil over high heat.

❷ Place the cream and chocolate in a large saucepan and cook over medium heat, stirring frequently, until the chocolate has thoroughly melted, the mixture is smooth, and a few puffs of steam rise from the surface, about 3 minutes.

❸ Meanwhile, whisk the egg yolks, sugar, and salt in a large bowl until creamy, smooth, and pale yellow, about 3 minutes. Set aside.

❹ Whisk the hot chocolate mixture in a slow, steady stream into the egg yolk mixture until smooth. Whisk in the vanilla.

❺ Ladle into six ½- or ¾-cup heat-safe ramekins or custard cups. Place these in a 13 × 9-inch baking pan or roasting pan.

❻ Take the teakettle off the heat so the water falls off the boil. Pull out the oven rack, set the baking pan or roasting pan with the cups on it, and slowly fill the pan from one corner with the near-boiling water until the water comes about halfway up the outsides of the cups or ramekins.

❼ Slide the rack back into the oven and bake until the custard is thickened but still movable when jiggled, about 20 minutes.

❽ Remove the ramekins or cups from the water bath and cool on a wire rack for 10 minutes. Refrigerate for at least 6 hours or for up to 3 days, covering with plastic wrap when chilled.

Baked Chocolate Espresso Cream: Whisk 1 teaspoon instant espresso powder into the egg yolks with the sugar.

Baked Mexican Chocolate Cream: Whisk 1 teaspoon ground cinnamon and ¼ teaspoon almond extract into the egg yolks with the sugar. Fold in ¼ cup toasted sliced almonds with the vanilla.

Baked Chocolate Cream Cake Filling: Make the chocolate cream as directed, chill, then scrape it out for a filling between two cake layers, such as the Buttery Vanilla Layer Cake (page 533) or the Banana Layer Cake (page 538). Or use it as the filling in a Vanilla Sponge Roll Cake (page 552).

Crème Caramel

Here, the custard sits over caramelized sugar, which slowly liquefies into a sauce as it bakes and cools. The custard itself is not as quite as rich as that for Crème Brûlée (page 637), but it is silkier because of a few egg whites and milk instead of cream. *Makes 6 servings*

> 1¼ cups sugar
> 2 tablespoons water
> 3 large eggs plus 6 large egg yolks, at room temperature
> ¼ teaspoon salt
> 2 cups whole or low-fat milk (do not use fat-free)
> 1 cup heavy cream
> 2 teaspoons vanilla extract

1. Position the rack in the center of the oven and preheat the oven to 350°F. Bring a teakettle of water to a boil over high heat.

2. Meanwhile, heat ½ cup sugar and the 2 tablespoons water in a small pan or skillet over medium-high heat, stirring almost constantly, until the sugar liquefies and turns golden brown, about 4 minutes. Divide this superhot sugar into six ¾-cup heat-safe ramekins or custard cups, tilting them quickly to coat the bottoms evenly. Set aside to cool.

3. Whisk the eggs, egg yolks, salt, and the remaining ¾ cup sugar in a large bowl until pale yellow and creamy, about 2 minutes. Whisk in the milk, cream, and vanilla until smooth.

4. Ladle the mixture into the custard cups, pouring it over the hardened sugar. Set these cups in a 13 × 9-inch baking pan or roasting pan.

5. Take the water off the heat so it stops boiling. Pull out the oven rack and set the baking pan on it. Slowly pour in the hot water at the pan's corner until the water comes about halfway up the outsides of the cups.

6. Slide the rack back into the oven and bake until the custards are set, with a slight wobble just at their centers when jiggled, about 50 minutes.

7. Remove the hot cups from the hot water bath and cool on a wire rack for 15 minutes. Cover with plastic wrap and continue cooling in the refrigerator for at least 2 hours—or store, covered, in the refrigerator for up to 3 days.

To serve: Run a sharp knife under the inside of the cups and invert them onto individual plates, shaking and jostling until the custard comes free and the sauce pours down over it.

To make a single Crème Caramel in a large bowl, pour the caramelized sugar syrup into a 1½-quart soufflé dish, tilting the dish a bit to get the sugar all over its bottom. Pour in the egg mixture, then bake in the water bath until a knife inserted into the center of the custard comes out clean, about 1 hour and 20 minutes. When cool, run a knife around the outside edge of the custard, invert onto a lipped platter, and jiggle out of its baking dish, letting the caramelized sugar sauce pour over the custard. Slice into wedges to serve, scooping up the sauce with each piece.

When a pudding is set is a matter of some debate. Some people like a thick pudding, one they can almost cut with a fork. Others like it spoonable and soft.

When you tap the pan in the oven, observe how the custard's surface moves. It should definitely be firm at the edges but not so firm as to appear solid. The center may still move a bit, but not in waves, more like in waggles, moving as a whole piece.

Baked Lemon Pudding

This pudding's actually halfway to being a cake: baked in a large dish, then sliced into wedges. Serve with fresh raspberries or blueberries for a springtime treat. *Makes 4 servings*

> 1½ tablespoons unsalted butter, melted, plus additional for greasing the baking dish
> ⅔ cup sugar
> ¼ cup plus 1 tablespoon all-purpose flour
> ¼ teaspoon baking powder
> ⅛ teaspoon salt
> 2 large eggs, separated (see page 19), at room temperature
> 1 cup milk (regular, low-fat, or fat-free)
> 3 tablespoons lemon juice
> 1½ teaspoons finely grated lemon zest

❶ Position the rack in the center of the oven; preheat the oven to 375°F. Bring a teakettle of water to a boil over high heat.

❷ Lightly butter a 1-quart, round, high-sided casserole dish; set aside. Whisk ⅓ cup sugar, the flour, baking powder, and salt in a medium bowl until uniform; set aside as well.

❸ Beat the egg whites in a large bowl with an electric mixer at high speed until foamy. Beat in the remaining ⅓ cup sugar in five or six additions, making sure each is dissolved before adding the next. Scrape down the sides of the bowl occasionally to make sure there are no undissolved granules. Continue beating until the egg whites have doubled in volume and form stiff, glossy peaks when lifted out of the mixture on the tip of a rubber spatula. Set aside.

❹ Clean and dry the beaters. Beat the egg yolks, milk, lemon juice, and lemon zest at medium speed in a large bowl until creamy, smooth, and very thick, about 3 minutes. Beat in the prepared flour mixture, making sure it is all dissolved in the egg yolks.

❺ Use a rubber spatula to fold in about half of the beaten egg whites, using long, even strokes to make sure they are incorporated without deflating them. Gently fold in the remainder of the beaten egg whites, using the same technique but stopping just after any white streaks have disappeared.

❻ Remove the boiling water from the heat. Pour and scrape the lemon mixture into the prepared baking dish, smoothing the top with a rubber spatula. Set it in a large baking pan or deep roasting pan. Fill the larger pan with hot water, pouring it into a corner so as not to douse the custard, until the water comes about halfway up the outside of the baking dish.

❼ Bake until the top is set when the dish is jiggled, until a knife inserted into the center of the pudding comes out clean, about 45 minutes. Transfer the very hot baking dish to a wire rack and cool for 10 minutes. This dessert is best served warm, within an hour of its coming out of the oven. However, you can cover the dish with plastic wrap and chill in the refrigerator for at least 2 hours or up to 3 days. To serve, cut the "pudding cake" into quarters, placing each on individual plates.

Serving Suggestions: Serve the wedges with fresh raspberries, fresh blackberries, finely chopped mint leaves, or sliced strawberries macerated for 15 minutes with a little sugar.

Baked Lemon Poppy Seed Pudding: Add ¼ cup poppy seeds with the lemon juice.

Baked Orange Pudding: Substitute orange zest for the lemon zest and frozen orange juice concentrate, thawed, for the lemon juice.

Baked Rice Pudding

Inspired by the rice pudding at New York delis, this is a baked custard; the rice slowly falls to the bottom and leaves a layer of custard on top. Cut it out of the pan in wedges like a cake. You don't need a water bath here because the starch in the rice protects the eggs. *Makes 6 servings*

Unsalted butter for greasing the baking dish
3 large eggs plus 3 large egg yolks, at room
   temperature
4 cups milk (regular, low-fat, or fat-free)
2 cups cold cooked rice (see Note)
½ cup sugar
½ cup raisins, preferably golden raisins
2 tablespoons vanilla extract
½ teaspoon salt

❶ Position the rack in the center of the oven and preheat the oven to 350°F. Lightly butter a 10-inch round or 9-inch square baking dish.

❷ Whisk the eggs and egg yolks in a large bowl until creamy. Whisk in the milk, rice, sugar, raisins, vanilla, and salt until the sugar has dissolved. Pour into the prepared baking dish.

❸ Bake until lightly browned and just set when jiggled, about 45 minutes. Transfer to a wire rack and cool for at least 15 minutes before serving; or continue cooling to room temperature, then cover and store in the refrigerator for up to 3 days.

Note: If you're making the rice from scratch, use ¾ cup white rice and 1½ cups water simmered over low heat, covered, until creamy, about 15 minutes.

Serving Suggestions: Pour Warmed Cream (page 631) or maple syrup over the top of each piece.

Variations: Reduce the sugar to ¼ cup; add ¼ cup honey with the remaining sugar.

Substitute dried cherries, dried blueberries, dried raspberries, chopped pitted dates, chopped dried apples, or chopped pitted prunes for the raisins. For a very easy dessert, stop by a Chinese restaurant and buy a carton of cooked white rice.

A Water Bath

Custards without a thickener like flour or cornstarch need protection because heat toughens eggs; a water bath (also called a "bain-marie") is the standard answer. Use a pan that's significantly larger than the baking dish or set of ramekins you've chosen, but not one that looks like a swimming pool in comparison. We use a copper roasting pan, the same we'd use for a rib roast—but a 13 x 9-inch baking dish can also work.

There are two rules: (1) make sure the water going into the bath is just below the boil (too hot and it can shock the custard) and (2) remove the custards from the water bath the moment they're set, remembering that both they and the water are very hot. Silicone baking gloves are particularly helpful here.

Some cooks put a thin kitchen towel in the large pan, setting the ramekins or baking dish on top, and then adding the hot water; the towel protects the bottoms of the custards from the baking pan's heat. We haven't found this necessary, but we use thick ceramic ramekins that insulate very well. If you're working with delicate custard cups or thin baking dishes, consider the towel trick if you find the bottoms of your custards are either a little chewy (slightly overbaked) or a little watery (seriously overbaked—the water has fallen out of suspension).

Zabaglione

More like a custard sauce, zabaglione can be poured over fresh berries, stone fruits (peaches, nectarines, plums, and such), or slices of cake (like Pound Cake, on page 511; One-Bowl Chocolate Buttermilk Loaf Cake, on page 510; or Semolina Cake with Ginger and Pine Nuts, on page 515). Although Marsala provides the authentic taste, the zabaglione is endlessly variable if you substitute another liqueur. *Makes 6 servings*

> 4 large egg yolks, at room temperature
> ¼ cup sugar
> ⅛ teaspoon salt
> ½ cup sweet Marsala, brandy, port, whiskey, an orange-flavored liqueur like Grand Marnier, a coffee-flavored liqueur like Kahlúa, a hazelnut-flavored liqueur like Frangelico, or brewed, cooled espresso

1 Use an electric mixer at medium speed to beat the egg yolks, sugar, and salt in the top half of a double boiler until thick, pale yellow, and creamy, about 3 minutes. Alternatively, beat them in a heat-safe medium bowl that you can later put over a saucepan of simmering water.

2 Bring about 1 inch of water to a boil over high heat in the bottom half of a double boiler or in a medium saucepan if you're using a bowl.

3 Meanwhile, beat the fortified wine, liqueur, whiskey, or espresso into the egg yolk mixture. When the water is boiling, set the top half of the double boiler or the bowl over it.

4 Immediately reduce the heat so the water simmers very slowly. Beat the mixture at medium speed, scraping down the sides of the pan or bowl so that no egg mixture solidifies there (be careful with the electrical cord around the heat and water) until the sauce has doubled in volume and is soft and fluffy, about 3 minutes.

5 Remove the pan from the heat and cool for at least 10 minutes before serving. If you want to make the sauce ahead, set the top half of the double boiler or the bowl in a larger bowl of ice water to cool quickly, stirring all the while; then scrape into a medium bowl, cover by pressing plastic wrap against the sauce's surface to seal it in, and refrigerate for up to 2 days.

Champagne Zabaglione: Substitute ¾ cup champagne for the liqueur.

Gratinéed Zabaglione: Spoon the sauce over sliced strawberries or other fresh berries in a heat-safe bowl and place about 6 inches from the heat source of a preheated broiler until browned and puffed, about 2 minutes.

Chestnut Flan

Chestnuts provide just the right amount of starch in a flan, turning this custard-style dessert into a rich, cakelike treat. The caramelized sugar creates a natural sauce as it melts a second time while baking. If you don't have a 2-quart soufflé dish, you can use a standard flan pan (larger in circumference and more shallow), but you'll have to watch the cooking time carefully, probably reducing it to about 45 minutes. *Makes 8 servings*

> 1 cup sugar
> 2 tablespoons water
> 2 cups whole or low-fat milk (do not use fat-free)
> ½ pound jarred roasted peeled chestnuts
> 3 large eggs plus 3 large egg yolks, at room temperature
> 2 teaspoons vanilla extract
> ¼ teaspoon salt

① Position the rack in the center of the oven and preheat the oven to 350°F. Bring a teakettle of water to a boil over high heat.

② Mix ½ cup sugar and the 2 tablespoons water in a large skillet over medium-high heat until the sugar has dissolved. Continue cooking, stirring almost constantly, until the melted sugar turns a deep caramel color.

③ Pour into a 2-quart soufflé dish, tilting the dish quickly to get the very hot liquid sugar into the corners and in as even a sheet across the bottom as you can. Set aside.

④ Place the milk and chestnuts in a large blender or a food processor fitted with the chopping blade. Blend or process until pureed.

⑤ Set a fine-mesh sieve or a colander lined with cheesecloth over a large bowl; pour in the puree and strain, making sure any solids are left behind.

⑥ Whisk in the remaining ½ cup sugar. Then whisk in the eggs, egg yolks, vanilla, and salt. Pour into the soufflé dish over the hardened sugar. Take the boiling water off the heat.

⑦ Set the soufflé dish in a deep roasting pan or baking dish. Place in the oven and pour in the hot water at the larger pan's corner until the water level comes about halfway up the outside of the smaller baking dish.

⑧ Bake until set, until the flan barely moves at its center when the dish is jiggled, about 1 hour and 15 minutes. Transfer the hot dish to a wire rack and cool for 10 minutes. Refrigerate for at least 4 hours, covering with plastic wrap when cool—or store, covered, in the refrigerator for up to 3 days.

⑨ To unmold, run a small knife around the inner rim of the dish, then set a serving platter over it. Invert, let the flan fall out, then remove the soufflé dish, letting the sauce run over the flan. Serve by slicing the flan into wedges like a pie.

Variations: Spice the flan by adding ½ teaspoon ground cinnamon, ¼ teaspoon grated nutmeg, and/or ¼ teaspoon ground mace with the vanilla. Or reduce the milk by 2 tablespoons and add 2 tablespoons liqueur with the remaining milk—whiskey, Cognac, rum, hazelnut-flavored liqueur like Frangelico, or coffee-flavored liqueur such as Kahlúa.

Fig and Honey Clafouti

A clafouti is fruit baked in a thickened custard. Ours is sweetened with honey for a rich dessert that needs no other fandango—except, perhaps, Sweetened Whipped Cream (page 522). *Makes 8 servings*

Unsalted butter for greasing the baking dish
8 ripe figs, preferably Black Mission figs, stemmed and halved
4 large egg yolks, at room temperature
¾ cup regular or low-fat sour cream (do not use fat-free)
⅓ cup honey
¼ cup whole or low-fat milk (do not use fat-free)
2 teaspoons vanilla extract
¼ teaspoon salt
½ cup all-purpose flour

① Position the rack in the center of the oven and preheat the oven to 400°F.

② Lightly butter a 9-inch square pan. Lay the fig halves, cut side up, in the bottom of the pan. Set aside.

③ Whisk the egg yolks, sour cream, honey, milk, vanilla, and salt in a large bowl until smooth. Whisk in the flour until smooth. Gently scrape and pour the mixture over the figs in the prepared pan, taking care not to dislodge them.

④ Bake until lightly browned, until a knife inserted into the cakelike custard without touching a fig comes out clean, about 25 minutes. Cool on a wire rack for 15 minutes before slicing, or cover and store in the refrigerator for up to 2 days.

Variations: Substitute 8 plums, pitted and halved; 8 apricots, pitted and halved; or 4 large peaches, pitted and quartered, for the figs.

❀ *Frozen Custards* ❀

A frozen custard is richer than ice cream or gelato. The former doesn't have as many egg yolks; the latter, little to no cream. Frozen custards taste best right out of the ice cream maker—or if frozen hard, when allowed to sit out on the counter for 10 or 15 minutes.

Vanilla Frozen Custard with Hot Fudge Sauce

This is a no-holds-barred, over-the-top, don't-give-it-another-thought treat. *Makes 1½ quarts*

9 large egg yolks, at room temperature
1½ cups sugar
2 cups whole milk
2¼ cups heavy cream
1½ tablespoons vanilla extract
½ teaspoon salt
Hot Fudge Sauce (recipe follows)

① Beat the yolks and sugar in a large bowl with an electric mixer at medium speed until thick, pale yellow, creamy, and doubled in volume, about 4 minutes, scraping down the sides of the bowl as necessary with a rubber spatula.

② Meanwhile, heat the milk in a large saucepan over medium heat until small bubbles pop up around the pan's inner rim.

③ Beat about half the hot milk into the egg yolk mixture in a small, steady stream until smooth; then beat this combined mixture back into the saucepan with the remaining egg yolk mixture.

④ Set the pan over low heat; if you're cooking with an electric stove, use a second burner just now turned to low. Cook, whisking constantly, until slightly thickened, until the mixture coats the back of a wooden spoon (see page 7), 2 to 3 minutes. Do not bring to a simmer or even the merest bubble.

⑤ Strain the custard into a large bowl through a fine-mesh sieve to remove any bits of inadvertently scrambled egg. Cool for 10 minutes; then stir in the cream, vanilla, and salt. Cover and refrigerate for at least 4 hours or preferably overnight.

⑥ Freeze the custard in an ice cream maker according to the manufacturer's instructions. Serve at once with Hot Fudge Sauce, if desired, or spoon into a plastic container, seal, and store on the floor of the freezer at the back for up to 3 days.

Vanilla Chocolate Chip Frozen Custard: Pour in 1 cup mini-chocolate chips during the last few churns in the ice cream maker, just so the chips are evenly distributed in the frozen custard.

Vanilla Chocolate Swirl Frozen Custard: After the custard has frozen in the machine, spoon or scoop it into a plastic container, layering chilled Hot Fudge Sauce between several layers to create ribbons. Place the container in the freezer to firm up for at least 2 hours.

Mint Chocolate Chip Frozen Custard: Substitute 1 teaspoon mint extract and several drops of green food coloring for the vanilla. Pour 1 cup mini-chocolate chips into the machine during the last few churns to get the chips evenly distributed in the frozen custard.

Hot Fudge Sauce

What would a frozen custard be without a thick, rich hot fudge sauce? Follow the cooking times here exactly. *Makes 2 cups*

- 1 cup half-and-half
- ¼ cup sugar
- ¼ cup light corn syrup
- 6 ounces bittersweet or semisweet chocolate, chopped
- 4 tablespoons (½ stick) unsalted butter, cut into chunks
- 1 teaspoon vanilla extract
- ¼ teaspoon salt

❶ Bring the half-and-half, sugar, and corn syrup to a low simmer in a medium saucepan set over medium heat; cook, whisking constantly, for 3 minutes.

❷ Add the chocolate and butter. Continue cooking, whisking all the while, until smooth. Bring to a very low simmer, the barest bubble;

then adjust the heat so the mixture bubbles just this slowly. Cook, whisking constantly, for 5 minutes.

❸ Whisk in the vanilla and salt. Set aside off the heat for 5 minutes before using; or seal in a glass jar or other heat-safe container and refrigerate for up to 2 weeks.

Chocolate Frozen Custard

In the end, semisweet chocolate is better for an ice cream served as an afternoon treat; bittersweet chocolate, with its sophisticated edge, for dessert after dinner. *Makes 1½ quarts*

- 4 large egg yolks, at room temperature
- ¾ cup sugar
- 10 ounces semisweet or bittersweet chocolate, chopped
- 2 cups whole milk
- ¼ cup unsweetened cocoa powder, preferably natural cocoa powder
- 2 cups heavy cream
- 1 tablespoon vanilla extract
- ½ teaspoon salt

❶ Beat the egg yolks and sugar in a large bowl with an electric mixer at medium speed until thick, pale yellow, and smooth, about 4 minutes. Set aside.

❷ Whisk the chocolate, milk, and cocoa powder in a medium saucepan set over medium-low heat until smooth. Continue whisking until a few puffs of steam rise off the surface.

❸ Beat half the chocolate mixture into the egg yolk mixture in a thin, steady stream until smooth; then beat this combined mixture into the remaining cocoa mixture in the pan.

4 Set the pan over low heat and cook, whisking constantly, until thickened and velvety but not boiling, until the mixture coats the back of a wooden spoon (see page 7), about 2 minutes.

5 Strain the custard through a fine-mesh sieve or a cheesecloth-lined colander into a large bowl. Cool for 10 minutes, then stir in the cream, vanilla, and salt until smooth. Cover and refrigerate for at least 4 hours or preferably overnight.

6 Freeze in an ice cream maker according to the manufacturer's instructions. Serve at once; or spoon the frozen custard into a plastic container, seal, and store on the floor of the freezer at the back for up to 3 days.

Variations: Add any of the following to the machine during its final few churns, just to get them mixed throughout the frozen custard: banana chips, chocolate chips, chopped Baby Ruth bars, chopped Butterfinger bars, chopped hazelnuts, chopped Junior Mints, chopped peanut brittle, chopped pecans, chopped pistachios, chopped Twix bars, chopped unsalted macadamia nuts, chopped unsalted peanuts, chopped walnuts, Cracker Jacks, crumbled biscotti, crumbled chocolate chip cookies, crumbled macaroons, crumbled peanut butter cream sandwich cookies, dried cherries, dried cranberries, M & M's Mini Baking Bits, malted milk balls, mint chocolate chips, peanut butter chips, shredded sweetened coconut, or white chocolate chips.

Or when the frozen custard comes out of the machine and is placed in a storage container, layer it with 1 cup purchased chocolate sauce, caramel sauce, or marshmallow cream sauce, spreading one of these sauces in three or four thin layers between the layers of frozen custard in the container.

Butter Pecan Frozen Custard

Butter pecan remains America's third favorite ice cream flavor, just behind vanilla and chocolate.
Makes 1½ quarts

1¾ cups pecan pieces
4 large egg yolks, at room
     temperature
3 tablespoons unsalted butter
⅔ cup packed light brown sugar
2 tablespoons granulated sugar
1 cup whole milk
2 cups heavy cream
½ teaspoon vanilla extract
½ teaspoon salt

1 Position the rack in the center of the oven and preheat the oven to 350°F. Bake the pecan pieces on a large lipped baking sheet until lightly browned and aromatic, about 5 minutes, stirring a few times. Set aside.

2 Whisk the egg yolks in a large bowl until creamy, about 1 minute. Set aside.

3 Melt the butter in a large saucepan over medium heat. Swirl the pan occasionally until the butter browns slightly, then stir in both sugars until melted.

4 Whisk in the milk, then bring to a gentle simmer, just a few bubbles, stirring often.

5 Whisk half the hot milk mixture into the egg yolks in a slow, steady stream until smooth; then whisk this combined mixture back into the remaining milk mixture in the pan.

6 Set the pan over low heat and cook, stirring constantly, until the mixture thickens and coats the back of a wooden spoon (see page 7), about 2 minutes.

7 Strain through a fine-mesh sieve or a colander lined with cheesecloth and into a clean, large bowl to remove any bits of egg that have scrambled by accident. Cool for 10 minutes, then stir in the cream, vanilla, and salt until smooth. Cover and refrigerate for at least 4 hours or overnight.

8 Freeze in an ice cream maker according to the manufacturer's instructions. A little over halfway through the freezing process, as the custard starts to firm up, add the toasted nuts and let them get churned into the machine. Serve at once—or spoon into a large container, seal well, and store in the coldest part of the freezer (in the back on the floor) for up to 3 days.

Strawberry Frozen Custard

Thawed, frozen strawberries make an easy puree.
Makes 1½ quarts

Two 10-ounce bags frozen strawberries, thawed
¼ teaspoon salt
1¼ cups whole milk (do not use low-fat or fat-free)
4 large egg yolks, at room temperature
½ cup sugar
1¼ cups heavy cream
1 teaspoon vanilla extract

1 Place the thawed strawberries and salt in a large blender or in a food processor fitted with the chopping blade. Blend or process until smooth. Set aside.

2 Heat the milk in a large saucepan over medium heat until a few wisps of steam rise off its surface, but not until it simmers in any way. Reduce the heat to keep the milk this hot.

3 Beat the eggs and sugar in a large bowl with an electric mixer at medium speed until thick and pale yellow, until ribbons can fall off the turned-off beaters and lie on top of the mixture without instantly dissolving back into it, about 4 minutes.

4 Beating at medium speed all the while, add half the hot milk to the egg mixture in a slow, steady stream. Continue beating until smooth, about 30 seconds.

5 Remove the pan from the heat and pour this combined mixture back into the hot milk, stirring with a wooden spoon. (Be careful of the electrical cord around the heating element.)

6 Reduce the heat to low and place the saucepan back over the heat. (If you're working on an electric stove, use a second burner, just now turned to low.) Stir over the heat until the mixture thickens slightly and can coat the back of a wooden spoon, about 2 minutes (see page 7).

7 Strain the custard into a large bowl through a fine-mesh sieve; stir in the strawberry puree as well as the cream and vanilla. Cover and refrigerate for at least 4 hours or preferably overnight.

8 Freeze the custard in an ice cream maker according to the manufacturer's directions. Serve at once or store in a separate container on the floor of the freezer for up to 1 month.

A dessert mousse is a chilled, intense but airy combination of eggs, sugar, and cream. Since these desserts use raw eggs, seek out in-shell pasteurized eggs if you're at all concerned. Admittedly, these recipes do involve quite a few bowls; you can't create a dessert this good without dirtying what you've got!

Chocolate Mousse

The best chocolate mousse is not too sweet; it's also made with high-quality chocolate. We prefer bittersweet chocolate with its higher percentage of cocoa solids; look for bars with around 72% of these solids. A background flavor (here, a liqueur) helps put the chocolate in the foreground. *Makes 6 servings*

> 8 ounces bittersweet chocolate, chopped
> ⅓ cup chocolate-flavored liqueur
> 4 large egg whites,
>   at room temperature
> ¼ teaspoon salt
> ⅔ cup heavy cream
> 4 large egg yolks, at room temperature

❶ Place the chocolate and liqueur in the top half of a double boiler. Alternatively, set them in a medium bowl that will eventually fit over a medium saucepan.

❷ Bring about an inch of water to a boil over high heat in the bottom half of the double boiler or in a medium saucepan that will snugly hold the bowl over the water. Set the top half of the double boiler or the bowl over the water, reduce the heat so the water simmers slowly, and stir until half the chocolate has melted.

❸ Remove the top half of the double boiler or the bowl from the heat and continue stirring until all the chocolate has melted. Set aside to cool for 10 minutes.

❹ Meanwhile, use an electric mixer at high speed to beat the egg whites and salt in a large bowl until soft peaks form under the beaters when they're turned off and lifted out, about 3 minutes. Set aside.

❺ Clean and dry the beaters. Beat the cream in a chilled bowl at medium speed until the mixture holds its shape in soft, smooth peaks on a rubber spatula, about 2 minutes. Set aside as well.

❻ Clean and dry the beaters one more time. Beat the egg yolks in a second large bowl with an electric mixer at medium speed until airy and pale yellow. Slowly beat in the melted chocolate mixture until smooth, scraping down the sides of the bowl with a rubber spatula as necessary.

❼ Remove the beaters and fold in the whipped cream with a rubber spatula, using large, smooth arcs so as not to deflate the cream.

❽ Fold in the beaten egg whites in the same way, mounding them on top, then gently pushing the spatula into the center and turning it up and over so as to fold the whites without their dissipating too much. The final mixture should have no white bits in it but can be a mélange of lighter and darker shades of brown. Scoop into individual serving bowls or wineglasses, cover, and chill for at least 2 hours or up to 2 days.

Variations: Substitute any sweet flavored liqueur you like: a coffee-flavored liqueur like Kahlúa, an orange-flavored liqueur like Cointreau, or a hazelnut-flavored liqueur like Frangelico.

White Chocolate Mousse

Look for white chocolate that isn't just flavored hydrogenated shortening. Instead, use one made from cocoa butter and vanilla. *Makes 8 servings*

8 ounces white chocolate, chopped
4 large egg yolks, at room temperature
¼ cup sugar
2 tablespoons gold or white rum
2 teaspoons vanilla extract
4 large egg whites, at room temperature
¼ teaspoon salt
½ cup heavy cream

❶ Stirring all the while, melt the white chocolate in the top half of a double boiler set over about an inch of simmering water or in a medium bowl that will fit over a medium saucepan with about the same amount of simmering water. Alternatively, melt the white chocolate in a medium bowl in the microwave, heating it on high in 15-second intervals and stirring after each. If you've used a double boiler, scrape the chocolate into a medium bowl; clean and dry the top half of the double boiler. In either case, set aside to cool for 10 minutes.

❷ Make sure there is enough water in the pot to continue simmering. Beat the egg yolks, sugar, rum, and vanilla with an electric mixer at medium speed in the cleaned top half of the double boiler or in a second bowl that will cover the saucepan. Set over the simmering water and continue beating (pay attention to the electric cord!) until thickened and lemon curd–like, about 3 minutes, scraping down the sides occasionally. Set aside to cool.

❸ Clean and dry the beaters. Beat the egg whites and salt at high speed in another bowl until they make light, fluffy but firm peaks off the tip of a rubber spatula, about 3 minutes. Set aside.

❹ Clean and dry the beaters again. Beat the cream in a chilled large bowl until it makes stable waves across the surface when pressed with a spatula, about 2 minutes.

❺ Fold the melted white chocolate into the egg yolk mixture until smooth. Fold this mixture into the whipped cream until smooth. Finally, fold half the beaten egg whites into the mixture with a rubber spatula, then work very gently to fold in the remaining egg whites, just until there are no white streaks or bits in the mixture.

❻ Spoon into 8 wineglasses or ramekins. Chill in the refrigerator for 2 days, then serve or cover and store in the refrigerator for up to 3 days.

Variations: Substitute any liqueur you like for the rum, including Cognac, whiskey, Calvados, or Armagnac.

Spiced White Chocolate Cherry Mousse: Whisk ¼ teaspoon ground cinnamon with the egg yolks; also fold ½ cup dried cherries, chopped, into the mousse with the beaten egg whites. For more zip, soak the dried cherries in a little brandy for 15 minutes before draining and chopping.

White Chocolate Macadamia Mousse: Fold in ½ cup chopped, salted macadamia nuts with the beaten egg whites.

Orange White Chocolate Mousse: Substitute Grand Marnier for the rum; also fold in 1 tablespoon finely grated orange zest with the beaten egg whites.

Black and White Chocolate Mousse: Make both the Chocolate Mousse (page 648) and the White Chocolate Mousse; layer these in wineglasses, white over dark. You can halve the recipe, if desired.

Peach Mousse

There's really little cooking here because gelatin provides most of the body, but you do have to prepare four separate ingredients, which are folded together to make a creamy mousse. *Makes 8 servings*

2½ teaspoons unflavored gelatin or one
   ¼-ounce package unflavored gelatin
¼ cup white or gold rum
3 large peaches, peeled, pitted and diced
¼ cup lemon juice
¼ teaspoon salt
1 cup cold heavy cream
4 large egg whites, at room temperature
4 egg yolks, at room temperature
½ cup sugar

1 Sprinkle the gelatin over the rum in a small bowl; set aside for 5 minutes.

2 Meanwhile, place the peaches, lemon juice, and salt in a blender; blend until pureed, scraping down the sides of the canister a few times.

3 Place the peach puree in the top half of a double boiler or in a medium bowl that will fit snugly over a saucepan. Bring about an inch of water to a simmer over high heat in the bottom of the double boiler or the saucepan. Set the top half of the double boiler or the bowl over the water, stir well, then add the coagulated gelatin and any remaining liquid in the bowl. Stir constantly over the heat until the mixture is smooth and the gelatin beads have dissolved, about 1 minute. Remove from the heat and set aside to cool for 10 minutes.

4 Meanwhile, use an electric mixer to beat the cream in a chilled medium bowl until soft, gentle peaks form when the turned-off beaters are dipped into the cream, about 2 minutes. Set aside.

5 Clean and dry the beaters. Beat the egg whites at high speed in a large bowl until they form firm, foamy peaks on the tip of a rubber spatula, about 3 minutes. Set aside.

6 Clean and dry the beaters one more time. Beat the egg yolks and sugar in a large bowl until thick and pale, until you can turn off the beaters, lift them out, and drizzle ribbons back into the mixture, ribbons that will not immediately dissolve into the mixture, about 3 minutes.

7 Fold the peach puree mixture into the egg yolk mixture with a rubber spatula until smooth. Fold the whipped cream into the mixture, using gentle, slow, long strokes.

8 Gently fold in half the beaten egg whites until smooth, then add the rest of the egg whites on top of the mixture and use very slow, long, careful arcs with the rubber spatula to fold in the remainder, just until there are no white streaks or specks visible.

9 Pour the mousse into a large bowl and smooth out the top with a spatula. Or spoon into 8 wineglasses or small ramekins. Chill in the refrigerator for 2 hours, then serve or cover and store in the refrigerator for up to 3 days.

Nectarine Mousse: Substitute nectarines for the peaches.

Apricot Mousse: Substitute about 6 peeled and pitted apricots for the peaches (you'll need to make about 1¼ cups puree).

Peach Melba Mousse: Substitute Amaretto or another almond-flavored liqueur for the rum; fold 1 cup fresh raspberries into the mousse with the beaten egg whites.

Peach Margarita Mousse: Substitute tequila for the rum and lime juice for the lemon juice.

❋ Dessert Soufflés ❋

A soufflé—from the French word for "to breathe"—is no more than a wisp of air, the lightest dessert imaginable: just beaten egg whites, flavored and baked until they rise up into nothingness. You'll need to serve them the moment they're out of the oven; scoop up airy mounds with a large spoon, place them in individual bowls, and top with a little Sweetened Whipped Cream (page 522), Ginger Cream (sweetened with a little sugar, page 476), or dessert liqueur, if desired.

Chocolate Soufflé

Makes 4 servings

4 large egg yolks, at room temperature
1 cup milk
¼ cup all-purpose flour
¼ cup cocoa powder, sifted through a fine-mesh sieve
¼ teaspoon salt
6 ounces bittersweet chocolate, chopped
6 large egg whites, at room temperature
½ cup sugar
1 prepared soufflé dish (see page 652)

❶ Position the rack in the center of the oven and preheat the oven to 400°F.

❷ Whisk the egg yolks in a large bowl until creamy, smooth, and pale yellow, about 2 minutes. Set aside.

❸ Clean the whisk. Whisk the milk, flour, cocoa powder, and salt in a medium saucepan set over medium heat until well blended.

❹ Add the chocolate; stir over the heat with a wooden spoon until the chocolate has melted and the mixture has just started to bubble and is thickened somewhat like pudding, perhaps 3 minutes.

❺ Using an electric mixer at medium speed, slowly beat this chocolate mixture into the egg yolks until smooth and light. Set aside to cool for 10 minutes.

❻ Clean and dry the beaters. Beat the egg whites at high speed in a large bowl until foamy. Begin adding the sugar in 1-tablespoon increments, scraping down the sides of the bowl as necessary. Continue beating until the mixture makes smooth, glossy, droopy peaks off the tip of a rubber spatula, about 3 minutes.

❼ Fold half the whites into the chocolate mixture until smooth, then plop the rest of the whites on top of the chocolate and gently fold in smooth, even arcs until there is no white visible but the eggs have maintained their height.

❽ Spoon the mixture into the prepared soufflé dish, smoothing the top gently with a rubber spatula.

❾ Bake until puffed, set, and slightly cracked, about 30 minutes. Serve without delay.

Grand Marnier Soufflé

Makes 4 servings

4 large egg yolks, at room temperature
½ cup sugar
1 cup milk (regular, low-fat, or fat-free)
¼ cup all-purpose flour
¼ cup Grand Marnier
1 tablespoon finely grated orange zest
1 teaspoon vanilla extract
¼ teaspoon salt
6 large egg whites, at room temperature
1 prepared soufflé dish (see box)

1 Position the rack in the center of the oven and preheat the oven to 400°F.

2 Beat the egg yolks and ¼ cup sugar in a large bowl with an electric mixer at medium speed until thick and pale yellow, about 2 minutes. Set aside.

3 Whisk the milk and flour in a medium saucepan until the flour is dissolved. Set over medium heat and continue whisking until the mixture is thickened and just bubbling, about 3 minutes.

4 With the mixer at medium speed, slowly beat this hot milk mixture into the egg yolk mixture until smooth, scraping down the sides of the bowl as necessary.

5 Beat in the Grand Marnier, orange zest, vanilla, and salt until smooth. Set aside.

6 Clean and dry the beaters. Beat the egg whites in a large bowl with the mixer at medium speed until frothy, about 1 minute. Raise the speed to high and continue beating, adding the remaining sugar 1 tablespoon at a time, until you can feel no sugar granules between your fingers and the mixture makes smooth, glossy, droopy but nonetheless firm peaks off the tip of a rubber spatula, about 2 minutes.

7 Use a rubber spatula to fold half the egg white mixture into the Grand Marnier mixture until smooth, then fold in the remainder of the beaten whites in smooth, long arcs just until there is no white visible. Spoon and spread this mixture into the prepared soufflé dish.

8 Bake until puffed, lightly browned, and set, about 30 minutes. Serve at once.

Raspberry Soufflé: Substitute raspberry-flavored liqueur, such as Chambord, for the Grand Marnier; substitute 1 teaspoon finely grated lemon zest for the orange zest.

Almond Soufflé: Substitute an almond-flavored liqueur such as Amaretto for the Grand Marnier and substitute ½ teaspoon almond extract for the vanilla. Omit the orange zest if desired.

Anise Soufflé: Substitute Sambuca for the Grand Marnier and substitute 1 teaspoon finely grated lemon zest for the orange zest.

To prepare a soufflé dish, lightly butter a 1½-quart, high-sided, round soufflé dish. Tear off a piece of aluminum foil about 10 inches long, fold it in half lengthwise, and butter one side. Wrap the foil around the soufflé dish butter side in so that 3 inches of foil stick up over the rim of the dish. Tape the foil together so it stays in a ring or tie it in place with butcher's twine. Sprinkle about 1 tablespoon sugar into the dish, then shake and roll it around a bit to coat the bottom, sides, and the inside of the foil with sugar. Knock out any excess.

Tools of the Trade

653

A Glossary for Some Ingredients

Adobo Sauce. See Chipotle Chiles.

Asiago. This Italian cheese from the Veneto was once made with sheep's milk but now is made almost exclusively with cow's milk. It's piquant, salty, and nutty, like a more intense version of Parmigiano-Reggiano (see page 660). Fresh varieties are occasionally—if rarely—available at high-end cheese counters, but we only call for aged Asiago, better for storage in the refrigerator over a couple of weeks if tightly wrapped.

Asian Red Chili Sauce. It's made from a fresh or fermented mixture of chiles, vegetables, and spices. Because there are hundreds of different kinds, experiment with various bottlings to discover which is right for your palate. Sambal Oelek is an Indonesian bottling, not quite as hot as others like Sriracha, a Thai or Thai-style sauce that's quite fiery. There are also Vietnamese bottlings with garlic added.

Baking Powder. Keep it dry; use only double-acting baking powder. Baking powder loses its efficacy over time as the acid and alkali react. As a rule, keep baking powder for 6 months. To check if yours if viable, dissolve 1 teaspoon in 1 cup lukewarm water. If it bubbles, you're good to go.

Baking Soda. Make sure to keep it dry. Even so, since ambient humidity compromises its effectiveness, replace it after 8 to 9 months. Never cook with baking soda that's been stored in the refrigerator to trap food odors.

Balsamic Vinegar. Technically made only from Trebbiano grapes (although most brands now are made with blends), this syrupy vinegar is low acid and a good match to greens. Aged balsamics are expensive and are only used as condiments.

White balsamic vinegar is milder and less sweet, a combination of white wine vinegar and grape juice.

Black Vinegar. This Chinese condiment is made from pressed, fermented glutinous rice; it's sweetened and flavored with aromatics, usually star anise. It's available in gourmet markets and Asian markets—or check out the source guide (see page 663) for mail-order suppliers. In every recipe, we also give a substitution formula that uses balsamic vinegar and Worcestershire sauce; the final concoction will not be the same, but close enough.

Bread Crumbs. Available in fresh or dried form, you cannot substitute one for the other. Fresh bread crumbs are made with, of course, fresh bread. Tear the crust off slices of stale white or wheat bread; pulse in a food processor fitted with the chopping blade a few times until the consistency of coarse sand. One ½-inch slice of bread will make a little more than ¼ cup fresh bread crumbs. One caveat: "whipped" bread will often yield only gummy crumbs because of the high-fat content. Dried bread crumbs are available seasoned or unseasoned (that is, plain); no recipe in this book calls for seasoned crumbs. If you'd like to make your own, bake crust-removed, ½ inch slices of bread on a lipped baking sheet in a preheated 275°F oven until brown and crisp, turning once, 25 to 35 minutes. Cool completely on the baking sheet, then pulse in a food processor fitted with the chopping blade until coarsely ground.

Broth. We recommend using reduced-sodium broth; you can thus control the salt in the dish. If you use standard canned broth, cut out the salt in the recipe and check again when the dish is done to see if you need more. In no case do we recommend bouillon cubes as a substitute for broth; these are mostly salt and a coloring agent.

Brown Sugar. See Sugar.

Butter. Our recipes only call for unsalted butter. If you use salted butter, reduce the salt in the recipe by half, then check at the end of cooking to see if you need to add more.

If you melt butter in a microwave, beware of splatters caused by the butter melting internally, superheating, and bursting out. To prevent this, cut the butter into 1-tablespoon sections, place in a small bowl, and microwave in 15-second increments, swirling the bowl after each heating. When almost all the butter has melted, remove the bowl from the microwave and let the residual heat melt any remainder.

Buttermilk. Here's one baking staple most of us don't keep on hand. One solution is to substitute powdered buttermilk, available at gourmet markets, specialty food stores, and from suppliers on the Web. Simply make the amount of buttermilk you need, based on the package instructions, then add it to the batter as indicated. Once opened, powdered buttermilk must be refrigerated for up to 1 year.

If you have neither fresh nor powdered, you can substitute 1 cup whole milk and 1 tablespoon lemon juice; stir together and set aside at room temperature for 5 minutes.

Cake Flour. See Flour.

Chili Oil. This Asian condiment is chile-steeped oil, tinted orange or red by the chiles' oils and infused with the chemical inferno in their membranes and seeds. By and large, Malaysian and Thai bottlings are hotter than Chinese. Because it goes rancid quickly after opening, store chili oil in the refrigerator. It should not be used as an oil for sautés.

Chipotle Chiles. Chipotles are smoked dried jalapeño chiles; they are often sold in larger supermarkets or Latin American markets. They should be toasted or softened before use, as the recipe indicates. Remove the inner membranes and seeds for a milder taste.

Chipotles are often canned in adobo sauce, a fiery mixture of chiles and vinegar; these can be used in place of dried chipotles if they are rinsed before seeding and chopping.

Chocolate. It usually comes in varieties like semisweet, bittersweet, and unsweetened. Basically, these indicate the ratio of cocoa solids to sugar: semisweet has more sugar than bittersweet; both have more sugar than unsweetened. Milk chocolate adds milk solids to the mix. High-end brands often have a percentage on the label: 66% or 71%, for example. This number represents the percentage of the mixture that is cocoa solids. As a rule, consider anything in the 40s or 50s to be semisweet, anything in the 60s and 70s to be bittersweet. We prefer bittersweet for almost all recipes because of its dark, sophisticated taste. Unsweetened chocolate (sometimes called "baking chocolate") should be at least 95% cocoa solids.

Store chocolate, tightly wrapped, in a cool, dark place. It can "bloom"—that is, develop a white coating on its surface from the cocoa butter falling out of suspension. A product of careless storage, the bloom will not affect a chocolate used for melting but will have seriously compromised one intended for eating.

Chorizo. This seasoned pork sausage is popular in Mexican and Spanish cooking. Mexican chorizo, or "Mexican-style chorizo," is fresh; it must be cooked thoroughly before use. Spanish chorizo is cured, usually smoked, and can be used as is.

Chutney. This jamlike, savory, East Indian condiment is made from a variety of fruits. The most common variety available in supermarkets is mango chutney; but often these bottlings are pale imitations of true Indian chutneys, which can range from sweet to fiery, depending on preference. If you can, buy chutney from an East Indian market or from one of the outlets listed in the source guide (see page 663).

Coarse-Grained Sea Salt. See Salt.

Cocoa Nibs. The quintessence of chocolate, these are coarsely ground, roasted cocoa beans. Store them sealed at room temperature for up to 9 months.

Cocoa Powder. To make cocoa powder, the cocoa butter is extracted from cocoa; the resulting solids (called "chocolate liquor") are dried, then ground. Unsweetened cocoa powder (the only kind called for in this book) is available in two forms: regular (sometimes called "natural") and Dutch process, which has been treated with an alkali to aid its ability to dissolve and to neutralize chocolate's natural acidity. A well-stocked pantry has both; if we have a preference, we indicate it in the recipe.

Coconut. Coconut flakes are available in two forms: (1) sweetened, sold in the baking aisle of most supermarkets, and (2) unsweetened or "desiccated," usually available at health food markets or at some gourmet stores in the bulk food section. Neither should be substituted for the other; a good pantry has both. To store, seal tightly in plastic bags for up to 6 months.

Coconut Milk. Made from cooking coconut flesh in water, then straining out the solids, this "milk" is thick and luxurious. From the can, coconut milk should be stirred before being added to a batter.

Light coconut milk is actually the second pressing of the same solids used for regular coconut milk, much of the fat having already been pressed out.

Cream of coconut is a sweetened concoction used for frozen drinks; it is not called for in this book and should not be substituted for coconut milk.

Confectioners' Sugar. Also called "powdered sugar" or "icing sugar," this sugar is ground finer than the standard granulated variety, with cornstarch added so the pulverized crystals do not clump.

Cornichons. French gherkins, these tiny pickles have a strong, vinegary bite. Never substitute bread-and-butter pickles.

Cornmeal. Commercial cornmeal is most often steel-ground, the hull and germ having been removed from the kernels; stone-ground cornmeal is usually a whole-grain product and is certainly more nutritious, if harder to dissolve in sauces and the like. Use either for these recipes, but use only yellow cornmeal unless otherwise indicated (not the more esoteric blue, purple, or white varieties) and use only fine or medium grinds (not the coarse ground, more common for making polenta).

Cream of Tartar. More accurately called "potassium bitartare," this acid is naturally found in grapes and is a by-product of winemaking, often scraped out of the casks. It stabilizes egg whites when beaten and makes some sugar mixtures creamy. It also changes the acidity of some cake batters to make them fluffier.

Crystallized Ginger. See Ginger.

Curry Powder. A mélange of up to twenty spices, no two brands are the same. Most bottled curry powders are yellow because they contain more turmeric by weight than any other spice. Madras curry powder is red from cayenne pepper—and much hotter. Look around the market and experiment with different bottlings.

Dried Bananas. Long and thin, like fresh bananas, these should be chopped before using. Those found in health food stores and gourmet markets are often dark brown because they lack preservatives. Don't confuse them with fried banana chips, which are too oily for successful baking.

Duck Confit. This is the meat from preserved duck legs. The heavily salted legs are slowly poached over very low heat in duck fat. They are cooled in the fat, then packed in it.

Eggs. We only call for large eggs. Mostly, they should be at room temperature. Cold eggs can shock batters and cause melted chocolate to seize (that is, come apart into tacky little threads and a thin liquid). To get cold eggs quickly to room temperature, submerge them in a bowl of warm (never hot!) water for 5 minutes. For tips on egg safety and egg anatomy, see pages 19 and 27.

Emmentaler. Most likely the original "Swiss cheese," this pale gold cow's milk cheese is slightly sweet with a nutty flavor. It is often served on its own after a meal. The brown rind is not edible.

Fish Sauce. Made from fermented fish parts, salt, and aromatics, this Southeast Asian condiment has a pungent smell that mellows beautifully when heated or combined with sugar and/or other fats. Don't be put off by the aroma: there is no substitute. But there are different varieties—nam pla (the very heady Thai bottlings), nuoc mam (the slightly sweeter Vietnamese bottlings), and fish gravy (the much milder Indonesian bottlings). You can buy fish sauce at almost all supermarkets these days; it is usually found in the Asian aisle, although the selection at Asian grocers will be larger. Once opened, store it in the refrigerator.

Flour. Flour is simply a finely powdered grain, seed, or nut. The most common type in Western cooking is, of course, wheat flour—and the only kind of flour called for in this book. In almost all the recipes, the flour isn't sifted; modern flour is aerated enough to make a tender cake without additional fuss. We also never call for self-rising flour, a mixture of flour, salt, and some kind of leavener, most often baking powder.

While all-purpose flour is made from only the wheat's endosperm, whole wheat flour has the bran and germ as well, all ground together.

Whole wheat pastry flour is a specialty flour, a more finely ground version of whole wheat flour and thus better for baking delicate cakes and breads that still need the extra body of whole wheat.

Cake flour is a high-starch, soft wheat flour, designed to give cakes better heft. A quick if somewhat unreliable substitution is 14 tablespoons all-purpose flour plus 1 tablespoon cornstarch.

For bread flour, see page 218.

Ginger. This rhizome should have a sweet smell, papery skin, and no wrinkled, mushy spots. Look for it in the produce section of the supermarket. Peel off the skin with a vegetable peeler or a knife, then either grate the ginger on a ginger board (available at cookware stores) or mince it very finely by rocking a knife back and forth through it until almost pureed. Jarred minced ginger is a convenience product, also often found in the produce section of a supermarket; once opened, store it in the refrigerator for months on end.

Crystallized ginger is strips of fresh ginger that have been cooked in a sugar solution and then dried. Sometimes called "candied ginger," it's available in the spice aisle.

Ground ginger is a powder made from dried ginger; it has a fairly short shelf life, perhaps only 6 months, after which it dulls and becomes rather like dry mustard.

Ginger Juice. This is the pressed juice from ginger. It's available in small bottles at most markets, usually alongside the condiments or sometimes in the Asian aisle. Make your own by placing small chunks of peeled fresh ginger in a garlic press and then extracting the juice. Freezing ginger before you juice it breaks down the fibers and makes the job easier.

Gorgonzola. This is a ripe, aged, Italian cow's milk blue cheese, often served with fruit for dessert.

Grana Padano. Sometimes considered a cheaper alternative to Parmigiano-Reggiano, this part–skimmed milk cheese is milder, with a fresh, less salty finish. It's best for grating and perfect when you don't want the spike of a heavier cheese.

Gruyère. This medium-fat cow's milk cheese was originally from Switzerland; it's now produced in most Western countries. Gruyère is somewhat hard, aged about 10 months. It grates well and is prized for its bitter, nutty flavor. One problem: it molds quickly, since it's not made with stabilizers. The solution: buy only as much as you need and store it wrapped in plastic in the refrigerator (not in the hydrator).

Half-and-Half. This is a mixture of half heavy cream and half whole milk. By and large, it has a fat content of between 10% and 12%.

Haricots Verts. These are a variety of French green beans, although the term has come to mean any tiny, thin string beans. They are darker and less fibrous than their larger American kin. In a pinch, substitute standard green beans but cut them into 2- or 3-inch sections.

Heavy Cream. The British and Canadian equivalent is double cream; some states sell heavy cream as "whipping cream." You can substitute light cream (or single cream) in any sauté or casserole but not in a baking recipe, dessert sauce, or emulsified (whipped) sauce.

Herbs. These are any number of leafy plants whose oils and natural flavor esters enhance a dish. Amounts in the recipes are usually given for both fresh and dried herbs unless either is necessary for the dish's success. For example, fresh herbs are better as a "finish"; dried herbs hold up better in deep-frying. In all recipes, fresh herbs are listed with an obvious marker, something that tells you what to do with the leaves: "2 teaspoons minced oregano leaves" or "1 teaspoon stemmed thyme." Dried herbs are listed as "dried." Don't forget that dried herbs have a shelf life; figure on 9 months as an easy guide, provided you store them in a cool, dark place.

Hoisin Sauce. This thick, sweet, ketchup-like, Asian condiment is made from soybeans, garlic, sugar, spices, and vinegar. It must be refrigerated once opened. Chouhee sauce is a slightly stronger version.

Honey. Its quality will dramatically impact your dish. In almost all recipes, don't be afraid to experiment with exotic varieties like orange blossom, chestnut, oak, or star thistle.

Horseradish. This root from a spiky green grass is highly prized in Central Europe for its pungent, nose-piercing flavor. In this book, we only specify bottled white horseradish, the grated white root seasoned with vinegar and salt and available most often in the dairy case of supermarkets.

Hot Red Pepper Sauce. Any bottled hot sauce will do, Tabasco being the most popular. We call for its use because of the bright, clean, puckering-hot bite it gives to a dish. Do not substitute salsa or smoked pepper sauces, such as those made from chipotles.

Kosher Salt. See Salt.

Lemongrass. This long, dry grass is naturally spiked with citral, an oil used to make citronella candles. Buy lemongrass stalks that are still tender, not brittle; remove the prickly outer leaves. To release the oils before adding a stalk to a dish, crush (but don't shatter) the stalk, using the smooth side of a meat mallet or the bottom of a heavy saucepan. In almost all cases, it should be removed before serving, like a bay leaf.

Maple Syrup. See page 30.

Marsala. This fortified Sicilian wine is available in two forms: sweet or dry. All recipes here call for dry Marsala; sweet is better for sipping after dinner. Once opened, it can be stoppered and stored in a cool, dry place at room temperature for several months.

Masa Harina. Literally "dough flour," this is the base ingredient for tortillas and tamales. It's made from dried corn kernels that have been cooked in limewater, then ground to a powder. Look for it in Mexican and Latin American markets, as well as in the Latin American section of almost all supermarkets.

Milk. In most recipes where milk is used, we've given you a choice among whole, low-fat, or fat-free. We've indicated a preference only if it's necessary to the final dish.

Mirin. This sweetened and seasoned rice wine is often used as a seasoning in Japanese dishes. It's sold in small bottles and can be stored in the pantry until it clouds, browns, or develops slimy whisps of particulate material. In a pinch, substitute sweet sherry or white wine plus a generous pinch of sugar.

Molasses. This thick syrup is made from sun-ripened sugar cane and prized for its aromatic, bright taste. We only call for unsulfured molasses. Sulfured varieties are made from immature canes from which the juice is extracted with the help of a noxious gas.

Montrachet. This soft white cheese is named for a town in Burgundy, France, and is probably the most accessible chèvre (or goat cheese) sold in the United States. Perishable, it loses its delicate taste over time, and should be stored no more than a few days in the refrigerator. Look for pure white varietals, not ones covered in ash, seeds, spices, or nuts.

Nuts. All nuts have a shelf life, the oils going rancid over time. To slow down this process, store nuts in the freezer in sealed plastic bags for up to 9 months. There's no need to thaw before using in recipes.

Onion. Unless otherwise stated, all onions specified are yellow onions. Consider chopping double the amount the recipe calls for and freezing half in a sealed plastic bag to be used in other recipes. You can also use packaged frozen chopped onion, although the quality of some convenience products can be greatly reduced (and mushy onions will definitely compromise a final dish).

Oyster Sauce. This molasses-like, dark red or brown thick condiment from China was once made only from oysters, salt, and sugar; today, almost all bottlings include thickeners and coloring agents. It's used mostly as a salt additive in Cantonese-style cooking. Cheaper bottlings can be laced with MSG.

Panko Bread Crumbs. A specialty, they're very coarse dried white bread crumbs, better for frying because of their thick texture, about like dried coconut. (The English name, in fact, is a redundancy since *panko* means "bread crumbs" in Japanese.) Look for them in the Asian aisle of most markets.

Paprika. Unless otherwise indicated, paprika in all recipes is mild (or sweet) paprika. Paprika is made from ground dried mild chiles; the oils react over time, robbing it of most of its flavor within about 9 months.

Spicy paprika, usually called "hot Hungarian paprika," is made from far hotter chiles.

Smoked paprika is simply made from smoked, dried, fairly mild chiles; it is an essential ingredient in Spanish and Portuguese cooking and can be found in many large markets in the spice aisle or from suppliers on the Web.

Parmigiano-Reggiano. There is no substitute for this hard, skimmed cow's milk Italian cheese. Grate it using a cheese plane, a cheese grater, or the small holes of a box grater. Buy small chunks, cut off larger wheels, with as little rind as possible to cut down on any waste. The rind should be stamped with the cheese's name and origin for authenticity.

Peanut Oil. Store this neutral cooking oil in the refrigerator because it goes rancid quickly, thanks in large part to its relatively high content of poly-unsaturated fats, which are free to hook up with just about anything that passes by in their environment. It will cloud and may solidify, but you can return it to its liquid state by placing the bottle in a bowl of warm (not hot) water for 5 or 10 minutes. Always smell peanut oil to make sure it hasn't turned rancid.

Pecorino Romano. There's a wide variety of Pecorino cheese, with Romano being the most common. It's a hard, dry, yellow, aged Italian grating cheese, sharper in taste than Parmigiano-Reggiano.

Pepper. Use only freshly ground pepper; keep a grinder out so it's always available.

White pepper is used largely for aesthetic reasons, so that black flecks don't dot a creamy dish.

Poblano Chiles. These long green chiles have an excellent balance of sour and hot; they are often used in chiles rellenos. Dried poblanos become anchos. There should be no substitute, although you can use a green bell pepper and a quarter or half of a jalapeño chile if you must.

Pomegranate Molasses. This sour Middle Eastern condiment is made from yellow or red pomegranates, boiled down with sugar until molasses-like. In a pinch, you can substitute frozen cranberry juice concentrate and balsamic vinegar in a 2-to-1 ratio.

Preserved Szechuan Vegetables. These small cans of salted, pickled mustard greens, cabbage, radishes, turnips, or mixed vegetables provide a musky, salty, distinctly Chinatown taste. Any variety can be used: preserved Chinese vegetables are salty; preserved Szechuan versions are, of course, much hotter, laced with chiles or chili oil. In a pinch, substitute wilted greens, seasoned with sugar, salt, and chili oil. Look for the cans in the supermarket Asian aisle, at Asian markets, or from mail-order suppliers (see page 663).

Rice Vinegar. Made from glutinous rice, this low-acid vinegar comes in two varieties: regular (often simply not marked as "seasoned" on the bottle) and seasoned (that is, with sugar added). Unless otherwise noted, we only call for the regular variety. Plain rice vinegar can be hard to track down except through Asian markets or suppliers. If you have to, you can substitute white wine vinegar or sherry vinegar but the taste will be sharper. There are aged rice vinegars—usually tan to brown in color—but they should be used only as condiments.

Rum. The difference between run-of-the-mill bottlings of gold rum and white rum is mostly just caramel coloring. Jamaican rums, however, must by law be colored with actual caramel (that is, caramelized sugar), not just food coloring. In even better bottlings, gold rum is aged in oak.

Dark rum, such as Myers's, is flavored, spiked with aromatics, and quite distinctive.

Salt. Unless otherwise specified, use table salt or other fine-grained salt. All amounts are actually to taste because the quantity of salt in a dish, unlike that for almost any other ingredient, is truly a matter of personal preference.

Kosher salt is a coarse-grained salt that does not contain magnesium carbonate and so will not make a brine solution murky. In these recipes, it's called for mostly because of its crunchy texture, a foil for soft vegetables and the like.

Coarse-grained sea salt is a highly specialized product, originally farmed on sea ledges in Brittany, France, but now produced all over the world; it is actually a condiment, prized for its mineral taste and delicate crunch.

Serrano Chile. A small, narrow chile that can be harvested green (in its immature stage), red, or even yellow. There is a subtle taste difference among the astringent green serranos, the more sour red ones, and the somewhat nuttier yellow ones. Always cut off the stem and discard the seeds as well as their fleshy membranes—unless you want the added heat. Work with rubber gloves to avoid skin irritation; if you don't use gloves, wash your hands thoroughly before you touch your face or eyes. You may substitute half a fresh jalapeño chile, seeded, for each serrano, but the dish will have a duller, more palate-drenching heat, rather than a bright spike.

Sesame Oil. It's sold in two varieties: toasted and untoasted. The former is what's called for again and again in this book for its nutty, aromatic taste. Store it in the refrigerator and sniff it before using to make sure it hasn't gone rancid.

Shaoxing. This is a salted Chinese rice wine (pronounced variously, but something like "Shoh-Shing" and also bottled as Shoa Shing, Shaohsing, or Huo Tiao). In a pinch, substitute dry sherry.

Smoked Paprika. See Paprika.

Soy Sauce. The condiment of northern Asia actually comes in many varieties—basically, from light to dark (not a reference to the sodium content but to how long it's aged after fermentation). Any soy sauce will do, depending on your taste. In general, we prefer low-sodium soy sauce; it doesn't have as bright a taste as some others, but it allows us to control the salt in the final dish. In any event, steer clear of thick, dark soy sauces and mushroom-based ones.

Sweet soy sauce is a sweet condiment, highly prized in Indonesian cooking. If you can't find it, make the sauce with 2 parts regular soy sauce and 1 part molasses, then use the amount of this mixture called for in the recipe.

Sugar. Always use granulated sugar unless otherwise indicated. Seal an open bag of sugar in a larger plastic bag for storage.

Brown sugar is made by processing granulated sugar with molasses. "Light" and "dark" simply indicate how much molasses is in the mix. Brown sugar clumps notoriously because the moisture evaporates over time, leaving the sticky crystals in rock-hard nodules. Soften brown sugar by placing it in a sealed, ziplock bag and heating it in the microwave on high in 10-second increments until usable.

Superfine sugar is finely ground sugar, better for dissolving—and also better for sifting onto the tops of cakes and the like.

For confectioners' sugar, see page 656.

Sweet Soy Sauce. See Soy Sauce.

Szechuan Peppercorns. Actually not true peppercorns at all, they are the outer pods of the fruit of a member of the citrus family. They have been variously banned and allowed in the United States, based on current citrus embargos and infections. The peppercorns have a sour, slightly mouth-numbing taste; there is no substitute, although Szechuan peppercorn oil can be sprinkled over the final dish for a certain reminiscence of the flavor.

Tamarind Paste. Made from the ultrasour fruit of a shade tree native to Asia, this condiment is often used as a thickener in Asian sauces. Look for it in Asian markets and from suppliers on the Web. Do not substitute tamarind syrup or pulp.

Tapioca. No recipe calls for tapioca per se, but many call for quick-cooking tapioca, a granulated version of the more familiar pellets made from the cassava root. Look for it in the baking aisle; store it in a sealed plastic bag at room temperature for months on end.

Thai Curry Paste. A convenience product, it comes in various heat levels. Look for either the green curry paste (with green chiles and aromatics) or red curry paste (with, obviously enough, red chiles). Be forewarned that some bottlings contain shrimp paste if you have health or dietary issues. All curry pastes should be refrigerated once opened to preserve their freshness. Do not substitute East Indian curry pastes, which are made with clarified butter.

Vanilla Beans. Look for moist, fat beans, a sign of good storage and lots of seeds. Wrap them in plastic, seal in a plastic bag, and refrigerate for up to 5 months.

Vanilla Extract. Use only pure vanilla extract, not an imitation flavoring. A double-strength extract will add more flavor.

Vermouth. This white wine has been fortified with spices; once, one of them was wormwood (*Wermut* in German—thus, "vermouth" in English). We often call for vermouth as an alternative to white wine because once opened, vermouth can stay on the shelf in a cool, dry place for several months—unlike wine, which begins to turn within hours of its opening. Vermouth comes in two varieties: dry (sold with a white label) and sweet (with a red). Don't confuse the two—use the one called for in the recipe. White wine can be substituted for dry vermouth; there is no substitute for sweet vermouth.

Wakame. This green, slightly bitter edible seaweed is most often sold fresh in Japan but is rarely available fresh in North America. Dried wakame is available in health food stores, Asian markets, and most gourmet supermarkets. To rehydrate it, place it in a large bowl, cover with hot water, and let stand for 10 minutes.

Wasabi. This prepared Japanese horseradish-type mixture is available in most supermarkets with the other Asian foods. It comes in paste and powder forms; use either as the recipe indicates. The powder can also be made into a paste with a little water.

White Balsamic Vinegar. See Balsamic Vinegar.

Whole Wheat Pastry Flour. See Flour.

Yogurt. Use only plain yogurt; but use regular, low-fat, or nonfat, based on your preference.

Source Guide

Artisanal Cheese
www.artisanalcheese.com
1 877 797-1200
The finest cheese selection online

Birchboy Syrups
www.birchboy.com
1 877 769-5660
Exotic syrups from Haines, Alaska, including elderberry, high-bush cranberry, spruce tip, and birch

Broadway Pan Handler
www.broadwaypanhandler.com
1 866 COOKWARE or 1 212 966-3434
65 E. 8th Street
New York, New York 10003
Kitchen gadgets, utensils, and appliances, including mixing bowls, knives, cookware, mixers, spatulas, wooden spoons, cutting boards, and sifters

D'Artagnan
www.dartagnan.com
1 800 327-8246
280 Wilson Avenue
Newark, New Jersey 07105
Meat and game drop-shipped, including pâté, foie gras, veal, pheasant, ostrich, and wild boar

Economy Candy
www.economycandy.com
1 800 352-4544
108 Rivington Street
New York, New York 10002
A dizzying array of dried fruits and nuts along with retro candy favorites at rock-bottom prices

The Fresh Lobster Company
www.thefreshlobstercompany.com
1 508 451-2467
Fresh seafood including (but not limited to) lobsters, oysters, and crabs

importfood.com
www.importfood.com
1 888 618-THAI
P.O. Box 2054
Issaquah, Washington 98027
Thai products including curry pastes and rice noodles

Kalustyans
www.kalustyans.com
1 800 362-3451
123 Lexington Avenue
New York, New York 10016
East Indian spices and oils, as well as chutneys, rice, and dried fruits

Kam Man Food Products
www.kammanfood.com
1 212 571-0330
200 Canal Street
New York, New York 10013
One of New York's finest Asian grocery and cookware stores with a comprehensive line of Asian oils, vinegars, sauces, and dried noodles

Kitchen Krafts
www.kitchenkrafts.com
1 800 298-5389
P.O. Box 442
Waukon, Iowa 52172

A complete line of candy-making and baking supplies

Kitchen Market
www.kitchenmarket.com
218 Eighth Avenue
New York, New York 10011
1 888 HOT-4433
A great source for Latin American and Mexican foods, including chiles and spices

Marshall's Honey Farm at the Flying Bee Ranch
www.marshallshoney.com
1 800 624-4637
155-159 Lombard Road
American Canyon, California 94503
Honey of all varieties from apiaries in northern California

Mexgrocer
www.mexgrocer.com
A full range of Mexican and Latin ingredients, including beans, rice, chiles, and spices

New York Cake and Baking Distributors
www.nycake.com
1 800 942-2539 or 1 212 675-CAKE
56 West 22nd Street
New York, New York 10010
Every baking tool imaginable

O & Co.
www.oliviersandco.com
1 877 828-6620
Some of the finest olive oil made—including flavored oils

Oasis Date Gardens
www.oasisdate.com
1 800 827-8017
P. O. Box 757
Thermal, California 92274
Dates of almost every variety

Pacific Rim Gourmet
www.pacificrim-gourmet.com
75-5660 Kopiko Street
Suite C7-210
Kailua-Kona, Hawaii 96740

Penzeys
www.penzeys.com
1 800 741-7787
Outlets throughout the United States as well as mail order. A wide selection of dried spices and extracts

Pike Place Fish Market
www.pikeplacefish.com
1 800 542-7732
86 Pike Place
Seattle, Washington 98101
Fresh fish and seafood shipped overnight

The Spanish Table
www.spanishtable.com
1 206 682-2827
1427 Western Avenue
Seattle, Washington 98101
Olives, oils, legumes, vinegars, and more

Taku
www.takusmokeries.com
1 800 582-5122
550 South Franklin Street
Juneau, Alaska 99801
Smoked Alaskan salmon, king crab legs, and other seafood specialties

The Wok Shop
www.wokshop.com
1 415 989-3797
718 Grant Avenue
San Francisco, California 94108
Woks, rice steamers, bamboo steamers, cleavers,
and other Asian cooking equipment

Williams-Sonoma
www.williams-sonoma.com
877 812-6237
Outlets throughout North America
Mixers, bowls, baking pans, and flavorings

Uwajimaya
www.uwajimaya.com
1 206 624-6248
600 Fifth Avenue South
Seattle, Washington 98104
An enormous Asian grocery store

www.ultimatecook.com
Recipes and information on Bruce and Mark,
our other books, and our magazine work, as well
as a list of links to some of our favorite mail-
order sources.

Quick Reference List for Sauces and Rubs

Pestos
Mint Pesto (page 443)
Pecan Pesto (page 179)
Sage Pesto (page 293)
Sun-Dried Tomato and Roasted Garlic Pesto
(page 48)

Savory Sauces and Condiments
Aïoli (page 45)
Apple-Cucumber Raita (page 409)
Apricot Relish (page 78)
Blackberry-Rhubarb Chutney (page 388)
Chile con Queso (page 16)
Chinese Black Bean Sauce (page 353)
Classic Cocktail Sauce (page 61)
Classic Tartar Sauce (page 121)
Cucumber-Apple Salsa (page 157)
Ginger Cream (page 476)
Grilled Pineapple Salsa (page 356)
Malty Sauce (page 74)
Mango Mayonnaise (page 121)
Mayonnaise (page 121)
Mignonette (page 74)
Peanut-Ginger Sauce (page 508)

Salsa (page 47)
Sesame Dipping Sauce (page 74)
Simple Asian Dipping Sauce (page 74)
Spiced Ketchup (page 405)
Streamlined Florentine Sauce (page 21)
Streamlined Hollandaise Sauce (page 20)
Sweet-and-Sour Sauce (page 353)
Szechuan Garlic Sauce (page 430)
Tomato-Cranberry Chutney (page 388)
Tzatziki (page 46)
Wasabi Mayonnaise (page 121)
Yellow Pepper Relish (page 374)

Barbecue Sauces
Beer Barbecue Sauce (page 437)
Blueberry Ginger Barbecue Sauce (page 277)
Maple Bourbon Barbecue Sauce (page 435)
Plum-and-Rum Barbecue Sauce (page 395)
Sweet-and-Spicy Barbecue Sauce (page 251)
Walnut Paprika Barbecue Sauce (page 350)

Glazes
Orange Marmalade Glaze (page 433)
Sesame Barbecue Glaze (page 332)

Spiced Molasses Glaze (page 433)
Sweet-and-Sour Barbecue Glaze (page 347)

Marinades
Apple Pomegranate Marinade (page 439)
Gin Marinade (page 439)
Honey-Orange Marinade (page 427)
Lemon Pepper Marinade (page 426)
Spiced Apple Marinade (page 427)
Teriyaki Marinade (page 426)
Yakitori (page 61)

Flavored Butters
Garlic Lemon Butter (page 276)
Ginger Butter (page 345)
Lemon Parsley Butter (page 346)
Mushroom Butter (page 346)
Parsley and Thyme Butter (page 276)
Smoked Paprika Butter (page 276)
Vanilla Butter (page 377)
Walnut Butter (page 346)
Wasabi Butter (page 346)

Rubs
Cajun Dry Rub (page 290)
Chili Rub (page 385)
Chinese Rub (page 308)
East Indian Rub (page 308)
Fennel Rub (page 308)

Fresh Herb Rub (page 440)
Garlic and Rosemary Rub (page 440)
Green Tea Rub (page 440)
Herb Butter Wet Rub (page 285)
Italian Wet Rub (page 285)
Jerk Dry Rub (page 290)
New England Rub (page 308)
Pepper Dry Rub (page 290)
Provençal Rub (page 308)
Rosemary-Garlic Rub (page 386)
Singapore-Inspired Rub (page 386)
Southwestern Wet Rub (page 286)
Szechuan Wet Rub (page 286)

Sweet Sauces and Condiments
Berry Jam (page 221)
Blueberry Maple Syrup (page 33)
Caramel Custard Sauce (page 628)
Chocolate Whipped Cream (page 546)
Crème Anglaise (page 599)
Fig Jam (page 221)
Hot Fudge Sauce (page 645)
Lemon Drizzle (page 520)
Orange Glaze (page 233)
Quince Jam (page 221)
Sweetened Whipped Cream (page 522)
Vanilla Cinnamon Maple Syrup (page 33)
Walnut Butter Rum Maple Syrup (page 33)
Zabaglione (page 642)

Charts, Conversions, and Substitutions

International Oven Temperatures

Fahrenheit	Celsius	Gas Equivalency	Description
225	110	1/4	Cool
250	120	1/2	
275	130	1	Very Slow
300	150	2	
325	160	3	Slow
350	180	4	
375	190	5	Moderate
400	200	6	Medium Hot
425	220	7	
450	230	8	Hot
475	250	9	

High Altitude Cooking and Roasting

Above 5,000 feet, increase the stovetop heat by a notch or increase the oven's heat by 5°F. Beans and grains will take longer to cook; sauces may take slightly longer to cohere, break down, or thicken. Larger roasts should be cooked to 5°F higher than the temperature given in the recipe. Above 7,500 feet, roast to 10°F higher.

High Altitude Baking

Do not change the oven temperature but make the following adjustments:

Above	Reduce the baking powder or baking soda by	Reduce the sugar by	Add this much more liquid, or this much milk with the egg(s)
3,000 feet	1/8 teaspoon	1/2 tablespoon	1 tablespoon
5,000 feet	1/4 teaspoon	1 tablespoon	2 tablespoons
7,500 feet	1/4 teaspoon	2 tablespoons	3 tablespoons

Quick Substitutions

1 teaspoon ground allspice = $1/2$ teaspoon ground cinnamon + $1/4$ teaspoon ground cloves

1 teaspoon baking powder = $1/4$ teaspoon baking soda + $1/2$ teaspoon cream of tartar

1 cup brown sugar = 1 cup granulated sugar + 1 tablespoon unsulfured molasses

1 cup buttermilk = 1 cup whole milk + 1 tablespoon lemon juice, mixed together and set aside at room temperature for 5 minutes

1 cup cake flour = 14 tablespoons all-purpose flour + 1 tablespoon cornstarch

1 cup confectioners' sugar = 1 cup granulated sugar + 1 tablespoon cornstarch, ground in a food processor with the chopping blade until finely powdered

1 cup milk = $1/2$ cup canned evaporated milk + $1/2$ cup water

1 ounce semisweet chocolate = 1 ounce unsweetened chocolate + 1 tablespoon sugar

Index